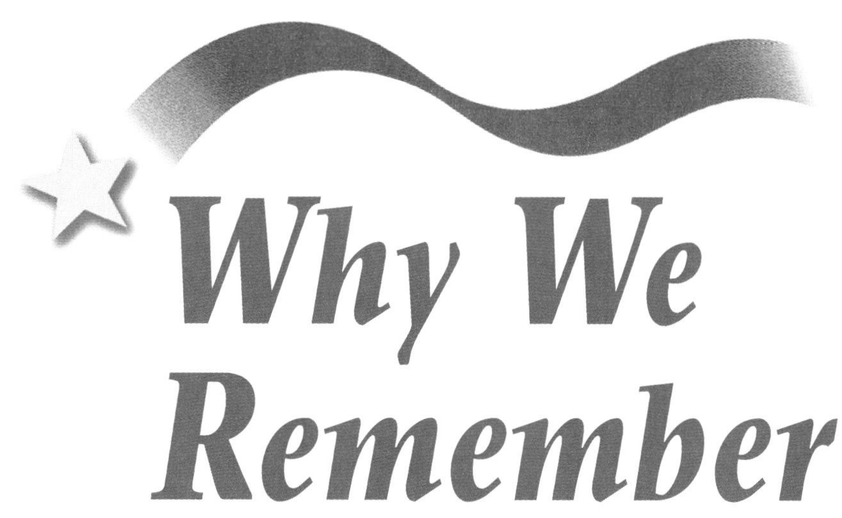

Why We Remember

United States History
Civil War to the Present

Teacher's Edition

Herman J. Viola

Contributing Authors
Helen Wheatley
Diane Hart

Scott Foresman
Addison Wesley

Editorial Offices: Glenview, Illinois • Menlo Park, California
Sales Offices: Reading, Massachusetts • Atlanta, Georgia • Glenview, Illinois
Carrollton, Texas • Menlo Park, California

http://www.sf.aw.com

Teacher's Edition Photo Acknowledgments

Terri Ashe: page T5
Jon Feingersh: page T4
Ken Karp: pages T16, T18, T20, T22, T24–T25 (top)

Jeopardy!® is a registered trademark of Jeopardy Productions.

Printed in the United States of America.

ISBN 0-201-33228-0

1 2 3 4 5 6 7 8 9 10 - RNT - 01 00 99 98 97

Why We Remember

United States History–Civil War to the Present

A Total Teaching Package

Why We Remember

An Interview with Dr. Herman Viola

by Ms. Bonnie White
Buzz Aldrin School
Reston, Virginia

Ms. White: When did you become interested in American history?

Dr. Viola: *I began to get interested in American history in elementary school. Both my parents were Italian immigrants who came to America as young adults. Neither of them had more than an eighth grade education, but they loved their adopted country even though they knew little about its past. I was the one who answered their questions about famous historical figures and explained the significance of our patriotic holidays. As I read about American history in school, I liked to go home and tell my family the stories I was learning about the country they had chosen to make their home.*

Ms. White: Many people enjoy reading about history. Why did you decide to make it your life's work?

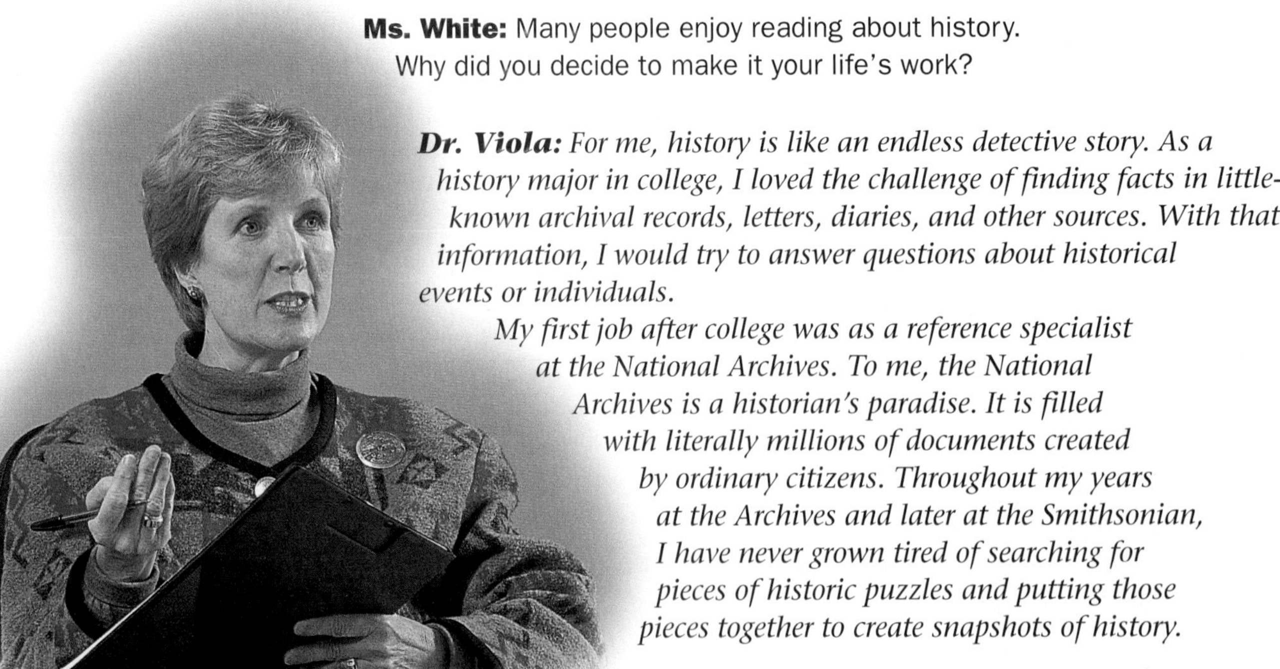

Dr. Viola: *For me, history is like an endless detective story. As a history major in college, I loved the challenge of finding facts in little-known archival records, letters, diaries, and other sources. With that information, I would try to answer questions about historical events or individuals.*

My first job after college was as a reference specialist at the National Archives. To me, the National Archives is a historian's paradise. It is filled with literally millions of documents created by ordinary citizens. Throughout my years at the Archives and later at the Smithsonian, I have never grown tired of searching for pieces of historic puzzles and putting those pieces together to create snapshots of history.

Ms. White: You've written many books and articles over the years. Why do you like to write?

Dr. Viola: *I have always liked to tell stories. Even before I finished my college training in history, I would tell history stories to anyone who wanted to listen. I learned that often people who said they hated history, like my Navy buddies, enjoyed listening to stories about the past.*

As I became a more seasoned historian, I knew that if I wanted to share my history stories with a wider range of people, I needed to write them down. So I started to write books based on the stories. One book just seemed to lead to another.

Ms. White: Writing a textbook for young adolescents seems very different from writing books for adults. Why did you decide to write *Why We Remember*?

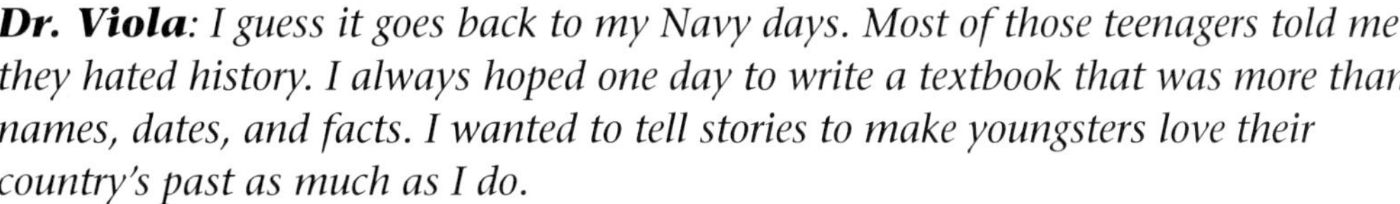

Dr. Viola*: I guess it goes back to my Navy days. Most of those teenagers told me they hated history. I always hoped one day to write a textbook that was more than names, dates, and facts. I wanted to tell stories to make youngsters love their country's past as much as I do.*

I decided I could employ some of the storytelling skills I use in trade book writing and in teaching to help solve the problem of uninspired history in textbooks. My goal in writing this text program has been to help students understand the intrigue and pleasure of history, as well as to help them learn the common core of knowledge that all Americans should know.

Ms. White: Some people contend that in our technological age learning history is not very important. Why do you think history is a meaningful study for young people?

Dr. Viola: *The best answer to that question is an inscription on a statue in front of the National Archives: "The Past is Prologue." For me, this epitomizes the reason every young person should leave school with a sense of the heritage that is his or hers as an American citizen. Without a grounding in the past—a knowledge of how we've gotten where we are—the next generations will not continue the legacy that our ancestors have passed along to us.*

Dr. Herman Viola

Ph.D. in American history, Indiana University
Nationally recognized authority on American Indians, the West, and the Civil War
Founder of the National Archives scholarly journal *Prologue*
Former Director of the National Anthropological Archives at the Smithsonian Institution
Curator of *Seeds of Change* and *Magnificent Voyager,* two highly acclaimed exhibitions at the Smithsonian Museum of Natural History
Author of more than 15 books and many articles on the history of the United States

Teaching the History You Want Students to Remember—

In Ways They'll Never Forget!

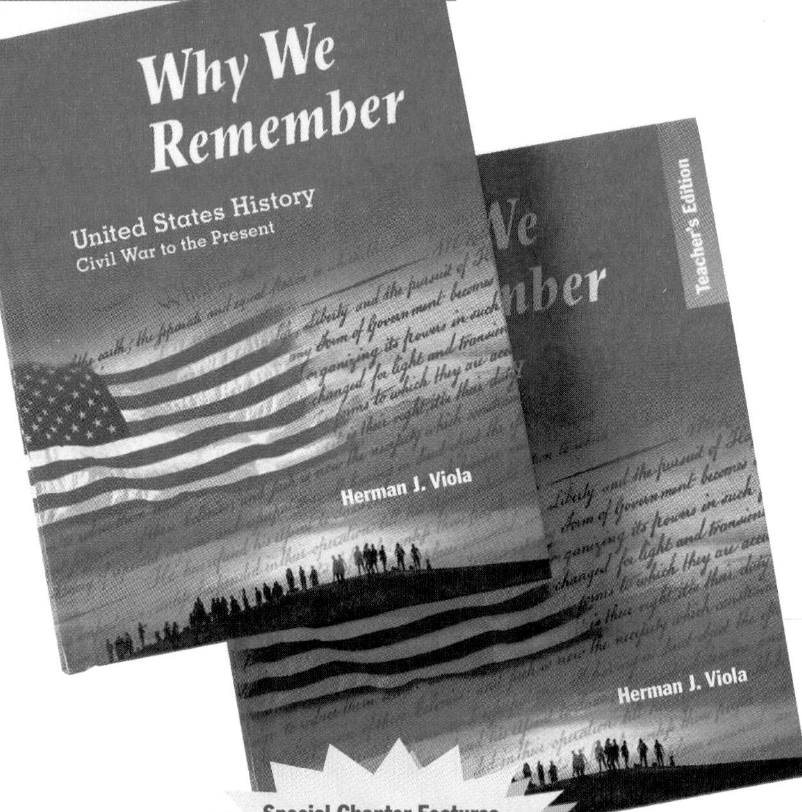

Student Text

Provides the young adolescent with a visual and conceptual road map for understanding and remembering our nation's past.

Teacher's Edition

Point-of-use information in a convenient format helps you bring new life to your history classroom.

Special Chapter Features

- 4-page *Citizenship Lab*
- 4-page literature excerpt, *American Readings*

Includes an 80-page review of history from North American beginnings to Civil War.

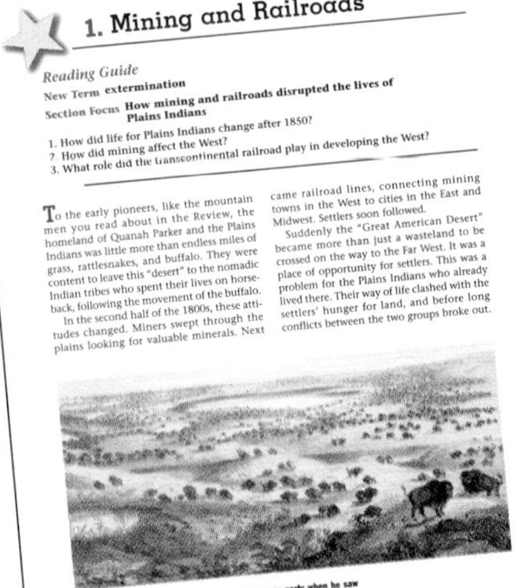

1. Mining and Railroads

Reading Guide

New Term extermination

Section Focus How mining and railroads disrupted the lives of Plains Indians

1. How did life for Plains Indians change after 1850?
2. How did mining affect the West?
3. What role did the transcontinental railroad play in developing the West?

To the early pioneers, like the mountain men you read about in the Review, the homeland of Quanah Parker and the Plains Indians was little more than endless miles of grass, rattlesnakes, and buffalo. They were content to leave this "desert" to the nomadic Indian tribes who spent their lives on horseback, following the movement of the buffalo.

In the second half of the 1800s, these attitudes changed. Miners swept through the plains looking for valuable minerals. Next came railroad lines, connecting mining towns in the West to cities in the East and Midwest. Settlers soon followed.

Suddenly the "Great American Desert" became more than just a wasteland to be crossed on the way to the Far West. It was a place of opportunity for settlers. This was a problem for the Plains Indians who already lived there. Their way of life clashed with the settlers' hunger for land, and before long conflicts between the two groups broke out.

John Mix Stanley was traveling with an army survey party when he saw this herd of bison. Such large herds had vanished by the 1880s.

224 • Chapter 4 1865–1900

Buffalo on the Plains

Before the settlers came, the Great Plains supported some 30 different Indian tribes. The region was also home to millions of bison, usually called "buffalo."

These large, shaggy creatures were the lifeblood of the Plains Indians. They provided the Indians with food, shelter, tools, ornaments, and even toys. When Plains Indians died they expected to go to a land teeming with buffalo. Some said the broad trail of stars across the sky that we call the Milky Way was dust raised by the hoofs of buffalo herds in the spirit world.

Government officials and Indian leaders met at Fort Laramie in 1851 and again in 1868, above, to try to bring peace to the plains.

The Fort Laramie Treaty

In the 1850s miners swarmed across the Great Plains on their way to the countless river valleys and mountains of the West. As they went they trespassed on Plains Indian land, trampling the buffalo range and killing the animals for food and sometimes just for sport. The Indians resented the miners and their disrespect for the Indian way of life. They began to wage war.

In an attempt to reduce conflict and protect the travelers, the government decided to strike a bargain with the Indians. In 1851 government officials met with between 8,000 and 12,000 Indians from 8 tribes at Fort Laramie, in what is now Wyoming. There the officials convinced the Indian representatives to sign the Treaty of Fort Laramie.

The treaty gave the government the right to build more roads and forts on the plains. It also defined geographical boundaries within which the Indian...

Western Mines

In the 1860s miners continued to cross the plains in full force, desperately hunting for gold. No spot was too hot, too dry, too cold, or too wet to discourage people hoping to strike it rich. Miners swarmed through the Rockies, the Sierra Nevada, and the Black Hills. They braved the scorching sands of Arizona and New Mexico as well as the frosty waters of Alaska.

The Comstock Lode One of the biggest finds was in Nevada in 1859. A group of miners had found a little gold on a hillside, but were frustrated...

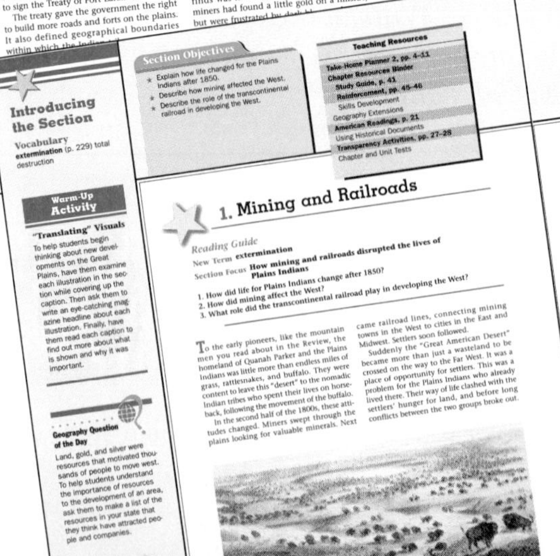

Teacher's Resource Package

Thoughtfully planned supplementary materials help ensure that students comprehend basic information *and* gain an in-depth understanding of history.

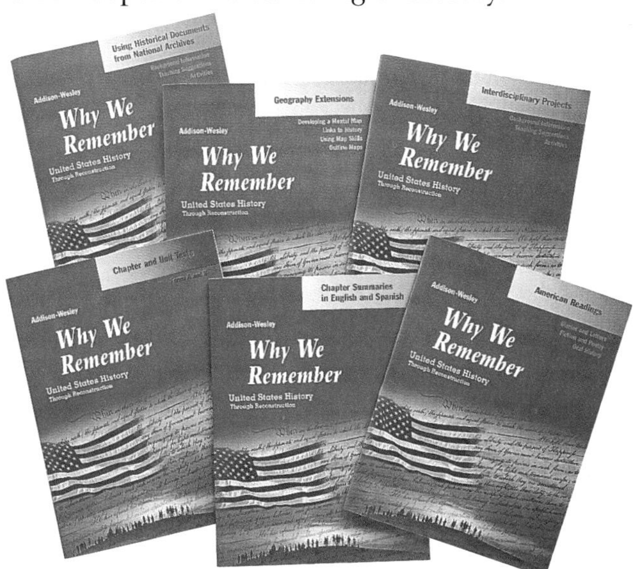

Take-Home Planner

For each chapter in a unit, an easy-to-carry guide previews content and teaching resources, describes options for in-class activities, and provides answers for grading.

Additional Resources

Special resources, designed specifically to be used with *Why We Remember,* are available for purchase.

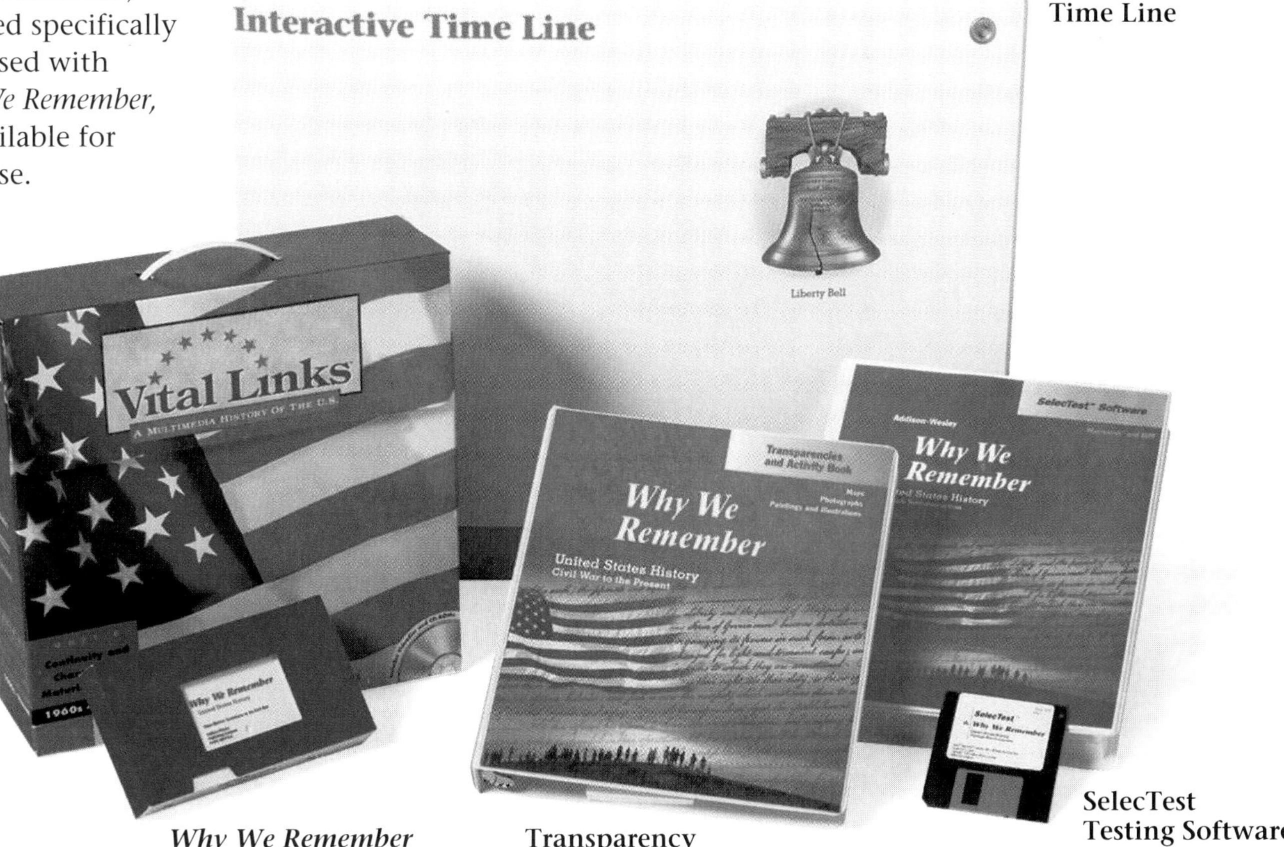

Wall Time Line

Vital Links™ Multimedia Program

***Why We Remember* Video Series**

Transparency Package

SelecTest Testing Software

Teaching Tools for Why We Remember

Chapter Planning Guide

The **Chapter Planning Guide** is your at-a-glance starting point for teaching each chapter of *Why We Remember.* The guide appears in both the Teacher's Edition and the Take-Home Planner. It highlights major teaching opportunities in the Student Text, Teacher's Edition, Teacher's Resource Package, and Take-Home Planner.

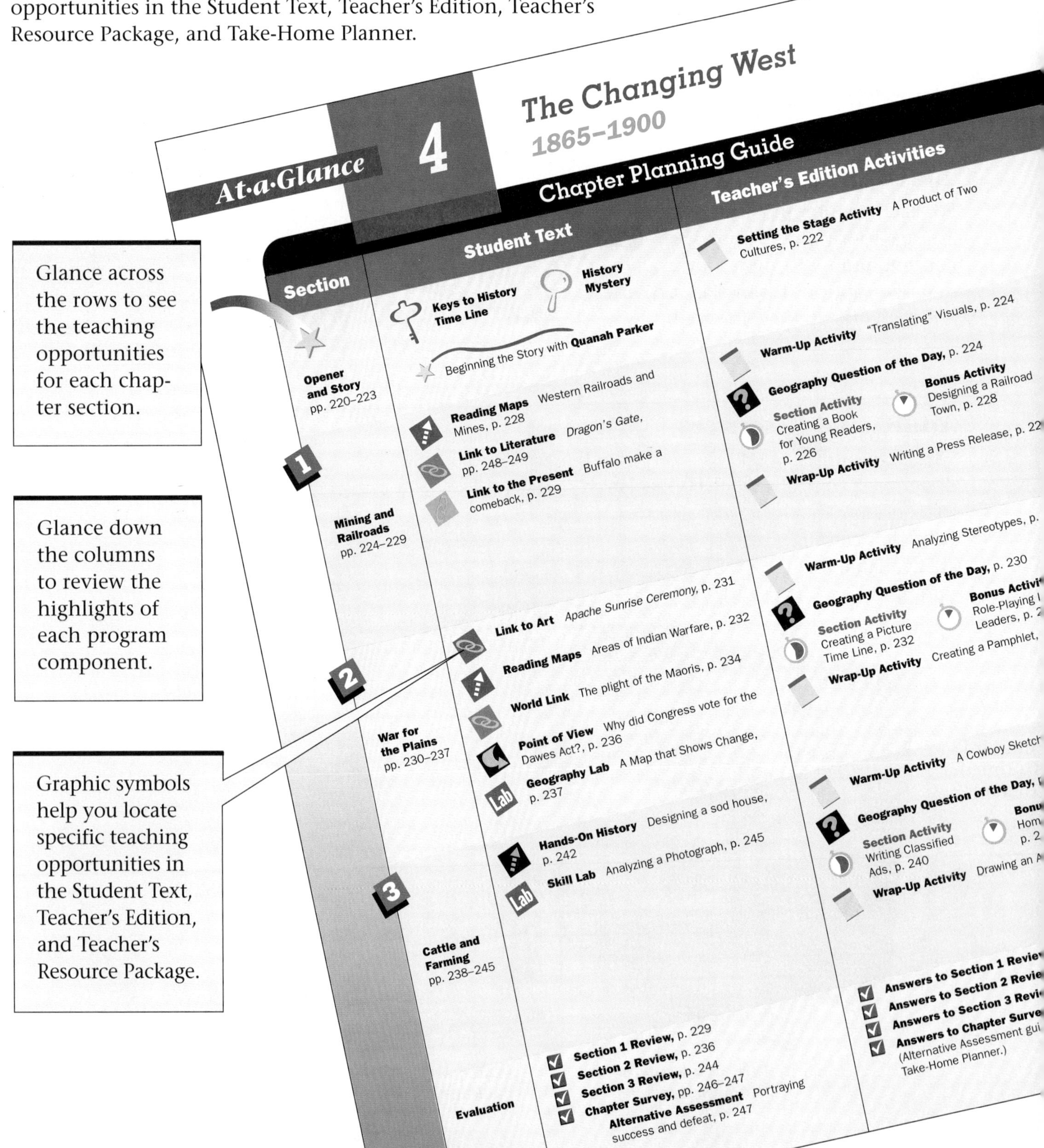

Glance across the rows to see the teaching opportunities for each chapter section.

Glance down the columns to review the highlights of each program component.

Graphic symbols help you locate specific teaching opportunities in the Student Text, Teacher's Edition, and Teacher's Resource Package.

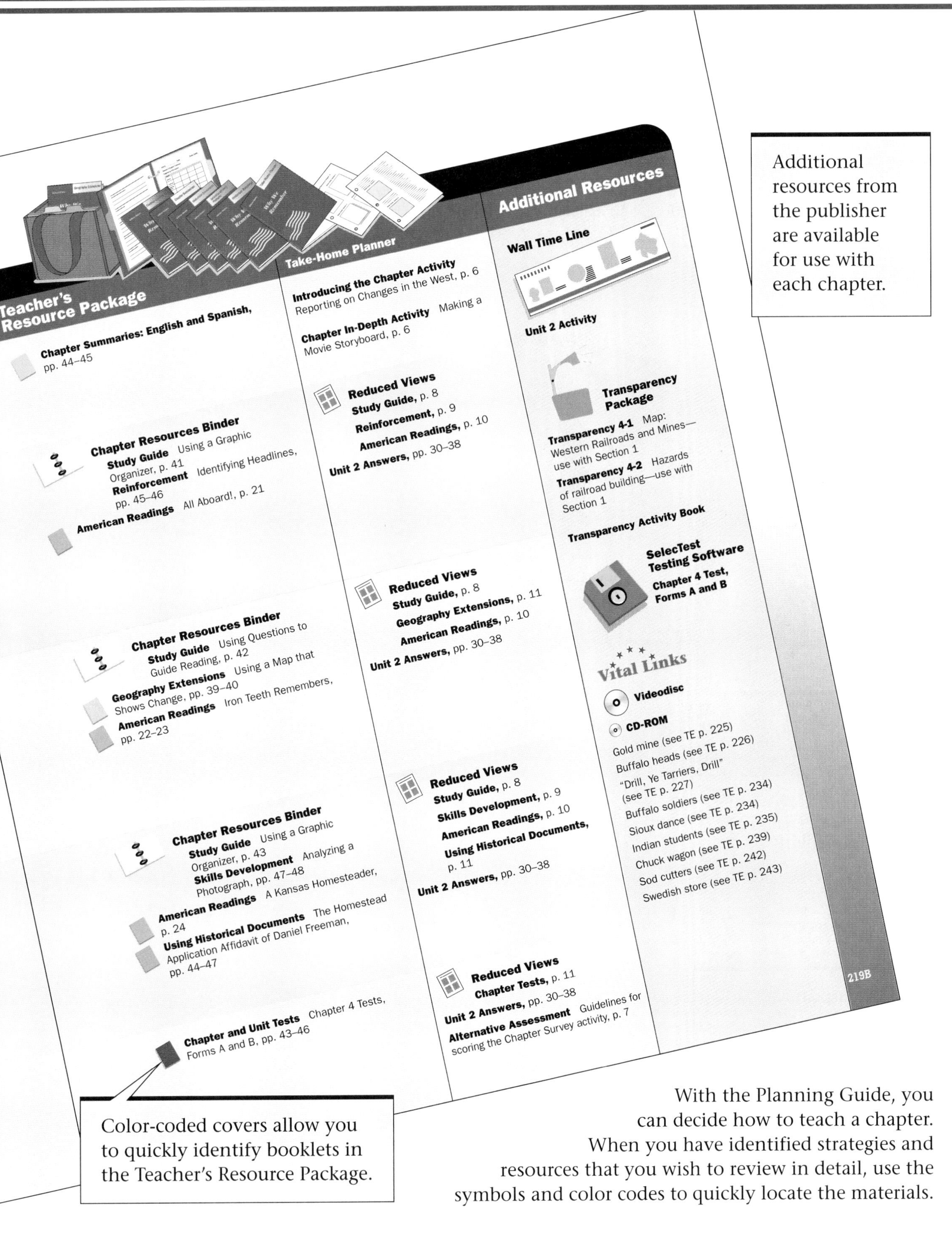

Additional resources from the publisher are available for use with each chapter.

Color-coded covers allow you to quickly identify booklets in the Teacher's Resource Package.

With the Planning Guide, you can decide how to teach a chapter. When you have identified strategies and resources that you wish to review in detail, use the symbols and color codes to quickly locate the materials.

Student Text

The student text of *Why We Remember* guides the young adolescent through history by identifying key people, events, and ideas—then connecting them to build a core of historical knowledge.

Each page organizes information conceptually and visually for maximum student retention.

State-of-the-art computer-generated maps enhance the chapter narrative while improving map-reading skills.

Frequent primary source excerpts are clearly identified with large quotation marks.

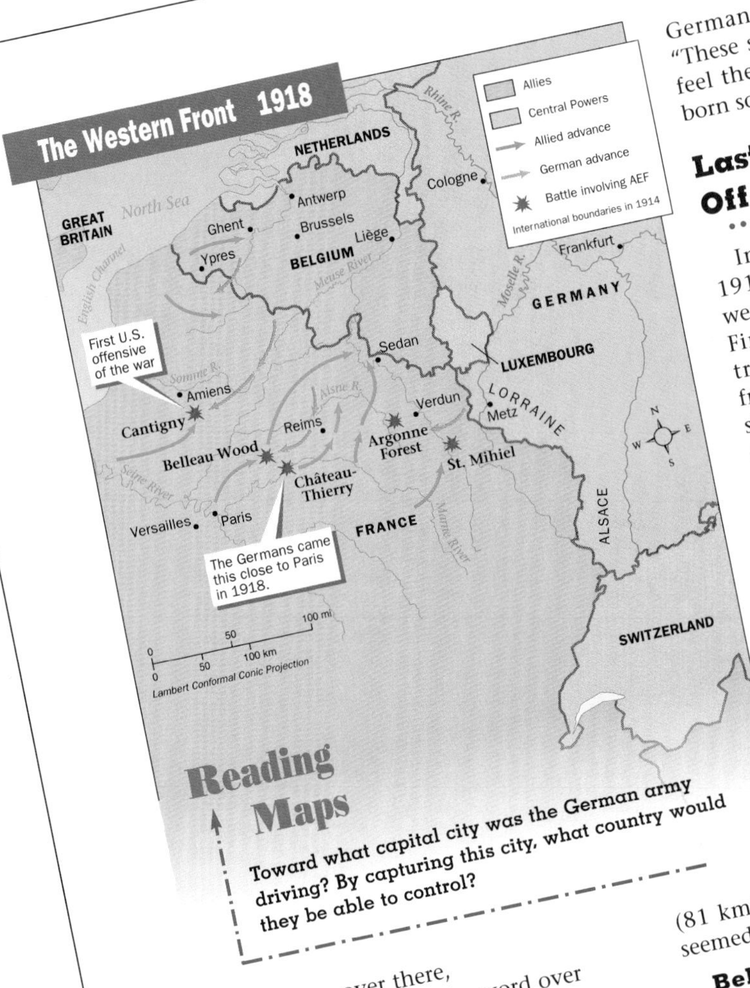

Reading Maps

Toward what capital city was the German army driving? By capturing this city, what country would they be able to control?

German officer marveled, "These semi-Americans . . . feel themselves to be true-born sons of their country."

Last German Offensive

In the winter of 1917–1918, the Central Powers were gaining an advantage. First they crushed Italian troops on the southern front. Then, in Russia, the short-lived democratic government fell to a wing of the Communist Party called the Bolsheviks, led by Vladimir Lenin. In 1918 the Bolsheviks signed a peace agreement with Germany and pulled out of the war.

With Russia out of th way, Germany could foc on the western front. In t spring of 1918 the Germa launched a massive ca paign to capture Paris the end of May, Ger troops were again a Marne River, only 50 (81 km) from Paris. The Allied situ seemed desperate.

Belleau Wood The Americans AEF arrived just in time. Frenchmen to fight drove thousands of doughbo front lines in trucks, taxicabs, and June 1 American troops had reache (bel-LŌ) Wood, a square mile between two hills.

For three weeks German and armies fought each other ove patch of blood-drenched soil become a symbol far beyond importance. The Americans we

"Over there, over there,
Send the word, send the word over there,
That the Yanks are coming, the Yanks are coming,
The drums rum-tumming ev'rywhere."

The extreme patriotism of the American soldiers puzzled the Germans. After all, many of the doughboys had not even been born in the United States. Indeed, the troops reflected the ethnic makeup of the United States. Their letters home were written in dozens of different languages. Yet, as a

Instructive pictures encourage valuable classroom discussion and learning.

(Right) Switchmen and signalmen run train traffic through a railroad yard in 1886. (Above) Dispatchers today control train traffic from huge video maps at computer centers.

Vocabulary words in bold type are easily recognized and are defined in context.

Railroad Competition

The railroad boom led to cutthroat competition. In the late 1870s, for example, there were 20 competing routes betweeen St. Louis and Atlanta.

Railroad companies that served the same area tried to drive one another out of business. Rate wars, in which competing railroads tried to charge less than their rivals, were common. The railroad that won a rate war then raised its rates to make up for lost revenue. Shippers had no choice but to pay the new rate.

Railroad companies also made secret deals with large shippers. They offered **rebates,** or refunds, of part of the shipping costs. In return, the shipper promised to use only that railroad.

Limiting competition To protect themselves from rate wars and rebate agreements, competing railroads sometimes combined to form "pools." The companies in a pool agreed to share freight business and fix prices at high levels. Pools did not always work, though. Members often broke agreements to make quick profits.

Another way to curb competition was by **consolidation.** In this method several companies were combined into one large company.

Cornelius Vanderbilt became a master at railroad consolidation. In the 1860s he began buying small railroad lines in New York. When the New York Central Railroad refused his offer, Vanderbilt stopped service between his lines and the Central. The loss of freight and passenger business forced the Central's directors to sell to Vanderbilt.

By 1873 Vanderbilt owned railroad lines that extended as far west as Chicago. Before his consolidation, passengers traveling from New York to Chicago had to change trains 17 times during a 50-hour trip. On Vanderbilt's lines, travel time was less than 24 hours.

A consolidated railroad could be run more efficiently and cheaply. With no competition, however, there was no reason to offer lower fares and shipping rates.

Regulating the Railroads

The main victims of cutthroat competition were the customers. Especially hard hit were

Bold headings create an outline of the chapter content.

Teaching Tools for Why We Remember

Take-Home Planner

A unique **Take-Home Planner** enables you to make teaching plans for each chapter in a unit and to grade students' work without carrying home the Teacher's Edition.

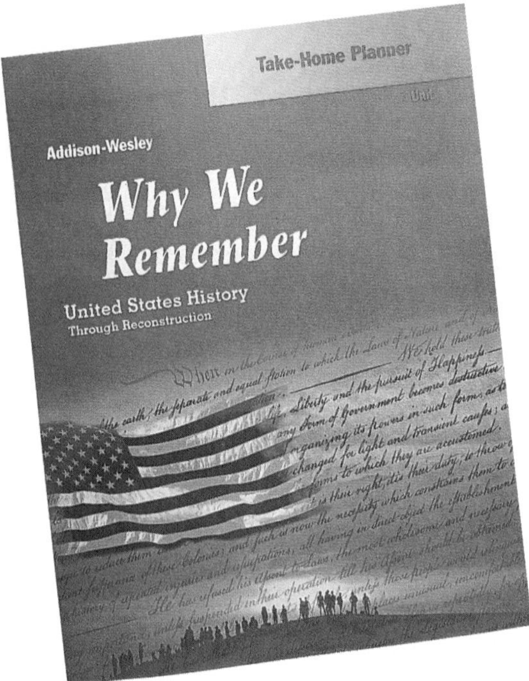

For each chapter, the Take-Home Planner provides

- a replica of the Chapter Planning Guide in the Teacher's Edition

Teaching Chapter 7

Chapter Overview

In the years after the Civil War, corruption reached into almost every level of government. Intense party competition, lax oversight during the Grant administration and those that followed, and the spoils system all contributed to corruption and misconduct. Public demand finally resulted in the passing of the Pendleton Act to create a competence-based civil service.

Beset by rising costs and falling incomes, farmers organized Farmers' Alliances and other groups to fight for their economic survival. Initial success led to the formation of the Populist Party on the national level. However, conflict over monetary and banking reform weakened the new party.

In cities and states Progressives gained power and worked to reform unresponsive governments, with help from muckraking journalists. In addition Progressives won reforms in areas such as worker protection, temperance, woman suffrage, and the rights of African Americans.

Progressive-influenced Presidents Roosevelt, Taft, and Wilson carried out reforms on the national level, in areas such as trust-busting, consumer protection, banking policy, and conservation.

Introducing the Chapter

Defining Reform Today
Students research present-day reformers and explain what reform means.
About 1 week

Tell students that in this chapter they will read about reformers, or people who tried to improve social, economic, and political conditions in the United States, for example, by helping the poor and fighting corruption in government. Reformers were creative in the many ways they worked to bring about change. One reformer, Lewis Hine, helped alert people to child labor problems by using photography. Women reformers, too, sometimes used unconventional methods to effect change, because traditional channels were blocked to them; they could not vote.

Ask students to list social problems today such as homelessness, hunger, crime, ineffective government, and so on. Write their suggestions on the chalkboard. Then ask them each to do research to find out about someone who is fighting these problems today. This present-day reformer may be someone in their family, in their community, or on the national or international scene; he or she may be well-known or unknown.

Have each student prepare a one-page report on a reformer, including information about the changes he or she hopes to bring about and the methods this reformer uses to create change. Put reports on a bulletin board for the class to review. Ask the class to discuss what the word "reform" means to them and to come up with a class definition.

Chapter In-Depth Activity

Getting the Message Across
Students orchestrate a campaign for Progressive reform.
2 class periods

Ask students to think about ways that people can make changes in the government and in business practices. (voting, petitions, protests, letters, laws, unions, boycotts) Tell students that in the late 1800s and early 1900s the Progressives relied on tactics like these to draw attention to their messages and

6 Unit 3 Planner • Chapter 7

© Addison-Wesley Publishing Company

- directions for
  - an introductory chapter activity
  - an in-depth chapter activity
  - scoring the chapter's alternative assessment

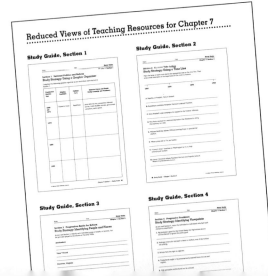

Reduced Views of Teaching Resources for Chapter 7

Study Guide, Section 1

Study Guide, Section 2

Study Guide, Section 3

Study Guide, Section 4

- reduced views of all activity sheets and tests for the chapter
- answers to all activity sheets and tests for the chapter

Teacher's Edition

The wraparound Teacher's Edition is designed for classroom use. Side columns provide instructional suggestions to guide daily teaching. Top margins provide organizational and background information, as well as suggestions for meeting special student needs.

Notes suggest appropriate times to use supplemental resources.

Tips for Teaching

Gifted Students

Ask musically gifted students to learn some immigrant songs in folk singer Jerry Silverman's *Immigrant Songbook* (Mel Bay Publications, 1992) and perform them. This book contains songs from more than 50 countries. Guitar chords, original-language lyrics, and English translations are included.

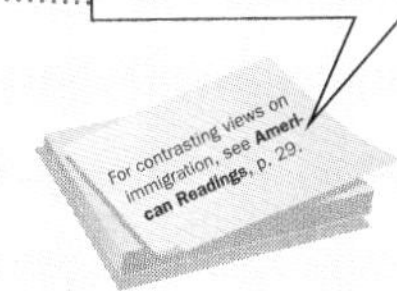
For contrasting views on immigration, see American Readings, p. 29.

Discussion

Checking Understanding

1. What were some of the hardships immigrants faced? (Crowded living quarters often shared with other families, poor pay, long working hours, discrimination.)

Stimulating Critical Thinking

2. Why do you think some immigrants regretted their decision to come to the United States? Explain. (Some possible reasons: discrimination, poor living and working conditions, difficult to understand the language, far from home and family.)

3. Do you think nativism still exists today? Explain with specific examples. (Answers will vary but should reflect current issues such as proposals to limit immigration from Latin American countries and to restrict immigrants' access to services.)

Vital Links

"My Little Son" (Song) Unit 4, Side 2, Search 18823, Play to 21162

See also Unit 4 Explore CD-ROM location 261.

Some cities became identified with certain nationalities. Milwaukee was known as a largely German city, Minneapolis a Scandinavian city, and Boston an Irish and Italian one. The South, with fewer cities and jobs, did not attract many immigrants.

Hardships and fears Bright dreams brought immigrants across the ocean. The reality they found was often far different. They crowded into tiny apartments, often with several other families, and worked long hours to earn barely enough to live on.

Meanwhile, they saw their children beginning to speak English and adopt American customs. Some parents encouraged their children to **assimilate**, which means to be absorbed into the main cultural group. Others, especially roundtrippers who planned to return to their homelands, feared losing their children to the new land.

The Nativist Reaction

The question of assimilating immigrants into American society worried many native-born Americans, too. Overwhelmed by the huge numbers of newcomers, they felt threatened by the different languages and religions. Sometimes they found themselves competing with immigrants for jobs and opportunities. The result was friction and a rebirth of nativism—hatred of immigrants, mostly the Irish and the Germans.

Irish looking for work were faced with signs that read "No Irish need apply." Jews, barred from renting in many neighborhoods, realized that anti-Semitism existed in the United States, too. Urged by nativists, Congress placed restrictions on immigration. For example, workers whose passage across the ocean was paid by American companies could not enter the country.

...n lived in Hawaii, where the labor of many ...ake sugar "king."

Engaging, motivational activities are easy to identify.

Helpful background information and teaching tips are provided.

Bonus Activity

Enlistment Posters

To help students understand why northerners and southerners were willing to fight in the war, have pairs create enlistment posters. Assign half the pairs to imagine they are recruiters for the Union army, and the other half that they are Confederate recruiters. They should focus on emotional appeals, using persuasive language and eye-catching images. Conclude by comparing persuasive techniques in the posters.

History Footnote

Several women served as spies in the war. Harriet Tubman knew many secret routes on the Underground Railroad, and she recruited other former slaves to find Confederate camps and report them to Union officers. She and the others were able to give information about the location of Confederate explosives to Colonel James Montgomery in South Carolina during a Union gunboat raid in 1863.

Another Union spy, Elizabeth Van Lew, lived in a mansion in Richmond. She provided hiding places in her home for Union soldiers who had escaped from Confederate prisons.

Rose O'Neal Greenhow was a society hostess in Washington, D.C., who spied for the South. She learned of the Union's planned attack on Manassas in 1861 and sent coded information to General Beauregard, who won an important victory at Manassas.

Link to Art

Sounding Reveille (1865) Almost every family North and South had someone in uniform. People at home were desperate for news of their loved ones. "Special artists" helped satisfy that demand. Hired by illustrated newspapers, special artists went to battlefields and camps to sketch what they saw. The most gifted of these artists was Winslow Homer, who worked for *Harper's Weekly* newspaper. In this painting of a Union camp by Homer, a bugler and two drummers sound reveille, a signal to wake the soldiers each morning. **Discuss** In what ways does this painting show the everyday life of soldiers?

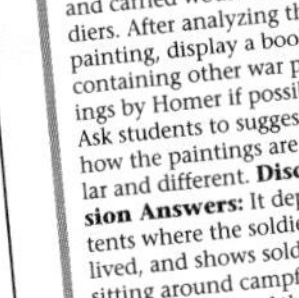

Teaching the Link to Art

Point out that drummers not only awakened soldiers and called them to meals but also communicated orders on smoke-filled battlefields. Drummers often became the target of enemy fire because of their importance in the field. They also cooked, cared for horses, and carried wounded soldiers. After analyzing this painting, display a book containing other war paintings by Homer if possible. Ask students to suggest how the paintings are similar and different. **Discussion Answers:** It depicts tents where the soldiers lived, and shows soldiers sitting around campfires and taking care of their equipment.

Although the Union and the Confederacy had rules banning boys from enlisting, many managed to join. Historians estimate that between 10 and 20 percent of all soldiers—250,000 to 420,000—were 16 years old or younger. John Mather Sloan of the 9th Texas was only 13 when he lost a leg in battle. He claimed his only regret was that "I shall not soon be able to ... at the enemy."

Women soldiers Hundreds of women, too, fought for the cause. Their exact number will never be known, for they had to change their names and disguise themselves as men. Rosetta Wakeman, who joined the 153d Regiment New York State Volunteers, called herself "Lyons Wakeman" and wore men's clothing. Some women even wore fake mustaches or charcoal "whiskers."

146

Symbols link teaching ideas to special Student Text features.

Teaching Resources

- Take-Home Planner 1, pp. 4–11
- Chapter Resources Binder
  - Study Guide, p. 17
  - Reinforcement, pp. 21–22
  - Skills Development
- Geography Extensions
- American Readings
- Using Historical Documents, pp. 27–31
- Transparency Activities
- Chapter and Unit Tests

Menus at the beginning of each section highlight appropriate resources.

Teacher's Resource Package

The Teacher's Resource Package has two kinds of resources—basic chapter teaching activities to ensure student comprehension, and fresh, innovative, in-depth activities to motivate and engage your students.

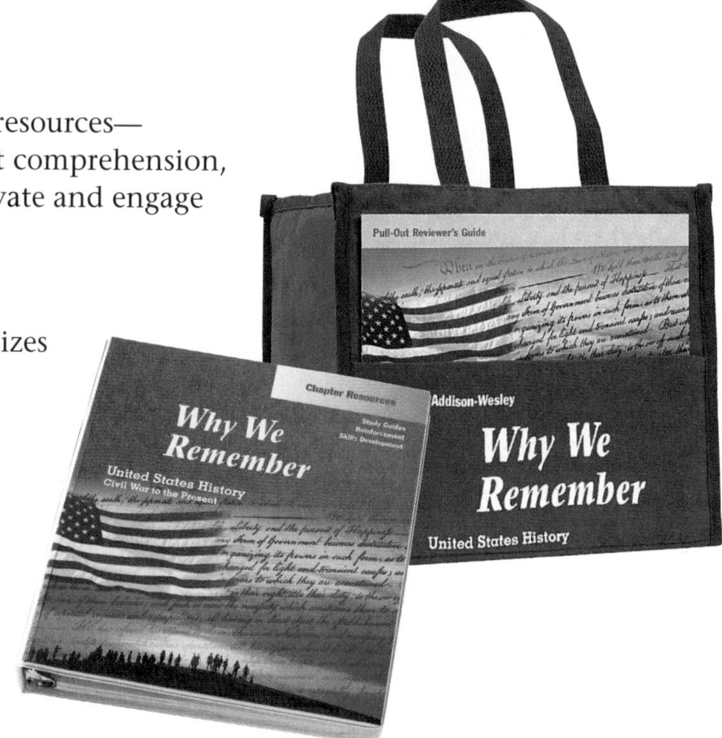

A **Chapter Resources Binder** conveniently organizes three basic resources by chapter:

- Study Guides
- Reinforcement Activities
- Skills Development Activities and Teaching Transparencies

Six separate booklets provide in-depth options for extending and assessing student learning

- Geography Extensions
- American Readings
- Using Historical Documents from National Archives
- Interdisciplinary Projects
- Chapter Summaries in English and Spanish
- Chapter and Unit Tests

Customize your own instructional notebook by removing activities from the in-depth booklets and inserting them into the Chapter Resources Binder.

Additional Resources

Available for purchase are five special resources specifically designed to add more instructional depth and student interest as you teach *Why We Remember.*

Wall Time Line

A 12-foot-long, laminated, foldable time line enables your students to create their own class time line of United States history. An activities guide suggests many creative ideas for continual use of the time line.

Transparency Package

Color transparencies, two for each chapter, help illustrate your lectures and stimulate discussion. The activities book contains suggestions for using transparencies to extend content.

SelecTest Testing Software

This computerized testing system (Macintosh and IBM) allows you to customize your own tests. The test file book contains a printed version of all test questions.

Vital Links Multimedia Program

See page T26 for information on this multimedia United States history program.

Why We Remember Video Series

Videotapes, one per unit, provide a motivational way to introduce each unit's content by engaging students in the story of one person from the time period. Videos can also be used for review and assessment.

Teaching the keys to history . . .

Teachers tell us . . .

"We want a U.S. history program that helps students to learn about important people, events, and ideas—the core history of our nation—and to understand their significance today."

Why We Remember responds . . .

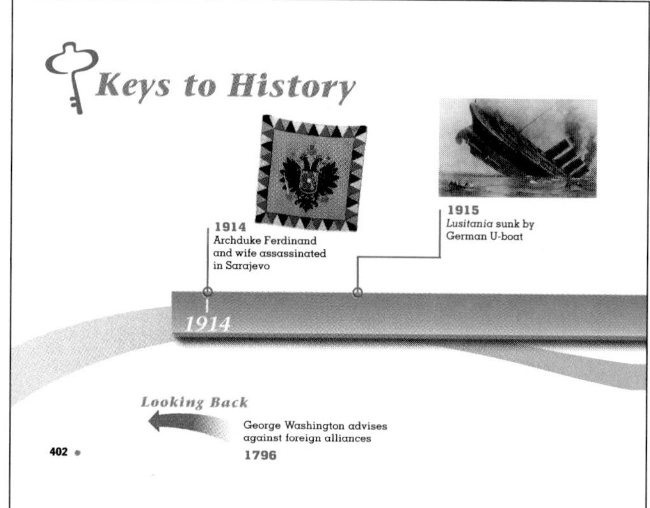

Keys to History

1914
Archduke Ferdinand and wife assassinated in Sarajevo

1915
Lusitania sunk by German U-boat

1914

Looking Back

George Washington advises against foreign alliances
1796

402 •

The **Student Text** provides a conceptual and visual road map that helps students identify and remember the key facts in understanding our nation's past.

Every entry in the **chapter time line** is a carefully chosen Key to History.

Teacher's Edition time line notes help you reinforce key learning.

As students read the chapter, they see the keys highlighted in **bold headings,** with their importance emphasized in the text.

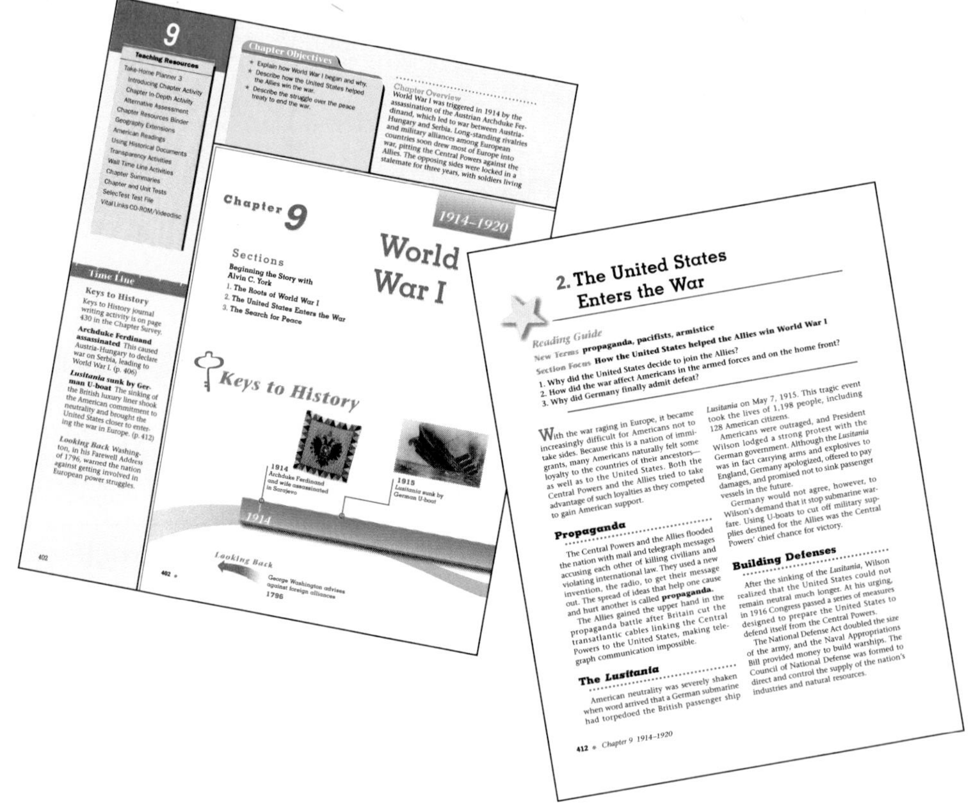

9

Teaching Resources

Take-Home Planner 3
Introducing Chapter Activity
Chapter In-Depth Activity
Alternative Assessment
Chapter Resources Binder
Geography Extensions
American Readings
Using Historical Documents
Transparency Activities
Wall Time Line Activities
Chapter Summaries
Chapter and Unit Tests
SelecTest Test File
Vital Links CD-ROM/Videodisc

Chapter Objectives

- Explain how World War I began and why.
- Describe how the United States helped the Allies win the war.
- Describe the struggle over the peace treaty to end the war.

Chapter Overview

World War I was triggered in 1914 by the assassination of the Austrian Archduke Ferdinand, which led to war between Austria-Hungary and Serbia. Long-standing rivalries and military alliances among European countries soon drew most of Europe into war, pitting the Central Powers against the Allies. The opposing sides were locked in a stalemate for three years, with soldiers living

Time Line

Keys to History

Keys to History journal writing activity is on page 430 in the Chapter Survey.

Archduke Ferdinand assassinated This caused Austria-Hungary to declare war on Serbia, leading to World War I. (p. 406)

***Lusitania* sunk by German U-boat** The sinking of the British luxury liner shook the American commitment to neutrality and brought the United States closer to entering the war in Europe. (p. 412)

Looking Back Washington, in his Farewell Address of 1796, warned the nation against getting involved in European power struggles.

402

Chapter 9

1914–1920

World War I

Sections

Beginning the Story with Alvin C. York
1. **The Roots of World War I**
2. **The United States Enters the War**
3. **The Search for Peace**

Keys to History

1914
Archduke Ferdinand and wife assassinated in Sarajevo

1915
Lusitania sunk by German U-boat

1914

Looking Back

George Washington advises against foreign alliances
1796

402 •

2. The United States Enters the War

Reading Guide

New Terms **propaganda, pacifists, armistice**

Section Focus **How the United States helped the Allies win World War I**

1. **Why did the United States decide to join the Allies?**
2. **How did the war affect Americans in the armed forces and on the home front?**
3. **Why did Germany finally admit defeat?**

With the war raging in Europe, it became increasingly difficult for Americans not to take sides. Because this is a nation of immigrants, many Americans naturally felt some loyalty to the countries of their ancestors—as well as to the United States. Both the Central Powers and the Allies tried to take advantage of such loyalties as they competed to gain American support.

Propaganda

The Central Powers and the Allies flooded the nation with mail and telegraph messages accusing each other of killing civilians and violating international law. They used a new invention, the radio, to get their message out. The spread of ideas that help one cause and hurt another is called **propaganda.**

The Allies gained the upper hand in the propaganda battle after Britain cut the transatlantic cables linking the Central Powers to the United States, making telegraph communication impossible.

The *Lusitania*

American neutrality was severely shaken when word arrived that a German submarine had torpedoed the British passenger ship *Lusitania* on May 7, 1915. This tragic event took the lives of 1,198 people, including 128 American citizens.

Americans were outraged, and President Wilson lodged a strong protest with the German government. Although the *Lusitania* was in fact carrying arms and explosives to England, Germany apologized, offered to pay damages, and promised not to sink passenger vessels in the future.

Germany would not agree, however, to Wilson's demand that it stop submarine warfare. Using U-boats to cut off military supplies destined for the Allies was the Central Powers' chief chance for victory.

Building Defenses

After the sinking of the *Lusitania*, Wilson realized that the United States could not remain neutral much longer. At his urging, in 1916 Congress passed a series of measures designed to prepare the United States to defend itself from the Central Powers.

The National Defense Act doubled the size of the army, and the Naval Appropriations Bill provided money to build warships. The Council of National Defense was formed to direct and control the supply of the nation's industries and natural resources.

412 • *Chapter 9 1914–1920*

Defeat of the Treaty

Twice an amended version of the Versailles Treaty came to a vote in the Senate. Both times Wilson refused to compromise. From his sickbed he instructed Senate Democrats to vote against it. If President Wilson had been willing to compromise, the Senate might have approved the treaty. Instead, in late November of 1919 the United States concluded a treaty of its own with the Central Powers.

Wilson in 1919

Meanwhile in Geneva, Switzerland, the League of Nations began its peace-keeping efforts. Without American membership, however, it had little hope of success.

3. Section Review

1. Define **self-determination** and **reparations.**
2. What influence did Wilson's Fourteen Points have on the Treaty of Versailles?
3. Why did the United States Senate refuse to ratify the treaty?
4. **Critical Thinking** Do you think that Wilson should have compromised with the Senate on the Treaty of Versailles? Why or why not?

Why We Remember

World War I

We remember World War I because it marked a sort of "coming of age" for Americans. When the United States declared war in 1917, Americans became involved in their first major overseas conflict. They took this step reluctantly but for the most honorable of reasons. President Wilson stated the nation's purpose in his address to Congress calling for war:

"The world must be made safe for democracy. Its peace must be founded upon the trusted foundations of political liberty."

World War I taught Americans that being peacemakers is never easy, especially when war inflames old hatreds and creates new ones. It also revealed that not everyone shares our reverence for democracy and freedom. There was another lesson as well. World War I reminded us once more that our strength as a nation rests on the willingness of ordinary people like Alvin York to do extraordinary things in defense of our ideals. As the *New York Times* wrote at the time of York's death in 1964, "One likes to think that the United States was built and protected by such . . . simple and pure men."

424 • *Chapter 9 1914–1920*

Each chapter ends with a **"Why We Remember" conclusion** explaining the significance of the time period for Americans today.

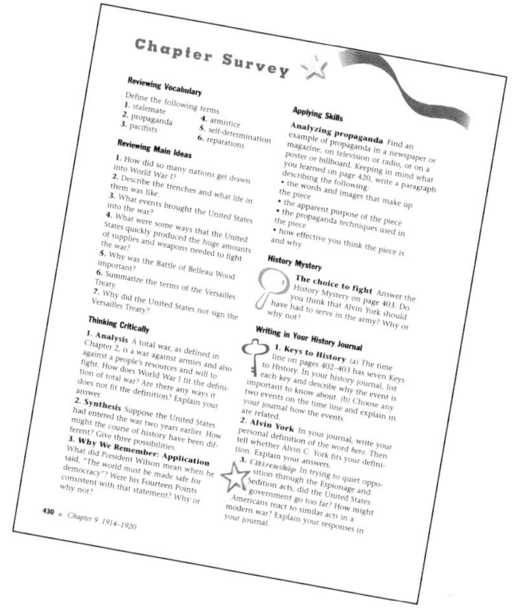

Chapter Survey

Reviewing Vocabulary

Define the following terms.

1. stalemate
2. propaganda
3. pacifists
4. armistice
5. self-determination
6. reparations

Reviewing Main Ideas

1. How did so many nations get drawn into World War I?
2. Describe the trenches and what life in them was like.
3. What events brought the United States into the war?
4. What were some ways that the United States quickly produced the huge amounts of supplies and weapons needed to fight the war?
5. Why was the Battle of Belleau Wood important?
6. Summarize the terms of the Versailles Treaty.
7. Why did the United States not sign the Versailles Treaty?

Thinking Critically

1. **Analysis** A total war, as defined in Chapter 2, is a war against armies and also against a people's resources and will to fight. How does World War I fit the definition of total war? Are there any ways it does not fit the definition? Explain your answer.
2. **Synthesis** Suppose the United States had entered the war two years earlier. How might the course of history have been different? Give three possibilities.
3. **Why We Remember: Application** What did President Wilson mean when he said, "The world must be made safe for democracy"? Were his Fourteen Points consistent with that statement? Why or why not?

Applying Skills

Analyzing propaganda Find an example of propaganda in a newspaper or magazine, on television or radio, or on a poster or billboard. Keeping in mind what you learned on page 420, write a paragraph describing the following:

- the words and images that make up the piece
- the apparent purpose of the piece
- the propaganda techniques used in the piece
- how effective you think the piece is and why

History Mystery

The choice to fight Answer the History Mystery on page 403. Do you think that Alvin York should have had to serve in the army? Why or why not?

Writing in Your History Journal

1. **Keys to History** (a) The time line on pages 402–403 has seven Keys to History. In your history journal, list each key and describe why the event is important to know about. (b) Choose any two events on the time line and explain in your journal how the events are related.
2. **Alvin York** In your journal, write your personal definition of the word *hero*. Then tell whether Alvin C. York fits your definition. Explain your answers.
3. *Citizenship* In trying to quiet opposition through the Espionage and Sedition acts, did the United States government go too far? How might Americans react to similar acts in a modern war? Explain your responses in your journal.

430 • *Chapter 9 1914–1920*

In a **journal writing activity** in the **Chapter Survey,** students describe in their own words the importance of the chapter's Keys to History.

The **Chapter Resources Binder** provides

- **Study Guides** that teach students a variety of study skills as they learn key information.
- **Reinforcement** activities that give students additional help in understanding and remembering key information.

The **Chapter Summaries** supplement offers

- a one-page summary of each chapter
- Summaries in Spanish as well as English

Chapter Tests assess student recall and comprehension of key information.

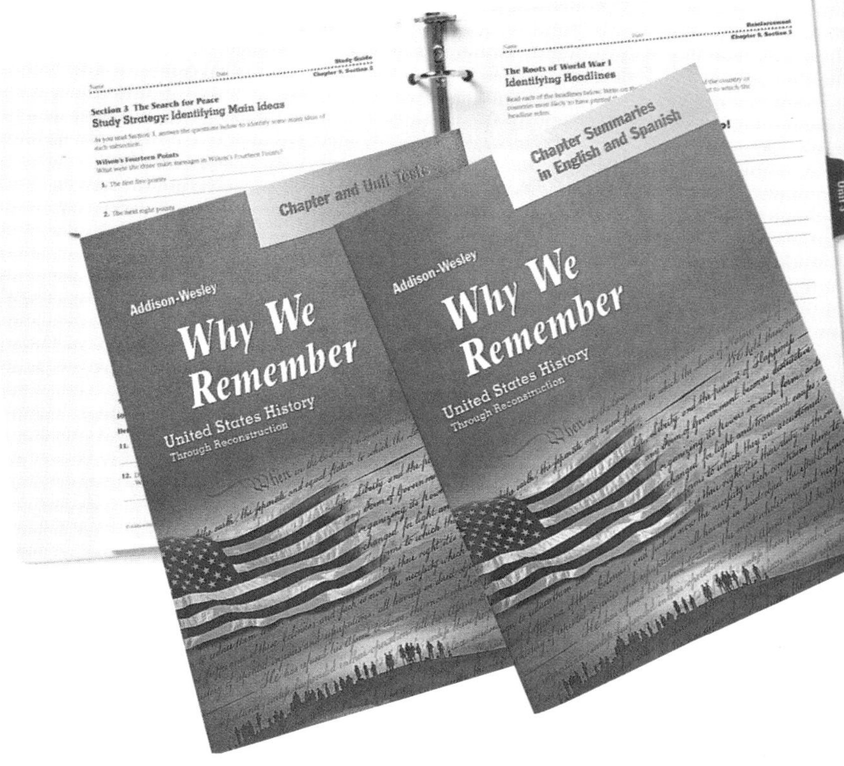

. . . the first step to historical literacy.

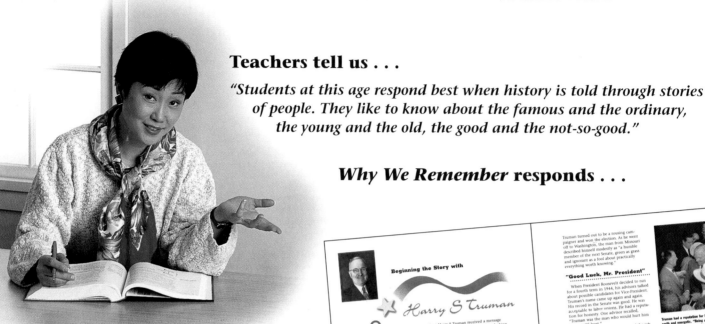

Teaching a history of people . . .

Teachers tell us . . .

"Students at this age respond best when history is told through stories of people. They like to know about the famous and the ordinary, the young and the old, the good and the not-so-good."

***Why We Remember* responds . . .**

In the **Student Text**, each chapter begins with an **introductory story** about a real person from the time period.

- The story tells a dramatic incident from the person's life.
- It focuses on an important decision the person had to make, often when he or she was an adolescent.
- The person reappears throughout the chapter and in the conclusion, putting a human face on historical events.

History Footnotes in the **Teacher's Edition** provide background information to help you personalize history. **Thinking Historically** questions help students put themselves in the place of people of the past.

Each chapter includes a **Point of View** feature, which helps students see that people have held differing opinions throughout our history.

- Focuses on issues of significance
- Incorporated into the ongoing text, so that students will not skip it

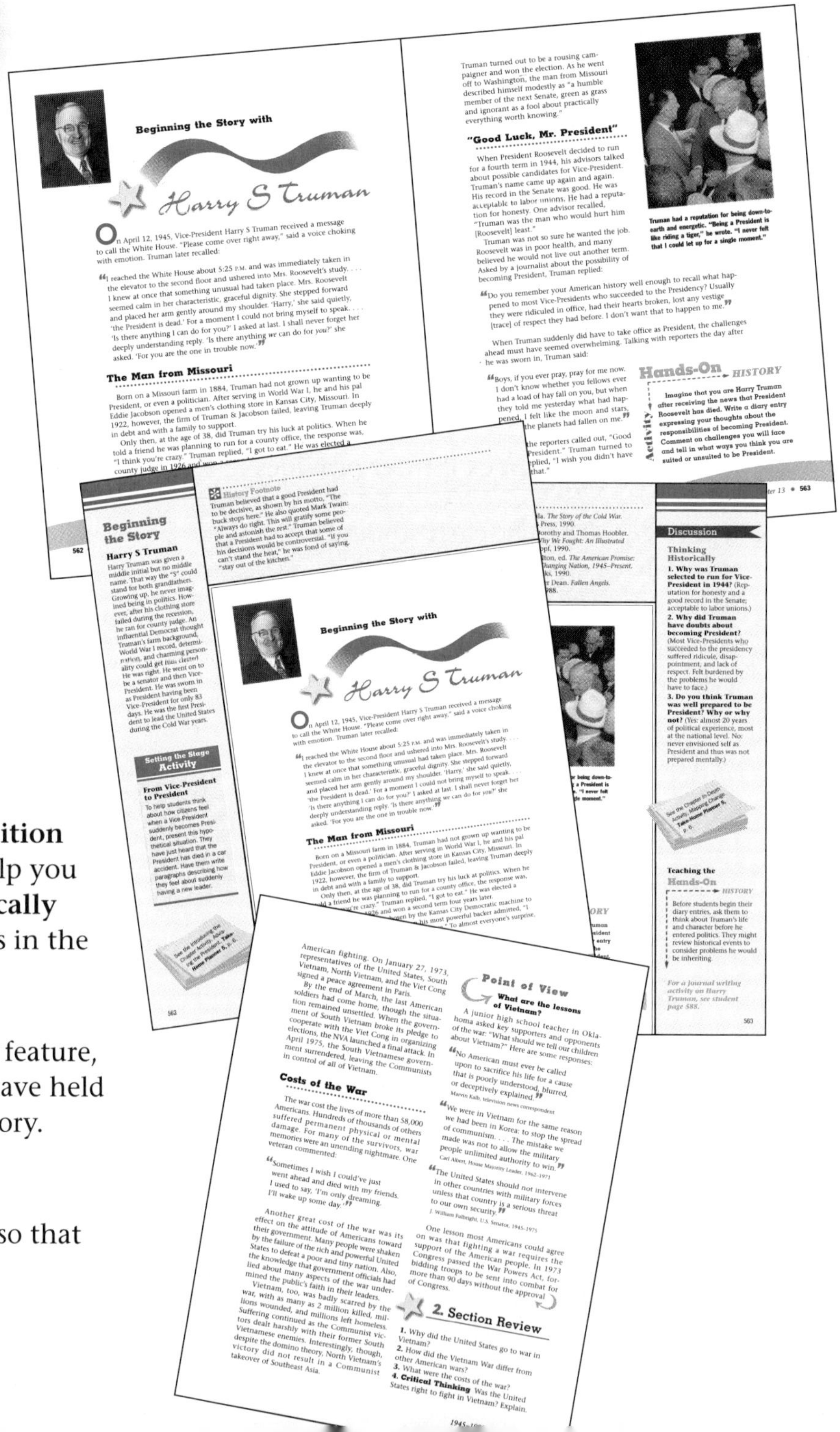

Scores of American voices are heard in the numerous **primary sources** woven throughout the narrative.

- Primary-source excerpts drawn from a wide range of historic figures
- Each chapter includes a 4-page literature excerpt, *American Readings.*

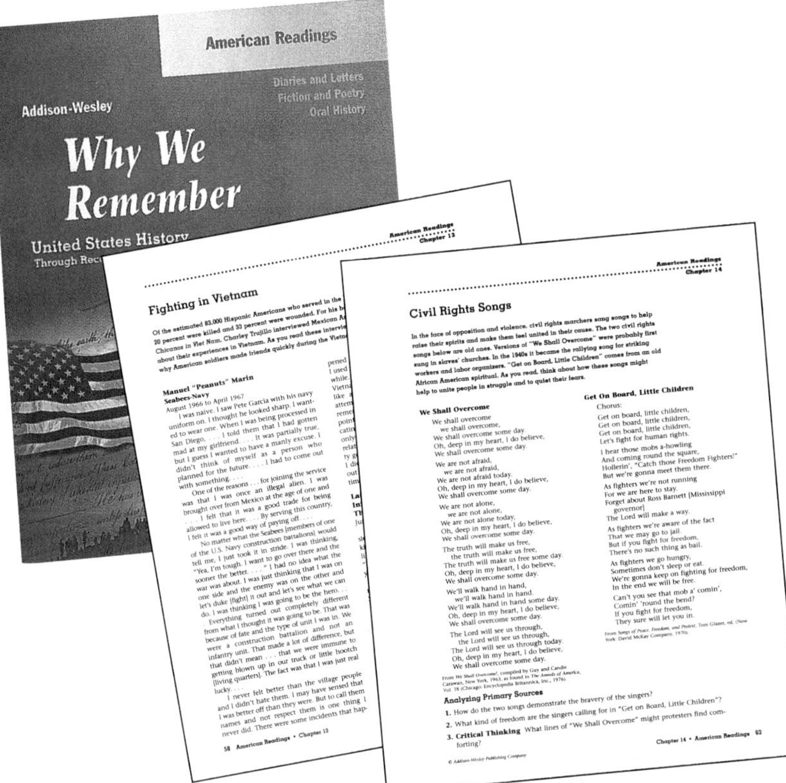

For every chapter, the **American Readings** supplement offers two or more opportunities for students to read firsthand what Americans have written about our past.

- Journal and diary entries and letters
- Excerpts from historical fiction and poetry
- Oral history

A unique ***Why We Remember*** **Video Series** offers a 10- to 12-minute video for each unit. Videos can be used to preview the unit content and to engage students by introducing them to a person from the time period.

- Each video tells a story of the time period through the eyes of a person from the era.
- Videos dramatize key events that students will read about as they study the unit.
- A video guide suggests strategies for using the videos for learning and motivation.

. . . that enables students to trace their American heritage.

Getting students involved . . .

Teachers tell us . . .

"We want students to like history—to see history as interesting, intriguing, and fun. We want to turn students on to history."

Why We Remember responds . . .

In the **Student Text**, each chapter begins with a **History Mystery**, which students can solve only by reading the chapter.

Hands-On History activities, two in each chapter, engage students in "doing history."

- Stimulate students' imaginations about the past.
  - Link past events with the present.
    - Encourage students to take responsibility for their own learning.

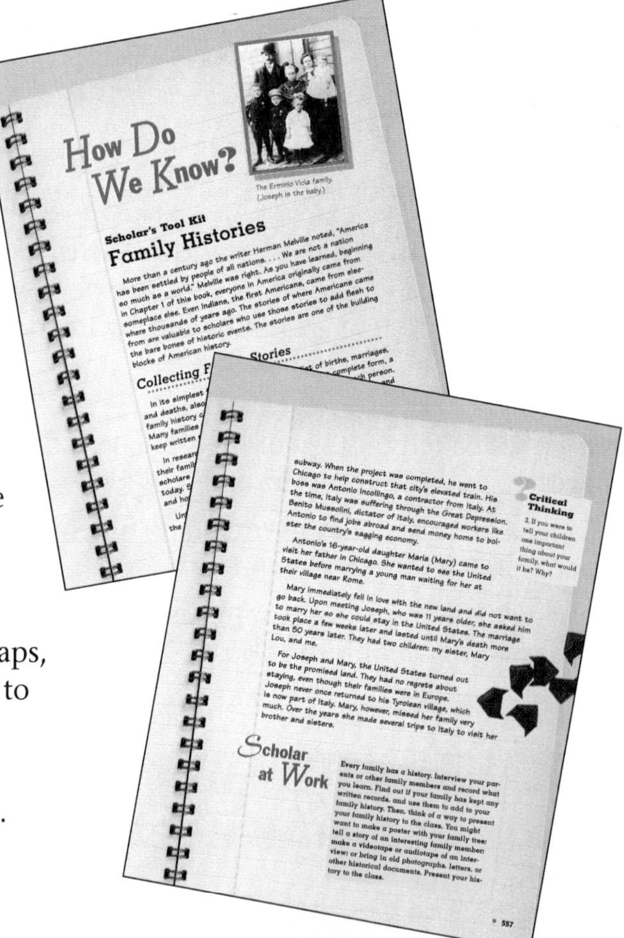

How Do We Know? Scholar's Tool Kits are a unique feature designed to help students learn about the "tools" historians use to understand history.

- Stories describe how historians use archaeology, maps, public records, pictures, oral history, and memoirs to learn about and interpret history.
- **Scholar at Work** activities let students become historians by practicing the use of historians' tools.

The **Teacher's Edition** helps you involve students in their learning.

- **Discussion questions** enable you to monitor student comprehension and stimulate critical thinking.
- A **Section Activity** and a **Bonus Activity** for each section give you the option of a full-period or a short activity each teaching day.
- Activities are innovative, practical, and engaging.
- Options allow you flexibility in meeting student needs as well as time constraints.

In the **Take-Home Planner** you will find two important activity options.

- An **Introducing the Chapter Activity** motivates students to dig into the upcoming chapter.
- A **Chapter In-Depth Activity** enables students to study a significant topic from the chapter in greater detail.

The **Teacher's Resource Package** offers even more resources for getting students involved.

- For example, **Using Historical Documents from National Archives** lets students analyze reproductions of actual documents from national archives in Washington, D.C.

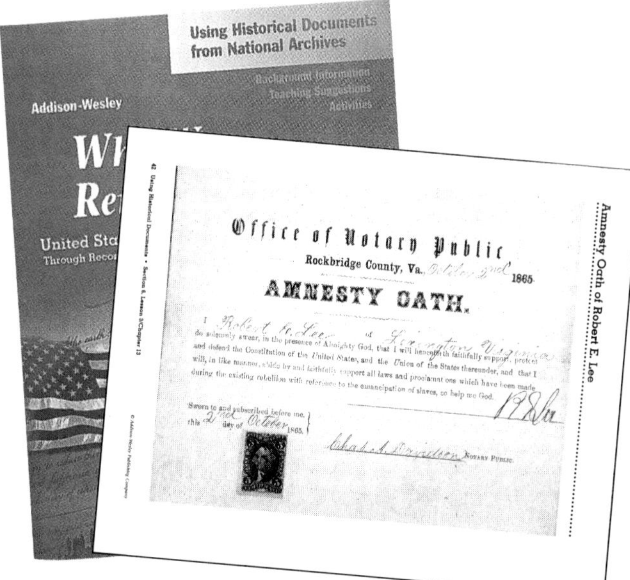

. . . in discovering the excitement and mystery of history!

Building geography knowledge . . .

Teachers tell us . . .

"Students this age need geography instruction combined with history."

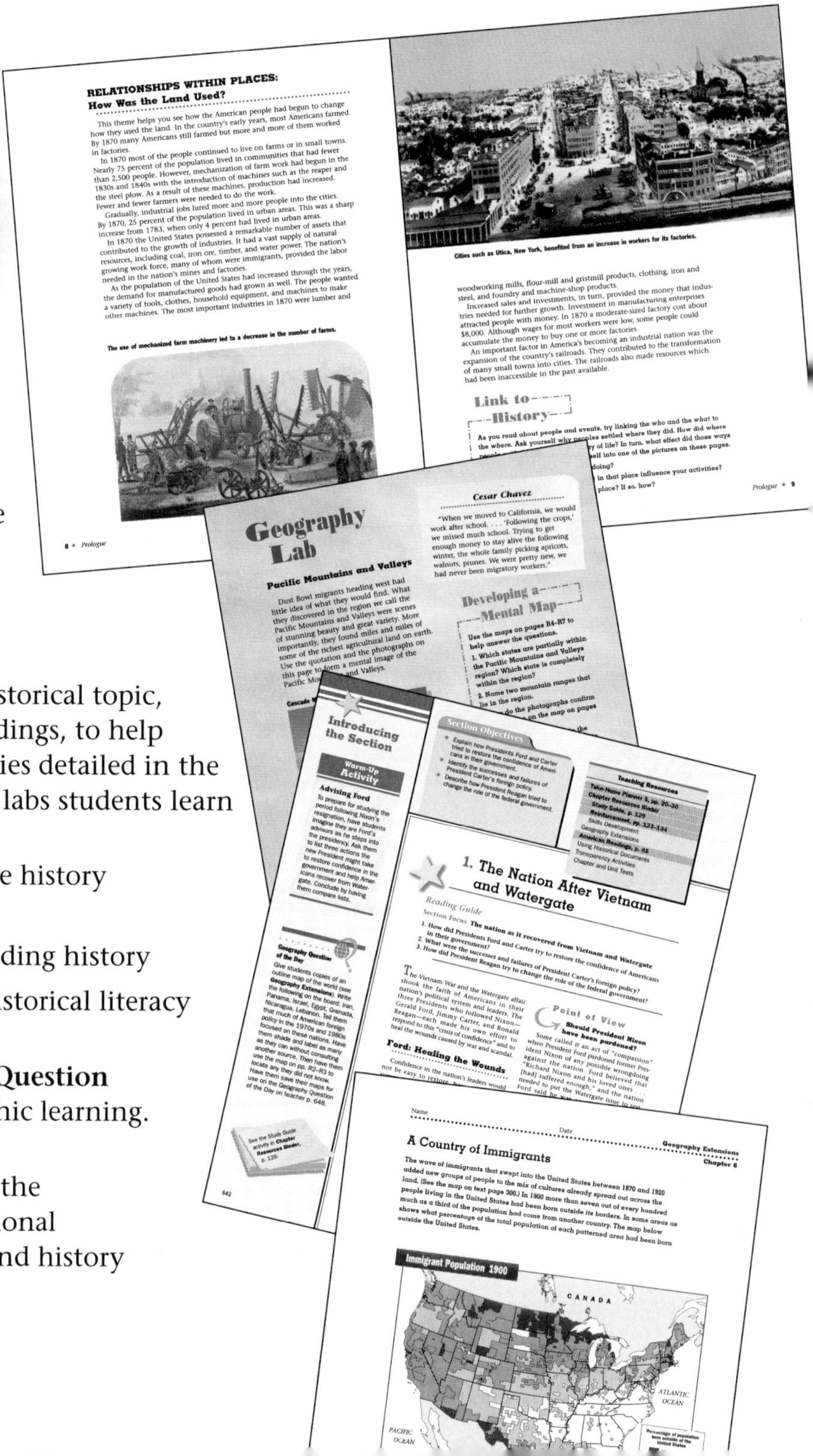

Why We Remember responds . . .

A **Prologue** in the student text describes the geographical setting of the United States in 1870 and introduces students to the use of map projections in the study of history.

A **Geography Lab** in each chapter uses a historical topic, often described through primary source readings, to help students achieve the geographic competencies detailed in the **National Standards for Geography.** In the labs students learn

- the geographic areas—"places"—where history happened
- why maps are important in understanding history
- how "mental maps" are essential to historical literacy

The **Teacher's Edition** offers a **Geography Question of the Day** to encourage continual geographic learning.

The **Geography Extensions** supplement in the **Teacher's Resource Package** presents additional geography learning opportunities that expand history understanding.

Applying social studies skills . . .

Teachers tell us . . .

"Students need practice in applying social studies skills to real problem-solving situations."

Why We Remember responds . . .

Skill Labs, one per chapter, systematically provide experiences in applying critical social studies skills as identified by the National Council for the Social Studies. Labs develop competencies in:

- Acquiring Information
- Thinking Critically
- Using Information

Each lab requires students to apply one or more skills to investigate an issue or question.

Throughout the text, students use **charts, diagrams, graphs,** and **maps** as they learn history.

To assist students who need review or remediation in social studies skills, the **Teacher's Resource Package** provides a series of **skills development activities** with accompanying **skills teaching transparencies** for you to use.

Citizenship Lab

Each chapter includes a 4-page **Citizenship Lab.** Based on Supreme Court cases, these labs engage students in thinking about how historic cases impact us yet today.

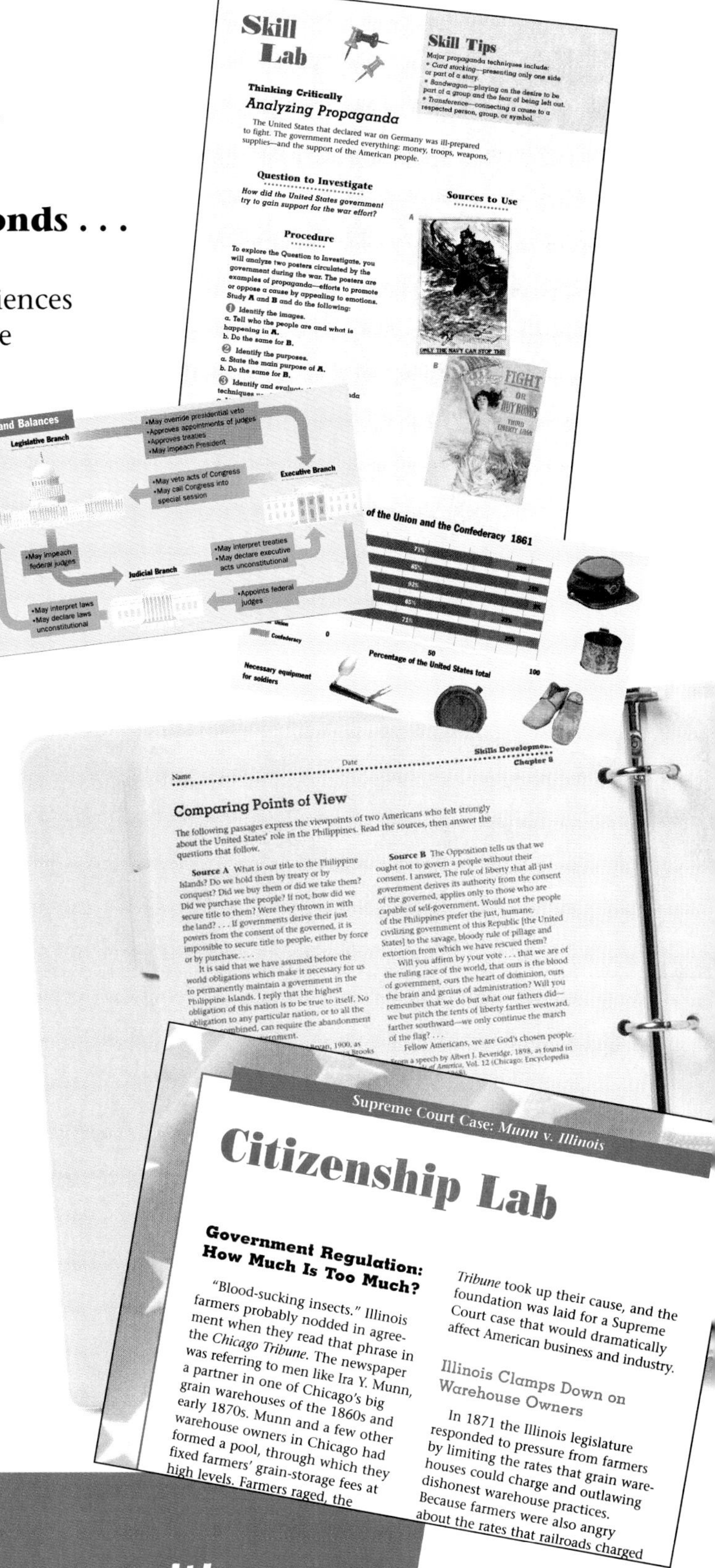

. . . to develop knowledgeable and competent young citizens.

Linking history to life . . .

Teachers tell us . . .

"We want students to understand how history relates to other subjects and to their everyday lives."

Why We Remember responds . . .

In the **Student Text**, each chapter presents a **Link to Art**, a **Link to the Present**, and a **World Link.**

The **Teacher's Edition** offers innovative strategies for using these links to broaden students' understanding of the world.

Links to Technology offer diagrams and cutaway drawings for students to examine as they study the role of technology in our nation's history.

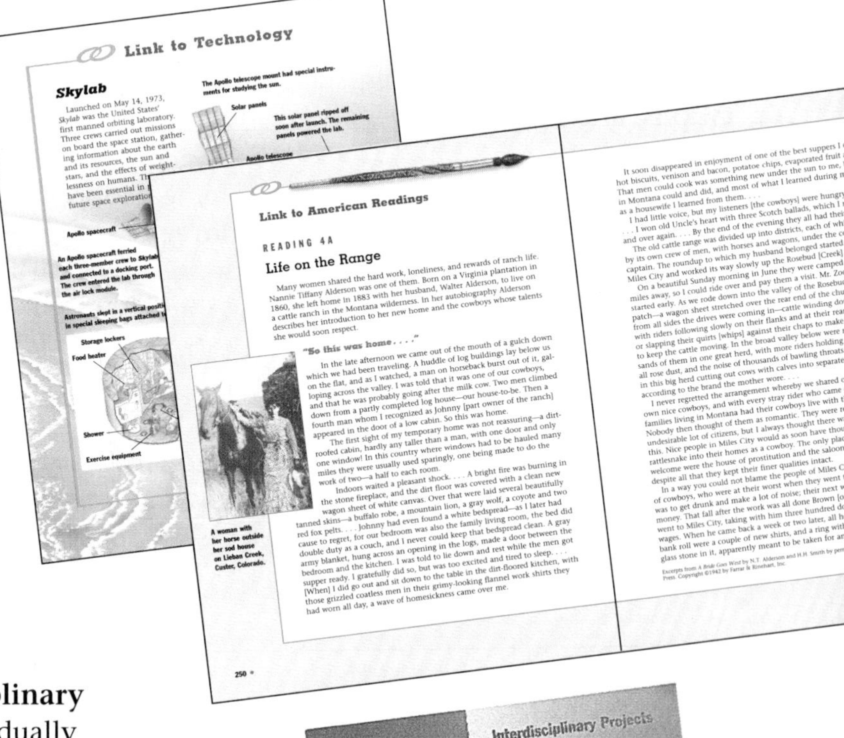

Literature as a way of knowing history is illustrated in each chapter's **Link to American Readings** selection, carefully chosen to stimulate interest in reading the book from which the selection is taken.

Why We Remember offers two options for **interdisciplinary projects.**

- Each **Unit Survey** provides an **interdisciplinary project** that students can complete individually or in groups.
- The **Interdisciplinary Projects** supplement in the **Teacher's Resource Package** provides all the resources and directions needed to direct four major interdisciplinary projects—peak learning experiences that students will never forget.

Assessing student performance . . .

Teachers tell us . . .

"We want options in how we assess students so that we can choose the best assessment for the chapter content and for the students."

Why We Remember responds . . .

Traditional Assessment Options

Section Reviews allow frequent comprehension checks.

Chapter and Unit Surveys provide a combination of comprehension and critical thinking questions appropriate for either teacher evaluation or student self-evaluation.

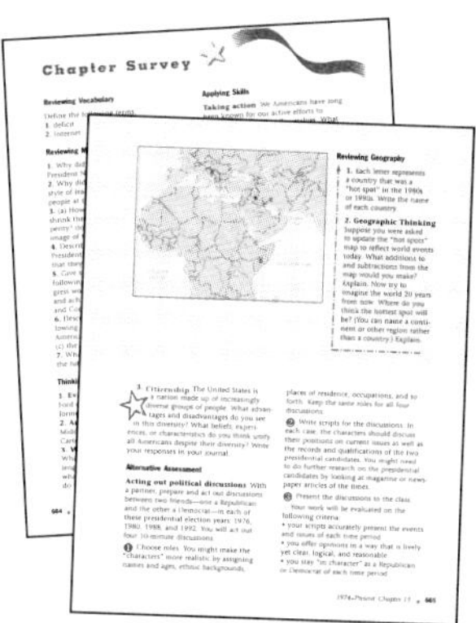

Chapter and Unit Tests, in the **Teacher's Resource Package,** enable you to assess levels of student understanding from factual recall to higher-order thinking. Two forms are provided for each test.*

*Also available as a computer software program, **SelecTest**.

The convenient **Take-Home Planner** lets you grade all student work without taking home the larger Teacher's Edition.

Alternative Assessment Options

Ideal for Portfolio Assessment, the **Writing in Your History Journal** activities in each **Chapter Survey** provide a continuous record of student comprehension and understanding.

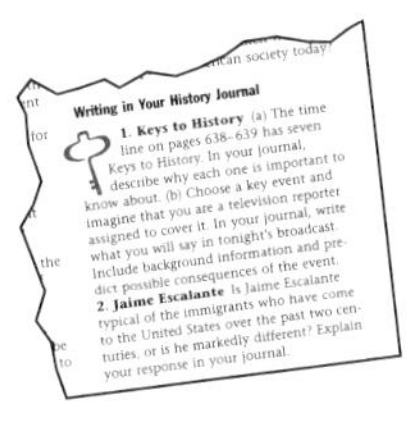
Writing in Your History Journal

1. Keys to History (a) The time line on pages 638–639 has seven Keys to History. In your journal, describe why each one is important to know about. (b) Choose a key event and imagine that you are a television reporter assigned to cover it. In your journal, write what you will say in tonight's broadcast. Include background information and predict possible consequences of the event.

2. Jaime Escalante Jaime Escalante is typical of the immigrants who have come to the United States over the past two centuries, or is he markedly different? Explain your response in your journal.

Alternative Assessment activities in each **Chapter Survey** and each **Unit Survey** offer opportunities to evaluate students' understanding through valid, reliable, performance-oriented assessment techniques.

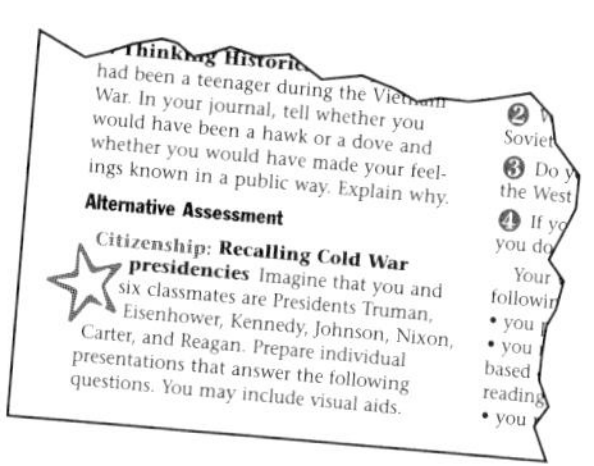
had been a teenager during the Vietnam War. In your journal, tell whether you would have been a hawk or a dove and whether you would have made your feelings known in a public way. Explain why.

Alternative Assessment

Citizenship: Recalling Cold War presidencies Imagine that you and six classmates are Presidents Truman, Eisenhower, Kennedy, Johnson, Nixon, Carter, and Reagan. Prepare individual presentations that answer the following questions. You may include visual aids.

For those teachers with limited experience in alternative assessment, the **Take-Home Planner** provides information on structuring each alternative assessment, developing appropriate evaluation criteria, and setting up a scoring rubric.

. . . to make history relevant to today's students.

Correlated with a Dynamic New Multimedia U.S. History Program

Vital Links is a project-based multimedia United States history program. It blends leading-edge technologies with sound instructional design to stimulate adolescent minds and meet unique learning needs. Each unit uses components to address different learning modes and expand opportunities for all students.

The Vital Links multimedia components include historical photographs, video, animation, and audio to capture students' attention and make learning history engaging and relevant. With Vital Links, teachers create a real-world learning environment. Available in Macintosh and Windows versions.

Vital Links is correlated through bar codes and CD-ROM address references throughout the Teacher's Edition of *Why We Remember.*

Each videodisc includes the Explore database of that unit's historical time period, giving students access to hundreds of video and audio primary sources. It also contains a Video Introduction of the unit themes.

Videotapes also provide the Video Introduction portion of the program, so that all classrooms have the technology to introduce unit themes to students.

***Vital Links Chronicle* newspapers** include articles, editorials, graphs, time lines, charts, and more for off-line historical reading and research.

CD-ROMs provide content and tools, including

Explore, a database with over 400 primary sources and an abundance of historical data.

Write, a desktop publishing tool that easily combines text and imported images into student documents.

Analyze, a spreadsheet tool for inputting, graphing, and evaluating historical and current data.

Present, a multimedia tool for producing dynamic video presentations with rich images and sound.

***Vital Links U.S. Heritage Music* audio-cassettes** provide 70 minutes of U.S. history through beautiful music and songs that span all time periods covered by the Vital Links program.

Enjoy the best of two worlds with the* Why We Remember *basal text program and Vital Links multimedia.

ORGANIZATION

The Teacher's Edition provides reductions of the pages of the student's text, plus lesson plans and teaching notes. The Teacher's Edition reflects the organization of the student's text, which consists of an optional 2-part review of history through Reconstruction and 15 chapters within 5 units. Each chapter is further divided into sections.

Why We Remember: Civil War to the Present provides you with flexibility regarding the content you wish to teach. Need to review material from last year? Only some of the content? The chart below shows some of the teaching options available to you.

Option/Coverage	Assignment Sequence
Option A *Review:* beginnings through Reconstruction *Full Coverage:* end of Reconstruction to present day	**1)** Review (pp. 20–103) **2)** Units 2–5 (pp. 218–end of text)
Option B *Review:* beginnings to the Civil War *Full Coverage:* Civil War to the present day	**1)** Sections 1–5 of Review (pp. 20–85) **2)** Units 1–5 (pp. 104–end of text)
Option C *Review:* None *Full Coverage:* Civil War to the present day	**1)** Units 1–5 (pp. 104–end of text)
Option D *Review:* None *Full Coverage:* end of Reconstruction to present day	**1)** Units 2–5 (pp. 218–end of text)

Side Notes

The basic teaching plan is located in blue-tinted columns along the sides of the student's text pages. The lesson plans are simple, easy to use, and flexible. Each lesson plan is made up of three parts: Introduce, Develop, and Close. Also in the blue side pages are menus highlighting appropriate Teaching Resources in each chapter, motivational activities, notes on when to use specific supplemental resources, bar-coded references to Vital Links—a project-based multimedia U.S. history program—and answers to review and special-feature questions.

Top Notes

The top margins of the Teacher's Edition also include a wealth of valuable information. Included are easy-to-read Section Objectives, menus highlighting important Teaching Resources in each section, Footnotes that provide valuable information about relevant topics in history, geography, economics, citizenship, and literature, and Connections notes that make important interdisciplinary links to math, art, science, economics, and geography. You will also find useful Tips for Teaching at-risk students, visual learners, auditory learners, gifted students, and students with limited English.

Chapter Planning Guides

Each chapter in the Teacher's Edition is preceded by a two-page insert containing a planning chart that highlights major teaching opportunities in the Student's Text, Teacher's Edition, Teacher's Resource Package, and Take-Home Planner. A table of contents for these pages follows:

Using the Internet for Social Studies Research

At the end of the Teacher's Edition (pp. R113–R116) you will find a valuable section devoted to using the Internet. Consult this handy guide whenever you assign students an Internet research project. It contains a glossary of Internet terms and sections on searching the net successfully, information literacy, bookmarks, and the Internet in your social studies classroom. In addition, Using the Internet for Social Studies Research contains a useful listing of web sites students can visit when doing social studies research.

About the Author

Dr. Herman J. Viola, curator emeritus with the Smithsonian Institution, is a distinguished historian, author, and curator. Dr. Viola received his Ph.D. in American history from Indiana University. He founded the scholarly journal *Prologue* at the National Archives. Dr. Viola also served as director of the National Anthropological Archives at the Smithsonian Institution. There he organized two major historical exhibitions: *Seeds of Change,* highlighting the cultural and biotic exchange after the Columbus voyages, and *Magnificent Voyagers,* chronicling the journey of the U.S. Exploring Expedition of 1838–1842, which sailed around the world and discovered Antarctica.

A nationally recognized authority on American Indians, the history of the American West, and the Civil War, Dr. Viola is the author of many historical works for both adults and young readers.

Books written or edited by Herman J. Viola

Thomas L. McKenney: Architect of America's Early Indian Policy

The Indian Legacy of Charles Bird King

Diplomats in Buckskins

The National Archives of the United States

Magnificent Voyagers: The U.S. Exploring Expedition, 1838–1841

Exploring the West

After Columbus: The Smithsonian's Chronicle of the Indians of North America Since 1492

Seeds of Change: A Quincentennial Commemoration

Ben Nighthorse Campbell: An American Warrior

The Memoirs of Charles Henry Veil

For young readers

Andrew Jackson

Giuseppe Garibaldi

Sitting Bull

After Columbus: The Horse's Return to America

Osceola

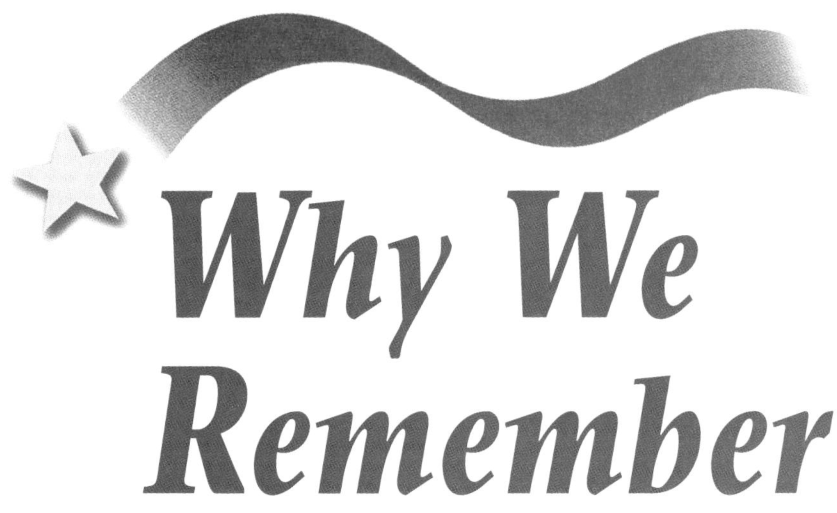

Why We Remember

United States History
Civil War to the Present

Herman J. Viola

Contributing Authors
Helen Wheatley
Diane Hart

Scott Foresman
Addison Wesley

Editorial Offices: Glenview, Illinois • Menlo Park, California
Sales Offices: Reading, Massachusetts • Atlanta, Georgia • Glenview, Illinois
Carrollton, Texas • Menlo Park, California

http://www.sf.aw.com

Contributing Authors

Dr. Helen Wheatley, Assistant Professor of History at Seattle University, specializes in United States, environmental, and world history. A former Fulbright fellow, she is active in promoting history education through the World History Association.

Diane Hart is a writer and consultant specializing in history and social studies. A former teacher and Woodrow Wilson Fellow, she has written a number of textbooks for middle school students.

Reviewers and Consultants

Dr. Pedro Castillo
Associate Professor of History and American Studies and Co-Director, Chicano/Latino Research Center, University of California, Santa Cruz

Dr. David Barry Gaspar
Professor of History, Duke University, Durham, North Carolina

Dr. Joseph E. Harris
Professor of History, Howard University, Washington, D.C.

LaDonna Harris
President, Americans for Indian Opportunity, Bernalillo, New Mexico

Tedd Levy
Teacher, Nathan Hale Middle School, Norwalk, Connecticut

Dr. Glenn Linden
Associate Professor of History and Education, Southern Methodist University, Dallas, Texas

Charlene Pike
Teacher, L'Ance Creuse Middle School South, Harrison Township, Michigan; past president, National Middle School Association

Esther Taira
Teacher Advisor, Division of Instruction, Los Angeles Unified School District, Los Angeles, California

Dr. Ralph E. Weber
Professor of History and Chair, Department of History, Marquette University, Milwaukee, Wisconsin

Acknowledgments

Susan P. Viola, literature consultant, is librarian at The Langley School in McLean, Virginia. She received her M.S.L.S. from The Catholic University of America.

Dr. Viola wishes to acknowledge **Jan Shelton Danis** for her research and editorial assistance and historians **Felix C. Lowe,** Smithsonian Institution, for drafting Chapter 9, **Roger A. Bruns,** National Archives and Records Administration, for drafting Chapter 10, and **Dr. George C. Chalou,** National Archives and Records Administration, for drafting Chapters 12 and 13.

Acknowledgments of permission to reprint copyrighted materials appear on page R104.

For information regarding permission, write to: Scott Foresman-Addison Wesley, 1900 East Lake Avenue, Glenview, Illinois 60025.
Printed in the United States of America.

ISBN 0-201-33227-2

1 2 3 4 5 6 7 8 9 10 - RNT - 00 99 98 97

Table of Contents

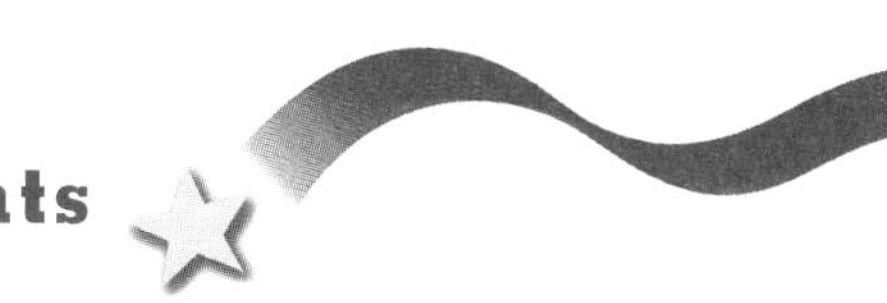

vii

Getting to Know This Textbook

To help you learn—and remember—history, the book has many special features. These features are explained on this page and the pages that follow.

Keys to History Time Line

As you glance through this text, you will see that each chapter begins with a two-page time line that shows the time period covered in the chapter.

Each time line entry is a **Key to History**—an important event, person, or idea from the period. The key symbol highlights these keys to the past.

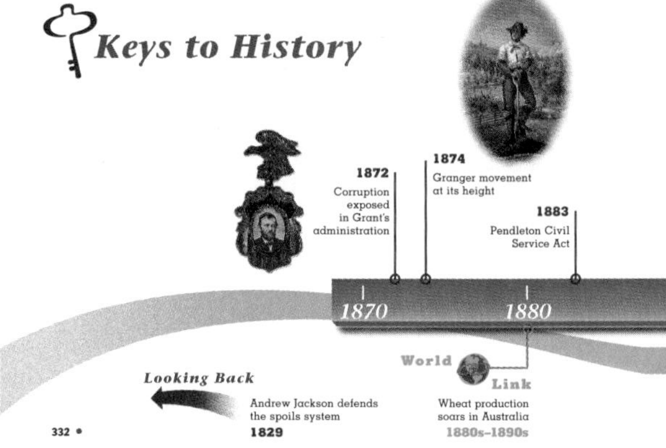

History Mystery

Historians sometimes think of history as a series of mysteries to be unraveled. The magnifying glass symbol at the start of each chapter points out a **History Mystery** feature. Read the feature and look for clues in the chapter to help you unravel the mystery.

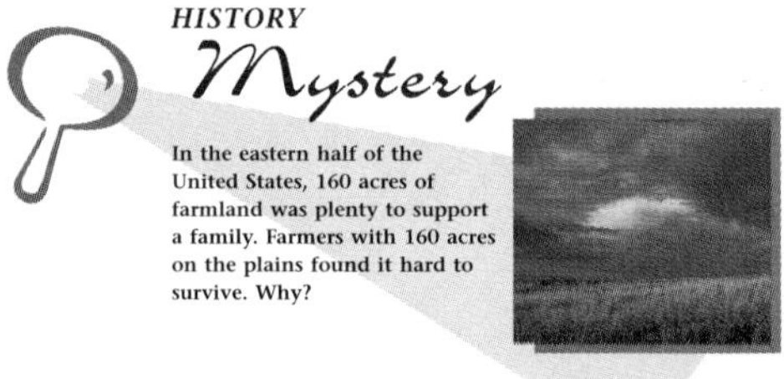

HISTORY
Mystery
In the eastern half of the United States, 160 acres of farmland was plenty to support a family. Farmers with 160 acres on the plains found it hard to survive. Why?

Citizenship Skills

Americans study our country's past to be better citizens today. In each chapter's Citizenship Lab, you will read about some of our nation's most important Supreme Court decisions and their effect on our everyday lives. In the Chapter Survey at the end of each chapter, you will see a star symbol. It points out an activity in which you can practice **Citizenship Skills** by applying information that you learned in the chapter.

Scholar's Tool Kit

How Do We Know?

How do we know what we know about history? Where does our knowledge of history come from? In this book you will learn about five different "tools" that historians use to uncover information about the past. Each tool is featured in a Scholar's Tool Kit, which comes before a new unit. You can recognize the tool kits by their notebook design.

How Do We Know?

Metal detectors played a crucial role in researching the true story of the Battle of the Little Bighorn.

Scholar's Tool Kit

Technology

One of the most dramatic incidents in American history is commonly known as Custer's Last Stand. On June 25, 1876, the U.S. Cavalry battled Sioux and Cheyenne warriors on the banks of the Little Bighorn River. For more than a century scholars have tried to understand how the warriors could destroy the elite 7th Cavalry led by the famous Civil War general, George Armstrong Custer. Recently, researchers using state-of-the-art metal detectors at the battle site have made discoveries that shed new light on the events of that fateful June day.

Custer's Last Stand?

Because none of the troopers with Custer survived the battle, the only witnesses were the victorious Indians. They reported that the attacking soldiers caught them by surprise. After some initial confusion, angry warriors urged by Sitting Bull, Crazy Horse, Two Moons, and Lame White Man rushed toward the soldiers to defend their families. The battlefield became a nightmare of dust, smoke, gunshots, and war cries. Arrows and bullets began to rain down on the soldiers, who had paused in their attack to look for a place to cross the river. Frightened cavalry horses started to break free from the soldiers holding them.

Perhaps surprised by the bold Indian counterattack, the soldiers with Custer failed to put up much of a defense. Instead, many panicked and ran away. According to Iron Hawk, a Sioux warrior, "Custer's

215

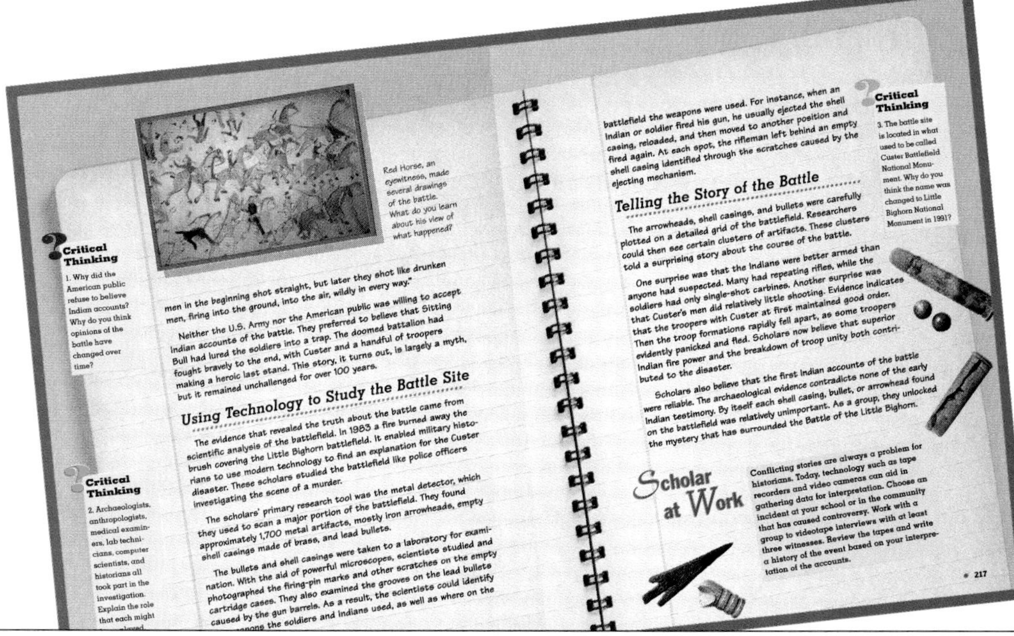

Red Horse, an eyewitness, made several drawings of the battle. What do you learn about his view of what happened?

Critical Thinking

1. Why did the American public refuse to believe Indian accounts? Why do you think opinions of the battle have changed over time?

men in the beginning shot straight, but later they shot like drunken men, firing into the ground, into the air, wildly in every way."

Neither the U.S. Army nor the American public was willing to accept Indian accounts of the battle. They preferred to believe that Sitting Bull had lured the soldiers into a trap. The doomed battalion had fought bravely to the end, with Custer and a handful of troopers making a heroic last stand. This story, it turns out, is largely a myth, but it remained unchallenged for over 100 years.

Using Technology to Study the Battle Site

The evidence that revealed the truth about the battle came from scientific analysis of the battlefield. In 1983 a fire burned away the brush covering the Little Bighorn battlefield. It enabled military historians to use modern technology to find an explanation for the Custer disaster. These scholars studied the battlefield like police officers investigating the scene of a murder.

The scholars' primary research tool was the metal detector, which they used to scan a major portion of the battlefield. They found approximately 1,700 metal artifacts, mostly iron arrowheads, empty shell casings made of brass, and lead bullets.

The bullets and shell casings were taken to a laboratory for examination. With the aid of powerful microscopes, scientists studied and photographed the firing-pin marks and other scratches on the empty cartridge cases. They also examined the grooves on the lead bullets caused by the gun barrels. As a result, the scientists could identify weapons the soldiers and Indians used, as well as where on the

Critical Thinking

2. Archaeologists, anthropologists, medical examiners, lab technicians, computer scientists, and historians all took part in the investigation. Explain the role that each might have played.

battlefield the weapons were used. For instance, when an Indian or soldier fired his gun, he usually ejected the shell casing, reloaded, and then moved to another position and fired again. At each spot, the rifleman left behind an empty shell casing identified through the scratches caused by the ejecting mechanism.

Telling the Story of the Battle

The arrowheads, shell casings, and bullets were carefully plotted on a detailed grid of the battlefield. Researchers could then see certain clusters of artifacts. These clusters told a surprising story about the course of the battle.

One surprise was that the Indians were better armed than anyone had suspected. Many had repeating rifles, while the soldiers had only single-shot carbines. Another surprise was that Custer's men did relatively little shooting. Evidence indicates that the troopers with Custer at first maintained good order. Then the troop formations rapidly fell apart, as some troopers evidently panicked and fled. Scholars now believe that superior Indian fire power and the breakdown of troop unity both contributed to the disaster.

Scholars also believe that the first Indian accounts of the battle were reliable. The archaeological evidence contradicts none of the early Indian testimony. By itself each shell casing, bullet, or arrowhead found on the battlefield was relatively unimportant. As a group, they unlocked the mystery that has surrounded the Battle of the Little Bighorn.

Critical Thinking

3. The battle site is located in what used to be called Custer Battlefield National Monument. Why do you think the name was changed to Little Bighorn National Monument in 1991?

Scholar at Work

Conflicting stories are always a problem for historians. Today, technology such as tape recorders and video cameras can aid in gathering data for interpretation. Choose an incident at your school or in the community that has caused controversy. Work with a group to videotape interviews with at least three witnesses. Review the tapes and write a history of the event based on your interpretation of the accounts.

217

Beginning the Story with

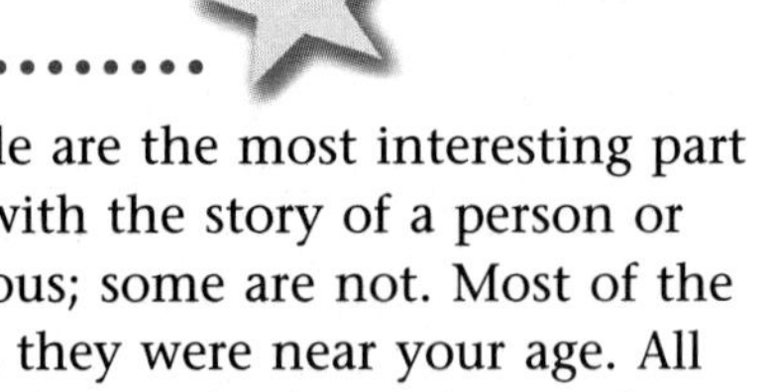

Most students find that stories about people are the most interesting part of history. Each chapter in this book begins with the story of a person or group of people. Some of the people are famous; some are not. Most of the stories tell something about the people when they were near your age. All the people in the stories are representative of those who lived during the time period. Remembering their stories will help you remember the significance of that period in history.

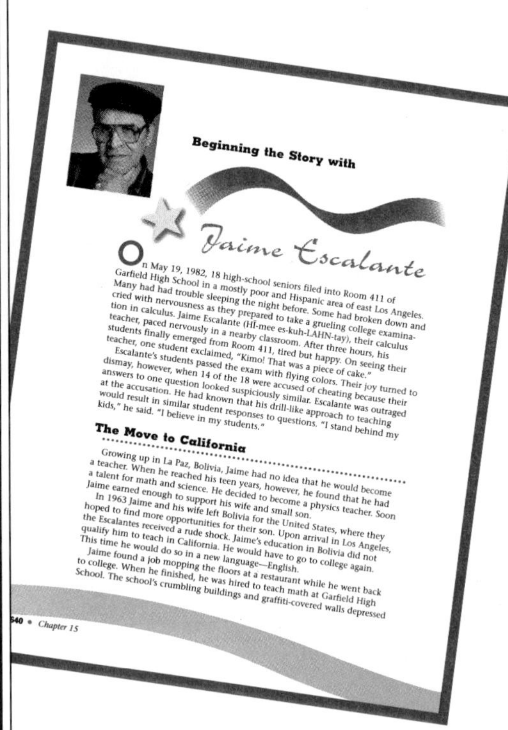

Beginning the Story with

Jaime Escalante

On May 19, 1982, 18 high-school seniors filed into Room 411 of Garfield High School in a mostly poor and Hispanic area of east Los Angeles. Many had had trouble sleeping the night before. Some had broken down and cried with nervousness as they prepared to take a grueling college examination in calculus. Jaime Escalante (HĪ-mee es-kuh-LAHN-tay), their calculus teacher, paced nervously in a nearby classroom. After three hours, his students finally emerged from Room 411, tired but happy. On seeing their teacher, one student exclaimed, "Kimo! That was a piece of cake."

Escalante's students passed the exam with flying colors. Their joy turned to dismay, however, when 14 of the 18 were accused of cheating because their answers to one question looked suspiciously similar. Escalante was outraged at the accusation. He had known that his drill-like approach to teaching would result in similar student responses to questions. "I stand behind my kids," he said. "I believe in my students."

The Move to California

Growing up in La Paz, Bolivia, Jaime had no idea that he would become a teacher. When he reached his teen years, however, he found that he had a talent for math and science. He decided to become a physics teacher. Soon Jaime earned enough to support his wife and small son.

In 1963 Jaime and his wife left Bolivia for the United States, where they hoped to find more opportunities for their son. Upon arrival in Los Angeles, the Escalantes received a rude shock. Jaime's education in Bolivia did not qualify him to teach in California. He would have to go to college again. This time he would do so in a new language—English.

Jaime found a job mopping the floors at a restaurant while he went back to college. When he finished, he was hired to teach math at Garfield High School. The school's crumbling buildings and graffiti-covered walls depressed

640 • Chapter 15

x

Link to Art

Apache Sunrise Ceremony (1890s) With vegetable dyes on doeskin, Naiche, son of Chief Cochise, preserved the memory of an Apache Sunrise Ceremony. At this coming-of-age celebration, people give thanks that young girls have reached womanhood safely. In the painting seven girls dance, each wrapped in a blanket with the older woman who is her guardian. Dancers on the far side of the fire represent spirits from a nearby mountain. **Discuss** What other times in peoples' lives are important enough to mark with special events, documents, or pictures?

The reservation system forced Plains Indians to change their way of life. Instead of living as nomads and hunting buffalo, they had to settle on specific pieces of land and raise crops. Many people expected the Indians to give up their old ways and learn the customs of the settlers. Beginning in 1867 a number of tribes, doomed without buffalo to hunt, signed treaties and tried to adapt to life on reservations.

1865–1900 Chapter 4 • **231**

Link to Art

Throughout our history, artists have expressed themselves in works that give us a sense of what life in America was like. Their drawings, paintings, sculpture, architecture, and other creations reflect America as they knew it, from important events to broad themes to images of daily life. The Link to Art feature found in each chapter provides us with a window on the past.

World Link

This book is primarily about United States history. Yet the history of our nation has always been linked to happenings in other parts of the world. In each chapter you will learn how events or people in other countries affected our nation's history.

Sit-in protestors bravely practiced nonviolent resistance as angry whites shouted abuse and smeared them with catsup, mustard, and sugar.

Freedom Riders A "sit-in on wheels" was equally successful. In May 1961 the Congress of Racial Equality (CORE), founded by James Farmer in 1942, sent a group of black and white "Freedom Riders" to ride interstate buses through the South.

Two buses left Washington, D.C., for New Orleans. They never got there. In Alabama mobs beat the riders and burned one of the buses. New riders arrived and were also attacked. The Freedom Riders won, though. President Kennedy ordered the integration of all buses, trains, and terminals.

Crisis in Birmingham

Nonviolence was met with violence again in Birmingham, Alabama, in April 1963. There King had launched peaceful demonstrations against discrimination in stores, restaurants, and workplaces. Birmingham police chief Eugene "Bull" Connor ordered fire hoses and police dogs turned on the protestors. Televised images of the police attacks helped turn public opinion against segregation.

World Link

Gandhi and nonviolence India offered dramatic proof of what nonviolence could achieve. There, Mohandas K. Gandhi used nonviolent resistance to force Britain to grant independence to India.

A lawyer, Gandhi became a leader of the independence movement about 1920. He and his followers refused to buy British goods. They stopped trains by lying down on the tracks. They sat in front of government buildings, forcing officials to climb over them. Gandhi was arrested many times, but India finally won its independence in 1947.

Howard Thurman, an African American teacher and minister, traveled to India in 1935 to learn about Gandhi's philosophy of nonviolence. Thurman later passed the philosophy on to his university students, who included James Farmer and Martin Luther King, Jr.

Point of View

Were the demonstrations in Birmingham necessary?

During the demonstrations Martin Luther King, Jr., was arrested. While he was in jail, a group of white Birmingham ministers criticized the demonstrations as "unwise and untimely." In a letter to the ministers, King defended the need for resistance. He wrote:

"Injustice must be exposed . . . to the light of human conscience and the air of national opinion before it can be cured."

1945–1974 Chapter 14 • 613

Link to the Present

Catalogs In 1993 Sears, Roebuck and Company stopped publishing its century-old catalog. Although shocking, the decision did not signal the death of the catalog business. In fact, today's catalog companies sell $60 billion in merchandise yearly.

Still, the industry has changed. Unlike Sears, companies today offer specialty goods and the convenience of toll-free numbers. They keep costs down by mailing catalogs only to people who are likely to buy. To target potential customers, they study purchase records and rent specialized electronic mailing lists.

1896 Sears Catalog

one-page list of items for sale. By 1874 his single sheet had grown to a 72-page catalog.

Ward soon had a competitor, Sears, Roebuck and Company. The Sears catalog, called "the Great Wish Book," came to include more than 1,000 pages of items, from children's shoes to tractors.

Madame C. J. Walker created a national market for her hair-care products both by sending them through the mail and by hiring young women to sell them door to door. Starting her company in the early 1900s with $1.50, she was the first African American woman in the nation to become a millionaire.

Improving railroad service With hundreds of companies building and running railroads, it was difficult to create an efficient rail system. For example, railroaders in the North used a narrower gauge, or distance between rails, than was used in the South. As a result, trains could not travel on all tracks.

Finally, the major railroads chose a standard gauge. Railroads in the South had to narrow almost 13,000 miles (20,800 km) of track. In one day—Sunday, May 30, 1886—frantic crews using crowbars and sledgehammers pushed thousands of miles of rail closer together.

Other developments also improved railroad service. The railway telegraph system developed by Granville T. Woods helped prevent collisions. Gustavus F. Swift and Philip D. Armour used refrigerated railcars to ship western beef safely from Chicago slaughterhouses to eastern butcher shops. George Westinghouse's air brakes and George M. Pullman's sleeping cars made rail travel safer and more comfortable.

Railroads and the environment The rapid expansion of the railroads came at a heavy cost to the environment. Lumber companies cut down whole forests for wood to make railroad ties and build bridges. Lumber was also used to build homes and furnish pulp for making paper. In 1901 one observer mourned the loss of forests in Georgia:

"In 1864 when I first went over the railroad from Savannah to Thomasville there was an almost unbroken forest of magnificent pines . . . but now one may go over that same route and scarcely see a [saleable] pine. From most of the visible land the timber is entirely gone."

Most Americans, though, were excited by the opportunities offered by expanding railroads and other industries. Furthermore, it was hard to believe that our vast natural resources would ever run out.

264 • Chapter 5 1865–1900

Link to the Present

Have you ever asked, "What does history have to do with my life?" As you read each chapter, you will find a Link to the Present that provides one example of how the past has influenced life today.

Point of View

What would you do if you were drafted?

In 1917 when President Wilson and Congress decided to have a draft, many citizens opposed the war. One group, called the Fellowship of Reconciliation, felt that the United States should not get involved in other countries' wars. They wrote:

"We are patriots who love our country and desire to serve her and those ideals for which she has stood . . . but we cannot believe that participation in war is the true way of service to America."

Other people, like Alvin York, were against the war because their religions opposed fighting for any reason. York explained his decision to join the army by saying:

"I loved and trusted old Uncle Sam and I have always believed he did the right thing. But I . . . didn't want to go and kill. I believed in my Bible. And it distinctly said, 'Thou shalt not kill.' And yet old Uncle Sam wanted me. And he said he wanted me most awful bad."

How would you feel if you were drafted? Can you make a list of three reasons why you would or would not fight?

Financing the War

From the beginning it was clear that the American war effort was going to be costly. To help finance this unexpected expense, in October 1917 Congress passed the War Revenue Act, increasing income taxes.

The government also raised money by selling liberty bonds. Politicians and movie stars gave speeches urging people to buy bonds. Some 21 million Americans bought

As the war took men away from home, women stepped in to take over their jobs. This young woman is filling shells in a munitions factory.

bonds—in effect, loaning money to the government. Through these measures, and by increasing taxes on corporations and on goods such as alcohol and tobacco, the government raised $10.8 billion.

"Use All Left-overs" Four years of war had laid waste to much of Europe. In addition to bullets and bombs, hunger and disease were killing thousands. The Liberty Loan Act of 1917 enabled the government to lend the Allies money to buy food and supplies from the United States.

President Wilson also set up an agency to make sure that there would be enough food for everyone, both at home and overseas. To head the Food Administration he chose Herbert Hoover, an engineer who had led relief efforts in Belgium. The Food Administration raised crop prices to encourage farmers to grow more, and it punished people who hoarded food.

1914–1920 Chapter 9 • 415

Point of View

Today's news reports often feature people expressing conflicting points of view. In the past, too, people had different opinions on the issues of the day. Furthermore, historians often disagree about how to interpret past events. In each chapter's Point of View feature, you will read about different perspectives on a historical issue.

xiii

Hands-On HISTORY

History is not just a subject for you to read. It is also something you can "do." The activities described in each Hands-On History feature will give you a chance to re-create or interact with some aspect of our nation's past. In addition to the Hands-On Histories listed here, you will also find them at the beginning of each unit and in the "Beginning the Story with . . ." feature at the start of each chapter.

Miracle on the Marne

In August 1914 Germany's plan was to attack first on the western front. It would roll through Belgium to crush France, then turn to the east and defeat Russia.

The plan worked well in the beginning, even though the Germans met unexpectedly stiff resistance from the outgunned and outnumbered Belgian army. The rapid German advance soon had French forces fleeing in disorder toward Paris. Confident of victory, the German commander in chief, Helmuth von Moltke, boasted that the war would be over in six weeks.

On September 6, however, just south of the Marne River and almost in sight of Paris, French and British forces finally overpowered the German troops and forced them to withdraw. The French called the victory "the Miracle on the Marne."

Stalemate on the Western Front

The German defeat on the Marne changed the character of the war. No longer was the conflict one of movement and maneuver. Instead, for three long years the opposing sides were stuck in a **stalemate**—deadlock—on the western front.

Trench warfare Soldiers on both sides of the stalemate dug trenches—long zigzag lines of ditches about 6 feet (1.8 m) deep and 3 feet (0.9 m) wide. Spaces dug into the sides of the trenches protected soldiers from enemy fire and provided room where they could eat and sleep.

Systems of trenches were barricaded with tangles of barbed wire. The stretch of ground between the opposing trenches was called "no man's land."

Hands-On HISTORY

Surviving life in a trench Describing the trenches he and fellow British soldiers dug during the war, Frank Richards wrote: "Little did we think when we were digging those trenches that we were digging our future homes for the next four years."

Activity With a group of five classmates, imagine living in a trench 6 feet deep by 3 feet wide by 20 feet long for a week. There is a lull in the fighting, but you must be alert. The enemy is less than 90 feet away, just across "no man's land." In your group of six, brainstorm answers to these questions:

1. If each of you could bring ten items into the trench—besides clothing and weapons—what would they be?
2. What are some activities you could do to pass the time in the trench?
3. What activities would not be a good idea? Why not?

American soldiers in a trench

Skill Lab

In science classes, you participate in labs where you practice skills used in scientific study. In this book, the Skill Lab in each chapter gives you a chance to learn and apply skills used by historians. The labs will help you develop skills in acquiring information, thinking critically, and using information. You can use these skills in everyday problem solving and decision making as well as in your study of history.

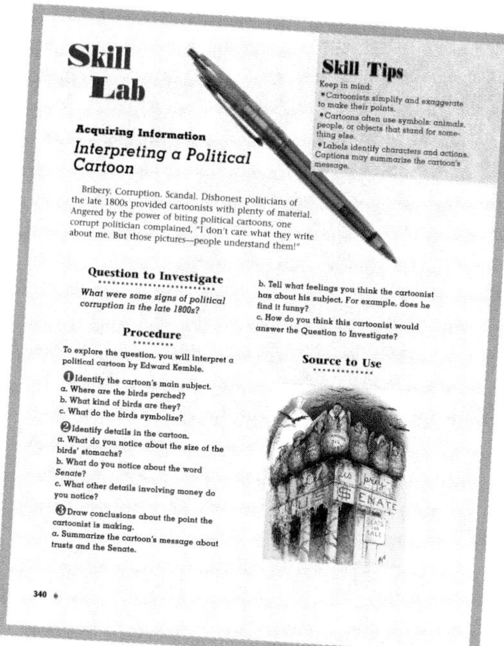

Skill Lab

Acquiring Information

Interpreting a Political Cartoon

Bribery. Corruption. Scandal. Dishonest politicians of the late 1800s provided cartoonists with plenty of material. Angered by the power of biting political cartoons, one corrupt politician complained, "I don't care what they write about me. But those pictures—people understand them!"

Skill Tips

Keep in mind:

• Cartoonists simplify and exaggerate to make their points.

• Cartoons often use symbols: animals, people, or objects that stand for something else.

• Labels identify characters and actions. Captions may summarize the cartoon's message.

Question to Investigate

What were some signs of political corruption in the late 1800s?

Procedure

To explore the question, you will interpret a political cartoon by Edward Kemble.

1. Identify the cartoon's main subject.
a. Where are the birds perched?
b. What kind of birds are they?
c. What do the birds symbolize?

2. Identify details in the cartoon.
a. What do you notice about the size of the birds' stomachs?
b. What do you notice about the word *Senate*?
c. What other details involving money do you notice?

3. Draw conclusions about the point the cartoonist is making.
a. Summarize the cartoon's message about trusts and the Senate.
b. Tell what feelings you think the cartoonist has about his subject. For example, does he find it funny?
c. How do you think this cartoonist would answer the Question to Investigate?

Source to Use

340

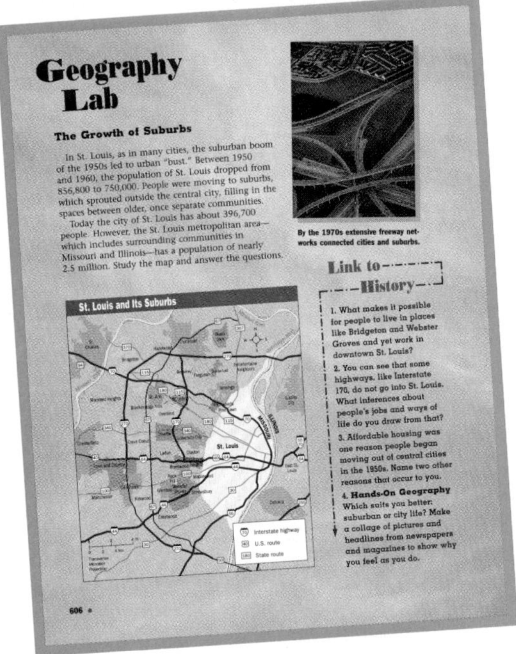

Geography Lab

The Growth of Suburbs

In St. Louis, as in many cities, the suburban boom of the 1950s led to urban "bust." Between 1950 and 1960, the population of St. Louis dropped from 856,800 to 750,000. People were moving to suburbs, which sprouted outside the central city, filling in the spaces between older, once separate communities.

Today the city of St. Louis has about 396,700 people. However, the St. Louis metropolitan area—which includes surrounding communities in Missouri and Illinois—has a population of nearly 2.5 million. Study the map and answer the questions.

By the 1970s extensive freeway networks connected cities and suburbs.

Link to History

1. What makes it possible for people to live in places like Bridgeton and Webster Groves and yet work in downtown St. Louis?
2. You can see that some highways, like Interstate 170, do not go into St. Louis. What inferences about people's jobs and ways of life do you draw from that?
3. Affordable housing was one reason people began moving out of central cities in the 1950s. Name two other reasons that occur to you.
4. **Hands-On Geography** Which suits you better: suburban or city life? Make a collage of pictures and headlines from newspapers and magazines to show why you feel as you do.

606 •

Geography Lab

You cannot fully understand history without also understanding geography. When you think of geography you may think of maps, but geography is much more than reading maps. The Geography Lab in each chapter has readings and pictures as well as maps to help you learn how geography influenced history—and how history influenced geography.

Citizenship Lab

To fully reap the benefits of our democracy, it is essential that you know about all of the rights, freedoms, and privileges that our Constitution provides you and every other citizen. It is also important to know about your duties and responsibilities as a citizen. The Citizenship Labs in each chapter, all of which feature an important Supreme Court case or cases, will provide you with an interesting and meaningful way to gain this knowledge.

Link to Technology

The Camera

A major development in technology around the time of the Civil War greatly changed the way we view past events. This development was the camera. While photographic technology had existed for many years, the early 1860s marked the beginning of the wide use of such technology. For the first time, even people far from the front lines could glimpse the grisly scenes of war. As a scholar's tool, photographs provide historians an important window to history—both the history of major events and of ordinary people.

Civil War photographers would rush to the battle scene, set up cameras, then develop the photos on the spot. Perhaps the most famous Civil War photographer was Mathew Brady, who is pictured above with his portable darkroom. The top picture shows the type of photo that made Brady famous. His 1860 camera is pictured at left.

1. A shutter opens quickly, allowing light reflected from the subject to pass through the lens and expose the film.
2. The film is coated with light-sensitive silver crystals. When the reflected light touches them, they turn dark. This process is called *exposure.*
3. Where the subject is dark, it reflects very little light. Where it is bright, it reflects more light. The exposure makes a reverse image, or *negative,* on the film.
4. When the film is developed, the image becomes fixed, and a positive image can be printed—the photograph.

152 • *Chapter 2 1861–1865*

Link to Technology

Some of the most dramatic changes in our nation have resulted from technological inventions. In each unit you will learn about one advance in technology, illustrated by diagrams or cutaway drawings.

Link to Literature

Just as artists give us visual pictures of the past, writers of literature give us word pictures of the past. Sometimes works of literature are based on true events, but often they are fiction. In each unit, you will read a short segment of a work of literature that will help you better understand the time period. Perhaps the segment will make you want to read the whole book from which it was taken.

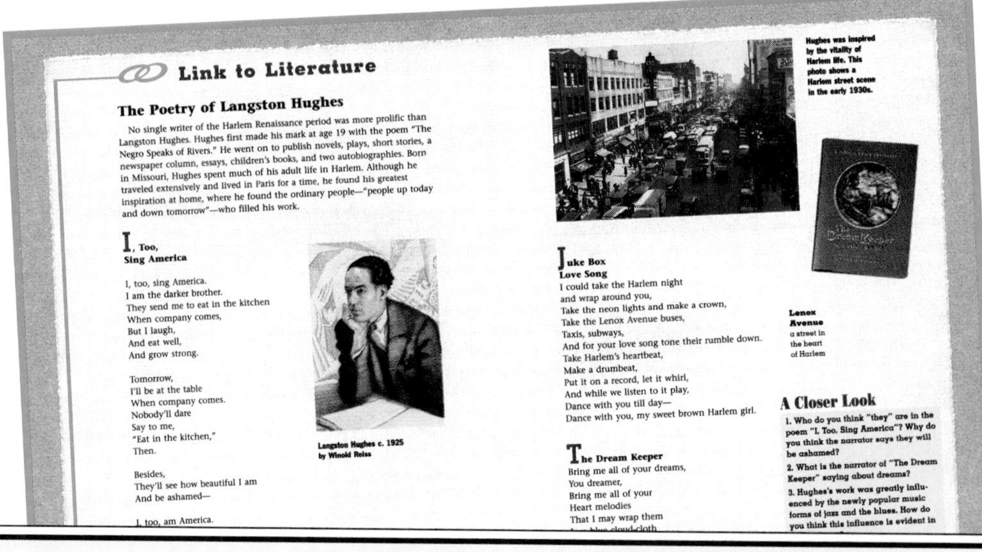

Link to Literature

The Poetry of Langston Hughes

No single writer of the Harlem Renaissance period was more prolific than Langston Hughes. Hughes first made his mark at age 19 with the poem "The Negro Speaks of Rivers." He went on to publish novels, plays, short stories, a newspaper column, essays, children's books, and two autobiographies. Born in Missouri, Hughes spent much of his adult life in Harlem. Although he traveled extensively and lived in Paris for a time, he found his greatest inspiration at home, where he found the ordinary people—"people up today and down tomorrow"—who filled his work.

I, Too, Sing America

I, too, sing America.
I am the darker brother.
They send me to eat in the kitchen
When company comes,
But I laugh,
And eat well,
And grow strong.

Tomorrow,
I'll be at the table
When company comes.
Nobody'll dare
Say to me,
"Eat in the kitchen,"
Then.

Besides,
They'll see how beautiful I am
And be ashamed—

I, too, am America.

Langston Hughes c. 1925 by Winold Reiss

Hughes was inspired by the vitality of Harlem life. This photo shows a Harlem street scene in the early 1930s.

Juke Box Love Song

I could take the Harlem night
and wrap around you,
Take the neon lights and make a crown,
Take the Lenox Avenue buses,
Taxis, subways,
And for your love song tone their rumble down.
Take Harlem's heartbeat,
Make a drumbeat,
Put it on a record, let it whirl,
And while we listen to it play,
Dance with you till day—
Dance with you, my sweet brown Harlem girl.

Lenox Avenue a street in the heart of Harlem

The Dream Keeper

Bring me all of your dreams,
You dreamer,
Bring me all of your
Heart melodies
That I may wrap them

A Closer Look

1. Who do you think "they" are in the poem "I, Too, Sing America"? Why do you think the narrator says they will be ashamed?
2. What is the narrator of "The Dream Keeper" saying about dreams?
3. Hughes's work was greatly influenced by the newly popular music forms of jazz and the blues. How do you think this influence is evident in

Link to American Readings

At the end of each chapter, you will find excerpts from documents, letters, journals, songs, and speeches that will enrich your study of American history.

Alternative Assessment

As you study history, you and your teacher will want to know how much you are learning. Your teacher will probably give you paper-and-pencil tests to assess your knowledge and skills. In the Chapter Survey, you will also have the opportunity to demonstrate what you have learned through an alternative assessment activity. To receive a good evaluation of your work, you will need to be sure to meet the criteria provided.

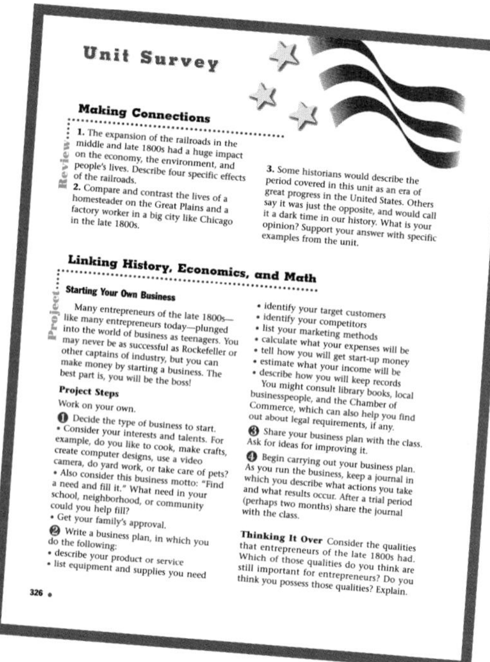

Unit Survey

Making Connections

Review

1. The expansion of the railroads in the middle and late 1800s had a huge impact on the economy, the environment, and people's lives. Describe four specific effects of the railroads.

2. Compare and contrast the lives of a homesteader on the Great Plains and a factory worker in a big city like Chicago in the late 1800s.

3. Some historians would describe the period covered in this unit as an era of great progress in the United States. Others say it was just the opposite, and would call it a dark time in our history. What is your opinion? Support your answer with specific examples from the unit.

Linking History, Economics, and Math

Project

Starting Your Own Business

Many entrepreneurs of the late 1800s—like many entrepreneurs today—plunged into the world of business as teenagers. You may never be as successful as Rockefeller or other captains of industry, but you can make money by starting a business. The best part is, you will be the boss!

Project Steps

Work on your own.

❶ Decide the type of business to start.
- Consider your interests and talents. For example, do you like to cook, make crafts, create computer designs, use a video camera, do yard work, or take care of pets?
- Also consider this business motto: "Find a need and fill it." What need in your school, neighborhood, or community could you help fill?
- Get your family's approval.

❷ Write a business plan, in which you do the following:
- describe your product or service
- list equipment and supplies you need
- identify your target customers
- identify your competitors
- list your marketing methods
- calculate what your expenses will be
- tell how you will get start-up money
- estimate what your income will be
- describe how you will keep records

You might consult library books, local businesspeople, and the Chamber of Commerce, which can also help you find out about legal requirements, if any.

❸ Share your business plan with the class. Ask for ideas for improving it.

❹ Begin carrying out your business plan. As you run the business, keep a journal in which you describe what actions you take and what results occur. After a trial period (perhaps two months) share the journal with the class.

Thinking It Over Consider the qualities that entrepreneurs of the late 1800s had. Which of those qualities do you think are still important for entrepreneurs? Do you think you possess those qualities? Explain.

326 •

Interdisciplinary Projects

Although this is a history book, you will discover that much of the information you learn relates to other subjects, such as science, math, and music. In each Unit Survey, you will find an interdisciplinary project that links history to one or more of these other subjects.

xx

Maps

Maps are the constant companions of historians. Maps are also tools you will use in everyday life. For many centuries maps were drawn by hand. Recently, however, map makers have begun to make maps with computers.

Most of the maps in this book have been created especially for this book using computers. Computers make it possible to include all the latest geographic information and reflect the most precise detailing possible. They also enable map makers to include color and explanations that are difficult to achieve with hand-drawn maps.

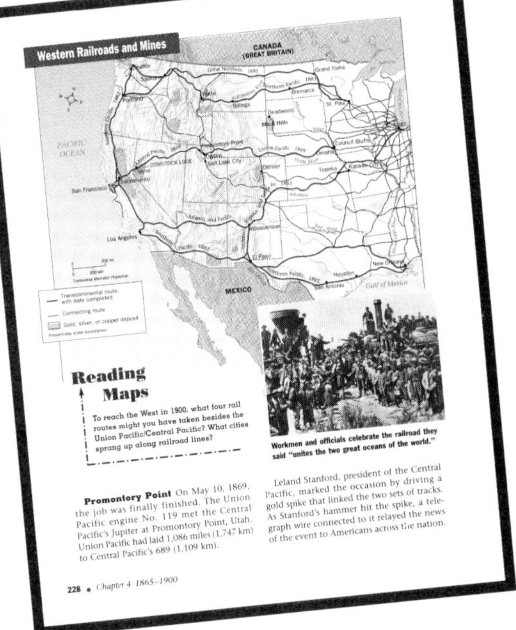

Reading Maps

To reach the West in 1900, what four rail routes might you have taken besides the Union Pacific/Central Pacific? What cities sprang up along railroad lines?

Workmen and officials celebrate the railroad they said "unites the two great oceans of the world."

Promontory Point On May 10, 1869, the job was finally finished. The Union Pacific engine No. 119 met the Central Pacific's Jupiter at Promontory Point, Utah. Union Pacific had laid 1,086 miles (1,747 km) to Central Pacific's 689 (1,109 km).

Leland Stanford, president of the Central Pacific, marked the occasion by driving a gold spike that linked the two sets of tracks. As Stanford's hammer hit the spike, a telegraph wire connected to it relayed the news of the event to Americans across the nation.

228 • *Chapter 4 1865–1900*

Maps

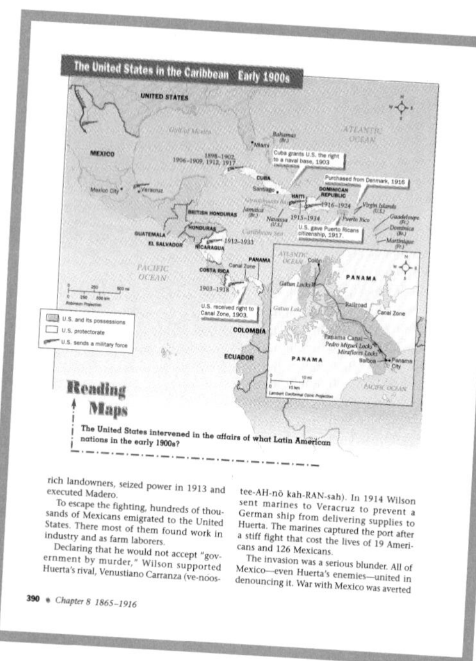
The United States in the Caribbean Early 1900s

Reading Maps

The United States intervened in the affairs of what Latin American nations in the early 1900s?

rich landowners, seized power in 1913 and executed Madero.

To escape the fighting, hundreds of thousands of Mexicans emigrated to the United States. There most of them found work in industry and as farm laborers.

Declaring that he would not accept "government by murder," Wilson supported Huerta's rival, Venustiano Carranza (ve-noos-tee-AH-nō kah-RAN-sah). In 1914 Wilson sent marines to Veracruz to prevent a German ship from delivering supplies to Huerta. The marines captured the port after a stiff fight that cost the lives of 19 Americans and 126 Mexicans.

The invasion was a serious blunder. All of Mexico—even Huerta's enemies—united in denouncing it. War with Mexico was averted

390 • *Chapter 8 1865–1916*

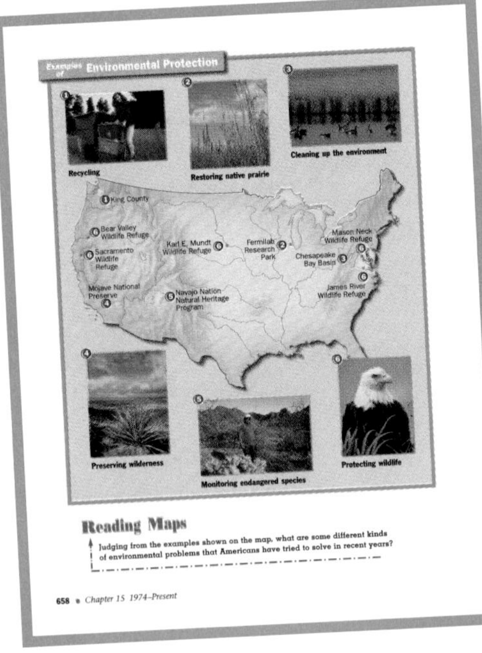
Examples of Environmental Protection

Reading Maps

Judging from the examples shown on the map, what are some different kinds of environmental problems that Americans have tried to solve in recent years?

658 • *Chapter 15 1974–Present*

Charts, Graphs, and Diagrams

Some information is easier to understand when it is presented in charts, graphs, and diagrams rather than in words. Throughout this book you will find these kinds of graphics. Like the maps in the text, these features are computer-generated and represent the latest techniques in data presentation.

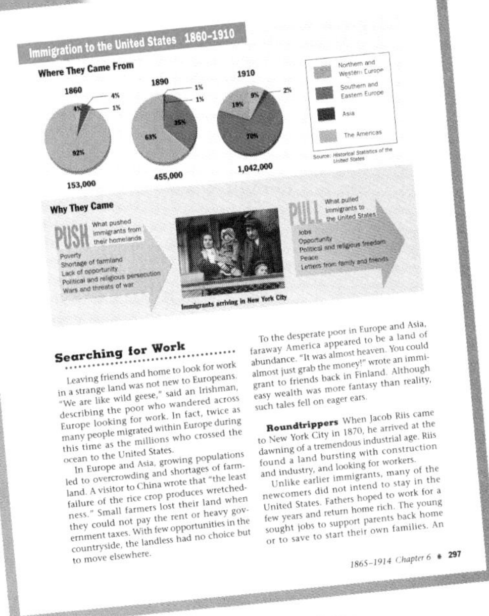

Searching for Work

Leaving friends and home to look for work in a strange land was not new to Europeans. "We are like wild geese," said an Irishman, describing the poor who wandered across Europe looking for work. In fact, twice as many people migrated within Europe during this time as the millions who crossed the ocean to the United States.

In Europe and Asia, growing populations led to overcrowding and shortages of farmland. A visitor to China wrote that "the least failure of the rice crop produces wretchedness." Small farmers lost their land when they could not pay the rent or heavy government taxes. With few opportunities in the countryside, the landless had no choice but to move elsewhere.

To the desperate poor in Europe and Asia, faraway America appeared to be a land of abundance. "It was almost heaven. You could almost just grab the money!" wrote an immigrant to friends back in Finland. Although easy wealth was more fantasy than reality, such tales fell on eager ears.

Roundtrippers When Jacob Riis came to New York City in 1870, he arrived at the dawning of a tremendous industrial age. Riis found a land bursting with construction and industry, and looking for workers.

Unlike earlier immigrants, many of the newcomers did not intend to stay in the United States. Fathers hoped to work for a few years and return home rich. The young sought jobs to support parents back home or to save to start their own families. An

1865–1914 Chapter 6 • **297**

xxiii

Epilogue

Into the Future

The Epilogue consists of an activity in which you and your classmates predict, based on the past and present, what the future holds for our nation and for you.

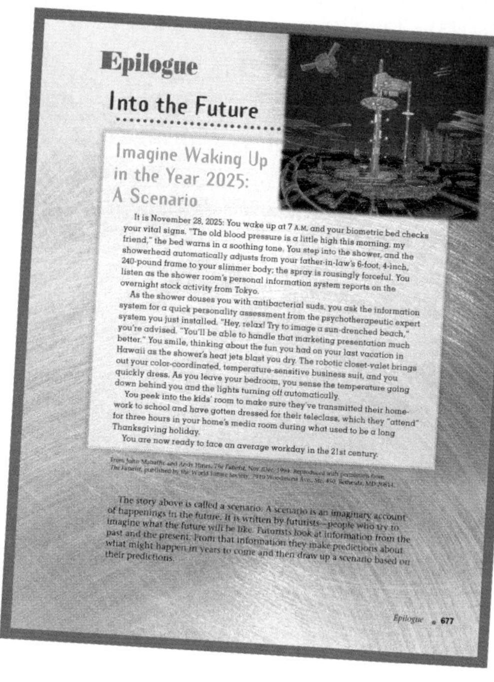

Epilogue

Into the Future

Imagine Waking Up in the Year 2025: A Scenario

It is November 28, 2025: You wake up at 7 A.M. and your biometric bed checks your vital signs. "The old blood pressure is a little high this morning, my friend," the bed warns in a soothing tone. You step into the shower, and the showerhead automatically adjusts from your father-in-law's 6-foot, 4-inch, 240-pound frame to your slimmer body; the spray is rousingly forceful. You listen as the shower room's personal information system reports on the overnight stock activity from Tokyo.

As the shower douses you with antibacterial suds, you ask the information system for a quick personality assessment from the psychotherapeutic expert system you just installed. "Hey, relax! Try to image a sun-drenched beach," you're advised. "You'll be able to handle that marketing presentation much better." You smile, thinking about the fun you had on your last vacation in Hawaii as the shower's heat jets blast you dry. The robotic closet-valet brings out your color-coordinated, temperature-sensitive business suit, and you quickly dress. As you leave your bedroom, you sense the temperature going down behind you and the lights turning off automatically.

You peek into the kids' room to make sure they've transmitted their homework to school and have gotten dressed for their teleclass, which they "attend" for three hours in your home's media room during what used to be a long Thanksgiving holiday.

You are now ready to face an average workday in the 21st century.

From John Mahaffie and Andy Hines, *The Futurist*, Nov./Dec. 1994. Reproduced with permission from *The Futurist*, published by the World Future Society, 7910 Woodmont Ave., Ste. 450, Bethesda, MD 20814.

The story above is called a scenario. A scenario is an imaginary account of happenings in the future. It is written by futurists—people who try to imagine what the future will be like. Futurists look at information from the past and the present. From that information they make predictions about what might happen in years to come and then draw up a scenario based on their predictions.

Epilogue • 677

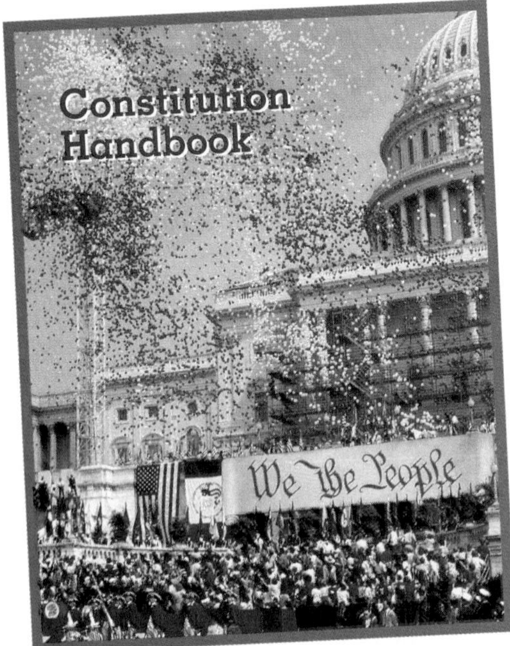

Constitution Handbook

In this text you will read about many important documents in our country's history. No document is as important for you to understand, though, as the United States Constitution. The Constitution Handbook includes the complete text of the Constitution as well as information that can help you better understand it and appreciate its importance in your life today.

Prologue

The United States in 1870: Geographical Setting

The ancient hunters who came into the Americas thousands of years ago found a land of forests, mountains, valleys, prairies, deserts, and swamps. The rivers were filled with fish. The prairies and forests teemed with bird and animal life. The first Americans learned to appreciate nature's gifts. These people and their descendants had little impact on the land and its resources.

The major changes to the American landscape began after the Columbus voyages of discovery at the close of the 15th century. Settlers from Europe carved out empires in North and South America giving little regard to the rights of the

Left: "Ther was neur seen amonge vs soe cunninge a way to take fish," wrote English artist John White of the Algonquins he painted in North Carolina in the late 1500s.

Below: Group of warehouses on Dan River in Danville, Virginia, in 1870

Introducing the Prologue:

The United States in 1870: Geographical Setting

In this Prologue, students explore the physical and cultural features of the United States in 1870 and reflect upon ways these features have both shaped and been shaped by human history. To introduce the Prologue, invite students to first thumb through the Prologue to look the pictures. Have them point out things that help them infer how the people in the 1870s lived. For example, they used vehicles pulled by horses or oxen.

Setting the Stage Activity

Listing the Land Acquisitions

To focus students' attention on the fact that the United States increased greatly in size between 1783 and 1870, make a chart on the chalkboard. In the first column, have volunteers list events and dates that led to the increase in the size of the United States. In the second column, have them describe what lands were added. If the students need help, have them refer to page R10. For example, the Louisiana Purchase of 1803—the Louisiana Territory; 1845—Texas.

Teaching

Introduction to the Prologue

Have students read the introduction to the Prologue and then look at the map on page 3. Ask what vast United States territory is not shown on the map. (Alaska) Ask students how many other territories were part of the United States. (ten)

Explain to students that the Prologue is divided into five sections, with each emphasizing one of the five themes of geography.

Teaching

LOCATION: Where Was It?

Explain to students that this theme identifies an area by giving its exact latitude and longitude or by describing its location in relation to a known landmark.

Bonus Activity

Locating a Place

To help students practice locating places, have them use the map on page 3 to describe the relative and absolute location of three states. Then use these locations to play "Where Am I? Divide the class into two teams. Have one team supply the location of a place where they are "marooned." Have the other team "rescue" them by naming their location. Judge winners by speed and accuracy.

Geography Footnote

William H. Seward, Secretary of State from 1861 to 1869, was an avid expansionist. The Civil War had prevented him from pursuing an aggressive expansionist policy, but with the war's end Seward began looking for lands to annex. At various times, Seward made plans to attempt the acquisition of Hawaii, Cuba, Puerto Rico, Greenland, Iceland, and even Canada.

The mood of the country, however, was not generally expansionist after the Civil War, and Congress reflected that mood. Without congressional backing, most of Seward's plans were frustrated. Besides Alaska, his only other significant acquisition was the annexation of the Midway Islands.

native peoples who had lived here for centuries. The Europeans cut down the forests for their plantations, farms, and ranches. They built cities and established countries. One of the countries that emerged after centuries of turmoil was the United States, which won its freedom from England in 1783.

By 1870, the United States had grown from a cluster of colonies on the eastern seaboard of North America to a large and powerful nation. Through wars, annexations, purchases, and international treaties, the boundaries of the United States now spanned the North American continent from the Atlantic Ocean to the Pacific Ocean. Thanks to the purchase of Alaska from Russia in 1867, its northwestern border reached to the arctic. According to the U.S. census of 1870, the country encompassed an area of three million square miles. This total did not include Alaska because no one knew the exact size of this huge and unexplored region.

With territorial expansion came great changes to the physical and political landscape. Americans constructed dams and canals. They dug mines. They built towns and cities linking them with highways, railroads, and telegraph wires. They also divided the country into states and territories. In 1870 there were 37 states. There were only 11 states west of the Mississippi River. The rest of the land in the West was divided into territories. Look at the map on page 3. Was your state part of the United States in 1870? Was it part of a territory?

In this Prologue you will explore the United States as it was around they year 1870. As you do so, you will see how the nation had developed since its early years. To do this, you will be using the five themes that geographers often employ to organize their investigations. These themes are location, place, movement, relationships with places, and regions.

Land to farm enticed many people to move West. The U.S. government annexed this land, a part of Texas, in 1845.

Geography Footnote

One of the basic tasks in geography is to describe exactly what is where on the earth. To do this, geographers must identify the absolute location, or the precise spot on the earth, of each place. The latitude and longitude of a place is called its *absolute location.*

The second part of the geographic theme of location is *relative location,* or the position of places in relation to other places on earth. The most common way to express relative location is in terms of direction.

Most of us use relative location every day to find the places where we need to go. Absolute location is used by navigators, meteorologists, and others who need to find exact locations.

LOCATION: Where Was It?

The location theme offers you a starting point for beginning your investigation of the United States in 1870. The country stretched across the North American continent between the Atlantic and Pacific oceans. It was located south of Canada and north of Mexico. The country was also east of the Pacific Ocean, west of the Atlantic Ocean, and north of the Rio Grande. In addition, the country included Alaska, in the northwestern corner of the continent.

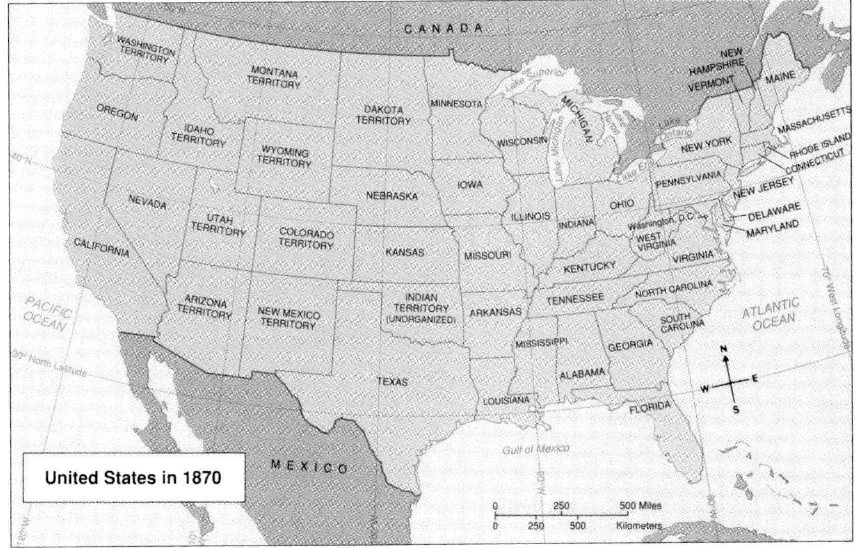

United States in 1870

Using Map Skills

To get the most out of maps, you need to use a variety of map skills. These skills include reading keys, locating features, and interpreting visual patterns. Locate the grid lines on this map. By using grid lines, you can pinpoint the country's exact location in 1870.

1. The main part of the country was located between what latitude lines?

2. The main part of the country was located between what longitude lines?

3. Find a state or territory on the map. Describe its exact location using latitude and longitude lines.

Discussion

Checking Understanding

1. What nations bordered the United States on the north and south in 1870? (Canada and Mexico)

2. What are lines of latitude and longitude? (Imaginary lines that circle the globe and are used to locate places on the earth.)

3. Pick any state or territory on the map on page 3. Describe its relative and absolution location. (Answers will vary.)

Stimulating Critical Thinking

4. Why is it important to have an understanding of latitude and longitude? (They make it possible to locate any place on the earth's surface.)

5. How do you use absolute and relative location in your own life? (Answers will vary, but most students will not use absolute location at all. Many students will use relative location for giving directions.)

Using Map Skills

Answers

1. Between 25º and 50º north latitude lines

2. Between 65º and 125º west longitude lines

3. Answers will vary.

Teaching

PLACE: What Was It Like?

Explain to students that the theme of *place* identifies an area by describing its physical and cultural features, such as plains or cities.

After students have read pages 4 and 5 about *place*, have them turn to the physical and political maps of the United States on pages R4–R5 and R6–R7. Then have them locate the following places mentioned in the text: Ohio Valley, Great Lakes, San Francisco, Rio Grande, Denver, and Salt Lake City.

Discuss with students the map showing United States settlement in 1870. Ask them why they think southern Florida, northwestern Maine, and upper Michigan, Wisconsin, and Minnesota were sparsely settled. (Southern Florida had a swampy terrain and a hot, humid, and unhealthy climate. The climate in northern Maine and upper Michigan, Wisconsin, and Minnesota was cold, and the growing season was short.) Have students compare the map on page 5 with the map on pages R4–R5. Point out that in some regions physical features account for the sparse population in 1870 and also today.

Role-Playing

Have small groups plan and role-play a guided tour to the United States in 1870. Describe both its physical and cultural features.

Geography Footnote

People's lives are grounded in particular places. You come from a place and you live in a place.

Places include continents, islands, countries, regions, states, cities, neighborhoods, villages, rural areas, and uninhabited areas. They usually have names and boundaries. Each place possesses a set of characteristics that helps to distinguish it from other places. Places are characterized by their physical and cultural features. Their physical features include climate, landforms, soils, vegetation, and animal life. Their cultural features include population distribution, language, religion, political systems, and economic systems.

PLACE: What Was It Like?

The place theme helps you investigate the cultural and physical features that gave our country its special identity. While the United States was adding vast territories in the West, its population was also growing. In 1870 the nation had almost 39 million people.

More than 95 percent of the population lived between the Atlantic coast and eastern Nebraska and Kansas. The 97th meridian, or longitude line, marked the limit of the continuously settled area. Find this line on the map on page 5. You can see that most of the population lived east of this line, or in the eastern half of the country.

However, great variations existed in the density of the population within the eastern settled area. The density was heaviest in the southern New England states, the central states along the Atlantic Ocean, westward through the Ohio Valley, and bordering the lower Great Lakes. New York, Pennsylvania, Illinois, and Ohio were the four largest states in number of people. Rhode Island was the most densely populated state. It had over 200 persons per square mile. On the other hand, places such as northwestern Maine, southern Florida, and parts of upper Michigan, Wisconsin, and Minnesota had less than two persons per square mile.

West of the 97th meridian lay one-half of the nation's area. However, in 1870 less than 5 percent of the population lived in the West. As you can see, areas of settlement were scattered over the western landscape. Most of the American Indians lived in the West on reservations.

To understand why the population was so widely dispersed, you must recall colonial settlement in the Southwest and in California. In those early years, colonization extended into present-day Texas, New Mexico, and the coastal valleys of the Pacific. Since that time, the population grew in those areas, especially in California following the gold rush of 1849. California's population in 1870 was nearly 600,000. San Francisco was one of the major cities in the country. About 150,000 people lived there.

Another major area of settlement existed along the northern part of the Rio Grande in present-day New Mexico. By 1870 this area had merged with the more recently developed gold- and silver-mining areas in and around Denver in the Colorado Territory.

The third major area of settlement in the West lay between Colorado and California. It was located in present-day Utah. Find this territory on the map on page 5. The Mormons, who were members of the Church of Jesus Christ of Latter-day Saints, chose this area for development in 1846. The Mormon settlement in what became Salt Lake City was one of the most successful in the West. The Mormons established a well-planned community. They were the first white settlers in America to use irrigation on a large scale. They built huge canals to carry water from the mountains to their fields in the valleys.

The Rio Grande formed part of the country's southern boundary.

Geography Footnote

Geographers identify four of the most common types of landforms as plains, plateaus, hills, and mountains. These surface features change only very slowly—over hundreds of thousands of years. The landforms of the United States have changed hardly at all since 1870.

Beyond these three major areas, settlements appear on the map as small scattered islands. Some of these were farming centers based on irrigation. Many were mining towns.

The yellow areas on the map had less than 2 people per square mile. Many people in these areas lived on cattle ranches, especially in the Great Plains. These ranches covered large areas. They contained many cattle but only a few people. Most of the rest of the yellow areas are mountainous. The rugged landscape, poor soil, and harsh climate conditions made them less desirable areas for settlement.

The 1870 census reported that there were almost an even number of men and women in the nation. However, their distribution was very uneven. In the sparsely populated West, men outnumbered women by almost two to one. On the other hand, women outnumbered men in the South, where so many men had died during the Civil War.

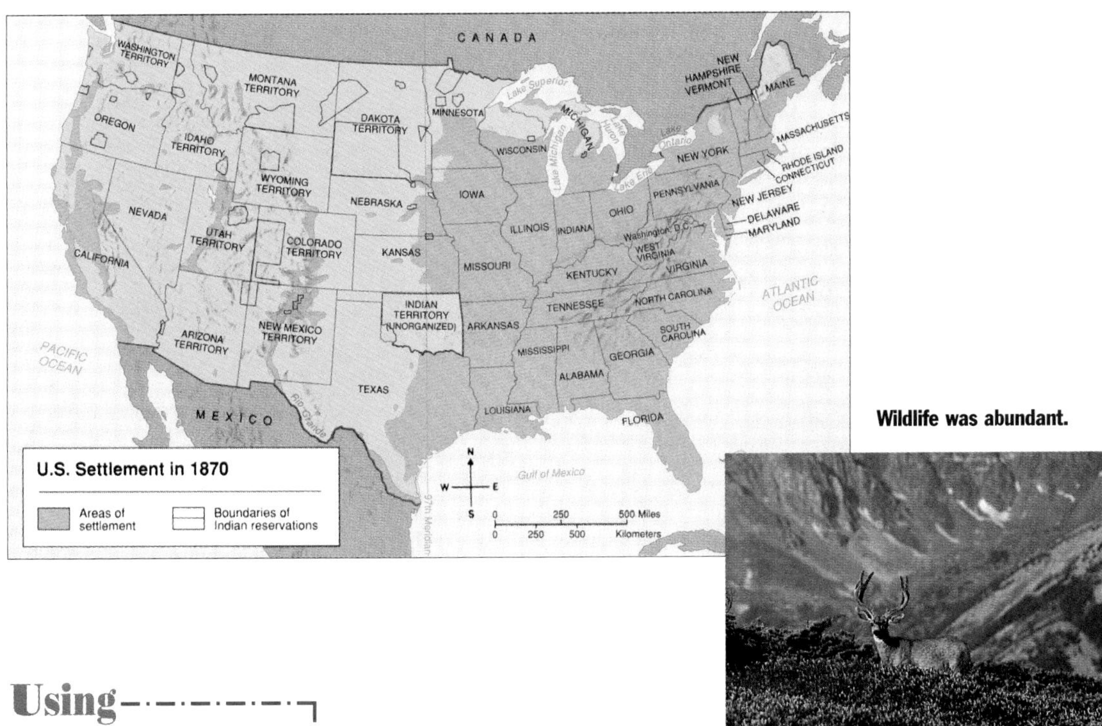

Wildlife was abundant.

Using Map Skills

Study the map. Then answer the questions. Refer to the map on pages R4–R5, if necessary.

1. Locate the Great Plains. What states and territories were in this area?

2. Locate the Rocky Mountains, the Cascades, and the Sierra Nevada. How does the map support the claim that mountains slowed down but did not stop Americans moving westward?

Discussion

Checking Understanding

1. Where did most of the U.S. population live in 1870? (Between the Atlantic coast and the 97th meridian)

2. Which areas of the West were major areas of settlement in 1870? (California; the area along the northern part of the Rio Grande in present-day New Mexico north to Denver in the Colorado Territory; and Utah, especially near Salt Lake City.)

Stimulating Critical Thinking

3. Using the population density map of the United States on page R11, choose one location that has many people living there and one that has few people. Which factor do you think is most important in causing the population level to be high or low in each location? (Answers will vary. Students might mention any geographical conditions that influence where people live, such as the nearness to fresh water and waterways, the ease of acquiring food and making a living, climate, type of elevation.)

Using Map Skills

Answers

1. Eastern Montana Territory, Wyoming Territory, Colorado Territory, New Mexico Territory; and western Dakota Territory, Nebraska, Kansas, Indian Territory, and Texas.

2. These three mountain ranges all run in a north-south direction and were difficult for the pioneers who were moving westward to cross.

Teaching MOVEMENT: What Were the East-West Networks?

Explain to students that the theme of *movement* explains how areas are connected by transportation, trade, and communication.

Have students read pages 6 and 7. Tell them that the drawing on page 6 shows telegraph wire being strung. By 1870 messages could be flashed over almost 100,000 miles of wire. Ask students what kinds of things might have hampered telegraph communication. (Wires could be cut or damaged in storms.)

Have students look at the map on page 6 showing railroads in the United States in 1870. Point out that in 1870 most of the railroad lines were concentrated in the northeastern and north-central states, and only one line reached the Pacific coast.

Bonus Activity

Making a Poster

Have students work in pairs to create posters enticing people to use the telegraph. Encourage students to use their imaginations and to be as persuasive as possible. Then as a class, discuss the effectiveness of the posters.

Geography Footnote

Prior to 1870 most pioneers traveling the trails to the West Coast left from Independence, Missouri, or from other towns on the Missouri River in the early spring, as soon as the rivers could be crossed safely. They traveled for six to seven months, across the Great Plains, the Rocky Mountains, and the Great Basin, hoping to reach the High Sierras before harsh weather and snow made crossing these rugged peaks impossible.

MOVEMENT: What Were the East-West Networks?

The movement theme helps you examine the communication and transportation networks that linked people and places. Such linkages connected the different parts of the country.

In 1860 the Pony Express had been started to speed up mail delivery. It began its operation with about 80 riders. They carried the mail from St. Joseph, Missouri, to Sacramento, California. Using a relay system of changing horses every 10 to 15 miles and riders every 75 miles, the Pony Express carried the mail in 10 days. Previously, it had taken several weeks for mail to go between Missouri and California. The system, however, only lasted a year and a half. It was then replaced by the telegraph and the railroads.

On May 24, 1844, Samuel F. B. Morse demonstrated the telegraph. Using a combination of dots and dashes that represented the letters of the alphabet, operators could send messages through wires attached to wooden poles. This system of dots and dashes eventually became known as the Morse code. By 1870 about 100,000 miles of wire connected every sizeable settlement. Telegraph lines stretched across the country. They carried people's messages rapidly from place to place.

From 1830 to 1870 the nation's railroads continuously expanded. By 1870 the country had around 50,000 miles of track. Look at the map below. All states east of the Mississippi River had railroad services.

Telegraph wires stretched from East to West all across the nation.

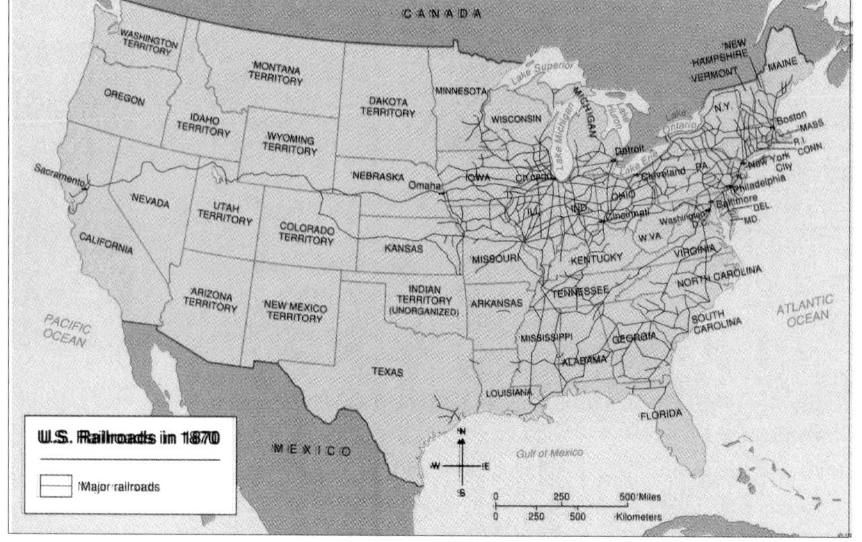

Geography Footnote
In 1869 two of the world's greatest engineering feats were completed. In the United States the first transcontinental railroad line was completed, enabling people to travel from New York to California in eight to ten days. In Egypt the Suez Canal was completed, which by connecting the Mediterranean Sea to the Red Sea eliminated the need to sail around Africa when going from Europe to East Asia. This reduced sailing time by many weeks.

In May 1869 the dream of a transcontinental railroad became a reality. This railroad connected Omaha, Nebraska, to Sacramento, California, helping to tie the East and West together.

In 1870 the nation stood "at the beginning" of a great period of economic growth. Up to this time, there had not been enough railroad lines. New routes were needed to accommodate existing traffic. Many new railroad lines would be built in the next 25 years.

Shipping on the Great Lakes was also important in 1870. Mounting demands for iron, copper, lumber, and wheat resulted in greatly increased tonnages passing from the upper lakes to the East. During 1870, 690,000 tons of cargo passed through the Soo Canal. Gradually Great Lakes navigation became integrated with railroad transportation. This meant that the cheapest way to haul goods from Chicago to New York City was partly by rail and partly by water.

Link to History

Use the text, map, and pictures on these pages to draw conclusions about how the new communication and transportation networks affected the growth of settlements.

1. Name five ocean ports that also were rail centers. Speculate why this happened.
2. Name three cities on the Great Lakes that had become rail centers by 1870. Speculate about why they became rail centers.
3. Write a sentence summarizing why railroad depots were becoming just as important centers of settlement as ocean ports and river landings.

By 1870 huge quantities of natural resources and finished goods were moved by rail and by ship.

Discussion

Checking Understanding

1. How was east-west communication and transportation improved by 1870? (By means of the telegraph, railroads, and shipping on the Great Lakes)

2. How were improved communication and transportation important to the nation? (Answers will vary but should include the following: sped up the rate at which people, goods, news, and mail traveled; changed trading patterns)

Stimulating Critical Thinking

3. Why wasn't the first transcontinental railroad built between New Orleans and Los Angeles? (Civil War was being fought in that part of the country.)

Link to History

Answers

1. Boston, New York, Philadelphia, Baltimore, and Washington, D.C.

2. Chicago, Cleveland, and Detroit. They became rail centers because farmers could send their crops by rail to these port cities and then by ship to the East.

3. Railroad depots were becoming just as important as centers of settlement as were ocean ports and river landings because more and more merchants and business people were locating there in order to ship and receive goods from other places.

Teaching

RELATIONSHIPS WITHIN PLACES: How Was the Land Used?

Explain to students that the theme of *relationships within places* defines an area by the way people interact with their surroundings.

Ask students to suggest ways in which people can use land. (agriculture, factories, mining, lumbering, commerce) Tell students that by 1870 the land of the United States was used in many ways, depending on climate, location, and available natural resources.

Have students read pages 8 and 9. Then ask them why 25 percent of the population of the United States lived in urban areas by 1870. (Industrial jobs lured rural people as well as immigrants to the cities.)

Bonus Activity

Create a Time Line

To present an overview of new inventions that affected how people used the land, groups of students can create time lines. They should do research to find out about at least five inventions from 1865 to 1880 (e.g., 1868—James Oliver developed new plow to cut through plains sod. After completing their time lines, they should display them for comparison and discussion of the significance of each invention.

Geography Footnote

Many of the important issues facing the world today are the consequences—intended and unintended, positive and negative—of human modifications of the land. To survive, people depend on the physical environment. They adapt to it and modify it to suit their changing need for such things as food, clothing, water, shelter, energy, and recreational facilities. As a result, people have altered the land in ways that have brought economic prosperity to some areas and created environmental crises in others.

The impacts vary in scope and scale. They can be local and small-scale (e.g., acid stream pollution from strip mining in eastern Pennsylvania) or global and large-scale (e.g., the clearing of the forests of North America for agriculture).

RELATIONSHIPS WITHIN PLACES: How Was the Land Used?

This theme helps you see how the American people had begun to change how they used the land. In the country's early years, most Americans farmed. By 1870 many Americans still farmed but more and more of them worked in factories.

In 1870 most of the people continued to live on farms or in small towns. Nearly 75 percent of the population lived in communities that had fewer than 2,500 people. However, mechanization of farm work had begun in the 1830s and 1840s with the introduction of machines such as the reaper and the steel plow. As a result of these machines, production had increased. Fewer and fewer farmers were needed to do the work.

Gradually, industrial jobs lured more and more people into the cities. By 1870, 25 percent of the population lived in urban areas. This was a sharp increase from 1783, when only 4 percent had lived in urban areas.

In 1870 the United States possessed a remarkable number of assets that contributed to the growth of industries. It had a vast supply of natural resources, including coal, iron ore, timber, and water power. The nation's growing work force, many of whom were immigrants, provided the labor needed in the nation's mines and factories.

As the population of the United States had increased through the years, the demand for manufactured goods had grown as well. The people wanted a variety of tools, clothes, household equipment, and machines to make other machines. The most important industries in 1870 were lumber and

The use of mechanized farm machinery led to a decrease in the number of farms.

Geography Footnote
The Erie Canal was finished in 1825. It made trade and travel across New York State much cheaper. As a result, towns on the canal, such as Buffalo, Rochester, Syracuse, Rome, and Utica, grew into cities as they became stops for travelers and trade.

Geography Footnote
Industries grew quickly in the United States after the Civil War because the nation had vast amounts of raw materials. For example, steel mills developed near coal or iron ore deposits, furniture factories and paper mills developed near hardwood forests, and textile-manufacturing plants developed near cotton fields.

Cities such as Utica, New York, benefited from an increase in workers for its factories.

woodworking mills, flour-mill and gristmill products, clothing, iron and steel, and foundry and machine-shop products.

Increased sales and investments, in turn, provided the money that industries needed for further growth. Investment in manufacturing enterprises attracted people with money. In 1870 a moderate-sized factory cost about $8,000. Although wages for most workers were low, some people could accumulate the money to buy one or more factories.

An important factor in America's becoming an industrial nation was the expansion of the country's railroads. They contributed to the transformation of many small towns into cities. The railroads also made resources which had been inaccessible in the past available.

Link to History

As you read about people and events, try linking the *who* and the *what* to the *where*. Ask yourself why peoples settled where they did. How did where people settled help shape their way of life? In turn, what effect did those ways of life have on the land? Put yourself into one of the pictures on these pages.

1. Who are you and what are you doing?
2. Where are you? How does being in that place influence your activities?
3. Are your activities changing the place? If so, how?

Discussion

Checking Understanding

1. Why were people lured to the cities? (Because of the prevalence of industrial jobs)

2. What assets contributed to the growth of industries in the United States? (A vast supply of natural resources and a growing work force)

3. Why were railroads important to the growth of industry? (They made resources that had been inaccessible in the past available.)

4. How do people change the land? (Answers will vary but could include altering the landscape to suit their needs by building cities, industries, and railroads.)

Stimulating Critical Thinking

5. List examples of human impact on the environment in your area. Explain whether the impact has been positive or negative. (Answers will vary.)

Link to History

Answers

Sample responses:

1. A farmer interested in purchasing mechanized farm machinery

2. In a farming area of the Great Plains; I live on a farm and if I buy a piece of mechanized farm machinery I will not have to hire as many people to help me.

3. Yes. I am able to plant more and more land and produce more. However, many of the people who used to work for me have moved to cities to work in factories.

Teaching

REGIONS: How Was the Country Divided?

Explain to students that the theme of *region* identifies an area according to its outstanding characteristics, such as climate, cultural traits, economic activities, or landforms.

Have students read page 10. Tell them that in 1870 the United States could be divided into three regions—the North, the South, and the West. Have them look at the chart showing the population of cities in 1870 on page 10 and the map on page 11. Ask students in which region most of the largest cities in the United States were located. (North) Ask which cities were located in the South. (New Orleans, Washington, D.C., and Louisville) Ask which city was located in the West. (San Francisco) Ask which state had the most large cities. (New York)

Bonus Activity

Mapping Sectional Differences

Organize the class into three groups. Have each group create a pictorial map showing one of the regions in the United States in 1870—the North, the South, or the West. It should show the boundaries of the particular region; important physical features; drawings or photocopies of pictures of economic activities, products, workers, and transportation.

Geography Footnote

A region is a part of the earth that has one or more common characteristics. Regions vary according to the characteristics that we use to identify them. A region can be characterized by a common human feature, such as the presence of people who share a particular language, religion, nationality, political identity, or culture, or by a common physical feature, such as the presence of a particular type of climate, landform, or vegetation.

Regions can be as small as a neighborhood or as vast as a territory covering thousands of square miles in which the people all speak the same language.

REGIONS: How Was the Country Divided?

The regions theme helps you divide the United States in 1870 into smaller units. A region is an area of land that has one or more features that make it different from neighboring areas. Regions may be defined by physical, cultural, political, or economic characteristics. In the 1870s the United States could be divided into three regions. These regions were the North, the South, and the West.

Locate each of the three regions on the map on the opposite page. List the states in each region. In what region would you have lived?

Population of Cities, 1870

City	Population
New York, New York	942,000
Philadelphia, Pennsylvania	674,000
Brooklyn, New York	396,000
St. Louis, Missouri	311,000
Chicago, Illinois	300,000
Baltimore, Maryland	267,000
Boston, Massachusetts	250,000
Cincinnati, Ohio	216,000
New Orleans, Louisiana	192,000
San Francisco, California	150,000
Buffalo, New York	117,000
Washington, D.C.	110,000
Newark, New Jersey	105,000
Louisville, Kentucky	100,000

Southern city, New Orleans, Louisiana (above); western mining town of Black Hawk Point (right); northern industrial city, Buffalo, New York (far right bottom)

Geography Footnote

One of the most important minerals in the North was coal, which was found underground in western Pennsylvania. Coal is a black mineral that is formed from plants that have lain buried deep in the earth for thousands of years.

One of coal's most important uses in 1870 was in the making of steel. Steelworkers needed coal to produce a fire hot enough to melt iron. When melted and mixed with other minerals, iron turned into an even harder metal called steel.

Have students list the states in the North in 1870. Tell them that New York, Pennsylvania, Illinois, and Ohio were the four largest Northern states in number of inhabitants in 1870. Have them use an almanac to determine if this is still true today. (Yes)

Ask students what was the largest city in the North in 1870. (New York City) Have them use an almanac to determine if it is still the largest city today. (Yes)

Bonus Activity

Comparing Cities

To identify how cities in the North (e.g., New York City, Boston, Baltimore, Philadelphia, Buffalo, Chicago, St. Louis) were alike and how they were different, have students write a different fact about each city on several cards. For example, they might note its size, its location along a certain latitude line, its location near or far from water, its location near or far from railroad lines or canals, its nearness to particular raw materials. They can then sort the cards to show similarities and differences.

Teaching
The South

Have students look at the map on page 11. Ask them which three bodies of water formed boundaries for the South. (Atlantic Ocean, Gulf of Mexico, and Rio Grande)

Have students look at the chart on page 10. Ask them what was the largest city in the South. (New Orleans) Ask them to describe its relative location. (New Orleans is located at the mouth of the Mississippi River near the Gulf of Mexico in southern Louisiana.)

Remind students that Texas was the largest state in land area in 1870. Then have them use an almanac to determine if that is true today. (No, Alaska is the largest state in land area.)

Bonus Activity

Making a Poster

Have students do research to find out about the cattle industry based on longhorns that developed in Texas. After they have finished their research, have them draw a poster illustrating their findings.

Geography Footnote

The Coastal Plain changes in width from only a few miles in New Jersey to more than 500 miles in Mississippi. Numerous rivers wind slowly across the plain and flow into the Atlantic Ocean or the Gulf of Mexico. These sites helped make many cities—e.g. Savannah, Charleston, and Mobile—important ports.

The South This region differed in many ways from the North. For one thing, landforms in the South were more varied. Many states were on the Gulf of Mexico and Atlantic coastal plains. Some states were within the Appalachians or the adjacent Piedmont. Western Texas was located on the Great Plains.

The most obvious difference between the North and South, however, was the climate. Most of the South had a humid subtropical climate. Its winters were far milder than in the North. Western Texas was semiarid. Elsewhere the South received plenty of rain for growing crops.

Vaqueros **who worked for Texas ranchers were careful guardians of their employers' longhorns (below).**

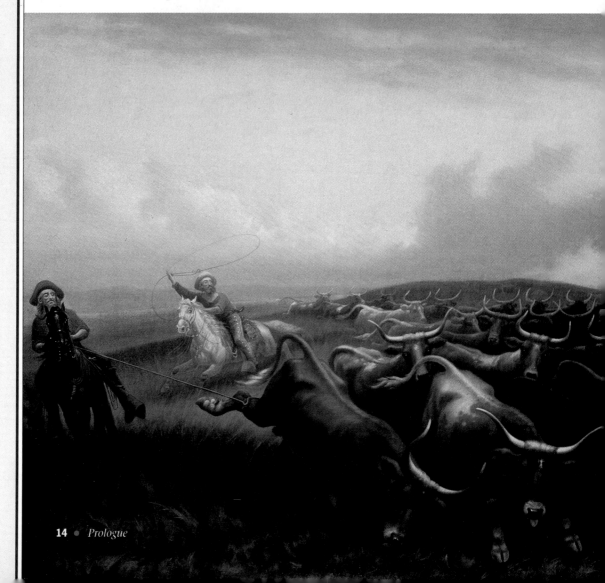

Geography Footnote

The Mississippi, the longest river in the United States, travels from near the Canadian border through the Midwest and the South. Many rivers, or tributaries, join the Mississippi along its trip to the Gulf of Mexico. The Mississippi becomes its widest after it is joined by the Missouri River. All along its course, the Mississippi picks up soil. When the river empties into the Gulf of Mexico, it leaves the soil behind. Over the years, the soil has built up into an area of land called a *delta*. Deltas make very rich farmland.

Point out to students that low-lying plains covered most of the South. The Coastal Plain (made up of the Atlantic Coastal Plain and the Gulf Coastal Plain) was and still is the predominant physical feature of the South. Have the students find these plains on the physical map on pages R4–R5 and describe their location. (They stretch from Maine along the Atlantic seaboard to Florida and then turn westward along the coasts of Alabama, Mississippi, Louisiana, and Texas.)

Bonus Activity

Value of Cotton

Have students keep a list of things they wear and of products or furnishings they use that are made of all or more than half cotton. Remind them to check labels of clothing to determine what the article is made from. Have the class make a master list of all of these products. Have students consider how important a part cotton plays in their daily lives.

Cotton farming continued to be as important as ranching. A cotton boll (inset) is ready to be harvested.

In 1870 the South was the most truly rural section of the United States. Before the beginning of the Civil War, most industries had been related to agriculture. The most important of which was the cotton industry. During the war, many of the South's cities, nearly all its industrial plants, and many miles of railroad lines were destroyed. Following the war, the South began to rebuild. The population increased. Most of its people were farmers and the raising of cotton continued to be important through the South as far west as east Texas.

Other people moved to the growing cities in the South. One striking example was Atlanta, Georgia. In the 1830s it was a railroad depot with only a few people. By 1870 Atlanta was a city of about 22,000 people. Other southern cities such as Mobile, Alabama; Nashville, Tennessee; and Vicksburg, Mississippi; began to show signs of renewal.

Teaching
The West

Point out to students that as the Great Plains stretch westward, they gradually slant upward to the Rocky Mountains. Much of the region is covered by mountains and plateaus.

The Rocky Mountains form the largest chain of mountains in North America. In 1870 they stretched across one western state—Nevada and several territories—Montana, Wyoming, Colorado, New Mexico, Idaho, Utah, and Arizona. Three states and territories in the West bordered the Pacific Ocean. Have the students find these on the map on page 3. (Washington Territory, Oregon, and California)

Ask students what was the largest city in the West in 1870. (San Francisco) Have them use an almanac to determine if it is still the largest city today. (No, Los Angeles is larger.)

Bonus Activity

Having a Mock Trial

People perceive using the land in different ways. Have students research the conflict in the west in 1870 among cattle ranchers, sheep herders, and farmers. Identify how each wanted to use the land. Then have some students present a mock trial in which the three groups are represented. The rest of the class can be the jury for settling the conflict and for determining how the land should be used or divided.

Geography Footnote

One of the most famous artists to portray the American West was John James Audubon. Best known for his paintings of North American birds, he also did extensive studies of mammals. He journeyed up the Missouri River, into the Rocky Mountains, and back to St. Louis, collecting specimens and making sketches of the scenery that served as the background for his books.

Geography Footnote

The West is known for its extremes. The lowest elevation in the Western Hemisphere is at Badwater, in California's Death Valley. It lies 282 feet (86 m) below sea level. Only 75 miles (120 km) from Death Valley rises Mt. Whitney. At 14,494 feet (4,418 m), it is the highest point in the conterminous United States.

Bill Pickett, the originator of steer wrestling, poses for the camera (above). A lone buffalo represents the end of the old Indian way of life (below).

The Baldwin Hotel and Theatre in San Francisco in 1874 (above). Fort Keogh, Montana, is one sign of the end of American Indians' freedom (right).

The West In 1870 this region covered about one-half of the country. After the Civil War, pioneers streamed into the West.

One difference between the West and the other two regions was that most of the West was sparsely populated. As you read earlier, San Francisco was the only city with a population of over 100,000 people. Most other settlements were towns. For example, Denver was a town of 5,000 people in the Colorado Territory. It was the largest place between Kansas City and the Rocky Mountains.

Another difference was the way in which many people made their living. Some were miners, others were cattle ranchers. However, many of the new settlers were farmers. On the Great Plains, farming families struggled because of the scarcity of rainfall. They had to develop new farming methods.

Another difference that made this region unique was that it had the largest number of American Indians. In 1870 about 175,000 Indians lived there. For many years settlers and Indians had been in conflict over the ownership of western lands. In the late 1860s the U.S. government devised a new Indian policy that confined the Indians to reservations. Major tribes reluctantly agreed to the new policy. The amount of land in reservations reached its greatest size in 1870. Find these reservations on the map on page 5.

The largest reservation was the Indian Territory, present-day Oklahoma. Within this territory were the greatest number of Indian tribes in America.

Geography Footnote

The Indian and white settlers had very different views of the value and ownership of the land. The Indians were proud of the land. It was to be cherished and shared by all people. The land belonged to everyone equally. Horses, hides, teepees, or cooking utensils could be owned but not the land. The white settlers did not understand the Indians' sentiments about the land. The whites wanted to sell the land. Moreover, they wanted to divide the land so that it could be owned by individuals as private property. The land was there to be planted, mined, and built upon for personal profit.

Eastern and Western tribes occupied different sections. The reservations north of Nebraska rivaled the Indian Territory in size, but not in the variety of inhabitants. Two of these reservations belonged to the Sioux and the Crows.

In Chapters 4–15, you will discover how these three regions—the North, the South, and the West—continued to develop. You will also read how the geography of the United States continued to change over time.

Developing a Mental Map

A mental map is a picture you carry in your head of how an area looks and where things are located. You use a mental map to find your way around your school and community. This year you will be expanding your mental map of the United States, beginning with your region.

1. Which of these three historical regions do you live in today?
2. Based on your own mental map, list five features of your region today.
3. **Hands-On Geography** Image that one morning you wake up somewhere in the United States in 1870. Of the three regions, on the map on page 11, where would you want to wake up? To help you decide, with a partner make a chart listing advantages and disadvantages of living in the three regions.

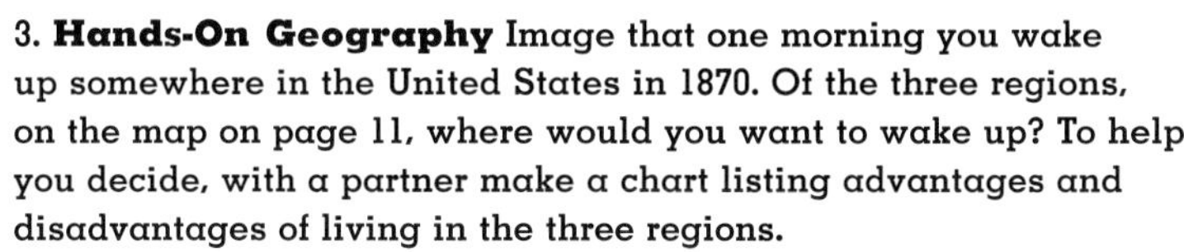

Discussion

Checking Understanding

1. In which region were most of the major cities of the United States located in 1870? (the North)

2. Which region of the United States was the most industrialized in 1870? (the North)

3. Which region of the United States was the most truly rural in 1870? (the South)

4. Which region of the United States was the most sparsely populated in 1870? (the West)

5. Which region contained the Indian Territory? (the West)

Stimulating Critical Thinking

6. What characteristics distinguished the three regions in 1870? (Answers will vary but should include location, distribution of population, kinds of landforms, types of land use.)

Developing a Mental Map

Answers

Answers will vary, depending upon the region. For example:

1. Eastern part of the West, e.g., the Great Plains

2. Flat land, few trees, large farms, few lakes, mostly rural areas

3. Lists will vary but may include advantages and disadvantages of different climates, kinds of landforms, and density of population.

Teaching

Types of Map Projections

Remind students that maps are critical in understanding the geography of a place, but they have limitations. Point out that a flat map that shows parallels and meridians is called a *map projection*. Have the students read and look at the different projections on pages 18 and 19.

Explain that a good way to check distortion is to study a map's arrangement of parallels and meridians. Tell them to keep the following facts in mind. On a globe with no distortions: (1) All meridians meet at the poles; (2) All parallels are exactly parallel to one another; (3) Parallels vary in length; and (4) All meridians are the same length.

Bonus Activity

Designing Advertisements

Have students design a 30-second television or radio commercial for either the Mercator or the Robinson projections. Students should point out the advantages of each kind of map, and perhaps criticize the disadvantages of the other map in their advertisements. Students should include as many uses for their type of projection as possible for an added sales feature.

Geography Footnote

Most world maps that are used today, including world maps used in this book, use equal-area projections. Such maps show land and water sizes accurately, but the shapes of the land are somewhat distorted.

Types of Map Projections

Because globes are round like the earth, they are the only true maps of the world. Globes give a true picture of the shapes and sizes of land and water areas. Globes, also, show true distances and true directions between two places.

Mapmakers have a problem, however. It is difficult to make a true likeness of the round earth on a flat sheet of paper. They can cut a globe apart along its meridians and flatten it, but this "unpeeling" of a globe is very hard to read.

To solve this problem, mapmakers have invented different projections. They admit, however, that each projection has to sacrifice something. Some projections are shown below and on the facing page. On the maps in this book, you will find the name of the projection under the scale bar. To find out what is distorted, refer back to these pages.

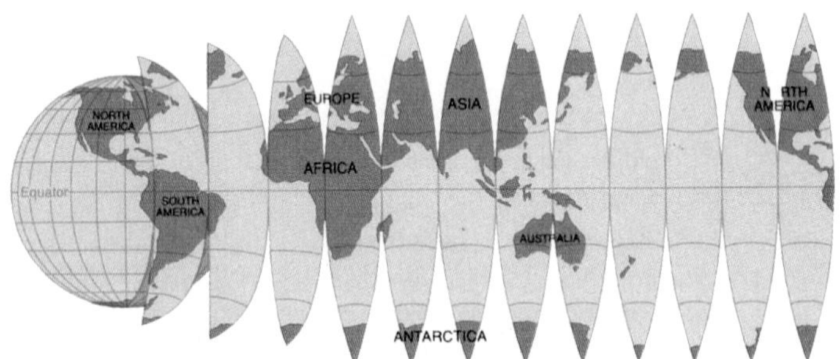

Interrupted Goode's Homolosine
This is one of several equal-area projections. As a result of being cut apart in the oceans, the shapes and sizes of most land areas are almost correct. These maps are useful for people who want to study land areas. Directions and distances between places are not true.

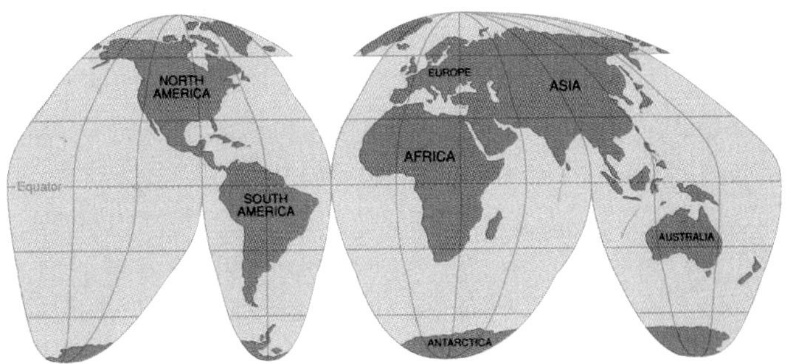

Robinson
This is another kind of equal-area projection, but it is not interrupted. The North and South poles appear as lines rather than points. This map shows the sizes of most large land and water areas correctly. However, around the edges, the shapes of some land and water areas are distorted. Distances are not true. In this book, many of the maps that show the world and continents use this projection.

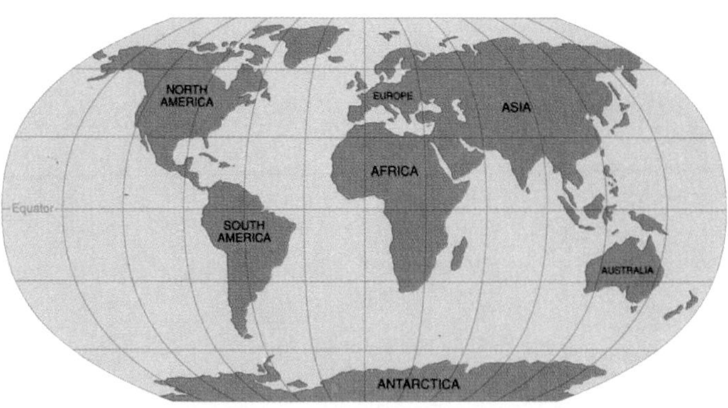

Geography Footnote

Geradus Mercator (1512-1594) was born in the Netherlands and educated at some of that country's best schools. He became the leading map maker of the 1500s. He won lasting fame because of his world map of 1569. It introduced a new way of show-ingthe roughly ball-shaped earth on a flat sheet of paper. This method, called the Mercator projection, proved ideal for navigation and is still used today.

Mercator

This kind of map projection was developed in the 16th century. In this map, the lines of latitude and longitude are stretched. Because the meridians do not meet at the poles as they do on a globe, the distances between the parallels become greater and greater as they approach the poles.

This stretching does several things. It keeps the shapes of land and water areas true, but their sizes are not true. On the earth, South America is much larger than Greenland. On Mercator maps, Greenland is much larger than South America. However, the shapes of both places are nearly true.

Mercator maps also show directions correctly. This gives sailors a way to plot a true course at sea. All they have to do is draw a straight line between two places. Mercator maps are still used for ocean travel today. In this book, many of the maps that show parts of the United States are Mercator projections.

Azimuthal Equidistant

Some maps show true distances from a central point. Any point of the earth's surface can be chosen as the center. The most well-known equidistant maps are polar maps. On this map, the North Pole is in the center. This means that if you are going from any point on the map toward the center, you are going north. Shapes at the edges of the map are not true.

Find the straight lines which go out from the center of the map. These lines are great circles. On polar maps, all great circles are straight lines. Airplane pilots like to use polar maps, because they often fly great-circle routes between places. You can find a polar map on page 571.

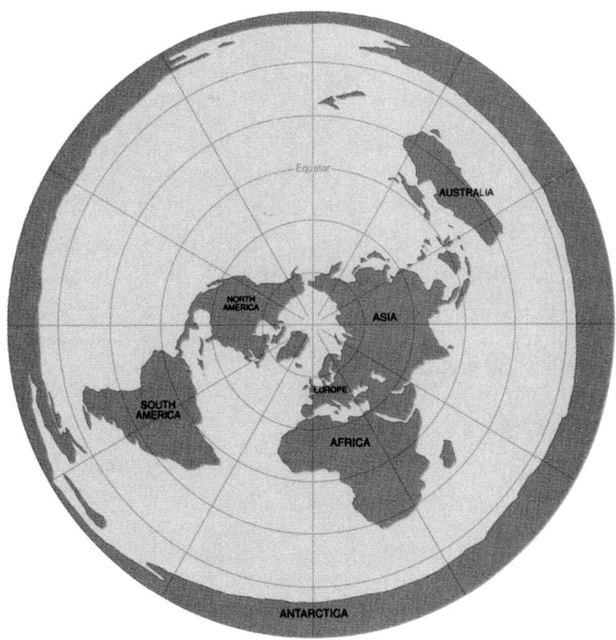

Discussion

Checking Understanding

1. Why is the globe the most accurate map of the earth? (Because globes are round like the earth)

2. Why do mapmakers accept untrue world maps as a problem that cannot be solved? (No matter how hard they try, they cannot make a true likeness of the round earth on a flat sheet of paper.)

3. What four features can be shown on a globe at one time, but not on a flat map? (True picture of the shapes and sizes of land and water areas and true distances and true directions between two places.)

4. What can you do to check to see if a map distorts reality? (Compare it with a globe; study the arrangements of parallels and meridians)

Stimulating Critical Thinking

5. Why is a polar projection more useful than a Mercator projection to airplane pilots? (Unlike the Mercator projection, the polar projection allows great circles to be drawn in straight lines across the map.)

6. Which of the fifty states of the United States is the most distorted in size on a Mercator map? Explain why. (Alaska, because it is farthest away from the Equator.)

At·a·Glance Review

Part 1

Beginnings to 1791

Review: Part 1 Planning Guide

Section	Student Text	Teacher's Edition Activities
Part 1 Opener pp. 20–21	**Link to the Present** *Indian* as a term, p. 20	**Answers to Captions,** p. 20, p. 21
1 **The Meeting of Worlds** pp. 22–33	Beginning the Story with **Christopher Columbus,** pp. 22–23 **History Mystery** p. 23 **Keys to History Time Line** pp. 24–25, pp. 28–29, pp. 30–31 **Hands-On History** Columbus's crew, p. 23 Recreating a temple treasure, p. 26 **Point of View** When did the first settlers migrate to America?, p. 25 **Link to the Present** The appeal of spices, p. 29	**Setting the Stage Activity** Effects of the Printing Press, p. 22 **Warm-Up Activity** Migration Then and Now, p. 24 Trading Goods, p. 28 Identifying Risk-Worthy Goals, p. 30 **Lesson Activity** Recording Aztec Tribute, p. 26 **Bonus Activity** Identifying Environments, p. 27 Identifying Exchanges Today, p. 32 **Wrap-Up Activity** Identifying Good and Bad Effects, p. 32
2 **The Planting of Colonies** pp. 34–45	Beginning the Story with **Pocahontas,** pp. 34–35 **History Mystery** p. 35 **Keys to History Time Line** pp. 36–37, pp. 38–39 pp. 42–43 **Hands-On History** Pocahontas rescues John Smith, p. 35 Planning a modern-day entrada, p. 37 Advertising the colonies, p. 41	**Setting the Stage Activity** Reacting to Strangers, p. 34 **Warm-Up Activity** A Conquistador Recruiting Poster, p. 36 Listing Reasons for Colonization, p. 38 Charting Diversity Today, p. 42 **Lesson Activity** A Puritan View of Settlement, p. 40 **Bonus Activity** "Best" and "Worst" Colonies, p. 40 **Wrap-Up Activity** An Indian Protest Letter, p. 41 Reporting on the Middle Passage, p. 44
3 **The Birth of a New Nation** pp. 46–59	Beginning the Story with **George Washington,** pp. 46–47 **History Mystery** p. 47 **Keys to History Time Line** pp. 48–49, pp. 52–53, pp. 56–57 **Hands-On History** Washington's letter home, p. 47 Joining the continental army, p. 53 **Reading Maps** European Claims, p. 49	**Setting the Stage Activity** How Much Do You Know?, p. 46 **Warm-Up Activity** Role-playing an Interview, p. 48 Preparing for War, p. 52 Views on National Government, p. 56 **Lesson Activity** Boston Tea Party News Reports, p. 50 Geography, p. 54 **Bonus Activity** Note from a Spy, p. 55 Class Constitutions, p. 58 **Wrap-Up Activity** Letters on the Coercive Acts, p. 51 Assessing a Defeat, p. 55 "Out of Many, One," p. 58
Evaluation	**Section 1 Survey,** p. 33 **Section 2 Survey,** p. 45 Alternative Assessment **Section 3 Survey,** p. 59 Alternative Assessment	**Answers to Section 1 Survey,** p. 33 **Answers to Section 2 Survey,** p. 45 **Answers to Section 3 Survey,** p. 59 (Alternative Assessment guidelines are in the Review Take-Home Planner.)

Teacher's Resource Package

American Readings, pp. 1–4

Geography Extensions, pp. 3–4

Using Historical Documents, pp. 8–17

Chapter Resources Binder
- **Study Guide,** p. 1
- **Reinforcement,** p. 4
- **Skills Development,** pp. 7–8

Chapter Summaries: English and Spanish, pp. 6–7, pp. 8–9, pp. 10–11

Chapter Resources Binder
- **Study Guide,** p. 2
- **Reinforcement,** p. 5

Chapter Summaries: English and Spanish, pp. 12–13, pp. 14–15, pp. 16–17

Chapter Resources Binder
- **Study Guide,** p. 3
- **Reinforcement,** p. 6

Chapter Summaries: English and Spanish, pp. 18–19, pp. 20–21, pp. 22–23

Chapter and Unit Tests

Section 1 Tests, Forms A and B, pp. 7–10

Section 2 Tests, Forms A and B, pp. 11–14

Section 3 Tests, Forms A and B, pp. 15–18

Take-Home Planner

Reduced Views
- **American Readings,** p. 11
- **Geography Extensions,** p. 13
- **Using Historical Documents,** p. 12

Reduced Views
- **Study Guide,** p. 9
- **Reinforcement,** p. 9
- **Skills Development,** p. 10

Section 1 Answers, pp. 24–30

Reduced Views
- **Study Guide,** p. 9
- **Reinforcement,** p. 10

Section 2 Answers, pp. 24–30

Reduced Views
- **Study Guide,** p. 9
- **Reinforcement,** p. 10

Section 3 Answers, pp. 24–30

Reduced Views
- **Section Tests,** p. 13

Alternative Assessment
Guideline for Scoring, pp. 7–8

Additional Resources

Wall Time Line

Transparency Package

Transparencies 1–3

Transparencies 4–7

Transparencies 8–11

SelecTest Testing Software

Review Section 1 Tests, Forms A and B

Review Section 2 Tests, Forms A and B

Review Section 3 Tests, Forms A and B

Vital Links

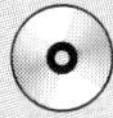

Videodisc **CD-ROM**

Columbus Lands (see TE p. 22)
Anasazi Indians (see TE p. 27)
American Indians (see TE p. 27)
Mohawk Indians (see TE p. 27)
Ancestry of African Americans (see TE p. 29)
Henry Hudson (see TE p. 30)
Cortéz (see TE p. 36)
Jamestown (see TE p. 38)
Life at Jamestown (see TE p. 39)
William Penn and Delaware Indians (see TE p. 41)
Voice of a Slave (see TE p. 44)
"African Song" (see TE p. 44)
French and Indian War (see TE p. 48)
"Revolutionary Tea" (see TE p. 50)
Voice of a Publisher (see TE p. 50)
Benjamin Franklin (see TE p. 58)

Introducing the Review: Part 1

Tell students that the Review is divided into two parts. The three sections of Part 1 are previewed on this and the following page.

Navajo Rock Painting

The painting depicts a procession of Spanish cavalry across Navajo land. It is thought that the painting shows soldiers led by Lieutenant Antonio Narbona, who attacked the Navajos at Massacre Cave in 1805.

Answers to Caption: Student responses will vary. By 1805, however, the Navajo had probably heard enough about the Spanish to view them as a threat to their way of life. The Spanish soldiers, in turn, probably regarded the Navajo as they had other Native American groups—as uncivilized savages who should be brought under Spanish control and converted to Christianity, by force, if necessary.

Teaching the

Link to the Present

Ask: **Why do you think most Indians prefer to be called by their tribe's name?** (To recognize each tribe has its own identity.)

History Footnote

For centuries the Indians of Canyon de Chelly have painted images on the cliffs. The Navajos were the most recent to do so. Most of their paintings probably date from the mid-1770s on. The rock painting shown is above the Standing Cow ruins in Canyon de Muerto, a side canyon within Canyon de Chelly. The black-robed central figure is about three feet (0.91 m) tall.

History Footnote

The *Van Bergen Overmantel* (1732–1733) is attributed to John Heaten. By the early eighteenth century, artists were at work in several parts of the colonies. But the most active school of painting was in the Hudson River valley, where the major landholders commissioned semitrained artists like Heaten to paint portraits for their Dutch-style manor houses.

Review

Part 1 Beginnings to 1791

The Meeting of Worlds

For thousands of years, the people of the Americas lived apart from the rest of the world. In that time they created complex cultures and great civilizations. With the arrival of Columbus in 1492, however, their splendid isolation vanished.

This rock painting from Canyon de Chelly, Arizona, shows Spanish soldiers entering the land of the Navajo. How do you think the Navajo saw the Spanish? As friends or threats? How did the Spanish see the Navajo?

Link to the Present

Indian as a term Europeans of the 1400s used the term *Indies* to refer to India, China, Japan, and the other Asian lands. When Christopher Columbus landed in the Bahamas in 1492, he was certain he had reached the Indies. He called the native people he met *Indians.*

Although Columbus was wrong about where he had landed, the name *Indian* stuck. Today many descendants of America's earliest people prefer *Indian* over terms like *Amer-Indian* or even *Native American.* However, the first preference for most is to be called by the name of their tribe or nation, such as Arapaho, Cherokee, Mandan, or Zuni. In most Indian languages, the tribal name means "the people."

History Footnote

John Trumbull (1756–1843), who had served in the Continental Army as an aide to George Washington, is best known for his scenes of the War of Independence. Encouraged by John Adams and Thomas Jefferson, he began in 1785 to work on a series of paintings glorifying the most famous Patriot leaders. First he made individual portraits of many of these men, painting them from life. Later he copied these portraits into larger revolutionary scenes. Several of his large paintings, including *The Declaration of Independence,* decorate the rotunda of the Capitol building in Washington, D.C. Jefferson called Trumbull's paintings "monuments of the tastes as well as the great revolutionary scenes of our country."

The Planting of Colonies

The men and women who followed Columbus to the Americas claimed, conquered, and colonized vast territories. Along the Atlantic shore, the English planted 13 colonies. Each had its own government, its own way of life.

This scene is part of a painting created for the Van Bergen farmhouse in New York in the early 1730s. Can you find signs of the meeting of worlds in this portrait of colonial farm life?

The Birth of a New Nation

In 1776 Great Britain's 13 American colonies declared their independence. With that bold act of rebellion, a new nation—the United States of America—was born.

Does this detail from *The Declaration of Independence, 4 July 1776* by John Trumbull look familiar to you? It would if you'd ever looked at the back of a $2 bill. How would this same scene be recorded for history if it were happening today?

Teaching Resources

- Review Take-Home Planner
  - Introducing Part 1 Activity
  - Part 1 In-Depth Activity
  - Alternative Assessment
- Chapter Resources Binder
- Geography Extensions
- American Readings
- Using Historical Documents
- Transparency Activities
- Wall Time Line Activities
- Chapter Summaries
- Chapter and Unit Tests
- SelecTest Test File
- Vital Links CD-ROM/Videodisc

Van Bergen Overmantel

This scene depicts the Van Bergen farmhouse and was hung above its mantel.

Answers to Caption:
The painting shows people from three worlds—Native Americans, Europeans, and an African—along with animals and a way of life brought from Europe.

The Declaration of Independence, 4 July 1776

The painting depicts the committee that drafted the Declaration presenting it to John Hancock, the president of Congress (seated). Committee members are (left to right) John Adams, Roger Sherman, Robert Livingston, Thomas Jefferson, and Benjamin Franklin.

Answers to Caption:
Today such a scene would be recorded in news photographs and on videotape.

Beginning the Story

Christopher Columbus

Students will read about the difficulties Columbus faced during his first voyage across the Atlantic Ocean. They will learn just how fine the line can be between success and failure when engaged in an enterprise of great risk and daring.

Setting the Stage Activity

Effect of the Printing Press

To help students see how the printing press helped spur exploration, have them create a cause-effect chain. Point out that Gutenburg invented his press around the time Columbus was born. Beginning with the event "Printing press invented," have students create a linked series of cause-effect statements that ends with "Many Europeans want to explore Asia and Africa." After discussing their cause-effect chains, lead into the story by asking them to imagine growing up in a seaport and reading the travel stories of Marco Polo.

Columbus landing in the Americas (Picture) Unit 1, Side 1, Search 20339

See also Unit 1 Explore CD-ROM location 185.

History Footnote

No portraits were made of Columbus during his lifetime. Fifty years after his death, when the significance of his voyages became apparent, likenesses of the Admiral were created by the dozens. Of course, by then, no one could be certain what Columbus looked like. His son Ferdinand reported that his father "was a well-made man, of a height above the medium, with a long face, and cheekbones somewhat prominent; neither too fat, nor too lean. He had an aquiline [hooked] nose, light-colored eyes, and a ruddy complexion." Many scholars believe that the portrait shown on this page most closely corresponds to written accounts.

Teaching Resources

Chapter Resources Binder
Study Guide, p. 1
Reinforcement, p. 4

Beginnings–1600

Section 1 The Meeting of Worlds

Beginning the Story with Christopher Columbus

"Tierra! Tierra!" "Land! Land!"

That cry sent Admiral Christopher and his crew rushing forward on the deck of their small ship. As they strained their eyes, all agreed that there was indeed land on the distant horizon. In the light of the dying sun, they could see a mountainous island rising up from the ocean's edge. Columbus knelt on the deck of the *Santa Maria* and gave thanks to God. The Italian mariner's dream of finding a sea route to Asia by sailing west across the Atlantic—a dream that had inspired King Ferdinand and Queen Isabella of Spain to back him with three ships and a crew of Spanish seamen—that dream now seemed just a day's sail from coming true.

Or was it? Columbus and his ships were but halfway across the Atlantic. By the next afternoon, their mountain—in reality a towering cloud—had vanished. What they had seen, Columbus admitted, was "Not land, but sky."

In 1992—500 years after Columbus set sail for the Americas—Spanish authorities built this replica of his flagship, the *Santa Maria*.

History Bookshelf

Meltzer, Milton. *Columbus and the World Around Him.* Franklin Watts, 1990. Meltzer gives a fascinating and balanced view of Columbus. He tells of the European culture that shaped him, how Columbus's desire for riches drove him, and how his unshakable belief in his superiority led to the exploitation of Indians. This book has been selected as a School Library Journal Best Book of the Year, an NCTE Outstanding Nonfiction Work for Children, and a Notable Children's Trade Book in the Field of Social Studies in 1990.

Also of interest:

Dor-Ner, Zvi. *Columbus and the Age of Discovery.* William Morrow, 1991.

Wilfor, John Noble. *The Mysterious History of Columbus.* Knopf, 1991.

HISTORY *Mystery*

Areas of land and bodies of water are often named for explorers. It was from the voyages of Christopher Columbus that Europeans first learned of the American continents. Why are these areas of land not called North and South Columbia?

"The Madness of a Foreigner"

This disappointment, coupled with the strain of sailing day after day across an empty sea began to tell on the men. Columbus wrote in his ship's log that;

"I am having serious trouble with the crew. . . . All day long and all night long those who are awake and able to get together never cease to talk to each other in circles, complaining that they will never be able to return home. They have said that it is insanity and suicidal on their part to risk their lives following the madness of a foreigner. . . . I am told by a few trusted men (and these are few in number!) that if I persist in going onward, the best course of action will be to throw me into the sea some night."

Columbus was lucky. He found land before his crew could toss him overboard or force him to turn back. On October 12, 1492, the Admiral waded ashore on a small island in the Bahamas and claimed the land in the name of God and of the King and Queen of Spain. Thinking that his ships had reached Asia, he called the people of the island *Indians.*

An Old "New World"

Columbus died in 1506 still thinking he had discovered a new route to Asia. The explorers who followed him across the Atlantic, however, soon learned that he had not reached Asia at all. Instead Columbus had found an "unknown world" that lay between Europe and Asia.

While the Americas may have been a new and strange world to Europeans, this was a very old and familiar world to its inhabitants. People had been living in the Americas for thousands of years before Columbus arrived. For these first Americans, the "new world" was simply their world, their home.

Hands-On *HISTORY*

Activity

Imagine that you are one of the crew sailing with Columbus from Spain in 1492. You have lost all confidence that the expedition will succeed. Write a petition on behalf of the crew asking the Admiral to end his insane quest by turning around and returning to Spain at once.

Discussion

Thinking Historically

1. Why did some members of Columbus's crew view their voyage as "suicidal"? (They believed they had risked their lives on a doomed plan promoted by a mad foreigner.)

2. What qualities made it possible for Columbus to complete the voyage? (Persistence, determination, optimism, courage, leadership ability, seamanship.)

3. Why did Europeans call the lands found by Columbus a "new world"? (Most Europeans had no knowledge of the existence of the American continents before Columbus's voyages. To them the lands Columbus found really did seem like a new and unknown world.)

Teaching the HISTORY *Mystery*

Students will find the answer on p. 31. See the Section Survey on p. 33 for additional questions.

Teaching the Hands-On HISTORY

Ask what arguments the crew might make for turning back. Students might mention the number of days at sea with no sight of land, dwindling supplies, fear of being lost at sea, or a loss of confidence in their mission. They should then incorporate the best of these arguments in their petitions.

Introducing the Lesson

Vocabulary

glacier
nomad
civilization
archaeologists
anthropologists
artifacts
culture

Note: Because these vocabulary terms should be familiar to most students, they are not boldfaced in the Review. Students will, however, find definitions of these terms in their glossary.

Warm-Up Activity

Migration Then and Now

Ask how many students have moved. Point out that moving has been a part of life for as long as 50,000 years. Have students list reasons why people move today and possible reasons why they moved thousands of years ago.

Time Line

Keys to History

Earliest Inhabitants The first people to migrate to the Americas followed herds of large animals across a land bridge from Siberia.

Agriculture The development of agriculture in the Americas was a turning point, leading to settled life and faster population growth.

Mayas The Mayas built one of the most advanced civilizations in the Americas.

Lesson Objectives

- ★ Explain how people may have first migrated to the Americas.
- ★ Describe the importance of agriculture in the rise of civilization in the Americas.
- ★ Identify the early civilizations of the Americas.
- ★ Describe the diversity of North American tribes and cultures in 1492.

Teaching Resources

Chapter Summaries
English, p. 6
Spanish, p. 7

Transparency Activities
p. 1

Beginnings–1492

Lesson 1 The First Americans

People first migrated to the Americas from Asia during the last ice age, when a third of the earth was buried under immense glaciers. So much water turned into ice that the level of the oceans fell, exposing a land bridge between Asia and North America. Geologists call this land bridge Beringia. Across the land bridge came musk oxen, elephants, caribou, and other large animals. They were followed by bands of hunters who depended on these animals for their survival. From Beringia, the descendants of these first Americans spread across North America and on into South America as well.

The first Americans were nomads. Their lives were an endless journey in search of animals to hunt and edible wild plants to eat. About 10,000 years ago, the earth began to warm, melting the glaciers. The land bridge disappeared, and with it many of the large animals the first Americans had hunted. As this happened, plants replaced meat at the center of the nomads' diet. Over time, the nomads learned how to plant and harvest foods such as corn, beans, squash, and potatoes.

The development of agriculture was a major turning point in American history. Once people began to grow their own food, they settled down in villages to tend their fields. In good years, farmers produced more than enough to feed themselves and their families. As food supplies increased, people lived longer and healthier lives. Populations began to grow. And villagers with special talents could be freed from farming to develop their skills as weavers,

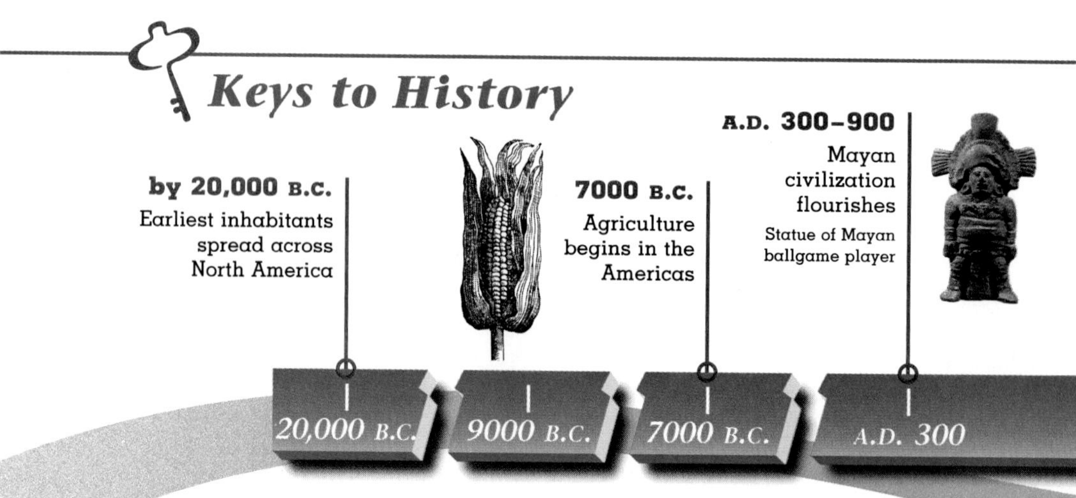

Connections to Science

The charcoal found at some ancient sites in South America is too old for its age to be determined by the traditional method of radiocarbon dating. However, archaeologists now have another tool for estimating the ages of some artifacts. With some substances, such as charcoal, they can measure the amount of light energy trapped inside. The older the artifact, the more light it has been exposed to. Scientists release the light energy by heating the object to a very high temperature. The amount of light energy released—called thermoluminescence—helps scientists estimate the artifact's age.

potters, or healers. The goods made by these skilled artisans, along with surplus crops, could be sold to other peoples. In time some of these trading villages grew into towns, then cities, and finally centers of civilizations.

Point of View

When did the first settlers migrate to America?

Archaeologists and anthropologists who study the first Americans are not sure just when they came to America. They do know from the discovery of giant bison bones alongside stone points used by ancient hunters that people were hunting ice-age mammals near Clovis, New Mexico, at least 12,000 years ago. But were the first Americans here far earlier than that?

Research done at other sites suggests that people were living in the Americans as long as 25,000, even 50,000 years ago. One problem with this research, however, is proving that the stone "tools" and campfire remains found at these ancient sites are really human artifacts. What one archaeologist sees as a stone tool may look to another like a rock shaped by nature. As for burned remains, archaeologist David Meltzer asks this question: "How do we know it was a piece of charcoal touched by human hands and not just a piece of burned tree?"

Migration Routes of First Americans

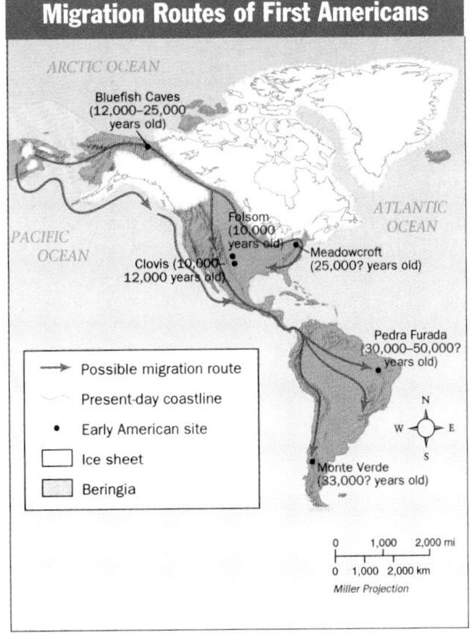

600
Mound builders establish the city of Cahokia
Figure from the ruins of Cahokia

1000s
Anasazis build cliff dwellings
Stone "apartments" at Mesa Verde

1300s
Aztecs establish their capital, Tenochtitlán
Turquoise and shell mosaic mask

1400s
Inca Empire dominates the Pacific Coast of South America

Alligator made of solid gold

A.D. 1000

A.D. 1500

Developing the Lesson

Discussion

Checking Understanding

1. Who were the first Americans? (The first Americans were nomadic hunters who probably followed ice-age mammals from Asia across Beringia to North America.)

Stimulating Critical Thinking

2. Farming is far more labor intensive than hunting and gathering. Why then might people begin to farm? (Answers might include food shortages, the need for a more reliable food supply, a desire to settle in one place.)

Time Line

Cahokia Cahokia, in present-day Illinois, was the largest Indian town in what is now the United States. At its peak around 1100, it had at least 10,000 people.

Anasazis The Anasazis of the Southwest built roads, irrigation canals and dams, and cliff dwellings.

Aztecs The Aztec empire controlled most of what is now central Mexico. The site of Tenochtitlán is within present-day Mexico City.

Incas The Inca empire of Peru was among the richest in the Americas.

Lesson Activity

Recording Aztec Tribute

The Aztecs used their military might to expand their empire and to exact tribute from conquered peoples.

To help students see how tribute was recorded, have them use symbols for amounts and types of goods, as the Aztecs did. Draw amount symbols on the chalkboard and explain that a circle equals 1, a square 20, a triangle 400, and an octagon 8,000. Have students invent their own symbols for different types of goods.

Then ask small groups to imagine they are Aztec leaders who have conquered a town. Have them make a tribute list of four types of goods. To represent 25 baskets of corn, for example, they could draw a square, 5 circles, and a basket. Have groups exchange and interpret the lists.

Teaching the Hands-On HISTORY

To provide a model, display items from each category, such as a small figurine or painting, an heirloom ring, a political poster or sign, a religious pin or pendant, a favorite pen or cup. Explain their significance to you.

History Footnote

The Aztec capitol of Tenochtitlán was a planned city, built over many centuries. Within its boundaries were hundreds of pyramids and workshop areas and about 2,000 apartment complexes, all laid out in a grid. Each area had its own plazas. There were different neighborhoods for production of different goods, such as pottery and cloth. The city's elaborate irrigation system enabled farmers to produce enough food to feed its huge population.

The city thrived mainly because it was a center of trade. It was located on a major trade route and controlled the major sources of obsidian, highly valued by stone workers for making sacrificial knives and mirrors. The city was also a major site for religious ceremonies.

Early Civilizations

Over the centuries, several civilizations rose and fell in the Americas. The first great American civilization was created by a people called the Olmecs in Mesoamerica. Olmec scientists invented a calendar based on their study of the solar system. They recorded their observations with an early form of writing.

After the decline of the Olmecs, the Maya, and then the Aztecs, created more advanced civilizations in Mesoamerica. The Maya excelled in mathematics, developing the concept of zero long before the rest of the world. The Aztecs were remarkable for their powerful and well-organized army and government.

In South America, the Incas established a remarkable civilization on the slopes of the Andes Mountains. Today the Incas are still famous for their monumental architecture as well as their advances in agriculture and medicine.

The Aztec writing system used pictures and symbols to represent ideas and sounds. This page from an Aztec book shows men playing a game. The curved symbols by two of the men represent speech.

Hands-On HISTORY

Recreating a temple treasure Ordinary activities sometimes lead to extraordinary discoveries. In Mexico City in 1978, a worker digging a trench came upon the buried ruins of *el Templo Mayor*—the "Great Temple" of the Aztecs.

As archaeologists uncovered the temple, they found thousands of items the Aztecs had buried as offerings to their gods. These included turtle shells, snake skins, jaguar skeletons, crocodile heads—and the remains of sacrificed humans. There were wonderful treasures too: gemstones, jewelry, masks, musical instruments, knives, pottery, statues of gods, and carvings of animals. Some items were made by Aztec artists. Others were antiques from previous civilizations, such as the Olmecs. Most came from peoples the Aztecs had conquered.

El Templo Mayor model

Activity

Suppose you wanted to bury a "treasure chest" containing items of special value to you. Make a list of what you would put in the chest. Include at least one item from each of these four categories: artworks, antiques or heirlooms, items with political or religious meaning, and special everyday objects. Explain each of your choices.

Connections to Language Arts

American Indians have a rich oral tradition of tales of creation and the Indian way of life and values. Many Northwest Coast Indians tell stories that involve Raven, who sometimes acts as a hero and sometimes as a trickster. The Navajos of the Southwest culture area relate their stories in chants. They combine the chants with dancing in their ceremonies.

History Footnote

The Algonquian cultures made excellent use of natural resources. From plants and trees they created homes, clothing, containers, firewood, dugout canoes, and medicines (bitterroot: chewed for sore throats; fuchsia: leaves applied to sores; gum plant: fluid used for stomachache, poison ivy rash, and toothache; watercress: leaves or juice used to treat acne and gallstones).

Cultures and Tribes in North America

While mighty civilizations were developing to the south, complex and diverse cultures were also thriving in the more northerly part of North America. In 1492, the year Columbus first crossed the Atlantic, the peoples of North America spoke nearly 550 different languages. From region to region, Indian groups had very different ways of life. Some lived in wooden houses, while others made homes out of animal skins. Some dug out logs to make boats. Others built boats out of bark or animal hides. In some tribes, men did the weaving. In other tribes, women were the weavers. Some Indian tribes honored their warriors. Others considered war a terrible thing and violence a form of insanity.

Peoples who lived near each other often had similar cultures. The regions in which tribes with similar ways of life lived are called culture areas. The map below shows where the main culture areas were located in North America in the 1400s.

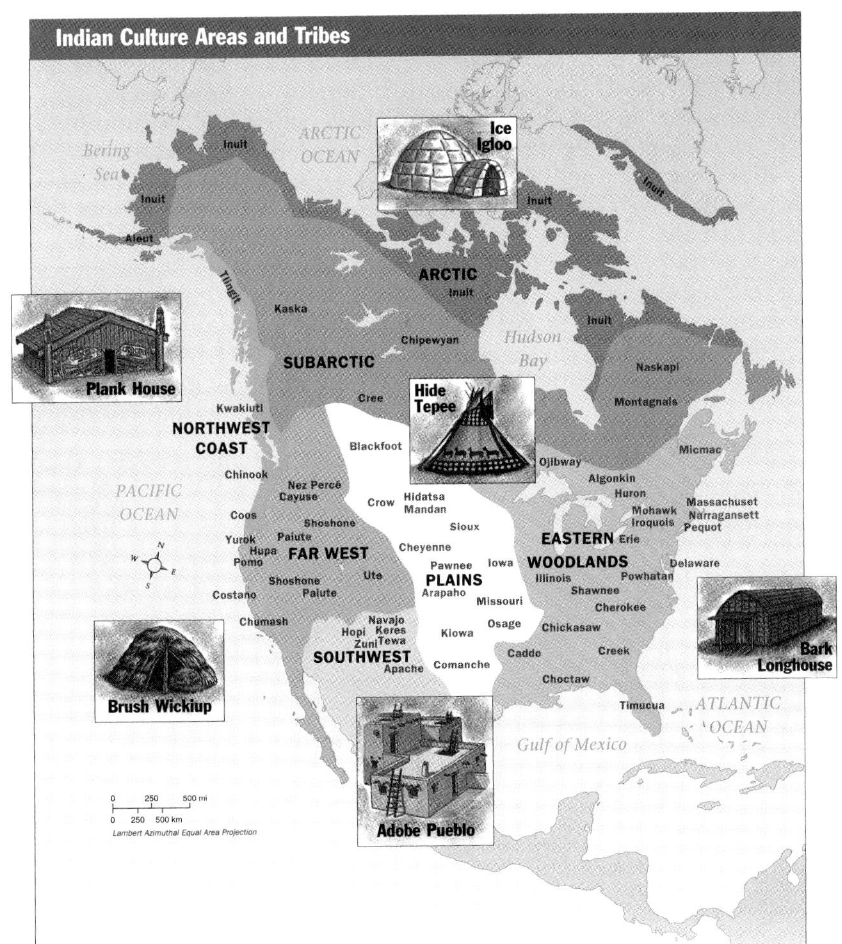

Bonus Activity

Identifying Environments

To identify environments and materials available for building shelters, have students examine the map on page R8 of the Atlas and the map on this page. Using their examination as a basis, have students write a description of the environments in which Indians built each of the shelters pictured on this page.

Vital Links

Anasazi Indians (Movie) Unit 1, Side 2, Search 11687, Play to 13007

See also Unit 1 Explore CD-ROM location 85.

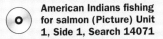

American Indians fishing for salmon (Picture) Unit 1, Side 1, Search 14071

See also Unit 1 Explore CD-ROM location 126.

Mohawk Indians farming (Picture) Unit 1, Side 1, Search 14049

See also Unit 1 Explore CD-ROM location 122.

Introducing the Lesson

Vocabulary

expedition

Warm-Up Activity

Trading Goods

To help students understand supply and demand, have them trade "goods." Provide five types: a large supply (about 60) of one, a small supply (about 5) of another, and a moderate supply (about 30) of each of the others. Some possible items are paper clips, folders, pencils, pens, and erasers. Divide the class into groups of three, distributing the large and moderate supplies equally. Give the "rare" item to one group. After the groups negotiate, discuss how scarcity affects trade.

Time Line

Keys to History

Fall of Roman Empire The Empire's fall led to division within Europe and a decline in trade.

Crusades Christian Europeans unsuccessfully fought to gain control of Palestine in a series of military expeditions against the Muslim Turks.

Lesson Objectives

- ★ Describe the relative isolation of Europe, Africa, and Asia from each other and from the Americas before the 1400s.
- ★ Explain how Europe's interest in trade and commerce gave birth to an age of exploration.

Teaching Resources

Chapter Summaries
English, p. 8
Spanish, p. 9

Transparency Activities
p. 2

1400–1460

Lesson 2 Africa, Asia, and Europe in the 1400s

For many thousands of years, the peoples of the Americas shaped their cultures and civilizations with no knowledge of other lands and peoples. The same was true for the peoples of Africa, Asia, and Europe. Most knew little or nothing about the world beyond their own horizon. A few Europeans might have heard about the spectacular journey of Mansa Musa, a powerful African ruler, to the holy Muslim city of Mecca in 1324. Yet they knew nothing about Africa and its diverse peoples. Or they might have read Marco Polo's account of his journey from Europe across Asia to China in the 1200s and still had no real knowledge of Asia's ancient cultures.

By 1400, however, Europeans had begun to look outward. Their curiosity was partly inspired by the Renaissance—a rebirth of interest in nature, the arts, ancient civilizations, and distant lands—that swept across Europe in the 1300s. It was also driven by a rising demand for such luxuries as silks and spices from Asia and gold from Africa. The trade routes along which these costly goods moved were tightly controlled by Arab merchants. Still, the profits of this trade were so great that Europeans dreamed of finding their own sea routes to the riches of Africa and Asia.

Prince Henry of Portugal led the way. Beginning in 1419, Henry sent ships south from Portugal to chart the west coast of Africa. By the 1440s, Portuguese

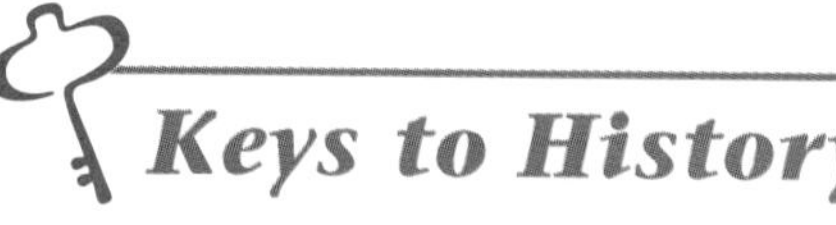

476
Fall of the Roman Empire
Bronze statue of Roman soldier

1095
Crusades begin
Battle between Christians and Muslims

400 | 1000

Connections to Art

The picture of silk spinning on this page is a detail of a porcelain vase made during the Ming dynasty (about A.D. 1368 to 1644). The Ming dynasty was well-known for improvements in porcelain. Painters made their designs with cobalt blue paint before the porcelain was glazed. They also used other kinds of paint to decorate porcelain pieces after they were glazed.

Connections to Economics

In Portugal, there was some criticism of Henry's expeditions. They were costing a lot and not producing any income. Then in 1441, one of Henry's caravels returned with Africans captured by the crew. These were the first enslaved people brought from West Africa to Europe. Soon Portugal was involved in a profitable slave trade and the criticism ended, but at a great human cost.

ships were returning from these expeditions with cargoes of gold and something else just as valuable—Africans to sell as slaves. Henry died long before Portuguese ships found their way around Africa to Asia. Even so, under his leadership Europe's age of exploration had begun.

Link to the Present

The appeal of spices Why were spices a driving force in European voyages of exploration? Spices did not just make food delicious. In the days before refrigeration, spices helped keep food from spoiling—and disguised the taste once spoilage occurred. They were also used as medicines.

In time, spices native to Asia came to be grown in other places, including the West Indies and South America. Today you can find the spices Europeans once prized in every grocery store.

Right: Silk was one of China's most prized items of trade. Here women unwind the delicate strands from silk-worm cocoons and form them into a long thread of raw silk.

1271
Marco Polo travels to China

1324
Mansa Musa journeys from Mali to Mecca

1419
Prince Henry's ships start to explore West African coast

1460s
Songhai is the most powerful trading empire in West Africa

1250 — *1460*

Teaching the

Link to the Present

Have students note similarities and differences in uses of spices then and now. Ask why Europeans of the 1400s valued spices so much more than we do today. Students should note that Europeans then used spices to preserve food, not just flavor it, and as medicine. Also, spices were new to most Europeans and were harder to obtain than they are today.

Time Line

Marco Polo Marco Polo's account of his travels inspired European interest in trade with Asia.

Mansa Musa As Europeans learned of his wealth, they became interested in African trade.

Prince Henry of Portugal He supported over 50 expeditions, which advanced European knowledge of geography and expanded trade.

Songhai By the time the Portuguese began sailing along the West African coast, Songhai had replaced Mali as the most powerful empire in the region.

Vital Links

Ancestry of African Americans (Map) Unit 1, Side 1, Search 06251

See also Unit 1 Explore CD-ROM location 31.

Introducing the Lesson

Vocabulary

colony
infectious diseases
invest

Warm-Up Activity

Identifying Risk-Worthy Goals

To focus on explorers' motivations, have students list goals they think are important enough to risk danger to achieve. They might rank the goals, beginning with the most risk-worthy. Conclude by comparing and discussing the goals.

Time Line

Keys to History

Columbus Christopher Columbus was the first European to have a lasting impact on the Americas.

Columbian Exchange The exchange of plants, animals, people, and diseases begun by Columbus transformed the world.

Vital Links

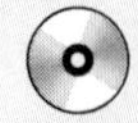

Henry Hudson (Picture) Unit 1, Side 1, Search 24474

See also Unit 1 Explore CD-ROM location 221.

Lesson Objectives

- ★ Explain how Europe's search for trade routes led to new discoveries.
- ★ Describe the Columbian Exchange.

Teaching Resources

Chapter Summaries
English, p. 10
Spanish, p. 11

Transparency Activities
p. 3

1450–1610

Lesson 3 Voyages of Exploration

Prince Henry's dream of finding a sea route to Asia finally came true when Vasco da Gama sailed around the tip of Africa and on to India in 1497. Portugal quickly became the center of thriving trade with Africa and Asia.

Meanwhile, an Italian sea captain named Christopher Columbus approached King Ferdinand and Queen Isabella of Spain with a radical plan. Rather than try to reach Asia by sailing south around Africa, Columbus proposed sailing due west across the Atlantic until he ran into Japan or China. After many delays, the Spanish monarchs agreed to sponsor his plan. It was the wisest investment they ever made.

On August 3, 1492, Columbus left Spain with three small ships. Ten weeks later his expedition reached a low island in the Caribbean Sea. Although the island hardly fit Marco Polo's descriptions of China or Japan, Columbus returned to Spain claiming to have reached Asia. The following year he crossed the Atlantic again, this time to set up a colony for Spain on a large Caribbean island. Later Columbus made two more voyages of exploration. Still, he died in 1506 not knowing just what he had found.

The many explorers who followed Columbus to America soon solved the puzzle. The first clue came from Amerigo Vespucci, an Italian trader. After searching the South American coast for a passage or opening leading to Asia, Vespucci concluded that a "new land" lay between Europe and Asia.

Keys to History

1492
Christopher Columbus reaches the Americas
Columbus's flagship

1492
Columbian Exchange begins
Columbus took chilies back to Europe

1450
1475

Connections to Geography

In sailing the Atlantic, navigators tried to take advantage of prevailing winds—those that usually blow from the same direction and travel long distances. Columbus traveled from northeast to southwest. In this region north of the equator, the prevailing winds flow from northeast to southwest. These "northeast trade winds" literally blew his ships to the Caribbean Islands.

Sailing into the northeast trade winds made the return trip slower. In time, navigators found prevailing winds further north that flowed from west to east. Another aid in sailing from America back to Europe was the discovery of the Gulf Stream—a strong ocean current moving northeast along the Atlantic coast of North America. With the Gulf Stream and the prevailing winds, explorers had a natural set of navigational aids.

In 1507 a German geographer published a map showing this new land, which he called America "since Amerigo found it." Other map makers copied the name, and the Western Hemisphere became known as the Americas, not the Columbias.

Key Voyages of Exploration, 1492–1610

While Spain and Portugal were the first to seek sea routes to Asia, other nations soon followed their example. Before long explorers from England, the Netherlands, and France were also searching for a western route to Asia. In an epic voyage begun in 1519, Ferdinand Magellan found a southwestern passage around the tip of South America. From there his expedition sailed west across the vast Pacific to Asia, and then finally back to Spain. Other explorers searched for a northern route, or Northwest Passage to Asia. While none of them succeeded, their voyages set the stage for the colonization of the Americas.

Key Voyages of Exploration, 1492–1610

Key
A = Magellan, Spain 1519–1521
B = Vasco da Gama, Portugal 1497–1498
C = Cabot, England 1497
D = Hudson, England 1610

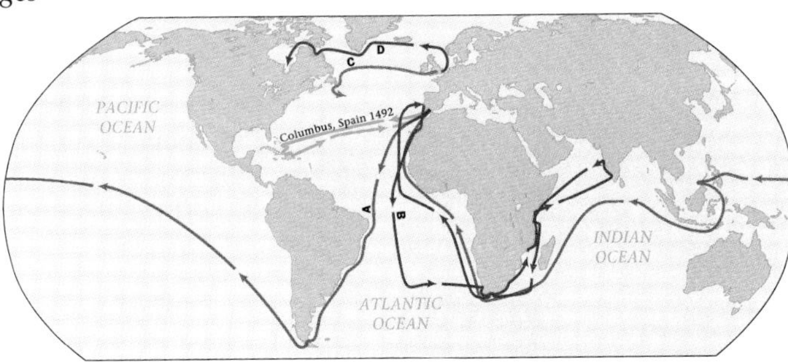

1497
Search for the Northwest Passage begins
Arctic iceberg

1519–1522
Magellan's expedition circles the globe

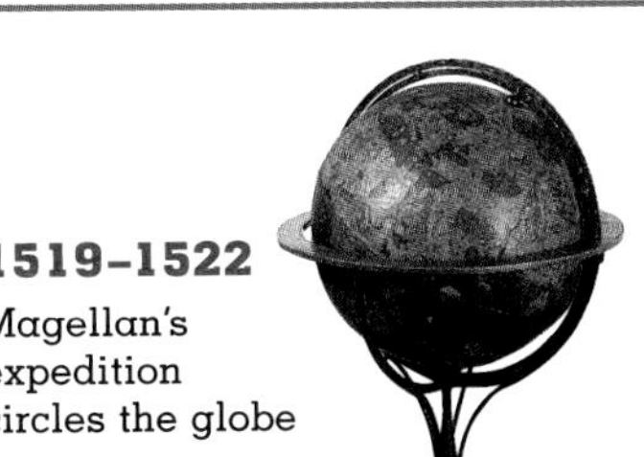

1607–1611
Henry Hudson explores for England and the Netherlands

1500 1525 1550 1600

Developing the Lesson

Discussion

Checking Understanding

1. How did Magellan realize Columbus's dream? (Magellan found the sea route to Asia that Columbus had been seeking.)

Stimulating Critical Thinking

2. How was Ferdinand and Isabella's investment in Columbus a wise one? (Answers might focus on benefits to Spain from Columbus's voyages ranging from geographic knowledge to the wealth Spain realized from its American colonies.)

Time Line

Northwest Passage Since Spain controlled waters off South America, her rivals looked for a northern route through the Americas to Asia.

"America" The land was named after the explorer Amerigo Vespucci who recognized that a "new world" unknown to Europeans lay between Europe and Asia.

Magellan Ferdinand Magellan proved that Columbus was right in saying Asia could be reached from Europe by sailing west.

Hudson Although Henry Hudson failed to find a Northwest Passage, his voyages established English claims to Canada and Dutch claims in New York.

Bonus Activity

Identifying Exchanges Today

To emphasize the continuing global exchange, have students identify trade examples today. Working in small groups, they should list four categories of exchange. Some possibilities are food, clothing, technology, art, music, and disease. Within each category, students should then list at least three examples, identifying the place of origin of each. Conclude by having students compare these examples with the Columbian Exchange.

Wrap-Up Activity

Identifying Good and Bad Effects

To review the impact of the Columbian Exchange, divide the class into groups to evaluate the effects. Half of the groups should identify examples of the positive and negative effects of the exchange on Native Americans. The other groups should identify the effects on Europeans.

Point out that the chart is a partial listing. For instance, the "From the West" list could include tobacco, discussed in Review Section 2, Lesson 2.

History Footnote

During the mid-1500s, explorers brought the potato to Europe. Potatoes grew easily in Ireland and soon became the chief crop and a mainstay in the Irish diet. In years when the potato crop failed, famine resulted. Later, students will learn about the devastating effects when a blight destroyed the crop in the mid-1800s.

History Footnote

Cattle, sheep, and pigs quickly adapted to the Americas. A time would come when they would play an important role on farms and ranches in both North and South America. Today, Texas is the top beef cattle-raising and sheep-raising state. Iowa is the top hog-raising state and ranks fifth for raising beef cattle. Wisconsin is the leading state for raising dairy cattle.

Seeds of Change

The voyages of Columbus marked the beginning of a great biological and human exchange between the Eastern and Western Hemispheres. As Columbus sailed back and forth to the Americas, he carried the beginnings, or "seeds," of great changes that would affect the whole world. Scholars call this transfer the Columbian Exchange.

Animals brought from Europe—cattle, sheep, goats, chickens, and especially horses—were the most beneficial part of this exchange for Native Americans. Indians quickly learned to value the strength and beauty of horses in both hunting and war.

Left: Indians hunting with bows and lances

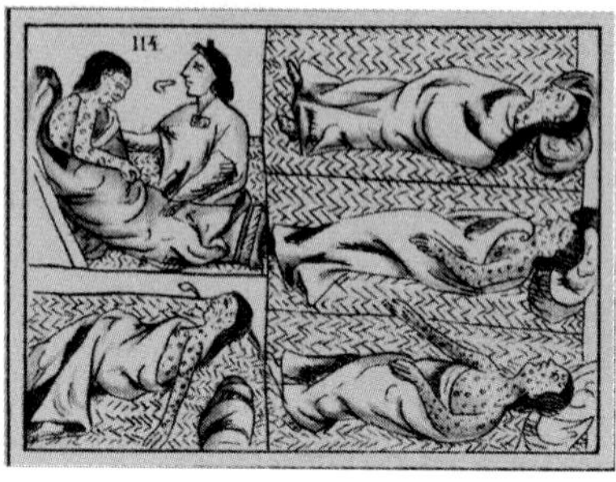

Disease was the most disastrous element of the Columbian Exchange for native peoples. Entire Indian tribes were wiped out by smallpox, measles, influenza, and other infectious diseases from Europe.

Left: Smallpox victims, from an old Aztec book

Plants moved both ways across the Atlantic. Two American plants—corn and potatoes—greatly improved food supplies in Europe and Asia. As a result, the population of those areas increased. Of all the plants that came from Europe, none had a greater impact than sugar. Wherever sugar plantations were established in the Americas, slavery soon followed.

From the West			From the East		
Corn	Pumpkins	Cashews	Grapes	Wheat	Watermelons
Potatoes	Squashes	Petunias	Olives	Sugar	Citrus fruits
Tomatoes	Pineapples	Wild Rice	Rice	Peaches	Daffodils
Chocolate	Peanuts	Peppers	Onions	Pears	Dandelions

Why We Remember

Thinking Critically

Divide the class into to six groups to complete the following sentence from the following six different points of view: "Columbus's chief contribution to history was. . . ." Have students share their answers with the class.

1. Columbus in 1506, the year of his death.
2. A European living in 1506.
3. An African brought to America as a slave.
4. Native American buffalo hunters on horseback
5. A Native American today.
6. A present-day historian.

Why We Remember

The Meeting of Worlds

Today we find it hard to picture America as it appeared to the first Americans. They arrived in their "new world" when ice covered much of the land and the rest was pathless wilderness. Even so, the first Americans learned how to use the land's gifts as they and their descendants spread across two continents. From the frozen Arctic shores to the steamy lowlands of Mesoamerica, they developed ways of life well-suited to America's varied environments.

For thousands of years, the Americas were a world apart, cut off from other lands and peoples by vast oceans. By the 1400s, however, forces were at work in Europe that would end that isolation. Motivated by equal measures of curiosity, ambition, and greed, Europeans had begun to explore beyond their known world. Portuguese explorers sailed south, making contact with first Africa, then Asia. Sailing for Spain, Christopher Columbus led the way across the Atlantic to encounter his first Americans. So began the meeting of once isolated worlds.

This meeting of worlds triggered a movement of people, plants, animals, and diseases between the Eastern and Western Hemispheres that continues to this day. According to historian Alfred Crosby, the Columbian Exchange "was the most important event since the end of the Ice Age." It is also where the story of America as we know it begins.

Section Survey

Reviewing Main Ideas

1. Why is the development of agriculture viewed as a major turning point in American history?
2. What motivated Europeans to begin making voyages of exploration in the 1400s?
3. What elements of the Columbian Exchange were most useful to Native Americans? most destructive?

History Mystery

Naming Places Answer the History Mystery on page 23. Did Vespucci deserve to have the Americas named after him? Why, or why not? What places in North and South America are named after Columbus?

Writing in Your History Journal

Citizenship For many years some states, cities, and private groups honored Columbus with a celebration in October. In 1971 Columbus Day—the second Monday in October—became a legal holiday. Now, some Americans say Columbus Day should be a day of sorrow or remembrance. How do you think Columbus Day should be remembered? In your journal write a letter to the editor of a newspaper in your state answering that question. Give your reasons.

Section Survey Answers

Reviewing Main Ideas

1. Once people began to farm, they could adopt a settled way of life, which led to the establishment of towns, cities, and civilizations.
2. Europeans were motivated to embark on voyages of exploration by their desire to find trade routes to Asia.
3. The most useful elements of the Columbian Exchange to Native Americans were horses and new European food crops. The most destructive elements were the deadly diseases brought from Europe.

History Mystery

Information on page 31 explains that a German cartographer named the land after Amerigo Vespucci because Vespucci first identified it as a "new land." Some students may think that Vespucci deserved the honor because of his explorations of the South American coast and his recognition that it was not Asia. Others may suggest that Columbus still deserved the honor because of the impact of his voyages on other explorers. Students might identify the city of Columbus, Ohio, and the country of Colombia.

Writing in Your History Journal

Opinions will vary, but letters should reflect an understanding of the positive and negative effects of the meeting of worlds sparked by Columbus's first voyage to America.

Beginning the Story

Pocahontas

Pocahontas was largely responsible for Jamestown's survival. She saved John Smith's life and brought the colonists food. When relations between Indians and settlers deteriorated, the settlers kidnapped Pocahontas. In Jamestown she learned about English culture. Her marriage to colonist John Rolfe resulted in several years of uneasy peace between the Indians and the colonists.

Setting the Stage Activity

Reacting to Strangers

To help students identify with the situation Pocahontas and her people faced, have them write about how they would react to the arrival of strangers. Divide the class into small groups and have them imagine that a gang from out of town is trying to take control of a local park. Ask them to discuss how they would react to these strangers and what the community should do. Each group should summarize their discussion in a short paragraph.

History Footnote

Pocahontas was the daughter of the leader of the Powhatan Confederacy. Her grandfather conquered five tribes and organized them into the confederacy. Her father, Wahunsenacawh, took the name Powhatan after becoming the confederacy's leader. He expanded the confederacy to include about 25 additional tribes. By the early 1600s, the small but powerful confederacy was made up of about 9,000 people. They lived in an area that extended from the Potomac River south to the Dismal Swamp (approximately from present-day southern Maryland to northern North Carolina).

Teaching Resources

Chapter Resources Binder
- Study Guide, p. 2
- Reinforcement, p. 5

1500–1750

Section 2 The Planting of Colonies

Beginning the Story with *Pocahontas*

Landfall for the three shiploads of English settlers came at dawn on April 26, 1607. As the sun rose skyward, they were awed by the beauty of this place they called Virginia. Captain James Smith, a hardened soldier and adventurer who had seen much of world, wrote that:

> "Heaven and earth never agreed better to frame a place for man's habitation. . . ."

The English planted their first colony on a low-lying peninsula wedged between two rivers, the James and the York, flowing into Chesapeake Bay. They called the small settlement Jamestown in honor of their king. But when the colony faced starvation, help came not from King James, but from an Indian princess named Pocahontas.

This detail from a map of Virginia prepared by John Smith shows Powhatan and his council deciding Smith's fate.

"The King's Dearest Daughter"

The coming of the English colonists did not go unnoticed by the Indians of Virginia. The settlers saw the Indians' smoke signals and heard their drums

History Bookshelf

Smith, Carter, ed. *The Explorers and Settlers: A Sourcebook on Colonial America*. The Millbrook Press, 1991. This overview of European exploration and colonization of North America is richly illustrated with period maps and drawings. The text offers background from the first European landings and explorations to the westward movement of the colonies. Time frames juxtapose world and colonial events.

Also of interest:

Bowen, Gary. *Stranded at Plymouth Plantation.* HarperCollins, 1994.

Fritz, Jean. *The Double Life of Pocahontas.* Putnam, 1983.

IlgenFritz, Elizabeth. *Anne Hutchinson.* Chelsea House, 1991.

HISTORY Mystery

The banjo was unknown in England and Europe, yet it was a well-known musical instrument in the English colonies. Where did the banjo come from?

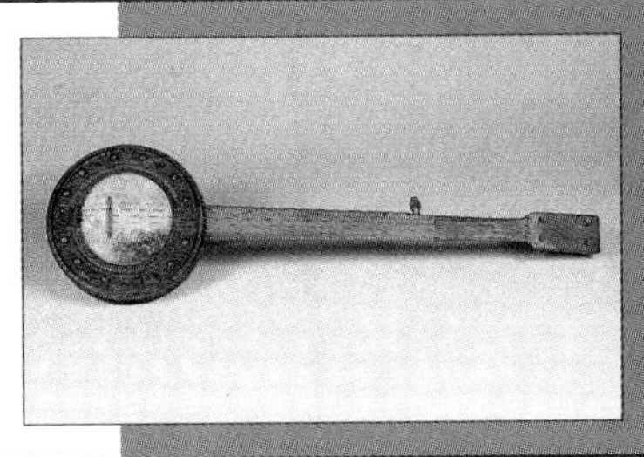

as reports of the strangers' arrival sped upriver. In his forest stronghold, Powhatan, the powerful ruler of the Virginia Indians, pondered what to do with the newcomers. Meanwhile, his daughter Pocahontas burned with curiosity about the light-skinned strangers and their white-winged ships.

Months later, one of those strangers was brought to Powhatan's village. John Smith had been captured while on a scouting expedition. Pocahontas listened as her father and his council debated his fate. Then she heard the decision: The white chief must die! Smith later recalled that:

> "Two great stones were brought before Powhatan. Then as many as could laid hands on [me], dragged [me] to them, and thereon laid [my] head, and being ready with their clubs to beat out [my] brains. . . ."

The Englishman steeled himself against the fatal blow. Instead he heard a girl's voice ring out, then felt the shock of her body thrown across his. It was, he later wrote, "Pocahontas, the King's dearest daughter . . . [who] got [my] head in her arms, and laid her own upon [mine] to save [me] from death." A few days later, Smith was safely back in Jamestown.

To save Smith, Pocahontas had followed a custom of her people and adopted him as a brother. Did she act out of curiosity? Or out of sympathy for the strangers? Who could say? Still, as the two became friends, Smith found that her "compassionate, pitiful heart . . . gave me much cause to respect her."

Adopting Smith was, for Pocahontas, a serious commitment. The following winter the colonists would have starved had she not often brought them food. "She, next under God," wrote Smith, "was . . . the instrument to preserve this colony from death, famine, and utter confusion."

Hands-On HISTORY

Activity

In his *Generall Historie of Virginia*, John Smith wrote about his rescue by Pocahontas, but we have no account of this event from her point of view. Write the story of her decision to save the white chief as you think she might have told it.

Discussion

Thinking Historically

1. Why did Smith respect Pocahontas? (She showed him and the other colonists compassion.)

2. Do you think Pocahontas was brave for trying to save Smith? (Some students may believe she was brave to disagree with her father and the council. Others may believe that because her father was chief, she knew no harm would come to her for intervening on Smith's behalf.

Teaching the HISTORY Mystery

Students will find the answer on p. 44. See Section Survey, p. 45, for additional questions.

Teaching the Hands-On HISTORY

Remind students that Pocahontas was only 12 years old when she saved Smith. Suggest that they write their story as a diary entry a young girl might make. Their stories should reflect Pocahontas's feelings about the event.

Introducing the Lesson

Vocabulary

conquistadors
plantation

Warm-Up Activity

A Conquistador Recruiting Poster

To help students understand why Spanish soldiers joined expeditions to the Americas, have groups create recruiting posters. After listing possible benefits (such as wealth, fame, adventure, or land), they can design posters that would point out these advantages and attract recruits.

Time Line

Keys to History

Ponce de León Juan Ponce de León led the first Spanish entrada into what is now the southern United States.

Cortés Hernán Cortés, the first famous conquistador, established Spain's empire in the Americas.

Las Casas Bartolomé de Las Casas was the leading Spanish protester against the mistreatment of Indians.

Vital Links

Cortés entering Mexico (Picture) Unit 1, Side 1, Search 21650

See also Unit 1 Explore CD-ROM location 195.

Lesson Objectives

- ★ Summarize how Spain conquered a vast empire in the Americas.
- ★ Identify Spain's primary objectives in organizing its American colonies.
- ★ Identify Spain's rivals in the race to colonize North America.

Teaching Resources

Chapter Summaries
English, p. 12
Spanish, p. 13
Transparency Activities
p. 4

1500–1700

Lesson 1 The Conquest of the Americas

Twenty-five years after Columbus's first voyage, Spain had settlements on many Caribbean islands. Next, Spaniards eagerly looked to the mainland. They had three goals: to win converts to Christianity, to gain gold for their king and themselves, and to bring glory to Spain. Holding to these goals, they carved out an empire in the Americas. The conquest began with the defeat of the Aztec and Inca empires by conquistadors led by Hernán Cortés and Francisco Pizarro. It was continued by explorers like Francisco Vásquez de Coronado, who led entradas—armed expeditions—into lands now part of the United States. By 1542, Spain claimed an empire stretching from present-day southern Oregon to the tip of South America, an area larger than all of Europe.

Spanish conquest was followed by colonization. Soldiers who had come to conquer settled down to run plantations, ranches, and mines. Missionaries arrived to bring the Catholic faith to Indians.

Other countries watched with interest and envy as Spain became the richest, most powerful nation in Europe. Hoping to find wealth to rival Spain's, the French explored and claimed nearly two-thirds of North America. Russia, the Netherlands, and Sweden all carved out smaller colonies in North America. The English, however, proved to be Spain's fiercest rivals. In 1588, Spain launched a mighty armada of warships to crush England. With the help of a timely storm, the English destroyed the Spanish fleet, and with the defeat of the armada, Spanish power began to decline.

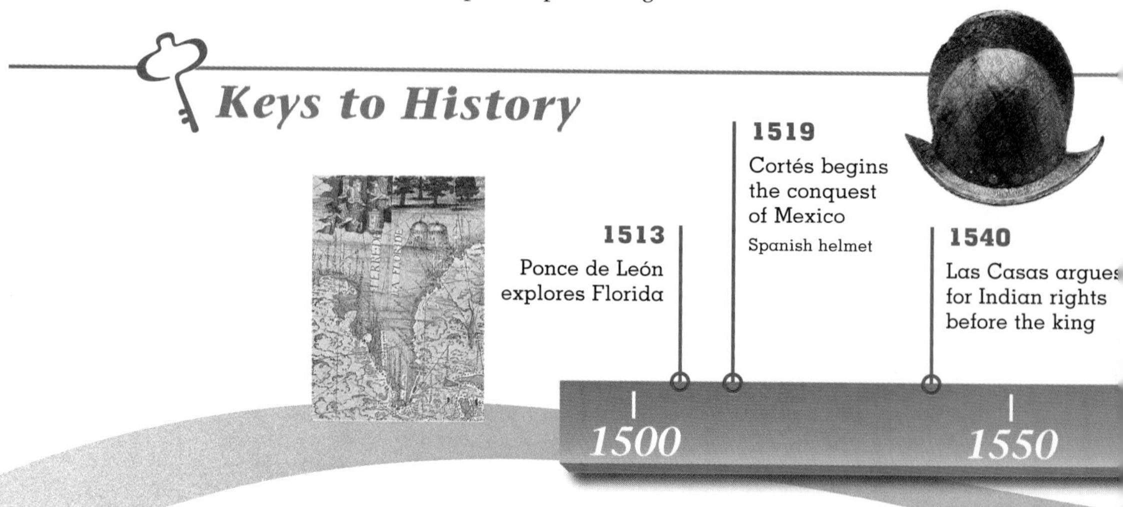

Connections to Art

Spanish influences can be seen today in art and architecture throughout the Southwest. A combination of Spanish and Indian influences are reflected in the work of artists José Clemente Orozco, Diego Rivera, and Frida Kahlo. The Spanish missions of California were restored and embellished, beginning in the late 1800s. Other Spanish-influenced architecture can be seen throughout the southwestern United States in buildings such as Scotty's Castle in Death Valley, California, and the San Xavier del Bac Mission near Tucson, Arizona.

Hands-On HISTORY

Planning a modern-day entrada Explorers tried to be prepared. They took foods like grain and beans, along with livestock and poultry for future slaughter. They carried items to trade with the native peoples, as well as armor, guns, and swords, in case the people proved to be unfriendly. For practical reasons, they packed shovels, hoes, and pans. For symbolic reasons, they carried flags, banners, and crosses.

Explorer unloading supplies

Imagine yourself as the leader or a modern-day entrada. You plan to take 50 people into a remote area to build 10 vacation cabins. There is a paved road for the first 50 miles, but you do not know what lies beyond. Your sponsors have asked you to list the items you need for 6 months and to explain why you need them. Answer this request in a letter. Keep these tips in mind:

- **If you use vehicles, they will need fuel. If you use animals, they will need food and water.**
- **You will be far from stores and hospitals.**
- **You may have to deal with a variety of weather conditions and geographic features.**

1565
Founding of St. Augustine
Fort in St. Augustine

1588
Defeat of the Spanish Armada

1608
Champlain founds Quebec

1682
La Salle explores the Mississippi
Detail from *La Salle Erecting a Cross and Taking Possession of the Land* by George Caitlin

1600 1650 1700

Developing the Lesson

Discussion

Checking Understanding

1. What were Spain's main objectives in founding colonies? (To enrich Spain, convert the Indians to Christianity, and bring glory to Spain by creating a colonial society that mirrored that of the mother country.)

Teaching the Hands-On HISTORY

Small groups of students can begin by brainstorming lists of difficulties they might encounter and possible necessary supplies. You may wish to assign categories such as food, transportation, and protective equipment to separate groups.

Time Line

St. Augustine St. Augustine is the oldest permanent European settlement in the United States.

Defeat of the Spanish Armada The English defeat of the Armada began Spain's decline and England's rise to world power.

Champlain Founds Quebec The French were interested in trade, not land, and so they were business partners with the Indians, not their conquerors.

La Salle The French built a chain of forts along the St. Lawrence and down the Mississippi.

Introducing the Lesson

Vocabulary

exports
representatives
proprietary colonies
persecution

Warm-Up Activity

Listing Reasons for Colonization
Have small groups list two or three reasons to colonize. They can later compare their reasons with those noted in the text.

Time Line

Keys to History

Jamestown The Jamestown settlers established the first permanent English colony in America.

House of Burgesses The Virginia House of Burgesses was the first elected legislature in the English colonies.

Mayflower Compact Passengers aboard the *Mayflower* established a voluntary government for the Plymouth colony.

Anne Hutchinson For openly disagreeing with the teaching of Puritan leaders, Hutchinson was forced to leave Massachusetts.

Vital Links

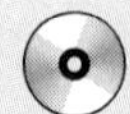
Jamestown (Picture) Unit 1, Side 1, Search 34169

See also Unit 1 Explore CD-ROM location 283.

Lesson Objectives

- ★ Describe the founding of Jamestown and Plymouth colonies.
- ★ Identify the colonies founded by the Puritans.
- ★ Describe the motives behind the founding of the proprietary colonies
- ★ Explain the attractions of William Penn's "Holy Experiment" in Pennsylvania.

Teaching Resources

Chapter Summaries
English, p. 14
Spanish, p. 15
Transparency Activities
p. 5–6

1600–1750

Lesson 2 Planting English Colonies

Jamestown was the first permanent colony planted by England on the shores of North America. It was founded by the Virginia Company as a business venture with the goal of finding precious metals. Built on low, swampy ground, Jamestown got off to a shaky start. Disease and hunger killed off the majority of settlers. Those who survived found no gold, but they did find something else of value—soil ideal for growing tobacco, a crop much in demand in Europe.

Even as its tobacco exports soared, the colony attracted few settlers until the Virginia Company made some important changes. One was to give colonists the right to own land and start their own plantations. The second was to bring women to Virginia so that the colonists might marry and start families. The third was to give male landowners the right to elect representatives, called burgesses, to a lawmaking assembly known as the Virginia House of Burgesses. With this right, the colonists in Virginia gained a degree of self-government unheard of at that time in the colonies of France or Spain.

As a result of these changes, the colony prospered and grew. When the settlers moved up the James River to clear more fields for tobacco, they came into conflict with local Indians. To protect their land and families, the Indians attacked the colony in March 1622, killing 347 settlers. Jamestown was left in ruins. The surviving colonists struck back with a vengeance. So began the tragic cycle of conflict between settlers and Indians that would be repeated again and again as English settlers planted more colonies along the Atlantic shore.

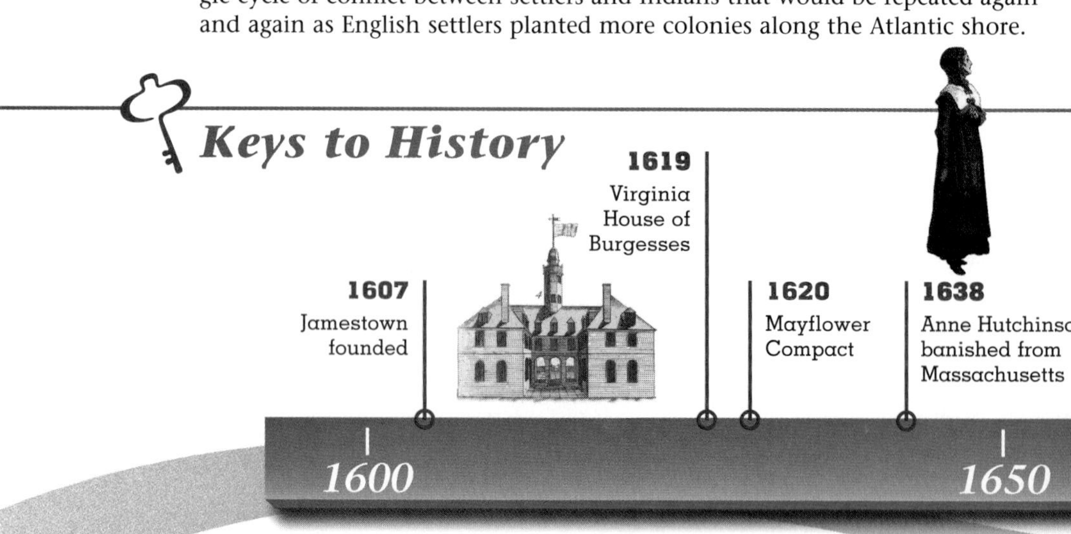

History Footnote

Tobacco cultivation became the mainstay of settlements in Virginia. Before long, the colonists were exporting vast quantities of tobacco to England. By 1618 they exported almost 50,000 pounds (22,680 kg). As Virginians grew more and more tobacco, they neglected to grow enough crops to feed themselves. The Virginia Company provided food supplies to the colonists in return for controlling the tobacco trade. Despite the high demand for tobacco, King James I of England hated the product. He noted that "Smoking is a custom loathsome to the eye, hateful to the nose, harmful to the brain, dangerous to the lungs." He even encouraged Parliament to ban the import of tobacco in 1621, but the members were persuaded by the Virginia Company not to do so.

No one knows what Jamestown looked like in 1607 because some of the site has been washed away by the James River. This artist's view shows how the colonist might have built a protective wall around their tents and huts.

Geographic Thinking In 1699 colonists moved the capital of Virginia from Jamestown to Williamsburg, a town that had been settled in 1633. Williamsburg is about 7 miles (11 km) from Jamestown, on a high ridge between the James and York rivers. What might be some advantages of Williamsburg's location over that of Jamestown? What might be some disadvantages?

1675
King Philip's War
Chief Metacomet, known as King Philip

1681
Penn plans "holy experiment" in Pennsylvania
Plate showing German settlers

1732
Georgia, the last English colony
James Oglethorpe, founder of Georgia

1700

1750

Developing the Lesson

Discussion

Checking Understanding

1. What factors led to the growth of the Virginia colony? (Demand for tobacco, settlers could own land and elect a legislature, women came to the colony.)

Geographic Thinking

Possible advantages: Williamsburg was not subject to flooding.
Possible disadvantages: Williamsburg was not a seaport, so people and goods probably had to move across land to a water route.

Time Line

King Philip's War Chief Metacomet led the Wampanoags in the most serious conflict between Indians and colonists.

Pennsylvania William Penn founded his colony as a refuge for Quakers and others persecuted for their religious beliefs.

Georgia James Oglethorpe founded the last English colony as a haven for debtors and a buffer against Spanish Florida.

Vital Links

Early home life at Jamestown (Picture) Unit 1, Side 1, Search 34187

See also Unit 1 Explore CD-ROM location 286.

Teaching Map Skills

Reading Map Keys

Ask: **What is the main purpose of the map on page 40?** (To show the extent and location of New England settlement in 1660.) **How does the map distinguish between names of colonies, towns, and Indian tribes?** (With light type, black dots, and dark type.)

Lesson Activity

A Puritan View of Settlement

Ask students to imagine being a Puritan leader who is planning a colony in New England. Have them write a speech explaining why they think they have a right to take Indian lands. Students' speeches should include both religious and economic arguments.

Bonus Activity

"Best" and "Worst" Colonies

To explore advantages and disadvantages of various colonies, have students imagine themselves as colonists. Ask them to write journal entries explaining which colony would be their first choice and which would be their last choice. Conclude by having students discuss their choices.

Connections to Geography

Before William Penn came to Pennsylvania, he began making plans for "a greene Countrie Towne, which will never be burnt, and allways be wholesome." Penn did not want his city to be destroyed by the fires and plagues he had seen in Europe. As a result, Penn's surveyor general, Thomas Holme, planned the layout of the city before building began. Holme plotted a grid extending out from a city square. This grid plan became a model for other cities. As part of the plan, streets were wider than in any other city. The two main streets were 100 feet (30.48 m) wide, and other streets were 50 feet (15.24 m) wide. Penn's planned city, Philadelphia, was nicknamed the "City of Brotherly Love" because *philadelphia* means "brotherly love" in Greek.

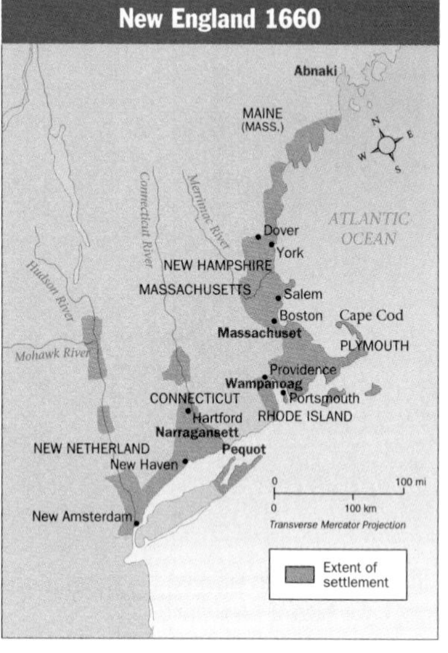

Plymouth Colony

The people who planted the next English colony were seeking not gold but something far different—the right to worship as they wished. They became known as Pilgrims because they made their journey for religious reasons.

In 1620 the Pilgrims left England in the *Mayflower,* bound for Virginia. Instead they landed in a region the English called New England. Before going ashore, the settlers signed an agreement known as the Mayflower Compact. In this compact they agreed to make laws for the colony and to obey those laws.

The early history of Plymouth is one of struggle and suffering. Half of the colonists died during the first year. Only with the help of a local Indian named Squanto did the Pilgrims survive. With them survived the belief that people have the right to create their own laws and to follow their own faith.

The Puritan Colonies

Like the Pilgrims, the Puritans had been harassed in England for following their religious beliefs. In 1629 a group of them came to New England determined to create a colony where they might live by God's law as they saw it.

The Puritans first settled on the shores of Massachusetts. As their numbers increased, so did conflicts over religious issues. Rhode Island and Connecticut were both founded by dissenters from Massachusetts. In search for good farmland, colonists from Massachusetts also moved north to found the colonies of New Hampshire and Maine.

As the Puritans spread across New England, they came into conflict with Indians who had lived there for thousands of years. In 1675 the Wampanoag chief Metacomet, also known as King Philip, rallied the New England tribes to drive the English out. King Philip's War was a tragedy for the colonists, but a disaster for the Indians. The colonists killed about 3,000 Indians, including Metacomet. They also sold hundreds of Indians into slavery in the West Indies.

As a child, Metacomet watched the Puritans take over Indian lands and force his people to obey English laws. After he became chief, he led New England tribes in resisting the English colonists.

History Footnote

When Oglethorpe arrived in Georgia, he promised the Indians that he would treat them fairly and justly. He kept his promise. He negotiated with the Creeks for land. They gave up almost all of the land between the Savannah and Altahama rivers to Oglethorpe. However, the Creeks did keep a small amount of land near Savannah so that they would have a place to camp when they visited the city. To prevent traders from cheating the Indians, Oglethorpe established a schedule of prices for which goods could be bartered. For example, the Indians could acquire a blanket for one buckskin and a gun for ten buckskins. (A buckskin is the hide of a deer and was valued as a material for shoes and clothing.)

The Proprietary Colonies

South of New England, seven colonies were founded by "royal favorites" on land given them by the English king. The motives of these owners, or proprietors, varied. Some sought wealth. Others wanted to help the persecuted or the poor.

Maryland was the first successful proprietary colony. It was founded in the 1630s by the Calvert family as a refuge for Catholics who, like other religious groups, faced persecution in England.

North and South Carolina were founded by a group of noblemen as a business venture. The proprietors had a difficult time making any money until rice growing was introduced in the 1690s.

King Charles II thought the Dutch colonists of New Netherland had no right to settle on what he believed was English territory. In 1664 he seized the Dutch colony and gave it to his brother James, Duke of York. In time, four proprietary colonies were carved out of this region—New York, New Jersey, Pennsylvania, and Delaware.

Pennsylvania was by far the best advertised of the English colonies. Its founder, a Quaker named William Penn, viewed his colony as a "holy experiment." Here, he hoped, not only persecuted Quakers like himself, but people of all faiths would live together in peace under laws of their own making. Penn distributed pamphlets in English, French, Dutch, and German offering all who came to his colony religious freedom, cheap land, and self-government. It was an offer many found hard to refuse.

The last proprietary colony, Georgia, was founded by James Oglethorpe in 1732. Oglethorpe worked to make Georgia a place where debtors and other poor people from England could make a fresh start.

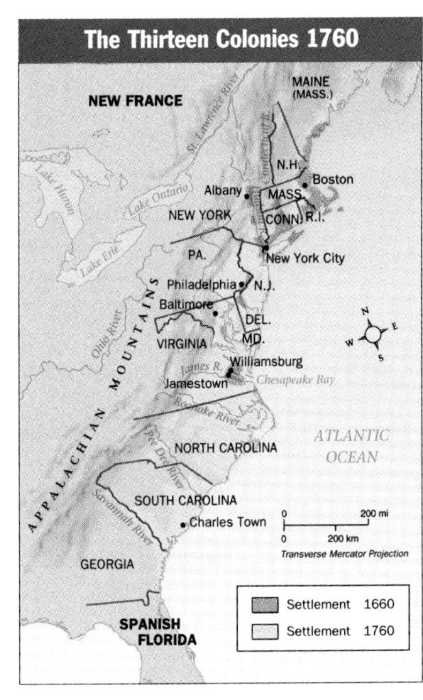

Hands-On HISTORY

Nova Britannia. OFFERING MOST Excellent fruites by Planting in Virginia. Exciting all such as be well affected to further the same.

1609 ad for Virginia

Advertising the colonies Imagine that you work for an advertising company. You are to come up with an ad to lure settlers to one of the 13 English colonies.

1. Choose a colony from the map and the type of ad you will create, such as a brochure, poster, or jingle.

2. Decide what makes your colony special. Why should people in the 1700s move there?

3. Create the ad and present it to your classmates. Are they ready to sail to North America?

Wrap-Up Activity

An Indian Protest Letter

To help students understand the Indian's point of view, ask them to imagine themselves as an Indian leader who wants to avoid fighting with the colonists. Have students write a protest letter to the governor of the colony outlining their grievances and asking for remedies.

Teaching the Hands-On HISTORY

Suggest that students prepare ads for the only medium that existed at the time—print. Their ads should not include reproductions of photographs. Point out that many advertisements emphasize distinguishing features of a product or service. For example, Pennsylvania could be distinguished by offering religious freedom to all people who believed in God.

Vital Links

William Penn and Delaware Indians (Picture) Unit 1, Side 1, Search 38993

See also Unit 1 Explore CD-ROM location 345.

Introducing the Lesson

Vocabulary

Tidewater
navigation
cash crops
diversity
tyranny
imports
indentured servants

Warm-Up Activity

Charting Diversity Today

By identifying the diversity of America today, students can gain insight into colonial life. Have them prepare a diversity chart for Americans today. The chart might include columns for country of origin, language, culture, and religion. As they read this section, students can compare the diversity of populations in the colonies with the diversity of the present-day population in the United States.

Time Line

Keys to History

First Africans The arrival of more than 20 Africans in Jamestown, some of whom were slaves, marked the beginning of black slavery in the English Colonies.

First College The Puritans founded Harvard College to train ministers.

Lesson Objectives

- ★ Compare the patterns of settlement in the English colonies.
- ★ Describe the growth of the colonies between 1600 and 1750.
- ★ Summarize how self-government worked in the colonies.
- ★ Describe the development of an African American culture in the colonies.

Teaching Resources

Chapter Summaries
English, p. 16
Spanish, p. 17

Transparency Activities
p. 7

1600–1750

Lesson 3 Life in the English Colonies

Visitors traveling through the English colonies were struck by how life varied from region to region. The way colonists lived depended in part on the land and resources they found. It also depended on the different religions, languages, customs, and ideas settlers brought with them to America.

In New England, with its thin soil and harsh climate, the best living came not from farms but from the forests and the sea. Most colonists lived in close-knit towns built near fishing harbors or pockets of fertile land. This pattern of settlement also supported the Puritans' goal of creating Christian communities in which people lived, worked, and worshiped together.

The good soil and climate of the Middle Colonies—along with William Penn's promise of religious liberty in Pennsylvania—attracted a diverse mix of nationalities and faiths. The newcomers dotted the land with small farms and villages. By 1750 this region also boasted the two largest colonial cities, Philadelphia and New York.

The warm and wet Tidewater region of the Southern Colonies was well-suited to the cultivation of cash crops, such as tobacco and rice. By the early 1700s, large plantations lined most Tidewater rivers. Neighbors lived so far from each other that each plantation had to be a self-sufficient community.

What may have been less obvious to visitors was just how fast the colonies were growing. In 1650 barely 50,000 colonists—most of them English—

Keys to History

TO BE SOLD,

A CARGO
OF
NINETY-FOUR
PRIME, HEALTHY
NEGROES,
CONSISTING OF
Thirty-nine MEN, Fifteen BOYS, Twenty-four WOMEN, and Sixteen GIRLS.
JUST ARRIVED,
In the Brigantine DEMBIA, *Francis Bare*, Master, from SIERRA-LEON, by
DAVID & JOHN DEAS.

1619
First Africans brought to Jamestown

Notice of sale of slaves

1636
First college in the English colonies

Embroidery of Harvard College

1600

1650

Connections to Economics

To avoid unfavorable British trade policies, colonists developed triangular trade routes. Some routes violated British law because they involved direct trade with other nations. Triangular trade also allowed colonists to barter rather than spend currency. One key route carried colonial fish, grain, and lumber to the West Indies in exchange for sugar and molasses. These were shipped to Britain and Europe and traded for manufactured goods. Another important route took New England rum to Africa and exchanged it for slaves. Slaves were sold in the West Indies for sugar and molasses, which were in turn sent to New England and made into rum. By the early 1700s, most slaves were taken directly from Africa to mainland colonies. Other triangular trade continued, however, bringing great profits to colonial merchants.

were clustered in Virginia and Massachusetts. By 1750 there were more than a million colonists spread from Maine to Georgia. While the majority were still English, large numbers had come from France, Germany, and other parts of Europe. Despite their differences, most colonists had one thing in common: a deep attachment to freedom and an equally deep hatred of tyranny.

Colonial Government

One of the freedoms the colonists valued most was the right of self-government. In no other country on earth, not even in Great Britain, did ordinary people have as much freedom to run their own affairs as did the colonists. By the 1750s, every colony had its own elected assembly. Each assembly had the power to pass laws and levy taxes.

The one area of life that colonists did not control was trade. Beginning in 1660, Parliament passed a series of laws known as the Navigation Acts to control trade with the colonies. The goal of these laws was for England to sell more to the colonies than it bought from them. Trade officials in London kept track of yearly exports and imports to see whether that goal was being met.

Colonial Trade with England 1750

Colony/Area	Exports	Imports
C	191,607	133,037
G	1,942	2,125
NE	48,455	343,659
NY/NJ	35,634	267,130
P/D	28,191	217,713
V/M	508,939	349,419
Total	814,768	1,313,083

Values in British pounds

Key:
C = The Carolinas
G = Georgia
NE = New England
NY/NJ = New York and New Jersey
P/D = Pennsylvania and Delaware
V/M = Virginia and Maryland

This table shows exports from the colonies to England and imports from England to the colonies for 1750—a typical year. Did the numbers bring smiles or frowns to the faces of London trade officials?

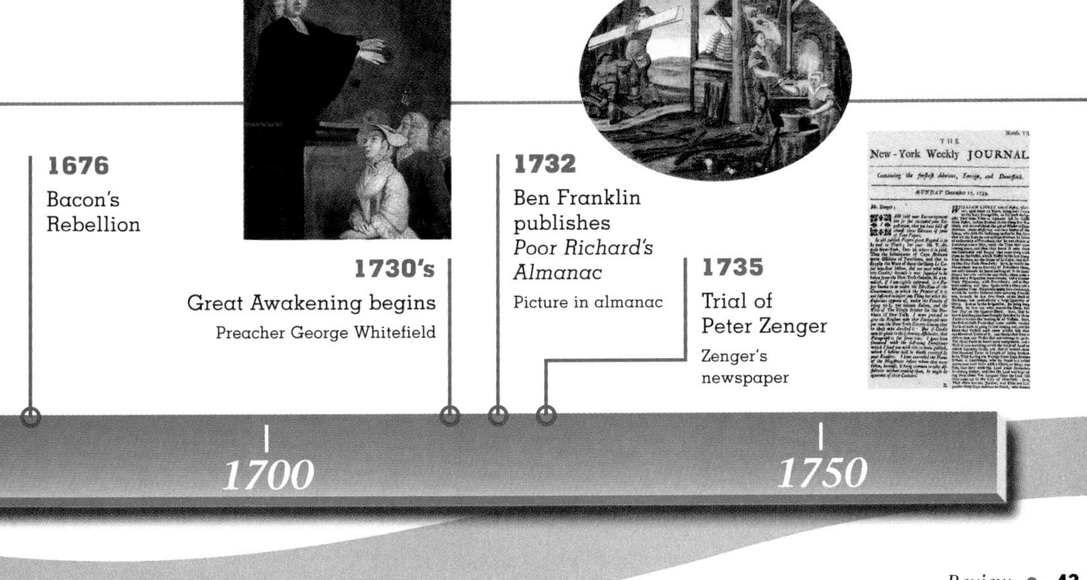

Developing the Lesson

Discussion

Checking Understanding

1. What rights and freedoms did the colonists value? (Religious liberty, the right to self-government.)

2. What was the main goal of the Navigation Acts? (To help England profit by selling more to the colonies than it bought from them.)

Answers to Caption:
The overall trade pattern in 1750 should have pleased London trade officials, as the colonies imported more than they exported to England.

Time Line

Bacon's Rebellion The revolt against Virginia's government reflected the tension between colonial governments and the backcountry settlers.

Great Awakening The Great Awakening revived interest in religion throughout the colonies.

Poor Richard's Almanac Benjamin Franklin's almanac, a compilation of advice and proverbs, became the second-most popular book in the colonies. The Bible was the most popular.

Trial of Peter Zenger The acquittal of Peter Zenger on the charge of libel inspired colonists to speak out for freedom of the press.

Wrap-Up Activity

Reporting on the Middle Passage

Students can gain insight into the horrors of the Atlantic slave trade by writing a news report. Tell them to imagine that they are doing an investigative report on the Middle Passage. Suggest that they describe the passage through the experiences of captured Africans. Remind them that a reporter would write a story that describes who, what, where, when, why, and how. Provide time for students to write and discuss their reports.

Vital Links

Voice of a slave on the Middle Passage (First Person Account) Unit 1, Side 1, Search 26432, Play to 27152

See also Unit 1 Explore CD-ROM location 249.

"African Song" (Song) Unit 1, Side 2, Search 02598, Play to 04227

See also Unit 1 Explore CD-ROM location 259.

History Footnote

Throughout the colonies Africans resisted slavery, usually by escaping. Many sought refuge among Indians or in Spanish Florida.

From 1733, the Spanish offered freedom to all slaves from the north. As a result, some Africans headed for St. Augustine. In September 1739, a leader named Cato gathered a group of slaves along the Stono River in South Carolina. Seizing weapons from an arsenal, they headed south. Before they were caught, they had killed about 30 whites. The Stono River uprising was one of several important slave revolts that occurred from the 1600s until the Civil War.

African Americans

The first Africans were brought to Virginia in 1619. Some worked as indentured servants and were later freed. By the late 1600s, southern planters decided that they could best meet their need for workers by adopting a system that had long been used on Caribbean sugar plantations—slavery.

By the early 1700s, enslaved Africans could be found in every English colony. The great majority, however, toiled on plantations in the Southern Colonies. Wherever they lived, slaves faced a lifetime of unrewarded toil. As one old African put it, "Slave young, slave long."

The Africans who were brought to America came from many different cultures, with different languages and traditions. Under the most difficult of conditions, they began to create a new African American culture. In doing so, they preserved much that they had brought with them from Africa.

The slaves' music and dances pulsed with African rhythms and the sounds of African instruments, such as the banjo. African designs showed up in their weavings, wood carvings, and quilts. African legends and stories survived as well. Br'er Rabbit, the wily hero of many slave tales, was based on the African trickster Shulo the Hare.

Enslaved Africans going to America were crammed so closely together in slave ships that they could barely move. After the voyage came the terror of sale.

Planters with large estates often hired overseers to supervise the work of slaves. The overseer in this picture probably got fired for doing more relaxing than overseeing. As one planter complained, "The overseer there is but a chattering fellow, promises much but does little." By the mid-1700s some large plantations no longer used overseers.

Why We Remember

Thinking Critically
Have students work in small groups to evaluate the effects of colonial heritage. Ask each group to determine which two or three colonial legacies it believes have had the most enduring impact on American life, either positive or negative. As each group reports its conclusions, record the students' answers. Then ask the class to come to a consensus on at least three main colonial legacies. (Possible responses include self-government, religious freedom, religious tolerance, racial prejudice, oppression of Indians and African Americans, and African American culture.)

Section Survey Answers

Reviewing Main Ideas
1. Economic: gain wealth; religious: convert the Indians or seek refuge; political: gain power.
2. As long as a colony was small, the Indians did not see the colonists as a threat. Once a colony expanded and colonists began taking over Indian lands, however, the Indians resisted, sparking conflict.
3. The colonists were united by a love of liberty and a hatred of tyranny.

History Mystery
West Africans brought the banjo. Sources on how the banjo has changed might include reference works on African American culture. Sources on modern uses are works on music and musical instruments.

Alternative Assessment
Allow one or two class periods for this activity, depending on how polished a result you would like to see. Have students work in pairs or small groups to prepare their plans. See the Review Take-Home Planner, p. 8, for suggestions and ideas for scoring rubrics for this activity.

Why We Remember

The Planting of Colonies

If you visit the Capitol building in Washington, D.C., take a moment to stand in the rotunda under the great dome. There you will see a mural showing scenes from the history of the United States. One of the earliest scenes shows Pocahontas being baptized in Jamestown.

At that moment, Powhatan's daughter could not have known what her efforts to help the English colonists in Jamestown would lead to. In little more than a century, her people would be almost wiped out, and the number of colonies would soar. By the time Georgia was founded in 1732, the English had a string of colonies stretching from Canada to Florida along the Atlantic coast. By then Spain and France had also colonized vast regions of North and South America.

We remember the planting of colonies because it was, in part, from those seeds that the United States would later grow. The society you live in today was shaped by the ideas, faiths, and cultures of Europeans, African Americans, and Native Americans.

Section Survey

Reviewing Main Ideas

1. What reasons did Europeans have for planting colonies in the Americas?
2. Why did early cooperation between the English colonists and Indians usually give way to conflict?
3. What common beliefs and values united the diverse settlers of the English colonies?

History Mystery

The banjo Answer the History Mystery on page 35. How would you go about learning how the banjo has changed since the 1600s? How would you find out what kinds of modern music use the banjo?

Alternative Assessment

Citizenship: Planning a colony Imagine that the English king has given your class a charter to start a proprietary colony in North America. How will you organize it?
1. With a group of three or four other proprietors, prepare a plan for the colony. Start deciding on the goals of the colony and how you expect to achieve them.
2. As you make your plan, consider these questions: What will you do to attract settlers to the colony? How will you avoid the problems that the Jamestown and Plymouth colonists had? How will you make the colony prosper? How will you govern the colony?

Beginning the Story

George Washington

Students may be surprised to learn that Washington was a staunch supporter of Britain as a young man. Like most colonists, Washington saw himself as a British citizen with a tradition of being loyal to "king and country." He hoped for a place of honor within the empire as a British officer. As students read further, they will see how his dream was denied. With his wounded pride, Washington can be seen to represent the growing colonial resentment of unfair treatment by the mother country.

Setting the Stage Activity

How Much Do You Know?

To check students' knowledge of Washington, have small groups list what comes to mind when they hear his name. They should note any images, characteristics, or stories that they recall. Make a list of students' responses on the chalkboard. Then ask students to summarize what kind of a person they think Washington was.

History Footnote

Despite his surrender at Fort Necessity, Washington was highly regarded by colonists and was appointed as head of Virginia's militia in the backcountry, where he served until 1758. When he attended the First and Second Continental Congresses, his impressive military air made him John Adams's choice for commander of the Continental Army.

History Footnote

The Continental Army enlisted many "citizen soldiers." Such soldiers might live at home much of the time, going out to fight only in emergencies, and returning home after a few weeks or months.

Teaching Resources

Chapter Resources Binder
- Study Guide, p. 3
- Reinforcement, p. 6

1750–1799

Section 3 The Birth of a New Nation

Beginning the Story with

George Washington

By the time he was 15, George Washington knew what he wanted in life—to be rich and respected. His problem was that he had no land, and in colonial Virginia, land was wealth. The best alternative, he decided, was to become an officer in the British army. As an officer and a gentleman, he would command respect, not to mention a handsome salary. The only problem was that most British officers believed that colonists made poor soldiers.

Washington set out to prove them wrong. In 1752, at the age of 20, he joined the Virginia colonial militia. The following year the eager young soldier volunteered to lead a small expedition north into French territory. In the dead of winter, he slogged across 1,000 miles of Ohio Valley wilderness to a French fort near Lake Erie. On his arrival, he delivered his blunt message that the Ohio Valley belonged to Virginia. The French should stay out.

The French officers at the fort received the Virginian politely, inviting him to dine with them. After dinner Washington wrote in his journal,

> "The wine, as they dosed them selves pretty plentifully with it, soon banished restraint. They told me it was their absolute design to take possession of the Ohio."

Washington's first military mission, in the winter of 1753, was nearly his last. He almost froze to death crossing an ice-clogged river.

History Bookshelf

Zall, P. M., ed. *Becoming American: Young People in the American Revolution.* Linnet Books, 1993. Students may enjoy reading about teenagers' experiences during the revolutionary period through diaries and letters.

Also of interest:

Asimov, Isaac. *The Birth of the United States.* Houghton Mifflin, 1974.

Davis, Burke. *Black Heroes of the American Revolution.* Harcourt Brace, 1976.

Kent, Deborah. *The American Revolution: "Give Me Liberty or Give Me Death."* Enslow Publishers, Inc., 1994.

McGovern, Ann. *The Secret Soldier: The Story of Deborah Sampson.* Four Winds Press, 1975.

Discussion

Thinking Historically

1. Why did Washington choose a military career? (He was unlikely to become respected and rich as a landowner or surveyor. As a British officer, he would earn respect and be well paid.)

2. How can you tell that Washington seized opportunity rather than waiting for it to come to him? (He took steps to gain military experience and quickly volunteered for a dangerous mission to prove himself.)

Teaching the HISTORY Mystery

Students will find the answer on page 55. See the Section Survey, page 59, for additional questions.

Teaching the Hands-On HISTORY

To help students imagine Washington's feelings, have them recall how they have felt after losing a contest or game. How might he have felt about losing an important battle? To help students get started, suggest beginning the letter, "Dear Family, Do you recall the letter in which I wrote you that I was charmed by the whistle of bullets? Well . . ."

HISTORY Mystery

General Washington's best spies in Philadelphia informed him that the British wanted their laundry returned immediately, "finished or unfinished." Why did Washington care about the British soldiers' laundry?

"I Heard the Bullets Whistle"

Washington rushed back to Virginia with this alarming news. In the spring of 1754, he was chosen to lead a small militia force back into the Ohio Valley. Their mission was to protect Virginians building a fort where the Allegheny and Monongahela rivers meet to form the Ohio River. They arrived too late. The French had already chased the Virginians away and were building their own fort on the same spot.

At that moment, Washington made one of the few mistakes in his military career. He attacked a small French force camped nearby, even though France and Britain were not at war. It was an easy victory. "I heard the bullets whistle," Washington wrote in a letter home, "and, believe me, there is something charming in the sound."

The charm of whistling bullets faded quickly when Washington found himself surrounded by angry French troops. His men quickly built a fort that they called Fort Necessity. After a ten-hour siege, which left a third of the Virginians dead, Washington realized his situation was hopeless. Reluctantly, he surrendered.

The French sent the Virginians home, where Washington was welcomed as a hero. He had, after all, stood up to the French against great odds. To British army leaders, however, his surrender was still more proof that colonials did not make good soldiers—much less good officers.

Hands-On HISTORY

Activity

You read what Washington wrote home after his victory over the French. Write another letter home from Washington after his surrender of Fort Necessity. Describe the feelings he might have had about his own future in the military and about the ability of the colonial militia.

Introducing the Lesson

Vocabulary

cede
proclamation
legislature
boycott
repeal
monopoly
militia
blockade

Warm-Up Activity

Role-playing an Interview
Have students imagine they are the young George Washington in an interview with British officers. Divide the class into small groups and have each list reasons why the British should train more colonial officers and why the British may oppose this.

Time Line

Keys to History

French and Indian War The war between France and Britain decided who controlled North America.

Stamp Act The stamp tax led to the first widespread colonial protests against British policies.

Vital Links

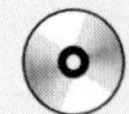

French and Indian War (Picture) Unit 1, Side 1, Search 40644

See also Unit 3 Explore CD-ROM location 366.

Lesson Objectives

- ★ Explain the problems Britain faced in the colonies after its victory in the French and Indian War.
- ★ Discuss why and how the colonists resisted efforts by Britain to tax them.
- ★ Identify the events that led Britain and the colonists to the brink of war.

Teaching Resources

Chapter Summaries
English, p. 18
Spanish, p. 19
Transparency Activities
p. 8

1754–1774

Lesson 1 The Years of Conflict

Washington's whistling bullets were the first shots of a conflict between France and Britain that was known in the colonies as the French and Indian War. When the war began in 1754, France controlled a large part of North America. When a peace treaty was finally signed in 1763, the map of North America looked very different. By then a defeated France had ceded Louisiana to Spain and Canada to Great Britain.

Two problems faced Britain as it tried to govern its new territory. One was how to deal with the Indian tribes that lived there. The other was whether to allow settlers to move west, turning Indian hunting grounds into farms. To prevent further conflict with the Indians, Parliament issued the Proclamation of 1763. It said that colonists could not settle west of the Appalachians. However, many ignored the proclamation.

To enforce the Proclamation of 1763, Britain planned to station 10,000 troops in North America. Parliament decided that the colonists should pay for their own defense. Over the next few years, Parliament passed a series of tax acts, each one designed to raise money in the colonies.

The colonists argued that they could only be taxed by their elected representatives in their colonial legislatures. When Parliament refused to back down, protesters calling themselves Sons and Daughters of Liberty staged demonstrations against tax collectors and boycotted British goods. In Boston, protest turned deadly when British troops opened fire on an unruly crowd. Many colonists saw the "Boston Massacre" as yet more proof that Britain would stop at nothing in its drive to crush their rights and freedoms.

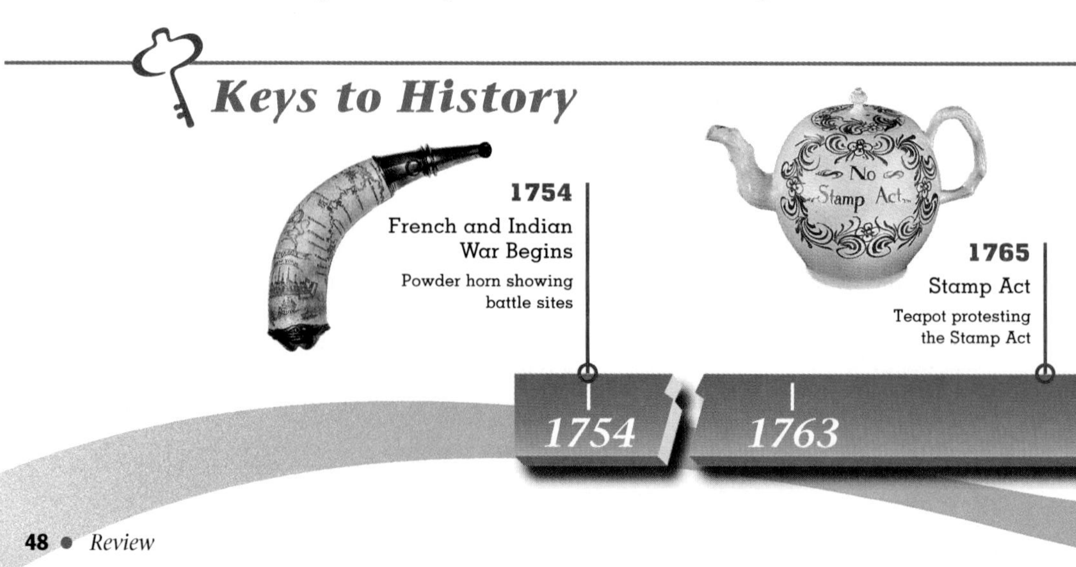

1754 French and Indian War Begins
Powder horn showing battle sites

1765 Stamp Act
Teapot protesting the Stamp Act

Connections to Literature

Henry Wadsworth Longfellow's narrative poem *Evangeline,* written in 1847, tells how the French and Indian War affected a young man and woman. The couple is separated when the British remove residents of French descent from Nova Scotia, known to the French as Acadia. Evangeline searches a lifetime for her friend, only to find him many years later as he is dying.

The relocation of the Acadians was spurred by British concern about controlling the large French population in the area. In 1775 Acadians were loaded on British ships and moved to other British colonies. Many made their way south to Louisiana to be near other French-speaking people. Today, their descendants are known as *Cajuns,* a word derived from *Acadians.*

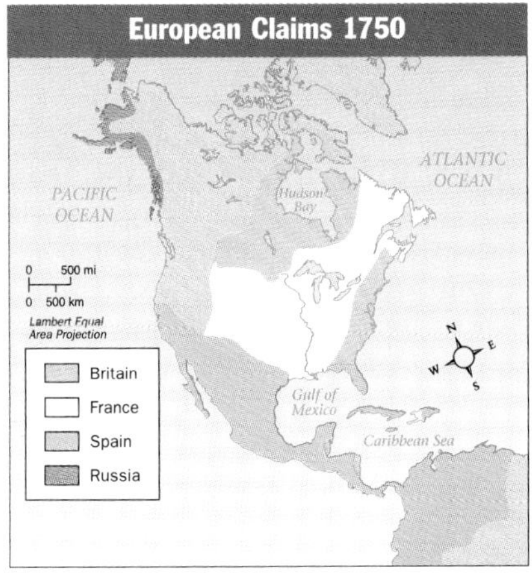

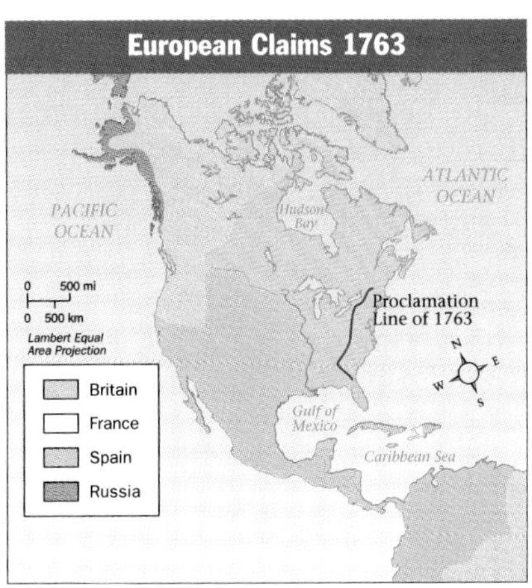

Reading Maps

1. What parts of North America did the four European powers claim in 1750?
2. Describe the large transfer of territory that took place as a result of the British victory in the French and Indian War.

1767
Sam Adams emerges as protest leader

1770
Boston Massacre
Coffin sketches with initials of some victims

1773
Boston Tea Party
British engraving made in 1789

1774
First Continental Congress

1769

1774

Developing the Lesson

Discussion

Checking Understanding

1. What was the purpose of the Proclamation of 1763? (To prevent conflicts between settlers and Indians until treaties could be signed.)

Teaching the Reading Maps

Answers: 1. Russia: Pacific Northwest; Spain: Florida, Southwest, Mexico, Central and South America; France: northeastern Canada, Midwest and Great Plains; Britain: Eastern seaboard, northern Canada. **2.** France ceded Canada and eastern North America to Britain and its claims in the west and south to Spain.

Time Line

Sam Adams Skill with words made Adams a leader of colonial protest against British taxation.

Boston Massacre News that British soldiers had fired upon a riotous crowd of colonists was used by protest leaders to stir anti-British feelings.

Boston Tea Party The dumping of tea into Boston Harbor challenged British authority, leading to the Intolerable Acts.

The First Continental Congress The meeting was an effort by the colonies to unite in response to the Intolerable Acts.

Lesson
Activity

Boston Tea Party News Reports

To compare British and colonial viewpoints on the Boston Tea Party, have students write newspaper articles. Each student should write one article that would appear in a British newspaper and one that would appear in a colonial newspaper. Each article should have a powerful headline, give a slanted description of the event, and state opinions about its causes and effects.

Vital Links

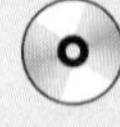

"Revolutionary Tea" (Song) Unit 2, Side 1, Search 13715, Play to 16138

See also Unit 2 Explore CD-ROM location 80.

Voice of newspaper publisher (First Person Account) Unit 2, Side 1, Search 12614, Play to 13271

See also Unit 2 Explore CD-ROM location 63.

Geography Footnote

Improvements in colonial roads were matched by the rapid rise in the spread of news by mail. Boston's 1772 Committee of Correspondence was joined by similar organizations in half of the more than 260 towns in Massachusetts. In 1773 Virginia's House of Burgesses proposed that each colony appoint a committee of correspondence. Within a year, almost every colony had such a network in place. By the time the Coercive Acts were imposed on Boston in 1774, the means were in place to rapidly inform the colonies of Boston's plight, thus paving the way for concerted action by the colonies. The First Continental Congress was a direct outgrowth of the committees.

The Intolerable Acts

On the very day of the Boston Massacre, Parliament met to discuss the Townshend Acts—the latest effort to tax the colonies. At the urging of King George III to show restraint, Parliament repealed all the taxes except the one on tea. For a time, tempers cooled.

The uneasy calm was shattered when Parliament passed the Tea Act in 1773. This law gave the British East India Company a monopoly of sales of British tea in the colonies. Colonial merchants thought this would put many of them out of business. When three tea ships arrived in Boston harbor, Sons of Liberty disguised as Indians boarded the vessels. As hundreds of Bostonians cheered from the docks, the "Indians" chopped open 342 chests of tea and tossed the contents into the sea. In both Britain and the colonies, most people saw the Boston Tea Party as a point of no return.

In Britain, a furious Parliament responded to this act of defiance by blockading Boston harbor and placing Massachusetts under military rule until the ruined tea was paid for. British leaders hoped that these Coercive Acts would frighten the colonies into accepting British authority.

Instead, angry colonists called these laws the "Intolerable Acts" and vowed to resist them. When Boston's port was closed, food donated by other colonies poured into the city. As a result, complained British officials, Boston's well-fed rebels grew "as sleek and as round as robins."

Members of the Sons of Liberty protested the Tea Act by dumping chests of tea into Boston harbor to make "salt-water tea."

History Footnote
The Irish term *boycott* originated in 1897 with a land agent named Charles C. Boycott. This English landlord mistreated his Irish tenants so badly that he was ostracized by them. The English ruling class was often inclined to regard the Irish as uncivilized and Ireland itself as a source of revenue. In this way, their circumstances were very much like those of American colonists.

History Footnote
The Coercive Acts included a law requiring the colonists to house British troops. It was a move guaranteed to inflame colonists' tempers. Prejudice amongst British soldiers against colonists had only worsened since the French and Indian War, and the colonists returned the dislike. If the British saw the colonists as bumpkins, the colonists saw the British as brutes.

On the Brink of War

In September 1774 delegates from all of the colonies except Georgia met in Philadelphia as the First Continental Congress. Their goal was to look for a peaceful way to resolve their conflict with Britain.

Politically, the Congress was split about equally into three groups: conservatives, moderates, and radicals. Despite their differences, the delegates all opposed the Coercive Acts and denied Parliament's right to tax the colonies. The Congress recommended a boycott of British goods. The delegates agreed to meet again the following May if Britain did not change its policies.

Across the colonies, towns formed committees to enforce the boycott. In case the boycott did not work, the colonists rushed to organize militias. After more than a decade of protest, the colonies stood on the brink of war.

Steps Toward the American Revolution 1763–1774

British Law	What It Did	Colonial Reaction
Proclamation of 1763	Prohibited settlement west of the Appalachians	Protests, defiance
Sugar Act (1764)	Lowered duties on molasses, but first time duties used to collect revenue; denied jury trial to accused smugglers	Protests, petitions
Stamp Act (1765)	Required all written materials to be printed on stamped paper; first direct tax to get revenue (repealed in 1766)	Stamp Act Congress, petitions, boycotts, demonstrations
Declaratory Act (1766)	Declared Parliament's right to impose any laws on colonies	Little notice because of Stamp Act repeal
Townshend Acts (1767)	Taxed tea, lead, glass, paint, and paper; governors to be paid by Parliament (most repealed in 1770)	Boycotts, riots, demonstrations
Tea Act (1773)	Required that only East India Company may import and sell tea	Boycotts, Boston Tea Party
Coercive Acts (1774) ("Intolerable Acts")	Closed Boston port until destroyed tea paid for; suspended town meetings; appointed military governor of Massachusetts; permitted trials of government officials to be in England	Other colonies sent food and money to Massachusetts; call for Continental Congress

Source: Oxford Book of Reference on English History

Developing the Lesson

Discussion

Checking Understanding

1. What was the economic motivation for the Boston Tea Party? (Colonial merchants thought the new Tea Act, which gave the British East India Company a monopoly, would put them out of business.)

Stimulating Critical Thinking

2. John Adams praised the Boston Tea Party, but Benjamin Franklin called it an act of violent injustice. With whom do you agree? Explain. (Those who agree with Adams may note that no person was injured and no property destroyed other than the tea. Those who agree with Franklin might argue that property was destroyed nonetheless and that the ship's crew were probably violently intimidated.)

Wrap-Up Activity

Letters on the Coercive Acts

To help students imagine colonists' reactions to the Coercive Acts, have them write letters to the editor of the *Boston Bugle* just before the meeting of the First Continental Congress. The letters should be written from the perspective of ordinary citizens telling how the Coercive Acts affect their lives and what should be done to try to solve the problem.

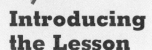

Introducing the Lesson

Vocabulary

minutemen
mercenaries
Patriots

Warm-Up Activity

Preparing for War

To help students understand how colonists prepared for war, have them write a speech explaining what steps to take. Ask them to imagine they are each the mayor of a small Massachusetts town in 1775. They are to write a speech to deliver at a town meeting. It should summarize events leading up to the "present" and explain what precautions and preparations people should make in case of war with Britain. (These might include hiding valuables, storing food, finding weapons, and so forth.)

Time Line

Keys to History

Lexington and Concord War broke out when shots were fired by British troops attempting to disarm the colonial militia.

Common Sense Thomas Paine's popular pamphlet convinced many doubtful colonists of the advantages of independence.

The Declaration of Independence Congress commissioned Thomas Jefferson to explain the colonies' reasons for separating from Britain.

Lesson Objectives

- ★ Identify the events that led Congress to declare independence in 1776.
- ★ Describe the strengths and weaknesses of each side in the war.
- ★ Summarize the turning points in the war.
- ★ Identify what the United States gained from the Treaty of Paris.

Teaching Resources

Chapter Summaries
English, p. 20
Spanish, p. 21
Transparency Activities
p. 9–10

1775–1783

Lesson 2 The War of Independence

When the Second Continental Congress met in May 1775, the long-feared war had already begun. Less than a month earlier, British troops stationed in Boston had clashed with colonial militias in nearby Lexington and Concord. The Congress elected George Washington to take command of the New England militiamen camped around Boston. In less than a year, Washington drove the British out of Boston. With that victory, many colonists hoped the war was over. In fact, it had just begun.

In spite of the fighting with the British, few colonists actually wanted independence from Britain. Many changed their minds, however, after reading *Common Sense*, a pamphlet published by Tom Paine early in 1776. Paine argued that Americans had much to gain and nothing to lose by breaking their ties with Britain. Suddenly the idea of independence began to seem sensible rather than unthinkable. On July 4, 1776, Congress approved a Declaration of Independence stating that "these united colonies are, and of right ought to be, free and independent states."

To British military leaders, the idea that the colonists might actually win their independence was laughable. Britain had a large well-trained army that would soon be joined by 30,000 mercenaries from Germany. The mighty British navy could land troops and supplies anywhere along the Atlantic coast.

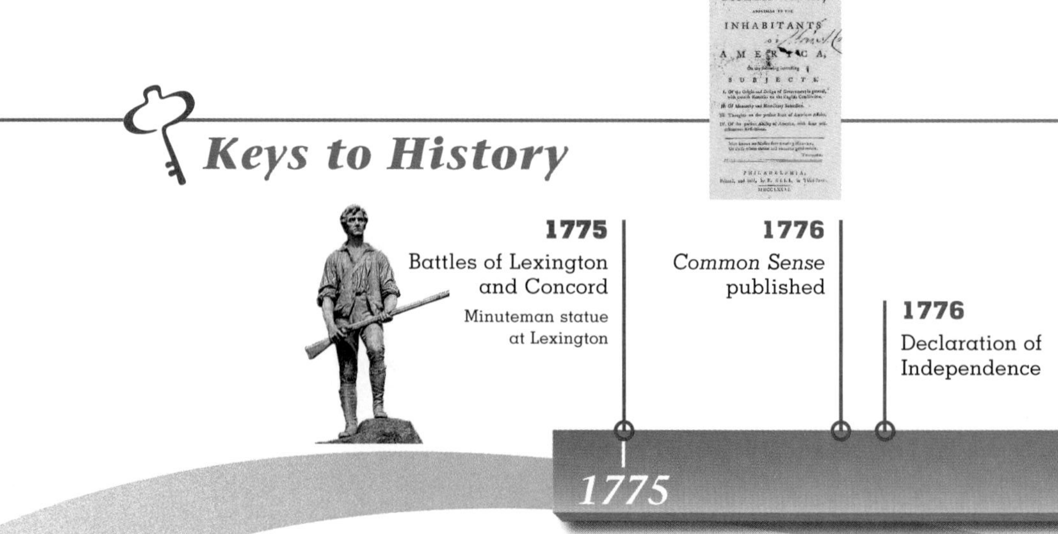

Minuteman statue at Lexington

History Footnote

Another Patriot strength was in weaponry. The firearm issued to British soldiers was a highly inaccurate musket with a smooth bore (inner surface of the barrel). The British usually stood in lines and fired all at the same time to increase their chances of hitting the enemy. Patriot troops increasingly made use of an American invention, the flintlock rifle. With a grooved (rifled) barrel, this weapon was much more accurate and easier to fire. This made it possible for Patriots to abandon fighting in ranks and firing together; they could now take cover and fire at their leisure, picking off the enemy one by one.

In contrast, the Americans began the war with a poorly trained army and almost no navy. Throughout the war, the Continental Army was always short of weapons, clothing, and food. The Patriots' strength was not in numbers but in the dedication of those who remained faithful through the darkest days of war. Without them, the struggle soon would have failed.

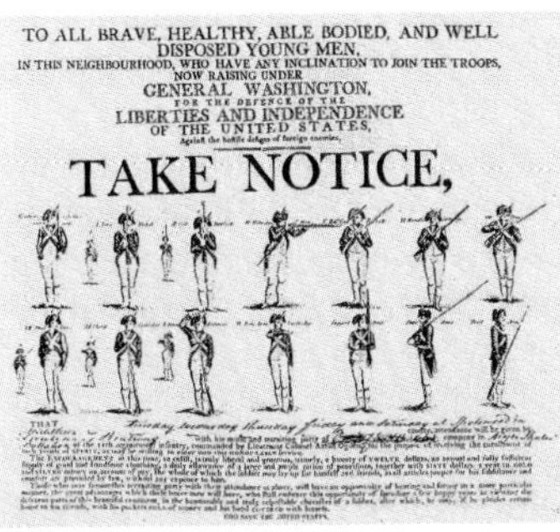

This recruiting poster shows how to fire a musket. Recruits were offered an annual wage of $60 and an opportunity for "honorable service."

Many Patriot women knew how to use muskets to defend their homes. Deborah Sampson even enlisted in the army disguised as a man.

Hands-On HISTORY

Activity

What would have convinced you to join the Continental Army in 1776? Patriotism? Love of Liberty? Bonus money? Thirst for adventure? Design your own recruiting poster aimed at persuading colonists your age to take up arms against Britain.

1777–1778

Winter at Valley Forge

General Lafayette and General Washington at Valley Forge

1781

British surrender at Yorktown

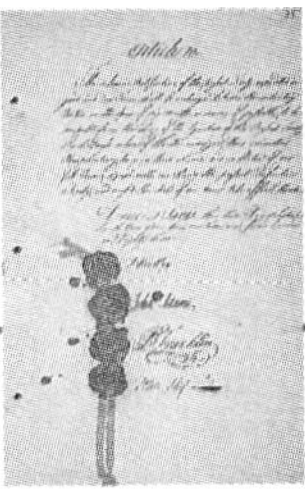

1783

Treaty of Paris recognizes American independence

779

1783

Developing the Lesson

Discussion

Checking Understanding

1. What were the two most important decisions made by the Second Continental Congress early in the war? (Appointing Washington to form a Continental Army and declaring independence.)

Teaching the Hands-On HISTORY

Remind students that recruiting posters, like commercials for the armed forces today, present military service as a learning experience or a patriotic duty. Ask: **What might a soldier learn in the Continental Army that would be useful later in life?** (Marksmanship, living off the land, discipline, perseverance.)

Time Line

Valley Forge At the low point of the war, Washington's troops endured a bitter winter of hunger, exposure, and desertion.

Yorktown The Patriot defeat of Cornwallis lead to the end of the war.

Treaty of Paris Britain recognized the United States as an independent nation and ceded its claims west to the Mississippi River.

Teaching Map Skills

Reading a War Map

Have students study the map on this page. Ask:

1. What do the bold lines on the map represent? The arrows? The splashes of color? (The bold lines represent the routes of the British and American armies; the arrows indicate the direction of movement; the splashes indicate either American or British military victories.)

2. Which side won the earliest battle shown on the map? (The British at New York City, on August 27, 1776.)

3. If you wanted to follow Washington's exact route from New York to Trenton today by car, could you do it using this map? Why or why not? (It would be better to have a map that shows paved roads and the historical route.)

Lesson Activity

Geography

Have students imagine that they are an aide to General Washington. The Continental Congress wants a summary of troop movements and important battles in 1777. Students should list the battles shown on the map for the year 1777 and include the circumstances of each battle. Students could draw a simple enlargement of the map area on this page and mark the locations of the relevant battles.

54

History Footnote

During the progress of Cornwallis's troops through the South, and especially during his slow retreat to Yorktown, ordinary citizens frequently fled before the British arrived in their towns. They wanted to avoid being robbed, beaten, or worse at the hands of British soldiers. Sixteen-year-old Betsy Ambler, daughter of Virginia's treasurer, wrote to a friend about her family's sudden exodus from Richmond, leaving home, friends, and belongings: "My father seemed to think we hadn't a moment to lose—such terror and confusion you have no idea of—governor, council, everyone scampering."

Keeping the Cause Alive

A few months after leaving Boston, the British invaded New York City with 32,000 British and Hessian troops. This time it was the Americans' turn to flee. As the weather turned cold and hopes faded, soldiers deserted. By December 1776, Washington commanded just 3,000 troops. Unless more recruits were found soon, he wrote, "I think the game will be pretty well up."

The Patriot army retreats across New Jersey, December 1776

In this desperate moment, Washington hatched a desperate plan. On Christmas night he ferried his troops across the ice-choked Delaware River in small boats. The next morning they captured a force of very surprised Hessians who were camped for the winter in Trenton, New Jersey.

As news of this victory spread throughout the colonies, thousands of volunteers joined the Continental Army. The Patriots' cause was still alive.

A Turning Point at Saratoga

In 1777 the British came up with a plan to end the war by dividing the colonies. General John Burgoyne would lead one army south from Canada to capture the upper Hudson River Valley. General William Howe would lead a second army upriver from New York City to conquer the lower valley. By controlling the Hudson River Valley, the British could cut off the flow of men and supplies from New England.

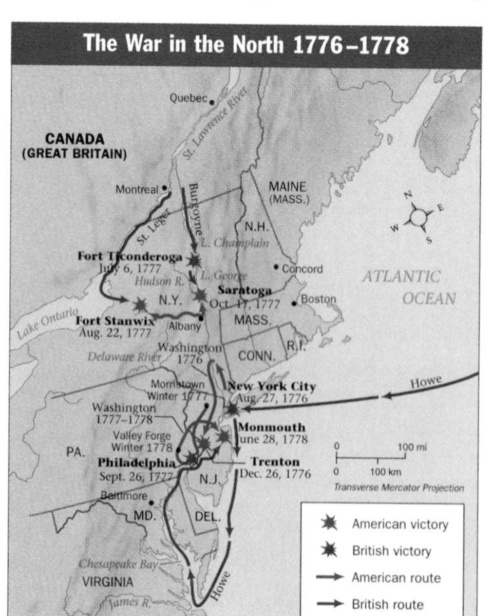

On paper it looked like a good plan. But Burgoyne misjudged how hard it would be to move an army through miles of wilderness. And Howe misjudged how long it would take him to capture Philadelphia before heading up the Hudson. When Burgoyne reached the Hudson River at Saratoga, he found a horde of hostile militia troops. Badly outnumbered, he was forced to surrender.

The victory at Saratoga was a turning point in the war for the Americans. Up to that time, their cause had looked hopeless. Even Britain's traditional enemies, France and Spain, had refused to get involved. With Burgoyne's surrender, the Americans no longer looked like losers. Over the next two years, both France and Spain entered the war against Britain. The American cause no longer looked hopeless.

History Footnote

The diary of Major Ebenezer Denny, 19, gives a gripping picture of Yorktown after the British surrendered. He notes that the British troops are left in confusion, and many riot throughout the day. At night some, in search of food, try to break into stores. The American patrols are kept busy trying to keep the British in line. He describes town life as filthy and shattered, noting "vast heaps of shot and shells lying about every quarter, which came from our works."

The War Moves South

In the spring of 1778, Washington received a message from his best spies in Philadelphia, the washerwomen. Their British customers had suddenly ordered all laundry to be returned at once, "finished or unfinished."

To Washington this could only mean one thing. The British were about to abandon Philadelphia. Weeks later, the British were back in New York City with Washington's troops camped nearby.

Having failed in the North, the British moved the war south. South Carolina fell to the British in 1780. A worried Washington sent General Nathanael Greene south to slow the British advance. Greene led British General Charles Cornwallis on an exhausting chase through the backcountry. Greene described his strategy in these words: "We fight, get beat, rise, and fight again."

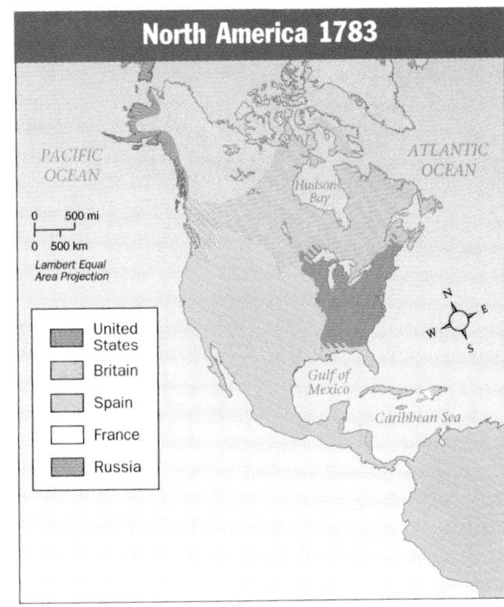

Victory at Yorktown

Greene's strategy worked. In 1781 General Cornwallis announced that he was "quite tired of marching about the country." He moved his army north to a sleepy tobacco port in Virginia called Yorktown. There he thought the British navy could keep his army supplied. Washington, however, moved most of his army south from New York to Virginia, surrounding Yorktown by land. Meanwhile, French warships sealed off the entrance to Chesapeake Bay, cutting Cornwallis off from the British fleet. On October 7, 1781, the Americans began to bombard Yorktown. Twelve days later, Cornwallis surrendered.

After their defeat at Yorktown, the British began peace talks with their former colonies. In 1783 both sides signed a peace treaty in Paris. In the Treaty of Paris, Britain recognized the United States as an independent nation. It also agreed to cede to the new nation all lands between the Atlantic Coast and the Mississippi River.

The Americans had won the freedom to shape their own future. Looking ahead, Washington was awed by the responsibility that came with that freedom. "With our fate," he wrote at war's end, "will the destiny of unborn millions be involved."

The original Declaration of Independence is preserved in a glass-and-bronze case at the National Archives in Washington, D.C. The case is filled with helium to protect the fragile, faded document from the air. The shatter-proof glass is tinted to protect it from the light. Each night the case is lowered into a reinforced vault beneath the floor. What do you think would have happened to the Declaration if the Americans had lost the war?

Bonus Activity

Note from a Spy

To help students understand the type of information that might be useful to a commander, have them write coded notes to General Washington. The code may be simple, such as substituting numbers for letters. Ask them to imagine being Patriots in Philadelphia during the winter of 1777–1778 and writing notes to Washington about British activity in the city. They should include information about numbers of troops, provisions, and status of weaponry.

Wrap-Up Activity

Assessing a Defeat

To help students understand why Yorktown was decisive, have them imagine themselves as British generals evaluating the military situation after the defeat. Ask students to make lists of reasons for and against continuing the war, followed by explanations of the decision to seek peace.

Answers to Caption: Opinions will vary, but most likely the Declaration would not have been preserved with such care had the Americans lost the war.

Introducing the Lesson

Vocabulary

constitution
confederation
legislative branch
executive branch
judicial branch
ratify
bill of rights
amendment
due process of law
federalism
checks and balances

Warm-Up Activity

Views on National Government

To help students predict what type of national government the states might accept, have small groups imagine themselves as state legislators shortly after the Declaration of Independence. Assign each group a state and have them discuss whether a national government is needed and, if so, what powers it should or should not have. After groups list ideas, have them share conclusions.

Time Line

Keys to History

State Constitutions By writing constitutions, the 13 former colonies declared themselves independent republics.

The Articles of Confederation The Articles were the first plan of government for the new nation, a loose alliance of independent states.

Lesson Objectives

- ★ Identify the problems the new nation faced under the Articles of Confederation.
- ★ Summarize the work of the Constitutional Convention.
- ★ Describe the origins of the Bill of Rights.
- ★ Summarize the ideas that have made the Constitution endure.

Teaching Resources

Chapter Summaries
English, p. 22
Spanish, p. 23
Transparency Activities
p. 11

1776–1791

Lesson 3 Creating the Constitution

During the War of Independence, the United States adopted a plan of government known as the Articles of Confederation. The Articles created a loose alliance of states, so loose that quarrels among states sometimes threatened to tear the new nation apart. Worse yet, the new government was powerless in the face of uprisings such as Shays' Rebellion.

In the spring of 1787, delegates from the states met in Philadelphia to revise the Articles. Instead, they decided to scrap the old plan altogether and create a new national government, one with real power and authority. They all agreed that this new government should have three branches—a legislative branch to make laws, an executive branch to carry out those laws, and a judicial branch to interpret the laws. Still, they spent months arguing about such issues as how to choose members of Congress, what powers the national government should have, and how to elect a president.

By summer's end, the hard work of debate and compromise was over. On September 17, 1787, the delegates met to sign their new Constitution. By late 1788, every state but one had approved the new plan. The following year elections were held for the first Congress and George Washington was elected the nation's first President.

During the ratification debates, supporters of the Constitution had promised to add a bill of rights to the document. When the first Congress met, it proposed twelve constitutional amendments. By 1791 the states had approved ten of these, which together formed the Bill of Rights. It guarantees

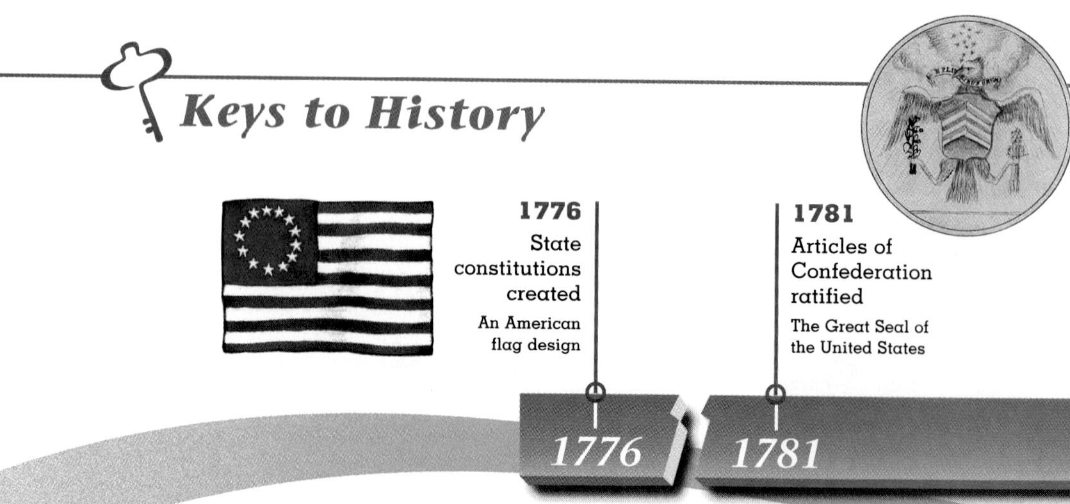

An American flag design

The Great Seal of the United States

History Footnote

The need for a bill of rights was by no means self-evident at the time. In fact, some feared including one because it might prove too limiting or might imply that any right not included did not exist. Madison said:

> My own opinion has always been in favor of a bill of rights; provided it be so framed as not to imply powers not meant to be included in the enumeration. At the same time I have never thought the omission a material defect, nor been anxious to supply it even by subsequent amendment. . . .

our most cherished freedoms, such as the freedoms of speech, the press, assembly, and worship. It provides such legal rights as trial by jury. It also prohibits the government from taking away "life, liberty, or property" without due process of law.

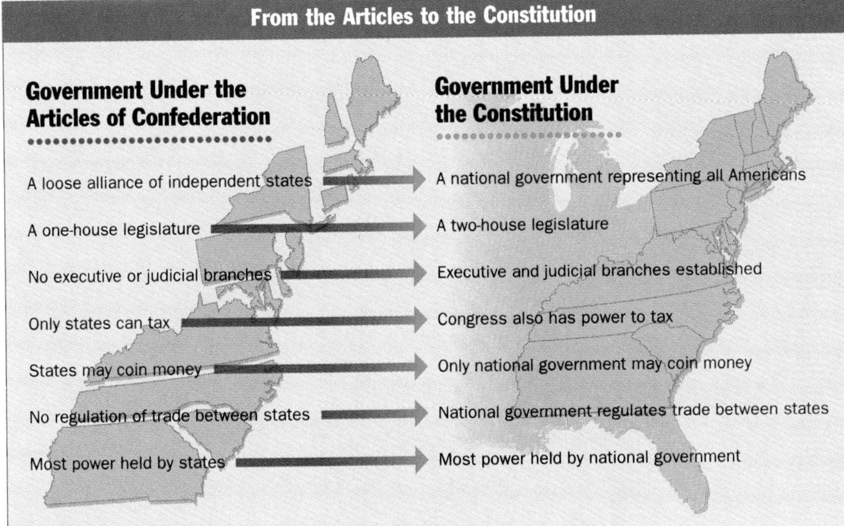

From the Articles to the Constitution
Government Under the Articles of Confederation
Government Under the Constitution
A loose alliance of independent states
A national government representing all Americans
A one-house legislature
A two-house legislature
No executive or judicial branches
Executive and judicial branches established
Only states can tax
Congress also has power to tax
States may coin money
Only national government may coin money
No regulation of trade between states
National government regulates trade between states
Most power held by states
Most power held by national government

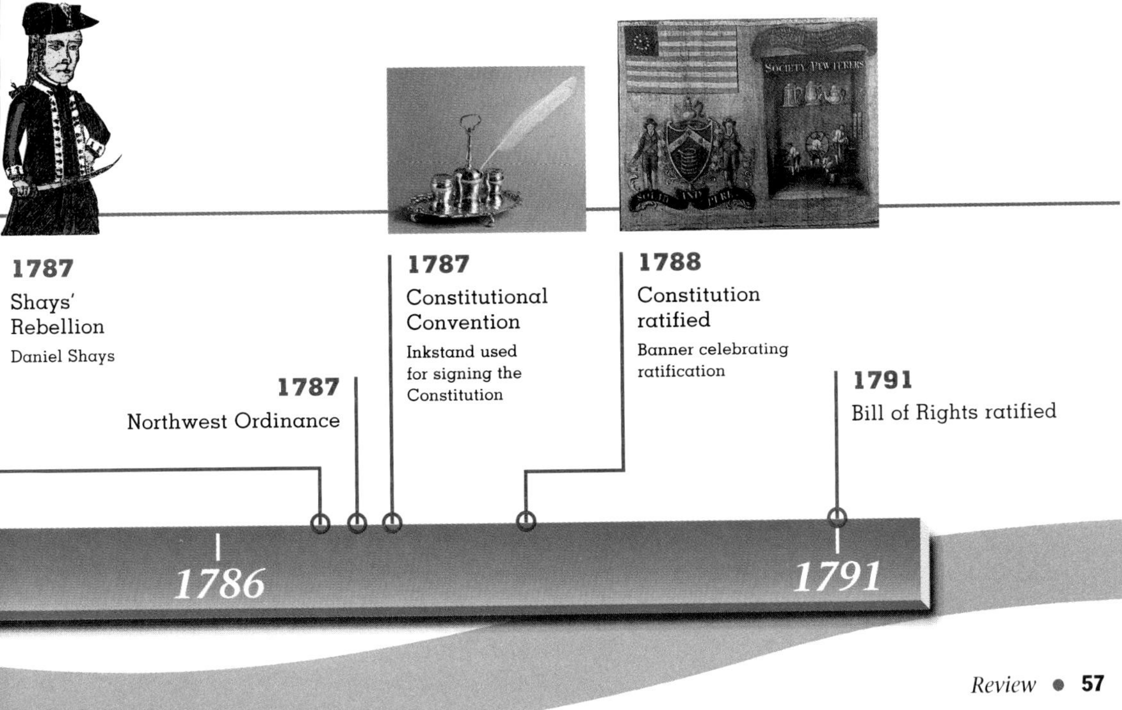

Developing the Lesson

Discussion

Checking Understanding

1. How did the Constitution make the national government stronger than the Articles of Confederation? (It gave Congress the powers to tax, coin money, and regulate interstate trade. It created the executive branch and judicial branch to carry out and enforce national laws.)

2. What kinds of rights are protected by the Bill of Rights? (Freedoms of speech, press, assembly, worship; basic legal rights such as trial by jury and the guarantee that the government cannot take away life, liberty, or property without due process of law.)

Time Line

Shays' Rebellion The revolt of Massachusetts farmers spurred states to send delegates to the Constitutional Convention.

Northwest Ordinance With this law, Congress planned how to divide the territory into states.

The Constitutional Convention The delegates drafted a plan for a strong national government.

Constitution Ratified When New Hampshire became the ninth state to ratify, the new plan of government was officially approved.

Bill of Rights The first ten amendments to the Constitution safeguard individual freedoms.

Bonus Activity

Class Constitutions

Divide the class into small groups. Assign each group the task of writing two class constitutions, one a list of very specific rules ("no student will call a classmate 'stupid'") and the other a list of general principles ("no student will insult a classmate"). Conclude by discussing the advantages of having general principles.

Wrap-Up Activity

"Out of Many, One"

Ask students to explain the meaning of our national motto, *e pluribus unum,* and have them find the words on coins and a dollar bill. Then ask them to write a description of what the motto meant when first adopted in 1782, how that meaning changed when the Constitution was ratified, and what the motto means to us today.

Vital Links

Voice of Benjamin Franklin (First Person Account) Unit 2, Side 1, Search 22014, Play to 23009

See also Unit 2 Explore CD-ROM location 122.

Connections to Civics

Although the United States may be the oldest republic still in existence today, it is not the longest enduring or the first. Rome was declared a republic in 509 B.C., after defeating the Etruscans. While its government was vastly different from ours, the ideas for our three-branch system are loosely based on the Roman Republic. The word "senate" comes from the Roman council of 300 senators, who acted as an advisory body to the chief executive. The republic, which lasted for 400 years, ended in 27 B.C., when Augustus declared himself emperor.

An Enduring Framework

Under the new Constitution, the United States not only survived but thrived. No other nation on earth has had such an enduring framework of government.

The men who framed the Constitution created a flexible plan that has allowed the government to adapt to changing needs. At the same time, they developed a plan that limits the government's power. They accomplished this in two ways. First they divided power between the national government and the states to create a system of government known as federalism.

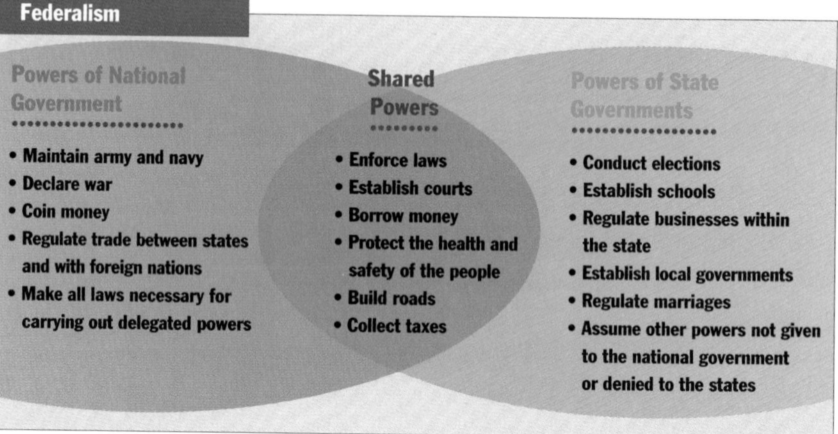

Federalism
Powers of National Government
• Maintain army and navy
• Declare war
• Coin money
• Regulate trade between states and with foreign nations
• Make all laws necessary for carrying out delegated powers
Shared Powers
• Enforce laws
• Establish courts
• Borrow money
• Protect the health and safety of the people
• Build roads
• Collect taxes
Powers of State Governments
• Conduct elections
• Establish schools
• Regulate businesses within the state
• Establish local governments
• Regulate marriages
• Assume other powers not given to the national government or denied to the states

Second, the framers created a system of checks and balances within the national government. Under this system, power is divided among the three branches of government, and each branch has the ability to check, or limit, the other two.

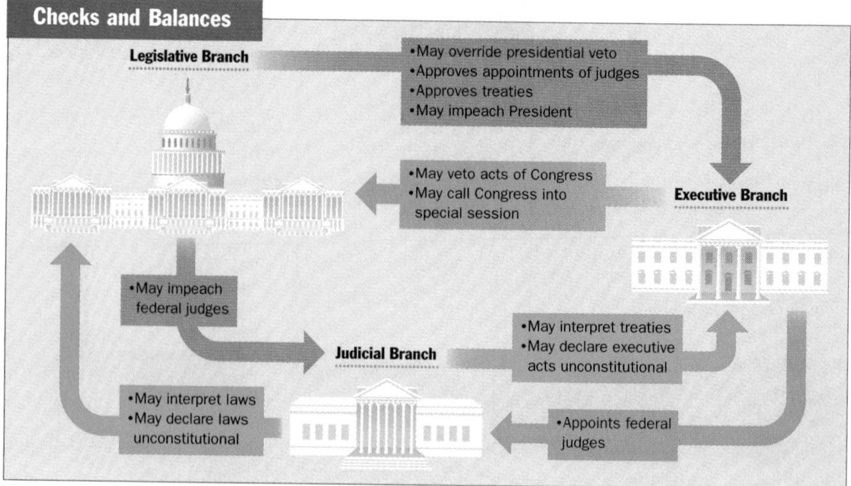

•May override presidential veto
•Approves appointments of judges
•Approves treaties
•May impeach President

•May impeach federal judges

•May interpret treaties

•May interpret laws

•Appoints federal judges

Why We Remember

Thinking Critically

1. In what way was the new Constitution an experiment? (In a world full of governments that were ruled by and for the strong, the Constitution created a government of limited power that was ruled by and for the people.)

2. Why was this experiment important to Americans in 1787? To the world? (In 1787 Americans were not sure that their new nation would survive. They needed to prove to themselves and to the world that a government ruled by and for the people could succeed. The success of the American experiment has given the world an alternative to rule by force.)

Why We Remember

The Birth of a New Nation

When George Washington was a boy growing up in Virginia, he often spoke of Britain as "home." So did most colonists. Then, as Britain tried to tighten its control over the colonies, such feelings began to change. Many colonists feared that the rights and liberties they most valued were suddenly at risk.

Washington and his fellow colonists faced a clear choice. They could ignore their fears. Or they could fight for their rights. Rich and poor, many chose to stand up to Britain. They fought back at first with protests and boycotts. When peaceful measures failed, many took up arms and went to war. In doing so, they risked everything, even life itself, to be free.

Today when we think about the birth of our nation, we remember the ideals and courage of those who fought for independence. We also remember their struggle to create a workable plan of government for the new United States. For thousands of years, nations had been built by the strong and ruled by force. In 1787 Americans set out to prove that a nation could be built instead on the consent of the people. That their experiment succeeded at all is remarkable. That it succeeded so well is truly amazing.

Section Survey

Reviewing Main Ideas

1. How did a British victory in the French and Indian war lead to conflict with the colonies?
2. When British troops surrendered at Yorktown in 1781, the band played "The World Turned Upside Down." Why do you think the Americans chose that tune?
3. How did the framers of the Constitution create a government with enough powers to unite the nation but still limit those powers?

History Mystery

British uniforms Answer the History Mystery on page 47. Now imagine yourself as a Patriot living in a city occupied by the British. What considerations would you have to weigh in deciding whether to spy on the British? As a spy, how might you gather information about the British?

Alternative Assessment

Explaining Founding Documents Our nation's two most important founding documents—the Declaration of Independence and the Constitution—are both on display at the National Archives in Washington, D.C. Each day visitors from around the world visit the Archives. However, some foreign visitors may not fully understand just why these documents are so honored by Americans. With a partner or small group, create a brief explanation of one of these two documents for foreign visitors. Your explanation can take the form of a brochure or a script for an audio-tape guide. It should explain the following:
- when and why the document was created.
- why the document was so important to Americans at the time of its creation and remains important today.

Section Survey Answers

Reviewing Main Ideas

1. The victory created new tensions when Britain issued the Proclamation of 1763, which closed the new territories won from France to Americans and tried to tax the colonies to enforce the Proclamation.
2. The Americans probably chose the tune because it symbolized the feeling that they had accomplished something remarkable.
3. The framers gave the national government enough power to bind the states together while still limiting its authority by leaving some powers with the states and by setting up a system of checks and balances.

History Mystery

The information about return of laundry indicated to Washington that the British had been suddenly ordered to leave Philadelphia. Accept any reasonable answer: some students might say they would consider the possibility they might be caught and hanged as a spy; others may feel they would be in a good position to gather information about the British.

Alternative Assessment

Allow one or two class periods for this activity, depending on how polished a result you would like to see. Have students work in pairs or small groups to prepare their guides. See the Review Take-Home Planner, p. 7, for suggestions and a scoring rubric for this activity.

Part 2
1789 to 1905

Review: Part 2 Planning Guide

Section	Student Text	Teacher's Edition Activities
Part 2 Opener pp. 60–61	**Link to the Present** Women in the workforce, p. 60	**Answers to Captions,** p. 60, p. 61
4 **The Early Years** pp. 62–73	Beginning the Story with **The Mill Girls,** p. 62 **History Mystery** p. 63 **Keys to History Time Line** pp. 64–65, pp. 66–67, pp. 70–71 **Hands-On History** Millworker dialogue, p. 63 Exploring unknown regions, p. 68	**Setting the Stage Activity** To Work Full-Time?, p. 62 **Warm-Up Activity** Defining Government's Role, p. 64 Letter to Europe, p. 66 Thinking About Machines, p. 70 **Bonus Activity** Making a Cause-Effect Chart, p. 72 **Wrap-Up Activity** Writing a Patriotic Poem, p. 69 Writing an Obituary, p. 72
5 **Expansion and Reform** pp. 74–85	Beginning the Story with **Frederick Douglass,** p. 74 **History Mystery** p. 75 **Keys to History Time Line** pp. 76–77, pp. 78–79, pp. 80–81, pp. 82–83 **Hands-On History** Writing a movie script, p. 75 Speaking to persuade, p. 83 **Reading Maps** Products of the North and South mid-1800s, p. 81	**Setting the Stage Activity** The Power of Reading, p. 74 **Warm-Up Activity** Points of View, p. 76 Writing About Moving, p. 78 Differences at a Glance, p. 80 Analyzing Reform, p. 82 **Bonus Activity** Letter to the Editor, p. 84 **Wrap-Up Activity** Newspaper Search, p. 84
6 **Civil War and Reconstruction** pp. 86–99	Beginning the Story with **Clara Barton,** p. 86 **History Mystery** p. 87 **Keys to History Time Line** pp. 88–89, pp. 92–93, pp. 96–97 **Hands-On History** War correspondents, p. 87 Commemorating the Civil War, p. 95 **Reading Maps** The Spread of Slavery, p. 90 Election of 1860, p. 91	**Setting the Stage Activity** *Help-Wanted* Ads, p. 86 **Warm-Up Activity** Anticipating Issues, p. 88 Off to War: Dialogues at Home, p. 92 Postwar Hopes, p. 96 **Bonus Activity** An *Uncle Tom's Cabin* Ad, p. 90 A Soldier's Letter Home, p. 94 **Wrap-Up Activity** Writing a News Release, p. 91 Interviewing Lee and Grant, p. 94 A Letter to a Former Master, p. 98
Evaluation	☑ **Section 4 Survey,** p. 73 ☑ **Section 5 Survey,** p. 85 Alternative Assessment ☑ **Section 6 Survey,** p. 99	☑ **Answers to Section 4 Survey,** p. 73 ☑ **Answers to Section 5 Survey,** p. 85 ☑ **Answers to Section 6 Survey,** p. 99 (Alternative Assessment guidelines are in the Review Take-Home Planner.)

Teacher's Resource Package

American Readings, pp. 5–8

Geography Extensions, pp. 5–6

Using Historical Documents, pp. 18–26

Chapter Resources Binder

Study Guide, p. 9

Reinforcement, p. 12

Skills Development, pp. 15–16

Chapter Summaries: English and Spanish, pp. 24–25, pp. 26–27, pp. 28–29

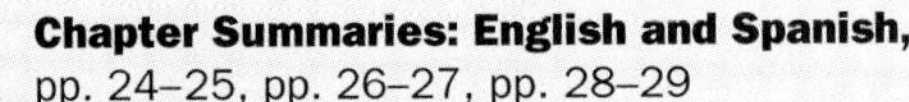

Chapter Resources Binder

Study Guide, p. 10

Reinforcement, p. 13

Chapter Summaries: English and Spanish, pp. 30–31, pp. 32–33, pp. 34–35, pp. 36–37

Chapter Resources Binder

Study Guide, p. 11

Reinforcement, p. 14

Chapter Summaries: English and Spanish, pp. 38–39, pp. 40–41, pp. 42–43

Geography Extensions, pp. 7–8, pp. 9–10, pp. 11–12

American Readings, pp. 9–12, pp. 13–16, pp. 17–20

Using Historical Documents, pp. 27–31, pp. 32–39, 40–43

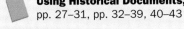

Chapter and Unit Tests

Section 4 Tests, Forms A and B, pp. 19–22

Section 5 Tests, Forms A and B, pp. 23–26

Section 6 Tests, Forms A and B, pp. 27–30

Take-Home Planner

Reduced Views

American Readings, p. 21

Geography Extensions, p. 23

Using Historical Documents, p. 22

Reduced Views

Study Guide, p. 19

Reinforcement, p. 19

Skills Development, p. 20

Section 4 Answers, p. 24–30

Reduced Views

Study Guide, p. 19

Reinforcement, p. 20

Section 5 Answers, p. 24–30

Reduced Views

Study Guide, p. 19

Reinforcement, p. 20

Section 6 Answers, p. 24–30

Reduced Views

Section Tests, p. 23

Alternative Assessment

Guideline for Scoring, p. 18

Additional Resources

Wall Time Line

Transparency Package

Transparencies 12–15

Transparencies 16–20

Transparencies 21–26

SelecTest Testing Software

Review Section 4 Tests, Forms A and B

Review Section 5 Tests, Forms A and B

Review Section 6 Tests, Forms A and B

Vital Links

Videodisc **CD-ROM**

Water Mills (see TE p. 62)
Whiskey Rebellion (see TE p. 64)
Nez Percé (see TE p. 68)
"The Star-Spangled Banner" (see TE p. 69)
"The Erie Canal" (see TE p. 70)
Plantation (see TE p. 74)
Nat Turner (see TE p. 75)
Andrew Jackson (see TE p. 76)
José Maria Sanchez (see TE p. 78)
McCormic Reaper (see TE p. 81)
Dorothea Dix (see TE p. 82)
Elizabeth Blackwell (see TE p. 84)
Voice of Elizabeth Cady Stanton (see TE p. 85)
Battle of Antietam (see TE p. 86)
Nurse Kate Cummings (see TE p. 87)
Uncle Tom's Cabin Poster (see TE p. 90)
Dred and Harriet Scott (see TE p. 91)
John Brown (see TE p. 91)
Segregated Jury (see TE p.98)

Introducing the Review: Part 2

The three sections of Part 2 of the Review are previewed on this and the following page.

A View of New Orleans Taken from the Plantation of Marigny, November, 1803

This painting celebrates the acquisition of New Orleans with the Louisiana Purchase of 1803. That landmark event doubled the size of the United States and ushered in an era of westward expansion and economic development.

Answers to Caption: Possible answers include: large stores and homes, cargo ships, lumber for construction, well-built roads, nicely dressed people.

Teaching the

Link to the Present

Discuss ways progress can be made in closing the wage gap between men and women. (Some possibilities are passing legislation, organizing women workers to demand equal pay, making the public aware of the pay gap, and educating women to compete for jobs traditionally held by men.)

History Footnote

French artist John L. Boqueto de Woieseri arrived in New Orleans in May of 1803, the month the Louisiana Purchase was signed. His painting, the first known view of New Orleans as an American city, reflects a mood of prosperity and expansion. He eventually published a set of aquatint engravings of six cities, titled *A View of the First Cities of the United States*.

History Footnote

Emanuel Gottlieb Leutze concentrated on American history subjects, including his famous *Washington Crossing the Delaware*. The detail below is from a 20- by 30-foot mural that the federal government commissioned for the Capitol building in Washington, D.C. In preparation, Leutze made the difficult journey to the Rocky Mountains to observe the landscape firsthand.

Part 2 1789–1905

The Early Years

After gaining their independence, Americans faced the challenge of organizing a new government at home while avoiding conflicts abroad. These early years saw dramatic growth—both in the size of the young nation and in its infant industries.

A View of New Orleans Taken from the Plantation of Marigny **was painted by Boqueto de Woieseri to celebrate the Louisiana Purchase in 1803. The banner reads: "Under My Wings Every Thing Prospers." What details in the painting suggest that this is true?**

Link to the Present

Women in the work force Ever since New England mills hired their first mill girls, large numbers of American women have been seeking jobs for pay. Today, about 60 percent of all American women work outside the home, many in jobs once held only by men. Almost half of the nation's accountants and bus drivers are now women. So are nearly 20 percent of doctors and lawyers.

Yet on average, modern women still earn only 72¢ for every dollar earned by men. The pay gap will probably not close until jobs traditionally held by women, such as nurse, secretary, and food server, pay as much as jobs for men with the same level of training.

History Footnote

The Battle of Shiloh (*shiloh* means "place of peace" in Hebrew) bears the name of a church located near the battle site. In the painting Grant and the Union army are shown at right. The Union troops, hidden among the thickets along the sunken road at the center, repelled repeated Confederate charges from a position that came to be known as the "Hornet's Nest." Though Grant's troops eventually drove back the Confederate forces, heavy losses made the victory a hollow one.

This lithograph was produced by McCormick Harvesting Machine Co. and included a caption: "The Machines Come Victoriously Out Of Every Contest, And Without A Scratch." Prominently placed in the shed at the lower left, surviving the surrounding destruction, is a McCormick reaper.

Expansion and Reform

Some Americans pushed westward in the mid-1800s, sparking conflicts with Native Americans and Mexico. Others put their energy into a religious revival and efforts to reform American society.

In his *Westward the Course of Empire Takes Its Way,* Emanuel Gottlieb Leutze shows pioneers looking out toward a vast and seemingly empty expanse of land. But was the West as empty as it looks in this mural?

Civil War and Reconstruction

As the United States expanded, Americans had to decide whether slavery would expand with it. In 1861 this question drew the nation into a long and bitter civil war. After the war, former enemies faced the difficult task of reconstructing the Union.

***The Battle of Shiloh—April 6th, 1862* depicts one of the bloodiest battles of the Civil War. More Americans died in this two-day battle than in the War of Independence, the War of 1812, and the war with Mexico combined. What made this war so deadly?**

Teaching Resources

- Review Take-Home Planner
  - Introducing Part 2 Activity
  - Part 2 In-Depth Activity
  - Alternative Assessment
- Chapter Resources Binder
- Geography Extensions
- American Readings
- Using Historical Documents
- Transparency Activities
- Wall Time Line Activities
- Chapter Summaries
- Chapter and Unit Tests
- SelecTest Test File
- Vital Links CD-ROM/Videodisc

Westward the Course of Empire Takes Its Way

This painting depicts a group of pioneers making their way across rough terrain, looking toward a vast expanse of seemingly uninhabited land. Leutze's mural expresses the mood of this era of exploration, expansion, and westward growth.

Answers to Caption: The West was home to American Indians, Mexican colonists, and a handful of American, German, French, and other adventurers.

The Battle of Shiloh—April 6th, 1862

This lithograph depicts a battle which left nearly 3,500 dead and more than 20,000 wounded. Although Confederate troops initially overran Union positions, reinforcements helped force the Confederates to retreat on the battle's second day.

Answers to Caption: New weapons, poor nutrition and medicine, as well as the fact that Americans were fighting other Americans, led to many casualties.

Beginning the Story

The Mill Girls

The first cotton mill opened in Massachusetts in 1815. Mill owners advertised for farm girls to work in the mills. The young women lived in boarding houses and worked long hours. Some, however, appreciated their independence and opportunities to pursue education and culture.

Setting the Stage Activity

To Work Full-Time?

Have pairs of students imagine making a choice between going to school, as they do now, or taking a full-time job (in a store, restaurant, or factory). Have one student write a letter describing two advantages of full-time work. The other replies in a letter pointing out its disadvantages and the advantages of staying in school. The pair should then exchange one more set of letters responding to each other and adding arguments. Allot about four minutes for each letter. Discuss major pros and cons with the class.

Vital Links

Water Mills (Movie) Unit 2, Side 2, Search 02616, Play to 03338

See also Unit 2 Explore CD-ROM location 174.

History Footnote

In their avid reading, the Lowell mill girls mainly patronized lending libraries, which dispensed novels for a subscription rate of about six cents a week. Reading was so popular among the young women that one factory sign read "No Reading in the Mills." One factory supervisor was said to have taken a drawerful of Bibles from his workers. The girls evaded the rule by putting pages from books on walls and loom frames. One girl wrote, "As well forbid us Yankee girls to breathe as read; we cannot help it."

The girls' literary learnings are reflected in *The Lowell Offering,* a factory magazine published during the 1840s. Contributors often wrote of the everyday life of mill workers.

Teaching Resources

Chapter Resources Binder
- Study Guide p. 9
- Reinforcement p. 12

1789–1830

Section 4 The Early Years

Beginning the Story with *the Mill Girls*

When the mill girls, as they were called, felt overworked, underpaid, or just plain homesick, they sang:

"Oh, isn't it a pity that a such a pretty girl as I
Should be sent to the factory to pine away and die?"

For most New England farm girls, going to work in the Lowell, Massachusetts, cotton mills was both an adventure and a trial. Few had ever been away

In mills owned by the Boston Associates, raw cotton was spun into thread. Then the thread was woven into cloth on power looms. This picture shows mill girls operating the machines that wound the thread onto huge bobbins, or spools, for weaving.

 History Bookshelf

Weisman, Joanne B. *Lowell Mill Girls: Life in the Factory.* Discovery Enterprises Ltd., 1991. The experiences of New England farm girls who became mill girls are reflected in their own accounts.

Also of interest:

Nirgiotis, Nicholas. *Erie Canal: Gateway to the West.* Watts, 1993.

Wormser, Richard. *The Iron Horse: How the Railroads Changed America.* Walker & Co., 1993.

Lacy, Dan Mabry. *The Lewis and Clark Expedition.* A Focus Book, 1974.

Meltzer, Milton. *Thomas Jefferson.* Franklin Watts, 1991.

Faber, Doris, and Harold Faber. *The Birth of a Nation.* Charles Scribner's Sons, 1989.

HISTORY Mystery

The greatest American victory in the War of 1812 was in a battle that need not have been fought. What was the battle, and why was it unnecessary?

from home before. Many liked living in the boarding houses provided by the mill owners—even with six boarders in a room, sleeping three to a bed. Compared to farm work, millwork was not hard. The hours, however, were long. Harriet Farley described her workday:

> "We go in at five o'clock; at seven we come out to breakfast; at half-past seven we return to our work, and stay until half-past twelve. At one . . . we return to our work, and stay until seven at night. Then the evening is all our own, which is more than some laboring girls can say."

"Another Payday"

Millwork offered young women a chance to exchange the isolation of the farm for the excitement of city life. In their precious evening hours, mill girls took classes, went to concerts, and read books from the Lowell library. For some book-starved farm girls, this library was almost as great a lure to millwork as a paycheck. Mill girls even wrote and published their own magazine, *The Lowell Offering.*

Then as now, however, the best day was payday. Being paid for their work was a new experience for most young women. So was having money of their own to spend. One millworker wrote to her sister:

> "Since I have wrote you, another payday has come around. I earned 14 dollars and a half, nine and a half dollars beside my board [payment for a room and meals]. The folks think I get along just first-rate. . . . I like it well as ever and Sarah don't I feel independent of everyone! The thought that I am living on no one is a happy one indeed to me."

Hands-On HISTORY

Activity

Imagine that you are a 15-year-old living on a New England farm in 1817. You and your parents have seen an ad seeking young women to work in a cotton mill. Create a dialogue between you and your parents about whether you should take a job as a millworker.

Discussion

Thinking Historically

1. Why do you think parents allowed or encouraged their daughters to work in mills? (They would not have to support them. The girls could make money and participate in cultural activities. There were more opportunities than on the family farm.)

2. What were disadvantages of factory work? (Girls were separated from families. Factory work was more regimented.)

3. What were advantages of factory work? (The girls were independent, earned money, and had cultural opportunities.)

Teaching the HISTORY Mystery

Students will find the answer on p. 69. See Section Survey, p. 73, for additional questions.

Teaching the Hands-On HISTORY

Before students begin writing dialogues, encourage them to consider different possibilities. One possibility might be parents encouraging a reluctant daughter to go to work. Alternatively, the daughter might be adventurous and independent, and the parents might be cautious or fearful.

Introducing the Lesson

Vocabulary

inauguration
cabinet
political parties
republic

Warm-Up Activity

Defining Government's Role
Have groups list functions and services the federal government should provide. Compare lists and discuss how different ideas about its role might affect its structure.

Time Line

Keys to History

Washington As president, Washington faced the challenge of turning the Constitution into a real government.

French Revolution Some Americans saw this as a victory for democracy, while others feared its violence.

Political Parties Although not foreseen by the Constitution's framers, political parties formed around different ideas.

Vital Links

Whiskey Rebellion (Picture) Unit 2, Side 1, Search 07863

See also Unit 2 Explore CD-ROM location 36.

Lesson Objectives

- ★ Identify some of the challenges of creating a new government for a new nation.
- ★ Describe the origins of political parties in the new republic.
- ★ Identify issues dividing the Federalist and Republican parties in the 1790s.

Teaching Resources

Chapter Summaries
p. 24
p. 25
Transparency Activities
pp. 12–13

1789–1801

Lesson 1 The First Years of the Republic

On April 30, 1789, a cheering crowd in New York City witnessed the inauguration of George Washington as the nation's first President. Washington did not share the crowd's enthusiasm. He knew how difficult it would be to turn the Constitution into a workable government.

The new Congress made a good start by organizing the executive branch and setting up a federal court system. On other issues—such as whether to establish a national bank or how to deal with the French Revolution—both Congress and Washington's cabinet were deeply divided. By the time Washington finished his second term, these divisions had hardened into the nation's first political parties, the Federalists and Republicans.

In 1796 John Adams, the Federalist candidate for President, won the election by just three electoral votes. Near the end of his term, the national government moved to Washington, D.C., the nation's new capital on the banks of the Potomac River. First Lady Abigail Adams wrote of the "President's House" that "not one room or chamber is finished." She used the East Room for hanging out laundry as it was fit for nothing else.

That same year, in an election campaign run more on insults than issues, Adams lost to his Republican rival Thomas Jefferson. For all its nastiness, however, the election of 1800 was a victory for the nation and its Constitution. In most countries at the time, power passed from one group to another through war or revolution. In the United States, power had passed peacefully from one party to another according to the will of the people.

Keys to History

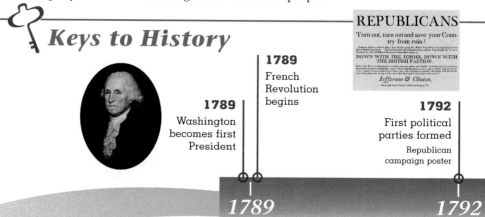

1789
Washington becomes first President

1789
French Revolution begins

REPUBLICANS
Turn out, turn out and save your Country from ruin!
DOWN WITH THE TORIES, DOWN WITH THE BRITISH FACTION.
Jefferson & Clinton,

1792
First political parties formed

Republican campaign poster

1789 *1792*

Connections to Civics

Neither the Federalists nor the Republicans claimed universal suffrage as a goal. Federalists in particular wanted to protect the voice of the propertied class. At that time most states limited the vote to adult white males with property. New Jersey's constitution did not specifically exclude women from voting, so until it was changed in 1807, some women did vote.

Amendments to the Constitution eventually forced all states to adopt universal adult suffrage. Women won the right to vote with the 19th Amendment in 1920. Though the 15th Amendment of 1870 stated the right to vote could not be denied based on race, some states continued to use poll taxes and literacy tests to exclude black voters. Poll taxes were finally outlawed in 1964 by the 24th Amendment.

The First Political Parties

	Federalists	Republicans
Leaders	Alexander Hamilton John Adams	Thomas Jefferson James Madison
Regions	strongest in northern towns and coastal south	strongest in northern farming areas and southern and western backcountry
Beliefs	rule by wealthy, educated people	rule by the common people
	strong national government	weak national government
	loose construction of the Constitution	strict construction of the Constitution
	limits on states' rights	protection of states' rights
	laws to help businesspeople	laws to help farmers
	high tariffs to protect manufacturers in the United States	low tariffs to keep goods cheap for farmers
	powerful national bank	no national bank
	pro-British	pro-French

Hamilton

Jefferson

1794
Whiskey Rebellion
Farmers tar and feather a tax collector

1796
Washington's Farewell Address

1798
Alien and Sedition Acts
Cartoon of battle in Congress

1800
Nation's capital moves to Washington, D.C.
Detail of design for Capitol building

1795 *1798* *1801*

Developing the Lesson

Discussion

Checking Understanding

1. What issues divided the Federalist and Republican parties?
(Who should rule; how strong the national government should be; strict vs. loose construction of the Constitution; limits on states' rights; tariffs; a national bank; a pro-British or pro-French foreign policy.)

Stimulating Critical Thinking

2. Why has the election of 1800 been hailed as a "peaceful revolution"?
(Power passed from one group to another without bloodshed or violence.)

Time Line

Whiskey Rebellion To show that federal laws must be obeyed, President Washington himself led troops to put down this tax rebellion.

Farewell Address Washington warned against party rivalry and advised against foreign alliances.

Alien and Sedition Acts Republicans charged that these laws, allowing the President to jail or deport suspicious aliens and banning anti-government writing and speech, violated the First Amendment.

Washington, D.C. Although still unfinished, Washington, D.C., became the official home of the federal government.

Introducing the Lesson

Vocabulary

embargo
nationalism

Warm-Up Activity

Letter to Europe

To help students review what they know about Thomas Jefferson, have them write a letter describing the nation's third President. Tell them to imagine that they are citizens of the United States in 1800 who are writing to relatives in Europe. Their letters should describe the President-elect in as much detail as the writer can recall. They might include the information that Jefferson was a wealthy Virginia planter, the main author of the Declaration of Independence, the leader of the Republican party, and a man of many interests and talents.

Time Line

Keys to History

Marbury* v. *Madison In this important decision, the Supreme Court and Chief Justice Marshall established the right of the Court to determine whether laws are constitutional or not.

Louisiana Purchase This purchase doubled the size of the United States and added 200,000 inhabitants.

Lewis and Clark Army officers Meriwether Lewis and William Clark explored beyond the Louisiana Territory westward to the Pacific Ocean.

Lesson Objectives

- ★ Explain how Jefferson doubled the size of the United States.
- ★ Describe Jefferson's efforts to protect American trade from British and French attacks.
- ★ Identify the first Americans to explore the Louisiana territory.
- ★ Summarize the main events of the War of 1812.

Teaching Resources

Chapter Summaries
p. 26
p. 27
Transparency Activities
p. 14

1801–1815

Lesson 2 The Jefferson Era

As President, Jefferson tried to live by his Republican ideals. However, when Napoleon Bonaparte, the ruler of France, offered to sell Louisiana Territory to the United States, he faced a dilemma. Jefferson believed in limited government power and in strictly following the Constitution. Yet the Constitution did not mention the purchase of foreign lands as one of the government's powers. Rather than lose this chance to double the size of the United States, Jefferson set his ideals aside and accepted Napoleon's offer.

During his second term, Jefferson faced a different sort of dilemma. France and Britain were once again at war with each other. In an effort to hurt each other's trade, both nations had begun seizing American ships bound for enemy ports. Worse yet, British sea captains were stopping American ships along the Atlantic coast to search for deserters from the Royal Navy. Any sailor who appeared to be English was in danger of being snatched away, even if he was an American citizen. "England has become a den of pirates," complained Jefferson, "and France has become a den of thieves."

Desperate to avoid war, Jefferson again put aside his ideals of limited government. In 1807 he imposed an embargo on all American trade. Under this policy, no ships could leave American ports and no foreign ships could enter them. Jefferson hoped the embargo would prove so painful to Britain and France that they would stop attacking American ships. Most of the pain, however, was felt by American sailors and merchants who were thrown out of work. Days before leaving office, Jefferson ended the hated embargo.

Keys to History

1803
Marbury v. *Madison*
Chief Justice John Marshall

1803
Louisiana Purchase

1804–1806
Lewis and Clark expedition
Compass used in expedition

1801 *1805*

Connections to Science

Jefferson invented a new type of plow and clock (see pictures below). These and other clever devices, such as the swivel chair, can be seen at his home, Monticello, near Charlottesville, Virginia. More importantly, perhaps, Jefferson supported other American inventors. He corresponded with and aided Oliver Evans, one of the pioneers of the high-pressure steam engine. He also influenced Eli Whitney with stories of an inventive British merchant named Honoré Blanc, who developed a system of interchangeable parts for gun-making. Whitney was the leader in a movement to design and use standardized parts in manufactured items in the United States. Jefferson, while serving as Secretary of State before he became President, was in charge of signing patents.

The Many Talents of Thomas Jefferson

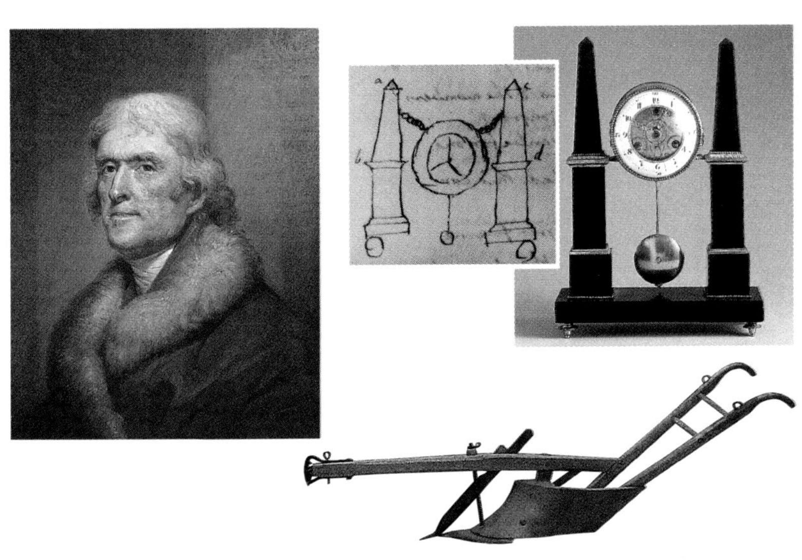

As an inventor, Jefferson designed a new type of clock and plow. He was also a musician, a farmer, and an architect, and he spoke many languages.

1811
Tecumseh's forces meet Harrison's troops at the Battle of Tippecanoe

1812–1815
War of 1812
An American sailor

1814
Francis Scott Key writes "The Star-Spangled Banner"
Flag that inspired Key

1815
Battle of New Orleans

1810 — 1815

Developing the Lesson

Discussion

Checking Understanding

1. When did Jefferson compromise his Republican ideals as President? (When he accepted Napoleon's offer to sell Louisiana and when he imposed an embargo on American trade.)

Stimulating Critical Thinking

2. How might the United States be different today if Jefferson had not approved the Louisiana Purchase? (Far less land, perhaps unfriendly neighbors to the west, no access to the Pacific, probably more focused on Europe than on Asia.)

Time Line

Tippecanoe While Tecumseh was away, his forces attacked, but failed to defeat, army troops camped near the Tippecanoe River.

War of 1812 Victories over Britain in the war gave Americans a new sense of national pride.

"The Star-Spangled Banner" Inspired by the American flag still waving over a besieged Fort McHenry, Francis Scott Key wrote the poem that would become the national anthem.

Battle of New Orleans Andrew Jackson became a popular hero after this victory in the War of 1812.

Teaching
Map Skills

Comparing Maps

The Louisiana Purchase provided territory for many future states. Have students compare the map on this page with the map on pages R6–R7 to determine which states would be carved from this area. If possible, have students note those states on an outline map of the United States. Students can use the list of states on pages R19–R23 to indicate which year each of these states joined the Union. (Louisiana, 1812; Missouri, 1821; Arkansas, 1836; Iowa, 1846; Minnesota, 1858; Kansas, 1861; Nebraska, 1867; North and South Dakota and Montana, 1889; Wyoming, 1890; Oklahoma, 1907.)

Teaching the
Hands-On HISTORY

Students may design medals that depict people, places, ideas, or events. Suggest that they think in terms of images that are simple, direct, and understandable regardless of the language spoken by their intended audience.

Vital Links

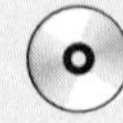

Nez Percé with Lewis and Clark (Movie) Unit 2, Side 2, Search 01585, Play to 02611

See also Unit 2 Explore CD-ROM location 284.

History Footnote

In 1805 Lewis and Clark hired a fur trader named Toussaint Charbonneau as a guide. The slow-witted Charbonneau proved to be a mixed blessing, but his young Shoshone wife Sacagawea made up for his failings. Sacagawea served as more than just an interpreter on the Lewis and Clark expedition. She expanded the company's diet of meat, bread, and flour pudding to include roots, wild onions, and berries. These foods provided vitamins that helped to keep the explorers healthy. Her presence signaled to Indians they encountered that this was a friendly expedition. In one instance, she saved much of the medicine, seeds, trade goods, and journals when the expedition's supply canoe almost capsized. She did all of this while caring for her infant son, who was just two months old when the journey began.

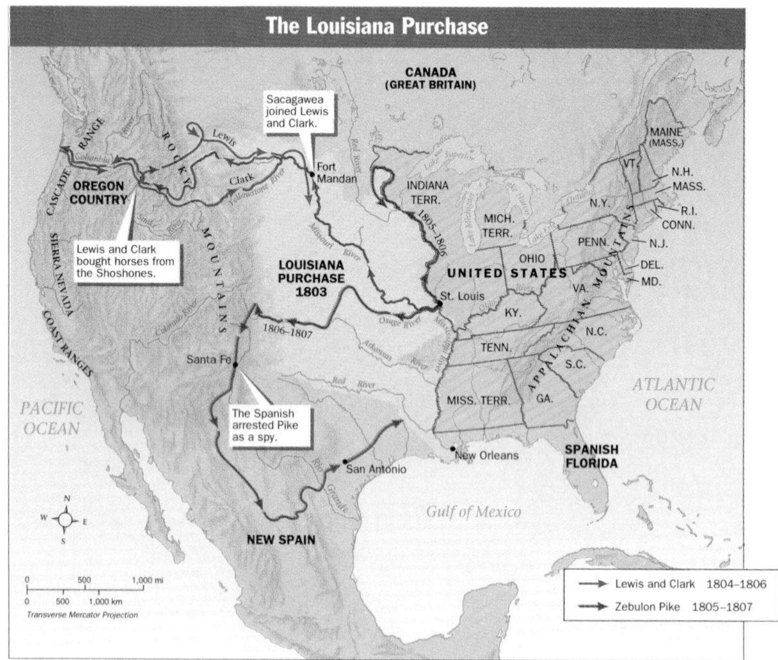

Exploring Louisiana

Americans knew little about Louisiana at the time of its purchase. In 1804 Jefferson asked Meriwether Lewis and William Clark to lead an expedition across Louisiana to the Pacific. Two years later, Zebulon Pike led another expedition into the purchase. From these explorers, Americans began to learn more about this region and its peoples.

On their journey to the Pacific, Lewis and Clark carried peace medals from President Jefferson to give as offerings of friendship to Indians they met along the way. One side of the medal featured an image of Jefferson. The other showed a handshake of peace.

Jefferson peace medal

Hands-On HISTORY

Activity

Imagine that you are to explore a region where you will encounter people who are unknown in the United States.

1. Design a medal to give to these people in friendship. What would you put on the front of your medal? On the back?

2. Draw the design on a surface large enough for the entire class to see.

3. When you present your design to the class, explain the images that you chose for the medal.

Connections to Music

There is some evidence that Key wrote his song to be sung to the tune of the old English drinking song "Anacreon in Heaven." The song was popular in that day, and the meter and verse forms of "The Star-Spangled Banner" are similar to those of the drinking song. As soon as Key reached Baltimore after the battle, he had handbill copies of his verse copied and distributed. The song became very popular in and around Baltimore, where it was sung by encamped military personnel. The song did not achieve national prominence until the Civil War. The U.S. Army started using it in 1895.

War Is Declared

In 1809 James Madison became the nation's fourth President. Like Jefferson, Madison tried to protect American ships from attack without going to war. Despite his efforts, Britain, continued to seize American vessels.

In 1812 Republican "War Hawks" persuaded Congress to declare war on Britain. Besides protecting American ships, the War Hawks hoped to drive the British out of Canada and add this colony to the United States. They also hoped to end the Indian threat in the Ohio Valley.

American efforts to invade Canada failed miserably when Canadians united to defend their land. The Americans were more successful against the Indians. In the Battle of the Thames and at Horseshoe Bend, Native Americans suffered disastrous defeats.

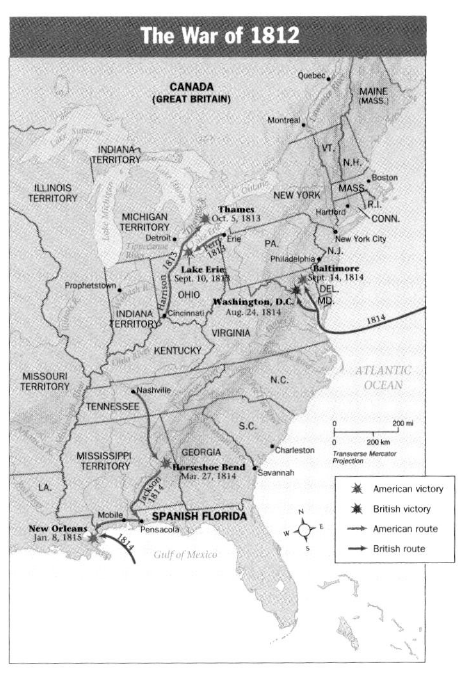

Britain Strikes Back

In 1814, Britain struck back by marching on Washington, D.C. When British troops reached the capital, they found it strangely empty. The troops enjoyed a splendid dinner left uneaten when Dolly Madison fled from the President's House. Then they set the house and other government buildings ablaze.

Next the British attacked nearby Baltimore. All day and night British ships bombarded Fort McHenry at the entrance to Baltimore's harbor. The fort's defenders bravely stood their ground, however, inspiring Francis Scott Key to write a poem called the "The Defense of Fort McHenry." Later set to music as the "The Star-Spangled Banner," it was adopted as the national anthem in 1931.

Victory at New Orleans

Early in 1815, the British launched a grand assault on New Orleans. They were stopped by a "backwoods rabble" of untrained troops, free African Americans, Indians, and pirates led by Andrew Jackson. The Americans greeted the invaders with a storm of gunfire. One soldier described the battlefield as a "sea of blood."

The result was a glorious victory for the American cause, but an unnecessary one. A peace treaty had been signed in Europe two weeks before the Battle of New Orleans.

Peace brought with it a new spirit of nationalism. "The people," wrote Treasury Secretary Albert Gallatin, "are more American. They feel and act more as a nation."

Teaching Map Skills

Reading a War Map

Have students study the map on this page to see the relationship between bodies of water and battle sites in the War of 1812. Ask:

1. What were the four areas where major battles took place during the War of 1812? (Lake Erie area, Washington/Baltimore area, Horseshoe Bend area, New Orleans area.)

2. How would you explain the relationship between battle sites and bodies of water in this war? (It was generally easier at that time to move troops by water than by land. This was especially true for Great Britain, which had to carry troops across the Atlantic Ocean by ship.)

Wrap-Up Activity

Writing a Patriotic Poem

To help students see why people felt "more American" after the War of 1812, have students write a patriotic poem celebrating some aspect of the conflict.

Vital Links

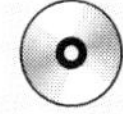

"The Star-Spangled Banner" (Song) Unit 2, Side 1. Search 00431, Play to 02988

See also Unit 2 Explore CD-ROM location 10.

Introducing the Lesson

Vocabulary

Industrial Revolution

Warm-Up Activity

Thinking About Machines

To help students understand the enormous changes that machines can cause, have them list several machines that make work easier at home, such as dishwashers or computers. They should write a short explanation of the work the machines do and how they save time and effort as compared to older ways of doing the work.

Time Line

Keys to History

Samuel Slater His invention of the spinning jenny began the Industrial Revolution—the shift of the production of goods from hand tools to machines and from homes to factories.

Eli Whitney The cotton gin made cotton a profitable cash crop in the South. It increased the demand for slave labor and led southerners to move west seeking more land for cotton.

Vital Links

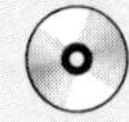

"The Erie Canal" (Song) Unit 2, Side 1, Search 25357, Play to 27575

See also Unit 2 Explore CD-ROM location 169.

Lesson Objectives

- ★ Identify new technology that began to change the way Americans lived.
- ★ Describe the new transportation that linked the nation together.
- ★ Summarize the new directions in foreign policy set by John Quincy Adams.
- ★ Describe growing sectional tensions over the expansion of slavery.

Teaching Resources

Chapter Summaries
p. 28
p. 29
Transparency Activities
p. 15

1816–1830

Lesson 3 The Confident Years

Wherever they looked after the War of 1812, Americans could see signs of economic progress. In New England, an English mechanic named Samuel Slater teamed up with Rhode Island merchant Moses Brown to build the nation's first spinning mill. The shift of spinning from homes to factories marked the beginning of America's Industrial Revolution.

Boston businessman Francis Cabot Lowell took the revolution a step further when he brought both spinning and weaving under one roof. Bales of raw cotton went into one end of Lowell's cotton mills. Yards and yards of mass-produced cotton cloth came out of the other end. To meet his labor needs, Lowell hired young farm women from the New England countryside.

A revolution in transportation helped mill owners move their goods to customers throughout the country. This revolution began with the construction of the National Road, a wide paved highway across the Appalachian Mountains. Meanwhile, river travel was revolutionized by Robert Fulton's invention of a steam-powered riverboat. Steamboats made traveling up rivers and across lakes almost as easy as floating downstream. Canals were the next major improvement in water transportation.

The future of transportation, however, lay not on water but on rails. In 1830 mechanic Peter Cooper mounted a steam engine on a wagon to create America's first steam locomotive, the *Tom Thumb*. When Cooper proved that his "teakettle on a truck" could move faster than horses and haul heavier loads, steam railway companies began laying tracks in several states. The United States had entered the railroad era.

Keys to History

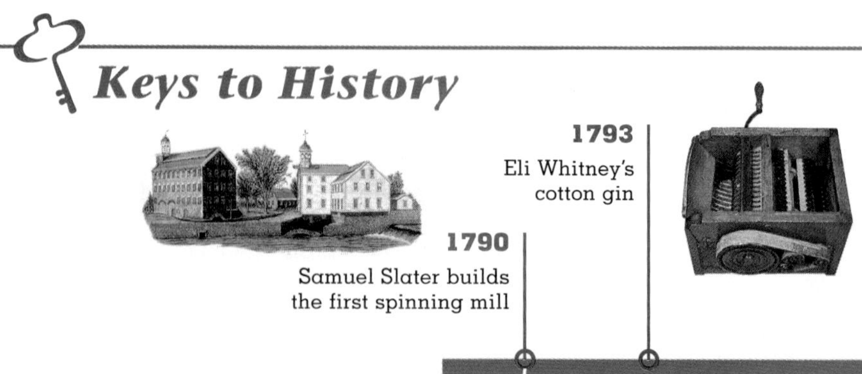

History Footnote
To build the Erie Canal, workers had to cut down trees and remove stumps without machinery. Using horses and mules, they cleared the way for the canal and its towpath. One challenging area was a swamp known as the Montezuma Marshes, which was full of malaria-carrying mosquitoes. One observer said that the insects "fell upon the diggers in hordes" and "the men came in with eyes swollen almost shut and hands so poisoned they could hardly wield tools." More than 1,000 workers became ill with malaria, and many died. Mud from the swampy area refilled the channels almost as soon as they were cleared. As they dug, the workers had to reinforce the channel sides with dry earth. Finally, a young engineer found a special limestone in the area that effectively sealed the canal's walls.

A Bold Foreign Policy

The growing confidence of the young nation could be seen in its foreign policy. Under President James Monroe and his brilliant Secretary of State John Quincy Adams, the United States quickly settled old boundary disputes with Britain. Adams also convinced Spain to cede Florida to the United States.

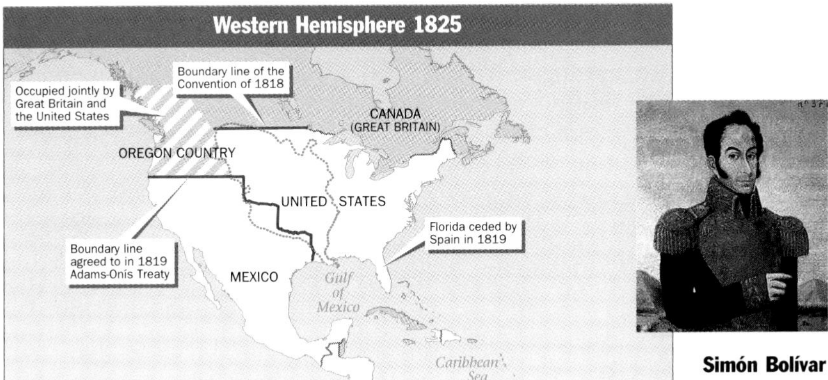

Simón Bolívar

José de San Martín

Meanwhile, a revolution was sweeping across Latin America. By 1823, Simón Bolívar and José de San Martín—the leaders of this war for independence—had liberated South America from Spanish rule. In a bold statement known as the Monroe Doctrine, President Monroe announced that the Americas were closed to "future colonization by any European powers." The Americas were for the Americans.

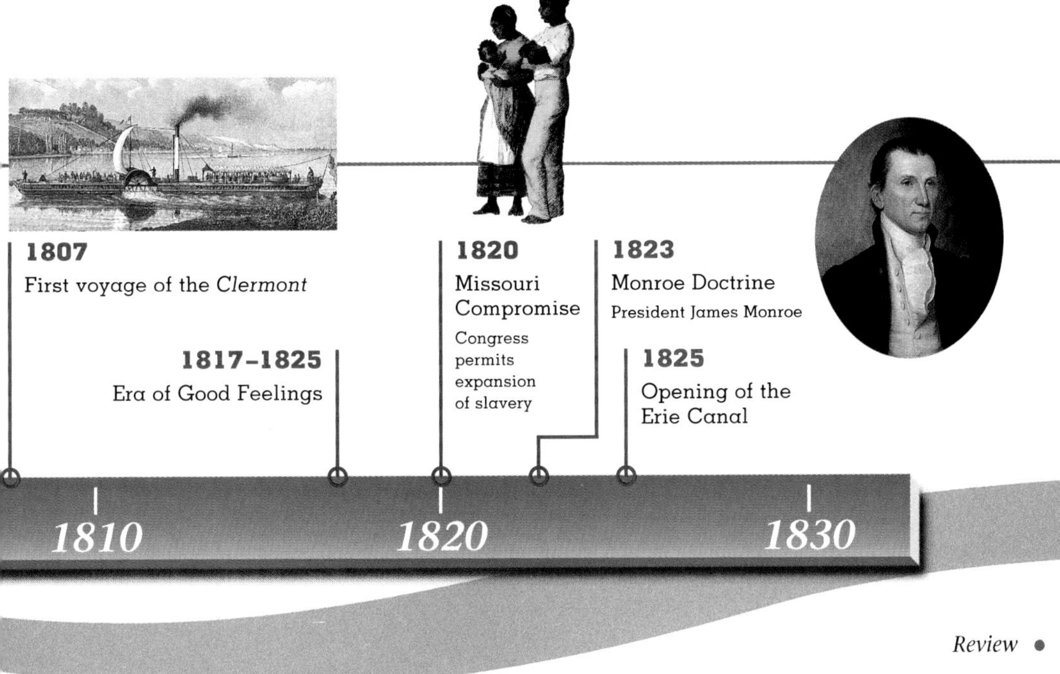

Developing the Lesson

Discussion

Checking Understanding

1. What marked the beginning of the Industrial Revolution in the United States? (Samuel Slater's construction of the first spinning mill.)

2. What was the main message of the Monroe Doctrine to the nations of Europe? (The Americas were closed to future colonization by other nations.)

Time Line

The *Clermont* Robert H. Fulton's steamboat revolutionized river travel.

Era of Good Feelings This term was used to describe James Monroe's presidency, referring to the sense of national unity following the War of 1812.

Missouri Compromise As sectional tensions increased over the issue of expanding slavery, Congress compromised by agreeing that Missouri would join the Union as a slave state and Maine as a free state, and by banning slavery north of latitude 36° 31′.

Monroe Doctrine President Monroe warned European countries against interfering with the nations in Latin America.

Erie Canal The canal created an all-water route from New York City to the Great Lakes, providing an inexpensive means of trade and travel.

History Footnote

Sectional differences on statehood for Missouri ran so deeply in Congress that the House Speaker Henry Clay observed, "The words *civil war* and *disunion* are uttered almost without emotion." Clay was known for his devotion to principle as well as for "the uncontrolled expression of violent feelings" in his oratory. His first speech on the Missouri question was a riveting four-hour performance. Clay foresaw that the argument over the expansion of slavery was potentially disastrous for the Union, and he fought desperately, using eloquence, charm, and threats, to solve it with a compromise. His success earned him the name the Great Compromiser. An appropriate quotation from one of Clay's speeches marks his grave: "I know no North—no South—no East—no West."

Teaching

Map Skills

Reading Map Keys

To help students focus on the map, have them study the key. Ask:

1. In which area of the United States do you find free states or territories? (Northeast, Old Northwest.)

2. In which area do you find slave states or territories? (South, small parts of Midwest.)

Bonus Activity

Making a Cause-Effect Chart

Have students create a cause-effect chart to show relationships between the expansion of slavery and the growth of the textile industry in the North, Eli Whitney's invention of the cotton gin, and the spread of cotton cultivation across the South.

Wrap-Up Activity

Writing an Obituary

Have students write an obituary for Eli Whitney, who died in 1825. Ask them to write their summaries of Whitney's life and achievements from different points of view. Suggest using the viewpoints of a southern reporter, a writer in Lowell, Massachusetts, and the editor of an African American newspaper.

The Expansion of Slavery

After the War for Independence, slavery seemed to be dying out in the United States. One by one, the northern states outlawed slavery. In the South, the price planters could get for their tobacco and rice dropped so low that it hardly paid to plant at all. As southerners planted less, their need for slave labor declined.

In 1792 Eli Whitney visited Georgia and saw slaves picking seeds out of raw cotton. It was such slow work, planters said, that no one could make money on cotton, despite a growing demand for cotton from the new spinning mills. Whitney's answer to this problem was to invent the cotton gin—a machine that could clean 50 times more cotton in a day than a slave working by hand.

Cotton production soared and with it a renewed demand for slaves. As southerners moved westward seeking more land for cotton, slavery went with them. Instead of dying out, slavery became an essential part of the South's growing "cotton kingdom."

The cotton gin was vital to the rapid expansion of cotton production in the South.

The Missouri Compromise

In 1819 Missouri asked to join the Union as a "slave state." Northerners in Congress who opposed slavery said no. In their eyes, the time had come to stop the expansion of slavery. Southerners were outraged by this response. What constitutional power, they asked, did Congress have to decide whether a state should be slave or free?

After a long and bitter debate, Congress reached a compromise in 1820. Missouri was allowed the join the Union as a slave state. At the same time Maine joined as a free state. In addition, a line was drawn from Missouri's southern boundary across the Louisiana Purchase. North of the line slavery was banned forever, except in Missouri. South of the line it was permitted.

Tempers cooled. But the debate on the expansion of slavery was just the beginning of a struggle that was to lead to a tragic civil war.

Why We Remember

Thinking Critically

Divide your class into groups of four or five to discuss the following question: Of the many American accomplishments during the early years of the new republic, which do you think was the most important for the survival and future growth of the United States? Ask each group to present its answer to the class along with reasons supporting their choice. (Possible answers include: the launching of the Industrial Revolution; the creation of a working national government; the linking together of the nation by new means of transportation; the physical growth of the United States; the development of political parties; and a willingness to seek and accept political compromise.)

Why We Remember

The Early Years

The early years of the young United States were growing years. During these decades the new nation more than doubled in size. Westward-moving settlers created new states. The nation's economy expanded as well, fueled by the growth of new industries in the North and the expansion of cotton production in the South.

During these same years, Americans struggled to transform the Constitution from a paper plan into a working government. From the beginning, the new republic was rocked by quarrels and complaints. Differing views of the purpose and power of the national government led to the formation of political parties and to nasty political campaigns.

In these early years, Americans learned important lessons. They learned how to use new technology to create new industries. They learned how to conquer distance with roads, canals, and railroads. But most important of all, Americans learned how to make government by the people work. They learned that it was better to fight for their interests and beliefs with political parties and votes than to die for them with armies and bullets.

Section Survey

Reviewing Main Ideas

1. Compare the views of the Federalists and the Republicans regarding (a) the power of the national government and (b) how to interpret the Constitution.
2. What problem did the purchase of Louisiana from France create for Jefferson? How did he solve it?
3. How did the spread of cotton mills across New England help speed the spread of slavery across the South?

History Mystery

The unnecessary battle Answer the History Mystery on page 63. How could you find out how news traveled at that time? How might such news travel today? What role did poor communications play in this unnecessary battle?

Writing in Your History Journal

Thinking Historically If you had been alive in 1800, which of the two political parties—Federalist or Republican—would you have favored? Why? What ideas do you like in both parties? Write your responses in your journal.

Citizenship The Missouri Compromise filled Thomas Jefferson with terror. John Quincy Adams thought it was "a title page to a great tragic volume." What did both leaders fear? Should northerners have continued to oppose the compromise? Why?

Section Survey Answers

Reviewing Main Ideas

1. The Federalists supported a powerful national government and a loose construction of the Constitution. The Republicans favored strict construction and a small national government with very limited powers.
2. Jefferson was torn between his desire to purchase Louisiana and his belief in a strict interpretation of the Constitution, which said nothing about buying new territory. Jefferson decided to approve the purchase of Louisiana.
3. The growth of cotton mills created a large demand for cotton, which was grown by slaves in the South.

History Mystery

Information on the Battle of New Orleans is found on page 69. To learn how news traveled then, students could research the history of communications. Methods today include phone, fax, radio, television, computers, and satellites. A peace treaty had been signed two weeks before the Battle of New Orleans, but the news did not reach the soldiers.

Writing in Your History Journal

Thinking Historically Responses should reflect an understanding of differences between the parties.

Citizenship Both feared slavery would destroy the Union. Some may think that taking a moral stand was more important than saving the Union; others, that it was more important to preserve the Union and hope that slavery would die out on its own.

Beginning the Story

Frederick Douglass

In 1845 Frederick Douglass wrote *Narrative of the Life of Frederick Douglass* to prove that he had been a slave. Some people simply refused to believe that a man so articulate and intelligent could have been a slave. As Douglass noted, "They said I did not talk like a slave, look like a slave, or act like a slave." Douglass helped lead the struggle to abolish slavery and gain equality for African Americans and he continues to inspire others.

Setting the Stage Activity

The Power of Reading

Point out that slave owners tried to prevent slaves from learning how to read. To help students understand why, have small groups discuss what advantages people who can read have over people who cannot read. Conclude by discussing these advantages with the class. Then note that they will see how Frederick Douglass used his ability to read and write to try to end slavery.

Vital Links

Plantation (Picture) Unit 3, Side 1, Search 32787

See also Unit 3 Explore CD-ROM location 164.

History Footnote

Once Frederick Douglass escaped to the North, he was considered a fugitive slave. In 1845 he traveled to Britain and Ireland to avoid possible capture and re-enslavement. He spent two years there, speaking to audiences about slavery. Douglass used the money he earned from speaking to buy his freedom when he returned to the United States.

Teaching Resources

Chapter Resources Binder
- **Study Guide p. 10**
- **Reinforcement p. 13**

1820–1850

Section 5 Expansion and Reform

Beginning the Story with Frederick Douglass

By the time he was 16, Frederick Augustus Washington Bailey was in trouble. Not only had the young slave learned to read and write, but he was caught teaching other slaves this forbidden skill. His owner decided that the time had some to send Frederick to Edward Covey, a professional slave breaker.

Frederick had not been on Covey's farm for a week before he received his first flogging. The lash left his body covered with bloody welts. After that, he later recalled, "aching bones and a sore back were my constant companions." So was exhaustion as Covey worked his slaves beyond endurance.

> "I was somewhat unmanageable when I first went there, but a few months of this discipline tamed me. Mr. Covey succeeded in breaking me. I was broken in body, soul, and spirit."

In this rare daguerreotype of an outdoor anti-slavery meeting, Douglass is seated at the right end of the table.

> "I appear before the immense assembly this evening as a thief and a robber. I stole this head, these limbs, this body from my master, and ran off with them."
>
> Frederick Douglass, from a speech to an antislavery audience in 1842

History Bookshelf

Hamilton, Virginia. *Many Thousand Gone: African Americans from Slavery to Freedom.* Knopf, 1993. In an interesting, lively style, the author describes the lives of Frederick Douglass, Harriet Tubman, and other well-know African Americans. Virginia Hamilton has received the Regina Award for lifetime achievement in children's literature.

Also of interest:

Lester, Julius. *To Be a Slave.* Dial Books, 1968.

Meltzer, Milton, ed. *Black Americans: A History in Their Own Words.* HarperCollins, 1984.

Walter, Mildred Pitts. *Mississippi Challenge.* Macmillan, 1992.

HISTORY Mystery

Dr. Blackwell graduated at the top of the class of 1849 from the medical school of Geneva College. Yet years earlier this brilliant student had been turned down by nearly a dozen schools. Why was Blackwell rejected?

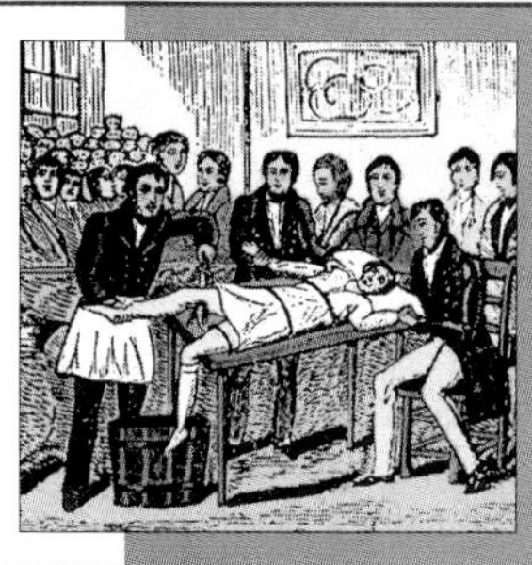

"The turning point in my life as a slave"

Frederick had sunk so low that he did the unthinkable. The next time Covey started to beat him, he fought back. "Whence came the daring spirit," he later wrote, "I do not know. . . . The fighting madness had come upon me, and I found my strong fingers firmly attached to the throat of my cowardly tormentor." For Frederick, this battle was "the turning point in my life as a slave." He wrote of that moment:

> "I had reached the point, at which I was *not afraid to die*. This spirit made me a freeman in *fact*, while I remained a slave in *form*. When a slave cannot be flogged he is more than half free."

In 1838 Frederick Augustus Washington Bailey escaped from slavery to become a free man in form as well as fact. He settled in Massachusetts where he took the name by which we know him today: Frederick Douglass. He threw himself into the abolitionist movement.

Douglass's antispeeches were so eloquent that some doubted he could ever have been a lowly slave. At one meeting, a heckler accused Douglass of being an educated northern black man posing as a slave. In reply, Douglass removed his shirt and turned around. The scars that Edward Covey had left on his back silenced all doubts.

Hands-On HISTORY

Activity

Imagine that you are writing the script for a movie about the young Frederick Douglass. Based on the story above, create a list of scenes to show on film. Give a brief description of the importance of each scene.

Discussion

Thinking Historically

1. Why do you think slave owners considered a slave who could read a threat? (They probably feared literacy would lead slaves to escape or to organize revolts.)

2. Why did Frederick Douglass feel "broken in body, soul, and spirit" after he was sent to the slave breaker? (The slave breaker used violence, fear, and overwork to destroy Douglass's independence.)

Teaching the HISTORY Mystery

Students will find the answer on p. 84. See Section Survey, p. 85, for additional information and questions.

Teaching the Hands-On HISTORY

To help students create scenes for their movies, ask them to list the people in the story. Then have them describe what took place between each person and Douglass.

Vital Links

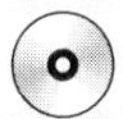

Nat Turner (Picture)
Unit 3, Side 1,
Search 37258

See also Unit 3 Explore CD-ROM location 205.

Introducing the Lesson

Vocabulary

spoils system

Warm-Up Activity

Points of View

To help students compare differing viewpoints, have them look at the painting *Westward the Course of Empire Takes Its Way* by Emanuel Gottlieb Leutze on page 61 from both the Indian and settler perspectives. For each perspective, have students write a title for the painting and prepare an explanation for that title.

Time Line

Keys to History

John Quincy Adams President Adams believed in a strong national government.

Tariff of Abominations South Carolina's leaders threatened to secede in response to the tariff, prompting a crisis for the Union.

Andrew Jackson President Jackson's election was seen as a victory for the common people.

Vital Links

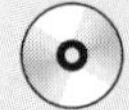

Andrew Jackson (Picture) Unit 2, Side 1, Search 06873

See also Unit 2 Explore CD-ROM location 21.

Lesson Objectives

- ★ Explain the meaning of "Jacksonian Democracy."
- ★ Describe how Jackson changed the role of the President.
- ★ Describe how the eastern Indians were forced onto lands west of the Mississippi.

Teaching Resources

Chapter Summaries
English p. 30
Spanish p. 31

Transparency Activities
p. 16

1824–1840

Lesson 1 The Age of Jackson

For most of two decades, Andrew Jackson, the hero of the Battle of New Orleans, dominated national politics. Unlike earlier Presidents, Jackson was not a polished, well-educated man of wealth. "Old Hickory" was a rough-cut, self-made champion of the "common people."

In 1824 Jackson lost his first bid to become President to John Quincy Adams. Jackson and his new Democratic Party came roaring back in 1828 to win the presidency. To his supporters, Jackson's election was a victory for the view that the government belonged to and should be run by the common people, not the well-born—an idea that became known as Jacksonian Democracy.

One of President Jackson's first acts was to replace some 900 government jobholders with loyal supporters. Critics accused him of creating a spoils system. Jackson replied that giving more of the common people a chance to hold government jobs strengthened democracy.

Jackson also changed the role of the President. Earlier Presidents had seen their job as carrying out the will of Congress. Jackson held that his job was to carry out the will of the people in national affairs. He was the first President to veto an act of Congress because he believed it went against the people's will. He would not be the last.

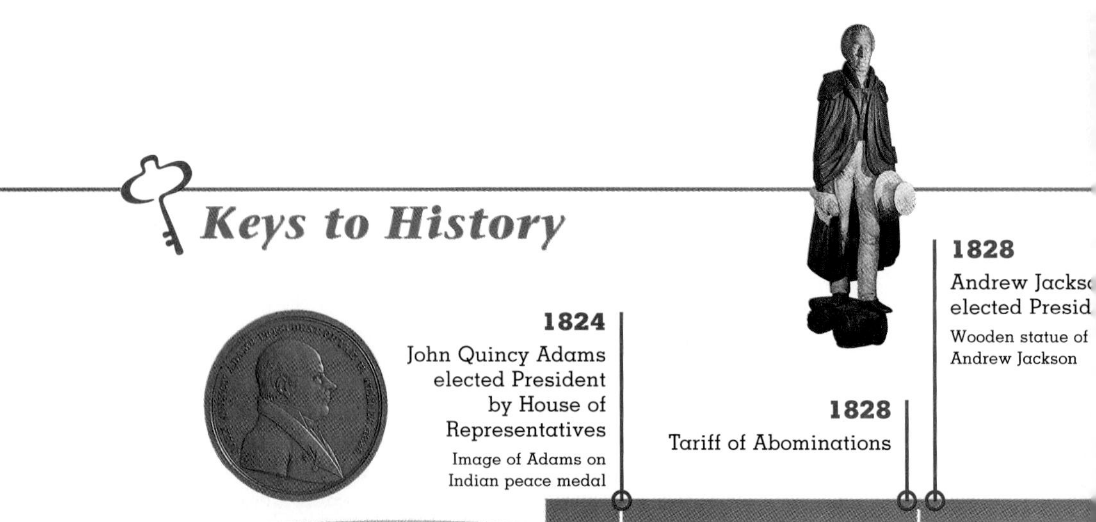

Image of Adams on Indian peace medal

Wooden statue of Andrew Jackson

Connections to Science

The settler's hunger for farmland was prompted in part by technological advances that made it possible for farmers to handle greater amounts of land. Eli Whitney's cotton gin had been improved and made widely available since its invention in 1792. Other inventors contributed to westward expansion as well. In 1838 John Deere perfected his design for a steel plow capable of turning the hard prairie soil. In that same period, Cyrus McCormick patented his extremely successful mechanical reaper, which greatly reduced the amount of labor needed to cut wheat.

Indian Removal

By 1830 the number of Indians living east of the Mississippi River had dwindled to 125,000 while the nation's population had grown to nearly 13 million. As Americans looked for new lands to settle, pressure mounted on the eastern tribes to move west to Indian Territory in present-day Oklahoma.

To hurry this process along, Jackson pushed the Indian Removal Act through Congress in 1830. Indian removal is a tragic chapter in American history. Most of the tribes accepted their fate with little or no resistance. They signed the treaties, packed belongings, and moved to the lands set aside for them across the Mississippi.

A few tribes, though, strongly resisted removal and had to be forcibly removed. In 1838 the Georgia militia rounded up 17,000 Cherokees and marched them west. As many as 4,000 Cherokees died on this terrible journey, which is remembered today as "The Trail of Tears."

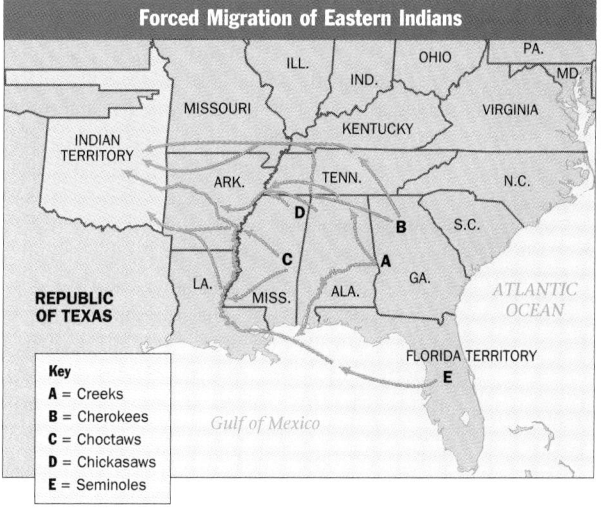

1830
Webster-Hayne debates
Daniel Webster (left) and Robert Hayne

1830
Indian Removal Act

1838
The Trail of Tears
Detail of *The Endless Trail* by Jerome Tiger

1840
"Tippecanoe and Tyler, too!"
An election campaign souvenir: a miniature log cabin

1832 1836 1840

Developing the Lesson

Discussion

Checking Understanding

1. How did Jackson justify his "spoils system"? (He argued that giving common people a chance to hold government jobs strengthened democracy.)

Stimulating Critical Thinking

2. What hardships do you think resulted from Jackson's Indian removal policy? (Indians had to leave their homes and travel long distances; many died on the journey west; their new territory was unfamiliar and may have had fewer natural resources.)

Time Line

Webster-Hayne Debates In one of the most dramatic debates in Senate history, these senators disagreed on whether or not states could nullify a federal law.

Indian Removal Act This act led to treaties that forced eastern Indians to move to land west of the Mississippi.

The Trail of Tears As many as 4,000 Cherokees died on the journey between Georgia and what is now Oklahoma, forced out of their homes by the Georgia militia.

"Tippecanoe and Tyler, too!" With campaign slogans like this, Whigs rallied popular support in their 1840 campaign for the presidency.

Introducing the Lesson

Vocabulary

annex

Warm-Up Activity

Writing About Moving

To underscore the personal issues involved in westward expansion, have students imagine that their family is moving to a new state. Ask them to write a letter to a friend or draw a picture that addresses the following questions: What things might you look forward to? What things might you miss about your old home? What things would you be glad to leave behind?

Time Line

Keys to History

Santa Fe Trail William Becknell opened the Southwest to American traders and settlers with the Santa Fe Trail.

Fur Trappers The rendezvous gave trappers a market for furs and a place to buy necessities.

Vital Links

Voice of José María Sánchez (First-Person Account) Unit 3, Side 1, Search 42623, Play to 43207

See also Unit 3 Explore CD-ROM location 275.

78

Lesson Objectives

- ★ Describe how Americans began to settle the far West.
- ★ Summarize how Texas became part of the United States.
- ★ Explain Manifest Destiny.
- ★ Summarize the events that culminated in the annexation of Oregon and the Mexican Cession.

Teaching Resources

Chapter Summaries
English p. 32
Spanish p. 33
Transparency Activities
p. 17

1820–1850

Lesson 2 The Westward Movement

The eastern Indians were not the only people moving west in the 1830s. Trappers and traders were also crossing the plains in search of furs and business opportunities in the Rocky Mountains and the Mexican territory of New Mexico.

Meanwhile, American cotton planters were moving into Texas, also part of Mexico. By 1835 there were more than ten times as many Americans as Mexicans in Texas—enough to declare and win their independence from Mexico a year later. Texas was annexed to the United States in 1845.

By then, Americans were venturing even further west into Mexican California and the Oregon Country, which the United States shared with Britain. Some went west by ship, but most traveled in wagon trains along the dusty and sometimes dangerous Oregon Trail. As more Americans made the Far West their home, the idea grew that it was the "Manifest Destiny" of the United States to acquire this vast and beautiful region.

In 1846 President James K. Polk, a strong believer in Manifest Destiny, reached an agreement with Britain to annex all of Oregon south of the 49th parallel to the United States. When Polk's efforts to buy California from Mexico failed, he provoked a war with Mexico. In the Treaty of Guadalupe Hidalgo, a defeated Mexico ceded New Mexico and California to the United States in return for $15 million. With both Oregon and the Mexican Cession, the United States now stretched "from sea to shining sea."

Keys to History

1821
William Becknell blazes the Santa Fe Trail
American merchants sight Santa Fe

1823
First fur trappers' rendezvous
Painting of a mountain man

1820 — 1830

History Footnote

In 1853 James Gadsen, the United States Minister to Mexico, negotiated the $10 million purchase of a strip of land south of the Mexican Cession. Gadsen was a businessperson before he joined the U. S. Army and took part in the War of 1812 and the Seminole Wars. He later served as the president of the South Carolina Railroad. In that position, he actively worked to unite small southern railroads and connect them to a transcontinental line. Although his efforts failed, he received support from his friend Jefferson Davis. In 1853 Davis, then the Secretary of War, encouraged the President to support Gadsen as Minister to Mexico. In the Senate many northerners objected to the Gadsen Purchase. They feared that slavery would be introduced to a new territory. The treaty was finally approved despite the opposition.

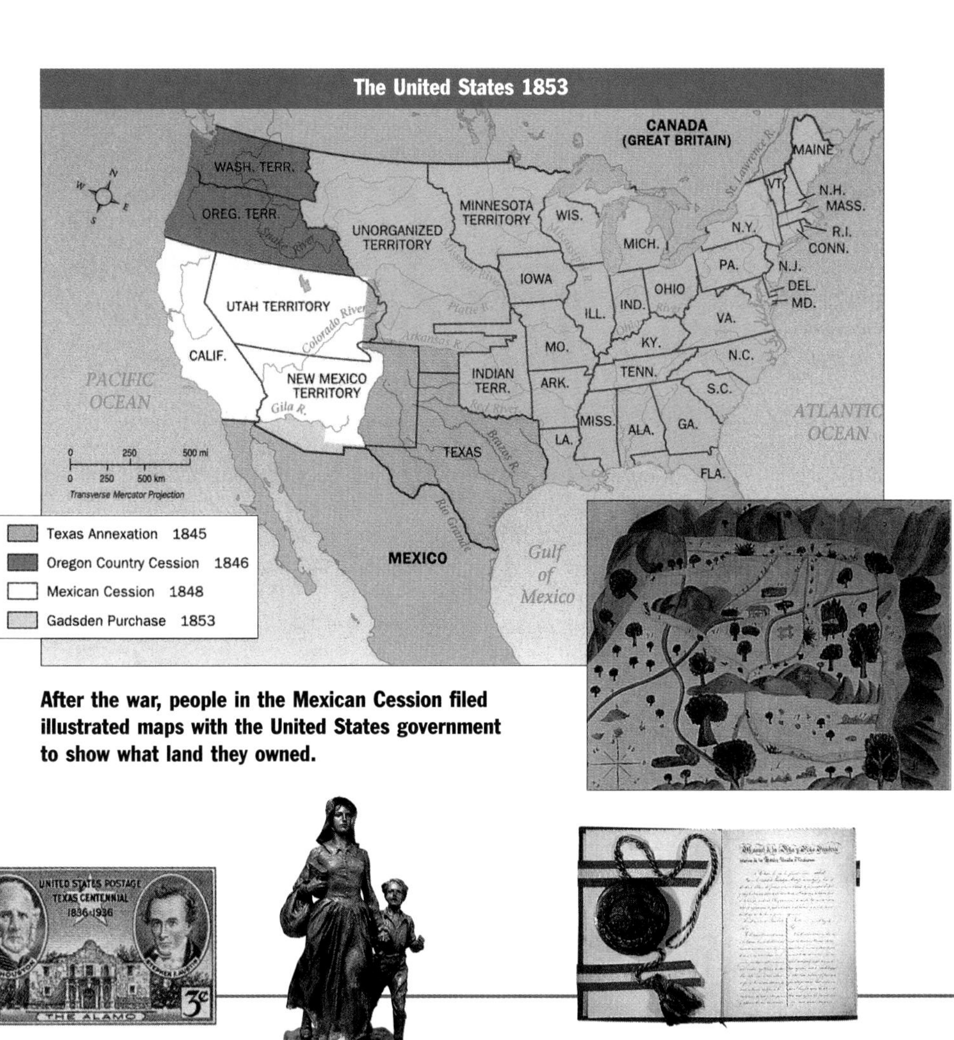

After the war, people in the Mexican Cession filed illustrated maps with the United States government to show what land they owned.

.835–1836
Remember the Alamo" ecomes Texas allying cry
tamp honoring the battle the Alamo

1836
Whitmans lead first families on the Oregon Trail
Monument to women pioneers

1846–1848
War with Mexico
Treaty of Guadalupe Hidalgo, ending the war

1849
Height of California gold rush

1840

1850

Developing the Lesson

Discussion

Checking Understanding

1. What did some people see as America's "Manifest Destiny"? (To expand westward to the Pacific.)

Teaching Map Skills

Comparing Maps

Have students compare the map of the territories with a political map of the United States today (pp. R6–R7), using the rivers of the territorial map as landmarks. Ask: **Which states were part of the Oregon Territory and which states came from the Mexican Cession?** (Oregon Territory: Oregon, Washington, and Idaho; Mexican Cession: California, Utah, Nevada, Arizona, and New Mexico.)

Time Line

"Remember the Alamo" This slogan was the rallying cry of Texans fighting for independence from Mexico.

Oregon Trail Following the Whitmans, thousands of settlers moved west on the Oregon Trail.

War with Mexico The Mexican Cession, gained as a result of the Mexican-American War, marked the final triumph of Manifest Destiny.

California Gold Rush Hopeful prospectors from around the world rushed to California.

Introducing the Lesson

Vocabulary

nativism
discrimination

Warm-Up Activity

Differences at a Glance

To preview the economic differences between regions, have students create a graphic organizer, beginning with two small circles labeled North and South. After they scan the time line, map, and pictures, have them draw lines radiating from the circles and write words or phrases describing each region's economy. Remind them that the Midwest is part of the North.

Time Line

Keys to History

Nat Turner Resistance to slavery sometimes took the form of open revolt. The revolt led by Nat Turner was so bloody that southern states passed stricter slave codes.

McCormick Reaper Cyrus McCormick revolutionized grain harvesting in the United States by creating a machine that cut as much grain in a day as three workers.

Workers' Strikes Faced with longer hours and wage cuts, workers organized unions and went on strike to try to improve their working conditions.

Lesson Objectives

- ★ Compare the economies of the North and the South.
- ★ Identify the link between the mid-century surge in immigration and the rise of nativism.
- ★ Summarize what life was like for African Americans, both enslaved and free.

Teaching Resources

Chapter Summaries
English p. 34
Spanish p. 35

Transparency Activities
pp. 18–19

1830–1850

Lesson 3 Americans at Mid-Century

When Frederick Douglass first escaped to the North in 1838, he thought the people there must be poor because they did not own slaves. It was a natural mistake for someone raised in the South. There, wealth was still measured in land and slaves.

Elsewhere, wealth came less from land and more from trade, industry, and invention. In the Northeast, enterprising Americans had long made money in fishing, whaling, and shipping. By mid-century, they were making new fortunes by building factories that churned out everything from rubber bands to ready-made clothes. In the agricultural Midwest, farmers still looked to the land for a living. With the invention of new farm machines like McCormick's reaper, many midwestern farmers were able to produce larger crops with many fewer workers.

By mid-century, the United States looked like a land of boundless opportunity to Europe's poor. After 1845 the number of Irish, Germans, English, and other Europeans coming to America rose rapidly. They were willing to accept low wages for factory jobs. As the number of newcomers grew, so also did an ugly streak of nativism among some native-born Americans.

For African Americans, mid-century America was more a land of oppression than of opportunity. The majority were slaves trapped in lives of bitter toil. Some, like Douglass, resisted slavery by rebelling or running away. Yet even when they were free, African Americans still faced discrimination in almost every aspect of their lives.

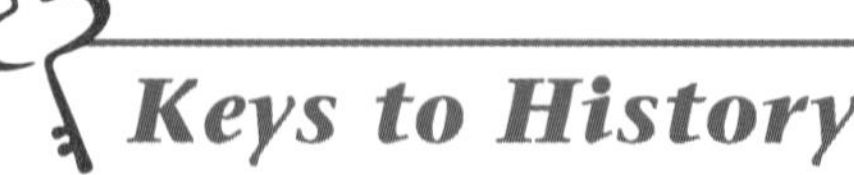

1831
Nat Turner's Revolt
Painting of execution of Nat Turner

1831
McCormick reaper invented

1835–1836
Workers protest wages and hours in 140 strikes

1830

Connections to Math

In the 1820s about 129,00 immigrants arrived in the United States, which had a population of about 12.9 million by 1830. Immigrants from the 1820s made up about 1 percent of the nation's population. In the 1850s about 2.8 million immigrants arrived. The U.S. population in 1860 was about 31.4 million. Immigrants from the 1850s made up about 9 percent of the 1860 population. For every immigrant who arrived in the 1820s, about 22 immigrants came in the 1850s.

Products of the North and South Mid-1800s

- Dairy cattle, hay
- Corn, wheat
- Rice, sugar
- Tobacco
- Cotton
- Iron
- Textiles
- Lumber, forest products
- Fish, whaling products
- Chief manufacturing cities

Whaling

Harvesting wheat

Picking cotton

Reading Maps

Using both the map and the pictures, describe economic differences between the North and the South in the 1850s.

1840s
Clipper ships speed overseas trade

1844
Samuel F. B. Morse demonstrates the telegraph
Early telegraph key

1846
Elias Howe invents the sewing machine

1849
Know-Nothing Party formed
Know-Nothing election poster

1840

1850

Developing the Lesson

Discussion

Checking Understanding

1. How was wealth measured in the South? (In land and slaves.)

2. Why would nativism grow along with the number of immigrants? (Native-born Americans may have felt that immigrants were taking jobs away from them.)

Time Line

Clipper Ships American clipper ships transported goods in such record time that they took over much of the China trade.

Morse Samuel F. B. Morse's invention of the telegraph created a new communications industry.

Howe The sewing machine, invented by Elias Howe, made mass production of clothing possible.

Know-Nothing Party Suspicious of new immigrants, some native-born Americans formed the Know-Nothing Party, which supported only white, Protestant, native-born candidates for office.

Vital Links

McCormick reaper (Picture) Unit 3, Side 1, Search 21879

See also Unit 3 Explore CD-ROM location 99.

Introducing the Lesson

Vocabulary

revival
social reform
temperance
abolition

Warm-Up Activity

Analyzing Reform

To introduce the topic of reform and help students understand the reform process, have them identify social problems of today in need of change or improvement. Write their suggestions on the chalkboard. Once potential areas of reform have been identified, help students analyze what these areas have in common.

Time Line

Keys to History

The Second Great Awakening The religious revivals of the early 1800s encouraged people to improve their personal lives and help others through social reform.

Public Schools Horace Mann led the movement to expand and improve public education, arguing that democracy required educated citizens.

Vital Links

Dorothea Dix (Hyperlink) Unit 3, Side 2, Search 21660, Play to 22465

See also Unit 3 Explore CD-ROM location 430.

Lesson Objectives

- ★ Identify the religious revivals and reform movements that swept the nation.
- ★ Describe the rise of the anti-slavery movement in the early 1800s.
- ★ Summarize the struggle for women's rights in the early 1800s.

Teaching Resources

Chapter Summaries
English p. 36
Spanish p. 37
Transparency Activities
p. 20

1820–1850

Lesson 4 Religion and Reform

In the early 1800s, a religious revival known as the Second Great Awakening spread across the United States. At huge camp meetings, traveling ministers urged their listeners to turn away from evil and receive God's love. Their words touched many hearts, and many people did change. "Drunkards, profane swearers, liars, quarrelsome persons, etc., are remarkably reformed," reported one preacher.

A major outcome of this religious revival was a new spirit of social reform. This spirit, combined with the political fervor of Jacksonian Democracy, inspired Americans to attack a number of social evils. Some reformers, such as Horace Mann, turned their energy toward improving public education. Scores of dedicated men and women gave over their lives to helping the deaf, blind, and disabled. Dorothea Dix led a crusade to build hospitals for the mentally ill and to create more humane prisons. Others attacked the problem of alcohol abuse by preaching temperance and pushing for laws banning the sale of "Demon Rum."

In this swell of reform efforts, the antislavery movement came to overshadow the rest. How could slavery be allowed, antislavery leaders thundered, in a nation dedicated to freedom and equality? Antislavery groups demanded the complete abolition of slavery. Until that day came, many abolitionists—both black and white—risked their lives helping runaway slaves reach freedom on the Underground Railroad.

Early 1800s
Second Great Awakening sweeps the nation
Carving of Henry Ward Beecher, a revival preacher

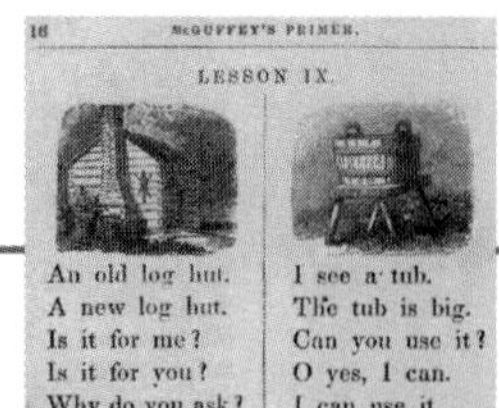

16 McGUFFEY'S PRIMER.

LESSON IX.

An old log hut.
A new log hut.
Is it for me?
Is it for you?
Why do you ask?

I see a tub.
The tub is big.
Can you use it?
O yes, I can.
I can use it.

1830s
Horace Mann urges spread of public schools
McGuffey reader, an early schoolbook

1820 1830

History Footnote

No reformer accomplished more than Dorothea Dix. She found her calling after teaching Sunday school in jail where women whose only crime was mental illness were locked away in dark, unheated cells. After studying jails and poorhouses, Dix appealed to the Massachusetts state legislature to improve prisons and create hospitals for the mentally ill. In one speech she said: "Men of Massachusetts, I beg, I implore, I demand pity and protection for these of my suffering, outraged sex. Become the benefactors of your race, the just guardians of the solemn rights you hold in trust. Raise up the fallen, succor the desolate, restore the outcast, defend the helpless, and for your eternal and great reward receive the benediction 'Well done, good and faithful servants, become rulers over many things.'"

Hands-On HISTORY

Activity

SPEAKING TO PERSUADE Speech can be a powerful tool. Revival preachers and reformers knew that power. A good speech, well delivered, can move an audience to laughter or tears, persuade them to change their beliefs or to join a cause, and leave them with words and ideas they never forget.

Think about the qualities of good speakers you have heard as you write and deliver a speech. Your goal is to persuade your classmates to join you in working for a cause.

Martin Luther King, Jr., an outstanding speaker

1. Choose a cause that people your age can do something about.
2. Decide what action you will ask the audience to take. This is the main point of your speech.
3. Do any research needed to make your speech more interesting and persuasive.
4. Write your speech. The introduction should catch your listeners' attention. The main part should describe the importance of your cause. The conclusion should state what you want your listeners to do.

833
merican Anti-Slavery
ociety established
illiam Lloyd Garrison

1845
Frederick Douglass publishes *Narrative of the Life of Frederick Douglass*

1848
Seneca Falls Convention on women's rights

1850s
Harriet Tubman makes heroic journeys as part of the Underground Railroad

1840 *1850*

Developing the Lesson

Discussion

Checking Understanding

1. What were two outcomes of the Second Great Awakening? (It inspired individuals to live better lives and gave rise to a spirit of social reform.)

2. What was the biggest reform effort to come out of the Second Great Awakening? (The anti-slavery movement.)

Teaching the Hands-On HISTORY

To provide a model of a persuasive speech, read aloud speeches by Sojourner Truth and Frederick Douglass, or use a more contemporary example, such as Martin Luther King's "I Have a Dream" speech.

Time Line

American Anti-Slavery Society Founded by William Lloyd Garrison, the society demanded the abolition of slavery.

Narrative of the Life of Frederick Douglass Douglass's popular autobiography supported the anti-slavery movement.

Seneca Falls Convention This meeting marked the beginning of the women's movement in America.

The Underground Railroad Harriet Tubman was one conductor on the Underground Railroad, a network of people who helped escaping slaves reach freedom.

Bonus Activity

Letter to the Editor

To help students use historical imagination, have them write letters to the editor of a newspaper in 1840, expressing support for the idea of admitting women to colleges and universities. Encourage them to imagine what arguments such a writer might use, and how he or she might refute arguments in opposition to education for women.

Wrap-Up Activity

Newspaper Search

To help students appreciate the long-term significance of the early women's rights movement, have groups search recent newspapers and magazines for articles about women. Have students identify different roles that women are playing today. Ask each group to write a paragraph identifying the different women and roles in their articles and telling why they think women would or would not have been playing those roles in the early 1800s.

Vital Links

Elizabeth Blackwell (Picture) Unit 3, Side 1, Search 41564

See also Unit 3 Explore CD-ROM location 252.

History Footnote

In 1840, the same year that the World Anti-Slavery Convention was held, Elizabeth Cady married Henry Brewster Stanton, a well-known abolitionist. Cady insisted that the word obey be omitted from the traditional marriage vow—"to love, honor, and obey." Throughout her marriage, she worked as a social reformer as well as a wife and mother. Stanton worked to promote women's rights for more than 40 years. Together with Susan B. Anthony, she led the women's rights movement and cofounded the National Women's Suffrage Association.

Neither Stanton nor Anthony would live to see the day when all women in the United States would be able to vote. Yet what they believed in was fulfilled some 70 years later by the 19th Amendment.

Working for Women's Rights

A number of women were active in the antislavery movement. As they fought to free the slaves, they became more and more aware of their own lack of freedom. Women in the early 1800s had few rights or opportunities. No colleges accepted women students. Women could not vote or hold public office. Most professions were closed to them. If a married woman worked, her earnings belonged to her husband.

One of the first areas that women worked to reform was education. Some reformers started their own schools for women. Others worked to break down barriers to women in colleges and professional schools. In 1849 Elizabeth Blackwell became the first woman to earn a medical diploma in the United States. She went on to start a nursing school and a hospital for women and children in New York City.

In 1848 antislavery activists Elizabeth Cady Stanton and Lucretia Mott organized a convention of women in Seneca Falls, New York. Some 300 people showed up, including 40 men. One of them was Frederick Douglass. After two days of spirited debate, the delegates issued a "Declaration of Sentiments" stating that "all men *and women* are created equal." The declaration asked that women be given full rights of citizens, including the right to vote. At the time, most newspapers and magazines scorned the convention and its demands. Today we look back on that meeting as the brave beginning of the women's movement in the United States.

When Elizabeth Cady Stanton's embarrassed son asked her not to come to his school in bloomers, she replied:

"Now suppose you and I were taking a long walk in the fields and I had on three long petticoats. Then suppose a bull should take after us. Why, you, with your arms and legs free, could run like a shot, but I, alas! should fall. . . .Then you in your agony, when you saw the bull gaining on me, would say, 'Oh! how I wish mother could use her legs as I can?' Now why do you wish me to wear what is uncomfotable, inconvenient, and many times dangerous?"

A woman's outfit typical of the 1850s included a whale-boned bodice, tight corset, and several petticoats. In 1851 Amelia Bloomer shocked the public with her comfortable short skirt and full "pants," which people called bloomers.

Why We Remember

Thinking Critically

Divide your class into small groups to discuss the following questions: **Do you agree with Douglass that "progress is still possible" in the United States? In what areas of American life is progress most needed?** Ask each group to share its conclusions with the class. (Students will differ in their confidence in the possibility of progress and in their opinions on what areas most need progress depending on their experiences and temperaments.)

Why We Remember

Expansion and Reform

In 1855 Frederick Douglass wrote a book about his life titled *My Bondage and My Freedom*. By this time, Douglass had experienced the harsh realities of slavery in the South as well as the injustices of racism in the North. Even so, despite "the ten thousand discouragements" facing African Americans, he wrote that "progress is yet possible."

This belief that life can be made better by our own efforts was widely shared by mid-century Americans. It brought the common people into the political system. It sent pioneers westward, expanding the nation from sea to sea. It inspired enslaved African Americans to seek freedom. It energized reformers to work for a more just society. And it lured millions of immigrants from lands where progress seemed a dim hope.

In the years since Douglass wrote his book, Americans' belief in progress has been battered and bruised. Yet it survives and still inspires us to work to make life better. Of all the gifts of the past to the present, surely the idea that "progress is still possible" is one of the most precious.

Section Survey

Reviewing Main Ideas

1. What was "Jacksonian Democracy"?
2. What new territories were added to the United States between 1820 and 1850?
3. What was the basis of wealth in the South at mid-century? In the North?

History Mystery

Medicine in the 1800s Answer the History Mystery on page 75. Elizabeth Blackwell had been turned down by every medical school in Philadelphia and New York City, as well as by Harvard, Yale, and Bowdoin. After she entered Geneva College, she learned that she was only admitted there because administrators and students thought her application was a prank by a rival school. Why do you think they expected her to fail?

Alternative Assessment

Working for reform Work with a group. Imagine that your group has been hired by the leaders of one of the reform movements of the 1800s. Your task is to develop a campaign to advance the reformers' cause.

1. Choose the reform movement.
2. Brainstorm a list of campaign tactics. For example, your list might include hanging posters in public places, giving speeches, and submitting petitions to Congress.
3. For each tactic, name the result you hope to achieve, such as changing the law or swaying public opinion.
4. When you have finished your list, choose two tactics and share them with the class in a concrete way. For example, you might make and display posters and write a petition to hand out for signatures.

Section Survey Answers

Reviewing Main Ideas

1. The belief that the national government belonged to and should be run by the common people, not the rich and well-born.
2. Texas, Oregon Country Cession (which became the Oregon and Washington Territories), and the Mexican Cession (which became California and the New Mexico and Utah Territories).
3. South: land and slaves to produce cotton, tobacco, rice, and sugar. North: trade, forest products, fishing, whaling, industry, and farming.

History Mystery

The answer to the History Mystery can be found on page 84. Blackwell had been turned down by nearly a dozen schools because they thought a woman would be unable to learn mathematics and science.

Alternative Assessment

Allow one or two class periods for this activity, depending on how detailed and polished a reform campaign you would like to see developed. See the Take-Home Planner Review, p. 18, for suggestions and ideas for scoring rubrics for this activity.

Vital Links

Voice of Elizabeth Cady Stanton (First Person Account) Unit 3, Side 1, Search 41201, Play to 41290

See also Unit 3 Explore CD-ROM location 249.

Beginning the Story

Clara Barton

Clara Barton overcame childhood shyness and fear to become a courageous nurse of injured Union soldiers during the Civil War. Known as "the angel of the battlefield," she accompanied the army and treated the wounded right at the battle site. She showed determination by personally obtaining needed supplies. Clara Barton went on to found the American Red Cross.

Setting the Stage Activity

Help-Wanted Ads

To help students consider the contributions made by both women and men during the Civil War, have them write help-wanted ads that might have been published around 1861. Have half of the class write ads asking for soldiers. Tell them to describe the kind of person needed to fight the war. Have the other half advertise for jobs done by women or young girls and boys. Ask several students to read their completed ads.

Vital Links

Battle of Antietam (Movie) Unit 3, Side 1, Search 28868, Play to 29319

See also Unit 3 Explore CD-ROM location 147.

History Footnote

Although normally not allowed to have female helpers, Clara Barton took three women with her to the Second Battle of Bull Run. The four women stayed up all night baking bread, serving soup, distributing shirts, and writing down names of wounded men. At Chantilly she slept in a tent sitting up because the floor was flooded with rainwater. She brought linen bandages to a field hospital where doctors had been dressing wounds in cornhusks. When a general who did not recognize her offered protection as she made her way through wounded soldiers at Fredericksburg, she replied, "Thank you very much, but I believe I'm the best protected woman in the United States."

Teaching Resources

Chapter Resources Binder
- Study Guide p. 11
- Reinforcement p. 14

1850–1905

Section 6 Civil War and Reconstruction

Beginning the Story with Clara Barton

On September 17, 1862, Confederate and Union troops clashed in a fierce battle along Antietam Creek in western Maryland. As the bullets flew, a lone woman appeared on the battlefield. Her face darkened by gun smoke, she moved from one wounded soldier to another. To some she gave a little food and water. To others she applied bandages. At times she had to stop and wring the blood from her skirt to keep moving.

The woman with the bloody skirt at Antietam was Clara Barton. Later generations would remember her as the founder of the American Red Cross. To Union troops on that day of death, she was simply "the lady," or, as a grateful army doctor put it, "the angel of the battlefield."

Women played many roles in the war. Women workers prepared cartridges for Union guns at the arsenal in Watertown, Massachusetts.

History Bookshelf

Stevens, Bryna. *Frank Thompson: Her Civil War Story.* Macmillan, 1992. Using the name Frank Thompson, Emma Edmonds disguised herself as a man and served in the Union army as a nurse, mail carrier, and spy.

Also of interest:

Archer, Jules. *A House Divided: The Lives of Ulysses S. Grant and Robert E. Lee.* Scholastic, 1995.

Chang, Ina. *A Separate Battle: Women and the Civil War.* Lodestar, 1991.

Freedman, Russell. *Lincoln: A Photobiography.* Clarion, 1991.

Keith, Harold. *Rifles for Watie.* Crowell, 1957.

Mettger, Zak. *Till Victory Is Won: Black Soldiers in the Civil War.* Lodestar, 1994.

HISTORY Mystery

More than 130,000 African Americans could vote in Louisiana in 1896. Four years later Louisiana had only 5,000 African American voters. What happened to all the other voters?

"I Remember Nothing but Fear"

As a child this fearless angel of mercy was painfully shy and filled with self-doubt. Looking back, Clara wrote, "I remember nothing but fear."

Her self-doubts followed her into adulthood. Still, they did not keep her for standing up for herself. Once Clara quit a teaching job because the school board hired a man to do the same job for more pay. "I may sometimes be willing to teach for nothing," she declared, "but if paid at all, I shall never do a man's work for less than a man's pay."

Clara finally conquered her doubts when the Civil War broke out and wounded soldiers began dying for lack of medical care. This waste of lives infuriated her. She collected medical supplies and followed the army into battle. Her place, she said, was "anywhere between the bullet and the battlefield."

Clara's courage in battle amazed all who knew her, and perhaps even herself. In the face of death and suffering, her old fears faded away. "I may be compelled to face danger," she once told an audience, "but never *fear* it. While our soldiers can stand and *fight,* I can stand and feed and nurse them."

Alice Buckner of Virginia tried—without success—to smuggle medicine in her petticoat to the Confederates.

Hands-On HISTORY

Activity

War correspondents traveled with the Union and Confederate armies to gather news for their papers. Imagine that you are a war correspondent with the Union army. Write a report of an interview with Clara Barton after the Battle of Antietam. Include at least three questions and her answers.

Discussion

Thinking Historically

1. What character traits do you see in Clara Barton? (She was courageous, independent, and persevering.)

2. What do you learn about the Civil War from Clara Barton's story? (It was brutal, with many casualties. Medical treatment was often primitive, and supplies were scarce.)

Teaching the HISTORY Mystery

Students will find the answer on p. 98. See Section Survey, p. 99, for additional questions.

Teaching the Hands-On HISTORY

To help students brainstorm questions, have them think about what people living during the Civil War would want to know about life on the battlefield. They should include questions about Clara Barton's personal feelings and what she witnessed on the battlefield.

Vital Links

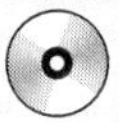

Voice of nurse Kate Cummings (First Person Account) Unit 3, Side 1, Search 26195, Play to 26465

See also Unit 3 Explore CD-ROM location 113.

Introducing the Lesson

Vocabulary

popular sovereignty
secede
sectionalism

Warm-Up Activity

Anticipating Issues

To help students see how westward expansion affected the slavery debate, divide the class into small groups, with group members evenly divided on both sides of the issue. Pose the question, "Should slavery be permitted in the new territories?" Ask groups to debate the issue and brainstorm ideas for resolving the conflict. Conclude by having groups share their ideas.

Time Line

Keys to History

Compromise of 1850 This compromise between proslavery and antislavery forces provided temporary relief to an unraveling Union.

Uncle Tom's Cabin Stowe's depiction of the brutality of slave life revitalized the abolitionists' cause.

Republican Party Former Whigs and Democrats formed a political party committed to antislavery.

"Bleeding Kansas" Violence between proslavery and antislavery forces erupted in a year-long battle.

Lesson Objectives

- ★ Describe how the conflict over slavery intensified as the nation expanded westward.
- ★ Identify the events during the 1850s that contributed to failed compromises over slavery.
- ★ Identify causes of the final break between the North and the South.

Teaching Resources

Chapter Summaries
English p. 38
Spanish p. 39

Transparency Activities
pp. 21–22

Geography Extensions
pp. 7–8

American Readings
pp. 9–12

Using Historical Documents
pp. 27–31

1846–1861

Lesson 1 The Gathering Storm

Clara Barton grew up during a time of increasing tension between the North and the South over the issue of slavery. As the antislavery movement gained strength in the North, proslavery southerners responded with equal force. Attempts by the North and South to find some middle ground did not solve the basic question: Did some people have the right to enslave others?

The slavery issue came to center stage after the war with Mexico. Antislavery forces wanted slavery banned from the new territories acquired from Mexico. Proslavery forces demanded that slavery be allowed to move into these lands. Moderates proposed giving voters in each territory popular sovereignty—the right to decide for themselves whether to allow slavery.

This argument came to a head in 1849 when California asked to join the Union as a free state. At that time the number of slave and free states was equal. As long as this was so, neither the North nor the South could win a vote in the Senate on laws related to slavery. California's bid for statehood threatened this balance of power between the two sections. It also triggered one of the greatest debates in the history of the Senate—a debate not only on the issue of slavery, but on the very survival of the United States.

The Compromise of 1850

The Senate debate on slavery in the territories revealed just how divided the nation was on this issue. South Carolina Senator John C. Calhoun threatened secession if slavery were not allowed to expand westward.

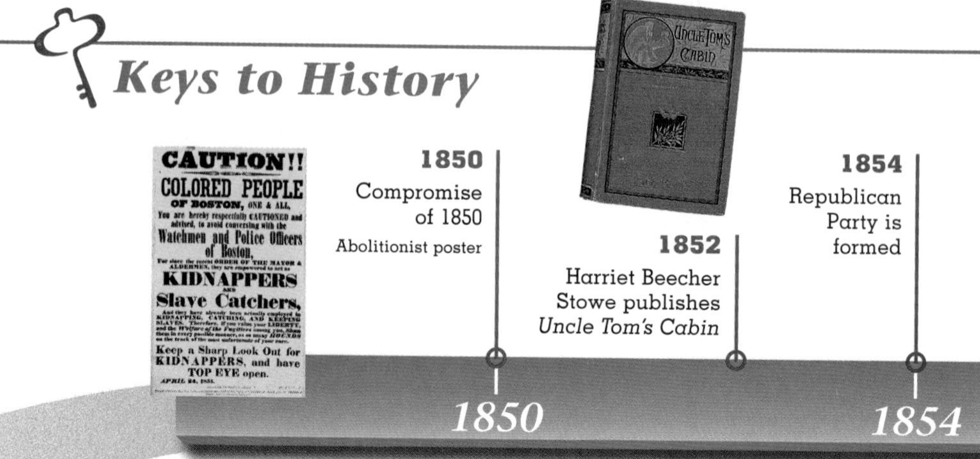

History Footnote

Daniel Webster was a known opponent of slavery. In his personal life, he supported the cause of freed slaves and donated money to help them buy freedom for their families. Yet in his political life, he valued moderation above all else. In a speech supporting the Compromise of 1850 he noted, "In all such disputes, there will sometimes be found men with whom everything is absolute; absolutely wrong, or absolutely right." Webster refused to take an absolute stand against slavery. For his willingness to compromise, he was seen as a traitor by northern radicals.

> "She [the South] has no compromise to offer. If you are unwilling [to meet our demands], we should part in peace."

John C. Calhoun

Senator Daniel Webster responded with an eloquent plea for national unity, only to be denounced by abolitionists as a traitor to their cause.

> "I wish to speak today, not as a Massachusetts man, nor as a northern man, but as an American. I speak today for the preservation of the Union."

Daniel Webster

After a long and stormy debate, Congress approved a compromise crafted by Senator Henry Clay of Kentucky. President Millard Fillmore praised the Compromise of 1850 as "the final settlement" of the slavery issue. It wasn't.

Henry Clay

Compromise of 1850

Provisions favoring proslavery forces	Provisions favoring antislavery forces
• New Mexico and Utah to become territories. The slavery question to be decided by popular sovereignty. • The new Fugitive Slave Law to require the return of escaped slaves, even slaves who had reached the North. • Slavery still legal in Washington, D.C.	• California to be admitted to the Union as a free state. • The slave trade to be abolished in Washington, D.C.

1854–1856
"Bleeding Kansas"

1857
Dred Scott decision

1859
John Brown leads raid on Harpers Ferry

1861
Confederate forces seize Fort Sumter—Civil War begins

Confederate Flag

1857

1861

Developing the Lesson

Discussion

Checking Understanding

1. How did the outcome of the War with Mexico trigger a new debate over slavery? (Antislavery forces wanted slavery banned in the territories acquired from Mexico. Proslavery sources wanted slavery allowed.)

Stimulating Critical Thinking

2. What position did moderates take in this debate? What are the advantages and disadvantages of taking a moderate position? (Moderates favored giving settlers in these territories the right to choose for themselves whether to permit or ban slavery. Moderates often reach an agreement more easily, but they must be willing to accept some solutions they may not like.)

Time Line

Dred Scott In denying this slave's petition for freedom, the Supreme Court ruled that African Americans were not citizens and slavery could not be banned in any territory.

John Brown Brown and his followers seized a federal arsenal at Harpers Ferry as part of their antislavery campaign. Brown was hanged for treason.

Civil War Southern states seceded after Lincoln's election, and the new Confederate States of America took Fort Sumter by force, beginning the Civil War.

Bonus Activity

An *Uncle Tom's Cabin* Ad

Have students create a poster for the stage play of *Uncle Tom's Cabin.* They should target a northern audience that thinks slaves were treated well. Suggest that they use ads for movies as models.

Teaching the Reading Maps

Review the map key with students to ensure that they understand how the four statuses differ.

Answer to Reading Maps: In 1820 Congress closed the part of Louisiana that became Kansas and Nebraska territories to slavery as part of the Missouri Compromise. The Compromise of 1850 left this region a free territory. In 1854 Congress opened these territories to slavery by popular sovereignty.

Vital Links

***Uncle Tom's Cabin* poster (Picture) Unit 3, Side 1, Search 32871**

See also Unit 3 Explore CD-ROM location 178.

Connections to Literature

In addition to the physical brutality suffered by slaves, Stowe attempted to show the emotional misery that results from families being separated by slaveholders. In a letter written soon after the publication of *Uncle Tom's Cabin,* she recounted her own heartache at the death of one of her seven children: "It was at his dying bed and at his grave that I learned what a poor slave mother may feel when her child is torn away from her." It is by this common thread of humanity that Stowe, in concluding remarks added to the novel, urged all women to take a stand against slavery. "I beseech you, pity those mothers that are constantly made childless by the American slave-trade!"

The Failure of Compromise

The Compromise of 1850 brought only temporary peace to the nation. Americans were still deeply divided over slavery, and it was not long until conflicts broke out again.

Three events shattered the calm. The first was enforcement of the Fugitive Slave Law of 1850. This law made it legal for slave hunters to track down runaway slaves in the North and return them to their masters. The sight of free blacks being sent back into slavery so upset northerners that they refused to enforce the law. Southerners, in turn, were outraged by the North's resistance to their one real gain from the Compromise of 1850.

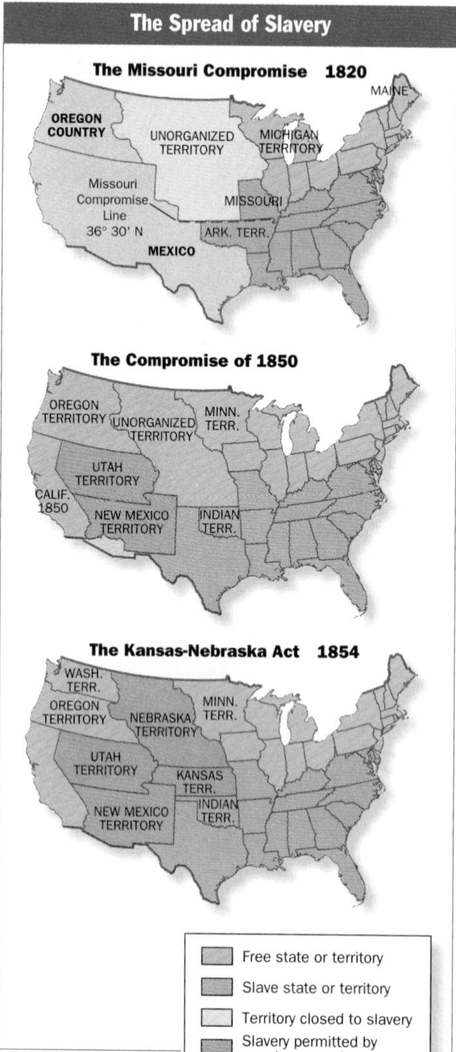

The second event was the publication of Harriet Beecher Stowe's antislavery novel *Uncle Tom's Cabin* in 1852. The book was an immediate best-seller. None who read it could continue to ignore the cruelties of slavery. Many southerners, however, complained that the novel was full of lies and denounced its author as that "wretch in petticoats."

The third event was an outbreak of warfare over slavery in Kansas. In 1854 Congress organized Kansas and Nebraska as territories with popular sovereignty. The Kansas-Nebraska Act overturned the Missouri Compromise, which had closed this region to slavery. Instead settlers in Kansas and Nebraska were to vote whether or not to allow slavery.

As election day drew near in Kansas, settlers on both sides of the slavery issue flooded into the territory. A proslavery band of "Border Ruffians" from Missouri attacked the antislavery town of Lawrence, Kansas, and set it ablaze. In revenge the antislavery fanatic John Brown and his sons attacked a proslavery settlement and murdered five men.

Two hundred lives were lost before federal troops finally brought order to "Bleeding Kansas" in late 1856.

Reading Maps

How did Congress define the status of slavery in the part of Louisiana that became Kansas and Nebraska territories in 1820? In 1850? In 1854?

History Footnote

While Lincoln campaigned for President in 1860, his appearance caught the attention of 11-year-old Grace Bedell. Grace wrote Lincoln a letter, advising him that his chances of winning the election would be improved if he were to "grow whiskers." It was said that Lincoln, a devoted father, had a great fondness for children. A week later, Grace received a letter from Lincoln; later that month Lincoln was photographed with the beginnings of a beard.

In February of 1861, the newly elected President stopped at the train station in Grace's hometown of Westfield, New York, and asked if his young correspondent was in the crowd. She nervously stepped forward. As she later recalled, "It seemed to me as the President stooped to kiss me that he looked very kind, yes, and sad."

On the Brink of War

By 1860 emotions had reached the boiling point in both the North and South. Northerners were seething over the Dred Scott decision of 1857. In this case the Supreme Court had ruled that slaves were property and that under the Constitution slaveowners had the right to take their property into any territory.

Southerners, meanwhile, were outraged by John Brown's recent raid on Harper's Ferry. Although the raid failed, Brown's plan to arm slaves and ignite a slave rebellion struck fear across the South.

The election of 1860 drove a final wedge between North and South. Of the four men who ran for President, only one, the Republican candidate Abraham Lincoln, spoke out against slavery. When Lincoln won the election with only 40 percent of the popular vote, many southerners decided it was time to leave the Union.

Within weeks of Lincoln's election, South Carolina had seceded from the United States. Alabama, Mississippi, Georgia, Florida, Louisiana, and Texas soon followed. Together they formed the Confederate States of America.

On taking office in 1861, Lincoln reached out to the South saying, "We are not enemies, but friends." In response, Confederate forces opened fire on Fort Sumter, a federal fort in South Carolina. The Civil War had begun.

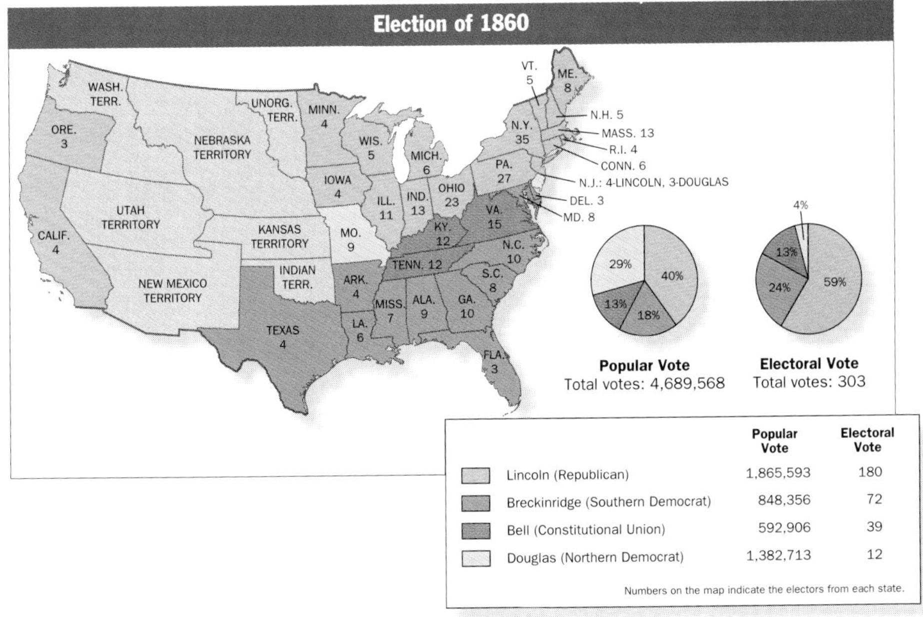

	Popular Vote	Electoral Vote
Lincoln (Republican)	1,865,593	180
Breckinridge (Southern Democrat)	848,356	72
Bell (Constitutional Union)	592,906	39
Douglas (Northern Democrat)	1,382,713	12

Numbers on the map indicate the electors from each state.

Source: *Historical Statistics of the United States*

Reading Maps

How does this map show that in 1860 people voted by sectional interests?

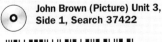

Wrap-Up Activity

Writing a News Release

To review the section, have students write short news releases summarizing events that led to the outbreak of the Civil War. Have them compare their releases with a partner.

Teaching the Reading Maps

Ask what the numbers in each state represent (electoral votes). As you discuss the Reading Maps question, ask if people vote according to sectional interests today. **Answer to Reading Maps:** Most free northern states supported Lincoln, who opposed the spread of slavery. Most southern states supported Breckinridge, a proslavery Southern Democrat.

Vital Links

Dred and Harriet Scott (Picture) Unit 3, Side 1, Search 32799

See also Unit 3 Explore CD-ROM location 166.

John Brown (Picture) Unit 3, Side 1, Search 37422

See also Unit 3 Explore CD-ROM Location 199.

Introducing the Lesson

Vocabulary

emancipation
total war

Warm-Up Activity

Off to War: Dialogues at Home

Have small groups create dialogues between parents and children. Assign each group a different scenario: a southern planter urging his reluctant son to enlist; a northern abolitionist urging her reluctant daughter to volunteer as a nurse; a southern farm woman trying to dissuade her daughter from volunteering as a nurse; a recent immigrant in the North trying to dissuade his son from enlisting. Conclude by having groups share their dialogues and summarize reasons for and against joining the war effort.

Time Line

Keys to History

First Battle of Bull Run The Union loss made northerners realize the war would not be won quickly.

Monitor* vs. *Merrimac In this battle between the first two ironclad steamships, neither side claimed victory, dashing the Confederates' hopes of breaking the blockade of Norfolk, Virginia.

Battle of Antietam A turning point, this battle destroyed one third of Lee's army and ruined the South's hopes of European aid.

Lesson Objectives

- ★ Summarize the expectations and war aims of both sides when the Civil War began.
- ★ Compare the resources of the Union and the Confederacy.
- ★ Identify the Union's changing war aims as the war dragged on.
- ★ Describe General Grant's strategy for crushing the Confederacy.

Teaching Resources

Chapter Summaries
English p. 40
Spanish p. 41

Transparency Activities
pp. 23–24

Geography Extensions
pp. 9–10

American Readings
pp. 13–16

Using Historical Documents
pp. 32–39

1861–1865

Lesson 2 The Civil War

The Confederate attack on Fort Sumter plunged the nation into civil war. It also forced the eight slave states that had not yet left the Union to take sides. Four of these "Border States" seceded to join the Confederacy. The other four stayed in the Union but were deeply divided. In many families, brothers, cousins, and even fathers and sons fought on opposite sides.

In the spring of 1861, most people believed the war would be quickly won. Northerners based their confidence on their section's size and economic strengths. The North had more people available to fight. It had more farmland and factories to produce food and equipment for an army. It also had more miles of railroad for moving troops and supplies into battle. The Confederacy had the edge in one key area: military leadership. The nation's best generals fought for the South. And they fought brilliantly.

Expecting a short, glorious war, volunteers rushed to enlist on both sides. Southerners joined to protect their homes and their way of life from an invading Union army. Northerners signed on to save the Union from the rebels. Hoping to strike a blow against slavery, African Americans flocked to Union recruiting centers—only to be turned away. For the first two years of the war, free blacks would have to fight for the right to fight for freedom.

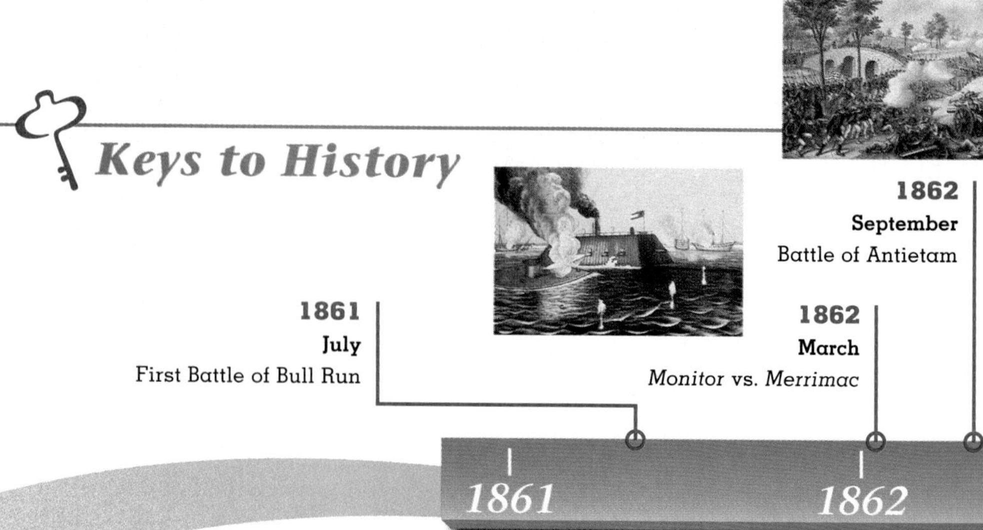

History Footnote

In 1857 Robert E. Lee inherited a large Virginia estate, including slaves, from his father-in-law. His father-in-law's will provided for the freedom of his slaves. As a lieutenant colonel in Texas in 1855, Lee was aware of the conflict between abolitionists and slave owners throughout the country. He wrote to his wife, "In this enlightened age, there are few, I believe, but what will acknowledge that slavery as an institution is a moral and political evil in any Country." With war looming in 1860, he said, "If the slaves of the South were mine, I would surrender them all without a struggle to avert this war." In 1862 he released the slaves on his plantation.

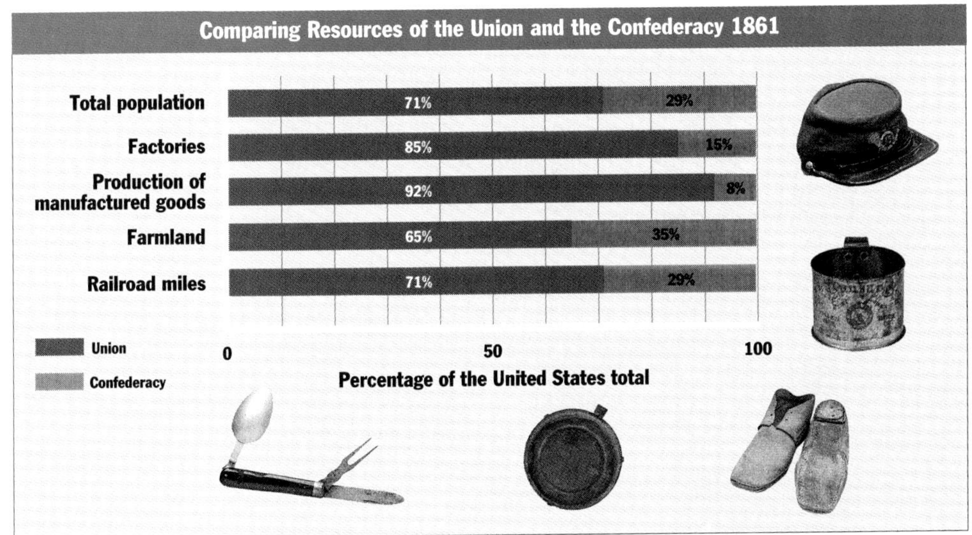

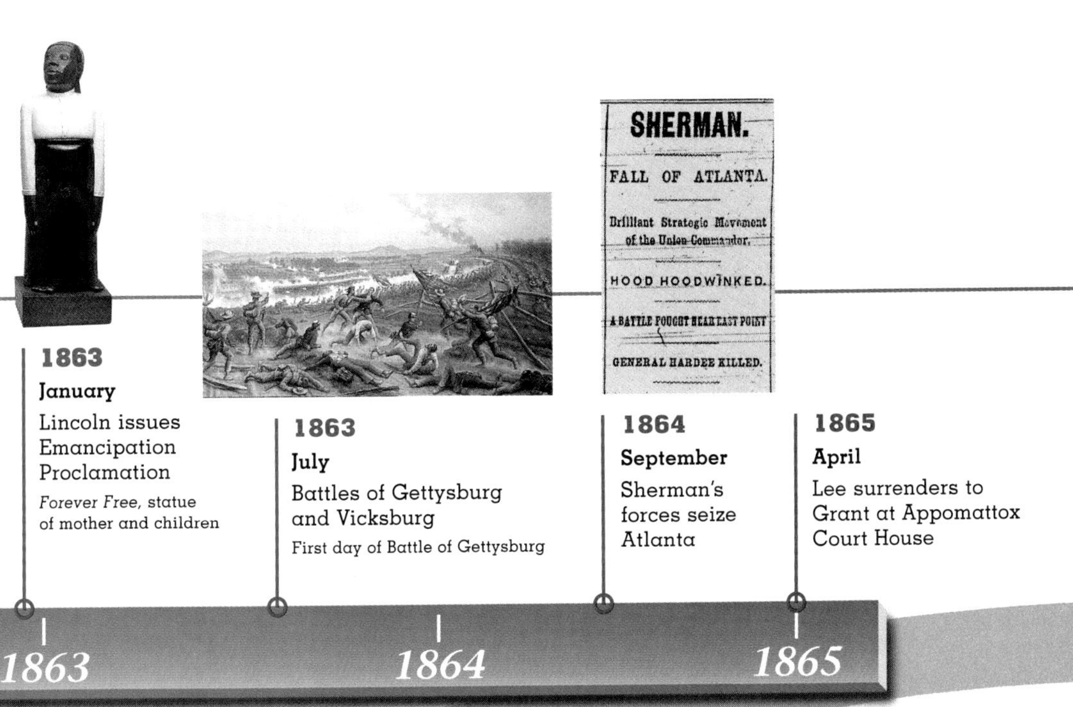

SHERMAN.
FALL OF ATLANTA.
Brilliant Strategic Movement of the Union Commander.
HOOD HOODWINKED.
A BATTLE FOUGHT NEAR EAST POINT
GENERAL HARDEE KILLED.
1863
1864
1865

1863
January
Lincoln issues Emancipation Proclamation
Forever Free, statue of mother and children

1863
July
Battles of Gettysburg and Vicksburg
First day of Battle of Gettysburg

1864
September
Sherman's forces seize Atlanta

1865
April
Lee surrenders to Grant at Appomattox Court House

Developing the Lesson

Discussion

Checking Understanding

1. What were the North's strengths when the war began? The South's? (The North had more farmland, factories, railroad lines, and population. The South had the best military leaders.)

Stimulating Critical Thinking

2. What were northerners fighting for? What were southerners fighting for? (Northerners were fighting to preserve the Union. Southerners were fighting to defend their homes and way of life.)

Time Line

The Emancipation Proclamation The plan freeing all slaves in the Confederate states changed the war into a fight for freedom as well as for the Union.

Battles of Gettysburg and Vicksburg The Confederate loss at Gettysburg turned the war into a defensive struggle on southern soil. The southern loss at Vicksburg led to Union control of the entire Mississippi River.

Sherman at Atlanta Use of total war by the Union raised spirits in the North and ensured Lincoln's re-election.

Lee Surrenders The bloodiest war in the history of the nation ended, having cost more than 620,000 lives.

Wrap-Up Activity

Interviewing Lee and Grant

To understand why the North won the war, have students prepare for an interview with the two commanding generals after Appomattox. Have them work in small groups, with half assigned to write questions for Grant, and half for Lee. As students share their questions with the class, discuss the answers they think each general would have been likely to give.

Bonus Activity

A Soldier's Letter Home

Ask students to imagine being participants in one of the Civil War battles described in this section. Have them choose a specific battle and review the facts about it. Then have them write letters home describing the sights, sounds, and feelings of the battle from the perspective of either a Union or a Confederate soldier. They should include their views on the war's prospects. Conclude by having volunteers read their letters aloud to compare perspectives.

Connections to Literature

The Fort Wagner attack inspired commemorations, like these excerpts from "The Old Flag Never Touched the Ground":

"The Old Flag never touched the ground!"
'twas thus brave Carney spoke—
A Negro soldier: words renowned that
Honor will invoke
Upon the records of the Race whose
heroes many are,
Records that Time cannot efface, and
Hate never can mar.
Those words were stamped with Carney's
blood upon our Country's scroll,
And though dislike, deep as a flood
against his Race may roll,
It cannot dim, nor wash away, its
crimson-written fame
Which History wrote on Wagner's day
without a tinge of shame.

The First Years of War

The war began badly for the Union. Most of its generals were reluctant to fight. And when they did go into battle, they lost.

In 1862 Confederate General Robert E. Lee boldly led his Army of Northern Virginia into Maryland. Lee hoped a successful invasion of the North would persuade France and Britain to aid the Confederacy.

On September 17 Lee's army met a Union force at Antietam Creek. Before darkness ended the fighting, 5,000 soldiers were killed and 18,500 were wounded. Lee lost a third of his army at Antietam, along with all hope of winning help from abroad.

Changing War Aims

By this time, President Lincoln had decided that what began as a war to save the Union should become a war to end slavery as well. On January 1, 1863, he signed the Emancipation Proclamation. It stated that all slaves in the Confederacy "are, and henceforward shall be, free."

Lincoln's proclamation turned the Civil War into a crusade for freedom and the Union army into a liberating force wherever it went in the South.

It also opened the door for more than 200,000 African Americans to fight in the Union army and navy.

This picture shows the 54th Massachusetts Infantry leading an assault on Fort Wagner, South Carolina. Although the attack failed, the 54th fought courageously, suffering almost 50 percent casualties.

From Defeat to Victory

The year 1863 started with still more Union defeats. In June, Lee decided to risk another invasion of the North. On July 1 Confederate soldiers met Union troops in the little town of Gettysburg, Pennsylvania. After two days of furious fighting, Lee risked everything on an infantry charge led by General George Pickett. Pickett's charge was a disaster. On July 4 Lee's battered army retreated to Virginia. From this point on the war would be fought on southern soil.

The Union triumph at Gettysburg came the same day as another victory in Mississippi. After a seven-week siege, Vicksburg had fallen to Union forces led

Connections to Music

The commemoration of the Civil War is in its music. The songs "The Battle Hymn of the Republic," "Bonnie Blue Flag," and "Marching Through Georgia" originated during the war, and have lived on. Music was an important part of life in the camps and battlefields. After the devastating fighting at Spotsylvania, for example, the Confederate bands are said to have struck up "Dixie" and Handel's "The Dead March," while the Yankees played "The Star-Spangled Banner" and "Home Sweet Home." Many songs were enjoyed by both sides and had titles such as "Cheer Boys, Cheer," "Just Before the Battle, Mother," and "Tramp, Tramp, Tramp." Out of the war grew a new music in which Irish, Scottish, English, Italian, German, and African American styles were combined.

by General Ulysses S. Grant. This victory gave the Union control of the Mississippi River, while dividing the Confederacy in two. It also gave President Lincoln a general who could win. "Grant is my man," he exclaimed, "and I am his for the rest of the war.

Total War

Grant believed in total war—war against both armies and civilians to break their will to fight. In 1864 he invaded Virginia with 120,000 troops. In a month, Grant had lost 50,000 men. Still he pressed on, replacing his losses with fresh troops.

Meanwhile, Union General William Tecumseh Sherman was waging total war in Georgia. First Sherman's troops burned Atlanta. Then they marched across Georgia to the sea at Savannah. Wherever he went, Sherman left a wide path of destruction and despair in his wake.

From War to Peace

On April 1, 1865, Grant's troops finally took Richmond, Virginia, the capital of the Confederacy. Nine days later, Lee surrendered at Appomattox Court House. Grant's terms were generous. Lee's troops could go home if they promised to fight no more.

The bloodiest war in America's history was over at last. The Union had been saved, but at the horrifying cost of more than 620,000 lives. Almost every family on both sides had lost a loved one. After the war, Clara Barton set up a "missing persons" office to help thousands of families search for missing relatives.

For President Lincoln, the end of the war was the happiest day of his life. "Thank God I have lived to see this," he said. "I have been dreaming a horrid nightmare for four years, and now the nightmare is over."

Hands-On HISTORY

Activity

Commemorating the Civil War Since the guns fell silent more than 130 years ago, Americans have continued to remember the Civil War. In paintings, monuments, and books, as well as in movies and television dramas, we have commemorated the people and events of that dramatic period in the nation's history.

You may never write a book or create a television drama about the Civil War, but you can plan a way to commemorate it.

1. Decide what part of the war to commemorate. It might be an event, a person or group of people, or a theme, such as life at home.

2. Decide what form to create—for example, a plaque, monument, play, pageant, or story.

3. Put your plan on paper. For example, draw a picture of a statue or write a program for a pageant. Share it with your classmates.

War monument

Discussion

Checking Understanding

1. How did the Emancipation Proclamation change the war? (It turned the war into a crusade against slavery and opened the way for African Americans to enlist in the Union army and navy.)

Stimulating Critical Thinking

2. Should the Emancipation Proclamation be the main thing Lincoln is remembered for? Why or why not? (Yes: It made part of the Union cause a fight against slavery; it was a brave moral stand. No: Lincoln's major accomplishment was saving the Union; the proclamation was simply a strategy to win the war.)

Teaching the Hands-On HISTORY

As an example of a Civil War monument, point out that in 1995 ground was broken in Washington, D.C. for a monument honoring the 178,000 African American soldiers who fought in the war. This memorial will be a curved stone wall holding stainless steel plaques listing the names of the black Union soldiers and the white officers who fought with them. Encourage students to create forms for their commemorations that fit their subjects.

Introducing the Lesson

Vocabulary

Reconstruction
impeachment
freedmen
Jim Crow laws
poll tax
segregation

Warm-Up Activity

Postwar Hopes

Have students imagine that they are a former Union soldier, Confederate soldier, or slave. Ask them to each write a short paragraph identifying who they are and what their expectations are for the future.

Time Line

Keys to History

Lincoln's Assassination Lincoln's death meant that Reconstruction would take place without his experience and wisdom.

Johnson's Impeachment The conflict between President Johnson and Congress over Reconstruction led to the only impeachment of a President in U.S. history.

14th Amendment The 14th Amendment was ratified in an effort to ensure that African Americans would have equal rights.

End of Reconstruction Following Hayes's election, Reconstruction ended and southern whites elected conservative Democratic governments.

Lesson Objectives

- ★ Contrast the views of Reconstruction held by the President and Congress.
- ★ Describe some accomplishments of the South's Reconstruction governments.
- ★ Explain the impact of the return to white man's rule on African Americans in the South.
- ★ Identify African American responses to segregation and Jim Crow laws.

Teaching Resources

Chapter Summaries
English p. 42
Spanish p. 43

Transparency Activities
pp. 25–26

Geography Extensions
pp. 11–12

American Readings
pp. 17–20

Using Historical Documents
pp. 40–43

1865–1905

Lesson 3 Reconstruction

After four long years of war, the entire nation longed for peace. But what kind of peace? One that punished the South or helped it to rebuild? In his second inaugural address, President Lincoln called on Americans to "bind up the nation's wounds" with "a just and lasting peace." The President was assassinated, however, before he could shape a such a healing peace.

For the next two years, President Andrew Johnson battled Republicans in Congress over how the Confederate states should be brought back into the Union. Johnson's plan for Reconstruction allowed the South's traditional leaders—wealthy white planters and Democrats—to keep control of their states. Congress favored a plan that shifted political power to poor whites and the freed slaves, who were more likely to vote Republican. This conflict finally ended when the House impeached Johnson in 1868. Johnson escaped removal from office, but his power was broken.

Under the Reconstruction Act of 1867, the army registered 635,000 white voters and 735,000 black voters across the South. These new voters chose delegates who wrote the most forward-looking state constitutions in the nation. Once these constitutions were ratified, the voters elected officials—some black, some white—to fill state and local offices. By 1870 all the former Confederate states had formed new state governments and been readmitted to the Union.

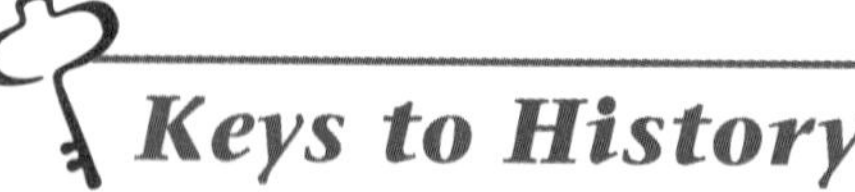

1868
President Johnson's impeachment and trial

Admission ticket for the President's trial

1865
President Lincoln is assassinated

1868
14th Amendment guarantees equality under law for all

1865 1870 1875

History Footnote

First organized in 1866, the Ku Klux Klan was officially disbanded in 1869, but many of its members went underground and formed other organizations under a variety of names throughout the South. Congress responded by enacting the Ku Klux Klan Act in 1871, giving the President wide powers to combat violence designed to disrupt elections. The name Ku Klux Klan was revived in 1915 when a new national organization was formed in Atlanta. The new organization did not limit its intimidation to African Americans, but also targeted Jews, Catholics, and immigrants. It reached its height, with more than three million members, in the late 1920s but was disbanded in 1944. A third Klan was formed in 1946 to combat the post-World War II demand for civil rights by African Americans. It still exists today.

Return to "White Man's Rule"

The new state governments set to work to build roads, schools, and hospitals. To pay for such projects, they raised taxes. Many whites resented the tax hikes. Even more they resented seeing former slaves voting, holding office, and trying to build a new society based on racial equality.

Klan members disguised themselves with hoods and robes. These men posed in a professional photography studio in 1868.

Resentful whites joined forces to return their states to "white man's rule." They formed secret societies, such as the White League and the Ku Klux Klan, to terrorize African Americans. Wearing long, hooded robes, they thundered across the countryside by night, warning blacks not to vote.

Such tactics worked. By 1877 the South's traditional Democratic leaders had regained power. A former slave observed:

> "The whole South—every state in the South . . . has got into the hands of the very men that held us as slaves."

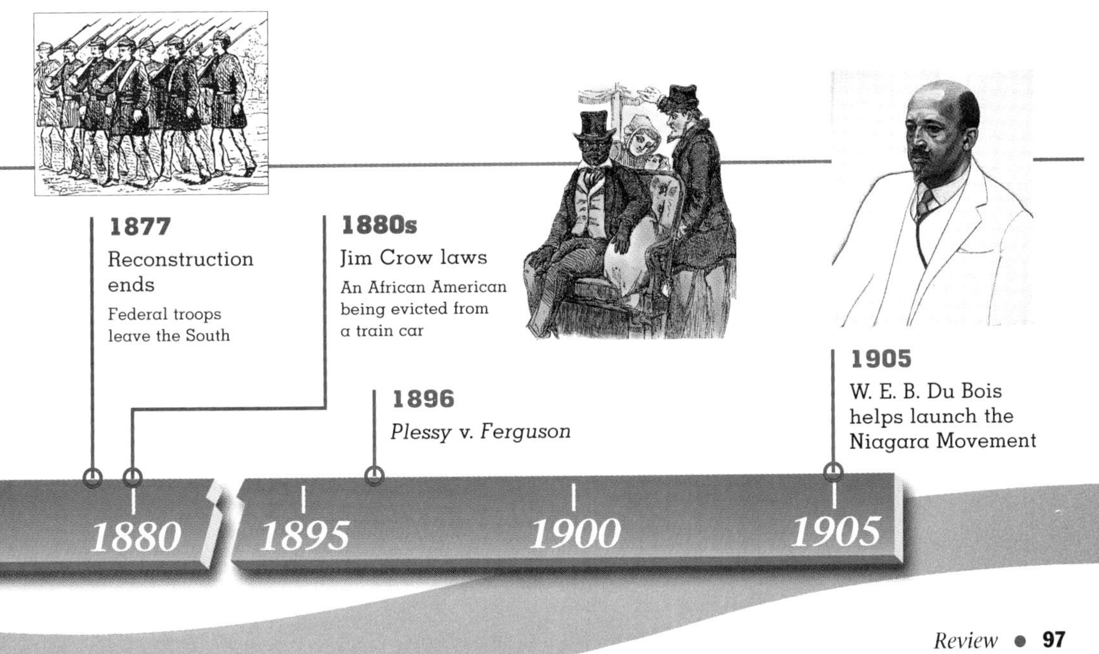

Developing the Lesson

Discussion

Checking Understanding

1. Why did most southern whites hate Reconstruction governments? (They resented the taxes imposed by Reconstruction governments as well as seeing African Americans voting and holding office.)

Stimulating Critical Thinking

2. What was the goal of the South's secret societies? Why were they so popular? (To return the South to "white man's rule." Many southerners may have felt unsure about the future and tried to return life to the way it was before the war.)

Time Line

Jim Crow Laws These segregation laws were passed by white-controlled southern state governments as part of their effort to undo the effects of Reconstruction.

Plessy* v. *Ferguson This landmark Supreme Court decision, with its "separate but equal" standard, made segregation legal for more than half a century, until the Court reversed itself in 1954.

Niagara Movement African Americans responded to discrimination by forming several self-help and activist organizations, including the Niagara Movement, which led to the founding of the National Association for the Advancement of Colored People (NAACP).

Checking Understanding

1. How were many African Americans prevented from voting? (By poll taxes and literacy tests enacted by southern states.)

Stimulating Critical Thinking

2. What effects do you think segregation had on African Americans? (Rising feelings of resentment; feelings of inferiority; denial of equal opportunities and services.) **On whites?** (Segregation reinforced prejudices because it resulted in fewer opportunities for people to understand each other.)

Wrap-Up Activity

A Letter to a Former Master

To point out the changed relationship between former slaves and masters, have students imagine themselves as freedmen writing a letter to a former master. The master has offered to hire the freedmen. In the letters they should explain why they will or will not accept. Conclude by having volunteers read their letters and compare their responses with the letter in *American Readings*, p. 20.

Vital Links

Segregated jury (Picture) Unit 3, Side 1, Search 38995

See also Unit 3 Explore CD-ROM location 215.

History Footnote

The South's new Reconstruction governments included a number of African American officials. In South Carolina, blacks held a majority of seats in the legislature for two years, and Jonathan J. Wright served for six years on the state supreme court. Sixteen African Americans served in Congress, fourteen in the House and two—Hiram R. Revels and Blanche K. Bruce—in the Senate. The conduct of these new legislatures impressed their white colleagues. Maine representative James G. Blaine, who knew most of the black Congressmen, observed that "The colored men who took their seats in both Senate and House did not appear ignorant or helpless. They were as a rule studious, earnest, ambitious men, whose public conduct . . . would be honorable to any race."

The Freedmen

For the four million African Americans freed from slavery, Reconstruction was a time of hope denied. While no longer slaves, most freedmen had no land or money to start new lives.

Black men were, however, given the right to vote. With their votes, they elected leaders who worked to make life better for all southerners, black and white.

Most freedmen pinned their hopes for a better life on education. In response, Reconstruction governments set up the South's first public school systems. When white Democrats regained control of their states, however, many of the new schools were closed.

Pictured at left are the seven African Americans who served in Congress in 1872. Twenty years later there was only one African American member of Congress.

Voting Rights and Jim Crow

Public education was not the only gain made by freedmen during Reconstruction that was lost after the return to "white man's rule." By 1900 most freedmen had lost the right to vote as well. They were kept from voting by poll taxes and literacy tests that were enacted in southern states to make it almost impossible for blacks to vote.

Southern Democrats also began passing segregation acts known as Jim Crow laws. These laws forced the separation of blacks and whites in public places such as schools and parks. In 1896 the Supreme Court ruled in *Plessy* v. *Ferguson* that segregation was constitutional so long as the facilities provided both races were roughly equal.

Despite these setbacks, southern blacks continued to struggle for a better future. Some black communities built their own schools and colleges for their children. By 1900 more than 1.5 million African American children were attending classes.

African Americans also continued to demand full equality. In 1905 William E. B. Du Bois and other black reformers launched the Niagara Movement, which later gave birth to the National Association for the Advancement of Colored People (NAACP). Du Bois said of their goals:

> "We claim for ourselves every single right that belongs to a freeborn American, political, civil, and social; and until we get these rights we will never cease to protest."

Jim Crow laws kept blacks and whites separated for many years. This photo of a public fountain was taken in 1950 in North Carolina.

Why We Remember

Thinking Critically
In his Gettysburg Address President Lincoln dedicated himself and all Americans to "the great task remaining before us . . . that this nation, under God shall have a new birth of freedom." Divide the class into groups to discuss the following questions and then share their answers with the class.

1. What did Lincoln do to complete his "great task" before his death in 1865? (He ended slavery forever.)
2. What did he leave undone? (He did not ensure that the freedmen would have full and equal rights.)
3. Does America today need a "new birth of freedom"? Why or why not? (Accept answers that students can support.)

Why We Remember

Civil War and Reconstruction

The Civil War years were a turning point for the nation. Again and again in the decade leading up to the war, Americans tried to find a lasting compromise on slavery. Each compromise, in turn, created new problems, new divisions. Abraham Lincoln understood why. Slavery was not simply a political issue to be worked out. It was a deeply moral issue. As Lincoln wrote in a letter to a friend, "If slavery is not wrong, nothing is wrong."

It took the nation four years of bloody combat to right that wrong. But when the guns fell silent, Americans had moved closer to that simple but powerful ideal on which our nation was founded: "We hold these truths to be self-evident, that all men are created equal."

After the war, the South's new Reconstruction governments worked to make African Americans full and equal citizens. Sadly, racism proved far stronger than ideals. With the return of "white man's rule," many of the gains southern blacks had made after the war were lost. Even so, the belief that all people deserve the same rights and opportunities was kept alive by black families, churches, and schools. Their faith in the ideal of equality would be the most hopeful legacy of the Civil War and Reconstruction.

Section Survey

Reviewing Main Ideas

1. What basic issue divided the North and South in the 1850s?
2. What was the Union's war aim when the Civil War began? How did that war aim change after 1863?
3. In what sense was Reconstruction a success for the freedmen? A failure?

History Mystery

Voting in the South Answer the History Mystery on page 87. How might such a decline in voting by African Americans after 1896 have been prevented?

Writing in Your History Journal

Thinking Historically A terrorist uses violence to advance a political cause. Would you call John Brown a terrorist or a hero? Explain why. How would you compare him with terrorists today? Write you response in your journal.

Citizenship Today, the growth of cities is threatening the sites of many famous Civil War battlefields, including Gettysburg and Petersburg. Imagine that you own property on the site of Gettysburg. A developer has offered to buy your land and plans to build a factory. In your journal write your thoughts about the offer.

Section Survey Answers

Reviewing Main Ideas

1. Americans were divided over whether slavery should be allowed to expand into new territories. It was hard to find a compromise because slavery was a deeply moral issue that provoked strong emotions.

2. The Union's initial war aim was to preserve the United States. After the Emancipation Proclamation, the Union's aim included ending slavery.

3. Reconstruction was a success for freedmen in that it gave them the right to vote and exercise political power for the first time. When Reconstruction ended, those gains were lost and segregation became a way of life in the South.

History Mystery

Information on voting is found on page 98. Poll taxes and literacy tests disqualified most African Americans from voting. The decline may have been prevented if the Supreme Court had declared these voting restrictions unconstitutional.

Writing in Your History Journal

Thinking Historically Accept answers that students can support. Brown was similar to terrorists today in that he used violent protest to draw attention to his cause.

Citizenship Accept reasonable answers. Students may mention a desire to preserve history, save open space, or honor the dead. If students feel that more should be done to protect Civil War battlefields, encourage them to think of ways to raise public awareness on this issue.

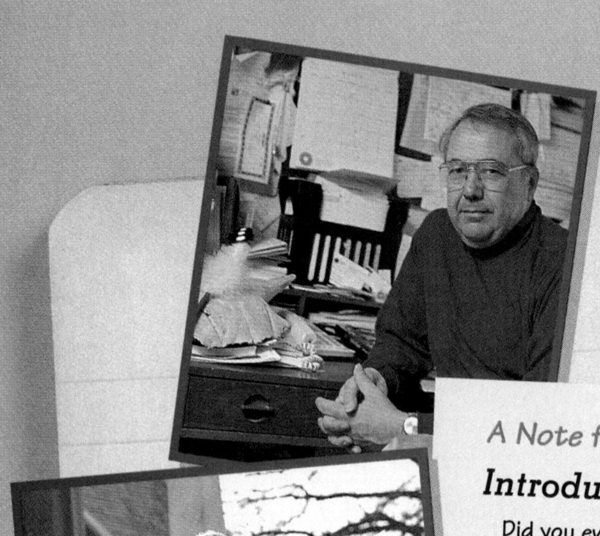

(Top) Dr. Viola in his home office, and (bottom) seeking out clues to history in the Congressional Cemetery.

A Note from the Author . . .

Introducing Scholar's Tool Kits

Did you ever wonder how historians are able to write about the past? It is not a secret. Anyone who has a curious mind, likes to solve mysteries, and knows how to use the "tools" of historical scholarship can "do" history.

Historians build knowledge much like carpenters build houses, only their tools are unlike anything a carpenter would use. A scholar's tools are ancient bones, pots, jewelry, and sculpture. They are drawings, maps, lithographs, and photographs. They are stories and remembrances passed down from person to person. They are letters, diaries, and newspapers. They are, in fact, anything that helps unlock the mysteries of history.

A scholar's tools, you will see, are easy to learn about and fascinating to use. The five Scholar's Tool Kits in this book each tell about how one tool is used, and give you a chance to try out "doing" history.

As you read the stories and information in this or any history book, think about the tools the historian who wrote the book used to learn about the past. What questions are still unanswered? What tools would you use to answer them? You will soon see that you, too, can use the tools of history to re-create the past.

Sincerely,

Herman J. Viola

Objectives

- ★ Understand what memoirs are.
- ★ Identify the kinds of information that historians can acquire from memoirs.
- ★ Understand the limitations of memoirs as a tool of history.

How Do We Know?

Charles Henry Veil

Scholar's Tool Kit

Memoirs

The Battle of Gettysburg, fought in July 1863, was one of the bloodiest battles of the American Civil War. Few battles in history caused more casualties. As many as 51,000 Confederate and Union soldiers failed to answer roll call after the three days of fighting.

A Crucial Moment

At a crucial moment early in the battle, Confederate forces were rushing through a cornfield to capture a key hill. Scrambling up the other side was a Union regiment. From atop his horse at the crest of the hill, Major General John Fulton Reynolds of the Union army watched as the two forces swept toward each other. With him were staff officers and his 21-year-old orderly, Private Charles Henry Veil.

As the Union infantry crested the hill, Confederate musket fire knocked down the first line of soldiers. Those behind them stopped and fell back in confusion. Anxious to prevent a terrible defeat, General Reynolds turned in his saddle and tried to rally the Union men.

"Forward!" he shouted. "Forward men! Drive these fellows out of there! Forward! For God's sake, forward!"

At that moment Reynolds slumped over and fell from his horse. A Confederate sharpshooter more than 200 yards (180 m) away had just made the shot of a lifetime. General Reynolds was the highest-ranking officer of the Union army killed during the Civil War.

Introducing How Do We Know?

Memoirs

Explain that a memoir is a form of autobiographical writing that presents recollections of significant events. It differs from autobiography in that it is less private and introspective and may focus on events and people other than the writer.

Ask why a historian might read memoirs about an event (to learn details from an eyewitness, to expand knowledge of an event by collecting different points of view). Point out that memoirs are not always completely reliable. Veil's, written many years after the Battle of Gettysburg, differs in important details from the account of the event in a letter he wrote soon after the battle. Ask students to speculate why Veil changed his story.

By reading about Veil's memoir and letter, students will better understand the importance of eyewitness accounts and of historians critically examining such accounts and cross-checking them with other evidence.

Setting the Stage Activity

Writing a Memoir

To prepare students to read about a memoir, have them write a brief account of an event they witnessed or took part in. Have them choose an event and describe what they saw and heard. Encourage them to include their reactions to the event.

Critical Thinking

Answers

1. Since the Battle of Gettysburg is often regarded as the turning point of the Civil War, it is important to have an accurate account of the battle and its effects.

2. Knowing the writer's identity and role in the situation helps the reader interpret the writer's point of view and evaluate the reliability of the account.

3. The accuracy of Veil's memoirs might be checked by reading other eyewitness accounts as well as historians' descriptions. By comparing several sources, students can piece together a more accurate account of what really happened.

Bonus Activity

Comparing Accounts

To help students see how easily information can be distorted as it is told and retold, have them play a game of "telephone." Write a brief account of an event on a piece of paper. Read it in a whisper to one student. Have that student repeat it word for word to another, and so on. When the final student has received the message, ask that student to tell the class what the message was. Then read the original message. Discuss how and why the message changed.

History Footnote

John Fulton Reynolds graduated from West Point in 1841 and saw action in the Mexican-American War. He was promoted twice during that war. In 1860 he became the commandant of cadets at West Point. Shortly after the outbreak of the Civil War, he served with distinction in a number of posts. In 1862 Reynolds became the commander of the First Corps of the Army of the Potomac. He was killed on July 1, 1863, the first day of the Battle of Gettysburg. To commemorate Reynolds and the battle, the state of Pennsylvania erected a monument on the spot where he fell.

Sketch of the death of Union General John Reynolds near Gettysburg

Critical Thinking

1. Why do you think historians care about knowing the accurate story of the Battle of Gettysburg?

That story is certain. What happened afterwards is not so certain. What we know is based largely on the testimony of Private Veil.

Veil Tells His Story

For Veil, the death of General Reynolds was such an important episode that he told and retold the story many times. He also described the event at length in his memoirs, which he wrote some 30 years later. **Memoirs** are a person's written remembrances of the events of his or her life.

Memoirs are key historical documents, but sometimes they pose dilemmas for historians. This was true in Veil's case. In a letter to a friend dated April 7, 1864—only months after the event—Veil wrote:

> "When the General fell, the only persons who were with him was Captain Mitchell & Baird and myself. When he fell we sprang from our horses. . . . We were under the impression that he was only stunned, this was all done at a glance. I caught the Gen[era]l under the arms while each of the Capt[ain]s took hold of his legs, and we commenced to carry him out of the woods. . . ."

Critical Thinking

2. When reading someone's memoirs, what information would you like to have about the person? Why?

Yet in his memoirs, written some 30 years after the event, Veil claimed that he was the only witness at the critical moment when General Reynolds was killed. Here is how Veil told the story then:

> "General Reynolds fell upon his face, his arms outstretched toward the enemy. I at once sprang from my horse and ran to his side, gave one glance at his body and seeing no wound or blood, turned his body upon its back. . . . My next impression was to save him from falling into the hands of the enemy. Not having any assistance, not

102

Connections to Literature

Michael Shaara's superb novel about Gettysburg, *The Killer Angels,* published in 1974, describes the shooting and death of General Reynolds. This novel has been praised by several historians, including James M. McPherson and Stephen B. Oates, and by Ken Burns, maker of the television documentary *The Civil War. The Killer Angels* was also the basis for the movie *Gettysburg.*

one of our men being near, I picked him up by taking hold under his arms and commenced pulling him backward toward our line. As I did so, the Confederates yelled 'Drop him! Drop him!' But I kept on backing off as fast as I could and finally got over the brow of the rise, where I found some men and where we were out of range of the enemy's fire."

Critical Thinking

3. Veil's memoirs are now published in book form. If you read the memoirs, how might you go about checking the accuracy of his accounts?

How Do Historians Know?

As time passed, Veil obviously enlarged his role in the event. He made himself more of a hero than he really was, failing to mention those who helped him take the body off the battlefield.

Certainly, Veil had no need to add to the facts. His role in saving the general's body from the enemy was widely known, and he was well rewarded—even by President Lincoln himself. The change in Veil's story could have been deliberate, or he could simply have forgotten. As people age, their memories sometimes fade or they have "selective memory"—remembering only the facts they want to remember.

Accounts of an event are more likely to be accurate when written closer in time to the event. In Veil's case, he gave a more believable account in his April 1864 letter. Because memories can be unreliable, scholars seek evidence from several sources in addition to memoirs. They go over all the descriptions of the event to figure out the facts. In this way, a scholar is like a detective. New discoveries of memoirs and other sources continue to affect the story we call history.

Scholar at Work

Anyone can write memoirs. Think of an important event that happened in your life. Write your memory of the event, telling the story with as many details as possible.

When your memoir is finished, share it with someone else—a parent, brother, sister, or friend—who was also a part of the event. Ask the person to point out any difference in his or her recollections. Working together, try to construct the most accurate story you can.

Discussion

Checking Understanding

1. What important event did Private Charles Henry Veil witness? (He witnessed the shooting of the highest-ranking officer of the Union army killed during the Civil War.)

2. What two accounts did Veil write of this event? (He wrote a letter describing the event and another account of the event in his memoirs.)

3. How do Veil's two accounts differ? (In his memoir, Veil enlarges his role in the event, neglecting to mention the others who helped him remove the body from the battlefield, whom he described in his letter.)

4. What does this suggest about the reliability of sources? (It suggests that memoirs can be unreliable, and historians must seek evidence from more than one source.)

Teaching the Scholar at Work

When you assign the activity, encourage students to list the differences between their versions and those of the others who took part in the events. When all students have completed their accounts, have them share the major differences they found. Can the class discover any pattern or make any generalizations about causes of the differences?

Unit 1

Introducing the Unit

Battle of Shiloh—April 6th, 1862

This lithograph depicts one of the bloodiest battles of the Civil War, which left nearly 3,500 dead and over 20,000 wounded. More Americans died in this two-day battle than in the War of Independence, the War of 1812, and the war with Mexico combined.

Throughout this unit, students will explore the divisions that erupted into the devastating Civil War, and how, through Reconstruction, those rifts in the nation began to heal.

Teaching the Hands-On HISTORY

Have students work in pairs or small groups to discuss the painting and identify details to include in their telegrams. Students should notice the casualties and great amount of physical destruction that has already occurred, as well as the ongoing violence. Ask students to imagine what sounds they might hear from the horses, the weapons, and from the fighters themselves.

Unit Overview

As the nation expanded westward, the conflict over slavery grew. The Compromise of 1850 brought only temporary relief. In April, 1861, the Civil War began.

With the Emancipation Proclamation, the war became a struggle for freedom as well as for preserving the Union. The year 1863 marked a turning point, as Lee was turned back at Gettysburg and Grant took command of the Union army. The South surrendered in 1865.

Reconstruction saw passage of the thirteenth, fourteenth, and fifteenth amendments. However, by 1877 white southerners had regained control of state governments, disenfranchised blacks, and created systems of rigid segregation. African American responses included migrating north, self-help, and open disobedience of Jim Crow laws.

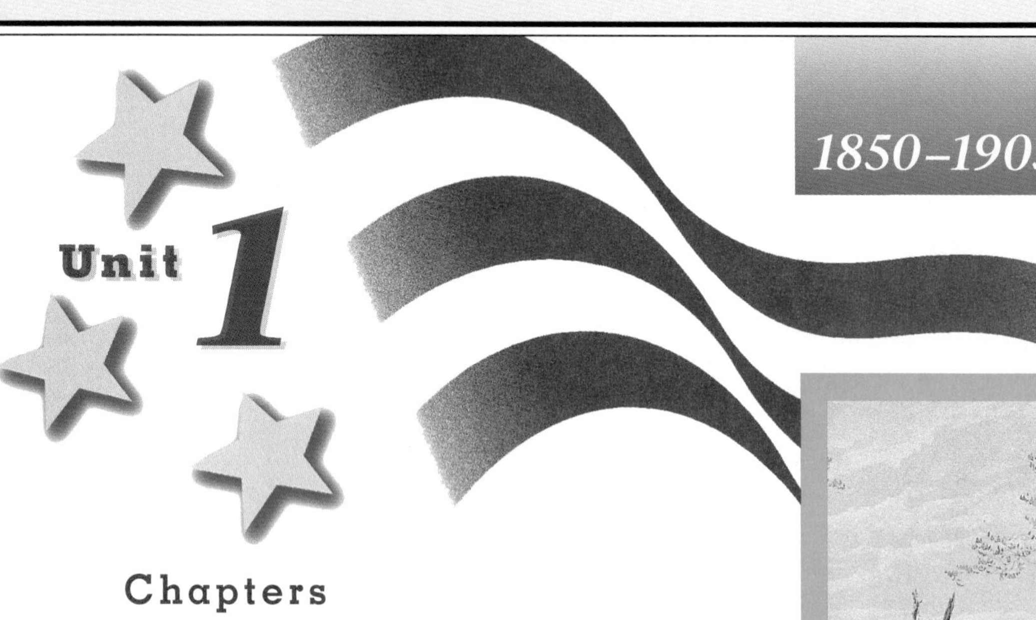

Unit 1

1850–1905

Chapters

Hands-On HISTORY

Activity

In the 1860s there was no radio, television, or Internet. People got their news mainly from newspapers. Imagine that it is 1862 and you are a journalist for a daily paper. You have just arrived at the Battle of Shiloh, in Tennessee, where both sides in the Civil War are suffering heavy losses. Send a telegram to your editor describing the sights and sounds of the battlefield.

Battle of Shiloh—April 6th, 1862 **(detail) published by the McCormick Harvesting Machine Co., Chicago, 1885**

History Footnote

The Battle of Shiloh bears the name of a church located near the battle site. *Shiloh* is a Hebrew word meaning "place of peace." In the painting, Grant and the Union army are shown at the right. The sunken road in the center became known as the "Hornet's Nest," as Union soldiers fired shots from the thickets along the road, confronting repeated Confederate attacks. Though Grant's troops drove back the Confederate forces, heavy losses made the victory a hollow one.

This lithograph, which documents a pivotal battle, served another purpose. McCormick Harvesting Machine Co. included on the print a caption: "The Machines Come Victoriously Out Of Every Contest, And Without A Scratch." Prominently placed in the shed in the lower left, surviving the destruction around it, is a McCormick reaper.

Civil War and Reconstruction

Discussion

Checking Understanding

1. What details suggest this is not a modern battle? (All men are on foot or on horseback; uniforms and guns are old-fashioned; no planes, tanks, or other motorized vehicles.)

Stimulating Critical Thinking

2. What do you think it felt like to be a soldier in this battle? (Students may suggest feelings of fear or confusion.)

3. Why do you think the artist chose to depict a vast number of soldiers, rather than just General Grant? (Accept reasonable responses. For example, the artist may have wanted to give a sense of the many who suffer in war, not just its heroes.)

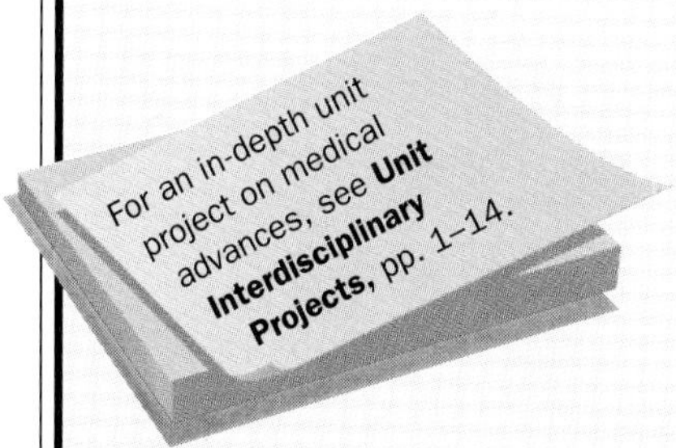

For an in-depth unit project on medical advances, see **Unit Interdisciplinary Projects**, pp. 1–14.

The Unit 1 episode of the *Why We Remember* video series focuses on Clara Barton.

At·a·Glance

1 The Gathering Storm
1846–1861

Chapter Planning Guide

Section	Student Text	Teacher's Edition Activities
Opener and Story pp. 106–109	**Keys to History Time Line** **History Mystery** Beginning the Story with **Abraham Lincoln**	**Setting the Stage Activity** Describing a Future President, p. 108
1 Efforts to Save the Union pp. 110–113		**Warm-Up Activity** Anticipating Issues, p. 110 **Geography Question of the Day,** p. 110 **Section Activity** Exploring the Art of Compromise, p. 112 **Bonus Activity** Protesting the Compromise of 1850, p. 112 **Wrap-Up Activity** Making a Venn Diagram, p. 113
2 The Failure of Compromise pp. 114–119	**Reading Maps** The Spread of Slavery, p. 116 **Hands-On History** Creating an advertisement for Kansas, p. 117 **Skill Lab** Asking Historical Questions, p. 119	**Warm-Up Activity** The Impact of Media, p. 114 **Geography Question of the Day,** p. 114 **Section Activity** Headlines on "Bleeding Kansas," p. 116 **Bonus Activity** An *Uncle Tom's Cabin* Ad, p. 115 **Wrap-Up Activity** Briefing Buchanan, p. 118
3 On the Brink of War pp. 120–127	**Link to the Present** Election campaigns today, p. 122 **Link to Art** *John Brown Going to His Hanging,* p. 123 **Reading Maps** Election of 1860, p. 124 **Point of View** Is secession ever justifiable?, p. 124 **World Link** Freedom for Russian serfs, p. 125 **Geography Lab** The Appalachian Mountains, p. 127	**Warm-Up Activity** Alternatives to Secession, p. 120 **Geography Question of the Day,** p. 120 **Section Activity** Arguing a Court Case, p. 121 **Bonus Activity** Descriptions of Fort Sumter, p. 124 **Wrap-Up Activity** Writing a News Release, p. 126
Evaluation	**Section 1 Review,** p. 113 **Section 2 Review,** p. 118 **Section 3 Review,** p. 126 **Chapter Survey,** pp. 128–129 **Alternative Assessment** Covering the 1860 election on TV, p. 129	**Answers to Section 1 Review,** p. 113 **Answers to Section 2 Review,** p. 118 **Answers to Section 3 Review,** p. 126 **Answers to Chapter Survey,** pp. 128–129 (Alternative Assessment guidelines are in the Take-Home Planner.)

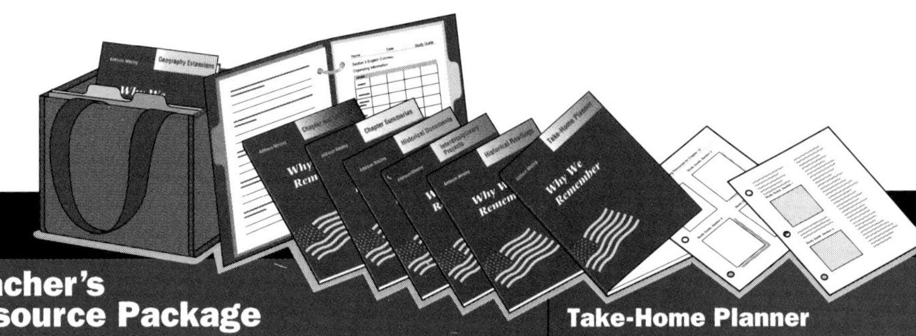

Teacher's Resource Package

Chapter Summaries: English and Spanish, pp. 38–39

Chapter Resources Binder

Study Guide Identifying Viewpoints, p. 17

Reinforcement Interpreting Election Results, pp. 21–22

Using Historical Documents The Compromise of 1850, pp. 27–31

Chapter Resources Binder

Study Guide Using a Time Line, p. 18

Skills Development Asking Historical Questions, pp. 23–24

Chapter Resources Binder

Study Guide Identifying Causes and Effects, p. 19

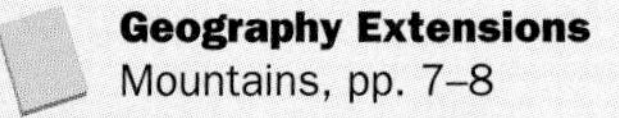
Geography Extensions Describing the Mountains, pp. 7–8

American Readings Lincoln on Slavery, pp. 9–10; Fort Sumter Under Attack, pp. 11–12

Chapter and Unit Tests Chapter 1 Tests, Forms A and B, pp. 23–26

Take-Home Planner

Introducing the Chapter Activity Arguing Against Slavery, p. 6

Chapter In-Depth Activity Examining the Republican Platform, p. 6

Reduced Views

Study Guide, p. 8

Reinforcement, p. 9

Using Historical Documents, p. 11

Unit 1 Answers, pp. 30–38

Reduced Views

Study Guide, p. 8

Skills Development, p. 9

Unit 1 Answers, pp. 30–38

Reduced Views

Study Guide, p. 8

Geography Extensions, p. 11

American Readings, p. 10

Unit 1 Answers, pp. 30–38

Reduced Views

Chapter Tests, p. 11

Unit 1 Answers, pp. 30–38

Alternative Assessment Guidelines for scoring the Chapter Survey activity, p. 7

Additional Resources

Wall Time Line

Unit 1 Activity

Transparency Package

Transparency 1-1 Map: The Spread of Slavery—use with Section 2

Transparency 1-2 *Dividing the National Map*—use with Section 3

Transparency Activity Book

SelecTest Testing Software

Chapter 1 Test, Forms A and B

Vital Links

Videodisc

CD-ROM

Slave auction (see TE p. 111)

Uncle Tom's Cabin poster (see TE p. 115)

Senator attack (see TE p. 117)

Dred and Harriet Scott (see TE p. 120)

Lincoln-Douglas debates (see TE p. 122)

John Brown (see TE p. 123)

Videotape Clara Barton: Eyewitness to the Civil War

1

Teaching Resources

Take-Home Planner 1
- Introducing Chapter Activity
- Chapter In-Depth Activity
- Alternative Assessment

Chapter Resources Binder
Geography Extensions
American Readings
Using Historical Documents
Transparency Activities
Wall Time Line Activities
Chapter Summaries
Chapter and Unit Tests
SelecTest Test File
Vital Links CD-ROM/Videodisc

Chapter Objectives

★ Describe how the conflict over slavery revived as the nation expanded westward.

★ Identify events in the 1850s that continued to divide the North and South.

★ Identify causes of the final break between North and South.

Chapter Overview

As the nation expanded, southerners and northerners had to confront the issue of slavery in the territories. The Compromise of 1850 temporarily calmed the Union. Proslavery forces were given a stronger Fugitive Slave Law and the possibility of new slave states. For slavery foes, California was admitted as a free state, and the slave trade was abolished in Washington, D.C.

Time Line

Keys to History

Keys to History journal writing activities are on page 128 in the Chapter Survey.

Compromise of 1850 This compromise between proslavery and antislavery forces provided temporary relief to an unraveling Union. (p. 112)

Uncle Tom's Cabin Stowe's depiction of the brutality of slave life revitalized abolitionists' cause. (p. 114)

Republican Party formed Former Whigs and Democrats formed this party committed to antislavery issues. (p. 118)

Looking Back This compromise, in which Missouri was admitted as a slave state and slavery was prohibited in the rest of the Louisiana Purchase north of 36° 30′, only temporarily answered the slavery question.

1846–1861

Chapter 1 The Gathering Storm

Sections

Beginning the Story with Abraham Lincoln
1. Efforts to Save the Union
2. The Failure of Compromise
3. On the Brink of War

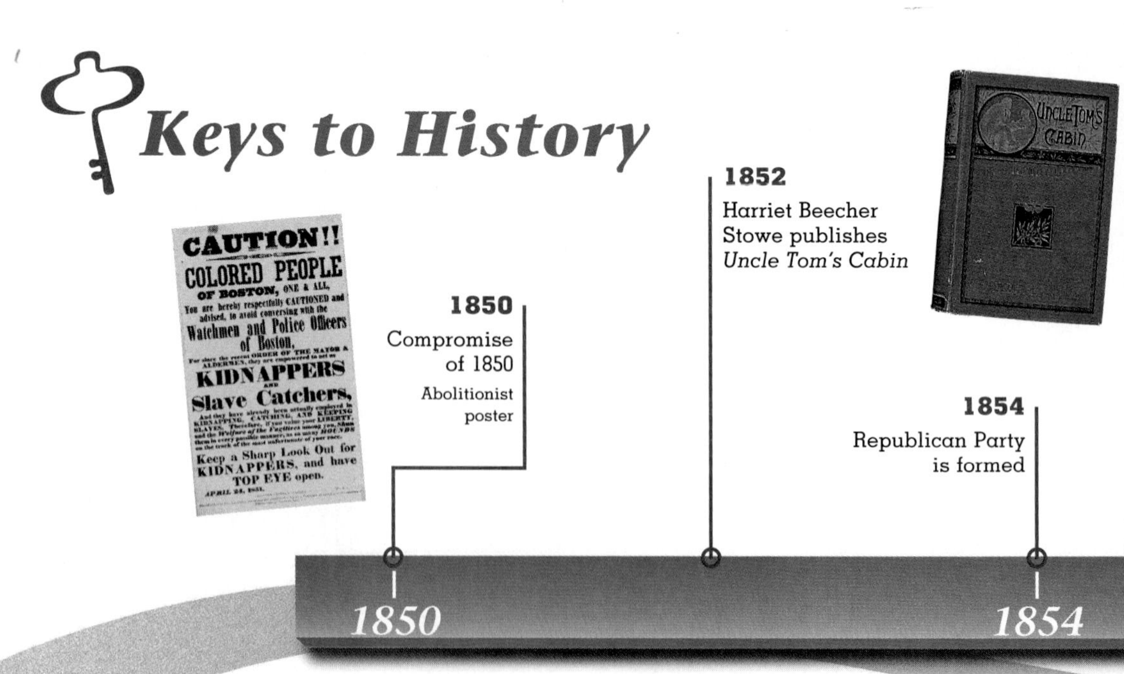

The Compromise of 1850 proved temporary as two key events gave northerners a closer look at slavery: the Fugitive Slave Law brought slave owners north to brutally kidnap escaped slaves, and the novel *Uncle Tom's Cabin* depicted the brutality of slavery. The slavery debate erupted in violence; "Bleeding Kansas" foreshadowed the Civil War. In 1854, former Democratic and Whig party members formed the Republican Party, dedicated to antislavery issues.

In the Dred Scott decision, the Supreme Court ruled that territories were open to slavery, ensuring that the issue dominated the 1860 election. A raid on Harpers Ferry by slavery opponent John Brown further convinced the public that the issue could no longer be ignored. Abraham Lincoln became the first Republican President and leader of a threatened Union: in 1861, the Civil War began.

HISTORY Mystery

In 1855 fewer than 3,000 voters lived in this territory. However, more than 6,000 people voted there in the March election that year. What was the territory, and how could so many people turn out on election day?

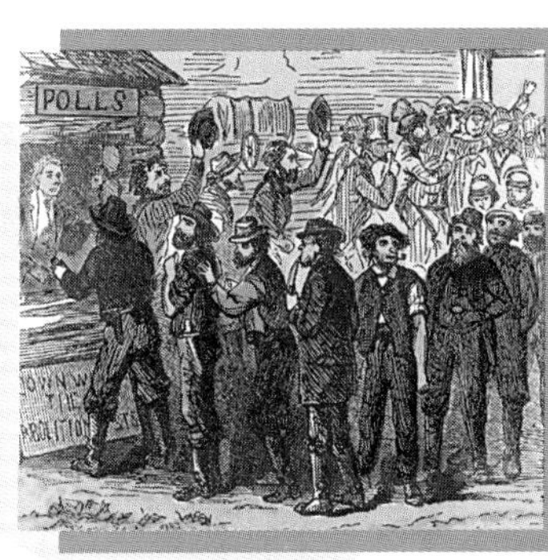

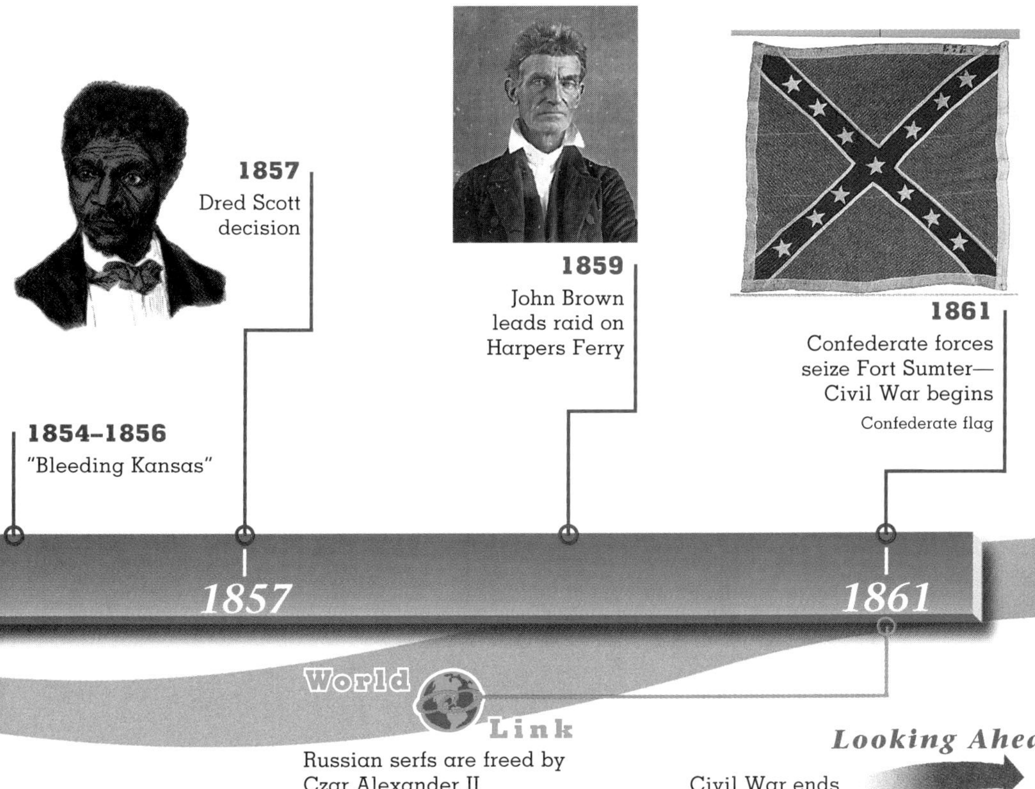

Teaching the *HISTORY* Mystery

Students will find further information on pp. 116–117. See Chapter Survey, p. 128, for additional questions.

Time Line

"Bleeding Kansas" Violence between proslavery and antislavery forces erupted in a year-long battle. (p. 116)

Dred Scott decision In denying this slave's petition for freedom, the Supreme Court ruled that African Americans were not citizens and slavery could not be banned in any territory. (p. 120)

John Brown's raid on Harpers Ferry Brown and his followers seized a federal arsenal as part of their antislavery campaign. Brown was hanged for treason, drawing more attention to the antislavery cause. (p. 122)

Civil War begins Southern states seceded after Lincoln's election, and the new Confederate States of America took Fort Sumter by force, beginning the Civil War. (p. 125)

World Link See p. 125.

Looking Ahead With the surrender of Confederate leaders, the Civil War drew to a close and restoration of the Union began.

Beginning the Story

Abraham Lincoln

Abraham Lincoln's humble early years gave little hint of the almost mythical stature he was to achieve. Largely self-educated, Lincoln became known for his love of reading, his honesty and devotion to justice, and his sense of humor. It is perhaps these very human qualities that made him a leader capable of believing in the equality promised in the Declaration of Independence, and of helping the nation to live up to that promise.

Setting the Stage Activity

Describing a Future President

To prepare students for learning about Lincoln's early years, ask them to imagine that they will be elected President in about 40 years. How would their childhood friends describe them to historians? Have students write short descriptions, from the point of view of a presidential historian, in which they describe how traits exhibited in childhood led to their success as President.

See the Introducing the Chapter Activity, Arguing Against Slavery. **Take-Home Planner 1,** p. 6.

History Footnote

Ralph Waldo Emerson described Lincoln as a man who

> . . . was at home and welcome with the humblest, and had a spirit and a practical vein in the times of terror that commanded the admiration of the wisest. His heart was as great as the world, but there was no room in it to hold the memory of a wrong.

Beginning the Story with

More than a century ago, the great Russian writer Leo Tolstoy visited his country's wild Caucasus Mountains. There, in the south of Russia, he met the chief of a mountain tribe. After listening to Tolstoy for a time, the chief said to him:

> "But you have not told us a syllable about the greatest general and greatest ruler of the world. We want to know something about him. He was a hero. He spoke with a voice of thunder, he laughed at the sunrise and his deeds were strong as the rock. . . . He was so great that he even forgave the crimes of his greatest enemies. . . . His name was Lincoln and the country in which he lived is called America. . . . Tell us of that man."

The Frontier Scholar

Perhaps no one at birth seemed so unlikely a candidate for greatness as Abraham Lincoln. He was born in Kentucky in 1809. His parents, Nancy and Thomas Lincoln, were frontier farmers who lived in a crudely built log cabin and barely knew how to read or write. Searching for a better life, Thomas moved his young family to Indiana, where Abe's mother died when Abe was just 9. The family later moved to Illinois. Bad luck and poverty, however, seemed to follow Thomas Lincoln wherever he went.

Living on the frontier, young Abe had very little education. All in all, he figured that his schooling "did not amount to a year." It was enough, however, to excite a craving for knowledge. Abe read everything he could lay his hands on. "My best friend," he said, "is the man who'll get me a book I ain't read." A cousin recalled, "Abe made books tell him more than they told other people."

History Bookshelf

Myers, Walter Dean. *Now Is Your Time: The African-American Struggle for Freedom.* HarperCollins, 1991. The author uses first-hand accounts and historical photographs and documents to weave the story of African Americans from the beginnings of slavery through the civil rights era. In 1992 he received the Coretta Scott King Award for *Now Is Your Time.*

Also of interest:

Fisher, Leonard Everett. *Tracks Across America: The Story of the American Railroad 1825–1900.* Holiday House, 1992.

Scott, John Anthony, and Robert Alan Scott. *John Brown of Harpers Ferry.* Facts on File, 1988.

"The Rail Splitter"

By the age of 17, Abe Lincoln had grown into a lanky giant well over 6 feet tall. He was amazingly strong and could handle an ax as well as any man. His skill at splitting logs into fence rails would earn him the nickname "The Rail Splitter." Still, Abe disliked physical labor:

> "My father taught me work, but not to love it. I never did like to work, and I don't deny it. I'd rather read, tell stories, crack jokes, talk, laugh—anything but work."

Lincoln tried a number of jobs, from running a store to surveying. As a shopkeeper, he earned a reputation for honesty that stuck with him for life. Stories were told of "Honest Abe" walking 6 miles to return a few cents to a woman who was overcharged for her goods. He finally found his career in the law, where he was paid for doing what he most loved—talking to people. Concerned more with gaining justice for his clients than with making money, Abe charged fees that fellow lawyers thought were laughably low.

As a young man, Abe Lincoln lived an active life. He split logs for fence rails, worked on a river flatboat on two trips to New Orleans, and fought in the Black Hawk War.

Lincoln's concern for justice was matched by his sense of humor, as revealed in the following story. One day, Lincoln said, he and a judge were talking about trading horses. They finally agreed to make a trade at nine o'clock the next morning. Neither man was to see the other's horse before that hour. The following morning the judge arrived leading a pathetic-looking creature not much bigger than a dog. A few minutes later, Lincoln appeared carrying a wooden sawhorse. Looking at the judge's puny horse, Lincoln said, "Well, Judge, this is the first time I ever got the worst of a horse trade."

During the stormy 1850s, Lincoln's sense of justice drew him into politics. At moments of frustration and even failure, his sense of humor saved him from despair. "I laugh," he once said, "because if I didn't I would weep." As Honest Abe became a national leader, he would need all the joy and comfort that laughter could bring.

Hands-On HISTORY Activity

Abe Lincoln loved to tell stories about his life in a down-to-earth way, spiced with humor. Think about some gift you received or something that happened to you that was funny or embarrassing. It could involve your family, perhaps, or a sports event. Then write or tell the story. Remember that you may be President someday and may use this story to help people get to know you.

Discussion

Thinking Historically

1. What qualities did young Lincoln show that may have helped him become a leader? (Craving for knowledge, honesty, concern for justice, sense of humor.)

2. How does Lincoln's background compare with those of most previous Presidents? (Most Presidents had more formal education and came from wealthy families.)

3. Is a sense of humor an important quality for a President? Why or why not? (Yes: humor helps in communicating with different kinds of people and in dealing with the stress of the presidency. No: it is a President's job to handle serious situations, and a sense of humor is irrelevant.)

See the Chapter In-Depth Activity, Examining the Republican Platform.
Take-Home Planner 1, p. 6.

Teaching the Hands-On HISTORY

If students are having difficulty thinking of a topic, remind them that the story does not have to be about a major event: describing a small act of kindness toward a classmate or sibling, for example, would be appropriate.

For a journal writing activity on Abraham Lincoln, see student pages 128–129.

Introducing the Section

Vocabulary

popular sovereignty (p. 110) the right of voters to decide an issue for themselves

Warm-Up Activity

Anticipating Issues

To help students see how westward expansion affected the slavery debate, have them role-play discussions between proslavery and antislavery forces. Divide the class into small groups, with group members evenly divided on both sides of the issue. Pose the question, Should slavery be permitted in the new territories? Ask groups to debate the issue and brainstorm ideas for resolving the conflict. Conclude by having groups share their ideas.

Geography Question of the Day

Ask students to create a two-column chart listing which states were free states and which were slave states as of 1848. Have them refer first to the Missouri Compromise map on page 116. Then have them refer to the list on pages R19–R23 to add the six states admitted between 1822 and 1848.

110

Section Objectives

★ Identify how southerners and northerners differed over the issue of slavery in the territories.
★ Describe the events that led to the Compromise of 1850.
★ Explain how the Compromise of 1850 dealt with the issue of slavery.

Teaching Resources

Take-Home Planner 1, pp. 4–11
Chapter Resources Binder
  Study Guide, p. 17
  Reinforcement, pp. 21–22
  Skills Development
Geography Extensions
American Readings
Using Historical Documents, pp. 27–31
Transparency Activities
Chapter and Unit Tests

1. Efforts to Save the Union

Reading Guide

New Term popular sovereignty

Section Focus Conflict over slavery revives as the United States expands westward

1. **How did southerners and northerners differ over the issue of slavery in the territories?**
2. **What events led to the Compromise of 1850?**
3. **How did the Compromise of 1850 deal with the issue of slavery?**

Abraham Lincoln entered politics during a time of increasing tension between the North and the South. The tension centered around the question of slavery. As the antislavery cause in the North grew in strength, proslavery southerners responded with equal force.

Attempts by the North and South to reach a middle ground did not solve the basic question: Do some people have the right to enslave others? A compromise would ease tensions only until a new crisis arose. In the 1850s the debate over slavery also brought into the open disagreements over states' rights—the idea that states can overrule federal laws—and secession.

Moderates and Radicals

In both North and South, people were divided over slavery. Northern moderates accepted slavery where it existed, but did not want it introduced into new states and territories. Northern radicals demanded an end to slavery everywhere in the United States.

Before the 1830s southern moderates viewed slavery as a necessary evil that would gradually give way to freedom for enslaved people. Southern radicals, however, insisted on the right to extend slavery into all new territories.

Slavery in the West

The slavery controversy came to center stage during the war with Mexico. In 1846 Congressman David Wilmot, a radical northerner, proposed that slavery be prohibited in all territory acquired from Mexico. Southern radicals fought back by demanding that slavery be permitted in all new territories.

To settle the conflict, some moderates from both regions suggested extending the Missouri Compromise line to the Pacific. Other moderates proposed giving voters in each territory **popular sovereignty**—the right to decide for themselves whether to allow slavery. To many people, popular sovereignty seemed the best way to end the debate over slavery in the territories.

The debate did not end, however. Although Wilmot's proposal was defeated in Congress, it exposed hostile feelings between the regions that continued to boil.

Balance of power An ongoing cause of tension was the balance of power in the Senate. As long as there were the same number of free states and slave states, neither North nor South could win a vote on laws related to slavery.

In 1848 slave and free states were, in fact, equal in number. However, Minnesota and

History Footnote
The antislavery Democrats led by Van Buren were called "barn burners." The term came from the story of the Dutch farmer who burned down his barn to get rid of the rats. Van Buren's followers were willing to burn down the barn—the Democratic Party—by forming their own Free Soil political party. They refused to put up with the rats—proslavery Democrats.

See the Reinforcement activity in **Chapter Resources Binder**, pp. 21–22.

Oregon, where residents opposed slavery, had applied for statehood. To avoid upsetting the balance of power, Congress put off admitting them to the Union.

The Election of 1848

During the 1848 presidential campaign both Democrats and Whigs avoided the topic of slavery. The Democrats chose a northern moderate, Senator Lewis Cass, as their candidate. The Whigs turned to General Zachary Taylor, a hero of the War with Mexico.

Angry that the two major parties were ignoring the slavery issue, antislavery forces formed the Free Soil Party. With former President Martin Van Buren as their candidate, the Free Soilers won enough northern votes away from the Democrats to throw the election to Taylor and the Whigs. The Free Soilers' success showed that the conflict over slavery in the territories was not over.

California and Popular Sovereignty

In 1849 the issue of slavery demanded fresh attention when California voters adopted a constitution banning slavery in their territory. President Taylor, who favored popular sovereignty, supported their decision and called for California statehood. People in present-day New Mexico and Utah also wanted their areas to become free states.

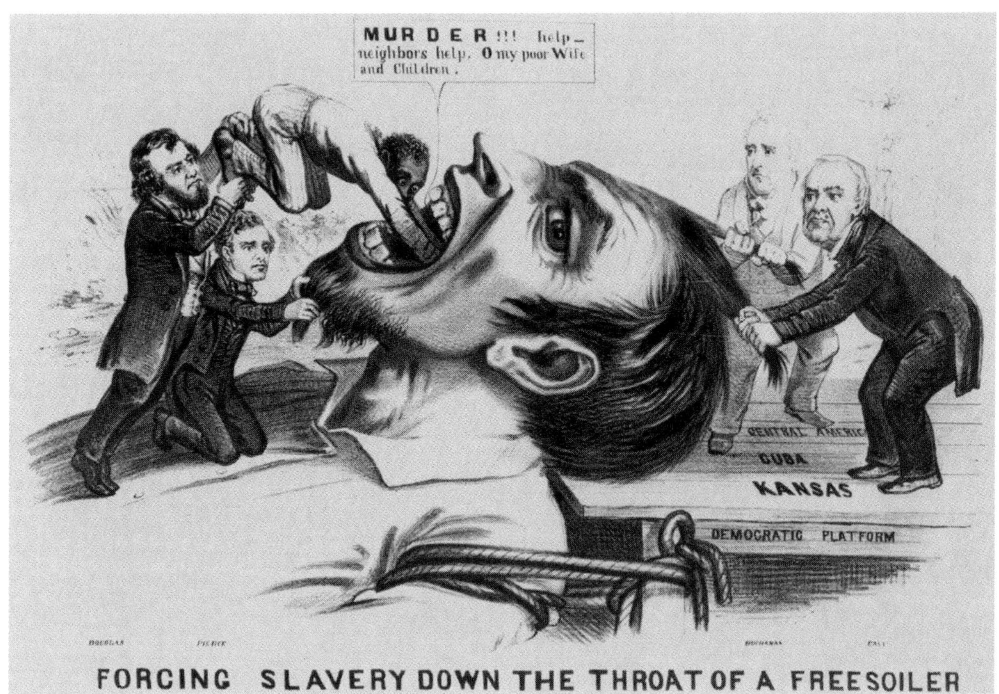

FORCING SLAVERY DOWN THE THROAT OF A FREESOILER

As this cartoon shows, Free Soilers feared that popular sovereignty would force the slave system down their throats.

Developing the Section

Discussion

Checking Understanding

1. How were northern and southern moderates similar? (Both were willing to accept slavery to some extent.)

2. Why was the Free Soil Party formed? (It was formed by antislavery forces who were angry that the Democrats and Whigs were avoiding the slavery issue.)

Stimulating Critical Thinking

3. Some moderates believed that slavery would eventually die out. Do you agree? Why or why not? (Yes: with increasing use of farm machines, slave labor would become less and less practical. No: southern economy had relied on slave labor too long to change; southern radicals were determined to preserve and spread slavery.)

Vital Links

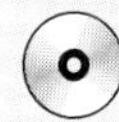
Slave auction (Picture)
Unit 3, Side 1, Search 32895

See also Unit 3 Explore CD-ROM location 182.

See the Study Guide activity in **Chapter Resources Binder**, p. 17.

Section Activity

Exploring the Art of Compromise

To help students understand the challenge of compromise, have them select a current controversial issue, such as welfare reform, prayer in schools, or the death penalty. Divide the class into small groups and provide time to discuss the topic. Within each group, members should state their opinions and provide supporting reasons. Then the group should try to arrive at a compromise acceptable to all members. Conclude by having each group report on the results, discussing why it was difficult to reach a compromise.

Bonus Activity

Protesting the Compromise of 1850

To underscore that the compromise did not settle the slavery issue, have students imagine themselves as either radical antislavery or proslavery protestors in 1850. Have them either write a letter to their senator or draw a cartoon criticizing the Compromise of 1850. Conclude by asking volunteers to share their protests.

History Footnote

Daniel Webster was a known opponent of slavery. In his personal life, he supported the cause of freed slaves and donated money to help them buy freedom for their families. Yet in his political life, he valued moderation above all else. In a speech supporting the Compromise of 1850 he noted, "In all such disputes, there will sometimes be found men with whom everything is absolute; absolutely wrong, or absolutely right." Webster refused to take an absolute stand against slavery. For his willingness to compromise, he was seen by northern radicals as a traitor.

Taylor's action launched one of the greatest debates in the Senate's history. This time, the argument went beyond the issue of slavery. It called into question the very future of the United States.

The Compromise of 1850

Two generations met on the Senate floor to debate the issue of slavery in the territories. Henry Clay, Daniel Webster, and John C. Calhoun represented the older generation. Among those who would lead the Senate in the future were Jefferson Davis, Stephen A. Douglas, and William H. Seward.

Clay Henry Clay, with a reputation for settling disagreements, led the Senate session. The "Great Compromiser" had prevented a showdown between the North and South in 1820 when he pushed through the Missouri Compromise. Many senators hoped that he could do it again.

Now 73 years old and in ill health, Clay fashioned a plan for dealing with the two main issues: slavery in the West and the return of escaped slaves. He called for admitting California as a free state, but not restricting slavery in the other territories gained from Mexico. He also proposed a more aggressive fugitive slave law.

Calhoun John C. Calhoun, a southerner, rejected Clay's plan. It would not guarantee the right to slavery in the territories, he claimed. He also demanded an even tougher fugitive slave law. Treat the South fairly, he warned the Senate, or the South would secede.

In his final role as the Great Compromiser, Henry Clay (center) tried to persuade the Senate to vote for the Compromise of 1850.

For an activity on analyzing the original text of the Compromise of 1850, see Using Historical Documents, pp. 27–31.

COMPROMISE OF 1850

Provisions favoring proslavery forces

- New Mexico and Utah to become territories. The slavery question to be decided by popular sovereignty.
- The new Fugitive Slave Law to require the return of escaped slaves, even slaves who had reached the North.
- Slavery still legal in Washington, D.C.

Provisions favoring antislavery forces

- California to be admitted to the Union as a free state.
- The slave trade to be abolished in Washington, D.C.

Weakened by throat cancer, Calhoun had another Senator read his speech:

> "How can the Union be saved? She [the South] has no compromise to offer. If you are unwilling [to meet our demands] we should part in peace."

Webster Daniel Webster, a northern moderate, pleaded for the nation's unity:

> "I wish to speak today, not as a Massachusetts man, nor as a northern man, but as an American. I speak today for the preservation of the Union."

Webster's plea fell on deaf ears as northern radicals took on southern radicals. William H. Seward saw compromise over slavery as "radically wrong." Representative Horace Mann believed that the world would view the United States "with disgust" for allowing slavery.

Agreement at last Events took a sudden twist when President Taylor—a staunch opponent of compromise—fell ill from cholera and died on July 9, 1850. The new President, Millard Fillmore, came out firmly for Clay's compromise. By this time Congress knew that voters in both the North and the South favored compromise. As a result, it passed the Compromise of 1850 (see chart to the left and map on page 116).

With the passage of the Compromise of 1850, President Fillmore claimed that the nation had found "the final settlement" that would end the arguments over slavery. In fact the nation did settle into a prosperous peace for the next few years. However, Fillmore had spoken too quickly. The crisis over slavery was far from ended.

1. Section Review

1. Define **popular sovereignty.**
2. Explain the positions of northern radicals and moderates on the issue of slavery.
3. What problem did President Taylor confront and how did he handle it?
4. **Critical Thinking** As a southern radical, how would you have voted on each measure in the 1850 Compromise and why?

Closing the Section

Wrap-Up Activity

Making a Venn Diagram

To review the different views on slavery, have students create a Venn diagram with two intersecting circles representing pro- and antislavery views. Where the circles overlap, they should place moderate views, such as, "accept slavery where it exists." Northern and southern radical views should be placed in the other two areas.

Section Review

Answers

1. Definition: *popular sovereignty* (110)

2. Northern radicals demanded an end to slavery everywhere in the U.S.; moderates accepted slavery where it existed, but did not want it in new territories.

3. By voting in 1849 to ban slavery, Californians brought renewed attention to the issue, which was ignored by major parties in the 1848 election. Since Taylor supported popular sovereignty, he called for California statehood.

4. A southern radical would probably support the new Fugitive Slave Law and continuation of slavery in Washington, D.C., and would oppose the other measures because they would curb slavery's expansion.

Introducing the Section

Vocabulary

transcontinental railroad (p. 115) a rail line across the continent, linking east and west

platform (p. 118) a statement of a political party's beliefs

Warm-Up Activity

The Impact of Media

To prepare for reading about *Uncle Tom's Cabin,* have students find current examples of how media brings attention to problems. Have the class select a problem such as drug abuse, gang violence, or poverty. Then ask them to identify ways that have been used recently to make the public more aware of the problem, such as specific movies, television shows, books, stories, billboards, and songs. Conclude by discussing which ways seem most effective and why.

Geography Question of the Day

Tell students they are to decide where 5,000 miles of railroad track are to be laid in the U.S. Have them trace on an outline map (from **Geography Extensions**) their ideas for routes, taking into consideration population density and terrain as indicated on the maps on pages R8 and R11.

Section Objectives

- ★ Explain how the Fugitive Slave Law and *Uncle Tom's Cabin* affected the slavery debate.
- ★ Describe how the Kansas-Nebraska Act increased tensions between the North and the South.
- ★ Explain why the Republican Party formed and describe its impact at that time.

Teaching Resources

Take-Home Planner 1, pp. 4–11
Chapter Resources Binder
Study Guide, p. 18
Reinforcement
Skills Development, pp. 23–24
Geography Extensions
American Readings
Using Historical Documents
Transparency Activities
Chapter and Unit Tests

2. The Failure of Compromise

Reading Guide

New Terms **transcontinental railroad, platform**

Section Focus **Events in the 1850s continue to divide the North and South**

1. How did the Fugitive Slave Law and *Uncle Tom's Cabin* affect the slavery debate?
2. How did the Kansas-Nebraska Act increase tensions between the North and the South?
3. Why did the new Republican Party form and what was its impact at the time?

The Compromise of 1850 brought only temporary relief to the nation. Americans were still deeply divided over slavery and states' rights, and it was not long before conflicts broke out again.

Three events shattered the calm. They were the enforcement of the new Fugitive Slave Law, the publication of the antislavery novel *Uncle Tom's Cabin,* and a violent struggle over slavery in Kansas. This time, efforts at compromise would fail.

The Fugitive Slave Law

Most northerners despised the Fugitive Slave Law of 1850. The law denied escaped slaves the right to have a jury trial and to testify in court on their own behalf. Anyone who helped a slave escape could be fined $1,000 and jailed for six months. Slave catchers received $10 for every African American they kidnapped in the North and brought to a slave owner in the South.

Before the new law, slavery had existed far from where most northerners lived. Now they had a firsthand look, as slave hunters came north, seeking escaped slaves. Almost 200 African Americans, even some free blacks who were not escaped slaves, were captured and sent to the South.

Northerners reacted against the kidnappings to the point of violence. A Pennsylvania mob killed a kidnapper. Frederick Douglass, himself an escaped slave, declared that "the only way to make the Fugitive Slave Law a dead letter [law] is to make half a dozen dead kidnappers."

The Fugitive Slave Law drove a deeper wedge between the North and the South. Southerners were outraged at northern resistance to it. They accused the North of breaking the Compromise of 1850. Northerners, on the other hand, were shocked by the cruelty of the law. It caused many of them to become more radical in their views of slavery.

Uncle Tom's Cabin

Northern outrage over the Fugitive Slave Law was mild, though, compared to the storm that arose when Harriet Beecher Stowe published *Uncle Tom's Cabin* in 1852. In this dramatic tale a religious and loyal old slave named Uncle Tom is beaten to death by orders of Simon Legree, one of the most hated villains in American literature.

Have you ever read a book that changed your way of thinking? Stowe's goal was to write such a book. By depicting the brutality

Connections to Literature

In addition to depicting the physical brutality suffered by the slaves, Stowe attempted in her work to show readers the emotional misery that results from families being separated by slaveholders. In a letter written soon after the publication of *Uncle Tom's Cabin,* she recounted her own heartache at the death of one of her seven children: "It was at his dying bed and at his grave that I learned what a poor slave mother may feel when her child is torn away from her." It is by this common thread of humanity that Stowe, in concluding remarks added to the novel, urged all women to take a stand against slavery. "I beseech you, pity those mothers that are constantly made childless by the American slave-trade!"

of slave life on a plantation, she wanted to awaken Americans to the evil in their midst.

Stowe succeeded beyond her wildest dreams. Within a year the book was a best-seller, outsold only by the Bible. As a play it shocked audiences around the world. People who read or saw *Uncle Tom's Cabin* could no longer close their eyes to slavery.

Many southerners, however, claimed that the story was full of lies. They feared that it would strengthen the influence of anti-slavery radicals in the North.

The Election of 1852

In the election of 1852, the Democrats nominated Franklin Pierce, who had promised to enforce the Compromise of 1850—including the Fugitive Slave Law. The Whig candidate, General Winfield Scott, took no stand on the compromise.

Pierce won almost every state. His landslide victory proved that despite the angry feelings caused by the Fugitive Slave Law and *Uncle Tom's Cabin,* most Americans still clung to the hope that the issue of slavery had been settled.

The Kansas-Nebraska Act

As it turned out, the 1852 election marked only a brief pause in the sectional conflict over slavery. The struggle started again when Senator Stephen Douglas of Illinois introduced a bill to be known as the Kansas-Nebraska Act.

A new railroad Douglas proposed that the nation build a **transcontinental railroad**—a rail line across the continent, linking east and west. He wanted it to begin at Chicago, in his home state of Illinois, and run to California. This transcontinental railroad would only succeed, Douglas thought, if the land west of the Mississippi was organized into territories.

Meanwhile, railroad boosters in the South wanted a southern route to California and the Pacific. They advised that their route would have several advantages. It would be much easier to lay tracks across the flat terrain of this route. In addition, the land needed for such a rail line—the Gadsden Purchase—had already been obtained from Mexico in 1853.

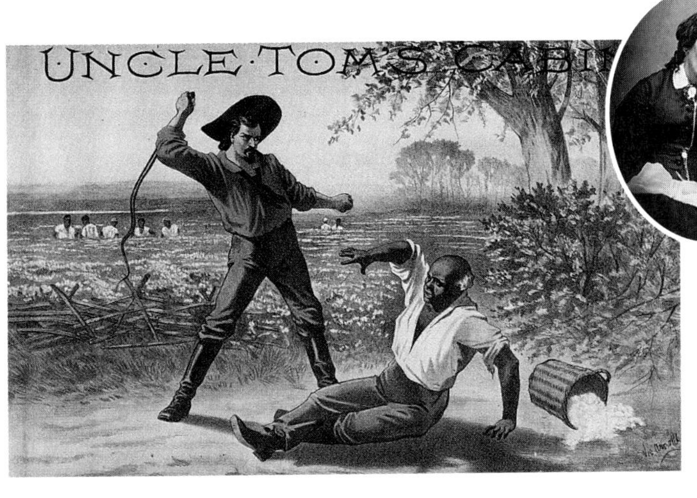

The cruelty and terror of slave life is captured by this poster for *Uncle Tom's Cabin.* Harriet Beecher Stowe (above) mistakenly feared that her future best-seller would be a failure.

Developing the Section

Discussion

Checking Understanding

1. How did the Fugitive Slave Law affect northern views on slavery? (By giving northerners a firsthand look at the cruelty of slavery it increased opposition.)

Stimulating Critical Thinking

2. Do you think slavery opponents were right in using violence against kidnappers? Why or why not? (Yes: need to prevent capture of those who escaped; best way to undercut Fugitive Slave Law. No: violence never justified; undercuts moral opposition.)

Bonus Activity

An *Uncle Tom's Cabin* Ad

Have students create a poster for the stage play of *Uncle Tom's Cabin.* They should target as their audience northerners who think slaves were treated well. Suggest that they use ads for movies as models.

Vital Links

***Uncle Tom's Cabin* poster (Picture) Unit 3, Side 1, Search 32871**

See also Unit 3 Explore CD-ROM location 178.

Section Activity

Headlines on "Bleeding Kansas"

To illustrate contrasting views of the Kansas conflict, have students create headlines for proslavery and antislavery newspapers. Divide the class into small groups, with half of them role-playing antislavery newspaper staffs and the other half proslavery newspaper staffs. Each group then plans a layout with headlines reflecting its bias, in choice of both words and topics emphasized. Possible topics include the Kansas-Nebraska Act, the election, laws passed by the proslavery legislature, the antislavery legislature, the attack on Lawrence, Brown's attack, and the killing of Brown's son. Conclude by having groups compare headlines and discuss how they reflect bias.

Teaching the Reading Maps

Point out the map key, ensuring that students understand how the four statuses differ. **Answer to Reading Maps:** Oregon Territory: closed to slavery by Compromise of 1850. Kansas Territory: closed to slavery in 1820 and 1850; in 1854 became open to slavery by popular sovereignty. Texas: by 1850 it had become a slave state.

History Footnote

The development of the railroad during the 1800s was pivotal to the economic development of the U.S. By 1860, the nation had more miles of railroad track than the rest of the world combined, making shipping freight by rail far more practical and affordable than by the former leading means of transportation, the steamboat. The railroad had a direct impact on urban growth, as well. Chicago, easily accessible by rail, saw its population nearly quadruple during the 1850s. With trains traveling at roughly 30 miles an hour, the trip from New York to Chicago was reduced from three weeks to just two days. The transcontinental railroad was finally authorized by Congress in 1862 and completed in 1869.

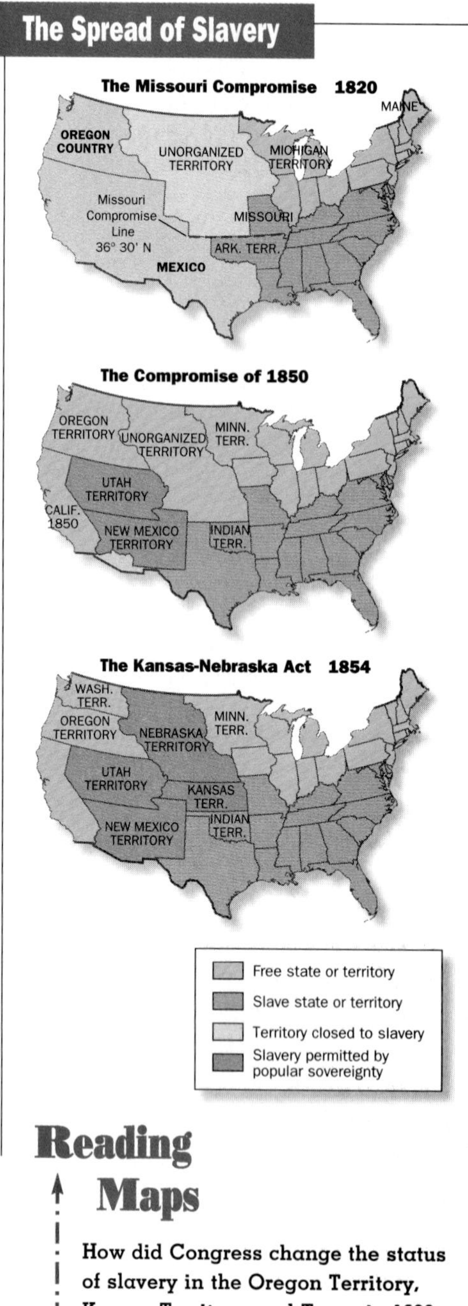

Reading Maps

How did Congress change the status of slavery in the Oregon Territory, Kansas Territory, and Texas in 1820, 1850, and 1854?

Kansas and Nebraska To win southern support for his northern route, Douglas called for popular sovereignty in lands to be organized as the Kansas and Nebraska territories (see map on this page).

Southerners supported the popular sovereignty idea because it allowed for the possibility of additional slave states. Northerners, however, were angry that the Kansas-Nebraska Act would overturn the Missouri Compromise of 1820, which barred slavery from that area.

What had begun as a proposal for a transcontinental railroad quickly turned into another crisis over slavery in the territories. Northern objections to Douglas's bill were loud and hostile. Still, with the support of southern congressmen and President Franklin Pierce, a Democrat, the Kansas-Nebraska bill became law in May 1854.

"Bleeding Kansas"

Douglas thought that the tempers that had flared during the Kansas-Nebraska debate would soon cool. Instead, the fight moved beyond the Senate floor to Kansas itself. The question of slavery there was to be decided by whichever side had the most voters. Senator William H. Seward of New York laid down the challenge:

> "Gentlemen of the Slave States, we will engage in competition for the virgin soil of Kansas, and God give victory to the side which is . . . right."

Antislavery settlers from the North raced to Kansas. They were met by proslavery settlers from the South, particularly from Missouri. Each group hoped to gain control of the territory in the upcoming election.

Two Kansas governments On election day in March 1855, nearly 5,000 Missouri residents crossed into Kansas. Their

History Footnote

Preston Brooks's vicious attack, in which he hit Charles Sumner over the head with a cane more than 30 times, heightened the level of anger between the North and the South. Even northerners who found Sumner's speech harsh denounced the attack as a symbol of southerners' mistreatment of slaves. Southerners treated Brooks as a hero who had acted nobly to defend the South's honor. Northerners in Congress tried to expel Brooks but failed because of southern support. Brooks resigned anyway and easily won re-election. His only punishment was a $300 fine. After the attack, supporters sent new canes to Brooks, some inscribed with mottoes such as "Hit Him Again." This enthusiastic show of support for Brooks only further angered northerners and widened the rift between the two regions.

illegal votes gave the victory to proslavery candidates. The new legislature quickly passed laws protecting slavery in Kansas.

Outraged antislavery settlers in Kansas refused to accept the proslavery legislature. They elected their own legislature and set up their own government.

John Brown in Kansas With sides now sharply drawn, Kansas became a dress rehearsal for the Civil War. In May 1856 a proslavery army of "Border Ruffians" from Missouri marched into the antislavery town of Lawrence and set it on fire.

The "sack of Lawrence" inspired an abolitionist named John Brown to seek revenge. Lean, strong, and "straight . . . as a mountain pine," Brown led four of his sons and several others to a proslavery settlement. There they murdered five men by splitting open their heads with swords. In retaliation, proslavery forces killed one of Brown's sons. Brown did not back down. He vowed:

> "I have only a short time to live [and] only one death to die, and I will die fighting for this cause."

These brutal deaths touched off a year-long war in Kansas. Two hundred lives were lost and many homes were burned before federal troops finally restored order to "Bleeding Kansas" in late 1856.

Violence in the Senate The violence in Kansas spilled over into the halls of Congress. In a speech in May of 1856, Charles Sumner, an abolitionist senator from Massachusetts, attacked slaveholders for the "crime [committed] against Kansas."

Three days later, Representative Preston Brooks of South Carolina broke his cane over Sumner's head while Sumner was seated at his desk. Brooks was furious that Sumner had insulted Brooks's uncle in the speech. Sumner, severely injured, did not return to the Senate for more than two years.

Hands-On HISTORY

Creating an advertisement for Kansas Has your family ever used a travel agent? Present-day travel agencies help people arrange vacation trips. In the 1850s, agencies in the North served another purpose: to help antislavery settlers move to the Kansas Territory so that it would become a free state.

Activity Imagine you are an agent working for a northern antislavery organization in 1854. Create an advertisement encouraging people to move to Kansas.

1. Design and write a full-page advertisement that appeals to your readers' feelings about slavery, and to their dislike for the opposing side. You will also want to highlight the attraction of Kansas itself: good soil and plenty of open land.
2. What illustrations might you use?
3. Share your finished ad with your classmates. Do they find it persuasive? Why or why not?

Poster promoting Kansas

Discussion

Checking Understanding

1. Why did Douglas propose popular sovereignty in the Kansas and Nebraska territories? (He wanted southerners to support his plan for a northern rail route.)

Stimulating Critical Thinking

2. Do you think antislavery settlers in Kansas had a right to set up their own government? Why or why not? (Yes: election results were obtained illegally. No: would be a disaster if a group set up a new government every time they lost an election.)

3. If you met John Brown in 1856, what would you tell him? (Accept reasonable responses, such as attempts to convince Brown to pursue his cause nonviolently or expressions of support for his antislavery views.)

Teaching the Hands-On HISTORY

In preparation for creating their advertisements, have students do research to find more information about Kansas. For example, they might identify natural resources that would be appealing to settlers.

Vital Links

Senator attack (Picture) Unit 3, Side 1, Search 37464

See also Unit 3 Explore CD-ROM location 206.

Closing the Section

Wrap-Up Activity

Briefing Buchanan

To review the events of the 1850s that further divided the Union, have pairs of students role-play a briefing between the newly elected President Buchanan and an advisor. The advisor should summarize factors that have increased tensions between the North and the South, identifying which are the major threats to national unity.

Section Review Answers

1. Definitions: *transcontinental railroad* (115), *platform* (118)
2. It allowed for the possibility of additional slave states.
3. Northerners who opposed the spread of slavery wanted a party that would commit itself to antislavery issues.
4. Accept reasonable responses. For example, students may think seeing a slave kidnapper in person may have been more powerful than reading a work of fiction, while others may find the story of Uncle Tom more moving.

See the Study Guide activity in **Chapter Resources Binder,** p. 18.

Tips for Teaching

Gifted Students

Gifted students benefit from exploring issues or topics in greater depth. Provide opportunities for independent projects or more elaborate treatments of activity suggestions. For instance, in addition to the Bonus Activity on creating an ad for *Uncle Tom's Cabin,* they might read the novel and write a review.

SOUTHERN CHIVALRY — ARGUMENT VERSUS CLUB'S.

Senator Sumner was praised by fellow New Englanders for his speech attacking slaveholders. Preston Brooks, a southern member of Congress, detested the speech, however. He is shown here beating Sumner on the Senate floor.

A New Republican Party

Meanwhile, northerners who opposed the spread of slavery had grown impatient with the Democratic and Whig parties. They wanted a party that would commit itself to antislavery issues. In 1854 such a party was formed. It was named the Republican Party, after the party founded by Jefferson.

The Republican Party **platform**—a statement of a political party's beliefs—took stands against the Kansas-Nebraska Act and the Fugitive Slave Law. Running on that platform, Republican candidates swept the 1854 elections in the North, especially in the Midwest. Soon, northern Whigs and Democrats were joining the new party, adding to its strength. As a result, the Democrats' main base of power shifted to the South.

The Election of 1856 The Republicans first attempted to gain the presidency in 1856. They selected John C. Frémont, western explorer and opponent of slavery, as their candidate. He campaigned with the slogan, "Free Soil, Free Speech, and Frémont." Abraham Lincoln, who had joined the Republicans, narrowly missed being nominated for Vice-President.

The Democrats were expected to nominate Stephen A. Douglas. However, they knew that the Kansas-Nebraska Act had made him unpopular with northern voters. Instead, the Democrats chose James Buchanan. He had been serving overseas as minister to England, and thus he had not taken a stand in the Kansas-Nebraska debate.

Although Frémont took 11 of the 16 free states, Buchanan won the election by carrying the southern states and 5 of the free states. As people became more alarmed that the nation might break apart, it remained to be seen if President Buchanan could hold the country together.

2. Section Review

1. Define **transcontinental railroad** and **platform.**
2. Why did southerners support the Kansas-Nebraska Act?
3. Why was the Republican Party founded?
4. Critical Thinking As a northerner, which would have affected your feelings about slavery more: the Fugitive Slave Law or *Uncle Tom's Cabin*? Explain why.

(Answers continued from side margin)
treated this way? Were other plantations similar? What was the purpose in writing? For Source B: Did the writer get information from slaves or masters? Might his point of view lead to proslavery bias? What is the evidence that women needed protection from husbands? For Source C: Were Legree and Tom based on real people? Where did the author get information on them? Are they stereotypes?

4. (a) Answers depend on questions. (b) Some possibilities: historians' descriptions, accounts by former slaves, anti- or proslavery writings or pictures.

For further application, have students do the Applying Skills activity in the Chapter Survey (p. 128).

If students need to review the skill, use the Skills Development transparency and activity in the Chapter Resources Binder, pp. 23–24.

Skill Lab

Using Information

Asking Historical Questions

Its promoters called it "The Greatest Book of the Age." It ranked second only to the Bible as a bestseller. *Uncle Tom's Cabin* awakened northerners to the cruelties of slavery—and enraged proslavery southerners. In essays, speeches, and even poems, southerners defended slavery as being good for both master and slave.

Question to Investigate

How were slaves treated?

Procedure

Imagine that you are a historian studying how slaves were treated. As you read the following sources, direct your research by asking historical questions.

1 **Write a sentence stating your goal.**

2 **Identify the information.**
a. Read sources A and B carefully.
b. Make a column for each source. List what each source says about the treatment of slaves.

3 **Identify questions to ask.**
a. Read the Skill Tips for examples.
b. List three questions about each source.

4 **Decide how to get the answers.**
a. Write the answers you know.
b. Name three ways you might get more information.

Is this Source believable?

Skill Tips

Ask yourself questions like these:
- Is this a statement of fact, opinion, or fiction?
- Is this a credible source?
- How might the author's background affect what he or she wrote?
- Are the claims supported by enough evidence?
- Are there signs of bias, overgeneralizations, or stereotypes?

Sources to Use

A "The negro slaves of the South are the happiest and, in some sense, the freest people in the world. . . . The women do little hard work, and are protected from the despotism [cruelty] of their husbands by their masters. The negro men and stout boys work, on the average, in good weather, not more than nine hours a day."

From an 1857 essay by the Virginia lawyer George Fitzhugh

B "'And now,' said Legree, 'come here, you Tom. . . . take this yer gal and flog her; ye've seen enough on't to know how.'

'I beg Mas'r's pardon,' said Tom, '. . . It's what I an't used to—never did—and can't do, no way possible.'

'Ye'll larn a pretty smart chance of things ye never did know before I've done with ye!' said Legree, taking up a cowhide and striking Tom a heavy blow across the cheek, and following up the infliction by a shower of blows. 'There!' he said, 'now will ye tell me ye can't do it?'

'Yes Mas'r,' said Tom, putting up his hand to wipe the blood that trickled down his face. 'I'm willin' to work night and day, and work while there's breath in me; but this yer thing I can't feel it right to do; and Mas'r, I *never* shall do it—*never!*'"

From Harriet Beecher Stowe's 1852 novel, *Uncle Tom's Cabin*

Introducing the Skill Lab

Point out that the goal is to find the truth, and that students will use skills applied in earlier labs. Direct attention to the Skill Tips, reviewing the meaning of fact, opinion, credibility, point of view, evidence, bias, generalization, and stereotype. Ask how each Skills Tips question is relevant to finding truth. Have students suggest specific questions similar to each one. (For example, on credibility: "Where did the writer get information?") Show how skills connect to each other. (For example, detecting bias may raise questions about point of view.)

Skill Lab

Answers

1. Goal should be realistically limited to the task, such as: I want to compare how these sources describe treatment of slaves.

2. Source A: beaten so often "aching bones" were constant; "never too hot or too cold" to force work; "broken in body, soul, and spirit." Source B: happiest, freest people; women do little hard work, protected by masters; men and boys work no more than nine hours a day. Source C: slaves ordered to flog others; flogged often.

3. Some questions for Source A: Were all the slaves

(Answers continued in top margin)

Introducing the Section

Warm-Up Activity

Alternatives to Secession

To focus attention on the secession issue, ask students to imagine that residents in your state today oppose a particular federal law. Have small groups brainstorm ideas for actions they might take, such as trying their case in court, rallying support of voters throughout the nation to oppose the law, or even moving to another country. Discuss the potential effects of each action.

Geography Question of the Day

Ask students to review the maps on page 116 and to write a paragraph giving a northern radical's view of the good and bad points of the changing status of slavery in the growing nation.

Vital Links

Dred and Harriet Scott (Picture) Unit 3, Side 1, Search 32799

See also Unit 3 Explore CD-ROM location 166.

Section Objectives

- ★ Describe how Dred Scott and the Lincoln-Douglas debates kept the slavery issue alive.
- ★ Explain how John Brown's raid and the 1860 election doomed hopes for compromise.
- ★ Describe the South's response to Abraham Lincoln's election.

Teaching Resources

Take-Home Planner 1, pp. 4–11
Chapter Resources Binder
Study Guide, p. 19
Reinforcement
Skills Development
Geography Extensions, pp. 7–8
American Readings, pp. 9–12
Using Historical Documents
Transparency Activities
Chapter and Unit Tests, pp. 23–26

3. On the Brink of War

Reading Guide

Section Focus The causes of the final break between North and South

1. How did Dred Scott and the Lincoln-Douglas debates keep the slavery issue alive?
2. How did John Brown's raid and the 1860 election doom hopes for compromise?
3. What was the South's response to Abraham Lincoln's election?

The 1856 election had avoided an all-out fight over the slavery question. However, whether it bubbled below the surface or exploded into open debate, slavery was an issue that would not go away.

James Buchanan had been President only two days when yet another crisis rocked the nation. On March 7, 1857, the Supreme Court announced its decision in the case of *Dred Scott* v. *Sandford*.

Dred Scott Decision

Dred Scott had been the slave of a Missouri surgeon, who had taken him to Illinois and the Wisconsin Territory. They lived there for several years before returning to Missouri. In 1846 Scott claimed in court that the years he had lived on free northern soil had made him a free man. The jury ruled in his favor, but the Missouri Supreme Court overruled the decision.

Soon after the Court ruled that Dred Scott must remain a slave, Scott finally gained his freedom from a new owner. He died just a year later.

Scott took his case to the United States Supreme Court. In *Dred Scott* v. *Sandford,* the Court ruled against Scott by a vote of 7 to 2. In the first place, the justices said, Scott did not have a right to a trial. African Americans—enslaved or free—were not citizens, and thus could not bring suits in federal court.

The Court also ruled that the Missouri Compromise was unconstitutional, and slavery could not be banned in any territory. Slaves were property, they reasoned, and the Fifth Amendment guaranteed the right to property. Slaveowners had the right to take slaves into any territory. Living in a free territory had not made Scott a free man.

Southern radicals praised the decision. Now all territories were open to slavery. Northerners were shocked. They accused the South of plotting with the Supreme Court and the new President to expand slavery. Buchanan had, in fact, encouraged the justices to rule in the South's favor. Instead of putting to rest the question of slavery in the territories, the Dred Scott decision only added fuel to the fire.

Lincoln-Douglas Campaign

Unhappy with the President's support of proslavery interests, Republicans wanted to "overthrow" the Democrats. In 1858 Abraham Lincoln agreed to help. He would run against Democrat Stephen A. Douglas, who was seeking re-election to the Senate from Illinois.

Connections to Science

Innovations in technology had a huge impact on the spread of information, giving voters more information than was previously possible. Samuel Morse's telegraph allowed for rapid transmittal of information. In 1848, several major newspapers formed the Associated Press to coordinate and share the expense of dispatches via telegraph. At the same time, advances in printing and papermaking, and the expansion of the rail system, made newspapers more affordable and widely available than ever before. Americans across the country could buy a newspaper and read the current news for one or two cents a copy.

Stephen A. Douglas Douglas felt up to the challenge. He was a short, sturdy man, whom admirers called the "Little Giant." Douglas had a strong, deep voice and a brilliant mind. Although his support for the Kansas-Nebraska Act had damaged his reputation in the North, he still hoped to become President in 1860.

Abraham Lincoln Illinois Republicans believed that Lincoln, a small-town lawyer in Springfield, had the best chance of defeating Stephen Douglas. Lincoln opposed the expansion of slavery into new territories, but he was not known as a northern radical. He had been a powerful speaker at the 1856 Republican convention. Douglas himself remarked:

> "I shall have my hands full. He [Lincoln] is the strong man of his party . . . the best speaker . . . in the West."

Still, the tall, gangly Lincoln seemed awkward beside the polished Douglas. Lincoln had a quick wit, but his voice sometimes squeaked and he used pronunciations like "git" for "get" and "thar" for "there."

Lincoln-Douglas Debates

Lincoln's strategy was to follow Douglas on the campaign trail. Douglas would arrive in a town in his private railroad car. He brought along a brass cannon to announce his arrival and to draw a large crowd. Riding as an ordinary passenger on the same train, Lincoln would address the crowd after Douglas had finished his speech.

Douglas supporters made fun of Lincoln, saying he could not attract crowds of his own. Lincoln responded by challenging Douglas to a series of debates.

Douglas accepted the challenge. He thought such debates would draw national attention

Lincoln and Douglas tried to win votes in their 1858 debates. Presidential candidates Bill Clinton, George Bush, and Ross Perot continued the tradition in their 1992 debates.

Developing the Section

Discussion

Checking Understanding

1. What were the Court's reasons for ruling against Dred Scott? (It declared African Americans were not citizens and therefore did not have a right to a federal trial. More importantly, it ruled slavery could not be banned in any territory and that under the Fifth Amendment slave owners could not be deprived of their property.)

2. For which office were Lincoln and Douglas running in 1858? (U.S. Senator from Illinois.)

Stimulating Critical Thinking

3. If you could have asked Lincoln and Douglas a question about slavery at the 1858 debates, what would it have been and why? (Responses should show understanding of the slavery issue.)

Section Activity

Arguing a Court Case

Divide the class into small groups, telling them they are teams of lawyers assigned to argue before the Supreme Court on behalf of Dred Scott. In their arguments, they might refer to the agreement made in the Missouri Compromise or documents such as the Declaration of Independence and the Bill of Rights.

History Footnote

Stephen Douglas's views on popular sovereignty earned him enemies in both the North and the South. Their criticism was sometimes expressed by burning him in effigy. After angry northerners protested his introduction of the Kansas-Nebraska Act, Douglas commented, "I could travel from Boston to Chicago by the light of my own effigies."

For excerpts from Lincoln's statements on slavery, see **American Readings**, pp. 9–10.

Teaching the

Link to the Present

Help students compile a list on the chalkboard of words and phrases describing the current President's ideas, background, appearance, and performance. Ask them to identify where this information might have come from, such as newspaper or television reports, or talking with family and friends. Accept reasonable responses in comparing Lincoln with the current President and assessing Lincoln's chances of being elected today.

Vital Links

Lincoln-Douglas debates (Picture) Unit 3, Side 1, Search 16801

See also Unit 3 Explore CD-ROM location 33.

Link to the Present

Election campaigns today In Lincoln's day, candidates traveled to picnics, rallies, and other gatherings to make speeches and hold debates. Modern-day candidates also travel widely and talk to as many voters as they can, but there are important differences.

Only a few thousand could see and hear the Lincoln-Douglas debates. Now television brings campaign speeches and debates into millions of homes. Yet critics claim that candidates today emphasize "sound bites"—short statements that people will easily remember—instead of solid information explaining their views.

Critics also complain that today's candidates work harder at looking attractive than at trying to address the nation's problems. Abe Lincoln was awkward and far from handsome, and he spoke in a high, squeaky voice. Do you think he could be elected today?

and boost his chances to become President. The two men met seven times in seven different Illinois towns.

In the debates, Lincoln appealed to antislavery voters by attacking Douglas's stand on slavery. Douglas did not care, Lincoln claimed, "whether slavery was voted down or voted up."

The Freeport Doctrine In the town of Freeport, Lincoln challenged Douglas to declare his position on slavery in the territories now that the Dred Scott decision had made it legal. Douglas was in a tight spot. His answer came to be called the Freeport Doctrine.

In the Freeport Doctrine, Douglas admitted that it was now legal for an owner to bring a slave into any territory. However, he said, a legislature could refuse to pass laws protecting slavery in their territory. Without such laws, slavery could not be enforced.

The result of the debates The seven debates were the highlight of a hard-fought campaign. Lincoln and Douglas spoke to crowds almost daily for four months. In the days before microphones, public speakers had to shout to be heard. By election day Douglas's throat was so sore he could barely talk.

Although Douglas narrowly defeated Lincoln, the election had broader results. The Freeport Doctrine turned many southern Democrats against Douglas, and would hurt his chances of becoming President in 1860. Lincoln, on the other hand, emerged as a national figure. His skill at challenging Douglas put the presidency within his reach.

Raid at Harpers Ferry

An event that terrified the South occurred on October 16, 1859. John Brown, the abolitionist from Kansas, appeared at Harpers Ferry, Virginia. With 21 followers he seized a federal arsenal there. He planned to give the guns to escaped slaves who in turn were to ignite a slave revolt across the South.

The plan had no hope of success. Brown never freed any slaves. Colonel Robert E. Lee led a force of marines who captured Brown and killed ten of his men, including two of his sons. Virginia authorities quickly convicted Brown of treason and of trying to start a rebellion. He was hanged six weeks later.

John Brown met his death with a dignity that made him a hero and "a new saint" for the antislavery cause. Brown also struck fear through the South. Would there be such raids in the future? Southerners were now convinced that the North would stop at nothing to destroy slavery.

Connections to Music

During the Civil War, Union soldiers composed and sang verses to a song called "John Brown's Body." One verse said:

His sacrifice we share! Our sword will victory crown! . . .
For freedom and the right remember old John Brown!
His soul is marching on.

African American soldiers added their own verses to the John Brown song. Referring to white southerners, they sang:

They will have to bow their foreheads to their colored kith and kin,
They will have to give us house-room or the roof will tumble in!
As we go marching on.

Link to Art

John Brown Going to His Hanging (1942) Most artists go to art school to develop their talent at painting. African American artist Horace Pippin did not. Instead, he taught himself. Pippin (1888–1946) painted many subjects, including landscapes, people, and historical scenes. In this painting, John Brown rides his coffin to the gallows. **Discuss** What is the mood in this scene? How does the artist use color and shapes to express the mood?

The Election of 1860

The presidential election of 1860 drove a final wedge between North and South. The Democratic Party split. Northern Democrats nominated Stephen A. Douglas and came out for popular sovereignty in the territories. Southern Democrats picked John C. Breckinridge, who supported slavery in all territories.

Discussion

Checking Understanding

1. What did Douglas state in the Freeport Doctrine? (It was legal for an owner to bring a slave into any territory, but a legislature did not have to pass laws to protect slavery.)

2. Why did John Brown raid Harpers Ferry? (To arm escaped slaves for a revolt.)

Stimulating Critical Thinking

3. Was John Brown a hero? (Yes: lost life for noble cause. No: killed innocent people and did not free any slaves.)

4. What else could John Brown have done to support abolition? (Perhaps nonviolent means such as distributing antislavery pamphlets, writing a book, or making speeches.)

Teaching the Link to Art

Tell students that Pippin's mother, who claimed to have been at the hanging, is shown in the lower right corner, facing the viewer.

Discussion Answers: The dark colors and bold images present a somber mood. Also, the perspective places the viewer in back of a faceless crowd.

Vital Links

John Brown (Picture)
Unit 3, Side 1,
Search 37422

See also Unit 3 Explore CD-ROM location 199.

Teaching the Reading Maps

Ask what the numbers in each state represent (electoral votes). As you discuss the Reading Maps question, ask if people vote according to sectional interests today. **Answer to Reading Maps:** Most free northern states supported Lincoln, who opposed the spread of slavery. Most southern states supported Breckinridge, a proslavery Southern Democrat.

Bonus Activity

Descriptions of Fort Sumter

To reflect viewpoints on the outbreak of war, have students write newspaper headlines about Fort Sumter. They should write two headlines describing the incident: one for a southern newspaper and another for a northern one. Conclude by comparing headlines and discussing how each section of the country viewed the outbreak of war.

Teaching the Point of View

Ask students to discuss whether a state should be able to legally secede. (Yes: may be necessary if federal government threatens citizens' rights and liberties, such as through unlawful imprisonment or unjust taxation. No: federal government is the most important protector of citizens' rights; states have adequate representation of interests within Congress.)

History Footnote

While Lincoln campaigned for President in 1860, his appearance caught the attention of 11-year-old Grace Bedell. Grace wrote Lincoln a letter, advising him that his chances of winning the election would be improved if he were to "grow whiskers." It was said that Lincoln, a devoted father, had a great fondness for children. A week later, Grace received a kind letter from Lincoln; later that month Lincoln was photographed with the beginnings of a beard.

In February of 1861, the newly elected President stopped at the train station of Grace's hometown of Westfield, New York, and asked if his young correspondent was in the crowd. She nervously stepped forward. As she later recalled, "It seemed to me as the President stooped to kiss me that he looked very kind, yes, and sad."

Election of 1860

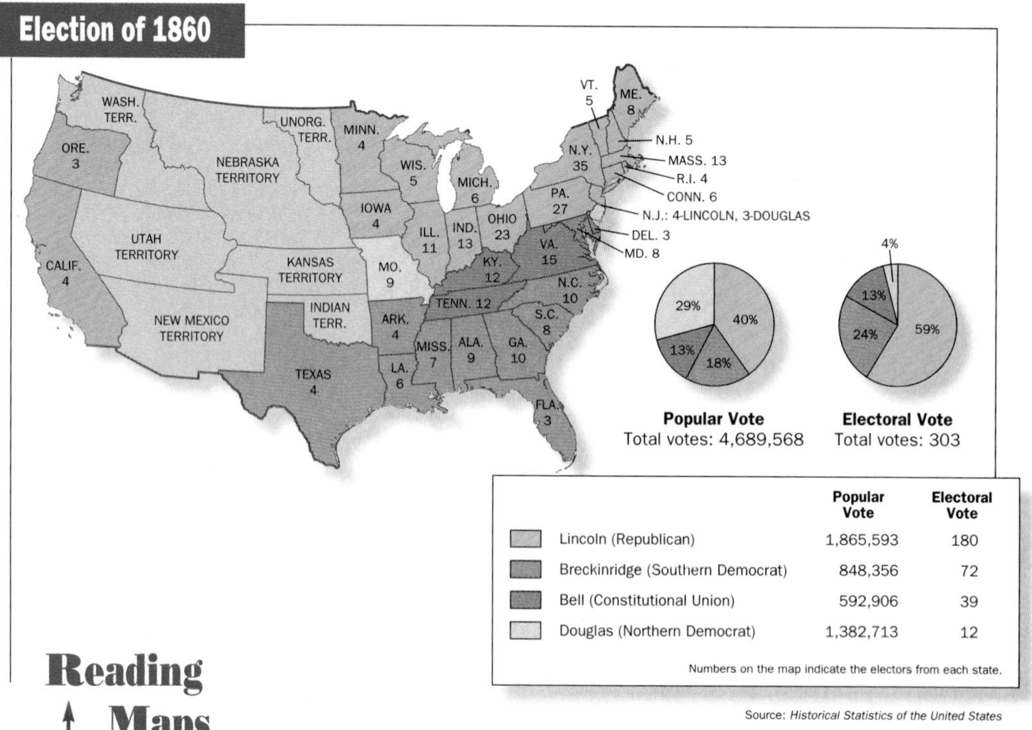

	Popular Vote	Electoral Vote
Lincoln (Republican)	1,865,593	180
Breckinridge (Southern Democrat)	848,356	72
Bell (Constitutional Union)	592,906	39
Douglas (Northern Democrat)	1,382,713	12

Numbers on the map indicate the electors from each state.

Source: *Historical Statistics of the United States*

Reading Maps

How does this map show that in 1860 people voted by sectional interests?

In a Chicago meeting hall packed with his supporters, Lincoln won the Republican nomination. The party did not call for the abolition of slavery. Rather, with Lincoln, it viewed slavery as "an evil not to be extended, but to be tolerated."

A fourth candidate, John Bell of Tennessee, was nominated by the Constitutional Union Party. This new party avoided the issue of slavery and supported the Union.

Lincoln's victory Although he won only 40 percent of the popular vote, Lincoln received a majority of the electoral votes. Thanks to the split in the Democratic Party, Abraham Lincoln was elected as the first Republican President.

The South Secedes

As Lincoln had predicted in 1858, "a house divided against itself cannot stand." Within weeks of his election, South Carolina left the Union. Alabama, Mississippi, Georgia, Florida, Louisiana, and Texas soon followed. Together they formed the Confederate States of America, with Jefferson Davis as their President.

Point of View

Is secession ever justifiable?

Many northerners agreed with Lincoln that "no state . . . can lawfully get out of the Union." Most southerners, however, believed

Tips for Teaching

At-Risk Students

To help students who are poor readers, focus first on understanding the "big picture." One way to do this is to provide opportunities to restate main ideas of the text in their own words, ideally with a partner or small group. Having a broader context will help them remember more specific details, such as dates and events.

that secession was justified. The Declaration of Independence, they pointed out, stated that people have the right to throw off an unjust government. Edmund Ruffin, a Virginia planter, declared:

> "Slaveholding states . . . [must proclaim] another declaration of independence [from the United States]. We, the children of those [founding] fathers . . . have submitted to oppression and wrong incalculably [far] greater than ever England inflicted."

Can a state ever legally secede from the nation? Under what conditions?

The Northern Response

At first few northerners took secession seriously. Some thought the South simply needed time to cool off. Others urged compromise again. Some abolitionists were happy to see the South go its separate way. Buchanan, still President in the months before Lincoln took office, hoped that Congress would reach a compromise. He did nothing, however, to help achieve one.

Lincoln's inaugural address Before his inauguration, Lincoln avoided making any statements. When he took office on March 4, 1861, though, he made his positions clear. He believed he had no legal right to interfere with slavery "in the States where it exists." However, he expressed his determination to hold the Union together:

> "The Union of these States is perpetual. . . . No state . . . can lawfully get out of the Union. . . . I therefore consider that . . . the Union is unbroken."

Lincoln would oppose all attempts at secession, but believed that there was no need for "bloodshed or violence." He concluded with the plea: "We are not enemies but friends. We must not be enemies."

The Outbreak of War

Southern radicals ignored Lincoln's plea. While the new President organized his government, Confederate leaders prepared for war. The first test came at Fort Sumter, in the harbor at Charleston, South Carolina.

Fort Sumter Fort Sumter—a federal fort—was running short of supplies. Trying to avoid armed conflict, Lincoln announced that while he would be sending food to the fort, he would send no soldiers.

World  Link

Freedom for Russian serfs In 1861 the slavery issue in the United States was coming to a crisis. In that same year 22 million Russian serfs gained their freedom with the stroke of a pen when Czar Alexander II signed the Emancipation Act.

Serfs were peasants who farmed pieces of land owned by lords. They gave part of their crop to the lord for rent and did many jobs for the lord as well. Unlike slaves in the United States, who had been forcibly brought from Africa, serfs were Russians like their lords. Like the slaves, though, they worked hard, lived in poverty, and were not allowed to move.

Under the Emancipation Act, Russian serfs could buy land, but few could find the money to pay for it. Most former serfs remained poor and discontented.

Discussion

Checking Understanding

1. What was Lincoln's view on slavery? (It was an evil not to be extended, but to be tolerated; he felt he had no right to interfere with slavery where it existed.)

Stimulating Critical Thinking

2. Do you think it is fair to compare the secession to the Declaration of Independence? Why or why not? (Yes: southern states, like the 13 colonies, were victims of abuse of government power. No: unlike the colonies, which were not represented in Parliament, southern states had representation in the national government; they should have abided by majority rule in Congress.)

Teaching the

World  Link

Ask students to compare the conditions of serfs and slaves. (Both worked for landowners, lived in poverty, and were not allowed to move. However, serfs were treated as people, not property.)

Closing the Section

Wrap-Up Activity

Writing a News Release

To review the section, have students write short news releases summarizing events that led to the outbreak of the Civil War. Have them compare their releases with a partner's.

Section Review Answers

1. The Court declared that African Americans did not have a right to a trial, and that no state or territory could ban slavery.

2. Lincoln followed Douglas on the campaign trail and challenged him to debates; he also forced Douglas to declare his position on slavery. The strategy worked, for even though he lost the race, he became a national figure and caused Douglas to lose some popular support. This helped Lincoln win the presidency.

3. He died fighting for his beliefs and drew attention to the cause of abolition.

4. Those who would vote against secession might focus on his statement that he would not interfere with slavery where it existed. Those who would vote for secession might focus on his view that slavery should not be extended.

To check understanding of "Why We Remember," assign Thinking Critically question 3 on student page 128.

History Footnote

In an 1858 speech at Edwardsville, Illinois, Lincoln asked:

> What constitutes the bulwark of our own liberty and independence? It is not our frowning battlements, our bristling sea coasts, the guns of our war steamers. . . . Our defense is in the preservation of the spirit which prizes liberty as the heritage of all men, in all lands, everywhere.

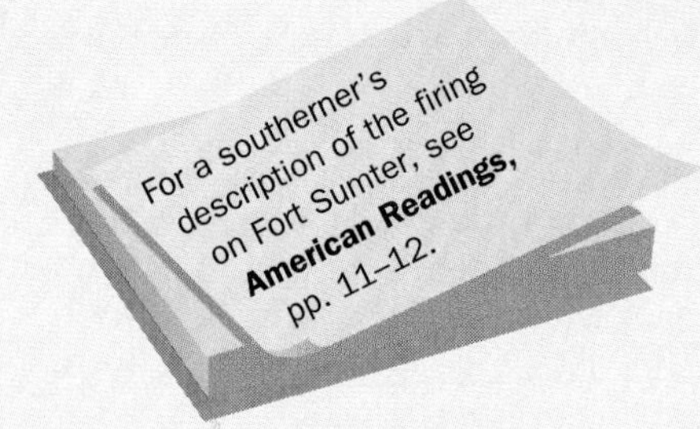

For a southerner's description of the firing on Fort Sumter, see **American Readings,** pp. 11–12.

Fort Sumter guarded one of the South's most important seaports. Thus, Confederate President Davis decided that the fort must not remain in Union hands. Confederate forces demanded that Major Robert Anderson, the commander of Fort Sumter, surrender immediately. Anderson refused.

Early in the morning of April 12, 1861, Confederate cannons opened fire. The fort withstood an intense artillery attack for over 30 hours. Anderson finally surrendered on April 13, 1861. He ordered a 50-gun salute to the United States flag as the Confederate army took the fort. The Civil War had begun.

3. Section Review

1. Why did the Supreme Court deny Dred Scott his freedom?
2. What were Lincoln's two strategies in challenging Douglas for the Senate? Did they work?
3. Why was John Brown a hero to the abolitionist cause?
4. Critical Thinking As a southerner, would you still have voted for secession if you had first heard Lincoln's inaugural address? Why or why not?

Why We Remember

The Gathering Storm

When Abraham Lincoln learned that he had been elected President in 1860, he said to reporters, "Well, boys, your troubles are over. Mine have just begun." As the dark clouds of secession rolled across the South, it became clear how serious those troubles would be. The survival of the United States, and the fate of 4 million enslaved people, rested in Lincoln's hands.

The stormy 1850s were a turning point for the nation. Again and again Congress tried to find a lasting compromise on slavery in the territories. Yet each compromise created new problems. Lincoln understood why. Slavery was not only a political problem, it was also a deeply moral issue. As he wrote in a letter to a friend, "If slavery is not wrong, nothing is wrong."

American democracy is based on the ideal that "all men are created equal." After his election, Lincoln declared his unshakeable belief in that ideal:

> "That sentiment [ideal of equality] in the Declaration of Independence . . . gave liberty not only to the people of this country, but hope to all the world. . . . I would rather be assassinated on this spot than surrender it."

As the gathering storm broke over Fort Sumter, the nation would finally decide whether or not to live and die by that simple but powerful ideal.

Geography Footnote

The Appalachian National Scenic Trail, covering 14 states from Mount Katahdin in Maine to Mount Oglethorpe in northern Georgia, is the longest marked, continuous footpath in the world. Benton MacKaye, a Massachusetts forester and author, proposed the idea for the trail in an article published in 1921. It was completed in 1937.

Wooden signposts and white paint markings on trees and rocks lead the way for hikers making the journey. The trail passes through some state and national parks, but is mainly on private property, by consent of the owners. In normal conditions, a hiker can complete the trail in about four months.

Geography Lab

The Appalachian Mountains

In the isolated valleys that twist and turn through the Appalachian Mountains, the issues that divided the North and South seemed far away. Most people who lived in the hollows and thick forests of the southern Appalachians—less rugged than the Rockies—did not own slaves. Farmers there did not want to secede from the Union. The photograph and readings that follow will help you form an image of the region.

The southern Appalachian Mountains

From James Paulding's Letters

"[W]e first caught a view of the distant undulating [wavy-looking] mountain, whose fading blue outline could hardly be distinguished from the blue sky. Between us and the mountain was spread a wide landscape—shade softening into shade . . . as blended the whole into a . . . harmony. Over all was spread that rich purple hue [color]."

From a Novel by William Simms

"Let the traveler . . . look down upon the scene below. Around us, the hills gather in groups on every side. . . . The axe has not yet deprived them of a single tree, and they rise up, covered with the honored growth of a thousand summers. . . . The leaves cover the rugged limbs which sustain them, with so much ease and grace, as if for the first time they were so green and glossy. . . . The wild flowers begin to flaunt [show off] their blue and crimson draperies [curtains] about us. . . . In the winding hollows of these hills, beginning at our feet, you see the first signs of as lovely a little hamlet [village] as ever promised peace to the weary and the discontent."

From *Charlemont* by William Simms

Developing a Mental Map

Refer to pages R4–R5 and R6–R7.

1. In what states do the Appalachian Mountains lie?
2. What are the highest peaks in the Appalachians and the Rocky Mountains? How do they compare?
3. How does the photograph of the Appalachians resemble the descriptions by Paulding and Simms?
4. **Hands-On Geography** Imagine that you have just completed a hike along the Appalachian Trail—a 2,000-mile footpath from Maine to Georgia. To show your friends and family what it was like to be in the Appalachians, create a diary with pictures. Write a list of topics, and a list of types of photographs, to include in the diary. You may need to look at some additional books before you begin.

Teaching the Geography Lab

To focus students' attention on the characteristics of mountains, ask volunteers who have visited or lived in the mountains to share their experiences. Encourage students to think about how the mountain landscape might affect people's way of life. For example, travel may be more difficult, making individuals more isolated.

Developing a Mental Map

Answers

1. Maine, New Hampshire, Vermont, Massachusetts, Rhode Island, Connecticut, New York, New Jersey, Pennsylvania, Ohio, Maryland, West Virginia, Virginia, Kentucky, North Carolina, Tennessee, Georgia, Alabama, and a small portion of South Carolina and Mississippi.

2. Appalachians: Mt. Mitchell, 6,684 feet (2,037 meters). Rockies: Mt. Elbert, 14,433 feet (4,400 meters), almost 8,000 feet higher than the highest Appalachian peak.

3. Possible answers: abundant trees and other vegetation, wavy-looking appearance.

4. Diaries might include descriptions of the mountains, feelings evoked by the landscape, details about length and difficulty of the journey, and descriptions of people encountered.

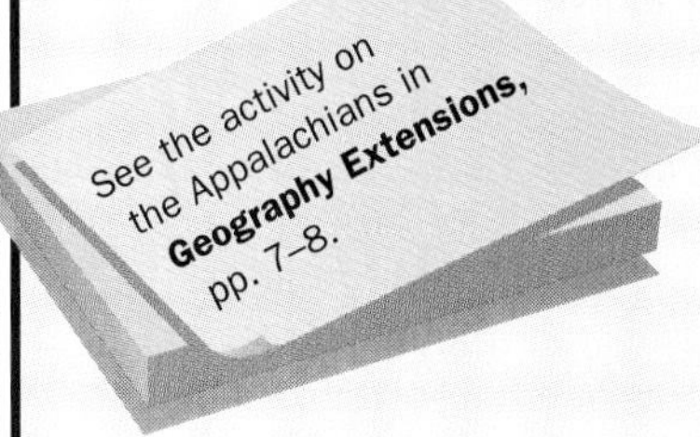

See the activity on
the Appalachians in
Geography Extensions,
pp. 7–8.

Survey Answers

Reviewing Vocabulary

Definitions are found on these pages: *popular sovereignty* (110), *transcontinental railroad* (115), *platform* (118).

Reviewing Main Ideas

1. Northern radicals wanted to prohibit slavery in the new territories, and southern radicals wanted to permit it. Moderates suggested extending the Missouri Compromise line to the Pacific Ocean or giving voters the right to decide whether to allow slavery.

2. California would be admitted as a free state; New Mexico and Utah would become territories in which the question of slavery would be decided by voters; the Fugitive Slave Law required the return of escaped slaves; the slave trade would be abolished in Washington, D.C., though slavery would remain legal there. Congress passed the Compromise because the President and most voters favored it.

3. Northerners were shocked as they watched kidnappers return African Americans to slavery, and some reacted violently. Southerners were angered by this reaction.

4. The Kansas-Nebraska Act created the Kansas and Nebraska territories, allowing voters there to decide the issue of slavery. Antislavery and proslavery settlers raced to Kansas to vote. Tensions erupted when a proslavery army set afire the antislavery town of Lawrence. Seeking revenge, John Brown and his followers killed five proslavery men, and proslavery forces retaliated. This touched off a war in which about 200 died.

5. (a) Antislavery issues.
(b) In 1854, the Republicans defeated many Democrats in the North and the Democrats'

(Answers continued in top margin)

main power base shifted to the South. The Whigs went into decline, with northerners switching to the Republicans and the Know-Nothings, and southerners shifting to the Democrats.

6. The Court said that the Missouri Compromise, which had banned slavery in certain territories, was unconstitutional. This ruling opened slavery to all the territories.

7. (a) As a result of his debates with Douglas during the 1858 campaign for the Senate. (b) The Democratic Party was split between northern and southern Democrats. (c) Seven states seceded from the Union.

Thinking Critically

1. Answers may vary, depending on how much weight students give each provision.

2. Students should understand that the Bill

Chapter Survey

Reviewing Vocabulary

Define the following terms.
1. popular sovereignty
2. transcontinental railroad
3. platform

Reviewing Main Ideas

1. What did the various groups of radicals and moderates want to do about slavery in territory acquired from Mexico?
2. What were the terms of the Compromise of 1850, and why did Congress pass it?
3. How did the Fugitive Slave Law increase the sectional conflict between the North and the South?
4. Describe how each event led to the next. (a) Kansas-Nebraska Act (b) settlers' race to Kansas (c) sack of Lawrence (d) "Bleeding Kansas"
5. (a) What was the focus of the Republican Party platform? (b) What happened to the Democratic and Whig parties as the Republicans gained support in the 1850s?
6. How did the Supreme Court's decision in *Dred Scott* v. *Sandford* affect the issue of slavery in the territories?
7. (a) How did Abraham Lincoln become a national figure? (b) Why did he win the election of 1860? (c) What was the South's immediate response to the election?

Thinking Critically

1. Evaluation Did the Compromise of 1850 favor the North, the South, or neither? Explain your answer.
2. Application Abolitionists attacked the Supreme Court for basing its Dred Scott decision on the Fifth Amendment in the Bill of Rights. Why would they be furious about such reasoning?
3. Why We Remember: Synthesis Could the conflict between North and South have been resolved peacefully after Lincoln's election? If yes, describe a solution that might have worked. If no, explain why war was unavoidable.

Applying Skills

Asking historical questions Slavery is rare in today's world, but other violations of human rights—such as torture of prisoners—still occur. Imagine that you are a reporter. You are to interview someone who claims to have witnessed a human rights violation in another country. Write a list of five questions to ask the person. For each question, write a sentence that tells why you would ask it. Keep in mind what you learned on page 119.

History Mystery

Kansas elections Answer the history mystery on page 107. How would you find out why more people voted in the election than lived in the territory? Why did so many people vote in the election and how might you have prevented them from voting?

Writing in Your History Journal

1. Keys to History (a) The time line on pages 106–107 has seven Keys to History. In your journal, describe why each one is important to know about.
(b) Choose one of the events on the time line. Write a paragraph in your journal that describes how the course of history might have been different if that event had not taken place.
2. Abraham Lincoln Imagine that you are Leo Tolstoy trying to reply to the

of Rights is designed to protect individual liberties, yet the Court used it to deny Scott his freedom.

3. Students who think war could have been avoided may suggest a new compromise, such as dividing western lands equally between free and slave territories. Those who think war was unavoidable may cite the repeated failures at finding a lasting compromise.

Applying Skills

Answers should reflect understanding of the Procedures and Skill Tips outlined on page 119.

History Mystery

Information on the election can be found on pages 116–117. Students may suggest examining the issues surrounding the election

(Answers continued in side margin)

to determine the reason for the increase. Implementing stricter voter registration guidelines would help prevent fraud.

Writing in Your History Journal

1. (a) Explanations should be similar to the time line notes on teacher pages 106–107. (b) Accept responses that reflect understanding of the effects of the event.

2. Accept any answers that reflect the characterization of Lincoln in this chapter and that students can support.

3. Accept answers that students can support. Students should consider Brown's actions in Kansas and at Harpers Ferry. He was similar to terrorists today in that he used violent protest as a way to draw attention to his cause.

Reviewing Geography

1. (A) Utah Territory
(B) Nebraska Territory
(C) Kansas Territory
(D) New Mexico Territory

2. There was still a huge area of unorganized land within the nation's boundaries. As long as the potential existed for new states, the slavery issue would not be resolved. Students may suggest that a decision was not reached because by postponing it Fillmore could avoid controversy. This land might have been simply divided in half to try to satisfy both sides.

Alternative Assessment

Teacher's Take-Home Planner 1, page 7, includes suggestions and scoring rubrics for the Alternative Assessment activity.

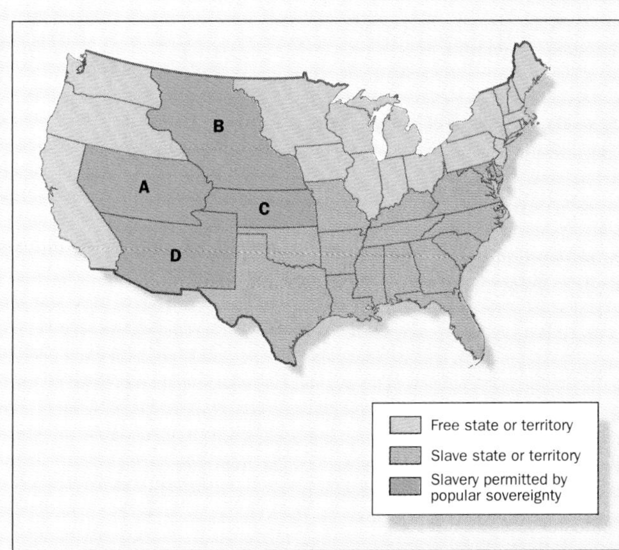

Reviewing Geography

1. Each letter on the map represents a territory as it existed after the Kansas-Nebraska Act. Write the name of each.

2. Geographic Thinking Look at the map on page 116. President Fillmore believed that the 1850 Compromise ended arguments over slavery in the territories. What territory did he ignore in his conclusion? Why was a decision not reached on the question of slavery there? How might this area be organized in a way that would appeal to both South and North?

mountain chief's request for information about Abraham Lincoln (see page 108). In your journal, write down three things about Lincoln that you believe are most important for the chief to know. Include a specific example from Lincoln's life to support each point.

3. Thinking Historically A terrorist uses violence to advance a political cause. Would you call John Brown a terrorist or a hero? Explain why. How would you compare him with terrorists today? Write your response in your journal.

Alternative Assessment

Citizenship: Covering the 1860 election on TV If television had existed in 1860, what might coverage of the presidential election have been like? With several classmates, act out an election-night broadcast as a television network might do.

In your broadcast:

1. Give a live report from the campaign headquarters of the candidates.
2. Interview two voters, one from the South and one from the North. Ask them who they think will win and what the result could mean for the nation.
3. After each live report and interview, give an election update on how many votes each candidate is receiving.
4. Include an election map, pictures, or some other visuals in your broadcast.

Your broadcast will be evaluated on the following criteria:

- it clearly presents the issues, the candidates, and the results of the 1860 election
- it resembles a television news show
- it is interesting to your audience

Teaching the

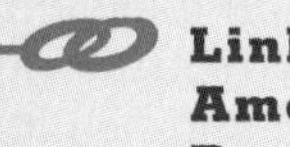

Link to American Readings

In this feature students learn about slavery from a primary source, the autobiography of James Pennington. His book advocates abolition and is written from the viewpoint of a former slave. The second reading is by John Greenleaf Whittier, an ardent abolitionist who wrote his poem from the perspective of one who fervently believes in justice for all, but who has never known life without justice.

Before students begin the lesson, review the material on the Fugitive Slave Law (page 114) and the secession of the South (pages 124–125). Have students read the entire feature before assigning the A Closer Look questions. The Setting the Stage Activity and Bonus Activity may then be introduced according to the needs and interests of the students. The information contained in the Discussion questions and the Footnotes may be used throughout the lesson as appropriate. Readers' Theater is ideal for students who might find the readings somewhat difficult. Use the Wrap-Up Activity for students who would enjoy taking a step beyond the core lesson.

Literature Footnote

The slave narrative is a distinctly American literary genre consisting of memoirs of daily life on southern plantations. Most typical are the stories of pain, both physical and emotional, of families separated when slaves were sold, of humiliation, and of both successful and failed attempts to escape to freedom. Wry humor can sometimes be found in anecdotes of the deception and pretenses that slaves assumed in order to survive the harsh realities of plantation life. There are also the stories of strong Christian faith that melded with familiar cultural practices. Throughout the stories runs a steady current of longing for freedom, dignity, and identity.

Link to American Readings

READING 1A

Escape from Slavery

James Pennington was born a slave in Maryland in 1809. At the age of 21, he escaped and fled to Pennsylvania. Educated by a Quaker family, Pennington eventually became a minister and a teacher. In 1849 he published his autobiography, *The Fugitive Blacksmith,* which sharply criticized slavery. In the following passage, he describes the painful event that prompted his decision to escape from slavery.

Once a slave, James Pennington became a minister, writer, and teacher.

A slave narrative by James W. C. Pennington, 1849

Three or four of our farm hands had their wives and families on other plantations. In such cases, it is the custom in Maryland to allow the men to go on Saturday evening to see their families, stay over the Sabbath, and return on Monday morning, not later than "half-an hour by sun." To overstay their time is a grave fault, for which, especially at busy seasons, they are punished.

One Monday morning, two of these men had not been so fortunate as to get home at the required time; one of them was an uncle of mine. Besides these, two young men who had no families, and for whom no such provision of time was made, having gone somewhere to spend the Sabbath, were absent. My master was greatly irritated, and had resolved to have, as he said, "a general whipping-match among them."

Preparatory to this, he had a rope in his pocket, and a cowhide in his hand, walking about the premises, and speaking to everyone he met in a very insolent manner, and finding fault with some without just cause. My father, among other numerous and responsible duties, discharged that of shepherd to a large and valuable flock of Merino sheep. This morning he was engaged in the tenderest of a shepherd's duties: a little lamb, not able to go alone, lost its mother; he was feeding it by hand. He had been keeping it in the house for several days. As he stooped over it in the yard, with a vessel of new milk he had obtained, with which to feed it, my master came along, and without the least provocation, began by asking, "Bazil, have you fed the flock?"

"Yes, sir."

insolent: overbearing, insulting

Merino sheep: a breed of sheep with long, fine wool

provocation: cause of irritation

Literature Footnote

Many historians consider *A Narrative of the Uncommon Sufferings and Surprising Deliverance of Briton Hammon, a Negro Man,* published in Boston in 1760, to be the first true slave narrative. Titles such as *A Narrative of the Lord's Wonderful Dealings with J. Murrant, a Black, Taken Down from His Own Relation* (1784) and *The Interesting Narrative of Olaudah Equiano, or Gustavas Vassa the African* (1789) were the next examples of slave narratives to be published. The most popular period for the genre was from about 1830 to 1860. The writing and publication of these books was strongly encouraged and often financially supported by abolitionists.

"Were you away yesterday?"

"No, sir."

"Do you know why these boys have not got home this morning yet?"

"No, sir, I have not seen any of them since Saturday night."

"By the Eternal, I'll make them know their hour. The fact is, I have too many of you; my people are getting to be the most careless, lazy, and worthless in the country."

"Master," said my father, "I am always at my post; Monday morning never finds me off the plantation."

"Hush, Bazil! I shall have to sell some of you; and then the rest will have enough to do; I have not work enough to keep you all tightly employed; I have too many of you."

All this was said in an angry, threatening, and exceedingly insulting tone. My father was a high-spirited man, and feeling deeply the insult, replied to the last expression, "If I am one too many, sir, give me a chance to get a purchaser, and I am willing to be sold when it may suit you."

"Bazil, I told you to hush!" and suiting the action to the word, he drew forth the cowhide from under his arm, fell upon him with most savage cruelty, and inflicted fifteen or twenty severe stripes with all his strength, over his shoulders and the small of his back. As he raised himself upon his toes, and gave the last stripe, he said, "By the *** I will make you know that I am master of your tongue as well as of your time!"

Being a tradesman, and just at that time getting my breakfast, I was near enough to hear the insolent words that were spoken to my father, and to hear, see, and even count the savage stripes inflicted upon him.

Posters such as this offered generous rewards for the capture and return of runaway slaves.

Setting the Stage Activity

Following the Road to Abolition

Help students understand that the road to the abolition of slavery was a long one. Have students create a time line using the dates listed below. Then have them add the details for each date in their own words. Discuss.

1712—Pennsylvania prohibits the importation of slaves.

1775—The first American abolition society is born in Pennsylvania.

1808—The United States prohibits the importation of slaves from Africa.

1809—James Pennington is born.

Abraham Lincoln is born.

Bonus Activity

Mapping Whittier

To help students understand the connection between literature and geography, have them use a map to locate Whittier, a city founded by Quakers in 1887. Named after the poet John Greenleaf Whittier, it is located southeast of Los Angeles, California. Today Whittier has a population of about 78,000.

Discussion

Stimulating Critical Thinking

1. Pennington asks this question about the beating his father experienced at the hand of the slave owner:

". . . how would you expect a son to feel at such a sight?" Answer the question posed by Pennington.

(Students might reply that they would feel humiliated or hurt. They might sympathize with the physical pain. They may also express anger, frustration at being unable to defend their father, or hate.)

2. Many slave owners and others who supported them believed that slavery was a social issue. John Greenleaf Whittier believed it was far more than that. Who or what does he believe supports the right to freedom for all? Do you agree with Whittier? What arguments can you give to support justice and the right to freedom for all people?

(Students will likely agree that Whittier has a strong faith in God. He believes that it is the God-given right of all people to live in freedom. Students' arguments to support freedom may vary greatly, depending on their personal and family experiences.)

Literature Footnote

Some people today consider education to be a right. For others, it is a privilege. But for James Pennington it was neither. Considering that it was a crime for slaves to learn how to read and write, it is amazing that some, such as Pennington, accomplished so much. After his escape, Pennington became a writer, teacher, and minister.

Literature Footnote

There are two sides to the prolific John Greenleaf Whittier. "The Kansas Emigrants" is written by the public, social, and civic-minded poet, an active abolitionist. A later work and perhaps his most famous, "Snow-Bound" (1866), is the creation of a much more private man who paints with words his portraits of rural New England life.

Let me ask any one of Anglo-Saxon blood and spirit, how would you expect a *son* to feel at such a sight?

This act created an open rupture with our family—each member felt the deep insult that had been inflicted upon our head; the spirit of the whole family was roused; we talked of it in our nightly gatherings, and showed it in our daily melancholy aspect. The oppressor saw this, and with the heartlessness that was in perfect keeping with the first insult, commenced a series of tauntings, threatenings and insinuations, with a view to crush the spirit of the whole family.

melancholy: sad, gloomy

Although it was some time after this event before I took the decisive step [to escape], yet in my mind and spirit, I never was a *Slave* after it.

Excerpts from James W. C. Pennington, *The Fugitive Blacksmith,* 1849.

Slaves often labored together in large, supervised groups. These women worked on a North Carolina rice plantation.

Readers' Theater

John Greenleaf Whittier's poem, "The Race to Kansas," became a rallying song for New England abolitionists who migrated to Kansas in the 1850s. Students might enjoy reading the poem as a small group. Encourage them to imagine that they are the abolitionists and that they gain strength and support from each other as they work for a common cause. The students then should work toward expressing the emotion of those deeply committed to a cause. They should practice the reading several times, until they are truly speaking as one voice. You might suggest that they mark their copies of the poem for short and long pauses, speed, and volume. This will promote unity in speaking.

READING 1B

The Race to Kansas

Poet John Greenleaf Whittier was born in Massachusetts and raised a Quaker. A writer who was active in politics, he attacked the Polk administration over its handling of the Mexican War and opposed the Compromise of 1850. He also helped found the Republican Party and spoke out against slavery. Whittier's "The Kansas Emigrants" became a rallying song for the thousands of New England abolitionists who migrated to Kansas in the 1850s.

The Kansas Emigrants

We cross the prairie as of old
The Pilgrims crossed the sea,
To make the West, as they the East,
The homestead of the free.

We go to rear a wall of men
On Freedom's southern line,
And plant beside the cotton tree
The rugged Northern pine!

We're flowing from our native hills
As our free rivers flow:
The blessing of our Motherland
Is on us as we go.

We go to plant her common schools
On distant prairie swells,
And give the Sabbaths of the wild
The music of her bells.

Upbearing, like the Ark of Old,
The Bible in our van,
We go to test the truth of God
Against the fraud of man.

Free-Soilers stand guard outside Lawrence, Kansas, in 1856.

No pause, nor rest, save where the
streams
That feed the Kansas run,
Save where our Pilgrim gonfalon
[banner]
Shall flout the setting sun!

We'll tread the prairie as of old
Our fathers sailed the sea,
And make the West, as they the East,
The homestead of the free!

"The Kansas Emigrants" by John Greenleaf Whittier, 1854.

fraud: deceit, trickery

flout: mock

A Closer Look

1. What event prompted James Pennington to plan his escape from slavery?
2. To whom does Whittier compare the Kansas pioneers? In what way are the two groups alike?
3. CRITICAL THINKING Pennington describes more than the physical suffering he and his family endured as slaves. What other hardship does he write about? How did it affect the family? Explain.

Wrap-Up Activity

Surviving Slavery

To extend the lesson, ask students to imagine that they have been enslaved by a conquering country. How would they adapt to slavery? What incident might make them willing to risk their life to escape to freedom? Students should respond in writing in their history journals.

A Closer Look

Answers

1. Pennington witnessed the beating and humiliation of his father at the hand of his owner. That his father had done nothing to deserve such treatment and that he and his father were both powerless to stop it, made the young Pennington determined to run for freedom.

2. He compares the Kansas pioneers to the early Pilgrims. They both searched for freedom—social, political, and religious.

3. Students may note the strong sense of humiliation and feeling of powerlessness that Pennington battled. The family was torn apart by the incident. It made them sad and dispirited.

Teaching the

Citizenship Lab

In this feature students learn about an important aspect of the Supreme Court's decision in *Dred Scott* v. *Sandford* (1857): the ruling that no African American could be a citizen of the United States. The ruling was eventually overturned through a constitutional amendment, but questions about who qualifies to be a U.S. citizen live on today.

Before students read the feature, review the information about the Dred Scott case on page 120. Have students read the entire feature before assigning the Understanding Civic Issues questions and the Hands-On Citizenship activity. The Bonus Activity in this Teacher's Edition may be used as an alternative to, or in addition to, the Hands-On Citizenship activity. The Discussion questions in this Teacher's Edition may be used at appropriate points during students' reading or afterward.

Objectives

- ★ Describe how the original Constitution left citizenship open to question.
- ★ Explain the Supreme Court's ruling on citizenship for African Americans in *Dred Scott* v. *Sandford.*
- ★ Describe how one modern-day proposal would change the requirements for U.S. citizenship.

Supreme Court Case: *Dred Scott* v. *Sandford*

Citizenship Lab

Who Can Be a Citizen?

If most Americans of 1857 had been asked to name the main significance of *Dred Scott* v. *Sandford*, they might have said, "It overturns the Missouri Compromise and opens all territories to slavery." To free African Americans, however, the Supreme Court's declaration that no black person could ever be a citizen of the United States was just as important—and just as horrifying.

How Things Stood Before the Dred Scott Decision

The question of African American citizenship might not have come before the Court if the Constitution's framers had handed down a precise definition of *citizen.* Instead, they created a Constitution that did not specify qualifications for citizenship nor offer a complete list of citizens' rights and duties.

Even without clear constitutional guidelines, free African Americans of the 1850s had some solid reasons to view themselves as citizens. For example, some held passports issued by the federal government. By definition, a passport identifies a person as a citizen of his or her nation. Free African Americans also could sue and be sued in state courts. In addition, free African American men could vote in elections in several northern states.

The Court Declares African Americans to Be Noncitizens

Chief Justice Roger B. Taney, who wrote the majority opinion in the Dred Scott case, was not impressed by such evidence. He believed that the important consideration was

Chief Justice Roger B. Taney

History Footnote

During one of his debates with Stephen A. Douglas in 1858, Abraham Lincoln expressed his reaction to the Dred Scott decision this way: "We believe . . . in obedience to, and respect for, the judicial department of government. We think its decisions on constitutional questions, when fully settled, should control not only the particular cases decided, but the general policy of the country, subject to be disturbed only by amendments of the Constitution as provided in that instrument itself. More than this would be revolution. But we think the Dred Scott decision is erroneous. . . ."

Among other things, the Scott case helped Lincoln get elected as President. And in an interesting twist of history, it was Chief Justice Taney who administered the oath of office to Lincoln in 1861.

whether African Americans were national citizens when the Constitution was adopted. Taney wrote:

"We think they . . . are not included, and were not intended to be included, under the word 'citizens' in the Constitution, and can therefore claim none of the rights and privileges which that instrument provides for and secures to citizens of the United States. On the contrary, they were at that time considered as a subordinate and inferior class of beings, who had been subjugated [controlled] by the dominant race, and whether emancipated [freed] or not, yet remained subject to their authority . . ."

Associate Justice Benjamin R. Curtis disagreed. He believed that the people who were citizens under the Articles of Confederation remained citizens under the Constitution. In his dissenting opinion, Curtis noted:

"At the time of the . . . Articles of Confederation, all free native-born inhabitants of the States of New Hampshire, Massachusetts, New York, New Jersey, and North Carolina, though descended from African slaves, were not only citizens of those States, but [some of them also] possessed the [right to vote], on equal terms with other citizens."

Curtis went on to declare that "every free person born on the soil of a State, who is a citizen of that State by force of its Constitution and laws, is also a citizen of the United States."

Dred Scott

African Americans React to Taney's Opinion

Of course, it was Taney's majority opinion that counted. The opinion "went across the land like a thunderclap," as one historian put it. African Americans in the North held meetings to discuss the "atrocious decision." One gathering in Philadelphia approved several resolutions, including these:

"*Resolved*, That though many of our fathers and some of us have . . . exercised the right of American citizenship; . . . the power to oppress us lurked all the time in the Constitution. . . ."

Setting the Stage Activity

Writing Diary Entries

To prepare students to read about citizenship issues, ask them to imagine that the Supreme Court has ruled that brown-eyed people cannot be U.S. citizens. Have students write diary entries in which they react to the ruling, stating whether or not it will affect them personally.

Bonus Activity

Thinking Like Justices

To help students understand the differences between Taney's and Curtis's opinions, have them take part in a role-play. First explain that before the justices of the Supreme Court reach a decision about a case, they discuss it among themselves. Next assign partners. Ask the partners to imagine the discussion about the Dred Scott case that took place between justices Taney and Curtis. Have them act out a few minutes of the discussion. If students will be performing their role-plays in front of the class, allow ample time for rehearsal.

Discussion

Checking Understanding

1. How did the original Constitution leave matters of citizenship open to question? (It did not define *citizen*, specify qualifications for citizenship, or offer a complete list of citizens' rights and duties.)

2. Why did Justice Curtis believe that free African Americans should be considered citizens? (Free African Americans had been citizens in some states under the Articles of Confederation, and Curtis believed they remained citizens under the Constitution. Justice Curtis also thought that every citizen of a state was also a national citizen.)

Stimulating Critical Thinking

3. Should citizenship be the birthright of every child born on American soil, or not? Explain your thinking. (Yes: it is a cherished tradition that has strengthened our country. No: it overburdens the nation's economy and government services to have so many citizens.)

Citizenship Footnote

The original Constitution implied the existence of two kinds of citizenship—state and national—but did not describe their relationship. Justice Curtis saw it this way: states are the basic source of citizenship, and state citizenship automatically means national citizenship. Chief Justice Taney disagreed. He wrote, "[N]o State can . . . introduce a new member into the political community created by the Constitution. . . . It cannot make him a member of this community by making him a member of its own." In other words, a state could bestow citizenship on anyone, including African Americans, but national citizenship did not necessarily follow. In time, the Fourteenth Amendment confirmed Taney's idea that the basic source of citizenship lies in the nation, not the states.

"*Resolved*, That . . . the only duty the colored man owes to a Constitution under which he is declared to be an inferior and degraded being, having no rights which white men are bound to respect, is to denounce and repudiate [reject] it. . . ."

Citizenship Is Debated Today

The Dred Scott decision has no legal force today. It was overturned by Amendments 13, 14, and 15, enacted after the Civil War. (See Chapter 3.) However, the question "Who can be a citizen?" continues to spark debate.

For example, *illegal aliens* are citizens of other countries who live in the United States without proper documents. Some illegal aliens give birth to children while here. As long ago as 1898, the Supreme Court ruled that such children are U.S. citizens. In other words, U.S. citizenship is the birthright of all children born on American soil. Now, a century later, a strong movement to reduce immigration and limit government benefits for aliens has developed. Some of the movement's supporters have called for a constitutional amendment to overturn the 1898 decision.

Congress may or may not pass such an amendment. If Congress does pass it, the states may or may not ratify it. But one thing is certain: As long as Americans wrestle with questions of citizenship, *Dred Scott* v. *Sandford* stands as more than just a dusty relic of some dim and distant past.

You Are a Citizen If . . .

- **You were born in the United States or its territories. (This is true even if your parents were not citizens, unless they were living in the United States as representatives of a foreign government.)**
- **At least one of your parents was a U.S. citizen when you were born.**
- **You have been naturalized, which means you have gone through the process of becoming a citizen.**
- **You were under age eighteen when your parents were naturalized.**

Connections to Geography

The justices in Dred Scott's case voted largely but not entirely along sectional lines. Five of the justices were from slave states: Taney, James M. Wayne, John Catron, Peter V. Daniel, and John A. Campbell. All five voted against Scott. The free-state justices were Curtis, John McLean, Samuel Nelson, and Robert C. Grier. Of the four, Nelson and Grier voted against Scott.

Because of the importance of the case, each of the justices wrote a separate opinion. Only two of the justices who voted with the majority—Wayne and Daniel, both from slave states—wrote that they agreed with Taney's idea that no black person could be a citizen. The other four justices—two from slave states, two from free states—kept silent on the subject.

Understanding Civic Issues

1. Why could free African Americans view themselves as citizens before the Dred Scott decision?
2. Why did Justice Taney believe the framers meant to exclude African Americans from citizenship?
3. **Critical Thinking** Choose one resolution approved at the Philadelphia meeting. Do you agree or disagree with its main point? Why?
4. **Hands-On Citizenship** You and two classmates have been asked to write a constitutional amendment to answer the question "Who can be a citizen?" once and for all.

- Discuss whether to delete, add, or change any items in the list titled You Are a Citizen If . . . As you talk, consider the rights and duties of citizens. If you need help, look up *citizen* in an encyclopedia or a civics textbook.
- Use existing amendments as guides to length and language style as you write. (See pages R59–R73.)
- Share your amendment. Can the class agree on which amendment is "best"? Why or why not?

Newly naturalized U.S. citizens

Citizenship Lab Answers

1. Passports, ability to sue and be sued in state courts, ability of men to vote in some states.

2. Because when the Constitution was written, white Americans dominated African Americans and considered them inferior.

3. Agree with first resolution: Constitution acknowledges and allows slavery. Disagree: Constitution does not prohibit citizenship for African Americans. Agree with second resolution: since the Declaration of Independence, Americans mistreated by their government have felt justified in opposing it. Disagree: blame should be placed on Taney and the justices who voted with him, not on the Constitution.

Teaching the Hands-On CITIZENSHIP

Have students recall what they know about citizenship issues from newspapers or other sources. Point out that people can be allowed to be citizens and yet have limited rights. For example, citizens must be at least 18 years old to vote.

To help students organize their thoughs about important issues, have them prepare a decision chart. At the top of the chart, students should write the main issue. In the next tier, students should indicate possible options. In the second tier, students should identify the positive and negative consequences of each alternative.

At·a·Glance

2 The Civil War 1861–1865

Chapter Planning Guide

Section	Student Text	Teacher's Edition Activities
Opener and Story pp. 138–141	**Keys to History Time Line** **History Mystery** Beginning the Story with **Clara Barton**	**Setting the Stage Activity** A Help-Wanted Ad, p. 140
1 **Preparing for War** pp. 142–147	**Reading Maps** The Union and the Confederacy, p. 143 **Link to Art** *Sounding Reveille*, p. 146 **Point of View** Should the Union have refused to enlist African Americans?, p. 147	**Warm-Up Activity** Off to War: Dialogues at Home, p. 142 **Geography Question of the Day,** p. 142 **Section Activity** Border State Stump Speeches, p. 144 **Bonus Activity** Enlistment Posters, p. 146 **Wrap-Up Activity** Writing Editorials, p. 147
2 **The First Two Years of War** pp. 148–153	**Link to Literature** *Bull Run*, pp. 170–171 **Reading Maps** The Civil War 1861–1862, p. 151 **Link to Technology** The Camera, p. 152	**Warm-Up Activity** War Then and Now, p. 148 **Geography Question of the Day,** p. 148 **Section Activity** War Dispatches, p. 150 **Bonus Activity** A Soldier's Letter Home, p. 152 **Wrap-Up Activity** A Battle Chart, p. 153
3 **The War Effort at Home** pp. 154–160	**Link to the Present** The American Red Cross, p. 156 **World Link** Britain stays neutral in Civil War, p. 158 **Skill Lab** Making a Hypothesis, p. 160	**Warm-Up Activity** Lincoln's Diary, p. 154 **Geography Question of the Day,** p. 154 **Section Activity** Newspaper Articles, p. 156 **Bonus Activity** Creating a Lincoln Collage, p. 158 **Wrap-Up Activity** War Problems: A Venn Diagram, p. 159
4 **From War to Peace** pp. 161–167	**Reading Maps** The Civil War 1863–1865, p. 163 **Hands-On History** Commemorating the Civil War, p. 164 **Geography Lab** Reading a Grid Map, p. 167	**Warm-Up Activity** A Military Report Card, p. 161 **Geography Question of the Day,** p. 161 **Section Activity** Interviewing Lee and Grant, p. 162 **Bonus Activity** Writing Song Lyrics, p. 164 **Wrap-Up Activity** Making a Time Line, p. 166
Evaluation	☑ **Section 1 Review,** p. 147 ☑ **Section 2 Review,** p. 153 ☑ **Section 3 Review,** p. 159 ☑ **Section 4 Review,** p. 166 ☑ **Chapter Survey,** pp. 168–169 **Alternative Assessment** Writing a play, p. 169	☑ **Answers to Section 1 Review,** p. 147 ☑ **Answers to Section 2 Review,** p. 143 ☑ **Answers to Section 3 Review,** p. 159 ☑ **Answers to Section 4 Review,** p. 166 ☑ **Answers to Chapter Survey,** pp. 168–169 (Alternative Assessment guidelines are in the Take-Home Planner.)

Teacher's Resource Package

Chapter Summaries: English and Spanish, pp. 40–41

Chapter Resources Binder
Study Guide Reading for Details, p. 25
Reinforcement Analyzing Primary Sources, pp. 29–30

Chapter Resources Binder
Study Guide Completing a Chart, p. 26

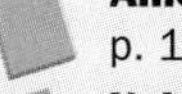
Chapter Resources Binder
Study Guide Completing an Outline, p. 27
Skills Development Making a Hypothesis, pp. 31–32
American Readings Celebrating Emancipation, p. 13
Using Historical Documents The Emancipation Proclamation, pp. 32–39

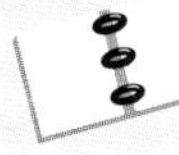
Chapter Resources Binder
Study Guide Completing a Graphic Organizer, p. 28

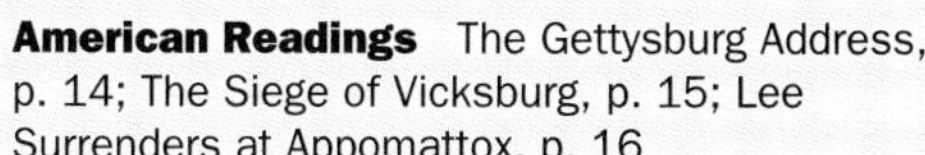
Geography Extensions Reading a Grid Map, pp. 9–10
American Readings The Gettysburg Address, p. 14; The Siege of Vicksburg, p. 15; Lee Surrenders at Appomattox, p. 16

Chapter and Unit Tests Chapter 2 Tests, Forms A and B, pp. 27–30

Take-Home Planner

Introducing the Chapter Activity Writing About War, p. 14

Chapter In-Depth Activity Creating a Civil War Magazine, p. 14

Reduced Views
Study Guide, p. 16
Reinforcement, p. 17
Unit 1 Answers, pp. 30–38

Reduced Views
Study Guide, p. 16
Unit 1 Answers, pp. 30–38

Reduced Views
Study Guide, p. 16
Skills Development, p. 17
American Readings, p. 18
Using Historical Documents, p. 19
Unit 1 Answers, pp. 30–38

Reduced Views
Study Guide, p. 16
Geography Extensions, p. 19
American Readings, p. 18
Unit 1 Answers, pp. 30–38

Reduced Views
Chapter Tests, p. 19
Unit 1 Answers, pp. 30–38
Alternative Assessment Guidelines for scoring the Chapter Survey activity, p. 15

Additional Resources

Wall Time Line

Unit 1 Activity

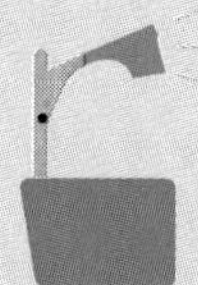

Transparency Package

Transparency 2-1 First Day of Gettysburg—use with Section 4
Transparency 2-2 Women in the Civil War—use with Section 3
Transparency Activity Book

SelecTest Testing Software
Chapter 2 Test, Forms A and B

Vital Links

Videodisc

CD-ROM

Irish regiment (see TE p. 144)
Lincoln on McClellan (see TE p. 150)
Battle of Antietam (see TE p. 153)
African American soldiers (see TE p. 154)
Voice of nurse Kate Cummings (see TE p. 157)
War refugees (see TE p. 159)
Voice of Major Sullivan Ballou (see TE p. 162)
Gettysburg Address (see TE p. 163)
"The Battle Hymn of the Republic" (see TE p. 164)
Atlanta (see TE p. 165)

Videotape Clara Barton: Eyewitness to the Civil War

2

Teaching Resources

- Take-Home Planner 1
  - Introducing Chapter Activity
  - Chapter In-Depth Activity
  - Alternative Assessment
- Chapter Resources Binder
- Geography Extensions
- American Readings
- Using Historical Documents
- Transparency Activities
- Wall Time Line Activities
- Chapter Summaries
- Chapter and Unit Tests
- SelecTest Test File
- Vital Links CD-ROM/Videodisc

Time Line

Keys to History

Keys to History journal writing activities are on page 168 in the Chapter Survey.

First Battle of Bull Run The Union loss shocked northerners into realizing that the war would not be quickly won. (p. 148)

Monitor* vs. *Merrimac In this battle between the first two ironclad steamships, neither side claimed victory, dashing the Confederates' hopes of breaking the Union blockade of Norfolk, Virginia. (p. 149)

Battle of Antietam This was a turning point in the war, destroying a third of Lee's army and ruining the South's hopes of European aid. (p. 153)

Looking Back Lincoln's election led seven states in the South to secede from the Union and form the Confederacy.

World Link See p. 158.

Chapter Objectives

- ★ Describe the resources of the Union and the Confederacy.
- ★ Explain the failure of either army to win a victory that would end the war.
- ★ Describe the Civil War's effect on northerners and southerners at home.
- ★ Describe the Union victories that finally ended the war.

Chapter Overview

After Fort Sumter, four Border States joined the seven Confederate states. Lincoln acted to keep the other four Border States in the Union. The North had an economic advantage in the war, but the Confederacy had great military leaders, such as Robert E. Lee.

To bring the Confederate states back into the Union, Lincoln ordered a naval blockade and planned to capture Richmond. But the

1861–1865

Chapter 2 The Civil War

Sections

Beginning the Story with Clara Barton

1. Preparing for War
2. The First Two Years of War
3. The War Effort at Home
4. From War to Peace

1862 September
Battle of Antietam

1862 March
Monitor vs. *Merrimac*

1861 July
First Battle of Bull Run

1861 — 1862

World Link
Britain stays neutral in Civil War
1861–1865

Looking Back
Lincoln elected President
1860

South won the first battle, at Bull Run. After several battles, neither side had a clear advantage. The Union realized there would be no quick victory.

In 1863 Lincoln signed the Emancipation Proclamation, and about 186,000 African Americans joined the Union army. Women helped the war effort as nurses and factory workers. However, Union citizens were protesting the draft and the income tax, while southerners were suffering from a poor economy.

In 1863 Lee's troops invaded the Union at Gettysburg; the battle resulted in a Union victory but huge losses for both sides. Grant then took Vicksburg, giving the Union control of the Mississippi. Meanwhile, Sherman waged total war through Georgia and South Carolina. On April 9, 1865, after the fall of Richmond, Lee surrendered at Appomattox Court House.

HISTORY *Mystery*

Although Lyons Wakeman enlisted in the Union army, family members kept this fact secret and hid the letters they received. Who was Lyons Wakeman, and what knowledge was the family hiding?

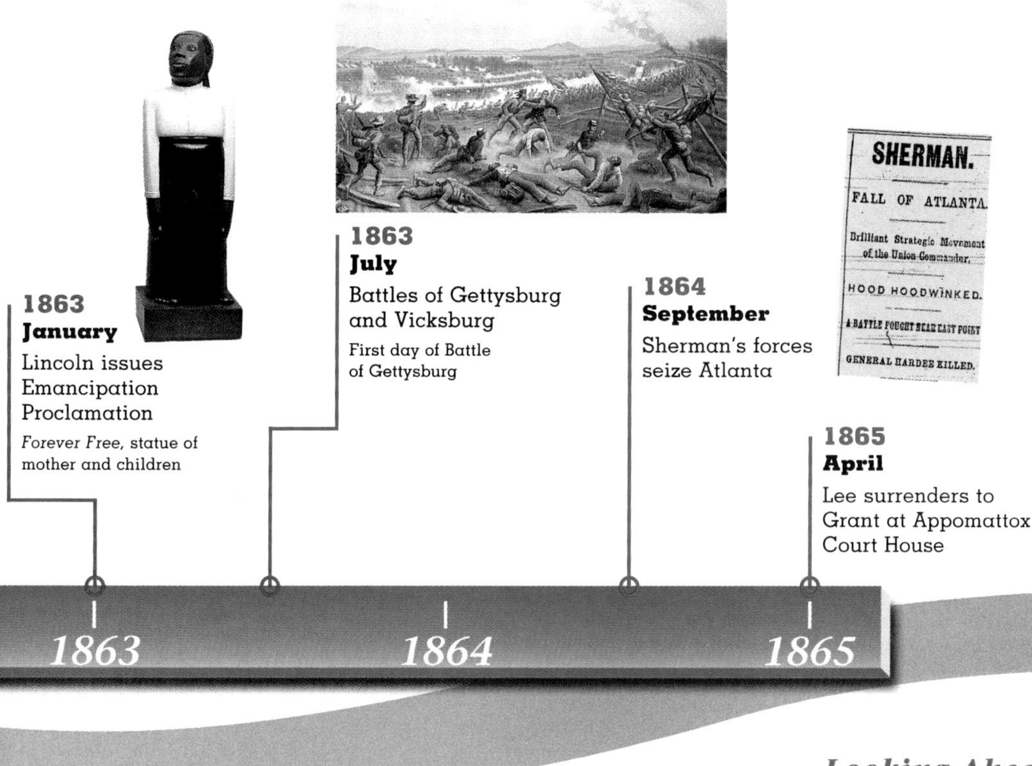

SHERMAN.
FALL OF ATLANTA.
Brilliant Strategic Movement of the Union Commander.
HOOD HOODWINKED.
A BATTLE FOUGHT NEAR EAST POINT
GENERAL HARDEE KILLED.
1863
1864
1865

1863
January
Lincoln issues Emancipation Proclamation

Forever Free, statue of mother and children

1863
July
Battles of Gettysburg and Vicksburg

First day of Battle of Gettysburg

1864
September
Sherman's forces seize Atlanta

1865
April
Lee surrenders to Grant at Appomattox Court House

Looking Ahead

14th Amendment guarantees equality

1868

Teaching the *HISTORY* *Mystery*

Students will find the answer on p. 146. See Chapter Survey, p. 168, for additional questions.

Time Line

Emancipation Proclamation The plan freeing all slaves in the Confederate states changed the war into a fight for freedom as well as for the Union. (p. 154)

Battles of Gettysburg and Vicksburg The Confederate loss at Gettysburg turned the war into a defensive war on southern soil. The southern loss at Vicksburg led to Union control of the entire Mississippi River. (pp. 161–164)

Sherman in Atlanta This Union use of total war raised spirits in the North and ensured Lincoln's reelection. (p. 165)

Lee surrenders to Grant The bloodiest war in the history of the nation ended, having cost more than 620,000 lives. (p. 166)

Looking Ahead The 14th Amendment, ratified in 1868, guaranteed equality to all men.

Beginning the Story

Clara Barton

Clara Barton overcame childhood shyness and fears to become a courageous nurse of injured Union soldiers during the Civil War. Known as "the angel of the battlefield," she followed the army from battle to battle and treated the men right on the battlefields. She showed determination in personally obtaining needed supplies. Clara Barton went on to found the American Red Cross. Her courage shines through the horrifying carnage of the Civil War.

Setting the Stage Activity

A Help-Wanted Ad

To help students consider the contributions made by both women and men during the Civil War, have them write help-wanted ads that might have been published around the beginning of the war in 1861. Have half the class write ads asking for soldiers. Tell them to describe specifically the kind of person needed to fight the war. Have the other half advertise for jobs that could be done by women or young girls or boys. Ask several students to read their completed ads.

See the Introducing the Chapter Activity, Writing About War. **Take-Home Planner 1,** p. 14.

History Footnote

Recorded in Clara Barton's journal and memoirs are some of her amazing war experiences. She took three women with her to the Second Battle of Bull Run. The four women stayed up all night baking bread, serving soup, distributing shirts, and writing down names of wounded men. On most other trips to the battlefield, she was not allowed to take female helpers. At Chantilly she slept in a tent sitting up because the floor was filled with rainwater. She brought linen bandages to a field hospital where doctors had been dressing wounds in corn husks. When a general who did not recognize her offered protection as she made her way through wounded soldiers at Fredericksburg, she replied, "Thank you very much, but I believe I'm the best protected woman in the United States."

Beginning the Story with Clara Barton

On September 17, 1862, Confederate and Union troops clashed in a fierce battle along Antietam (an-TEET-uhm) Creek in western Maryland. As the bullets whizzed past and the cannon balls crashed, a lone woman appeared on the battlefield. Her face darkened by gun smoke, she moved from one wounded soldier to another. To some she gave a little food and water. To others she applied bandages. Once she dug a bullet out of flesh with her pocketknife.

All through that long day the bodies piled up. At times the woman had to stop and wring the blood from her skirt to keep moving. She was so close to the raging battle that as she bent over one man a bullet clipped her sleeve and killed him. Later, after darkness fell and the pitiful cries of the wounded replaced the din of combat, she continued to help the injured and dying.

The woman helping wounded soldiers on that day of death was Clara Barton. Later generations would remember her as the founder of the American Red Cross. To the Union troops at the Battle of Antietam, she was simply "the lady" or, as a grateful army doctor put it, "the angel of the battlefield."

"I Remember Nothing But Fear"

As a young child, this fearless angel of mercy had been anything but bold. Born on Christmas Day in 1821 in Massachusetts, the youngest of five children, Clara never felt comfortable with herself. She thought she was too short and too fat. She preferred studying "boys' subjects," such as mathematics and science, to such "womanly" tasks as cooking and sewing.

Clara was also painfully shy. To help overcome her self-doubts, her parents encouraged her to excel at sports and horseback riding. Doing exciting things helped Clara hide her inner fears. So did helping others. Their praise made her feel better about herself. Nonetheless, looking back on her childhood, Clara said, "I remember nothing but fear."

History Bookshelf

Stevens, Bryna. *Frank Thompson: Her Civil War Story*. Macmillan, 1992. Using the name Frank Thompson, Emma Edmonds disguised herself as a man and served in the Union army as a nurse, mail carrier, and spy.

Also of interest:

Archer, Jules. *A House Divided: The Lives of Ulysses S.Grant and Robert E.Lee.* Scholastic, 1995.

Chang, Ina. *A Separate Battle: Women and the Civil War.* Lodestar, 1991.

Freedman, Russell. *Lincoln: A Photobiography.* Clarion, 1991.

Keith, Harold. *Rifles for Watie.* Crowell, 1957.

Mettger, Zak. *Till Victory Is Won: Black Soldiers in the Civil War.* Lodestar, 1994.

Discussion

Thinking Historically

1. What attitudes do you see in Clara Barton's life before the Civil War that help explain her actions during the war? (She liked "boys' subjects," she pursued active hobbies, she liked to help people, and she rebelled against sexist job and pay policies.)

2. What character traits do you see in Clara Barton? (She was courageous, independent, and persevering.)

3. What do you learn about the nature of the war from Clara Barton's story? (It was brutal, with many casualties. Medical treatment was often primitive, and supplies were scarce.)

Clara Barton wanted to "go to the rescue of the men who fell." She treated them right on the battlefield rather than in hospitals behind the lines. This picture shows wounded Union soldiers in a field near Fredericksburg, Virginia.

See the Chapter In-Depth Activity, Creating a Civil War Magazine. **Take-Home Planner 1,** p. 14.

"Between the Bullet and the Battlefield"

Clara Barton's self-doubts followed her into adulthood. She did not, however, let them keep her from standing up for herself. Once she quit a teaching job because the school board hired a man to do the same work at a higher salary. "I may sometimes be willing to teach for nothing," she declared, "but if paid at all, I shall never do a man's work for less than a man's pay."

Clara also stood her ground when she took a job as a clerk in the United States Patent Office in 1854. As one of the first women hired by the federal government, she was resented by the male clerks. They called her names, blew cigar smoke in her face, and spit tobacco juice at her feet. Their insults, she told a friend, made "about as much impression upon me as a sling shot would upon the hide of a shark."

It was as a volunteer nurse in the Civil War that Clara completely overcame her childhood fears. When the war began, neither side was prepared to care for wounded soldiers. Countless men died for lack of medical treatment. This waste of lives infuriated Clara, and she began to collect medical supplies to care for the wounded herself. In spite of the disapproval of Union officers, she followed the army into battle after battle. Her place, she said, was "anywhere between the bullet and the battlefield."

Clara's courage in battle amazed all who knew her, and perhaps even herself. In the face of death and suffering, her old fears faded away. "I may be compelled to face danger," she once told an audience, "but never *fear* it. While our soldiers can stand and *fight,* I can stand and feed and nurse them."

Hands-On HISTORY

Activity

War correspondents traveled with the Union and Confederate armies to gather news for their papers. Imagine that you are a war correspondent with the Union army. Write a report of an interview with Clara Barton after the Battle of Antietam. Include at least three questions and her answers.

Teaching the Hands-On HISTORY

To help students brainstorm questions, have them think about what people living during the Civil War would want to know about life on the battlefield. They should include some questions about Clara Barton's personal feelings, and some about what she witnessed on the battlefield.

For a journal writing activity on Clara Barton, see student page 168.

Introducing the Section

Vocabulary

habeas corpus (p. 142) a right that protects people from being held in prison unlawfully

martial law (p. 142) rule by the army instead of by the usual government officials

Warm-Up Activity

Off to War: Dialogues at Home

To help students imagine different reactions to the war, have small groups create dialogues between parents and children. Assign each group a different scenario: a southern planter urging his reluctant son to enlist; a northern abolitionist urging her reluctant daughter to volunteer as a nurse; a poor southern farm woman trying to dissuade her son from enlisting; a recent immigrant in the North trying to dissuade his daughter from volunteering as a nurse. Conclude by having groups share their dialogues and summarize reasons for and against joining the war effort.

Geography Question of the Day

Ask students to refer to the map on page 143 and list the Union and Confederate states when the war began.

Section Objectives

- ★ Identify the slave states that did not join the Confederacy.
- ★ Explain why volunteers rushed to join the Union and Confederate armies.
- ★ List the advantages each side had as the war began.

Teaching Resources

Take-Home Planner 1, pp. 12–19
Chapter Resources Binder
Study Guide, p. 25
Reinforcement, pp. 29–30
Skills Development
Geography Extensions
American Readings
Using Historical Documents
Transparency Activities
Chapter and Unit Tests

1. Preparing for War

Reading Guide

New Terms habeas corpus, martial law

Section Focus The resources of the Union and the Confederacy

1. Which slave states did not join the Confederacy?
2. Why did volunteers rush to join the Union and Confederate armies?
3. What advantages did each side have as the war began?

The Confederate attack on Fort Sumter on April 12, 1861, plunged the nation into civil war. In Washington, D.C., Clara Barton witnessed the confusion and fear. Rumors spread wildly. The city was torn between supporters of the Union and of the Confederacy. In the Patent Office, where Clara worked, some people openly supported the Confederate cause.

Clara was a staunch Republican. In this crisis, she looked to President Lincoln to take action against "those who have dared to raise the hand of rebellion." Lincoln responded quickly and firmly. On April 15 he called for 75,000 volunteers for 90 days to put down the rebellion in the 7 Confederate states.

Taking Sides in the War

Lincoln's action had a powerful effect on the eight slave states of the Upper South. These "Border States" had not yet decided whether to join the Confederacy or stay in the Union. After Lincoln's call for volunteers, Virginia, Arkansas, North Carolina, and Tennessee seceded from the Union. Richmond, Virginia, became the capital of the Confederacy.

People in the mountainous western part of Virginia, however, remained loyal to the Union. They broke away to form the new state of West Virginia, which joined the Union in 1863.

Slave states in the Union Of the other four Border States, Delaware voted unanimously to stay in the Union. Maryland, Kentucky, and Missouri, though, were deeply divided. Lincoln knew he had to keep Maryland in the Union because the state surrounded Washington, D.C., on three sides.

When a pro-Confederate mob attacked Union soldiers traveling through Maryland on their way to Washington, Lincoln sent troops to keep order. He had pro-Confederate leaders arrested. Then he used his constitutional power to suspend the right of **habeas corpus,** which protects people from being held in prison unlawfully. Maryland stayed in the Union.

At first, Kentucky tried to stay neutral. However, when fighting broke out between pro-Confederate and pro-Union groups, Kentucky sided with the Union.

In Missouri, Union and Confederate supporters fought each other fiercely. Lincoln kept Missouri in the Union by putting the state under martial law. **Martial law** is rule by the army instead of by the usual government officials.

The war brought special anguish to people in the Border States. Brothers, cousins, and even fathers and sons fought on different sides. Clifton Prentiss of Maryland fought for

History Footnote

Indians in the war were known as excellent fighters, but the customs of wearing uniforms, standing at attention, and marching in formation were foreign to them. One Confederate account of a group of Cherokee soldiers describes their painted faces, ponytails, and buckskin clothing. Many continued to use their traditional weapons, bows and arrows and tomahawks.

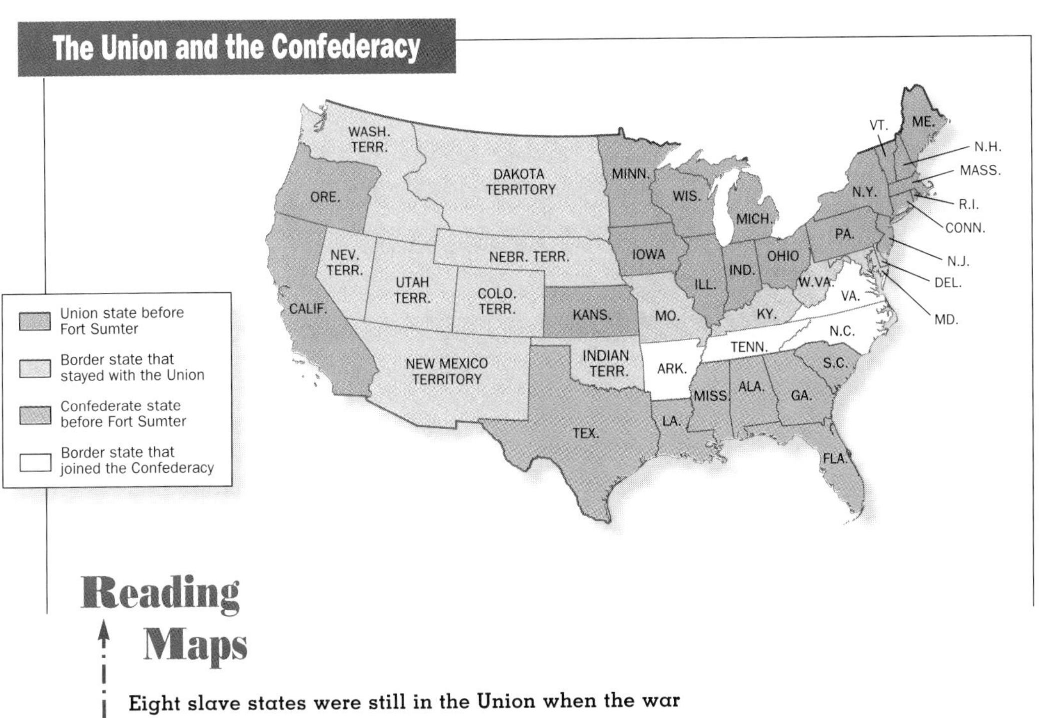

Reading Maps

Eight slave states were still in the Union when the war began. Which ones joined the Confederacy?

the Union while his brother, William, was in the Confederate army. In 1865 the two brothers finally met again on their deathbeds in a hospital in Washington, D.C.

Far West states and territories Most of the states and territories of the Far West were loyal to the Union from the beginning. Early in the war, however, Union and Confederate forces struggled for control of the huge New Mexico Territory.

Texas, a Confederate state, feared a Union invasion from New Mexico, so it sent troops into the territory in 1861. They defeated the main Union forces and captured Tucson, Albuquerque, and Santa Fe.

Their victory was short-lived, though. In March 1862 Union volunteers from Colorado and New Mexico smashed a Confederate force at Glorieta Pass. The Confederates retreated to Texas, their hopes of conquering the Southwest shattered.

The Confederates had more success winning the support of the Cherokees, Creeks, Choctaws, Chickasaws, and Seminoles. Now living in Indian Territory, these southern tribes had been resettled in the West under the Indian removal policy of President Andrew Jackson. Many of these groups of Indians owned slaves and leaned strongly to the South's cause.

All five tribes signed alliances with the Confederacy. In return for their support, they received the right to send delegates to the Confederate Congress. About 15,000 Indian soldiers fought in the Confederate army.

At least 3,000 Indians fought for the North, including 135 Oneida volunteers from Wisconsin. Ely S. Parker, a New York Seneca, served as Ulysses S. Grant's military secretary.

Developing the Section

Discussion

Checking Understanding

1. How was the new state of West Virginia formed? (After Virginia joined the Confederacy, people in the western part remained loyal to the Union and formed a new state.)

Stimulating Critical Thinking

2. Was Lincoln right to suspend habeas corpus and declare martial law? Why or why not? (Yes: in wartime President should have power to take steps to save nation. No: violates democratic principles.)

Teaching the Reading Maps

To help students visualize the division of the nation, have them refer to the map as you point out that South Carolina's secession was quickly followed by Mississippi, Florida, Alabama, Georgia, Louisiana, and Texas. After war was declared, Virginia, Arkansas, Tennessee, and North Carolina seceded. West Virginia, Delaware, Maryland, Kentucky, and Missouri stayed with the Union, as did states and most territories of the West. **Answer to Reading Maps:** Virginia, Arkansas, North Carolina, Tennessee.

Section Activity

Border State Stump Speeches

To focus on issues facing citizens at the outbreak of the Civil War, have pairs of students imagine they are representatives of the North or South traveling through the Border States. Assign half the pairs to write speeches to persuade the citizens to secede, while the other pairs write speeches to convince the states to remain in the Union. Speeches should include a mixture of moral, political, and economic reasons. They should include both rational and emotional appeals. Conclude by asking volunteers to read their speeches and having the class compare arguments.

Vital Links

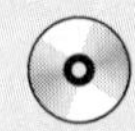

Irish regiment (Picture)
Unit 3, Side 1,
Search 28862

See also Unit 3 Explore CD-ROM location 142.

Tips for Teaching

Students With Limited English

Visuals are helpful for providing clues to meaning. Discuss the graph on page 144. For example, have a student define the word *population.* Then ask: What percentages of the population lived in the North and in the South? How is a greater population an advantage in a war? Ask similar questions for each entry on the graph.

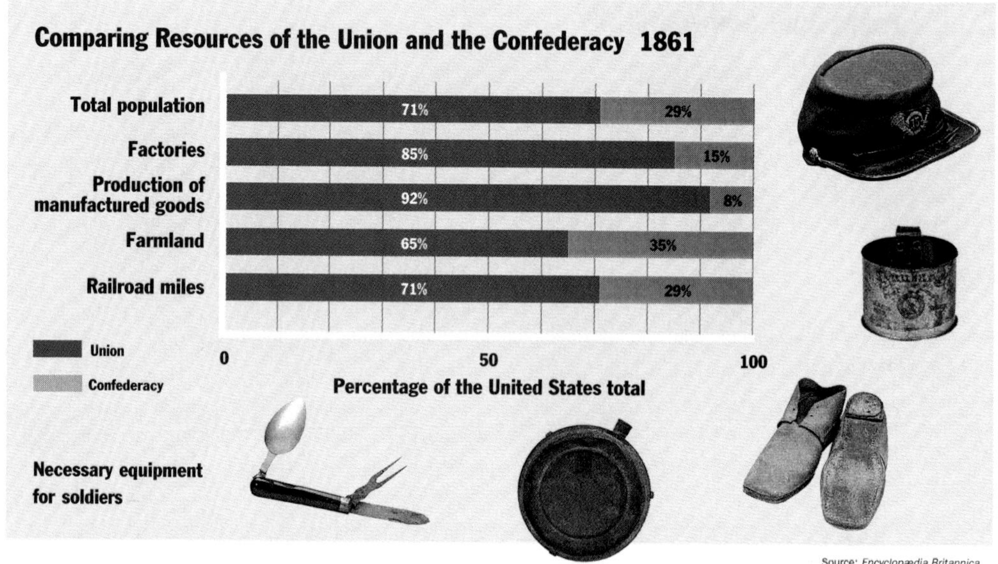

Source: *Encyclopædia Britannica*

Resources for Waging War

In the spring of 1861 most people expected a short war. Northerners felt sure they would defeat the South in a few battles. Southerners were equally optimistic. An Alabamian predicted peace by 1862 because "we are going to kill the last Yankee [northerner] before that time. . . . I think I can whip 25 myself." In fact, each side had advantages it was counting on to bring it victory.

Economic strengths Northerners were confident of their greater economic strength. The Union had almost twice as much farmland as the Confederacy and would be better able to feed its armies as well as the people at home.

The graph above shows that 85 percent of the nation's factories were in the North. These factories produced almost all of the nation's manufactured goods, including guns, cloth, boots, and shoes.

The Union also had 71 percent of the nation's railroad lines, which would be essential for moving troops and supplies. The Union had a navy, too, and nearly all the nation's shipbuilding took place in the North. The Confederacy had few shipyards and no navy.

Finally, the Union had more than twice as many people as the Confederacy. This greater population made little difference at first, when the two armies were fairly equal in size. Later, however, having twice as many men available to fight would turn out to be a great advantage to the Union.

Military strengths In one area the Confederacy clearly had the edge at the start of the war—it had the nation's best military leaders. One of them was Robert E. Lee of Virginia, who had graduated from the United States Military Academy at West Point and served in the Mexican-American War. During that war, Lee had been described by General Winfield Scott as "the very best soldier that I ever saw in the field."

Lee had opposed secession. When Virginia joined the Confederacy, however, everything

History Footnote

In 1857 Robert E. Lee inherited a large Virginia estate, including slaves, from his father-in-law. His father-in-law's will provided for the freedom of his slaves. As a lieutenant colonel in Texas in 1855, Lee had been aware of the conflict between abolitionists and slave owners throughout the country. He wrote to his wife, "In this enlightened age, there are few, I believe, but what will acknowledge that slavery as an institution is a moral and political evil in any Country." With war looming in 1860, he said, "If the slaves of the South were mine, I would surrender them all without a struggle to avert this war." In 1862 he released the slaves on his plantation.

changed. "I must side either with or against my section," he told a friend. With a heavy heart, Lee declined President Lincoln's offer of command of the Union army. "I cannot raise my hand against my birthplace, my home, my children," he explained.

Raising Armies

Expecting a short, glorious war, volunteers rushed to enlist. Southerners, who were called Johnny Rebs (for rebels), were determined to defend their homes, their loved ones, and the South's way of life from an invading Union army. One southerner wrote, "Our men *must* prevail [win] in combat, or lose their property, country, freedom, everything."

Northerners, called Billy Yanks or Yankees, fought to preserve the Union. Ted Upson of Indiana joined the army when he was barely 16. He told his father: "This Union your ancestors and mine helped to make must be saved from destruction."

Interest in having an adventure or earning a paycheck also led young men to join the army. Benjamin F. Chase joined the 5th Volunteer Infantry of New Hampshire to see the country and help his parents, who had 11 children to support. "i don't buy eny of the foolish stuff," he assured his parents when sending money home. "You may think i do but i certain don't."

Like many recruits in 1861, Chase was delighted with his new experiences and confident of a brief war. "What a good ride we shall have going south," he boasted in one of his first letters home. Even after three months in uniform, he was still enthusiastic. On January 8, 1862, he wrote:

> "All of the boys in our tent are very well indeed and enjoying their health first rate. i hant been a mite home sick sense we ben out hear and have not ben a mite sick ether. Mother don't worrough a bout me a mite for i think we shall be home before long."

Like many recruits, these soldiers posed for portraits before marching off to war: (left) Johnny Clem, 11-year-old Union drummer, 22d Michigan Regiment; (center) unidentified Union soldier from New York; (right) Confederate Private Edwin Jennison, 2d Louisiana Cavalry.

Discussion

Checking Understanding

1. What were the North's strengths when the war began? The South's? (The North had more farmland, factories, railroad lines, and population. The South had the best military leaders.)

2. What were northerners fighting for? What were southerners fighting for? (Northerners were fighting to preserve the Union. Southerners were fighting to defend their homes and way of life.)

Stimulating Critical Thinking

3. Robert E. Lee decided not to lead the Union army. Do you agree with his decision? Why or why not? (Yes: loyalty to family and home come before loyalty to the nation. No: Lee had been trained as an officer in the United States Army and should have remained loyal to that commitment; loyalty to the nation should be more important than loyalty to one's state, otherwise there is no basis for having a nation.)

For selections from Lee's letters, see the Reinforcement activity in **Chapter Resources Binder**, pp. 29–30.

Bonus Activity

Enlistment Posters

To help students understand why northerners and southerners were willing to fight in the war, have pairs create enlistment posters. Assign half the pairs to imagine they are recruiters for the Union army, and the other half that they are Confederate recruiters. They should focus on emotional appeals, using persuasive language and eye-catching images. Conclude by comparing persuasive techniques in the posters.

Teaching the Link to Art

Point out that drummers not only awakened soldiers and called them to meals but also communicated orders on smoke-filled battlefields. Drummers often became the target of enemy fire because of their importance in the field. They also cooked, cared for horses, and carried wounded soldiers. After analyzing this painting, display a book containing other war paintings by Homer if possible. Ask students to suggest how the paintings are similar and different. **Discussion Answers:** It depicts tents where the soldiers lived, and shows soldiers sitting around campfires and taking care of their equipment.

History Footnote

Several women served as spies in the war. Harriet Tubman knew many secret routes on the Underground Railroad, and she recruited other former slaves to find Confederate camps and report them to Union officers. She and the others were able to give information about the location of Confederate explosives to Colonel James Montgomery in South Carolina during a Union gunboat raid in 1863. Another Union spy, Elizabeth Van Lew, lived in a mansion in Richmond. She provided hiding places in her home for Union soldiers who had escaped from Confederate prisons.

Rose O'Neal Greenhow was a society hostess in Washington, D.C., who spied for the South. She learned of the Union's planned attack on Manassas in 1861 and sent coded information to General Beauregard, who won an important victory at Manassas.

Link to Art

Sounding Reveille (1865) Almost every family North and South had someone in uniform. People at home were desperate for news of their loved ones. "Special artists" helped satisfy that demand. Hired by illustrated newspapers, special artists went to battlefields and camps to sketch what they saw. The most gifted of these artists was Winslow Homer, who worked for *Harper's Weekly* newspaper. In this painting of a Union camp by Homer, a bugler and two drummers sound reveille, a signal to wake the soldiers each morning. **Discuss** In what ways does this painting show the everyday life of soldiers?

Although the Union and the Confederacy had rules banning boys from enlisting, many managed to join. Historians estimate that between 10 and 20 percent of all soldiers—250,000 to 420,000—were 16 years old or younger. John Mather Sloan of the 9th Texas was only 13 when he lost a leg in battle. He claimed his only regret was that "I shall not soon be able to get at the enemy."

Women soldiers Hundreds of women, too, fought for the cause. Their exact number will never be known, for they had to change their names and disguise themselves as men. Rosetta Wakeman, who joined the 153d Regiment New York State Volunteers, called herself "Lyons Wakeman" and wore men's clothing. Some women even wore fake mustaches or charcoal "whiskers."

History Footnote

Many African Americans were disappointed that they were not allowed to serve in the war. However, they were convinced that they would be invited to join eventually, so they actively drilled and prepared for battle. Some light-skinned African Americans became Union soldiers by pretending they were white. Others helped in any way they could, by cooking for the army, acting as servants for officers, or performing manual labor. Women did laundry, sewed, and served as nurses. In the South, African Americans served as guides and spies for the Union. Escaped slaves who sought refuge in Union camps were sometimes returned to owners who came for them, according to the government's official policy. However, some officers allowed the escaped slaves to stay and render support services.

Many of the women who enlisted were patriotic or adventurous. Some joined to be with husbands, boyfriends, or brothers. At the Battle of Antietam, Clara Barton tended a soldier, shot in the neck, whose real name turned out to be Mary Galloway. Later she helped to reunite Mary and her wounded boyfriend. After the war, Mary and her husband named their first daughter Clara, after Clara Barton.

Point of View

Should the Union have refused to enlist African Americans?

From the moment the war began, free African Americans flocked to recruiting centers in the North. During the first two years of war, though, the Union refused to enlist African Americans.

Lincoln's reasons for the ban were political. He feared that the slave states still in the Union would view the enlistment of black soldiers as a threat to slavery. Using African American soldiers, he argued, might drive the Border States, especially Kentucky, out of the Union and into the Confederacy. He wrote to a friend:

> "I think to lose Kentucky is nearly the same as to lose the whole game. [With] Kentucky gone, we cannot hold Missouri, nor, as I think, Maryland. These [states] all against us, and the job on our hands is too large for us. We would as well consent to separation at once, including the surrender of this capital."

Many white northerners thought that African Americans had no right to fight in the war. When a group of African Americans asked to form a regiment, Governor David Todd of Ohio refused, saying:

> "Do you know that this is a white man's government; that the white men are able to defend and protect it; and that to enlist a Negro soldier would be to drive every white man out of the service?"

Frederick Douglass was outraged by such racist talk. He urged the government to focus on the goal of winning the war. He said:

> "Why does the government reject the Negro? Is he not a man? Can he not wield a sword, fire a gun, march and countermarch, and obey orders like any other? . . . Men in earnest don't fight with one hand, when they might fight with two, and a man drowning would not refuse to be saved even by a colored hand."

At the start of the war, most northerners were too confident of victory to listen to Douglass's advice. Only later, as the war turned long and bloody, would the Union decide to fight with two hands instead of one.

1. Section Review

1. Define the terms **habeas corpus** and **martial law.**
2. Why did Maryland, Kentucky, and Missouri decide to stay in the Union during the Civil War?
3. Give at least three reasons why volunteers rushed to join the Union and the Confederate armies.
4. **Critical Thinking** A Confederate said, "The longer we have them [northerners] to fight, the more difficult they will be to defeat." What do you think the Confederate meant? Explain why you agree or disagree with this view.

Teaching the Point of View

Ask students to identify reasons for and against African American enlistment. (For: black men as competent as white men to be soldiers; blacks needed to win war. Against: keep border slave states loyal; war was white man's fight; would cause whites to leave army.)

Closing the Section

Wrap-Up Activity

Writing Editorials

Have students imagine writing editorials in 1861 predicting which side will win the war and why. Encourage them to think historically about how citizens of the time would have seen the situation.

Section Review Answers

1. Definitions: *habeas corpus* (142), *martial law* (142)
2. In Maryland, Lincoln had opposition leaders arrested and suspended habeas corpus; Kentucky dropped neutrality after fighting broke out there; Lincoln imposed martial law on Missouri.
3. Patriotism, adventure, and money.
4. With stronger industry and more people, Union could keep its war machine running longer. Agree: Union's physical advantages would be decisive. Disagree: Motivation is determining factor, and southerners were defending own land.

Introducing the Section

Vocabulary

casualties (p. 150) soldiers killed, wounded, captured, or missing

Warm-Up Activity

War Then and Now

To help visualize how battles were fought during the Civil War, have students make a chart with the headings "War today" and "War in 1861." Have them list weapons and methods used today, such as planes, submarines, bombs, missiles, tanks, and automatic weapons. Then have them list the Civil War counterparts, such as horses, wooden and ironclad ships, rifles, swords, and cannons.

Geography Question of the Day

Ask students to suppose that the main map on page 151 was the only information they had on the war. Have them write paragraphs explaining what they could conclude about the war based on that map alone. (Confederate states were apparently on the defensive since almost all the battles were fought on their territory. Union had much stronger navy, as evident in blockade. Blockade also indicates foreign trade by sea was important to Confederacy. Control of the Mississippi also seems important because several battles were fought there.)

Section Objectives

- ★ Describe the Union and Confederate strategies for winning the war.
- ★ Explain why these strategies failed to end the war quickly.

Teaching Resources

Take-Home Planner 1, pp. 12–19
Chapter Resources Binder
- **Study Guide, p. 26**
- Reinforcement
- Skills Development

Geography Extensions
American Readings
Using Historical Documents
Transparency Activities
Chapter and Unit Tests

2. The First Two Years of War

Reading Guide

New Term casualties

Section Focus The failure of either army to win a victory that would end the war

1. **What were the Union and Confederate strategies for winning the war?**
2. **Why did these strategies fail to end the war quickly?**

From the first, many people in both the Union and the Confederacy believed that the war would be a short one. No one, in 1861, could imagine that it would drag on for four long, bloody years.

Strategies for Victory

In Washington and Richmond, Presidents Lincoln and Davis planned their strategies. Davis's goal was to defend the Confederacy against invasion. "All we ask," he declared, "is to be left alone."

To achieve their goal, the Confederates would just push back invading Union forces. They hoped to make the war so costly that the North would give up. In this struggle, the Confederates expected help from Britain and other nations that needed the South's cotton.

Lincoln's goal was to bring the Confederate states back into the Union. His first strategy was to prevent supplies from reaching the Confederacy. He took the first step on April 19, 1861, when he ordered a naval blockade of southern seaports (see map, page 151). In a second step a year later, he ordered Union troops to take control of the Mississippi River.

Lincoln's second strategy was to capture Richmond, the Confederate capital, which was only 100 miles (160 km) from Washington. There had not been time to train an army, but northerners were anxious to end the war quickly. "On to Richmond!" they urged, and Lincoln agreed.

First Battle of Bull Run

Lincoln sent General Irvin McDowell with 30,000 soldiers into northern Virginia. Their orders were to crush the Confederate forces at the town of Manassas and then move on to Richmond.

At Manassas, McDowell found General Pierre G. T. Beauregard and a Confederate force of 21,000 in the hills above Bull Run,* a small stream. Certain of a Union victory, congressmen, reporters, and curious Washingtonians drove the 26 miles (42 km) to enjoy a picnic and watch the battle.

On the morning of July 21, 1861, the Union troops attacked, and the Confederate line began to crumble. Thomas J. Jackson and his brigade of Virginians, however, stood firm. "There is Jackson, standing like a stone wall! Rally around the Virginians!" yelled a Confederate officer.

The bravery of Stonewall Jackson—as he was called from then on—stopped the Union advance. Now the Confederates rushed forward. The Union soldiers retreated in panic. Some even stole horses and carriages from the onlookers.

*Union forces usually named a battle for the natural feature nearest the fighting, such as a stream or hill. The Confederates named the battle for a nearby town. Thus, the Battle of Bull Run was known in the South as the Battle of Manassas.

History Footnote

In terms of weapons and military tactics, the Civil War straddled two eras. It was the last of the traditional wars that featured massed columns of infantry, horse cavalry, swords, single-shot rifles, front-loaded cannons, and wooden ships. At the same time, it was the first of the modern wars because it saw the introduction of metallic cartridges, breech-loaded rifles and cannons, rapid-fire machine guns, ironclad warships, the telegraph, railroads, and other hallmarks of mechanized warfare. According to James McPherson in *The Battle Cry of Freedom,* "the old-fashioned cavalry charge against infantry . . . became obsolete in the face of rifles that could knock down horses long before their riders got within saber or pistol range."

In 1864 a Union fleet led by Admiral David G. Farragut, shown in the ship's rigging, captured the Confederate port at Mobile Bay, Alabama.

The First Battle of Bull Run shocked northerners into realizing that the war would not be quickly won. Lincoln immediately called for a million volunteers to serve in the army for three years. At the same time, the easy victory gave southerners a false sense of confidence. Maybe, they thought, 1 rebel could whip 25 Yankees after all.

The War at Sea

President Lincoln had more success with his strategy of blockading southern seaports. The blockade crippled the South's ability to trade its cotton in Europe for the supplies needed to support its war effort.

In a desperate attempt to break the blockade of Norfolk, Virginia, the Confederates developed an "ironclad" warship. They covered a wooden steamship—the *Merrimac*—with iron plates and attached a large iron beak to its prow to ram and sink the ships blockading Norfolk's harbor.

Renamed the *Virginia,* the ironclad sank two Union ships and ran another aground. However, the Union, too, had built an ironclad, the *Monitor.* On March 9, 1862, the two ships battled for hours, with neither able to claim victory. The battle dashed Confederate hopes of breaking the Norfolk Harbor blockade.

Confederate sea raiders In an effort to hurt northern sea trade, the Confederacy had several warships built in England. These ships, including the *Florida* and the *Alabama,* destroyed 250 northern merchant ships. However, the loss had little effect on the Union's ability to wage the war.

Developing the Section

Discussion

Checking Understanding

1. **How would a successful naval blockade by the Union help defeat the Confederacy?** (It would keep the South from sending its cotton to Europe in exchange for war supplies.)
2. **How did the First Battle of Bull Run change the northerners' attitude toward the war?** (The Confederate victory made northerners realize the war would not be quickly won.)

Stimulating Critical Thinking

3. **Why do you think the Confederates' destruction of 250 northern merchant ships had little effect on the Union's ability to wage war?** (The North had plentiful resources and was not depending on trade with Europe to win the war.)

See the Study Guide activity in **Chapter Resources Binder,** p. 26.

For a fictional account of the First Battle of Bull Run, see the Link to Literature feature on pp. 170–171.

Section Activity

War Dispatches

To analyze the first two years of the war, divide the class into five groups, each to write a dispatch to President Lincoln on a particular battle or campaign. Dispatches should include an explanation of its purpose, the outcome, and a prediction about the outcome's effects on the war. The events are the First Battle of Bull Run; the battle between the *Monitor* and the *Virginia;* the war along the Mississippi; the campaign to seize Richmond; and Lee's invasion of the North and the Battle of Antietam. Conclude by having group representatives read their dispatches. Then have the class discuss this question: By the end of 1862, which side was winning?

Vital Links

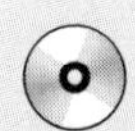

Lincoln on McClellan (First Person Account) Unit 3, Side 1, Search 15714, Play to 15985

See also Unit 3 Explore CD-ROM location 30.

History Footnote

In August 1864, 63-year-old Admiral Farragut led his fleet past three defending Confederate forts to close Mobile, Alabama, the last remaining major southern port on the Gulf of Mexico. Farragut had himself lashed to his ship's rigging so that he would not fall to his death if wounded while commanding the battle. The Confederates had scattered mines across the channel. One mine blew up a Union ship, bottling up the whole fleet under the guns of a fort guarding the entrance to Mobile Bay. Farragut refused to retreat, and shouted what became a famous battle cry: "Damn the torpedoes! Full speed ahead." He took his ship through the minefield safely, followed by the rest of the fleet, and defeated the rebel fleet.

The Fight for the Mississippi

President Lincoln gave the task of gaining control of the Mississippi River to General Ulysses S. Grant. Grant was one of many officers who had left the army after the Mexican-American War. He quickly rejoined with the outbreak of the Civil War.

Grant proved to be an able leader. In February 1862 he captured Fort Henry and Fort Donelson. These two Confederate posts guarded the upper approaches to the Mississippi River at the Tennessee border. Grant showed his fierce determination to win by refusing to discuss terms for the Confederate surrender at Donelson. After that, U. S. Grant was sometimes known as "Unconditional Surrender" Grant.

The Battle of Shiloh With the surrender of Donelson, Confederate troops retreated south. Grant and his army followed. On April 6 the Confederates surprised them near a church named Shiloh. By the end of the day, Grant's forces were close to defeat.

Some Union officers advised retreat. "Retreat? No!" Grant replied. "I propose to attack at daylight and whip them." The next day, Grant did just that, driving the Confederates farther south.

The Battle of Shiloh gave the Union control of much of Kentucky and Tennessee. Now Union forces advanced to Memphis, Tennessee, taking the city in early June.

Farragut Meanwhile, Captain David G. Farragut led a fleet up the Mississippi River. On April 29, 1862, New Orleans surrendered. Baton Rouge, Louisiana, fell a few weeks later.

The next target was the well-defended town of Vicksburg, which was vital to Union success. Lincoln declared, "Vicksburg is the key. The war can never be brought to a close until the key is in our pocket."

Farragut was unable to take Vicksburg, and the Union's Mississippi strategy stalled. It was to be more than a year before Grant could finally capture that important Confederate stronghold.

Campaign to Seize Richmond

In the East, Lincoln now renewed the effort to capture Richmond. To command the new Army of the Potomac he chose General George B. McClellan.

McClellan took months training his raw recruits. At last, in March 1862 he landed 100,000 men on the Virginia Peninsula and advanced slowly toward Richmond. Confederate troops under General Joseph E. Johnston were waiting. They stopped the Union army at the Battle of Seven Pines on May 31 and June 1.

At this point, Robert E. Lee took over command of the Army of Northern Virginia from the wounded Johnston. In late June Lee launched a series of attacks against the Union army that drove them off the peninsula (see map, page 151).

Second Battle of Bull Run Before the Union forces could regroup, Lee surprised them on August 29 in a second battle at Bull Run. **Casualties**—soldiers killed, wounded, captured, or missing—were enormous. Clara Barton was horrified by the casualties. "The men were brot down from the [battle]field and laid on the ground beside the train . . . 'till they covered acres," she wrote. One Union soldier later recalled:

> "Long rows of wounded men were lying around. . . . The surgeons were cutting off arms, feet, hands, limbs of all kinds. As an arm or leg was cut off, it was thrown out an open window. It was an awful sight."

History Footnote

The Battle of Shiloh (see also pp. 104–105) was devastating to both sides, with about 20,000 killed and wounded. During the battle, General Grant rested under a tree because he was suffering from a leg wound received a few days earlier. He finally went to a makeshift field hospital, but he said that the sight of wounded and suffering men there "was more unendurable than encountering the enemy's fire, and I returned to my tree in the rain." The Confederates' fierce resistance ended Grant's hopes for a quick victory on the Mississippi, and made him realize that the entire South, and not just its army, would have to be defeated. "I gave up all idea of saving the Union except by complete conquest," he said.

Discussion

Checking Understanding

1. What qualities made Grant an effective general? (He was fiercely determined, insisting on complete and unconditional surrender at Fort Donelson. He was persevering, refusing to retreat.)

2. Why was the capture of Vicksburg so important to the Union? (It was a well-defended town on the Mississippi; Union needed it, along with New Orleans and Baton Rouge, to control the river.)

Stimulating Critical Thinking

3. What do you think caused the terrible medical conditions described by Barton? (Both sides unprepared for enormous casualties; not enough trained medical personnel or equipment; medical techniques relatively primitive.)

Teaching the Reading Maps

To help students focus on the map, ask them to identify the two main geographic areas where Union forces were attacking the Confederates (Mississippi River and Richmond). **Answers to Reading Maps: 1.** Arkansas, Texas, and Louisiana. **2.** The Battle of Seven Pines and the Seven Day's Battles. Confederate forces went from Richmond north to Manassas and then north to Antietam in Maryland.

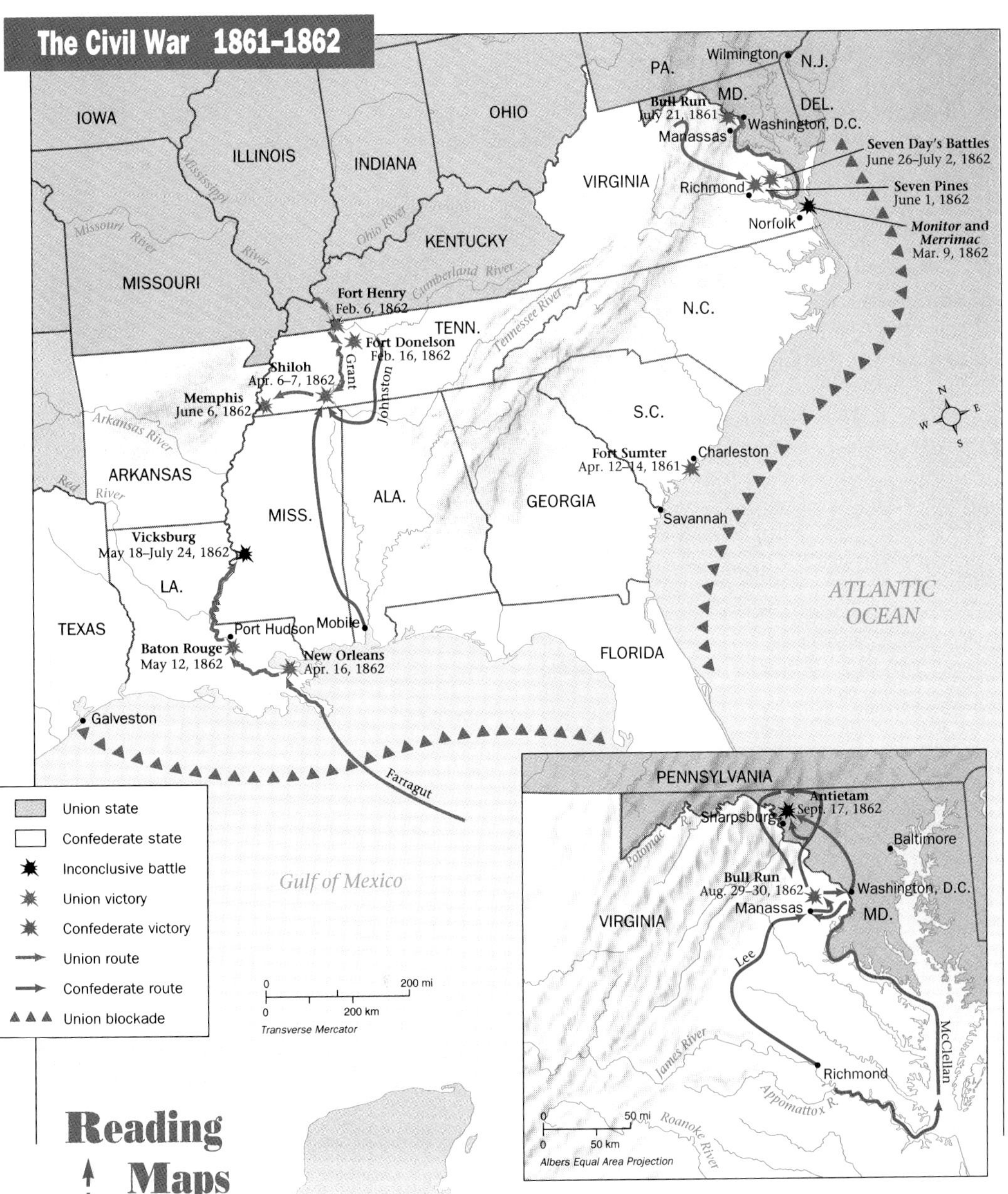

Reading Maps

1. What Confederate states would be cut off from the rest of the Confederacy if the Union controlled the entire Mississippi River?
2. What Confederate victories forced McClellan to retreat from Richmond? What route did Confederate forces under Lee take to invade the Union?

Teaching the

Link to Technology

Point out that many of the photographs taken during the war were of the dead lying on the battlefield. Ask students how they think the extensive photographs taken and published affected people's perceptions of the war. (People were able to see fully the horrors of war as they never had before unless they had been on a battlefield; they would probably be more active in trying to put an end to the war.)

Bonus Activity

A Soldier's Letter Home

Ask students to imagine being participants in one of the Civil War battles described in this section. Have them choose a specific battle and review the facts about it. Then have them write letters home describing the sights, sounds, and feelings of the battle from the perspective of either a Union or a Confederate soldier. They should include their views on the war's prospects. Conclude by having volunteers read their letters aloud to compare perspectives.

History Footnote

The first war photographs were taken in the war with Mexico, from 1846 to 1848. A portable darkroom was needed for battlefield photography, which consisted of a horse-drawn wagon with a hooded canopy that allowed no light to enter. Inside the wagon were built-in containers for chemicals, and compartments for cameras, lenses, and other equipment. Mathew Brady went to the First Battle of Bull Run in a wagon such as this, along with a newspaper reporter and a sketch artist. While attempting to take photographs of soldiers and civilians fleeing the battle site, Brady got caught up in the turmoil. His wagon was overturned, and his equipment was ruined. Although he was able to save some of the exposed glass plates, no Bull Run photographs by Brady have been found.

Link to Technology

The Camera

A major development in technology around the time of the Civil War greatly changed the way we view past events. This development was the camera. While photographic technology had existed for many years, the early 1860s marked the beginning of the wide use of such technology. For the first time, even people far from the front lines could glimpse the grisly scenes of war. As a scholar's tool, photographs provide historians an important window to history—both the history of major events and of ordinary people.

Civil War photographers would rush to the battle scene, set up cameras, then develop the photos on the spot. Perhaps the most famous Civil War photographer was Mathew Brady, who is pictured above with his portable darkroom. The top picture shows the type of photo that made Brady famous. His 1860 camera is pictured at left.

1 A shutter opens quickly, allowing light reflected from the subject to pass through the lens and expose the film.

2 The film is coated with light-sensitive silver crystals. When the reflected light touches them, they turn dark. This process is called ***exposure.***

3 Where the subject is dark, it reflects very little light. Where it is bright, it reflects more light. The exposure makes a reverse image, or ***negative,*** on the film.

4 When the film is developed, the image becomes fixed, and a positive image can be printed—the photograph.

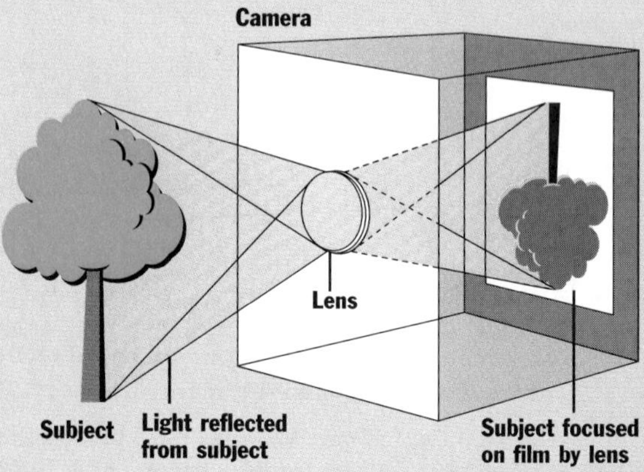

Vital Links

Battle of Antietam (Movie)
Unit 3, Side 1, Search
28868, Play to 29319

See also Unit 3 Explore CD-ROM location 147.

Antietam was the first Civil War battlefield to be photographed before the dead had been buried. Arriving soon after the battle ended, photographer Alexander Gardner took this photo of Confederate dead. Photographs like this captured the horror of war for Americans.

The Battle of Antietam

With the Union forces in chaos, Lee boldly crossed into Maryland in September 1862. He hoped a successful invasion of the North would encourage Britain and France to give aid to the Confederacy.

With a little luck, Lee's gamble might have worked. However, a copy of his orders fell into Union hands, and McClellan learned the exact position of Lee's forces.

On September 17 the two armies clashed at Antietam Creek. It was to be the bloodiest day of the war, but neither side could claim victory. Lee slipped back into Virginia. McClellan, ignoring Lincoln's orders, did not pursue him.

Close to 5,000 soldiers died at Antietam, and 18,500 were wounded. One soldier who survived was Benjamin Chase. His letter home was filled with sadness and fear for the future:

> "i was so lucky to get out of it alive. i thought to myself if thear mothers could only see . . . [their dead sons] they would be crasy."

Chase prayed for the "happy day" when he could talk to his mother again. "When will that day come?" he wondered. "i cant tell that, . . . perhaps never."

The Battle of Antietam was a turning point in the war. The battle ended Lee's invasion of the North, destroyed a third of his army, and shattered Confederate hopes of getting aid from abroad.

As 1862 drew to a close, neither side held a clear advantage over the other. Lee's failure at Antietam, however, gave President Lincoln the chance to take a bold step that would change the course of the war.

2. Section Review

1. Define **casualties.**
2. What was the basic goal of the Confederacy? The Union?
3. What brought Union advances to a standstill in 1862?
4. **Critical Thinking** How might the outcome of the war have been different if Lee had won a decisive victory at the Battle of Antietam?

Closing the Section

Wrap-Up Activity

A Battle Chart

To summarize the first two years of the war, have students create a chart of the major battles and campaigns. The chart should include the name, date, strategic importance, and result of each.

Section Review Answers

1. Definition: *casualties* (150)
2. The Confederacy wanted to defend the South against the Union's invasion. The Union wanted to bring the Confederate states back into the Union.
3. The Union's failure to take Vicksburg stalled the strategy to control the Mississippi River in 1862.
4. Answers might include that Lee's army would have continued the invasion of the North and received aid from Europe. With this help, the Confederates might have ultimately defeated the Union.

Introducing the Section

Vocabulary

draft (p. 158) a system that requires men to serve in the military

income tax (p. 159) a tax on money people earn from work or investments

Warm-Up Activity

Lincoln's Diary

Have students imagine that they are President Lincoln writing a diary entry following the Battle of Antietam. The entries should express what hopes and fears Lincoln might have felt upon reviewing the events of the first two years of the war.

Geography Question of the Day

Ask students to make a chart of the geographic advantages and disadvantages of the Union and the Confederacy. They should consider such factors as agriculture, transportation, and use of resources.

Vital Links

African American soldiers (Picture) Unit 3, Side 1, Search 28748

See also Unit 3 Explore CD-ROM location 123.

Section Objectives

- ★ Describe the effect of the Emancipation Proclamation.
- ★ Explain how women contributed to the war effort.
- ★ Identify the challenges Lincoln and Davis faced as wartime leaders.

Teaching Resources

Take-Home Planner 1, pp. 12–19
Chapter Resources Binder
Study Guide, p. 27
Reinforcement
Skills Development, pp. 31–32
Geography Extensions
American Readings, p. 13
Using Historical Documents, pp. 32–39
Transparency Activities
Chapter and Unit Tests

3. The War Effort at Home

Reading Guide

New Terms **draft, income tax**

Section Focus **The Civil War's effect on northerners and southerners at home**

1. **What was the effect of the Emancipation Proclamation?**
2. **How did women contribute to the war effort?**
3. **What challenges did Lincoln and Davis face as wartime leaders?**

From the start of the Civil War, President Lincoln had resisted pleas to abolish slavery. Although Lincoln personally hated slavery, the purpose of the war, he said, "*is* to save the Union, and is *not* either to save or to destroy slavery."

As hopes for peace dimmed, however, Lincoln changed his mind. He came to see that emancipation—freeing all slaves—was "essential to the preservation of the Union."

Moving Toward Emancipation

Several factors led Lincoln to favor emancipation. One was that it made sense from a military point of view. The Confederacy was using enslaved African Americans to build fortifications, haul supplies, and grow crops. If Lincoln freed the slaves, the Confederates would lose a vital source of labor—and the Union would gain one.

In fact, since the war began, thousands of enslaved African Americans had sought freedom by fleeing to join Union forces invading the South. Union commanders paid the escaped slaves to work as cooks, carpenters, guides, and drivers. Some commanders also accepted escaped African Americans as soldiers, forming regiments in South Carolina and Louisiana.

A second reason for emancipation was to keep European nations from helping the Confederacy. Slavery had long been abolished in Europe. Lincoln believed that emancipation would win public support for the Union in those countries.

A third factor in Lincoln's decision was pressure from abolitionists. More and more people were coming to believe that it was time to settle the slavery issue once and for all. "This rebellion has its source . . . in slavery," a Republican told the House of Representatives. Defeating the South would be useless "if slavery shall be spared to canker [infect] the heart of the nation anew."

The Emancipation Proclamation

By the summer of 1862, Lincoln's emancipation plan was ready. The President decided not to announce it, though, until Union forces had won a victory. He did not want it to seem like an act of desperation.

When the Union army turned back Lee's troops at Antietam, Lincoln saw his chance. On September 22, 1862, he issued a warning to the Confederate states: Unless they returned to the Union by January 1, 1863, he would free their slaves. The Confederacy ignored the warning.

Tips for Teaching

Gifted Students

In-depth activities provide opportunities to develop research and critical thinking skills. For instance, gifted students might explore the history of Lincoln's emancipation policy and his responses to criticism of it. They might research the moral, political, economic, and constitutional arguments for and against emancipation.

For an activity on analyzing the text of the Emancipation Proclamation, see **Using Historical Documents**, pp. 32–39.

True to his word, on January 1, 1863, Lincoln signed the Emancipation Proclamation. It stated that all slaves in the Confederate states "are, and henceforward shall be, free." Slaves in areas loyal to the United States or under Union control were not affected. Lincoln had no constitutional power to act against slavery there.

The Emancipation Proclamation changed the war into a struggle for freedom as well as for the Union. It turned the Union army into a liberating army wherever it went in the South. It won European approval for the Union cause. It was also a giant step toward abolishing all slavery. Lincoln believed that it was the "one thing that will make people remember I ever lived."

African American Troops

After the Emancipation Proclamation, African Americans could join the Union army as soldiers. About 186,000 African Americans, most of them former slaves, enlisted to fight for the Union and for their own freedom. Another 30,000 joined the navy, which had been accepting black sailors since 1861.

Even though they were risking their lives, African American soldiers were discriminated against. They were assigned to all-black regiments commanded by white officers. Most were given more than their share of digging trenches and building fortifications and bridges.

This picture shows the 54th Massachusetts Infantry leading an assault on Fort Wagner, South Carolina. Although the attack failed, the 54th fought courageously, suffering almost 50 percent casualties.

Developing the Section

Discussion

Checking Understanding

1. Why did Lincoln finally favor emancipation? (He wanted to prevent Confederacy from using slaves to help military effort, to keep European nations from supporting Confederacy, and to respond to increasing pressure from abolitionists.)

2. How were African American soldiers discriminated against? (They were placed in segregated regiments led by white officers, and were often assigned an unfair share of physical labor.)

Stimulating Critical Thinking

3. Should the Emancipation Proclamation be the main thing Lincoln is remembered for? Why or why not? (Yes: made the Union cause a fight against slavery also; in effect, Union was now committed to abolishing slavery if it won the war. No: major accomplishment was saving the Union; proclamation was a strategy to win the war rather than a moral stand, and did not itself free any slaves.)

For Charlotte Forten's account of a celebration of emancipation, see **American Readings**, p. 13.

Teaching the

Link to the Present

Have students name some specific examples of how the American Red Cross has provided assistance. Explain that although the Red Cross is highly respected today, Clara Barton had a hard time persuading the United States to join the international organization in 1881. She had learned of the International Red Cross in 1869 when she was informed by its president that the United States had refused three times to join the organization. Lobbying in Washington in 1877, she learned that the United States' refusal to join was part of its policy of isolating itself from Europe. Barton finally convinced President Garfield in 1881 that the Red Cross could help people in times of peace, such as during natural disasters, as well as during international wars.

Section Activity

Newspaper Articles

To explore aspects of the war effort at home, have groups imagine they are newspaper staffs in the North and South. Have them create front pages containing articles reflecting their regional biases. Topics include the Emancipation Proclamation, the 54th Massachusetts Regiment, opposition at home, the war's effect on the economy, and contributions of women to the war effort. Conclude by having groups compare articles.

Connections to Literature

The Fort Wagner attack inspired commemorations, like these excerpts from "The Old Flag Never Touched the Ground":

"The Old Flag never touched the ground!"
'twas thus brave Carney spoke—
A Negro soldier: words renowned, that
Honor will invoke
Upon the records of the Race whose
heroes many are,
Records that Time cannot efface, and
Hate can never mar.
Those words were stamped with Carney's
blood upon our Country's scroll,
And though dislike, deep as a flood
against his Race may roll,
It cannot dim, nor wash away, its
crimson-written fame
Which History wrote on Wagner's day
without a tinge of shame.

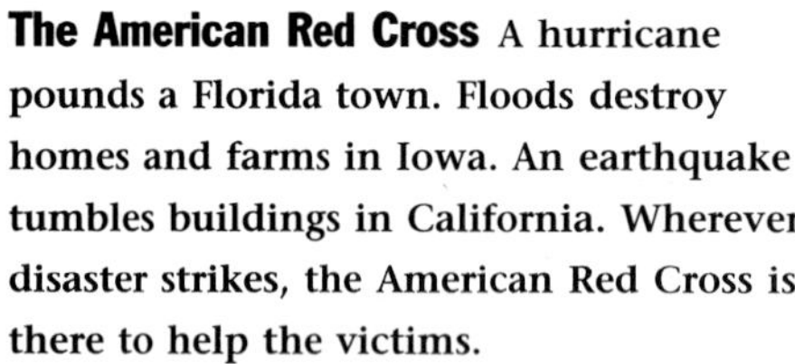

Link to the Present

The American Red Cross **A hurricane pounds a Florida town. Floods destroy homes and farms in Iowa. An earthquake tumbles buildings in California. Wherever disaster strikes, the American Red Cross is there to help the victims.**

While in Switzerland in 1869, Clara Barton learned of the International Committee of the Red Cross, a group of volunteers who aided wounded soldiers. Impressed by its work, she founded the American branch of the Red Cross in 1881.

Barton soon expanded Red Cross activities to include disaster relief. Today the Red Cross also collects and distributes blood and teaches first aid. Most workers are volunteers, and programs are funded by private—not government—contributions.

At first, African American troops were paid as laborers, not soldiers, and all received the same pay no matter what their rank. To protest such unequal treatment, many soldiers refused to accept any pay at all. In a letter to President Lincoln, Corporal James Henry Gooding of the 54th Massachusetts Infantry asked:

> "The main question is, are we soldiers, or are we laborers? . . . We have done a soldier's duty. Why can't we have a soldier's pay?"

In 1864 Congress finally granted black soldiers equal pay, including all back pay.

Some northerners doubted that African Americans would make good soldiers. Such doubts were quickly put to rest in battle. For example, in a suicidal attack on Fort Wagner, South Carolina, in 1863, the 54th Massachusetts Infantry lost its commander, most of its officers, and almost half of its troops. Although terribly wounded, Sergeant William Carney carried the regiment's flags to safety. He was the first of 20 African American soldiers to win the Congressional Medal of Honor.

New Challenges for Women

Until the Civil War, women had few choices of jobs outside the home other than teacher, factory worker, or house servant. With thousands of men fighting in the war, though, women took over family farms and businesses. They also had the chance to tackle jobs usually closed to them.

Women worked in mints making coins and in offices copying documents, as Clara Barton did in the Patent Office. Women also worked in arsenals making ammunition. This was a dangerous business. After 21 women were killed in an explosion in Washington, D.C., President Lincoln led the funeral procession to Congressional Cemetery. There the victims, mostly Irish immigrants, were buried in a common grave.

Setting up hospitals When the war began, there were almost no large military hospitals. Medical officers scrambled to convert barns, tobacco warehouses, schools, and even large boats into hospitals.

Conditions in most hospitals were terrible. They lacked ways to treat water and sewage to prevent the spread of disease. In fact, twice as many soldiers died of disease as of combat wounds. Mary Boykin Chesnut described her visit to a hospital in Richmond:

> "I can never again shut out of view the sights I saw of human misery. . . . Long rows of ill men on cots. Ill of typhoid fever, of every human ailment."

Connections to Science

At the time of the Civil War, doctors had not discovered the importance of using antiseptic conditions to prevent infection. Not until 1865 did Joseph Lister, a British surgeon and professor, realize that infection was caused by microorganisms, which were present not only in the air but also on a surgeon's hands and instruments. Even minor wounds to soldiers' arms and legs could result in amputation, because of the threat of infection. Sanitary conditions in camps and prisons were horrendous. Food and water were often contaminated, leading to outbreaks of dysentery and diarrhea. Malaria, pneumonia, bronchitis, scurvy, and measles were also rampant. Twice as many soldiers died from disease as were killed in combat.

Women played many roles in the war. Women workers prepared cartridges for Union guns at the arsenal in Watertown, Massachusetts. Alice Buckner of Virginia tried—without success—to smuggle medicine in her petticoat to the Confederates. Captain Sally Tompkins founded one of the best small hospitals for soldiers in the South.

Many women took wounded soldiers into their homes. Sally L. Tompkins set up a hospital in a Richmond house where she treated more than 1,300 patients. Jefferson Davis rewarded her services by appointing her a captain of cavalry.

Nursing the wounded Many noted women reformers threw themselves into the effort to nurse the wounded. Dorothea Dix, who had reformed mental hospitals, worked with Dr. Elizabeth Blackwell to set up a training program for female nurses. Dix's rules were so strict that she became known as "Dragon Dix."

Clara Barton felt "cramped" in hospitals. She preferred being on the battlefield. There she treated wounded soldiers, some of whom had gone for days without food or water.

Harriet Tubman also helped tend the wounded, working with Clara Barton in the Sea Islands off the coast of South Carolina. Sojourner Truth worked in Union hospitals and in camps for escaped slaves. She also recruited black soldiers for the Union army. Two were her sons.

Opposition at Home

Not everyone was as patriotic and eager to serve as the brave women working in the arsenals and hospitals of the Union and the Confederacy. As the war dragged on and hopes for a quick victory faded, Presidents Davis and Lincoln both faced growing opposition at home.

States' rights A serious problem for Davis was lack of cooperation by the states in the Confederacy. Holding fast to the idea of states' rights, they resisted paying taxes and cooperating on military matters. At one point, Georgia even threatened to secede from the Confederacy.

Discussion

Checking Understanding

1. What job opportunities outside the home were open to women before the Civil War? (Teacher, factory worker, house servant.)

2. How did the war open up some opportunities for African Americans and women? (Because of the growing need for soldiers, African American men were finally allowed to join the Union army and were eventually given equal pay. Meanwhile, many women had to take over family farms and businesses, and some worked at government jobs traditionally denied to them.)

Stimulating Critical Thinking

3. If you were a reformer in the early 1860s, why might you be cautious in hoping for equal rights for women and African Americans? (A reformer might suspect that the changing roles for these two groups were more a result of wartime necessity than of any basic change in the attitudes of white men.)

Vital Links

Voice of nurse Kate Cummings (First Person Account) Unit 3, Side 1, Search 26195, Play to 26465

See also Unit 3 Explore CD-ROM location 113.

History Footnote

The Copperheads objected to Lincoln's policies on the draft, military arrests, African Americans in the military, and emancipation. On all these issues, Lincoln stood firm. He supported the jailing of those who obstructed the draft, and by the summer of 1863 more than 13,000 of these objectors had been imprisoned. When Lincoln was criticized for jailing a prominent Ohio Democrat for denouncing the draft, he said, "Must I shoot a simple-minded soldier boy who deserts while I must not touch a hair of the wily agitator who induces him to desert?" In response to calls to revoke the emancipation policy, Lincoln replied, "I am a slow walker, but I never walk backward."

Teaching the World Link

Explain that gaining British support was a reasonable expectation for the South at the beginning of the war. In fact, a satirical rhyme in the British magazine *Punch* said: "Though with the North we sympathize / It must not be forgotten / That with the South we've stronger ties / Which are composed of cotton." Point out that economic considerations concerning both sides played a large part in Britain's eventual neutrality, but so did the Emancipation Proclamation. The northern writer Henry Adams wrote from London, "The Emancipation Proclamation has done more for us here than all our former victories and all our diplomacy."

Bonus Activity

Creating a Lincoln Collage

Have students make a collage illustrating some of the facts they have learned about Abraham Lincoln. Suggest that they begin with a drawing or silhouette of Lincoln and then write and/or illustrate some of the important actions and words of his presidency. They may also want to include an original poem or paragraph describing Lincoln's qualities.

World Link

Britain stays neutral in Civil War

"No power dares . . . to make war on cotton. Cotton is king." So said Senator James Hammond of South Carolina in 1859. When the Civil War broke out, southern leaders expected British support. They thought Britain would want to protect the supply of cotton flowing to its textile mills.

What went wrong? Between 1860 and 1862, bad weather ruined Europe's grain crops while Union farmers were having record harvests. Britain needed northern grain more than southern cotton.

Meanwhile, in 1861 British mills had a surplus of cotton. By the time it ran out, they had found new sources of cotton in India and Egypt. Thus, Britain could afford to stay neutral in the Civil War.

Copperheads For his part, Lincoln led a Union that was far from united. Many northern Democrats were more interested in restoring peace than in saving the Union or ending slavery. Republicans called these Democrats "Copperheads," after the poisonous snake.

The draft The hottest issue faced by both the Union and the Confederacy was the **draft**—a system that requires men to serve in the military. At first both armies had more than enough volunteers. As casualties mounted, though, enlistments dropped.

In 1862 the Confederacy passed the first draft law in United States history. With a few exceptions, all white men aged 18 to 35 could be called for military service for 3 years. A draftee could avoid serving by paying for a substitute to take his place. Anyone who owned 20 slaves or more was excused from the draft. Angry southerners protested that it was "a rich man's war and a poor man's fight."

Soon the Union had to resort to the draft as well. Its draft act applied to all men aged 20 to 45. As in the South, a draftee could pay for a substitute. The Union's draft act was passed only 2 months after the Emancipation Proclamation. Copperheads accused the government of forcing white workers to fight to free the slaves, who would then compete for their jobs after the war.

When the first draft was held in July 1863, riots broke out. The worst was in New York City. There a mob, mostly Irish Americans, went on a 4-day rampage, burning draft offices and lynching African Americans. At least 105 people were killed.

Years of war aged President Lincoln, as this 1865 portrait shows, but he never doubted his war aims.

History Footnote

During the Civil War thousands of boys under the age of 18—some as young as 10—managed to join the military. Rather than lie to the recruiters by swearing they were at least 18 years old, some young boys would scribble the number 18 on a piece of paper and place it in the sole of their shoe. Then, when they appeared before the recruiters, they could truthfully say, "I am over 18."

See the Study Guide activity in Chapter Resources Binder, p. 27.

Economic Strains of the War

The war placed a great strain on the economies of both sides. To pay for the Union war effort, Congress passed the nation's first **income tax**—a tax on money people earn from work or investments. The Union also raised millions of dollars through the sale of war bonds. People who bought bonds were, in effect, lending money to the government.

Unable to raise enough money to pay their bills, both governments printed money. Union notes were called "greenbacks" because of their color. Since paper money was not backed by gold or silver, it lost value during the war. Between 1862 and 1865, the value of a one-dollar Union note dropped to half that amount in gold. A similar Confederate note was worth about two cents.

Getting supplies The Union economy was up to the challenge of supplying both troops and people at home during the war. Aided by the McCormick reaper, farmers produced large crops of wheat and corn. Labor-saving machines enabled factories to keep soldiers well clothed and armed.

The Confederacy, however, suffered increasingly from shortages. Its economy, based largely on cotton and with few industries, was ill-suited to supporting a war effort.

Early in the war, southerners had made a serious mistake. They stopped shipping cotton abroad, hoping to force Britain to aid the Confederacy. The plan backfired. As you have seen, Britain did not help the South—and the South lost an important source of income.

Meanwhile the Union blockade made it increasingly difficult for the Confederacy to import supplies. After southern victories, desperate Confederate soldiers stripped dead and wounded Union soldiers of their weapons, shoes, and even uniforms.

President Davis had the heavy responsibility of organizing a new nation and guiding it in war.

The Union's naval blockade was working. It was strangling the southern economy and, with it, the Confederate war effort. As a Confederate officer later admitted, the blockade "shut the Confederacy out from the world, deprived it of supplies, [and] weakened its military and naval strength."

3. Section Review

1. Define **draft** and **income tax.**
2. Why did Lincoln wait to issue the Emancipation Proclamation?
3. Describe at least two contributions made by women to the war effort.
4. Critical Thinking How might public opposition in the Union and the Confederacy have weakened the war effort?

Vital Links

War refugees from the South (Picture) Unit 3, Side 1, Search 28802

See also Unit 3 Explore CD-ROM location 132.

Closing the Section

Wrap-Up Activity

War Problems: A Venn Diagram

Have students create Venn diagrams identifying the problems faced by the North and the South. The overlapping portion should identify shared problems, such as opposition to the draft. Conclude by drawing a large diagram on the chalkboard and calling on students to fill in examples.

Section Review Answers

1. Definitions: *draft* (158), *income tax* (159)

2. He did not want to issue it until the Union had won a victory, so it would not seem like an act of desperation.

3. Answers may include nursing wounded, setting up hospitals, making ammunition, running farms and businesses, working in mints, copying documents.

4. Answers might include that public opposition made soldiers less likely to join the army, and less likely to risk their lives if they did join.

If students need to review the skill, use the Skills Development transparency and activity in the **Chapter Resources Binder**, pp. 31–32.

Introducing the Skill Lab

Begin by asking students why they think it might be important for a historian to make hypotheses (to help understand why events happened as they did, and perhaps to learn lessons from those events that can be applied to the present). Point out that after forming a hypothesis there is always a danger that a historian will look only at evidence that seems to support that theory, and ignore contrary evidence. A good historian will revise his or her hypothesis if necessary to fit the facts.

Skill Lab

Answers

1. Students' notes should reflect an ability to extract preliminary hypothesis ideas from the sources. For example, notes for source B might include the following possible reasons for issuing the proclamation: to encourage slaves to leave plantations, and to give the North a stronger moral cause.

2. (a) Lincoln wanted to weaken the South by depriving it of slave labor. He also wanted to cut off European support for the South. In addition, he was responding to pressure from abolitionists. (b) Sources B and C suggest the hypotheses mentioned in A. In addition,

(Answers continued in top margin)

source B suggests that Lincoln wanted the North to have a stronger moral cause, and Source C suggests that he wanted to hurt the South as much as possible and to open up extensive recruitment of black soldiers into the Union army.

3. (a) As the sources indicate, Lincoln probably had several reasons, and therefore no one hypothesis completely explains his action. Students might give more weight to hypotheses mentioned by more than one source, such as Lincoln's desire to weaken the South. (b) Accept any reasonable ideas for further research—for example, studying Lincoln's own words on the subject.

For further application, have students do the Applying Skills activity in the Chapter Survey (p. 168).

Skill Lab

Using Information

Making a Hypothesis

"All persons held as slaves within any [rebellious] state . . . shall be . . . forever free." With those words, Abraham Lincoln ensured his place in history as the "Great Emancipator." Historians have long disagreed, however, about Lincoln's reasons—and timing—for the Emancipation Proclamation.

Question to Investigate

Why did President Lincoln issue the Emancipation Proclamation?

Procedure

Any answer to that question is a hypothesis—a theory to explain the event. Part of a historian's job is to develop hypotheses for events and situations. Then each hypothesis must be tested against available information.

❶ Gather information.
a. Read sources A, B, and C.
b. As you read, take notes on possible reasons for the proclamation.

❷ Develop several hypotheses.
a. Write the hypotheses suggested by source A.
b. Write two more hypotheses that sources B and C suggest to you.

❸ Test each hypothesis.
a. From what you know, does each hypothesis give an adequate explanation for why Lincoln issued the proclamation? Is one hypothesis more valid? Explain.
b. What can you do to test how reasonable each hypothesis is?

Skill Tips

Keep in mind:

- To qualify as a hypothesis, a theory must be able to be tested.
- There may be more than one reasonable hypothesis to explain an event.
- Even the best hypothesis may need to be tested again if new information is available.

Sources to Use

A Reread pages 154–155.

B "Thousands of jubilant [joyful] slaves, learning of the proclamation, flocked to the invading Union armies, stripping already rundown plantations of their work force. . . . The North now had much the stronger moral cause. In addition to preserving the Union, it had committed itself to freeing the slaves."

From Thomas A. Bailey and David M. Kennedy, *The American Pageant* (D.C. Heath: 1991)

C "Three developments caused Lincoln to change his mind [and to abolish slavery]. First, the bloody fighting made many northerners want to hurt the South as much as possible. Abolishing slavery would help do that. Second, slavery helped the southern war effort. Slaves helped to build military fortifications, and they produced food. Third, slavery was a crucial issue on the Union's diplomatic front with Britain. Britain's leaders would not support a war whose aim was to keep the United States together. However, British public opinion would back a war against slavery. . . . The Emancipation Proclamation also encouraged the recruitment of black soldiers into the Union army. . . . All told, nearly 300,000 blacks served in the Union army."

From Winthrop D. Jordan et al., *The Americans* (McDougal, Littell: 1991)

Section Objectives

- ★ Explain why the Battles of Gettysburg and Vicksburg were turning points in the war.
- ★ Describe Grant's strategy for winning the war.
- ★ List the events that led to Lee's surrender at Appomattox.

Teaching Resources

Take-Home Planner 1, pp. 12–19
Chapter Resources Binder
Study Guide, p. 28
Reinforcement
Skills Development
Geography Extensions, pp. 9–10
American Readings, pp. 14–16
Using Historical Documents
Transparency Activities
Chapter and Unit Tests, pp. 27–30

4. From War to Peace

Reading Guide

New Term **total war**

Section Focus **Union victories that finally ended the war**

1. Why were the Battles of Gettysburg and Vicksburg turning points in the war?
2. What was Grant's strategy for winning the war?
3. What events led to Lee's surrender at Appomattox?

The year 1862 ended in despair for the Union. The war effort in Virginia and on the Mississippi had stalled. Many northerners began to speak openly about letting the Confederacy have its independence. President Lincoln kept his sights on his goal—to win the war. He knew, however, that he needed a general he could count on to "fight battles and win victories."

Two Confederate Victories

After the Battle of Antietam, Lincoln fired General McClellan for refusing to attack Lee's retreating army. He gave command to General Ambrose E. Burnside. In December 1862 Lee soundly defeated Burnside's forces at Fredericksburg, Virginia. Benjamin Chase died that day. He was only 18 years old.

Next Lincoln turned to General Joseph Hooker. Lee stopped Hooker, too—at Chancellorsville, Virginia, in May 1863. Lee's victory was clouded, however, by the death of Stonewall Jackson. "I know not how to replace him," confessed Lee.

After Chancellorsville, Lee decided to invade the Union again. He thought that another victory, this time on northern soil, would prove to northerners and Europeans that the Confederacy could win the war. His invasion might also draw Union troops away from Vicksburg on the Mississippi.

The Battle of Gettysburg

In June 1863 Lee led his confident troops across Maryland and into Pennsylvania. On July 1 Confederate soldiers met Union soldiers in the little town of Gettysburg. General George C. Meade, the new commander of the Army of the Potomac, had been following Lee's forces. He rushed his army to Gettysburg and forced Lee to take a stand.

Courtesy of the R. W. Norton Art Gallery, Shreveport, Louisiana

The greatest loss to the South at Chancellorsville was the death of Stonewall Jackson, Lee's "right arm." Jackson was accidentally shot by his own men.

Introducing the Section

Vocabulary

total war (p. 164) war against armies and also against a people's resources and will to fight

Warm-Up Activity

A Military Report Card

To review the status of the war at the end of 1862, have students work in pairs to grade the performance of each side's military forces. They should write reports assessing the outcomes of the First Battle of Bull Run, the war at sea, the fight for the Mississippi, the Richmond campaign, and the Battle of Antietam. They should conclude the reports by assigning each side a letter grade for its military performance, explaining how they arrived at the grades.

Geography Question of the Day

Have students refer to the large map on page 163 to identify which states Sherman's troops marched across, and explain how it is apparent from the map that his campaign was successful. (Sherman marched through Georgia, South Carolina, and North Carolina. His path was not interrupted by Confederate victories and resulted in Union victories in Atlanta, Savannah, and Columbia.)

Developing the Section

Section **Activity**

Interviewing Lee and Grant

To analyze why the North won the war, have students imagine interviewing the two commanding generals following Appomattox. Have them work in small groups, assigning half the groups to write a Lee interview script and half to write a Grant interview script. Each script should include questions regarding military strategy and key victories and defeats, with answers they think the general would be likely to give. Conclude by discussing what each general might see as the key factors determining the war's outcome.

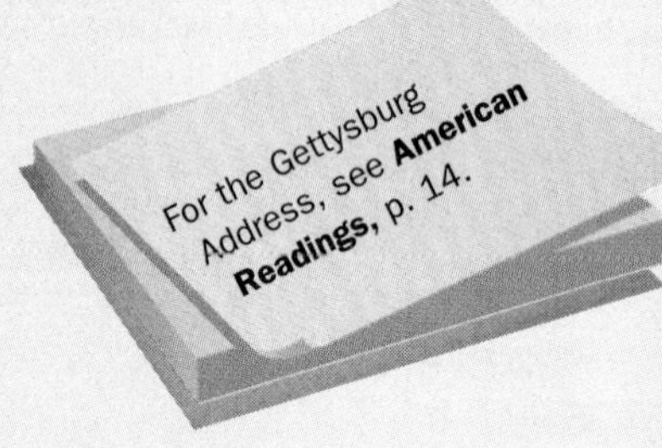

For the Gettysburg Address, see **American Readings**, p. 14.

Vital Links

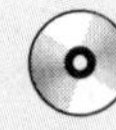

Voice of Major Sullivan Ballou (First Person Account) Unit 3, Side 1, Search 26469, Play to 27413

See also Unit 3 Explore CD-ROM location 114.

History Footnote

Although the Gettysburg Address is remembered as one of the great speeches in American history, its initial reception was less than enthusiastic. Lincoln had intended to use the occasion to discuss the meaning of the war as a whole, but his speech was not completed when he set out for Gettysburg. He did not finish writing it until the morning of the ceremony. The crowd of 15,000 grew restless as Edward Everett, a famous orator, preceded Lincoln and spoke for two hours. Lincoln's speech, consisting of 270 words, lasted for two minutes. His address was so unexpectedly short that a photographer who had planned to record the event was still adjusting his camera when Lincoln finished. Many people were disappointed in the speech, including many listeners, opposition newspapers, and Lincoln himself.

On the first day of the Battle of Gettysburg, Confederate troops attacked Union lines. Union forces, though, had more troops, greater firepower, and a strong defensive position on high ground.

For two days Union and Confederate forces fought furiously. Finally, on July 3, Lee risked everything on an infantry charge led by General George E. Pickett. About 15,000 Confederates hurled themselves at the center of the Union line on Cemetery Ridge. Pickett's Charge was a disaster. Half of his men were struck by Union fire as they rushed uphill. More fell in hand-to-hand combat when they reached the ridge.

The Battle of Gettysburg was a turning point in the war. On July 4 Lee, who had lost a third of his army, retreated to Virginia. From this point on, he would be fighting a defensive war on southern soil.

The Gettysburg Address The casualties at Gettysburg were staggering—23,000 for the Union and 28,000 for the Confederates. The bloodshed was so appalling that a national cemetery was created for the soldiers who died there. At the dedication ceremony on November 19, 1863, President Lincoln delivered a brief speech.

The Gettysburg Address is one of the most eloquent statements of American democracy. In it Lincoln vowed:

> "We here highly resolve that these dead shall not have died in vain; that this nation, under God, shall have a new birth of freedom; and that government of the people, by the people, for the people shall not perish from the earth."

Victory on the Mississippi

The Union victory at Gettysburg was quickly followed by good news from the Mississippi. After failing to storm the hilltop stronghold of Vicksburg, General Grant had surrounded it while Union gunboats bombarded it. The starving citizens held out for

History Footnote

After the Battle of Gettysburg, Lee blamed himself for the disastrous assault to the center of the Union line by General Pickett's troops. Most of Pickett's men were Virginians like Lee himself. In addition to the 7,500 soldiers cut down, all thirteen colonels in the division and all three brigade commanders were killed or injured. Lee realized that his gamble in taking the offensive on northern soil had failed miserably. He said to Pickett later, "Upon my shoulders rests the blame. The men and officers of your command have written the name of Virginia as high today as it has ever been written before." He said to another man, "It is I who have lost this fight and you must help me out of it the best way you can."

The Civil War 1863–1865

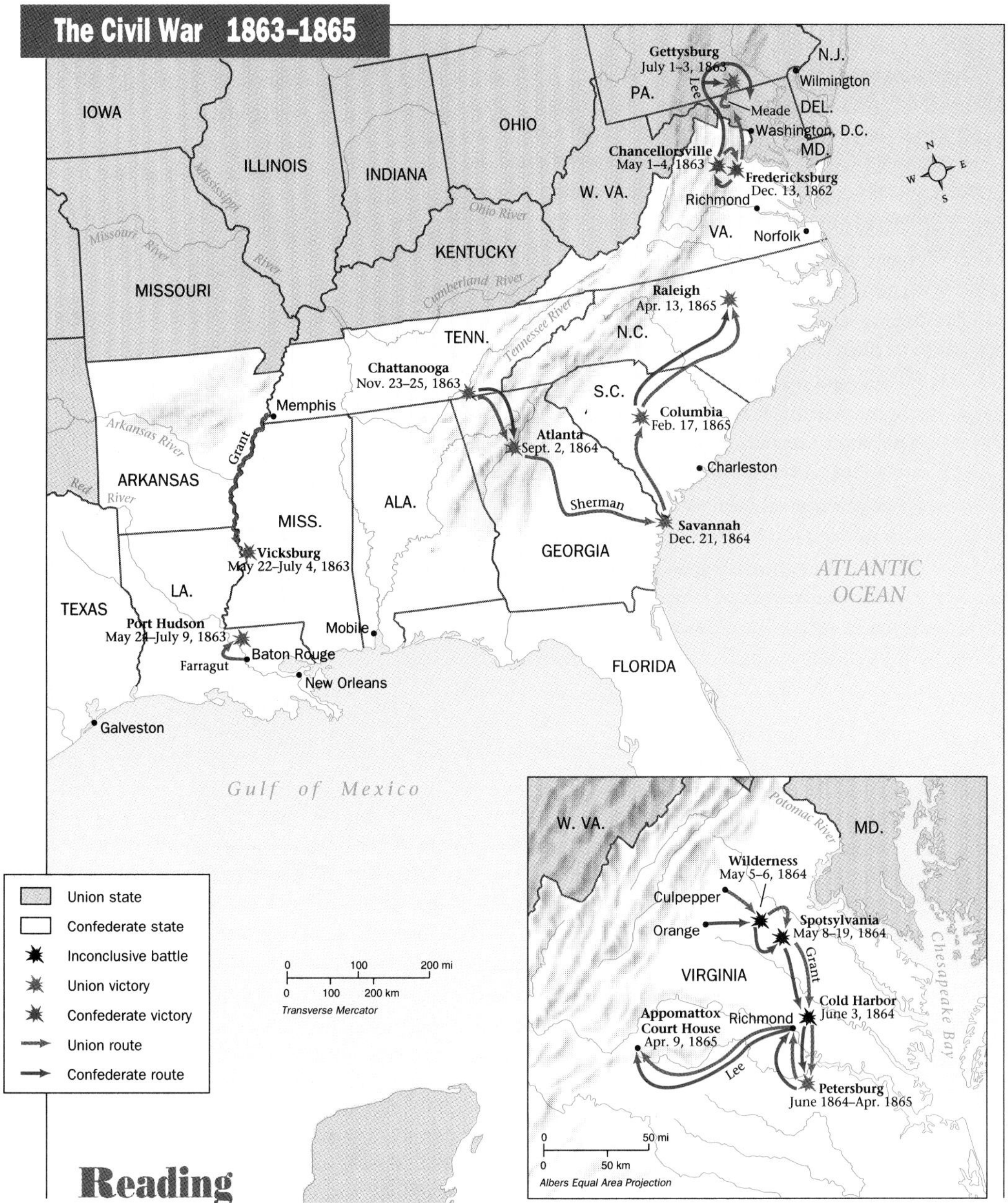

Reading Maps

For each of the years 1863, 1864, and 1865, write a newspaper headline that describes a campaign near one of the two capitals.

Discussion

Checking Understanding

1. Why were Union troops victorious at the Battle of Gettysburg? (They had more soldiers, greater firepower, and a good defensive position on a hill.)

Stimulating Critical Thinking

2. Why do you think the Gettysburg Address is so celebrated? (It states America's democratic philosophy in a simple, straightforward, graceful style. Its dignified manner fit the occasion. It honors people who died to save the nation.)

Teaching the Reading Maps

To help students focus on the maps, ask: **Which battles were fought near Washington, D.C.?** (Gettysburg, Wilderness, Spotsylvania, Chancellorsville, Fredericksburg) **Which were fought near Richmond?** (Cold Harbor, Petersburg) **Answer to Reading Maps:** Some possible headlines: 1863—Jackson Dies in Confederate Victory at Chancellorsville; 1864—Grant Persists in Spotsylvania; 1865—Union Batters Rebel Defenses at Petersburg.

Vital Links

Gettysburg Address (First Person Account) Unit 3, Side 1, Search 25295, Play to 26191

See also Unit 3 Explore CD-ROM location 112.

Teaching the Hands-On HISTORY

As an example of a Civil War monument, point out that ground was broken in 1995 in Washington, D.C., for a monument honoring the 178,000 black soldiers who fought. The African American Civil War Memorial will be a curved stone wall holding stainless steel plaques listing the names of the black Union soldiers and the white officers who led them. Encourage students to create forms for their commemorations that fit their subjects.

Bonus Activity

Writing Song Lyrics

Have students write a song about a person, battle, or other event of the war. Encourage them to choose subjects that have a strong impact for them, and to use specific words and images. Some possible subjects are Clara Barton, the death toll of a battle such as Gettysburg, the leadership of Lincoln, or the surrender at Appomattox.

Vital Links

"The Battle Hymn of the Republic" (Song) Unit 3, Side 2, Search 02045, Play to 04844

See also Unit 3 Explore CD-ROM location 143.

Connections to Music

One commemoration of the Civil War is its music. The songs "The Battle Hymn of the Republic," "Bonnie Blue Flag," and "Marching Through Georgia" originated during the war, and have lived on. Music was an important part of life in the camps and battlefields. After the devastating fighting at Spotsylvania, for example, the Confederate bands are said to have struck up "Dixie" and Handel's "The Dead March," while the Yankees played "The Star-Spangled Banner" and "Home Sweet Home." Other popular songs had titles such as "Cheer Boys, Cheer," "Just Before the Battle, Mother," and "Tramp, Tramp, Tramp." Many were enjoyed by both Union and Confederate troops. Out of the war grew a new music in which Irish, Scottish, English, Italian, and German styles were combined and influenced by African American styles.

Hands-On HISTORY

Commemorating the Civil War Since the guns fell silent more than 130 years ago, Americans have continued to remember the Civil War. In paintings, monuments, and books, as well as in movies and television dramas, we have commemorated the people and events of that dramatic period in the nation's history.

Activity You may never write a book or create a television drama about the Civil War, but you can plan a way to commemorate it.

1. Decide what part of the war to commemorate. It might be an event, a person or group of people, or a theme, such as life at home.
2. Decide what form to create—for example, a plaque, monument, play, pageant, or story.
3. Put your plan on paper. For example, draw a picture of a statue or write a program for a pageant. Share it with your classmates.

War monument

almost seven weeks, living in caves and eating rats, cats, dogs, and mules.

Vicksburg finally surrendered on July 4, 1863—another turning point in the war. Port Hudson, the last Confederate stronghold on the Mississippi, gave up five days later. Union forces now controlled the entire river. Lincoln was thrilled. "Grant is my man," he exclaimed, "and I am his for the rest of the war."

President Lincoln named Grant commander of all western forces. Grant responded by capturing Chattanooga, a key railroad center in Tennessee, in November 1863.

Total War

At last, Lincoln had found a general who could win battles. In March 1864 he gave Grant command of all Union forces.

The new commander had a commonsense way of looking at war. He wrote:

"The art of war is simple enough. Find out where your enemy is. Get at him as soon as you can. Strike at him as hard as you can and as often as you can, and keep moving on."

Grant believed in **total war**—war against armies and also against a people's resources and will to fight.

Now Grant mapped out a strategy to end the war. He would lead the Army of the Potomac against Lee and capture Richmond. Meanwhile, he ordered General William Tecumseh Sherman to invade Georgia and take Atlanta.

The battle for Richmond On May 4, 1864, Grant invaded northern Virginia with 120,000 troops. They clashed with Lee's army of 61,000 in the Wilderness, a dense forest. In 2 days of fighting, Grant's troops suffered 18,000 casualties. Instead of turning back, though, Grant pressed on toward Richmond.

The two armies next met at Spotsylvania Court House. Again Grant suffered heavy losses but would not retreat. "I propose to fight it out along this line if it takes all summer," he said. The two armies clashed at Cold Harbor, again with high casualties.

In a month, Grant's army had lost 50,000 soldiers, compared with about 30,000 Confederate losses. The greater population of the North meant that Grant could get more troops. Lee, however, could not replace his losses. By the time the Confederate Congress decided to use African American troops in March 1865, it would be too late to make a difference.

History Footnote

Atlanta was a major target of Union forces for several reasons. It had become an important symbol of the Confederacy, equal only to Richmond. It was one of the South's most important manufacturing centers, and it was an important railroad link to the Carolinas and Virginia. However, the state capital of South Carolina, Columbia, also received harsh treatment by Sherman's troops. Many northerners considered South Carolina especially at fault in the war since the first shot had been fired at Fort Sumter. Sherman telegraphed Lincoln, "The truth is the whole army is burning with an insatiable desire to wreak vengeance upon South Carolina."

Lee moved on to defend Petersburg, an important rail center 20 miles (32 km) from Richmond. If Petersburg fell, the Confederates could not hold Richmond.

The capture of Atlanta Meanwhile, Sherman moved toward Atlanta. The Confederates made Union forces pay for every advance, but by mid-July of 1864 Sherman had surrounded Atlanta.

The Confederates hoped to hold out until the Union's presidential election. They thought that war-weary northerners would reject Lincoln and elect General George McClellan, who called for an end to the war. However, on September 2, 1864, Atlanta fell. News of Sherman's victory raised spirits in the North and ensured Lincoln's reelection.

Sherman now put into effect Grant's idea of total war. To break the South's will to continue fighting, his troops burned Atlanta. Then they marched almost unopposed across Georgia. Along the way they torched barns and houses and destroyed railroad tracks, crops, and livestock.

In December Sherman reached the sea at Savannah. Then, leaving destruction in his wake, he marched north through South Carolina and into North Carolina. From there he drove on toward Richmond.

Lee Surrenders

For nine months Grant's forces battered Lee's defenses at Petersburg, the gateway to Richmond. They finally broke through on April 1, 1865. Two days later, Union troops marched into Richmond.

Lee fled with 30,000 soldiers. Grant followed. At this point, other Union forces

This painting commemorates the end of the Civil War. General Lee (left) signs the agreement surrendering his army to General Grant (right).

Discussion

Checking Understanding

1. In what way was Grant a solution to one of Lincoln's ongoing problems? (He was a successful general after many ineffective ones.)

2. How did Sherman put Grant's ideas about war into effect? (He waged total war—against the people's resources and will to fight—as he invaded Georgia and took Atlanta. His troops burned houses, barns, and factories; destroyed railroad tracks; and ruined crops and livestock.)

Stimulating Critical Thinking

3. What role do you think Sherman's march through Georgia played in Lee's surrender? (Answers might include that it was an important part of the northern victory because it warned of the ongoing destruction if war continued.)

Vital Links

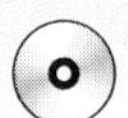

Atlanta (Picture) Unit 3, Side 1, Search 38977

See also Unit 3 Explore CD-ROM location 212.

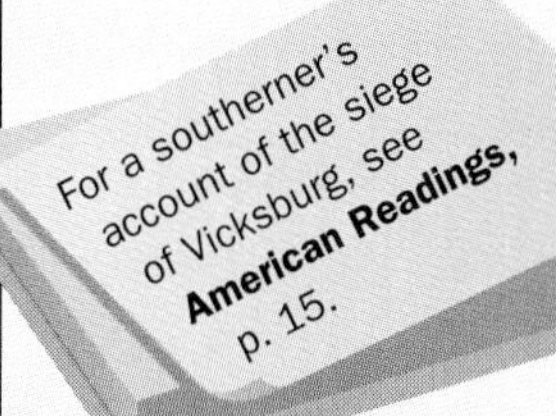
For a southerner's
account of the siege
of Vicksburg, see
American Readings,
p. 15.

Closing the Section

Wrap-Up Activity

Making a Time Line

To review the section, have students work in groups to create a detailed time line for the years 1863–1865. Each key event for the period should include the date and a sentence identifying it and stating its importance.

Section Review Answers

1. Definition: *total war* (164)

2. The Battle of Gettysburg forced Lee to begin fighting a defensive war on southern soil. After the Battle of Vicksburg, Union forces controlled the entire Mississippi River.

3. Grant had more troops and so was able to surround Lee's armies in Richmond.

4. No: farms and cities were devastated and caused economic ruin for innocent citizens. Yes: it helped to put an end to the war and save the Union.

To check understanding of "Why We Remember," assign Thinking Critically question 3 on student page 168.

History Footnote

After the war, Clara Barton spent more than two years helping thousands of families frantically seek missing relatives. Such searches were difficult because few soldiers carried identification. Sometimes before battle, a soldier might pin a slip of paper with his name to his uniform so he could be identified. Benjamin Chase etched his name on a coin, a forerunner of military dog tags.

For Grant's account of the surrender at Appomattox, see **American Readings**, p. 16.

cut off Lee's escape route. Outnumbered and surrounded, Lee decided that further fighting would be useless.

On April 9, 1865, Lee surrendered at Appomattox Court House. Grant gave generous terms. Lee's troops could go home if they promised to fight no more. All soldiers could keep their own horses. Grant also provided food for Lee's starving soldiers. In the next few days, all Confederate forces followed Lee's lead. The last general to surrender was Stand Watie of the Cherokee Nation. On May 10, Jefferson Davis was captured.

Costs of war The bloodiest war in the history of the nation had finally ended. The Union had been saved, but at the horrifying cost of more than 620,000 Union and Confederate dead.

Almost every family on both sides had lost a friend or loved one. Benjamin Chase's mother never overcame the shock of his death. Daniel and Rebecca Hite of Virginia had watched five sons go off to war. Only two came home. Clara Barton set up a "missing persons" office to help thousands of families searching for missing relatives.

For President Lincoln, the end of the war was the happiest day of his life. "Thank God I have lived to see this," he said. "I have been dreaming a horrid nightmare for four years, and now the nightmare is over."

4. Section Review

1. Define **total war.**

2. Why were the Battles of Gettysburg and Vicksburg turning points in the war?

3. What Union advantage helped Grant defeat Lee in 1865?

4. Critical Thinking Do you think Sherman should have used total war in Georgia and the Carolinas? Give reasons for your answer.

Why We Remember

The Civil War

The Civil War, wrote the *New York Times* after the guns fell silent, "leaves us a different people forever." Nowhere was this truth easier to see than in the longstanding issue of slavery. The Union's victory in the war destroyed the system of slavery and paved the way to freedom for 4 million African Americans. Many of them had helped win that freedom on the battlefield. To Clara Barton, each one was a "soldier of freedom."

The Civil War also changed how Americans viewed their country. Before the war, most Americans thought of the United States as a loose union of separate states. When talking of their country, they said, "The United States *are*." Afterward, people in both the North and the South saw the country as a single nation and began to say, "The United States *is*."

Geography Footnote

Many sites of Civil War battles are now part of the National Park system. Some, such as Gettysburg, Fredericksburg and Spotsylvania, and Shiloh are national military parks. Others, such as Antietam, Manassas, and Petersburg, are national battlefields; and others, such as Appomattox Court House, are national historical parks. All are run by the National Park Service, which is a bureau of the United States Department of the Interior. The sites have been restored to look as much as possible as they did during the Civil War, and they include relics such as cannons and other weapons.

Geography Lab

Reading a Grid Map

Each year close to 1.5 million people visit the Gettysburg National Military Park in Pennsylvania. There they can trace the events of the battle by car or on foot.

The map shows the site of the Battle of Gettysburg. As with road maps, this map has a grid of intersecting lines. Note that the spaces between horizontal lines are labeled with letters, while the spaces between vertical lines are labeled with numbers. Thus, the squares in the grid can be referred to as A-1, A-2, and so on. The labeled grid makes it easy to find sites and describe their location on the map.

Gettysburg National Cemetery, Pennsylvania

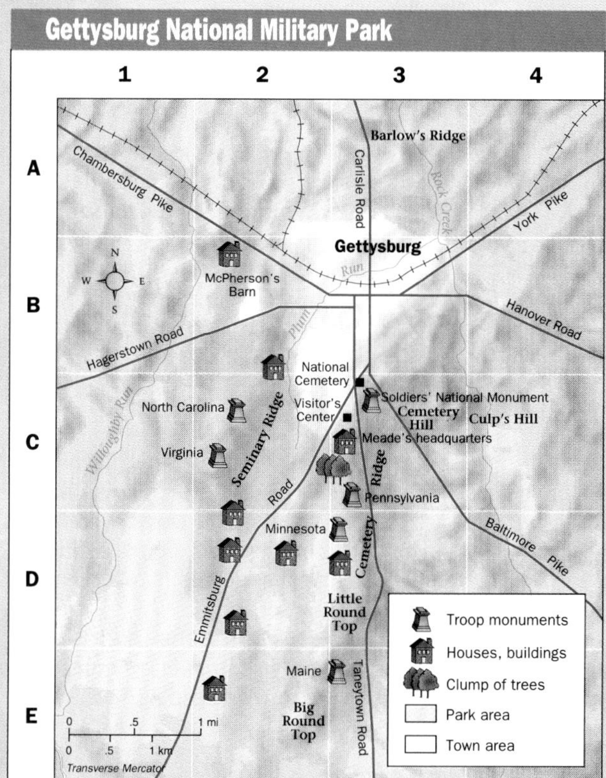

Using Map Skills

1. Confederates approached Gettysburg on a road that passes through grid locations A-1, A-2, and B-2. What is the name of the road?
2. A Union line curled around what two hills in C-3 and C-4?
3. Confederate troops lined Seminary Ridge. From there Pickett's men charged Union troops atop Cemetery Ridge. To keep their sense of direction, they focused on a clump of trees. Give its grid location.
4. President Lincoln delivered his address where Soldier's Monument is today. Give its grid location.
5. **Hands-On Geography** Use the map to plan a tour of the Gettysburg battle site. Begin at the Visitor's Center and end at McPherson's Barn, with five stops in between. Imagine a path through the park. Write instructions for the tour, using grid locations and compass directions to describe the route and the stopping points along it.

Teaching the Geography Lab

To help students read the grid map, ask them to point to the area within A-3 and name the road indicated there (Carlisle Road). Have them look at the key and tell what kind of structure is located in E-3 (a troop monument). Point out that on a road map, names of streets and buildings are alphabetized next to the map with locations indicated by grid area (A-1,B-2, etc.). Suggest that students bring in road maps and practice locating streets.

Using Map Skills

Answers

1. Chambersburg Pike
2. Cemetery Hill and Culp's Hill
3. C-2, C-3
4. C-3
5. Tour instructions will vary but may include going east to Culp's Hill in C-3, south to Cemetery Hill in C-3, south to Little Round Top in D-3, north to the Minnesota Troop Monument in D-3, and northwest to Seminary Ridge in C-3.

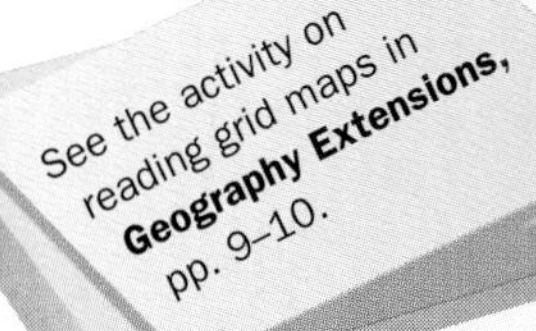

Survey Answers

Reviewing Vocabulary

Definitions are found on these pages: *habeas corpus* (142), *martial law* (142), *casualties* (150), *draft* (158), *income tax* (159), *total war* (164).

Reviewing Main Ideas

1. (a) the Union (b) the Union (c) the Confederacy (d) the Union (e) the Union

2. Davis planned to push back invading forces, making the war so costly that the Union would give up. Lincoln planned to blockade seaports, gain control of the Mississippi River, and capture Richmond.

3. Lincoln had mixed success. His blockade prevented importation of supplies. On the Mississippi, Union troops captured many key sites, but they failed to gain complete control of the river. They also failed to capture Richmond.

4. (a) The proclamation freed all slaves in the Confederate states, but slaves in areas loyal to the Union were not freed. (b) The war became, in part, a struggle to abolish slavery; the Union gained European support; African American soldiers bolstered the Union army.

5. Lincoln's problems included opposition from Copperheads, resistance to the draft, and raising money. Davis's problems included lack of cooperation from states, opposition to the draft, raising money, and getting supplies. Each faced the problem of a loss of value of paper money.

6. The Union victory at Gettysburg: Lee's forces were too weak to invade the North again, and European nations did not help the South. The Confederate surrender of Vicksburg led to the surrender of Port Hudson. The Union controlled the entire Mississippi River.

(Answers continued in top margin)

7. Grant's army broke through Lee's lines at Petersburg. Lee fled but was quickly surrounded and decided to surrender.

Thinking Critically

1. As a result of the Battle of Saratoga, France became a U.S. ally, and Spain entered the war against Britain. Their support helped make victory possible. Antietam was a turning point in the Civil War. It weakened Lee's army and hurt Confederate hopes of European aid.

2. Answers may include that he wanted to reunite the nation as quickly and as peacefully as possible. Students' opinions on terms will vary.

3. Lincoln was referring to abolishing slavery. The Emancipation Proclamation was the first step.

Chapter Survey

Reviewing Vocabulary

Define the following terms.

1. habeas corpus
2. martial law
3. casualties
4. draft
5. income tax
6. total war

Reviewing Main Ideas

1. When the Civil War began, which side had the advantage in the following areas? (a) farmland (b) factories (c) military leadership (d) population (e) transportation
2. How did President Davis plan to win the war? How did President Lincoln?
3. By the end of 1862, how successful had Lincoln been in achieving his war goal? Give supporting examples.
4. (a) What were the provisions of the Emancipation Proclamation? (b) How did the proclamation affect the war?
5. What were two problems faced at home by President Lincoln? By President Davis?
6. Describe two events that took place in the first week of July 1863 that changed the course of the war.
7. What led Lee to surrender his Army of Northern Virginia in April 1865?

Thinking Critically

1. Analysis The Battle of Saratoga was a turning point in the American War of Independence. The Battle of Antietam was a turning point in the Civil War. Compare the results of the two battles.
2. Synthesis Why do you think Grant's terms of surrender at Appomattox were so generous? If you had been in his place, what terms would you have offered? Why?
3. Why We Remember: Analysis In the Gettysburg Address, President Lincoln vowed that "this nation, under God, shall have a new birth of freedom." What do you think he meant?

Applying Skills

Making a hypothesis When Lincoln issued the Emancipation Proclamation, he was using a power of the presidency. A presidential proclamation—also called an executive order—does not require any action by Congress.

Look in newspapers and magazines to find a recent example of an executive order. Then use what you learned on page 160 to do the following:
1. Create three hypotheses to explain why the President issued the executive order.
2. Test each hypothesis against the information available to you.
3. List your hypotheses and tell which of them best explains the President's action. If you cannot choose one, explain why not. What might you do next?

History Mystery

An army recruit Answer the History Mystery on page 139. Where might you find information about Lyons Wakeman's experiences? Where would you look for evidence that Wakeman was, in fact, a soldier?

Writing in Your History Journal

1. Keys to History (a) The time line on pages 138–139 has seven Keys to History. In your journal, list each key and describe why it is important to know about. (b) Imagine that you are a reporter or "special artist" covering the Civil War. If you could cover only one event on the time line, which one would you choose? In your journal, explain the reasons for your decision.
2. Clara Barton During the Civil War, thousands of women felt the same urge to help as Clara Barton had. Imagine that

Applying Skills

Answers should show a knowledge of the definition of *hypothesis* and an understanding of the steps involved in hypothesizing. Those steps can be found in the Procedure and Skill Tips sections on page 160.

History Mystery

Information is found on page 146. Students should note the National Archives as a source of information on Lyons Wakeman.

Writing in Your History Journal

1. (a) Explanations should be similar to the time line notes on teacher pages 138–139. (b) Choices should be supported by reasons that tell why the event is important or particularly interesting.

(Answers continued in side margin)

2. Answers might include being a soldier, a nurse, or a factory worker; setting up hospitals; and helping escaped slaves.

3. Accept reasonable answers. If students feel the government should take the responsibility for protecting Civil War battlefields, encourage them to think about how to raise the necessary funds. They might mention the desire to preserve the environment or to promote racial or cultural pride as possible reasons.

Reviewing Geography

1. (A) Atlanta, (B) Vicksburg, (C) Washington, D.C., (D) Gettysburg, (E) Appomattox Court House

2. Students should consider Montgomery's location and the need to divide forces to fight in different arenas. The Union might attack Alabama from the Gulf of Mexico or move forces down the Mississippi and across the state of Mississippi. The strategy of having a blockade and controlling the Mississippi would remain the same. Fighting in Virginia would also continue.

Alternative Assessment

Teacher's Take-Home Planner 1, page 15, includes suggestions and scoring rubrics for the Alternative Assessment activity.

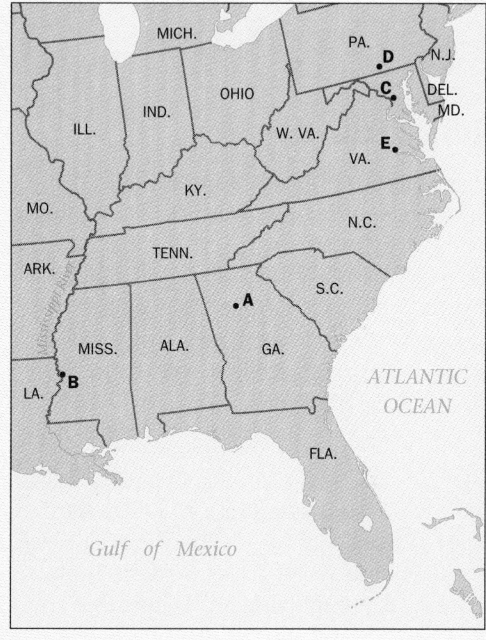

Reviewing Geography

1. For each letter on the map, write the name of a town or city that was important during the Civil War.

2. Geographic Thinking One of the major Union strategies was to capture Richmond, which was only 100 miles (160 km) from Washington, D.C. As a result, many battles took place on Virginia soil.

The Confederate capital was originally at Montgomery, Alabama (see the map on pages R6–R7). Imagine that Montgomery had remained the Confederate capital. How do you think Union strategy might have changed? How might it have remained the same?

you are living then. Choose a role for yourself—man or woman, old or young. Describe what you would like to do to help in the war effort.

3. Citizenship Today, the growth of cities is threatening the sites of many famous Civil War battlefields, including Gettysburg and Petersburg. Imagine that you own property on the site of Gettysburg. A developer has offered to buy your land and plans to build a factory. In your journal, write your thoughts about the offer.

Alternative Assessment

Writing a play Divided loyalties, especially in the Border States, led brothers, cousins, and fathers and sons to fight on different sides in the Civil War. With several classmates, write a one-act play about the reunion of a divided family after the war.

❶ Decide who the family members are, where they live, what they did before the war, and what role they played on which side in the war.

❷ As part of the play, have each person describe an event in which he or she took part. It might be a battle, an aspect of the war effort at home, or Lee's surrender. Use the information in the text and do additional research as needed to provide background.

❸ When your play is complete, present it to the class.

Your work will be evaluated on the following criteria:

• you describe historical events and attitudes accurately
• you include both Union and Confederate views in the dialogue
• you present the characters and action in believable ways

Teaching the

Link to Literature

Remind students of the First Battle of Bull Run, to which onlookers from Washington traveled to observe the first battle of the Civil War. Point out that the civilians had no idea how serious the battle would be or how long the war would last. Encourage students to look for contrasts between the onlookers' expectations and what happens in reality as they read. Have them look for details that express this contrast, such as the contrast of the linen tablecloths and the eventual carnage of the battle.

Literature Footnote

Paul Fleischman's novel is told by 16 different characters. All the characters are fictional, except one: Union General Irvin McDowell. However, the novel realistically presents officers' points of view. Confederate Colonel Oliver Brattle contemplates "what shells do to living flesh" as those around him look with excitement toward the battle. General McDowell reveals nervousness about commanding an army of 30,000. The soldiers reveal how pride and excitement turn to horror after they see the devastation of their first battle. With a wide array of characters, including an 11-year-old boy who wants to play the fife in the Confederate army and a young Minnesota girl who watches her brother go off to battle, the novel is suited to readers' theater performances.

Link to Literature

Bull Run by Paul Fleischman

Bull Run, the first battle of the Civil War, took place 26 miles (42 km) outside of Washington, D.C. In his novel, *Bull Run,* author Paul Fleischman creates "eyewitnesses" who tell a vivid story of the battle—a doctor, an enslaved woman, a photographer, two soldiers, and Edmund Upwing, an African American carriage driver. In the following passage, Upwing tells of driving two congressmen and their wives to watch the Union army crush the Rebels. Like the scores of other picnickers who come to watch the "fun," Upwing's passengers experience the shock of their lives.

Morning

'Twas dark as Hell's cellar when we left for Washington. I'd thought they would sleep, but they chattered like sparrows. I caught a good deal of it, as usual. Cabmen dull witted as their nags? Don't be daft! They know more of Washington than the President. Though whenever a question is put to me, I ignore it until it's asked a fourth time, that my passengers mightn't suspect I have ears.

nags: worn-out horses

daft: foolish

There were plenty of other spectators heading south. The shooting commenced as we neared Centreville. We passed through the village and found a fine grassy spot on a hill overlooking Bull Run. Every last horse and buggy for hire in Washington seemed to be there. Linen tablecloths were spread out and people of quality spread out upon 'em. My passengers were in a merry mood—all but one of the men who let out that McDowell had been given command for no better reason than that he'd come from Ohio, whose governor had Lincoln's ear and had whispered "McDowell" in it constantly. 'Tis a fact. I feigned deafness, but took the precaution of noting our fastest route of retreat.

feigned: pretended

Afternoon

The shout went 'round, "The Rebels are upon us!" The words struck the picnickers like a storm, sent them shrieking into their coaches, and sent every coach bolting toward the road. My riders commanded that I put on all speed. Every driver heard the same demand. The road was narrow and choked with coaches. This mass of wheels and whips blocked the soldiers, who seemed even more eager than we to be gone. They were furious with us. How their teamsters swore! Those on foot rushed around us like an April torrent. They were bloody, dusty, and wild-eyed as wolves. "The Black Horse Cavalry is coming!" one bellowed. The air rang with rumors of hidden batteries, heartless horsemen, rivers

teamsters: wagon drivers who hauled goods

Literature Footnote

Historical fiction such as Paul Fleischman's *Bull Run* portrays the facts about a historical event, adding fictional characters and details that remain true to the event's character. He realistically portrays the doubts soldiers had before entering into battle. *Bull Run* won the 1994 Scott O'Dell Award for Historical Fiction.

This sketch of the chaos as Union forces fled Bull Run appeared in a British newspaper, the *Illustrated London News.* Illustrated newspapers sent out "special artists" to cover events of the war.

red with blood, and visions worthy of the Book of Revelation. One frantic soldier cut a horse free from a wagon's team and took off bareback. Another fugitive tried to unseat me. I drove him off with my whip. 'Tis a fact. Then there came a terrific boom. Women screamed. A Rebel shell had fallen on the road. The caravan halted. The way was blocked by a tangle of overturned wagons. The soldiers scattered or froze in fear. Men fled their buggies. A second shell struck. Then a young officer galloped up, leaped down, and dragged the vehicles away. His courage was acclaimed. We jerked forward afresh. My sharp ear learned that the man's name was Custer. All predicted that he was destined for great deeds.

Book of Revelation: the last book of the Bible, which tells about the end of the world

Night

Rain came on during the night. It soaked the men, turned the roads to muck, and added more misery to the retreat. It was past midnight when we reached Washington. . . . How my passengers railed against the soldiers! And their know-nothing officers, and the profiteers, and the press, and the generals, and the President. I learned later that week that Jeff Davis and Beauregard were pulled to pieces the same way for not pressing on toward Washington. A few days after the battle, Lincoln sent McDowell packing. This raised spirits some, but not everyone's. I heard that Horace Greeley himself, the most powerful editor in the land—who'd first told Lincoln to let the South secede, then insisted that Richmond be taken—now had sent Lincoln a letter stating that the Rebels couldn't be beaten! The winds blew fickle about the President, but he had his feet on the ground. I'm proud to say he ignored the letter.

fickle: changeable in loyalty

A Closer Look

1. How does the author's portrayal of Upwing and his passengers help paint a picture of the scene?
2. Do you think Upwing shares his passengers' expectation that the Union will win quickly? Explain.
3. How does Upwing view public opinion about the war?

Discussion

Stimulating Critical Thinking

1. If you had been a soldier at the battle, how do you think you would have felt? (Frightened and confused because it was the first battle; annoyed or angry because civilians were making soldiers' jobs more hazardous.)

2. How do you think the event described in the selection shows what the next four years will be like? (The chaos and destruction foreshadow the shocking devastation of the entire war.)

A Closer Look

Answers

1. Upwing is a sensible narrator who gives an accurate picture of the scene. The description shows the public's attitudes toward the war and explains why the battle was so chaotic: they are foolish and do not view the event seriously.

2. Upwing seems to have a clearer understanding of the seriousness of the event as a whole, and he supports Lincoln in standing firm in his fight against the Confederates.

3. Upwing seems to recognize that everyone has opinions about the war based on personal interests and that few people understand the real issues. He seems to discount public opinion.

Teaching the

Link to American Readings

In this feature students learn that history is comprised of facts—but facts are interpreted by historians. Here they will read differing views of the causes of the Civil War. They will also read a poem that became a marching song for Confederate troops.

Before students begin the lesson, review the material in Taking Sides in the War (page 142) and Why We Remember (page 166). Have students read the entire feature before assigning the A Closer Look questions. The Setting the Stage Activity and Bonus Activity may then be introduced according to the needs and interests of the students. The information contained in the Discussion questions and the Footnotes may be used throughout the lesson as appropriate. Readers' Theater is ideal for students who might find the readings somewhat difficult. Use the Wrap-Up Activity for students who would enjoy taking a step beyond the core lesson.

Literature Footnote

It is a movie about the Civil War that has been America's favorite historical film since it was first released in 1939. *Gone with the Wind,* based on Margaret Mitchell's novel by the same name, garnered an unprecedented 13 Academy Award nominations and 8 Oscars. However, life for "southern belles" on plantations in 1863 was quite different from that of the pampered Scarlett O'Hara in the movie. Most young girls from plantation families married by the time they were 20. They immediately assumed the responsibilities of plantation management. The mistress was to oversee the care, feeding, and clothing of her own family and that of her husband's slaves. She supervised the gardens, dairy barn, and medicine chest, and was expected to keep the estate running smoothly.

Link to American Readings

READING 2A

Why Did the Civil War Occur?

Historians have debated this question for more than a century. Some believe it was an unavoidable clash between two societies with different value systems. Others have argued that better leaders would have been able to settle even major issues, such as slavery, in a peaceful manner. In the following selections, four twentieth-century historians present their views.

Historians debate the causes of the Civil War

Charles and Mary Beard argue that abolition was not widely accepted in the North. Therefore, slavery was not the root cause of the conflict.

No other [political] party organized between that time [1844] and the clash of arms attempted to do more than demand the exclusion of slavery from the territories and not until the Democrats by repealing the Missouri Compromise threatened to extend slavery throughout the West did any party poll more than a handful of votes on that issue. . . .

Even the Republican party, in the campaign of 1856, coming hard on the act of defiance which swept away the Missouri compact, won little more than one-third the active voters to the cause of restricting the slavery area. . . .

Moreover, not a single responsible statesman of the middle period [1820–1860] committed himself to the doctrine of immediate and unconditional abolition to be achieved by independent political action. . . .

Since, therefore, the abolition of slavery never appeared in the platform of any great political party, since the only appeal ever made to the electorate on that issue was scornfully repulsed, since the spokesman of the Republicans emphatically declared that his party never intended to interfere with slavery in the states in any shape or form, it seems reasonable to assume that the institution of slavery was not the fundamental issue during the epoch preceding the bombardment of Fort Sumter. . . .

fundamental: basic, primary

The roots of the controversy lay elsewhere—in social groupings founded on differences in climate, soil, industries, and labor systems.

Literature Footnote

Margaret Mitchell (1900–1949) was a writer for *The Atlanta Journal.* For ten years after she left her job as a journalist, Mitchell worked on what would be her only novel, *Gone with the Wind* (1936). This book about the Civil War and Reconstruction from the southern point of view became the largest selling novel in U.S. history up to that period.

Literature Footnote

"My Maryland" has a strong rhythm that makes it an ideal marching song. Also note the strong sense of patriotism that pervades the poem. It is a patriotism not just for a country, but for a way of life.

A modern painting details the Battle of Gettysburg.

Avery Craven argues that each faction created a distorted view of the other. As passions became enraged, leaders lost their ability to compromise. Clear-thinking politicians would have been able to resolve the conflict.

The significant thing about the antislavery men and movements and those who developed the abstract defense of the South is the picture of slavery and of society which they created. They were too extreme for any great following. Conservative men of the day dismissed them as fanatics and hastened to assure their friends in other sections [of the country] that such voices did not represent the true opinions and feelings of their people. But these fanatics, unrestrained by fact, were creating clear-cut pictures of slavery, slaves, slaveholders, and southern and northern life positive enough to suit the needs of those engaged in conflict. When politicians became enraged in debate, when the sections became entangled in strife, then these pictures were to serve wider purposes. The time would come when opponents needed just such distorted weapons—when false propaganda could take the place of truth. Then the conceptions of men and societies woven by these intense emotional voices of heaven would pass as sober truth. Enemies would become devils; friends, the incarnation of right and justice. Blood would have to be spilled.

Setting the Stage Activity

Friend Against Friend

To reinforce the importance of emotion and patriotism in the Civil War, have students do a role play. Remind students that especially in the border states, where feelings ran high for both the Union and the Confederacy, families were torn apart and friends became enemies when one chose the North and the other supported the South. Ask pairs of students to portray either friends or family being split by North-South politics. What issues would they argue? How might they try to resolve their differences? Which would prove stronger, family and friendship or patriotism?

Bonus Activity

Illustrating Lincoln

To demonstrate to students the relevancy of history, ask them to give a contemporary example of the following quote by Abraham Lincoln. "In giving freedom to the slave, we assure freedom to the free—honorable alike in what we give and what we preserve." (1862) You may wish to have students work in small groups to complete this activity.

Discussion

Stimulating Critical Thinking

1. One raging debate that drove the nation toward civil war was the question of who should have the final determination regarding issues such as slavery. Should the states or the federal government be responsible for making and enforcing human rights laws? What do you think? Explain.
(Students who believe that the states should determine human-rights issues might say that because the country is so large, and situations vary, each state should make and enforce its own laws. Those who support federal power might say that as a country of united states, all citizens should adhere to and support the same human-rights laws.)

2. What purpose do you think songs such as "My Maryland" served for the soldiers of the Civil War?
(They provided inspiration; gave the soldiers a sense of fighting for a common cause; offered some distraction from the very real danger and hardship that they would face in battle.)

Literature Footnote
The poetry of James Randall is invigorating, uplifting, and inspiring. However, it had little to do with the realities of the Civil War battlefield. There are numerous fine primary sources, including many written by women, that do address those realities. Diaries and memoirs are some of the most enlightening and at the same time shocking sources. Students might like to read some of those and compare the differing viewpoints. Suggested reading includes: the diary of Mary Boykin Chesnut; the memoirs of Ulysses S. Grant; Louisa May Alcott's accounts of her work as a volunteer nurse in a Civil War hospital; "C. Aytch" by Sam Watkins, a private in the Confederate army; and the memoirs of Susie King Taylor, a slave who escaped at age 14 and later volunteered to work with the wounded in a black regiment in Georgia.

James McPherson argues that southerners seceded to preserve their vision of liberty.

When secessionists protested that they were acting to preserve traditional rights and values, they were correct. They fought to protect their constitutional liberties against the perceived northern threat to overthrow them. The South's concept of republicanism had not changed in three-quarters of a century; the North's had. With complete sincerity the South fought to preserve its version of the republic of the founding fathers—a government of limited powers that protected the rights of property and whose constituency comprised an independent gentry and yeomanry of the white race undisturbed by large cities, heartless factories, restless free workers, and class conflict. The accession to power of the Republican party, with its ideology of competitive, egalitarian, free-labor capitalism, was a signal to the South that the northern majority had turned irrevocably toward this frightening, revolutionary future. Indeed, the Black Republican party appeared to the eyes of many Southerners as "essentially a revolutionary party.". . . Therefore secession was a pre-emptive counterrevolution to prevent the Black Republican revolution from engulfing the South.

republicanism: political system in which power belongs to those entitled to vote

pre-emptive: action taken to stop another action before it takes place

---

READING 2B

Before the Battle

Maryland, one of the border slave states, wavered when the war began. As Union troops marched through Baltimore in the first days of the war, they were attacked by southern sympathizers. Still, the state did not secede. The Baltimorean James R. Randall, who urged secession, wrote the famous song "My Maryland." Sung to the tune of "O Tannenbaum," it became the most popular marching song of the Confederate soldiers. The opening and closing stanzas follow.

Readers' Theater

To emphasize the power of rhythm and sound in poetry, have students practice reading "My Maryland" in a group. One student in each group might act as the "conductor" for the reading. This person should be someone familiar with leading music. The conductor can tap the beat or rhythm of the poem as the group reads. Encourage students first to pay close attention to the leader, just as they would if they were members of a band or a chorus. Next, work with students to achieve understanding of the text. Expression will be more effective if students truly understand what they are reading.

Wrap-Up Activity

Evaluating Human Rights Issues

To extend the lesson, tell students that the enormity of the Civil War tended to overshadow other problems. For example, Cheyenne and Arapaho Indians were massacred at Sand Creek, Colorado, in 1864. Ask students to read about this massacre on page 230 and then to respond in their journals. In what way were human rights violated?

My Maryland

The despot's heel is on thy shore,
    Maryland!
His torch is at thy temple door,
    Maryland!
Avenge the patriotic gore
That flecked the streets of Baltimore,
And be the battle-queen of yore,
    Maryland, My Maryland!

Hark to an exiled son's appeal,
    Maryland!
My Mother State, to thee I kneel,
    Maryland!
For life and death, for woe and weal,
Thy peerless chivalry reveal,
And Gird thy beauteous limbs with steel,
    Maryland, My Maryland!

Thou wilt not yield the Vandal toll,
    Maryland!
Thou wilt not crook to his control,
    Maryland!
Better the fire upon thee roll,
Better the shot, the blade, the bowl,
Than crucifixion of the soul,
    Maryland, My Maryland!

I hear the distant thunder hum,
    Maryland!
The Old Line's bugle, fife, and drum,
    Maryland!
She is not dead, nor deaf, nor dumb;
Huzza! she spurns the Northern scum!
She breathes! She burns! She'll come! She'll come!
    Maryland, My Maryland!

despot: tyrant

avenge: seek revenge

weal: injury

The Civil War, like most wars, inspired the creation of sentimental and patriotic songs. The troops sang about home, mother, and sweethearts.

A Closer Look

1. According to the Beards, what issues triggered the Civil War?

2. Summarize Randall's sentiments about his home state of Maryland. How does he feel about the Civil War?

3. CRITICAL THINKING With which historian do you most closely agree about the cause of the Civil War? Explain.

A Closer Look Answers

1. The cause of the Civil War was not slavery; it was issues such as differences in climate, soil, industries, and labor.

2. Randall loves Maryland. He feels that it has been invaded and that it is being forced to adopt a social system that it neither believes in nor wants. He encourages the people of Maryland to fight.

3. Students' answers will vary. Some students might agree with the Beards because slavery was not one of the major political issues prior to the war. Others might say that political debates concerning freedom and state sovereignty were really about preserving the institution of slavery.

Teaching the Citizenship Lab

In this feature students learn about *Ex Parte Milligan* (1866), in which the Supreme Court ruled that civilians cannot be tried by military courts as long as civil courts remain open. The ruling helped set the boundaries of presidential and military authority in wartime.

Before students read the feature, have them look up *circuit court* and *grand jury* in a civics text or other source. Have students read the entire feature before assigning the Understanding Civic Issues questions and the Hands-On Citizenship activity. The Bonus Activity in this Teacher's Edition may be used as an alternative to, or in addition to, the Hands-On Citizenship activity. The Discussion questions in this Teacher's Edition may be used at appropriate points during students' reading or afterward.

Objectives

- ★ Define the term *writ of habeas corpus* and explain its importance.
- ★ List some ways President Lincoln exceeded or stretched his constitutional authority during the Civil War.
- ★ Explain the Supreme Court's ruling on the rights of civilians in wartime in *Ex Parte Milligan.*

Supreme Court Case: *Ex Parte Milligan*

Citizenship Lab

The Rights of Civilians in Wartime

"The Constitution of the United States is a law for rulers and people, equally in war and in peace, and covers with the shield of its protection all classes of men, at all times, and under all circumstances." So said Associate Justice David Davis, writing for the majority in the 1866 Supreme Court case known as *Ex Parte Milligan* ("On Behalf of Milligan"). In this landmark case, the Court limited the military's power over civilians during times of war. The case had grown out of the Civil War and some of the extraordinary measures that President Lincoln and his military leaders took to win it.

Lambdin Milligan's Case

Lambdin P. Milligan was a resident of Indiana and an antiwar Democrat. In 1864 U.S. Army officials arrested Milligan and several other "Copperheads." The officials charged that the Copperheads were involved in a conspiracy to steal weapons from Union arsenals and to free Confederate prisoners being held in northern prison camps. Indiana was not a war zone. The civil courts still functioned there, and the Milligan defendants could have been tried for treason (betrayal of country) in such a court. But the army officials did not trust civilians to be reliable jurors in a treason trial. They brought the defendants before a military commission. The commission found Milligan and two others guilty and sentenced them to die by hanging.

Believing that a military court had no right to try a civilian like him, Milligan petitioned the U.S. circuit court in Indianapolis to issue a *writ of habeas corpus.* This is an order from a court to an officer who is holding someone prisoner. The writ requires the officer to produce the prisoner and submit to the court's judgment as to whether the prisoner has been wrongfully held. As you have read, President Lincoln had first suspended the right of habeas corpus in Maryland in 1861. That same year, Chief Justice Roger B. Taney declared in *Ex Parte Merryman* that only Congress has the power to suspend habeas corpus. Lincoln refused to follow Taney's ruling. In 1863 he decided that habeas corpus must be suspended for anyone who resisted the draft or was suspected of "affording aid to the rebels." Congress passed a law confirming the President's power to take such action.

It was against this background that the judges of the circuit court received Milligan's petition. Milligan

History Footnote

In May 1861 a secessionist named John Merryman was arrested and imprisoned at Fort McHenry in Baltimore. Because Supreme Court justices had to spend part of each year in the lower federal courts, Chief Justice Taney was sitting in the U.S. circuit court in Baltimore at the time. Taney issued a writ of habeas corpus directing Fort McHenry's commander to bring Merryman to court. The commander refused, citing Lincoln's suspension of habeas corpus. Taney responded with the *Ex Parte Merryman* opinion. *Dred Scott* had brought Taney scathing criticism, and *Merryman* only increased northerners' anger at him. One observer wrote: "He had outlived his epoch, and was shunned and hated. . . ." Taney died in 1864 at age 87.

hoped that if he was brought before the circuit court, the judges would either turn him over to a civil court for trial or set him free. Not surprisingly, the circuit court judges could not agree on whether to issue a writ of habeas corpus. They sent Milligan's case to the Supreme Court.

How the Court Ruled

By the time the Court announced its decision, the Civil War was over and President Lincoln was dead. But it was still important to settle the issues involved in the case. Justice Davis put it this way: "This nation, as experience has proved, cannot always remain at peace, and has no right to expect that it will always have wise and humane rulers, sincerely attached to the principles of the Constitution."

All nine justices agreed that the military commission that had tried the Milligan defendants did not have jurisdiction (authority) in the case. However, the justices disagreed about the reasons for their decision. Because of this disagreement, Justice Davis wrote the majority opinion, while Chief Justice Salmon P. Chase

As depicted in this painting by David G. Blythe, President Lincoln's political enemies in the North, who called on him to strictly adhere to the Constitution in an effort to bring about "peace at any price," made it difficult for the President to make wartime decisions without stretching his powers.

Setting the Stage Activity

Writing to the President

To prepare students for reading about *Ex Parte Milligan*, have them imagine they are northern civilians during the Civil War, arrested by soldiers for conspiracy against the Union and pronounced guilty by a military court. Students should consider what seems unfair about this and then write protest letters to President Lincoln.

Bonus Activity

Creating Political Cartoons

The Supreme Court's ruling in *Ex Parte Milligan* can be viewed as a posthumous criticism of some of Lincoln's wartime actions. To help students grasp that, have them create political cartoons about the Court's ruling. Students should imagine themselves as political cartoonists living in 1866, but they can choose to be either supporters or critics of Lincoln. Provide background by explaining that during the war, some northerners—especially antiwar Democrats—had believed Lincoln was taking too much power into his own hands. Lincoln's use of power was a major issue in the presidential campaign of 1864.

Discussion

Checking Understanding

1. Why did Milligan petition the U.S. circuit court to issue a writ of habeas corpus? (He believed a military court had no right to try a civilian; he hoped that if he was brought before the circuit court, he would get a civil court trial or be set free.)

2. How did the fifth and sixth amendments support the Supreme Court's majority opinion? (The Fifth Amendment guarantees civilians the right to indictment by a grand jury, and Milligan had not been indicted by a grand jury. The Sixth Amendment guarantees trial by jury, and Milligan had not been tried by jury.)

Stimulating Critical Thinking

3. As in many cases that come before the Supreme Court, the question of Milligan's actual guilt or innocence was not considered. Why is that? (Because the Supreme Court's main task is not to rule on the facts of a particular case but rather to decide whether a law or an executive action is constitutional or not.)

Citizenship Footnote

Although Chief Justice Chase agreed with the majority, he rested his conclusion on the Habeas Corpus Act of 1863 rather than the Constitution. The 1863 law authorized the President to suspend habeas corpus, but it required the secretaries of state and war to give federal judges the names of all political prisoners. If a federal grand jury then failed to indict, the prisoners had to be freed.

Chase disagreed with the majority on another point. Although the majority took it upon itself to declare that Congress also lacked the power to authorize military trials of civilians, under the Constitution, Chase wrote, Congress could pass laws to carry out war. Thus, if Congress ever found the civil courts incapable of dealing with treason, it could indeed authorize military trials.

Lincoln and the Constitution

President Lincoln, for the most part, acted within constitutional guidelines as Commander-in-Chief during the Civil War. However, as the chart shows, he exceeded or stretched his authority on several occasions. Although Congress ultimately gave its approval to most of Lincoln's wartime actions, the Supreme Court ruled in *Ex Parte Milligan* that civilians could not be tried in military courts as long as the civil courts were open.

The Constitution States:	President Lincoln's Actions:
• Congress is given the power to raise and support armies.	• Without congressional approval, he increased the size of the army.
• No money can be taken from the Treasury unless approved by law.	• He withdrew $2 million from the Treasury without authorization.
• A *writ of habeas corpus* shall not be suspended except if necessary in cases of rebellion or invasion; this is mentioned in Article 1, which deals with the legislative branch.	• He arrested and jailed anti-Unionists, providing no reason for doing so and failing to obtain permission from Congress.
• No law shall be made abridging freedom of speech or the press.	• He censored some anti-Union newspapers and had editors and publishers arrested.
• Accused persons have the right to a speedy trial and impartial jury in the state or district where the alleged act was committed.	• Although U.S. civil courts were operating, he set up military courts to try Confederate sympathizers.

(joined by three other justices) wrote a concurring opinion in which he detailed his own reasoning.

In the majority opinion, Davis declared that neither the President nor Congress could authorize trials of civilians by military courts as long as civil courts remained open. No matter how severe the national emergency, Davis wrote, the Constitution is not suspended.

Davis cited the Fifth Amendment: "No person shall be held to answer for a capital or otherwise infamous crime unless on a presentment or indictment of a grand jury, except in cases arising in the land or naval forces, or in the militia, when in actual service in time of war or public danger. . . ." Milligan, Davis noted, had never been indicted (charged) by a grand jury, even though he was not a member of the military. Davis also quoted the Sixth Amendment: "In all criminal prosecutions, the accused shall enjoy the right to a speedy and public trial by an impartial [unbiased] jury. . . ."

Connections to Language Arts

Historian James M. McPherson contends that no President, except FDR, has used language as effectively as Abraham Lincoln did. Lincoln's defense of his suspension of habeas corpus provides an example. Noting that the Confederate states were breaking all federal laws, he asked, "[A]re all the laws but *one* to go unexecuted, and the government itself go to pieces lest that one be violated?"

Lincoln frequently used colorful metaphors. Responding to fears that suspension of habeas corpus would carry over into peacetime, Lincoln said he no more believed that could happen than he believed "a man could contract so strong an appetite for emetics [medicines that cause vomiting] during temporary illness, as to persist in feeding upon them through the remainder of his healthful life."

Davis called trial by jury "a vital principle, underlying the whole administration of criminal justice" that could not "be frittered away on any plea of state or political necessity." Milligan, of course, had not been tried by a jury.

Results of the Milligan Decision

As a result of the Court's ruling, Lambdin Milligan was freed from military prison. He then sued the Army for false imprisonment. The jurors in his case apparently lacked sympathy for the former Copperhead. They awarded Milligan damages of only five dollars.

Some critics have charged that the Court's decision in Milligan could someday hurt the government's ability to protect national security. Others say that unless another civil war occurred, the military would have no reason to seek to bypass civilian courts in treason cases. In any event, most Americans probably would not want to subject civilians to the same rules and procedures that govern the lives of members of the military. In 1969 Supreme Court Justice William O. Douglas noted, "A civilian trial . . . is held in an atmosphere conducive [favorable] to the protection of individual rights, while the military trial is marked by the age-old [policy] of retributive justice [punishment]." The Milligan decision recognizes that difference.

Understanding Civic Issues

1. Why was Lambdin Milligan arrested and tried?
2. Summarize the Supreme Court's ruling.
3. **Critical Thinking** Habeas corpus is considered a basic guarantee of personal freedom in American law. Why is it so important? What might happen if citizens had no right of habeas corpus?
4. **Hands-On Citizenship** Imagine the United States has plunged into a second civil war. The President believes he needs to go beyond his constitutional powers to save the nation. With a partner, take on the roles of the President and one of his advisors.
   - List six or seven emergency powers the President might want to use. (See the chart on page 178 for some actions Lincoln took during the Civil War.)
   - List arguments for and against use of each power.
   - After all pairs present their lists, take a class vote on the question of what special powers, if any, the President should use in a national emergency.

Citizenship Lab Answers

1. Army officials believed Milligan and several other Copperheads were involved in a conspiracy to steal weapons from Union arsenals and to free Confederate prisoners held in northern prison camps.

2. The Supreme Court ruled that the military commission that had tried Milligan did not have jurisdiction in the case. In the majority opinion, Justice David Davis said neither the President nor Congress could authorize trials of civilians by military courts as long as civil courts remained open.

3. Habeas corpus ensures that people will not be imprisoned unlawfully. If citizens had no right of habeas corpus, the police could hold people in jail for any reason, with or without proper evidence.

Teaching the Hands-On *CITIZENSHIP*

Students might get ideas for presidential emergency powers by reading the following parts of the Constitution: Article 1, Section 8 (pages R43–R45); Article 2, Section 2 (page R50); and the Bill of Rights, (pages R59–R62).

In teaching this activity, emphasize to students the need to justify their choices. In order to develop higher-order thinking skills, it is necessary to ask not just "what" questions, but also "why" and "how" questions. What's really important is not the specific answers, but that the answers reflect real thinking, analysis, and evaluation.

At·a·Glance 3

Reconstruction

1865–1905

Chapter Planning Guide

Section	Student Text	Teacher's Edition Activities
Opener and Story pp. 180–183	**Keys to History Time Line** **History Mystery** Beginning the Story with **Susie King Taylor**	**Setting the Stage Activity** Freedom Strategies, p. 182
1 **Rebuilding the Union** pp. 184–189	**Link to the Present** Juneteenth, p. 187	**Warm-Up Activity** Postwar Hopes, p. 184 **Geography Question of the Day,** p. 184 **Section Activity** Deciding as Freedmen, p. 186 **Bonus Activity** Anti-Johnson Protest Signs, p. 188 **Wrap-Up Activity** Comparing Reconstruction Plans, p. 189
2 **The South Under Reconstruction** pp. 190–195	**Hands-On History** Getting out the vote, p. 191 **Skill Lab** Making Decisions, p. 195	**Warm-Up Activity** Factors Affecting Elections, p. 190 **Geography Question of the Day,** p. 190 **Section Activity** Planning a Political Cartoon, p. 192 **Bonus Activity** Reconstruction Headlines, p. 193 **Wrap-Up Activity** Time to End Reconstruction?, p. 194
3 **The Legacy of Reconstruction** pp. 196–203	**Reading Maps** African Americans in Congress 1876, 1896, p. 198 **Link to Art** *Aspects of Negro Life: From Slavery Through Reconstruction,* p. 199 **Point of View** Were Jim Crow laws to be taken seriously?, p. 199 **World Link** Europeans divide up Africa, p. 200 **Geography Lab** The Civil War and Southern Agriculture, p. 203	**Warm-Up Activity** Postwar Problems, p. 196 **Geography Question of the Day,** p. 196 **Section Activity** A Postwar Collage, p. 198 **Bonus Activity** A Letter to a Former Master, p. 201 **Wrap-Up Activity** Steps Forward and Backward, p. 202
Evaluation	☑ **Section 1 Review,** p. 189 ☑ **Section 2 Review,** p. 194 ☑ **Section 3 Review,** p. 202 ☑ **Chapter Survey,** pp. 204–205 **Alternative Assessment** Improving on Reconstruction, p. 205	☑ **Answers to Section 1 Review,** p. 189 ☑ **Answers to Section 2 Review,** p. 194 ☑ **Answers to Section 3 Review,** p. 202 ☑ **Answers to Chapter Survey,** pp. 204–205 (Alternative Assessment guidelines are in the Take-Home Planner.)

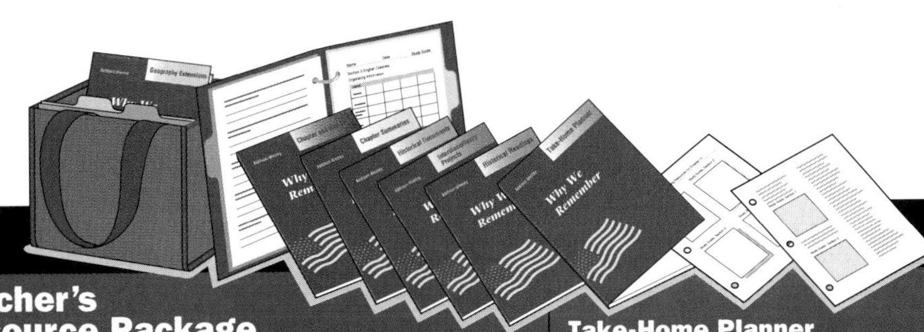

Teacher's Resource Package

Take-Home Planner

Additional Resources

Chapter Summaries: English and Spanish, pp. 42–43

Introducing the Chapter Activity Understanding Freedom, p. 22

Chapter In-Depth Activity Writing Historical Fiction, p. 22

Wall Time Line

Unit 1 Activity

Chapter Resources Binder

Study Guide Reading for Details, p. 33

Reinforcement Making a Graphic Organizer, pp. 37–38

American Readings "O Captain! My Captain!," p. 17

Using Historical Documents Amnesty Oath of Robert E. Lee, pp. 40–43

Reduced Views

Study Guide, p. 24

Reinforcement, p. 25

American Readings, p. 26

Using Historical Documents, p. 27

Unit 1 Answers, pp. 30–38

Transparency Package

Transparency 3-1 Aaron Douglas's mural *Aspects of Negro Life: From Slavery through Reconstruction*—use with Section 3

Transparency 3-2 Building African American Communities—use with Section 3

Transparency Activity Book

Chapter Resources Binder

Study Guide Identifying Main Ideas, p. 34

Skills Development Making Decisions, pp. 39–40

American Readings The War-Torn South, pp. 18–19

Reduced Views

Study Guide, p. 24

Skills Development, p. 25

American Readings, p. 26

Unit 1 Answers, pp. 30–38

SelecTest Testing Software

Chapter 3 Test, Forms A and B

CD-ROM

Freedman's shop (see TE p. 186)
Freedmen's Bureau (see TE p. 188)
Hiram Revels (see TE p. 192)
Farm family (see TE p. 197)
Segregated jury (see TE p. 200)
Howard University (see TE p. 201)

Chapter Resources Binder

Study Guide Using Visual Images to Preview, p. 35

Geography Extensions Rich States and Poor States 1860 vs. 1880, pp. 11–12

American Readings A Letter to a Former Master, p. 20

Reduced Views

Study Guide, p. 24

Geography Extensions, p. 27

American Readings, p. 26

Unit 1 Answers, pp. 30–38

Videotape Clara Barton: Eyewitness to the Civil War

Chapter and Unit Tests Chapter 3 Tests, Forms A and B, pp. 31–34

Reduced Views

Chapter Tests, p. 27

Unit 1 Answers, pp. 30–38

Alternative Assessment Guidelines for scoring the Chapter Survey activity, p. 23

3

Teaching Resources

Take-Home Planner 1
- Introducing Chapter Activity
- Chapter In-Depth Activity
- Alternative Assessment

Chapter Resources Binder
Geography Extensions
American Readings
Using Historical Documents
Transparency Activities
Wall Time Line Activities
Chapter Summaries
Chapter and Unit Tests
SelecTest Test File
Vital Links CD-ROM/Videodisc

Chapter Objectives

- ★ Explain the views of Reconstruction held by the President and Congress.
- ★ Describe what Radical Reconstruction was and how it ended.
- ★ Identify how the return of power to southern Democrats affected black southerners.

Chapter Overview

After Lincoln's death the task of Reconstruction fell to Andrew Johnson. Republicans in Congress objected that his plan did not give blacks voting rights and allowed white Democrats to control southern states, passing restrictive black codes. After gaining control of Congress in 1866, Republicans passed their own plan: to rejoin the Union, southern states would have to allow black men to

Time Line

Keys to History

Keys to History journal writing activities are on page 204 in the Chapter Survey.

Lincoln's assassination Lincoln's death meant that Reconstruction would take place without his experience and wisdom. (p. 184)

Johnson's impeachment The conflict between President Johnson and Congress over Reconstruction led to the only impeachment of a President in U.S. history. (p. 189)

14th Amendment The 14th Amendment was ratified in an effort to ensure that African Americans would have equal rights. (p. 188)

Looking Back With the secession of the southern states and the firing on Fort Sumter, the Civil War began.

1865–1905

Chapter 3

Reconstruction

Sections

Beginning the Story with Susie King Taylor

1. **Rebuilding the Union**
2. **The South Under Reconstruction**
3. **The Legacy of Reconstruction**

Keys to History

1865
President Lincoln is assassinated

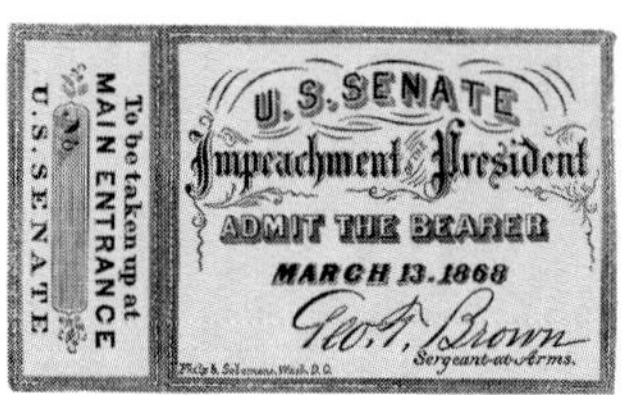

1868
President Johnson's impeachment and trial

Admission ticket for the President's trial

1868
14th Amendment guarantees equality under the law for all

1865 — 1870 — 1875

Looking Back

Civil War begins
1861

vote, elect new governments, and ratify the Fourteenth Amendment.

Under Radical Reconstruction, many black voters were registered, the Fourteenth and Fifteenth Amendments were ratified, and efforts were made to improve roads and schools. However, Ku Klux Klan terrorism and opposition to increased taxes helped white Democrats regain control of most southern states by 1876. Reconstruction ended in 1877.

Despite the goal of an industrialized "New South," most southerners remained poor farmers. Meanwhile, state governments reversed effects of Reconstruction by passing Jim Crow segregation laws and poll taxes to undermine the Fourteenth and Fifteenth Amendments. Some blacks migrated north, but most remained. Some hoped equality would come through education, while others stressed protesting discrimination.

Students will find the answer on pp. 197–198. See Chapter Survey, p. 204, for an additional question.

HISTORY *Mystery*

More than 130,000 African Americans could vote in Louisiana in 1896. Four years later Louisiana had only 5,000 African American voters. What happened to all the other voters?

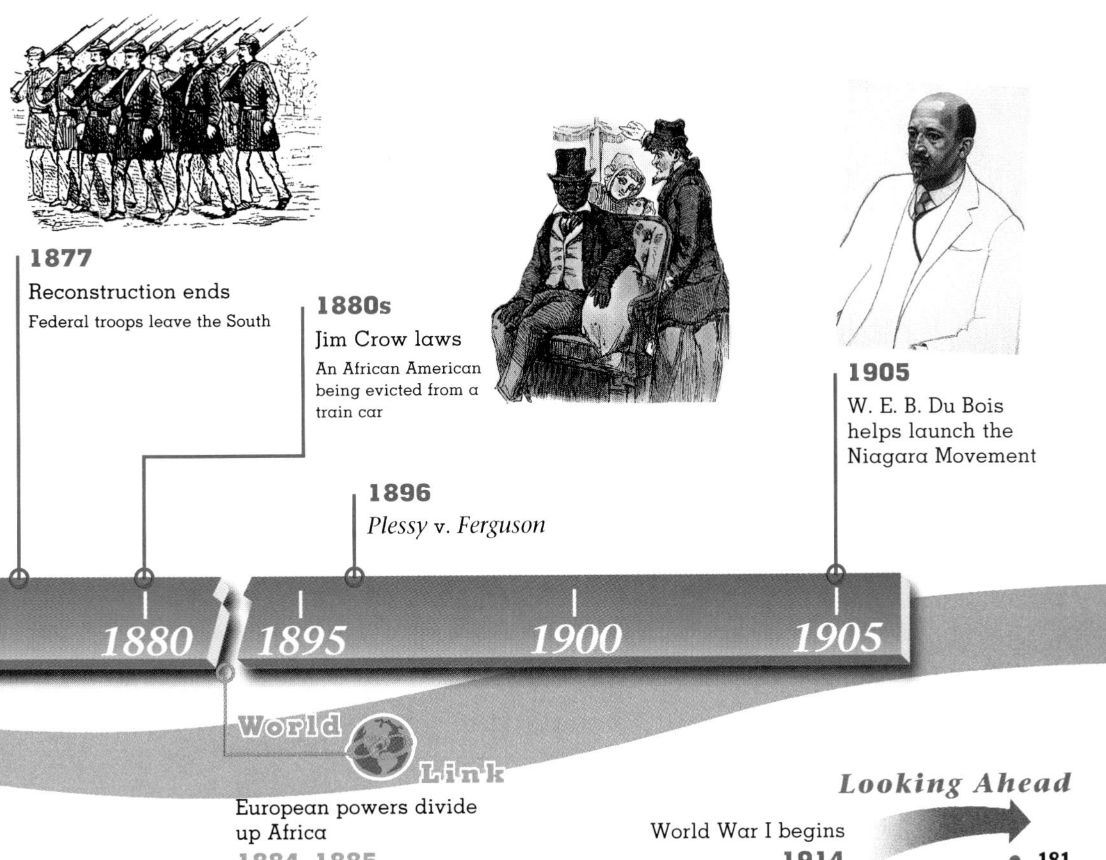

Time Line

Reconstruction ends Following Hayes's election, Reconstruction ended and southern whites elected conservative Democratic governments. (p. 194)

Jim Crow laws These segregation laws were passed by white-controlled southern state governments as part of their effort to undo effects of Reconstruction. (p. 198)

Plessy* v. *Ferguson This landmark Supreme Court decision, with its "separate but equal" standard, made segregation legal for more than half a century, until the Court reversed it in 1954. (p. 200)

Launch of Niagara Movement African Americans responded to discrimination by forming several self-help and activist organizations, including the Niagara Movement, which led to the founding of the National Association for the Advancement of Colored People (NAACP). (p. 201)

World Link See p. 200.

Looking Ahead The reintegration of the South was shown when the entire nation faced the external threat of World War I as a united country.

Beginning the Story

Susie King Taylor

Born into slavery in Georgia, Susie King Taylor was a teenager when the Civil War began. Her experiences during and after the war were like those of many other African Americans in the South. She represents the hope with which former slaves greeted the end of the war and their new status as freedmen. Her life also reflects the subsequent struggle to try to make that hope a reality in the face of resistance from many white southerners.

Setting the Stage Activity

Freedom Strategies

To focus on challenges of moving from slavery to freedom, divide the class into small groups and ask them to imagine that they are freed slaves at the end of the Civil War. Have each group write a strategy for the best way to survive and improve their situations. Conclude by discussing the proposed strategies and how practical they are.

See the Introducing the Chapter Activity, Understanding Freedom. **Take-Home Planner 1**, p. 22.

History Footnote

Whitelaw Reid, a reporter who traveled throughout the South after the war, visited freedmen settlements on the Sea Islands. Though whites had told him that "the poor, shiftless creatures will never be able to support themselves," what he saw proved otherwise. By 1865 the Sea Island farmers had built a bank, churches, and schools. Teachers there told Reid that they saw no difference "in the facility with which these students and ordinary white children . . . learn to read." Reid left certain that "the question about [former] slaves being self-supporting is a question no longer."

Beginning the Story with Susie King Taylor

Susie King Taylor wrote about her fellow African Americans during the Civil War, "Oh, how those people prayed for freedom!" Indeed, for the 4 million enslaved people in the United States, the meaning of the war was bound up in that one precious word—freedom. It was dangerous, though, to speak that word aloud. Susie, who was 13 years old and living in Savannah, Georgia, when the war began, remembered when her grandmother went to a church meeting one night. The people gathered at this meeting fervently sang an old hymn that spoke of their longing for freedom. "Yes," they said, "we shall all be free when the Lord shall appear."

At that moment the police burst in and arrested the churchgoers, accusing them of plotting to escape from slavery. The police claimed that when the slaves sang about being free "when the Lord shall appear," they really meant that they would be set free when the Yankees appeared. Although it was the last such meeting that Susie's grandmother attended, she never forgot that night. Susie, too, did not forget her grandmother's story. From that time forward she dreamed of meeting the Yankees herself.

Freedom on the Sea Islands

Susie's chance came in 1862 when Union ships bombarded Fort Pulaski at the entrance to Savannah's harbor. After Union troops captured the fort, General David Hunter promised freedom to all slaves in the area who could escape and reach the Union-controlled Sea Islands off the Georgia coast. Susie later wrote:

> "Two days after the taking of Fort Pulaski, my uncle took his family of seven and myself to St. Catherine Island. We landed under the protection of the Union fleet, and remained there two weeks. . . . At last, to my unbounded joy, I saw the 'Yankee.'"

History Bookshelf

Gaines, Ernest J., *The Autobiography of Miss Jane Pittman.* Dial Press, 1971. Gaines's novel explores the experiences of Miss Pittman's life from Reconstruction to the civil rights movement of the 1960s. The novel helps put the Reconstruction era into perspective for students.

Also of interest:

Foner, Eric and Olivia Mahoney, *America's Reconstruction: People and Politics After the Civil War.* HarperCollins, 1995.

Hurmence, Belinda, *Tancy.* Clarion, 1984.

Mettger, Zak, *Reconstruction: America After the Civil War.* Lodestar, 1994.

Myers, Walter Dean, *The Glory Field.* Scholastic, 1994.

On the Sea Islands, Susie met an escaped slave named Edward King. They fell in love and were soon married. Edward King enlisted with other former slaves to form the Union army's first African American regiment, the 33rd U.S. Colored Troops. Susie King joined her new husband, serving as a nurse and laundress in the regiment. Having learned how to read and write as a child, Susie was also in great demand as a teacher. She later wrote of her war years:

> "I taught a great many of the comrades in Company E to read and write, when they were off duty. Nearly all were anxious to learn. . . . I gave my services willingly . . . without receiving a dollar."

African Americans, freed from slavery, are shown here in front of their log cabin after the Civil War. Susie King Taylor lived in a similar home along the coast of Georgia.

"Every prospect before you is full of hope"

After the war ended, Commander C. T. Trowbridge disbanded the African American regiment to which Susie's husband belonged. In the commander's final message to the troops, he asked them

> "to harbor no feelings of hatred toward your former masters. . . . The church, the school-house, and the right forever to be free are now secured to you, and every prospect [chance for success] before you is full of hope and encouragement. The nation guarantees you full protection and justice."

Susie and Edward King returned to Savannah full of hope. "A new life was before us now," Susie wrote, "all the old life left behind." Still, they could not help but wonder what that new life would hold. Most of all, they wondered how white southerners would now treat their former slaves.

For decades, most white southerners claimed that blacks were an inferior people. With slavery swept away, would whites change their often racist views? Or would the end of slavery be just the first stage of a long struggle for equality?

Hands-On HISTORY

Activity

In the story above, you have read several quotes from Susie King Taylor's own detailed account of her life. Imagine that you are Susie and that you want to write three more entries in your diary. Choose three events in Susie's life from the story you just read and from the chapter to follow. Write what Susie might have felt and thought at these three different moments in her life.

Discussion

Thinking Historically

1. Why was learning to read and write so important to African Americans? (It was the main tool for bettering themselves economically and being independent of former masters.)

2. If you were in Trowbridge's regiment, what might you have thought upon hearing "the nation guarantees you full protection and justice"? (There might be a strong desire to believe this promise, but knowledge that racism was deeply rooted might temper that hope.)

See the Chapter In-Depth Activity, Writing Historical Fiction. **Take-Home Planner 6,** p. 22.

Teaching the Hands-On HISTORY

Point out that some events suggested are the church meeting, going off to war with her husband, and hearing of Trowbridge's statement. Later events include running a school (p. 186), the effect of black codes on her husband (p. 187), becoming a household servant (p. 196), and moving to Boston (p. 201).

For a journal writing activity on Susie King Taylor, see student page 204.

Introducing the Section

Vocabulary

freedmen (p. 184) former slaves

Reconstruction (p. 187) bringing Confederate states back into the Union

black codes (p. 187) laws that set limits on the rights and opportunities of African Americans

impeach (p. 189) to accuse of wrongdoing and bring to trial

Warm-Up Activity

Postwar Hopes

To focus on hopes following the Civil War, have students imagine that they are either a former Union soldier, a Confederate soldier, or a slave. Ask them to each write a short paragraph identifying who they are and what their expectations are for the future.

Geography Question of the Day

Ask students to identify the 11 states that had made up the Confederacy. Have them note which state was geographically different in 1865 than it had been in 1861 and explain why. (Virginia; West Virginia had seceded from eastern Virginia in 1861.)

Section Objectives

- ★ Identify the challenges white and black southerners faced after the Civil War.
- ★ Describe how President Johnson's plan for Reconstruction affected southerners.
- ★ Explain why Congress and Johnson fought for control of Reconstruction policy.

Teaching Resources

Take-Home Planner 1, pp. 20–27
Chapter Resources Binder
Study Guide, p. 33
Reinforcement, pp. 37–38
Skills Development
Geography Extensions
American Readings, p. 17
Using Historical Documents, pp. 40–43
Transparency Activities
Chapter and Unit Tests

1. Rebuilding the Union

Reading Guide

New Terms **freedmen, Reconstruction, black codes, impeach**

Section Focus **The President and Congress differ over the reconstruction of the South**

1. **What challenges did white and black southerners face after the Civil War?**
2. **What effect did President Johnson's Reconstruction plan have on southerners?**
3. **Why did Congress fight Johnson for control of Reconstruction policy?**

Susie and Edward King were not the only people thinking about the future as the war ended. The entire nation longed for peace. But what kind of peace? A peace that would punish the South for starting the war, or one that would help rebuild the southern states? In his second inaugural address in 1865, President Lincoln spoke of a healing peace:

> "With malice [ill will] toward none, with charity for all, with firmness in the right as God gives us to see the right, let us . . . bind up the nation's wounds . . . [and] do all which may achieve and cherish a just and lasting peace."

Lincoln Is Assassinated

The country would never know how Lincoln might have achieved such a "just and lasting peace." On April 14, 1865, only days after the war ended, the President was shot while watching a play at Ford's Theater in Washington, D.C. When Lincoln died the following morning, Andrew Johnson was sworn in as the new President.

Lincoln had been assassinated by John Wilkes Booth, an actor and southerner who sought revenge against Lincoln and the North. Soldiers tracked Booth to a barn in Virginia where he was fatally shot.

The North reacted with sorrow to Lincoln's death. Never before had so many people "shed tears for the death of one they had never seen," wrote poet James Russell Lowell. However, sorrow soon turned to rage. Northerners blamed the South both for the war and for Lincoln's death. From across the North came the cry: "The South must be punished!"

The Defeated South

Northerners did not realize how much the South had already suffered. In addition to the staggering loss of human life, the southern economy had been destroyed. Wherever armies had marched, they had left behind smoking cities, ruined farms, and deserted plantations.

Confederate money was now worthless. Planters, without slaves, did not know how to go on. "There is nothing else I know anything about," said one, "except managing a plantation." With their society shattered, many white southerners found it hard to see a future for themselves.

The Freedmen

Black southerners, on the other hand, were overjoyed by the arrival of peace. For these former slaves, now called **freedmen**

History Footnote

John Wilkes Booth had been plotting the President's murder for about a month—since attending Lincoln's second inauguration. Booth, a southern sympathizer and white supremacist, was convinced that Lincoln was trying to make himself dictator. Booth did not appear in the English comedy *Our American Cousin* that the Lincolns went to see, but friends told him Lincoln would attend the performance. After shooting Lincoln, Booth leaped to the stage, breaking his leg in the fall. Lincoln, shot in the head, never regained consciousness. He was taken across the street to a boarding house, where he died at 7:00 A.M. the next day. Booth was on the run for ten days before being trapped in a Virginia barn and shot by a soldier.

(a term that applied to both women and men), peace meant freedom.

The Emancipation Proclamation had abolished slavery in the Confederate states. In 1865 the Thirteenth Amendment freed slaves everywhere in the nation. Until the last day of their lives, freedmen would remember that precious moment when the "freedom sun shone out." Houston Holloway recalled that when he was freed:

"I felt like a bird out of a cage. Amen. Amen. Amen. I could hardly ask to feel any better than I did that day."

The dilemma of freedom Freedom appeared to open up a new world for former slaves. In the past, a husband and wife could be sold to different owners, never to see each other again. Freedom now meant that marriage could last "until death do us part." It also meant that African Americans could be paid for their work and could choose how to spend their money.

Freedmen now had the freedom to move, but to where? Some took to the road in a painful search for family members sold away during slavery. Others moved to towns and cities. Susie and Edward King went to Savannah after the war. There they joined a community of freedmen struggling to build new lives.

Wherever they lived, though, most freedmen faced huge problems. Few knew much about the world beyond the plantation. Frederick Douglass described the freedman's desperate situation:

"He had neither money, property, nor friends. . . . He was turned loose, naked, hungry, and destitute [poor] to the open sky."

After the Civil War, the streets and buildings of Richmond, Virginia, lay in ruins. Many southern cities suffered similar destruction.

Developing the Section

Discussion

Checking Understanding

1. What were the rights that freedom brought to the former slaves? (To live where they wanted, to stay with spouses and families, to be paid for work.)

2. What was the most important problem that they faced? (Without money or land, newly freed slaves were responsible for their own economic survival and well-being.)

Stimulating Critical Thinking

3. Based on the excerpt on p. 184 from Lincoln's second inaugural address, do you think he would have required equal rights for African Americans? Why or why not? (Yes: his reference to "firmness in the right" and a "just and lasting peace" indicate he would insist on equal rights. No: the tone of his speech indicates he did not want to punish former Confederates. Giving equality and political power to African Americans would be seen by former Confederates as a punishment.)

See **American Readings**, p. 17, for Walt Whitman's "O Captain! My Captain!"

Section Activity

Deciding as Freedmen

To help students understand the situation facing freedmen, have them imagine being former slaves discussing whether to stay in the South or move to the North. Divide the class into groups, with each group listing pros and cons of staying or leaving. They should consider factors such as family and community life, work opportunities, housing, and climate. Conclude by discussing the pros and cons as a class.

Vital Links

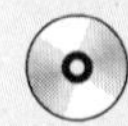

Freedman's shop (Picture) Unit 3, Side 1, Search 39043

See also Unit 3 Explore CD-ROM location 223.

See the Study Guide
activity in **Chapter Resources Binder,**
p. 33.

For an activity on Robert
E. Lee's amnesty oath,
see **Using Historical Documents,** pp. 40–43.

It did not take long for the 4 million freedmen to realize that their freedom was very limited. Most were unable to read or write, and had no land or money. Some were even driven from the only home they knew. One angry planter told his former slaves as he pushed them off his land, "The Yankee freed you. Now let the Yankee feed you."

The Freedmen's Bureau

Shortly before the war ended, Congress established the Freedmen's Bureau. This government agency was to give food and medical care to both blacks and whites in the South. Above all else, however, newly freed slaves wanted land and an education. The Bureau tried to provide both.

Schools and land The Freedmen's Bureau worked with educated former slaves and northern churches and charities to open up more than 4,300 schools in the South. Susie King, for example, ran a school for black children in Savannah. The educator and author Booker T. Washington later described the hunger for learning as "a whole race trying to go to school."

Freedmen were also desperate to get land of their own to farm. Congressman Thaddeus Stevens proposed breaking up the South's plantations and giving every freedman "forty acres and a mule." He argued:

The federal government helped African Americans build thousands of schools like this one in the years following the Civil War. Before the war, it had been illegal to teach slaves how to read.

History Footnote

Andrew Johnson was as much a self-made man as Abraham Lincoln. His family was poor, and he worked as a young man as a tailor. He did not learn to read and write until after he was married, when his wife taught him. He worked his way up in politics, serving in both houses of Congress and as governor of Tennessee. A lifelong Democrat, he was the only U.S. senator from the South to remain loyal to the United States. As a reward, Lincoln named him military governor of the parts of Tennessee occupied by Union forces from 1862. The Republicans chose him to run with Lincoln in 1864 in order to attract Democratic support.

"We have turned . . . loose 4 million slaves without a . . . cent in their pockets. . . . This Congress is bound to provide for them until they can take care of themselves."

Congress, however, refused to take plantations from their owners. Doing so, most congressmen believed, would violate the Constitution's protection of property. As a result, few black southerners were able to obtain land.

Johnson's Plan for the South

After Lincoln's assassination, the task of **Reconstruction**—bringing Confederate states back into the Union—fell to President Johnson. A former Democrat from Tennessee, he favored an easy and smooth return to the Union for the southern states.

In May 1865 Johnson announced his Reconstruction plan. Each southern state could rejoin the Union once it had:

- written a new state constitution
- elected a new government
- repealed its act of secession
- canceled its war debts
- ratified the Thirteenth Amendment, which outlawed slavery in the United States (see page 185)

Republicans in Congress asked the new President to add one more requirement to his list. They wanted freedmen to be guaranteed the right to vote. Johnson ignored their request. "White men alone," he said, "must manage the South."

The First Effort at Reconstruction

By the fall of 1865, every southern state had rejoined the Union under President Johnson's plan. Not surprisingly, leaders of the new state governments were often the same men who had held power in the South before the Civil War.

Link to the Present

Juneteenth On June 19, 1865, the Civil War had been over for more than two months. The Emancipation Proclamation had been law for more than two years. But until Union soldiers landed in Galveston on that day, slaves in Texas had no idea they were free. Their owners had not told them.

Juneteenth is the name given to the day when the last slaves discovered they were free. From Houston to San Francisco, people now celebrate Juneteenth with parades, concerts, and barbecues. It is a way to look back on the struggle and remember that slavery did not end overnight.

The black codes Once in office, these leaders did their best to bring back the way of life of the old South. They passed laws called **black codes** that set limits on the rights and opportunities of African Americans. Black codes also helped planters find workers to replace their freed slaves. An African American without a job could be arrested and sent to work for a planter.

In fact, the codes barred African Americans from any jobs but farm work and unskilled labor. As a result, Susie King's husband, Edward, could not continue to work as a carpenter after the war. The only job he could find was unloading boats in Savannah's harbor.

The black codes did give certain rights to freedmen: the right to marry, own property, work for wages, and sue in court. Other

Discussion

Checking Understanding

1. What were the purposes of the Freedmen's Bureau? (To provide food and medical care to both blacks and whites; to give freedmen education and land.)

2. Why did Republicans in Congress criticize President Johnson's Reconstruction plan? (They believed that African Americans should have been given the right to vote.)

Stimulating Critical Thinking

3. Should Congress have taken plantation land from owners and divided it among freedmen? (Yes: would help make up for slavery; best way to help ensure that freedmen could make a living. No: would violate constitutional protection of property; would anger owners, resulting in more resistance to Reconstruction.)

Teaching the

Point out that Juneteenth is celebrated by African Americans throughout the state of Texas. In 1980, June 19 became an official state holiday. Interest in it has grown in the last 20 years. Juneteenth is the most well-known of freedom celebrations, but African Americans in other states and localities celebrate emancipation on different dates. Students might find out if your state or locality has such a celebration.

Bonus Activity

Anti-Johnson Protest Signs

To explore reasons for opposing Johnson, have students imagine preparing to protest one of the President's appearances during his northern tour in 1866. Ask them to work in pairs to create protest signs. Some possible topics are his stand on black suffrage, his opposition to the Fourteenth Amendment, and his support of the black codes. Conclude by having students display and compare their signs.

Vital Links

Freedmen's Bureau (Picture) Unit 3, Side 1, Search 38989

See also Unit 3 Explore CD-ROM location 214.

See the Reinforcement activity in **Chapter Resources Binder,** pp. 37–38.

History Footnote

Thaddeus Stevens had long supported equal rights for African Americans, arguing that "there can be no state rights against human rights." Stevens declared, "I am for Negro suffrage in every rebel state. If it be just, it should not be denied; if it be necessary, it should be adopted; if it be punishment to traitors, they deserve it."

basic rights, such as serving on juries and owning weapons, were denied in most southern states. No southern states allowed freedmen the right to vote.

Black codes also barred black children from attending the new public schools in the South. According to a Louisiana lawmaker, it made no sense to use public money to educate "any but the superior race of man—the white race."

Johnson vs. Congress

As 1865 came to a close, President Johnson announced that Reconstruction was over. The former Confederate states were once again part of the Union.

Northerners and black southerners were stunned. What Johnson called Reconstruction, critics said, was "no reconstruction at all." They were outraged that the same southern men who had led the nation into its bloodiest war were now back in power. Worse yet, they feared that the black codes in the South would bring back the horrors of slavery in all but name.

Representative Thaddeus Stevens (left) and Senator Charles Sumner (right) introduced many bills in Congress meant to protect the rights of African Americans.

Radical Republicans A group of Republicans in Congress, called Radicals, demanded that the southern states meet stricter requirements for coming back into the Union. In contrast to Johnson's plan, they insisted on full and equal rights for freedmen—a revolutionary idea in both the North and the South in 1865.

Early in 1866 the Radical Republicans, led by Representative Thaddeus Stevens of Pennsylvania and Senator Charles Sumner of Massachusetts, pushed two bills through Congress. One bill extended the life of the Freedmen's Bureau and gave it power to build more schools. A second bill, the Civil Rights Act, declared that freedmen were full citizens with the same rights as white citizens. Johnson vetoed both bills.

The Radical Republicans fought back. They persuaded Congress to act against the President's wishes. For the first time in the nation's history, a two-thirds majority in Congress voted to override a President's vetoes. Both the Freedmen's Bureau Act and the Civil Rights Act became law.

The Fourteenth Amendment Worried that the Supreme Court might overturn the Civil Rights Act, Republicans put the protections of the act into a Fourteenth Amendment. The proposed amendment gave all people born in the United States, including African Americans, the right to "equal protection of the laws." No state could deprive a citizen of "life, liberty, or property without due process of law."

Johnson opposed the amendment. In 1866 congressional elections were to be held. Johnson took his case to the people by touring northern cities and urging voters to elect Democrats. Wherever he spoke, however, he ended up in shouting matches with hecklers. The tour was a disaster. Republicans won control of both houses of Congress. They, not the President, now controlled Reconstruction.

History Footnote

In 1875 Johnson returned to the capital as a senator from Tennessee. When he entered the Senate chamber, there was at first an embarrassed silence. Then other senators came up to shake his hand. Later, a friend visited him at his hotel and commented that his lodgings were not as spacious as those he had had in the White House. "No," said Johnson, "but they are more comfortable."

This sketch shows an African American election judge and voters in Washington, D.C., in 1867.

Radical Reconstruction

In 1867 the Radical Republicans passed their own Reconstruction Act. State governments in the South were declared illegal. The region, except Tennessee, was divided into five districts under the control of the army.

To rejoin the Union, each state would have to do the following:

- adopt a constitution guaranteeing all male citizens, black and white, the right to vote
- elect a new government
- ratify the Fourteenth Amendment

No white southerners who had served as Confederate soldiers or officials could vote on the new state constitutions.

Radical Republicans had hoped for more. They wanted to divide up plantations into small farms for black and white southerners and build enough schools for every child in the South. However, these ideas were rejected by the full Congress.

To keep Johnson from stopping the new Reconstruction plan, Congress passed two laws to reduce his power. The Command of the Army Act limited the President's power over the army. The Tenure of Office Act barred Johnson from firing certain federal officials, including those who supported Congress instead of him, without Senate approval.

The Impeachment of Johnson

President Johnson believed both laws were unconstitutional. In February 1868 he fired Secretary of War Edwin Stanton. The House promptly voted to **impeach**—to accuse of wrongdoing and bring to trial—the President. It charged him with violating the Tenure of Office Act.

The President's lawyers argued that the Tenure of Office Act was unconstitutional. His only "crime," they said, had been to disagree with Congress. A two-thirds vote by the Senate was needed to remove him from office. Seven Republicans joined the Senate's Democrats in voting "not guilty." The President escaped removal from office by just one vote. He finished his term, but his power was broken.

1. Section Review

1. Define **freedmen, Reconstruction, black codes,** and **impeach.**
2. How did the Freedmen's Bureau try to help former slaves start a new life?
3. Why did Congress overturn President Johnson's Reconstruction plan?
4. Critical Thinking As an African American, explain why you might have been disappointed by President Johnson's Reconstruction plan.

Closing the Section

Wrap-Up Activity

Comparing Reconstruction Plans

To review differences between the Reconstruction plans of President Johnson and Congress, have students grade each plan from the perspective of African Americans. Working in pairs, they should create two-column charts listing characteristics of each plan. After placing a plus or minus next to each characteristic, they should assign each plan a letter grade, explaining how they evaluated the characteristics.

Section Review

Answers

1. Definitions: *freedmen* (184), *Reconstruction* (187), *black codes* (187), *impeach* (189)

2. The Freedmen's Bureau provided food and medical care, set up schools, and tried—but failed—to give land to freedmen.

3. Northern Republicans in Congress thought Johnson was too lenient on the former Confederates in allowing them to control state governments and pass black codes.

4. Students might suggest disappointment that they still did not have equal rights, that they could not vote, and that Johnson declared the end of Reconstruction though restrictive black codes were still in effect.

Introducing the Section

Vocabulary

scalawags (p. 190) white southerners considered traitors or scoundrels for joining the Republicans

carpetbaggers (p. 191) northerners who moved south after the war, voting as Republicans and seeking opportunities

corruption (p. 193) using public office for illegal purposes

Warm-Up Activity

Factors Affecting Elections

Ask students to imagine that the class will be voting on the following proposal: Homework will be collected from odd-numbered rows three days a week, but from even rows only two days. Have them identify factors affecting whether it would pass. Then ask them to predict how different groups in the South might try to win elections.

Geography Question of the Day

Write the following claim on the chalkboard: "The states farthest south were the last to reenter the Union." Ask students to write paragraphs explaining whether the claim is valid. They should refer to the chart on p. 192 and map on pp. R6–R7. (Invalid: in both 1868 and 1870 a mixture of states in the middle and deep South were readmitted.)

Section Objectives

- ★ Describe the new groups of voters in the South and how Congress protected them.
- ★ Identify the accomplishments of the Reconstruction governments.
- ★ Explain how the Democratic Party was able to regain control of the South.

Teaching Resources

Take-Home Planner 1, pp. 20–27
Chapter Resources Binder
Study Guide, p. 34
Reinforcement
Skills Development, pp. 39–40
Geography Extensions
American Readings, pp. 18–19
Using Historical Documents
Transparency Activities
Chapter and Unit Tests

2. The South Under Reconstruction

Reading Guide

New Terms scalawags, carpetbaggers, corruption

Section Focus Radical Reconstruction in the South and why it ended

1. **Who were the new voters in the South and how did Congress protect them?**
2. **What did the southern Reconstruction governments accomplish?**
3. **How was the Democratic Party able to regain control of the South?**

Radical Republicans had clear goals for Reconstruction in the South. With the slave system now dead, they believed they had a rare opportunity to shape "a more perfect Union." They wanted to build a new society based on the equality of all citizens.

The key to equality, Radical Republicans argued, was the right to vote. African Americans could use the ballot to protect their rights. Therefore, ensuring voting rights was central to the Republicans' bold new Reconstruction plan.

The South's New Voters

Under the Reconstruction Act, the army returned to the South in 1867. Its first job was to register voters. Three groups of men registered to vote: African Americans, white southerners who could swear that they had opposed the war, and northerners now living in the South. The law barred from voting anyone who had fought against, or otherwise been disloyal to, the Union.

Freedmen African Americans made up the largest group of new voters. Most joined the Republicans, whom they saw as their protectors. As with new white voters in Andrew Jackson's time, many blacks had no experience in politics. Yet they knew what they wanted. An Alabama convention of freedmen declared:

> "We claim exactly the same rights . . . as are enjoyed by white men—we ask for nothing more and will be content with nothing less."

"Scalawags" The army also registered a sizable group of white southerners who swore they had not supported the Confederacy. Some were small farmers who lived in the pro-Union hill areas and had never voted before. Others were southern businessmen who lived in the towns.

A large number of the new white voters joined the Republicans, too. They saw the southern Democrats as the party of wealthy planters, while the Republicans were the party of opportunity and equality.

The South's planters were shocked that they had lost control of the political system. To them, white southerners who joined the party of Lincoln and emancipation were traitors to the South. They scorned such people, calling them **"scalawags,"** or scoundrels.

"Carpetbaggers" The last group of new voters were northerners who had moved south after the war. Some were teachers, ministers, or Freedmen's Bureau agents. Others

History Footnote

In the election of 1868, Grant won the electoral vote by a large margin of 214 to 80, but he got only 52.7 percent of the popular vote. The Democrat, Horatio Seymour, took Louisiana and Georgia, but Grant won Tennessee, North Carolina, South Carolina, Florida, Alabama, and Arkansas, thanks to the African American vote. Mississippi, Virginia, and Texas could not vote because they had not been readmitted to the Union. Without the black vote, Grant would have had a minority in the popular vote even though he still would have won the electoral vote.

Hands-On HISTORY

Getting out the vote Did you know that voter turnout in the United States today is much lower than in most democracies? Only about half of all possible voters actually vote. Those who fail to vote may think their votes do not matter. However, voting does matter. For example, African Americans, voting for the first time, helped President Grant win the 1868 election.

Activity Create a presentation that will persuade people in your community to vote.

1. First, choose the best way to convince people in your area to vote. You might make posters and brochures to display at a mall, or produce a commercial for radio or television.
2. Next, plan your presentation. If you have a registration table, make an attention-getting sign and a brochure explaining why voting counts. If you do a radio or television commercial, write one or make an audio or video tape of one.
3. Show your sign and brochure to the class. If you have a commercial, act it out or play it on audio or video tape for the class.

Young people work to get out the vote.

were businessmen or former Union soldiers looking for new opportunities. Most of them also registered as Republicans.

Yankee-hating southerners called these newcomers **"carpetbaggers,"** after a type of travel handbag. They saw carpetbaggers, often unfairly, as fortune hunters who had come south "to fatten on our misfortunes."

Grant Elected President

The army registered about 635,000 white voters and 735,000 black voters across the South in time for the 1868 election. That year the Republicans nominated Union war hero Ulysses S. Grant. He supported the Republicans' Reconstruction experiment.

The Democrats chose Horatio Seymour, the former governor of New York, as their candidate. Seymour wanted to return power in the South to its traditional leaders—white Democrats.

Grant won the election with the help of an estimated 500,000 African Americans who cast their first votes for the Republican candidate. The Republican Party learned a valuable lesson from the 1868 election—African Americans could contribute heavily to its election victories.

The Fifteenth Amendment Shortly after Grant's election, Congress passed the Fifteenth Amendment guaranteeing former slaves the right to vote. It states that a citizen's right to vote "shall not be denied . . . on account of race, color, or previous condition of servitude." At the time, the right of women to vote was not advanced.

Radical Republicans supported the amendment for two reasons. First, they wanted to make sure that African Americans would retain their right to vote even if the Democrats someday regained power in the South.

Second, many northern states at the time still barred African Americans from voting.

Developing the Section

Discussion

Checking Understanding

1. How were scalawags and carpetbaggers similar? (Both voted Republican and were scorned by white southern Democrats.) **Different?** (Scalawags were native southerners. Carpetbaggers were northerners who had moved south.)

2. How did Grant win the 1868 election? (The army registered many African Americans, scalawags, and carpetbaggers as Republican voters in the South.)

Stimulating Critical Thinking

3. In what ways do you think criticisms of carpetbaggers might have been fair? In what ways might they have been unfair? (Fair: some businessmen took advantage of poor southerners. Unfair: most teachers, ministers, and Freedmen's Bureau agents were probably not motivated by personal gain.)

Teaching the Hands-On HISTORY

Point out that "get out the vote" campaigns often appeal to voters' self-interest. Signs and brochures should focus on how voting can benefit the target audience, perhaps by referring to issues that directly affect their lives.

Section Activity

Planning a Political Cartoon

To explore perspectives on Reconstruction, have small groups plan editorial cartoons. Each should select a topic and a point of view. Some topics are white Democratic governments, black codes, the Ku Klux Klan, the Freedmen's Bureau, scalawags, carpetbaggers, Radical Reconstruction governments, and northern Radical Republicans. Each group should decide on the general scene to illustrate, elements within it, labels, and a caption, if needed. For example, a cartoon from a white Democrat point of view might criticize carpetbaggers by showing a rich businessmen taking money from poor white southern farmers and stuffing it into a large travel bag. Conclude by having groups sketch and share cartoons.

Vital Links

Hiram Revels (Picture) Unit 3, Side 1, Search 50420

See also Unit 3 Explore CD-ROM location 149.

For a description of the devastation in the South, see American Readings, pp. 18–19.

Tips for Teaching

Gifted Students

Gifted students interested in extra credit might write brief biographies of African Americans who served in Congress during Reconstruction. They should find out their backgrounds, education, how they were elected, how long they served, what they accomplished in Congress, and the circumstances of their defeat.

See the Study Guide activity in Chapter Resources Binder, p. 34.

Reconstruction Begins and Ends

State	Readmitted to the Union	Reconstruction government falls
Tennessee	1866	1869
Alabama	1868	1874
Arkansas	1868	1874
Florida	1868	1877
Louisiana	1868	1877
North Carolina	1868	1870
South Carolina	1868	1877
Georgia	1870	1871
Mississippi	1870	1875
Texas	1870	1873
Virginia	1870	1870

Radical Republicans wanted voting rights granted to all men throughout the country. "We will have no peace," wrote one, "until this right is made national."

The Reconstruction Governments

Meanwhile, southern Reconstruction was under way. The first task was to rebuild state governments. Delegates were elected to constitutional conventions in each state. Many were African Americans—mostly educated men such as preachers and teachers.

New constitutions The conventions wrote the most forward-looking state constitutions in the nation. These constitutions outlawed racial discrimination and guaranteed the right to vote to every adult male, regardless of race. They also called for public schools that would be, according to Georgia's constitution, "forever free to all the children of the state."

With the new constitutions ratified, elections were held to fill state offices. To no one's surprise, but to the disgust of the South's traditional leaders, a majority of those elected were Republicans. The new southern legislatures quickly passed the Fourteenth and Fifteenth Amendments.

By 1870 all the former Confederate states had met the requirements of Congress for coming back into the Union. Reconstruction seemed complete, and federal troops withdrew from the South.

African American officeholders The South's new Reconstruction governments included a number of African American officials. In South Carolina, blacks made up a majority of the legislature for two years, and Jonathan J. Wright served for six years on the state supreme court.

Sixteen African Americans served in Congress as well. Of these, 14 men served as representatives in the House, while Mississippi sent Hiram R. Revels and Blanche K. Bruce to the Senate. The conduct of these new legislators impressed Maine's Representative James G. Blaine, who observed:

> "The colored men who took their seats in both the Senate and House . . . [were] earnest, ambitious men, whose public conduct . . . would be honorable to any race."

History Footnote

First organized in 1866, the Ku Klux Klan was officially disbanded in 1869, but many of its members went underground and created other organizations under a variety of names throughout the South. Congress responded by enacting the Ku Klux Klan Act in 1871, giving the President wide powers to combat violence designed to disrupt elections. The name Ku Klux Klan was revived in 1915 when a new national organization was formed in Atlanta. The new organization did not limit its intimidation to African Americans but also targeted Jews, Catholics, and immigrants. It reached its height, with over three million members, in the 1920s but was disbanded in 1944. A third Klan was formed in 1946 to combat the post–World War II demand for civil rights by African Americans. It still exists.

Most whites in the South detested the Reconstruction governments. They resented having had these governments "forced" on them by the much-hated Yankees. Even more they resented seeing former slaves holding public office and talking about equality.

Despite such resentment, Reconstruction governments set to work rebuilding roads and bridges and expanding the South's railroads. They built badly needed schools, as well as hospitals, orphanages, and prisons. Of course, such projects were expensive. To pay for them, the states had to raise taxes.

Pictured above are the seven African Americans who served in Congress in 1872. Twenty years later there was only one African American member of Congress.

Return to "White Man's Rule"

To win support and return their states to "white man's rule," Democrats blamed Republicans for the higher taxes. They also accused them of **corruption**—using public office for illegal purposes. While some officials did line their pockets with tax money, most were honest and capable. Still, as taxes increased, so did resentment of white and black Republican officeholders.

White terrorism Certain whites were willing to use any means necessary to stop blacks from voting and thus return the South to its traditional leaders. They formed secret organizations, such as the White League and the Ku Klux Klan, to terrorize African Americans. The White League declared that "this should be a white man's government, [and] as far as our efforts go, it shall be."

Wearing long, hooded robes, Ku Klux Klan members spread terror by night. They thundered across the countryside on horseback, warning both black and white Republicans not to vote.

The Klan burned down the homes of Republicans who ignored their threats. African Americans were often beaten and murdered. To combat Klan terrorism Congress passed the Enforcement Acts in 1870 and 1871. These laws directed President Grant to send federal troops back into the most violent areas to protect black voters. Witnesses, however, feared the Klan's revenge and refused to testify. Few terrorists were convicted.

Democrats back in power In 1872 the Amnesty Act forgave former Confederates and gave them back the right to vote. By then, white Republicans were returning to the Democratic Party. The Democrats began to win elections in state after state.

By 1876 Democrats had regained control of all but three southern states. Republicans clung to power in South Carolina, Louisiana, and Florida, but only with the help of federal troops.

Discussion

Checking Understanding

1. Why did most southern whites hate Reconstruction governments? (They resented blacks voting and serving in government. Many resented having their own right to vote denied because they had supported the Confederacy, and they thought that Reconstruction violated states' rights.)

Stimulating Critical Thinking

2. Should federal troops have remained in the South after 1870? Why or why not? (No: states had met Congress's requirements; military expenses too much of a burden on North. Yes: Reconstruction governments needed continued support because white Democrats resented having black leaders in government.)

Bonus Activity

Reconstruction Headlines

To imagine biases in newspaper coverage during Reconstruction, have small groups create lists of headlines. They should include some that might appear in Republican-controlled papers and some in Democrat-controlled papers. Some topics are Grant's election, the Fifteenth Amendment, new state constitutions, the Ku Klux Klan, and the Compromise of 1877. Conclude by having students read headlines and identify biases.

Closing the Section

Wrap-Up Activity

Time to End Reconstruction?

To review effects of Reconstruction, have students imagine themselves writing letters to the editor during the election of 1876. Assign half to write letters arguing for an end to Reconstruction and the other half to write letters arguing against ending it. Each letter should include at least three reasons. Ask some students to read their letters aloud. Conclude by summarizing arguments.

Section Review Answers

1. Definitions: *scalawags* (190), *carpetbaggers* (191), *corruption* (193)

2. African Americans, white southerners who had not fought for the Confederacy, and northerners who moved to the South could vote. Those who had supported the Confederacy could not vote.

3. In 1876 Republicans agreed to return control to white southerners in return for enough electoral votes to make Rutherford B. Hayes President.

4. The federal government might have made Klan membership a federal crime, sent marshals to protect witnesses, and moved trials of Klansmen to communities where the Klan would not have support and where witnesses would be less afraid to testify.

194

Connections to Civics

Samuel Tilden was one of three candidates (Andrew Jackson in 1824 and Grover Cleveland in 1888 were the others) who lost the White House even though they received the most popular votes. Tilden got 4.3 million votes to Hayes's 4 million. Tilden needed 185 electoral votes to win, but he got 184. The votes in three southern states that still had Republican administrations—South Carolina, Louisiana, and Florida—were overturned, although it appeared that Tilden had a majority in all three. One Oregon vote was disputed on a technicality. The entire dispute was referred to an electoral commission of seven Republicans, seven Democrats, and one independent. Shortly before it was to meet, the independent quit and was replaced by a Republican. The commission decided 8–7 in favor of Hayes.

Klan members disguised themselves with hoods and robes. These men posed in a professional photography studio in 1868.

The End of Reconstruction

While white terrorism was increasing and Republican power weakening in the South, the North was losing interest in the task of Reconstruction. The Civil War had been over for a decade. It was time, many northerners argued, to "let the South alone."

The disputed 1876 election In 1876 Americans went to the polls to vote for a new President. The Democrats had nominated Governor Samuel J. Tilden of New York. Rutherford B. Hayes from Ohio headed the Republican ticket. Hayes knew that most voters were tired of thinking about Reconstruction, the Klan, and "the everlasting Negro question." In his campaign he had said little about these issues.

When the election returns came in, Hayes was 20 electoral votes short of victory, but 20 electoral votes from 4 states remained in dispute. The Republican-controlled Congress awarded all the disputed electoral votes to Hayes. The Democrats cried foul and threatened to block his inauguration. As Inauguration Day drew near, the nation was without a new President.

The Compromise of 1877 At the last moment, the two parties worked out a compromise. The Democrats agreed to accept Hayes as President. In return, Hayes agreed to give the southern states the right to control their own affairs.

True to his word, President Hayes removed all federal troops from the South. With the army gone, Democrats quickly gained control of the last three southern states. "This is a white man's country," boasted Senator Ben Tillman of South Carolina, "and white men must govern it."

While white southerners cheered the end of Reconstruction, African Americans feared what the future might hold. Henry Adams, a Louisiana freedman, observed sadly:

> "The whole South—every state in the South . . . has got into the hands of the very men that held us as slaves."

2. Section Review

1. Define **scalawags, carpetbaggers,** and **corruption.**
2. Under the Republican Reconstruction plan, who could vote in the South and who could not?
3. How did white southern Democrats regain control of state government?
4. Critical Thinking Describe at least two more actions that the government or citizens might have taken to stop the rise of the Klan in the South.

(Answers continued from side margin)
war. Possible good results of Congress's plan: blacks will have legal protection as they strive to improve their conditions; blacks will have power to elect officials who represent their interests. Possible bad results: white southerners may be uncooperative; disruption may result from having inexperienced people govern.

4. Accept any decision in line with the stated goal and reflecting careful consideration of possible outcomes.

For further application, have students do the Applying Skills activity in the Chapter Survey (p. 204).

If students need to review the skill, use the Skills Development transparency and activity in the **Chapter Resources Binder**, pp. 39–40.

Skill Lab

Using Information
Making Decisions

If President Lincoln had not been assassinated on April 14, 1865, he might have gone down in history as "the Great Reconstructor" as well as "the Great Emancipator." Instead, the question of how to rebuild the Confederate states was left to a new President and to a Congress opposed to that new President's ideas.

Question to Investigate

What was the best way to rebuild the South?

Procedure

Although historical events may seem inevitable to us, many have resulted from deliberate decisions that people have made. Imagine that you are a member of Congress after the Civil War. You must decide whether to support the President's Reconstruction plan or one offered by the Radical Republicans.

1 Identify the problem and your goal.
a. State the problem to be solved.
b. State your goal—what you hope to achieve.

2 Identify the options.
a. Read source A.
b. Summarize the two plans.

3 Evaluate each option.
a. Read sources B and C.
b. List the possible good and bad results of each plan.

4 Choose one option and explain why you chose it.

Skill Tips

Keep in mind:
- When making decisions people often have several options, some better than others. However, there is almost never a perfect solution.
- People base decisions partly on the available facts and partly on their biases, or slanted views.

Sources to Use

A Reread the two plans on pages 187–189.

B "Let us go down to Louisiana. . . . We find the Negro downtrodden. Men are imprisoned for speaking their opinions about Negro suffrage. The worst features of the slave laws are revived. The Rebels . . . are rapidly pushing their state back to the terror and gloom of the [pre-Civil War] period. They know full well that if we [northerners] leave the Negro in their hands . . . they will have little trouble in perpetuating [continuing] a system more degrading than slavery."

From Horace Greeley, *New York Daily Tribune*, November 15, 1865

C "I think if the whole regulation of Negroes, or freedmen, were left to the people of the communities in which they live, it will be administered for the best interest of the negroes as well as of the whites. I think there is a kindly feeling [by white southerners] towards the freedmen. . . . I think there is a willingness to give them every right except the right of suffrage. . . . They will eventually be endowed with that right. It is only a question of time; but it will be necessary to prepare for it by slow and regular means, as the white race was prepared. . . . It would be disastrous to give the right of suffrage now."

By James D. B. De Bow, editor of the New Orleans-based *De Bow's Review* from 1846 to 1867

Option 1
+
Option 2
+
–

Introducing the Skill Lab

Point out to students that in making their decision they need to place themselves in the shoes of a member of Congress in 1865. There is no right answer. They should not rely on hindsight but instead consider the information available at the time. In gathering information from sources B and C, they should consider the possibility of bias.

Skill Lab
Answers

1. (a) "The South needs to be rebuilt." (b) Goals will vary. Some possibilities: "To bring the South back into the Union with as little disruption as possible." "To bring the South back into the Union with equality for all its people guaranteed."

2. Summaries should reflect the plans' main points. The main difference is that Johnson's did not mention legal equality or voting rights for freedmen.

3. Some possible good results of Johnson's plan: South governed by experienced leaders; less disruption if South moves slowly toward equal rights. Possible bad results: without legal protection or the right to vote, blacks will be powerless; South may return to political and economic system like the one before the

(Answers continued in top margin)

Introducing the Section

Vocabulary

tenant farmers (p. 197) farmers who pay rent for the use of land on which they grow crops

sharecropping (p. 197) system in which tenants give part of crop as rent

poll tax (p. 198) fee for voting

grandfather clause (p. 198) clause in a voting law saying it did not apply to a man whose father or grandfather could have voted before January 1, 1867

segregation (p. 198) forced separation of races in public places

Jim Crow laws (p. 198) segregation laws

Warm-Up Activity

Postwar Problems

To identify challenges facing the South, have pairs make lists of postwar recovery tasks. They should consider such factors as physical effects on southern farms and cities, conditions of refugees, and the need for jobs. Conclude by compiling a "to do" list on the chalkboard.

Geography Question of the Day

To illustrate how tenant farming and the end of slavery changed southern plantations, have students draw layouts before and after the war. They should label buildings and divisions of land. (Before: large, undivided field area, clustered slave quarters. After: small plots, sharecropper cabins.)

Section Objectives

★ Explain why the South remained mostly rural and poor after Reconstruction.
★ Describe how the rights and conditions of black southerners changed after Reconstruction.
★ Identify ways in which African Americans responded to segregation and violence.

Teaching Resources

Take-Home Planner 1, pp. 20–27
Chapter Resources Binder
Study Guide, p. 35
Reinforcement
Skills Development
Geography Extensions, pp. 11–12
American Readings, p. 20
Using Historical Documents
Transparency Activities
Chapter and Unit Tests, pp. 31–34

3. The Legacy of Reconstruction

Reading Guide

New Terms **tenant farmers, sharecropping, poll tax, grandfather clause, segregation, Jim Crow laws**

Section Focus **The return to power of southern Democrats and its impact on the lives of black southerners**

1. Why did the South remain mostly rural and poor after Reconstruction?
2. What happened to the rights and conditions of black southerners after Reconstruction?
3. In what ways did African Americans respond to segregation and violence?

As Reconstruction ended, southern leaders vowed to build a "New South" that would hum with industry. Under the slogan "Bring the cotton mills to the cotton," they expanded the region's textile industries by nine times between 1880 and 1900. Meanwhile, Birmingham, Alabama, became a major iron-making center.

In 1886 Georgia newspaper editor Henry Grady bragged:

> "We [the South] have . . . put business above politics. We have challenged your spinners in Massachusetts and your iron-makers in Pennsylvania."

Despite Grady's boasts, industry in the South did not develop as he had hoped. In the decades following the war, the North would emerge as an industrial giant. Most southerners—both black and white—would remain trapped, however, in a region that was mostly rural and poor.

Life in the "New South"

The South was still staggering from the effects of the Civil War when Reconstruction ended. The average income of southerners was just 40 percent that of northerners. Many whites had lost everything in the conflict—homes, farms, and businesses. Rebuilding crushed lives would be slow work.

Freedmen under freedom For most freedmen, poverty was the unwelcome companion of freedom. They began their new lives, as Frederick Douglass noted, "empty-handed, without money . . . without a foot of land on which to stand."

For Susie King, the struggle to survive was made more difficult by her husband Edward's death. Unable to support herself and her baby on the tiny salary of a teacher, she was forced to find other work. Despite her education, the only job she could get was as a household servant.

Other freedmen also supported themselves as best they could on the pitiful wages they earned. Virginia tobacco workers reported:

> "It is impossible to feed ourselves and family—starvation is certain unless a change is brought about."

Tenant farming Once-wealthy planters also faced hard times. With little cash to pay workers, planters had to divide their land into small plots, which they rented to tenant

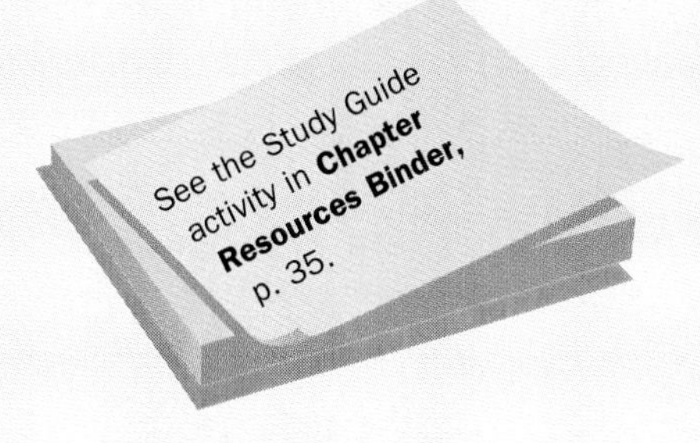
See the Study Guide activity in Chapter Resources Binder, p. 35.

farmers. **Tenant farmers** pay rent for the use of land on which they grow crops. Rather than pay cash, some tenant farmers paid a part—or share—of their crop as rent. This system is known as **sharecropping.**

To landless southerners—both black and white—tenant farming looked promising at first. They hoped to save enough money to buy the land. First, though, they had to borrow money to buy seeds and tools.

Had crop prices been high after the war, these farmers might have been able to repay their loans. Instead, prices fell. By 1900 two-thirds of southern farmers found themselves buried in debts and trapped in the tenant-farming, sharecropping system.

Education in the "New South"

During Reconstruction, many African Americans pinned their hopes for a better future on education. Reconstruction governments responded by opening thousands of public schools in the South.

However, when white southern Democrats regained control of their states, they cut spending on education. "Free schools are not a necessity," explained the governor of Virginia, "they are a luxury . . . to be paid for, like any other luxury, by the people who wish their benefits."

Many southern schools closed down for lack of funds. Others charged fees. By the 1880s, less than 60 percent of white children and 49 percent of black children still attended school in the "New South."

Reversing Reconstruction

Free public education was not the only Reconstruction program that the new southern leaders ended. They also found ways to rob African Americans of what remained of their political power. Freedmen still voted in the South, but white election officials refused to count their votes. A black voter in Georgia observed:

> "We are in a majority here, but . . . there's a hole gets in the bottom of the boxes some way and lets out our votes."

New voting laws Still not satisfied, southern whites passed laws in the 1890s that made it even harder for African Americans

Sharecroppers who could not read relied on the landowner to keep records of how much money they owed. Even when harvests were good, they were often told that they owed more to the landowner than they had the year before.

Developing the Section

Discussion

Checking Understanding

1. Why did most southerners become tenant farmers, and why did they remain poor? (They could not afford to buy land. Low crop prices left them unable to pay off their debts.)

Stimulating Critical Thinking

2. How was life in the "New South" much like life in the old South? (Despite some growth in industry, the region remained mostly rural and poor. Reconstruction efforts to provide free schools and guarantee voting rights to blacks were reversed by post-Reconstruction governments.)

3. Why do you think most of the South remained rural and poor? (Lack of money to finance industries, competition from established northern industries, difficulty of changing traditional economy by retraining work force.)

Vital Links

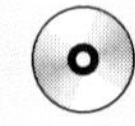

Farm family (Picture)
Unit 3, Side 1,
Search 39019

See also Unit 3 Explore CD-ROM location 219.

Connections to Literature

Some white southern writers protested the treatment of African Americans. For instance, George Washington Cable of New Orleans wrote *Silent South,* one of the strongest indictments of southern racial policies. Lewis H. Blair of Richmond wrote *The Prosperity of the South Dependent Upon the Elevation of the Negro,* an attack on the notion of black inferiority.

Teaching the Reading Maps

Ask students to compare the numbers of African American representatives and senators in 1876. (6 representatives, 1 senator) How might they explain the difference? (More difficult to get statewide support for a black candidate.) **Answers to Reading Maps:** There were 6 in 1876, but only 1 in 1896. During Radical Reconstruction, African Americans were a powerful voting bloc, but later restrictions denied suffrage to most of them.

Section Activity

A Postwar Collage

To give an overview of life in the South, have small groups create layouts for collages. The goal is to compare life during and after Reconstruction. Each group should decide which topics to show, sizes of images in relation to each other, labels needed, and how best to arrange images to highlight differences or similarities. For example, an image of a long line of African American voters might be juxtaposed with an image of one person being denied suffrage because of a poll tax. Images of poor white and black tenant farmers might be positioned to show that their economic condition was the same during and after Reconstruction. Conclude by having groups present and explain layouts.

to vote. All citizens now had to pay a **poll tax**—a fee for voting. The tax was set high to make voting, like schooling, a luxury that very few black southerners could afford.

Some southern states also made potential voters pass a literacy test to prove that they could read. A person who failed the test could not vote.

Lawmakers claimed that these laws did not violate the right to vote, since they applied to white voters, too. Whites, though, were protected by a **grandfather clause** in the laws after 1898. This clause said that voting laws did not apply to a man whose father or grandfather could have voted before January 1, 1867. Before that day, of course, only whites had been able to vote.

African Americans appealed to the Supreme Court in 1898 to protect their right to vote under the Fifteenth Amendment. To their shock, the Court ruled against them. The Court accepted the argument that the voting laws were constitutional because they applied equally to blacks and whites.

Jim Crow Laws

During Reconstruction most southern state governments had outlawed **segregation**—the forced separation of races in public places. Once back in power, however, white southern Democrats began to pass segregation laws that whites called **Jim Crow laws.** Whites used the term Jim Crow

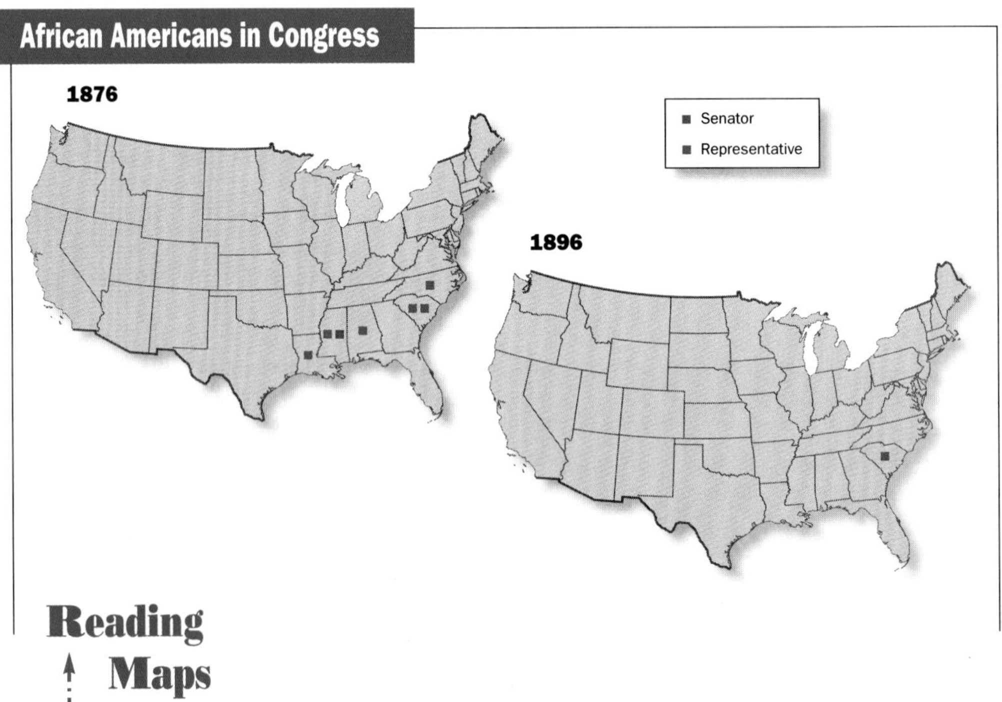

Reading Maps

Compare the number of African Americans in the House of Representatives in 1876 and 1896. Explain the difference.

Tips for Teaching

Students with Limited English
Students with limited English often benefit from relating a graphic representation to ideas in the text. Using Aaron Douglas's mural, have them identify images representing events described in the text. For instance, ask what the dancing and broken chains represent, why the soldiers leave, and why the left side is darker.

Link to Art

Aspects of Negro Life: From Slavery through Reconstruction (1934)
In Aaron Douglas's striking mural, the story unfolds from right to left. On the right side the Emancipation Proclamation is read in 1863. In response to the news, an enslaved man has broken his chains. The center section pays tribute to black leaders in the South from 1867 to 1876. On the left side black figures fall and the sky darkens as the Ku Klux Klan terrorizes black people after the 1870s. **Discuss** What symbols does Douglas use in "telling" the story? How does he use light and color to enhance the story?

to refer to blacks in an insulting way. In the 1880s one state after another drew a "color line" between blacks and whites.

Point of View

Were Jim Crow laws to be taken seriously?

Most whites in the South welcomed Jim Crow laws. The brave editor of the *News and Courier* in Charleston, South Carolina, was an exception. To convince his readers that segregation was unjust, he tried poking fun at Jim Crow laws. He wrote an article drawing what he thought was an extreme picture of where Jim Crow laws might lead:

"If there must be Jim Crow cars on railroads, there should be Jim Crow cars on the street railways . . . on all passenger boats. . . . Jim Crow waiting saloons [rooms]. . . . Jim Crow eating houses. . . . Jim Crow sections of the jury box, and a . . . Jim Crow Bible for colored witnesses to kiss."

What seemed absurd to the editor was not so ridiculous to other white southerners, and it turned out to be a tragedy for African Americans. In the years to come, nearly all of the editor's ideas actually became law as segregation tightened its grip on the South.

Discussion

Checking Understanding

1. How were many blacks prevented from voting? (Poll taxes and literacy tests, both declared legal by the Supreme Court.)

Stimulating Critical Thinking

2. What effects do you think segregation had on blacks? (Rising feelings of resentment; feelings of inferiority; denial of equal opportunities and services.) **On whites?** (Reinforced prejudices because segregation resulted in fewer opportunities for people to understand each other.)

Teaching the Link to Art

Ask students to explain whether the overall mood is hopeful or gloomy. (Gloomy: the hopeful beginnings give way to terrorism.) **Discussion Answers:** Some symbols: cotton, broken chains, trumpet. Concentric circles act like a spotlight to focus on sections of the mural. The left side is darker to represent bleakness at the end of Reconstruction. Silhouettes make human figures stand out as representations.

Teaching the Point of View

Ask students why they think the article had the opposite effect of what was intended. (Most whites welcomed Jim Crow, so any step to achieve segregation seemed reasonable to them.)

History Footnote

In addition to Liberia and Ethiopia, there was one other independent black-ruled nation in the world at the end of the nineteenth century. Haiti won its independence from France in a long struggle from 1791 to 1804, making it the second oldest independent republic in the western hemisphere, and the oldest black republic in the world. The United States is the oldest independent republic in the hemisphere. Because of southern objections to having a black ambassador in Washington, the United States did not establish diplomatic relations with Haiti until 1862.

Teaching the World Link

Point out that Europeans saw Africa as a key source of raw materials for industry and that the race for colonies was part of a competition between European nations for political and economic power. They were able to colonize most of Africa because of advantages in weaponry and because many African societies had been weakened by the slave trade. Nonetheless, many Africans resisted colonial rule. Ask students to consider how European nations might have tried to justify their colonization of Africa. (Belief in white superiority and in a mission to "civilize" non-white peoples.)

Segregated jury (Picture)
Unit 3, Side 1,
Search 38995

See also Unit 3 Explore CD-ROM location 215.

World Link

Europeans divide up Africa In 1884 European nations were racing frantically to acquire more colonies. That year the European powers met in Berlin, Germany, to carve up Africa. Soon the continent was under European control. Only Ethiopia and Liberia escaped colonization.

Ethiopia remained an independent kingdom after it defeated an invading Italian army in 1896. Liberia, founded as a home for freed American slaves in 1821, had been a republic since 1847. Whenever Europeans threatened to take over Liberia, the United States would speak up and the Europeans would back down.

Plessy* v. *Ferguson Many Americans believed that Jim Crow laws violated the Fourteenth Amendment's guarantee of "equal protection of the laws." When Homer Plessy was arrested for riding in a "whites-only" railroad car in Louisiana, he appealed his case to the Supreme Court.

In 1896 the Supreme Court handed down its decision in *Plessy* v. *Ferguson.* It ruled that segregation laws did not violate the Fourteenth Amendment. Facilities for both races could be separate as long as they were roughly equal.

Only one justice, John Marshall Harlan, disagreed. "Our Constitution is color blind," he wrote. He also warned that Jim Crow laws were deeply destructive. "What can more certainly arouse race hate," he asked, than these laws?

The Supreme Court's support for segregation in *Plessy* v. *Ferguson* led to a flood of new Jim Crow laws. Despite the "separate but equal" rule, though, schools and parks for whites were always better than those set aside for blacks.

The color line drawn between black and white southerners was to remain firmly in place for decades. In fact, segregation was the law of the South until 1954, when the Supreme Court finally ruled in *Brown* v. *Board of Education* that racial segregation is unconstitutional.

Responses to Segregation

As the noose of segregation tightened in the South, African Americans responded in a variety of ways. Some bravely disobeyed segregation laws. Others left the South for new homes in the North and West. Still others looked for ways to work together to improve opportunities and protect the rights of African Americans.

Open disobedience Some African Americans refused to obey Jim Crow laws. To do so, however, was dangerous. Almost 3,000 black southerners were lynched—killed by mobs—between 1892 and 1903. Most were lynched because they refused to accept segregation and "white rule."

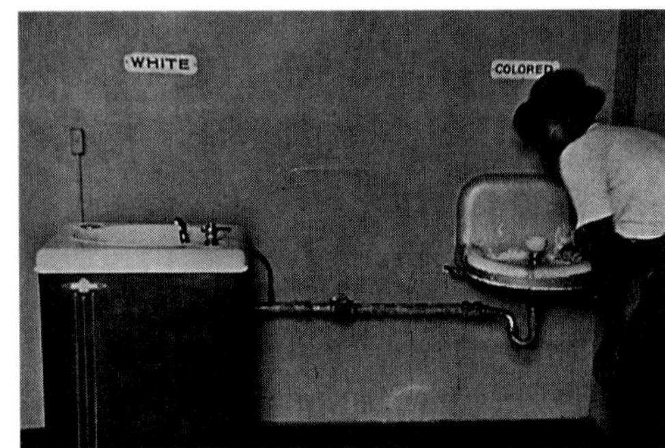

Jim Crow laws kept blacks and whites separated for many years. This photo of a public fountain was taken in 1950 in North Carolina.

History Footnote

Booker T. Washington and William E. B. Du Bois were personally as well as ideologically hostile. Du Bois started out admiring the older Washington. In 1900 Washington offered Du Bois a job at the Tuskegee Institute, but Du Bois wanted to be superintendent of African American schools in the District of Columbia. He did not get the job and thought it was due to Washington's influence; he turned down the Tuskegee offer. After Washington published his autobiography, *Up From Slavery,* in 1901, Du Bois wrote *The Souls of Black Folk* in 1903 as a rebuttal. In it he called Washington the greatest southern leader since Jefferson Davis; he did not mean it as a compliment. The two met in 1904 to form a united black political organization. However, Du Bois quit after it was taken over by Washington supporters.

Bonus Activity

A Letter to a Former Master

To point up the changed relationship between former slaves and masters, have students imagine themselves as freedmen writing letters to a former master. The master has offered to hire the freedmen. In the letters they should explain why they will or will not accept. Conclude by having volunteers read their letters and compare reasons. Students might also compare their responses with the letter in **American Readings,** p. 20.

Migration Rather than put up with segregation and violence, many thousands of African Americans left the South. Some moved to the North. Susie King, for example, moved to Boston with her son. There she met and married her second husband, Russell Taylor.

A teacher and his students work in a laboratory at the Tuskegee Institute in 1903. The college continues to serve African Americans, with over 3,000 students enrolled today.

Some freedmen headed west. Benjamin "Pap" Singleton organized the "Exodus of 1879"—a migration of black southerners to Kansas. Within two years close to 40,000 African Americans had moved to Kansas. Life on the plains had its hardships, but as one "Exoduster" put it, "We had rather suffer and be free."

In 1878 a group of 200 freedmen decided that "the colored man had no home in America." They chartered a ship and sailed to Liberia, a West African nation founded by freed American slaves in the 1820s. Still, few African Americans chose to leave the United States. "We are not Africans now," wrote one, "but colored Americans, and are entitled to American citizenship."

Self-help The majority of black southerners remained in the South where they had the support of their families, churches, and a close-knit community. Believing that their best hope lay in education, they built many schools and colleges. By 1900 more than 1.5 million African American children were attending school. In the South's 29 black colleges, students were preparing to become teachers, lawyers, and doctors.

Two approaches to change No African American believed more strongly in the power of education and self-help than the educator Booker T. Washington. In 1881 he founded the Tuskegee Institute in Alabama to teach practical skills such as farming and carpentry. Washington urged his students to worry less about the injustice of segregation and racial violence, and more about getting education and jobs.

Other African Americans disagreed. They were led by another outspoken black educator, William E. B. Du Bois [doo-BOYS] of Atlanta University. Unlike the more cautious Washington, Du Bois urged blacks to stand up against discrimination and demand equality. Black southerners needed leaders who would demand equal opportunities, Du Bois argued, or many jobs would remain out of their reach.

In 1905 Du Bois met with other African American reformers to form a national organization called the Niagara Movement. Five years later, this movement gave birth to the National Association for the Advancement of Colored People (NAACP).

Vital Links

Howard University (Picture)
Unit 3, Side 1,
Search 30139

See also Unit 3 Explore CD-ROM location 160.

Closing the Section

Wrap-Up Activity

Steps Forward and Backward

To summarize the failure of Reconstruction, have students create charts with 2 columns and 3 rows. Column heads: "How promoted," "How prevented." Row heads: "Political equality," "Economic opportunity," "Social equality." Students should fill in one example for each square, such as "free schools" to promote economic opportunity. Conclude by having volunteers fill in a chart on the chalkboard.

Section Review Answers

1. Definitions: *tenant farmers* (197), *sharecropping* (197), *poll tax* (198), *grandfather clause* (198), *segregation* (198), *Jim Crow laws* (198)

2. By imposing poll taxes and literacy tests.

3. Washington urged a focus on getting education and jobs rather than protesting discrimination. Du Bois said no progress could come unless blacks demanded equal rights.

4. Answers may include leaving the South, working to get an education and skilled job, and contesting unfair laws politically. Students should consider what was feasible after Reconstruction.

To check understanding of "Why We Remember," assign Thinking Critically question 3 on student page 204.

History Footnote

In public, Booker T. Washington supported accommodation in order to "cement the friendship of the races and bring about hearty cooperation between them." In light of the reversal of Reconstruction, Washington believed that this was the only policy that could be really effective. In private, however, he worked to stop racial discrimination. For example, he raised funds to challenge cases in the federal courts against disenfranchisement and Jim Crow laws, and he argued against discrimination in the allocation of funds to white and black schools.

The Failure of Reconstruction

Du Bois could not know how long and difficult the struggle would be. In the decades that followed Reconstruction, white southerners had erected cruel barriers of segregation to strip African Americans of their rights and opportunities.

During the same period, most white southerners, too, had failed to prosper. Only many years later would opportunity and equality finally come to the South.

3. Section Review

1. Define **tenant farmers, sharecropping, poll tax, grandfather clause, segregation,** and **Jim Crow laws.**

2. Explain how the right to vote was denied to black southerners.

3. How did Booker T. Washington's ideas for bettering African American lives differ from those of William E. B. Du Bois?

4. Critical Thinking As a black southerner, how would you have responded to Jim Crow laws, and why?

Why We Remember

Reconstruction

In 1898 Susie King Taylor returned to the South after many years in Boston. On that journey she rode in Jim Crow railroad cars, and heard stories about African Americans being beaten and murdered. "Each morning you can hear of some Negro being lynched," a porter told her. "We have no rights here." Taylor was outraged. "Was the [Civil] war in vain?" she asked. "Has it brought freedom, in the full sense of the word, or has it not made our condition hopeless?"

Looking back at Reconstruction, it is easy to understand and even share Taylor's bitterness. After the Civil War, the world had seemed full of hope to Taylor and her fellow freedmen. With support from the Republican Congress until 1876, the South's Reconstruction governments had built schools and granted voting rights to help make African Americans full and equal citizens.

Still, racism proved stronger than Congress's laws. The chance to breathe new life into the nation's ideals of freedom and equality was lost. These ideals were not, however, forgotten. The belief that all people deserve the same opportunities and rights was kept alive by black families, churches, and schools. Even in the worst moments, Taylor believed that some day blacks and whites would live as equal citizens in America. "I know I shall not live to see the day," she wrote, "but it will come." This faith that the nation could overcome racism and live up to its ideals would be Reconstruction's most hopeful legacy.

Geography Footnote

In 1860 there were about two million farms in the United States, with fewer than 1 percent of them in the West. Therefore, the West is not included in the graphs below. However, during the 1870s alone, some 170 million acres of western farmland were added. Growth was so rapid that by 1890 the Superintendent of the Census wrote, "there can hardly be said to be a frontier line."

Geography Lab

The Civil War and Southern Agriculture

Visitors to the South at the end of the Civil War described it as "almost a desert." The farmland was a ruin of burned buildings, trampled crops, and dead livestock. Use the photo and the tables to understand some of the war's effects on southern agriculture.

Union troops dig into the hillside of a plantation.

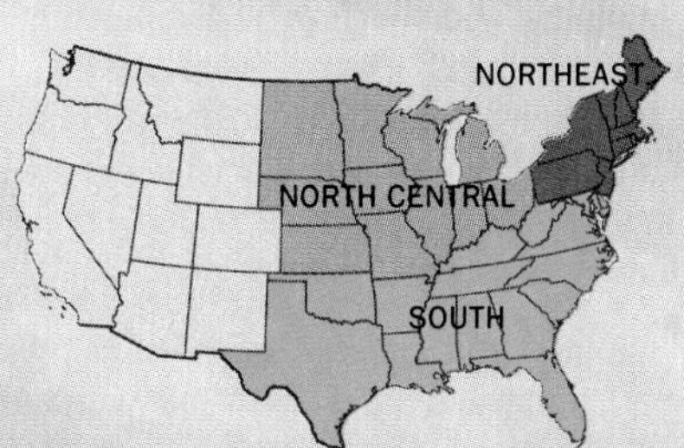

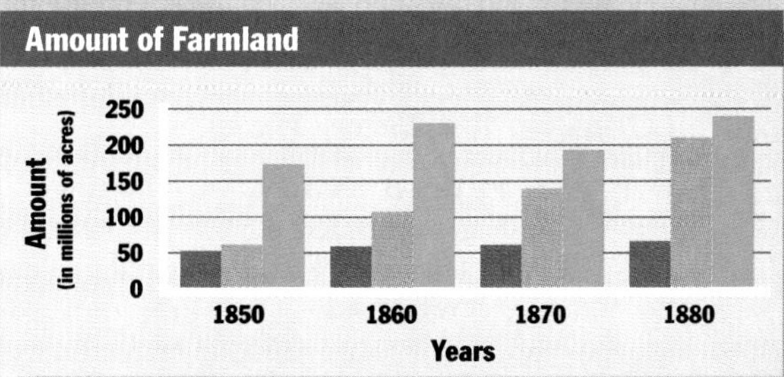

Source: *Historical Statistics of the United States*

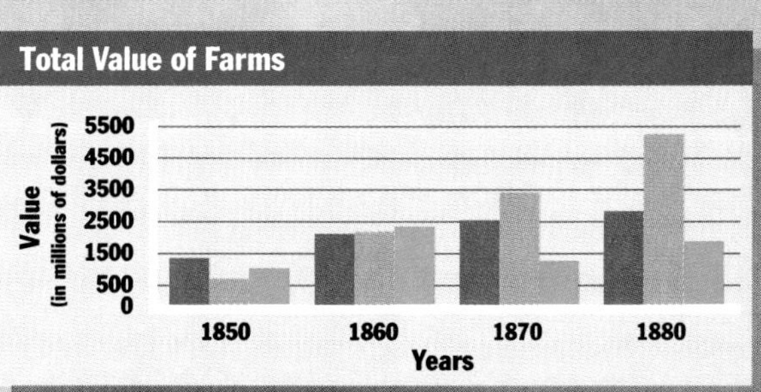

Source: *Historical Statistics of the United States*

Link to History

1. How did farm values change between 1850 and 1880 in the Northeast and North Central regions?
2. How did the value and amount of farmland in the South change between 1860 and 1870? Give at least three reasons for the change.
3. From 1850 to 1880 which region had the largest increase in the amount of farmland?
4. **Hands-On Geography** Imagine that you and your family must turn the land shown in the photo back into productive farmland. You have very little cash. Create a three-step plan to restore your farmland. Explain the plan and the reasons that you chose this plan.

Teaching the Geography Lab

Explain that the physical devastation of the war and lack of money made it very difficult for southerners—both black and white—to make a living.

Link to History

Answers

1. From 1850 to 1880, Northeast farm values roughly doubled, from about $1,400 million (or $1.4 billion) to about $2,800 million ($2.8 billion). North Central values increased from about $700 million to a little over $5,000 million ($5 billion).

2. South farm value declined from about $2,300 million (or $2.3 billion) in 1860 to about $1,300 million ($1.3 billion) in 1870. Reasons include the physical damage from the war, the loss of part of the labor force, and the loss of markets.

3. North Central

4. Steps should take into account the hillside terrain. Steps might include borrowing money, buying wood for retaining walls to create terraces, and plowing the terraces.

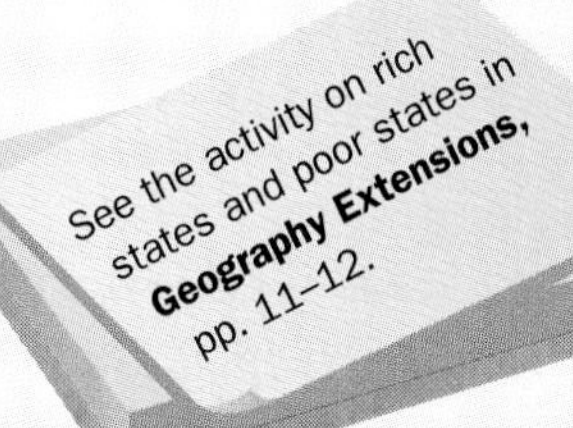

Survey Answers

Reviewing Vocabulary

Definitions are found on these pages: *freedmen* (184), *Reconstruction* (187), *black codes* (187), *impeach* (189), *scalawags* (190), *carpetbaggers* (191), *corruption* (193), *tenant farmers* (197), *sharecropping* (197), *poll tax* (198), *grandfather clause* (198), *segregation* (198), *Jim Crow laws* (198).

Reviewing Main Ideas

1. Their lives were very difficult and insecure because they did not have the education, land, or money to take full advantage of their freedom and rights.

2. (a) They believed Johnson had been too lenient, and the black codes were oppressing African Americans.
(b) Congress passed the Freedmen's Bureau Act and the Civil Rights Act, overriding the President's veto. After the election of 1866 gave the Republicans control of Congress, they passed their own Reconstruction Act. When Johnson tried to stop their plan, they broke his power by nearly removing him from office.

3. (a) African Americans, carpetbaggers, and scalawags. (b) Set up schools for former slaves and began the process of giving African Americans full civil rights.

4. Departure of federal troops from the South, election of Democratic state governments, and the Compromise of 1877.

5. Planters could not afford to pay wages for labor, so they rented plots of land to tenant farmers. Some tenants could not afford to rent the land, so they paid a share of their crop as rent. Most were unable to earn enough to buy land or repay loans for seeds and tools. Low crop prices left them trapped in debt.

(Answers continued in top margin)

6. Jim Crow laws, laws limiting public education, and poll taxes.

7. Some left the South for other parts of the country; some tried to educate themselves and improve skills. Some also fought unjust laws.

Thinking Critically

1. White southerners resented the changed position of former slaves and wanted to regain economic and political power. Northerners may have realized how hard it was going to be for African Americans to get the skills and resources they needed, and that white southerners were being alienated.

2. Answers will vary. Some might share Washington's view that it was more productive to accept the power structure as it was and to try to work within it. Others might agree with Du Bois that unjust laws should be contested.

Chapter Survey

Reviewing Vocabulary

Define the following terms.

1. freedmen
2. Reconstruction
3. black codes
4. impeach
5. scalawags
6. carpetbaggers
7. corruption
8. tenant farmers
9. sharecropping
10. poll tax
11. grandfather clause
12. segregation
13. Jim Crow laws

Reviewing Main Ideas

1. What was life like for freedmen immediately after the Civil War?
2. (a) Why did the Radical Republicans want to take control of Reconstruction? (b) How did they get that control?
3. (a) Who were the South's new voters and officeholders? (b) What did the Reconstruction governments accomplish?
4. Describe the events that led to the return of "white man's rule" in the South.
5. Why did southern farmers turn to sharecropping, and what were the results?
6. What were three ways that southern Democrats reversed the gains that African Americans made during Reconstruction?
7. How did African Americans respond to their treatment after Reconstruction?

Thinking Critically

1. Analysis Most white southerners resented Reconstruction, while many white northerners gave up on it. Why did the two groups take these positions?
2. Evaluation If you had been an African American in the South in the late 1800s, how might you have responded to the rising tide of segregation? Why?
3. Why We Remember: Synthesis Susie King Taylor once asked, "Was the [Civil] war in vain?" How would you have responded at the time, and today?

Applying Skills

Making decisions The specific problems that people face today are different from those faced by people in the United States after the Civil War. However, the basic need to solve problems by making decisions has never changed. Think about a problem you need to solve in your own life. It does not have to be a big problem, but its solution should require careful thought. Use what you learned on page 195 to decide on the best solution to the problem. Then write the following:

- a description of the problem
- steps you took in making the decision
- why you made the decision you did

History Mystery

Voting in the South Answer the History Mystery on page 181. How might such a decline in voting by African Americans after 1896 have been prevented?

Writing in Your History Journal

1. Keys to History (a) The time line on pages 180–181 has seven Keys to History. In your journal, describe why each one is important to know about. (b) What three events from the chapter would you add to the time line? Write those events and their dates in your journal, and tell why you think each event should be added.

2. Susie King Taylor People often "vote with their feet" rather than stay in a difficult or dangerous situation. In your journal, describe the times when Taylor did this. Then write responses to the following questions: What do her choices tell you about Taylor as a person? Did she make the right choice in each case? Why or why not?

3. Answers may vary, but students will probably see Taylor's bitterness as understandable in light of the dashed hopes. Nevertheless, the war did destroy slavery and open the possibility of equality. Today, most would probably still argue that the war was not in vain because the end of slavery was the necessary first step toward equal rights.

Applying Skills

Answers should reflect an understanding of the steps listed on student page 195, as well as ability to make a final choice in line with the goal to be achieved.

History Mystery

Information on voting is found on pages 197–198. Poll taxes and literacy tests

(Answers continued in side margin)

disqualified most African Americans from voting. The decline might have been prevented if the Supreme Court had declared these voting restrictions unconstitutional.

Writing in Your History Journal

1. (a) Explanations should be similar to the time line notes on teacher pages 180–181.
(b) Accept additions that are accurately described and dated and that reflect an understanding of what makes an event historically important.

2. Students should mention the times when Taylor fled to the Sea Islands, returned to Savannah, and moved to Boston. In saying whether these were good choices, they should discuss her options. Answers should reflect that she was a brave person who took risks.

3. Editorials should show an understanding that the editor opposed Jim Crow laws. Notes might agree that all people deserve equal rights.

Reviewing Geography

1. (A) Virginia; (B) North Carolina, South Carolina; (C) Alabama, Georgia, Florida; (D) Arkansas, Mississippi; (E) Texas, Louisiana.

2. The major factor was the change in labor systems—from slavery to tenant farming and sharecropping. Other factors included destruction of property during the war, lack of capital for rebuilding and improvements, depletion of land from overfarming, opening up of lands in the West, and loss of markets.

Alternative Assessment

Teacher's Take-Home Planner 1, p. 23, includes suggestions and scoring rubrics for the Alternative Assessment activity.

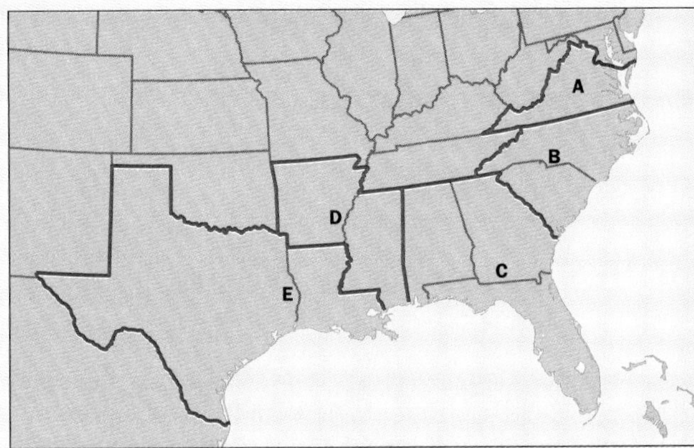

Reviewing Geography

1. Each letter on the map represents one of five military districts in which former Confederate states, except Tennessee, were divided. After each letter, write the name of the state or states in the district.

2. Geographic Thinking In looking back at Chapters 1 and 3, what factors determined the organization and use of farmland in the South before and after the Civil War? Give at least three reasons why these changes occurred.

3. Thinking Historically Reread the editor's opinions in the Point of View on page 199 and review the Supreme Court's decision in *Plessy* v. *Ferguson* on page 200. In your journal, write down the thoughts and ideas that you would want to express to the editor and to all southerners about Jim Crow laws and the Court's decision.

Alternative Assessment

Citizenship: Improving on Reconstruction Imagine that a few days from now, you will travel back through time to the Washington, D.C., of 1867. There, you will present to the members of Congress a "new and improved" Reconstruction plan. The purpose of your plan is to answer the critics of Johnson's 1865 plan while preventing the problems that you have learned will result if the Radical Republicans have their way.

Work with a partner to develop the Reconstruction plan and present it to Congress (your classmates).

In your presentation:

1. Explain what roles former Confederate soldiers, officials, and supporters will play.
2. Tell what rights freedmen will gain.
3. Explain how those rights will be protected under your plan.
4. Describe what will be done to improve the lives of all southerners.
5. Tell what the federal government will do to make your Reconstruction a success.
6. Include the costs of your Reconstruction and how they will be paid.

Your presentation will be evaluated on the following criteria:

- it shows a knowledge of Reconstruction
- it offers creative yet practical solutions to the challenges of the historical period
- it is clear and convincing

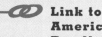

Teaching the

Link to American Readings

In this feature students will read excerpts from a speech by Frederick Douglass, a former slave, who campaigned for black suffrage in the years following the Civil War. They will also hear from three historians whose views of Reconstruction and its relative success and failure are quite different.

Before students begin the lesson, review the material in The South's New Voters (pages 190–191), The Reconstruction Governments (pages 192–193), and Return to "White Man's Rule" (page 193). Have students read the entire feature before assigning the A Closer Look questions. The Setting the Stage Activity and Bonus Activity may then be introduced according to the needs and interests of the students. The information contained in the Discussion questions and the Footnotes may be used throughout the lesson as appropriate. Readers' Theater is ideal for students who might find the readings somewhat difficult. Use the Wrap-Up Activity for students who would enjoy taking a step beyond the core lesson.

Literature Footnote

After English friends helped him purchase his freedom in 1847, Frederick Douglass established the *North Star* in Rochester, New York. He edited the publication for 17 years, advocating abolition through political activism. Douglass urged African Americans to join Union troops during the Civil War. Then, during and after Reconstruction, he held several government positions.

Literature Footnote

Traditionalist theories of Reconstruction (Bowers and others) dominated scholarly work for many years. In the 1930s W. E. B. DuBois published a history that attacked the traditionalists. Historians ignored DuBois, however, and it was not until the civil rights movement that some historians once again began putting Reconstruction in a positive light.

Link to American Readings

READING 3A

"What the Black Man Wants"

In an illustration from an 1870 issue of *Harper's Weekly*, a freedman registers to vote in Richmond, Virginia's first municipal election after the end of the Civil War.

Born a slave, Frederick Douglass escaped in 1838 and settled in Massachusetts. There he educated himself and became an outspoken critic of slavery. When the Civil War ended and slavery was abolished, he began to campaign for African American suffrage and civil rights. In the following speech, delivered before the Massachusetts Anti-Slavery Society in 1865, Douglass argues that freedom is meaningless without the right to vote.

A speech by Frederick Douglass, 1865

I am for the "immediate, unconditional, and universal" enfranchisement of the black man, in every state in the Union. Without this, his liberty is a mockery; without this, you might as well almost retain the old name of slavery for his condition; for, in fact, if he is not the slave of the individual master, he is the slave of society, and holds his liberty as a privilege, not as a right. . . .

We may be asked, I say, why we want it. I will tell you why we want it. We want it because it is our right, first of all. No class of men can, without insulting their own nature, be content with any deprivations of their rights. . . . By depriving us of suffrage, you affirm our incapacity to form an intelligent judgment respecting public men and public measures; you declare before the world that we are unfit to exercise the elective franchise, and by this means lead us to undervalue ourselves, to put a low estimate upon ourselves, and to feel that we have no possibilities like other men.

Again, I want the elective franchise, for one, as a colored man, because ours is a peculiar government, based upon a peculiar idea, and that idea is universal suffrage. . . . [Here], where universal suffrage is the rule, where that is the fundamental idea of the government, to rule us out is to make us an exception, to brand us with the stigma of inferiority, and to invite to our heads the missiles of those about us; therefore, I want the franchise for the black man.

Excerpts from Frederick Douglass, "What the Black Man Wants," 1865.

enfranchisement: right to vote

suffrage: right to vote

stigma: mark of disgrace

History Footnote

Frederick Douglass championed women's as well as black suffrage. At the same time, women were beginning to speak for themselves. The following excerpt is by Victoria Woodhull, from her testimony before the House Judiciary Committee in 1871. "Women have the same invaluable right to life, liberty, and the *pursuit* of happiness that men have. Why have they not this right politically as well as men? Women constitute a majority of the people of this country—they hold vast portions of the nation's wealth and pay a proportionate share of the taxes. . . . The American nation, in its march onward and upward, cannot publicly choke the intellectual and political activity of half its citizens by narrow statutes."

READING 3B

Historians Look at Reconstruction

Although history does not change, scholars' interpretations of events do change. The Reconstruction era is a case in point. In the following selections, three historians examine Reconstruction. Each interprets the era in a different way.

Three views of Reconstruction

Writing in the 1920s, and supporting a philosophy dating back to the 1890s, Claude G. Bowers views Reconstruction as a tragic era. He argues that the Radical Republicans were self-serving and corrupt politicians who imposed unfair policies on the South. Only after southern governments were "redeemed" and southern civilization was preserved, did the tragic era end.

They were years [1865–1877] of revolutionary turmoil. . . . The prevailing note was one of tragedy. . . . Never have American public men in responsible positions, directing the destiny of the Nation, been so brutal, hypocritical, and corrupt. The Constitution was treated as a doormat on which politicians and army officers wiped their feet after wading in the muck. Never has the Supreme Court been treated with such ineffable contempt, and never has that tribunal [court] so often cringed before the clamor of the mob. . . .

That the Southern people literally were put to the torture is vaguely understood, but even historians have shrunk from the unhappy task of showing us the torture chambers. . . . Brutal men, inspired by personal ambition or party motives, assumed the pose of philanthropists and patriots, and thus deceived and misguided vast numbers of well-meaning people in the North.

ineffable: unspeakable

philanthropist: one who helps others

The Civil Rights Act of 1875 was designed to protect the social equality of the freedmen. Shortly after it was enacted, Thomas Nast made an engraving in which Columbia, the symbol of American liberty, gives a civil rights document to the freedman. In 1883 the Supreme Court declared the Civil Rights Act unconstitutional.

Setting the Stage Activity

What is "Right"

To introduce the lesson, have students open their history journals and write their own definitions of "right" and "privilege." Then read aloud the opening paragraph of the Douglass speech. Discuss his argument that without black suffrage, the former slaves hold their "liberty as a privilege, not as a right. . . ." Ask students to explain this statement.

Bonus Activity

Writing a Definition

To continue the lesson, have students open their history journals and reread their own definitions of "right." How do theirs compare to those of Douglass? Ask students whether they would now consider revising their definitions, and if so, how. Have students make revisions to their definitions in their journals.

Discussion

Stimulating Critical Thinking

1. After reading this speech, what do you think Douglass would say about giving women the right to vote?

(Douglass, in fact, was in favor of suffrage for women. "I hold that women, as well as men, have the right to vote, and my heart and my voice go with the movement to extend suffrage to woman; . . ."[from "What the Black Man Wants"])

2. What do you think Douglass would say about social justice in today's society? Would he be happy with the advancements, or would he be frustrated? Explain. (Douglass would most likely be pleased with the fact that both African Americans and women have the right to vote. However, he might be disappointed in the social inequalities that still exist.)

Literature Footnote

Although people such as Frederick Douglass and Victoria Woodhull made progress in their fight for equality, there were many who undercut their efforts. One of those was Thomas Dixon, Jr. After his ordination in 1886, Dixon became popular in the North as a preacher of the Social Gospel. His novel *The Leopard's Spots* (1902) pushed for the segregation and repression of blacks. *The Clansman* (1905) dramatized his version of Reconstruction and would become the inspiration for the D. W. Griffith film *The Birth of a Nation*. This film version of Dixon's book, which premiered in 1915, was especially vicious in its attack on African Americans.

Kenneth Stampp is a historian who wrote an essay in 1965 arguing that traditionalists distorted Reconstruction by exaggerating the corruption and harsh policies of the Radicals. Instead, Stampp emphasizes the important accomplishments of the era.

Rarely in history have the participants in an unsuccessful rebellion endured penalties as mild as those Congress imposed upon the people of the South, and particularly upon their leaders. After four years of bitter struggle costing hundreds of thousands of lives, the generosity of the federal government's terms was quite remarkable. . . .

[Traditionalists] are guilty of distortion by exaggeration, by a lack of perspective, by superficial analysis, and by overemphasis. They make corruption a central theme of their narratives, but they overlook constructive accomplishments. . . .

Radical idealism was in part responsible for two of the most momentous enactments of the Reconstruction years: the Fourteenth Amendment to the federal Constitution which gave Negroes [African Americans] citizenship and promised them equal protection of the laws, and the Fifteenth Amendment which gave them the right to vote. The fact that these amendments could not have been adopted under any other circumstances, or at any other time, before or since, may suggest the crucial importance of the Reconstruction era in American history. Indeed, without Radical Reconstruction, it would be impossible to this day for the federal government to protect Negroes from legal and political discrimination.

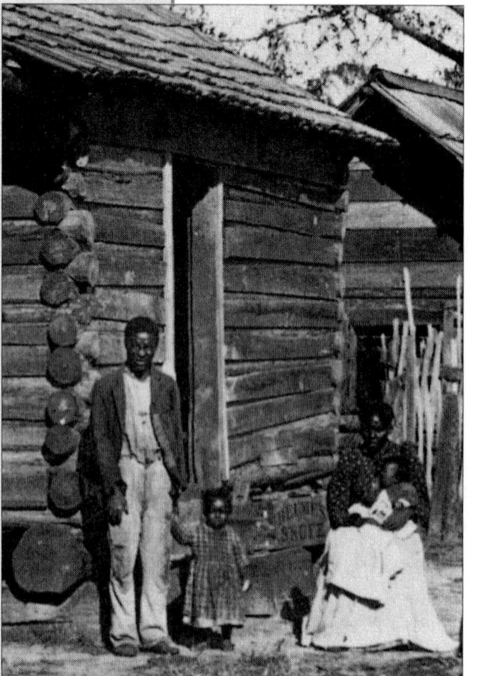

Georgia sharecroppers pose in front of their cabin in the 1890s.

Readers' Theater

Although "What the Black Man Wants" is written in the first person, students can stage it using mixed voices. Have them analyze the speech carefully to determine where logical breaks in thought will allow a change of voice. Be sure that girls are not given lines with first person pronouns, (I . . . as a colored man), which might result in an unintentional humorous effect. Students should need no props for this reading. They may sit or stand, and should direct their lines to the audience. Allow enough time for at least one complete run-through before the group makes its presentation to the class. Students should be familiar enough with their lines to be comfortable and to sound natural in their presentation.

Historian Eric Foner has praised the work of historians such as Stampp, but he argues that they have failed to consider all aspects of Reconstruction. He addresses the social, political, and economic issues of the era. In Reconstruction: America's Unfinished Revolution *(1988), Foner concludes that the defeat of Reconstruction deeply affected the future of race relations in America.*

Black participation in Southern public life after 1867 was the most radical development of the Reconstruction years, a massive experiment in interracial democracy without precedent in the history of this or any other country that abolished slavery in the nineteenth century. . . . As illustrated by the small but growing number of black landowners, businessmen, and professionals, the doors of economic opportunity that had opened could never be completely closed. Without Reconstruction, moreover, it is difficult to imagine the establishment of a framework of legal rights enshrined in the Constitution that, while flagrantly violated after 1877 [the formal end of Reconstruction], created a vehicle for future federal intervention in Southern affairs. . . .

precedent: something that comes first

For the nation as a whole, the collapse of Reconstruction was a tragedy that deeply affected the course of its future development. If racism contributed to the undoing of Reconstruction, by the same token Reconstruction's demise and the emergence of blacks as a disenfranchised class of dependent laborers greatly facilitated racism's further spread, until by the early twentieth century it had become more deeply embedded in the nation's culture and politics than at any time since the beginning of the antislavery crusade and perhaps in our entire history.

demise: end

A Closer Look

1. According to Douglass, what effect did disenfranchisement have on African Americans?

2. Explain the traditional view of Reconstruction. What is the view of historians such as Kenneth Stampp?

3. CRITICAL THINKING How does Foner find the middle ground between Bowers and Stampp? Do you agree or disagree with his ideas? Explain.

Wrap-Up Activity

Making Changes

To encourage students to think beyond what happened to what might have been, have them respond to the following question in their history journals. Imagine that you are a government official during the Reconstruction era. What three changes do you think are most important and should be addressed first? Explain.

A Closer Look

Answers

1. According to Douglass, disenfranchisement robbed the black man of true freedom. If he did not have the right to vote, then neither did he have real freedom or control over his life. He was still at the mercy of the white voter, and in that sense, still a slave.

2. The traditional view holds that corruption reigned during Reconstruction; that unfair punishments were placed on the South. Historians such as Stampp argue that the corruption of the period was exaggerated; that many accomplishments marked the era.

3. Foner says that African Americans were active in Reconstruction and that its defeat set back race relations for decades to come.

Teaching the
Citizenship Lab

In this feature students learn more about the Supreme Court's decision in *Plessy* v. *Ferguson* (1896), which legalized "separate but equal" treatment of racial groups. The Court finally overturned the *Plessy* ruling with its decision in *Brown* v. *Board of Education* (1954).

Before students read the feature, have them study Section 1 of the Fourteenth Amendment on page R64. Have students read the entire feature before assigning the Understanding Civic Issues questions and the Hands-On Citizenship activity. The Bonus Activity in this Teacher's Edition may be used as an alternative to, or in addition to, the Hands-On Citizenship activity. The Discussion questions in this Teacher's Edition may be used at appropriate points during students' reading or afterward.

Objectives

- ★ Explain why Homer Plessy and others considered a Louisiana segregation law to be unconstitutional.
- ★ Explain the Supreme Court's ruling on racial segregation in *Plessy* v. *Ferguson.*
- ★ Describe how the Supreme Court's decision in *Brown* v. *Board of Education* affected the "separate but equal" rule.

Supreme Court Case: *Plessy* v. *Ferguson*

Citizenship Lab

Can Separate Ever Be Equal?

Considering the impact of Homer Plessy's Supreme Court case, it seems odd that we know so little about the man himself. We do know that Plessy was young and that he had worked as a carpenter. We also know that although he appeared white, he was classified as "colored" under Louisiana law because one of his great-grandparents had been an African American. Finally, we know that Plessy's arrest for riding in a "whites only" railroad car was no accident: it was a carefully staged event with a definite purpose.

How the Plessy Case Came About

In 1890 Louisiana had passed a law "to promote the comfort of passengers" that ordered railroads in the state to provide "equal but separate" cars for white and black passengers. Railroad owners disliked the law, because providing separate cars meant extra costs. With this in mind, a group of African Americans in New Orleans formed a Citizens' Committee to Test the Constitutionality of the Separate Car Law. The committee raised money, hired a lawyer, and asked Homer Plessy to initiate a test case.

And so, on June 7, 1892, Plessy boarded an East Louisiana Railway train in New Orleans. He deliberately took a seat in a car reserved for white passengers. The conductor, who had been brought in on the plan ahead of time, asked Plessy to move to the "coloreds" car. Plessy refused and was arrested by a detective who had been alerted to stand by for the occasion.

In court, Plessy argued that the Louisiana law violated the Fourteenth Amendment to the Constitution, which guarantees citizens "equal protection of the laws." John H. Ferguson, the local judge in the case, overruled Plessy and fined him twenty-five dollars. The Louisiana Supreme Court agreed with Ferguson. Plessy then appealed to the Supreme Court of the United States.

The Supreme Court Rules

Nearly four years after Plessy's arrest, the Supreme Court handed down its decision. Associate Justice Henry B. Brown wrote the majority opinion upholding the Louisiana law:

"We consider the underlying fallacy [error] of [Plessy's] argument to consist in the assumption that the enforced separation of the two races

History Footnote

"[I]n the eye of the law, there is in this country no superior, dominant, ruling class of citizens. . . . Our Constitution is color-blind, and neither knows nor tolerates classes among citizens. In respect of civil rights, all citizens are equal before the law. The humblest is the peer of the most powerful." Justice Harlan's ringing dissent in the Plessy case is especially noteworthy in light of his background. A Kentucky slaveholder, Harlan had joined the Union army during the Civil War because he viewed preserving the nation as more important than defending slavery. He opposed the Thirteenth Amendment but later came to believe in equal rights for African Americans. In 1871 Justice Harlan publicly stated his change of heart, declaring he would "rather be right than consistent."

stamps the colored race with a badge of inferiority. If this be so, it is . . . solely because the colored race chooses to put that construction [interpretation] upon it. . . . [Plessy's] argument also assumes that social prejudices may be overcome by legislation, and that equal rights cannot be secured to the negro except by an enforced commingling [mingling together] of the two races. We cannot accept this. . . . Legislation is powerless to eradicate [eliminate] racial instincts or to abolish distinctions based upon physical differences. . . . If one race be inferior to the other socially, the Constitution of the United States cannot put them upon the same plane."

Only Justice John Marshall Harlan, a former slaveholder, dissented:

"It was said in argument that the statute [law] of Louisiana does not discriminate against either race. . . . But . . . [e]veryone knows that the statute in question had its origin in the purpose . . . to exclude colored people from coaches occupied by . . . white persons. . . . The thing to accomplish was, under the guise of giving equal accommodation for whites and blacks, to compel the latter to keep to themselves. . . . The fundamental objection, therefore, to the statute, is that it interferes with the personal freedom of citizens. . . . If a white man and a black man choose to occupy the same public conveyance [vehicle] . . . it is their right to do so, and no government . . . can prevent it without infringing the personal liberty of each. . . ."

The Louisiana segregation law tested by Homer Plessy in 1892 was representative of many such laws passed in the 1880s and 1890s. Such laws were neither new nor confined to the South. This 1856 engraving documents the expulsion of an African American from a railway car in Philadelphia.

Plessy Decision Overturned

In *Plessy* v. *Ferguson,* the Supreme Court gave its blessing to a pattern of segregation that would last for nearly sixty years. The pattern was finally broken when the Court agreed to review the "separate but equal" rule as it applied to public schools. In 1954 the Court announced its unanimous decision in *Brown* v. *Board of Education:* segregated schools were, by nature,

Setting the Stage Activity

Listing Observations

To prepare students to read about segregation cases, have small groups list any modern examples of racial or ethnic segregation they have observed in your community or the nation. Have them list examples of integration as well. Then have groups share their lists in a class discussion on the extent of segregation today.

Bonus Activity

Demonstrating Against Segregation

To focus on opposition to segregation, have students imagine they are preparing to demonstrate outside the Supreme Court as it considers the Brown case in 1954. (You might point out that such demonstrations are common.) Have students make signs that call on the justices to overturn the Plessy decision and end legalized segregation. Encourage students to go beyond such obvious messages as "End Segregation Now." Students might derive slogans from the Brown and Harlan opinions in Plessy, including the quotes on pages 211 and 212 of this Teacher's Edition. Also encourage students to employ rhyme, wordplay, and other creative uses of language in their signs.

Discussion

Checking Understanding

1. What did the Supreme Court decide in the Plessy case? (It decided Louisiana's railroad segregation law did not violate the Fourteenth Amendment; the law was upheld as constitutional.)

Stimulating Critical Thinking

2. How did Justice Brown contradict himself when he wrote about racial "inferiority"? (On the one hand, he said that if black people felt separation branded them as inferior, it was only because they chose to interpret it that way. On the other hand, he acknowledged that African Americans were considered socially inferior when he said the Constitution could not "put them upon the same plane" with white Americans.

3. How were the Dred Scott and Plessy cases similar? (Some possibilities: Both decisions reflected prevailing views of white southerners. Both decisions had negative effects on African Americans. Both decisions were overturned, though by different means: constitutional amendment versus a later Court decision.)

Citizenship Footnote

Justice Brown's interpretation of the Fourteenth Amendment sounds tortured to modern ears: "The object of the amendment was undoubtedly to enforce the absolute equality of the two races before the law, but in the nature of things it could not have been intended to abolish distinctions based upon color, or to enforce social, as distinguished from political, equality. . . ." Brown, like many others of his era, believed that racial prejudice (a term he would not have used) was inborn. Surely, he thought, the amendment's writers knew that to be true and therefore did not expect the amendment to wipe out racial "instincts." Brown's own "instincts" made him unable to accept that African Americans deserved equal treatment in all areas of life.

unequal and therefore unconstitutional. It did not matter, wrote Chief Justice Earl Warren, that the schools in question were fairly equal in terms of teacher qualifications, curriculum, and quality of facilities. Instead, Warren wrote, "To separate [African American children] . . . solely because of their race generates a feeling of inferiority as to their status in the community that may affect their hearts and minds in a way unlikely ever to be undone." (You will read more about this case and about the civil rights movement in Chapter 14.)

By overturning the Plessy decision, the Court declared that legal segregation—also called *de jure segregation* —could no longer exist. However, *de facto segregation*—segregation that exists in fact but is not supported by law—persists to this day. For example, about one-third of African American public school students attend schools where 90 to 100 percent of the students are members of minority groups. One reason for continued segregation is "white flight"—the tendency for white people to move to the suburbs, while African Americans and other minorities remain in the cities. Many people believe de facto segregation is harmful, and they want to continue efforts to end it. But other people—both black and white Americans—feel differently. Rather than try to force integration, they prefer to concentrate their efforts on improving the quality of existing neighborhoods and schools.

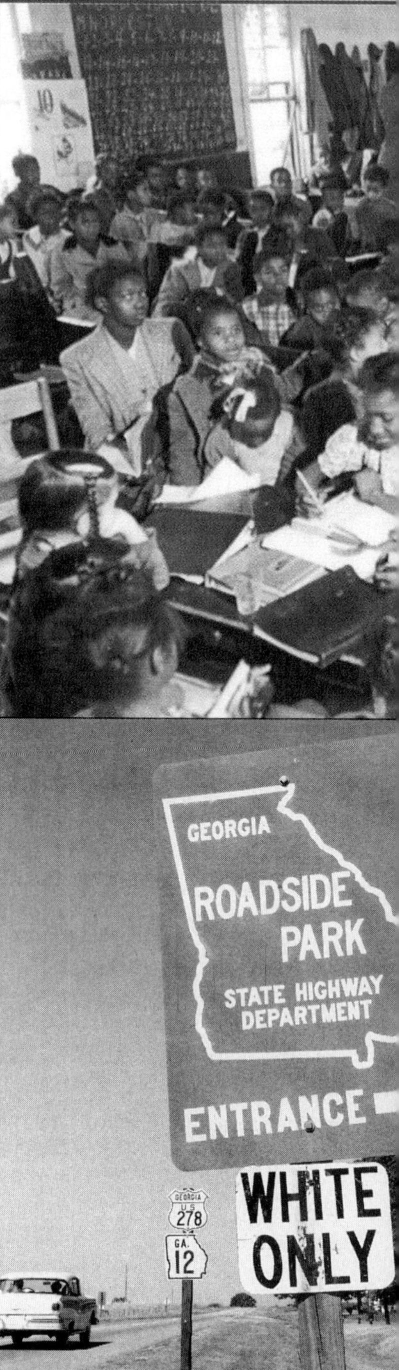

Connections to Economics

Economics played a role in the growth of legalized segregation in the South. For some time after the Civil War, the desperate poverty of most black southerners separated them from white southerners in housing and other areas of life. But as some black southerners improved their economic situation and took advantage of amenities like railroad travel, they came in more frequent contact with white southerners. Louisiana's 1890 railroad law was a typical response. The law offered railroads two ways to achieve racial separation: "by providing two or more passenger coaches for each passenger train, or by dividing the passenger coaches by a partition so as to secure separate accommodations." Black nurses caring for white children, however, were exempted.

***Plessy* v. *Ferguson* served to reinforce policies of racial segregation and eventually resulted in the institution of "separate but equal" facilities like the ones in these photographs.**

Understanding Civic Issues

1. Describe how the Plessy case came about.
2. The quotes from justices Brown and Harlan each make two main points. Summarize those points.
3. **Critical Thinking** Justice Warren's idea that segregated schools are always unfair remains controversial. For example, Supreme Court Justice Clarence Thomas, an African American, says, "It never ceases to amaze me that the courts are so willing to assume that anything that is predominantly black must be inferior." What is your opinion of the reasoning behind the *Brown* v. *Board of Education* decision?
4. **Hands-On Citizenship** Throughout our history, Americans have disagreed about whether the Supreme Court should reflect society (as the Plessy decision reflected southern attitudes) or try to change society (as the Brown decision did).
   - Poll six adults and six teenagers on this question.
   - Present your findings. Include at least one graph. Are there clear differences in attitudes between generations? If so, how do you explain them?

Citizenship Lab Answers

1. In 1892 Homer Plessy was arrested for refusing to leave a "whites-only" train car. When lower courts overruled his idea that Louisiana's railroad segregation law violated the Fourteenth Amendment, he appealed to the Supreme Court.

2. Brown: Forced separation does not brand black people as inferior. Laws cannot create social equality. Harlan: The point of this law is to make black people keep to themselves. The law interferes with personal freedom.

3. Students should realize Warren did not mean a school was inferior because its students were black; he meant segregation was viewed as implying inferiority and thus was unfair. However, some students may believe separate schools can benefit African Americans.

Teaching the Hands-On Citizenship

To avoid overlaps in polling, have students interview their own relatives and neighbors rather than teachers or fellow eighth-graders.

Discuss some of the methodological problems involved in gathering information as you review the results of the polls. Ask the class if their respondents are representative of all Americans? What sort of biases might they have? Would the poll's results have been different if they were taken in a different community? at a shopping center? at a sports event? at a traffic court?

Unit Survey

Making Connections

Answers

1. Students might suggest compromise and negotiation as alternatives. They might choose key events such as the Dred Scott decision, firing on Fort Sumter, Gettysburg, or the assassination of Lincoln, and consider effects if these events ended differently.

2. White southerners based their stand on the principle of self-determination, just as the colonists claimed the right to determine whether they wanted to be part of the British Empire. They ignored that slavery was based on oppression. Northerners may have stressed that the states had chosen to be part of the country and were obliged to remain part of it.

3. Legislative branch more powerful during 1850s and Reconstruction; executive branch stronger during the war. Easier to lead a war effort with strong President. Personalities and skills of Presidents affected which branch was stronger.

Teaching the Unit Project

Have students determine whether their state was directly involved. Suggest that they read the text and encyclopedias for background and also examine state and local history books.

Evaluation Criteria

The project can be evaluated according to the criteria listed below, using a scale for each: 4 = exemplary, 3 = good, 2 = adequate, 1 = poor.

(Continued in top margin)

Completing the task The map is well executed and accurate. Accompanying materials are relevant.

Knowing content Map presents a clear theme or fact about the state's role.

Thinking critically The materials are appropriate to the message illustrated.

Communicating ideas Map an aspect of the state's involvement.

Thinking It Over

Students' responses may show an interest in the fact that the war was between Americans, with some family members taking different sides, and that it was one of the first wars to have detailed photographs depicting it. Students may be fascinated by a particular battle, military strategy, or war-related document.

Unit Survey

Making Connections

Review

1. From 1850 to 1876, the nation struggled over the issues of slavery, secession, and Reconstruction. Could these issues have been solved in any other way than they were? Use examples to explain your answer.

2. What similarities do you suppose Southerners saw between secession and the American Revolution? What differences might Northerners have seen?

3. Although the Constitution balances the powers of the legislative and executive branches, at different times one or the other has been stronger. Which branch was stronger during the 1850s? During the Civil War? During Reconstruction? Why do you think these shifts occurred?

Linking History, Geography, and Art

Project

Your State in the Civil War

Did armies clash on the soil of your state between 1861 and 1865? Or was your state less directly involved in the war that split our nation? Even if your state was not yet a state, it was somehow affected by the Civil War. Find out how. Present what you learn in a pictorial map.

Project Steps

Work with a group.

❶ Choose one or two topics on which to focus. Here are some possibilities:
- battles that were fought in your state
- production of food, weapons, or other supplies in your state
- military or political leaders who came from your state
- citizens of your state who went to war
- contributions to the war effort by various organizations in your state
- effects of fighting, blockades, etc.

❷ Gather information about your topics. Start with this book. Then check your school or local library or the local historical society. Some students' families might have information—even photographs, letters, or other items to copy.

❸ Draw a large map of your state as it existed during the Civil War. Draw the map to scale, and include cities, land and water features, and any war-related features, such as battle sites or supply routes. Display the map on the bulletin board.

❹ Prepare pictorial or descriptive items and arrange them around the state map. Here are some possibilities:
- graphs
- drawings, paintings, or photographs
- letters or diary entries
- newspaper or magazine headlines, articles, or political cartoons
- descriptions of the events or the effects of the war

If an item relates to a specific place, use pushpins and yarn to connect the item to the correct spot on the map.

Thinking It Over How would you explain the fascination that the Civil War has for modern-day Americans? What aspect of the war do you find most interesting? Why?

Objectives

- ★ Describe the technological tools and methods used by historians.
- ★ Identify the kinds of information historians can acquire by using technology.
- ★ Explain how historians can use modern technology to draw conclusions about past events.

How Do We Know?

Metal detectors played a crucial role in researching the true story of the Battle of the Little Bighorn.

Scholar's Tool Kit

Technology

One of the most dramatic incidents in American history is commonly known as Custer's Last Stand. On June 25, 1876, the U.S. Cavalry battled Sioux and Cheyenne warriors on the banks of the Little Bighorn River. For more than a century scholars have tried to understand how the warriors could destroy the elite 7th Cavalry led by the famous Civil War general, George Armstrong Custer. Recently, researchers using state-of-the-art metal detectors at the battle site have made discoveries that shed new light on the events of that fateful June day.

Custer's Last Stand?

Because none of the troopers with Custer survived the battle, the only witnesses were the victorious Indians. They reported that the attacking soldiers caught them by surprise. After some initial confusion, angry warriors urged by Sitting Bull, Crazy Horse, Two Moons, and Lame White Man rushed toward the soldiers to defend their families. The battlefield became a nightmare of dust, smoke, gunshots, and war cries. Arrows and bullets began to rain down on the soldiers, who had paused in their attack to look for a place to cross the river. Frightened cavalry horses started to break free from the soldiers holding them.

Perhaps surprised by the bold Indian counterattack, the soldiers with Custer failed to put up much of a defense. Instead, many panicked and ran away. According to Iron Hawk, a Sioux warrior, "Custer's

Introducing *How Do We Know?*

Technology

Ask students to name technological advances that may have improved historians' abilities to learn about the past (computers that make processing large amounts of data much easier and faster, x-ray and other technologies that allow historians to examine items without destroying them, carbon dating that allows historians to reliably date artifacts). Point out that technology does not replace the skills a historian needs such as knowledge, background research, and creativity.

Setting the Stage Activity

Using Technology

To prepare students to read about the use of metal detector technology in analyzing "Custer's Last Stand," have them think of the site of a recent major event. It might be a large sporting event, a rally, or an outdoor concert. It might also be a natural or human-caused disaster. Have them list advantages of examining the site with a technological tool that allows them to find everything left at the site. What information could they obtain? What conclusions could they draw?

Critical Thinking

Answers

1. The American public was conditioned to believe stories of Indian treachery and cavalry heroism. However, knowledge about and sympathy for Native Americans has increased enormously over the last century, making people more willing to believe their accounts of the battle.

2. Archaeologists found the objects, anthropologists helped explain their significance, medical examiners studied human remains, lab technicians examined and tested the artifacts, computer scientists helped process the data, and historians assembled, interpreted, and published the information.

3. People felt that it was unfair to place so much emphasis on one person, especially since the Indians won the battle. The new name reflects an objective viewpoint.

Bonus Activity

Future Digs

Ask students to imagine they are living 100 years from now and are using a metal detector (or other modern technological tool) to find artifacts in your community from the past. What sorts of objects might they discover and what information would these items reveal about our times? As students brainstorm, have a volunteer write the lists on the chalkboard.

Connections to Science

The instrument that made possible the in-depth examination of the battlefield at Little Bighorn is a state-of-the-art version of the common metal detector. These devices, common among hobbyists, all operate the same way. Radio waves are transmitted from the head of the instrument through an antenna. Metal objects, even those buried or behind walls, absorb some of the radio waves and reflect them back. A receiving circuit amplifies the returning signal and gives the user an audible warning that it has found a metal object. Many metal detectors have a circuit that can distinguish valuable materials, such as gold or silver, from nonvaluable material. Most of the objects on the Little Bighorn battlefield were less than six inches underground, making them easy for archaeologists to find.

Red Horse, an eyewitness, made several drawings of the battle. What do you learn about his view of what happened?

Critical Thinking

1. Why did the American public refuse to believe Indian accounts? Why do you think opinions of the battle have changed over time?

men in the beginning shot straight, but later they shot like drunken men, firing into the ground, into the air, wildly in every way."

Neither the U.S. Army nor the American public was willing to accept Indian accounts of the battle. They preferred to believe that Sitting Bull had lured the soldiers into a trap. The doomed battalion had fought bravely to the end, with Custer and a handful of troopers making a heroic last stand. This story, it turns out, is largely a myth, but it remained unchallenged for over 100 years.

Using Technology to Study the Battle Site

The evidence that revealed the truth about the battle came from scientific analysis of the battlefield. In 1983 a fire burned away the brush covering the Little Bighorn battlefield. It enabled military historians to use modern technology to find an explanation for the Custer disaster. These scholars studied the battlefield like police officers investigating the scene of a murder.

Critical Thinking

2. Archaeologists, anthropologists, medical examiners, lab technicians, computer scientists, and historians all took part in the investigation. Explain the role that each might have played.

The scholars' primary research tool was the metal detector, which they used to scan a major portion of the battlefield. They found approximately 1,700 metal artifacts, mostly iron arrowheads, empty shell casings made of brass, and lead bullets.

The bullets and shell casings were taken to a laboratory for examination. With the aid of powerful microscopes, scientists studied and photographed the firing-pin marks and other scratches on the empty cartridge cases. They also examined the grooves on the lead bullets caused by the gun barrels. As a result, the scientists could identify the weapons the soldiers and Indians used, as well as where on the

Connections to Literature

Perhaps the best account of the Battle of the Little Bighorn and the career and personality of George Custer is *Son of the Morning Star: Custer and the Little Bighorn* (San Francisco: North Point Press, 1984). The author is the distinguished American novelist Evan S. Connell. He focuses on the human side of the battle and on its significance in the war against the Plains Indians and the westward expansion of the United States. According to Connell, few events have had as powerful an impact on the American popular consciousness as the Battle of the Little Bighorn, and few still retain as much power to haunt us today.

battlefield the weapons were used. For instance, when an Indian or soldier fired his gun, he usually ejected the shell casing, reloaded, and then moved to another position and fired again. At each spot, the rifleman left behind an empty shell casing identified through the scratches caused by the ejecting mechanism.

Telling the Story of the Battle

The arrowheads, shell casings, and bullets were carefully plotted on a detailed grid of the battlefield. Researchers could then see certain clusters of artifacts. These clusters told a surprising story about the course of the battle.

One surprise was that the Indians were better armed than anyone had suspected. Many had repeating rifles, while the soldiers had only single-shot carbines. Another surprise was that Custer's men did relatively little shooting. Evidence indicates that the troopers with Custer at first maintained good order. Then the troop formations rapidly fell apart, as some troopers evidently panicked and fled. Scholars now believe that superior Indian fire power and the breakdown of troop unity both contributed to the disaster.

Scholars also believe that the first Indian accounts of the battle were reliable. The archaeological evidence contradicts none of the early Indian testimony. By itself each shell casing, bullet, or arrowhead found on the battlefield was relatively unimportant. As a group, they unlocked the mystery that has surrounded the Battle of the Little Bighorn.

Critical Thinking

3. The battle site is located in what used to be called Custer Battlefield National Monument. Why do you think the name was changed to Little Bighorn National Monument in 1991?

Scholar at Work

Conflicting stories are always a problem for historians. Today, technology such as tape recorders and video cameras can aid in gathering data for interpretation. Choose an incident at your school or in the community that has caused controversy. Work with a group to videotape interviews with at least three witnesses. Review the tapes and write a history of the event based on your interpretation of the accounts.

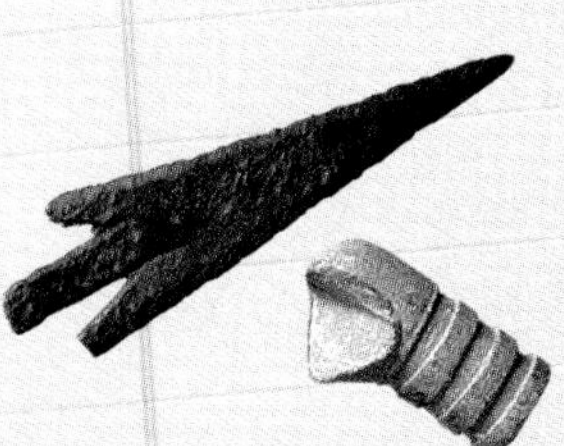

Discussion

Checking Understanding

1. Who were the only eyewitnesses to the Battle of the Little Bighorn and how did this affect the American public's understanding of the event? (Indians were the only survivors. Because the American public had prejudices against them, they did not believe the Indian accounts.)

2. What natural event made it possible to study the battlefield with metal detectors? (A fire burned away the brush covering the battlefield.)

3. What types of artifacts did the scholars find and how did they use them? (Mostly arrowheads, empty shell casings, and lead bullets. With them, they were able to determine who fired, how much, from where, and how often. This knowledge enabled them to accurately reconstruct the movements on the battlefield and dispel the myth of a valiant "last stand" by Custer and his men.)

Teaching the Scholar at Work

After students have videotaped the eyewitnesses and examined the testimony, have them analyze the differences in the accounts. Ask them to discuss reasons for the varying accounts and interpretations. Finally, ask students if they can find any pattern or make any generalizations about the different interpretations of the event.

Unit 2

Introducing the Unit

Panoramic View, City of Cincinnati, U.S.A., 1900

Point out that bird's-eye views of cities were very popular during the 1800s and early 1900s. As in this lithograph, they usually showed an appealing scene of urban life, reflecting the optimism of the times. Ask students how the lithograph relates to the topic of the unit. (It shows a large mid-west city, reflecting the urban growth and confidence characteristic of the period.)

Teaching the Hands-On HISTORY

Suggest that before students begin their maps they make a list of the important features they want to include. If they are not sure where certain features are located, have them consult a map of the area. After they draw their maps, have them list what features, if any, they included that are not on the maps in the book. Ask them what are the reasons for these differences.

Unit Overview

As the nation expanded westward in the second half of the 1800s, increased mining, ranching, and farming, along with the spread of railroads, led to conflicts between the settlers and the Indians. The West took on a new look, with former open spaces replaced by homesteads and crisscrossed by train tracks.

The growing power of big business soon resulted in attempts by the government to regulate business excesses. Meanwhile workers began to organize into unions in an attempt to improve wages and working conditions.

This period also saw the great wave of immigration to the United States. Both immigrants and native-born Americans flocked to the cities, spurring their growth. This growth created numerous problems, but it also spawned opportunities.

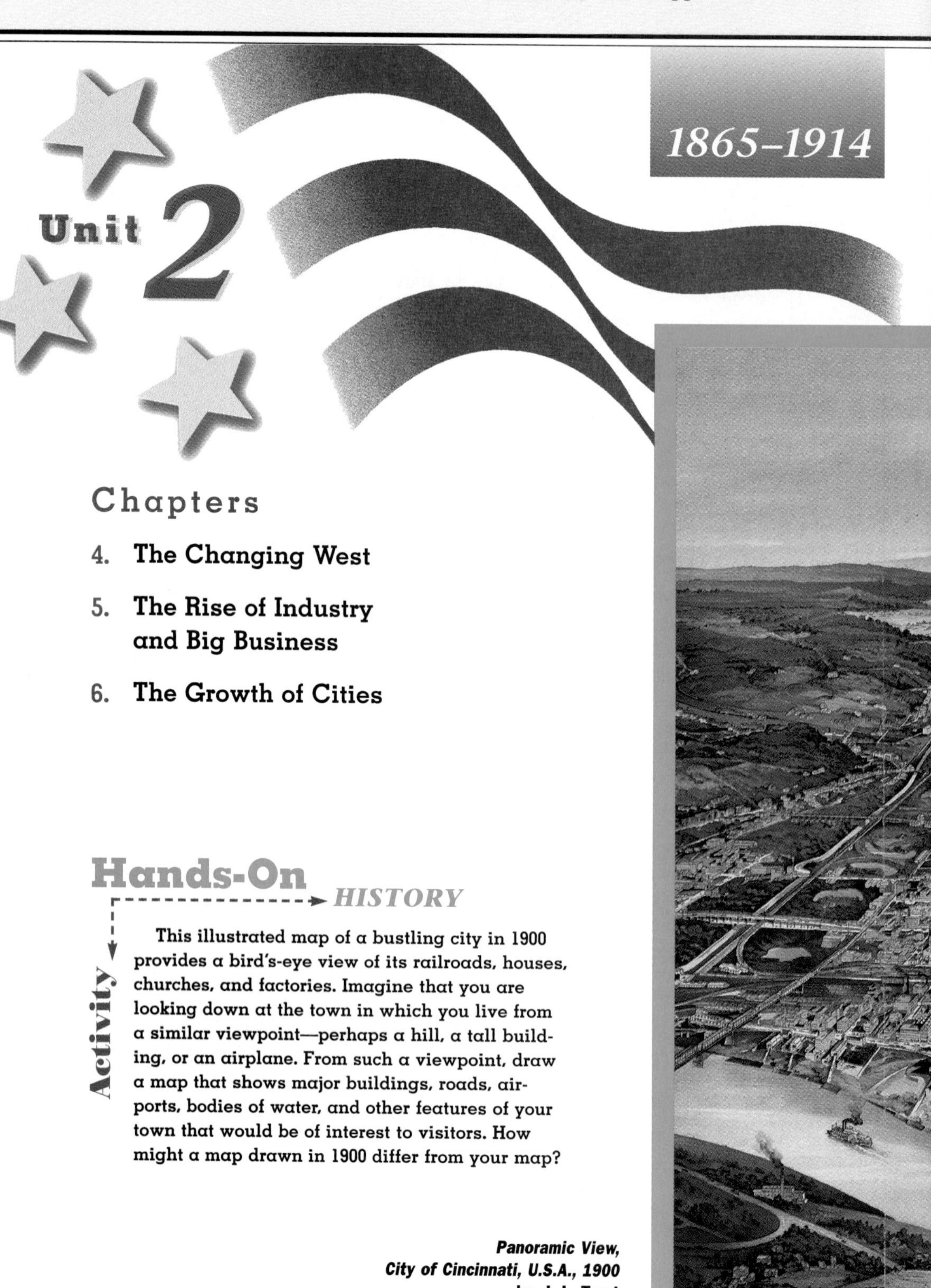

Unit 2

1865–1914

Chapters

Hands-On HISTORY

Activity

This illustrated map of a bustling city in 1900 provides a bird's-eye view of its railroads, houses, churches, and factories. Imagine that you are looking down at the town in which you live from a similar viewpoint—perhaps a hill, a tall building, or an airplane. From such a viewpoint, draw a map that shows major buildings, roads, airports, bodies of water, and other features of your town that would be of interest to visitors. How might a map drawn in 1900 differ from your map?

Panoramic View, City of Cincinnati, U.S.A., 1900 **by J. L. Trout**

History Footnote

As the United States expanded westward, bird's-eye views of new towns became one of the most popular subjects for lithographs. The lithographs were inexpensive yet beautiful and finely detailed prints that many Americans framed to hang in their homes. Each town had a distinctive look, and every artist had his or her own style of portraying it. Often, these lithographs showed idealistic views of cities and towns on perfect summer days, with steam rising from factories, trains, and ships, all symbols of progress and expansion. While these lithographs tend to idealize their subjects, they also serve as accurate historical records of the location of buildings and roads in many cities and towns.

New Horizons

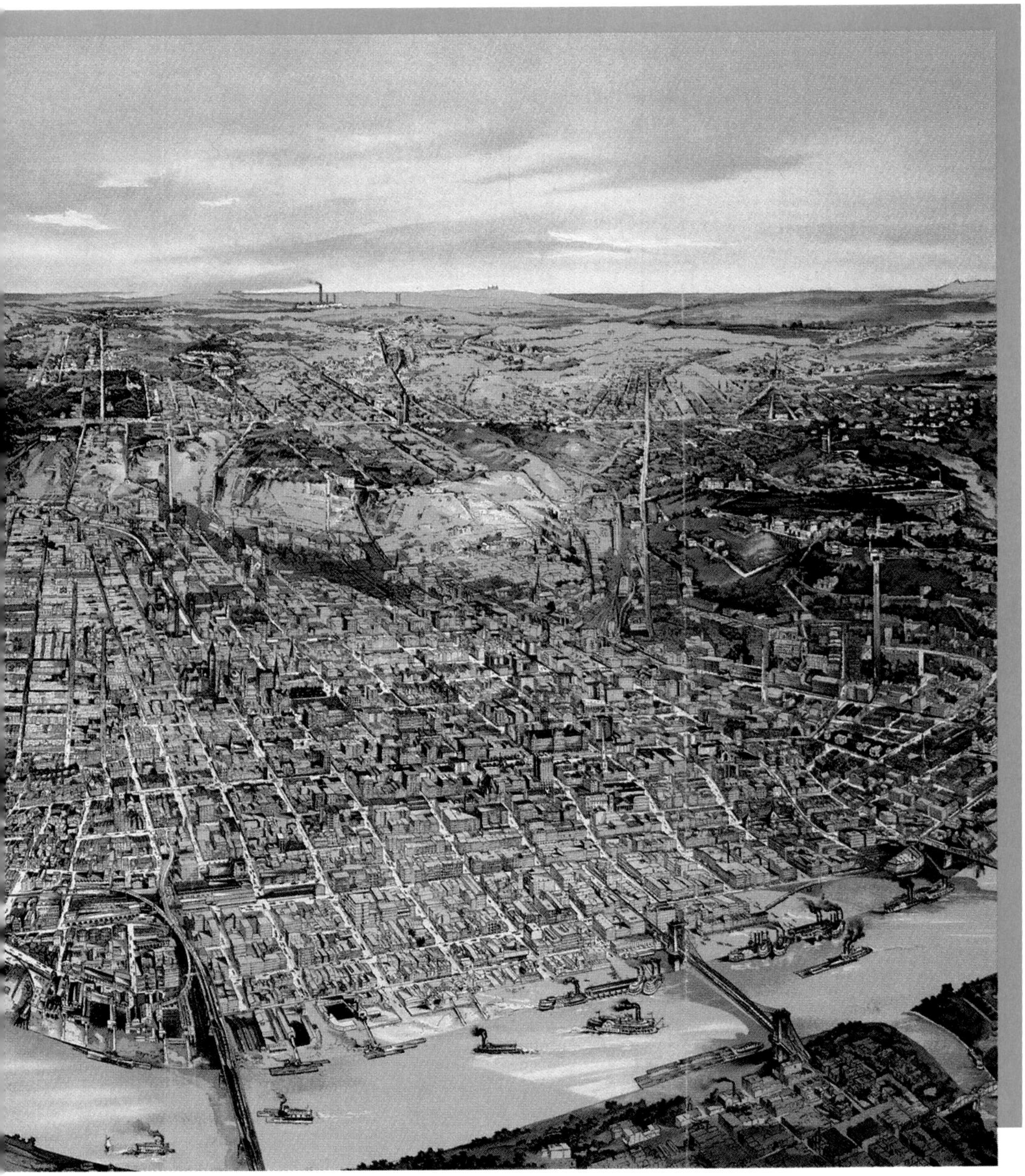

Discussion

Checking Understanding

1. What impression does this lithograph give of Cincinnati in 1900? (Prosperous, huge, expanding, beautiful.)

2. Why is it called a "bird's-eye view"? (The perspective is from a great height, as a bird overhead might see it.)

Stimulating Critical Thinking

3. Would this lithograph be a reliable primary source for a historian who wanted to learn more about the city's layout? Explain. (Yes: it probably shows buildings and streets accurately. No: artist may have changed things to show the city at its best; it is not a photograph.)

4. If you were a resident of Cincinnati in 1900, would you want to buy this print? Explain. (Probably yes—the print displays pride in the city.)

For an in-depth unit project on inventions, see **Interdisciplinary Projects**, pp. 15–24.

See the Unit 2 activity in **Wall Time Line Activities.**

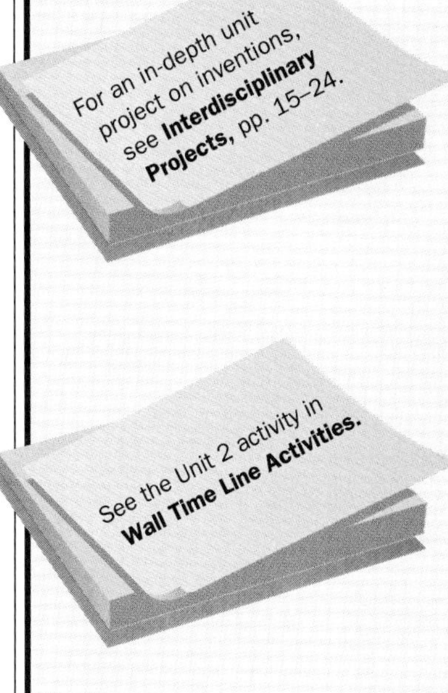

At·a·Glance

4 The Changing West

1865–1900

Chapter Planning Guide

Section	Student Text	Teacher's Edition Activities
Opener and Story pp. 220–223	**Keys to History Time Line** **History Mystery** Beginning the Story with **Quanah Parker**	**Setting the Stage Activity** A Product of Two Cultures, p. 222
1 **Mining and Railroads** pp. 224–229	**Reading Maps** Western Railroads and Mines, p. 228 **Link to Literature** *Dragon's Gate,* pp. 248–249 **Link to the Present** Buffalo make a comeback, p. 229	**Warm-Up Activity** "Translating" Visuals, p. 224 **Geography Question of the Day,** p. 224 **Section Activity** Creating a Book for Young Readers, p. 226 **Bonus Activity** Designing a Railroad Town, p. 228 **Wrap-Up Activity** Writing a Press Release, p. 229
2 **War for the Plains** pp. 230–237	**Link to Art** *Apache Sunrise Ceremony,* p. 231 **Reading Maps** Areas of Indian Warfare, p. 232 **World Link** The plight of the Maoris, p. 234 **Point of View** Why did Congress vote for the Dawes Act?, p. 236 **Geography Lab** A Map that Shows Change, p. 237	**Warm-Up Activity** Analyzing Stereotypes, p. 230 **Geography Question of the Day,** p. 230 **Section Activity** Creating a Picture Time Line, p. 232 **Bonus Activity** Role-Playing Indian Leaders, p. 233 **Wrap-Up Activity** Creating a Pamphlet, p. 236
3 **Cattle and Farming** pp. 238–245	**Hands-On History** Designing a sod house, p. 242 **Skill Lab** Analyzing a Photograph, p. 245	**Warm-Up Activity** A Cowboy Sketch, p. 238 **Geography Question of the Day,** p. 238 **Section Activity** Writing Classified Ads, p. 240 **Bonus Activity** Homestead Posters, p. 241 **Wrap-Up Activity** Drawing an Aerial View, p. 244
Evaluation	**Section 1 Review,** p. 229 **Section 2 Review,** p. 236 **Section 3 Review,** p. 244 **Chapter Survey,** pp. 246–247 **Alternative Assessment** Portraying success and defeat, p. 247	**Answers to Section 1 Review,** p. 229 **Answers to Section 2 Review,** p. 236 **Answers to Section 3 Review,** p. 244 **Answers to Chapter Survey,** pp. 246–247 (Alternative Assessment guidelines are in the Take-Home Planner.)

Teacher's Resource Package

Chapter Summaries: English and Spanish, pp. 44–45

Chapter Resources Binder

Study Guide Using a Graphic Organizer, p. 41

Reinforcement Identifying Headlines, pp. 45–46

American Readings All Aboard!, p. 21

Chapter Resources Binder

Study Guide Using Questions to Guide Reading, p. 42

Geography Extensions Using a Map that Shows Change, pp. 39–40

American Readings Iron Teeth Remembers, pp. 22–23

Chapter Resources Binder

Study Guide Using a Graphic Organizer, p. 43

Skills Development Analyzing a Photograph, pp. 47–48

American Readings A Kansas Homesteader, p. 24

Using Historical Documents The Homestead Application Affidavit of Daniel Freeman, pp. 44–47

Chapter and Unit Tests Chapter 4 Tests, Forms A and B, pp. 43–46

Take-Home Planner

Introducing the Chapter Activity
Reporting on Changes in the West, p. 6

Chapter In-Depth Activity Making a Movie Storyboard, p. 6

Reduced Views

Study Guide, p. 8

Reinforcement, p. 9

American Readings, p. 10

Unit 2 Answers, pp. 30–38

Reduced Views

Study Guide, p. 8

Geography Extensions, p. 11

American Readings, p. 10

Unit 2 Answers, pp. 30–38

Reduced Views

Study Guide, p. 8

Skills Development, p. 9

American Readings, p. 10

Using Historical Documents, p. 11

Unit 2 Answers, pp. 30–38

Reduced Views

Chapter Tests, p. 11

Unit 2 Answers, pp. 30–38

Alternative Assessment Guidelines for scoring the Chapter Survey activity, p. 7

Additional Resources

Wall Time Line

Unit 2 Activity

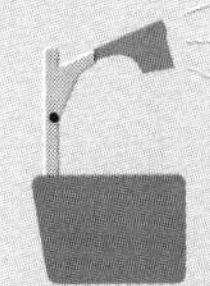

Transparency Package

Transparency 4-1 Map: Western Railroads and Mines—use with Section 1

Transparency 4-2 Hazards of railroad building—use with Section 1

Transparency Activity Book

SelecTest Testing Software

Chapter 4 Test, Forms A and B

Vital Links

Videodisc

CD-ROM

Gold mine (see TE p. 225)

Buffalo heads (see TE p. 226)

"Drill, Ye Tarriers, Drill" (see TE p. 227)

Buffalo soldiers (see TE p. 234)

Sioux dance (see TE p. 234)

Indian students (see TE p. 235)

Chuck wagon (see TE p. 239)

Sod cutters (see TE p. 242)

Swedish store (see TE p. 243)

4

Teaching Resources

Take-Home Planner 2
- Introducing Chapter Activity
- Chapter In-Depth Activity
- Alternative Assessment

Chapter Resources Binder
Geography Extensions
American Readings
Using Historical Documents
Transparency Activities
Wall Time Line Activities
Chapter Summaries
Chapter and Unit Tests
SelecTest Test File
Vital Links CD-ROM/Videodisc

Chapter Objectives

★ Explain how mining and railroads disrupted the lives of Plains Indians.
★ Describe how the Plains Indians tried to hold onto their land.
★ Identify how the Great Plains region was settled by ranchers and farmers.

Chapter Overview

After 1850, miners in search of valuable minerals, and settlers seeking a new life, swept into the Great Plains. Their hunger for land clashed with the nomadic way of life of the Plains Indians, leading to conflict between the two groups. The transcontinental railroad brought more people and supplies, giving rise to new towns. The newcomers' slaughter of millions of buffalo threatened

Time Line

Keys to History
Keys to History journal writing activity is on page 246 in the Chapter Survey.

Homestead Act This law encouraged western settlement by granting 160 acres to anyone who worked the land for five years. (p. 241)

Chisholm Trail Cattle were herded north on trails such as the Chisholm to railroad towns where they were shipped to eastern cities. (pp. 238–239)

Transcontinental railroad completed The linking of eastern and western railroads accelerated the development of the West with easy, cheap transportation. (pp. 226–229)

Looking Back The Georgia militia forced 17,000 Cherokees to move to Indian Territory, the present state of Oklahoma.

World Link See p. 234.

1865–1900

Chapter 4
The Changing West

Sections

Beginning the Story with Quanah Parker
1. Mining and Railroads
2. War for the Plains
3. Cattle and Farming

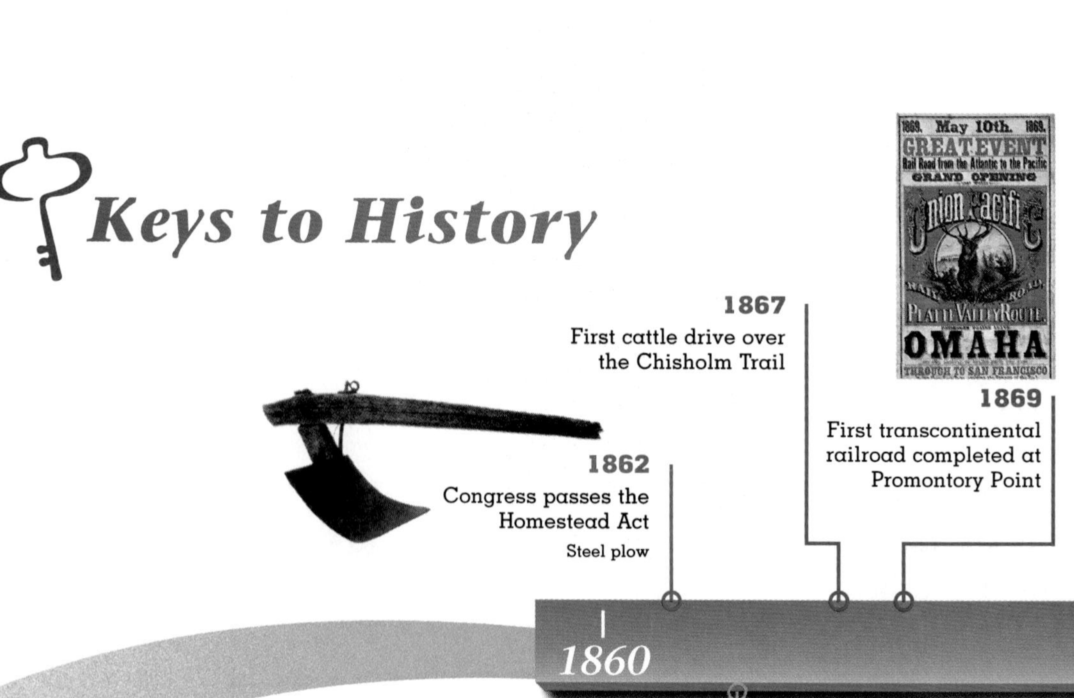

the survival of the Plains Indians.

The government made many treaties with the Plains Indians, but settlers and miners continued to trespass on Indian lands. In 1867 Congress decided to move the Indians to reservations, where they had to change their way of life. Many groups resisted relocation and fought to defend their homelands, but by 1890 the Plains Indians were defeated.

The grasslands of the plains attracted cattle ranchers, who established a booming cattle industry on the plains. Cowhands herded longhorn cattle on long drives across unfenced range to be shipped east at railroad towns. Homesteaders battled severe winters and crop-eating insects as they transformed the dry grassland into farmland, using new farming techniques and inventions.

HISTORY Mystery

In the eastern half of the United States, 160 acres of farmland was plenty to support a family. Farmers with 160 acres on the plains found it hard to survive. Why?

1876
The Battle of the Little Bighorn
Sioux quiver with bow and arrows

1887
Congress passes the Dawes Act

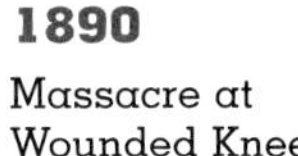

1890
Massacre at Wounded Knee

1895
Only about 1,000 buffalo left in North America

1880

1900

Looking Ahead

Panama Canal opens
1914

Teaching the *HISTORY* Mystery

Students will find the answer on p. 241. See Chapter Survey, p. 246, for additional information and questions.

Time Line

Battle of the Little Bighorn This most famous battle of the Indian Wars was the Indians' last victory. (pp. 232–233)

Dawes Act This law gave plots of land to individual Indian families to farm, in a failed attempt to change their ways of life. (pp. 235–236)

Massacre at Wounded Knee The Seventh Cavalry's slaughter of a small group of Sitting Bull's followers marked the end of more than two decades of resistance by the Plains Indians. (p. 234)

Only 1,000 buffalo left The buffalo were the lifeblood of the Plains Indians. Miners, railroad workers, and settlers killed millions of them for food and sport, almost exterminating the once vast herds. (p. 229)

Looking Ahead In 1914, the Panama Canal made travel from coast to coast much faster and easier, just as the transcontinental railroad did in 1869.

Beginning the Story

Quanah Parker

Quanah Parker was a Comanche chief who took his last name from his white mother. Respected for his wisdom and skill in dealing with white people, he obtained income for his people by allowing Texas cattle ranchers to graze their herds on Comanche lands. A product of two peoples, Quanah became a bridge between two worlds. Today there is a town in Texas named after him.

Setting the Stage Activity

A Product of Two Cultures

To help students consider factors that increase understanding between people of different cultures, have them write a response to this question: How might being raised by parents of two different cultures (or races or religions) affect a person's attitude toward those cultures? Some students can write from personal experience on this topic. Allow five minutes for writing. Then have students share their responses in a class discussion.

See the Introducing the Chapter Activity, Reporting on Changes in the West. **Take-Home Planner 2**, p. 6.

History Footnote

When the Comanches entered the reservation, their only wealth was their horses. In Quanah's vision of the future, cattle would become his people's source of wealth. He planned to raise cattle and lease his land to others to pasture their herds on. He began to learn about cattle raising from experts such as Charles Goodnight. He also developed strong personal friendships with the cattle barons.

The idea of leasing land to the cattlemen led to much discussion among the Kiowa, Comanche, and Apache tribes, who all resided on the same reservation. After their leaders finally agreed to the arrangement—which would provide cash income for the land leased and employment for 54 Indians—Quanah led an Indian delegation to Washington, D.C., to lobby for its approval.

Beginning the Story with Quanah Parker

When Cynthia Ann Parker was a little girl living in Texas in 1836, a Comanche raiding party swooped down on the Parker ranch and carried her off. The Comanches raised Cynthia Ann, calling her Naudah, and in time she forgot her former life. She married a Comanche warrior and had three children. One of them she named Quanah.

When Quanah was still a young boy, Texas Rangers attacked his village and recaptured his mother. Although Cynthia Ann wanted to return to her Comanche family, she was forced to stay with her white relatives in Texas. Several years later she died, some say of a broken heart.

A Comanche Chief

Quanah grew up to become a famous warrior and a chief of his tribe. Although he fought to keep his people free, the Comanches were eventually forced to move onto a reservation in Oklahoma.

Indians looked up to Quanah because he learned how to deal with white people. Speaking of Quanah's wisdom a Comanche man said, "He has things, as it were, written on his tongue. What he learns from the government he writes on his tongue, and we learn from him." Another Comanche said of Quanah, "He is just like light. You strike a match in a dark room and there is light. That is the way with Quanah. Wherever he is there is light."

Although Quanah valued many of the ways of white people, he remained true to Comanche culture. He wore his hair in braids. He also kept several wives, even though the government wanted him to have only one. "You pick out the one who should be my only wife," he challenged when government officials pressed the issue. "I have had children by all my wives. I love them equally and I love my children and care for them equally."

Quanah earned the respect of the government officials. One official said:

History Bookshelf

Smith, Carter. *Native Americans of the West: A Sourcebook on the American West.* Millbrook Press, 1992. This book contains period descriptions and illustrations of the Indians of the West from the collection of the Library of Congress.

Also of interest:

Chu, Daniel, and Bill Shaw. *Going Home to Nicodemus: The Story of an African American Frontier Town and the Pioneers Who Settled It.* Julian Messner/Silver Burdett, 1994.

Elish, Dan. *The Transcontinental Railroad: Triumph of a Dream.* Millbrook Press, 1993.

Neeley, Bill. *The Last Comanche Chief: The Life and Times of Quanah Parker.* Wiley, 1995.

Worcester, Don. *The Chisholm Trail: High Road to the Cattle Kingdom.* University of Nebraska Press, 1980.

Discussion

Thinking Historically

1. In what ways was Quanah Parker a man of two worlds? (Comanche father and white mother; lived among the Comanches but also learned ways of whites.)

2. How did Quanah Parker help his people? (Defended his reservation; obtained income by charging cattlemen for grazing their herds on Comanche land.)

3. What do you think Quanah meant when he said, "We are all the same people anyway"? (Possible answer: we are all human beings, with similar emotions and desires.)

Quanah Parker stands with his wife Tonarcy on the porch of their Oklahoma ranch house.

"If ever nature stamped a man with the seal of headship, she did it in this case. Quanah would have been a leader and a governor in any circle where fate might have cast him. It is in his blood."

Although Quanah had fought to keep settlers off the Comanche reservation, the white people of Texas and Oklahoma respected him, too. They admired his honesty and pride. They saw that he had adapted to changes in the West, yet he always spoke up for his people.

Texas ranchers were especially grateful to Quanah because he allowed them to pasture their livestock on the rich grass of the Comanche reservation. The arrangement gave the Comanches a much-needed income. In appreciation the ranchers built Quanah a large ranch house on the reservation. There he welcomed Indian and white visitors alike.

See the Chapter In-Depth Activity, Making a Movie Storyboard. **Take-Home Planner 2,** p. 6.

A Man of Two Worlds

Quanah's name comes from the Comanche word *kwaina*, which means fragrant. As an adult and after his tribe moved onto the reservation, he added Parker to his name in honor of the mother he had lost. Thereafter, he was known as Quanah Parker, a man of two peoples, a man of two worlds.

Quanah never forgot his mother. He asked to visit her grave in Texas, but her family kept him away. At last, however, the Parker family allowed him to move Cynthia Ann's remains to his home in Oklahoma. There she was reburied in a graveside service conducted by Baptists and Mennonites.

Quanah gave a brief speech of thanks to the many Comanche and white friends who had come to witness the ceremony. He spoke first in Comanche and then in English. Quanah told the hushed crowd that his mother loved Indians so well, she did not want to go back to her white folks. That was all right, he said, because "we are all the same people anyway."

Hands-On HISTORY

Activity

Quanah was the last Comanche chief to surrender to life on a reservation. He became the most successful of Indian chiefs at negotiating with the whites for favorable conditions for his people. As he gave up the skills of the warrior, what new skills do you think Quanah had to develop? List or describe three such skills and explain how each might have been useful to Quanah.

Teaching the Hands-On HISTORY

Before listing skills, have students list the kinds of people that Quanah dealt with and the actions he took.

For a journal writing activity on Quanah Parker, see student page 246.

Introducing the Section

Vocabulary

extermination (p. 229) total destruction

Warm-Up Activity

"Translating" Visuals

To help students begin thinking about new developments on the Great Plains, have them examine each illustration in the section while covering up the caption. Then ask them to write an eye-catching magazine headline about each illustration. Finally, have them read each caption to find out more about what is shown and why it was important.

Geography Question of the Day

Land, gold, and silver were resources that motivated thousands of people to move west. To help students understand the importance of resources to the development of an area, ask them to make a list of the resources in your state that they think have attracted people and companies.

See the Study Guide activity in **Chapter Resources Binder,** p. 41.

Section Objectives

- ★ Explain how life changed for the Plains Indians after 1850.
- ★ Describe how mining affected the West.
- ★ Describe the role of the transcontinental railroad in developing the West.

Teaching Resources

Take-Home Planner 2, pp. 4–11
Chapter Resources Binder
Study Guide, p. 41
Reinforcement, pp. 45–46
Skills Development
Geography Extensions
American Readings, p. 21
Using Historical Documents
Transparency Activities, pp. 27–28
Chapter and Unit Tests

1. Mining and Railroads

Reading Guide

New Term **extermination**

Section Focus **How mining and railroads disrupted the lives of Plains Indians**

1. How did life for Plains Indians change after 1850?
2. How did mining affect the West?
3. What role did the transcontinental railroad play in developing the West?

To the early pioneers, like the mountain men you read about in the Review, the homeland of Quanah Parker and the Plains Indians was little more than endless miles of grass, rattlesnakes, and buffalo. They were content to leave this "desert" to the nomadic Indian tribes who spent their lives on horseback, following the movement of the buffalo.

In the second half of the 1800s, these attitudes changed. Miners swept through the plains looking for valuable minerals. Next came railroad lines, connecting mining towns in the West to cities in the East and Midwest. Settlers soon followed.

Suddenly the "Great American Desert" became more than just a wasteland to be crossed on the way to the Far West. It was a place of opportunity for settlers. This was a problem for the Plains Indians who already lived there. Their way of life clashed with the settlers' hunger for land, and before long conflicts between the two groups broke out.

John Mix Stanley was traveling with an army survey party when he saw this herd of bison. Such large herds had vanished by the 1880s.

History Footnote

The Plains Indians used virtually every part of the buffalo for most of their daily needs. The meat of one large buffalo could feed 100 people. Much of the meat was preserved by cutting it into strips and hanging it in the sun. Liver, brains, and other organs spoiled quickly, so were eaten at the site of the kill.

The hide, which belonged to the hunter, was made into items such as winter coats, caps, pants, tepees, shoes, and saddlebags. Rawhide from the neck of the buffalo was stretched to make tough war shields. Muscles were made into strings for bows and thread, and hair was braided into rope. Buffalo stomachs could be used to carry water, and tails were fashioned into fly swatters. Hooves were boiled to make soap and glue. Even buffalo droppings were used as fuel for cooking fires.

Buffalo on the Plains

Before the settlers came, the Great Plains supported some 30 different Indian tribes. The region was also home to millions of bison, usually called "buffalo."

These large, shaggy creatures were the lifeblood of the Plains Indians. They provided the Indians with food, shelter, tools, ornaments, and even toys. When Plains Indians died they expected to go to a land teeming with buffalo. Some said the broad trail of stars across the sky that we call the Milky Way was dust raised by the hoofs of buffalo herds in the spirit world.

The Fort Laramie Treaty

In the 1850s miners swarmed across the Great Plains on their way to the countless river valleys and mountains of the West. As they went they trespassed on Plains Indian land, trampling the buffalo range and killing the animals for food and sometimes just for sport. The Indians resented the miners and their disrespect for the Indian way of life. They began to wage war.

In an attempt to reduce conflict and protect the travelers, the government decided to strike a bargain with the Indians. In 1851 government officials met with between 8,000 and 12,000 Indians from 8 tribes at Fort Laramie, in what is now Wyoming. There the officials convinced the Indian representatives to sign the Treaty of Fort Laramie.

The treaty gave the government the right to build more roads and forts on the plains. It also defined geographical boundaries within which the Indian tribes could hunt. The government agreed to make yearly payments to the Indians, and promised the tribes that they could live and hunt on this land forever. As you will read, Fort Laramie was the first of many treaties that the United States government made with the Plains Indians—but did not honor.

Government officials and Indian leaders met at Fort Laramie in 1851 and again in 1868, above, to try to bring peace to the plains.

Western Mines

In the 1860s miners continued to cross the plains in full force, desperately hunting for gold. No spot was too hot, too dry, too cold, or too wet to discourage people hoping to strike it rich. Miners swarmed through the Rockies, the Sierra Nevada, and the Black Hills. They braved the scorching sands of Arizona and New Mexico as well as the frosty waters of Alaska.

The Comstock Lode One of the biggest finds was in Nevada in 1859. A group of miners had found a little gold on a hillside, but were frustrated by dark blue sand and a gummy soil that slowed their work. When they had the soil tested, the men got the shock of their lives. The soil was almost pure silver. The gold and silver ore in the deposit was worth $3,200 to $4,800 a ton.

The find was called the Comstock Lode for Henry Comstock, a prospector who bragged that he had discovered it all. Comstock's

Developing the Section

Discussion

Checking Understanding

1. Why was the buffalo vital to the Plains Indians' way of life? (It provided for many of their needs, including food, shelter, and tools.)

2. What were two promises that the U.S. government made to the Plains Indians in the Fort Laramie Treaty? (It promised yearly payments for land and that the tribes could live and hunt on the land forever.)

Stimulating Critical Thinking

3. If you had been one of the Indian representatives at the Fort Laramie meeting, would you have supported the treaty? Why or why not? (Yes: defined boundaries could help prevent trespassing; conflict would be reduced; government is trustworthy. No: hunting lands would be limited; new roads and forts would bring more settlers and miners; government is not trustworthy.)

Vital Links

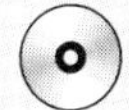

Gold mine (Picture)
Unit 3, Side 1,
Search 41648

See also Unit 3 Explore CD-ROM location 266.

Connections to Economics

Most prospectors did not get rich from mining, but many storekeepers did. As thousands of hopeful miners streamed west, the combination of too many people and too few supplies made prices skyrocket. Storekeepers sold pork, which cost about 50¢ a pound in the East, for $5 a pound or more. A loaf of bread that cost a few cents back East went for $2. A pair of boots cost $20 as opposed to $2.50, and a mule to haul supplies could set a miner back as much as $200. Most miners considered a half ounce to an ounce of gold a day as the bare minimum required to support themselves. Gold sold for $16 an ounce, so any profits were used up quickly in food and supplies.

Section Activity

Creating a Book for Young Readers

To underscore effects of mining and railroads on the Plains Indians, have small groups create a nonfiction book for first- or second-graders. Have each group write and illustrate a chapter for the book, based on one of the section headings. Members should divide up the tasks—art, research, writing, and editing. Then have all the groups work together to organize their chapters into a book and to create a cover and a title. Have students share the book with a first- or second-grade class.

See the Reinforcement activity in **Chapter Resources Binder,** pp. 45–46.

Vital Links

Buffalo heads (Picture)
Unit 3, Side 1,
Search 43373

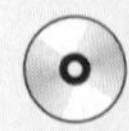
See also Unit 3 Explore CD-ROM location 303.

claims were only a small part of one of the richest mineral fields ever found in the West. Comstock sold one claim for only $11,000 and another for two mules. Eventually, the Comstock Lode made others very wealthy. It produced more than $300 million in gold and silver.

Comstock's story was not unusual. Individual prospectors—people who search for gold and silver and other precious ores—rarely got rich. It took expensive machinery and skilled mining engineers to extract the valuable minerals that lay like gigantic spider webs within the mountains of the West. The people who made the great mining fortunes were investors in large companies that bought the rights to the mines from the prospectors who discovered them.

Boomtowns

Despite the odds against striking it rich, hordes of hopeful prospectors rushed to each new site. Within days, mining camps would spring up in areas that had been mostly barren and desolate land. The camps were little more than tents and shacks built in a matter of days. They were known as "boom and bust" towns, because when the gold or silver was gone they disappeared as quickly as they had appeared.

The cycle of boom and bust repeated itself over and over. In 1857 newspaperman J. Ross Browne described the creation of Gila City in present-day Arizona:

> "Enterprising men hurried to the spot with barrels of whiskey and billiards tables, . . . ready-made clothing, and fancy wares. Traders crowded in with wagons of pork and beans. Gamblers came with cards and Monte [gambling] tables. There was everything in Gila City within a few months but a church and a jail."

Seven years later Gila City was a ghost town. All that remained, Browne wrote, were "three chimneys and a coyote."

Although most prospectors got little more than calluses on their hands for their efforts, they did leave behind a legacy of colorful place names such as Ground Hog's Glory, Miller's Defeat, Bogus Thunder, Poverty, and Deadman's Bar. A few of these boomtowns, such as Denver and Reno, survived the cycle and grew into cities.

Justice in the mining camps Keeping order in the mining camps was a challenge. Gold strikes meant quick money, which attracted gamblers, thieves, and outlaws. Crime and fighting were common. Many towns had no jails, so the options for punishment were often banishment, whipping, or death. One young man in California wrote a letter describing his fate:

> "Dear Friend:
> I take this opportunity of writing these few lines to you hoping to find you in good health me and Charley is sentenced to be hung today at 5 o'clock for a robbery good by give my best to Frank and Sam and Church.
> John Bucroft"

Placerville, California, held so many hangings it was called "Hangtown." In Montana, citizens hanged a sheriff when they learned he was the leader of an outlaw gang. They also hanged 24 members of the gang.

The Transcontinental Railroad

As more and more Americans settled in the West, they needed fast and reliable transportation to carry people and supplies back and forth. In 1862 President Lincoln signed the Pacific Railway Bill. It called for a

Tips for Teaching

Visual Learners

Visual learners benefit from drawings or diagrams that illustrate a concept. As you discuss the transcontinental railroad, draw a large outline map of the United States on the chalkboard. Ask a student to draw a train track that runs from east to west and to place and label a Central Pacific train on the western track and a Union Pacific train on the eastern track. Ask questions to elicit facts about the construction of each railroad. Have volunteers take turns writing the facts under the appropriate portion of track. If information applies to both sides, have them write it in a central area between the two trains.

In 1860—two years after prospectors discovered gold in the area—Denver's population was 4,500. A railroad line completed in 1870 helped the town grow as a supply center for nearby mines. Today, Denver is the chief commercial city of the Rocky Mountain area.

transcontinental railroad linking the Atlantic and Pacific coasts. Trains on this line could cross the country in just one week instead of taking a whole month, as stagecoaches had.

The transcontinental railroad was to be built by the Union Pacific and the Central Pacific railroad companies. To help the companies pay for the huge project, the government donated the land for the tracks and gave the companies sections of free land in return for every mile of track they laid. The government also loaned the companies money at low interest rates.

The Union Pacific began building westward from Omaha, Nebraska. The Central Pacific started in Sacramento, California. The two companies raced to see which could lay the most track—and earn the most free land from the government.

Building the railroad Building the transcontinental railroad was dangerous, backbreaking, and low-paying work. The two crews laid from 2 to 5 miles (3 to 8 km) of track each day, and it took them 6 years to finish the project.

Most of the workers were immigrants to the United States, eager for work. The Union Pacific employed as many as 10,000 laborers from Ireland. They had to fight off numerous attacks by Plains Indians who resented the workers for trespassing. They also had to cut through the Rocky Mountains.

The Central Pacific hired about 10,000 men as well, most of whom were Chinese. They learned about the project through pamphlets the company handed out in China. Central Pacific workers dynamited tunnels through solid rock. They marked their progress in inches a day as they laid track across the snowcapped Sierra Nevada. One winter they shoveled a path through drifts of snow 50 feet (15 meters) deep to lay track on the frozen ground.

Discussion

Checking Understanding

1. How did mining create a need for railroads in the West? (Miners needed faster and more reliable transportation to bring food and supplies from the East.)

2. Why was it easier for mining companies to make more money than individual prospectors? (Companies could mine on a large scale and also afford the equipment and labor needed to mine large areas.)

Stimulating Critical Thinking

3. Why do you think some boomtowns survived and some did not? (Answers will vary but should include that resources other than minerals, such as water, fertile farmland, and so on, were most likely available in towns that survived.)

For a fictional account of a 15-year-old Chinese boy's experiences as a railroad worker in California, see the Link to Literature on pages 248–249.

Vital Links

"Drill, Ye Tarriers, Drill" (Song) Unit 3, Side 2, Search 11145 Play 13322

See also Unit 3 Explore CD-ROM location 340.

Bonus Activity

Designing a Railroad Town

To convey how the building of railroads led to the growth of towns, divide the class into groups and give each group chart paper to design a railroad town. Tell students to assume that the town started as a boomtown, but soon grew due to the railroad. Each group should brainstorm businesses and services to include and where to locate them. Then have students draw the railroad tracks, label locations of businesses, and create a name for their town. Have groups compare and discuss their designs and town names.

Teaching the Reading Maps

To help students understand the orientation of railroad routes, ask: **Does it look like more miles of track go east-west or north-south? Why do you think this is so?** (East-west; demand for travel from the eastern part of the country to the West was much higher than demand for north-south travel within the less-developed West.) **Answers to Reading Maps:** Great Northern; Northern Pacific; Atlantic and Pacific/Atchison, Topeka, and Santa Fe; Southern Pacific. Students should name every city on map.

History Footnote

When Americans learned that the last spike had been hammered into the transcontinental railroad, church bells rang, cannons fired, and people danced in the streets. In cities across the nation, from New York to San Francisco, happy crowds celebrated the new unity of the nation. It was one of the biggest nationwide celebrations since the British surrendered at Yorktown, Virginia, in 1781.

Western Railroads and Mines

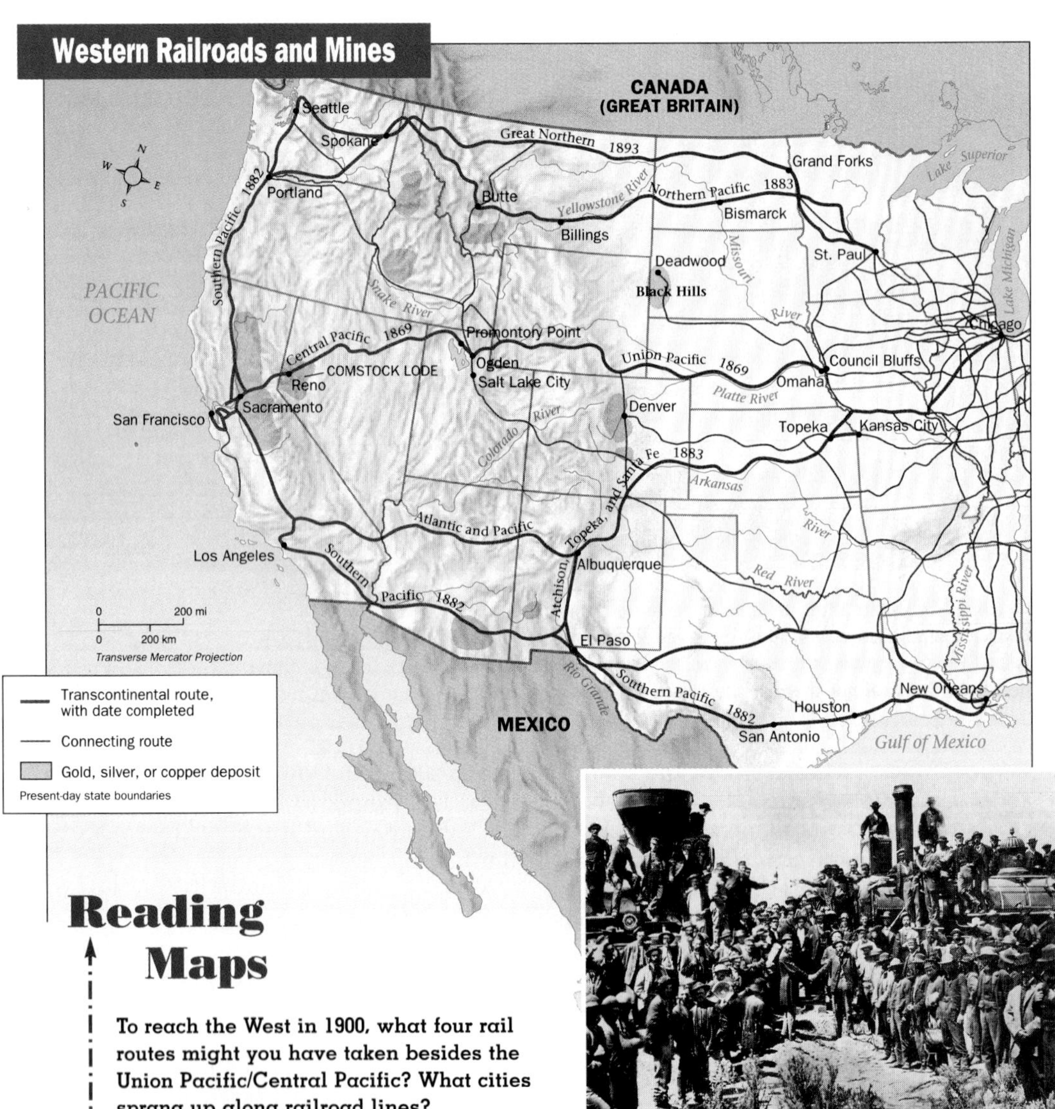

Workmen and officials celebrate the railroad they said "unites the two great oceans of the world."

Reading Maps

To reach the West in 1900, what four rail routes might you have taken besides the Union Pacific/Central Pacific? What cities sprang up along railroad lines?

Promontory Point On May 10, 1869, the job was finally finished. The Union Pacific engine No. 119 met the Central Pacific's Jupiter at Promontory Point, Utah. Union Pacific had laid 1,086 miles (1,747 km) to Central Pacific's 689 (1,109 km).

Leland Stanford, president of the Central Pacific, marked the occasion by driving a gold spike that linked the two sets of tracks. As Stanford's hammer hit the spike, a telegraph wire connected to it relayed the news of the event to Americans across the nation.

History Footnote

Travelers on the transcontinental railroad could travel economically or in high style. The basic fare from Omaha to Seattle was about $40. The cheapest cars, called "emigrant cars," were fitted with bare wooden seats. Each car had a wood stove as well as toilets and sinks. Trains stopped for meals at railroad stations where passengers often dined on buffalo meat.

"First-class" fare was about $35 more and offered padded seats and more room for sleeping. For a few dollars more, passengers could make the trip in a luxurious Pullman Palace Car where they could relax in compartments with padded seats that converted to beds. Each compartment was furnished with reading lamps and carpeting. Dining cars served elegant meals and some even offered entertainment.

Settlers on the plains Railroad lines transformed the country. They offered easy, inexpensive transportation to a new life and new opportunities. Thousands of settlers took advantage of these opportunities, moving their families from crowded eastern cities to the great empty spaces of the Great Plains. Settlements and towns quickly sprang up along the tracks.

The End of the Buffalo

The Plains Indians depended on the buffalo. Yet as miners, railroad workers, and settlers traveled across the Great Plains, they slaughtered millions of the animals.

Railroad companies hired hunters to shoot buffalo to feed their workers. William F. Cody earned his nickname, "Buffalo Bill," by slaughtering 4,000 buffalo in 8 months. Sometimes passengers on the trains would shoot buffalo from the windows just for amusement, leaving the remains to rot.

By 1895 the buffalo faced **extermination**—total destruction. Where once there had been 50 million buffalo in North America, only about a thousand were left. The extermination of the buffalo was disastrous for the Plains Indians. A Lakota Sioux warrior said of the white hunters:

> "Our living was their sport, and if you look at it one way, they might as well have been killing us as the buffalo."

The Plains Indians could not stop the government, which had parceled out more than 150 billion acres of land to the railroad companies, nor the settlers, who were building homes on the plains. Government officials and settlers often ignored the Fort Laramie Treaty and other agreements. As a result, Indian tribes lost much of their land. As you will read, the conflict led to decades of warfare on the plains.

Link to the Present

Buffalo make a comeback Thanks to the efforts of early conservationists, the buffalo were not completely wiped out. Today about 200,000 live on public lands and private ranches. Ranchers have discovered that buffalo are hardy and easy to raise. Consumers have discovered that buffalo meat tastes good and has less fat and cholesterol than some other meats.

To modern-day Lakotas and other Plains Indians, the buffalo is sacred, as it was to their ancestors. Members of the InterTribal Bison Cooperative raise buffalo for ceremonial purposes as well as for food and income.

The cooperative, which represents more than 30 tribes in 15 states, is also working to save the buffalo at Yellowstone National Park. The herd is threatened with slaughter because nearby ranchers fear it will spread disease to cattle, though there have been no proven cases.

1. Section Review

1. Define **extermination.**
2. What problems did Plains Indians face in the 1870s?
3. Why did so few miners strike it rich? Who did become rich from mining?
4. How did the transcontinental railroad change the way people thought about moving west?
5. Critical Thinking Imagine that you lived in a boomtown in the 1860s. What are some ways, besides mining for gold, that you could make a living?

Teaching the

Link to the Present

Point out that buffalo exist in national parks, ranches, preserves, and zoos. Ask how ranchers, Native Americans, and conservationists each might view the importance of buffalo. (Selling meat; ceremonial uses, food; preservation, education.)

Closing the Section

Wrap-Up Activity

Writing a Press Release

To review the railroad's impact, have students write press releases about the gold spike. Have one-third write as railroad employees, another third as settlers or miners, and the others as Plains Indians.

Section Review Answers

1. Definition: *extermination* (229)

2. Miners trespassing; building of roads, forts, railroads, and towns on hunting grounds; settlers claiming land; slaughter of buffalo.

3. Few could afford machinery or pay engineers. Investors who bought rights became rich.

4. Railroads made it easy and inexpensive to travel.

5. Run a clothing or food store, own a saloon, sell prospecting supplies.

Introducing the Section

Vocabulary

reservations (p. 230) areas of land set aside for Indian nations

Warm-Up Activity

Analyzing Stereotypes

To help students distinguish fact from fiction when thinking about the Plains Indians, have them list examples of negative images and stereotypes of Indians in the popular media. Then have them analyze how their examples are stereotypic. They may consider Hollywood movies, TV, novels, advertising, sports logos, and so on.

Geography Question of the Day

To introduce students to the geographical area covered by this section, have them look at the map on page 232 and list the present-day states that make up the Great Plains. Have them place a star by the name of each state where Indian battles took place.

See the Study Guide activity in **Chapter Resources Binder**, p. 42.

Section Objectives

- ★ Identify the events that threatened the survival of the Plains Indians.
- ★ Explain why people trespassed on Indian land and describe how the Indians reacted.
- ★ Describe the government's policies toward Plains Indians.

Teaching Resources

Take-Home Planner 2, pp. 4–11
Chapter Resources Binder
Study Guide, p. 42
Reinforcement
Skills Development
Geography Extensions, pp. 13–14
American Readings, pp. 22–23
Using Historical Documents
Transparency Activities
Chapter and Unit Tests

2. War for the Plains

Reading Guide

New Term reservations

Section Focus How the Plains Indians tried to hold onto their land

1. **What events threatened the survival of the Plains Indians?**
2. **Why did people keep trespassing on Indian land and how did Indians react?**
3. **What were the government's policies toward Plains Indians?**

In 1874 Quanah Parker and 700 Indian warriors attacked a group of hunters camped in a deserted Texas trading post called Adobe Walls. The hunters had been killing buffalo by the thousands for their hides, which they sold for leather.

The hunters had such superior weapons that they won the fight easily. Quanah Parker was wounded in the shoulder, and his horse was killed. This battle was just one of many conflicts that raged across the plains for the next two decades. Sometimes called the Indian Wars, they pitted Plains Indians, fighting for their land, against the United States Army, sent to make the plains safe for travelers and settlers.

The Sand Creek Massacre

The extermination of the buffalo was one thing that destroyed the way of life of the Plains Indians. Miners passing through the plains was another. In 1859 miners found gold near Pikes Peak in Colorado. By the end of that year, 100,000 miners were trespassing on land promised to the Cheyenne and Arapaho Indians in the Fort Laramie Treaty eight years before.

The government tried to negotiate a new treaty, but the Indians were filled with resentment over the broken treaty. They refused to sell their land. Parties of Cheyennes and Arapahos attacked wagon trains, stagecoaches, and mining camps.

Hoping to restore order, the governor of the Colorado Territory put together a military force. In November 1864 Colonel John Chivington led his soldiers in a surprise attack on a peaceful Cheyenne village camped at Sand Creek. Chief Black Kettle waved an American flag and then a white flag of truce, but Chivington attacked.

General Nelson A. Miles later called the Sand Creek Massacre the "foulest and most unjustifiable crime in the annals [history] of America." More than 200 Cheyenne men, women, and children were brutally slaughtered. Word of the massacre spread among the Indians, stiffening their determination to resist the oncoming settlers.

Reservations

Wars raged across the Great Plains throughout the 1860s. Indians continued to raid white settlements and wagon trains, and settlers continued to ignore boundaries and pass through areas set aside for Indians.

In 1867 Congress decided that the best way to end the fighting was to separate Indians and settlers. To do this the federal government would create **reservations**—areas of land set aside for Indian nations—and force Indians to move onto them.

Connections to Civics

A *treaty* is a binding agreement between two nations covering governmental rights, human rights, and property rights. By signing treaties, the federal government of the United States recognized the sovereignty (self-rule) of Indian tribes.

Today the limited sovereignty of tribes is much like that of states. The tribes have powers to govern themselves, but only under federal regulations. Tribes have the right to regulate membership; make laws; establish courts and police; enforce laws and administer justice; remove nonmembers from tribal property; levy taxes on members; and regulate land use, including resource development, environmental protection, and hunting and fishing. Most govern by a form of council, and many have written constitutions and legal codes.

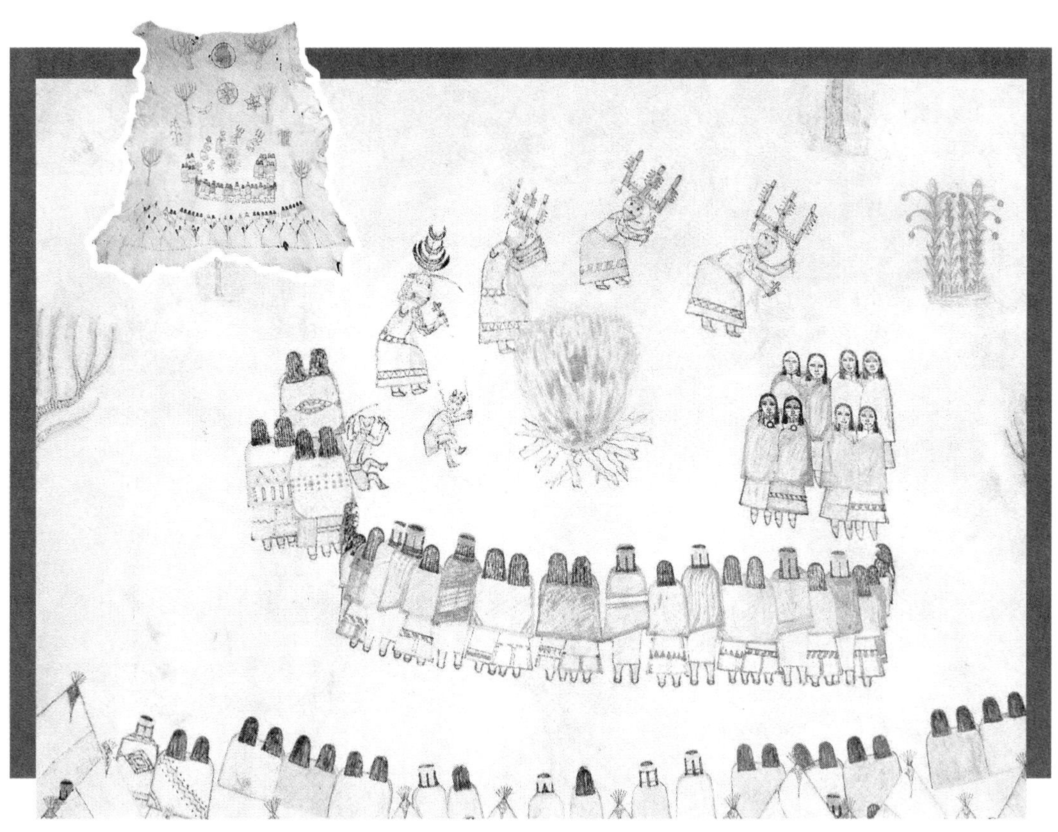

Link to Art

Apache Sunrise Ceremony (1890s) With vegetable dyes on doeskin, Naiche, son of Chief Cochise, preserved the memory of an Apache Sunrise Ceremony. At this coming-of-age celebration, people give thanks that young girls have reached womanhood safely. In the painting seven girls dance, each wrapped in a blanket with the older woman who is her guardian. Dancers on the far side of the fire represent spirits from a nearby mountain. **Discuss** What other times in peoples' lives are important enough to mark with special events, documents, or pictures?

The reservation system forced Plains Indians to change their way of life. Instead of living as nomads and hunting buffalo, they had to settle on specific pieces of land and raise crops. Many people expected the Indians to give up their old ways and learn the customs of the settlers. Beginning in 1867 a number of tribes, doomed without buffalo to hunt, signed treaties and tried to adapt to life on reservations.

Developing the Section

Discussion

Checking Understanding

1. How did the Pikes Peak gold rush affect the Plains Indians? (Miners trespassed on Cheyenne and Arapaho lands; Cheyennes and Arapahos retaliated; Sand Creek Massacre followed.)

Stimulating Critical Thinking

2. How do you think Plains Indians of the 1860s might have defined the word *reservation*? (Definitions may reflect the confining nature of being forced to stay on a reservation, the different way of life, or safety from the U.S. Army.)

Teaching the Link to Art

Point out that the ceremony depicted celebrates the time when a young person becomes an adult. Such celebrations often occur around the age of 13, or when a child reaches maturity. Point out that many cultures, both ancient and modern, have coming-of-age rituals. Ask students to think of different ways that coming of age is marked in our society (for example, the Jewish bar mitzvah). Then have them describe details of the Apache ritual as shown in the doeskin painting. **Discussion Answers:** Some possibilities are birthdays, graduation, marriage, births of children, and death.

Section
Activity

Creating a Picture Time Line

To present an overview of the struggle of the Plains Indians and its outcome, groups of students can create picture time lines. Students should include at least seven events mentioned in this section and cover the period from 1850 to 1900 (setting benchmark years every ten years). After placing each event in its appropriate place on the time line, they should draw pictures depicting each event. Have them display their time lines for comparison and discussion.

Teaching the Reading Maps

To help students focus on the map, ask: **What landforms were the Indian Wars fought on?** (mountains, plains) **Answer to Reading Maps:** 1854–1890.

For a Cheyenne woman's account of encounters with settlers, see **American Readings,** pp. 22–23.

History Footnote

Sitting Bull was an influential and respected Sioux leader who strongly defended the Indian way of life and felt total distrust and hostility toward white people. From the age of 14 he fought bravely in numerous battles and became known for his courage and wisdom. His role later became that of medicine man, and the Sioux intently listened to everything he said. While he did not actually fight at the Battle of the Little Bighorn, he prepared the Indians for the battle by performing a sun dance during which he entered into a deep trance and saw soldiers attacking. He remained at the village during the battle, but it was his inspiration and his warning to fight to kill that helped the Indians to win the battle.

Red Cloud's War

In 1863 gold was discovered in Montana, and miners poured in. Most took the Bozeman Trail, which branched off of the Oregon Trail. It led to the mines by cutting through the homeland of the Teton Sioux Indians. Angry Teton Sioux warriors attacked mining parties as they trespassed on Sioux land. To guard the Bozeman Trail, the government built three forts.

Red Cloud, a capable and strong-willed chief, was determined to protect the Teton Sioux homeland at all costs. He, as well as Crazy Horse, led his warriors in repeated attacks on travelers along the trail. After months of conflict and the death of 80 soldiers, the federal government finally agreed to abandon the forts. In 1868, as soldiers left the forts, Red Cloud signed a peace agreement—the Second Treaty of Fort Laramie.

Although Red Cloud's War was a victory for the Plains Indians, the treaty he signed established a reservation for northern Plains Indians that covered much of present-day Montana, Wyoming, and the Dakotas—the Great Sioux Reserve. Red Cloud hated to move his people onto a reservation, but he was satisfied that he had accomplished the goal of saving his people's homeland for all time.

Areas of Indian Warfare

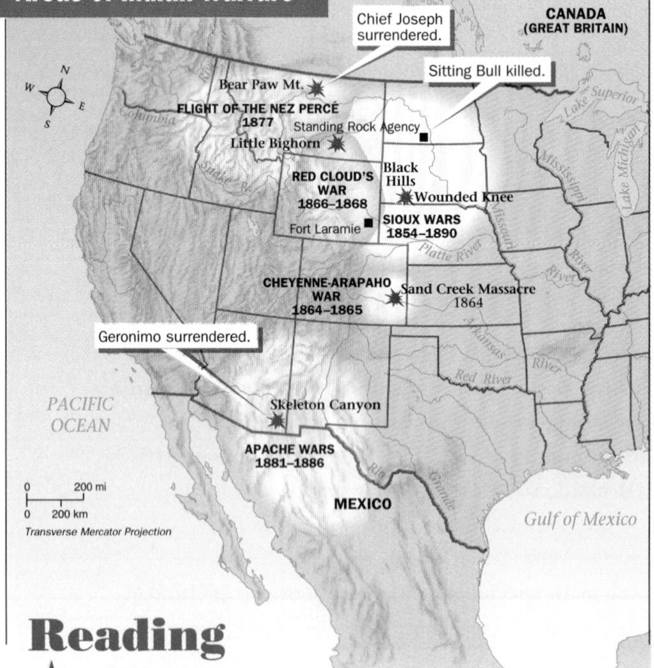

Reading Maps

The map represents some of the many conflicts in the wars for the West. During what period of time did those conflicts take place?

The Battle of the Little Bighorn

The peace brought by the Second Treaty of Fort Laramie was short-lived. When prospectors found gold in the Black Hills in 1874, hundreds of miners flocked to the site even though it was on Sioux and Cheyenne hunting grounds. Angry warriors attacked mining camps, so the government ordered all the Sioux and Cheyenne bands onto reservations. When leaders of the several Indian bands refused, the government sent the United States Army against them.

Custer's Last Stand The result of this poorly thought-out campaign was the Battle of the Little

Connections to Geography

The original homeland of the Nez Percés was a huge area bounded on the west by the Cascades, on the east by the Bitterroots, and on the south by the 44th and 46th parallels. Since the Nez Percés lived by hunting and gathering, they often traveled far beyond these bounds as well.

Food gathering was an activity shared by the whole family. Generally, men hunted for large animals while women and children trapped small ones, fished, and gathered roots and berries. The most important food was the fat root of the camas, a type of lily. These nutritious bulbs could be eaten raw or roasted, mashed, and formed into loaves.

One of the major hunting trails of the Nez Percés followed the Salmon River. It was here that miners discovered gold, leading to an invasion of Nez Percé lands.

Bighorn, on June 25, 1876. Along the banks of the Little Bighorn River, in present-day Montana, Sioux and Cheyenne warriors led by Sitting Bull, Crazy Horse, Two Moons, and Lame White Man destroyed the 7th Cavalry commanded by Lieutenant Colonel George Armstrong Custer.

The Battle of the Little Bighorn is the most famous battle of the Indian Wars. It was a great victory for the Indians—but it was their last. Before another year had passed, most of the Sioux and Cheyennes had been defeated in battle or had moved onto reservations. Crazy Horse was captured and murdered, while Sitting Bull escaped to Canada with a handful of followers.

Chief Joseph's Retreat

The next year the Nez Percé Indians of Oregon, Washington, and Idaho found themselves under increasing pressure from settlers who wanted their land. Although most of the Nez Percés eventually signed a treaty and moved to a reservation, some refused to do so. A group of young Nez Percés, resentful at being forced off their land, attacked and killed four settlers.

The Nez Percés' Chief Joseph, though, wanted to avoid war. Joseph, with White Bird and Looking Glass, led some 800 men, women, and children in an amazing retreat. For three and a half months and almost 2,000 miles (3,218 km) they traveled the Lolo Trail over the Bitterroot Range—the route Lewis and Clark had taken 75 years earlier to reach the Pacific. The Nez Percés hoped to reach Canada to join Sitting Bull.

Chief Joseph

Throughout their ordeal the Nez Percés behaved with honor, paying for supplies and doing little harm to settlers. They might have made it all the way had they not stopped to rest some 40 miles from the border. It was there that federal troops caught up with them. About 300 of the Nez Percés managed to escape into Canada. On a bitterly cold October day, the rest, including Chief Joseph, surrendered. He told the soldiers:

> "I am tired of fighting. My heart is sick and sad. From where the sun now stands, I will fight no more forever."

The Nez Percés who surrendered were sent to Oklahoma. A few years later they were allowed to join their relatives on the Nez Percé reservation in Idaho.

Geronimo's Maneuvers

By 1881 most Indians were living on reservations. An exception was a small group of Apaches who were determined to hold onto their freedom. Led by Geronimo, the band roamed the mountains of Arizona and New Mexico, as well as northern Mexico. Although government soldiers tracked this group closely, it took them five years to capture the Indians.

By 1886 Geronimo's group had declined from 150 to a few dozen men, women, and children. These Apaches had successfully evaded 5,000 United States troops and 3,000 Mexican soldiers.

End of the Indian Wars When Geronimo's group finally surrendered in 1886, a generation of Indian wars ended. The group moved onto a reservation. Geronimo himself was imprisoned for two years and lived out the rest of his life in exile in Florida and Oklahoma, never to return to his homeland.

Discussion

Checking Understanding

1. What caused Red Cloud's War and what was the result? (Cause: miners traveled on a trail through the homeland of the Teton Sioux. Result: Red Cloud forced government troops to leave area. He saved his homeland by signing a treaty that set up a large reservation in the Northwest.)

Stimulating Critical Thinking

2. If you were an Apache in 1881, would you have joined Geronimo in fighting for your freedom? Explain. (Yes: reservation system is unfair; it is better to stand up for one's freedom. No: reservations offer the only way to survive.)

Bonus Activity

Role-Playing Indian Leaders

To explore the dilemma of the Plains Indians—to continue fighting or to accept reservation life—have small groups role-play a meeting of Sioux or Cheyenne leaders in 1870. Encourage students to support their opinions with facts from the text. Role-plays should reflect diverse ideas, and groups should report to the class any conclusions they reached.

Teaching the

World  Link

Help students find New Zealand on a world map. Ask if they can think of other times in history when a greatly outnumbered people with less-sophisticated weapons stood up against powerful people who wanted their land. Have them discuss how religion might help people during times like this.

Vital Links

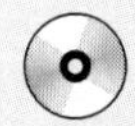
Buffalo soldiers (Picture) Unit 3, Side 1, Search 43559

See also Unit 3 Explore CD-ROM location 334.

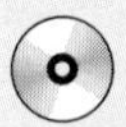
Sioux dance (Picture) Unit 3, Side 1, Search 47372

See also Unit 3 Explore CD-ROM location 361.

History Footnote

According to a Lakota Sioux who witnessed the Ghost Dance, the participants danced without rest until dizzy and exhausted. When they fell "dead," they had visions of a great encampment where they were joyfully reunited with all of their relatives who had died.

Settlers, military leaders, and government officials believed the Ghost Dance was a war dance. Fearing a huge, unified uprising, the government decided to halt the dances. Red Cloud, who now lived on the Pine Ridge reservation in South Dakota, understood the true meaning of the dances: "The people were desperate from starvation—they had no hope."

World Link

The plight of the Maoris After New Zealand became a British colony in 1840, the native Maoris (MAH-ō-reez) found themselves in a position much like that of the Plains Indians. Pressured by land-hungry settlers, they fought back against the British.

A movement similar to the Ghost Dance arose. Called Pai Marire, which means "Good and Peaceful Religion," the movement was founded in 1864 by Te Ua Haumene. Inspired by a vision of the angel Gabriel, Te Ua Haumene convinced his followers that they would be protected against British bullets by shouting in battle "Pai Marire, hau, hau!" For this reason, followers of Pai Marire came to be called Hauhau. Despite the bravery of Hauhau warriors, the Maoris were defeated in 1872 and lost most of their land to the British.

The Ghost Dance Religion

More than two decades of fighting and bloodshed had left the Plains Indians defeated and depressed. Most were living in poverty on barren and isolated reservations where they were forced to accept a way of life they neither understood nor wanted.

Looking for a miracle to help them improve their situation, in the late 1880s many Indians turned to a new religion that swept across the West. The religion was founded by a Paiute named Wovoka. He had a vision of a deliverer coming to rescue the Indians and give them back their lands.

Believers in this new religion wore shirts and dresses of white cotton or buckskin. They danced, chanted, and prayed for dead friends and relatives to come back to life and the buffalo to return to the plains. Settlers named the new religion the Ghost Dance because of its emphasis on the living reuniting with the dead.

The Death of Sitting Bull

Sitting Bull, who returned from Canada in 1881, became a believer in the Ghost Dance religion. Afraid that he might try to lead other believers to war, the government tried to talk Sitting Bull into banning the religion. When the chief refused, the government decided to arrest him.

In December 1890, 43 Indian policemen surrounded Sitting Bull's cabin at Standing Rock Reservation in North Dakota and told him he was under arrest. At first Sitting Bull agreed to go with them, but when he got outside he changed his mind, shouting, "I will not go." In the scuffle that followed he was killed, along with seven of his followers and six policemen.

The massacre at Wounded Knee Alarmed by the death of their chief, Sitting Bull's followers fled. Some disappeared into the Badlands of South Dakota, an area of deep gullies and steep hills. There they joined other believers in the Ghost Dance religion led by Chief Big Foot.

It was bitterly cold, and Big Foot's group decided to go to the Pine Ridge Reservation. Near Wounded Knee Creek they met troops of the Seventh Cavalry.

On December 29, 1890, the cavalrymen decided to disarm the Indians. When someone discharged a rifle, nervous soldiers fired into the group. Many Indians ran for cover. In the bloody struggle that followed at least 150 Indian men, women, and children and 25 soldiers lost their lives.

Tips for Teaching

Gifted Students

Trying to solve a seemingly unsolvable problem is a challenge gifted students enjoy. Pose this question: What other plan or policy could have allowed settlement but prevented the Indian wars and allowed the Plains Indians to maintain their way of life? Have students present their proposals in the form of letters to the President of the United States in 1870, Ulysses S. Grant. They should give clear descriptions of their plans and explain how they would benefit not only Native Americans but other Americans as well. Have students post their solutions on a bulletin board for the class to read.

Sitting Bull, above, hoped that the Ghost Dance religion would bring about a just and beautiful new world. Believers made special clothing for Ghost Dance ceremonies, such as the Arapaho dress, left, and Sioux shirt, right. Some Sioux made their shirts of muslin flour sacks.

Reformers

Even before the massacre at Wounded Knee the public was waking up to the tragic situation of Native Americans. Reservations were becoming more crowded and living conditions were growing worse.

Furthermore, the government kept breaking promises to provide Indians with food, supplies, and money. Eventually, dedicated people, both Indian and white, began to protest and call for reforms.

One reformer was Helen Hunt Jackson. In 1879 she heard speeches by Standing Bear, a Ponca chief, and Susette La Flesche, an Omaha. Horrified by their accounts of mistreatment of Indians, Jackson decided to devote herself to their cause.

In 1881 she published *A Century of Dishonor*. In it she documented the many broken promises made to Indians. Her most famous book, *Ramona*, was a fictional account of Indians treated unfairly by settlers. *Ramona* stirred public sympathy for the plight of Indians much as Harriet Beecher Stowe's *Uncle Tom's Cabin* had caused anger at the cruelty of slavery.

Another influential reformer, Sarah Winnemucca, was the daughter of a Paiute chief from Nevada. While living with a trader's family, Sarah learned to read and write English. She spent her life speaking out to audiences in the East for the Paiutes' right to their land.

The Dawes Act

Some reformers believed that the only way to help the Plains Indians was to convince them to adapt to American culture. Congress responded to this idea by passing the Dawes Act in 1887. The goal of the act was to end

Discussion

Checking Understanding

1. Why were many Plains Indians attracted to the Ghost Dance religion? (They were depressed and disheartened by their life of poverty on the reservation. The new religion offered a vision of rescue and return to their old way of life.)

2. How did reformers respond to the tragic situation of Native Americans? (They wrote about how the Indians had been mistreated, and they spoke out for Indian rights.)

Stimulating Critical Thinking

3. If you were Sitting Bull, would you have banned the Ghost Dance? (No: the Ghost Dance was the last source of hope for a starving poor people; Sitting Bull may have been powerless to stop this religion. Yes: to save the people from further massacre.)

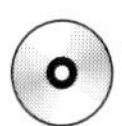

Indian students (Picture) Unit 3, Side 1, Search 47501

See also Unit 3 Explore CD-ROM location 382.

Teaching the Point of View

Ask what the two people quoted hoped the Dawes Act would do. Ask students to identify differing opinions here about land Indians should be given, and discuss how quality of land might affect results of the Dawes Act.

Closing the Section

Wrap-Up Activity

Creating a Pamphlet

To sum up effects of war and reservation life, have students create headlines and pictures for a pamphlet to be handed out at a speech by a reformer. They should identify the speaker, and refer to what happened to Plains Indians between 1850 and 1900.

Section Review Answers

1. Definition: *reservations* (230)
2. Extermination of buffalo, confinement on reservations, massacres and war, broken treaties, trespassing miners and settlers.
3. To end conflict by separating Indians and settlers.
4. It ended tribal ownership by giving plots to individual families. It did not help because few wanted to farm, land was poor, and many were cheated.
5. Give them better land, teach them how to farm, pass laws forbidding settlers to kill buffalo.

Connections to Literature

Bury My Heart at Wounded Knee, by Dee Brown, tells the story of the settling of the West from the Indians' point of view. Brown used the Indians' own words as much as possible—a difficult task since they had an oral culture. Among his sources were a few accounts of the history of the West by Indians, recorded in pictographs or in translated English, and newspaper articles from the late 1800s containing interviews with chiefs and warriors. However his richest sources of first-person statements were the records of treaty councils and other formal meetings with government and military representatives. Most Indian leaders spoke frankly at such meetings through official interpreters. Some gave eyewitness accounts of events and even summed up the histories of their peoples.

tribal ownership of lands and give plots of land to individual Indian families to farm.

Point of View

Why did Congress vote for the Dawes Act?

Members of Congress had different reasons for supporting the Dawes Act. Some felt that they were doing the right thing for Indians. Like the reformers, these politicians wanted to "Americanize" Indians by dealing with them as individuals, rather than as tribes. Carl Schurz, the Secretary of the Interior, agreed that

> "[land ownership would] inspire the Indians with a feeling of assurance as to the permanency of their ownership of the lands they occupy and cultivate. . . . It will be the most effective measure to place the Indians and white men upon an equal footing as to the protection and restraints of law common to both."

Other members of Congress who voted for the act had no interest in supporting the rights of Indians. They wanted to isolate Indians on out-of-the-way plots of land. They realized that this solution was cheaper and safer than fighting Indians for the good farmland. One government official explained it this way:

> "[Giving Indians plots of land would not] cause any considerable annoyance to the whites. . . . [The pieces of land] consist, for the most part, of ground unfitted for cultivation, but suited to the peculiar habits of the Indians."

Reformers rejoiced over the passage of the Dawes Act. However, in the long run the act failed to benefit Indians.

Failure of the Dawes Act Although Plains Indian families were assigned plots of land, few of them wanted to farm. Farming was not part of their tradition.

To make matters worse, the land they were given was often the poorest farmland on the plains. Unable to raise enough food to live on, Indians were forced to rely on weekly food rations from the government.

Because they had never officially owned land as individuals before, Indians did not understand how much money it was worth to the advancing settlers. Some settlers took advantage of this lack of knowledge and talked Indians into selling their land for a fraction of its value. In 1887 Indians owned 138 million acres of land. By 1934 they owned only close to 49 million acres.

Changes on the Great Plains

With Indians confined to reservations, buffalo nearly extinct, and railroads reaching westward across the continent, the Great Plains was a different place by 1880 than it had been 20 years earlier. As you will read, over the next few decades cattle ranchers and farmers moved onto the plains, and with them came new ways of life.

2. Section Review

1. Define **reservations.**
2. Give two examples of situations that threatened the Plains Indians' way of life in the last half of the 1800s.
3. Explain why Congress established the reservation system.
4. What was the Dawes Act? Did it help Indians?
5. Critical Thinking If you were a reformer in the 1880s, how would you try to help the Plains Indians?

Geography Footnote

The original Sioux reservation included the Black Hills. Today most of this mountainous region is preserved as the Black Hills National Forest. Located between the Cheyenne and Bell Fourche Rivers, the hills rise approximately 3,000 feet (914 m) above the Great Plains. They include Harney Peak, the highest point in South Dakota at 7,242 feet (2200 m); Mount Rushmore; and Devil's Tower.

The Black Hills get their name from the dark appearance of their well-forested slopes when viewed from a distance.

To the Sioux of the late 1800s, the Black Hills, which they called *Paha Sapa,* were a sacred place where their people withdrew to fast and pray and renew themselves spiritually.

Geography Lab

A Map that Shows Change

The Second Treaty of Fort Laramie established a huge reservation as a permanent home for the Sioux. Before long, though, miners, railroaders, and farmers were demanding parts of the Great Sioux Reserve.

Senator Henry Dawes of Massachusetts introduced a bill that would let the government take pieces of the reservation, paying the Sioux for their land. Reformers thought the Sioux Bill offered the best terms the Sioux were likely to get. They pressured the tribe into accepting the bill.

Pine Ridge Reservation, South Dakota, shown in 1890, was once part of the Great Sioux Reserve.

Dakota Reservations 1875 and 1900

Yellowstone River
Little Missouri River
Cannonball River
Cedar Creek
Grand River
Moreau River
Belle Fourche River
Missouri River
Sheyenne River
Red River
James River
Big Sioux River
Vermillion River
White River
Cheyenne River
Black Hills
GREAT SIOUX RESERVATION

Indian reservations 1875
Indian reservations 1900
Present-day state boundaries

0 50 100 mi
0 50 100 km
Lambert Conformal Conic Projection

Using Map Skills

1. What are the colored areas? What do the heavy lines stand for? What change does the map show?
2. Describe what happened to the Great Sioux Reserve over time. Include information about the Black Hills, which the Sioux hold sacred.
3. How does the photograph add to what you can learn from the map?
4. **Hands-On Geography** Find out how the boundaries of your community have changed in the past century. Then make a map of your community 100 years ago and today.

Teaching the Geography Lab

After students answer the questions, have them use the map scale to figure out the approximate area in square miles or kilometers of the reservation land in 1875 and in 1900. Then have them express the size of the land area in 1900 as a percentage of the original Sioux land area.

Using Map Skills

Answers

1. Boundaries of the Sioux reservations in 1875; the reservations in 1900; the change in size of the reservations because of the Sioux Bill.

2. The Great Sioux reservation was greatly reduced in size and broken into parts. The Sioux lost the Black Hills entirely.

3. It shows the flat barren terrain and the poverty.

4. Possible sources for boundary information: local history archives at the public library, the Chamber of Commerce, local residents with knowledge of the community's early history.

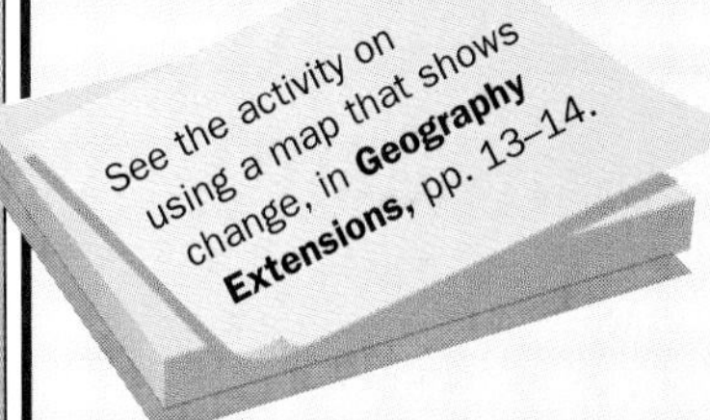

See the activity on using a map that shows change, in **Geography Extensions**, pp. 13–14.

Introducing the Section

Vocabulary

open range (p. 238) unfenced grassland

homesteaders (p. 241) people who took advantage of the Homestead Act by claiming free land in the West

prairie (p. 241) the eastern part of the plains where the grasses grow tall

sod (p. 241) the mat of roots and earth beneath the prairie grasses

Warm-Up Activity

A Cowboy Sketch

To help students better understand cowboy life in the 1860s and 1870s, have them write brief sketches of cowboy life based on their own knowledge. Most will have some prior knowledge, as well as misconceptions, about cowboys in the old West. As they read the section, they will be able to extend and correct their impressions.

Geography Question of the Day

To review the physical geography of the Great Plains, have students study the maps on pages R4–R5 and R8–R9 and then have them describe the physical environment of the Great Plains.

Section Objectives

- ★ Explain why cattle ranching developed on the Great Plains and then collapsed.
- ★ Explain why farmers were attracted to the Great Plains.
- ★ Describe the homesteaders and the challenges they faced.

Teaching Resources

Take-Home Planner 2, pp. 4–11
Chapter Resources Binder
Study Guide, p. 43
Reinforcement
Skills Development, pp. 47–48
Geography Extensions
American Readings, p. 24
Using Historical Documents, pp. 44–47
Transparency Activities
Chapter and Unit Tests, pp. 43–46

3. Cattle and Farming

Reading Guide

New Terms **open range, homesteaders, prairie, sod**

Section Focus **How the Great Plains region was settled by ranchers and farmers**

1. Why did cattle ranching rise and then collapse on the plains?
2. What attracted farmers to the Great Plains?
3. Who were the homesteaders and what challenges did they face?

For settlers in the 1860s and 1870s, the Great Plains was a place of both opportunity and hardship. Some people fared better than others. Still, everyone who tried life on the plains faced new challenges.

The Cattle Industry

While Indians were being forced onto reservations, enterprising cattle ranchers were bringing herds of longhorn cattle onto the plains. Longhorn cattle got their name because of the wide span of their horns—up to 7 feet (2 m) across. They were hardy descendants of the cattle the Spaniards brought to America in the early 1700s.

Originally from Texas and other parts of the Southwest, the cattle ranchers were attracted by the **open range**—thousands of miles of unfenced grassland. Longhorns thrived on this lush grass. Ranchers would claim cattle as their own by putting special marks, called brands, onto their hides with hot branding irons. Then they would let the animals roam free on the open range.

The market for beef, however, was not in the sparsely populated Great Plains, but in the crowded cities to the east. Cows worth $3 or $4 a head in Texas brought as much as $50 in Chicago, New York, or Philadelphia. The problem was getting them there.

Cow Towns

Railroads provided the solution. In 1867 Joseph G. McCoy established the first cow town—Abilene, Kansas—a sleepy cluster of log huts along the Kansas Pacific Railroad. That summer McCoy built stockyards, pens, loading chutes, and a hotel.

That year, 35,000 longhorns were herded to Abilene and shipped east. Four years later Abilene shipped 700,000. From 1867 to 1887 some 5.5 million head of cattle were herded north to Abilene and other cow towns, such as Wichita and Dodge City, that grew up along the tracks.

The Long Drive

Herding cattle across the plains to the cow towns was known as the "long drive." It was a two-month adventure for a dozen or so cowboys with herds of about 3,000.

On the long drive cowboys herded the cattle along trails known to have grass and water. The best-known trail—the Chisholm Trail—was named for Jesse Chisholm, a part-Cherokee trader. With no fences or barriers, the cowboys could let the herds graze wherever they wanted along the way.

Comanche lands Of course most of the range land was, in fact, private property.

Connections to Language Arts

Other cowboy words derived from Spanish include the word *mustang,* from the Mexican Spanish *mestengo,* which in turn is derived from the Spanish word *mesteño,* meaning "strayed." The mustangs were small, hardy, wild horses descended from those brought by the Spanish. They were so spirited they were often called *broncos,* a Spanish word meaning "rough" or "wild." A really tough bronco might be called *loco,* Spanish for "crazy."

A cowboy might catch a mustang with a lasso or *lariat,* a long, light rope tied into a noose. The word comes from the Spanish *la* or "the" plus *reata,* "tied again."

Cowboys might show off their lariat skills at a *rodeo.* This word was originally used in Spanish and English to describe a roundup. The Spanish word comes from *rodear,* "to surround."

The federal government had given much of it to various Indian tribes for their reservations. For example, the Comanches, whose chief was now Quanah Parker, were blessed with especially fertile grazing land.

In June 1876 ranchers drove several herds across the Comanche reservation in Oklahoma. Parker quickly realized the value of the land. He began charging the ranchers a dollar per head to let their cattle cross. With the money the tribe bought their own cattle.

Later Quanah Parker leased land to the ranchers, which allowed their cattle to graze on the reservation. These agreements provided cash for Comanche families and encouraged ranchers to hire Indians to tend the herds.

The Cowboy

In people's imaginations, the cowboy is one of the most romantic characters in American history. In reality, the cowboy led a difficult, lonely, and dangerous life. Longhorn cattle were ornery and touchy. A clap of thunder or a gunshot could send thousands off in a mad rush called a stampede.

The life of the cowboy revolved around the long drive. After two or three months on the trail, cowboys arrived in the cow towns eager to let off steam by drinking, gambling, and fighting. Many towns had a cemetery known as "boot hill," for men who had "died with their boots on."

Cowboy life appealed to men from many different backgrounds. In fact, nearly one in three cowboys was either African American or of Mexican or Spanish ancestry.

One African American cowboy named Jack Spicer, of the Loomis-Ostrander ranch in Texas, was a noted broncobuster. His job was to train young horses to be ridden. When the owner of the ranch asked him how he learned to ride so well, Jack replied:

> "When I was a boy my old master made me ride pitching [bucking] horses. When I was thrown off he used to give me a licking and make me get back on the horse until I rode him. That's the way I learned to stay on."

Spanish origins The American cowboy owes his clothes, gear, and some of his vocabulary to the Spanish and Mexican vaqueros. The cowboy's hat, lasso, and chaps (SHAPS)—leather leggings that protect his legs from thorns—were first used by vaqueros. Many cowboy terms are English versions of Spanish words, such as chaps from *chaparreras* and stampede from *estampida.*

Cowboys rode specially trained ponies for cutting out—or separating—a single cow from the rest of the herd.

Discussion

Checking Understanding

1. How did cattle herds get to the railroad towns to be shipped east? (Cowboys drove the herds across the open range on two-month-long drives.)

2. How did the Comanche chief Quanah Parker take advantage of the long drive? (He charged ranchers for driving their herds across Comanche grasslands.)

Stimulating Critical Thinking

3. Do you think cowboys today face the same challenges as cowboys in the old West? Explain. (No: improved transportation has made the long cattle drive obsolete. Yes: cowboys still have difficult chores, such as calf roping and controlling stampedes.)

Vital Links

Chuck wagon (Picture)
Unit 3, Side 1,
Search 43403

See also Unit 3 Explore CD-ROM location 308.

Section Activity

Writing Classified Ads

To focus on the new economy of the West in the late 1800s, have groups create classified sections for an 1870s newspaper from the Great Plains. They can write listings for cowboys, farmers, sheepherders, and homesteaders; "position wanted" ads; and advertisements for new farming equipment, land, livestock, and other items for sale. Encourage students to think of what kinds of jobs would be available and what people would need and want. If possible, groups should type their classified sections and post them for others to see.

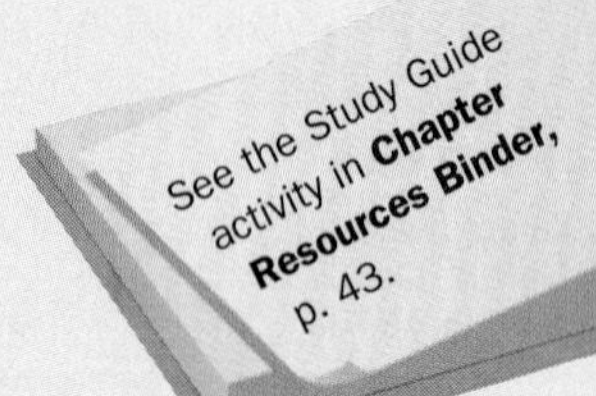
See the Study Guide activity in **Chapter Resources Binder**, p. 43.

History Footnote

Between 1865 and 1900 more than 15 million sheep grazed on the Great Plains. Cattle ranchers and sheepherders fought over rights to land and water. Cattle ranchers often refused to recognize sheepherders' rights to graze their sheep on land that was public domain. They often tried to intimidate sheepherders by causing their cattle to stampede or by killing sheep. Thousands of sheepherders were injured or killed in the process. Fighting between the rival groups broke out most often in Wyoming and Colorado, especially as settlement made public land more scarce. However, as the cattle business weakened and wool prices rose, cattle ranchers themselves took to raising sheep, sometimes pasturing them alongside their cattle on the range.

Collapse of the Cattle Industry

No one could have predicted the huge impact the cattle industry had on the plains. By the mid-1880s, millions of cattle grazed freely on the plains. The very success of the open-range cattle industry, however, was what finally led to its collapse.

The main problem was the number of cattle. As the number increased, cattle prices fell. Still, ranchers bred more, hoping prices would rise. Soon there were too many cattle for the amount of open range.

The next problem was the weather. The winter of 1885–1886 was cold and blustery. Many cattle froze to death. The summer that followed was hot and dry, burning away much of the grass. Longhorns had trouble finding enough food to survive.

By the fall of 1886, ranchers could see that the herds were in trouble. Steers that had been worth $30 a head the year before were now lucky to bring $10.

Those who sold their cattle—even at low prices—were wise. The next winter was worse. When spring arrived a ghastly sight awaited ranchers. Cattle had died by the thousands. Those animals that survived were little more than walking skeletons.

Sheepherders Even before the cattle industry collapsed, sheepherders had begun to compete for the open range. For years cattle and sheep ranchers fought bitter wars—with guns and in the courts—over rights to water and land. In time, though, attitudes softened. Sheep, it turned out, were easier to raise and more profitable than longhorns. Some cattle ranchers even decided to raise sheep.

In 1886 *Harper's Weekly*, a popular news magazine, showed the effects of the terrible blizzards that had swept across the plains that winter. The next winter was just as bitterly cold. Hundreds of thousands of cattle died. The two terrible winters changed cattle ranching. Ranchers began to keep smaller herds and raise hay as feed for winter instead of letting the cattle graze on the open range.

History Footnote

Scientists have theorized that the migrations of locusts are a response to overcrowding as well as to temperature and weather conditions. The worst years for locust plagues on the Great Plains were 1874 to 1877. One swarm at this time in Nebraska was studied with surveying instruments. The dense cloud of insects was estimated to be half a mile high, 100 miles wide, and 300 miles long. Another swarm may have contained over 120 billion insects. The damage from the great plagues was so serious that Nebraska's original constitution was rewritten to respond to economic problems caused by it. The new document was dubbed "The Grasshopper Constitution."

The collapse of the cattle industry meant many lost dreams and fortunes. Ranchers who survived the crash reduced their herds and fenced their pastures. Many cowboys took more stable but less exciting jobs on the new ranches.

Homesteaders

As the cattle industry was shrinking, a new industry—farming—was growing on the plains. In the East, cheap farmland was in short supply. To help farmers acquire land in the West, in 1862 Congress passed the Homestead Act.

Under the act a person could claim 160 acres of free land for a small registration fee. If they built a house and worked the land for at least five years, it became theirs. Between 1862 and 1900 some 500,000 **homesteaders**—people who took advantage of the Homestead Act—moved to the Great Plains, where they claimed 80 million acres of land.

Challenges of homesteading Homesteaders faced many challenges when they tried to turn grasslands into farmlands. One challenge was having too little land.

The Homestead Act did not take into account the difference between farming in the East, where rainfall was plentiful, and farming on the **prairie**—the eastern part of the plains where the grasses grow tall. A family could support itself on 160 acres in the East. On the dry prairie a greater number of acres were needed.

The dry climate created another problem. In summer, lightning could start fires in the dry prairie grasses as readily as a careless match. Raging prairie fires could outrun horses. The fires left everything in their paths in charred and smoking ruins.

Winter brought its own terrors. Perhaps worst were the blizzards with their winds, sleet, and snow. Farmers strung ropes between buildings to keep from getting lost walking from their houses to their barns.

A Kansas woman collects buffalo chips to use for fuel. With little wood available, settlers burned dried hay, corncobs, and sunflower stalks, too.

Homesteaders also had to contend with the locust, a large grasshopper that thrived on the plains. Huge clouds of locusts would darken the sky and eat everything edible in their path, even laundry on the line.

Sod houses Building shelter on the treeless plains was another challenge. Lumber from the East was expensive. Instead, homesteaders built with chunks of **sod**—the mat of roots and earth beneath the prairie grasses.

Sod houses could be snug in winter and cool in summer, but they leaked terribly. Emma Brown, a Kansas homesteader, described one heavy rainstorm:

> "When nearly everything in the house was soaked and the fuel gone, I went to a neighbor's . . . dugout. But before morning there was six inches of water in it so we had to make another move."

Discussion

Checking Understanding

1. What were the reasons for the collapse of the cattle industry? (Success led cattle ranchers to buy more cattle. As the numbers increased, cattle prices fell because the supply was greater than the demand. Then many cattle froze to death during the cold winters of the mid-1880s.)

2. How did the cattle industry change after 1886? (Ranchers who survived kept smaller herds and fenced their pastures. Many cowboys took jobs on ranches.)

Stimulating Critical Thinking

3. Why do you think the government encouraged farmers to move west? (To provide more food for the nation's population, to establish the dominant culture in the West, to ensure claims on resources in the West.)

Bonus Activity

Homestead Posters

To help students understand reasons why people wanted to become homesteaders, have them imagine they work for the federal government during the late 1800s. Their job is to create posters/flyers to distribute in the East to persuade people to move west and farm the land. They should work in groups to create original, colorful posters with persuasive slogans.

History Footnote

Another more efficient plow invented in the 1870s was the sulky plow, which allowed the farmer to sit on the plow and control cutting depth with levers, instead of pushing the plow from behind. Plows became wider, cutting more soil with each pass. Such gang plows, or double plows, were pulled by teams of horses, and later by steam engines.

Harvesting, a task requiring twice as many workers as plowing and seeding, became faster. The twine binder freed five workers to perform threshing tasks. After 1880 a new machine called the combine allowed farmers to cut the grain and thresh it at the same time. Pulled by 20 horses or mules, the steam-powered combine had a 20- to 50-foot cutting bar. Threshing was automatic, so the job of the small, four-person crew was to toss the sacked grain into wagons.

Teaching the Hands-On HISTORY

Remind students that homesteaders usually could not afford to bring much furniture with them when they traveled west. In smaller quarters, they conserved space by sleeping several to a bed, using trundle beds, or storing bedding on a single bed frame and spreading it on the floor at night. Suggest that students draw their floor plans on $\frac{1}{4}$" graph paper. For flexibility in trying out different arrangements, have them cut out simple shapes (to scale) for each piece of furniture and move them around on base drawings.

For an account of homesteading in Kansas, see **American Readings**, p. 24.

Vital Links

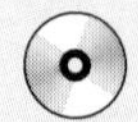

Sod cutters (Picture)
Unit 3, Side 1,
Search 43283

See also Unit 3 Explore CD-ROM location 288.

Hands-On HISTORY

Designing a sod house "Soddies," as sod houses were called, could be built in a week for the cost of a little lumber, a few windowpanes, door and window hardware, and nails. A typical soddy was one story high, with a rectangular floor plan and inside dimensions of about 16 feet by 20 feet (5 m × 6 m), though many soddies were smaller than that. The sod walls usually were 2 to 4 feet thick.

Sod house in the Dakotas, about 1885

Activity Imagine you are part of a family preparing to build a soddy on the Great Plains. Make a scale drawing (1/2 inch = 1 foot) of the floor plan. Include a door, at least two windows, and furniture. Keep the following in mind:

1. Your family has three adults and three children, one of whom is an infant.
2. You can divide your soddy into rooms, but interior walls take up precious space.
3. You own a wood-burning stove for cooking and heating, though you will have to burn corncobs and dried manure because so little wood is available.
4. You will be fetching water from an outside well.
5. All your possessions, except for tools that can go in the barn, must fit in the soddy.

Solving the Problems

Most homesteaders were used to the moist climates of the East. Defeated by the problems of farming on the dry and treeless plains, many gave up in despair. Gradually, however, using new techniques and inventions, those who stayed adapted to their difficult new environment.

Dry farming Over much of the Great Plains, less than 20 inches (50 cm) of rain falls each year, usually not enough for wheat and other grains. Farmers put the wind to work by using windmills to pump water from underground streams.

A Nebraskan named Hardy W. Campbell found that if he plowed deeply, he reached moist soil. The moisture would rise through the plowed soil to the plants' roots. To keep the moisture from rising to the surface and evaporating, he packed the topsoil firmly.

Campbell experimented with this technique on grains that require little water. His method, called dry farming, let plains farmers raise crops even in times of drought.

Farming inventions Plains farmers also benefited from new inventions. In 1838 John Deere of Illinois had developed the steel plow. In 1868 James Oliver patented a plow modified to cut through plains sod. Oliver's

Connections to Literature

Novelist Willa Cather (1873–1947) was born in Virginia and moved to the Nebraska prairie when she was 9 years old. There, she grew up among European immigrant homesteaders from many countries. She experienced firsthand the hardships of pioneer life, which she later depicted in many of her novels. *O Pioneers!* (1913) tells the story of courageous and tough, yet sensitive, immigrant women working hard to make a life on the American plains. In *My Ántonia* (1918), a girl from an immigrant homesteading family who lives in a dugout and a boy from a more prosperous ranch grow up together as best friends. Both books portray the beauty and simplicity of prairie life as well as the hardships and bitterness the settlers endured.

Discussion

Checking Understanding

1. What was dry farming and why was it used? (Plowing deeply and packing topsoil firmly to conserve the limited moisture in the soil.)

Stimulating Critical Thinking

2. Do you think poor farmers benefited from the new farming inventions? Explain. (No: they most likely could not afford expensive machinery, such as the combine, and did not own the animals needed to pull some of the new inventions. Yes: some inventions, such as barbed wire, were most likely fairly cheap; poor farmers might be able to borrow or lease the new equipment, which in turn would lead to bigger harvests and more income.)

plow made it easier for "sodbusters," as plains farmers were called, to plow the plains.

In 1874 Joseph Glidden patented barbed wire. It was advertised as "light as air, stronger than whiskey, and cheaper than dirt." Farmers across the plains fenced off their land to protect it from grazing cattle.

In 1879 John Appleby introduced the twine binder, a reaper that gathered and tied bundles of wheat automatically. An acre of wheat that took 60 hours to reap by hand could be harvested and bundled in 3 hours by machine.

Windmills, dry farming, and the new inventions made huge farms possible. Some of the largest were more than 30,000 acres.

Opportunities on the Plains

Homesteading was a hard, often lonely life. Still, it offered opportunities not available in the East.

Women homesteaders On homesteads women did everything men did. They ran machinery, hitched horses, and handled guns. Living far from towns they had to be teachers, nurses, cooks, laundresses, and seamstresses. For many women, homesteading was an opportunity to prove themselves equal to men even though they might not have had as much physical strength. As Harriet Strong of Wyoming announced:

> "It takes brains, not brawn, to make farms pay. We need more women farmers!"

Under the Homestead Act a woman could apply for her own land grant. By 1890, a quarter of a million women ran farms and ranches. By 1910, 10 percent of all homesteaders were women. Elinore Pruitt Stewart, who filed for a homestead in Wyoming in 1909, shared her feelings in a letter to a friend:

> "I realize that temperament has much to do with success in any undertaking, and persons afraid of coyotes and work and loneliness had better let ranching alone. At the same time, any woman who can stand her own company, can see the beauty of the sunset, loves growing things, and is willing to put as much time at careful labor as she does over a washtub, will certainly succeed."

Exodusters Former slaves also found opportunities on the plains. They called themselves "Exodusters," for the Bible's book of Exodus, which tells the story of Jews leaving Egypt for the Promised Land of Israel.

Within a few years African Americans had established homesteads and towns in Kansas. They called one community Nicodemus, the name of the first slave in the United States to buy his freedom.

In 1878 Nicodemus boasted 700 residents, two hotels, a barber shop, several general

The Shores family poses in front of their sod house near Westerville, Nebraska, in 1887.

For an activity on a homestead application, see **Using Historical Documents**, pp. 44-47.

Vital Links

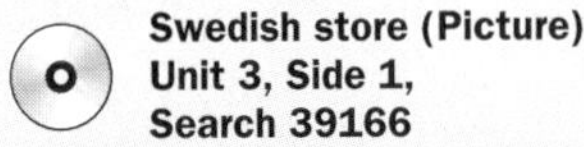

Swedish store (Picture)
Unit 3, Side 1,
Search 39166

See also Unit 3 Explore CD-ROM location 244.

Closing the Section

Wrap-Up Activity

Drawing an Aerial View

To see how the plains were transformed during the late 1800s, have students draw two aerial views of a part of the plains in 1865 and in 1900. They can refer to the description on this page or the section as a whole. Have them label the "before" and "after" views with appropriate headings.

Section Review Answers

1. Definitions: *open range* (238), *homesteaders* (241), *prairie* (241), *sod* (241)

2. Severe winters; hot, dry summers; too many cattle, which led to lower prices. Farmers faced dry soil, prairie fires, blizzards, locusts, lack of trees for building.

3. Congress passed the Homestead Act in 1862. It gave settlers free land, which became theirs if they worked the land for at least five years.

4. Free land, a chance for a better life than back east, and pride in being self-reliant.

To check understanding of "Why We Remember," assign Thinking Critically question 3 on student page 246.

History Footnote

The early settlers of Nicodemus were ill-equipped to turn the prairie into farmland. Most owned only the simplest farm tools. They also had no horses and lacked the skills to catch and tame wild ones. Because they broke the prairie sod by hand, using axes and hoes, the size of the average farm was small, about eight acres.

Since their farms were meager, settlers had to find other sources of income. Some men hired themselves out for odd jobs. Others repaired railroad track, a job that often required long periods away from home. Some families earned money by gathering buffalo bones left from the slaughter of the great herds. The bones, which were shipped east to be ground up and converted to fertilizer, could be sold for $6 to $8 a ton.

stores, a wagon shop, a drug store, a bank, a blacksmith shop, and a lumber dealer. It had a baseball team, a literary society, and two newspapers.

The West in 1900

An eagle flying over the West in 1900 would have seen a vastly different landscape than it would have only a quarter-century earlier. The Great Plains was no longer a vast sea of grass dotted with Indian camps and herds of buffalo. Instead, the region was crisscrossed by railroad tracks and barbed-wire fences, scattered with towns, ranches, and farms. The Indians, now on reservations, had been replaced by millions of settlers.

The Great American Desert was no more. In its place was the "Breadbasket of America," a rich agricultural area.

3. Section Review

1. Define **open range, homesteaders, prairie,** and **sod.**
2. What problems did ranchers face on the plains? What problems did farmers face?
3. How did the United States government encourage farmers to move to the plains?
4. Critical Thinking Homesteaders faced many challenges. If you had chosen the life of a homesteader, what might your reasons have been?

Why We Remember

The Changing West

Quanah Parker was a witness to the changes that reshaped the West. During his life he made a remarkable transition from Comanche warrior to cattle rancher and leader of his people. By the time he died in 1911, Quanah had ridden in trains and automobiles and visited the President. For him, as for countless Americans today, the West was a land of opportunity.

We remember other changes, too. Vast herds of buffalo were reduced to an endangered species—showing how fragile nature can be. Some people also saw that plowing the plains could damage the soil. Quanah Parker warned:

> "We love the white man, but we fear your success. This [was] pretty country you took away from us, but see how dry it is now. It is good only for red ants, coyotes, and cattlemen."

Finally, it was in the West that many Indians died trying to preserve their way of life. The survivors lived with the bitterness of defeat. Still, Nez Percés, Comanches, Sioux, and others endured. In doing so, they preserved a valuable cultural heritage, not only for themselves, but for all Americans.

(Answers continued from side margin)
funeral arrangers—undertaker sign; (b) Possible reasons for needs: legal advice—to help settle conflicting land claims; town park—to have a place with trees to get out of the sun; help in buying and selling land—because Oklahoma was the site of a land rush; funeral arrangers—to assist people with burying the dead.

For further application, have students do the Applying Skills activity in the Chapter Survey (p. 246).

If students need to review the skill, use the Skills Development transparency and activity in the **Chapter Resources Binder**, pp. 47–48.

Skill Lab

Acquiring Information

Analyzing a Photograph

Skill Tips

Keep in mind:

- Most photographs show things as they really are, or were. There is little or no exaggeration, as there often is in a painting.
- The captions that accompany some photographs can be helpful. Usually, though, you need to go beyond the caption to draw reasonable conclusions.

Western towns sprang up with incredible speed. In one day, Guthrie, Oklahoma, changed from a tiny railroad stop to a city of more than 10,000 people. How did it happen? Bowing to pressure from would-be homesteaders, the U.S. government declared that on April 22, 1889, almost 2 million acres of Indian Territory (present-day Oklahoma) would be open for settlement. At noon, the Oklahoma Land Rush began as thousands raced to stake claims in Guthrie and elsewhere.

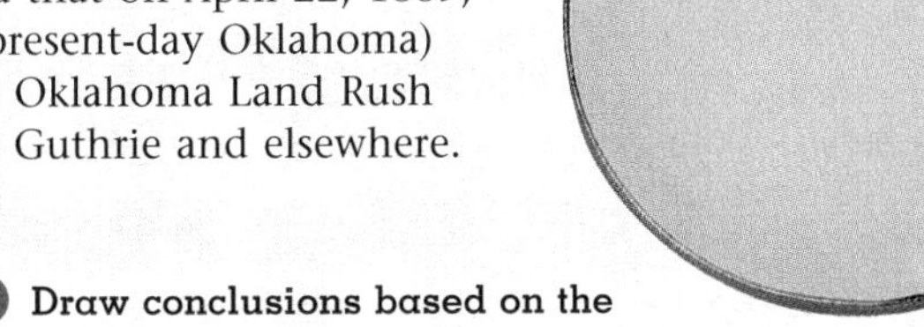

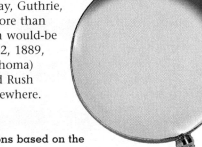

Question to Investigate

What needs did people in the new western towns have?

Procedure

Like paintings, photographs can be valuable sources of information about people and events of the past. Analyze this photograph to explore the Question to Investigate.

❶ Identify the main subject of the photograph.
a. Identify where and when the photograph was taken. Does the photograph itself provide any clues? Explain.
b. Identify in general what the photograph shows.

❷ Identify details in the photograph.
a. What will the sign at the far right be used for?
b. What service is the long sign at the far left advertising?
c. Which signs do not advertise services?

❸ Draw conclusions based on the photograph.
a. Name four needs that people had in western towns. For each one, explain how you can tell from the photograph.
b. Why do you think people in western towns had these needs?

Source to Use

Shop in Guthrie, Oklahoma, 1889

Introducing the Skill Lab

Point out that early photographs generally presented their subject matter in a straightforward way. For example, photographers generally did not use unusual camera angles or employ special effects. For this reason they offer a reliable source of information about the past. Ask students if they think photographs today are as "trustworthy" and have them give reasons for their answers. (Images can be manipulated through technology; photographers often compose a picture to convey a distinct point of view toward the subject.)

Skill Lab

Answers

1. (a) In front of a sign shop in Guthrie, Oklahoma, 1889. Clues: clothing, style of signs and buildings. (b) Two men, probably Walker and McCoy, in front of their shop where they make a variety of signs.

2. (a) Lawyers who were available for hire. (b) Undertaker sign—provided burial and funeral services. (c) North Park sign.

3. (a) Needs: Legal advice—attorney and counselor at law sign; a town park—North Park sign; help in selling and buying land—real estate brokers sign;

(Answers continued in top margin)

Survey Answers

Reviewing Vocabulary

Definitions are found on these pages: *extermination* (229), *reservations* (230), *open range* (238), *homesteaders* (241), *prairie* (241), *sod* (241).

Reviewing Main Ideas

1. To end warfare between miners and Indians, to gain the right to build more roads and forts on the plains, to limit the movement of Indians.

2. Investors who bought the rights to mines made fortunes. Prospectors usually did not because they sold their rights to the mines or could not afford to invest in large-scale mining.

3. Positive: created construction jobs on the railroads and in railroad towns, provided fast and inexpensive transportation for supplies and settlers. Negative: near extermination of buffalo, trespassing on Indian lands, increased conflicts between settlers and Indians.

4. Attacked mining camps, wagon trains, railroads, and settlements; fought the United States Army; migrated to other areas; followed the Ghost Dance religion.

5. They thought that introducing individual ownership of land would make the Indians feel more secure and would "Americanize" them.

6. Oversupply caused prices to drop; harsh winters and summer droughts killed livestock; sheep herds competed for water and land.

7. They built houses from sod, used dry farming, and took advantage of inventions such as windmills, stronger plows, barbed wire, and the twine binder.

Thinking Critically

1. Railroads brought more settlers and miners and led

(Answers continued in top margin)

to the destruction of the buffalo herds. Mining machinery allowed large-scale mining. Sod-busting plows, windmills, and other inventions made farming easier.

2. Yes: They could have united to resist settlers or to negotiate more successfully with the government. No: They were outnumbered, the pressure to settle and exploit their lands was too great, and most settlers did not respect their way of life.

3. Positive: opportunities for newcomers made possible by transcontinental railroad, mining, farming technology, and the cattle industry. Negative: near extermination of the buffalo, Indian wars, reservations, damage to soil by plowing, impact of mining and the railroad on Indians.

Chapter Survey

Reviewing Vocabulary

Define the following terms.

1. extermination
2. reservations
3. open range
4. homesteaders
5. prairie
6. sod

Reviewing Main Ideas

1. Why did the government present the Treaty of Fort Laramie to the Plains Indians in 1851?
2. In general, who made fortunes in mining? Who did not? Why?
3. Name one positive effect and one negative effect of the building of transcontinental railroads.
4. List three ways that the Plains Indians reacted to pressure from trespassers and the government.
5. Why did people who believed in doing the right thing for Indians support the Dawes Act?
6. What led to the collapse of the cattle industry?
7. Give two examples of how homesteaders met the challenges of living and farming in a dry, treeless environment.

Thinking Critically

1. Analysis How did technology change the West? Include at least three examples in your answer.
2. Synthesis Is there something that the Plains Indians could have done to successfully resist the pressures exerted by settlers and the United States government? If so, what? If not, why not?
3. Why We Remember: Evaluation If you were going to write an article emphasizing positive changes that reshaped the West after 1865, what topics would you include? In an article on negative changes, what topics would you include?

Applying Skills

Analyzing photographs Bring in several photographs from home, preferably a mix of posed portraits and casual shots. Exchange photographs with a classmate. Imagine that you are a historian 100 years from now, studying the photographs as historical records. Write a paragraph describing the conclusions about life in the past that you draw from the photographs. Keep in mind what you learned in the Skill Lab on page 245.

History Mystery

The arid Great Plains Answer the History Mystery on page 221. As you travel westward from 100° of longitude, the climate becomes drier. Average yearly rainfall ranges from between 40 and 50 inches (100–125 cm) near the Mississippi to less than 10 inches (25 cm) between the Rockies and the Sierra. Why might some people prefer a rainy climate and others prefer a dry one?

Writing in Your History Journal

1. Keys to History (a) The time line on pages 220–221 has seven Keys to History. In your journal, describe why each one is important to know about. (b) If you could travel back in time and prevent one of the events on the time line, which would you choose? Why? Write about it in your journal.
2. Quanah Parker Imagine that you have just heard Quanah Parker speak at his mother's burial service. A stranger standing next to you criticizes Parker for accepting both the white and the Indian worlds. "He ought to choose one and stick to it," the stranger says. In your journal, write your reaction.

Applying Skills

Paragraphs should reflect an understanding of the steps in the Procedure section of the Skill Lab on p. 245. Students should support their conclusions with specific details from the photos.

History Mystery

Information on Great Plains land is found on page 241. With much less rainfall than in the East, the land was much drier and therefore not as productive. Students can cite various reasons for preferring rainy or dry climate, such as health factors, occupations, and favorite leisure activities.

Writing in Your History Journal

1. (a) Explanations should be similar to the time line notes on teacher pages 220–221.
(Answers continued in side margin)

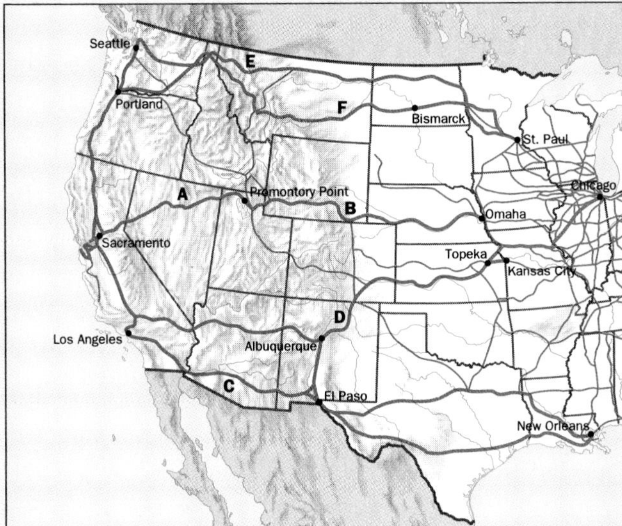

Reviewing Geography

1. Each letter on the map represents a western railroad. Name each railroad.

2. Geographic Thinking Some boomtowns went on to become big cities. Looking at the map on page 228, what reasons can you give for the growth of Denver and Reno? Why do you suppose Deadwood never did become a large city? Think about other cities you have been in or heard about. What kinds of locations or other physical characteristics help a small town become—and remain—a large city?

3. Citizenship Some people have the idea that, until recently, the United States government played only a minor role in the country's economic and social development. After reading this chapter, do you agree or disagree with that idea? Why? Write your responses in your journal.

Alternative Assessment

Portraying success and defeat One historian has said, "The West is the place where everybody was supposed to escape failure, but it didn't happen that way." With classmates, create a bulletin-board display that portrays both the successes and the defeats that people experienced in the West.

❶ Divide into two groups, one to portray the successes and one to portray the defeats in the settlement of the West.

❷ With the rest of your group, decide who and what you will portray. Think of events you have read about—for example, Indians, railroad workers and owners, prospectors, ranchers, and homesteaders. Also think of places, such as ranches, farms, mining sites, boomtowns, ghost towns, and so on.

❸ Gather materials for your display. These might include drawings or other artwork, interesting quotes, maps, charts, and so on. You may want to do research in sources besides the text.

❹ Assemble the display. Give it a title.

Your display will be evaluated on the following criteria:

- it shows understanding of the positive or negative aspects of the changing West
- it provides accurate information
- it presents the information in clear, attractive, inviting ways

(b) Accept any answer that shows understanding of negative consequences.

2. Students who defend Quanah Parker might point out the positive results he achieved by acting as a bridge between two worlds. Those who agree with the critic might say he made it difficult for his family by trying to blend both worlds.

3. Opinions will vary. Students should recognize the government's influence on Indian culture through the reservation system and the Dawes Act; its encouragement of western settlement through the Homestead Act; and its support of the transcontinental railroad through land grants and loans.

Reviewing Geography

1. (A) Central Pacific, (B) Union Pacific, (C) Southern Pacific, (D) Atchison, Topeka and Santa Fe, (E) Great Northern, (F) Northern Pacific

2. Both Denver and Reno are on railroads and rivers. Deadwood is not on a railroad or a major body of water. Locations: on a river, body of water, railroad, or highway. Physical characteristics: fertile farmland, deep harbors, natural resources such as forests and mines.

Alternative Assessment

Teacher's Take-Home Planner 2, p. 7, includes suggestions and scoring rubrics for the Alternative Assessment activity.

Teaching the

Link to Literature

Introduce *Dragon's Gate* by giving some background about the vocabulary word T'ang. Chinese railroad workers called themselves T'ang men after the great T'ang dynasty (618–907), known for its wealth and artistic achievements. Tell students that Chinese railroad workers, like most Chinese immigrants in the late 1800s, were males who came from impoverished areas in southern China. They sent their families the money they earned, and most intended to return to China. Otter's intentions change, however, through his experiences in the railroad camp. Eventually, he finds a way to leave the railroad, but he vows to remember the sacrifices of the T'ang men and to hold on to the promise of human equality in the United States.

Literature Footnote

Laurence Yep is the author of science fiction and fantasy books as well as several books about Chinese American history. His novel *Dragonwings,* which won the Newbery Award in 1976, is based on the true story of Fung Joe Guey, a Chinese American who designed and flew his own flying machine in 1909. Yep, a Chinese American who was raised in a black neighborhood in San Francisco, attended school in Chinatown but did not speak Chinese. His Chinese American books, he says, are "a way of stepping into the shoes of members of my family." Among his other books for young adults are *Child of the Owl, Dragon of the Lost Sea,* and *The Rainbow People.*

Link to Literature

Dragon's Gate by Laurence Yep

In the novel *Dragon's Gate,* author Laurence Yep tells the story of Otter, a 15-year-old boy who travels from China to California to join his father and uncle at work on the transcontinental railroad. Otter finds the two men in the Sierra Nevada, where the Chinese crew is laboring to build tunnels through the solid rock of the mountains. Shocked and angered by the miserable conditions, the barbaric treatment of the workers, and the danger of the work itself, Otter asks his friend Sean to find out whether the "western"—white—crews work under similar conditions. In the following scene, he discusses a letter from Sean with other members of the Chinese crew.

It was a surprise to learn what the western crews earned. Each westerner earned thirty-five dollars a month while we earned only thirty; and the railroad paid for their food as well while we had to pay out of our own pockets. Moreover, it was official company policy that no one should work in the tunnels for more than eight western hours at a time—a policy that was applied to westerners but not T'ang crews.

When I read it to the crew, Dandy did some figuring. "When you deduct the charges for food, we make a third as much."

Honker was waiting patiently on his bunk for his turn to wash. Though it was hot now, he wore his scarf against the dust. "It kind of sticks like a bone in your throat, doesn't it?" he asked. By now, I could understand even his scarf-muffled words. "I mean, we do all the dirty work."

Curly glanced at me and then said, "And all the dangerous jobs. Like when they want to stop an avalanche."

"When we were at Cape Horn," a wispy little voice said, "Kilroy didn't even try to ask his western crews." The voice sounded raspy, as if it had not been used in a long time. We all turned to see; it was Shaky. His head nodded up and down constantly as he spoke the only words I had ever heard from him. "He came to my crew. We were all

T'ang crews: a reference to the Chinese railroad workers

Cape Horn: name given to a part of the Sierra Nevada that was especially treacherous for the railroad workers

Kilroy: an overseer of the railroad workers

Railroad worker, Sierra Nevada

Literature Footnote

In *Dragon's Gate,* Otter travels to the United States, the "Land of the Golden Mountain," dreaming of learning about American technology in order to return to help modernize China. Instead, Otter is trapped in the transcontinental railroad work camp, and must fight for survival. This dramatic coming-of-age story is based on the lives of Chinese railroad workers in the 1800s.

Railroad construction in the Sierra Nevada involved tunneling through solid rock and building trestles like the one shown here.

young and fresh off the boat. What did we know?" He looked around the cabin. "We wound up dangling over a cliff in a basket, swaying on a rope while we hammered away with a chisel, with only the basket bottoms between us and a fall into forever. And sometimes after we packed the holes and lit the fuses, the fuses were too short or the crew took too long to haul us up. We were lucky if there was enough to bury. Even when the rest of my crew was dead, he kept ordering me to go over. Remember. Someone please remember."

We stared in astonishment as Shaky lapsed into his usual silence; but he was lost now in his own terrifying memories, and the nodding of his head changed into a gentle rocking of his whole torso.

With a sigh, Bright Star started to strip. "The westerners' history books will write about what a big hero Kilroy was."

"And us?" Dandy asked. As the headman, Bright Star got to wash first. When he rose from the bucket, his face was scarlet from the hot water. "They're their history books. And the T'ang historians won't care a thread what happens in this barbaric land."

A Closer Look

1. What does Otter learn from the letter he receives? What effect does the information have on the men?
2. Why do you think Shaky says "Remember. Someone please remember"? How does his plea affect the others?
3. Why do you think Bright Star refers to America as "this barbaric land"?

Discussion

Stimulating Critical Thinking

1. Why were T'ang crews treated differently from western crews? Could T'ang workers have done anything to improve their situation? Why or why not? (Because they were newly arrived, poor immigrants. Yes: they could have organized together to demand better pay and conditions. No: they needed work and could not risk losing their jobs.)

2. What does Bright Star imply about historians and history books? Do you agree? (That books are biased in favor of the main culture of a country. Opinions should be supported with evidence.)

A Closer Look

Answers

1. He learns that because of lower wages, longer shifts, and having to pay their own expenses, T'ang workers actually make a third as much as western railroad workers. The men are surprised, angry, and discouraged.

2. He knows about the bravery and hardships of the Chinese workers and wants them to be acknowledged. The others talk about how history books will ignore their contributions and the injustices they endured.

3. He is referring to the fact that western bosses are willing to endanger and mistreat Chinese workers.

Teaching the

Link to American Readings

In this feature students see the American cowboy from two different viewpoints. In the first reading, an excerpt from the diary of Nannie Alderson, the cowboy's good points and bad points are illuminated. In the second reading, an excerpt from a dime novel, the cowboy is stereotyped and romanticized.

Before students begin the lesson, review The Cowboy (page 239) and Homesteaders (page 241). Have students read the entire feature before assigning the A Closer Look questions. The Setting the Stage Activity and Bonus Activity may then be introduced according to the needs and interests of the students. The information contained in the Discussion questions and the Footnotes may be used throughout the lesson as appropriate. Readers' Theater is ideal for students who might find the readings somewhat difficult. Use the Wrap-Up Activity for students who would enjoy taking a step beyond the core lesson.

Literature Footnote

Wyatt Earp may have been one of the few western figures who was both real and a dime-novel hero. In real life, Earp was a rather minor figure. He was arrested for horse stealing, was a buffalo hunter, gambler, and eventually a deputy marshal of Dodge City. He was married once and then took common-law wives. He lived a life of violence where the strong ruled the weak.

The heroic and honorable Wyatt Earp of the movies was a character created by popular writer Stuart Lake. In 1931 Lake wrote *Wyatt Earp: Frontier Marshal*. In this book Earp was a marshal whose purpose in life was to clean up the worst towns on the western frontier. Lake's "biography" of Earp became the authority for film makers. Although it contained just enough fact to lend it credibility, the book was a hoax.

Link to American Readings

READING 4A

Life on the Range

Many women shared the hard work, loneliness, and rewards of ranch life. Nannie Tiffany Alderson was one of them. Born on a Virginia plantation in 1860, she left home in 1883 with her husband, Walter Alderson, to live on a cattle ranch in the Montana wilderness. In her autobiography Alderson describes her introduction to her new home and the cowboys whose talents she would soon respect.

A woman with her horse outside her sod house on Lieban Creek, Custer, Colorado.

"So this was home. . . ."

In the late afternoon we came out of the mouth of a gulch down which we had been traveling. A huddle of log buildings lay below us on the flat, and as I watched, a man on horseback burst out of it, galloping across the valley. I was told that it was one of our cowboys, and that he was probably going after the milk cow. Two men climbed down from a partly completed log house—our house-to-be. Then a fourth man whom I recognized as Johnny [part owner of the ranch] appeared in the door of a low cabin. So this was home.

The first sight of my temporary home was not reassuring—a dirt-roofed cabin, hardly any taller than a man, with one door and only one window! In this country where windows had to be hauled many miles they were usually used sparingly, one being made to do the work of two—a half to each room.

Indoors waited a pleasant shock. . . . A bright fire was burning in the stone fireplace, and the dirt floor was covered with a clean new wagon sheet of white canvas. Over that were laid several beautifully tanned skins—a buffalo robe, a mountain lion, a gray wolf, a coyote and two red fox pelts. . . . Johnny had even found a white bedspread—as I later had cause to regret, for our bedroom was also the family living room, the bed did double duty as a couch, and I never could keep that bedspread clean. A gray army blanket, hung across an opening in the logs, made a door between the bedroom and the kitchen. I was told to lie down and rest while the men got supper ready. I gratefully did so, but was too excited and tired to sleep. . . . [When] I did go out and sit down to the table in the dirt-floored kitchen, with those grizzled coatless men in their grimy-looking flannel work shirts they had worn all day, a wave of homesickness came over me.

History Footnote

The American cowboy had a variety of duties to complete during his day. He kept the cattle together in the herd, collected strays, led them to pastures and water, protected them from rustlers, branded them, and drove them to the shipping points. Because of the lack of regular and efficient law enforcement in the West, the cowboy also provided security for the ranch and the herd. He was most important to the ranchers from the end of the Civil War through the 1890s, when transportation in the West was meager. Herds had to be driven over long distances to reach shipping points, and moving the herd was the cowboy's job. It was work that required strength, physical endurance, and tenacity.

It soon disappeared in enjoyment of one of the best suppers I ever ate—hot biscuits, venison and bacon, potatoe chips, evaporated fruit and coffee. That men could cook was something new under the sun to me, but the men in Montana could and did, and most of what I learned during my first years as a housewife I learned from them. . . .

I had little voice, but my listeners [the cowboys] were hungry for music. . . . I won old Uncle's heart with three Scotch ballads, which I murdered over and over again. . . . By the end of the evening they all had their favorites. . . .

The old cattle range was divided up into districts, each of which was worked by its own crew of men, with horses and wagons, under the command of a captain. The roundup to which my husband belonged started May 1 near Miles City and worked its way slowly up the Rosebud [Creek] toward us. . . .

On a beautiful Sunday morning in June they were camped only a few miles away, so I could ride over and pay them a visit. Mr. Zook, Hal and I started early. As we rode down into the valley of the Rosebud we saw a white patch—a wagon sheet stretched over the rear end of the chuck wagon. And from all sides the drives were coming in—cattle winding down from the hills, with riders following slowly on their flanks and at their rear, singing, calling or slapping their quirts [whips] against their chaps to make a noise; anything to keep the cattle moving. In the broad valley below were more cattle, thousands of them in one great herd, with more riders holding them, and over it all rose dust, and the noise of thousands of bawling throats. Men were at work in this big herd cutting out cows with calves into separate bunches, each according to the brand the mother wore. . . .

I never regretted the arrangement whereby we shared our home with our own nice cowboys, and with every stray rider who came our way. . . . Few families living in Montana had their cowboys live with them as we did. Nobody then thought of them as romantic. They were regarded as a wild and undesirable lot of citizens, but I always thought there was much injustice in this. Nice people in Miles City would as soon have thought of inviting a rattlesnake into their homes as a cowboy. The only places that made them welcome were the house of prostitution and the saloon. The wonder is that despite all that they kept their finer qualities intact.

In a way you could not blame the people of Miles City for their opinion of cowboys, who were at their worst when they went to town. Their first idea was to get drunk and make a lot of noise; their next was to squander their money. That fall after the work was all done Brown [one of the cowboys] went to Miles City, taking with him three hundred dollars in accumulated wages. When he came back a week or two later, all he had to show for his bank roll were a couple of new shirts, and a ring with an enormous purple glass stone in it, apparently meant to be taken for an amethyst.

venison: deer meat

amethyst: semi-precious purple gem

Setting the Stage Activity

A New Home in The West

To help students understand what it might have been like for Nannie Alderson to leave her familiar Virginia plantation and move to the West, have them work in pairs to write a first-person narrative. They might imagine that they are leaving their current home to move to an unknown wilderness. How would they feel? What would they take? What would they miss the most?

Bonus Activity

Art and Music

Cowboys have inspired art and music from the time they first began to work the range. One of the most famous artists who painted subjects of the West was Frederic Remington. Others include Charles M. Russel and Henry F. Farny. Songs such as "Streets of Laredo" and "Leaving Cheyenne" were popular. Bring samples of art or cowboy music to class. Ask students to comment on which works they prefer and why.

Discussion

Stimulating Critical Thinking

1. Although Nannie Alderson's life was not an easy one, she obviously adapted well to the changes and for the most part loved the challenges and the people of the West. Do you think her experience was typical? What problems might ranchers and homesteaders have encountered that she did not mention? (Students might list problems such as extreme weather, illness, and the unpredictability of a steady labor source to work the herds.)

2. Alderson writes that the cowboy was far from a revered figure in town. When he was so respected by the ranch owners, and worked such long and hard hours at his job, why do you think the cowboy caused such problems when he went into town? (Cowboys worked a very hard and lonely job. Their entire existence revolved around the cattle they cared for. When the men went to town, many felt entitled to spend their money and "socialize." There were no such opportunities on the range.)

History Footnote

The cowboy led a nomadic life, and all that he owned served a purpose. The hat shielded him from sun and rain, while the kerchief kept dust from his nose and mouth and served as everything from a bandage to hot pad. Leather chaps protected legs from brush, the boots held feet in the stirrups, and the saddle was large and comfortable. A revolver and lasso were essential.

Literature Footnote

The cowboy's adventurous life style and his renowned skills in horsemanship and marksmanship, which were necessary for survival, made him a perfect subject for books, movies, and television. Some of the best-known westerns include *The Virginian* by Owen Wister and the novels of the prolific Zane Grey. Students will likely have their own favorite western movies or shows.

READING 4B

The West

Misnamed "dime novels" (they actually cost less), these thin volumes were popular reading 100 years ago. Some of the colorful titles included: *Bess, the Female Trapper; Boy Trappers of Oregon; Buffalo Bill's Buckskin Braves; Dead Shot Ned, The Kansas Kid; Marked Men of Arizona; Reckless Rider of the Rockies;* and *Texan Terror.* Like most of the men and women who wrote dime novels, Prentiss Ingraham had spent a short time in the West. He based his exciting tales on this limited experience. The following excerpt from one of his books typifies the text of dime novels.

From *Wild Bill, the Pistol Dead Shot; or, Dagger Don's Double*

At the shot of the ruffian, Wild Bill's pistol dropped from his hand, and it was evident that he was wounded; but, without an instant's hesitation, he raised his left hand, which held a revolver, and at the report the man fell dead, a bullet in his brain, while his two comrades, who were rushing upon their foe, believing him at their mercy, stopped short with a suddenness that was ludicrous [absurd], and cries that were piteous for him to spare them.

"I've got a mind to kill you both," he said, sternly.

"Don't do it, pard, for we hain't no weapons hid."

"Shuck yourselves quick, so that I can see."

With astounding rapidity they obeyed, shaking their woolen shirts violently to show that no deadly weapons were concealed within their folds.

"All right, put on your rig again, or you might catch cold and die, and I prefer that you should live to be hanged."

rig: clothes and riding gear

"Oh pard, what hev we don?" cried one innocently.

"Where is the maiden you stole from her home?"

"Up the ravine yonder."

ravine: large, deep gully

"Oh! Is she alone?"

"Ther horses are with her."

"Why did you kidnap her?"

"Orders, pard."

"From whom?"

"The boss."

"Remove those bodies," and Wild Bill pointed to the dead men he had slain.

"Where shall we put 'em, pard?"

"Out of sight anywhere."

Readers' Theater

Students are sure to enjoy doing a reading of the excerpt from *Wild Bill, the Pistol Dead Shot; or, Dagger Don's Double*. Students might choose a narrator to set the stage and to introduce the characters. The characters can then follow the dialogue in the excerpt fairly closely. Because this scene is from a dime novel, it is comparable to what students might recognize as a melodrama. Encourage the readers to emphasize this melodramatic aspect of the script. They should rehearse several times until they are comfortable with the material, and above all, have fun with it.

The men obeyed, throwing their dead comrades into a clump of bushes.

A few steps had they gone . . . [and] beneath a scrub pine near by, and securely bound to it, was a maiden, attired in a dark blue riding-habit.

She glanced quickly up with a look of terror, at beholding the two ruffians, and half-sprung to her feet, as she caught sight of the splendid looking man following them.

One glance into his face, and she seemed to read there that she had a friend, for she cried earnestly:

"Oh sir, you have come to save me from those wretches."

Excerpt from *Wild Bill, the Pistol Dead Shot; or, Dagger Don's Double* by Prentiss Ingraham. Number 168 of Beadle's Dime Library. (New York: Beadle & Adams). 1882.

"Wild West" shows, such as the Miller Brothers circus, popularized exciting and glamorous images of the West. Circus performers Annie Oakley and Buffalo Bill became American folk heroes.

A Closer Look

1. Describe the Aldersons' first home in the Montana wilderness.

2. How did the picture of the cowboy in dime novels differ from that given by Nannie Alderson? Which do you think is more accurate? Why?

3. CRITICAL THINKING A genre is a particular literary type or style, such as short story or poem. The "dime novel" had its own particular characteristics. What contemporary genres have a similar style or approach to their subjects? Give at least one example and explain the similarities.

Wrap-Up Activity

Cowboys in the Media

To demonstrate to students how important a figure the cowboy is in many books, movies, and television programs, have them compare Alderson's cowboys to those in books or shows with which they are familiar. Have them record their comments in their history journals.

A Closer Look

Answers

1. The Aldersons' home was made of logs, had a dirt roof, and was only slightly higher than a man. It had one door and one window. Inside was a large stone fireplace and the dirt floor was covered with white canvas. Tanned animal skins covered the canvas, and the bed, which was also the couch, was covered with a white spread. An army blanket was hung to create a private area.

2. Alderson's cowboy was a hard worker, but had faults. He was kind and a good cook but could be rowdy and irresponsible. The cowboy of the dime novel was always good, brave, heroic, and gallant. Alderson's cowboy is closer to reality.

3. Certain types of TV shows, such as situation comedies or soap operas, use stock characters.

Teaching the Citizenship Lab

In this feature students learn about *Reynolds* v. *United States* (1879), in which the Supreme Court handed down its first ruling on the First Amendment's free exercise clause. The Court held that the free exercise clause protects only religious beliefs, not practices—a position on which it has wavered since then.

Before students read the feature, have them study the first part of the First Amendment on page R59. Have students read the entire feature before assigning the Understanding Civic Issues questions and the Hands-On Citizenship activity. The Bonus Activity in this Teacher's Edition may be used as an alternative to, or in addition to, the Hands-On Citizenship activity. The Discussion questions in this Teacher's Edition may be used at appropriate points during students' reading or afterward.

Objectives

- ★ Identify the constitutional issue involved in *Reynolds* v. *United States*.
- ★ Describe the Supreme Court's ruling in the Reynolds case.
- ★ Summarize the Court's decisions regarding the First Amendment's free exercise clause since the Reynolds case.

Supreme Court Case: *Reynolds* v. *United States*

Citizenship Lab

What Happens When Law and Religion Collide?

Following a route that began in Illinois and paralleled the Oregon Trail, 148 settlers arrived in an isolated valley near the Great Salt Lake in what is now Utah. It was the summer of 1847 and the settlers were members of the Church of Jesus Christ of Latter-day Saints, or Mormons.

Life in the desert was difficult at first, but hard work and a well-planned irrigation system soon led the Mormon colony to grow and prosper. Within ten years their population would swell to more than 20,000.

The Mormons had come West in hopes of being left alone to practice their religious beliefs in peace. Since Joseph Smith had founded the church in New York in 1830, the Mormons had been driven out of several places by neighbors who regarded their beliefs and practices as dangerously different. Non-Mormons were especially distressed by the fact that some Mormon men had more than one wife, a practice known as *polygamy*.

In the 1850s thousands of other Mormons joined the original 148 settlers in Utah.

History Footnote

Five years before the Morrill Act, the American public's distaste for polygamy had led President Buchanan to replace Brigham Young with a non-Mormon territorial governor. When Buchanan sent federal troops to Utah to enforce the appointment, Young mobilized a militia to block the soldiers' route. The so-called Mormon War ended in 1858 when the Mormons accepted the new governor and Buchanan issued a general pardon. Clearly, though, animosity to Mormon ways was not dead. After the Supreme Court upheld the Morrill Act, Congress intensified its attack on polygamy. The 1887 Edmunds-Tucker Act, which was especially harsh, was upheld by the Court in 1890. With that blow, the church president officially advised Mormons to give up polygamy, opening the door to statehood.

A Mormon poses with his five wives and five children at Echo City, Utah Territory, in 1868.

Congress Opposes Polygamy

The Compromise of 1850 created Utah Territory. Brigham Young, the church leader who had brought the Mormons to the Great Salt Lake, became the first territorial governor. The people of the territory wanted statehood, but Congress repeatedly turned them down because of polygamy.

In 1862 Congress passed the Morrill Act, which stated that no person having a living husband or wife should "marry any other person, whether married or single, in a Territory of the United States." Those who broke the law could be fined and imprisoned. For 12 years after the law's passage, the federal government failed to enforce it. Finally, George Reynolds—Brigham Young's secretary—was indicted under the Morrill Act in 1874. He was convicted by the territorial district court, but the Utah Territorial Supreme Court reversed the conviction on a technical point.

Reynolds was indicted a second time in 1875. Again he was convicted, and again he appealed to the Utah Territorial Supreme Court. This time, though, the court upheld his conviction. Reynolds appealed to the Supreme Court of the United States.

The Supreme Court Distinguishes Between Belief and Practice

In presenting Reynolds's case, his attorneys spent most of their time on technical points. But the importance of *Reynolds* v. *United States* lay in the constitutional issue it involved.

Setting the Stage Activity

Defining Religious Freedom

To prepare students to read about Court cases involving religion, ask them to think about what the American ideal of religious freedom means to them. Have students write journal entries on the topic. Students need not share their entries.

Bonus Activity

Describing Church-State Relations

To focus on the relationship between government and religion in the United States, have small groups brainstorm examples of that relationship from daily life and the news. Ask each group to use its list of examples to develop generalizations about the nature of church-state relations in our country. Conclude by having groups share their generalizations with the rest of the class. If groups need help getting started with their lists, suggest some of the following ideas. Examples from daily life: the motto on paper money and coins; the words "under God" in the Pledge of Allegiance; swearing of oaths on the Bible in court; national holidays that are religious in nature.

Discussion

Checking Understanding

1. Who was George Reynolds, and why was he indicted? (He was secretary to Mormon leader Brigham Young and was indicted for polygamy, which was against the Morrill Act.)

2. What constitutional issue did Reynolds's case involve? (Did the Morrill Act deprive Reynolds of his First Amendment right to free exercise of religious beliefs?)

Stimulating Critical Thinking

3. How would you explain the fact that the federal government failed to enforce the Morrill Act for 12 years? (Possible answers: Civil War and Reconstruction took most of the government's attention. Remoteness of Utah from Washington, D.C., also may have played a role.)

4. Why do you suppose Chief Justice Waite used the example of human sacrifice in the Reynolds case, and what is your opinion of his use of it? (Waite probably referred to human sacrifice because no one could argue with it as an example of a practice that must be outlawed. Students may feel the implied comparison of polygamy and human sacrifice was extreme and somewhat unfair.)

Citizenship Footnote

Some of the hottest debates about religious freedom involve the First Amendment's establishment clause, rather than the free exercise clause. Clearly, the framers wanted to prohibit government-supported churches like the Church of England. This fact aside, does the establishment clause mean that the government must give no support to any religion or only that it must not favor one religion over another?

School prayer is especially controversial. In *Engel* v. *Vitale* (1962), the Supreme Court ruled that voluntary prayer, done as part of classroom exercises in public schools, violated the establishment clause. Although the decision angered many Americans, the Court has held firm. Some religious and political leaders advocate a constitutional amendment permitting school prayer.

Brigham Young

The First Amendment to the Constitution begins, "Congress shall make no law respecting an establishment of religion or prohibiting the free exercise thereof. . . ." Legal experts refer to the first part of that statement as the establishment clause; the principle is also referred to as separation of church and state. The second part of the statement is called the free exercise clause. It was this clause that the justices had to consider in *Reynolds* v. *United States*. Polygamy was part of Mormon belief; George Reynolds was a Mormon. Did the Morrill Act deprive him of his constitutional right to the free exercise of his religious beliefs?

The Court handed down its unanimous ruling in 1879: the Morrill Act was constitutional, and Reynolds's conviction was upheld. Chief Justice Morrison R. Waite wrote the opinion.

Waite said that while laws "cannot interfere with mere religious belief and opinions, they may [interfere] with practices. Suppose one believed that human sacrifices were a necessary part of religious worship, would it be seriously contended that the civil government . . . could not interfere to prevent a sacrifice? . . . Can a man excuse [illegal practices] because of his religious belief? To permit this would be to make the . . . doctrines of religious belief superior to the law of the land, and in effect permit every citizen to become a law unto himself. Government could exist only in name under such circumstances."

In the years after the Reynolds case, about 1,000 Mormons were fined and sent to prison for polygamy. Then, in 1895, Utah submitted to Congress a new constitution that outlawed polygamy. The next year Utah became a state.

"Free Exercise" Questions Continue

Reynolds v. *United States* was the Supreme Court's first ruling on the free exercise clause, but not its last. By the mid-1900s, the Court seemed to abandon the idea embraced in the Reynolds case that the free exercise clause protects only beliefs, not practices. Instead, the Court made rulings based on whether the government truly had a "compelling interest" to punish religion-based practices or to force people to obey laws against their religious beliefs.

Connections to Economics

Congress was determined not only to wipe out polygamy but also to break the social, political, and economic power of the Mormon church. In keeping with that last goal, a section of the Morrill Act prohibited religious organizations in the territories from owning real estate worth more than $50,000. The Edmunds-Tucker Act (see page 255 in this Teacher's Edition) went further, providing for confiscation of Mormon church property unless the church gave up polygamy. When the question of that law's constitutionality came before the Supreme Court, church lawyers focused on economic issues and did not even try to defend polygamy as free expression of religion. When the church gave up polygamy in the wake of the Court's 1890 ruling, much of its confiscated property was returned.

Recently, though, the Court backtracked on the "compelling interest" idea. In *Employment Division* v. *Smith* (1990), two Native Americans lost their jobs because they used an illegal drug as part of their tribal religious practices. The state of Oregon refused to pay them unemployment benefits. The Supreme Court upheld the state's decision and cited *Reynolds* v. *United States* as its precedent.

Many Americans regarded the Employment Division ruling as a threat to religious freedom. Congress agreed, and it passed the Religious Freedom Restoration Act of 1993. This law calls for government to follow the "compelling interest" idea in matters relating to free exercise of religion. The Court has not yet ruled on the constitutionality of that law, which goes against its decision in the Employment Division case. But it seems likely that the struggle to interpret and apply the free exercise clause will occupy courts and legislative bodies at every level for a long time to come.

Understanding Civic Issues

1. What were the provisions of the Morrill Act?
2. Restate Chief Justice Waite's opinion in *Reynolds* v. *United States* in your own words.
3. **Critical Thinking** "The Constitution never gets settled! The same kinds of cases keep coming up and are never decided the same way! Why?" How do you respond?
4. **Hands-On Citizenship** Act out this imaginary Supreme Court case: A state legislature has passed a law requiring recitation of the Pledge of Allegiance at sports events sponsored by public schools and universities. Several religious groups are challenging the law on the grounds that reciting the pledge goes against their beliefs.
   - Assign roles: nine Supreme Court justices plus lawyers to represent the state and the religious groups.
   - Establish the procedures you will follow. For example, in real Court cases, justices often interrupt lawyers' arguments with questions.
   - After the lawyers prepare their roles, act out the Court scene. Then have the justices meet to discuss the case. Keep in mind that Supreme Court cases are decided by majority vote.

A member of the Bahai faith leading a procession that opened a religious conference in Chicago attended by thousands of people representing hundreds of religious faiths.

Citizenship Lab Answers

1. Anyone in a U.S. territory who already had a spouse and yet married another person could be fined and imprisoned.

2. Possible answer: People can believe whatever they choose, but the government must have the ability to outlaw religious practices it considers harmful. Otherwise, chaos could result.

3. Possible answer: This does seem to be true, but it reflects two facts: the Constitution was deliberately written in broad terms to ensure flexibility, and such flexibility is needed because social, economic, and other situations and attitudes change constantly.

Teaching the Hands-On Citizenship

Ideally there should be at least 2 students on each legal team. If a group smaller than 13 students is more practical for your situation, make sure the number of justices is uneven (3, 5, or 7) to allow for a majority decision.

Evaluation of simulations are often a concern for teachers. You may want to evaluate student preparation for the role play, attention to following the rules, and seriousness of effort. Debriefing the activity is important. Be sure to involve all the students and not just those who had key roles in the simulation.

At·a·Glance

5 The Rise of Industry and Big Business 1865–1900

Chapter Planning Guide

Section	Student Text	Teacher's Edition Activities
Opener and Story pp. 258–261	**Keys to History Time Line** **History Mystery** Beginning the Story with **Andrew Carnegie**	**Setting the Stage Activity** To Be a Millionaire?, p. 260
1 **Railroads Spur Industrial Growth** pp. 262–267	**Reading Maps** Resources for American Industry, p. 263 **Link to the Present** Catalogs, p. 264 **Geography Lab** The Canadian Shield, p. 267	**Warm-Up Activity** Thinking About Competition, p. 262 **Geography Question of the Day,** p. 262 **Section Activity** A Railroad Regulation Hearing, p. 264 **Bonus Activity** Writing Railroad Songs, p. 265 **Wrap-Up Activity** Writing Editorials, p. 266
2 **The Growth of Big Business** pp. 268–274	**Hands-On History** Choosing worthy causes, p. 269 **Link to Technology** The Suspension Bridge, pp. 270–271 **World Link** Japan becomes an industrial nation, p. 273 **Skill Lab** Analyzing a Flowchart, p. 274	**Warm-Up Activity** Forming a Monopoly, p. 268 **Geography Question of the Day,** p. 268 **Section Activity** Starting a Business, p. 270 **Bonus Activity** A Meeting of Minds, p. 271 **Wrap-Up Activity** Conducting an Interview, p. 273
3 **Workers Struggle for a Better Life** pp. 275–281	**Point of View** Should unions use the strike?, p. 278 **Link to Art** *The Ironworkers' Noontime,* p. 280	**Warm-Up Activity** Analyzing Visuals, p. 275 **Geography Question of the Day,** p. 275 **Section Activity** A Workers' Dialogue, p. 278 **Bonus Activity** Setting Workers' Priorities, p. 276 **Wrap-Up Activity** Writing an Editorial, p. 281
Evaluation	**Section 1 Review,** p. 266 **Section 2 Review,** p. 273 **Section 3 Review,** p. 281 **Chapter Survey,** pp. 282–283 **Alternative Assessment** Participating in a round table, p. 283	**Answers to Section 1 Review,** p. 266 **Answers to Section 2 Review,** p. 273 **Answers to Section 3 Review,** p. 281 **Answers to Chapter Survey,** pp. 282–283 (Alternative Assessment guidelines are in the Take-Home Planner.)

Teacher's Resource Package

Chapter Summaries: English and Spanish, pp. 46–47

Chapter Resources Binder

Study Guide Previewing Headings, p. 73

Geography Extensions The Canadian Shield, pp. 15–16

American Readings The Railroad Octopus, pp. 25–26

Chapter Resources Binder

Study Guide Telling *What, When,* and *Where,* p. 74

Skills Development Analyzing a Flowchart, pp. 79–80

American Readings The Oil Boom, p. 27

Chapter Resources Binder

Study Guide Supplying Supporting Evidence, p. 75

Reinforcement Gathering Information, pp. 77–78

American Readings Breaker Boys and Trapper Boys, p. 28

Using Historical Documents The Manifest of the *London,* pp. 48–51

Chapter and Unit Tests Chapter 5 Tests, Forms A and B, pp. 47–50

Take-Home Planner

Introducing the Chapter Activity A Paper Airplane Factory, p. 14

Chapter In-Depth Activity Illustrating Steps in the Manufacturing Process, p. 15

Reduced Views

Study Guide, p. 16

Geography Extensions, p. 19

American Readings, p. 18

Unit 2 Answers, pp. 30–38

Reduced Views

Study Guide, p. 16

Skills Development, p. 17

American Readings, p. 18

Unit 2 Answers, pp. 30–38

Reduced Views

Study Guide, p. 16

Reinforcement, p. 17

American Readings, p. 18

Using Historical Documents, p. 19

Unit 2 Answers, pp. 30–38

Reduced Views

Chapter Tests, p. 19

Unit 2 Answers, pp. 30–38

Alternative Assessment Guidelines for scoring the Chapter Survey activity, p. 15

Additional Resources

Wall Time Line

Unit 2 Activity

Transparency Package

Transparency 5-1 A suspension bridge—use with Section 2

Transparency 5-2 The Brooklyn Bridge—use with Section 2

Transparency Activity Book

SelecTest Testing Software

Chapter 5 Test, Forms A and B

Vital Links

Videodisc

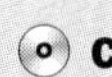
CD-ROM

Carnegie castle (see TE p. 269)

Rockefeller cartoon (see TE p. 272)

Voice of "Mother" Jones (see TE p. 277)

"Don't Forget the Union Label" (see TE p. 279)

Voice of Eugene Debs (see TE p. 280)

5

Teaching Resources

Take-Home Planner 2
- Introducing Chapter Activity
- Chapter In-Depth Activity
- Alternative Assessment

Chapter Resources Binder
Geography Extensions
American Readings
Using Historical Documents
Transparency Activities
Wall Time Line Activities
Chapter Summaries
Chapter and Unit Tests
SelecTest Test File
Vital Links CD-ROM/Videodisc

Chapter Objectives

- ★ Explain how railroads spurred industrial growth in the nation.
- ★ Describe the growth of big business.
- ★ Describe how American workers responded to changes brought about by industrialization.

Chapter Overview

The railroads expanded rapidly after the Civil War. Abundant natural resources fueled this growth, which created a national market for raw materials and finished goods. The railroad boom also led to cutthroat competition and the spread of unfair business practices. As a result, Congress passed the Interstate Commerce Act in 1887, an attempt to regulate the railroad industry.

Time Line

Keys to History

Keys to History journal writing activity is on page 282 in the Chapter Survey.

Carnegie and steel The efficient production of steel spurred the growth of railroads and heavy industry. (p. 268)

Vanderbilt's railroad empire Vanderbilt's huge railroad network made shipping more efficient. However, without competition, shipping costs went up. (p. 265)

Looking Back The demonstration of a steam locomotive spurred the beginning of the railroad era in the United States.

1865–1900

Chapter 5

The Rise of Industry and Big Business

Sections

1873
Andrew Carnegie builds modern steel mill

1873
Cornelius Vanderbilt extends railroad empire to Chicago

1865 — 1875

Looking Back

Tom Thumb, successful railroad steam engine
1830

World Link
Japan becomes an industrial nation
1868–1900

As the railroads expanded, so did industry. Business leaders formed corporations and combined corporations into trusts to gain better control of their businesses. Andrew Carnegie and John D. Rockefeller built business empires in steel and oil by improving production and buying out their competitors. In response to growing alarm at the monopoly power of trusts, Congress passed the Sherman Antitrust Act. The law banned trusts but was hard to enforce.

Low wages and unsafe working conditions were widespread. To improve their situation, industrial workers organized into unions such as the Knights of Labor and the American Federation of Labor. Several strikes led to violent clashes between employers and workers. Although the labor movement was hurt, union membership continued to grow.

HISTORY *Mystery*

Some people called her "Mother." Others said she was "the most dangerous woman in America." Who was she? What did she do to earn such different reputations?

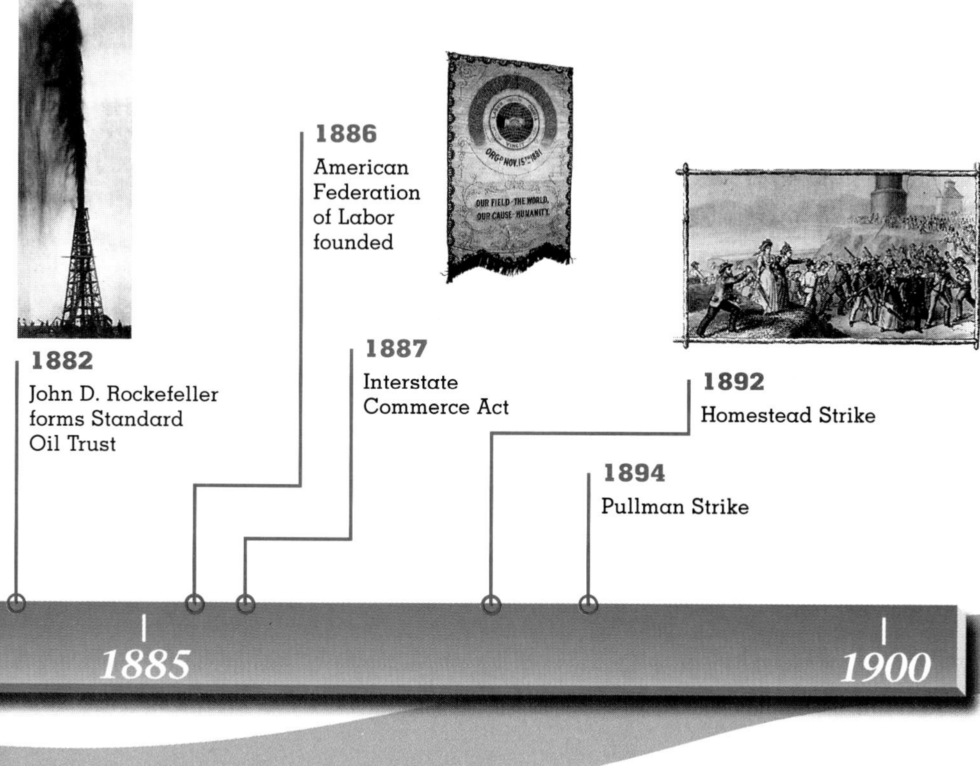

Looking Ahead

Wagner Act guarantees workers the right to join unions

1935

Teaching the HISTORY *Mystery*

Students will find the answer on p. 277. See Chapter Survey, p. 282, for additional information and questions.

Time Line

Rockefeller and Standard Oil Rockefeller created a powerful monopoly in the new oil industry. (p. 272)

American Federation of Labor Many skilled workers joined this large union, which often used collective bargaining and strikes to try to achieve better pay and working conditions. (p. 278)

Interstate Commerce Act With this law, Congress gained the power to regulate the railroad industry. (p. 266)

Homestead Strike Employers defeated this strike at a Carnegie steel plant by using force and hiring replacement workers. (p. 278)

Pullman Strike American Railway Union workers staged a general strike that brought national railroad lines to a halt. It ended in violent rioting and the imprisonment of union leaders. (p. 279)

World Link See p. 273.

Looking Ahead The Wagner Act established a National Labor Relations Board (NLRB), which ordered employers to end antiunion actions, arbitrated grievances, and reinstated workers who were fired for joining unions.

Beginning the Story

Andrew Carnegie

Enterprising individuals like Andrew Carnegie spearheaded the rapid industrial growth of the late 1800s. Establishing his first steel mill in 1872, Carnegie hired scientists to improve his steel, purchased iron mines to supply his factories, and bought ships and railroads to transport iron ore. By making steel production more efficient and buying out rival companies, he rapidly expanded his company and amassed millions of dollars.

Setting the Stage Activity

To Be a Millionaire?

To help students appreciate Carnegie's meteoric rise from "rags to riches," ask this question: "What do you think you would need to do today to become a millionaire through your own efforts?" Give students ten minutes to write a response. Then ask volunteers to share their wealth-building scenarios.

See the Introducing the Chapter Activity, A Paper Airplane Factory. **Take-Home Planner 2**, p. 14.

History Footnote

Andrew Carnegie's knowledge of human nature helped him to succeed. In 1858, Carnegie became a part owner of a railroad sleeping car company established by the inventor Theodore T. Woodruff. He later discovered that George M. Pullman had developed a better sleeping car. One day he met Pullman by accident in a hotel. Carnegie suggested that the two unite and form a company. When Pullman asked him what he would call the company, he said, "Let's call it the Pullman Palace Car Company."

The compliment worked. Pullman's name became famous (and is still used to refer to sleeping berths on trains). Carnegie, meanwhile, had enlarged his empire and expanded his personal fortune. Commenting on the company's success, he said, "Blessed be the man who invented sleep."

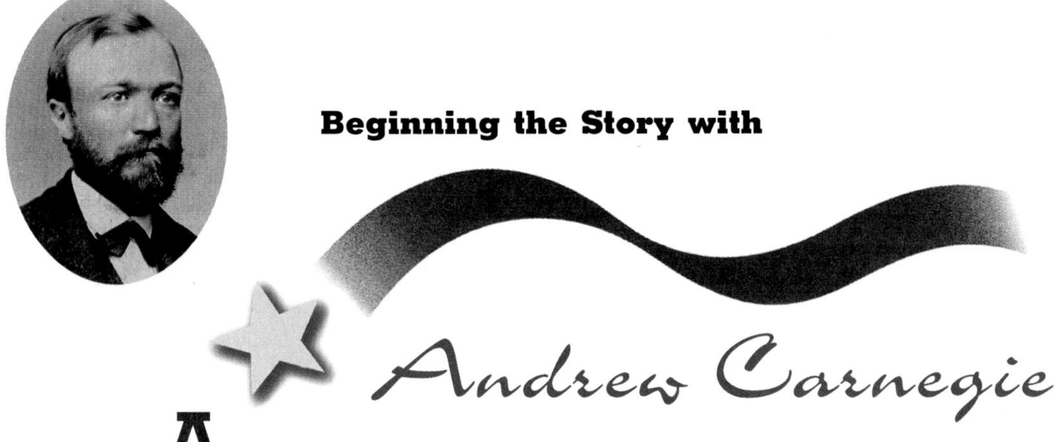

Although he missed his home in Scotland, 17-year-old Andrew Carnegie knew his future lay in the United States. In a letter to his uncle, he wrote:

> "Although I sometimes think I would like to be back in Dunfermline, working at the loom, it's very likely I would have been a poor weaver all my days, but here, I can surely do something better than that. If I don't it will be my own fault, for anyone can get along in this country."

Andrew certainly got along. While many immigrants in the United States struck it rich, few enjoyed Carnegie's success. Born the son of a poor weaver, Andrew grew up to be one of the richest men in the world.

Becoming a "Bread Winner"

Life in Scotland had been difficult for Andrew's family. His father, William, toiled endless hours over a hand loom in their little cottage. His mother, Margaret, repaired shoes. Together they barely eked out a living. Then came power looms, which put cottage weavers like William out of work. Rather than face a life of poverty, Margaret insisted the family emigrate to the United States, where her two sisters already lived. The Carnegies arrived in 1848 and settled near Pittsburgh.

Andrew, now 13, found a job in a textile mill as a "bobbin boy." He worked 12 hours a day, 6 days a week for $1.20 per week. "I have made millions since," he later said, "but none of these gave me so much happiness as my first week's earnings. I was now a helper of the family, a bread winner."

After a year of millwork, Andrew found a job as a messenger for a telegraph office. There he earned $2.50 a week, delivering telegrams to customers. To Andrew, the job seemed like heaven, "with newspapers, pens, pencils, and sunshine about me."

History Bookshelf

Fisher, Leonard Everett. *Tracks Across America: The Story of the American Railroad, 1825–1900.* Holiday House, 1993. Period photographs, maps, and drawings enhance this account of the burgeoning railroad industry; includes chapters on the Indian resistance and immigrant workers.

Also of interest:

Bowman, John. *Andrew Carnegie: Steel Tycoon.* Silver Burdett, 1989.

Coffey, Ellen Greeman. *John D. Rockefeller, Empire Builder.* Silver Burdett, 1989.

Kraft, Betsy Harvey. *Mother Jones: One Woman's Fight for Labor.* Clarion, 1995.

Lens, Sidney. *Strikemakers and Strikebreakers.* Lodestar, 1985.

When not delivering telegrams, Andrew learned the language of the telegraph. Messages came into the office in the form of dots and dashes punched into narrow strips of paper. The dots and dashes represented letters of the alphabet translated into Morse code.

Most telegraph operators would then "read" the strips of paper to translate the coded message back into words. Not Andrew. He trained himself to decode the dots and dashes by listening to the sound they made as the message clicked over the telegraph key. Astonished customers stood around the telegraph office just to watch him take messages.

Andrew Carnegie became the greatest American steelmaker by using new technology to produce inexpensive, durable steel.

A Teenage Capitalist

One of the people most impressed by Carnegie's skill was Thomas A. Scott, superintendent of the Pennsylvania Railroad. Scott hired Andrew as his personal assistant. The teenager's primary job was to send telegraph orders to trains moving between Philadelphia and Pittsburgh.

One day Scott asked Carnegie if he could find $500 to invest. Without knowing where the money would come from, Andrew replied, "Yes, sir; I think I can." Scott said, "Very well, get it; a man has died who owns ten shares in the Adams Express Company which I want you to buy."

Andrew turned to his mother for help. Determined "to give our boy a start," she raised the $500 by borrowing on the family's home. Carnegie was now the proud owner of ten shares of Adams Express stock, which paid a monthly dividend (part of the company's profits). When he showed his first check for $5 to his friends, they were astonished. They had never received money except from work. Carnegie later recalled:

> "How money could make money . . . led to much speculation upon the part of the young fellows; and I was for the first time hailed as a 'capitalist.'"

Carnegie quickly learned how to use his money to make money. He built this first investment into a fortune.

Hands-On HISTORY

Activity

In the early 1850s Andrew Carnegie invested $500 in Adams Express stock. If you wanted to make a similar investment today, you would need to raise $9,000. Write a plan describing how you would raise the money and what investments you would make.

Discussion

Thinking Historically

1. What personal qualities and talents played a part in Andrew Carnegie's rise to success? (He was a hard worker, even at low-paying jobs. He learned a new skill, decoding telegraph messages by ear. He was charming.)

2. How did personal contacts contribute to Carnegie's financial success? (His abilities and personal charm were noticed by an influential railroad executive who offered him a better job. That person also steered him toward profitable investments.)

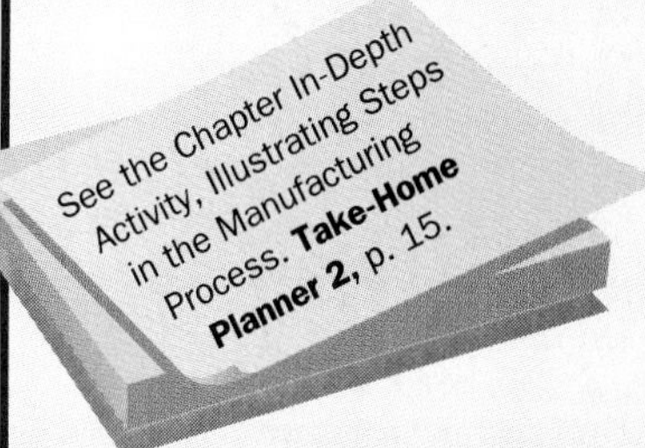

See the Chapter In-Depth Activity, Illustrating Steps in the Manufacturing Process. **Take-Home Planner 2**, p. 15.

Teaching the Hands-On HISTORY

Have students brainstorm in groups. For fund-raising ideas, they could think about products or services they might provide, as well as special events they could hold. For ideas on where to invest, they could consider community projects, new technologies, and successful companies they have heard about.

For a journal writing activity on Andrew Carnegie, see student page 282.

Introducing the Section

Vocabulary

rebates (p. 265) refunds of part of the cost of something

consolidation (p. 265) the combining of several companies into one large company

regulate (p. 266) make rules for

free enterprise (p. 266) economic system in which businesses are free to compete without government rules

interstate commerce (p. 266) business between states

Warm-Up Activity

Thinking About Competition

To focus on how competition affects business practices, have students imagine running a bicycle messenger service in a large city. Their company is the largest of several but has one major competitor. Each student should write a strategy memo to his or her business partners presenting a plan for gaining a larger share of the bicycle messenger business in the city.

Geography Question of the Day

Have students review the map on page 228. Ask: What cities located along major railroads probably experienced tremendous growth beginning in the late 1860s? the early 1890s?

Section Objectives

- ★ Describe the causes and effects of the rapid expansion of the railroads.
- ★ Explain how railroad companies limited competition and increased profits.
- ★ Identify the events that led to the passage of the Interstate Commerce Act.

Teaching Resources

Take-Home Planner 2, pp. 12–19
Chapter Resources Binder
Study Guide, p. 49
Reinforcement
Skills Development
Geography Extensions, pp. 15–16
American Readings, pp. 25–26
Using Historical Documents
Transparency Activities
Chapter and Unit Tests

1. Railroads Spur Industrial Growth

Reading Guide

New Terms **rebates, consolidation, regulate, free enterprise, interstate commerce**

Section Focus **How railroads spurred industrial growth in the nation**

1. **What were the causes and effects of the rapid expansion of railroads?**
2. **How did railroad companies limit competition and increase profits?**
3. **What led to the passage of the Interstate Commerce Act?**

Andrew Carnegie's rise from bobbin boy to businessman took place during a time of rapid industrial growth in the United States. The forces behind this change can be traced to the Industrial Revolution that began in the early 1800s (see page 70 in the Review). By 1860, machines, mass production, the factory system, and railroads had all made their appearance.

Reasons for Growth

After the Civil War, enterprising individuals like Andrew Carnegie brought these elements of industry together on a larger scale than Americans had ever seen before. Machines took over much of the nation's work. Factories, rather than small workshops, now produced most of the nation's manufactured goods.

Abundant natural resources A wealth of natural resources made such growth possible. The nation's many rivers carried freight and served as sources of power. Forests supplied wood for railroad ties and bridges. Coal deposits provided fuel for steam engines and the furnaces of the iron industry. Ample supplies of iron ore kept steel mills booming. Fuels made from oil became widely used for light, heat, and power.

Statistics tell the story of the United States' coming of age as an industrial nation. Between 1865 and 1900, the number of factories increased from 140,000 to 510,000. The number of people who worked in factories and mills swelled from 1.3 million to 5.1 million. The value of manufactured goods leaped from \$2 billion to over \$18 billion. By 1900 the United States had become the world's leading industrial nation.

Railroads expand The driving force behind the industrial growth of the United States was the booming railroad industry. In 1865 the nation had about 30,000 miles (48,000 km) of track. By 1900, 200,000 miles (320,000 km) of track covered the nation like a giant spider web. It was the biggest railroad system in the world.

While some railroaders were laying track in the West, others were building lines in the East and the Midwest. The South repaired lines wrecked during the Civil War and added seven times as many miles of track. When a railroad reached Harrison, Arkansas, people welcomed it with booming cannons. The local newspaper declared, "Harrison Is a Railroad Town at Last."

Connections to Geography

A major challenge for the early railroads was to operate efficiently without any standardized time zones. Every community decided its own time based on its own calculations, making it impossible for railroads to make uniform schedules. In 1883 American and Canadian railroads solved the problem by dividing the countries into four time zones.

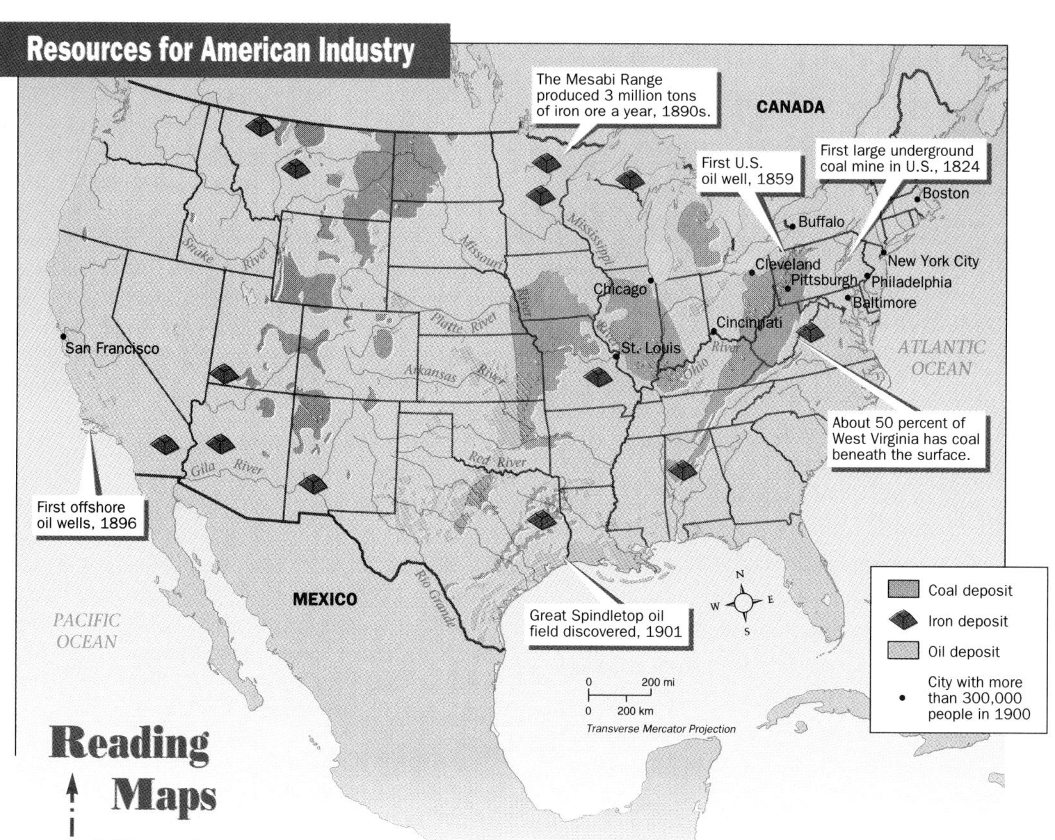

Reading Maps

1. For each resource, name the areas of the United States where major deposits are found.

2. What characteristics besides being close to resources contribute to making a city an industrial center?

Railroads Link the Nation

As railroad lines crisscrossed the United States, they created a national market for the nation's raw materials and manufactured goods. Railroads carried coal from the mines of West Virginia, Kentucky, and Pennsylvania to factories in Chicago, Cleveland, Buffalo, and Pittsburgh. "Minnesota flour and Iowa lard," a historian wrote, "went into pies baked in Ohio-made ovens by Vermont matrons."

With so many new customers, manufacturers could increase production. They opened new and bigger factories, bought better machines, and hired more workers.

Mail-order businesses Now that merchants could ship goods to locations across the country, shopping by mail began. In 1872 Aaron Montgomery Ward, a young salesman, had an idea for giving farmers a greater selection of goods than they could find in local stores. That year he sent out a

Developing the Section

Discussion

Checking Understanding

1. What natural resources made railroad expansion possible? (Rivers, forests, coal deposits, iron ore deposits.)

Stimulating Critical Thinking

2. How do you think the typical American benefited from the national market created by railroads? (Answers might include that people had a wider range of products to choose from and that they could buy unusual or high-quality goods not available locally.)

Teaching the Reading Maps

Ask students what they notice about the location of large cities in 1900. Then ask why there is only one large city west of the Mississippi River despite the availability of resources. (Answers will vary but should include the fact that the East was settled first and the West was still in the process; San Francisco may have grown because immigrants settled there after crossing the Pacific Ocean and because of railroad access. **Answers to Reading Maps: 1.** Coal: East, Midwest; Iron: North, Southwest; Oil: South. **2.** Being near major means of transportation such as airports, railroads, rivers, and highways.

Teaching the

Link to the Present

Point out that originally the Sears catalog targeted people in rural areas. Ask students if they think people in rural areas today rely on catalogs as much as they did in the past. Why or why not? Why do people today in urban areas shop by catalog, even when they live near a wide variety of stores?

Discussion Answers: Answers will vary but should mention that people in remote areas often drive to towns or cities to shop. People in cities, on the other hand, might choose to shop by catalog to save time or gas, or to avoid traffic and crowds.

Section Activity

A Railroad Regulation Hearing

To help students understand controversies surrounding government regulation of railroads, have them role-play a congressional hearing. Divide the class into three groups. One will favor regulation, another oppose it, and the third will be the congressional committee. Students should identify themselves by profession (farmer, small business owner, large shipper, railroad executive, and so on) and support their positions persuasively. The committee should keep order, listen to both sides, and ask questions. Finally, have the class summarize the role-play.

Connections to Science

The invention of the air brake by George Westinghouse in 1869 marked a landmark in railroad safety. Before the air brake, trains were stopped by brakemen, who climbed on top of each car and, at the whistle of the engineer, turned a wheel to apply the brake. This method of braking was a common cause of worker injuries as well as of train wrecks.

With air brakes, the engineer has complete control of the brakes for each car. When the engineer engages the brake, compressed air shoots out and pushes on the pistons, which in turn push the brakes against the wheels. Air brakes became widely used on railroad cars beginning in 1872.

Link to the Present

Catalogs In 1993 Sears, Roebuck and Company stopped publishing its century-old catalog. Although shocking, the decision did not signal the death of the catalog business. In fact, today's catalog companies sell $60 billion in merchandise yearly.

1896 Sears Catalog

Still, the industry has changed. Unlike Sears, companies today offer specialty goods and the convenience of toll-free numbers. They keep costs down by mailing catalogs only to people who are likely to buy. To target potential customers, they study purchase records and rent specialized electronic mailing lists.

one-page list of items for sale. By 1874 his single sheet had grown to a 72-page catalog.

Ward soon had a competitor, Sears, Roebuck and Company. The Sears catalog, called "the Great Wish Book," came to include more than 1,000 pages of items, from children's shoes to tractors.

Madame C. J. Walker created a national market for her hair-care products both by sending them through the mail and by hiring young women to sell them door to door. Starting her company in the early 1900s with $1.50, she was the first African American woman in the nation to become a millionaire.

Improving railroad service With hundreds of companies building and running railroads, it was difficult to create an efficient rail system. For example, railroaders in the North used a narrower gauge, or distance between rails, than was used in the South. As a result, trains could not travel on all tracks.

Finally, the major railroads chose a standard gauge. Railroads in the South had to narrow almost 13,000 miles (20,800 km) of track. In one day—Sunday, May 30, 1886—frantic crews using crowbars and sledgehammers pushed thousands of miles of rail closer together.

Other developments also improved railroad service. The railway telegraph system developed by Granville T. Woods helped prevent collisions. Gustavus F. Swift and Philip D. Armour used refrigerated railcars to ship western beef safely from Chicago slaughterhouses to eastern butcher shops. George Westinghouse's air brakes and George M. Pullman's sleeping cars made rail travel safer and more comfortable.

Railroads and the environment The rapid expansion of the railroads came at a heavy cost to the environment. Lumber companies cut down whole forests for wood to make railroad ties and build bridges. Lumber was also used to build homes and furnish pulp for making paper. In 1901 one observer mourned the loss of forests in Georgia:

> "In 1864 when I first went over the railroad from Savannah to Thomasville there was an almost unbroken forest of magnificent pines . . . but now one may go over that same route and scarcely see a [saleable] pine. From most of the visible land the timber is entirely gone."

Most Americans, though, were excited by the opportunities offered by expanding railroads and other industries. Furthermore, it was hard to believe that our vast natural resources would ever run out.

History Footnote

Before 1875, live cattle had to be shipped to and then slaughtered in the destination city. Only in winter was it occasionally possible to ship slaughtered meat without it spoiling. Gustavus Swift, a butcher and cattle dealer, hoped to extend the market for meat by using refrigerator cars. He knew that butchered beef would take up much less space than live animals, enabling much more beef to be shipped at once to eastern markets. No railroad companies, however, would invest in Swift's idea. They had already built loading docks and feeding stations for shipping live cattle. Swift plunged ahead, using his own limited capital. By 1881 the refrigerator car was in use, and Swift was on his way to becoming a wealthy man in industry.

(Right) Switchmen and signalmen run train traffic through a railroad yard in 1886. (Above) Dispatchers today control train traffic from huge video maps at computer centers.

Railroad Competition

The railroad boom led to cutthroat competition. In the late 1870s, for example, there were 20 competing routes betweeen St. Louis and Atlanta.

Railroad companies that served the same area tried to drive one another out of business. Rate wars, in which competing railroads tried to charge less than their rivals, were common. The railroad that won a rate war then raised its rates to make up for lost revenue. Shippers had no choice but to pay the new rate.

Railroad companies also made secret deals with large shippers. They offered **rebates,** or refunds, of part of the shipping costs. In return, the shipper promised to use only that railroad.

Limiting competition To protect themselves from rate wars and rebate agreements, competing railroads sometimes combined to form "pools." The companies in a pool agreed to share freight business and fix prices at high levels. Pools did not always work, though. Members often broke agreements to make quick profits.

Another way to curb competition was by **consolidation.** In this method several companies were combined into one large company.

Cornelius Vanderbilt became a master at railroad consolidation. In the 1860s he began buying small railroad lines in New York. When the New York Central Railroad refused his offer, Vanderbilt stopped service between his lines and the Central. The loss of freight and passenger business forced the Central's directors to sell to Vanderbilt.

By 1873 Vanderbilt owned railroad lines that extended as far west as Chicago. Before his consolidation, passengers traveling from New York to Chicago had to change trains 17 times during a 50-hour trip. On Vanderbilt's lines, travel time was less than 24 hours.

A consolidated railroad could be run more efficiently and cheaply. With no competition, however, there was no reason to offer lower fares and shipping rates.

Regulating the Railroads

The main victims of cutthroat competition were the customers. Especially hard hit were

Discussion

Checking Understanding

1. In what ways did railroad companies improve their services? (The major railroads agreed to use a standard gauge track so trains could travel on all tracks. The railway telegraph system and the invention of air brakes helped to make train travel safer. Refrigerator cars made it possible to ship fresh meat. Sleeping cars made passengers more comfortable during long trips.)

Stimulating Critical Thinking

2. Do you think offering rebates to large-volume customers is a good business practice? Explain. (Yes: rebates reward the best customers and help ensure steady income for the company. No: rebates hurt smaller customers; unequal rates are basically unfair.)

Bonus Activity

Writing Railroad Songs

Point out that some of the nation's most beautiful country ballads, blues, work songs, and spirituals were inspired by the early railroads. Have each student write a song or poem about one aspect of the early railroads. If they are musically inclined, encourage them to put the words to music and perhaps perform the song for the class.

History Footnote

As a boy, Cornelius Vanderbilt, the son of New Jersey farmers, enjoyed boats more than anything else. He often spent afternoons gazing at ships sailing in and out of New York Bay and had the job of taking farm produce to New York in the family's sailboat. At 16, determined to have a boat of his own, he struck a "deal" with his mother. She would lend him $100 if he plowed and sowed a rocky family field. He persuaded his friends to help him with the task by promising them rides on the new boat. Vanderbilt used his boat to set up a ferry business. At the end of the first year, he had repaid his loan and earned an additional $1,000.

Vanderbilt made his fortune after entering the steamboat business in 1839. By age 40, he had accumulated wealth of more than $500,000.

Closing the Section

Wrap-Up Activity

Writing Editorials

To review the main concepts of the section, have each student choose three of the vocabulary words and write a brief editorial about each. Ask half of the class to write from the viewpoint of a big business tycoon and the other half from the viewpoint of a small farmer. Have students read aloud editorials from both viewpoints for each vocabulary word chosen.

Section Review

Answers

1. Definitions: *rebates* (265), *consolidation* (265), *regulate* (266), *free enterprise* (266), *interstate commerce* (266)

2. Railroads expanded and became safer, more efficient, and more comfortable. Effects: national market for raw materials and manufactured goods, damage to environment, faster and more pleasant train travel.

3. Rate wars, rebates, pools, and consolidation.

4. For: Small farmers and small business owners do not have to pay higher rates. Against: Railroads important to economic progress.

For a passage from The Octopus, see American Readings, pp. 25–26.

After some fierce competition, a small number of companies gained control of the railroads, sometimes by unfair means. This cartoon shows the "railroad barons" carving up the United States and even seeking to expand into Europe. The cartoon is entitled, "Let them have it all, and be done with it!"

small farmers and small business owners, who did not get rebates. To farmers, wrote novelist Frank Norris, the railroad was

> "the [sea monster] with tentacles of steel clutching into the soil, . . . the Master, the Colossus, the Octopus."

Faced with unfair shipping rates, they demanded that government **regulate**—make rules for—the railroads.

Up to this time, most Americans believed that government should not interfere with **free enterprise,** the economic system in which businesses are free to compete without government rules. Many people saw free enterprise as the reason for the nation's economic progress. Now, though, some Americans began to complain that free enterprise did not always serve the common good.

In the 1870s several midwestern states passed laws to halt unfair railroad practices. However, in 1886 the Supeme Court ruled that a state could not regulate the rates of railroads that crossed state lines. Only Congress had the power to regulate **interstate commerce**—business between states.

The Interstate Commerce Act The Court's decision led Congress to pass the Interstate Commerce Act in 1887. This act declared that all railroad rates must be "reasonable and just." It also set up the Interstate Commerce Commission (ICC) to investigate charges of unfair railroad practices. Railroads that refused to stop such practices could be taken to court by the ICC.

Although the courts usually sided with the railroads against the ICC, an important step had been taken. Congress had established a commission to regulate an industry. In the future such commissions would be created to oversee other industries.

1. Section Review

1. Define **rebates, consolidation, regulate, free enterprise,** and **interstate commerce.**
2. How did railroads change in the late 1800s? What effects did the changes have?
3. Describe two ways railroad companies tried to force competitors out of business.
4. Critical Thinking If you were in a debate about government regulation of railroad rates, what is one argument you would use for it? Against it?

Geography Footnote

The Canadian Shield was formed during the most recent ice age, about 2.5 million years ago. As huge ice sheets moved across the region, they scraped away soil, deposited rock debris, and carved out lake basins and riverbeds. Mining occurs primarily in the southern part of the shield. Not only iron ore but also copper, nickel, zinc, uranium, gold, silver, platinum, and molybdenum are mined.

Geography Lab

The Canadian Shield

Glaciers once ground across the rocky landscape of the Canadian Shield, leaving thousands of lakes behind. One of Minnesota's early governors, William R. Marshall, described the area as a "forest region of rocks, swamps, and marshes . . . accessible only by travel through the woods on foot, or by canoe on the rivers."

Much of the iron ore that fed the Industrial Revolution came from the Canadian Shield. In 1890 Leonidas Merritt and his brothers discovered huge deposits of iron ore there, in the Mesabi Range. The Merritts turned to business leader John D. Rockefeller to finance their mining operations. Rockefeller soon owned it all, though he leased most of the mines to Andrew Carnegie. Study the photos on this page to learn more about the Canadian Shield.

Lake Superior shoreline, Minnesota

Open pit mine in the Mesabi Range

Developing a Mental Map

Use the maps on pages R4–R8 and R11 to help answer the questions.

1. The Canadian Shield covers parts of which states? In what state is the Mesabi Range?

2. We often think of rocky regions as being mountainous. Is that the case in the Canadian Shield? Explain.

3. What characteristics of the Canadian Shield do the photographs portray?

4. The Canadian Shield is a popular vacation destination. Does that surprise you? Explain.

5. Hands-On Geography Imagine that it is 1892 and you have just arrived at the Mesabi Range to work in the mines. Write a diary entry describing your impressions of your new surroundings.

Teaching the Geography Lab

Point out that *shield* is not only a metaphor for the landform described but also a geologic term. It refers to a large, generally lowland area where the ancient bedrock of the earth is exposed at the surface. Ask students what image and associations the word *shield* brings to mind (a smooth, nearly flat surface; something hard and protective). Then ask them to use the text and upper photograph to distinguish the physical appearance of a shield from that of a plain. (Plain: uniformly flat, treeless region. Shield: large, low-lying region with some tree cover and some areas of higher elevation.)

Developing a Mental Map

Answers

1. Michigan, Wisconsin, Minnesota; Minnesota.

2. No. The region is rocky but low in elevation.

3. They show that the natural vegetation of the area is forest.

4. Answers will vary but may include that the Canadian Shield is an area of great natural beauty that would attract campers, canoeists, and so on.

5. Entries should include impressions based on the Mesabi Range geography, such as mountains, rocks, forest, and swamps.

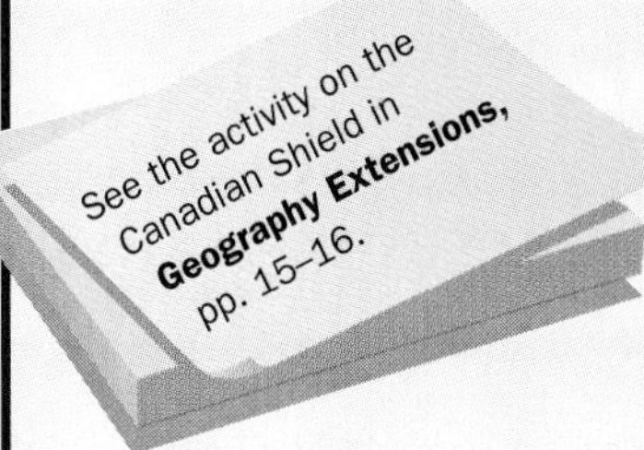
See the activity on the Canadian Shield in **Geography Extensions,** pp. 15–16.

Introducing the Section

Vocabulary

capital (p. 269) money used to produce goods

corporation (p. 269) a form of business that raises money by selling shares of stock to investors

stockholders (p. 269) investors who buy shares of stock in a business

dividends (p. 269) the part of a corporation's profits that is distributed to shareholders

trust (p. 272) a form of business combination in which member corporations are controlled by a board of trustees

Warm-Up Activity

Forming a Monopoly

To introduce the concept of a monopoly, ask one-half of the class to stand. Each student represents a large business. Those left seated are "out of business." Have businesses take turns to either buy assets (by telling a seated student to join them) or drive a competitor out of business (by telling another business with the same number or fewer people to sit down). Soon a class monopoly will form.

Geography Question of the Day

Have students look at the map on p. 263 and predict which big businesses might grow in the late 1800s as a result of these natural resources.

Section Objectives

- ★ Explain why businesspeople organized corporations in the late 1800s.
- ★ Describe new ways that business leaders found to combine businesses.
- ★ Explain why and how government tried to regulate big business.

Teaching Resources

Take-Home Planner 2, pp. 12–19
Chapter Resources Binder
Study Guide, p. 50
Reinforcement
Skills Development, pp. 55–56
Geography Extensions
American Readings, p. 27
Using Historical Documents
Transparency Activities, pp. 29–30
Chapter and Unit Tests

2. The Growth of Big Business

Reading Guide

New Terms capital, corporation, stockholders, dividends, trust

Section Focus Why new ways to organize businesses developed

1. **Why did businesspeople organize corporations in the late 1800s?**
2. **What new way did business leaders find to combine businesses?**
3. **Why and how did government try to regulate big business?**

The booming railroad industry spurred growth throughout the American economy. The railroads' demand for coal, iron, and wood boosted the mining and timber industries. Steel mills expanded, as did factories producing rails, ties, and cars.

As industries in the United States grew, farsighted business leaders found new ways to organize and control them. In the process, some became very rich.

Carnegie and Steel

Andrew Carnegie pioneered many of the changes in American business. He followed a simple formula for success: "Adopt every improvement, have the best machinery, and know the most" about your business. That formula made Carnegie into what admirers called a "captain of industry."

Carnegie's first venture was building iron bridges. From a friend, he had learned that wooden bridges would have to be replaced. The sparks from steam engines set them on fire and the trains were too heavy for wooden trestles. In 1865 Carnegie and four partners formed the Keystone Bridge Company.

The Bessemer process Carnegie knew that steel was better than iron for large construction projects because it was stronger and more flexible. However, making iron into steel was expensive.

In 1872 Carnegie went to Britain to see a process invented by Henry Bessemer. It greatly reduced the cost of making steel. Upon his return, Carnegie announced, "The day of iron has passed. Steel is king!"

A year later, Carnegie and several partners chose Pittsburgh, Pennsylvania, as the site for a steel mill that used the Bessemer process. Now steel could be used for rails, locomotives, railroad cars, and bridges.

Carnegie's steel empire Between the 1870s and 1890s, steel production in the nation rose rapidly. Competition for customers was fierce. Carnegie was determined to win out by selling a better product at a lower cost than other companies. He hired scientists to improve his steel and the best managers he could find to produce it.

Carnegie also set out to control every step in the steelmaking process. He did not want to pay outsiders for work his own company could do at a lower cost. By the 1890s Carnegie's company was mining all the ore it needed from its own iron mines. His own ships and railroad transported the ore to his Pittsburgh mill.

Carnegie was also gaining control of the steel industry through consolidation. In the 1870s and 1880s he bought out several rival companies. In 1892 he combined them to form the giant Carnegie Steel Company. It produced 25 percent of the nation's steel.

History Footnote

In 1906 Woodrow Wilson, then president of Princeton University, invited Carnegie to visit his campus, hoping for a donation. Wilson proudly showed Carnegie the playing fields, not knowing that Carnegie thought football was dangerous and stupid. When Carnegie was about to leave, he told Wilson he knew just what Princeton needed—a lake. "That would take the young men's minds off football!" Carnegie said. Carnegie gave Princeton $400,000 to build a 3.5-mile-long lake.

After ten years of philanthropy, Carnegie decided the job of giving away all his money was too hard for him to do alone. He set up the Carnegie Corporation in New York with an endowment of $125 million. It was the first modern philanthropic foundation administered by trustees skilled in business.

Corporations

To build and operate big businesses, owners like Andrew Carnegie needed large amounts of **capital**—money used to produce goods. To get it, they formed corporations. A **corporation** is a type of business that raises money by selling shares of stock to investors. The investors, who are known as **stockholders,** then own part of the business. They elect the board of directors that runs the business.

If a corporation is profitable, its stockholders earn **dividends,** or part of the profits. At the same time, they are protected if the corporation goes bankrupt. They lose only the amount they invested.

Morgan and Banking

To manage the huge sums of money obtained from investors, corporations came to rely on investment bankers. The bankers sold stock, arranged loans, and gave advice on how to run profitable businesses.

In the late 1800s the most powerful investment banker in the United States was J. Pierpont Morgan. Believing that cutthroat competition was wasteful, he bought failing railroads and consolidated them.

Next Morgan decided to merge his railroads with steel companies into a single large corporation. Only Andrew Carnegie stood in his way. Instead of challenging Carnegie, the wily Morgan offered to buy him out. The idea appealed to Carnegie, who was now 66 years old. He sent Morgan a scrap of paper with his price on it: $480 million. Morgan agreed on the spot.

In 1901 Morgan formed the United States Steel Corporation. The largest corporation in the world at the time, it made three-fifths of the nation's steel.

The "Gospel of Wealth"

The sale of his company made Carnegie one of the richest people in the world, with a fortune of $500 million. He already knew what he was going to do with it.

Hands-On HISTORY

Choosing worthy causes "Pity the poor millionaire, for the way of the philanthropist is hard." So wrote an exhausted Andrew Carnegie after more than a decade of philanthropy—donating money to worthy causes. Carnegie gave away more than $300 million, mostly to causes that he listed in the following order of worthiness.

1. universities
2. free libraries
3. hospitals
4. parks
5. concert and meeting halls
6. swimming baths [pools]
7. churches

Activity Imagine that you have a fortune to give away. Choose seven causes to which you will make donations. List the causes in order of importance to you. Share the list with your classmates, giving reasons for your choices.

Carnegie with libraries

Developing the Section

Discussion

Checking Understanding

1. How did investment bankers help corporations? (They sold stock, arranged loans, and gave advice on how to run profitable businesses.)

Stimulating Critical Thinking

2. Why do you think someone in 1892 would purchase shares in the Carnegie Steel Company? (Confidence because of past success; huge demand for steel; desire to make money.)

Teaching the Hands-On HISTORY

To brainstorm causes for their list, have students think about problems they would like to solve. These could be local, national, or global. Have them list organizations that might help solve these problems or suggest new organizations to fit needs on their lists.

Vital Links

Carnegie castle (Picture) Unit 4, Side 1, Search 15052

See also Unit 4 Explore CD-ROM location 132.

Section Activity

Starting a Business

To help students understand the dynamics of starting a business, have small groups each assume that they have formed a new company with a new product or service. Have each group decide whether to become a corporation and seek outside investors or keep control of the company themselves. Have them list the advantages and disadvantages of each and share their decisions with the class.

Teaching the

Explain that in the design of a suspension bridge, the weight of the *roadway* is supported by two main *cables* that pass over *towers* on each side and have ends that are securely anchored. Ask students to draw a simple sketch of a suspension bridge based on the picture here, and to label the parts. They should also label the *main span* between the towers. Remind students that the concept of a suspension bridge was not new—the Incas, for example, built them in the 1500s out of straw rope—but the use of steel made it possible to build longer and stronger bridges.

Tips for Teaching

Gifted Students

Political cartoonists of the late 1800s depicted wealthy business leaders as both admirable and despicable. Have gifted students present an important aspect of Andrew Carnegie's or John D. Rockefeller's career in a political cartoon. Have them first study other cartoons, such as those printed in the front of news magazines or in daily newspapers. Point out that such cartoons usually focus on a single aspect of the subject, use simplified images that are often labeled, and employ exaggeration to make a point.

In an 1889 article called "The Gospel of Wealth," Carnegie had pointed out the wide gap between the mass of Americans struggling to make a living and business leaders who had gained great wealth. Such wealth, he argued, carried with it the social responsibility to "help those who will help themselves."

Practicing what he preached, Carnegie devoted the rest of his life to giving much of his fortune to worthy causes. He gave 7,689 organs to churches, built more than 1,900 libraries for towns throughout the United States, and supported colleges.

Rockefeller and Oil

While Carnegie and Morgan were building empires in steel, a new industry was being born. Before the Civil War, the petroleum industry did not exist. In fact, no one valued

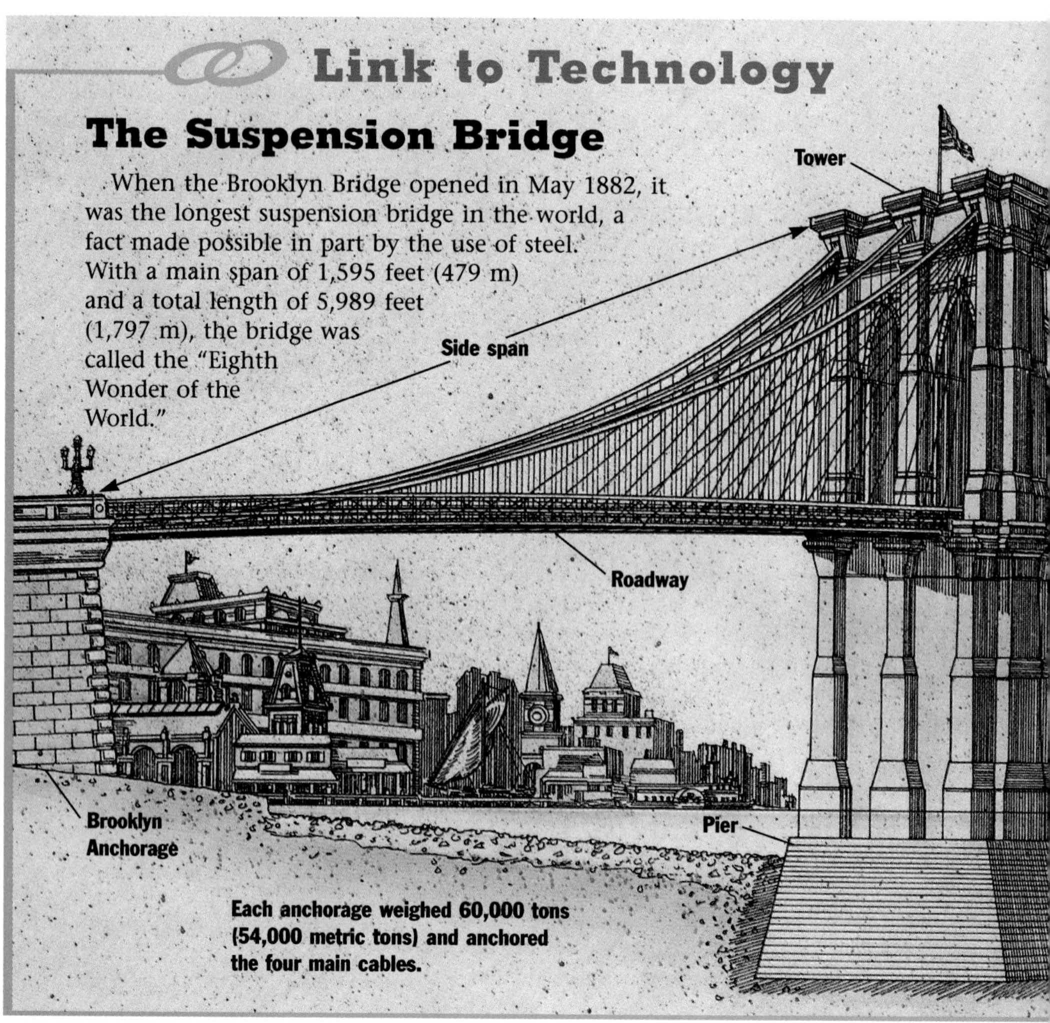

Link to Technology
The Suspension Bridge
When the Brooklyn Bridge opened in May 1882, it was the longest suspension bridge in the world, a fact made possible in part by the use of steel. With a main span of 1,595 feet (479 m) and a total length of 5,989 feet (1,797 m), the bridge was called the "Eighth Wonder of the World."
Tower
Side span
Roadway
Brooklyn Anchorage
Pier
Each anchorage weighed 60,000 tons (54,000 metric tons) and anchored the four main cables.

History Footnote

The business of selling petroleum began in Titusville, Pennsylvania. For many years, Seneca Indians collected petroleum to use as medicine. The settlers called it "Seneca Oil."

In the early 1850s, a businessman named Samuel Kier bottled and sold the oil, cheaper and brighter-burning than whale oil, to be used in lamps. Demand for it grew, and the first petroleum company—Brewer, Watson and Company—was formed. At first, they bottled only three to six gallons a day.

As supplies of the surface oil diminished, entrepreneur Edwin L. Drake formed the Seneca Oil Company and began to drill for oil in the area, using new drilling techniques and equipment, such as a drill powered by a stationary steam engine. The machine, which could dig only three feet a day, took several months to strike oil.

petroleum, often called oil, except to grease wagon axles or to take as medicine.

Then in 1855 a scientist reported that oil was a good lubricant for machinery. Refined oil, called kerosene, also made an excellent source of light and heat. Kerosene soon replaced whale oil as the main fuel for lamps.

In 1859 the nation's first oil well was drilled in Pennsylvania, spurring a frantic rush for "black gold." Soon oil wells were pumping in Kentucky, Ohio, Illinois, Indiana, and West Virginia. By the early 1900s huge new oil fields had been discovered in Texas, California, and Oklahoma.

Rockefeller's oil empire One of the early visitors to Pennsylvania's oil fields was John D. Rockefeller. Growing up in Cleveland, Ohio, he had started a business to sell farm produce when he was 20 years old.

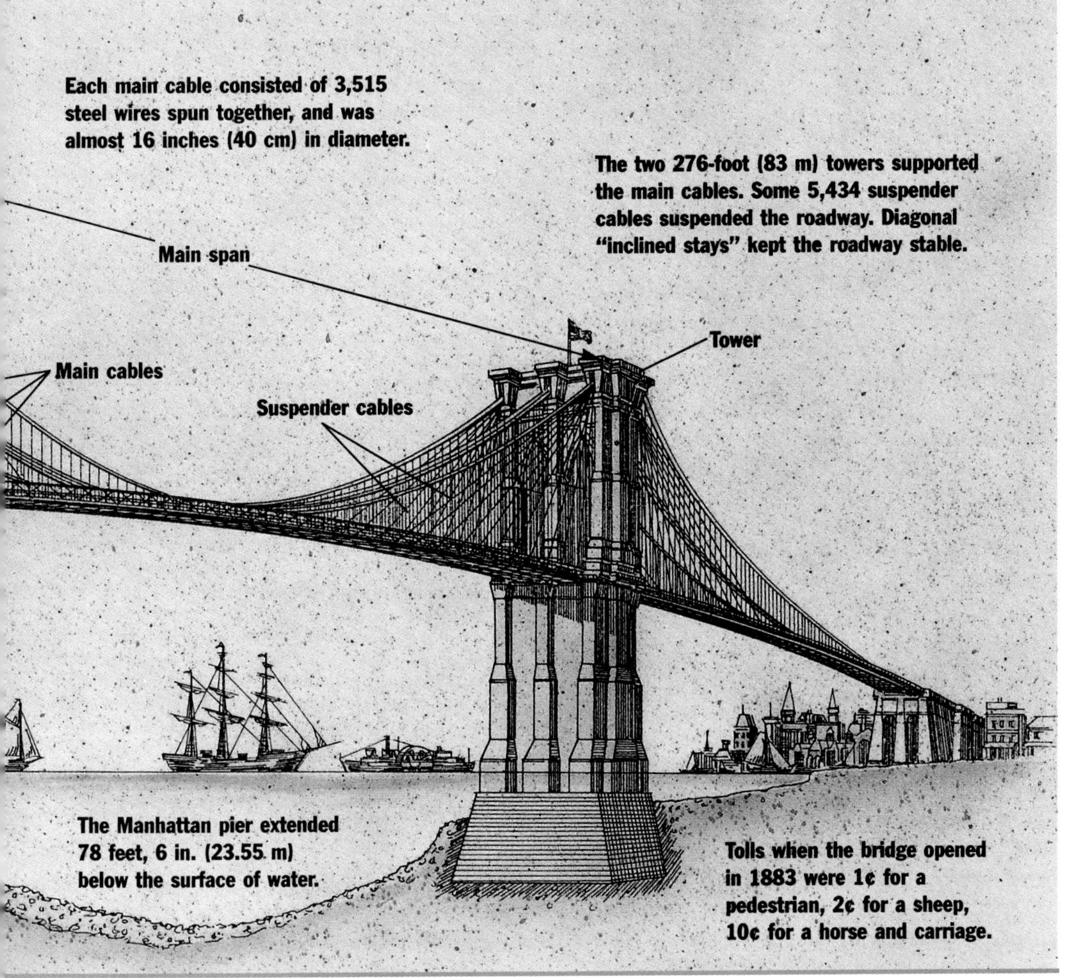

Each main cable consisted of 3,515 steel wires spun together, and was almost 16 inches (40 cm) in diameter.
The two 276-foot (83 m) towers supported the main cables. Some 5,434 suspender cables suspended the roadway. Diagonal "inclined stays" kept the roadway stable.
Main span
Tower
Main cables
Suspender cables
The Manhattan pier extended 78 feet, 6 in. (23.55 m) below the surface of water.
Tolls when the bridge opened in 1883 were 1¢ for a pedestrian, 2¢ for a sheep, 10¢ for a horse and carriage.

Discussion

Checking Understanding

1. How did the new oil industry affect the average household? (People used kerosene, a refined oil, in place of whale oil in lamps.)

Stimulating Critical Thinking

2. How do you think business leaders might best help the poor—by donating to charities, such as colleges and homeless shelters, or by paying employees higher wages? Explain. (Charities: help the poor directly by providing for basic necessities and the opportunity to improve their economic condition through education. Higher wages: low-income people gain financial independence and the freedom to use increased income at their own discretion to improve their lives without having to depend on outside charity.)

Bonus Activity

A Meeting of Minds

To reinforce understanding of Carnegie's and Rockefeller's business methods and attitudes, have pairs of students role-play conversations between the two in which they compare notes about their business methods and their attitudes toward wealth and success. The role-plays should bring out similarities as well as differences.

Teaching the World Link

Remind students that technology, such as the spinning jenny that spurred the Industrial Revolution in the United States, was often "imported" from Great Britain, when inventors such as Samuel Slater shared their knowledge with American business owners. Ask why Europe and the United States might have wanted to share technology with countries such as Japan in the late 1800s. (Would offer new markets and investment opportunities for western corporations.)

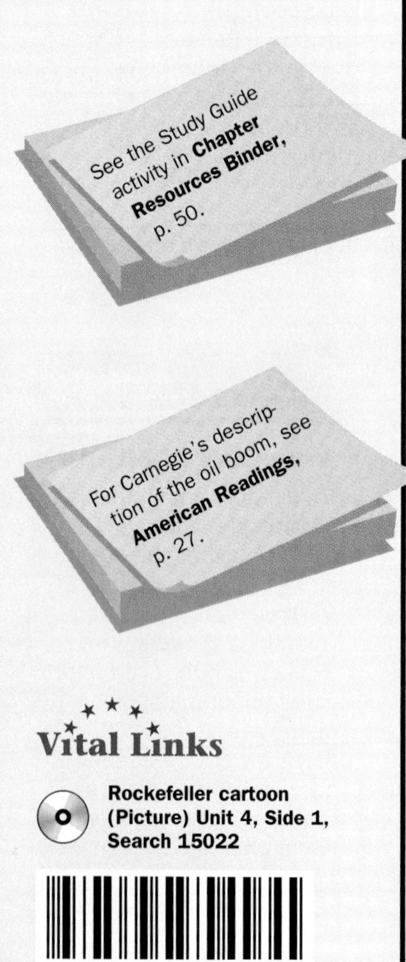

See the Study Guide activity in **Chapter Resources Binder,** p. 50.
For Carnegie's description of the oil boom, see **American Readings,** p. 27.

Vital Links

Rockefeller cartoon (Picture) Unit 4, Side 1, Search 15022

See also Unit 4 Explore CD-ROM location 128.

History Footnote

In 1922 the Supreme Court ruled that baseball was exempt from antitrust laws. In its ruling the Court declared that baseball was a business involving state exhibitions, not interstate commerce. Baseball's special status was challenged in 1953 and 1972, but the Court took no action, arguing that Congress should be the one to lift the exemption.

The issue surfaced again in 1994 when owners refused to agree to player demands. Players went on strike. When the World Series was canceled, some lawmakers argued for lifting the exemption, thus allowing the courts to intercede in the labor dispute. It was not lifted, however. The players and owners eventually reached an agreement, but the bad public relations hurt the popularity of the sport.

Instead of fighting in the Civil War, he paid for a substitute and expanded his business.

In 1862 Rockefeller established an oil-refining business in Cleveland. Eight years later he reorganized the business as a corporation, Standard Oil of Ohio.

John D. Rockefeller

Faced with intense competition and falling prices, Rockefeller set out to gain control of the oil-refining industry. He made deals with railroads to give rebates to Standard Oil. He could then lower his prices and force rival refineries out of business. In a depression that began in 1873, he bought the bankrupt companies.

To keep costs down, Rockefeller also set out to control each step of production. He bought pipelines and ships for moving oil. He built his own warehouses and made his own barrels. He even counted the drops of solder required to seal oil containers.

By 1880 Standard Oil controlled 90 percent or more of the nation's refining and almost all oil transportation. That made it a monopoly—a single business with the power to control prices in the market.

Organizing Trusts

To manage his empire better, in 1882 Rockefeller combined all the corporations he controlled into the Standard Oil Trust. A **trust** was a new form of business combination in which a board of trustees, or managers, controlled the member corporations.

Stockholders of Standard Oil's member corporations still owned their stock. However, the board of the Standard Oil Trust, headed by Rockefeller, managed the corporations. In return, stockholders received "trust certificates" that paid dividends from Standard's profits.

The Standard Oil Trust ensured that the oil industry would operate more efficiently than it had in the past. The danger was that, as a monopoly, it had the power to set high prices for oil and oil products. The free-enterprise system depended on competition to keep prices fair. By getting rid of competition, Standard seemed to threaten the free-enterprise system itself.

The Sherman Antitrust Act Meanwhile, other business leaders saw the advantages of the Standard Oil Trust. Soon they had formed trusts in other industries,

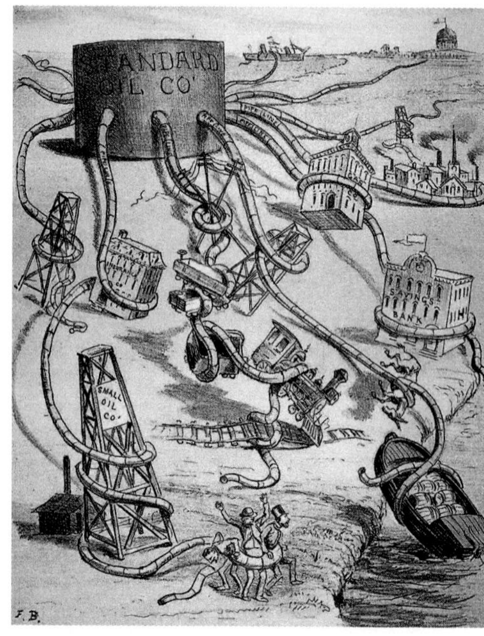

This 1884 cartoon, "The Monster Monopoly," attacked John D. Rockefeller's Standard Oil Company, which almost completely controlled the oil industry in the United States.

History Footnote

The Vanderbilts and other wealthy industrial families spent their summers in a colony of the rich on the rocky coast of Newport, Rhode Island. Their days were occupied with formal picnics and luncheons, dinners and balls, polo matches and yachting races. At "summer cottages," which were actually palatial mansions, they pursued a way of life that was so luxurious that even visiting royalty were astonished. One family bedded its horses on linen sheets bearing the family monogram. Many threw exquisite, richly costumed balls that cost up to $200,000. At one dinner party, guests gathered around a sandbox centerpiece and were invited to use tiny pails and shovels made of sterling silver to dig for rubies, diamonds, and sapphires.

including sugar, meatpacking, leather, copper, and farm machinery. The growth of monopoly power alarmed many Americans. They demanded reasonable prices and the chance for smaller businesses to compete in any market.

In response to public pressure, Congress passed the Sherman Antitrust Act in 1890. The act declared that

> "every contract, combination in the form of trust or otherwise, or conspiracy in restraint of trade . . . is hereby declared to be illegal."

However, the Sherman Act proved difficult to enforce because it did not define what a trust or a monopoly was. In fact, the act was not enforced until the early 1900s, when the courts finally broke up two trusts for using unfair business practices. One was the Standard Oil Trust.

Captains of Industry or Robber Barons?

As companies grew, so did the wealth of their owners. There had been very few millionaires in the United States before the Civil War. By the 1890s, however, there were more than 4,000 of them. Most of them were entrepreneurs—people who start businesses—who had made their fortunes by driving their competitors out of business, sometimes by unfair methods. Critics called them "robber barons."

At the same time, many people could not help but admire what entrepreneurs like Carnegie, Morgan, and Rockefeller had accomplished. By seeing opportunities and forming large business combinations, these captains of industry had made the steel and oil industries grow and prosper. In so doing they had helped the United States become the leading industrial nation in the world.

Japan becomes an industrial nation Half a world away from booming American factories, Japan's leaders were creating another industrial giant. Their efforts were spearheaded by Emperor Meiji (MAY-jee), who was only 15 years old when he came to the throne in 1867. A year later he announced his plan to make Japan an industrial nation.

To achieve his goal, Emperor Meiji looked outward. "Knowledge shall be sought throughout the world," the emperor declared. He sent groups of Japanese to Europe and the United States to study modern industrial technology. During the late 1800s, Japan built railroads, telegraph lines, shipyards, seagoing vessels, and factories.

2. Section Review

1. Define **capital, corporation, stockholders, dividends,** and **trust.**
2. Name two forms of business organization that developed in the late 1800s and describe how they operated.
3. How did Andrew Carnegie and John D. Rockefeller deal with fierce competition?
4. Why did Congress pass the Sherman Antitrust Act? Explain why the act was not successful.
5. **Critical Thinking** Captains of industry argued that consolidated companies were more efficient than many small, competing companies. As the owner of a small business, how would you have responded?

Closing the Section

Wrap-Up Activity

Conducting an Interview

To help students review how entrepreneurs shaped entire industries, have them prepare questions for an interview with John D. Rockefeller or Andrew Carnegie. Questions should focus on early careers, business strategies, and public images.

Section Review Answers

1. Definitions: *capital* (269), *corporation* (269), *stockholders* (269), *dividends* (269), *trust* (272)
2. Corporation—business that raised money by selling shares to investors and bought out bankrupt companies to increase its profits. Trust—group of corporations managed by a board of trustees, which held a monopoly in an industry and controlled prices.
3. Controlled every step in steelmaking and oil refining businesses, and bought out rival companies until they had a monopoly.
4. To ensure reasonable prices and open up competition; it was hard to enforce because it did not define trust or monopoly.
5. While consolidated companies might be more efficient because they operated under the same set of guidelines and had more resources, smaller companies had to manage resources more efficiently to survive the competition.

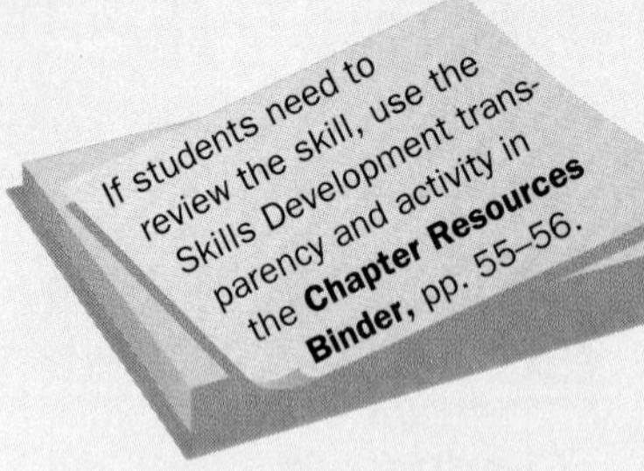

If students need to review the skill, use the Skills Development transparency and activity in the **Chapter Resources Binder**, pp. 55–56.

Introducing the Skill Lab

Explain that a process is much easier to comprehend if it is presented as a set of steps. A flowchart isolates and links each step graphically, showing both sequence and cause–effect relationships. After students have followed the procedure, suggest that they check their statements for brevity and clarity. They should use consistent terms throughout the flowchart. For example, instead of using both *company* and *corporation* to refer to a business, they should use just one of these terms.

Skill Lab

Answers

1. (b) Descriptions of each relationship should be similar to the following: each of the two events in the first sentence (reduced production costs and opening of new markets) is a cause of the event in the second sentence (profits rose). That is, the event in the second sentence is an effect of the two events in the first sentence.

(Answers continued in top margin)

2. (b) Possible rest of flowchart: → New businesses enter field. → Competition increases. → Surplus of goods is produced. → Businesses cut prices. → Profits fall. → Smaller businesses fail. → Surviving firms buy failing companies.

3. Businesses rose and fell as profits rose and fell, due to cheaper production methods, increased competition, market surpluses, and the opportunity to buy failed businesses.

For further application, have students do the Applying Skills activity in the Chapter Survey (p. 282).

Skill Lab

Skill Tips

- Use present tense for statements in flowchart boxes.
- Use as few words as possible.
- Any step may be both a cause (with one or more effects) and an effect (with one or more causes).

Acquiring Information

Analyzing a Flowchart

In 1865 dozens of companies were building oil wells and refineries. Within 15 years, though, Standard Oil had gobbled up most of them, gaining almost complete control over the industry. The oil industry is a dramatic example of the fact that few businesses could survive the fierce competition of the late 1800s.

Question to Investigate

Why did many businesses rise and fall in the late 1800s?

Procedure

One way to explore the Question to Investigate is by creating a **flowchart**—a diagram that uses words and arrows to show steps in a process. A box indicates an individual step. Arrows connect the steps in order. By showing at a glance how one step leads to another, a flowchart is useful for showing cause–effect relationships.

1 Identify the cause–effect relationships.
a. Read source **A**.
b. State each cause–effect relationship in a few words.

2 Arrange the causes and effects into a flowchart.
a. Study **B** as a model and copy it to begin your flowchart.
b. Add arrows and statements in boxes to show the causes and effects described in **A**. Refer to the Skill Tips.

3 Analyze the flowchart in order to answer the Question to Investigate.

Sources to Use

A "Briefly, then, machinery reduced production costs and expansion opened new markets. Profits rose. New entrepreneurs were attracted into the field, competed vigorously with each other, produced a surplus and, under the necessities of business warfare, slashed prices. Profits fell. There was then a general mortality [death] among marginal firms—those that could not push their costs of production down beneath new low prices. Finally, the assets of the deceased [dead] organizations were taken over by a reduced number of survivors. Competition had yielded concentration as one of its fruits."

From Bernard Weisberger et al., *The Life History of the United States*, Vol. 7 (Time-Life Books, 1974).

B

Machinery reduces production costs. ↘
Expansion opens new markets. ↙
Profits rise.

Section Objectives

- ★ Describe the conditions that led workers to organize unions after the Civil War.
- ★ Identify the methods that workers used to improve their wages and working conditions.
- ★ Evaluate the success of workers in achieving their goals.

Teaching Resources

Take-Home Planner 2, pp. 12–19
Chapter Resources Binder
Study Guide, p. 51
Reinforcement, pp. 53–54
Skills Development
Geography Extensions
American Readings, p. 28
Using Historical Documents, pp. 48–51
Transparency Activities
Chapter and Unit Tests, pp. 47–50

3. Workers Struggle for a Better Life

Reading Guide

New Terms **collective bargaining, arbitration, injunction, socialism**

Section Focus **How American workers responded to changes brought about by industrialization**

1. **What conditions led workers to organize unions after the Civil War?**
2. **What methods did workers use to try to improve their wages and working conditions?**
3. **How successful were workers in achieving their goals?**

In 1874 a brakeman applied for a job at a railroad yard. The yardmaster asked,

> "'When will you be ready to go to work?'
> 'Right away,' I said.
> The yardmaster looked at his watch.
> 'Well, you had better get your dinner first. There's no use of your getting killed on an empty stomach.'"

That afternoon a co-worker was crushed to death between two cars.

Changes in the Workplace

Such accidents occurred frequently on the railroads—and in other industries as well. It seemed as if the safety and well-being of workers were of little or no concern to the captains of industry.

In fact, the rapid industrial growth in the late 1800s greatly changed the relations between employers and their workers. Gone were the days when most goods were produced in small shops where owners knew their workers and took an interest in their welfare. Instead, as Andrew Carnegie wrote, "all [communication] between them is at an end . . . and often there is friction between the employer and the employed."

Gone, too, were the days when skilled workers were in demand. In many factories now, workers endlessly repeated one or two tasks that called for little skill or training. They could be replaced as easily as the parts in their machines.

To make matters worse, there were plenty of workers available. Immigrants and people from rural areas streamed into the cities, eager to take any job at any wage. With many workers to choose from, business owners could pay very low wages.

Working Families

Indeed, wages were so low that the average man could not earn enough to support his family. Wives and children, too, had to get jobs. Employers were glad to hire them at lower wages than men.

In 1900 as many as 2 million children went to work instead of to school. They sold newspapers and shined shoes. They worked in mills, factories, and mines. At the Triangle Shirtwaist Company, Pauline Newman remembered:

Introducing the Section

Vocabulary

collective bargaining (p. 278) process by which representatives of a union and a business discuss and reach agreement

arbitration (p. 278) using a third party to settle a dispute

injunction (p. 280) a court order

socialism (p. 281) the belief that government, rather than individuals, should own a nation's major industries

Warm-Up Activity

Analyzing Visuals

To preview the labor movement, have students write three statements about the lives of workers, supporting each with evidence from the photographs and illustrations in the section. Some possible observations: crowded and dangerous conditions, child labor, poor wages.

Geography Question of the Day

Ask students to imagine they are living in the 1870s and decide to move from a rural area to take a factory job in one of the cities shown on the map on p. 263. Ask them to write about the adjustments they would need to make and the difference between city life and country life.

Developing the Section

Bonus Activity

Setting Workers' Priorities

To help students understand the issues that led workers to form unions, have groups brainstorm the different issues and objectives. They should assume they are young women who work for the Triangle Shirtwaist Company. (See description on this page.) Groups should write specific objectives for bettering working conditions and then rank their objectives in order of importance. Have them each circle the change that their employer might be most willing to accept. Compare groups' lists and have a volunteer make a master list on the chalkboard.

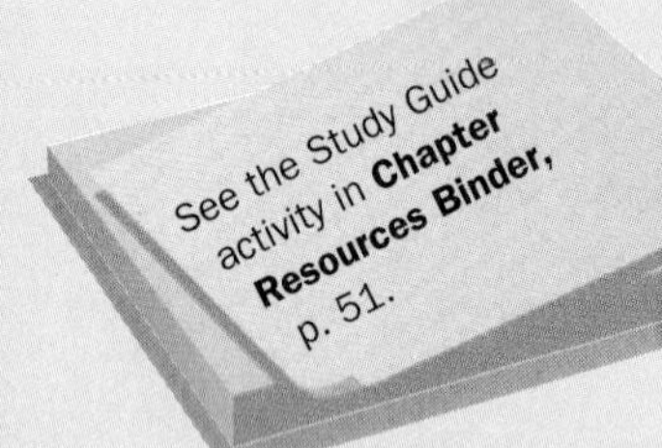

See the Study Guide activity in **Chapter Resources Binder,** p. 51.

Connections to Economics

By 1900, 20 percent of American women were in the work force. They were most numerous in textile mills and tobacco factories, where they made up more than half of the workers. They also worked in the shoe industry, in meatpacking and canning, in heavy industries such as foundries (where metal is melted and poured into molds to make machinery parts, for example), in cablemaking and hinge factories, and in the new electrical industry. Most jobs open to women required little skill. When women were able to obtain more skillful jobs, they typically earned a third to a half of what men did for the same work.

In many industries, wages were so low that two working parents could not support a family. Children, too, were sent to work. Here men and boys work in a mine and in a glass factory. Women (top) labor in a "sweatshop" in the garment industry. A family (left) works at home making artificial flowers.

"We were young, eight, nine, ten years old. . . . The hours were from 7:30 in the morning to 6:30 at night when it wasn't busy. When the [busy] season was on we worked until 9 o'clock. No overtime pay, not even supper money. . . . My wages were $1.50 for a seven-day week."

Many women worked in the garment industry, making clothes in factories or in crowded rooms called "sweatshops." Their pay was based on the number of pieces they produced. In 1885 a New York City seamstress received $1.50 for a dozen pairs of trousers, 15¢ for a vest, and 90¢ for a dozen pairs of gloves.

History Footnote

From the age of 50 until she died at age 100, Mother Jones made the labor struggle her life's work. Having lost her entire family in a yellow fever epidemic in 1867, she went to Chicago and worked as a dressmaker. There she became deeply concerned about economic inequality and began to attend meetings of the Knights of Labor. After 1880 she traveled tirelessly to industrial troublespots. She organized unions among coal miners in West Virginia, joined striking machinists of the Southern Pacific Railroad, and protested child labor by leading child workers on a march from textile mills in Pennsylvania to the home of President Theodore Roosevelt. When she received congratulations from former adversary John D. Rockefeller, Jr., on her 100th birthday, she said, "He's a damn good sport. I've licked him many times."

The Growth of Labor Organizations

Compared to the manager of a large mill or factory, an individual worker had little power. Desperate workers began to realize that they could improve wages and working conditions only if they organized into groups to fight for common goals.

Working people in the United States had begun forming trade unions in the early 1800s. The rapid rise of industry after the Civil War led to another upsurge in workers trying to organize unions.

As before, employers tried to kill the union movement. They offered jobs to workers who promised never to join unions. They fired union members and put them on "blacklists," ensuring that other businesses would not hire them. Despite this opposition, many brave workers did join labor organizations.

The Knights of Labor One of the most important new unions was the Knights of Labor, which was founded in 1869. Unlike earlier unions, the Knights accepted any worker, skilled or unskilled, male or female, of any race.

Growth was slow until Terence V. Powderly, a machinist recently elected mayor of Scranton, Pennsylvania, became the leader of the Knights in 1879. An idealist, Powderly attracted members by calling for an eight-hour workday, equal pay for equal work by men and women, and an end to child labor.

One of the most successful organizers for the Knights—and other unions—was a seamstress named Mary Harris Jones. From the 1870s through the 1920s, she traveled around the country urging workers to join unions. Most of her work was with coal miners, but she also helped metal and railroad workers and women garment workers, and led protests against child labor. She later said,

> "My life work has been to stir up the oppressed to a point of getting off their knees and demanding that which I believe is rightfully theirs."

Grateful miners called Mary Harris Jones "Mother" Jones. Mine owners, however, regarded her as "the most dangerous woman in America."

The Great Railroad Strike

As unions gained strength, they were able to organize strikes to force employers to make changes. In 1877 workers on the Baltimore and Ohio Railroad went on strike to protest pay cuts. Railroad workers across the country joined them, setting off the first nationwide strike.

Bloody battles broke out when state and federal troops were called in to put down the strike. By the time the workers gave up, more than 100 had been killed.

The Great Railroad Strike failed, but between 1884 and 1886 the Knights held a series of successful strikes against wage cuts. Their victories attracted new members to the union. By 1886 the Knights had more than 700,000 members.

The Haymarket Bombing

Then, at the height of their success, a violent incident dealt a fatal blow to the Knights of Labor. On May 3, 1886, striking workers in Chicago clashed with police. Several strikers were killed.

A mass meeting to protest the killings was held the next evening in Haymarket Square. As the meeting was ending, the police arrived. Suddenly a bomb exploded. The police responded by opening fire. Altogether eight policemen and seven or eight people in the crowd were killed. About a hundred were wounded.

Discussion

Checking Understanding

1. Why did many children go to work in the factories? (Because wages were low the average man and woman could not earn enough to support a family, so children also worked.)

Stimulating Critical Thinking

2. Why do you think many women worked in the garment industry? (Most learned domestic skills such as sewing as part of their upbringing. Employers probably assumed that women were more skillful sewers than men. Also, they could pay women lower wages.)

3. Why do you think the federal government helped put down the Railroad Strike of 1877? (It was a nationwide strike, and railroads were the nation's economic lifeline. Railroad owners had enough power to influence government officials.)

Vital Links

Voice of "Mother" Jones (First Person Account) Unit 4, Side 1, Search 11592, Play to 12337

See also Unit 4 Explore CD-ROM location 87.

For Mother Jones's description of child labor in the mines, see **American Readings**, p. 28.

Tips for Teaching

Students with Limited English

Allow students with limited skills in speaking or writing English to demonstrate their understanding of the main points of the section by creating recruitment posters for a labor union. The posters should focus on the concerns, goals, or tactics of the union as well as successes (perhaps "before and after" pictures). Posters should include a brief message or slogan and the name of the union. Students should also target their posters to specific groups of workers such as seamstresses, railroad workers, or steel workers.

Section Activity

A Workers' Dialogue

To underscore conditions that led workers to organize unions, have small groups write dialogues between two workers. First, each group should develop an identity for the worker (name, age, sex, job, work setting, job-related concerns, attitude toward unions, and so on) and decide on a context for the dialogue (possibilities: an after-work talk, a union meeting). When the writing is completed, have one member of each group introduce the characters and setting to the class. Then ask two group members to read the dialogue aloud. After each group has presented its dialogue, conclude with a discussion of observations and comments.

Teaching the Point of View

Ask students what they think Gompers meant by "all else" when he once said he thought strikes were useful "if all else failed." Have students discuss how far apart or similar these men's beliefs really were. Then ask students to discuss the pros and cons of collective bargaining or arbitration vs. strikes. (Strikes might draw negative response from employers but force them to take quick action to improve workers' conditions. Collective bargaining or arbitration might not force quick action but might help maintain better long-term worker-employer relations.)

Although no evidence linked the Knights to the bombing, the Haymarket affair turned public opinion against them. From 1886 on, membership in the Knights dropped rapidly.

The American Federation of Labor

As the Knights declined, a new national union was gaining strength. In 1886 representatives of many trade unions formed the American Federation of Labor (AFL). The AFL admitted only skilled workers, and most of its member unions barred women, African Americans, and immigrants.

The guiding spirit of the AFL was its president, Samuel Gompers. Born in London of Dutch-Jewish parents, Gompers came to the United States in 1863, when he was 13. At the age of 14, he became a member of the Cigarmakers' International Union. There he quickly showed his talent as a writer, speaker, and labor organizer.

Under Gompers, the AFL grew rapidly. By 1900 it claimed a million members. As head of the AFL, Gompers focused on practical issues. He fought for higher wages, shorter hours, and better working conditions.

Gompers believed that the best way to obtain these goals was through **collective bargaining**—the process by which the representatives of a union and a business discuss and reach agreement about wages and working conditions. However, if collective bargaining failed, Gompers did not hesitate to call a strike.

Samuel Gompers

Point of View

Should unions use the strike?

The question of whether to use the strike divided organized labor. Terence Powderly of the Knights of Labor believed that "strikes are a failure." He preferred **arbitration**—using a third party to settle a dispute. One of the Knights' major goals, Powderly wrote, was to

> "[substitute] arbitration for strikes, whenever and wherever employers and employees are willing to meet on [equal] grounds."

AFL leader Samuel Gompers was more enthusiastic about strikes. He saw them as a useful tool to achieve goals if all else failed. He also believed workers have the right to strike. In a letter in 1894, he wrote:

> "What shall workers do? Sit idly by and see the vast resources of nature and the human mind be used and monopolized for the benefit of the . . . few? No. The laborers must learn to think and [strike, so that] . . . their rights to life can be secured."

In the years to come, the question of whether to strike would be on the minds of workers, employers, and the public as strikes wracked the nation.

The Homestead Strike

Several violent strikes shook the labor movement in the 1890s. One of the worst involved Andrew Carnegie.

In 1892 the Carnegie steel plant at Homestead, Pennsylvania, cut wages. The Amalgamated Association of Iron and Steel Workers, one of the most powerful trade unions in the country, called a strike.

History Footnote

Pullman believed that by building an all-new town for his workers, he could prevent the problems associated with industrialism—slums, crime, and especially labor disorders. Pullman, however, did not claim to be a philanthropist, saying that the scheme was "strictly a business proposition." Some writers praised the "beauty and convenience" of the all-brick town as well as the absence of saloons. Critics said the idea was undemocratic: "It is benevolent, well-wishing feudalism, which desires the happiness of the people, but in such a way as shall please the authorities."

In this illustration from *Harper's Weekly*, armed guards surrender to striking workers at the Carnegie steel plant in Homestead, Pennsylvania. Soon after, the state militia drove the strikers out of the plant, and strikebreakers began work.

Henry Clay Frick, the Homestead manager, decided to break the union. He locked the workers out of the plant and hired 300 armed guards to protect the strikebreakers—outside workers to replace those on strike—he planned to hire.

When the guards arrived on July 6, 1892, thousands of angry men and women were waiting for them. A battle broke out. Four guards and ten strikers were killed.

The strike dragged on until November. By then, strikebreakers had reopened the mill and the union was dead. Forty years would pass before a successful union was organized in the steel industry.

No one acted more upset at the turn of events than Carnegie. "The works [mill] are not worth a drop of human blood," he wrote. "I wish they had sunk." In fact, though, he had supported Frick throughout the strike.

The Pullman Strike

In 1894 an even more violent clash between unions and employers erupted in Pullman, Illinois, just outside of Chicago. The Pullman Palace Car Company required its workers to live in this company-owned town, where they had to pay more for rent and food than in nearby towns. Pullman workers bitterly joked,

> "We are born in a Pullman house, fed from the Pullman shop, taught in the Pullman school, catechized in the Pullman church, and when we die, we shall be buried in the Pullman cemetery and go to the Pullman hell."

When a depression hit the nation in 1893, the company cut workers' wages but refused to lower the rents in Pullman. In May 1894 desperate workers went on strike, demanding higher wages or lower rents.

Discussion

Checking Understanding

1. How did the manager of the Homestead steel plant respond when workers called a strike? (He locked the workers out and hired non-union workers to take their place. He protected the replacement workers with armed guards.)

Stimulating Critical Thinking

2. Would you have liked living in a Pullman town? Why or why not? What would have been the advantages? Disadvantages? (Answers will vary but should be supported with valid reasoning. Advantages: security, convenience, attractive setting, neighbors who have a lot in common. Disadvantages: decrease in freedom and individuality, more costly, less diverse population.)

Vital Links

"Don't Forget the Union Label" (Song) Unit 4, Side 2, Search 14383, Play to 16500

See also Unit 4 Explore CD-ROM location 107.

For an activity on Samuel Gompers and strikes, see **Using Historical Documents**, pp. 48–51.

Teaching the

Link to Art

To see how the painting differs in content from more typical paintings of the period, have students look at the Prendergast and Cassatt paintings on pages 313 and 386. Emphasize the difference in subject matter—the rich leisure class painted by Prendergast and Cassatt as opposed to the poor working class painted by Anshutz. **Discussion Answers:** The artist may have chosen this subject because of the growing importance of industry and industrial workers. The artist wants viewers to appreciate and respect the workers, who are shown as tired and strong. He may also want viewers to sympathize with the workers' situation since he reveals their unpleasant work environment, shown as smoky and dirty.

Vital Links

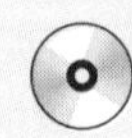

Voice of Eugene Debs (First Person Account) Unit 4, Side 1, Search 12455, Play to 13019

See also Unit 4 Explore CD-ROM location 108.

Connections to Music

The campaign for the eight-hour day produced numerous songs and ballads. One popular song was "Eight Hours," by I. G. Blanchard, published in the *Labor Standard* in 1878. The song begins with these lines:

We mean to make things over,
  we are tired of toil for naught,
With but bare enough to live upon,
  and never an hour for thought;
We want to feel the sunshine,
  and we want to smell the flowers,
We are sure that God has will'd it,
  and we mean to have eight hours.

Often sung at union meetings and rallies, such songs drew support to labor causes and inspired union members.

Link to Art

The Ironworkers' Noontime (1880) Vulgar. Crude. Shocking. These were some of the reactions to Thomas Anshutz's painting of ironworkers. Unlike most painters in the late 1800s, Anshutz did not paint portraits of the rich or murals of idealized landscapes. Instead, he was interested in realistic scenes of day-to-day life. **Discuss** Why might Anshutz have chosen to paint industrial workers? What does the artist want you to think about the workers and their lives?

The American Railway Union Many Pullman workers belonged to the American Railway Union (ARU), founded by Eugene V. Debs. When the Pullman workers struck, 150,000 ARU members nationwide supported them. They derailed railroad cars and blocked tracks. Soon the 24 railroad lines leading out of Chicago stood idle.

The federal government then entered the conflict. In July 1894 a federal court issued an **injunction**—a court order—based on the Sherman Antitrust Act. The court charged the union with interfering with interstate commerce because the trains could no longer deliver mail. The injunction ordered the strikers back to work.

History Footnote

Eugene V. Debs worked for the railroads until he was 19, leaving after a friend was killed falling from a locomotive. He later returned to take a job as a railroad billing clerk and joined a railroad brotherhood. Although a union member, he opposed the strikes of 1877, saying there was no "necessary conflict between capital [business owners] and labor." As the railroad workers' struggle intensified over the next 15 years, however, he gradually changed his mind. By 1893 he had concluded: "To escape the . . . clutch of these monsters [the capitalists] constitutes a standing challenge to organized labor." His ardent convictions led him to run for President on the Socialist ticket five times between 1900 and 1920.

When they refused, federal troops were sent to Chicago. Days of rioting followed, with 34 lives lost. After Debs and other union leaders were sent to prison, both the strike and the ARU collapsed.

During his six months in jail, Debs learned about **socialism,** the belief that government, rather than individuals, should own a nation's major industries. He became the leader of the Socialist Party of America, founded in 1901.

Most workers, though, did not want to destroy the nation's system of free enterprise. Instead, they wanted to make it fairer. Indeed, union membership continued to grow. More and more workers had learned the lesson in the Knights of Labor motto, "An injury to one is the concern of all."

3. Section Review

1. Define **collective bargaining, arbitration, injunction,** and **socialism.**
2. Describe two ways that industrial growth affected the conditions of workers.
3. Critical Thinking If you had been a union member in the late 1800s, would you have agreed to go on strike? Why or why not?

Why We Remember

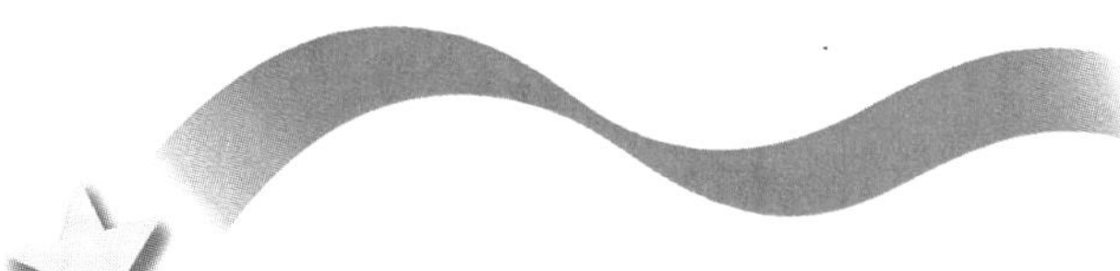

The Rise of Industry and Big Business

One day a friend asked Andrew Carnegie how he was doing. "I'm rich, I'm rich," he replied. In his spectacular rise from rags to riches, Carnegie and the other pioneers of big business reshaped the American dream.

Ever since colonial times, the United States had been a place where dreams of freedom, cheap land, and a decent reward for hard work came true. Never before, however, had a few business leaders amassed such great wealth. The hope of getting rich became part of the American dream—and still inspires ambitious entrepreneurs today.

The Carnegies, Morgans, and Rockefellers are not the only reasons for remembering the rise of industry and big business, however. Their great business empires could not have been built without the brains and brawn of millions of laboring men, women, and children.

Toiling under conditions most of us would find intolerable, these workers built the nation's industries. Many of them also organized to demand what Americans had always dreamed of—a decent reward for hard work. In doing so, they kept the American dream alive for all us.

Closing the Section

Wrap-Up Activity

Writing an Editorial

To reinforce the different points of view presented in the chapter, have groups of students write editorials from the point of view of one of the following individuals: worker at the Triangle Shirtwaist Company, mine owner, union organizer, railroad worker, or Pullman Company executive. Make sure all five perspectives are assigned. Have each group share its editorial with the class.

Section Review Answers

1. Definitions: *collective bargaining* (278), *arbitration* (278), *injunction* (280), *socialism* (281)

2. Possible answers: Employers had little personal interest in their workers, many jobs were repetitious and required little skill, working conditions were often unsafe, wages were low and hours long, children had to hold jobs to help support their families.

3. Yes: make employers value their role more and agree to their demands. No: risk being fired or replaced by other workers.

To check understanding of "Why We Remember," assign Thinking Critically question 3 on page 282.

Survey Answers

Reviewing Vocabulary

Definitions are found on these pages: *rebates* (265), *consolidation* (265), *regulate* (266), *free enterprise* (266), *interstate commerce* (266), *capital* (269), *corporation* (269), *stockholders* (269), *dividends* (269), *trust* (272), *collective bargaining* (278), *arbitration* (278), *injunction* (280), *socialism* (281).

Reviewing Main Ideas

1. Merchants could ship goods across the country by train.

2. Helped: Owners of consolidated railroads because they could run their businesses more cheaply; passengers because train travel became faster and easier. Hurt: Small railroad owners who were driven out of business; passengers, small business owners, and small farmers because less competition meant higher fares and shipping rates.

3. All viewed competition as something to be conquered. They tried to buy competitors out or run them out of business.

4. It did not define what a trust or monopoly was.

5. Conditions were terrible: Accidents were common, the work was repetitious and dull, wages were extremely low, hours were long, and many children had to work instead of going to school.

6. They organized strikes, used arbitration, engaged in collective bargaining.

7. (a) People were killed and wounded; public opinion turned against the Knights of Labor; membership in the Knights dropped rapidly. (b) People were killed in a battle between strikers and guards of strikebreakers; mill was reopened by strikebreakers; Amalgamated Association

(Answers continued in top margin)

of Iron and Steel Workers shut down.
(c) Strikers derailed railroad cars and blocked tracks; a federal court issued an injunction ordering strikers back to work; federal troops fought in riots in Chicago and 34 people were killed; Eugene V. Debs and other union leaders were imprisoned; the strike failed and the American Railway Union collapsed.

Thinking Critically

1. Low wages kept production costs down and thus increased profits. Profits used to expand the business would create more jobs for workers and strengthen the United States economically. Any worker can get ahead, even if starting out in a low-wage job.

2. Agree: The Homestead and Pullman strikes were a failure; strikes often led to violence.

Chapter Survey

Reviewing Vocabulary

Define the following terms.

1. rebates
2. consolidation
3. regulate
4. free enterprise
5. interstate commerce
6. capital
7. corporation
8. stockholders
9. dividends
10. trust
11. collective bargaining
12. arbitration
13. injunction
14. socialism

Reviewing Main Ideas

1. Why did shopping by mail become practical in the late 1800s?
2. Who was helped by the consolidation of railroads, and how? Who was hurt, and how?
3. How did Andrew Carnegie, J. Pierpont Morgan, and John D. Rockefeller view competition? Explain.
4. What was the major flaw in the Sherman Antitrust Act?
5. Describe industrial working conditions in the late 1800s.
6. Give at least two examples of how labor unions tried to improve wages and working conditions.
7. What was the outcome of each of the following events? (a) Haymarket bombing (b) Homestead strike (c) Pullman strike

Thinking Critically

1. Analysis What arguments might captains of industry have used to keep the wages of workers low?
2. Evaluation Terence Powderly of the Knights of Labor believed that strikes were not a good way for workers to achieve their goals. Do you agree or disagree? Give evidence from the chapter to support your answer.
3. Why We Remember: Application Imagine that you are a teenager in the late 1800s. Who are your role models: entrepreneurs like Carnegie and Rockefeller, union leaders like Gompers and Debs, or factory workers like your parents? Explain.

Applying Skills

Making a flowchart Find a newspaper or magazine article about a recent business event, such as a merger (consolidation) or a sharp rise or fall in the value of a company's stock. Make a flowchart to show the causes and effects described in the article. Keep in mind what you learned in the Skill Lab on page 274.

History Mystery

"The most dangerous woman in America" Answer the History Mystery on page 259. A writer said of Mary Harris Jones: "With one speech she often threw a whole community on strike and she could keep the strikers loyal month after month on empty stomachs and behind prison bars." How does this description help to explain her reputation among mine owners?

Writing in Your History Journal

1. Keys to History (a) The time line on pages 258–259 has seven Keys to History. In your journal, list each key and describe why it is important to know about. (b) Choose one of the events on the time line. Imagine you were an ordinary American when the event occurred. Write a diary entry as that person, describing your reactions to the event.

2. Andrew Carnegie An obituary is a notice of a person's death that appears in a

Disagree: Some strikes by railroad workers in the Knights of Labor were effective. Strikes are a powerful tool if used under the right circumstances.

3. Students should support their choice of role model by citing aspects of the person's behavior they admire.

Applying Skills

Flowcharts should clearly show the cause–effect relationship between steps; statements should be concise, as discussed on page 274.

History Mystery

Mary Harris Jones—known as "Mother" Jones—was a very influential and successful union organizer. Mine owners thought she was dangerous because she could inspire workers to take action that might destroy the mine owners' fortunes.

(Answers continued in side margin)

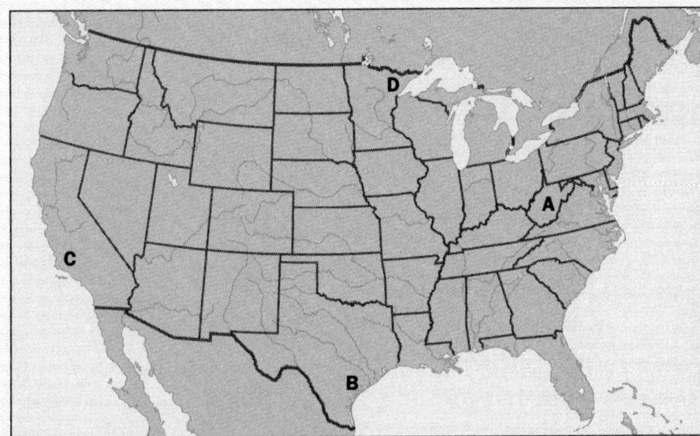

Reviewing Geography

1. For each letter on the map, write the major mineral resource—iron, coal, or petroleum—found in the area.

2. Geographic Thinking How did the environment in the United States make rapid industrial growth possible? How did rapid industrial growth, in turn, affect the environment? Support your answers with evidence from the text as well as your own observations.

newspaper. Many obituaries give a short account of the person's life and achievements. Imagine that you are the obituary editor at a major newspaper in 1919, when Andrew Carnegie died. In your journal, write the obituary that will appear in the newspaper.

3. Citizenship Did the government "do the right thing" in regulating business in the late 1800s? Do you think that the government should have done more? Should the government have done less? Write your thoughts in your journal.

Alternative Assessment

Participating in a round table
Imagine that you live in 1895, and a round table (conference) sponsored by a group of concerned citizens is about to take place. The topic for discussion is "Big Business: Fair or Unfair." With five classmates, participate in the round table.

❶ Meet as a group to assign roles: Andrew Carnegie, J. Pierpont Morgan, John D. Rockefeller, a person who owns a small business, a farmer, and a factory worker.

❷ Develop a plan for the round table. For example, you might begin by having each participant briefly answer the question, giving examples from the chapter. Then you might take turns reacting to one another's answers.

❸ Act out the round table for the class.

Your work will be evaluated on the following criteria:

- you cover a wide variety of issues, including consolidation in railroads and other industries, the growth of trusts, government regulation, working conditions, the growth of labor organizations, and conflict between workers and employers
- you present your positions clearly
- you stay "in character" in your roles

Writing in Your History Journal

1. (a) Explanations should be similar to the time line notes on teacher pages 258–259. (b) Entries will vary but should incorporate accurate facts and show a personal response to the event.

2. Obituaries should mention Carnegie's birth in Scotland, early work experiences, rise to fortune, pioneering role in the steel industry, sale of his company to J. Pierpont Morgan, and his philanthropy.

3. Answers will vary depending on how strong a role students think government should take in protecting the welfare of citizens. Answers will most likely reflect modern concepts of workers' rights.

Reviewing Geography

1. (A) coal, (B) oil, (C) oil, (D) iron

2. Vast natural resources, such as rivers, forests, coal, iron ore, and oil, made rapid industrial growth possible. Forests were cut down to build railroads as well as homes. Students may also mention air pollution from factories, trains, and ships; landscape scarring from mining; and water pollution from the dumping of industrial waste.

Alternative Assessment

Teacher's Take-Home Planner 2, p. 15, includes suggestions and scoring rubrics for the Alternative Assessment activity.

Teaching the

Link to American Readings

In this feature students learn about the problems and progress created by rapid industrial growth in the late nineteenth century. For most factory workers, conditions were grim at best—for children, there was little, if any, future. For many of these workers, unions were the answer. But unions could be the source of some problems too. In the end, there was no easy answer.

Before students begin the lesson, review Workers Struggle for a Better Life (pages 275–276). Have students read the entire feature before assigning the A Closer Look questions. The Setting the Stage Activity and Bonus Activity may then be introduced according to the needs and interests of the students. The information contained in the Discussion questions and the Footnotes may be used throughout the lesson as appropriate. Readers' Theater is ideal for students who might find the readings somewhat difficult. Use the Wrap-Up Activity for students who would enjoy taking a step beyond the core lesson.

Literature Footnote

In 1870 Jacob Riis (1849–1914) came to the United States from Denmark to work as a carpenter. Seven years later he was a police reporter for the *New York Tribune*. In his work, Riis witnessed the worst of New York City—the crime, the poverty, the criminals, and the victims. He began documenting life in the slums and tenements as it really was, not as people liked to pretend it was. His book *How the Other Half Lives* (1890) was one of the first popular social documentary books in the United States. It was instrumental in gaining the support of Theodore Roosevelt, who was then police commissioner of the city, to initiate reform programs. Riis's other books include *Out of Mulberry Street* (1896), *The Making of an American* (1901), and *Neighbors: Life Stories of the Other Half* (1914).

Link to American Readings

READING 5A

Working in a Sweatshop

Sadie Frowne was a Jewish girl who, at the age of 13, emigrated from Poland to New York City with her mother. Shortly after moving in with her Aunt Fanny, Sadie's mother died. Fanny encouraged Sadie to earn money at a trade so she could afford to attend night school. Sadie got a job making skirts by machine in a sweatshop—a workplace where employees work at a fast pace for long hours at low pay. Here she describes her work and life.

Sadie Frowne in New York City, around 1900

I get up at half-past five o'clock every morning and make myself a cup of coffee on the oil stove. I eat a bit of bread and perhaps some fruit and then go to work. Often I get there soon after six o'clock so as to be in good time, though the factory does not open till seven. . . .

At seven o'clock we all sit down to our machines and the boss brings to each one the pile of work that he or she is to finish during the day, what they call in English their "stint." This pile is put down beside the machine and as soon as a skirt is done it is laid on the other side of the machine. Sometimes the work is not all finished by six o'clock and then the one who is behind must work overtime. Sometimes one is finished ahead of time and gets away at four or five o'clock, but generally we are not done till six o'clock.

The machines go like mad all day, because the faster you work the more money you get. Sometimes in my haste I get my finger caught and the needle goes right through it. It goes so quick, though, that it does not hurt much. I bind the finger up with a piece of cotton and go on working. We all have accidents like that. Where the needle goes through the nail it makes a sore finger, or where it splinters a bone it does much harm. Sometimes a finger has to come off. (Generally, though, one can be cured by a salve.)

salve: healing ointment

Workers toil by gaslight in the sewing room of a garment factory around 1910.

Literature Footnote
Upton Sinclair (1878–1968) was an outspoken socialist who was active in politics for most of his adult life. This author of more than 80 books wove his tales around the themes of social and industrial reform. Perhaps the most famous is *The Jungle* (1906), a stark, harsh portrayal of the life and job of a Chicago stockyard worker. Sinclair described the filthy conditions under which cattle were slaughtered and the means used by the meat packers to exploit their workers. The book became a best seller, and President Theodore Roosevelt responded by ordering a government investigation that led to federal meat inspection and the passage of the Pure Food and Drug Act of 1906. Other Sinclair books include *King Coal* (1917), *Oil!* (1927), *Little Steel* (1938), and *Dragon's Teeth* (1942), winner of the Pulitzer Prize.

All the time we are working the boss walks about examining the finished garments and making us do them over again if they are not just right. So we have to be careful as well as swift. But I am getting so good at the work that within a year I will be making $7 a week, and then I can save at least $3.50 a week. I have over $200 saved now.

The machines are all run by foot-power, and at the end of the day one feels so weak that there is a great temptation to lie right down and sleep. But you must go out and get air, and have some pleasure. So instead of lying down I go out, generally with Henry. Sometimes we go to Coney Island, where there are good dancing places, and sometimes we go to Ulmer Park to picnics. . . .

We recently finished a strike in our business. It spread all over and the United Brotherhood of Garment Workers was in it. . . . We struck for shorter hours, and after being out four weeks won the fight. We only have to work nine and a half hours a day and we get the same pay as before. So the union does good after all in spite of what some people say against it—that it just takes our money and does nothing.

I pay 25 cents a month to the union, but I do not begrudge that because it is for our benefit. The next strike is going to be for a raise of wages, which we all ought to have.

begrudge: feel resentment

Excerpts from *The Life Stories of Undistinguished Americans: as Told By Themselves* edited by Hamilton Holt. New York: James Pott & Company, 1906.

READING 5B

Dreary Lives

The growth of industry just before and after the turn of the century was rapid, unregulated, and often earned at the expense of the workers. The following two excerpts reveal what life was like behind the factory walls, and what waited for the workers at home.

A Machinist, 1865

Take the average operative or mechanic employed by a corporation 14 hours a day. His labor commences at half-past four in the morning, and does not cease until half-past seven p.m. How many newspapers or books can he read? What time has he to visit or receive visits? to take baths? to write letters? to cultivate flowers? to walk with his family? Will he not be quite as likely to vote in opposition to his real interests as in favor? What is his opinion good for? Will anyone ask his advice? What will he most enjoy, works of art or rum? Will he go to [religious services] on Sunday? Does

Setting the Stage Activity

Charting Changes

To help students understand the impact of changes that were taking place in the United States, have them complete this exercise. Divide the class into groups of three or four. Give them five minutes to brainstorm technological changes that influenced life styles in the late nineteenth century. Then, call the class together and ask them to share ideas from their lists. Next, ask what changes they think will come about in their life time. How do they think these changes might impact their lives? Do they think that life will ever again be as difficult as it was for the workers described in the readings?

Bonus Activity

Picturing Reality

To help students visualize living and working conditions in late-nineteenth-century urban areas, bring to class photographs by Jacob Riis. The photos force the viewer to acknowledge the extent of the urban poverty of the time. Additional information can be found in the Literature Footnote at the top of page 284.

Discussion

Stimulating Critical Thinking

1. What do Sadie Frowne, the machinist, and the breaker boys have in common? How do their lives differ? (All work very long hours for little pay. Working conditions range from poor to deplorable. There are differences. Sadie is able to have some time for entertainment. She is also saving money for school and belongs to a union. She has hope for her future. The machinist sees no hope, no control over his work situation or life. The breaker boys do dirty, exhausting work for money that is hardly enough to keep them alive. They also have, or will have, health problems from breathing coal dust.)

2. Respond to this statement by Samuel Gompers: "Whoever or whatever controls economic power directs and shapes development for the group or the nation." Do you agree or disagree? Explain, using examples from your own experience. (Students who agree might cite examples of large corporations or makers of popular products. Those who disagree might point to the democratic process as controlling economic growth and development.)

History Footnote

In 1859 English scientist Charles Darwin published his theory of evolution and natural selection. Darwin argued that plants and animals produce more offspring than can survive. Those best suited to their environment will survive and reproduce. English philosopher Herbert Spencer applied Darwin's "survival of the fittest" theory to human life. According to Spencer, only the fittest individuals, businesses, and nations survived. Although losers suffered, civilizations progressed. Andrew Carnegie and John D. Rockefeller praised Social Darwinism. They believed that the government should not regulate working conditions or other business practices. Government involvement would prevent natural selection from weeding out inefficient businesses and unfit workers, thus impeding progress.

society care whether he is happy or miserable? sick or well? dead or alive? How often are his eyes tempted by the works of art? His home means to him his food and his bed. His life is work . . . for his work means bread! "Only that and nothing more." He is debased by excessive toil! He is almost without hope!

debased: lowered in quality or value

Children sort slate from coal, 1877

In a little room in this big, black shed—a room not twenty feet square—forty boys are picking their lives away. The floor of the [breaker room] is an inclined plane, and a stream of coal pours constantly in. They work here, in this little black hole, all day and every day, trying to keep cool in summer, trying to keep warm in winter, picking away among the black coals, bending over till their little spines are curved, never saying a word all the livelong day. These little fellows go to work in this cold dreary room at seven o'clock in the morning and work till it is too dark to see any longer. For this they get $1 to $3 a week.

breaker room: room where coal is broken into pieces and separated

Excerpts from "Fincher's Trades' Review," Oct. 14, 1865. Cited in *Bread and Roses:* "Labor Standard," 1877.

Breaker boys work the coal chutes around 1900.

READING 5C

The Controversy over Unions

Many workers believed that the only way to improve their wages and working conditions was to join together in a union. As individuals they could earn only what their employers were willing to pay. As a union they negotiated as a group on wages and working conditions. Unions, however, were bitterly opposed by employers. Factory and railroad owners believed that they had the right to determine the wages and working conditions of their workers. Because each side believed so passionately in its cause, the fight to win union representation in the last half of the nineteenth century was often a violent one.

Samuel Gompers, president of the American Federation of Labor, 1886–1924

My earliest official efforts were concentrated in promoting stability of labor organizations. This had to be done by making the idea an inseparable part of the thought and habits of trade unionists by establishing a business basis for unionism and then driving home the fallacy of low dues. Cheap unionism cannot maintain effective economic activity. . . .

fallacy: untruth, lie

Readers' Theater

Readings from this section might be staged with the following characters: Sadie Frowne, the machinist, and one or two breaker girls or boys. Suggest that the students in each group work together to write a dialogue for these characters based on what they have learned through their reading and discussions. The young workers might discuss their jobs, their living conditions, their leisure time, and their family life. They might offer hope, encouragement, or empathy for each other. Tell students to write dialogue that sounds natural and believable for the characters they are playing. They should rehearse sufficiently so that the dialogue is not choppy or forced. Students should try to become their characters, if only for a short time.

Economic betterment—today, tomorrow, in home and shop, was the foundation upon which trade unions have been built. Economic power is the basis upon which may be developed power in other fields. It is the foundation of organized society. Whoever or whatever controls economic power directs and shapes development for the group or the nation.

Excerpts from *Seventy Years of Life and Labor* by Samuel Gompers. Copyright 1925 by E.P. Dutton & Co., Inc.: renewal ©1953 by Gertrude Gleaves Gompers. Reprinted by permission of the publishers.

Army cavalry troopers clear the way for a train to pass through the strikers' lines during the 1895 Pullman strike in Chicago.

George F. Baer, president of a Pennsylvania coal and iron company and a railroad, 1902

Is liberty to work less desirable than liberty to worship? Can the one live without the other? Are we freemen in the sense of the Declaration of Independence, whose liberties are vouchsafed [protected] by the Constitution, if there be any power in this broad land to control our choice of labor? Shall we be denied the right to work in the lawful vocations of man because we do not belong to a particular labor organization? . . .

[What] moral or legal right has a labor organization to deprive [a worker] of his inalienable liberty to work? Yet it is being done every day. Men are driven from work, threatened, abused, called all manner of harsh names, their wives and children are insulted. . . .

Work will not be [worshipped] in this country until it is universally conceded that no man shall be deprived of his right to work, by law, by force, by threats . . . by boycott, or by insult . . . no man shall be denied the right to work as many hours as he pleases, and at any price he pleases, and no man shall be boycotted or injured in his business because he employs non-union labor.

conceded: agreed upon

Excerpts from *Addresses and Writings of George F. Baer* collected by William N. Appel. (Lancaster, PA: Privately printed). 1916

A Closer Look

1. Why does Sadie Frowne support the union?
2. What are the goals of the unions? What do the employers want?
3. CRITICAL THINKING Rarely is one side or one point of view all right or all wrong. Explain which union complaints and goals you think were justified. Which employer arguments were reasonable? With which group do you most strongly agree? Why?

Wrap-Up Activity

Taking Another Look at Unions

For students who would like to further explore the pros and cons of unions in the late nineteenth century, suggest the following activity. Have students write an editorial that either supports the presence of a union in a garment factory or argues against it. Students should state the name of their persona, their job, and their position in the factory. All editorials should state specific reasons and examples. Students may do additional research for this project if they wish.

A Closer Look

Answers

1. The union has improved working hours and will strike for increased wages.
2. The unions want to improve working conditions and wages. The employers believe they have the right to control pay and working conditions.
3. Students should support opinions with examples from the text. Many will agree that working conditions and pay were unfair, and because employers did not make changes, regulation was necessary.

Teaching the

Citizenship Lab

In this feature students learn about *Munn* v. *Illinois* (1877), in which the Supreme Court upheld an Illinois law regulating grain warehouses and railroads. The ruling opened the door to far-reaching government regulation of business and industry.

Before students read the feature, review the information about railroad regulation on pages 265–266. Have students read the entire feature before assigning the Understanding Civic Issues questions and the Hands-On Citizenship activity. The Bonus Activity in this Teacher's Edition may be used as an alternative to, or in addition to, the Hands-On Citizenship activity. The Discussion questions in this Teacher's Edition may be used at appropriate points during students' reading or afterward.

Objectives

- ★ Explain why owners of grain warehouses considered the Illinois regulatory law of 1871 unconstitutional.
- ★ Summarize the Supreme Court's ruling on state regulation of business in *Munn* v. *Illinois.*
- ★ Identify modern-day arguments for reducing government regulation of business and industry.

Supreme Court Case: *Munn* v. *Illinois*

Citizenship Lab

Government Regulation: How Much Is Too Much?

"Blood-sucking insects." Illinois farmers probably nodded in agreement when they read that phrase in the *Chicago Tribune.* The newspaper was referring to men like Ira Y. Munn, a partner in one of Chicago's big grain warehouses of the 1860s and early 1870s. Munn and a few other warehouse owners in Chicago had formed a pool, through which they fixed farmers' grain-storage fees at high levels. Farmers raged, the *Tribune* took up their cause, and the foundation was laid for a Supreme Court case that would dramatically affect American business and industry.

Illinois Clamps Down on Warehouse Owners

In 1871 the Illinois legislature responded to pressure from farmers by limiting the rates that grain warehouses could charge and outlawing dishonest warehouse practices. Because farmers were also angry about the rates that railroads charged

This 1866 print shows several grain houses in Chicago, including one operated by Munn & Scott at the right.

History Footnote

In the wake of the Munn decision, states felt free to place controls on virtually any business operating within their borders, even if the business also operated outside the state. For example, Illinois passed a law prohibiting railroads from charging higher rates for short hauls than for more competitive long hauls. The state sued one railroad for violating the law, and the case reached the Supreme Court as *Wabash, St. Louis and Pacific Railway Co.* v. *Illinois* in 1886. By this time, most shipments by railroad were interstate. Thus, the Wabash railway argued, regulations had to come from Congress. Otherwise, a railroad might meet conflicting rules in every state through which it passed. A majority of the Court agreed and ruled the Illinois law unconstitutional.

them, the legislature set maximum railroad rates too.

Enforcing the law proved difficult. Warehouse owners simply ignored it. Ira Munn and his partner George L. Scott refused to take out the license required by the new law; they also refused to allow state officials to inspect their warehouses. The state sued the firm of Munn & Scott, but the trial was delayed by the Chicago fire of 1871. When the state won its case in 1872, Munn & Scott appealed to the Illinois Supreme Court.

While all this was going on, Munn & Scott took part in some complicated financial mischief that pushed the partners into bankruptcy. The men who took over the Munn & Scott properties continued to defy state law and to press their case in court. They argued, as Munn himself had, that the Illinois regulatory law interfered with Congress's power to regulate commerce (Article 1, Section 8 of the Constitution).

The warehouse owners and their lawyers also argued that the law went against the recently ratified Fourteenth Amendment. Part of that amendment reads, "[N]or shall any state deprive any person of life, liberty, or property without due process of law." The warehouse owners claimed that Illinois was taking away their property rights—that is, their right to set fees for use of their warehouses—without due process. The Illinois Supreme Court disagreed, and the warehouse owners appealed to the Supreme Court of the United States.

This 1885 cartoon satirizes railroad monopolists and points out the need for federal regulation of the railroad industry. The "robber baron" astride his iron horse brandishes his weapons—land grants and federal funds—and shoots down workers and farmers.

Munn's Case Goes to the Supreme Court

Munn v. *Illinois* reached the Supreme Court along with seven cases in which railroad owners challenged recent regulatory laws passed by several midwestern states. Together the cases became known as the Granger cases, named for a farmers' movement of the time. (You will read about the Granger movement in Chapter 7.)

Unfortunately for the warehouse and railroad owners, Chief Justice Morrison R. Waite had a strong faith in representative democracy—a faith that made him tolerant of legislative experiments like the midwestern

Setting the Stage Activity

To prepare students to read about government regulation, have groups list events in a typical morning, up to their arrival at school. Then have them list all the ways they can think of in which government regulates those events (for example, setting rules for cereal labels). Ask for a generalization about the scope of regulation.

Bonus Activity

Arguing Before the Supreme Court

To help students understand arguments for and against government regulation, ask them to imagine that—through the wonders of time travel—they have found themselves in the courtroom during oral arguments in the Munn case. Although the justices and lawyers are surprised at the sudden appearance of an oddly dressed teenager, they are willing to hear what this visitor from the future has to say about the case. Ask each student to prepare a brief argument to deliver before the Court. Encourage students to include information about what has happened in the dozen-plus decades since the Munn decision.

Discussion

Checking Understanding

1. What were the provisions of the 1871 Illinois regulatory law? (Provisions limited storage rates that grain warehouses could charge, outlawed dishonest warehouse practices, set maximum railroad rates.)

2. What did Justice Field predict would happen if laws like the Illinois regulatory law were upheld? (Predicted government regulation of business would increase to the point of ridiculous interference.)

Stimulating Critical Thinking

3. If you had been a justice of the Supreme Court, how would you have voted in the Munn case? Why? (In favor of state law: Without some government regulation, big business owners have an unfair advantage over farmers and others; regulation is needed to promote the common good. Against state law: Government interference in business can harm the nation's economy; a little regulation may lead to a burdensome amount.)

Citizenship Footnote

Due process of law is a basic principle of the American legal system. In its simplest usage, the term refers to fair and proper procedures that governments must follow in dealing with individuals. For example, accused persons must be informed of the charges against them.

Some lawyers and judges have put forth a broader theory of due process. Under this theory, called *substantive due process,* courts have the power to overturn laws if their content, or substance, conflicts with a right protected by the Constitution. In the 1800s the theory was most often applied to property. Thus, lawyers in the Munn case argued that by restricting the warehouse owners' property rights, the Illinois law inherently violated due process.

states' regulatory laws. Waite and six other justices decided to uphold the state laws in all eight cases. Waite assigned himself to write the opinions, and he chose *Munn* v. *Illinois* for his main opinion, which he delivered in March 1877.

Waite declared that the Illinois law did not conflict with Article 1 of the Constitution. Because Munn's business was not directly involved in interstate commerce, the Chief Justice wrote, regulation of the business fell within the police power of the Illinois legislature, not of Congress.

Waite also said that the Illinois law did not violate due process. Instead, he wrote, when a person "devotes his property to a use in which the public has an interest, he, in effect, grants to the public an interest in that use, and must submit to be controlled by the public for the common good. . . ." In such a case, Waite said, creation of laws requiring the person to use his property in ways that do not harm others "is the very essence of government."

Associate Justice Stephen J. Field wrote a fierce dissent. He labeled the Munn decision "subversive of the rights of private property." He predicted it would lead to far-reaching government regulation of business, in which "the prices of everything, from a calico gown to a city mansion, may be the subject of legislative direction."

Regulation Leads to Calls for Deregulation

In general terms, Field's prediction proved correct. The Court backed down from the Munn decision a bit in an 1886 ruling that a state could not regulate interstate railroads. But

Selected Regulatory Commissions

Interstate Commerce Commission (ICC) (1887)	Regulates transportation between states.
Federal Reserve System (FRS) (1913)	Directs the nation's banking system by managing the money supply.
Federal Trade Commission (FTC) (1914)	Protects consumers from unfair or misleading business practices.
Securities and Exchange Commission (SEC) (1934)	Enforces laws that regulate the sale of stocks and bonds.
National Labor Relations Board (NLRB) (1935)	Works to correct or prevent unfair labor practices by either employers or unions.
Equal Employment Opportunity Commission (EEOC) (1964)	Enforces laws against job discrimination based on race, color, religion, sex, national origin, age, or disability.

Connections to Geography

It seems fitting that the principal Granger case had its roots in Illinois and, especially, in Chicago. Thanks to moderate precipitation and rich black soil covering nearly level land, Illinois was, and is, a major grain producer. By 1870 Illinois also was the nation's leader in railroad mileage, and its largest city—Chicago—was not only the nation's but the world's busiest railroad hub. Each year, rail lines like the Chicago & North Western brought millions of bushels of wheat, corn, and other grains into Chicago from downstate Illinois and neighboring midwestern states. Some of the grain was used in Chicago, but much of it was destined for points east. The need to store the grain between its trips into and out of Chicago gave rise to the grain warehouse business.

Federal regulatory agencies often provide fodder for political cartoonists. What point do you think the cartoonist is trying to make in this cartoon?

that decision resulted in more regulation, not less, by leading Congress to establish the Interstate Commerce Commission. (See page 266.) From then on, government regulation of business and industry mushroomed.

Today many Americans believe that such regulation has gone too far. They say that excessive regulation raises the prices that consumers pay for goods, makes American business less competitive in the world market, and contributes to cumbersome, inefficient government. In response to such concerns, Congress has deregulated some industries, such as the airline industry. More deregulation may be on the way, reversing a trend that began when angry Illinois farmers took on companies like Munn & Scott more than a century ago.

Understanding Civic Issues

1. What made the Illinois warehouse-regulation law unconstitutional, according to the warehouse owners?
2. How did Chief Justice Waite answer the warehouse owners' arguments?
3. **Critical Thinking** Why might farmers of the 1870s feel government was their only hope in dealing with railroad and warehouse owners?
4. **Hands-On Citizenship** Has government regulation gone too far, or not? With a partner, present a debate on that question.
   - Narrow your focus by choosing one federal regulatory agency to talk about. See the list on page 290 for a few possibilities.
   - Together, do some research to learn about the agency's purposes and methods. Your librarian can help. You may want to write to or call the agency too. (See the U.S. government pages of your local telephone book.)
   - Decide which of you will defend the "too-far" position and which will defend the "not-too-far" position. Work on your own to prepare your arguments. Try to make them convincing, even if you do not personally agree with the position.
   - Present your debate to the class.

Citizenship Lab Answers

1. The law allegedly interfered with Congress's power to regulate commerce and deprived warehouse owners of property rights without due process of law.

2. Waite said regulation of the business was within the state's power because the business was not directly involved in interstate commerce; also, businesses that affect the public are subject to government control.

3. Possible answer: Farmers knew that, without government on their side, they had little or no power. For example, they could not raise prices to cover their costs but instead had to take what the market would give them for their products. They also had no alternative railroads and warehouses to turn to because the existing ones controlled the industry.

Teaching the Hands-On *CITIZENSHIP*

Explain that the list of federal agencies is only a sampling; students may choose other federal agencies to talk about, or they might focus on state or local regulatory agencies. In any case, students need not do in-depth research.

To involve the whole class, be sure to follow the debates with a discussion. What were the most convincing arguments? Which side was best in drawing logical conclusions? You might try using peer evaluation, stressing the fact that the students are to evaluate the arguments and reasoning, not the personalities of the debaters.

At·a·Glance

6 The Growth of Cities

1865–1914

Chapter Planning Guide

Section	Student Text	Teacher's Edition Activities
Opener and Story pp. 292–295	**Keys to History Time Line** **History Mystery** Beginning the Story with **Jacob Riis**	**Setting the Stage Activity** Through an Immigrant's Eyes, p. 294
1 **Land of Promise** pp. 296–303	**World Link** Russian pogroms begin, p. 298 **Hands-On History** Discussing a move to America, p. 299 **Reading Maps** Ethnic Diversity, p. 300 **Geography Lab** A West Side Chicago Neighborhood, p. 303	**Warm-Up Activity** Describing Immigration Today, p. 296 **Geography Question of the Day,** p. 296 **Section Activity** Presenting an Immigrant Talk Show, p. 297 **Bonus Activity** Describing "America Fever," p. 298 **Wrap-Up Activity** A Modern Immigration Poem, p. 302
2 **The Rise of American Cities** pp. 304–308	**Link to Art** Chicago Style, p. 306 **Point of View** Were political machines helpful or harmful?, p. 307	**Warm-Up Activity** Examining City Problems, p. 304 **Geography Question of the Day,** p. 304 **Section Activity** Planning Mayors' Campaigns, p. 306 **Bonus Activity** Running a Settlement House, p. 307 **Wrap-Up Activity** An Urban-Rural Dialogue, p. 308
3 **Cities and a New Way of Life** pp. 309–315	**Link to the Present** The new "downtowns," p. 310 **Skill Lab** Creating Appropriate Graphs, p. 315	**Warm-Up Activity** Living in the City, p. 309 **Geography Question of the Day,** p. 309 **Section Activity** Creating an "Arts and Leisure" Page, p. 311 **Bonus Activity** Designing a City Park, p. 312 **Wrap-Up Activity** Judging Impacts on City Life, p. 314
Evaluation	**Section 1 Review,** p. 302 **Section 2 Review,** p. 308 **Section 3 Review,** p. 314 **Chapter Survey,** pp. 316–317 **Alternative Assessment** Planning a city guide, p. 317	**Answers to Section 1 Review,** p. 302 **Answers to Section 2 Review,** p. 308 **Answers to Section 3 Review,** p. 314 **Answers to Chapter Survey,** pp. 316–317 (Alternative Assessment guidelines are in the Take-Home Planner.)

Teacher's Resource Package

Chapter Summaries: English and Spanish, pp. 48–49

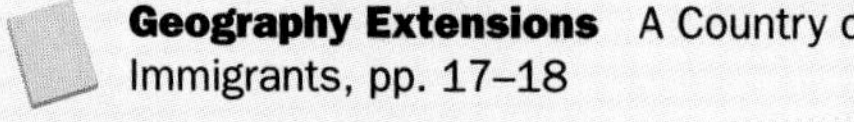

Chapter Resources Binder

Study Guide Supplying Supporting Evidence, p. 57

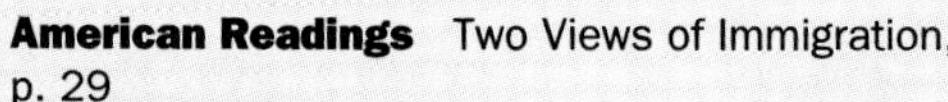

Geography Extensions A Country of Immigrants, pp. 17–18

American Readings Two Views of Immigration, p. 29

Using Historical Documents Granite City School for Americanism poster, pp. 52–55

Chapter Resources Binder

Study Guide Reading for Details, p. 58

Reinforcement Organizing Information, pp. 61–62

American Readings Tenement Life, p. 30

Chapter Resources Binder

Study Guide Relating Cause and Effect, p. 59

Skills Development Creating Appropriate Graphs, pp. 63–64

American Readings "Casey at the Bat," pp. 31–32

Chapter and Unit Tests Chapter 6 Tests, Forms A and B, pp. 51–54

Take-Home Planner

Introducing the Chapter Activity Entering the Golden Door, p. 22

Chapter In-Depth Activity Art as a Historical Record, p. 22

Reduced Views

Study Guide, p. 24

Geography Extensions, p. 27

American Readings, p. 26

Using Historical Documents, p. 27

Unit 2 Answers, pp. 30–38

Reduced Views

Study Guide, p. 24

Reinforcement, p. 25

American Readings, p. 26

Unit 2 Answers, pp. 30–38

Reduced Views

Study Guide, p. 24

Skills Development, p. 25

American Readings, p. 26

Unit 2 Answers, pp. 30–38

Reduced Views

Chapter Tests, p. 27

Unit 2 Answers, pp. 30–38

Alternative Assessment Guidelines for scoring the Chapter Survey activity, p. 23

Additional Resources

Wall Time Line

Unit 2 Activity

Transparency Package

Transparency 6–1 Immigration to the United States—use with Section 1

Transparency 6–1 Entering the United States—use with Section 1

Transparency Activity Book

SelecTest Testing Software

Chapter 6 Test, Forms A and B

Vital Links

Videodisc

CD-ROM

Voice of Lee Chew (see TE p. 300)

"My Little Son" (see TE p. 301)

Steel-framed skyscraper (see TE p. 305)

Child health exhibit (see TE p. 308)

Telephone operators (see TE p. 310)

"Take Me Out to the Ball Game" (see TE p. 312)

High wheelers (see TE p. 313)

Coney Island amusement park (see TE p. 313)

Vaudeville (see TE p. 313)

6

Teaching Resources

Take-Home Planner 2
- Introducing Chapter Activity
- Chapter In-Depth Activity
- Alternative Assessment

Chapter Resources Binder
Geography Extensions
American Readings
Using Historical Documents
Transparency Activities
Wall Time Line Activities
Chapter Summaries
Chapter and Unit Tests
SelecTest Test File
Vital Links CD-ROM/Videodisc

Time Line

Keys to History
Keys to History journal writing activity is on page 316 in the Chapter Survey.

Edison invents lightbulb Electricity became an inexpensive source of light for city people. (p. 310)

Chinese Exclusion Act Prejudice against Chinese workers led to this act banning the entry of Chinese immigrants. (p. 302)

First metal-frame skyscraper New construction techniques allowed cities to expand upward. (p. 304)

Looking Back The Irish were one of the largest and most influential immigrant groups.

World Link See page 298.

Chapter Objectives

- ★ Identify the new immigrants who came to this country after the Civil War and describe their experiences.
- ★ Explore the effects of immigration and industry on cities.
- ★ Describe the new ways of living that developed in American cities.

Chapter Overview
In the years following the Civil War, immigrants from Europe and Asia came in greater numbers than ever before. Driven by poverty and persecution, they sought opportunity and freedom. Many settled in ethnic neighborhoods in cities. Faced with the challenge of assimilating to American culture, some preferred to return home. Nativist fears and prejudice led to attempts to exclude some

1865–1914

Chapter 6 The Growth of Cities

Sections

Beginning the Story with Jacob Riis
1. Land of Promise
2. The Rise of American Cities
3. Cities and a New Way of Life

Keys to History

1884–1885
First metal-frame skyscraper is built
Home Insurance building in Chicago

1879
Edison invents electric lightbulb

1882
Chinese Exclusion Act

1865 — 1875 — 1885

Looking Back

Great Famine drives Irish immigrants to United States
1845

World Link

Russian pogroms begin
1881

immigrants, but the dream of a new life remained strong.

Industrialization attracted immigrants, as well as people from rural areas, to the growing cities. But overcrowding led to problems such as fires and poor housing and sanitation. Political machines helped solve some urban problems, but corruption led reformers to try to clean up politics as well as to find ways to help the poor.

Cities presented new opportunities and a new way of life. Inventions such as electric lighting, the telephone, and other conveniences created more leisure time for ordinary people. The growth of free time led to an explosion of new interests and pastimes available to city dwellers. These included newspapers and books, sports and recreation, and new entertainment choices, as well as a new focus on culture.

Teaching the *HISTORY* Mystery

Students will find the answer on p. 298. See Chapter Survey, p. 316, for additional questions.

Time Line

Electric streetcars This new transportation method led to the growth of suburbs. (p. 304)

San Francisco earthquake and fire Thousands of buildings were destroyed, demonstrating the danger of fire in crowded cities. (p. 306)

Peak year for immigration Between 1870 and 1920 nearly 27 million immigrants arrived in the United States, with 1907 being the peak year. (p. 296)

Triangle Shirtwaist factory fire Deaths of 146 workers, mostly immigrants, focused attention on wretched factory conditions. (p. 306)

Looking Ahead The quota law was the first restriction on immigration.

HISTORY Mystery

Although she never actually swam across the ocean, the "Atlantic swimmer" well deserved her title. Who was she and how did she earn her nickname?

1888
Electric streetcar system built in Richmond, Virginia
Restored streetcar in Seattle

1907
Peak year for immigration
Ellis Island

1906
San Francisco earthquake and fire

1911
Triangle Shirtwaist factory fire in New York City

1895 *1905* *1915*

Looking Ahead

Congress sets first quotas on immigration
1921

Beginning the Story

Jacob Riis

In many ways Jacob Riis was typical of the immigrants in the late 1800s, but his talent as a writer and photographer was not typical. Throughout his long career as a journalist and social reformer, Riis never lost his sympathy for the weak and helpless. His study of poverty in New York City's teeming immigrant neighborhoods, *How the Other Half Lives,* influenced reform legislation.

Setting the Stage Activity

Through an Immigrant's Eyes

To help students understand what immigrants in 1870 might have experienced on their first day in the United States, have them work in pairs to write a first-person narrative of a new immigrant who has just arrived in New York. Have them describe the sights and sounds of the area through the new immigrant's eyes, as well as the immigrant's hopes and fears about the future. Students may choose any country they wish as the immigrant's homeland. Ask for volunteers to read their narratives aloud.

See the Introducing the Chapter Activity, Entering the Golden Door. **Take-Home Planner 2,** p. 22.

History Footnote

A clean and healthy environment was one of Jacob Riis's special concerns. He believed that physical and emotional health were almost impossible to attain in the ugly, polluted, overcrowded environment in which many immigrants lived. He especially worried about the health of children raised in squalid big-city tenements. He wrote letters to New York's newspapers asking people to donate flowers that he could distribute to poor children. Riis received so many flowers that he had to enlist the help of a women's organization, the King's Daughters, to distribute them. The distribution of flowers to beautify poor neighborhoods soon led to more substantial improvements. The King's Daughters hired a public health nurse to visit poor families and opened a settlement house.

Beginning the Story with

Jacob Riis

It was a wet and windy October night in New York City. A hungry young immigrant from Denmark named Jacob Riis (rees) sat along the banks of the river, gazing into its dark waters. Winter would soon be coming and he had no money, no home, no job, not even a winter coat to wear. Numb with cold and filled with an aching loneliness, how could he go on? No one would know or care if he threw himself into the river to end his misery, he told himself.

Suddenly, another shivering body pressed close to his. A little dog that had been following Jacob for days had found him again. As Jacob reached down to pet it, the dog climbed into his lap and licked his face. "The love of the faithful little beast thawed the icicles in my heart," he later wrote. Jacob picked up the dog and walked back into the city to seek shelter for the night.

The only place he could find was a lodging room at the police station. Jacob was caught trying to smuggle the dog in under his jacket, and the police forced him to leave it outside. There the dog shivered through the night alone.

During the night, a man stole a gold locket that Jacob kept hidden beneath his shirt. The locket was given to him by Elisabeth—the girl back home in Denmark whom he loved and hoped someday to marry. Even with an ocean between them, Elisabeth's face still haunted his dreams.

In the morning, tearful and angry, Jacob told the police sergeant that he had been robbed. When the sergeant did not believe that a poor man like Jacob Riis could have owned something as valuable as a gold locket, Jacob yelled at him. Following the sergeant's order, a guard kicked Jacob down the steps and out into the city street. The furious Jacob was then marched out of the neighborhood and forced onto the first ferry leaving New York City.

History Bookshelf

Meyer, Edith P. *Not Charity, But Justice: The Story of Jacob Riis*. New York: Vanguard Press, 1974. The author tells the story of Jacob Riis—immigrant, social reformer, muckraking journalist, and pioneering photographer.

Also of interest:

Benton, Barbara. *Ellis Island: A Pictorial History*. Facts on File, 1985.

Gorm, Elliot, and Warren Goldstein. *A Brief History of American Sports*. Hill and Wang, 1993.

Takaki, Ronald. *A Different Mirror: The Making of a Multicultural America*. Little, Brown, 1993.

Seeking to show the terrible living conditions of immigrants in the late 1800s, Riis photographed this courtyard at 22 Baxter Street in New York City. In such tenements "piles of garbage [were] fairly alive with diseased odors, [with] numbers of children filling every nook."

Homeless in a New World

The year was 1870 and Jacob Augustus Riis was one of hundreds of thousands of European immigrants pouring into the United States each year. Unable to find work as a carpenter in his hometown in Denmark, Jacob had left for the United States at the age of 21.

When he arrived, Jacob discovered that many other young men were also seeking work. He took whatever jobs he could find, from picking vegetables to hauling bricks. He wandered the streets, moving from job to job.

Sometimes Jacob had money to buy a meal. At other times he rummaged through garbage cans for food.

Jacob lived in the worst neighborhoods of New York City. He stayed in cheap lodging houses, where at best he could rent a tiny bedroom with a cot, and at worst sleep on a musty mattress along with a dozen or more other lodgers.

Jacob Riis Becomes a Reporter

Not long after that terrible night at the police station, though, Jacob's luck began to change. A friend told him about a reporting job on a New York City newspaper. To his amazement, he got the position.

As a reporter, Jacob Riis covered the daily dramas of the city, from terrible fires to everyday life in the slums. His stories were known for their accuracy and compassion—rare qualities in the newspaper business at the time. Even with his success, Riis never forgot how difficult life had been for him, and how difficult it continued to be for millions of others.

Hands-On HISTORY Activity

Jacob Riis wrote stories about people living in a strange new land. As a television reporter, you have been sent back in time to explore the lives of immigrants in Jacob Riis's time. What scenes would you show in your television special? What four questions might you ask to help immigrants describe their lives to your audience?

Discussion

Thinking Historically

1. What are some obstacles Riis faced as an immigrant? (English not his native language; lonely, penniless, unable to find steady work; forced to live in worst neighborhoods; crime victim.)

2. What was the police sergeant's attitude toward immigrants? (Seemed to dislike them; also may have been prejudiced—could not believe someone like Riis could have a gold locket.)

3. What qualities helped Riis succeed? (Willingness to take any job and tolerate bad living conditions; kind and thoughtful; accurate, compassionate reporter; sympathy for the poor.)

See the Chapter In-Depth Activity, Art as a Historical Record. **Take-Home Planner 2**, p. 22.

Teaching the Hands-On HISTORY

To help students brainstorm scenes and questions, have them think about what might seem unfamiliar about the 1870s to people today. Ask them to consider what scenes would be most typical of immigrants' lives and what questions best convey the reality of immigrants' lives to TV viewers.

For a journal writing activity on Jacob Riis, see student page 316.

Introducing the Section

Vocabulary

anti-Semitism (p. 298) hatred and persecution of Jews

ethnic neighborhoods (p. 299) areas in cities where people share the same languages and culture

assimilate (p. 301) to be absorbed into the main cultural group

Warm-Up Activity

Describing Immigration Today

To focus on issues surrounding immigration, have small groups brainstorm responses for the following topics: reasons immigrants come to the United States today, types of jobs open to newcomers who speak no English, problems new immigrants experience, and the meaning of "Americanization." Then have each group write three responses for each topic and share them with the class.

Geography Question of the Day

Have students use the map on p. 300 to identify the nationalities of immigrants settling in the United States. Ask them what kinds of patterns they see in the map—for example, that the majority of Asian immigrants settled on the West Coast.

296

Section Objectives

- ★ Identify the new immigrants to the United States after the Civil War and explain why they came.
- ★ Describe immigrants' experiences on the way to the United States and after they arrived.
- ★ Discuss how native-born Americans responded to the new arrivals.

Teaching Resources

Take-Home Planner 2, pp. 20–29
Chapter Resources Binder
Study Guide, p. 57
Reinforcement
Skills Development
Geography Extensions, pp. 17–18
American Readings, p. 29
Using Historical Documents, pp. 52–55
Transparency Activities, pp. 31–32
Chapter and Unit Tests

1. Land of Promise

Reading Guide

New Terms anti-Semitism, ethnic neighborhoods, assimilate

Section Focus The great new wave of immigrants to the United States

1. **Who were the new immigrants after the Civil War and why did they come?**
2. **What experiences did immigrants have in making their way to the United States and after they arrived?**
3. **How did native-born Americans respond to the new arrivals?**

To a 13-year-old boy, departing for the United States from his homeland of Macedonia, it appeared as if

> "the whole world had discovered America at the same time . . . and was in a hurry to get there."

Everyone, it seemed, had "America fever." After the Civil War the number of Europeans crossing the Atlantic—and Asians crossing the Pacific—skyrocketed. Millions of people were now on the move. Who were these new immigrants? How did they differ from earlier newcomers? What forces pushed them from their homes and attracted them to the United States?

The New Wave of Immigrants

To the poor farmers of Europe and Asia, America meant jobs and freedom. Between 1870 and 1920 nearly 27 million people arrived. They were seeking new lives—or at least the opportunity to make and save money to take back to their homelands.

European immigrants Europeans made up 21 of the 24 million people who came to the United States between 1880 and 1920. This wave of Europeans, though, differed from earlier ones. Before, most had come from northern Europe—Britain, Ireland, Germany, and Scandinavia. Now many came from southern and eastern Europe.

Italians, Poles, and eastern European Jews made up some of the larger groups of the new immigrants. Nearly 5 million Italians came during this time, and 3 million Jews. Greeks, Serbs, Czechs, and Slovaks also joined the migration. In cities throughout the nation, a chorus of languages—including Polish, Italian, and Yiddish—filled the air. Jewish synagogues and Catholic and Eastern Orthodox churches sprang up.

These immigrants differed from earlier ones in another important way. Few had money to buy land and start farms. Instead, most settled in cities and took whatever jobs they could find.

Asian immigrants The new wave of immigrants also included Asians. In 1849, 325 Chinese joined the California gold rush. They were followed by more than 300,000 Chinese who crossed the Pacific in the next 50 years. Japanese began migrating to the United States in the 1870s. Almost 400,000 had made their way here by the 1920s. Koreans and Filipinos also arrived from Asia, while Armenians, Lebanese, and Syrians came from the Middle East.

History Footnote
The countries of origin for immigrants in the 1990s have some similarities to those of the 1890s, but the differences are more striking. Here are the top 15 countries of origin for a recent year: Mexico, China, the Philippines, Vietnam, the states of the former Soviet Union, the Dominican Republic, India, El Salvador, the United Kingdom (England, Wales, Scotland, and Northern Ireland), South Korea, Jamaica, Canada, Taiwan, Cuba, and Ireland. From 1921 to 1965, a quota system was in effect to regulate immigration. U.S. immigration law, which was revised in 1990, is now based on uniting families of citizens. Today, almost two-thirds of legal immigrants to the United States are relatives of people already living in the country.

Developing the Section

Discussion

Checking Understanding

1. How did growing populations in Europe and Asia affect immigration to the United States? (It led to overcrowding and shortages of farmland, and pressured people to leave.)

Stimulating Critical Thinking

2. Why do you think fewer immigrants came from northern Europe in the late 1800s, compared with southern and eastern Europe? (Life for poor people may have improved in countries that sent fewer immigrants; more may have moved within the country or to other countries; immigrants from southern and eastern Europe may have suffered religious and political persecution.)

Immigration to the United States 1860–1910

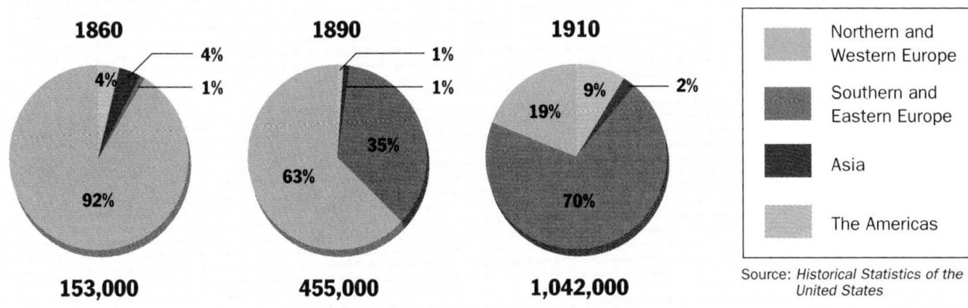

Source: *Historical Statistics of the United States*

Why They Came

PUSH What pushed immigrants from their homelands
- Poverty
- Shortage of farmland
- Lack of opportunity
- Political and religious persecution
- Wars and threats of war

Immigrants arriving in New York City

PULL What pulled immigrants to the United States
- Jobs
- Opportunity
- Political and religious freedom
- Peace
- Letters from family and friends

Section Activity

Presenting an Immigrant Talk Show

To explore immigrants' feelings about their journeys and new lives, have the class role-play a talk show. Roles include several immigrant families, a host, and an audience. The host and audience members should prepare questions to ask the family members. Families should prepare profiles of their characters' backgrounds and views to use in answering questions. Encourage a wide range of questions and responses.

Searching for Work

Leaving friends and home to look for work in a strange land was not new to Europeans. "We are like wild geese," said an Irishman, describing the poor who wandered across Europe looking for work. In fact, twice as many people migrated within Europe during this time as the millions who crossed the ocean to the United States.

In Europe and Asia, growing populations led to overcrowding and shortages of farmland. A visitor to China wrote that "the least failure of the rice crop produces wretchedness." Small farmers lost their land when they could not pay the rent or heavy government taxes. With few opportunities in the countryside, the landless had no choice but to move elsewhere.

To the desperate poor in Europe and Asia, faraway America appeared to be a land of abundance. "It was almost heaven. You could almost just grab the money!" wrote an immigrant to friends back in Finland. Although easy wealth was more fantasy than reality, such tales fell on eager ears.

Roundtrippers When Jacob Riis came to New York City in 1870, he arrived at the dawning of a tremendous industrial age. Riis found a land bursting with construction and industry, and looking for workers.

Unlike earlier immigrants, many of the newcomers did not intend to stay in the United States. Fathers hoped to work for a few years and return home rich. The young sought jobs to support parents back home or to save to start their own families. An

Teaching the World Link

Explain that while many Jewish immigrants of the late nineteenth century came from Eastern Europe, earlier Jewish immigrants were mostly German. Many German American Jews wanted to assimilate to American ways, while the eastern European Jews hoped to continue their traditional ways of living. Despite these differences, they shared a common heritage and supported one another. Ask students if they think Jews escaping pogroms were likely to be roundtrippers. Why or why not? (Because they were fleeing for their lives, it is unlikely they would have considered returning.)

Bonus Activity

Describing "America Fever"

To help students understand the reasons for immigration in the late 1800s, have them write clinical descriptions of the symptoms of the "disease" called "America fever," and who was likely to be affected by it. Then have them prescribe the "cure" and why they, as "doctors," believe the cure will work.

History Footnote

Pogrom is the Russian word for "devastation." Pogroms became more common in Russia in the years leading up to the 1917 Revolution. An increasingly embattled government tried to deflect public resentment and revolutionary rumblings by making Jews scapegoats. During the civil war that followed the Bolshevik victory, another large pogrom occurred.

See the Study Guide activity in **Chapter Resources Binder,** p. 59.

Russian pogroms begin "I feel that every cobblestone in Russia is filled with Jewish blood," mourned a Jew who fled to the United States during the organized attacks on Jews that began in Russia in 1881. These attacks—called pogroms (po-GRAHMS)—were touched off by rumors that Jews were involved in the assassination of Czar Alexander II.

In fact, the rumors were false. The czar had been killed by revolutionaries. Fearing that revolution would spread, the government tried to convince discontented Russians that Jews were to blame for their problems. It whipped up anti-Jewish feelings in Russia, then looked the other way when mob violence against Jews took place.

The pogroms ended in 1884. Then in 1903 a second wave began, driving hundreds of thousands of Jews to escape to the United States.

Irishwoman known as "the Atlantic swimmer" made six round trips by ship between Ireland and the United States.

Longing for Freedom

While many immigrants were seeking work, others were longing for freedom. Harsh laws and religious persecution pushed them from their homelands.

For centuries **anti-Semitism**—hatred and persecution of Jews—had simmered in Europe. In the 1880s treatment of Jews turned cruel and violent. Laws forced Jews to live in certain areas and barred them from owning land. They suffered from mass killings and destruction of their homes.

Jews were not alone in their suffering. Throughout Europe religious persecution, tyranny, wars, and threats of war drove people from their lands.

Dreams of America satisfied other yearnings for freedom, too. Many young people wanted to begin new lives. They believed that by moving to the United States they could "escape from the priest's eye and from the parent's eye."

The Journey

Compared to the days of sailing ships, the journey was easier for these immigrants. They traveled by rail from their homes in Europe and Asia to ports where they boarded steamships. Steamships shortened the Atlantic voyage from 7 weeks to 12 days.

Eager to fill their ships, steamship companies paid agents up to $8 for each person they brought aboard. Thousands of agents combed China and Europe for passengers, sometimes emptying entire villages of their populations. Agents provided clothing for the trip and loaned passengers money for tickets—to be repaid once they found work.

Steerage Still, the voyage could be a nightmare. Few immigrants could afford private rooms. Instead, they crammed together in steerage—large compartments below deck, just in front of the rudder that steered the ship. Jacob Riis traveled in steerage, enduring the cramped, dirty quarters, rotten meat, and foul drinking water.

Given the hardships of the voyage, it is easy to understand the excitement immigrants felt as they arrived at their destination. Riis recalled:

> "As I looked over the rail at the miles of ferryboats and pleasure craft on the

Connections to Music

Songs about the heartaches caused by leaving one's homeland are common in many cultures. The traditional music of Ireland, for instance, includes a large number of emigration ballads. Here are some lines from a typical ballad, "Paddy's Green Shamrock Shore."

Then fare thee well, sweet Liza dear,
and likewise Derry town,
And twice farewell to my comrades brave,
who dwell on that sainted shore.
If fame or fortune shall favor me,
and I have money in store,
I'll come back and I'll wed that lassie I
left on Paddy's green shamrock shore.

Hands-On HISTORY

Discussing a move to America One immigrant wrote to his brother back in Poland, "[I]f you want to come to America, then come. You could . . . earn some money so that you could pull yourself out from under that misery and be a man." Watching their younger son eagerly read the letter, his parents may have wished they had hidden it from him.

Two immigrant boys in 1896

Activity Create and act out a conversation that might have taken place between members of a poor family in Europe in 1890. The children, ages 13 and 16, want to move to the United States. Their parents oppose the idea.

1. Working with three classmates, write a script for the conversation. How might the teens persuade their parents to let them go? For example, how might they compare conditions in Poland to those in the United States? What objections might the parents raise?
2. When finished writing, assign roles and rehearse until you have memorized the script.
3. Present the conversation—"live" or on videotape—to the class.

river, my hopes rose high that somewhere in this teeming hive there would be a place for me."

Making a New Life

Many immigrants first stepped onto American soil at one of two entry stations—Ellis Island in New York or Angel Island in San Francisco. Inspectors checked their identification documents and their health.

A person with tuberculosis or other contagious disease could be refused entry. Officials who could not pronounce foreign names gave immigrants new, more simple spellings of their names, whether they wanted them or not.

Once admitted to the United States, the newcomers faced the challenge of finding work and a place to live. Jacob Riis had difficulty at first, even though he spoke some English and was a carpenter. Luckily, a Danish diplomat helped him get a job.

Ethnic neighborhoods Like Riis, immigrants often relied on people from their homelands to help them get started. They clustered in **ethnic neighborhoods**—areas where people shared the same languages and culture. There they found familiar foods, newspapers in their native languages, and help from earlier arrivals.

For example, Jewish immigrants settled in large numbers on New York City's Lower East Side and worked in the garment industry. Chicago's meatpacking industry attracted Polish immigrants. In western cities, Chinese established neighborhoods called Chinatowns. Japanese who worked in Hawaii's sugar cane fields opened Japanese-language schools and built Buddhist temples.

Immigrants transformed American cities. In 1890 nearly 80 percent of New Yorkers were foreign-born or children of the foreign-born. By 1900 they made up over 30 percent of the populations of Chicago, Cleveland, Minneapolis, and San Francisco.

Discussion

Checking Understanding

1. What was the role of agents in immigration to the United States? (Hired by steamship companies to increase the number of immigrants, provided clothing, lent money to passengers for tickets, drummed up enthusiasm.)

2. At which two places did most immigrants enter the United States? (Ellis Island in New York and Angel Island in San Francisco.)

Stimulating Critical Thinking

3. Do you think living in ethnic neighborhoods was beneficial for immigrants? Support your opinion. (Yes: they provided support networks and the psychological comfort of familiar surroundings. No: their cultural and linguistic segregation was a barrier to assimilation and had the potential for limiting economic advancement.)

Teaching the Hands-On HISTORY

Suggest that students focus on push-pull factors, objections to emigration, and specific conditions in Poland or whatever country they choose. If appropriate, change the nationality of the family to reflect the ethnic makeup of your class.

Teaching the Reading Maps

Ask students to generalize about the distribution of different ethnic groups around the country. (East Asian immigrants were most common in the West; Scandinavians gravitated toward the Upper Midwest and Plains; eastern European Jews were centered in cities.) Ask students why this general distribution took place. (For example, the West is closest to East Asians' point of entry; Scandinavians may have preferred a climate similar to their own countries'; Jews depended on the support provided by urban ethnic neighborhoods.)
Answers to Reading Maps: Africa, Asia, Europe. Answers will vary.

Vital Links

Voice of Lee Chew (First Person Account) Unit 4, Side 1, Search 31732, Play to 32312

See also Unit 4 Explore CD-ROM location 263.

Connections to Geography

A study in toponymy (origin of place names) reveals that names from immigrants' home countries abound in the United States. Here is a sampling from the Midwest and Plains states: Lindsborg and Galva, Kansas, are named after Swedish towns; Minnesota has New Ulm, settled by Germans, and New Prague, settled by Czechs; Ohio has Macedonia, named after the Balkan territory, Toledo, named after the city in Spain, and London and Lancaster, named after the city and county in England. South Dakota has Aberdeen, named for the Scottish city; and many states have a Dublin, Berlin, Vienna, Warsaw, or Belfast. Examining a map of Indiana reveals well over 100 towns named after foreign cities, counties, and countries.

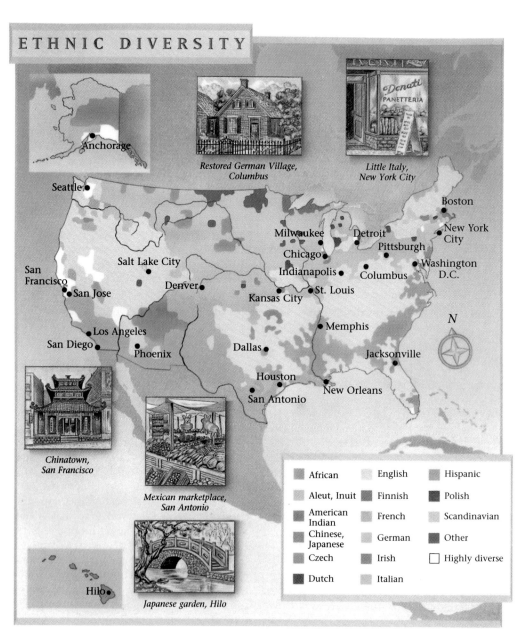

ETHNIC DIVERSITY

Anchorage, Seattle, San Francisco, San Jose, Los Angeles, San Diego, Salt Lake City, Denver, Phoenix, Kansas City, Dallas, Houston, San Antonio, Milwaukee, Chicago, Detroit, Indianapolis, St. Louis, Memphis, New Orleans, Columbus, Pittsburgh, Washington D.C., New York City, Boston, Jacksonville, Hilo, N

Restored German Village, Columbus

Little Italy, New York City

Chinatown, San Francisco

Mexican marketplace, San Antonio

Japanese garden, Hilo

African	English	Hispanic
Aleut, Inuit	Finnish	Polish
American Indian	French	Scandinavian
Chinese, Japanese	German	Other
Czech	Irish	Highly diverse
Dutch	Italian	

Reading Maps

Ancestors of Americans came from what continents? What groups settled in your area? (Not every group is shown on the map.)

Tips for Teaching

Gifted Students

Ask musically gifted students to learn some immigrant songs in folk singer Jerry Silverman's *Immigrant Songbook* (Mel Bay Publications, 1992) and perform them. This book contains songs from more than 50 countries. Guitar chords, original-language lyrics, and English translations are included.

For contrasting views on immigration, see **American Readings**, p. 29.

Discussion

Checking Understanding

1. What were some of the hardships immigrants faced? (Crowded living quarters often shared with other families, poor pay, long working hours, discrimination.)

Stimulating Critical Thinking

2. Why do you think some immigrants regretted their decision to come to the United States? Explain. (Some possible reasons: discrimination, poor living and working conditions, difficult to understand the language, far from home and family.)

3. Do you think nativism still exists today? Explain with specific examples. (Answers will vary but should reflect current issues such as proposals to limit immigration from Latin American countries and to restrict immigrants' access to services.)

Some cities became identified with certain nationalities. Milwaukee was known as a largely German city, Minneapolis a Scandinavian city, and Boston an Irish and Italian one. The South, with fewer cities and jobs, did not attract many immigrants.

Hardships and fears Bright dreams brought immigrants across the ocean. The reality they found was often far different. They crowded into tiny apartments, often with several other families, and worked long hours to earn barely enough to live on.

Meanwhile, they saw their children beginning to speak English and adopt American customs. Some parents encouraged their children to **assimilate,** which means to be absorbed into the main cultural group. Others, especially roundtrippers who planned to return to their homelands, feared losing their children to the new land.

The Nativist Reaction

The question of assimilating immigrants into American society worried many native-born Americans, too. Overwhelmed by the huge numbers of newcomers, they felt threatened by the different languages and religions. Sometimes they found themselves competing with immigrants for jobs and opportunities. The result was friction and a rebirth of nativism—hatred of immigrants, mostly the Irish and the Germans.

Irish looking for work were faced with signs that read "No Irish need apply." Jews, barred from renting in many neighborhoods, realized that anti-Semitism existed in the United States, too. Urged by nativists, Congress placed restrictions on immigration. For example, workers whose passage across the ocean was paid by American companies could not enter the country.

Lee Wai She and her children lived in Hawaii, where the labor of many Chinese Americans helped make sugar "king."

Vital Links

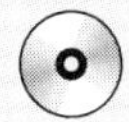

"My Little Son" (Song) Unit 4, Side 2, Search 18823, Play to 21162

See also Unit 4 Explore CD-ROM location 261.

Closing the Section

Wrap-Up Activity

A Modern Immigration Poem

To focus on changes in immigration over time, have small groups write new poems for the base of the Statue of Liberty. Refer them to the first stanza of Emma Lazarus's poem on this page. They should consider how the country has changed since the 1880s and what message would be appropriate today. Conclude by having the poems read aloud.

Section Review Answers

1. Definitions: *anti-Semitism* (298), *ethnic neighborhoods* (299), *assimilate* (301)

2. Many newer immigrants came from southern and eastern Europe rather than from northern Europe; most settled in cities rather than on farms; many were roundtrippers.

3. Push: overcrowding, lack of opportunity, poverty, shortages of farmland, war, harsh laws, religious and political persecution. Pull: freedom, wealth, peace, abundant land, jobs, opportunity, and letters from family and friends.

4. Their farm and railroad labor seemed to be in strong demand, yet native-born Americans were expressing hatred toward them. This resentment may also have puzzled them because they had been told that the United States had limitless opportunities.

Connections to Language Arts

Immigrants often expressed their hopes and fears in poetry and other forms of written language. Here are two poems written by Japanese immigrants. The first is a haiku, a traditional Japanese poetry form. This poem expresses the immigrant's hopes for the future:

Huge dreams of fortune
Go with me to foreign lands,
Across the ocean.

A second poem reflects the harsher reality of an immigrant's life in the new land:

Hawaii, Hawaii,
Like a dream.
So I came.
But my tears
Are flowing now
In the canefields.

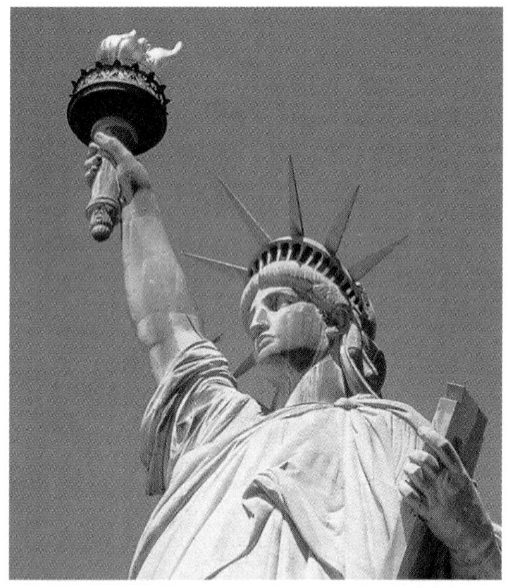

The Statue of Liberty, which has become a symbol of freedom and hope to immigrants, was given to the United States by the people of France in 1884.

The Chinese Exclusion Act Nativists were most successful in their attacks on Asians. Nativists in California accused the Chinese of working for lower wages. They pushed for laws that unfairly taxed Chinese immigrants and kept the children of Chinese from attending public schools. In 1882 they persuaded Congress to pass the Chinese Exclusion Act, which banned Chinese laborers from coming to the United States.

With Chinese workers unable to enter the country, California farmers and businesses hired Japanese to work in the fields, on the railroads, and in canneries. In 1907 and 1908, under nativist pressure, the United States negotiated the Gentlemen's Agreement with Japan by which Japan agreed to limit immigration to the United States.

Nativists in California and other states were not satisfied. They soon passed laws that banned Japanese Americans from owning or even renting farmland.

A Lamp Beside the Golden Door

In 1883, amid the nativist outcry, a poet lifted her voice with a different message for the immigrants struggling to make a life in the United States. In a poem now inscribed at the base of the Statue of Liberty, Emma Lazarus painted a picture of the United States as a beacon of freedom and a land of hope:

> "Give me your tired, your poor,
> Your huddled masses yearning to breathe free,
> The wretched refuse of your teeming shore.
> Send these, the homeless, tempest-tossed to me:
> I lift my lamp beside the golden door!"

Whether they came and then returned home, or came and made the United States their home, millions of people responded to that promise. One immigrant, Emmanuel Goldenberg, expressed the feeling of many who stayed to start new lives: "At Ellis Island I was born again."

1. Section Review

1. Define **anti-Semitism, ethnic neighborhoods,** and **assimilate.**
2. Describe two ways in which immigrants after the Civil War differed from earlier immigrants to the United States.
3. What factors pushed and pulled people from their homelands to the United States?
4. Critical Thinking As an immigrant from Asia, why might you have been confused by the various reactions of Americans to your arrival?

Geography Footnote

As immigrants arrived in Chicago during the last decades of the 1800s, they frequently settled in neighborhoods near employment opportunities. Not far from the neighborhood portrayed in the Geography Lab were the massive Union Stockyards, which opened in 1865. Within a year, 1.5 million cows, hogs, and sheep were slaughtered and packed there. By 1900, almost 15 million head of livestock were processed annually. Tens of thousands of workers, many of them recent immigrants, found work in the stockyards. The immigrants' low-paying jobs and substandard living conditions were documented in the famous 1906 muckraking novel by Upton Sinclair, *The Jungle,* best known for its grisly portrait of the meatpacking industry.

Geography Lab

A West Side Chicago Neighborhood, 1895

In 1893 Agnes Sinclair Holbrook, a worker at Hull House (page 308), studied the ethnic mix of a Chicago neighborhood made up mainly of immigrants. She used the results of a house-to-house survey to create a map like the one on this page. The colors reflect the percentages of people of various ethnic backgrounds living in each building, not the actual number of people. English-speaking residents were usually the children of immigrants who spoke another language.

Link to History

1. What group made up the largest percentage of the households on each street?
2. On the map, what evidence can you find that Germans had lived in the neighborhood for several decades while Italians had begun coming very recently?
3. **Hands-On Geography** Imagine that you live with your parents in this neighborhood in 1895. Write a letter to a friend in the old country. Describe your neighbors and the sights, sounds, and scents of your surroundings.

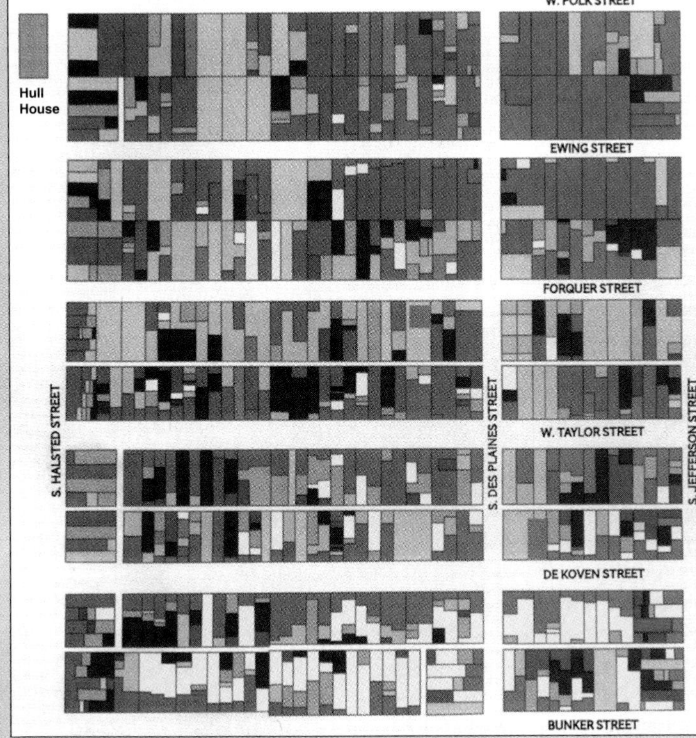

Non-housing lots are not colored

Hull House, see page 308

Source: National Geographic Society rendering of data from *Hull House Maps and Papers*

Teaching the Geography Lab

To focus on the concept of relationships within places, ask students to identify problems people living in this neighborhood could face (cultural tensions, overcrowding), as well as opportunities (diversity of people, cultures, and ideas). Discuss factors that may have kept residents apart (language and culture) and those that may have given a sense of solidarity (shared immigrant experience, religion, physical proximity, common problems).

Link to History

Answers

1. W. Polk: Italian; Ewing: Italian; Forquer: Irish; W. Taylor: German; De Koven: Czech; Bunker: Czech.

2. Germans were more widely scattered and more mixed in with English speakers.

3. Have students decide the nationality of their fictional parents and place themselves in one of the dwellings. Letters should include street names and descriptions of people, places (apartment houses, places of worship, ethnic grocery stores and cafes, newspaper stands), smells, speech, music, and so on.

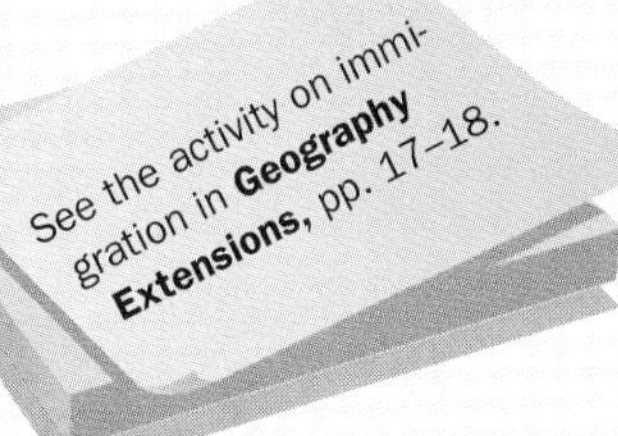

Introducing the Section

Vocabulary

urbanization (p. 304) the movement of people into cities

tenements (p. 305) apartment houses where large families shared one or two rooms, often without heat or water

political machine (p. 307) the organization of a political party to grant favors in return for votes

settlement house (p. 308) a community center providing services to the poor

Warm-Up Activity

Examining City Problems

To start students thinking about urban problems, have small groups list those facing your city or a large city nearby. Have students rank the problems in order of seriousness. After reading the section, they can compare their lists with the problems in the late 1800s.

Geography Question of the Day

Have students locate the three largest cities in the United States in 1900—New York, Chicago, and Philadelphia—on a map. Ask them to make a list of possible reasons why each one would have grown so large.

Section Objectives

- ★ Explain why cities grew so quickly in the decades following the Civil War.
- ★ Describe the problems growing cities faced and how political leaders responded.
- ★ Describe how reformers and immigrants tried to solve the problems of cities.

Teaching Resources

Take-Home Planner 2, pp. 20–29
Chapter Resources Binder
Study Guide, p. 58
Reinforcement, pp. 61–62
Skills Development
Geography Extensions
American Readings, p. 30
Using Historical Documents
Transparency Activities
Chapter and Unit Tests

2. The Rise of American Cities

Reading Guide

New Terms **urbanization, tenements, political machine, settlement house**

Section Focus **The effects of immigration and industry on American cities**

1. **Why did cities grow so quickly in the decades following the Civil War?**
2. **What problems did growing cities face, and how did political leaders respond?**
3. **How did reformers and immigrants try to solve the problems of cities?**

As a boy in Denmark, Jacob Riis had listened carefully to stories of the American West told by a man who had dug for gold there. With those stories filling his head, Riis arrived in New York City in 1870. He half expected to meet cowboys and see buffalo charging through the streets. Instead, he found a city "quite as civilized as Copenhagen," with paved streets, electric lights, and tall buildings.

The Growth of Cities

Riis had landed in New York at a time when the industrial age was transforming the United States from a nation of farmers to a nation of city dwellers. Cities with good transportation links to the outside world—large harbors, railroads, and steamships—grew into industrial centers. Their factories attracted immigrants as well as American migrants from farms and small towns.

The nation was undergoing **urbanization**—the movement of people into cities. In 1860 only one-fifth of Americans lived in cities with more than 2,500 people. By the dawn of the twentieth century, almost one-half of Americans were city dwellers.

From coast to coast, cities now dotted the American landscape. In 1900 three cities had over 1 million people—New York, Chicago, and Philadelphia—and 35 others had more than 100,000 residents.

Outward and Upward

American cities before the Civil War were "walking cities"—compact and easily crossed on foot or in horse-drawn carriages. Now, as urbanization put pressure on cities to expand, new technologies made it possible for them to grow outward and upward.

Streetcars In 1890 the main form of public transportation was the horse-drawn streetcar. Tons of horse manure clogged the streets and filled the air with foul smells. Also, crowded streetcars cruelly strained the horses. In New York City alone, 15,000 horses died each year on the streets.

The solution was found in the electric streetcar or trolley, which was powered by an overhead electric wire. In 1888 Frank J. Sprague built a 12-mile (19-km) streetcar line for Richmond, Virginia. Three years later, 50 cities had electric streetcars.

Streetcar tracks radiated outward like spokes from the downtown hub. With an easy way to get to work, middle-class people—businesspeople and highly skilled workers—moved to quieter neighborhoods beyond the busy city core.

Skyscrapers Cities not only expanded outward. They grew upward, too, thanks to improved materials and to electricity. Buildings with walls framed in steel or iron were

Tips for Teaching

Gifted Students

Gifted students can learn through long-term projects that let them use artistic methods. They may enjoy constructing cardboard models or making architectural draftings or computer graphics of the building discussed on page 306. Students may use the photos in the textbook as a reference, or a library book about Chicago Style architecture. Have them paint the models, add trees and contemporary vehicles, pedestrians, and other details. Have them share the models or drawings with the class.

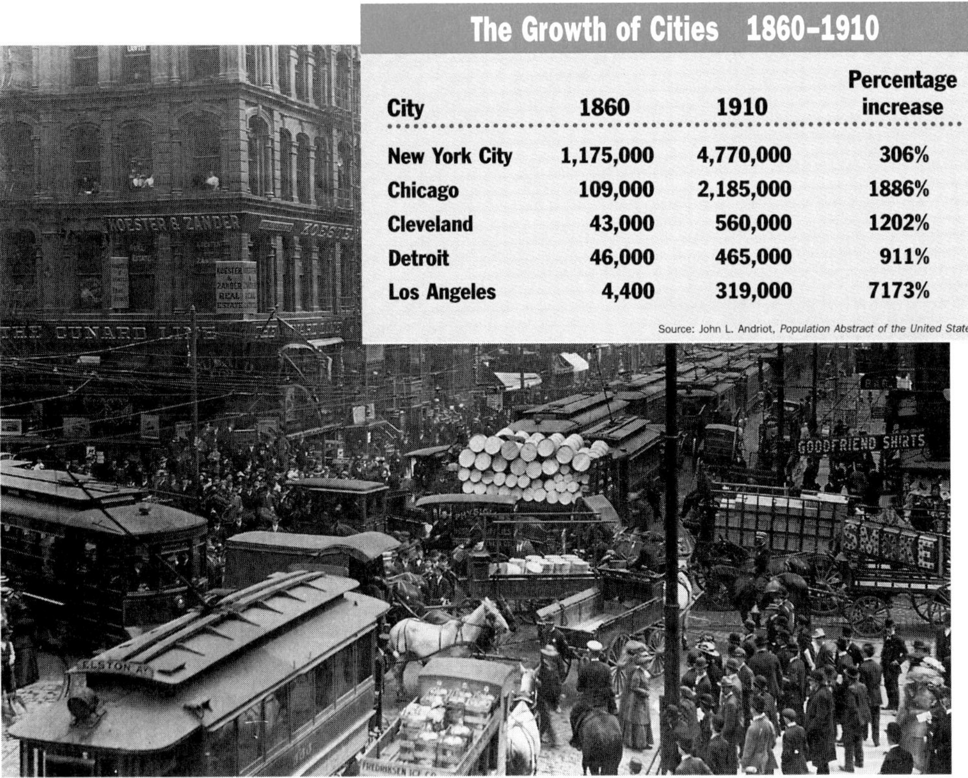

KOESTER & ZANDER
GOODFRIEND SHIRTS

The Growth of Cities 1860–1910

City	1860	1910	Percentage increase
New York City	1,175,000	4,770,000	306%
Chicago	109,000	2,185,000	1886%
Cleveland	43,000	560,000	1202%
Detroit	46,000	465,000	911%
Los Angeles	4,400	319,000	7173%

Source: John L. Andriot, *Population Abstract of the United States*

In 1909 streetcars, wagons, and people jammed the streets of Chicago—a city bursting with new construction and industry.

strong enough to reach higher than the old limits of four or five stories. Electric lights and elevators made it possible for people to live and work in the new "skyscrapers" sprouting up in cities across the country.

Problems in Cities

These new modes of transportation and construction encouraged urbanization. With urbanization, though, came new problems.

Tenements One serious problem was overcrowding. Cities were filling with immigrants and newcomers from American farms and small towns. Too poor to rent their own apartments, they crammed together into **tenements**—apartment houses where large families shared one or two rooms, often without heat or water.

The tenement areas of American cities were among the most densely populated places in the world. An observer in 1888 described tenements as

> "great prison-like structures of brick, with narrow doors and windows, cramped passages and steep rickety stairs. . . . In case of fire they would be perfect death-traps."

Fire In fact, fire was a major threat in the cities. In 1871 the great Chicago fire

Developing the Section

Discussion

Checking Understanding

1. What did a city need to grow into an industrial center in the late 1800s? (Good transportation links to the outside world.)

2. By the end of the 1800s, what percentage of Americans were city dwellers? (Almost 50 percent.)

Stimulating Critical Thinking

3. If you lived on a farm in the late 1800s, would you want to move to a city? Explain. (Yes: conveniences such as street cars and skyscrapers, availability of jobs. No: too crowded, might have to live in a tenement.)

See the Study Guide activity in Chapter Resources Binder, p. 58.

Vital Links

Steel-framed skyscraper (Picture) Unit 4, Side 1, Search 08477

See also Unit 4 Explore CD-ROM location 54.

History Footnote

The Triangle Shirtwaist factory was on the eighth, ninth, and tenth floors of the Asch building. Eighth-floor workers tried to douse the fire using water buckets and the building's fire hose, but the hose was defective. The phone on the ninth floor did not work. Finally, a worker on the tenth floor was able to call the fire department.

Those on the tenth floor could reach the roof, where people in the building next door helped them to safety with ladders. Workers from the two lower floors crammed into elevators, which broke after a few trips, and onto the fire escape, which twisted from the heat and soon also broke. Firefighters put up ladders for those trapped by the windows, but they reached only to the sixth floor; they held out safety nets but the falling bodies ripped through the nets.

Section Activity

Planning Mayors' Campaigns

To broaden understanding of the problems facing cities of the late 1800s, have the class prepare two mayoral campaigns for an election in 1890. Have half of the class divide into small groups to design posters, create slogans, and write short speeches for a machine mayor already in office. Have the other half do the same for a reform challenger. Campaigns should propose appropriate solutions for problems. Ask groups to present their campaigns.

Teaching the Link to Art

Discuss ways the architecture of the newly-constructed Guaranty building may have affected those working in and around it. (Possibilities are: more light from larger windows and decorative exterior make people happier and more productive.)

Discussion Answers: Answers should reflect an understanding of how shape and color affect a building's appeal.

For a description of dangers of tenement life, see **American Readings**, p. 30.

Link to Art

Chicago Style After the Chicago fire the city embarked on a massive rebuilding effort. Architects were needed, and Louis Sullivan became one of the finest. Sullivan rejected the old style of dark, thick-walled skyscrapers. He wanted them to be pieces of art. He designed thinner walls to make them more graceful, with larger windows to let in more light. Then Sullivan adorned the walls with elaborate decoration. Like a sculptor, he shaped buildings "into new forms of use and beauty." Sullivan's style, shown here in the Guaranty building in Buffalo, New York, came to be called the Chicago Style. **Discuss** What building in your area would you redesign to make more beautiful? What shapes, colors, or construction materials might you use?

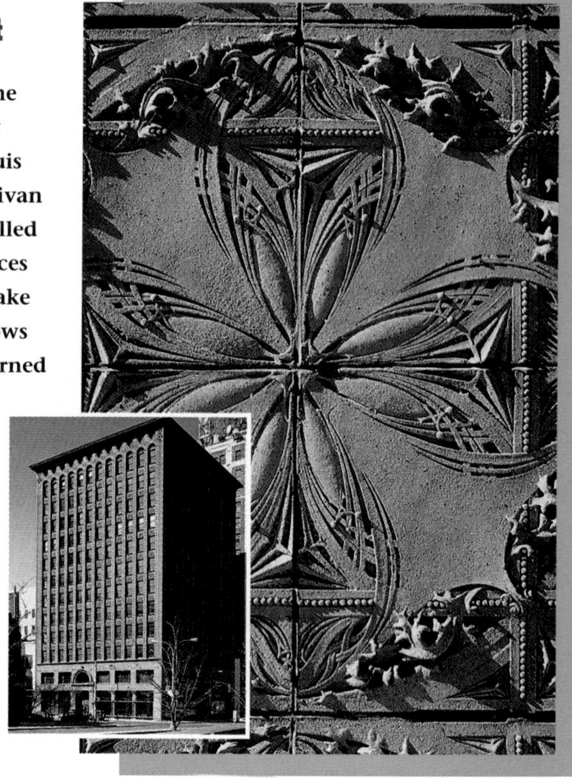

destroyed the heart of that city. When San Francisco was shaken by its 1906 earthquake, the fires that followed did more damage than the quake itself. Thousands of buildings burned to the ground.

Fire was a constant danger to factory workers. The most famous factory fire broke out in 1911 in the ten-story Triangle Shirtwaist factory in New York City. Many of the 146 workers who died in that tragedy were young immigrant women. They could not escape because exits were locked and stairways were too narrow. Frances Perkins, a social worker, described the tragedy:

> "We saw the smoke pouring out of the building. We got there just as they started to jump. . . . They came down in twos and threes, jumping together in a kind of desperate hope."

Sanitation In the overcrowded cities, sanitation was also a problem. Water systems were unable to supply enough water to swelling city populations. Ill-planned sewers emptied waste into rivers and harbors.

Jacob Riis feared that raw sewage was getting into New York City's drinking-water supply. With a notebook and camera, he set out to document the source of the city's water. Riis found sewage from nearby cities pouring into the rivers. Garbage piled up on riverbanks as well as on city streets. It was not surprising, then, that city dwellers were plagued by diseases such as typhus, tuberculosis, dysentery, and cholera.

Connections to Math

The 1906 San Francisco earthquake is estimated to have been magnitude 7.9 on the Richter scale, an extremely strong tremor. Seismologists—scientists who study earthquakes—use the Richter scale to measure the severity of earthquake tremors. Most people have heard of this scale, named after the American seismologist Charles Francis Richter. The scale runs from 1 to 9. Unlike the familiar Fahrenheit temperature scale in which 78 degrees is one degree warmer than 77 degrees, the Richter scale increases by a factor of 10 for each whole number on the scale. This means that an earthquake measuring 7 on the Richter scale is 10 times more powerful than one measuring 6. It is 100 times more powerful than a magnitude 5 quake, and 1,000 times more powerful than a magnitude 4 quake.

Seeking Solutions

The explosive growth of cities made it hard for city governments to keep up with demands for services such as fire protection and sanitation. As problems mounted, elected officials struggled to solve them.

Shocked by disasters like the Triangle Shirtwaist fire, cities passed new laws and building codes. They hired and trained firefighters to replace volunteer firemen. They required building owners to install fire extinguishers and to improve fire escapes. Builders also began to use brick, concrete, and steel instead of wood.

Meanwhile, journalists like Jacob Riis were having an effect. Riis's reports helped push cities to install safer water and sewage-disposal systems.

Machine Politics

To force city officials and landlords to address their problems, citizens had to take action. However, it was hard for the poor—especially immigrants who spoke little English and did not understand the American political system—to make their needs known. Seeing an opportunity, local politicians stepped in.

Many cities were divided into small districts called wards. Voters in a ward elected an alderman to represent them on the city council. The person who ran the Democratic or Republican Party in the ward was called the ward boss.

If a tenement was without heat, if garbage went uncollected, or if a street needed to be paved, people turned to the alderman and the ward boss for help. In exchange for votes at election time, ward bosses tried to give people what they needed.

The organization of a political party that granted favors in return for votes was called a **political machine.** In the cities, political machines worked hard to help solve the problems of the poor in their districts. That was how they gained power—and kept it.

Corruption Political machines, however, were also corrupt. Bosses bought votes and gave city jobs to their supporters, whether they were qualified or not. If a streetcar company wanted to run a trolley in a certain ward, it would bribe the ward boss to let it do so. Tenement owners could keep fire inspectors out of their buildings by paying off the political machine.

Point of View

Were political machines helpful or harmful?

In spite of their corruption, political machines had their defenders. The journalist Frederick Howe reported approvingly that ward bosses

> "were kindly, tolerant; good companions. Their system was human and simple, something any one could understand. It took graft [bribes] . . . and gave help to neighbors when sick or in need."

Others condemned the system. Senator Carl Schurz worked tirelessly to wipe out machine politics. He claimed that

> "it attracts to . . . politics the worst elements of our population. . . . The people of some of our great municipalities [cities] are crying out that they have been scandalously misgoverned and robbed and oppressed [by political machines]."

Political machines continued to dominate the politics of many cities well into the twentieth century. However, reformers and journalists did their best to expose and destroy them.

Discussion

Checking Understanding

1. How did city officials respond to health and safety problems? (Passed new laws and building codes, hired firemen, required building owners to provide fire escapes and extinguishers.)

Stimulating Critical Thinking

2. Why do you think exit doors were locked at the Triangle Shirtwaist factory? (Possible answers: Employers did not want workers to sneak out, or inspectors to come in.)

Bonus Activity

Running a Settlement House

To underscore the importance of settlement houses, have small groups list services that might be offered, such as child care and instruction in reading, music, math, and cooking. Then have groups designate one student to role-play a visitor seeking help, with the rest of the group describing the available services.

Teaching the Point of View

After students have read the two quotations, have them discuss whether people would rather have government help when in need or have honest government, and whether they should have to choose between the two.

Closing the Section

Wrap-Up Activity

An Urban-Rural Dialogue

To review urban living conditions, ask pairs of students to imagine it is 1895 and they are visiting their old rural home after having moved to a large city. Have them take turns to write or act out a conversation, with their partners playing a family member back home. They should include descriptions and questions about urban scenery, work, and living conditions.

Section Review Answers

1. Definitions: *urbanization* (304), *tenements* (305), *political machine* (307), *settlement house* (308)

2. Overcrowded and unsafe tenements, fire, poor sanitation, corrupt politicians.

3. Answers should reflect problems from the text and their importance.

Vital Links

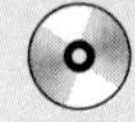

Child health exhibit (Picture) Unit 4, Side 1, Search 13059

See also Unit 4 Explore CD-ROM location 115.

History Footnote

The YMCA was founded in 1844 in England to help young men from rural areas cope with temptations of urban and industrial life, such as gambling and drinking. Bible study was the most popular activity. The first American "Y" opened in Boston in 1851. By 1916, membership in American YMCAs had grown to 600,000. Members could read in libraries, swim, listen to educational programs, attend summer camps, and live in hotel-type rooms. They could also play games in gymnasiums, including basketball. James Naismith, a Canadian native and physical education teacher at the YMCA in Springfield, Massachusetts, invented it to provide indoor exercise during the cold winter months. The Young Women's Christian Association was founded in 1858 to provide similar services to young women in urban areas.

Early Reformers

Some citizens were shocked by corrupt political machines. They claimed that officials were more interested in taking bribes than in protecting health and safety. Cleaning up cities, they realized, required cleaning up politics as well. (You will read more about political reform in Chapter 7.) Meanwhile, many private citizens—well-educated and middle class—felt it their duty to help the suffering poor.

Women reformers Women played a leading role in these efforts. They formed associations such as the Women's Municipal League to pressure local leaders to build schools and provide other services. Some women worked as teachers and nurses in city neighborhoods. Others became social workers, collecting information on living conditions and working to promote the well-being of poor city dwellers.

Settlement houses On Mulberry Street in New York City, an organization called the King's Daughters helped improve a neighborhood by planting trees and flowers. Realizing that people needed more serious help, they opened a **settlement house**—a community center providing services to the poor.

During the 1880s and 1890s, settlement houses sprang up everywhere. One of the best known was Hull House on Chicago's West Side. Started in 1889 by Jane Addams and Ellen Starr, it provided everything from English-language classes to hot meals. Settlement houses were also places for the poor to meet and discuss problems.

Help for children Settlement houses took a special interest in children. Streets were filled with children—orphans as well as those left to look after themselves while their parents struggled to earn a living. Unable to get into overcrowded schools, some joined gangs. Many toiled in sweatshops to help their families. As many as 350,000 homeless children were put on "orphan trains" and sent to live with families outside the big cities.

Settlement houses ran day nurseries for the children of working parents. Reformers pressed cities to make public schools available to all, and to build playgrounds to provide places for children to play and breathe fresh air.

Religious groups The plight of the poor was of concern to religious groups, too. In the 1880s the Salvation Army began providing the poor with food and shelter. The Young Men's and Women's Christian Associations (YMCA and YWCA) set up clubs and activities for youth. In 1891 James Naismith nailed a peach basket to a wall in a YMCA gymnasium and invented basketball.

Many Protestants worked in settlement houses because they accepted an idea known as the Social Gospel—the belief that the teachings of Jesus require Christians to help the poor. Catholic churches became community centers for immigrants from Catholic regions such as Italy, Poland, and Bohemia.

Self-help Immigrants themselves organized to deal with the hardships of city life. The Hebrew Immigrant Aid Society helped Jewish newcomers. Chinese formed family and neighborhood associations. Immigrants published newspapers in their native languages and joined unions to fight for better wages and working conditions. When they became citizens, they joined political parties in order to have a voice in improving their lives.

2. Section Review

1. Define **urbanization, tenements, political machine,** and **settlement house.**
2. Describe three problems that cities faced.
3. Critical Thinking If you had been an early reformer, what city problem would you have tried to solve first? Why?

Section Objectives

- ★ Explain how American cities changed to become more exciting places to live.
- ★ Describe new inventions and products that changed daily life for city dwellers.
- ★ Describe how people spent their leisure time in the cities.

Teaching Resources

Take-Home Planner 2, pp. 20–29
Chapter Resources Binder
Study Guide, p. 59
Reinforcement
Skills Development, pp. 63–34
Geography Extensions
American Readings, pp. 31–32
Using Historical Documents
Transparency Activities
Chapter and Unit Tests, pp. 51–54

Introducing the Section

Vocabulary

leisure (p. 311) free time

vaudeville (p. 312) a stage show that combined songs, dance, opera, and comedy

Warm-Up Activity

Living in the City

To start students thinking about advantages of city life, have pairs compile a list of three or four reasons why people enjoy living in cities today. Some reasons are choice of free time activities; nearness to entertainment, sports, restaurants, and shopping; cultural attractions; variety of people; and job opportunities. Have them refer to their lists after they have finished the section and learned why people of the late 1800s flocked to cities.

Geography Question of the Day

Ask students to identify what they think of as the "center" of their city or town. Have them list the buildings (e.g. city hall, shopping center) that make them think of that location as the center.

3. Cities and a New Way of Life

Reading Guide

New Terms leisure, vaudeville

Section Focus New ways of living that developed in American cities

1. How did American cities change to become more exciting places to live?
2. What new inventions and products changed daily life for city dwellers?
3. How did people spend their leisure time in the cities?

As you have seen, American cities changed dramatically in the late 1800s—and not simply in size and shape. The American way of life itself was changing. Indeed, cities offered more than jobs for the poor from far and near. They became centers of new ideas, activities, and expectations.

The Excitement of City Life

When people left the countryside for the city, they found a whole new world there. This world included a downtown center with its tall buildings, theaters, stores, and busy streets. Looking back, the author Hamlin Garland described the effect of Chicago's bright lights and bustle on newcomers like him and his brother:

> "Everything interested us. The business section so sordid [dirty] to others was grandly terrifying to us. . . . Nothing was commonplace; nothing was ugly to us."

So many people, in fact, flocked downtown that the streets were choked by traffic. To decrease congestion, Boston, Philadelphia, and other cities built underground tunnels—called subways—for their streetcars. Wealthier families, meanwhile, often preferred the quiet, tree-shaded avenues of suburbs, where homes and apartment houses lined streetcar routes.

City Planning

Amid the bustle and excitement of city life, a new idea was taking root. People began to realize that beauty and open space were vital to the well-being of city people.

Until now, cities had grown without plan. Builders threw up tenements and homes as fast as possible. The more families they squeezed onto a lot, the more profits landlords made. They did not provide open spaces where people could escape from the bustle of the streets and breathe fresh air.

Frederick Law Olmstead was convinced of the importance of open spaces to city dwellers. In 1858 he designed Central Park as a green refuge in the middle of New York City. He went on to draw up plans for city parks, elegant boulevards, and entire suburbs from Seattle to Atlanta.

The urban planner Daniel Burnham had even grander plans. He dreamed of making American cities as attractive as London and Paris and the other great capitals of Europe. He would do so by proposing magnificent public buildings, parks, and tree-lined waterfronts. Cleveland, San Francisco, and other cities hired Burnham to lay out plans for them.

Developing the Section

Teaching the

Link to the Present

Ask students to name some similarities between large malls of today and the downtowns of the late 1800s. (Large selection of stores of different types, exciting or glamorous atmosphere, different kinds of entertainment and restaurants, place to meet friends.) Point out that the two have social and economic differences, and encourage students to name examples of these differences. (Malls become identified with a neighborhood and an economic class; stores and shoppers might be economically varied in a downtown; malls might be safer.)

See the Study Guide activity in **Chapter Resources Binder**, p. 59.

Vital Links

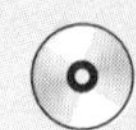

Telephone operators (Picture) Unit 4, Side 1, Search 16419

See also Unit 4 Explore CD-ROM location 148.

Connections to Science

When inventor Thomas Edison got an idea into his head, there was no stopping him. In the 1870s, he knew that finding a cheap, household alternative to the gaslight depended on finding the right material for the filament in an electric bulb. This tiny strand carries the electric current and glows, producing the light. The inventor and his staff tried all sorts of materials, from metals like platinum and chromium to paper, hemp, tree bark, cork, and lemon peel. Edison even tried a hair he plucked from a friend's beard. He moved on to carbonized cotton sewing thread, then cardboard. Both worked, but not well enough. Edison then tested 6,000 vegetable fibers. Finally, a type of Japanese bamboo burned for 1,000 hours in a vacuum container. The lightbulb was born. Today's lightbulb filament is made of tungsten steel.

Link to the Present

The new "downtowns" Where do people go when they are in the mood to spend money and have fun? In the late 1800s a city dweller would have said, "Downtown." Today, millions of Americans would say, "The mall." The 1980s saw malls popping up all over the country.

After a few years, however, people began to be bored with malls. In response, owners rebuilt their malls to serve as centers of entertainment as well as shopping. An extravagant example, The Mall of America in Minnesota, has more than 400 stores, 50 restaurants, 9 music and dance clubs, 14 movie theaters, and a 7-acre amusement park with roller coasters.

Even as new malls flourish, though, cities are reviving their old downtowns. Now people are rediscovering the excitement of shopping and even living there.

Inventions

Meanwhile, new inventions were bringing great changes to the lives of city dwellers. The energy that powered most of these inventions was electricity.

Thomas Edison The genius behind many of the new inventions was Thomas A. Edison. One of his early triumphs was the first phonograph, or record player, in 1877. Edison's big breakthrough, however, came in 1879 when he invented the first practical lightbulb. Then he developed light switches, fuse boxes, and underground electric cables. Edison made electricity an inexpensive source of light for city people.

By 1900 Americans were using over 25 million lightbulbs. Dubbed by admirers the "Wizard of Menlo Park"—the site of his laboratory in New Jersey—Edison dismissed such labels. He credited his achievements, such as the storage battery and the motion picture camera, to hard work, not wizardry. "Genius," he declared, "is one percent inspiration and ninety-nine percent perspiration."

The Bell telephone Equally important in changing daily life was the telephone. Although not the first to believe that electricity might transmit the human voice, Alexander Graham Bell was the first to invent a workable telephone. Investors, slow to provide money for Bell's invention, could not imagine people preferring verbal messages to written ones. By 1890, however, every major city had a telephone system.

Housework Made Easier

New technologies and products also made housework easier. People who had coal and oil stoves no longer had to chop wood for fuel. City dwellers who installed plumbing could replace chamber pots and hand-filled washtubs with toilets and running water.

Housewives could now buy factory-canned fruits and vegetables instead of depending on foods they preserved in jars at home. Thanks to refrigerated railroad cars and steamships, the well-to-do could enjoy oranges from California, fresh meat from Illinois, and bananas from the West Indies.

Meanwhile, clothing—once made at home—was now produced more cheaply in factories. Soiled clothing could be sent to a laundry instead of washed by hand.

Department and chain stores Even shopping was made easier. Instead of going to different stores for each item, shoppers went to department stores, where they could find everything from clothing to furniture in

History Footnote

Brothers Erastus Flavel Beadle and Irwin P. Beadle, encouraged by the success of their pamphlet called *The Dime Song Book,* moved to New York City in 1858 in hopes of selling dime books. They formed I. P. Beadle and Company, which first published joke books, handbooks, songbooks, and biographies. Most were small paperback books, about six inches tall by four inches wide. Their success attracted other publishers to the industry, which soon expanded to serial magazines.

The dime-novel industry published mostly historical, romance, western, and detective fiction, often with larger-than-life heroes. Some titles were *Roaring Ralph Rockwood, the Reckless Ranger; Captain Cool Blade—or the Man-Shark of the Mississippi;* and *Alice Wilde, the Raftsman's Daughter: A Forest Romance.*

Alexander Graham Bell invented the telephone in 1876. The first long-distance service began in 1887 when telephone lines were connected between New York City and Philadelphia. Cellular telephones (inset) are now used without any telephone lines.

one place. In the 1890s Macy's store in New York employed 3,000 workers—as many as Carnegie's biggest steel plant.

Shoppers looking for bargains could find them in chain stores—stores owned by one company, with branches in many towns and cities. Chains such as Woolworth's and J. C. Penney could buy items in great quantities and thus offer them at low prices.

The New Leisure

Changes in housework and shopping meant that middle-class families—and poorer families, too—spent less time on daily chores. For the first time in history, ordinary people as well as the rich had a significant amount of **leisure**—free time. As leisure increased, city dwellers began to seek new and different ways to enjoy life.

Newspapers and pulp fiction Reading was one favorite form of entertainment. New ways to make paper, set type, and produce illustrations lowered the cost of newspaper and book production, while the spread of public schools increased literacy. Publishers rushed to satisfy the appetites of the reading public.

By 1900 immigrant communities supported over 1,000 foreign-language newspapers. Daily papers in English thrived, too. Joseph Pulitzer's newspapers appealed to readers with cartoons and sports pages as well as news articles. Reporters like Jacob Riis competed to get the "scoop" on scandals.

Writers followed formulas to churn out detective novels and magazine stories. Such stories became known as "pulp fiction" because they were printed on cheap paper made of wood pulp. They were also called "dime novels" because they cost so little.

Literature Other readers turned to more serious literature. Samuel Clemens, who used the name Mark Twain, wrote of small-town life along the Mississippi River. His humorous portrayal of characters such as Huck Finn and Tom Sawyer made his stories bestsellers.

Twain and other writers of the time were called Realists because they wrote about real life, even if it meant criticizing American society. Stephen Crane's novel *The Red Badge of Courage* evoked the horrors of the Civil War, while Theodore Dreiser described the tragic fates of people who tried to rise out of the working class.

Amusement parks and circuses In search of entertainment, people thronged to

Discussion

Checking Understanding

1. Name developments that made housekeeping easier. (Coal and oil stoves, indoor plumbing, factory-canned fruits and vegetables, inexpensive clothing, department and chain stores.)

Stimulating Critical Thinking

2. Do you agree with Edison's definition of genius? Explain. (Yes: good ideas need hard work to become reality. No: a less intelligent person might work hard and not invent anything.)

3. If you ran a foreign-language newspaper, what kinds of information might you include? (News from the Old Country, local news about the ethnic community, advice about how to survive in an American city.)

Section Activity

Creating an "Arts and Leisure" Page

To illustrate the impact of new inventions, products, and trends in the late 1800s, have small groups create a page from the "arts and leisure" section of a big-city newspaper. Bring in sample arts and leisure sections. Each page should include at least two ads (for new products, theaters, museums, and so on) and two reviews (of books, performances, or sports events). Then have groups compare their pages.

Bonus Activity

Designing a City Park

To help students understand the importance of open spaces and free-time activities, have them imagine being asked to design a large city park. Have them draw the layout for the park, including ponds, forests, buildings, access points, and attractions. They can then name the park and write a paragraph to accompany the drawing, explaining why they included the features they designed.

Vital Links

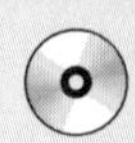

"Take Me Out to the Ball Game" (Song) Unit 4, Side 2, Search 05065, Play to 07116

See also Unit 4 Explore CD-ROM location 394.

For the poem "Casey at the Bat," see **American Readings**, pp. 31–32.

History Footnote

Phineas Taylor Barnum's long career as a showman, museum operator, and circus owner began in 1835. In 1841, his American Museum opened in New York City. The museum was famous for its good-natured jokes and tricks. In one exhibit, museum-goers paid an extra fee to see an oddity labeled "The Cherry-colored Cat." When they entered the room, they saw an ordinary black cat with a sign that read, "Some cherries are black." But instead of getting angry, people enjoyed the jokes and obvious fakes. In 1871, Barnum organized his traveling circus. Ten years later, his circus merged with one owned by James Bailey. Barnum's circus lives on today, in the famous Ringling Brothers and Barnum & Bailey Circus.

P. T. Barnum's circus traveled across the country by train. Its colorful posters attracted crowds to its shows at every stop.

amusement parks, fairs, and circuses. One young woman, visiting New York's Coney Island with a friend, described it as a "wonderful and beautiful place" with exciting rides and amusements. She recalled:

> "When we had been on the razzle-dazzle, the chute and the loop-the-loop . . . I asked her how she liked it. She said: 'It is just like what I see when I dream of heaven.'"

P. T. Barnum opened a museum that specialized in exhibits such as the "Feejee Mermaid," with the body of a fish and the head of a monkey. The museum was so successful that Barnum took it on the road as part of his circus, "The Greatest Show on Earth."

One of the most popular forms of entertainment was **vaudeville**—a stage show that combined songs, dance, opera, and comedy. Vaudeville grew in popularity because people could watch it while they talked and socialized.

Baseball and bicycles Beginning in the big cities, baseball soon became a favorite sport. In 1876 teams in eight cities formed baseball's National League. To encourage family attendance, the league banned Sunday games, beer, and gambling.

Prohibitions on beer and Sunday games turned off some fans. A rival organization, the American League, loosened the rules. Together, the two leagues appealed to a broad spectrum of fans and turned baseball into "the national pastime."

By the 1890s women, too, had begun to play sports, including basketball, baseball, and tennis. When turned down by men's athletic clubs, women established their own.

Meanwhile, a craze for bicycling swept the nation. Riders were attracted by the new "safety bicycle," which now had air-filled tires instead of solid ones. Millions of adults and children took to the streets with this new form of recreation.

Dance halls Young people with leisure and a little extra money liked to gather at dance halls. At first, members of the same sex danced with one another, for the custom of dating was almost unknown. Gradually, however, customs changed, and boys began to "treat" girls to a night at the dance hall.

The Blossoming of Culture

Working people, who had rarely had leisure time before, loved the entertainment of dance halls, amusement parks, and sports events. At the same time, people with more wealth and education increasingly turned to

History Footnote

New York City's Central Park was one of the first American parks to be developed using landscape architecture techniques. Alarmed by the increasing rate of urbanization in Manhattan, people began calling for a large public park in the 1840s. In 1856, the city bought most of the park's land for $5 million. A contest to design the park was announced with a $2,000 prize.

Out of 33 plans submitted, the one designed by Frederick Law Olmstead and Calvert Vaux won. It called for clearing the land and sculpting it into ravines, hills, open grassy areas, forests, and lakes, with a system of pathways, roads, and bridges. Besides moving tons of earth to fit this plan, workers planted about 5 million trees and constructed a water supply system. The completed park opened in 1876.

"high culture" for entertainment. In cities across the country, bankers and industrialists gave money to establish art museums, symphonies, and opera companies.

The first museums were private and run for profit. Soon, however, universities and cities opened museums devoted to painting, sculpture, and other fine arts. These museums were supported by rich Americans who scoured the collections of Europe, buying masterpieces and hurrying home to show off their treasures.

Meanwhile, American artists began to make their marks on the art world. Thomas Eakins, Mary Cassatt, and Maurice Prendergast painted scenes of Americans at work and play, while Frederic Remington and Charles Russell portrayed the drama and life of American Indians and cowboys in the West.

In vaudeville, opera singers performed alongside juggling acts. Now, however, business leaders built opera houses and concert halls where performances of classical music could be enjoyed without interruption.

The intent was to educate the public to appreciate art and classical music. The effect, however, was to isolate the rich from the poor. A night at the symphony or opera became an occasion to display one's wealth and status by dressing in fine clothes and jewels. Working people could not afford to buy tickets—nor did they feel at home in

In this 1901 painting, Maurice Prendergast showed well-to-do Americans enjoying a day in New York City's Central Park. How did their lives compare to the lives of the immigrants shown on page 295?

Discussion

Checking Understanding

1. What were some things Americans did with their increased leisure time? (Thronged to parks, fairs, dance halls, and circuses, read books and newspapers, went to vaudeville shows, played sports such as baseball and tennis, attended concerts, and went to museums.)

Stimulating Critical Thinking

2. Do you think the "new leisure" of Americans had a good or bad effect on the economy? Explain. (Good: provided more jobs for people in the entertainment and appliance industries. Bad: Instead of saving, people spent their money on entertainment.)

Vital Links

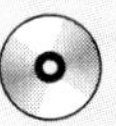

High wheelers (Picture) Unit 4, Side 1, Search 43472

See also Unit 4 Explore CD-ROM location 381.

Coney Island amusement park (Picture) Unit 4, Side 1, Search 43496

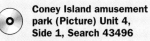

See also Unit 4 Explore CD-ROM location 385.

Vaudeville (Picture) Unit 4, Side 1, Search 43502

See also Unit 4 Explore CD-ROM location 386.

Closing the Section

Wrap-Up Activity

Judging Impacts on City Life

To reinforce understanding of the impact of inventions on city life, have pairs discuss which invention or development described in this section had the greatest impact on city life and why. Have each pair explain briefly why they made the choice they did. Keep a tally on the chalkboard.

Section Review Answers

1. Definitions: *leisure* (311), *vaudeville* (312)

2. Provide open spaces and beauty to promote the well-being of city people, make American cities as beautiful as European cities; they tried to meet these goals by designing parks, drawing up plans for suburbs and elegant boulevards, and building magnificent public buildings and tree-lined waterfronts.

3. Answers could include coal and oil stoves, electric lights, plumbing, telephones, canned foods, cheap clothing and laundry service, chain and department stores.

4. To show that their culture was equal to that of wealthy Europeans, to express a higher social and economic status than that of working-class people, or in an effort to develop sophisticated tastes.

To check understanding of "Why We Remember," assign Thinking Critically question 3 on page 316.

314

History Footnote

The word *vaudeville* comes from the French *vau-de-vire,* which means "valley of Vire," a town in northwest France where popular satirical songs were composed. Before television or movies, people could find inexpensive evening entertainment at vaudeville shows. In the late 1800s a vaudeville show consisted of several acts featuring singers and musicians, comedians, jugglers, magicians, acrobats, and trained animals. At vaudeville's height in the early 1900s, an estimated 2 million people a day watched a show in one of 1,000 vaudeville theaters across the country. Among the famous entertainers who traced their roots to vaudeville are W. C. Fields, Fanny Brice, Red Skelton, Bert Lahr (*The Wizard of Oz*'s Cowardly Lion), Groucho Marx, Jack Benny, and George Burns.

the elegant halls, where talking, laughter, and baskets of food were frowned upon.

Poverty Amid Plenty

Reformers took some pride in city improvements. Better transportation and building codes made life safer. Parks and entertainment provided pleasure for even the poorest families.

Still, much work remained to be done. For many reformers the luxuries and displays of wealth by the rich seemed a waste of money that could be better spent on meeting the needs of the poor. Jacob Riis worried that "the gap between the classes . . . is widening day by day." How could cities cope with the surging tide of eager but penniless newcomers? Said Riis:

> "I know of but one bridge that will carry us over safe—a bridge founded upon justice and built of human hearts."

As a new century dawned, reformers would take on the challenge of bridging the gap between the rich and the poor.

3. Section Review

1. Define **leisure** and **vaudeville.**

2. What were the goals of city planners and how were they accomplished?

3. What developments gave people more leisure? Give at least three examples.

4. Critical Thinking Why do you think wealthy Americans began to collect art and support concert halls and opera companies?

Why We Remember

The Growth of Cities

Some 25 years after that terrible night in the police station, Jacob Riis showed his friend Theodore Roosevelt around New York City's neighborhoods. Arriving at the police station where he had spent the night so long ago, Riis pointed to a man asleep on a plank. "I was like this once," he told Roosevelt. At that moment, it seemed as though nothing had changed. However, the nation had undergone enormous change. In 1870 the United States was still largely rural. Forty years later, it was a nation of cities. As a reporter, Riis knew the dark side of cities. He also knew their attractions—beautiful parks, splendid museums, and tall buildings that people still enjoy today.

Riis also witnessed another great change. Before 1865 most immigrants had come from northern Europe. By 1900 most arrived from eastern and southern Europe and from Asia. Never had the nation been more diverse—or faced more decisions about how to absorb so many peoples and cultures. Jacob Riis, as a reporter and photographer, helped to bring greater knowledge and understanding to the decisions that Americans made.

(Answers continued from side margin)
of the urban line on the graph chosen for step 1(b). The increase in urban population percentage is reflected in the circle graphs chosen for step 1(a) (the urban piece of the pie is larger for 1910 than for 1860) and in the line graph chosen for step 1(c) (urban percentage line slopes up, while rural percentage line slopes down).

For further application, have students do the Applying Skills activity in the Chapter Survey (p. 316).

If students need to
review the skill, use the
Skills Development trans-
parency and activity in the
Chapter Resources
Binder, pp. 63–64.

Skill Lab

Acquiring Information

Creating Appropriate Graphs

Between 1860 and 1910 the increase in city populations was staggering. Los Angeles, for example, grew from 4,400 to 319,000 people. Meanwhile, Chicago's population soared from 109,000 to more than 2 million. New York grew from 1 million to nearly 5 million.

Question to Investigate

In what ways did population distribution change in the late 1800s and early 1900s?

Procedure

Create three appropriate graphs for exploring the question. Look at the Skill Tips and study A, B, and C.

1 Decide on the best type of graph to make for each purpose.
a. Decide how to compare urban population percentages in 1860 and 1910.
b. Decide how to show which population—urban or rural—increased faster between 1860 and 1910.
c. Decide how to show the change in percentages of rural and urban populations between 1860 and 1910.

2 Make the three graphs.
a. Use the statistics in A.
b. Refer to B and C as models.

3 Analyze your graphs in order to write an answer to the Question to Investigate.

Skill Tips

- Line graphs show changes at a glance, while circle graphs show percentages.
- On a line graph, the vertical axis indicates frequency or amount, while the horizontal axis indicates categories, such as years.

Sources to Use

A

U.S. Urban and Rural Populations 1830–1910

Year	Urban Population	Urban % of Total Population	Rural Population	Rural % of Total Population
1830	1,127	9	11,739	91
1840	1,845	11	15,224	89
1850	3,544	15	19,648	85
1860	6,217	20	25,227	80
1870	9,902	26	28,656	74
1880	14,130	28	36,026	72
1890	22,106	35	40,841	65
1900	30,160	40	45,835	60
1910	41,999	46	49,973	54

Population in thousands (rounded)
Source: *Historical Statistics of the United States*

B

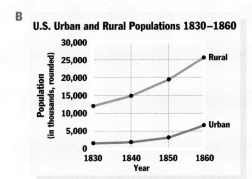

U.S. Urban and Rural Populations 1830–1860

Population (in thousands, rounded): 0, 5,000, 10,000, 15,000, 20,000, 25,000, 30,000
Year: 1830, 1840, 1850, 1860
Rural
Urban

C

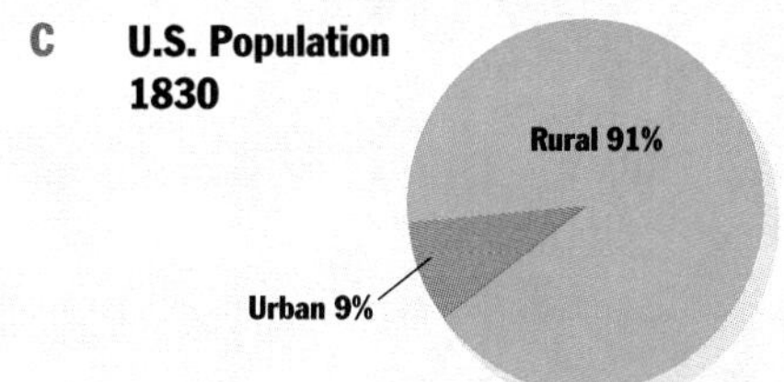

Introducing the Skill Lab

Discuss advantages of graphs in general. (Quick way to express much information visually in compact form, good for showing changes and relationships between data.) Ask students to compare purposes of a circle graph (show percentages/parts of a whole), a line graph (show trends/progression over time), and a bar graph (compare).

Skill Lab

Answers

1. (a) Two circle graphs similar to C, for 1860 and 1910. (b) Line graph similar to B in format. (c) Line graph with labels 1860–1910 on horizontal axis, label *Percentage of Total Population* on vertical axis, and two lines plotted—for urban and rural percentages.

2. Graphs should accomplish their purposes, reflect the statistics in A, and resemble B and C in format.

3. While both urban and rural populations increased in the late 1800s and early 1900s, urban population increased faster. While the percentage of the total population in urban areas increased greatly, it was still slightly lower than the percentage of those living in rural areas in 1910. The faster increase in urban population is reflected in the steep slope

(Answers continued in top margin)

Survey Answers

Reviewing Vocabulary

Definitions are found on these pages: *anti-Semitism* (298), *ethnic neighborhoods* (299), *assimilate* (301), *urbanization* (304), *tenements* (305), *political machine* (307), *settlement house* (308), *leisure* (311), *vaudeville* (312).

Reviewing Main Ideas

1. To find work and freedom.

2. They expected to find good jobs and to make a lot of money. In reality, they lived in poor, crowded tenements; worked long, hard hours; and faced problems of prejudice and assimilation.

3. Discrimination in workplace and housing; pushed Congress to restrict immigration; pushed for taxes for Chinese immigrants and separation of Asian children in schools.

4. Railroads and improved roads increased travel to cities; technologies such as electricity, modern amenities, and new methods of entertainment all helped lure people to the cities.

5. People in the growing cities, especially the poor, faced such problems as unsafe buildings and unsanitary water supply. Local politicians provided help in exchange for votes.

6. Possible answers: Formed associations to pressure local leaders to provide needed services; worked as teachers, nurses, and social workers in city neighborhoods; opened settlement houses; pressured city governments to make public schools and playgrounds available to all children.

7. (a) New technologies, products, and developments made work and shopping quicker and easier. (b) Read newspapers, pulp fiction, and other literature; went

(Answers continued in top margin)

to amusement parks, fairs, circuses, museums, and dance halls; attended vaudeville performances, operas, and symphony performances; played sports and attended sporting events; bicycled.

Thinking Critically

1. They had no money to buy passage back; they had fled far worse conditions in their homelands, such as pogroms, persecution, and starvation; they felt that bettering one's condition was easier in the United States.

2. Support: life was more healthful away from the cities; children would have a better chance to succeed; overcrowding in the inner cities would be eased. Oppose: they would be unhappy in strange, unsympathetic surroundings; they would lose their ethnic heritage and culture; children could be placed

Chapter Survey

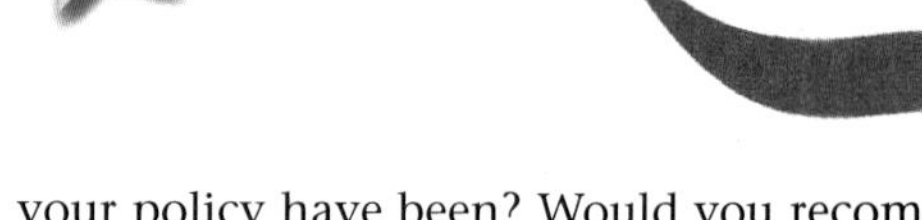

Reviewing Vocabulary

Define the following terms.

1. anti-Semitism
2. ethnic neighborhoods
3. assimilate
4. urbanization
5. tenements
6. political machine
7. settlement house
8. leisure
9. vaudeville

Reviewing Main Ideas

1. What were two main reasons for immigration to the United States after 1865?
2. Compare immigrants' expectations of life in the United States with their experiences once they arrived.
3. How did nativists respond to the new immigrants from Europe and Asia?
4. Why did American cities grow after 1865 and what role did new technologies play in helping them to grow?
5. How did political machines respond to city problems?
6. Describe four ways in which early reformers tried to improve city life.
7. (a) Why did people have significant amounts of leisure time in the late 1800s? (b) Give three examples of how city people made use of their newfound leisure.

Thinking Critically

1. Evaluation Given the terrible conditions that many immigrants encountered, why do you think that so many of them decided to remain in the United States?
2. Synthesis Thousands of homeless city children were put on "orphan trains," which took them to new lives in small towns and on farms. Give arguments for and against the idea.
3. Why We Remember: Synthesis If you had been responsible for developing the nation's immigration policy during the period covered in the chapter, what would your policy have been? Would you recommend following the same policy today, or a different one? Explain.

Applying Skills

Creating appropriate graphs You want to show the following in graph form:
• the change in population of your state's largest city since 1890
• the percentages of people in that city today who belong to various ethnic groups

Keeping in mind what you learned in the Skill Lab on page 315, decide what kind of graph would be most appropriate for each purpose. Find the information you need in the library. Make the graphs and write a paragraph that summarizes what your graphs show.

History Mystery

Crisscrossing the Atlantic Answer the History Mystery on page 293. How might you find more information about the "Atlantic swimmer"? Why do you think most immigrants did not cross the ocean as many times as she did?

Writing in Your History Journal

1. Keys to History (a) The time line on pages 292–293 has seven Keys to History. In your journal, describe why each one is important to know about. (b) Imagine that, like Jacob Riis, you are a reporter at that time. What two events from the chapter would you add to the time line? Write the events and their dates in your journal. Tell why you think each should be added.
2. Jacob Riis Imagine that you are Jacob Riis. Look at the photographs in the chapter. Choose four of them and write

in uncaring homes seeking cheap labor.

3. Answers should attempt to remedy unfair practices spurred by nativism such as the Chinese Exclusion Act. At the same time, students might suggest limitations they consider fair, to cut down on unemployment.

Applying Skills

Students should make a line or bar graph to show changes in population and a circle graph to show percentages of ethnic groups. Paragraphs should accurately reflect graphs.

History Mystery

Information on the Atlantic swimmer is found on page 298. An encyclopedia or book on Irish immigration to the United States could provide more information. Answers might include: could not afford to return,

(Answers continued in side margin)

were committed to remaining, or could not return because of persecution.

Writing in Your History Journal

1. (a) Explanations should be similar to the time line notes on teacher pages 292–293. (b) Entries should be accurately named and dated. Explanations should reflect understanding of the events' historical importance.

2. Captions should reflect events' importance as Riis might have seen them.

3. Students should identify similarities and differences with past problems. They may suggest similar solutions, or new ones.

Reviewing Geography

1. (A) San Francisco—Chinese, (B) Hilo—Japanese, (C) New York City—Italian, (D) Columbus—German, (E) San Antonio—Hispanic. Based on the map and text, students may give other answers.

2. Answers to the first question will depend on familiarity with urban ethnic neighborhoods that have changed or not changed over time. Reasons for change include assimilation and dispersion of families, arrival of new groups, loss of native language, and impoverishment of the neighborhood while immigrants became more prosperous and moved to better areas. Reminders may include foreign languages still spoken; ethnic restaurants, churches, newspapers, and signs; foreign-language street names; flags; and cultural centers. Accept any reasonable ideas, especially those based on actual observation.

Alternative Assessment

Teacher's Take-Home Planner 2, p. 23, includes suggestions and scoring rubrics for the Alternative Assessment activity.

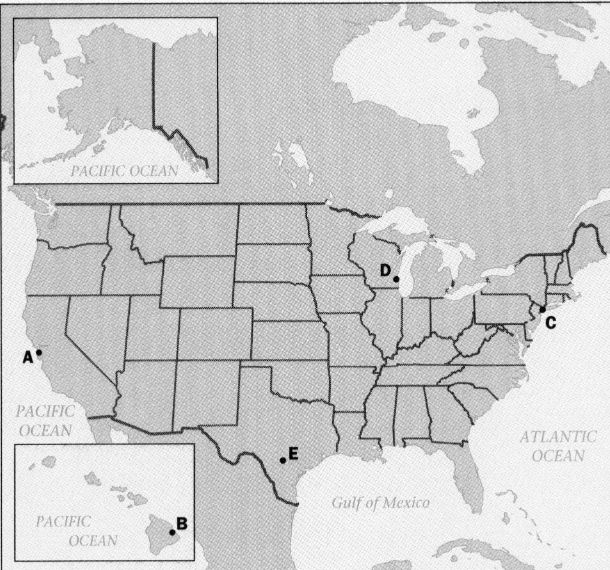

Reviewing Geography

1. For each letter on the map, write the name of the city and of an immigrant group with which it became identified.

2. Geographic Thinking Suppose you visited a modern-day city neighborhood that had been home to one or more immigrant groups in the late 1800s. Would you expect the ethnic groups now living in the neighborhood to be the same as they were back then, or different? If different, why? Even if the new ethnic groups were quite different, what reminders of earlier groups might you find?

new captions that you think Riis might have written. The captions should each be at least two sentences in length, though they may be longer if you wish.

3. Citizenship Think of a problem that modern-day cities face. Is it different from or similar to a problem faced by cities in the late 1800s and early 1900s? What should today's citizens do to try to solve the problem? Write your responses in your journal.

Alternative Assessment

Planning a city guide Today, people who plan to visit or move to a large city can find a variety of helpful guides on bookstore shelves. Imagine that you have been hired to create a newcomers' guide to an imaginary city of the late 1800s.

With a partner, plan the guide. Write a detailed outline of topics and a descriptive list of illustrations, such as maps and photographs. Write a six-paragraph introduction to the city and create an illustration to accompany your introduction.

Keep the following in mind:

1. The city is New Metropolis, a Midwest industrial and transportation center.
2. Rural Americans and two groups of immigrants (you choose which two) have flooded into the city in recent years.
3. New Metropolis has the same kinds of problems and attractions as do cities like New York, Chicago, and San Francisco.

Your work will be evaluated on the following criteria:

- your materials reflect a broad, realistic view of city life at the time
- you arrange topics logically
- you write in appealing, easy-to-understand language

Literature Footnote

Between 1836 and 1857, William Holmes McGuffey, a college professor and minister, published a series of school textbooks known as *McGuffey's Eclectic Readers*. These books became enormously popular and were revised and enlarged several times. The books included selections from such great writers as William Shakespeare, Thomas Jefferson, and Ralph Waldo Emerson. The *Readers* not only introduced millions of children to literature, but also emphasized the virtues of patriotism and practical morality. For example, a lesson on the moral "Where there is a will, there is a way" was based on a story about a boy who wanted a grammar book, but whose mother could not afford it. He shoveled snow to earn money, and thereafter was first in his class. More than 122 million copies of the books were sold.

Teaching the

Link to American Readings

In this feature students learn about the immigrants of the late nineteenth and early twentieth centuries. There are the physical hardships and the dreams that dissipate as so many bubbles in the wind. Then there is the anguish over whether to "melt" into the American society in hopes of finding acceptance or to retain one's own familiar culture as a source of comfort in an unfamiliar land.

Before students begin the lesson, review Making a New Life (pages 299–301), The Nativist Reaction (pages 301–302), and Problems in Cities (pages 305–306). Have students read the entire feature before assigning the A Closer Look questions. The Setting the Stage Activity and Bonus Activity may then be introduced according to the needs and interests of the students. The information contained in the Discussion questions and the Footnotes may be used throughout the lesson as appropriate. Readers' Theater is ideal for students who might find the readings somewhat difficult. Use the Wrap-Up Activity for students who would enjoy taking a step beyond the core lesson.

Link to American Readings

***Hairdresser's Window* by John Sloane. The artist found his subject matter in the crowded tenements and streets of early twentieth-century cities.**

READING 6A

Problems in the New Land

Most immigrants first arrived in New York City. Many settled in one of New York's ethnic neighborhoods. The Lower East Side, in downtown Manhattan, became the refuge for generations of Poles, Chinese, Puerto Ricans, Dominicans, and most predominantly, Jews. The following letters were sent by Jewish immigrants to a local newspaper, the *Jewish Daily Forward.*

Letters to the Editor, 1906–1910

Worthy Editor,

I am eighteen years old and a machinist by trade. During the past year I suffered a great deal, just because I am a Jew. . . .

I worked in a shop in a small town in New Jersey, with twenty Gentiles. There was one other Jew besides me, and both of us endured the greatest hardships. That we were insulted goes without saying. At times we were even beaten up. . . . After that I went to work on a job in Brooklyn. As soon as they found out that I was a Jew they began to torment me so that I had to leave the place. I have already worked at many places, and I either have to leave, voluntarily, or they fire me because I am a Jew. . . .

Lately I've been working on one job for three months and I would be satisfied, but the worm of anti-Semitism is beginning to eat at my bones again.

Your reader, E. H.

Answer: In the answer, the Jewish machinist is advised to appeal to the United Hebrew Trades and ask them to intercede for him and bring up charges before the Machinist Union about this persecution. His attention is also drawn to the fact that there are Gentile factories where Jews and Gentiles work together and get along well with each other.

intercede: act on one's behalf

Gentile: non-Jew

Dear Editor,

Since I do not want my conscience to bother me, I ask you to decide whether a married woman has the right to go to school two evenings a week. My husband thinks I have no right to do this.

I admit that I cannot be satisfied to be just a wife and mother. I am still young and I want to learn and enjoy life. My children and my house are not

Literature Footnote

As a 19-year-old in 1885, Nellie Bly became the first full-time female reporter for a big-city newspaper, the *Pittsburgh Dispatch*. While working for the paper, Bly went to Mexico to do a story about the large numbers of Americans who were going there to work in the mines and on the railroads. The articles earned her the wrath of the Mexican government. In addition, she wrote a series exposing inhumane conditions in a New York City mental hospital, gaining access by pretending to be insane. Bly continued to assume new identities to get the facts for her crusading stories. She even got herself arrested in order to investigate the abuses women suffered in prison. Bly had pioneered what has become known as "investigative reporting."

neglected, but I go to evening high school twice a week. My husband is not pleased and when I come home at night and ring the bell, he lets me stand outside a long time intentionally, and doesn't hurry to open the door. . . .

When I am alone with my thoughts, I feel I may not be right. Perhaps I should not go to school. I want to say that my husband is an intelligent man and he wanted to marry a woman who was educated. The fact that he is intelligent makes me more annoyed with him. He is in favor of the emancipation of women, yet in real life he acts contrary to his beliefs.

Awaiting your opinion on this, I remain,
Your reader,
The Discontented Wife

Answer: Since this man is intelligent and an adherent of the women's emancipation movement, he is scolded severely in the answer for wanting to keep his wife so enslaved. Also the opinion is expressed that the wife absolutely has the right to go to school two evenings a week.

Worthy Editor,

My husband . . . deserted me and our three small children, leaving us in desperate need. I was left without a bit of bread for the children, with debts in the grocery store and the butcher's, and last month's rent unpaid.

I am not complaining so much about his abandoning me as about the grief and suffering of our little children, who beg for food, which I cannot give them. I am young and healthy, I am able and willing to work in order to support my children, but unfortunately I am tied down because my baby is only six months old. . . .

It breaks my heart but I have come to the conclusion that in order to save my innocent children from hunger and cold I have to give them away.

I will sell my beautiful children to people who will give them a home. I will sell them, not for money, but for bread, for a secure home where they will have enough food and warm clothing for the winter.

Impoverished immigrant families often lived in tiny, windowless rooms in crowded tenement districts such as this one in New York City's Lower East Side.

Setting the Stage Activity

Recognizing Basic Human Rights

To help students understand the deprivation that many immigrants endured, have them note the specific negative living conditions and situations cited in the first reading. Then, as a contrast, have them create a list of basic healthful living conditions that every American should have a right to expect. The items listed can include environmental, social, and political rights. For example, the letter from E. H. might prompt a response of "freedom from prejudice."

Bonus Activity

Tracing Origins

To help students understand the changing face of immigration, have them complete this short exercise. First, explain that most nineteenth- century immigrants were European. Before 1880 they came chiefly from northern and western Europe. Have students take about ten minutes to research the southern and eastern European countries that were home to many post-1880 immigrants.

Discussion

Stimulating Critical Thinking

1. Refer to the three letters to the editor in the first reading. Identify the basic social or political issue that is presented in each letter. Then discuss the extent to which that problem has been resolved in today's society. (The first letter addresses prejudice, the second cites the right to an education, and the third poses the problems of a single mother who is unable to work to support her children because she has no one to care for them. Students' responses will vary, depending on their personal experience, but they will most likely agree that these problems still exist to varying degrees. Students should cite specific examples as part of their responses.)

2. What is one important step that could be taken to eliminate each of the social problems listed in the first question? (Students' responses will vary, depending on personal experience. All answers should be practical. For example, they might suggest government-subsidized day care for single parents.)

Literature Footnote

Theodore Dreiser (1871–1945) also wrote about the horrors of the cities and their poor immigrants. However, his was not the objective reporting of Nellie Bly. As a pioneer of naturalism in American literature, Dreiser wrote novels that reflected his mechanistic view of life. He believed that everyone is governed by uncontrollable forces such as nature, heredity, environment, economics, and even chance. Therefore, according to Dreiser, the poor are destined to remain poor, no matter how hard they try to overcome their situation. Dreiser's works include *Sister Carrie* (1900), *Jennie Gerhardt* (1911), and *The Financier* (1912). *An American Tragedy* (1925), considered his best work, is the story of a young man's futile attempts to escape his poverty. Dreiser also wrote short stories and commentaries.

I, the unhappy young mother, am willing to sign a contract, with my heart's blood, stating that the children belong to the good people who will treat them tenderly. Those who are willing and able to give my children a good home can apply to me. Respectfully,

Mrs. P.
Chicago

Answer: What kind of society are we living in that forces a mother to such desperate straits that there is no other way out than to sell her three children for a piece of bread? Isn't this enough to kindle a . . . fire of hatred in every human heart for such a system? . . .

We also ask our friends and readers to take an interest in this unfortunate woman and to help her so that she herself can be a mother to her children.

READING 6B

The Americanization of Immigrants

Today, the Americanization of immigrants is an important national issue. To what extent should immigrants be expected to leave behind their culture and languages? Should they become part of the great "melting pot" of America, or should they be encouraged to retain and nourish their own cultures? These issues were no less pressing in the early part of the twentieth century. Two different views follow.

Professor Grover G. Huebner on the role of public schools in the Americanization of immigrant children, 1906

1. It [public school] at once throws the children of different nationalities into mutual relationship. This inevitably breaks up the habits of any one of the foreign nationalities. . . . [The] immigrant child necessarily loses its foreign ideas and unconsciously adopts the thoughts and activities of the American companions. . . .

2. The public school teaches the children the English language. . . .

3. The public school tends to break up hostility between nationalities. . . .

4. It teaches American traditions and the history of our institutions. . . .

5. The public school is the first and chief trainer of the immigrant child's mind to fit it for originality and inventiveness. . . .

6. . . . The public school, in training the minds of the children, fits them to meet this versatility in American industry.

Readers' Theater

Students will find that the first reading adapts well to readers' theater. A group of four students can prepare this reading. Three students should each assume the role of one of the letter writers. The first letter should most realistically be read by a boy and the last two by girls. The person who assumes the role of the editor can be either a girl or boy. The letter readers are free to follow the script as closely as they like, taking care to put themselves in the place of their characters and to present the reading accordingly. The editor may write a personal and complete answer to each letter. The group might work together to write the dialogue for the editor. Allow the group time enough to rehearse so that they become familiar with their parts and can make adjustments in the editor's responses.

7. The American characteristic of aspiration to reach a higher plane of production is transmitted to the immigrant child. This Americanizes the thoughts of the immigrant.

aspiration: ambition

Journalist Marcus E. Ravage on the immigrants' view of Americanization. An excerpt from *An American in the Making*, 1917

It seems to be assumed by the self-complacent native that we immigrants are at once and overwhelmingly captivated by America and all things American. . . . Why should we not be happy? Have we not left our own country because we were in one way or another discontented there? . . . If the alien were dissatisfied with America, would he not be taking back the first steamer instead of inviting his friends and family to follow him? . . .

self-complacent: smug

. . . To begin with, the alien who comes here from Europe is not the raw material that Americans suppose him to be. He is not a blank sheet to be written on as you see fit. He has not sprung out of nowhere.

Quite the contrary. He brings with him a deep-rooted tradition, a system of culture and tastes and habits—a point of view which is as ancient as his na-tional experience and which has been engendered in him by his race and his environment. And it is this thing—this entire Old World soul of his—that comes in conflict with America as soon as he has landed. . . .

. . . My good friends are unwilling to see that the alien has as much to teach as to learn, that the readjustment is inevitably a matter of give and take, and that he only begins to feel at home in this new country when he has succeeded in blending his own culture and ideas and mode of life with those of the people that came here before him.

Your self-complacent native takes stock of the Americanized alien and cries, delightedly: "See how America has changed him." But I suppose he would be greatly astonished if the immigrant were to answer, with equal truth: "Look how I have changed America!"

The Hedlund family celebrates Independence Day, 1911. Courtesy, Minnesota Historical Society.

Excerpts from *An American in the Making* by Marcus E. Ravage. (New York: Harper & Bros.), 1917.

A Closer Look

1. Choose one of the letters to the editor. Write a response that will truly help the individual.

2. Summarize Huebner's philosophy on the Americanization of immigrant children. How did Ravage differ in his opinion?

3. CRITICAL THINKING What role do you think the American schools or government should take in the Americanization of immigrants today? Explain.

Wrap-Up Activity

Responding to Jane Addams

To extend the lesson, ask students to respond in their history journals to the following quote from Hull House founder Jane Addams: "In time it came to seem natural to all of us that the Settlement [Hull House] should be there. If it is natural to give pleasure to the young, comfort to the aged, and to minister to the deep-seated craving for social intercourse that all men feel."

A Closer Look

Answers

1. Students' responses to the letters will vary. However, all suggestions should be practical.

2. Huebner believed that all children should be educated so that they could be "Americanized," in order to blend into society and have a better chance at success. Ravage believed that retaining elements of one's culture was important.

3. Some will say that the government should not interfere, that every American should be allowed to nurture his or her own culture. Others might say that having common elements and standard education is important for everyone.

Teaching the

Citizenship Lab

In this feature students learn about *Muller* v. *Oregon* (1908), in which the Supreme Court upheld a worker-protection law despite overturning a similar law in *Lochner* v. *New York* (1905). The feature also traces child-labor debates from *Hammer* v. *Dagenhart* (1918) to the present day.

Before students read the feature, review the information on reformers on page 308. Have students read the entire feature before assigning the Understanding Civic Issues questions and the Hands-On Citizenship activity. The Bonus Activity in this Teacher's Edition may be used as an alternative to, or in addition to, the Hands-On Citizenship activity. The Discussion questions in this Teacher's Edition may be used at appropriate points during students' reading or afterward.

Objectives

- ★ Explain how the Supreme Court was persuaded to uphold a state worker-protection law in *Muller* v. *Oregon*.
- ★ Describe the differences between the Muller case and an earlier worker-protection case, *Lochner* v. *New York*.
- ★ Summarize the controversies over child-labor laws from the time of *Hammer* v. *Dagenhart* to the present.

Supreme Court Case: *Muller* v. *Oregon*

Citizenship Lab

Protecting Workers: How Far Should Government Go?

Some reformers of the late 1800s and early 1900s took a special interest in improving the lives of industrial workers. Reformers who persuaded state legislatures to pass worker-protection laws soon learned that the struggle did not end there. Many of the laws were challenged in the courts; some cases even reached the Supreme Court.

When that happened, the results were mixed. For example, in *Lochner* v. *New York* (1905), the Court held that a New York law setting maximum working hours for bakers was invalid. The law was based on the theory that inhaling large amounts of flour could cause lung disease in bakers and thus contaminate the dough they made. The Court called the connection between working hours and health "too shadowy and thin to build any argument for the interference of the legislature [in private business]." Three years later, however, the Court took a very different position in a similar case.

Carl Muller Breaks the Law

That case began one day in September 1905, when the foreman at Curt Muller's Grand Laundry in Portland, Oregon, required an employee named Mrs. Elmer Gotcher to work more than ten hours. The problem was that Oregon had passed a law in 1903 setting a maximum of ten hours of work per day for women in factories and laundries. A local court found Carl Muller guilty of breaking that law and fined him ten dollars.

Muller knew about the recent *Lochner* decision, and he appealed his conviction. In 1906 the Oregon Supreme Court upheld the constitutionality of the ten-hour law. Muller then appealed to the Supreme Court of the United States.

Louis Brandeis Defends the Law

The National Consumers League, an organization dedicated to worker and consumer protection, took an interest in *Muller* v. *Oregon*. Florence Kelley, who had worked with Jane Addams, headed the league. With the permission of Oregon's attorney general, the league hired Louis D. Brandeis to defend the state law before the Supreme Court.

Brandeis, a prominent Boston lawyer, was known as the "People's Attorney" because he often took on cases in which ordinary people

History Footnote

Born in Kentucky, Louis Brandeis entered Harvard Law School at the age of 18 with no previous college education. While at Harvard, he supported himself by tutoring other students. Yet he completed the law program in only 2 years with the highest grades in the school's history, an academic record that still stands. After graduation, Brandeis achieved great financial success with his Boston law practice, but he drew his greatest personal satisfaction from cases for which he charged no fee.

Brandeis became an associate justice of the Supreme Court in 1916, the first Jewish person to do so. Brandeis and Associate Justice Oliver Wendell Holmes, Jr., held similar views on constitutional law. They joined in writing various opinions supporting social legislation and freedom of speech.

challenged business interests. With Kelley's encouragement and help, Brandeis decided on an unusual approach to the Muller case. He presented to the Court a very abbreviated *legal brief,* a statement or summary of the facts and points of law in a case. Attached to the brief, however, was about 100 pages of authoritative information supporting the theory that women's health could be harmed by long hours of work.

The justices were impressed with the lawyer's strategy. All nine voted to uphold the Oregon law. Associate Justice David J. Brewer wrote the Court's opinion, in which he took the unusual step of referring to Brandeis and noting with approval the "very copious collection" of information he had submitted. Thus, the Court established that information on social conditions, as well as strictly legal arguments, could be considered when making decisions. Since the Muller decision, so-called Brandeis briefs have been effective tools for lawyers defending reform laws or attacking social problems.

Louis Brandeis

Brandeis brief had proved to the Court's satisfaction that women have special health needs; therefore, a state could give special protection to women in the workplace.

From Protection of Women to Protection of Children

One might suppose that the Court's ruling in *Muller* v. *Oregon* overturned its decision in *Lochner* v. *New York*. But this was not true, according to Brewer. The difference between the cases, he wrote, lay in the fact that the Lochner case involved male workers while the Muller case involved females. The

The Muller decision raised reformers' hopes that the Court might be sympathetic to another of the reformers' concerns: outlawing child labor. In the early 1900s, many states passed laws against child labor, but enforcement efforts were uneven. Reformers persuaded Congress to pass the Keating-Owen Child Labor Act in 1916. It clamped down on child labor by prohibiting interstate sales of goods produced by young workers.

Setting the Stage Activity

Deciding on Protections

To prepare for reading about worker-protection cases, have students make two lists: (1) groups they believe need special workplace protection and (2) kinds of protection needed. Have students compare lists and discuss differences. For example, if some put women in the first list and others did not, what are their reasons?

Bonus Activity

Covering the Muller Decision on TV

To help students focus on the issues involved in *Muller* v. *Oregon*, ask the class or smaller groups to imagine that television existed in 1908 and to act out TV newscasts about the Muller decision.

Assigned roles should include one or more television reporters, Carl Muller, Muller's lawyer, Mrs. Elmer Gotcher, Louis Brandeis, Florence Kelley, and Justice Brewer. Allow students time to plan the newscast, which might include a brief introduction by a reporter, interviews outside the Supreme Court with the lawyers and Justice Brewer, and off-site interviews with Muller, Gotcher, and Kelley.

Discussion

Checking Understanding

1. What is a "Brandeis brief"? (A legal argument that includes information on social conditions, named for attorney Louis Brandeis.)

2. According to Justice Brewer, why did the Muller ruling have no effect on the earlier Lochner ruling? (Brewer said the cases were different because they involved opposite sexes; women's health needs warranted special protection in the workplace.)

Stimulating Critical Thinking

3. Do you suppose people who want child-labor laws relaxed would agree with Roland Dagenhart's reasoning? Explain. (Economic need may be a consideration, but other arguments might include these: current laws are too protective and intrusive; wider variety of jobs will increase young people's opportunities to learn responsibility and skills; longer working hours will keep young people out of trouble.)

4. How would you explain a decline in school performance among working teens? (Possible answer: working teens may lack time and energy for studying, cut classes to work or sleep, or miss out on extracurricular activities that could aid school performance.)

Citizenship Footnote

The Fourteenth Amendment was central to the Lochner and Muller cases. In *Lochner,* the Court said the right to make a contract to buy or sell labor is a liberty protected by the Fourteenth Amendment. By limiting working hours, the New York law deprived both Joseph Lochner (a bakery owner) and his employees of their liberty without due process. In *Muller,* the Court refined this idea, holding that liberty of contract is not absolute and that some conditions (such as women's health needs) require limitations on it.

Because his case involved a federal law, Roland Dagenhart cited the Fifth Amendment in arguing that his sons were deprived of their liberty of contract without due process. He also said the Keating-Owen law violated the Tenth Amendment.

In the early 1900s many children worked 14-hour days. The girl (far right) worked at a loom in a textile factory. The boys (right) picked out pieces of slate from the coal in the mines. Accidents were common.

A North Carolina man named Roland Dagenhart challenged the law. He had two young sons who worked in a cotton mill, and he felt his family could not live without the boys' wages. Dagenhart sued W. C. Hammer, a U.S. district attorney, to halt enforcement of the Keating-Owen law. Dagenhart argued that under the Tenth Amendment to the Constitution, the power to regulate child labor belongs to the states, not the federal government. When the federal district court found the federal law unconstitutional, Hammer appealed to the Supreme Court. In 1918 the Court upheld the district court's decision.

The ruling in *Hammer* v. *Dagenhart* was a setback for reformers, but they continued their fight against child labor and eventually won. Today both state and federal laws set minimum ages for employment and maximum hours that young people may work. Some people want tighter laws, citing studies that show a decline in school performance among teens who work. Other people want child-labor laws relaxed to allow young people to work longer hours at a wider variety of jobs. Whether the dispute will reach the Supreme Court remains to be seen.

Connections to Literature

Edwin Markham (1851–1940) was a popular American poet who first achieved fame with a powerful poem of social protest called "The Man with the Hoe" (1899). In addition to writing poetry, Markham traveled throughout the country, visiting cities and lecturing on the social ills caused by industrialization. The following passages about child labor are from an article Markham wrote for *Cosmopolitan Magazine* in 1907: "In New York City alone 60,000 children are shut up in the home sweatshops. . . . Many . . . will never sit on a school bench. Is it not a cruel civilization that allows little hearts . . . to strain under these grown-up responsibilities, while in the same city a pet [dog] is jeweled and pampered and aired on a fine lady's velvet lap on the beautiful boulevards?"

Understanding Civic Issues

1. Summarize the Supreme Court's rulings in *Lochner* v. *New York*, *Muller* v. *Oregon*, and *Hammer* v. *Dagenhart*.
2. How did Louis Brandeis win his case in *Muller* v. *Oregon*?
3. **Critical Thinking** Do you agree with the distinction that the Court made between the New York case and the Oregon case? Explain.
4. **Hands-On Citizenship** Imagine that you and a small group of classmates have been asked to write a teen-labor law to submit to Congress.
   - Discuss what you know about teen employment in your community. What kinds of jobs do working teens commonly hold? How much time do they devote to their jobs? Do their jobs seem harmful in any way?
   - Decide what limits, if any, your law will place on teen employment. You may find it helpful to first list all the "pros" and "cons" of teen employment that you can think of.
   - Write your ideal teen-labor law. Make sure it covers the minimum age for holding a job; kinds of jobs, if any, that are off-limits for teens; and limits, if any, on hours per day, per night, and per week that teens may work.

Teens working at a fast-food restaurant

Citizenship Lab Answers

1. *Lochner:* Overturned a New York law setting maximum working hours for bakers. *Muller:* Upheld an Oregon law setting maximum working hours for women in factories and laundries. *Hammer:* Overturned the federal Keating-Owen Child Labor Act.

2. Presented many pages of authoritative information supporting the theory that women's health could be harmed by long hours of work.

3. Because students live in an era that stresses equal treatment of the sexes in employment and other areas, they may disagree with the distinction. However, some may think physical differences between the sexes have been downplayed too much and thus may see merit in the distinction.

Teaching the Hands-On Citizenship

Less prepared students generally display short attention spans, a deficiency in basic language skills, and difficulty in grasping abstract concepts and ideas. Activities such as this one are usually quite effective with less prepared students because it is not abstract and involves something they are likely to have experienced or at least are interested in. They may not be as good as other students in expressing their opinion in writing, but they are sure to have strong opinions on this topic. Encourage their participation and make sure they feel a part of the class.

show evidence of careful thought and planning.

Thinking critically Students show good judgment in planning and operating the business.

Communicating ideas Journal entries are up-to-date and perceptive.

Thinking It Over

Answers will vary but may include ability to spot opportunities, self-confidence, determination, discipline, willingness to work hard and take risks, and intelligence.

Unit Survey

Making Connections

Answers

1. Answers will vary, but students may mention jobs provided for immigrants; transportation for miners and western crops and cattle; settlement of the West and connection of remote areas creating new towns, destroying forests, and nearly exterminating buffalo and Indian civilizations.

2. Answers will vary, but may include how each struggled to survive. Students may note that the city had more modern conveniences; the country was safer and less polluted.

3. Answers will depend on which evidence students cite from the textbook.

Teaching the Unit Project

Begin by creating a class list of possible types of businesses based on needs in the community. Have students select possibilities that appeal to them. Suggest they then make a list of their talents and abilities and match these with the business possibilities.

Evaluation Criteria

The project can be evaluated according to the criteria listed below, using a scale for each:
4 = exemplary, 3 = good,
2 = adequate, 1 = poor.

Completing the task The business is chosen, the plan is carefully written and researched, the business is running, and the journal entries are made.

Knowing content The plan and conduct of the business

(Continued in top margin)

Unit Survey

Making Connections

Review

1. The expansion of the railroads in the middle and late 1800s had a huge impact on the economy, the environment, and people's lives. Describe four specific effects of the railroads.

2. Compare and contrast the lives of a homesteader on the Great Plains and a factory worker in a big city like Chicago in the late 1800s.

3. Some historians would describe the period covered in this unit as an era of great progress in the United States. Others say it was just the opposite, and would call it a dark time in our history. What is your opinion? Support your answer with specific examples from the unit.

Linking History, Economics, and Math

Project

Starting Your Own Business

Many entrepreneurs of the late 1800s—like many entrepreneurs today—plunged into the world of business as teenagers. You may never be as successful as Rockefeller or other captains of industry, but you can make money by starting a business. The best part is, you will be the boss!

Project Steps

Work on your own.

❶ Decide the type of business to start.
• Consider your interests and talents. For example, do you like to cook, make crafts, create computer designs, use a video camera, do yard work, or take care of pets?
• Also consider this business motto: "Find a need and fill it." What need in your school, neighborhood, or community could you help fill?
• Get your family's approval.

❷ Write a business plan, in which you do the following:
• describe your product or service
• list equipment and supplies you need
• identify your target customers
• identify your competitors
• list your marketing methods
• calculate what your expenses will be
• tell how you will get start-up money
• estimate what your income will be
• describe how you will keep records

You might consult library books, local businesspeople, and the Chamber of Commerce, which can also help you find out about legal requirements, if any.

❸ Share your business plan with the class. Ask for ideas for improving it.

❹ Begin carrying out your business plan. As you run the business, keep a journal in which you describe what actions you take and what results occur. After a trial period (perhaps two months) share the journal with the class.

Thinking It Over Consider the qualities that entrepreneurs of the late 1800s had. Which of those qualities do you think are still important for entrepreneurs? Do you think you possess those qualities? Explain.

Objectives

- ★ Identify the kinds of information historians can acquire from photographs.
- ★ Explain how historians can use photographic evidence to draw conclusions about life in the past.

How Do We Know?

Lewis Hine photographed this young coal miner at work in West Virginia.

Scholar's Tool Kit

Photographs

In 1900 as many as 2 million children under the age of 16 went to work instead of school. Thousands of children only 12 or younger worked in mills and factories at night. Some as young as 3 picked cotton. How do we know the sad stories of these child laborers? In part we know about their lives through the photographs of reformer Lewis Hine.

A Zealous Reformer

Lewis Hine was one of the most zealous opponents of child labor. As a schoolteacher in New York, Hine became concerned about the abuse of child workers. He became an investigative reporter, using his camera to document children at work. "Seeing is believing," Hine would say.

Hine quit teaching and joined the staff of the National Child Labor Committee. "I felt that I was merely changing my educational activities from the classroom to the world." He hoped his photographs would stir the hearts and consciences of concerned citizens, and help bring about reform.

A shy, slender man, Hine risked his life for the cause of social justice. Factory and mill owners wanted to keep wages low and saw Hine as a threat to their profits. To get his pictures, Hine sometimes had to resort to trickery. He would pretend to be a fire inspector or an insurance salesman. Sometimes he claimed he was

Introducing How Do We Know?

Photographs

Ask students if they agree that a picture is worth a thousand words and have them explain in what ways that might be true. Then have them imagine seeing a photograph of the Pilgrims landing at Plymouth or a video of Lincoln giving his Gettysburg Address. Explain that for past events such as these we depend on paintings or eyewitness accounts, which can be colored by the artist's or eyewitness's bias or point of view.

Explain that for more recent events we do have documentary evidence, and that this feature focuses on one type—photography. Ask students to name characteristics of photography that make it more reliable than more subjective types of evidence. (Records what was actually present with less interpretation or bias.)

Setting the Stage Activity

Evaluating Photographs

To prepare students for examining the photographs of Lewis Hine and assessing their value as historical documents, ask them to make a short list of what we can learn from a photograph that we cannot learn from a work of art or written account. Write items from their lists on the chalkboard.

Critical Thinking
Answers

1. Answers will vary based on values and preferences.

2. They tell the story of the cruelties of child labor. Viewers can see effects of deplorable working conditions. The photos may motivate students to want to know more about the subjects.

3. He kept accurate records about his photos. He had a special way to measure heights of children he photographed. He never retouched or faked photos. Other photographers may not have his integrity. Also, photographs used in fashion photography and for various special effects are routinely retouched and edited.

Bonus Activity

Documenting the Past

To illustrate the role of photography in learning about history, have students imagine traveling into the past to make a photodocumentary on an event in American history. Have them make a "shoot list" of scenes. For example, a shoot list for the winter at Valley Forge might include soldiers keeping warm at fires, General Washington brooding alone, Baron von Steuben drilling the troops, and the bleak winter landscape. Have them explain their choices.

History Footnote

Lewis Hine began taking pictures after he moved to New York from his native Wisconsin in 1901. Trained as a sociologist, he took his first photographs of immigrants arriving at Ellis Island. Rather than looking for abstract, artistic values in a photograph, Hine sought the human story and truthfulness of the scene. His Ellis Island photographs caught the attention of the National Child Labor Committee, which sent him on a cross-country tour to document the horrors of child labor. He took about 5,000 photographs of children working and thousands more of other subjects. Thanks to Hine's artistry, each of these photographs is not only a mini-documentary of its time and place, but also an individual human-interest story.

One mill owner observed that children made good workers because their hands were small enough to reach into the machinery. Unfortunately those small hands sometimes got caught in the machines. (Above) Boys changing bobbins; (right) girl picking cotton.

Critical Thinking

1. Hine left his job to work full time as a reformer. If you were to devote your life to a cause, which cause would you choose? Why?

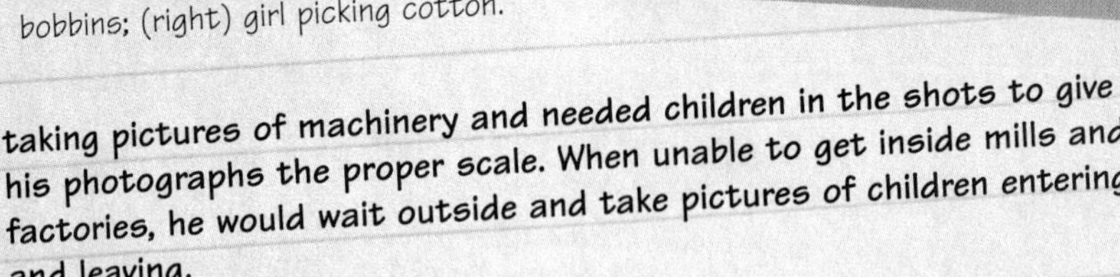

taking pictures of machinery and needed children in the shots to give his photographs the proper scale. When unable to get inside mills and factories, he would wait outside and take pictures of children entering and leaving.

Employers had tricks of their own. When inspectors like Hine came to her shirt factory, one girl recalled, "we children [had to] climb into the big boxes the finished shirts were stored in. Then some shirts were piled on top of us, and when the inspectors came—no children."

Critical Thinking

2. Hine called his pictures "photo stories." What stories do the photos here tell?

Recording History

Hine was a careful researcher. He kept accurate records and documented each photograph. He even secretly recorded the height of children by having them stand next to him. He could measure their height because he knew the height from the floor to each button on his vest. "All along," he said, "I had to be double-sure that my photo data was 100 percent pure—no retouching or fakery of any kind."

Connections to Science

The camera that Lewis Hine used to take his striking documentary photographs was very different from today's point-and-shoot models, although the basic technology is similar. Hine was able to take advantage of the 1883 invention of roll film, which consisted of a light-sensitive chemical, called an emulsion, on a plastic-like tape. Before this advance, photographers needed to haul around heavy glass plates coated with various chemicals to capture the light image. The famous Civil War photographer Mathew Brady used these plates to photograph that war. The inventor of roll film, George Eastman, helped make photography more accessible to millions. The company he founded in Rochester, New York, is now synonymous with popular photography—Kodak.

Hine crisscrossed the country in his crusade. He traveled as many as 50,000 miles (80,000 km) a year by train and automobile. Even he was shocked at what he learned. One in 4 millworkers was a child between the ages of 10 and 15. Children under 10 were not counted as employees.

Hine's pictures of little boys and girls laboring in mines, sweatshops, and cotton fields exposed a shocking side of life hidden from most Americans. His photographs were so striking and effective they helped change child labor laws. After seeing his photographs, one reporter wrote:

"There has been no more convincing proof of the absolute necessity of child labor laws . . . than these pictures showing the suffering, the degradation, the immoral influence, the utter lack of anything that is wholesome in the lives of these poor little wage earners. They speak more eloquently than any work—and depict a state of affairs which is terrible in its reality—and terrible to encounter, terrible to admit that such things exist in civilized communities."

The photographs Hine took as an investigative reporter are now important historical records. Hine documented a part of history that was hidden to many Americans. Today many of these photographs are in the National Archives in Washington, D.C. There they form part of an immense collection of government photographs open for research to all Americans.

Critical Thinking

3. What made Hine's photographs a reliable source of information? Are photographs always a reliable source of information? Why or why not?

Scholar at Work

Lewis Hine knew that "seeing is believing." As an investigative reporter he used his camera to show the public evidence of child labor. With a group, think of a problem in your school or community and become investigative reporters yourselves. Use a camera to document the problem. Then arrange your photos for a magazine article and write captions explaining the problem. Present your findings to the class.

Discussion

Checking Understanding

1. **What was Lewis Hine's goal in taking photographs?** (He hoped they would stir the hearts of Americans about the plight of child laborers and bring about reform.)
2. **Why did mill owners, mine bosses, and farm overseers try to keep Hine from photographing child workers?** (They knew the photographs would create an outrage among the general public, which could result in losing the cheap source of labor they wanted.)
3. **What effect did the photographs of Lewis Hine have on the nation's laws?** (They helped bring about laws restricting and outlawing child labor.)

Teaching the Scholar at Work

Ask students who have cameras to volunteer to take a variety of pictures of a certain topic. To help them think of topics that would be of human interest and be visually stimulating, have groups list problems they encounter in their everyday lives and determine what aspects they could photograph. Some topics are the environment, homelessness, littering, and traffic. Have students bring in their photographs and group them by topic to make collages.

Unit 3

Introducing the Unit

The Fleet Entering the Golden Gate, May 6, 1908

One of the best-known examples of President Theodore Roosevelt's foreign policy motto, "Speak softly and carry a big stick," was the Great White Fleet. Reuterdahl's painting, seen today in the United States Naval Academy Museum, shows the Great White Fleet returning to San Francisco at the end of its tour. Roosevelt sent the fleet on a world tour in 1907 to showcase the new warships. The fleet's visit showed that the United States was firmly taking its place on the world stage. In Unit 8 students will learn about this new world role.

Teaching the Hands-On HISTORY

Begin by asking students to imagine how people in each of the three countries may have felt when they saw the Great White Fleet sail into the harbor. While Brazilians, Australians, and Japanese would have been impressed, would they have also felt threatened? Flattered? Suspicious? Remind students to consider earlier interactions between the United States and the country they choose and how these relations would have influenced peoples' opinions about the arrival of the fleet in 1907. Have them incorporate this information into their magazine covers and article titles.

Unit Overview

The many challenges facing American society in the late 1800s were met by rural and urban reformers on the local, state, and national levels. Reformers managed to elect three Presidents who shared their zeal: Roosevelt, Taft, and Wilson.

The United States also joined the worldwide race for colonies. Expansionists looked abroad for new markets and increased prestige. With victory in the Spanish-American War, the United States became a world power.

The empires of Europe soon clashed. The result was World War I. As millions died in the trenches, the United States tried to remain neutral. In 1917, however, the nation joined the Allies. On the battlefield and on the home front, Americans helped the Allies triumph. However, Wilson's idealistic hopes for a just and lasting peace were thwarted.

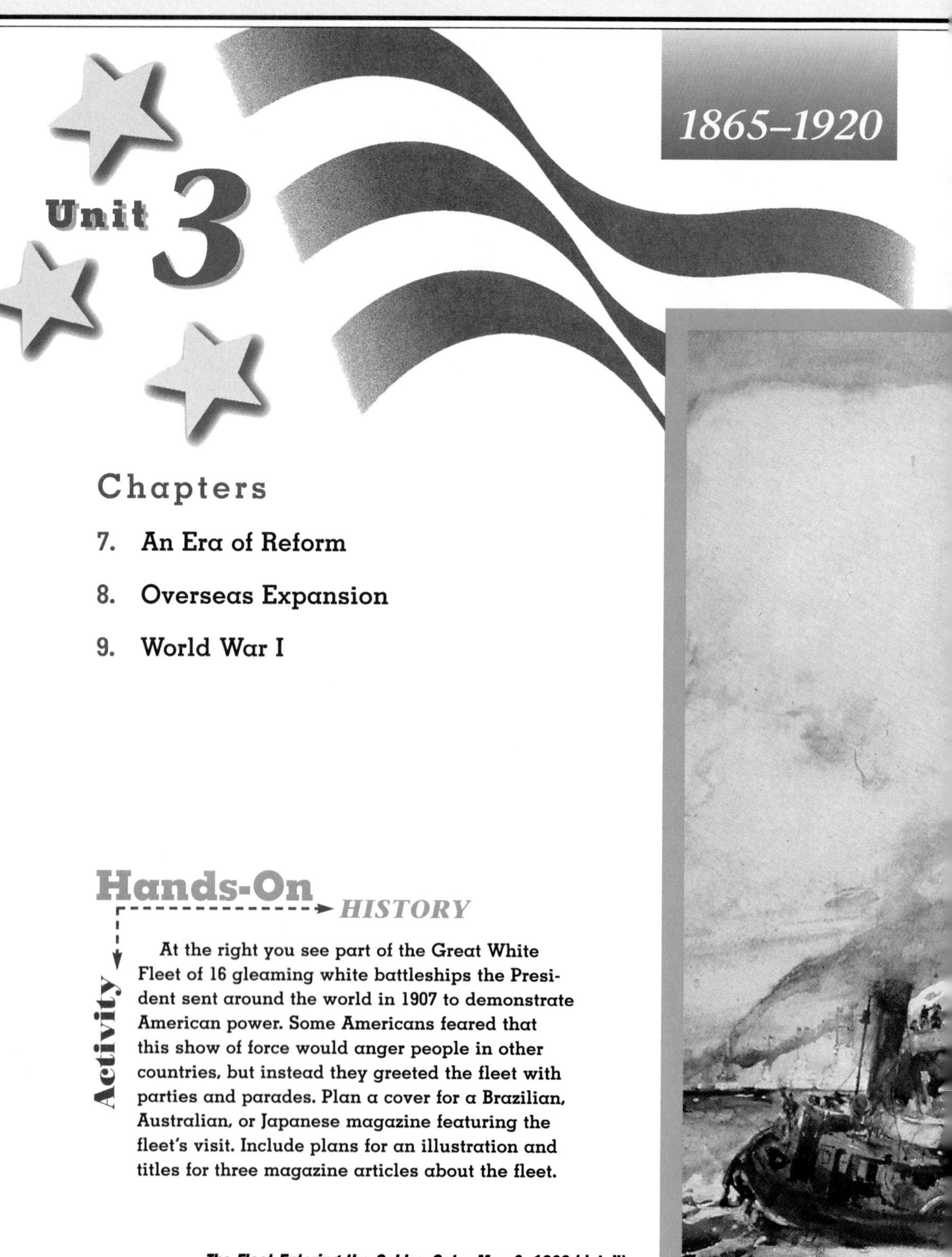

Unit 3

1865–1920

Chapters

Hands-On HISTORY

Activity

At the right you see part of the Great White Fleet of 16 gleaming white battleships the President sent around the world in 1907 to demonstrate American power. Some Americans feared that this show of force would anger people in other countries, but instead they greeted the fleet with parties and parades. Plan a cover for a Brazilian, Australian, or Japanese magazine featuring the fleet's visit. Include plans for an illustration and titles for three magazine articles about the fleet.

The Fleet Entering the Golden Gate, May 6, 1908 **(detail)**
by Henry Reuterdahl, about 1908

History Footnote

Ironically, when the Great White Fleet was visiting ports around the world in 1907, 44 nations were gathered at the Hague in the Netherlands to talk peace. As the painting implies, huge warships were the most devastating weapons of the era. Delegates at the Hague wrestled with how to restrict the building of bigger and more powerful battleships. That same year Britain launched the world's biggest battleship, the HMS *Dreadnought* (literally, "fear nothing"). This mammoth warship was more powerful than those of Britain's arch-rival Germany and the gleaming new United States fleet. Even though the painting shows an atmosphere of celebration and national pride, the deadly spiral of the naval arms race was continuing. Just six years later, it would help plunge the world into war.

Questions of Power

Discussion

Checking Understanding

1. If you were a Japanese, Australian, or Brazilian seeing these ships for the first time, what would catch your attention? (Students may mention the large guns, the unfamiliar flag, the sheer number and size of the ships, or other striking elements.)

2. What do you think are the feelings of the boatloads of American sightseers greeting the fleet? What are some details in the painting that support your answer? (The sightseers are proud of their fleet and country; they are giving the ships a heroic welcome.)

Stimulating Critical Thinking

3. How would it feel to be a sailor on one of the ships of the Great White Fleet? (Students may cite feelings of national pride, confidence in the fighting strength of the United States fleet, and fascination with foreign countries.)

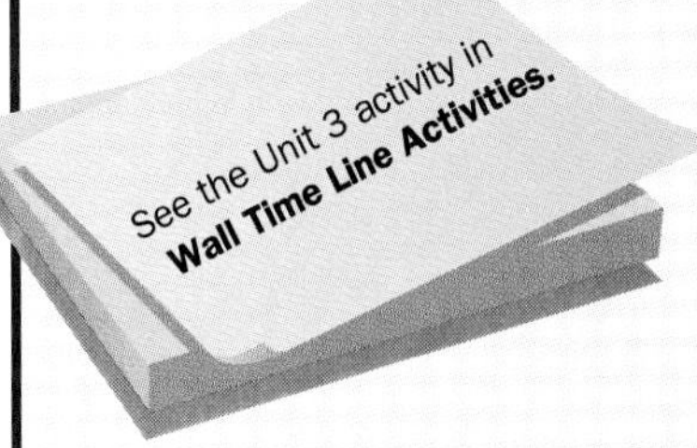

See the Unit 3 activity in
Wall Time Line Activities.

At·a·Glance 7

An Era of Reform
1870–1914

Chapter Planning Guide

Section	Student Text	Teacher's Edition Activities
Opener and Story pp. 332–335	**Keys to History Time Line**; **History Mystery**; Beginning the Story with **Jane Addams**	**Setting the Stage Activity** Point/Counterpoint, p. 334
1 **National Politics and Reform** pp. 336–340	**Hands-On History** Interviewing a civil-service worker, p. 338 **Skill Lab** Interpreting a Political Cartoon, p. 340	**Warm-Up Activity** Looking at Military Heroes, p. 336 **Geography Question of the Day,** p. 336 **Section Activity** Presenting a News Report, p. 337 **Bonus Activity** Preparing a Job Interview, p. 338 **Wrap-Up Activity** Creating a Cartoon, p. 339
2 **Farmers Take Action** pp. 341–346	**World Link** Wheat from "Down Under," p. 341 **Link to the Present** *The Wizard of Oz,* p. 344 **Reading Maps** Election of 1896, p. 345 **Geography Lab** The Great Plains, p. 346	**Warm-Up Activity** Focusing on Farming, p. 341 **Geography Question of the Day,** p. 341 **Section Activity** Role-Playing a Farm Family, p. 342 **Bonus Activity** A Populist Pamphlet, p. 343 **Wrap-Up Activity** Making a Crossword Puzzle, p. 345
3 **Progressives Battle for Reform** pp. 347–352	**Link to Art** Thomas Nast, p. 349 **Reading Maps** Spread of Woman Suffrage, p. 351	**Warm-Up Activity** Solving Society's Problems, p. 347 **Geography Question of the Day,** p. 347 **Section Activity** A Roundtable Discussion, p. 348 **Bonus Activity** Describing a Protest, p. 350 **Wrap-Up Activity** Creating a Reforms Chart, p. 352
4 **Progressive Presidents** pp. 353–357	**Point of View** How should labor disputes be resolved?, p. 354	**Warm-Up Activity** Evaluating the Power of Trusts, p. 353 **Geography Question of the Day,** p. 353 **Section Activity** Creating a Roosevelt Song or Poem, p. 355 **Bonus Activity** Writing Campaign Slogans, p. 356 **Wrap-Up Activity** Guessing an Identity, p. 357
Evaluation	☑ **Section 1 Review,** p. 339 ☑ **Section 2 Review,** p. 345 ☑ **Section 3 Review,** p. 352 ☑ **Section 4 Review,** p. 357 ☑ **Chapter Survey,** pp. 358–359 **Alternative Assessment** Creating public-service announcements, p. 359	☑ **Answers to Section 1 Review,** p. 339 ☑ **Answers to Section 2 Review,** p. 345 ☑ **Answers to Section 3 Review,** p. 352 ☑ **Answers to Section 4 Review,** p. 357 ☑ **Answers to Chapter Survey,** pp. 358–359 (Alternative Assessment guidelines are in the Take-Home Planner.)

Teacher's Resource Package	Take-Home Planner
Chapter Summaries: English and Spanish, pp. 50–51	**Introducing the Chapter Activity** Defining Reform Today, p. 6 **Chapter In-Depth Activity** Getting the Message Across, p. 6
Chapter Resources Binder **Study Guide** Using a Graphic Organizer, p. 65 **Skills Development** Interpreting a Political Cartoon, pp. 71–72	**Reduced Views** **Study Guide,** p. 8 **Skills Development,** p. 9 **Unit 3 Answers,** pp. 29–38
Chapter Resources Binder **Study Guide** Using a Time Line, p. 66 **Geography Extensions** Farmers of the Great Plains, pp. 19–20	 **Reduced Views** **Study Guide,** p. 8 **Geography Extensions,** p. 11 **Unit 3 Answers,** pp. 29–38
 **Chapter Resources Binder** **Study Guide** Identifying People and Places, p. 67 **Reinforcement** Determining Cause and Effect, pp. 69–70 **American Readings** Lynchings in the North, pp. 33–34 **Using Historical Documents** The Nineteenth Amendment	 **Reduced Views** **Study Guide,** p. 8 **Reinforcement,** p. 9 **American Readings,** p. 10 **Using Historical Documents,** p. 11 **Unit 3 Answers,** pp. 29–38
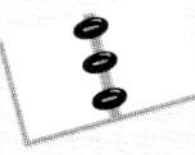 **Chapter Resources Binder** **Study Guide** Identifying Viewpoints, p. 68 **American Readings** *The Jungle,* pp. 35–36	 **Reduced Views** **Study Guide,** p. 8 **American Readings,** p. 10 **Unit 3 Answers,** pp. 29–38
 **Chapter and Unit Tests** Chapter 7 Tests, Forms A and B, pp. 63–66	 **Reduced Views** **Chapter Tests,** p. 11 **Unit 3 Answers,** pp. 29–38 **Alternative Assessment** Guidelines for scoring the Chapter Survey activity, p. 7

Additional Resources

Wall Time Line

Unit 3 Activity

Transparency Package

Transparency 7-1 Map: Spread of Woman Suffrage—use with Section 3

Transparency 7-2 The Woman Suffrage Movement—use with Section 3

Transparency Activity Book

SelecTest Testing Software

Chapter 7 Test, Forms A and B

Videodisc

CD-ROM

Coxey's Army (see TE p. 344)

Tweed Ring cartoon (see TE p. 348)

Suffragists' march (see TE p. 350)

Slaughterhouse (see TE p. 354)

The Jungle (see TE p. 354)

Theodore Roosevelt in Yosemite (see TE p. 356)

7

Teaching Resources

Take-Home Planner 3
Introducing Chapter Activity
Chapter In-Depth Activity
Alternative Assessment
Chapter Resources Binder
Geography Extensions
American Readings
Using Historical Documents
Transparency Activities
Wall Time Line Activities
Chapter Summaries
Chapter and Unit Tests
SelecTest Test File
Vital Links CD-ROM/Videodisc

Time Line

Keys to History

Keys to History journal writing activity is on page 668 in the Chapter Survey.

Corruption in Grant's administration Despite his personal honesty, Grant was unable to prevent the spread of corruption. (p. 337)

Grange movement In an attempt to control their economic destinies, farmers formed a society to market their products. (p. 342)

Pendleton Civil Service Act This act struck at the heart of the spoils system by mandating tests to determine the most competent civil servants. (p. 339)

Looking Back President Andrew Jackson rewarded his supporters with government jobs.

World Link See page 341.

Chapter Objectives

- ★ Explain why political reforms became an important national issue in the late 1800s.
- ★ Discuss how American farmers responded to changes brought about by industrialization.
- ★ Summarize how Progressives tried to solve problems facing cities and states.
- ★ Discuss reforms the federal government carried out under Progressive Presidents.

Chapter Overview

In the years after the Civil War, corruption reached into almost every level of government. Intense party competition, lax oversight during the Grant administration and those that followed, and the spoils system all contributed to corruption and misconduct. Public demand finally resulted in the passing of the Pendleton Act to create a competence-based civil service.

1870–1914

Chapter 7 An Era of Reform

Sections

Beginning the Story with Jane Addams

1. National Politics and Reform
2. Farmers Take Action
3. Progressives Battle for Reform
4. Progressive Presidents

1872 Corruption exposed in Grant's administration

1874 Granger movement at its height

1883 Pendleton Civil Service Act

1870 1880

World Link Wheat production soars in Australia **1880s–1890s**

Looking Back

Andrew Jackson defends the spoils system **1829**

Beset by rising costs and falling incomes, farmers organized Farmers' Alliances and other groups to fight for their economic survival. Initial success led to the formation of the Populist Party on the national level. However, conflict over monetary and banking reform weakened the new party.

In cities and states, Progressives gained power and worked to reform unresponsive governments, with help from muckraking journalists. In addition Progressives won reforms in areas such as worker protection, temperance, woman suffrage, and the rights of African Americans.

Progressive-influenced Presidents Roosevelt, Taft, and Wilson carried out reforms on the national level, in areas such as trust-busting, consumer protection, banking policy, and conservation.

HISTORY *Mystery*

As Vice-President, Chester A. Arthur opposed civil-service reform. After he became President in 1881, he supported it. What caused President Arthur to change his mind?

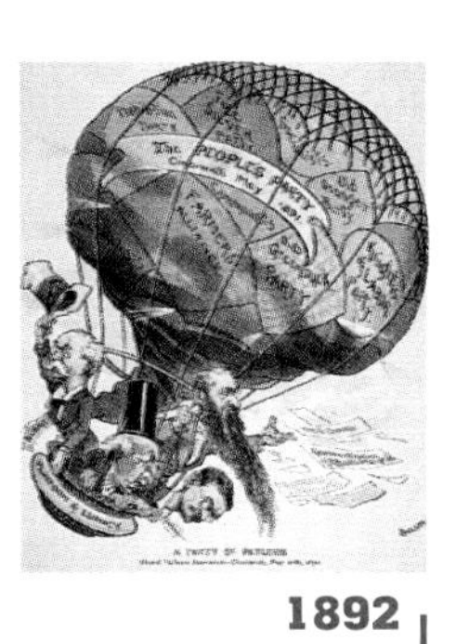

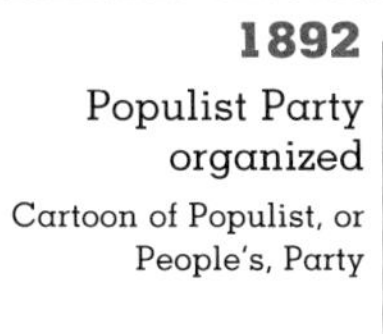

1892
Populist Party organized
Cartoon of Populist, or People's, Party

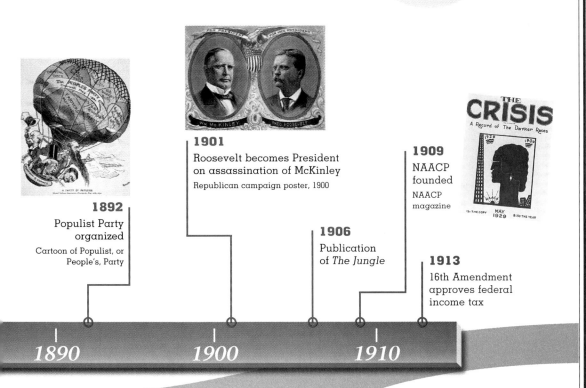

1901
Roosevelt becomes President on assassination of McKinley
Republican campaign poster, 1900

1906
Publication of *The Jungle*

1909
NAACP founded
NAACP magazine

1913
16th Amendment approves federal income tax

1890 1900 1910

Looking Ahead

19th Amendment gives women the right to vote
1920

Teaching the HISTORY *Mystery*

Students will find the answer on p. 338. See Chapter Survey, p. 358, for additional information and questions.

Time Line

Populist Party organized Appealing mainly to farmers, the Populists proposed a series of reforms that would influence later reform movements. (p. 343)

Roosevelt becomes President A reform-minded leader moved into the White House. (p. 353)

Publication of *The Jungle* Horrified reactions to the novel led to adoption of federal laws regulating food and drug production. (p. 355)

NAACP founded Black leaders formed the organization that became an important voice for the rights of African Americans. (p. 352)

16th Amendment approves federal income tax Originally called for by Populists, this amendment gave the federal government an important new source of revenue. (p. 356)

Looking Ahead The federal government followed the lead of the states in granting woman suffrage.

Beginning the Story

Jane Addams

Like many Americans of her time, Jane Addams was appalled by the dreadful living conditions of many of the poor in American cities. From early childhood, Jane wondered why such conditions had to exist and sympathized with those who had to endure them. After the death of her father, she quit medical school, battled depression, and searched for a new purpose in her life. She found it one day in the slums on the west side of Chicago. An old mansion she bought was transformed into Hull House, one of the earliest and the most famous community settlement houses.

Setting the Stage Activity

Point/Counterpoint

To help students understand the conditions into which Addams plunged, have pairs imagine they are friends of the young Jane Addams, to whom she has confided her plan to create Hull House. Have one think of arguments to dissuade her from her plan. The other should provide answers to the arguments. Ask for volunteers to share their arguments and answers.

See the Introducing the Chapter Activity, Defining Reform Today. **Take-Home Planner 3,** p. 6.

History Footnote

One of the dreadful conditions poor people faced in the neighborhood of Hull House was the lack of garbage collection. Sanitation problems were made even worse, Addams wrote, "by decayed fruit and vegetables discarded by . . . fruit peddlers and by piles of rags of the rag pickers." In 1895, Addams pressured political leaders to appoint her garbage inspector for her ward. She supervised garbage collectors, followed them to the dump to make sure they did not drop their loads in the streets, took careless landlords to court, and fought bribery and corruption. She was paid $1,000 a year, the only paid job she ever held. Many politicians in her area were outraged that a woman, therefore a non-voter, had this job.

Beginning the Story with

Jane Addams

It was just a moment in a young girl's life. Jane Addams was 6 years old. Her father, a businessman in Cedarville, Illinois, had taken her to visit one of his mills. There she caught her first sight of poverty. She asked her father why people lived in such "horrid little houses." Jane's father patiently explained that people lived in such conditions out of necessity, not by choice.

Jane reflected on this interesting information. She decided that when she grew up, she was going to have a large house right in the middle of horrid little houses like these. All the children who had no place to play at home, she said, "could come and play in my yard."

An "Ugly, Pigeon-Toed Little Girl"

The moment passed. At the time, Jane later confessed, she was far more worried about feeling like an "ugly, pigeon-toed little girl, whose crooked back obliged her to walk with her head very much upon one side."

Jane, whose mother died when Jane was just 2 years old, loved and admired her "Pa," a free-thinker who hated injustice. Jane would later write of her father that "he was the uncompromising enemy of wrong doing."

John Addams encouraged his daughter to read, think, and be true to her own beliefs. He also taught her compassion. One Sunday morning when it was time to go to church, Jane appeared in a new coat that she was eager to show off to her friends. Her father told her how pretty it looked on her, but suggested she not wear it to Sunday school. It might, he said, make the other children feel unhappy because they could not afford anything so nice.

Jane asked her father why other children did not have new coats like hers. Again he explained that some families did not have enough money to buy all the things they might want. Jane was not satisfied with this reply. "Then what can be done about it?" she asked. John Addams had no good reply. Jane would spend a lifetime trying to find an answer.

History Bookshelf

Twain, Mark, and Charles Dudley Warner. *The Gilded Age*. NAL-Dutton, 1985. A quirky, yet savagely satirical look at the excesses of the 1870s and 1880s by the quintessential American writer.

Also of interest:

Meigs, Cornelia. *Jane Addams: Pioneer for Social Justice*. Little, 1970.

Sinclair, Upton. *The Jungle*. Harper & Row, 1951.

Wertheimer, Barbara. *We Were There: The Story of Working Women in America*. Pantheon, 1977.

Jane Addams and other reformers took a special interest in children's welfare. This rooftop nursery provided day care for children of working parents.

Finding "Life's Purpose"

Jane grew up, went to college, and graduated with her "life's purpose" clearly fixed in her mind. She was going to become a doctor and live with the poor. Then real life stepped in to shatter her dreams. In 1881, shortly before Jane turned 21, her beloved father died. His death was "the greatest sorrow that can ever come to me," Jane wrote to her school friend Ellen Starr.

While still in mourning, Jane entered medical school. She tried to throw herself into her studies, but she disliked her classes and felt she was a failure. After seven months, she collapsed and dropped out of school.

For the next few years Jane battled health problems as well as bouts of depression. If she was not to be a doctor, then just what was she to do with her life? The only careers thought suitable for educated young women in the late 1800s were marriage and teaching. Neither of these appealed to her.

Then it came to her—the long-ago idea of having a big house among all the horrid little houses and being a friend to the people who lived in them.

While wandering through a tenement area of Chicago, Jane found her house, a mansion built by Charles Hull. On September 14, 1889, Hull House opened its doors to the public. Just as Jane had imagined, among her first visitors were children who needed someplace to play. In its first year of operation, Hull House would welcome 50,000 visitors. Jane Addams had found her life's work.

Hands-On HISTORY

Activity

Imagine that you are writing a biography of Jane Addams. Based on the story above, create a list of turning points—points at which significant change occurred in her life. Write a brief description of the importance of each turning point.

Discussion

Thinking Historically

1. What are some ways John Addams influenced his daughter? (Instilled compassion for the poor and hatred of injustice; encouraged her to read, think, and follow own beliefs; probably provided money for her activities.)

2. What traits do you see in Jane Addams that helped make Hull House a reality? (Sympathetic to poor; self-confidence; wanted to help people.)

3. How might her own problems have influenced her attitude about the poor? ("Crooked back," depression, and loss of parents may have made her more sympathetic to others' problems.)

See the Chapter In-Depth Activity, Getting the Message Across. **Take-Home Planner 3**, p. 6.

Teaching the Hands-On HISTORY

To help students identify turning points in Jane's life, have them list events and her reactions. Remind them that turning points can be caused by both internal and external elements or conditions. Ask them to consider what her life might have been like if the event had not occurred.

For a journal writing activity on Jane Addams, see student page 359.

Introducing the Section

Vocabulary

civil service (p. 338) the body of government workers who are hired rather than elected

Warm-Up Activity

Looking at Military Heroes

To encourage students to think about the qualifications of military leaders such as Grant to be President, have them list reasons why generals might and might not be effective Presidents. Have them compare and discuss their lists.

Geography Question of the Day

Ask students to review p. 194 and list states that would probably be mostly Democratic and those that would probably be mostly Republican in the late 1800s.

See the Study Guide
activity in Chapter
Resources Binder,
p. 65.

Section Objectives

- ★ Describe how party competition affected politics after the Civil War.
- ★ Discuss why government corruption increased during Grant's presidency.
- ★ Explain how Congress tried to reform the spoils system.

Teaching Resources

Take-Home Planner 3, pp. 4–11
Chapter Resources Binder
- **Study Guide, p. 65**
- Reinforcement
- **Skills Development, pp. 71–72**

Geography Extensions
American Readings
Using Historical Documents
Transparency Activities
Chapter and Unit Tests

1. National Politics and Reform

Reading Guide

New Term **civil service**

Section Focus **Why political reform became a national issue in the late 1800s**

1. **How did party competition affect politics after the Civil War?**
2. **Why did government corruption increase during Grant's presidency?**
3. **How did Congress try to reform the spoils system?**

In 1905 Jane Addams became a member of the Chicago Board of Education. To her surprise, she found corruption in the schools. Politicians, she wrote,

> "received a rake-off in the contract for every new building or coal supply or the adoption of school books."

Since the Civil War, such corruption had reached into every level of government.

The Grant Years

After the Civil War and the bitter struggle over Reconstruction (see Chapter 3), Americans were tired of conflict. In the presidential election of 1868, they elected General Ulysses S. Grant, whose campaign slogan was "Let us have peace."

Grant seemed an ideal leader to unite the nation. Bearded, muscular, and overly fond of cigars, he was admired as the Civil War general who had faced down Confederate General Robert E. Lee. He was also known for his generous terms of surrender to the Confederate armies.

A gentle, modest man, Grant brought a quiet dignity to the White House. During the Civil War, he had disliked the fancy trappings of high military rank. As President he refused to take advantage of his position. When he received a $20 speeding ticket for driving his carriage too fast, he paid it.

Yet Grant was not able to impose his standards on other members of the Republican Party. Despite his promise of peace, Grant's presidency was plagued by political conflicts, corruption, and scandal.

Party Competition

In the years after the Civil War, Republicans and Democrats struggled fiercely for power. As the North and the South gingerly knit themselves together again, the parties took advantage of the passionate memories that remained.

Republicans were quick to remind voters that theirs was the party of Abraham Lincoln. They gained the loyalty of African American voters as well as their traditional northern supporters.

Democrats accused the Republicans of "waving the bloody shirt"—stirring up wartime feelings to appeal to voters even when the issues had nothing to do with the Civil War. Yet Democrats, too, appealed to wartime passions. In the South, where white resentment of Radical Reconstruction still rankled, most whites belonged to the Democratic Party. For years the party would be able to count on the votes of the "Solid South."

Connections to Civics

While Grant's presidency was surrounded by corruption, he himself took many positive actions to help the nation. He signed a law insuring that money printed during the Civil War would retain its value, he established a national park system, and he negotiated a treaty with Great Britain to settle a hostile financial dispute. To help ease the tense conflicts with Native Americans, he appointed his friend Ely Parker, a Seneca Indian, as head of Indian Affairs. To try to ensure African Americans' voting rights, he supported the Fifteenth Amendment, passed by Congress in 1870, which guaranteed all men (not women) the right to vote regardless of "race, color, or previous condition of servitude."

The nation as a whole was almost evenly divided between the Democrats and Republicans. Presidential elections were often very close. There were divisions within the parties, too. Thus neither party dared to take too strong a stand on issues for fear of scaring away voters.

Corruption in Government

Corruption tarnished Grant's presidency. Although honest himself, Grant appointed a number of people who used their offices to enrich themselves. The Secretary of War, for example, accepted bribes for contracts to run Indian trading posts in Oklahoma. Whiskey companies owned by government officials bribed Grant's personal secretary to help them avoid paying taxes.

Later Grant apologized for giving appointments to the wrong people. In his last annual message to Congress, he wrote:

> "It was my . . . misfortune to be called to the office of Chief Executive without any previous political training. . . . Errors of judgment must have occurred."

Despite Grant's own honesty, political corruption became known as "Grantism."

The Crédit Mobilier scandal The biggest scandal of Grant's presidency involved the Crédit Mobilier (cray-DEE mō-BEEL-YAY) construction company. In the 1860s the federal government had offered special payments to encourage the building of the Union Pacific Railroad. Crédit Mobilier, which built the railroad, exaggerated the construction costs and received much higher payments than it deserved.

The company then bribed members of Congress and even the Vice-President to try to prevent an investigation. Finally, in 1872, the *New York Sun* newspaper exposed Crédit Mobilier as the "king of frauds," leading Congress to investigate.

The spoils system Other levels of the federal government were also guilty of corruption. Since the 1820s, Presidents had used the spoils system to reward political supporters with government jobs. After the Civil War, the sharp competition between Democrats and Republicans encouraged the growth of the spoils system.

In this 1872 cartoon, politicians and businessmen beg President Grant for government jobs and work contracts. In his 1868 election campaign, Grant had called for *peace* between northerners and southerners. However, office and contract seekers seemed more interested in getting a *piece* of "government cake."

Developing the Section

Discussion

Checking Understanding

1. Give three examples of corruption during the Grant administration. (Bribes taken by the Secretary of War, Crédit Mobilier scandal, growth of spoils system.)

Stimulating Critical Thinking

2. Do you think the corruption affected average citizens? Explain. (Yes: citizens without money or connections could have no part in government and had difficulty getting work contracts; government catering to big business made it hard for small businesses to survive. No: government officials accepted bribes and executives pocketed money, but this did not affect most citizens.)

Section Activity

Presenting a News Report

To explore government corruption and reform in the late 1800s, have small groups create television news reports on the theme, "Corruption in Government: How Bad Is It and What Can Be Done?" Possible formats include an interview program, a reporters' roundtable, or an undercover account. Have them use information from their textbooks and possibly from the library. Encourage them to make their reports lively.

Bonus Activity

Preparing a Job Interview

To reinforce understanding of the corruption in politics in the late 1800s, have pairs write two scripts for government job interviews—one before the civil service reform, and one after the civil service reform. Have some pairs act out their interviews.

Teaching the Hands-On HISTORY

Have pairs look in the government listings in the telephone book to find names of government offices in your area. They could also interview relatives, friends, or neighbors who work for the federal government. Tell them to either take notes during the interview or record it, but before recording they must ask the interviewee's permission. Suggest they ask the interviewee to compare work in the private sector with work as a federal employee, citing advantages and disadvantages of each.

Tips for Teaching

Students with Limited English

Students benefit from examining roots of words and other words based on the same roots. Explain that *gilded* means both to overlay with gold and to make something seem more valuable. Discuss words related to *gilded (gold, golden, gilt-edged).* Ask why the Gilded Age is a good name for the era.

Officeholders in each party gave government jobs, as well as work contracts, to their supporters. Unfortunately, loyal party members often had no training for their work. Even worse, many were dishonest.

The Gilded Age Novelists Mark Twain and Charles Dudley Warner thought that the golden wealth of the nation masked corruption and greed. They described the years after the Civil War as the Gilded Age.

Civil-Service Reform

The widespread greed and corruption in government enraged many Americans. In the presidential election of 1876, voters chose Rutherford B. Hayes, the respected Republican governor of Ohio. Hayes proposed a system of tests to determine who was best qualified for jobs in the **civil service**—the body of government workers who are hired rather than elected. Congress ignored the proposal, however.

In the presidential election of 1880 the Republicans again captured the presidency. This time, though, the party was split in two. One side sought reform of the civil service, while the other opposed it. The new President, James A. Garfield of Ohio, represented the reformers. Vice-President Chester A. Arthur supported the spoils system.

In July 1881, four months after taking office, President Garfield was shot to death. The assassin was seeking revenge because he had not been given a government job.

Dismayed by the tragedy, Chester Arthur, now President, changed his opinion. He threw his support behind efforts to reform the spoils system.

Hands-On HISTORY

Interviewing a civil-service worker More Americans work for the federal government than for any other employer. In order to get their jobs, most of those 2 million civilian (nonmilitary) employees had to take a civil-service test or other form of evaluation to show that they were qualified for the job.

Activity To find out what it is like to work for the government, rather than for a private business, interview a federal government worker in your community. For example, you might talk to a postal worker or someone who works for the Social Security Administration. Ask questions about the following topics:

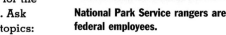

National Park Service rangers are federal employees.

- hiring and promotion procedures
- job requirements and responsibilities
- vacations and other benefits
- restrictions, such as limits on collective bargaining

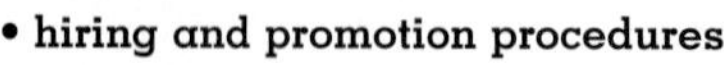

Share what you learn with the rest of the class.

History Footnote

New York lawyer and women's rights advocate Belva Ann Lockwood ran for President in 1884 and 1888 with the endorsement of the Equal Rights Party. She was the author of several congressional bills concerning women's issues: one mandated equal pay for women federal employees, another granted the vote to women in the territories of Oklahoma, Arizona, and New Mexico, and a third allowed women to argue cases before the Supreme Court. In fact, she was the first woman lawyer to practice her profession before the U.S. Supreme Court. Representing a North Carolina Cherokee group in a lawsuit against the U.S. government for treaty violations concerning land rights, she won $5 million for the Indians.

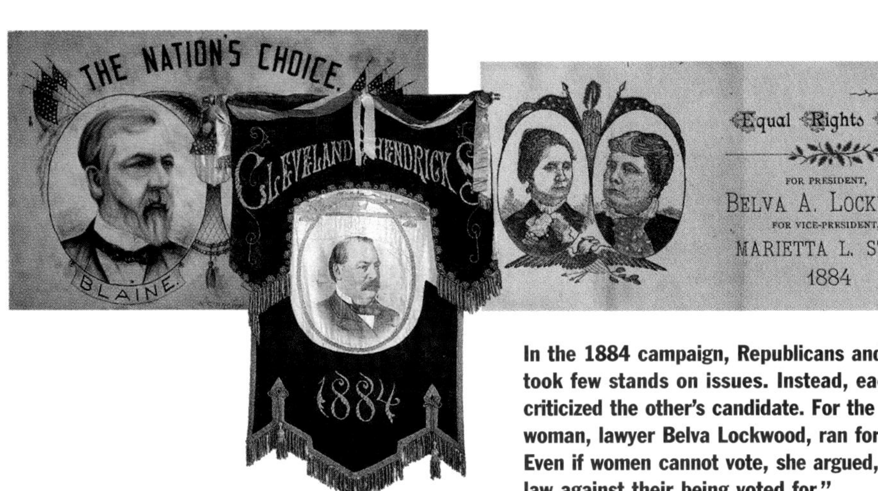

In the 1884 campaign, Republicans and Democrats took few stands on issues. Instead, each party criticized the other's candidate. For the first time a woman, lawyer Belva Lockwood, ran for President. Even if women cannot vote, she argued, "there is no law against their being voted for."

In 1883 Congress passed the Pendleton Civil Service Act. It set up a commission to prepare tests for civil-service jobs. New workers would be chosen from among those with the highest scores. Once hired, they could not be fired for political reasons.

At first, the Civil Service Act applied to only about 10 percent of all government jobs. Over the years, however, Presidents expanded the civil service to cover most government jobs.

The election of 1884 Even with the passage of the Civil Service Act, corruption continued to be an issue. In the presidential election of 1884, Democrat Grover Cleveland, the governor of New York, campaigned for "clean government." His supporters attacked the Republican candidate, James G. Blaine of Maine, for taking bribes when he served in Congress. They chanted: "Blaine, Blaine, James G. Blaine, the continental liar from the state of Maine!"

In a close, bitterly fought election, Cleveland defeated Blaine. Cleveland was the first Democrat to be elected President since the Civil War.

Cleveland came into office committed to civil-service reform. However, after so many years of Republican rule, job-hungry Democrats poured into the nation's capital. "The Washington hotels are crowded," one journalist wrote, "and office seekers are as thick as shells on the beach."

Caught between civil-service reformers and party supporters, Cleveland tried to please both. He rewarded thousands of Democratic Party members with government jobs. At the same time, though, he almost doubled the number of federal jobs covered by civil-service laws.

1. Section Review

1. Define **civil service.**
2. Why did the two political parties avoid taking stands on issues after the Civil War?
3. Why did corruption in the federal government grow during Grant's presidency?
4. How did civil-service reform change the way that workers in the federal government were hired?
5. **Critical Thinking** How do you think Grant should be judged for the increase of corruption during his presidency? Give evidence to support your answer.

Closing the Section

Wrap-Up Activity

Creating a Cartoon

To demonstrate their understanding of the issues discussed in the section, ask students to create political cartoons on any issue of the period, using the information in the textbook. Have them label their cartoons as necessary. Ask volunteers to discuss their cartoons, and display them around the classroom.

Section Review Answers

1. Definition: *civil service* (338)
2. Both parties were locked in a fierce struggle for power, so they were reluctant to take a stand on issues for fear of alienating voters.
3. Although Grant was honest, many of his appointees enriched themselves by taking bribes.
4. Before the Pendleton Act, government workers often got their jobs as rewards for political support; after the act, workers had to pass a test to be considered for government jobs.
5. Answers will vary, but students should recognize Grant's responsibility for appointing people who used their offices to enrich themselves.

If students need to review the skill, use the Skills Development transparency and activity in the **Chapter Resources Binder**, pp. 71–72.

This is evident in the threatening sky, the birds' ugliness, and their droppings on the Capitol. The artist seems to feel contempt and disgust for the trusts because he has portrayed them as birds that many people find repulsive. The artist may blame the trusts more than the senators because the latter do not appear in the cartoon. (c) Answers may include rampant bribery, disrespect of the institution of government, power of the trusts, and dishonesty of lawmakers.

For further application, have students do the Applying Skills activity in the Chapter Survey (p. 358).

Introducing the Skill Lab

Ask students to read the Skill Tips and examine the cartoon with the tips in mind. Have them point out examples of exaggeration in the drawing (trusts are portrayed as vultures, not as people). Ask them to describe the feelings most people have for the type of bird in the cartoon (disgust and repulsion). Finally, ask them to read the labels in the cartoon to make sure they understand what is represented in the drawing.

Skill Lab

Answers

1. (a) On a building labeled *U.S. Senate;* the U.S. Capitol, where the Senate meets. (b) They are vultures, as seen from their distinctive faces and the punning legend "Let us prey." (c) Each bird symbolizes a trust, with Standard Oil the most prominent.

2. (a) Their stomachs are large. (b) The *S* has been replaced by a dollar sign. (c) There is a bag of money with a dollar sign on it and a sign on the Senate that reads "Seats for Sale."

3. (a) The trusts buy or bribe members of the Senate and grow fat on the rewards their bribery produces. (b) Despite humor in the cartoon, such as the pun *prey/pray,* the artist takes the issue very seriously.

(Answers continued in top margin)

Skill Lab

Skill Tips

Keep in mind:

- Cartoonists simplify and exaggerate to make their points.
- Cartoons often use symbols: animals, people, or objects that stand for something else.
- Labels identify characters and actions Captions may summarize the cartoon's message.

Acquiring Information

Interpreting a Political Cartoon

Bribery. Corruption. Scandal. Dishonest politicians of the late 1800s provided cartoonists with plenty of material. Angered by the power of biting political cartoons, one corrupt politician complained, "I don't care what they write about me. But those pictures—people understand them!"

Question to Investigate

What were some signs of political corruption in the late 1800s?

Procedure

To explore the question, you will interpret a political cartoon by Edward Kemble.

1 Identify the cartoon's main subject.
a. Where are the birds perched?
b. What kind of birds are they?
c. What do the birds symbolize?

2 Identify details in the cartoon.
a. What do you notice about the size of the birds' stomachs?
b. What do you notice about the word *Senate*?
c. What other details involving money do you notice?

3 Draw conclusions about the point the cartoonist is making.
a. Summarize the cartoon's message about trusts and the Senate.
b. Tell what feelings you think the cartoonist has about his subject. For example, does he find it funny?
c. How do you think this cartoonist would answer the Question to Investigate?

Source to Use

Section Objectives

- ★ Describe the problems farmers faced in the late 1800s.
- ★ Discuss the actions farmers took to improve their economic conditions.
- ★ Evaluate how successful farmers were in achieving their goals.

Teaching Resources

Take-Home Planner 3, pp. 4–11
Chapter Resources Binder
Study Guide, p. 66
Reinforcement
Skills Development
Geography Extensions, pp. 19–20
American Readings
Using Historical Documents
Transparency Activities
Chapter and Unit Tests

2. Farmers Take Action

Reading Guide

Section Focus **How American farmers responded to changes brought about by industrialization**

1. **What problems did farmers face in the late 1800s?**
2. **What actions did farmers take to improve their economic conditions?**
3. **How successful were farmers in achieving their goals?**

As politicians squabbled over power and business and industry expanded, the nation's farmers were suffering. Frustrated and angry that political leaders were paying little attention to their concerns, they organized to demand help from government. Mary Elizabeth Lease, a leader of the movement, sounded a warning:

> "The people are [cornered], let the blood-hounds of money who have dogged us thus far beware."

Farmers' Troubles

As cities grew after the Civil War, so did the farms that fed their hungry people. Between 1860 and 1910, the number of farms tripled. Farmers bought new machines that allowed them to plant more acres and harvest bigger crops. They concentrated on raising cash crops—such as corn, wheat, cotton, and rice—to supply growing markets at home and overseas.

Falling farm prices The expansion of farms did not guarantee prosperity for farmers, however. In fact, farm prices began to fall because farmers were growing more than the American market demanded.

American farmers tried to sell their surplus crops abroad, but other countries were also flooding the world's markets with their crops. In the early 1880s farmers received 80¢ a bushel for their wheat. By 1890 they were lucky to get 71¢.

Although prices were falling, the costs of doing business were not. Farmers paid high interest rates on loans for machinery and land. They paid high prices to merchants for handling and storing their crops. They paid

World Link

Wheat from "Down Under" **American wheat farmers of the 1890s faced stiff competition from a place that many had never heard of. The place was Australia, a British colony.**

To help farmers, Australia set up experimental farms and agricultural colleges in the 1880s and 1890s. There, improved varieties of wheat were developed and methods of preventing diseases were put into practice. Farmers also began using a superphosphate fertilizer.

The result was greatly increased yields and booming wheat exports. Half a world away, American farmers felt the pinch.

Introducing the Section

Warm-Up Activity

Focusing on Farming

Ask students to list elements that affect a farmer's livelihood. (Weather, diseases and pests, land prices, transportation costs, no control over prices.) Make a master list on the chalkboard.

Geography Question of the Day

Have students refer to the map on p. 345. Ask why large states such as Montana and Wyoming have so few electoral votes. How would this distribution affect an election?

Teaching the World Link

Tell students that wheat is still an extremely important crop throughout the world. In 1992 the following countries were the leading wheat exporters (figures in metric tons): United States (35,205,000), Canada (23,878,000), France (19,761,000), Australia (8,203,000), and Argentina (6,268,000). Write this information on the chalkboard and have students create bar graphs, using either computer software or pencil and paper.

Developing the Section

Section Activity

Role-Playing a Farm Family

To explore farmers' problems and possible solutions, have small groups role-play the following scenario: A farm family is gathered around the kitchen table. Falling prices for crops have put them at the edge of financial ruin. A son has learned about the local Farmers' Alliance and is trying to convince his father to support it and the new Populist Party. The father is a Republican because of Lincoln's role in preserving the Union. Other family members should join in the discussion. Have groups prepare and present role-plays.

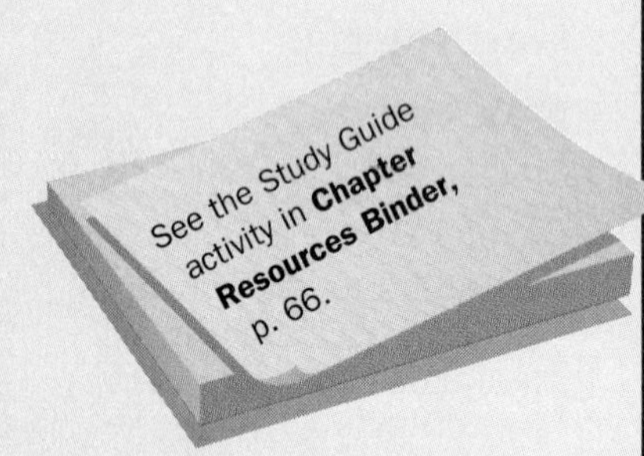

See the Study Guide activity in **Chapter Resources Binder,** p. 66.

History Footnote

Mary Elizabeth Lease was known as one of the most colorful and controversial Populist reformers. Born in Pennsylvania in 1850, the daughter of Irish immigrants, she moved to Kansas in 1870. There she married and quickly became known as a spirited and hypnotic speaker at Farmers' Alliance meetings. Lease's abrasive personality and intensity led her to break with the Populists, and she opposed the nomination of William Jennings Bryan in 1896. She moved on to other causes later in her life, including the annexation of Cuba, Canada, and the West Indies; nationalization of the railroads and telegraph system; high tariffs on foreign goods; woman suffrage; birth control; and prohibition.

Farmers formed cooperatives to try to lower business costs. In this photo men, women, and children work together on the apple harvest.

high railroad rates to get their crops to market. The editor of a farmers' newspaper angrily declared:

> "There are three great crops raised in Nebraska. One is a crop of corn, one a crop of freight rates, and one a crop of interest. One is produced by farmers who by sweat and toil farm the land. The other two are produced by men who sit in their offices and behind their bank counters and farm the farmers."

High or low tariffs? To raise farm prices, farmers sought to increase foreign demand for American crops. They reasoned that if people in the United States bought more foreign goods, then foreigners would have more dollars to spend on American farm products.

To encourage Americans to buy more foreign goods, farmers asked Congress to reduce tariffs. The Democrats supported the farmers' demands. The Republicans, on the other hand, wanted to keep tariffs high in order to protect American industry from foreign competition.

Republicans won the argument in 1888, when their candidate, Benjamin Harrison, was elected President. Farmers would have to find another solution to their problems.

Grangers and Farmers' Alliances

In 1867 Oliver Kelley, a clerk in the United States Department of Agriculture, had an idea. If the government would not help farmers, he thought, farmers must help themselves. Kelley organized a society called the Patrons of Husbandry. He traveled throughout the nation seeking members. By 1874, nearly 1 million people had joined.

Members called their new society the Grange, based on an old English word for farm buildings. Grangers formed cooperatives to market their products themselves instead of having to pay middlemen. There were cooperative creameries, warehouses, and banks. Grangers also experimented with making their own farm equipment.

A depression in the 1870s caused many Grange cooperatives to fail. Disheartened, many farmers left the Grange.

Rise of Farmers' Alliances As the Grange declined, farmers organized local, state, and then regional Farmers' Alliances to demand help from government. By the late 1880s there were the Northern Farmers' Alliance and the Southern Farmers' Alliance. African Americans formed the Colored Farmers' National Alliance in the South.

In 1890 the Farmers' Alliances plunged into politics. A leader in Kansas was the fiery Mary Elizabeth Lease, known as "the Kansas Pythoness." She traveled tirelessly

History Footnote

Grange founders modeled the Grange on the Masonic order, complete with degrees or ranks, signs, passwords, and secret rituals. They divided Grange membership into seven degrees. Four were low, or subordinate, degrees. For men these were Laborer, Cultivator, Harvester, and Husbandman; the corresponding degrees for women were Maid, Shepherdess, Gleanor, and Matron. The state Grange awarded the fifth degree to masters of subordinate granges and their wives; it was called Pomona, or Hope. The National Grange awarded to masters of state granges the sixth degree, called Flora, or Charity. Members of this degree made up the National Council, and, after serving one year, they could be awarded the highest degree—Demeter or Ceres—Faith. The head of this degree held the title of High Priest.

Mary Elizabeth Lease was such an effective speaker, one journalist reported, that "she set the crowd hooting or hurrahing at her will."

across the state, whipping up support in more than 160 speeches.

In the elections of 1890, Alliance candidates swept into power across the South and in several midwestern states. More than 50 Alliance candidates were elected to Congress.

The Populist Party

Encouraged by their success, in 1892 the Farmers' Alliances met in Omaha, Nebraska, and formed their own political party. They called it the Populist, or People's, Party.

In the presidential campaign of 1892, the Populist Party proposed a series of reforms. They wanted the government to own and run the railroads "in the interest of the people." They called for a graduated income tax to tax higher incomes more heavily than lower incomes. To win workers' support, they called for an eight-hour workday.

The Populists also thought that people had a right to participate more directly in politics. They proposed that senators be elected by the people, not by state legislatures. They also believed that citizens should be able to vote to approve or disapprove of laws and to propose new ones.

The Populist message appealed to farmers. Their message was not as popular with other groups, though. Business people disliked the demand for a government takeover of railroads. Immigrants resented the call for restricting immigration and limiting land ownership to American citizens.

The election of 1892 In the 1892 election Grover Cleveland received 5.5 million votes, defeating both President Benjamin Harrison and the Populist candidate, James B. Weaver of Iowa. Although Weaver made a strong showing, with 1 million votes, Cleveland ignored the Populists' ideas. He did not believe that government should take a more active role in the nation's economy.

The Panic of 1893

Soon after Cleveland regained the White House, the Panic of 1893 pushed the nation into a depression that threatened to bring the economy to a wrenching halt. Thousands of businesses failed. Unemployment soared. In Chicago, Jane Addams recalled:

> "When the first cold weather came, the police stations and the very corridors of the city hall were crowded by men who could afford no other lodging."

By 1894, nearly 3 million workers had been thrown out of work. Debt drove farmers off their land.

Silver or gold? Democrats, Republicans, and Populists all agreed that to end the depression, the nation's money system must be reformed. They disagreed passionately, however, about how to do it.

Populist farmers wanted the government to make more money available. Then they could pay their debts and buy more land and

Discussion

Checking Understanding

1. What were the positions of the Republicans and Democrats on tariffs? (Republicans favored high tariffs; Democrats wanted to lower them.)

2. Why did many farmers leave the Grange movement? (A depression in the 1870s caused many cooperatives to fail.)

Stimulating Critical Thinking

3. Which Populist proposals do you think were good? Which were not? Explain. (Opinions should be based on sound reason-ing and facts. Students may approve of the graduated income tax as fair and the eight-hour workday as humane; they may or may not approve of government ownership of the railroads or restrictions on immigration.)

Bonus Activity

A Populist Pamphlet

To reinforce understanding of Populist ideas, have small groups create a pamphlet for a Populist rally in a farm state, using art materials or graphics software. Have them choose speakers, themes for speeches, and appropriate entertainment for the rally. Encourage them to use eye-catching graphics and appealing slogans. Display the pamphlets around the classroom.

Teaching the

Link to the Present

Tell students that in the original book Dorothy's magic slippers were silver, not ruby, and ask what significance this fact might have. (Populists saw the free coinage of silver as the way to improve the nation's economy.) Then ask about Baum's attitude toward the government, based on his portrayal of the Wizard and on Baum's Populist sympathies. (He felt that the government was a fraud and that it ruled the people by deception.) Also, ask what they think the wicked witches represent. (Big banks and corporations.) Point out that "oz." is also the abbreviation for ounce, the standard measure for gold.

Vital Links

Coxey's Army (Picture)
Unit 4, Side 1,
Search 12377

See also Unit 4 Explore CD-ROM location 93.

 **History Footnote**

Jacob Coxey's army of marchers included many colorful and eccentric figures. One of the organizers was a painter and philosopher from California named Carl Browne, who liked to dress in fringed buckskin clothes with silver-dollar buttons. Another marcher was Dr. Cyclone Kirkland, who claimed to be able to predict hurricanes with astrology. He wrote an epic poem about the march based on Homer's *Odyssey.* A black minstrel performer, Professor C. B. Freeman, claimed to be the loudest singer in the world. "Dr." Pizarro, a traveling medicine man, was accompanied by a band of Indians. At the head of this ragtag army rode the small, mild-looking "General" Coxey along with his wife and baby son, Legal Tender Coxey.

Link to the Present

The Wizard of Oz

"We're off to see the Wizard!" Whether they have seen the movie or read the book, most American children love *The Wizard of Oz* as much today as when L. Frank Baum wrote it in 1900.

Few realize, though, that the story is an allegory. Beneath the fantasy of Dorothy in the land of the Munchkins, Baum was writing about the problems of farmers and industrial workers.

To Baum, the Scarecrow stood for farmers and the Tin Woodsman for workers. With Dorothy, who stands for ordinary people, and the loud but powerless Cowardly Lion (William Jennings Bryan), they follow the yellow brick road (the gold standard) to the Emerald City, or Washington, D.C.

Like Coxey's Army, they hope that the Wizard—the President—will solve their problems. When they get there, though, they discover that the Wizard is a fraud who can give them no help at all.

machinery. They urged the government to buy and turn into money all the silver now being mined in the West. This group was called "silverites."

Most business leaders feared American money would lose its value if there was too much of it available. They believed money should be based on the value of gold. President Cleveland and many members of Congress, both Democrats and Republicans, agreed. They were called "goldbugs."

As political leaders wrestled with the money question, the depression grew worse. Millions of people fell into deeper distress. Thousands of unemployed men rode the rails from town to town, searching for work.

"Coxey's Army" Jacob Coxey, a farmer in Ohio, decided that something had to be done to help the jobless. In 1894 he organized an "army" of unemployed workers to march to Washington, D.C. He hoped to persuade Congress to put the unemployed to work building roads. Thousands of jobless men from as far away as California responded to his call.

Despite bad weather and other hardships, Coxey and about 1,000 marchers reached the capital. Looking for an excuse to arrest Coxey, police charged him with walking on the grass on his way to make a speech at the Capitol steps. Coxey's army melted away, but the seed of an idea had been planted. The next century would see many marches on Washington, D.C., to protest injustice.

The Election of 1896

When it came time for the presidential election of 1896, the Democrats were in trouble. They were deeply divided over the silver issue. They could not nominate President Cleveland, for he was widely blamed for the depression that still gripped the nation. Could they agree upon a candidate to oppose the Republican, Governor William McKinley of Ohio?

At their convention in Chicago, the Democrats found their leader when William Jennings Bryan, a congressman from Nebraska, stepped up to deliver a speech. Taking a stand for farmers, Bryan electrified his audience as he thundered:

History Footnote

After three unsuccessful campaigns for President in 1896, 1900, and 1908, William Jennings Bryan served as Secretary of State under President Woodrow Wilson from 1913 to 1915. He continued to rally support for his favorite causes—prohibition, woman suffrage, and popular election of United States senators. But he is best remembered for his role in the 1925 trial of teacher John Scopes, who was tried for teaching evolution in the classroom. Bryan, a religious fundamentalist, helped the prosecution convict Scopes. However, Bryan was subjected to an embarrassing cross-examination by the defense attorney Clarence Darrow. Bryan's ignorance of modern science was revealed, and the brutal questioning may have been a cause of Bryan's sudden death only five days after the end of the trial.

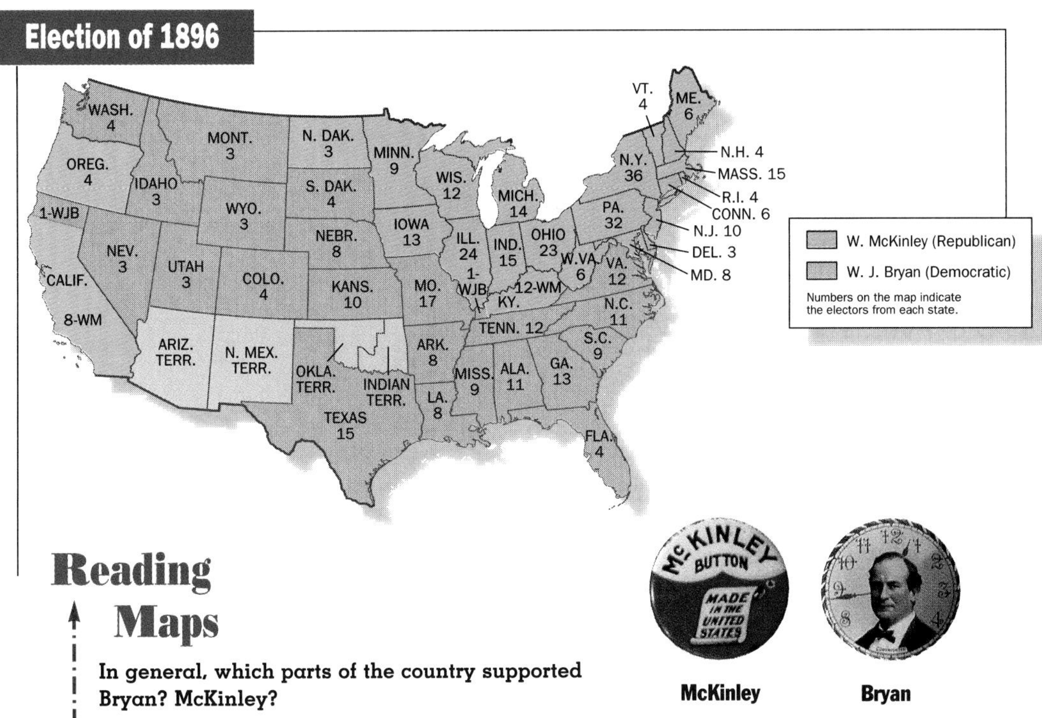

McKinley

Bryan

Reading Maps

In general, which parts of the country supported Bryan? McKinley?

"Burn down your cities and leave our farms, and your cities will spring up again as if by magic. But destroy our farms and the grass will grow in the streets of every city in the country."

To the goldbugs in his audience, Bryan, a silverite, proclaimed: "You shall not crucify mankind upon a cross of gold."

The crowd went wild. Shouting, "Amen!" the convention delegates gave Bryan the nomination. He also won the support of the Populist Party.

Bryan vs. McKinley Rarely had Americans faced such a sharp contrast between candidates. Bryan was for silver. McKinley was for gold. Bryan stormed across the country giving dozens of speeches a day. McKinley campaigned from his front porch.

More people voted in the 1896 election than ever before. The majority, from the more populated industrial states, voted for McKinley.

The election of 1896 spelled the decline of the Populists, but it did not mean defeat for their ideas. Their demand for "equal rights to all, special privileges to none" was soon taken up by a new group of reformers.

2. Section Review

1. Describe three problems that farmers faced in the late 1800s.
2. Why did the Populist Party develop, and what were its goals?
3. Critical Thinking If you had lost your job in the depression that began in 1893, would you have joined Coxey's Army? Give reasons for your answer.

Teaching the Reading Maps

Have students identify the kind of information the map provides (results of 1896 presidential election). Have them discuss why the vote was split.

Answer to Reading Maps: Most states in the South and West supported Bryan and in the East and Midwest, McKinley.

Closing the Section

Wrap-Up Activity

Making a Crossword Puzzle

To review issues discussed in the section, have pairs create crossword puzzles. Ask them to include at least ten clues and answers based on the major issues. Have students exchange puzzles and solve them.

Section Review Answers

1. Falling farm prices due to overproduction and foreign competition; high cost of business due to interest rates; high cost of storage, handling, crop transport.

2. Created by Farmers' Alliances to demand government help; wanted government ownership of railroads, graduated income tax, eight-hour workday, more direct participation in politics.

3. Yes: right to petition the government, a feeling of desperation with nothing to lose. No: fear of being arrested.

Teaching the

Geography Lab

To help students understand the influence of familiar landscapes on our own personal preferences, ask them to discuss what type of landscape they find most appealing. Then ask why a person such as Willa Cather, who had grown up on the Great Plains, might find it more appealing than would a person from New York City. (It is familiar and therefore not threatening; good memories may be associated with life there.) Discuss how immigrants may have felt on first seeing the wide expanses and featureless terrain. (Intimidated, repelled, or attracted to openness and possibilities.)

Developing a Mental Map

Answers

1. N. Dakota, S. Dakota, Nebraska, Kansas, eastern Colorado, Oklahoma, Texas, New Mexico, Wyoming, and Montana; no.

2. Between 500,000 and 750,000 square miles.

3. The elevation gradually increases from east to west.

4. The soil is extremely fertile. The Willa Cather quote supports this: "green and billowy," "stifled in vegetation," "heavy harvests."

5. Those who leave may cite difficulties of making a living and the isolation. Those who stay may cite freedom and independence of farm life.

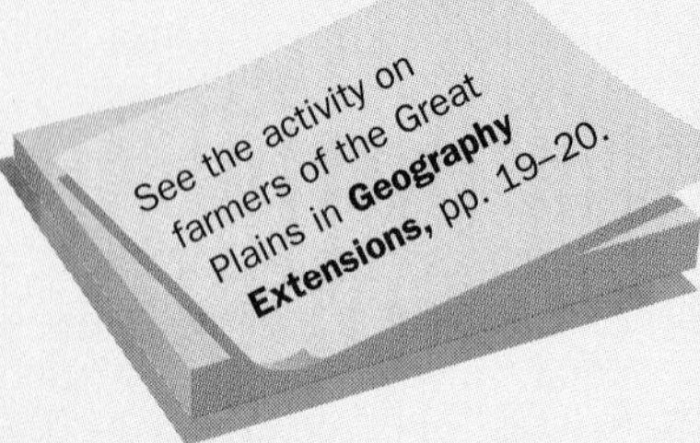

See the activity on farmers of the Great Plains in **Geography Extensions**, pp. 19–20.

Geography Footnote

Many varieties of wheat are grown in the United States. The majority of the wheat is grown in the "Wheat Belt," extending through the Great Plains region. Hard red winter wheat grows in the southern plains, while hard red spring wheat and durum spring wheat grow in the northern plains. Hard red wheat is used mostly for bread flour and durum wheat is used to make pasta. Winter wheat is planted in mild climates in the fall and harvested the next spring. Spring wheat, grown in cold climates, is planted in the spring and harvested in late summer.

Other types of wheat include soft red wheat, used for cakes and cookies, grown mainly in the Midwest, and white wheat, used for cereals and pastries, grown in Michigan, New York, California, and the Northwest.

Geography Lab

The Great Plains

Many of the farmers who were the backbone of the Populist Party lived in the Great Plains region. Wheat covers much of the region, while cattle and sheep graze in the drier areas. The climate of the plains varies, with years of abundant moisture followed by years of drought.

The year 1886 began a decade of especially hot, dry summers. Crops failed and farm families left the land in droves. One wagon heading east carried a sign that read "In God we trusted, in Kansas we busted." Other farmers refused to give up. Author Willa Cather expressed the feelings of those who still found satisfaction in life on the Great Plains. Use her description and the photograph to add to your knowledge of the Great Plains region.

Ripened wheat, Nebraska

Willa Cather's Description

"We were talking about what it is like to spend one's childhood in little towns like these, buried in wheat and corn, under stimulating extremes of climate; burning summers when the world lies green and billowy beneath a brilliant sky, when one is fairly stifled in vegetation, in the color and smell of strong weeds and heavy harvests; blustery winters with little snow, when the whole country is stripped bare and gray as sheet-iron. We agreed that no one who had not grown up in a little prairie town could know anything about it."

Developing a Mental Map

Use the maps on pages R4–R7 and R11 to help answer the questions.

1. Through which states do the Great Plains extend? Does any state lie wholly within the Great Plains?

2. Estimate the area of the Great Plains.

3. If you were driving from east to west over the Great Plains, what would you notice about the elevation?

4. What conclusion about the soil of the Great Plains do you draw from the photograph? What evidence do you find on this page to support the idea that the soil of the Great Plains is extremely fertile?

5. Hands-On Geography Imagine that it is 1892, and you are a farmer on the Great Plains. Your relatives in Chicago want you to leave your farm and move to the city. Write a letter to them, giving your answer and explaining your decision.

Section Objectives

- ★ Explain how Progressives built support for reform.
- ★ Discuss the problems that existed in city and state governments and the solutions that Progressives proposed.
- ★ Discuss how African American leaders worked to influence public affairs.

Teaching Resources

Take-Home Planner 3, pp. 4–11
Chapter Resources Binder
Study Guide, p. 67
Reinforcement, pp. 69–70
Skills Development
Geography Extensions
American Readings, pp. 33–34
Using Historical Documents
Transparency Activities
Chapter and Unit Tests

3. Progressives Battle for Reform

Reading Guide

New Terms direct primary, initiative, recall, referendum, suffragists

Section Focus Progressive efforts to reform city and state governments

1. **How did Progressives build support for reform?**
2. **What problems existed in city and state governments and how did Progressives try to solve them?**
3. **How did African American leaders work to influence public affairs?**

Jane Addams was shocked by the neighborhood in Chicago in which Hull House was situated. She wrote:

> "The streets are inexpressibly dirty, . . . the street lighting bad, [and] the paving miserable. . . . Hundreds of houses are unconnected with the street sewer. . . . Many houses have no water supply save the faucet in the backyards."

Finding that neighborhoods of poor people throughout the city lacked the public services required by law, she set out to force city officials to take action.

Like Jane Addams, people all across the United States were trying to correct injustices. In the early 1900s, their reform efforts blossomed into the Progressive movement.

Progressive Goals

Progressives tackled many problems. They tried to end government corruption and the monopoly power of big business. They fought to improve the conditions of factory workers and to end child labor. They looked for ways to end alcoholism. They struggled to gain woman suffrage.

Whatever their particular interests, Progressives were united in a desire to bring order and fairness to the chaos of a rapidly growing nation. They also believed that people's lives could be improved by putting the public good above self-interest.

The muckrakers Newspapers and magazines helped to make Americans aware of the problems that worried the Progressives. As early as the 1870s, reporter Jacob Riis had described the horrors of New York City slums in his newspaper articles.

In 1902 and 1903 *McClure's Magazine* caused a sensation with a series of articles on John D. Rockefeller's Standard Oil Company. The articles, written by Ida Tarbell, revealed the cutthroat practices that Standard Oil used. "Mr. Rockefeller," Tarbell concluded, "has systematically played with loaded dice."

That same year, Lincoln Steffens uncovered a network of political corruption in St. Louis. Other reporters investigated unsafe factory conditions, especially for working children. David Graham Phillips exposed senators who took thousands of dollars from industrial interests.

Journalists who dug out the dirty secrets of American life earned the name "muckrakers." They bore the title proudly.

Sounding the alarm was just the first step, though. To reform the system, Progressives needed political power.

Introducing the Section

Vocabulary

direct primary (p. 350) election open to all members of a party to choose candidates to run for office

initiative (p. 350) issue placed on the ballot by citizens' petition, to be voted on by the people

recall (p. 350) election held to remove a public official from office

referendum (p. 350) election in which a law passed by the legislature is either approved or disapproved by the voters

suffragists (p. 351) people who supported the right of women to vote

Warm-Up Activity

Solving Society's Problems

To allow students to assume the role of social reformer, write the following problems on the chalkboard: illegal drug use, low voter turnout, bad housing for poor people. Ask them to choose one of the problems and write down three ways society could try to solve it. Have them compare suggestions.

Geography Question of the Day

Tell students that during the late 1800s, millions moved to cities and towns from the countryside. Have them write a paragraph explaining ways this would have made problems facing urban areas harder to solve.

Developing the Section

Section Activity

A Roundtable Discussion

To help students grasp the wide range of issues that reformers addressed during this period, have them create a roundtable discussion featuring reformers. Divide the class into groups of suffragists, NAACP founders, muckraking journalists, temperance workers, and city- and state-level political reformers. Have the groups list issues important to them and strategies for convincing politicians to listen. Then have each group choose a representative to the round table, where reformers can discuss their goals and methods. Ask the class to identify points of common interest as well as disagreements.

Vital Links

Tweed Ring cartoon (Picture) Unit 4, Side 1, Search 15028

See also Unit 4 Explore CD-ROM location 129.

Connections to Language Arts

The term *muckrakers* comes from the seventeenth century English religious parable *Pilgrim's Progress,* by John Bunyan. In this work, the man with the muckrake is so obsessed with worldly things that he cannot look up to heaven. A muckrake is a rake used to spread muck, or manure. Some sources claim Theodore Roosevelt first applied the term to journalists and social reformers.

See the Study Guide activity in **Chapter Resources Binder,** p. 67.

City Government

Cities presented the first real challenge to Progressives. As you read in Chapter 6, most of the nation's major cities were controlled by corrupt political machines.

Jane Addams knew machine politics well. She lived in Chicago's Nineteenth Ward. Garbage collectors in the ward saw their jobs as a reward for political loyalty, not as an important service. To get the garbage off the streets, Addams herself took on the job of garbage inspector.

The Tweed Ring One of the most corrupt political machines in the nation was run by "Boss" William Marcy Tweed. Between 1869 and 1871, members of the Tweed Ring stole more than $75 million from New York City. They made millions more by accepting bribes from private contractors.

The Tweed Ring controlled the mayor, the city council, the district attorney, and municipal judges. Tweed's power reached to the state legislature and even to the governor.

In 1871 muckraking articles in *Harper's Weekly* exposed the corrupt practices of the Tweed Ring. Boss Tweed was arrested and sent to jail, and the ring broke up.

Reforming the cities Gradually, in one city after another, groups of reformers organized to end corruption. Often the groups united behind a candidate who promised to fight the city's political machine. Between 1889 and 1901, reform mayors were elected in Detroit, Toledo, San Francisco, Cleveland, and New York City.

Reformers also experimented with new forms of city government. After a hurricane destroyed Galveston, Texas, in 1900, citizens set up a commission form of government to rebuild the city. Instead of a mayor and council, voters elected a group of commissioners. Each commissioner took charge of a single department, such as sanitation or finance, and hired experts to run it.

Even more popular was the city-manager form of government. It was first established in Staunton, Virginia, in 1908. There, voters elected a city council to pass laws. The council then hired a city manager—an expert in urban government—to take care of day-to-day city business.

This scene of garbage on a New York City street could have been found in any of the nation's overcrowded cities. Trash, ashes from stoves, and horse manure piled up on streets and in empty lots. It was not surprising that city dwellers were plagued by the stench as well as by diseases.

History Footnote

William Marcy Tweed and Thomas Nast will forever be linked, based on Nast's famous cartoons attacking the Tweed ring and its widespread corruption. However, as a boy growing up in New York City, Nast idolized Tweed, who was the dashing commander of the local fire department. The fire engine had a fierce tiger painted on its side. Both the boy and the fire department captain went on to bigger things. Tweed stole millions of dollars from the city as head of the corrupt Tammany Hall political machine. Nast became one of Tweed's worst foes. Remembering the tiger on the fire engine, he created the "Tammany tiger" as his symbol for the ferociously corrupt Tweed and his henchmen. After Tweed escaped to Europe with his stolen money, he was caught by Spanish police who recognized him from a Nast cartoon.

Link to Art

Thomas Nast As chief cartoonist for *Harper's Weekly* from 1862 to 1886, Thomas Nast used his skills as an artist to carry the message of reform to the magazine's readers. At a time when newspapers and magazines were Americans' main source of information, Nast made the cartoon an important political force. This 1871 cartoon was one of a series that helped bring about the downfall of Boss Tweed. **Discuss** In this cartoon, what does Nast want you to think about the power of the Tweed Ring? How does he accomplish his goal?

State Government

Unfortunately, corrupt state governments often blocked the Progressives' reforms in the cities. In many states, the governor and the legislature were in the hands of a political machine controlled by the major state industry, such as the railroads in California and the lumber industry in Wisconsin.

Robert La Follette In trying to reform state governments, Democratic and Republican Progressives often worked together. They found a champion in Robert M. La Follette of Wisconsin. Twice defeated by the state's political machine, "Fighting Bob" finally won election as governor in 1900.

La Follette hired experts to help solve the state's problems. They advised him on

Discussion

Checking Understanding

1. Why was the Tweed ring so powerful? (It controlled most of New York's city government and also had influence in the state government.)

Stimulating Critical Thinking

2. Which level of government would you have chosen to reform first—city or state? Explain. (Those choosing cities may cite the nature of city services, such as garbage collecting and sanitation, which have more of an immediate impact on people's lives, as well as the more manageable size of cities. Those choosing states may cite greater need to reform the larger arena affecting more people.)

Teaching the Link to Art

Have students identify the cartoon's setting and what the setting refers to (ancient Rome; Romans unleashing wild animals on early Christians and others). Ask why this situation fits Nast's purpose. (He sees New Yorkers as innocent victims of the corrupt "Emperor" Tweed.) Point out that Boss Tweed is sitting in the emperor's place, above the seal on the wall. **Discussion Answers:** Answers should reflect understanding of Nast's opposition to Tweed, as well as the techniques of cartoonists to attack opponents.

Bonus Activity

Describing a Protest

To focus on reform movements, ask students to write eyewitness accounts of a protest by one of the reform groups discussed in the section: suffragists, African Americans, temperance workers, or municipal or state reformers. Remind them to make their accounts as vivid as possible, to set the stage appropriately, and to provide information on the cause, people involved, and results of the protest. Have volunteers read their accounts to the class.

Vital Links

Suffragists' march (Movie) Unit 4, Side 1, Search 22245, Play to 22753

See also Unit 4 Explore CD-ROM location 212.

Connections to Civics

Until the end of the 1800s, voting procedures in the United States were vulnerable to all sorts of confusion and fraudulent practices. Starting in the early 1800s, political parties provided voters with their own ballots, which were often distinctly colored. This allowed illiterate voters to support the party of their choice. However it also made privacy impossible, so political bosses could pay people to vote their way. In 1888 Massachusetts became the first state to adopt the "Australian ballot," first used in that country in 1856. The Australian ballot featured voter lists and a single official ballot, with the names and party affiliations of all candidates, marked in the privacy of a voting booth. This method of voting was soon adopted by all states.

Direct Democracy Reforms

Reform	Effect
Direct election of senators (17th Amendment)	The voters of each state, instead of the legislature, elect their senators.
Direct primary	An election, open to all party members, is held to choose the party's candidates for office.
Initiative	Citizens who want a law that the legislature will not pass can petition to put it on the ballot.
Recall	An elected official can be removed from office by a vote of the people before the end of his or her term.
Referendum	Citizens who do not like a law that was passed by the legislature can petition to put it on the ballot.
Secret ballot	Voters receive an official ballot and vote in a private booth.

reforming the civil service, regulating railroads, and conserving natural resources.

Direct democracy To break the power of Wisconsin's political machine and make the legislature more responsive to the voters, La Follette urged reforms. For example, Wisconsin adopted the **direct primary**—an election, open to all members of a party, to choose candidates to run for office. No longer would party bosses choose candidates behind closed doors.

Encouraged by La Follette's success, Progressives throughout the nation pushed for reforms that forced legislatures to share power with ordinary citizens. By 1916, more than half the states had adopted at least one of the reforms described in the table above.

Laws to Protect Workers

Once they had elected their candidates to governorships and state legislatures, Progressives worked toward their goal of improving people's lives. High on their list was the health and safety of factory workers.

In 1892 Florence Kelley, who worked at Hull House, visited garment factories and sweatshops, collecting evidence on the danger of long hours and unsafe machinery. As a result of her investigations, Illinois passed laws banning child labor and limiting the hours of factory work for women. As the state's first chief factory inspector, Kelley later enforced the laws.

In 1902 Maryland passed the first workers' compensation law to provide income for workers injured on the job. Oregon set limits on the hours women could work. Soon other states passed similar laws.

Temperance Movement

Some Progressives, disturbed by poverty and crime, placed the blame on liquor. They joined the temperance movement, which since the 1830s had been calling attention to the evil effects of alcohol.

In 1873 women in Ohio began to hold prayer meetings at saloons. A year later they formed the Women's Christian Temperance Union (WCTU). It became the largest women's organization in the world, with hundreds of thousands of members.

Tips for Teaching

Kinesthetic Learners

Kinesthetic learners benefit from lessons illustrated by physical activity. Use this procedure to dramatize the issue of suffrage in the early 1900s. Have all students stand. Then ask all students whose birthdays are in January through June to sit down. Then ask students who are wearing an item of green clothing to sit down. Ask seated students how they would feel if only those standing were allowed to vote.

Remind them that in 1900 not every citizen had the right to vote. Voting rights were denied to women, and although African American men gained the right to vote in 1870, they were intimidated to keep them away from the polls.

Discussion

Checking Understanding

1. What kinds of laws were passed to protect workers? (Banning of child labor; limited hours women could work in factories; workers' compensation for those injured on job.)

2. Why did some Progressives want to ban the consumption of alcoholic beverages? (Blamed alcohol for poverty and crime.)

Stimulating Critical Thinking

3. Do you think women are more likely than men to support reformers? Explain. (Yes: tend to be more sympathetic to needs of underprivileged. No: no difference in inclinations to favor liberals or reformers.)

Teaching the Reading Maps

Have students examine the map and identify the major information it provides. (Spread of suffrage granted to women by states.) Ask: **What do the states that granted suffrage to women before 1915 have in common?** (They are all western states.) **Answers to Reading Maps:** Woman suffrage began in Utah and Wyoming. It spread throughout the West and began to spread east.

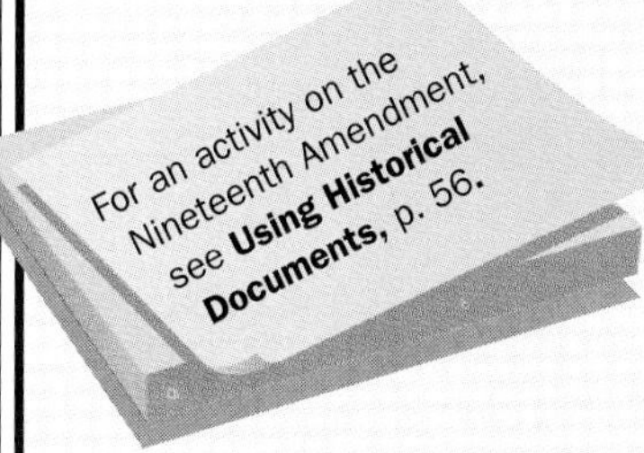

Spread of Woman Suffrage

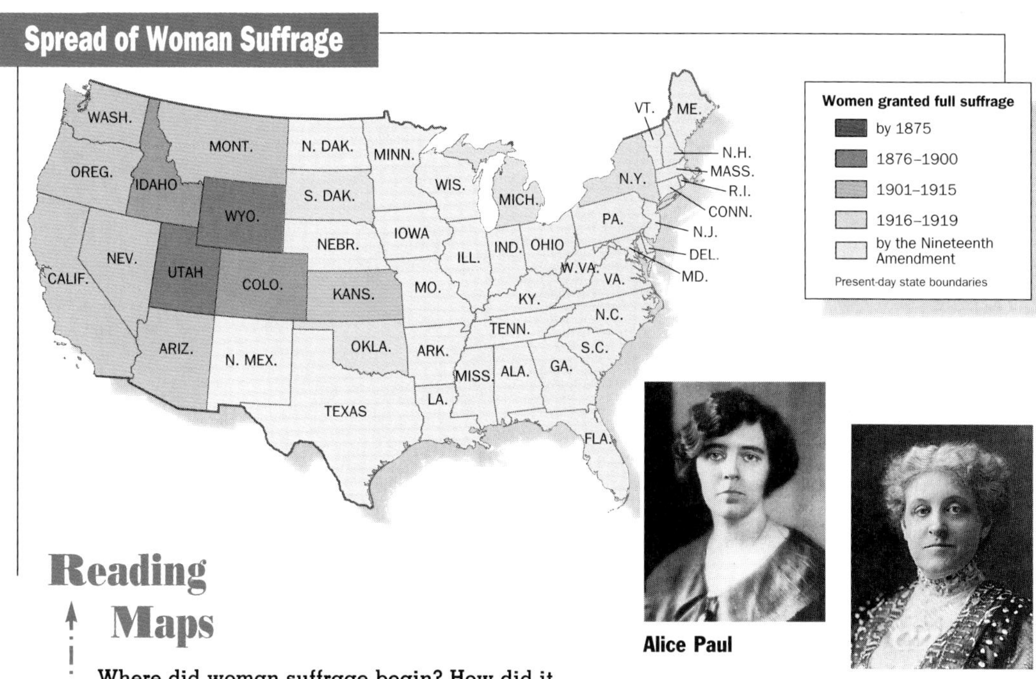

Alice Paul

Carrie Chapman Catt

Reading Maps

Where did woman suffrage begin? How did it spread between 1875 and 1920?

Frances Willard led the WCTU. She traveled tirelessly throughout the country, calling for laws to control the sale of liquor. By 1914, one-fourth of the states had banned the sale of alcoholic beverages.

Woman Suffrage

Like Frances Willard, many Progressives were **suffragists**—people who supported the right of women to vote. If women could vote, suffragists argued, they could help to elect reform candidates.

The battle for woman suffrage had been going on since Elizabeth Cady Stanton's Seneca Falls Declaration of July 1848. Still, by 1915, only 11 states had granted full voting rights to women.

Progressives like Jane Addams brought new energy to the suffrage movement. In 1916 a spirited young woman named Alice Paul formed the National Woman's Party to demand that Congress pass a constitutional amendment giving women the vote. She led parades and even picketed the White House.

Meanwhile, Carrie Chapman Catt led the National American Woman Suffrage Association in a campaign to flood Congress with petitions. Suffragists took to the streets, urging people to sign their petitions.

Finally in 1919 Congress approved the Nineteenth Amendment, granting equal suffrage to women. The next challenge was to win ratification by at least 36 of the 48 states.

In August 1920 the 36th state, Tennessee, considered the suffrage amendment. The state senate quickly passed it, but the house was deadlocked for ten days.

Finally, the house ratified the amendment by a margin of only two votes. One of

Closing the Section

Wrap-Up Activity

Creating a Reforms Chart

To summarize reform movements, have students fill in a chart with columns headed *Group, Reform Sought, Issues, Outstanding Figures,* and *Successes.* Answers for the temperance movement, for example, might include prohibition of manufacture and sale of alcohol; drinking as cause of crime and poverty; Frances Willard; one-fourth of states banned alcohol by 1914.

Section Review

Answers

1. Definitions: *direct primary* (350), *initiative* (350), *recall* (350), *referendum* (350), *suffragists* (351)

2. Muckrakers helped make Americans aware of Progressives' concerns and built support for the movement.

3. Progressives united behind a candidate who promised to fight the city machine; they experimented with new forms of city government.

4. White and black reformers used speeches and the press to highlight problems. Blacks worked with whites on issues such as woman suffrage but often had to work alone against segregation and lynching. Few white reformers took an interest in black issues.

History Footnote

The term *lynching* is generally believed to be derived from a Virginia judge, Charles Lynch, who allowed Patriots to punish British sympathizers during the Revolution without due process of law. During the settlement of the West, pioneers often resorted to lynching to punish murder, horse theft, and other crimes. However, lynching is most closely associated with the South. Before the Civil War, victims were usually white abolitionists. After the war, most lynchings were committed against blacks.

For Ida Wells-Barnett's description of lynchings in the North, see **American Readings**, pp. 33–34.

IS THIS CIVILIZATION?

The anti-lynching crusade that Ida Wells-Barnett began grew to include protest marches and legal action by the NAACP.

those votes was cast by Representative Harry Burn. His district opposed ratification, but Burn had taken the advice of his mother, who wrote to her son, "Don't forget to be a good boy and help Mrs. Catt."

African Americans Seek Equality

Many African American women had supported woman suffrage as part of their larger struggle for equality. Mary Church Terrell, president of the National Association of Colored Women, was a favorite speaker at suffrage conventions.

Few Progressives, however, took an interest in the issues that most concerned black Americans. It was up to African Americans themselves to raise their voices against the injustices of segregation and the violence of lynching they faced in both the South and the North.

Crusade against lynching Between 1892 and 1903, nearly 3,000 African Americans were lynched, mostly by southern mobs. Ida Wells-Barnett, the African American editor of the *Memphis Free Speech,* spoke out fearlessly against lynchings. When a white mob lynched three black men in 1892, she urged black citizens to

> "leave a town which will neither protect our lives and property, nor give us a fair trial in the courts."

Taking her advice, 2,000 African Americans moved out of Memphis.

An angry mob wrecked Wells-Barnett's presses and threatened her life. She simply moved north and continued her crusade by writing and speaking against lynching.

The NAACP In 1909 black leaders, including W. E. B. Du Bois, Ida Wells-Barnett, and Mary Church Terrell, formed the NAACP to fight for racial justice (see page 201). A number of white Progressives joined them in their efforts. One who did was Jane Addams.

The NAACP won several legal battles, and membership grew rapidly. Although it failed to get Congress to pass an anti-lynching law, the NAACP became an important voice for the rights of black Americans.

3. Section Review

1. Define **direct primary, initiative, recall, referendum,** and **suffragists.**
2. What was the relationship between muckrakers and the Progressive movement?
3. What are two ways that Progressives brought about change in city government?
4. Critical Thinking What similarities can you find between the issues and methods of white and black reformers? What differences?

Section Objectives

- ★ Explain how President Roosevelt increased the power of the federal government.
- ★ Discuss ways President Taft followed Roosevelt's policies.
- ★ Explain how President Wilson extended Progressive reform.

Teaching Resources

Take-Home Planner 3, pp. 4–11
Chapter Resources Binder
Study Guide, p. 68
Reinforcement
Skills Development
Geography Extensions
American Readings, pp. 35–36
Using Historical Documents
Transparency Activities
Chapter and Unit Tests, pp. 63–66

4. Progressive Presidents

Reading Guide

New Term conservation

Section Focus The reforms that the federal government carried out under Progressive Presidents

1. How did President Roosevelt increase the power of the federal government?
2. In what ways did President Taft follow Roosevelt's policies?
3. How did President Wilson extend Progressive reform?

Theodore Roosevelt, the reform governor of New York, had a decision to make. President William McKinley, who was running for re-election in 1900, had asked him to be the vice-presidential candidate. Vice-Presidents had little to do, though. "I could not *do* anything," Roosevelt worried, "and yet I would be seeing continually things I would like to do." Very reluctantly, he accepted.

McKinley and Roosevelt won the election. Then, on September 6, 1901, only six months into his new term, McKinley was killed by a man later judged to be insane. Theodore Roosevelt became President. The nation now had a reform-minded leader.

Trustbusting

Like most Republicans, Roosevelt believed that big business was good for the United States. Unlike them, he realized that big business often ignored the needs of the public. Therefore, he argued, it was government's reponsibility to regulate business—especially trusts. He declared:

> "We do not want to destroy corporations, but we do wish to make them [serve] the public good."

The Northern Securities case Regulating railroads was high on Roosevelt's list. When Congress refused to pass new laws to control the railroads' monopoly power over shipping rates, the President took action.

First, he had the Attorney General gather evidence that the Northern Securities Company, a railroad trust, was using unfair business practices. Then in 1902 the federal government sued the Northern Securities Company for violating the Sherman Antitrust Act of 1890.

The business world was amazed. It was like "a thunderbolt out of a clear sky," reported the *New York Tribune*. Roosevelt's career as a "trustbuster" had begun. During his presidency the government filed suit against dozens of trusts. In two major victories, it broke up the Northern Securities Company and John D. Rockefeller's oil trust.

The Coal Strike

President Roosevelt's actions reflected his belief that the government should play an important role in the economic affairs of the nation. He had the opportunity to expand that role when a coal strike threatened the nation's fuel supply. In the spring of 1902, 150,000 coal miners in Pennsylvania went on strike for higher wages and an eight-hour workday.

The representative of the mine owners, George Baer, refused to negotiate with the

Introducing the Section

Vocabulary

conservation (p. 355) protecting natural resources and using them wisely

Warm-Up Activity

Evaluating the Power of Trusts

To introduce the topic of the power of trusts, have students imagine that one company—MegaFood—owns all the fast food chains in the country. Ask them how they think prices and quality of MegaFood's restaurants would compare to those they eat at today. Have them discuss their ideas.

Geography Question of the Day

Ask students to list natural resources, such as water, forests, and oil. Then have them explain whether they think the federal government should have some control over these resources.

See the Study Guide activity in **Chapter Resources Binder**, p. 68.

Developing the Section

Teaching the Point of View

Ask students to consider why each side may have held the opinion it expressed. Then have them discuss whether, as the owners claim, unions have no right to interfere with their management, or, as the union claims, workers must unite in order to protect their jobs, rights, and incomes.

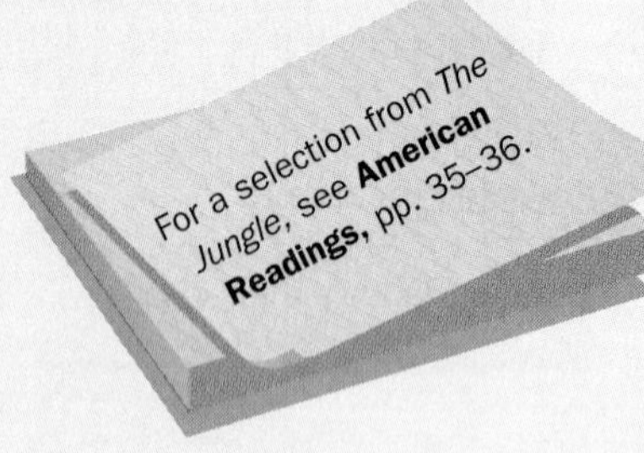
For a selection from The Jungle, see American Readings, pp. 35–36.

Vital Links

Slaughterhouse (Picture) Unit 4, Side 1, Search 09421

See also Unit 4 Explore CD-ROM location 62.

The Jungle (Picture) Unit 4, Side 1, Search 12341

See also Unit 4 Explore CD-ROM location 88.

History Footnote

In 1902 Theodore Roosevelt, famous for his conservation sentiments and love of the outdoors, took a hunting trip. While on this trip, he refused to shoot a captured grizzly bear cub. The incident was featured in a popular editorial cartoon. Soon after, a New York couple, Rose and Morris Michtom, began manufacturing a stuffed toy bear, which they named "teddy bear" in honor of the President.

As coal became scarce during the 1902 strike, the price soared. This photo shows poor New Yorkers lined up to buy coal by the bag.

United Mine Workers (UMW), led by John Mitchell. The strike continued, and the nation began to run out of coal.

President Roosevelt invited both sides to the White House, but even there, mine owners refused to talk to UMW leaders. Roosevelt, furious at Baer's attitude, later said:

> "If it wasn't for the high office I hold, I would have taken him by the seat of the breeches and the nape of his neck and chucked him out of that window."

Roosevelt threatened to send troops to take over the mines. Alarmed, the mine owners agreed to government arbitration. The result was a wage increase and shorter workday for the miners.

For the first time the federal government had stepped in, not to break up a strike, but to bring about a peaceful settlement. Later Roosevelt said he had simply been trying to be fair—giving both miners and owners "a square deal."

Point of View

How should labor disputes be resolved?

Efforts to resolve the 1902 coal strike showed the wide gap between business and labor. The mine owners refused to accept unions as legal organizations. At the hearings on the coal strike, George Baer declared:

> "We do not admit the right of an organization [a union] to . . . interfere with our management."

UMW lawyer Clarence Darrow asserted that miners had the right to organize. Unless they had a union, the miners would have to

> "come to [the owners] with their hat in their hand, each one in a position to be [fired] . . . if they raise their voice."

In the years to come, unions would continue to grow. More and more, business and organized labor would sit down together to work out their differences.

Connections to Geography

Even before he became President, Theodore Roosevelt was strongly committed to conservation. The two years he spent in the 1880s ranching and hunting in the Dakota Territory gave him a love and respect for the natural wonders of the American West. In seven years Roosevelt placed 194 million acres under federal protection. Several of the country's most beloved national parks became the property of all Americans during his presidency. These include Crater Lake in Oregon and Mesa Verde in Colorado. Theodore Roosevelt National Park in North Dakota's Badlands became a National Park in 1978. The park includes Roosevelt's Elkhorn Ranch, his residence from the 1880s.

The Square Deal

In the election of 1904, Roosevelt campaigned for "a square deal all around." Americans liked what they heard and elected him President by a large margin. A happy Roosevelt told his wife, "I am no longer a political accident." Meanwhile, Progressives like "Fighting Bob" La Follette were being elected to Congress. There they offered Roosevelt support for further reforms.

Curbing railroad rates Roosevelt continued to strengthen the power of the federal government by persuading Congress to pass new regulatory laws. To curb high railroad rates, he supported the Hepburn Act. Passed by Congress in 1906, it gave the Interstate Commerce Commission (ICC) the power to set the maximum rates that railroads could charge.

Regulating food and drugs For years reformers had urged Congress to pass food-inspection laws. Then in 1906 the muckraker Upton Sinclair published *The Jungle*. Sinclair's novel described the filthy conditions in the Chicago meatpacking industry. To kill rats, Sinclair wrote,

> "the packers would put poisoned bread out for them, they would die, and then rats, bread, and meat, would go into the hoppers together."

Horrified by *The Jungle*, Roosevelt demanded action. In 1906 Congress passed the Meat Inspection Act, setting sanitary standards for meatpacking and requiring federal inspection of meats sold in interstate commerce.

That year Congress also passed the Pure Food and Drug Act. This law required manufacturers to list the ingredients they used and to tell the truth about what medicines could do.

Conservation

President Roosevelt was also committed to **conservation**—protecting natural resources and using them wisely. He worried that the nation was using its natural resources at too rapid a rate. He asked the nation's leaders to think about

> "what will happen when our forests are gone, when the coal, the iron, the oil, and the gas are exhausted."

With the help of his friend Gifford Pinchot (PIN-shō), the chief of the United States Forest Service, Roosevelt set out to protect the nation's remaining forests. During his presidency he turned 150 million acres of government-owned timberlands into forest reserves, where logging was regulated.

John Muir (right), shown here with President Roosevelt at Yosemite National Park, rallied support for preserving the nation's wilderness areas.

Discussion

Checking Understanding

1. What was the significance of Roosevelt's intervention in the coal strike of 1902? (It was the first time the federal government had intervened, not to break a strike, but to bring about a peaceful settlement.)

2. Name three areas in which Roosevelt helped pass reform laws. (Curbing railroad rates, regulating food and drugs, and promoting conservation.)

Stimulating Critical Thinking

3. Why do you think a novel like *The Jungle*, or other work of art such as a film, poem, painting, or photograph, can have such a powerful influence on people's opinions? (Creative works can grip our imaginations more strongly than dry facts; adding a story and human interest to social issues makes them come alive.)

Section Activity

Creating a Roosevelt Song or Poem

To help students understand Roosevelt's reforms and the reasons for and against those reforms, have groups write two folk songs or poems—one from the point of view of a Roosevelt supporter, and one from the point of view of a Roosevelt opponent. Ask groups to share their songs or poems with the class.

Bonus Activity

Writing Campaign Slogans

To reinforce students' understanding of the main views of each Progressive President, have them imagine they are campaign managers for Roosevelt, Taft, and Wilson, working individually to create catchy and convincing campaign slogans for each man. Have volunteers present their slogans to the class, and have the class conclude which slogans best reflect each candidate.

Theodore Roosevelt in Yosemite (Picture) Unit 4, Side 1, Search 07467

See also Unit 4 Explore CD-ROM location 25.

History Footnote

William Howard Taft holds two quite different distinctions. He is the only person to have served as both President of the United States and Chief Justice of the Supreme Court. An enthusiastic sportsman, at a 1910 Washington Senators game Taft became the first President to throw out the ceremonial first ball to open the baseball season.

Roosevelt achieved other victories as well. At the urging of naturalist John Muir, he created national parks to preserve some areas of wilderness in their natural states.

From Roosevelt to Taft

Roosevelt yearned to do battle for more reforms, but he had promised to serve only two terms. In 1908 he asked his Secretary of War, William Howard Taft of Ohio, to be the Republican candidate for President. Roosevelt's great popularity with the voters helped Taft win the election.

Calm and easygoing, President Taft was a very different man from Roosevelt. "I don't like politics," Taft wrote. "I don't like the limelight." Instead, he preferred to work quietly, behind the scenes.

Taft carried on Roosevelt's policies, urging Congress to pass new regulatory laws. In 1910 Congress passed the Mann-Elkins Act, which gave the ICC the power to regulate telephone and telegraph companies. Taft also used the Sherman Act even more vigorously against trusts than Roosevelt had.

During Taft's presidency, Congress approved the Sixteenth Amendment, which was ratified by the states in 1913. Originally called for by the Populists, it gave Congress the power to enact a federal income tax. Also ratified in 1913, the Seventeenth Amendment called for direct election of senators by the voters instead of by state legislatures.

Still, some of Taft's actions enraged Progressives. He supported high protective tariffs, forcing Americans to pay more for imported goods. He also fired Gifford Pinchot for disloyalty.

Wilson and Reform

By the presidential election of 1912, the Republicans were badly split. When the party nominated Taft for a second term, the Progressives walked out. They formed the new Progressive Party and nominated Roosevelt, who declared he was "fit as a bull moose . . . and ready for the fight." The party became known as the "Bull Moose" Party.

Roosevelt won more votes than Taft, but neither could defeat the Democratic candidate, Woodrow Wilson. As a native of the South and the reform governor of New Jersey, Wilson had wide appeal.

Lower tariffs Soon after taking office, Wilson proposed reforms long called for by Populists and Democratic Progressives. His first goal was to reduce tariffs. At his urging, Congress passed the Underwood Tariff in 1913. It lowered tariff rates for the first time since the Civil War.

The Federal Reserve System Next, Wilson set out to reform the nation's banking and currency system. Problems with the system had helped cause the Panic of 1893 (page 343) and another in 1907.

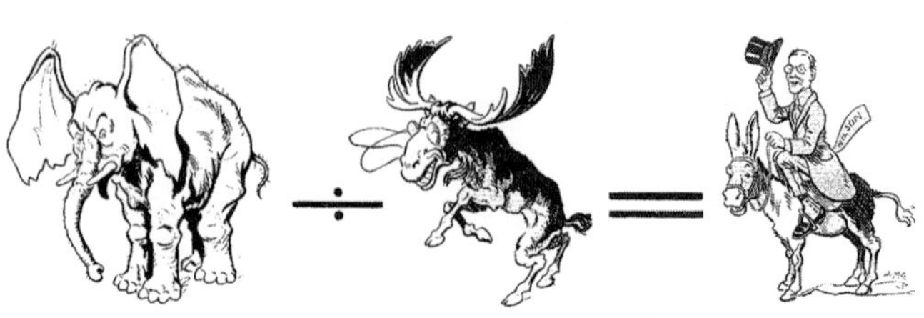

Before the election of 1912, a cartoonist predicted the results of the split in the Republican Party caused by Roosevelt's Bull Moose Party.

Connections to Economics

Federal Reserve notes were created by President Woodrow Wilson's bank reforms of 1913, and have remained the most common type of United States currency. Another type of currency, the silver certificate, was created by an act of Congress in 1890. Silver certificates were in circulation until 1968. These bills, along with bills backed by gold, were redeemable until 1934 for a set amount of gold or silver money. Coins actually containing gold were circulated in the United States until 1934, when the federal government put a stop to the coining of gold and its use as legal tender. Silver dollars were issued until 1965.

In 1913 Congress passed the Federal Reserve Act, which created the Federal Reserve System. New government banks took control of the nation's currency by issuing Federal Reserve notes. These bills make up nearly all the paper money issued in the United States today.

Antitrust laws When it came to breaking up the power of trusts, Wilson took even stronger action than had Roosevelt or Taft. In 1914 Wilson pushed Congress to create the Federal Trade Commission, which had power to control unfair trade practices. Congress also armed the President with the Clayton Antitrust Act of 1914, which allowed him to enforce antitrust rules against more companies than any President before him.

At the end of his first term, Wilson could say with pride: "We have . . . come very near to carrying out the platform of the Progressive Party as well as our own, for we also are Progressives."

4. Section Review

1. Define **conservation.**
2. In what ways did Taft follow Roosevelt's policies?
3. Give two examples of how Wilson extended Progressive reform.
4. **Critical Thinking** What benefits do you see in the government trying to intervene in strikes? What dangers?

Why We Remember

An Era of Reform

Today we look back on the Gilded Age and the Progessive Era as a time of corrupt politicians and earnest reformers. It was more than that, though. In many ways it was a testing time for democracy.

For much of this period after the Civil War, it seemed to many Americans that democracy was not working well. The two major political parties ignored the most important issues of the day. At the same time, business interests and political machines wielded far more power than ordinary voters at every level of government. Jane Addams found corruption not only in Chicago's city hall, but also in city schools.

Instead of giving up on democratic government, Americans set to work to fix what was wrong. Sometimes their efforts ended in disappointment and sometimes in success. Most important, the people made their voices heard, and government began to respond. Looking back on this era, Jane Addams wrote, "At moments we believed that we were witnessing a new pioneering of the human spirit." It was that spirit that kept democracy alive through discouraging times.

Closing the Section

Wrap-Up Activity

Guessing an Identity

To review accomplishments of the three Presidents discussed in the section, have students work in pairs and write "Who Am I?" profiles. One student will prepare a list of statements about a President, beginning with harder clues and moving on to easier ones. When the identity of the President is guessed, students trade roles.

Section Review Answers

1. Definition: *conservation* (355)

2. Pushed Congress to regulate telephone and telegraph companies; broke up monopolies.

3. Reduced tariffs, reformed banking and currency systems, created Federal Trade Commission, pushed passage of Clayton Antitrust Act.

4. Benefits: strikes may be settled more quickly, limiting economic hardship and loss of business; government can affect outcome for public good. Dangers: government may favor one side; may cause ill will because of tactics to force settlement; issues may not be fully resolved.

To check understanding of "Why We Remember," assign Thinking Critically question 3 on student page 358.

Survey Answers

Reviewing Vocabulary

Definitions are found on these pages: *civil service* (338), *direct primary* (350), *initiative* (350), *recall* (350), *referendum* (350), *suffragists* (351), *conservation* (355).

Reviewing Main Ideas

1. The spoils system had filled government jobs with loyal party supporters who were often unqualified and/or dishonest.

2. Farmers, who were growing more than the United States market needed, faced tough competition from abroad. The resulting falling prices, coupled with high interest rates and high transportation and storage costs, led to higher expenses, even though they were earning less.

3. In 1892, the Farmers' Alliances formed the Populist Party. Populists proposed reforms that appealed to farmers, but not to businesspeople and immigrants. Although the Populist candidate did well in the 1892 election, Cleveland was elected and ignored Populist ideas. The Panic of 1893 led to major disagreements between Populists and members of other parties on how to reform the nation's money system. Bryan, supported by both Democrats and Populists, lost the election of 1896 to McKinley, a goldbug. The Populist Party declined.

4. (a) Commission and city manager forms of government. (b) Ordinary citizens gained political power once held by machine politicians and state legislatures.

5. (a) Child labor laws, laws limiting hours of work for women, workers' compensation. (b) Ban in some states on the sale of alcoholic beverages. (c) Adoption of the Nineteenth Amendment.

6. Regulated trusts, arbitrated

(Answers continued in top margin)

the 1902 coal strike, urged Congress to regulate railroad rates and pass food and drug regulations, adopted conservation policies.

7. Urged Congress to lower tariffs, helped create the Federal Reserve system, increased antitrust enforcement, helped create the Federal Trade Commission.

Thinking Critically

1. Many Populist policies were adopted, including reducing tariffs; government regulation, although not ownership, of railroads; a graduated income tax; workplace protection; and more direct participation in politics through direct election of senators, initiative, and referendum.

2. It is a fight for the ideals on which the nation was founded, as expressed in the Declaration of Independence.

3. There can be legitimate differences of

Chapter Survey

Reviewing Vocabulary

Define the following terms.

1. civil service
2. direct primary
3. initiative
4. recall
5. referendum
6. suffragists
7. conservation

Reviewing Main Ideas

1. Why was civil-service reform an important issue in the Gilded Age?
2. How did falling farm prices contribute to farmers' troubles?
3. Trace the development of the Populist Party from its birth in 1892 through the presidential election of 1896.
4. (a) What new forms of city government did Progressives introduce? (b) What was the overall effect of Progressive reforms in state government?
5. What achievements could Progressives point to in each of the following areas? (a) protection of workers (b) temperance (c) woman suffrage
6. Give three examples of how President Roosevelt increased the power of the federal government.
7. How did President Wilson help to achieve Progressive goals?

Thinking Critically

1. Analysis Support the following statement with three examples from the chapter: Populist ideas triumphed even though the Populist Party declined.
2. Evaluation W. E. B. Du Bois said that the African American battle for equality was "not for ourselves alone but for all true Americans." What do you think he meant? Do you agree? Why or why not?
3. Why We Remember: Application Progressives like Jane Addams and Robert La Follette had faith that the American people would always do what was right. Was that faith justified, or not? Support your answer with evidence from the chapter and your own observations.

Applying Skills

Interpreting a political cartoon Find a political cartoon about a person or a current issue in government. Keeping in mind what you learned on page 340, identify the main subject and details of the cartoon. Then write the following:

- a brief summary of the cartoon's message
- a statement of how you think the cartoonist feels about the subject

History Mystery

President Arthur changes his mind Answer the History Mystery on page 333. Chester Arthur had been appointed collector of import duties for the Port of New York in 1871. In this position he used the spoils system to reward Republican Party workers with government jobs. In 1878 Arthur was removed by President Hayes for violating an executive order banning federal officials from taking part in political party activities. Why do you think such a ban was a good idea?

Writing in Your History Journal

1. Keys to History (a) The time line on pages 332–333 has eight Keys to History. In your journal, describe why each is important to know about. (b) Choose a key event and imagine yourself as a newspaper reporter assigned to cover it. In your journal, write an article about the event, including its causes and possible effects.

opinion over what is "right." Yes: prohibition, election of candidates pledged to end corruption, and passage of reform legislation in many areas. No: the election of corrupt officials and lack of interest in civil rights issues. Students may also cite current issues to back up their opinions.

Applying Skills

Answers should reflect understanding of the Procedure steps and Skill Tips on page 340, as well as the ability to recognize and interpret specific devices such as symbols and caricatures.

History Mystery

Arthur changed his mind after President Garfield was killed by someone who wanted a government job and did not get it. The ban was a good idea because it curbed corruption.

(Answers continued in side margin)

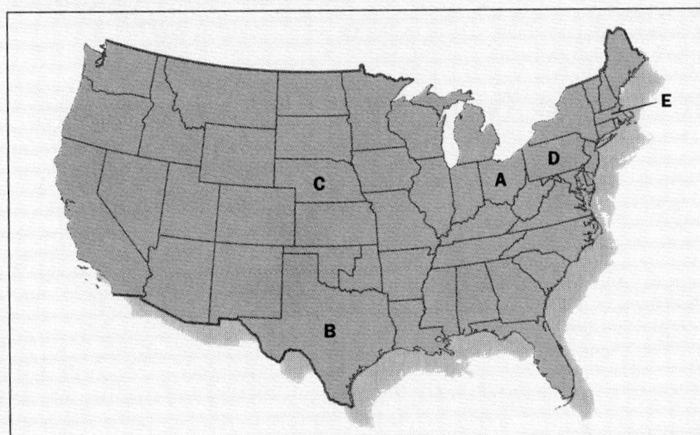

Reviewing Geography

1. For each letter on the map, name the state, tell whether its electoral votes in 1896 went to William McKinley or William Jennings Bryan, and explain why.

2. Geographic Thinking The first 12 national parks were all located in the West. How might you explain this fact? Do you think these areas could have remained wilderness without government action? Explain, using evidence from the chapter and your own observations.

2. Jane Addams In your journal, reflect on how Jane Addams was representative of the Progressives.

3. Citizenship Some people criticized the muckrakers for writing about nothing but problems in American life. In a 1906 speech, President Roosevelt argued that the people "with the muck-rakes are often [necessary] to the well-being of society, but only if they know when to stop raking the muck." Do you think this criticism was valid? Do modern-day muckrakers help or harm the nation? Write your response in your journal.

Alternative Assessment

Creating public-service announcements If you listen to the radio, you probably have heard announcements that inform listeners about a problem, offer a solution, and call on the public to take part in solving the problem. Work with three classmates to create four public-service announcements that reformers in the late 1800s and early 1900s might have used to gain support.

1. Choose four areas of reform discussed in the chapter.
2. Brainstorm ideas for a script for a one-minute public-service announcement for each reform.
3. Write first drafts of the four announcements, evaluate the drafts, and then produce final scripts.
4. Take turns presenting the public-service announcements to the class. Your presentations can be "live," or you can make an audiotape and play it for the class.

Your announcements will be evaluated on the following criteria:

- they accurately describe the concerns and goals of reformers of the time period
- they offer specific ways that the public can help, based on the reformers' methods
- they are clear, striking, and persuasive

Writing in Your History Journal

1. (a) Explanations should be similar to the time line notes on teacher pages 332–333. (b) Articles should reflect an understanding of the event's historical importance and context.

2. She understood and attacked the problems of poverty, corruption, and political power. She reflected the Progressive desire to create order and fairness, putting the public good above self-interest.

3. Answers will vary, but most students will feel the criticism was not valid because the muckrakers' job was to draw attention to serious problems. Most will respond that modern-day muckrakers (such as Ralph Nader) perform a valuable service. Accept all thoughtful answers on the help vs. harm question.

Reviewing Geography

1. (A) Ohio, McKinley—industrial state; (B) Texas, Bryan—farm state; (C) Nebraska, Bryan—farm state; (D) Pennsylvania, McKinley—industrial state; (E) Massachusetts, McKinley—industrial state

2. Most of the available land, as well as the most dramatic scenery, was in the West. Students who feel government intervention was necessary will probably cite development pressures. Others may feel that the land would have remained wilderness even without government intervention because much of it was inaccessible to development.

Alternative Assessment

Teacher's Take-Home Planner 3, p. 7, includes suggestions and scoring rubrics for the Alternative Assessment activity.

Teaching the

Link to American Readings

In this feature students learn about reformers and the social changes that they instituted in the late nineteenth and early twentieth centuries. Perhaps those in greatest need of champions for their cause were the children, and it was primarily women who came to their aid. The readings in this section introduce some of those women.

Before students begin the lesson, review Jane Addams (pages 334–335) and African Americans Seek Equality (page 352). Have students read the entire feature before assigning the A Closer Look questions. The Setting the Stage Activity and Bonus Activity may then be introduced according to the needs and interests of the students. The information contained in the Discussion questions and the Footnotes may be used throughout the lesson as appropriate. Readers' Theater is ideal for students who might find the readings somewhat difficult. Use the Wrap-Up Activity for students who would enjoy taking a step beyond the core lesson.

Literature Footnote

Hull House was just one of Jane Addams's efforts to improve the world. She also played a prominent role in the formation of the National Progressive Party in 1912 and of the Women's Peace Party in 1915. In the same year she was elected president of the International Congress of Women at The Hague, Netherlands, and president of the Women's International League for Peace and Freedom. Addams was a delegate to similar conferences around the world over the next 15 years. In 1931 she received the Nobel Peace Prize. Her published works include *Democracy and Social Ethics* (1902), *Newer Ideals of Peace* (1907), *Twenty Years at Hull House* (1910), and *The Second Twenty Years at Hull House* (1930).

Link to American Readings

READING 7A

Hull House: A Haven for Immigrants

In the 1890s and early 1900s, many reformers argued that the American dream could be achieved by one and all. However, changes first had to be made, and those changes were monumental. Jane Addams was one who tried to repair social problems, especially those created by the new industrial system. In 1889 she founded Hull House, the first settlement house in the United States.

Jane Addams at work, 1889

According to its charter, Hull House set out "to provide a center for a higher civic and social life; to institute and maintain educational and philanthropic enterprises, and to investigate and improve the conditions in the industrial districts of Chicago." . . .

When Hull House opened its doors on September 18, 1889, the neighborhood [Halsted and Polk streets in Chicago] was a conglomerate of immigrant colonies of Italians, Germans—including German Jews—Polish and Russian Jews, Bohemians, Irish, and first-generation Americans. Immediately surrounding Hull House were mostly frame houses originally built as one-family units but now occupied by several families. . . .

conglomerate: cluster; grouping

. . . At first some of the neighboring women came just to see, but they came back with others, again and again, for at Hull House they found warmth and friendship; people who cared and understood one's problems, who were ready to listen and to help. Here adults and children could play and learn, as there were classes in English, music, painting, drama, crafts. . . .

From the start, Hull House was prepared to perform a variety of services. Many hours were spent to get "support for deserted women, insurance for bewildered widows, damages for injured operators, furniture from the clutches of the installment store." . . .

A major problem in the Hull House neighborhood was poor sanitary conditions in the alleys. The [infrequent] garbage collections made the area particularly unhealthy and dangerous because of the large amounts of decayed fruit and vegetables thrown out by the . . . peddlers who lived there. Added to this were the disease-ridden piles of filthy rags which the rag pickers would pull out of the city dumps and bring home for further sorting and washing. Sickening odors came from the wooden boxes in the alleys. These conditions led to many deaths each year.

Literature Footnote

A socialist when he arrived in the United States in 1882, Lithuania-born Abraham Cahan helped to organize the first garment workers unions, taught English, and worked as a reporter. In 1897 he helped found a Yiddish-language newspaper, the *Jewish Daily Forward.* He served as its editor from 1903 to 1951. The paper's goal was to promote socialism and to help immigrant Jews to Americanize. The most widely read Yiddish newspaper in the world, its "bundle of letters" column and pertinent news items made it especially popular with immigrants. In addition to many short stories, Cahan wrote one of the first and most respected immigrant novels, *The Rise of David Levinsky* (1917), the story of the costs of assimilation. The 1975 film *Hester Street* was based on Cahan's short story "Yekl."

To help relieve the situation, talks on sanitation were arranged for the immigrants. The housewife was told she must keep not only her own house clean but also the streets. Though in her native village she might sweep the refuse into the street and then let it decay in the open air, this was not healthy in the crowded quarters in which she now lived. . . .

Among the activities at Hull House were the meetings held by the fledgling labor unions. Jane Addams encouraged labor organizations in their struggles against long hours, unsafe working conditions, and the sweatshops of the garment industry. Since Chicago was a center of the garment trades and many of the workers in the industry lived around Hull House, the cloakmakers and the shirtmakers organized their unions at the settlement. . . .

fledgling: new; young

In their investigation of the poverty of the neighborhood, Hull House residents found sweatshops where women sewed for twelve to fourteen hours a day. They had little or no time to care for their children, who in many instances were left with neighbors already overburdened with the care of their own children. Sometimes youngsters were left alone, locked in a room in their tenement apartment. To fill the need for child care for working mothers, Hull House opened a day nursery.

Young children themselves worked long hours in factories. . . . Jane Addams became acquainted with the pledges signed by parents of children working in factories, which promised that the parents would make no claim for damages resulting from "carelessness" at work. Three boys from a Hull House club were injured at a machine in a neighboring factory. One of the boys died. The machine needed only an inexpensive protective guard to avoid such accidents, but the manufacturer refused to provide this. . . .

A typical neighborhood near Hull House at the turn of the century. Jane Addams encouraged proper sanitation in the streets as well as in the home. Her efforts helped to reduce deaths related to the disease-ridden refuse that had lined streets and alleys.

Courtesy: Chicago Historical Society

Setting the Stage Activity

Charting Social Reform

To help students visualize the course of social reform, have them complete a time line with the following data.

1836—Massachusetts prohibits employment of children under 15 who had less than 3 months schooling the previous year.

1848—Pennsylvania establishes minimum age of 12 years for workers in mills.

1853—Several states adopt ten-hour workdays for children.

1900—One-fifth of all U.S. children are employed.

1910—Efforts of social welfare organizations such as the NCLC result in a sharp reduction in number of children employed in industry.

Bonus Activity

Planning Reform

To help students understand that the answers to social problems were complex, have them form small groups and role play the part of city planning commissioners. What steps would they take to improve their city? Which problems are most urgent? How might these be addressed?

Discussion

Stimulating Critical Thinking

1. In addition to the practical services such as day care and education, what benefits did Hull House offer to the people of its neighborhood? (It provided a place for people to gather, talk, and share common experiences. People learned that they were not alone with the problems they faced as immigrants.)

2. Why did Florence Kelley believe that it was important for women to vote? How do you think Kelley's speech would have affected her audience? (She believed that if women had the vote, they would pass laws that would prevent children from working long hours in factories. Her speech probably would have been effective because it appealed to the consciences and emotions of the listeners.

Literature Footnote

Just as immigrants struggled to find their place in American society, so did African Americans. To this end, the American Negro Academy, which was founded in 1897, promoted "higher education, the publication of scholarly work and the defense of the Negro against vicious assault." W. E. B. Du Bois was one of the black scholars active in the Academy. He believed that blacks must organize and trust in their own abilities to overcome disadvantages they faced in the new century. In 1910 Du Bois was elected as one of the founding officers of the National Association for the Advancement of Colored People (NAACP). He was also named editor of *The Crisis*, the organization's magazine. Two of his most important books include *Black Reconstruction* and his autobiography, *Dusk of Dawn* (1940).

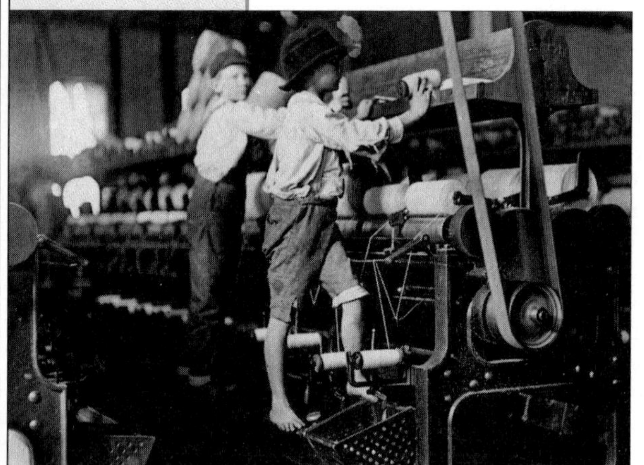

International Museum of Photography at George Eastman House.

In an effort to abolish some of these problems, Hull House lobbied for labor legislation, including an eight-hour workday law for women. Out of the experiences and activities of the Hull House residents, the first juvenile court was set up in Chicago, the city's first public playground was built, and public baths were opened because such facilities were missing in most tenement apartments in the area. . . .

These young boys had to stand on boxes or on the machine itself to change spools. Many were maimed or lost their lives as they worked.

READING 7B

"For the Sake of the Children . . ."

Before becoming the first woman Chief Inspector of Factories in Illinois in 1893, Florence Kelley was a lawyer. A leading advocate of women's suffrage, Kelley became vice-president of the National American Woman Suffrage Association. She grew increasingly concerned about the harsh working conditions endured by children in factories. In her following speech, Kelley argues that if mothers had the vote, they would not let their young children work endless nights in textile mills.

A speech by Florence Kelley, 1903

To-night while we sleep, several thousand little girls will be working in textile mills, all the night through, in the deafening noise of the spindles and looms spinning and weaving cotton and woolen, silks and ribbons for us to buy. . . . If the mothers and the teachers in Georgia could vote, would the Georgia Legislature have refused at every session for the last three years to stop the work in the mills of children under twelve years of age? . . .

Until the mothers in the great industrial States are enfranchised, we shall none of us be able to free our consciences from participation in this great evil. No one in this room to-night can feel free from such participation. The children make our shoes in the shoe factories; they knit our stockings, our

Readers' Theater

Either reading in this section may be easily adapted to readers' theater. The Jane Addams story may be read by a boy with little modification of the original text. The account could be read as if the boy were a friend of Addams's who is recounting her accomplishments. A girl might wish to change the text to first person (substituting "I" for "she") and to assume the identity of Jane Addams. Because the second reading is written from a female perspective, it might be a better choice for interpretation by a girl rather than by a boy. A girl might assume the persona of Florence Kelley and prepare the speech as written. The delivery of the reading should be in the mode of a speech. Encourage students doing this reading to practice emphasis and pauses for maximum effectiveness.

International Museum of Photography at George Eastman House.

A young girl at work in a Carolina cotton mill.

knitted underwear in the knitting factories. They spin and weave our cotton underwear in the cotton mills. Children braid straw for our hats, they spin and weave the silk and velvet wherewith we trim our hats. They stamp buckles and metal ornaments of all kinds, as well as pins and hat-pins. . . . [Tiny] children make artificial flowers and neckwear for us to buy. They carry bundles of garments from the factories to the tenements, little beasts of burden, robbed of school life that they may work for us.

wherewith: which with

We do not wish this. We prefer to have our work done by men and women. But we are almost powerless. Not wholly powerless, however, are citizens who enjoy the right of petition. For myself, I shall use this power in every possible way until the right to the ballot is granted, and then I shall continue to use both.

What can we do to free our consciences? There is one line of action by which we can do much. We can enlist the workingmen on behalf of our enfranchisement just in proportion as we strive with them to free the children. No labor organization in this country ever fails to respond to an appeal for help in the freeing of the children.

enfranchisement: the vote

appeal: request

For the sake of the children, for the Republic in which these children will vote after we are dead, and for the sake of our cause, we should enlist the workingmen voters, with us, in this task of freeing the children from toil.

Excerpts from Florence Kelley's address to the Massachusetts Woman Suffrage Association, 1903.

A Closer Look

1. How did Hull House serve the immigrant families of its surrounding neighborhoods?

2. Describe Kelley's plan to halt child labor practices.

3. CRITICAL THINKING Although the services provided by Hull House have evolved over the years, the need for this and other service organizations is still strong. What service organizations are helping those in your community? Include both public and private groups. What can you do to become a volunteer to use your talents to help others? Formulate a plan.

Wrap-Up Activity

Responding to Du Bois

To extend this lesson on immigrants and their place in America, have students respond in their history journals to the following statement by W. E. B. Du Bois. "We are Americans, not only by birth and by citizenship, but by our political ideals, our language, our religion. Farther than that, our Americanism does not go."

A Closer Look Answers

1. Hull House provided a gathering place for children and adults, classes in English and other subjects, support and insurance for those who needed it, lectures on subjects such as sanitation, and legal support.

2. Kelley wanted women to have the right to vote, and she wanted to enlist the help of the unions and their members to push for legislation to decrease the number of children who worked in industry.

3. Students should identify real problems in their neighborhood and consider carrying out the plan they formulate.

Teaching the
Citizenship Lab

In this feature students learn about *Minor* v. *Happersett* (1875), in which the Supreme Court ruled that under the Constitution, states could deny women the right to vote. It would be 45 years before the decision was overturned by the Nineteenth Amendment.

Before students read the feature, review Woman Suffrage on pages 351–352. Have students read the entire feature before assigning the Understanding Civic Issues questions and the Hands-On Citizenship activity. The Bonus Activity in this Teacher's Edition may be used as an alternative to, or in addition to, the Hands-On Citizenship activity. The Discussion questions in this Teacher's Edition may be used at appropriate points during students' reading or afterward.

Objectives

- ★ Explain how the Constitution as it stood in 1872 could be interpreted as giving women the right to vote.
- ★ Summarize the Supreme Court's ruling on the connection between citizenship and the right to vote in *Minor* v. *Happersett.*
- ★ Explain why the Court's ruling made a constitutional amendment on woman suffrage necessary.

Supreme Court Case: *Minor* v. *Happersett*

Citizenship Lab

Should the Law Treat Men and Women Differently?

For decades during the 1800s, the story of the woman suffrage movement was one of great struggles and few gains. A favorable decision by the Supreme Court would have helped the cause. Instead, in 1875 the Court dealt the movement a severe blow. In *Minor* v. *Happersett,* the justices unanimously upheld the power of the states to deny women the right to vote.

Virginia L. Minor

Virginia and Francis Minor: Woman Suffrage Activists

Virginia L. Minor lived in St. Louis, Missouri, with her husband, Francis Minor, a lawyer. After the Civil War, Virginia Minor began devoting her time to woman suffrage. In 1867 she petitioned the Missouri state legislature to extend voting rights not only to newly freed African American men but to women as well. The legislature rejected her proposal by a vote of 89 to 5. But Minor had no intention of giving up. She founded the Woman Suffrage Association of Missouri and became an active member of the National Woman Suffrage Association.

Francis Minor supported his wife's efforts. His legal studies had convinced him that the Constitution already gave women the right to vote. He noted that, for the most part, the Constitution referred to "citizens" and "persons," not "men" and "women." Minor regarded the state laws that prohibited women from voting as *bills of attainder*—that is, laws aimed at punishing particular persons or groups. Article 1, Section 9 of the Constitution specifically prohibits such laws.

Perhaps most important, Minor believed women's right to vote was supported by the newly ratified Fourteenth Amendment, especially

History Footnote

Although the Supreme Court's ruling in *Minor* v. *Happersett* was a setback, suffragists could take some encouragement from it. For one thing, the Court had given dignity to the Minors' case simply by agreeing to consider it. And nowhere in his opinion did Chief Justice Waite imply that woman suffrage was an unjust or unworthy cause, or that it was doomed to failure. Instead, he wrote this: "We have given this case the careful consideration its importance demands. If the law is wrong, it ought to be changed; but the power for that is not with us. The arguments addressed to us . . . may, perhaps, be sufficient to induce those having the power to make the alteration. . . ."

the part that reads, "No state shall make or enforce any law which shall abridge the privileges or immunities [freedoms] of citizens of the United States. . . .

A number of legal experts and judges agreed with Minor's arguments and said so publicly. Even more encouraging, Chief Justice Salmon P. Chase suggested that women should initiate court cases to test whether the Constitution did indeed give them the right to vote.

The Minors Test the Constitution

The Minors decided to act. On October 15, 1872, Virginia Minor tried to register to vote in St. Louis. The registrar, a man named Reese Happersett, refused to sign her up on the grounds that only male citizens could vote under Missouri law. The Minors then sued Happersett. They acted together because the law did not allow married women to file lawsuits alone.

The Minors' case reached the Supreme Court in 1875. By this time, Chief Justice Chase had died and been replaced by Morrison R. Waite. He and the other justices rejected the Minors' appeal and upheld the Missouri law.

The Court stated that women "may be citizens" but that citizenship means "membership of a nation, nothing more." "[T]he Constitution, when it conferred citizenship, did not necessarily confer the right of suffrage," Chief Justice Waite said. Furthermore, he said, the Fourteenth Amendment had nothing to do with suffrage; it did not grant suffrage to anyone. After all, if the Fourteenth Amendment had granted suffrage, the Fifteenth Amendment protecting the voting rights of former slaves would not have been needed.

Suffragist Carrie Chapman Catt (center) leads a march in New York City in 1918.

Setting the Stage Activity

Writing About Voting

To prepare for reading about *Minor* v. *Happersett*, ask students to consider the fact that they will be eligible to vote a few years from now. How do they feel about the prospect of voting? Do they view the right to vote as important, or not? Have students write paragraphs explaining their answers. Volunteers can share their paragraphs.

Bonus Activity

Comparing Women's Lives Then and Now

To help students understand changes in women's lives and status since 1875, have them create a bulletin-board display on the topic. Break the class into two groups. One group collects materials for the section of the display titled "Women Then," while the other group collects materials for the section titled "Women Now." Materials can include art and photos; newspaper and magazine headlines, ads, and articles; quotes; and so on. Remind students to include inability/ability to vote in the display. Encourage students to avoid stereotyping the past as uniformly negative and the present as uniformly positive.

Discussion

Checking Understanding

1. Why did Francis Minor think women's right to vote was already in the Constitution? (Constitution mostly used gender-neutral language; state laws prohibiting women from voting could be seen as bills of attainder, which the Constitution does not allow; the Fourteenth Amendment says no state can abridge the privileges and freedoms of citizens.)

2. Why did Virginia Minor come to believe that a constitutional amendment on woman suffrage was necessary? (Supreme Court had upheld the power of the states to deny women the right to vote. But the Court could not overturn a constitutional amendment.)

Stimulating Critical Thinking

3. Why do you suppose the Equal Rights Amendment did not win enough support to be ratified? (Possible answers: Some people may have felt it was not needed because women's rights were protected by the Constitution. Some people may have felt it would force equality to the point that women would be forced to fight in wars, could not take time off from work after giving birth, and so on.)

Citizenship Footnote

Alice Paul submitted the first version of the Equal Rights Amendment (ERA) to Congress in 1923. Nearly 50 years later, in 1972, Congress finally passed the amendment. The ERA was then sent to the state legislatures. Congress set a standard seven-year deadline for ratification.

At first it seemed as if the ERA was destined for success. It moved quickly through a number of state legislatures. But then opposition to the ERA began to mount, mostly from people who wanted to protect women's traditional roles. When it became clear that the deadline would not be met, Congress extended it until 1982. Even by the second deadline, only 35 of the necessary 38 states had ratified. Since then, the ERA has been reintroduced periodically, but Congress has not passed it.

Aftermath of the Minor Case

Although she lost her case, Virginia Minor became a national hero of the woman suffrage movement. She was an honored guest at National Woman Suffrage Association conventions and went on speaking tours throughout the country. Her experience led her to believe that trying to gain the vote on a state-by-state basis was hopeless. Only a constitutional amendment, to which the Supreme Court could not say no, would accomplish the goal of suffrage for all American women.

As you have read, that goal was achieved when the Nineteenth Amendment was ratified in 1920. Since that time, American women have made tremendous educational, economic, and social gains as well.

However, women still encounter discrimination and other barriers. The Equal Rights Amendment, which would have banned all discrimination on the basis of gender, was passed by Congress in 1972 but never ratified. Without such an amendment, it took a 1996 Supreme Court ruling to force the nation's two state-funded, all-male military colleges—the Virginia Military Institute and the Citadel—to admit women students. In that ruling, the Court cited the Fourteenth Amendment—a part of the Constitution that the Court of 1875 considered irrelevant to the issue of women's rights.

Connections to Language Arts

When the Fourteenth Amendment was first proposed, women's rights activists such as Susan B. Anthony and Elizabeth Cady Stanton were outraged by the language of Section 2. Up to that point, except for references to the President as *he*, the Constitution's language had been gender-neutral. Now, for the first time, the word *male* would appear in the document. Unable to get the amendment's wording changed, the activists next sought to have *sex* added to the Fifteenth Amendment's list of improper limits on voting: *race, color*, and *previous condition of servitude*. Failing once more, Anthony and Stanton came to the grim realization that yet another amendment would be needed to achieve woman suffrage. Neither would live to see the realization of their goal.

The Equal Rights Amendment

"Equality of rights under the law shall not be denied or abridged by the United States or any state on account of sex."

Understanding Civic Issues

1. What actions did Virginia and Francis Minor take to try to win woman suffrage?
2. In the *Minor* v. *Happersett* decision, did the justices define citizenship broadly or narrowly? Explain.
3. **Critical Thinking** Why do you suppose it took women so long to gain the right to vote?
4. **Hands-On Citizenship** During the long campaign for woman suffrage, activists used various tactics, or methods, to promote their cause. You read about a few of these tactics, including the filing of test lawsuits. Think about a modern-day cause that you believe in, and imagine you are in charge of planning a student campaign for that cause.
   - Brainstorm a list of possible tactics. Make sure they are realistic for students to carry out. Also be sure that they are legal.
   - Create a poster asking for volunteers to help carry out your ideas.
   - Present your poster to your classmates. Does it spark their interest and motivate them to join you in your cause? Why or why not?

Cadets at the Citadel in 1996.

Citizenship Lab Answers

1. Virginia petitioned Missouri legislature to extend voting rights to women, founded Woman Suffrage Association of Missouri, worked for National Woman Suffrage Association, tried to register to vote; Virginia and Francis sued the St. Louis voting registrar, taking their case to the Supreme Court.

2. Narrowly: the justices said citizenship means only "membership of a nation" and does not necessarily give a person the right to vote.

3. Possible answer: Because women were half the population, their gaining the right to vote could result in huge changes in politics and legislation. Men felt threatened by this potential power. Women were divided on whether they wanted such power.

Teaching the Hands-On CITIZENSHIP

Structure this cooperative learning activity by having the group select a chairperson, a recorder, a reporter who has primary responsibility for presenting the group's findings, and one or two artists who will prepare the poster.

One of the aims of cooperative learning is to make students dependent on each other. Therefore, it is important to evaluate them as a group. Later, perhaps in a testing situation, you will have ample opportunity to assess the content learning that took place.

At·a·Glance

8 Overseas Expansion
1865–1916

Chapter Planning Guide

Section	Student Text	Teacher's Edition Activities
Opener and Story pp. 368–371	**Keys to History Time Line**; **History Mystery**; Beginning the Story with **Theodore Roosevelt**	**Setting the Stage Activity** Discussing Childhood Hardships, p. 371
1 **The Roots of Overseas Expansion** pp. 372–376	**Point of View** Should the United States have an empire?, p. 374 **World Link** Olympic Games, p. 375 **Geography Lab** Understanding a Map's Point of View, p. 376	**Warm-Up Activity** Discussing Power, p. 372 **Geography Question of the Day,** p. 372 **Section Activity** Imperialist Images, p. 373 **Bonus Activity** A Foreign-Policy Report Card, p. 374 **Wrap-Up Activity** Debating Imperialism, p. 375
2 **The Spanish-American War** pp. 377–384	**Hands-On History** Writing yellow journalism, p. 378 **Reading Maps** United States Overseas Possessions 1858–1900, p. 381 **Link to the Present** Puerto Rico: The 51st state?, p. 383 **Skill Lab** Comparing Points of View, p. 384	**Warm-Up Activity** Reasons for War, p. 377 **Geography Question of the Day,** p. 377 **Section Activity** Writing Letters Home, p. 380 **Bonus Activity** Writing a Song or Poem, p. 382 **Wrap-Up Activity** Making a Time Line, p. 383
3 **A New Role in the World** pp. 385–391	**Link to Art** *The Letter; Okita Carrying a Teacup*, p. 386 **Reading Maps** The United States in the Caribbean Early 1900s, p. 390	**Warm-Up Activity** Discussing "World Power," p. 385 **Geography Question of the Day,** p. 385 **Section Activity** Speaking Softly and Carrying a Big Stick, p. 388 **Bonus Activity** Drawing a Comic Strip, p. 389 **Wrap-Up Activity** Playing *Jeopardy!*®, p. 391
Evaluation	☑ **Section 1 Review,** p. 375 ☑ **Section 2 Review,** p. 383 ☑ **Section 3 Review,** p. 391 ☑ **Chapter Survey,** pp. 392–393 **Alternative Assessment** Putting expansionism on trial, p. 393	☑ **Answers to Section 1 Review,** p. 375 ☑ **Answers to Section 2 Review,** p. 383 ☑ **Answers to Section 3 Review,** p. 391 ☑ **Answers to Chapter Survey,** pp. 392–393 (Alternative Assessment guidelines are in the Take-Home Planner.)

Teacher's Resource Package

Chapter Summaries: English and Spanish, pp. 52–53

Chapter Resources Binder

Study Guide Identifying People and Places, p. 73

Geography Extensions Maps and Point of View, pp. 21–22

Chapter Resources Binder

Study Guide Skimming to Locate Information, p. 74

Skills Development Comparing Points of View, pp. 79–80

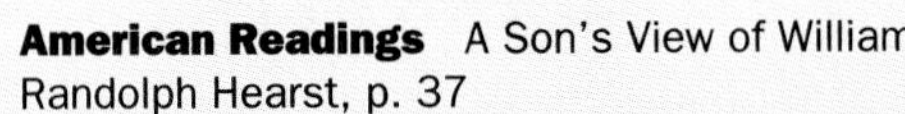

American Readings A Son's View of William Randolph Hearst, p. 37

Chapter Resources Binder

Study Guide Using Questions to Guide Reading, p. 75

Reinforcement Making a Graphic Organizer, pp. 77–78

American Readings An American Describes the Boxer Rebellion, p. 38; The Roosevelts Take Over the White House, pp. 39–40

Using Historical Documents A Chinese Nationalist Map, pp. 60–63

Chapter and Unit Tests Chapter 8 Tests, Forms A and B, pp. 67–70

Take-Home Planner

Introducing the Chapter Activity Pros and Cons of Expansionism, p. 14

Chapter In-Depth Activity Looking Into the Future, p. 14

Reduced Views

Study Guide, p. 16

Geography Extensions, p. 19

Unit 3 Answers, pp. 29–38

Reduced Views

Study Guide, p. 16

Skills Development, p. 17

American Readings, p. 18

Unit 3 Answers, pp. 29–38

Reduced Views

Study Guide, p. 16

Reinforcement, p. 17

American Readings, p. 18

Using Historical Documents, p. 19

Unit 3 Answers, pp. 29–38

Reduced Views

Chapter Tests, p. 19

Unit 3 Answers, pp. 29–38

Alternative Assessment Guidelines for scoring the Chapter Survey activity, p. 15

Additional Resources

Wall Time Line

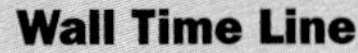

Unit 3 Activity

Transparency Package

Transparency 8-1 Japanese Influence on the West—use with Section 3

Transparency 8-2 Western Influence on Japan—use with Section 3

Transparency Activity Book

SelecTest Testing Software

Chapter 8 Test, Forms A and B

Vital Links

Videodisc

CD-ROM

"Aloha Oe" (see TE p. 373)

"Guantanamera" (see TE p. 378)

USS *Maine* (see TE p. 378)

Dewey in Manila Bay (see TE p. 379)

Marines in Cuba (see TE p. 380)

Voice of Charles Young (see TE p. 380)

Cuban freedom fighters (see TE p. 381)

Filipino village (see TE p. 382)

Japanese immigrants (see TE p. 387)

Panama Canal (see TE p. 388)

Workers at the Panama Canal (see TE p. 388)

8

Teaching Resources

Take-Home Planner 3
- Introducing Chapter Activity
- Chapter In-Depth Activity
- Alternative Assessment

Chapter Resources Binder
Geography Extensions
American Readings
Using Historical Documents
Transparency Activities
Wall Time Line Activities
Chapter Summaries
Chapter and Unit Tests
SelecTest Test File
Vital Links CD-ROM/Videodisc

Chapter Objectives

- ★ Explain why the United States became interested in overseas expansion.
- ★ Describe the causes and effects of the Spanish-American War.
- ★ Discuss how the United States took a more active role in Asia and Latin America.

Chapter Overview

During the late 1800s, the United States became interested in acquiring overseas possessions, as well as in expanding its trade with foreign countries. It strengthened its influence in the Pacific region through increased trade with China and Japan, the purchase of Alaska, and increased control over Hawaii and other territories.

Time Line

Keys to History

Keys to History journal writing activity is on page 392 in the Chapter Survey.

Alaska Purchase Acquisition of Alaska expanded American territory farther into the Pacific. (p. 372)

Hawaii annexed The United States gained strategically important islands. (p. 379)

Spanish-American War The American victory led to an overseas empire. (pp. 377–383)

Open Door policy in China The United States declared open trade with China. (p. 385)

Looking Back Commodore Perry's visit opened Japanese contact with the West.

World Link See page 375.

1865–1916

Chapter 8 Overseas Expansion

Sections

Keys to History

1867 Alaska Purchase
Russian copy of purchase treaty

1898 Spanish-American War

1898 Hawaii annexed

1900 Open Door policy in China declared

Looking Back Commodore Perry opens trade with Japan **1854**

World Link Olympic Games revived **1896**

The expansionist mood in the country helped lead to the Spanish-American War, in which the United States gained several important territories, eliminated Spain as a colonial power, and became a world power. Debates about the proper role of the United States on the world stage pitted expansionists like Theodore Roosevelt against those who felt that imperialism was a betrayal of the country's values.

Through aggressive military intervention, diplomacy, and trade, the United States increased its influence and power in Asia and Latin America. It built the strategically important Panama Canal. However, its interventions in various countries led to resentment abroad and controversy at home.

HISTORY *Mystery*

In 1898 the United States went to war to help Cuba gain its independence. Why, then, did the first battle of that war take place on the other side of the world?

1907
Great White Fleet tours the world

1916
Wilson sends troops into Mexico

1914
Panama Canal opens

1905

1915

Looking Ahead

The United States enters World War I
1917

Teaching the *HISTORY* *Mystery*

Students will find the answer on p. 379. See Chapter Survey, p. 392, for an additional question.

Time Line

Great White Fleet President Roosevelt sent 16 warships on a world tour to emphasize U.S. naval strength. (p. 387)

Panama Canal opens It took 43,000 workers 7 years to link the Atlantic and Pacific Oceans. (pp. 387–388)

Wilson sends troops into Mexico United States military intervention in Mexico led to tensions and the loss of American lives. (pp. 389–391)

Looking Ahead The United States' entry into World War I was the nation's first involvement in a major overseas war.

Beginning the Story

Theodore Roosevelt

The assassination of William McKinley in 1901 made Roosevelt the youngest President ever, and his youthful energy and exuberance matched the nation's mood. His exploits as a cowboy, outdoorsman, and Rough Rider were famous and made the young aristocrat seem larger than life. His willingness to use American strength to extend the nation's overseas influence caught the imagination of the American people.

Setting the Stage Activity

Discussing Childhood Hardships

To help students understand how Theodore Roosevelt's early experiences helped shape his adult life and personality, have pairs discuss how overcoming ill health or other hardships in childhood can lead to greater self-confidence as an adult. Then ask them to cite examples from Roosevelt's life and career, covered in the last chapter, that show his self-confidence.

See the Introducing the
Chapter Activity, Pros and
Cons of Expansionism.
Take-Home Planner 3,
p. 14.

History Footnote

From an early age, Roosevelt was interested in natural history and science. He kept a detailed diary of the plants and animals he observed on family vacations in the Adirondack Mountains of New York state, and he collected "museum" specimens. His family would find "field mice in the ice chest, a snapping turtle tied to the leg of the sink, or a snake in a water pitcher." While at Harvard he and another student wrote and published *The Summer Birds of the Adirondacks in Franklin County, N.Y.*, based on their observations of 97 species of birds.

Later, as President, those same interests led him to take conservationist measures. Working with naturalist John Muir, Roosevelt began a large-scale conservation program, including setting aside 148 million acres for forest reserves.

Beginning the Story with

Theodore
Roosevelt

Theodore Roosevelt is often described as the first modern President. When he was born, in 1858, the United States was a nation of 33 states. When he died, in 1919, there were 48 states stretching from sea to sea. The nation and its 26th President came of age together.

When Roosevelt was a child, it seemed doubtful he would come of age at all. Born to a wealthy family in New York City, "Teedy"—as his parents called him—suffered terribly from asthma attacks. Some attacks were so severe that his father would bundle up his wheezing son and ride around the streets of New York in an open carriage, hoping the brisk air would help the boy breathe more easily.

"You Must *Make* Your Body"

Due to his poor health, Teedy never went to school but was instead tutored at home. He was a bright boy who loved studying nature. At the age of 9 he wrote a book about insects. When his mother asked the maid to throw out some dead mice he was preserving in her icebox, Teedy cried, "Oh, no! The loss to science! The loss to science!"

One day his father sat him down for a serious talk. "Teedy," he said, "you have the mind, but you have not the body. Without the help of the body, the mind cannot go as far as it should. You must *make* your body." Teedy took this advice to heart. At his grandfather's country estate he learned to ride horseback and became an expert rifle shot. He also began a vigorous exercise program that included boxing and wrestling. Because of poor eyesight he often took a licking in the boxing ring, but he never quit. He eventually lost the sight in his left eye as the result of a boxing match.

History Bookshelf

Fritz, Jean. *Bully for You, Teddy Roosevelt!* Putnam, 1991. This is one of dozens of popular biographies by a perennial favorite. It captures Roosevelt's energy and accomplishments.

Also of interest:

Fleischman, Paul. *Coming-and-Going Men: Four Tales*. Harper, 1985.

Meltzer, Milton. *Theodore Roosevelt and His America*. Watts, 1994.

St. George, Judith. *Panama Canal: Gateway to the World*. Putnam, 1989.

Whitelaw, Nancy. *Theodore Roosevelt Takes Charge*. Albert Whitman, 1992.

An Unlikely Cowboy

As a young man Roosevelt fell in love, married his sweetheart, and was beginning a career in politics when tragedy struck. His young wife died suddenly. In his grief Roosevelt decided to start life anew in the West, becoming a cattle rancher in Dakota Territory.

The New Yorker made an unlikely cowboy. His neighbors called him "four-eyes" because of his glasses. They laughed at his squeaky voice and strange way of speaking. No rancher they knew exclaimed "By Godfrey!" or ordered ranch hands to "Hasten forward quickly there!" Yet the Dakotans admired this eastern tenderfoot for being honest and hard-working.

As the Republican candidate for Vice-President in 1900, Theodore Roosevelt was already a famous public figure—more popular in the eyes of many Americans than President William McKinley.

President "Teddy"

Perhaps haunted by memories of boyhood weakness, Roosevelt still exercised constantly after he became President. He did so much presidential business while hiking, riding horses, or playing tennis that the Congressmen who shared these sports with him were called the "tennis cabinet."

Many a White House visitor fell prey to Roosevelt's enthusiasm for exercise. One day the French ambassador arrived in formal clothes, expecting to go for a dignified "walk" with the President. Instead, he was taken on a rigorous cross-country hike. When Roosevelt asked the hikers to take off their clothes to keep them dry while wading a deep creek, the ambassador insisted on continuing to wear his fancy gloves. The British ambassador, a veteran of similar adventures, once warned a colleague, "You must always remember that the President is about six years old."

Americans, however, loved their energetic leader. They called him "Teddy" and embraced him as warmly as the stuffed animal named for him, the "teddy bear." He was, most felt, the right leader for a new century in which the United States would flex its muscles as a world power.

Hands-On HISTORY

Activity

Imagine that you are Theodore Roosevelt and have just become President. You have been asked to speak to a group of 12- and 13-year-olds about setting and reaching goals. Prepare a short speech to give them, using your experiences as examples.

Discussion

Thinking Historically

1. From what disease did Theodore Roosevelt suffer and how did he overcome his early health problems? (He had asthma and began a rigorous program of exercise and outdoor activities to build up his body.)

2. What impression do you think President Roosevelt made on European diplomats? (He probably impressed them with his energy, but they may have disapproved of his undignified behavior and worried about his plans to make the United States a stronger world power.)

Teaching the Hands-On HISTORY

Before students begin to write their speeches, have them list significant events and experiences from Roosevelt's young life. Then have them incorporate these lists into their speeches, remembering to write from Roosevelt's point of view and to make the talk inspiring for an audience of 12- and 13-year-olds.

For a journal writing activity on Theodore Roosevelt, see student page 392.

Introducing the Section

Vocabulary

imperialism (p. 372) the policy of taking control of governments and resources of other countries to build an empire

Warm-Up Activity

Discussing Power

To encourage students to begin thinking about issues surrounding imperialism, write on the chalkboard: "Might makes right." Ask students to discuss in groups of four what makes a country strong. Then ask which countries might be likely to use this slogan and why. Finally ask them to discuss whether they agree or disagree with the statement and under what circumstances.

Geography Question of the Day

Have students work in pairs to write down as many ways as they can think of that a territory could be seen as an important acquisition for a country. To get them started, say that a piece of land or territory can be important because of its location.

See the Study Guide activity in **Chapter Resources Binder,** p. 73.

Section Objectives

- ★ Discuss why and how the United States increased its influence in the Pacific.
- ★ Explain arguments for and against an overseas empire.
- ★ Explain why the United States almost went to war with Britain.

Teaching Resources

Take-Home Planner 3, pp. 12–19
Chapter Resources Binder
Study Guide, p. 73
Reinforcement
Skills Development
Geography Extensions, pp. 21–22
American Readings
Using Historical Documents
Transparency Activities
Chapter and Unit Tests

1. The Roots of Overseas Expansion

Reading Guide

New Term **imperialism**

Section Focus **Why the United States became interested in overseas expansion**

1. **Why and how did the United States increase its influence in the Pacific?**
2. **What were arguments for and against an overseas empire?**
3. **Why did the United States almost go to war with Britain?**

By 1850 the United States stretched from the Atlantic to the Pacific. For most Americans, the Manifest Destiny "to overspread the continent" had been fulfilled.

Some expansionists, though, wanted more. They believed that the country should look beyond its coasts—particularly westward across the Pacific Ocean. Future prosperity, they argued, would come from strengthening trade with Asia.

Opening Trade with Japan

By the mid-1800s American ships were already crisscrossing the Pacific. American merchants were competing with Europeans in the China trade. They also wanted to trade with Japan, which had kept itself almost completely shut off from the outside world since the 1600s. The United States government decided to try to convince Japan to open its ports.

Four warships led by Commodore Matthew Perry arrived in Japan in 1853. The Japanese were impressed by Perry's modern, steam-powered vessels and by his gifts, which included various machines. The following year they agreed to allow limited trade with American merchants.

Britain, Russia, France, and the Netherlands pressured Japan into similar agreements. Recognizing its weakness, Japan quickly began to change itself from a farming society into an industrialized nation. It also built up a modern army and navy, the first Asian country to do so.

The Purchase of Alaska

In 1867 Secretary of State William H. Seward took another step to increase American power in the Pacific. He convinced Congress to buy Alaska from Russia for $7.2 million, or 2¢ an acre.

Many Americans ridiculed the deal as "Seward's Folly," saying that "Seward's Icebox" would never be worth what it cost. Seward, however, saw potential in Alaska's resources of fur, timber, and fish.

Also, Alaska included the Aleutians, a string of islands stretching halfway across the Pacific. These islands could serve as supply bases where American ships could take on food for their crews and coal to fuel their steam engines. For the same reason, Seward persuaded Congress to annex the tiny Midway Islands, located in the central Pacific between Hawaii and Japan.

History Footnote

The first European to land on Hawaii was British explorer James Cook, in 1778. By the early 1800s, American missionaries, whalers, and other settlers had arrived and brought with them their religions, ways of life, diet, and diseases. Many native Hawaiians died. The shrinking of the native population, combined with the rise of American sugar plantations and arrival of Chinese and Japanese field workers, signaled the end for native Hawaiian self-government. King Kalakaua and Queen Liliuokalani were unable to stop the wealthy and powerful plantation owners, who seized power and called their quickly-formed government "the Committee on Safety." The government was headed by Sanford Dole, the son of an American missionary and a member of the famous fruit-growing family.

Interest in Hawaii

Seward and other expansionists were especially interested in annexing Hawaii. As one newspaper editorial declared, "It will give us command of the Pacific."

Since the early 1800s Hawaii had been a favored port for American whaling and merchant ships. In their wake came missionaries eager to convert the native Hawaiians to Christianity. By mid-century the islands were home to a thriving community of Americans—mainly descendants of the missionaries, many of whom had become wealthy sugar planters.

In 1887 the planters forced Hawaii's King Kalakaua (kah-LAH-KAH-oo-ah) to give them control of the Hawaiian legislature. When Kalakaua died in 1891, his sister Liliuokalani (lih-LEE-OO-Ō-kah-LAH-nee) inherited the throne. Strong-willed, proud, and fiercely independent, "Queen Lil" rallied her people to oppose foreign rule. Her slogan was "Hawaii for the Hawaiians."

Fearful of losing their plantations, the American planters overthrew Queen Lil in 1893. They set up their own government and quickly sent a treaty of annexation to the United States Senate. They hoped to discourage any movement by native Hawaiians to restore Queen Lil to the throne. Becoming part of the United States would increase the planters' profits because Hawaiian sugar would no longer be taxed as an import.

Before the Senate could act, though, President Grover Cleveland withdrew the treaty. He was convinced that the planters had behaved dishonorably. Declaring that Queen Lil should be restored to power, he opposed efforts to annex Hawaii.

Queen Liliuokalani of Hawaii tried to free the islands from the control of American sugar planters.

An American Empire?

Events in Hawaii sparked the first widespread public debate among Americans about **imperialism**—the policy of taking control of governments and resources of other countries in order to build an empire. Britain, Germany, and France were already racing to grab up colonies in Africa and the Middle East. Should the United States, too, extend its power to people and lands beyond its borders?

Arguments for expansion Expansionists offered a variety of reasons to justify imperialism. Appealing to national pride, they declared that the United States needed to take its place among the world powers. European nations were already gobbling up chunks of real estate around the world. If the United States did not annex the Hawaiian Islands, they argued, some other nation would surely do so.

Developing the Section

Discussion

Checking Understanding

1. Why did Seward think Alaska was valuable? (Fur, timber, and fish; strategic location.)

2. What group was behind the overthrow of Queen Liliuokalani? (American plantation owners.)

Stimulating Critical Thinking

3. If the United States had not bought Alaska in 1867, would you support its purchase today? (Yes: natural resources; strategic location; tourism. No: national debt too high for this expense; no need to defend against Russia.)

Section Activity

Imperialist Images

To focus on characteristics of imperialism, have students create visual or written metaphors for it. For example, imperialist nations might be described as octopuses. Students should explain how their comparisons reflect imperialism.

Vital Links

"Aloha Oe" (Song)
Unit 4, Side 2, Search 16504, Play to 18819

See also Unit 4 Explore CD-ROM location 404.

History Footnote

The establishment of the Naval War College (where Mahan was a professor) in 1884, the forming of the Naval Reserve in 1888, and the decision in 1886 to resume construction of battleships marked the true beginnings of the "New Navy."

In 1890 Benjamin Tracy, an ardent supporter of Mahan, convinced Congress to authorize the building of three new 10,000-ton armored battleships—the *Indiana,* the *Massachusetts,* and the *Oregon,* the latter to be built on the West Coast. The *Indiana* is considered to have been the first modern battleship. When numbers were assigned to battleships in 1920, the *Indiana* was designated BB1, the *Massachusetts* BB2, and the *Oregon* BB3. This numbering system kept ships organized by class (BB stands for battleship).

Bonus Activity

A Foreign-Policy Report Card

To focus on the purpose of the Monroe Doctrine, have students prepare a report card grading the United States on how well it lived up to that doctrine's ideals during the period discussed in this section. Suggest they begin by listing several events, such as the Alaska Purchase, annexation of Midway and proposed annexation of Hawaii, and the dispute with Britain in South America. Have students discuss and justify their report cards.

Teaching the Point of View

Ask students to imagine they are native Hawaiians, Alaskans, or Midway Islanders of the late 1800s. Have them read Lodge's statement and underline words or phrases they find offensive or with which they disagree. Then have them give reasons for their reactions.

Some expansionists spoke of a duty to bring democracy and Christianity to "uncivilized" peoples. The clergyman Josiah Strong declared that white Americans represented "the largest liberty, the purest Christianity, the highest civilization."

Expansionists also argued that American factories and farms produced more than could be sold at home. They needed overseas markets. Island bases in the Pacific and Caribbean would help American merchants increase trade with China and Latin America.

Arguments against expansion Critics argued that imperialism violated the nation's democratic beliefs. The United States, they declared, had no right to impose its rule on other peoples.

Some critics also argued that expansion would hurt the economy. They feared that people from American colonies would take jobs away from American workers. An empire would be expensive, too, because it would need a larger army and navy to protect it.

Point of View

Should the United States have an empire?

One leading expansionist was Senator Henry Cabot Lodge of Massachusetts. In 1892 he declared:

> "The great nations are rapidly absorbing for their future expansion and their present defense all the waste places of the earth. It is a movement which makes for civilization and the advancement of the race. As one of the great nations of the world, the United States must not fall out of the line of march."

Like other expansionists, Lodge believed that the nation had a new Manifest Destiny to be a world power.

Building a Stronger Navy

If Lodge had called the United States "one of the great nations" just a few years earlier, his boast would have seemed ridiculous. As late as 1880, its navy ranked only 12th in the world. After the Civil War, most of its ships had been scrapped or left to rot. Congress, seeing no need for a large navy in peacetime, had spent little on new ships.

In 1890, though, expansionists convinced Congress to approve funds for a modern fleet of steel battleships. By 1900 the United States had the world's third largest navy, behind only Britain and Germany.

Credit for this turnabout belongs largely to Navy Captain Alfred T. Mahan. His 1890

This 1881 American cartoon criticizes the weak United States Navy for having too many officers and an outdated fleet of old wooden ships.

History Footnote

It was not only in the United States that the ideas of Alfred T. Mahan captured the imaginations of government leaders. Mahan had a devoted European disciple in Wilhelm II, the Kaiser of Germany. After reading *The Influence of Sea Power Upon History,* the ambitious Kaiser decided that Germany needed a navy powerful enough to challenge Britain's. Wilhelm was so impressed with Mahan's ideas that he invited the American to dinner aboard his royal yacht in 1894. He also ordered that Mahan's book be placed on every ship in the German navy. The Japanese were also impressed by Mahan and adopted the book as a text in their military and naval colleges. They also translated his later works on naval strategy into Japanese.

Olympic Games While European nations competed to build overseas empires, another kind of competition was being revived. Forgotten for almost 1,500 years, the Olympic Games were held in Athens, Greece, in 1896.

The first Olympic competition—a footrace—took place in Olympia, Greece, in 776 B.C. In time, other events were added. Every four years all wars were halted while the athletes competed. Roman rulers ended the games in A.D. 394. An earthquake later destroyed the stadium in Olympia.

Centuries passed. Then in 1875 archaeologists found the long-buried ruins. Fascinated by the finds, a French educator, Baron Pierre de Coubertin (koo-bayr-TAN), saw an opportunity to promote peace through international athletic competition. As a result of his efforts, the Olympics were reborn.

book *The Influence of Sea Power Upon History* argued that a nation's strength depends on a large battle-ready navy and many merchant ships, served by bases around the globe. He pointed to Britain as an example of success through sea power.

Mahan urged quick action to stake claims in the Pacific before Britain and Germany got all the bases. As an example, he pointed to a near-battle in 1889 between American and German warships over the Samoan Islands. The United States finally agreed to share control of Samoa with Britain and Germany. Mahan warned that the navy must be ready for such "dangerous germs of quarrel."

Defending the Monroe Doctrine

Expansionists also feared that quarrels would arise over Latin America if European nations tried to test the Monroe Doctrine. This doctrine, issued in 1823, had warned Europe against interfering in Latin American affairs.

In 1895 such a test seemed likely to occur when a boundary dispute erupted between the British colony of Guiana and the nation of Venezuela. When the United States warned Britain not to use force against Venezuela, tempers flared on both sides of the Atlantic. Excited by the idea of taking part in a war, Theodore Roosevelt wrote, "Let the fight come if it must. . . . This country needs a war."

In the end, Britain backed down, and the dispute was settled peacefully. Still, many Americans hailed it as a victory for the Monroe Doctrine. Meanwhile, expansionists saw the beginnings of a more active foreign policy. Mahan wrote approvingly:

> "It indicates the awakening of our countrymen to the fact that we must come out of our isolation . . . and take our share in the turmoil of the world."

1. Section Review

1. Define **imperialism.**
2. What were early steps toward American expansion in the Pacific?
3. What were reasons for and against overseas expansion?
4. How did the United States defend the Monroe Doctrine?
5. **Critical Thinking** How were some of the arguments in favor of imperialism similar to reasons given to justify taking Indian lands?

Teaching the World Link

Have students compare athletic competition and war. Then discuss whether international athletic competition promotes peace.

Closing the Section

Wrap-Up Activity

Debating Imperialism

To review the issue of imperialism, have students imagine themselves as senators in 1893. Have them list arguments for and against annexing Hawaii.

Section Review Answers

1. Definition: *imperialism* (373)
2. Opening trade with Japan in 1854, purchasing Alaska, annexing Midway, considering the annexation of Hawaii.
3. For: need to gain territories before other powers did so; bring democracy and Christianity to "uncivilized" peoples; need for overseas markets and bases. Against: would violate democratic beliefs, hurt our economy, and require costly army and navy.
4. Intervened in boundary dispute between British Guiana and Venezuela.
5. Both stressed fulfilling destiny, civilizing "uncivilized" peoples, and protecting economic interests.

Geography Footnote

The science of map making is at least 4,000 years old, and the need to map one's known world seems to be universal. The earliest known maps are from Babylonia and date from 2,300 B.C. These maps are land surveys for tax purposes, cut on clay tiles. Ancient Chinese maps have been found, drawn on silk and dating from the second century B.C. In the sixth century B.C., the Greek philosopher Anaximander made a circular map with the Aegean Sea at the center, the first known map of the world. About 400 years later, another Greek, Eratosthenes, created a map that represented the known world from England to India, the first with parallel lines to show equal latitudes.

Teaching the Geography Lab

Explain that all maps distort size, shape, and distance in some way. Some make countries near the equator appear relatively larger, or make polar regions appear bigger than they are. Others make certain areas appear farther or closer than they are. Discuss what impressions maps can give about places whose size, shape, or location is distorted.

Using Map Skills

Answers

1. Most: countries in northern South America, northwestern Africa, or western Europe. Least: in southern South America, eastern and southeastern Asia, Pacific islands, and Australia and New Zealand, based on distance from North America.

2. Because of apparent isolation caused by orientation of first map, countries deemed least likely now seem more likely.

3. Russia, because it is close to these countries.

4. Location at "crossroads" of Pacific is key to economic and military power in region.

5. Maps should be accurate. Summaries should reflect that countries at a map's center seem more important than those on its edges.

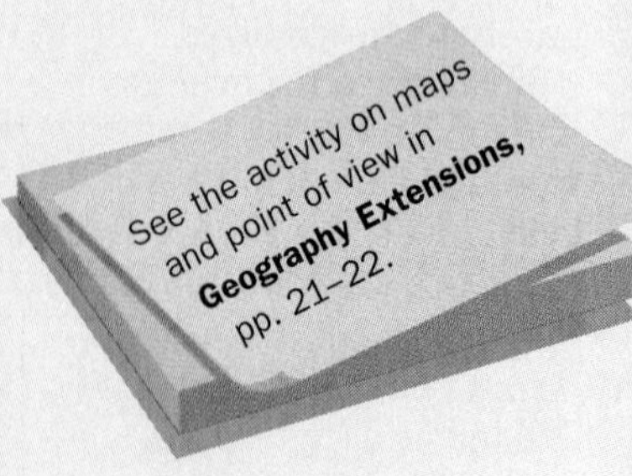

Geography Lab

Understanding a Map's Point of View

Did you know that every map, like every person, has a point of view? A map's point of view is the place at or near the center of the map. It reflects the background and interests of the mapmaker and the people who will use the map. Because we are Americans and our nation has origins in Europe, most world and hemisphere maps that we use have North America, Europe, or the linking Atlantic Ocean at their center. The world map on pages R2–R3 is a good example.

The map on this page has a different point of view—one that reflects the interests of the expansionists you have been reading about. Perhaps Senator Albert J. Beveridge of Indiana was picturing a map like this one when he stated, "The Pacific is our Ocean."

Senator Henry Cabot Lodge, 1895

"[F]or the sake of our commercial supremacy in the Pacific we should control the Hawaiian Islands and maintain our influence in Samoa."

The View from the Pacific

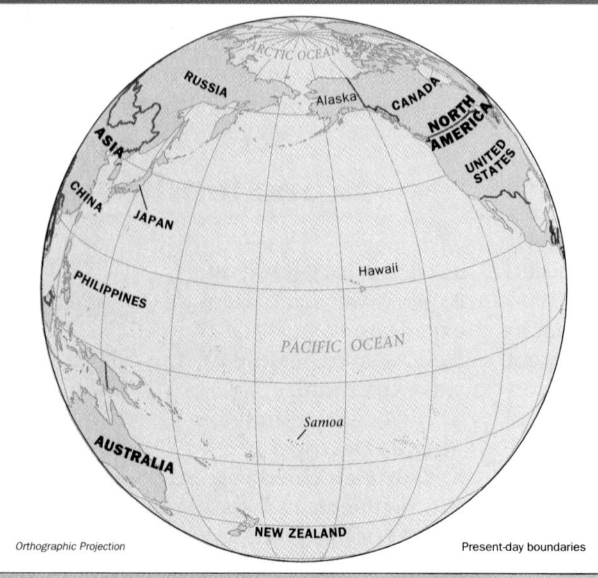

Using Map Skills

1. Look at the map on pages R2–R3. List six countries not in North America that the United States would be most likely to trade with. List six it would be least likely to trade with. Explain.
2. Look at the map on this page. Does your view of likely trading partners change? Explain.
3. What country might Americans see as their chief rival for trade with China and Japan? Why?
4. Suppose someone ridiculed Senator Lodge by saying, "Those islands are mere dots! Why bother?" How might Lodge use this map to defend his position?
5. **Hands-On Geography** Draw a world map centered on a country (not the United States) from which one of your ancestors came. Put it next to the map on pages R2–R3. Write a summary of the different views of the world that the two maps provide.

Section Objectives

- ★ Explain why the United States went to war with Spain.
- ★ Identify the results of the Spanish-American War.
- ★ Discuss how the United States governed its new empire.

Teaching Resources

Take-Home Planner 3, pp. 12–19
Chapter Resources Binder
Study Guide, p. 74
Reinforcement
Skills Development, pp. 79–80
Geography Extensions
American Readings, p. 37
Using Historical Documents
Transparency Activities
Chapter and Unit Tests

Introducing the Section

Vocabulary

protectorate (p. 383) a nation controlled and protected by another nation

Warm-Up Activity

Reasons for War

To focus on causes of war, have students list reasons for declaring war on another nation. (Some possibilities: expand territory, gain new markets, control resources, enhance national pride, punish wrongdoing, flex muscles, try out new weapons, gain revenge, warn other countries, spread religion, satisfy public opinion, distract citizens from economic hardship or political oppression.) Have students keep their lists and refer to them at the end of this section to see if they named reasons that apply to the American declaration of war against Spain.

Geography Question of the Day

Have students color in the following islands on an outline map of the world (see **Geography Extensions, p. 21**): Cuba, Puerto Rico, the Philippines, Hawaii. Refer them to the map on p. 381 if necessary. Ask which of the islands are closest to the United States. Farthest?

2. The Spanish-American War

Reading Guide

New Term **protectorate**

Section Focus **The causes and effects of the war with Spain**

1. **Why did the United States go to war with Spain?**
2. **What were the results of the war?**
3. **How did the United States govern its new empire?**

In looking toward Latin America, expansionists had long hoped to end Spain's rule over Cuba and Puerto Rico. These island colonies—along with Guam (gwahm) and the Philippines in the Pacific—were the remains of Spain's once-mighty empire.

Expansionists argued that taking over Cuba and Puerto Rico would help the United States control trade in the Caribbean. In 1895 a Cuban revolt against Spain provided an opportunity for the United States to expand its influence in the region.

Tensions over Cuba

Since the 1850s several Cuban patriots operating from American soil had tried to organize rebellions against Spain. Although the Spaniards brutally suppressed these revolts, they could not crush the Cubans' desire for independence. In 1895 the Cubans rebelled again, under the leadership of José Martí (mahr-TEE). Spain responded by sending an army under General Valeriano Weyler.

Although Martí was soon killed, the revolution spread rapidly. To choke off support for the rebels, Weyler ordered all Cubans into camps. Any Cuban found outside the camps would be executed.

Disease and starvation quickly turned the camps into death camps. As many as 200,000 Cubans lost their lives. Weyler's plan had worked, though. By the end of 1896, the rebels were in retreat and the revolution seemed lost.

The yellow press Newspaper accounts of events in Cuba aroused tremendous sympathy in the United States. Calls to help the rebels were widespread. American newspapers fed these feelings, as stories of Spanish cruelty appeared daily. The more horrible the story—true or not—the more newspapers were sold. Soon most Americans knew about "Butcher Weyler."

Two rival big-city newspapers—William Randolph Hearst's *New York Journal* and Joseph Pulitzer's *New York World*—fed the hysteria. More interested in selling papers than in providing unbiased news, they competed to find and print the most sensational stories and pictures.

Exaggerated news stories that were meant to appeal to emotion became known as "yellow journalism." The name came from a popular cartoon character in the *Journal* and the *World* called "The Yellow Kid."

Theodore Roosevelt was delighted as public anger over Cuba swelled into calls for war. In a private letter he wrote:

> "Until we definitely turn Spain out of the island (and if I had my way that would be done tomorrow) we will always be menaced by trouble there."

Developing the Section

Teaching the Hands-On HISTORY

Bring in a few issues of a tabloid newspaper as examples of contemporary yellow journalism. Also discuss examples of television counterparts to yellow journalism. Ask students to brainstorm a list of emotionally charged words to substitute for more neutral ones, such as *slash* for *cut,* *plead* for *ask,* and *clash* for *debate.* Have them pinpoint potential areas to exaggerate in a typical news story.

Vital Links

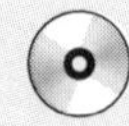
"Guantanamera" (Song)
Unit 4, Side 2, Search 11836, Play to 14379

See also Unit 4 Explore CD-ROM location 356.

USS *Maine* (Picture)
Unit 4, Side 1, Search 42339

See also Unit 4 Explore CD-ROM location 350.

Connections to Language Arts

In 1883 Joseph Pulitzer bought the *New York World.* In 15 years its circulation climbed from 15,000 to 1.5 million, the largest circulation of any newspaper in the country. His newspaper appealed to the masses by adding sports, color comics, and human-interest stories—all with lively headlines and clearly and interestingly written. The large circulation enabled him to help expose corruption in government, an important goal for him.

Because of his love of journalism, and to encourage talented writers, Pulitzer left money in his will to establish a graduate school of journalism at Columbia University. He endowed a special fund for Pulitzer Prizes to be given for achievements in journalism, literature, and music. The first Pulitzer Prizes were awarded in 1917.

Hands-On HISTORY

Writing yellow journalism The practice of writing exaggerated, emotional news stories did not end with the Spanish-American War. The headlines in the papers you see at supermarket checkout lines today are proof that yellow journalism is still alive and well.

Activity Try your hand at writing a piece of yellow journalism.

1. Look in a daily newspaper for an article about an event or person. Choose an article that seems straightforward and factual.
2. Rewrite the article to turn it into a piece of yellow journalism. To do so, exaggerate some of the information and add emotionally charged words.
3. Exchange articles with a classmate. Then identify the differences between the two versions. Conclude by discussing what might happen if regular daily newspapers adopted the style of yellow journalism.

$50,000 REWARD.—WHO DESTROYED THE MAINE?—$50,000 REWARD.

NEW YORK JOURNAL AND ADVERTISER

DESTRUCTION OF THE WAR SHIP MAINE WAS THE WORK OF AN ENEMY

$50,000! $50,000 REWARD! For the Detection of the Perpetrator of the Maine Outrage!

Assistant Secretary Roosevelt Convinced the Explosion of the War Ship Was Not an Accident.

The Journal Offers $50,000 Reward for the Conviction of the Criminals Who Sent 258 American Sailors to Their Death. Naval Officers Unanimous That the Ship Was Destroyed on Purpose.

$50,000! $50,000 REWARD! For the Detection of the Perpetrator of the Maine Outrage!

***New York Journal* headline two days after the *Maine* explosion**

President Cleveland, however, feared that a war would open the door to American imperialism. Responding to his critics in Congress, he said:

> "There will be no war with Spain over Cuba while I am President. . . . It would be an outrage."

"Remember the *Maine!*" When William McKinley became President in 1897, it appeared that he, too, would try to avoid a war. Roosevelt, who had been named Assistant Secretary of the Navy, expressed his disgust in a private letter. The President, he wrote, had "no more backbone than a chocolate éclair."

Hopes for a peaceful solution received a sudden blow on February 15, 1898. An explosion destroyed the battleship U.S.S. *Maine* in Havana harbor. The ship had been sent to protect Americans in Cuba. Some 260 American sailors died in the blast.

Although the cause of the explosion remains a matter of debate to this day, popular opinion at the time blamed Spain. "Remember the *Maine*!" became the watchword for war supporters in and out of government. Roosevelt called it "an act of dirty treachery on the part of the Spaniards." As the yellow press fanned the flames, Hearst told one of his artists, "You furnish the pictures. I'll furnish the war."

The United States declares war If President McKinley had been made of sterner stuff, he would have stood firm against those who were calling for the United States to fight Spain. Instead, he bowed to the pressure and asked Congress to declare war. On April 20 Congress passed a resolution declaring the independence of Cuba and demanding the withdrawal of all Spanish forces from the island.

To calm the fears of anti-expansionists, Congress passed the Teller Amendment declaring that the United States would not annex Cuba. Two days later McKinley ordered a naval blockade of Cuba. Roosevelt and Hearst had their war.

History Footnote

The Battle of Manila Bay was typical of most action in the Spanish-American War: It was quick, decisive, and one-sided, and American losses were minimal against the demoralized, badly trained, and ill-equipped Spaniards. These facts did not take away from the glee many Americans felt at the victory. One anonymous poet of the time was moved to heights of punning merriment:

Oh, dewy was the morning,
Upon the first of May,
And Dewey was the admiral,
Down in Manila Bay.
And dewy were the Spaniards' eyes,
Them orbs of black and blue,
And dew we feel discouraged?
I dew not think we dew!

The War in the Philippines

The United States began the war with a spectacular victory—not in Cuba, but halfway around the world in the Philippines. Expansionists already had their eyes on those islands as a possible prize of winning a war with Spain.

In fact, just ten days after the *Maine* explosion, Roosevelt had taken steps to prepare for war. The Secretary of the Navy made the mistake of leaving his office for a few hours, allowing Roosevelt to be in charge. Without consulting anyone, Roosevelt gave orders readying the navy for a possible conflict. He sent a telegraph message to Commodore George Dewey of the Asian Fleet:

> "Order the squadron . . . to Hong Kong. Keep full of coal. In the event [of a] declaration of war [with] Spain, your duty will be to see that the Spanish squadron does not leave the Asiatic Coast, and then [to conduct] offensive operations in Philippine Islands."

The battleship *Maine* mysteriously exploded in Cuba's Havana harbor on February 15, 1898. This illustration was designed to stir up public support for declaring war on Spain.

The shocked Secretary of the Navy wrote in his diary, "Roosevelt has come very near causing more of an explosion than happened to the *Maine*." However, he let the order to Dewey stand.

At dawn on May 1, Commodore Dewey surprised the Spanish fleet anchored in Manila Bay in the Philippines. The American battleships sank all ten Spanish ships without the loss of a single American sailor. In one blow, the United States had crushed Spanish naval power in the Pacific.

With word of Dewey's dramatic victory, the army scrambled to organize a force to fight Spanish soldiers in the Philippines. As war fever swept the nation, the Senate finally voted to annex Hawaii, responding to the argument that the American army and navy needed the islands as a halfway station to the Philippines.

The War in the Caribbean

The Spanish fleet in Cuba, meanwhile, made the mistake of sailing into Santiago harbor. There a stronger American fleet blockaded it. The path was clear for sending in American troops. On June 22 they landed on Cuba's southern coast.

Unlike the navy, the army was woefully unprepared. The thousands of volunteers who rushed to join the war lacked guns, tents, and blankets. Soldiers received heavy woolen uniforms completely inappropriate for the tropics. Their food, leftover canned rations from the Civil War, was disgusting and sometimes even poisonous.

The army camps lacked proper sanitary facilities, and soon the troops suffered

Discussion

Checking Understanding

1. Why was the destruction of the *Maine* a lucky event for those who favored war? (They could blame the Spaniards for the explosion, even though there was no proof.)

2. What was the effect of the Teller Amendment and why was it passed? (Declared that the United States would not annex Cuba; passed to calm fears of anti-expansionists.)

Stimulating Critical Thinking

3. Should newspapers report news objectively, or should they support a nation's war effort? Explain. (Most students will say newspapers should provide objective coverage, letting people decide for themselves the merits of the cause. Others may say all citizens should support the nation's leaders in war, even if they have doubts about its rightness.)

4. Do you think Roosevelt was wrong to order the navy to prepare for possible conflict in the Philippines? Explain. (Yes: took a drastic step without permission. No: helped lead to the dramatic victory at Manila Bay.)

Vital Links

Dewey in Manila Bay (Picture) Unit 4, Side 1, Search 43945

See also Unit 4 Explore CD-ROM location 354.

Section Activity

Writing Letters Home

To reinforce understanding of the causes and effects of fighting in Cuba and the Philippines, have each student write two letters "home." One should be from the point of view of an American soldier just before returning home from fighting in Cuba. The other should be from one preparing to return from fighting against Aguinaldo's rebels in the Philippines. Tell students to include reasons for being there, battle experiences, attitudes of the natives toward the United States, and results of the fighting. Ask them to include dates and locations on the letters.

Tips for Teaching

Auditory Learners

Auditory learners often grasp ideas better through speaking and hearing than reading. Have pairs role-play an interview with a figure of the Spanish-American War, such as Dewey, Roosevelt, McKinley, or Aguinaldo. Then have them choose another figure and switch roles so that the interviewer becomes interviewee.

See the Study Guide activity in **Chapter Resources Binder**, p. 74.

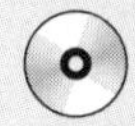

Vital Links

Marines in Cuba (Picture) Unit 4, Side 1, Search 42345

See also Unit 4 Explore CD-ROM location 351.

Voice of Charles Young (First Person Account) Unit 4, Side 1, Search 41171, Play to 41376

See also Unit 4 Explore CD-ROM location 347.

from plague and yellow fever. All told, 5,462 Americans lost their lives. Of those deaths, only 379 were the result of combat.

"Rough Riders," "Smoked Yankees" Among the volunteers who landed in Cuba in June was Theodore Roosevelt. He had quit the Navy Department to become second in command of a volunteer regiment nicknamed the "Rough Riders."

"Rough" was a good name for them because they came from all walks of life—from wealthy socialites to cowhands, Indians, and even a few outlaws. As things turned out, though, few were "riders." A mix-up sent most of their horses elsewhere, so they had to walk into battle.

The key battles in Cuba were the assaults on the hills overlooking the city of Santiago. The main American force attacked San Juan Hill on July 1, 1898.

Meanwhile, the Rough Riders and two regiments of black soldiers, whom the admiring Spaniards called "Smoked Yankees," charged bravely up nearby Kettle Hill. Calling it a "bully fight," Roosevelt claimed that he "would rather have led that charge than served three terms in the U.S. Senate."

In one of the key battles in Cuba, American troops braved heavy fire to seize the Spanish fort on San Juan Hill above the city of Santiago. The soldiers are wearing their thick woolen uniforms in the sweltering heat.

Connections to Literature

In February 1899, in the midst of the national debate over what to do with the former Spanish colonies, including Cuba and the Philippines, a poem by English author Rudyard Kipling appeared in *The Nation,* an American magazine. Kipling's poem urged Americans to

> Take up the White Man's burden
> Send forth the best ye breed
> Go bind your sons in exile
> To serve your captive's need.

The poem charged the United States with the duty of "Fill[ing] full the mouth of Famine / And bid the sickness cease." Kipling's presentation of imperialism as an unselfish mission spurred on by noble destiny influenced many to be less hesitant about annexing new territories.

United States Overseas Possessions 1858–1900

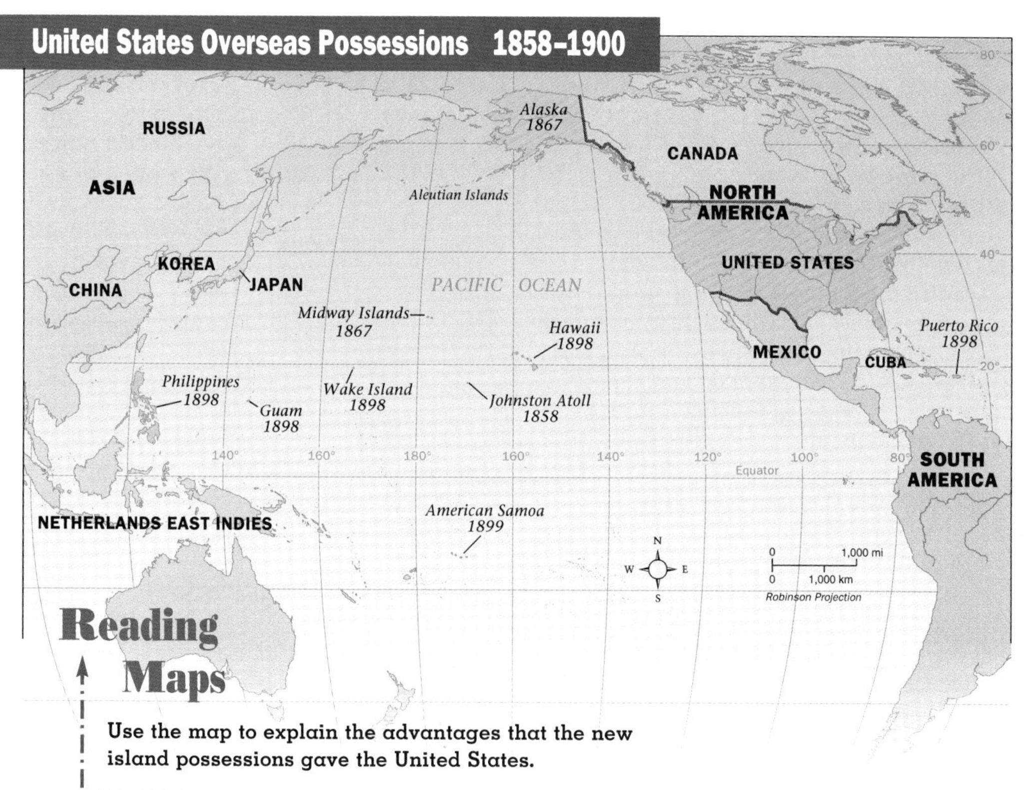

Reading Maps

Use the map to explain the advantages that the new island possessions gave the United States.

With American troops above the city and American ships blocking the harbor, the Spanish ships tried desperately to escape. On the morning of July 3 they went down in a blaze of glory. All were sunk or run aground. Nearly 1,800 Spanish sailors were captured; 474 were killed or wounded. Only one American sailor was killed and two wounded. The stunning victory gave Americans much to celebrate the next day, the Fourth of July.

The Peace Settlement

The Spanish troops in Santiago surrendered on July 17. After American forces landed on neighboring Puerto Rico a week later, Spain began negotiating for peace. A truce was finally signed on August 12, only four months after the war began. The next day American troops, aided by Filipino rebels under Emilio Aguinaldo (ah-gee-NAHL-dō), captured the Philippine capital of Manila.

By the terms of the peace treaty, signed December 10, 1898, Spain gave up Cuba, and the United States took control of Puerto Rico, Guam, and the Philippines. For Spain, the war marked the end of the great empire that Columbus had launched 400 years earlier. For the United States, the victory in what one diplomat called "a splendid little war" marked the arrival of a new world power.

Debate on the Philippines

Before the treaty could become law, though, it had to be ratified by the Senate. Many senators were troubled by its terms.

Discussion

Checking Understanding

1. Who were the "Rough Riders" and "Smoked Yankees"? (Volunteer regiment that included Roosevelt; regiments of African American soldiers.)

Stimulating Critical Thinking

2. Do you think any war could be a "splendid little war"? Explain. (Yes: wars that cost few lives and gain much could be considered so by those who do not fight or die in them. No: no war is such for those who endure its hardships or die.)

3. Could negotiation have prevented the Spanish-American War? (Answers will vary, but students should support their opinions with sound reasoning.)

Teaching the Reading Maps

Ask students to identify the main feature of the area shown. (It is mostly empty sea.) Where might the United States ships stop on their way to Japan? To the East Indies? To Australia?

Answer to Reading Maps: Provided refueling and supply stops for American navy and merchant ships, as well as military bases.

Vital Links

Cuban freedom fighters (Picture) Unit 4, Side 1, Search 42357

See also Unit 4 Explore CD-ROM location 353.

History Footnote

Emilio Aguinaldo was the leader of a revolutionary group that fought bitterly to win independence from Spain. In 1897 he signed a pact with Spain agreeing to go into exile in Hong Kong if Spain would offer the Philippines money and reforms. While in Hong Kong, he arranged to help the United States fight Spain. He returned to the Philippines in 1898. As relations with the United States worsened in 1899, the Filipinos established the Philippine Republic with Aguinaldo as president. After his capture by American troops in 1901, Aguinaldo took an oath of allegiance to the United States and retired to private life, later working toward the improvement of relations between the Philippines and the United States.

Bonus Activity

Writing a Song or Poem

To focus on varying perspectives of the Spanish-American War, have students write poems or songs about some aspect of the conflict. Songs could be heroic ballads or protest songs, and poems could either celebrate a battle or hero, criticize the war, or portray the life of a common soldier or sailor on either side. Have volunteers read their poems or perform their songs.

Teaching the

Link to the Present

Have students help you prepare a chart of the advantages and disadvantages of independence, statehood, and commonwealth for Puerto Rico. If you have Puerto Rican students in your class, ask for volunteers to voice their opinions about statehood, independence, or commonwealth status.

Vital Links

Filipino village (Picture)
Unit 4, Side 1,
Search 35739

See also Unit 4 Explore CD-ROM location 289.

The war had been fought for the stated purpose of freeing a colony from Spain. Now it looked as if the United States was about to grab colonies of its own.

When the treaty came up for a vote early in 1899, it prompted bitter debate within the Senate and by the public. The hottest issue was whether to annex the Philippines.

Leading opponents of expansion, who called themselves anti-imperialists, included labor leader Samuel Gompers, industrialist Andrew Carnegie, social worker Jane Addams, and Grover Cleveland. Author Mark Twain commented:

> "There must be two Americas, one that sets the captive free, and one that takes a once-captive's new freedom away."

Many anti-imperialists shared Twain's view that the United States was violating its belief in democracy. They wanted the Philippines to become independent.

Expansionists countered that the Filipinos were "unfit" to govern themselves, and that if the islands were left alone another country might seize them. They also appealed to national pride. Where once the American flag goes up, they insisted, it must never come down.

The treaty was finally ratified on February 6, 1899, by a vote of more than two to one. The Senate split, however, on a proposal by anti-imperialists to give the Philippines immediate independence. It took a tie-breaking vote of the Vice-President to defeat the proposal. It was, admitted Senator Lodge, the "hardest fight I have ever known."

The Filipino uprising Little did Lodge suspect that the real fight had just begun. The Filipino people were angry at the idea of replacing one foreign ruler with another. Filipino leader Emilio Aguinaldo immediately launched a spirited campaign to rid his homeland of the Americans.

Filipino rebel leader Emilio Aguinaldo

In the resulting war of ambush, massacre, and torture, the American forces were sometimes as brutal as the Spanish soldiers had been against rebels in Cuba. Even after Aguinaldo was captured in March of 1901, his followers continued to fight. The three-year struggle, which ended in 1902, cost the lives of more than 4,000 Americans and more than 20,000 Filipinos.

An Overseas Empire

Taking control of its new empire posed a problem for the United States. The islands it had acquired were useful as overseas bases. However, what would be the status of the native peoples there? If they were given independence, the United States would no longer control the islands. Making them colonial subjects would be un-American. Should they be made American citizens?

In 1901 the Supreme Court declared that new territories could be considered either incorporated or unincorporated. People in incorporated territories would be American citizens. Also, such territories could eventually become states. People in unincorporated territories would not be granted citizenship but might eventually be given independence. The Court left it up to Congress to decide the status of each new territory.

The Philippines To control the Philippines, the United States set up a civil, or nonmilitary, government under an American commission headed by a governor, William Howard Taft. However, it promised the Filipinos independence in the future.

Connections to Science

The elimination of deadly yellow fever from Cuba is one of the great successes in the history of medicine. The theory that the disease was carried by mosquitoes was first suggested by a Cuban doctor, Carlos Juan Finlay. The American Yellow Fever Commission met with Finlay in Havana, Cuba, in 1900 and he convinced them of the validity of his theory. U.S. Army physician Walter Reed further investigated Finlay's theory and proved that the disease was caused by a virus carried by a type of mosquito. Based on Reed's findings, William Gorgas designed a successful plan that destroyed mosquito breeding areas in Cuba. Swamps, marshes, stagnant pools, and other bodies of standing water were drained and filled.

Puerto Rico: The 51st state? To be or not to be a state—that is a question for the Caribbean island of Puerto Rico. In 1993 Puerto Ricans narrowly voted against statehood, but the debate continues.

Some Puerto Ricans strongly favor complete independence from the United States. However, most are satisfied to remain a commonwealth. They think it is "the best of both worlds." They get some benefits that states enjoy, such as economic aid and military protection. At the same time, the island keeps its cultural identity separate from the United States. Meanwhile, Puerto Rican leaders continue to negotiate with Congress to change the definition of commonwealth in ways that will help the island.

In 1902 Congress made the islands an unincorporated territory and allowed Filipinos to elect the lower house in the legislature. Taft's commission served as a senate. In 1916 Congress replaced the commission with a Filipino senate but kept an American governor. The Philippines did not receive independence until July 4, 1946.

Puerto Rico The United States did not promise independence to Puerto Rico. It did, however, gradually give Puerto Ricans a greater voice in their government. In 1917 Congress granted Puerto Ricans citizenship. It gave them control over both houses of the legislature but kept an American governor. In 1952 Puerto Rico became a commonwealth of the United States, subject to federal laws but without the rights that a state has to be represented in Congress.

Cuba The Teller Amendment had pledged that the United States would not annex Cuba. Still, American leaders did not want to give Cuba independence until the island had recovered from the war. Under an American military government, troops distributed food, built roads and schools, and improved sanitation.

Crucial to Cuba's future success was finding a cure for yellow fever. Thanks to the efforts of army doctors led by Walter Reed and William Gorgas (GOR-guhs), the disease was traced to a species of mosquito. Once the carrier was discovered, it was possible to bring the terrible plague under control.

By 1901 the Cubans had adopted a constitution and declared themselves ready for self-government. To guard against another foreign power taking over Cuba, Congress added the Platt Amendment to Cuba's constitution, making Cuba a protectorate of the United States. A **protectorate** is a nation protected and controlled by another nation. Reluctantly, the Cubans agreed.

The Platt Amendment gave the United States the right to intervene militarily to maintain order. American forces did so four times before the amendment was finally repealed in 1934. As a result of a treaty signed in 1903, the United States still has a naval base at Guantánamo Bay.

2. Section Review

1. Define **protectorate.**
2. Why did war break out between the United States and Spain?
3. How did the United States benefit from the Spanish-American War?
4. Did people in former Spanish colonies become American citizens? Explain.
5. **Critical Thinking** Should the United States have given immediate independence to the former Spanish colonies? Explain.

Closing the Section

Wrap-Up Activity

Making a Time Line

To review the major events of the section, have students create a time line beginning with the Cuban revolt against Spain and concluding with the end of the Filipino uprising. Have them include each important event and draw a picture to represent it on the time line.

Section Review Answers

1. Definition: *protectorate* (383)

2. Desire of many Americans, including government leaders, for an expansion of American influence; outrage over Spanish cruelty in Cuba and Puerto Rico; inflammatory reports in the yellow press; sinking of the *Maine.*

3. Gained Puerto Rico, Guam, and Philippines; strengthened influence in Cuba and became a world power.

4. Those in Puerto Rico became citizens, while those in Cuba and the Philippines did not. The Supreme Court left it up to Congress to determine the status of each protectorate.

5. Yes: hypocritical not to grant immediate independence. No: residents of former colonies were not ready for self-government, and territory could be seized by another power.

and way of life. He sees positive aspects of American life and wants to extend them to Filipinos, while enriching United States economically and increasing its prestige. (b) Aguinaldo is a Filipino who has fought against Spanish colonial rule and resents idea of Spain being replaced by another colonial power.

For further application, have students do the Applying Skills activity in the Chapter Survey (p. 392).

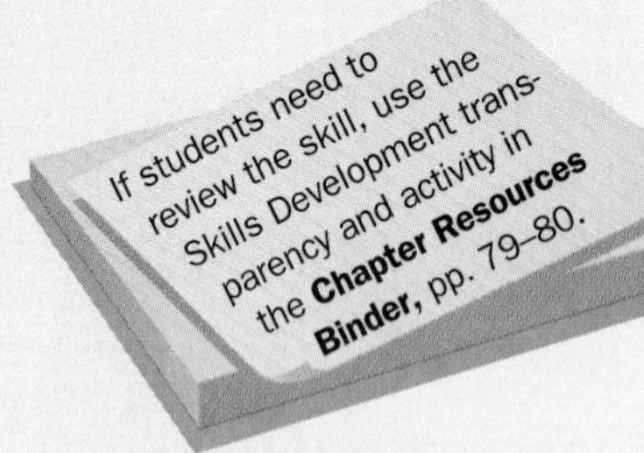

If students need to review the skill, use the Skills Development transparency and activity in the Chapter Resources Binder, pp. 79–80.

Introducing the Skill Lab

Make sure students know the definitions of *point of view* and *bias*. Ask for suggestions on how to neutralize effects of point of view and bias when examining an historical event. (Consulting multiple sources, examining the source's background for signs of bias.)

Skill Lab

Answers

1. (a) Annexing Philippines will help increase trade with China; United States has mission to "civilize" Filipinos. (b) Tried to avoid war in attempt to achieve independence, but American arrogance provoked conflict. (c) Beveridge—yes, Aguinaldo—no.

2. (a) Yes: refers to United States as God's trustee of civilization and to Americans as chosen people. (b) Focuses on benefits to the United States, such as trade advantages, and to Filipinos of American "civilizing" influence, while ignoring American belief in self-government. (c) No: sees them as arrogant, mean, underhanded, and to blame for provoking hostilities. (d) Focuses on denial of independence and self-government, ignoring possible benefits of American rule.

3. (a) Beveridge is an American who believes in superiority of American values

(Answers continued in top margin)

Skill Lab

Thinking Critically

Comparing Points of View

Upon returning from a tour of the war-torn Philippines, Senator Albert J. Beveridge of Indiana made a name for himself by arguing in favor of annexation. His ideas were opposed by some Americans and, most importantly, by Filipino rebel leader Emilio Aguinaldo.

Question to Investigate

Did the United States have the right to rule the Philippines?

Procedure

Read A and B. Then do the following.

1 Summarize the speakers' statements.
a. What main points does Beveridge make?
b. What main points does Aguinaldo make?
c. How would each speaker answer the Question to Investigate?

2 Identify the bias of each speaker.
a. Does Beveridge think Americans are superior to Filipinos? Explain.
b. What effects of annexation does Beveridge focus on? What effects does he seem to ignore?
c. Does Aguinaldo think Americans are as fair and honest as he is? Explain.
d. What possible effects of a fight for independence does Aguinaldo focus on? What does he seem to ignore?

3 Consider how point of view can cause bias.
a. Imagine that you are Senator Beveridge. What has led you to feel the way you do?
b. Imagine that you are Emilio Aguinaldo. What has led you to feel the way you do?

Skill Tips

Keep in mind:

- Point of view grows out of such influences as family background, nationality, experiences, and beliefs.
- Point of view can lead to bias. A biased statement may be emotional, exaggerated, or inaccurate. It may focus on some aspects of an issue and ignore others.

Sources to Use

A "The Philippines are ours forever. . . . And just beyond the Philippines are China's illimitable markets. We will not retreat from either. We will not repudiate [reject] our duty in the archipelago [group of islands]. We will not abandon our opportunity in the Orient.

We will not renounce our part in the mission of our race, trustee [supervisor], under God, of the civilization of the world. And we will move forward to our work . . . with gratitude for a task worthy of our strength, and thanksgiving to Almighty God that He has marked us as His chosen people. . . ."

From a speech by United States Senator Albert J. Beveridge, January 9, 1900

B "By my proclamation of yesterday I have published the outbreak of hostilities between the Philippine forces and the American forces of occupation in Manila, unjustly and unexpectedly provoked by the latter. . . . I have tried to avoid, as far as it has been possible for me to do so, armed conflict. . . .

But all my efforts have been useless against the measureless pride of the American Government and of its representatives in these islands, who have treated me as a rebel because I defend the sacred interests of my country and do not make myself an instrument of their dastardly intentions."

From a speech by Filipino leader Emilio Aguinaldo, February 5, 1899

Section Objectives

- ★ Explain how the United States tried to prevent rivals from gaining power in Asia.
- ★ Discuss how and why the United States built a canal through Panama.
- ★ Discuss ways the United States intervened in Latin America.

Teaching Resources

Take-Home Planner 3, pp. 12–19
Chapter Resources Binder
Study Guide, p. 75
Reinforcement, pp. 77–78
Skills Development
Geography Extensions
American Readings, pp. 38–40
Using Historical Documents
Transparency Activities
Chapter and Unit Tests, pp. 67–70

Introducing the Section

Vocabulary

spheres of influence (p. 385) areas of a country in which other countries claim exclusive rights to trade and invest

diplomacy (p. 387) conducting relations with other nations

Warm-Up Activity

Discussing "World Power"

To prepare students for reading about the new role of the United States, have them write about what they think it means to become—and remain—a "world power." After reading the section, they can determine if the United States at the time matched their definition.

Geography Question of the Day

Have students list geographic features and other conditions that would simplify the task of digging a canal. (Short distance between bodies of water; hospitable climate; plentiful supplies; easy access for supplies, workers, and machinery; loose soil and few rocks; level terrain; assistance from local government.) Have them keep their lists to see how many of these conditions were met in Panama.

3. A New Role in the World

Reading Guide

New Terms **spheres of influence, diplomacy**

Section Focus **How the United States took a more active role in Asia and Latin America**

1. How did the United States try to prevent rivals from gaining power in Asia?
2. How and why did the United States build a canal through Panama?
3. In what ways did the United States intervene in Latin America?

As a result of annexing Hawaii and winning the war with Spain, the United States had firm footholds in the Pacific and the Caribbean. Americans now saw themselves as having a new, more important role in the world. The nation was ready to flex its muscles and take steps to protect and expand its overseas interests.

The Open Door Policy

The United States soon saw a threat to its trade with China. In 1899 the European powers and Japan were rushing to carve China into **spheres of influence**—areas in which each country claimed exclusive rights to trade and invest. The Philippines had given American merchants a base at China's doorstep. Now it seemed that the door might be slammed in their faces.

In 1899 Secretary of State John Hay sent letters to each of the great powers asking them to agree that China's ports would remain open to all nations. Although none made a definite commitment, the next year Hay boldly declared that this "Open Door policy" was in effect.

Meanwhile, many Chinese resented foreign control of their trade. Chinese patriots known as "Righteous and Harmonious Fists" (or "Boxers") called for the destruction of all "foreign devils." The Boxers stormed the capital city of Peking (now called Beijing), killing more than 300 foreigners.

The foreign powers used the Boxer Rebellion as an excuse to invade China and extend their spheres of influence. To make sure that the United States had a hand in settling the

An American cartoon in 1900 shows Uncle Sam opening China to free trade with all nations. Figures representing Britain (left) and Russia look on.

Developing the Section

Teaching the

Link to Art

Begin by asking students to describe the subject matter of each painting. Ask how this subject matter differs from that of such illustrations as the ones on pages 379 and 380. (These paintings show unknown people in everyday scenes, rather than well-known military or political events.) Then have them compare the Cassatt and Utamaro paintings and answer the discussion question. **Discussion Answer:** In both paintings, the figures appear flat rather than multi-dimensional, and make a strong silhouette against the background. Cassatt used floral patterns like the dress in Utamaro's painting for both the dress and the background. Both paintings show women performing everyday domestic tasks.

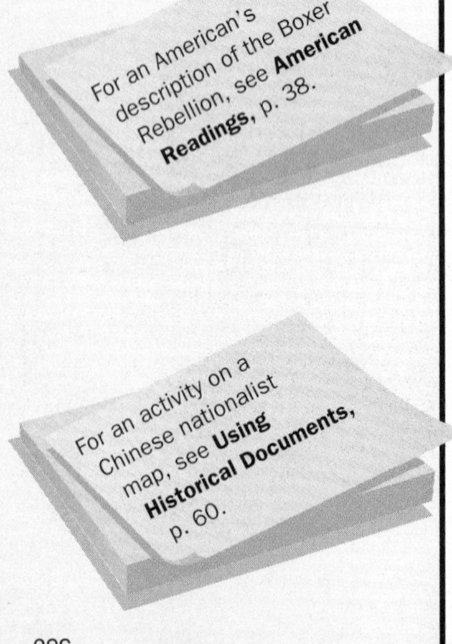
For an American's description of the Boxer Rebellion, see **American Readings**, p. 38.
For an activity on a Chinese nationalist map, see **Using Historical Documents**, p. 60.

Connections to Art

After Pennsylvania-born Mary Cassatt studied art in Philadelphia, she moved to France in 1866, just as the Impressionist school of painting emerged. She settled in Paris, where her work attracted the attention of painter and sculptor Edgar Degas, who invited her to exhibit her work with his and that of other Impressionists. Beginning in 1882 Cassatt's style changed as her work became influenced by Japanese woodcuts. She emphasized line instead of mass and experimented with asymmetrical composition. Cassatt frequently chose as her subjects members of her family. She portrayed them in domestic settings, often showing mothers and children in informal gestures and positions. Her adopted country awarded her the Legion of Honor for outstanding artistic achievement in 1904.

Honolulu Academy of Arts

Link to Art

The Letter (Mary Cassatt, 1891), ***Okita Carrying a Teacup*** (Kitagawa Utamaro, about 1790) The growing trade with Japan introduced many Americans to Japanese art. Impressionist painters such as Mary Cassatt experimented with Japanese styles. Instead of showing depth, the Japanese divided pictures into large flat surfaces. They showed glimpses of everyday life, using silhouettes and decorative patterns. **Discuss** Compare the two paintings. How does Cassatt's painting reflect Japanese influence?

crisis, President McKinley sent troops to help crush the rebellion. Meanwhile, Hay convinced the other powers not to take over Chinese territory and to maintain an "open door" for trade.

Tensions with Japan

As you read in Chapter 7, McKinley's assassination in 1901 made Theodore Roosevelt President. Only 42 years old, Roosevelt was the youngest person to have held the office—and he intended to thoroughly enjoy using his powers as President. He said to his friend Senator Henry Cabot Lodge:

> "It is a dreadful thing to come into the Presidency this way, but it would be a far worse thing to be morbid [gloomy] about it."

Connections to Music
The arrival of the American fleet in Japanese ports around the turn of the twentieth century has furnished the story for one of the most popular Italian operas, *Madame Butterfly.* American playwright David Belasco wrote a melodrama about an American naval officer named B. F. Pinkerton who weds a beautiful, young Japanese girl in the port city of Nagasaki. The story ends in tragedy as Pinkerton abandons his Japanese wife and later returns with his American bride to take his half-Japanese child back to the United States. Heartbroken, Butterfly commits suicide with her father's sword as the baby, named Trouble, waves a little American flag. The story was turned into an opera by the great Italian composer Giacomo Puccini in 1904. *Madame Butterfly* has remained a popular opera to this day.

As President, Roosevelt took firm control of **diplomacy**—conducting relations with other nations. He believed that the United States needed to take a strong role to protect its investments and trade. In looking toward Asia, for instance, he wanted to make sure that no other country became powerful enough to control trade there.

In 1905 Roosevelt stepped in to help end a war between Russia and Japan. For more than a year, they had been locked in a bloody conflict over Korea and the Chinese province of Manchuria. Japan won all the battles but was running low on money, and Russia refused to quit. Roosevelt invited both nations to a peace conference in Portsmouth, New Hampshire.

In the Treaty of Portsmouth, Russia recognized Japan's control of Korea, and both nations agreed to withdraw from Manchuria. For his effective diplomacy in ending the Russo-Japanese War, Roosevelt received the 1906 Nobel Peace Prize. Many Japanese, however, resented Roosevelt because he had not supported Japan's demand for large cash payments from Russia.

Tensions with Japan were increased by racist attitudes in the United States. Japanese especially resented a decision by the San Francisco School Board in 1906 to segregate Asian students. In 1907 Roosevelt arranged a "Gentlemen's Agreement" with Japan. In return for Roosevelt getting the school board to give up its plans to segregate Asian students, Japan promised to limit immigration to the United States.

The Great White Fleet Roosevelt, meanwhile, worried about Japan's rising spirit of imperialism. He decided to make a show of naval strength by sending 16 gleaming white warships on a round-the-world tour in 1907.

The tour was a grand success. At every port cheering crowds met "the Great White Fleet." Japan gave the fleet its warmest welcome, as children waved American flags and sang "The Star-Spangled Banner." For the time being, tensions between the two nations eased, and they promised to respect each other's overseas possessions.

The Panama Canal

Meanwhile, Roosevelt had taken steps to fulfill a dream in the Caribbean—building a canal linking the Atlantic and Pacific oceans. Such a canal would greatly reduce the time and cost of trade with Asia. Also, warships could travel more quickly between the oceans to defend the nation's new islands.

During the Spanish-American War, the battleship *Oregon* had to steam 12,000 miles (19,312 km) from San Francisco, around the tip of South America, arriving in Cuba just in time for the battle of Santiago Bay. The trip took 68 days. A canal would have shortened the distance to 4,000 miles (6,437 km).

A canal across Central America was not a new idea. In fact, a French company had begun building one in Panama, then a part of Colombia. When the company went bankrupt, the United States bought its construction equipment.

Then, in 1903, John Hay negotiated a treaty with Colombia for a strip of land across Panama. At the last minute the Colombian Senate rejected an offer of $10 million and $250,000 in annual rent, asking instead for $25 million. This demand threw Roosevelt into a rage.

Meanwhile, Panamanians who were angry at Colombia's rejection of the treaty prepared to rebel against Colombia. They were sure the United States would help them.

On November 2, 1903, the American gunboat U.S.S. *Nashville* arrived in Panama. The next day the rebels struck. When Colombian troops arrived by sea to try to stop the revolt, the *Nashville* turned them back. The United States quickly signed a canal treaty with the new Republic of Panama.

Discussion

Checking Understanding

1. What was President Roosevelt's view of diplomacy? (Believed the United States needed to take a strong role to protect its investments and trade.)

2. Why was a canal needed? (To reduce time and cost of trade with Asia, and allow warships to move more quickly between Atlantic and Pacific Oceans.)

Stimulating Critical Thinking

3. Do you think Japanese leaders were happy about the "Gentlemen's Agreement"? Explain. (Yes: it assured Japanese children's education in the United States. No: were aware of racist attitudes of many in the U.S. and may have felt pressured into the agreement.)

For a description of the lively Roosevelt White House, see **American Readings**, pp. 39–40.

Vital Links

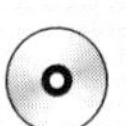
Japanese immigrants (Picture) Unit 4, Side 1, Search 35655

See also Unit 4 Explore CD-ROM location 273.

Section Activity

Speaking Softly and Carrying a Big Stick

To help students understand this important theme of United States foreign policy, have them create a world map of American diplomatic and military interventions in the first decade of the 1900s. They should mark countries such as Panama, the Philippines, China, Japan, Nicaragua, Mexico, Haiti, and the Dominican Republic on the map. Have them include the date and type of intervention (military or diplomatic) and draw or find a picture or cartoon to illustrate each event.

Vital Links

Panama Canal (Picture) Unit 4, Side 1, Search 43915

See also Unit 4 Explore CD-ROM location 402.

Workers at the Panama Canal (Picture) Unit 4, Side 1, Search 43939

See also Unit 4 Explore CD-ROM location 403.

History Footnote

The dream of carving a channel to connect the Atlantic and Pacific Oceans was centuries old. In the 1500s, Cortés had suggested a canal across southern Mexico. In 1523 Holy Roman Emperor Charles V ordered a survey of the Panama isthmus but did not attempt to build a canal. It was not until 1819 that the Spanish government formally authorized a company to begin canal construction. However, the revolt of Spain's Latin American colonies put an end to this attempt. The California gold rush of 1849 stimulated the United States' interest in finding a faster route to the West Coast, but progress on this idea moved slowly. A French attempt and an international attempt in the late 1800s both ended in bankruptcy. The United States government finally created an Isthmian Canal Commission in 1899.

Theodore Roosevelt visited the Panama Canal construction site in 1906, taking time to try out a steam shovel. He was the first President to travel outside the United States while in office. Above, a ship enters one of the canal locks.

No one was more pleased than President Roosevelt. Although critics accused him of encouraging the revolt, he felt no shame or guilt. Indeed, he later boasted, "I took the Canal Zone."

Building the canal Although Roosevelt was anxious to "make the dirt fly," construction proceeded at a snail's pace. First, it was necessary to rid the area of mosquitoes carrying malaria and yellow fever. This task fell to William Gorgas, who had helped eliminate yellow fever in Cuba. Gorgas's workers drained the swamps and ponds where the mosquitoes laid their eggs.

Then a team of army engineers led by George Goethals (GŌ-thuhlz) tackled the immense task of carving a channel through 40 miles (64 km) of solid rock and tropical rain forest. Some 45,000 workers labored on the "big ditch" for seven years. Its completion in 1914 was hailed as a monumental achievement.

"Big Stick Diplomacy"

In conducting diplomacy, Roosevelt followed the advice of an African proverb: "Speak softly and carry a big stick: you will go far." He believed that the threat of military force was the most effective way to deal with other countries.

Roosevelt had waved the "big stick" to stop Colombia from crushing the revolt in Panama. He continued to wave it to warn European nations not to intervene in Latin America.

Many Latin American nations were badly governed and owed huge debts to European investors. Roosevelt feared that European powers might use military force to collect these debts. He warned them that such interference would violate the Monroe Doctrine of 1823. He then went a step further to argue that the United States had a right to intervene in the affairs of Latin American nations if necessary:

Tips for Teaching

At-Risk Students

At-risk learners often benefit from hands-on learning experiences. Ask students to build models or create detailed drawings of the Panama Canal. They may include explanations of how locks work, as well as descriptions of total length, depth, and other information.

> "If we intend to say 'Hands off' to the powers of Europe, sooner or later we must keep order ourselves."

This policy became known as the "Roosevelt Corollary" to the Monroe Doctrine.

The Roosevelt Corollary was first applied in the Dominican Republic in 1905. To settle a financial crisis there, Roosevelt sent officials to take over customshouses and pay off foreign debts. This intervention, and others that followed, caused bitter resentment among Latin Americans.

Taft's "Dollar Diplomacy"

William Howard Taft, who followed Roosevelt as President in 1909, tried a different way to reduce European influence in Latin America. He encouraged United States businesses to invest there as owners of mines, plantations, railroads, and banks.

Taft's "dollar diplomacy" also angered Latin Americans, who resented American control of their industries and banks. When protests erupted in Nicaragua, Taft fell back on Roosevelt's policy and sent in the marines. They remained until 1933, making Nicaragua a United States protectorate.

Wilson's "Moral Diplomacy"

President Woodrow Wilson, who took office in 1913, rejected both Roosevelt's and Taft's policies. He considered big stick diplomacy too aggressive and thought dollar diplomacy mainly served the interests of big business. Wilson offered a new approach to relations with Latin American nations—"moral diplomacy." He declared, "We must prove ourselves their friends and champions upon terms of equality and honor."

In fact, however, Wilson was unable to rely only on a policy based on moral principle. To protect American business interests he, too, ended up sending troops—to Cuba, the Dominican Republic, and Haiti. "The marines have landed" became a common newspaper headline. By the end of Wilson's presidency, Latin America would be dotted with United States protectorates.

THE BIG STICK IN THE CARIBBEAN SEA

A 1904 American cartoon shows Roosevelt using military force—the "big stick"—to intervene in Latin American countries.

Wilson's intervention in Mexico The greatest failure of Wilson's moral diplomacy was in Mexico. In the Mexican Revolution of 1911, Francisco Madero (frahn-SEES-kō mah-DE-rō) overthrew the dictator Porfirio Díaz (pōr-FEE-ryō DEE-ahs). However, Victoriano Huerta (VEEK-tō-RYAH-nō WAYR-tah), an ally of the

Discussion

Checking Understanding

1. What was the Roosevelt Corollary to the Monroe Doctrine? (The idea that if the United States forbade European involvement in Latin America it would have to step in to keep order itself.)

2. Define dollar diplomacy and moral diplomacy. (Dollar diplomacy was President Taft's emphasis on American investment and ownership of banks and properties in Latin America, while moral diplomacy was President Wilson's policy of approaching Latin America on terms of equality and honor.)

Stimulating Critical Thinking

3. Which of the three types of diplomacy toward Latin America do you think was best for the period? Why? (Answers will vary but should reflect knowledge of the different policies and the historical context.)

Bonus Activity

Drawing a Comic Strip

To examine United States policy toward either Asia or Latin America, have students create comic strips. The strips should reflect the point of view of an ordinary citizen in one of the countries in which intervention took place and should describe some aspect of the country's relationship with the United States. Display the finished comic strips around the classroom.

History Footnote

An incident in the city of Tampico, several hundred miles up the coast from Veracruz, lit the spark that led to the armed clash in 1914. A United States Navy boat was temporarily seized by Mexican authorities and its crew arrested. The American commander demanded within 24 hours an apology and punishment for those who seized the ship. Most galling to the Mexicans, he required the Mexican army to raise the American flag and give it a 21-gun salute. The Mexican government, which was not even recognized by the United States at the time, refused to humiliate itself over what it saw as a trivial incident. In spite of his distaste for "big stick" diplomacy, President Wilson felt it necessary to support the navy and defend the honor of the United States. He ordered marines to capture Veracruz, which led to the brink of war.

Teaching the Reading Maps

Have students look at the map and identify the types of information it provides. (United States protectorates, territories of other nations, independent countries of the Caribbean, the Canal Zone, and sites and dates of United States interventions.)

Answer to Reading Maps: Mexico, Panama, Nicaragua, Cuba, the Dominican Republic, and Haiti.

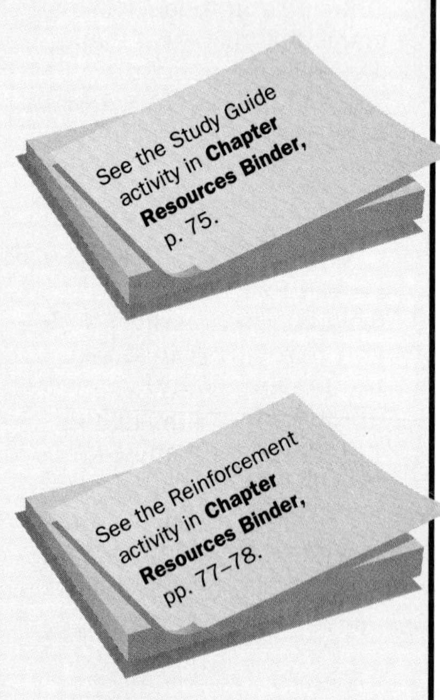

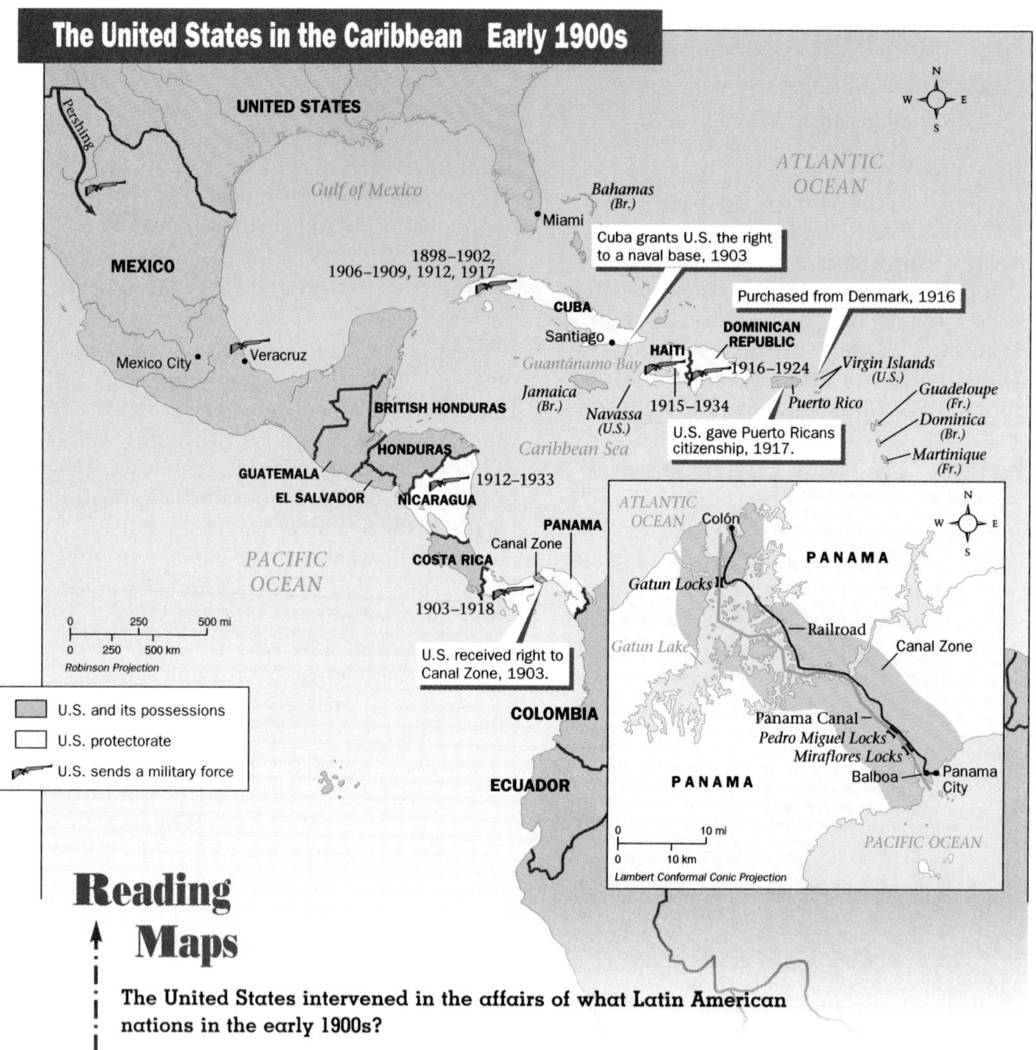

Reading Maps

The United States intervened in the affairs of what Latin American nations in the early 1900s?

rich landowners, seized power in 1913 and executed Madero.

To escape the fighting, hundreds of thousands of Mexicans emigrated to the United States. There most of them found work in industry and as farm laborers.

Declaring that he would not accept "government by murder," Wilson supported Huerta's rival, Venustiano Carranza (ve-noos-tee-AH-nō kah-RAN-sah). In 1914 Wilson sent marines to Veracruz to prevent a German ship from delivering supplies to Huerta. The marines captured the port after a stiff fight that cost the lives of 19 Americans and 126 Mexicans.

The invasion was a serious blunder. All of Mexico—even Huerta's enemies—united in denouncing it. War with Mexico was averted

History Footnote

On March 15, 1916, President Wilson sent a 3,000-man expedition into Mexico to capture Pancho Villa and his scattered band. However, Villa retreated deep into the Chihuahua Mountains, which he knew very well. He was sighted on several occasions and was shot in the knee, but even with the help of Apache Indian scouts his pursuers could not catch him. His ability to elude them for 11 months made him a Mexican folk hero.

Even while being pursued, Villa continued guerrilla activities. In the fall of 1916, he attacked a Carranza military force and raided Chihuahua City, freeing 1,600 prisoners and massacring the city's Chinese population. By January 1917 President Wilson, concerned about growing tensions with Mexico, ordered Pershing to withdraw his forces.

only when Argentina, Brazil, and Chile offered to mediate.

Carranza soon forced Huerta from power with the help of Francisco "Pancho" Villa (VEE-yah). When Villa then turned against Carranza, Wilson supported Carranza. Villa retaliated by raiding the town of Columbus, New Mexico, killing American citizens.

With Carranza's permission, Wilson sent an army in 1916 under General John J. Pershing to get Villa "dead or alive." When the troops were deep into Mexico, Carranza changed his mind and ordered an end to the search. Tensions between the two nations eased when Wilson withdrew the troops in 1917.

3. Section Review

1. Define **spheres of influence** and **diplomacy.**
2. How did the United States try to limit the power of its rivals in Asia?
3. How did the United States get permission to build a canal across Panama?
4. How were the policies of Roosevelt, Taft, and Wilson toward Latin America similar? How were they different?
5. Critical Thinking Do you think the United States was right to intervene in Latin America? Why or why not?

Why We Remember

Overseas Expansion

As a candidate for Vice-President in 1900, Theodore Roosevelt addressed the Republican National Convention with these words:

> "We stand on the threshold of a new century big with the fate of mighty nations. It rests with us now to decide whether in the opening years of that century, we shall march forward to fresh triumphs or whether at the outset we shall cripple ourselves for the contest. Is America a weakling to shrink from the work of the great world powers? No. The young giant of the West stands on a continent and clasps the crest of an ocean in either hand. Our nation, glorious in youth and strength, looks into the future with eager eyes and rejoices as a strong [athlete] to run a race."

We remember the years of overseas expansion because they mark a shift toward active involvement in the affairs of other nations. Under Roosevelt's influence, the United States began to act like one of "the great world powers."

Now, as we enter the twenty-first century, Roosevelt's words still have meaning for Americans. In the uncertain times ahead, will the United States "shrink from the work of the great world powers"? In this age of global communications and trade, just what should that work be?

Closing the Section

Warm-Up Activity

Playing *Jeopardy!*®

To review main concepts and events, have pairs write *Jeopardy!*®-style answers and questions. (For example, the answer "Taft's policy of encouraging investment in Latin America" should elicit the question, "What is dollar diplomacy?") Have students take turns reading answers and supplying questions.

Section Review Answers

1. Definitions: *spheres of influence* (385), *diplomacy* (387)

2. Declaring Open Door policy in China, mediating end to Russo-Japanese War, sending Great White Fleet.

3. Helped Panama gain independence, signed treaty with new Panama government.

4. All intervened in Latin American economies and governments and sent troops. Roosevelt's policies were more militarily imperialistic, while Taft encouraged financial imperialism and Wilson encouraged equal and honorable relations.

5. Answers should reflect historical context and sound reasoning about economic, moral, and political results of interventions.

To check understanding of "Why We Remember," assign Thinking Critically question 3 on student page 392.

Survey Answers

Reviewing Vocabulary

Definitions are found on these pages: *imperialism* (373), *protectorate* (383), *spheres of influence* (385), *diplomacy* (387).

Reviewing Main Ideas

1. Opened trade with Japan, purchased Alaska, annexed Midway Islands, considered annexation of Hawaii.

2. For: national pride and Manifest Destiny, need to control areas before other powers do, need to protect trade and deal with United States surpluses, desire to "civilize" other peoples. Against: violation of American beliefs and values, may lead to more immigration and loss of jobs to immigrants, requires expensive army and navy.

3. Tensions were rising over Spanish mistreatment of Cuba, expansionists called for annexation, explosion on *Maine* was blamed on Spanish, and Congress and media pressured McKinley to ask for war declaration.

4. Spain lost last colonies and world-power status, while United States gained colonies and became a world power.

5. (a) After uprising was suppressed, United States set up government under its control. Filipinos gained right to elect legislature in 1916 but had American governor.
(b) Puerto Ricans gained greater voice in government, U.S. citizenship, and control over both houses in 1917, but with American governor.
(c) United States maintained military government until 1901; Platt Amendment made Cuba a protectorate.

6. (a) United States declared Open Door policy to increase United States' influence and keep China open to trade with United States.

(Answers continued in top margin)

(b) Tensions rose over Japanese dissatisfaction with treaty that Roosevelt mediated ending war with Russia and over racist attitudes toward Japanese immigrants. "Gentlemen's Agreement" and tour of Great White Fleet eased tensions.

7. Protect U.S. business interests, prevent other powers from gaining influence, spread American civilization.

Thinking Critically

1. Some students will say racism played a large role, such as desire to spread democracy and Christianity to "uncivilized" peoples. Others will say economics played larger role in expansionism, with desire to increase overseas trade.

2. Yes: from perspective of most Americans, it was short, inexpensive, successful, and

Chapter Survey

Reviewing Vocabulary

Define the following terms.
1. imperialism
2. protectorate
3. spheres of influence
4. diplomacy

Reviewing Main Ideas

1. How did the United States increase its influence in the Pacific during the middle and late 1800s?
2. Summarize the arguments for and against the idea of an American empire.
3. Describe the events that led up to the Spanish-American War.
4. How did the outcome of the war affect both Spain and the United States?
5. Describe the relationship between the United States and each of the following during the first 20 years after the war.
(a) the Philippines (b) Puerto Rico (c) Cuba
6. (a) What policy did the United States pursue in China, and why? (b) Why did tensions arise between the United States and Japan? How did President Roosevelt try to ease those tensions?
7. Why did the United States become increasingly involved in the affairs of Latin American nations?

Thinking Critically

1. Analysis What role did racism play in American expansion overseas?
2. Evaluation Do you think the Spanish-American War was indeed a "splendid little war"? Explain.
3. Why We Remember: Evaluation Reread the quotation from Theodore Roosevelt on page 391. What kinds of attitudes and actions do you think Roosevelt would regard as signs of a "weakling" nation? Do you agree with his view? Explain.

Applying Skills

Comparing points of view Look through newspapers or magazines to find expressions of two points of view about a foreign policy issue. Keeping in mind what you learned on page 384, write three paragraphs in which you do the following:
1. Summarize the two writers' statements.
2. Identify the bias, if any, in each statement and tell how the writer's point of view might have contributed to it.
3. State your own opinion on the issue. Then identify your own bias, if any, and explain what has led you to feel the way you do.

History Mystery

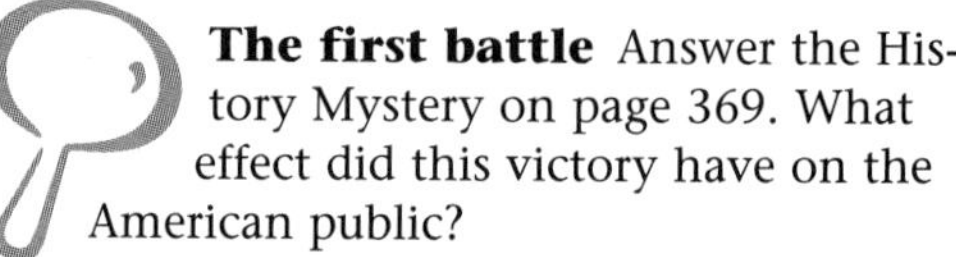

The first battle Answer the History Mystery on page 369. What effect did this victory have on the American public?

Writing in Your History Journal

1. Keys to History (a) The time line on pages 368–369 has seven Keys to History. In your journal, describe why each one is important to know about. (b) If you could go back in time, which one of the events on the time line would you most like to observe, take part in, or try to prevent? Why? Write about it in your journal.
2. Theodore Roosevelt Mount Rushmore in South Dakota is a memorial to four Presidents: George Washington, Thomas Jefferson, Abraham Lincoln, and Theodore Roosevelt. Some people think Roosevelt does not belong. Based on what you have learned about him in this chapter and in Chapter 7, do you agree or disagree? Why? Write your responses in your history journal.

had few casualties. No: war was not splendid for those on either side who died or suffered and for those who came under American control against their will.

3. Isolationism, refusal to acquire territories, hesitation to use force. Agree: weak actions or inaction might cause disrespect for the United States; strong nations should influence world. Disagree: moral strength, gained through refusal to use force; greater power in international affairs.

Applying Skills

Paragraphs should reflect an understanding of how point of view can lead to bias.

History Mystery

The United States fought, in part, for expansionist motives and hoped to take over Spain's

(Answers continued in side margin)

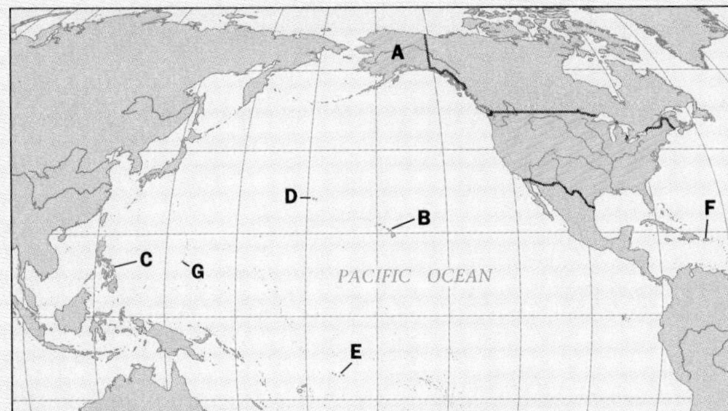

Reviewing Geography

1. Each letter on the map represents an American possession. Name each one.

2. Geographic Thinking Nicaragua was the first site favored by most people who dreamed of a canal through Central America. Look at the map on page 390. Where might a Nicaraguan canal have started? What major disadvantage of a Nicaraguan canal site is apparent? If the Panama Canal had not been built when it was, do you think it would be built today? Explain.

3. Thinking Historically Imagine that you are a Hawaiian, a Filipino, a Cuban, or a Puerto Rican during the period of U.S. intervention. Write a letter to the President of the United States in which you describe your feelings about the fact that your homeland is under American control.

Alternative Assessment

Citizenship: Putting expansionism on trial Conduct a "trial" to determine whether American expansionism did more harm or more good for the United States and the world.

❶ Decide on a role for each class member. You will need a judge, a jury of 12, a lawyer for the prosecution (seeking a "Guilty" verdict), a lawyer for the defense (seeking a "Not Guilty" verdict), and the following witnesses:

- Theodore Roosevelt and other American expansionists
- Mark Twain and other American anti-expansionists
- people from the places affected by American expansionism, including Queen Liliuokalani and Emilio Aguinaldo

❷ Have at least one pretrial planning meeting. Plan to have the prosecution present its case first, followed by the defense. Allow time for preparing roles.

❸ Conduct the trial. Then give the jury time to review and discuss the evidence.

Your work will be evaluated on the following criteria:

- you offer evidence that reflects real events and the viewpoints of historical figures
- you present your position and arguments clearly and logically
- you stay "in character"

colonies. The victory spread war fever throughout the nation.

Writing in Your History Journal

1. (a) Explanations should be similar to the time line notes on teacher pages 368–369. (b) Entries will vary but should reflect an understanding of the event's historical importance and context.

2. Does: tremendous energy and popularity; major reforms; dedicated to conservation; roles in Spanish-American and Russo-Japanese wars; building Panama Canal; making United States respected world power. Does not: not equal to others there; "big stick" diplomacy not admirable.

3. Letters should demonstrate understanding of events chosen, as well as ability to imagine goals and desires of various peoples.

Reviewing Geography

1. (A) Alaska, (B) Hawaii, (C) the Philippines, (D) Midway Islands, (E) Samoa, (F) Puerto Rico, (G) Guam

2. Should note large lake in southern Nicaragua as a starting point. The fact that Nicaragua is wider than Panama would be a disadvantage. Yes: today there exists advanced construction equipment and need to carry certain raw materials and products by ship. No: air shipping more important than sea transport.

Alternative Assessment

Teacher's Take-Home Planner 3, p. 15, includes suggestions and scoring rubrics for the Alternative Assessment activity.

Teaching the

Link to American Readings

In this feature students learn about American imperialism. In the first reading, Grover Cleveland explains that the United States has a duty to maintain a moral and honorable code of conduct in international affairs. However, the ideal is not always the reality. Stephen Crane's poem chronicles those realities—the ravages he witnessed while a war correspondent during the Spanish-American War.

Before students begin the lesson, review Interest in Hawaii (page 373) and The Spanish-American War (pages 377–383). Have students read the entire feature before assigning the A Closer Look questions. The Setting the Stage Activity and Bonus Activity may then be introduced according to the needs and interests of the students. The information contained in the Discussion questions and the Footnotes may be used throughout the lesson as appropriate. Readers' Theater is ideal for students who might find the readings somewhat difficult. Use the Wrap-Up Activity for students who would enjoy taking a step beyond the core lesson.

History Footnote

Even before he was elected to the presidency, Grover Cleveland pushed the ideals of trust and justice within and among governments. His 1884 campaign slogan was "A public office is a public trust." This slogan reminded voters that the opposing candidate, James G. Blaine, allegedly took bribes from a railroad while serving as speaker of the House of Representatives in the 1870s.

History Footnote

Although Grover Cleveland was a man who preached justice for all, he was not loved by all. What follows is a good example. "[Cleveland is] a man of force & stubbornness with no breadth of view, no training in our history & traditions & essentially coarse fibred & self sufficient." —*Henry Cabot Lodge, 1896.*

Link to American Readings

READING 8A

A Moral Standard in Foreign Policy

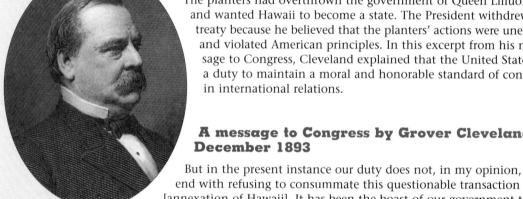

In 1893 President Grover Cleveland withdrew a Hawaiian annexation treaty submitted to the U.S. Senate by American planters in Hawaii. The planters had overthrown the government of Queen Liliuokalani and wanted Hawaii to become a state. The President withdrew the treaty because he believed that the planters' actions were unethical and violated American principles. In this excerpt from his message to Congress, Cleveland explained that the United States has a duty to maintain a moral and honorable standard of conduct in international relations.

Grover Cleveland

A message to Congress by Grover Cleveland, December 1893

But in the present instance our duty does not, in my opinion, end with refusing to consummate this questionable transaction [annexation of Hawaii]. It has been the boast of our government that it seeks to do justice in all things without regard to the strength or weakness of those with whom it deals. I mistake the American people if they favor the odious doctrine that there is no such thing as international morality; that there is one law for a strong nation and another for a weak one, and that even by indirection a strong power may with impunity despoil a weak one of its territory.

By an act of war, committed with the participation of a diplomatic representative of the United States and without authority of Congress, the government of a feeble but friendly and confiding people has been overthrown. A substantial wrong has thus been done which a due regard for our national character as well as the rights of the injured people requires we should endeavor to repair. The Provisional Government [the new Hawaiian government] has not assumed a republican or other constitutional form, but has remained a mere executive council or oligarchy, set up without the assent of the people. It has not sought to find a permanent basis of popular

consummate: complete

odious: offensive

impunity: freedom from punishment

oligarchy: government in which power is held by a small number of people

History Footnote

Liliuokalani (1838–1917) was born in Honolulu, the daughter of Hawaii's royal family. As a member of the royal family, she attended an American missionary school, where she studied English and learned American ways. She later married an American, John Owen Dominis. However, Liliuokalani's association with America did not change her belief that Hawaii should be governed by native Hawaiians. When Liliuokalani became queen in 1891, she was determined to reign over her country. Her attempts failed, but she continued to live in Honolulu, where she wrote songs and frequently hosted important guests. Liliuokalani became an honored link between Hawaii's past and present. She is also remembered for writing Hawaii's well-known song, "Aloha Oe."

Windjammers, loaded with a sugar cargo, docked in Honolulu Harbor, 1892.

support and has given no evidence of an intention to do so. Indeed, the representatives of that government assert that the people of Hawaii are unfit for popular government and frankly avow that they can be best ruled by arbitrary or despotic power.

The law of nations is founded upon reason and justice, and the rules of conduct governing individual relations between citizens or subjects of a civilized state are equally applicable as between enlightened nations. . . . [The] United States, in aiming to maintain itself as one of the most enlightened nations, would do its citizens gross injustice if it applied to its international relations any other than a high standard of honor and morality.

Excerpts from James D. Richardson, ed., *A Compilation of the Messages and Papers of the Presidents 1789–1897* (Washington, 1899) 9: 460–472.

Setting the Stage Activity

Connecting to Geography

To help students understand the importance of place and the strategies involved in the acquisition of territories, have them complete this exercise. Have students find Hawaii on the world map on page R2. Ask students why they think the United States might want to control the affairs of the islands. Divide the class into two groups and have them hold a debate on whether the United States should acquire Hawaii.

Bonus Activity

Understanding the Importance of Place

Once again have students locate Hawaii on the world map on page R2. Then ask them to estimate the distance between Hawaii and California. Give students about ten minutes to work in small groups to research and discover what resources, physical characteristics, and culture Hawaii had at the time the United States debated its annexation. Of what importance were those resources to the United States?

Discussion

Stimulating Critical Thinking

1. What American ideal does Cleveland defend in his speech? Has the United States ever strayed from that ideal? If so, how? (The ideal he speaks about is the treatment of all governments, strong and weak, with justice. Hawaii is a good example of failure to live up to the ideal.)

2. What does Cleveland describe as the basis for the "law of nations"? Based on what you have learned in studying American history, what is the result when this law is broken? (The law of nations is reason and justice. Without it, there exists the rule of the strong over the weak, there is forever a struggle to be the strongest, and eventually there is war.)

3. Explain how the irony in Paul Nash's painting is similar to that in Crane's poem. (The irony in Crane's poem can be found in the title, "War Is Kind." As Crane describes it, war is anything but kind. Nash's painting is titled "We Are Making a New World." In this case the new world is built on the ashes, corpses, and destruction of the old world—a new world that would not have been needed if the old had not been destroyed.)

Literature Footnote

Stephen Crane published *The Red Badge of Courage*, a novel about a young man's experiences in the Civil War, in 1895. Although the book became a classic, he was criticized because he had never seen a battle. Later, Crane became a war correspondent and experienced real battles. The change in his writing is most evident in the tone of pessimism that blankets his later work.

Literature Footnote

Poet and novelist Stephen Crane belonged to an American school of writing called *naturalism*. Naturalists attempted to portray everyday scenes, but they went beyond that in facing up to the coarse and brutal aspects of life. Naturalists were often also pessimists, and they frequently used symbolism in their writing.

READING 8B

"A Field Where a Thousand Corpses Lie"

Stephen Crane was a foreign correspondent as well as a writer of fiction. He was hired to cover the Cuban revolt in Spain, but his ship sank off the Florida coast. He barely survived, reaching shore in the ship's dinghy. He later covered the Greco-Turkish War and the Spanish-American War. The following poem was published in 1899 and expresses his view of war. Crane died at the age of 28, having never fully recovered from his ordeal when shipwrecked.

Stephen Crane

War Is Kind

Do not weep, maiden, for war is kind.
Because your lover threw wild hands toward the sky
And the affrighted steed ran on alone,
Do not weep.
War is kind.

Hoarse, booming drums of the regiment,
Little souls who thirst for fight,
These men were born to drill and die.
The unexplained glory flies above them,
Great is the battle-god, great, and his kingdom—
A field where a thousand corpses lie.

Do not weep, babe, for war is kind.
Because your father tumbled in the yellow trenches,
Raged at his breast, gulped and died,
Do not weep.
War is kind.

affrighted: frightened

Title page of *War Is Kin*

Literature Footnote

Stephen Crane was hired to cover the Cuban revolt against the Spanish, but his ship sank off the coast of Florida. He survived the disaster and reached shore in the ship's dinghy. This experience served as the basis for his most famous short story, "The Open Boat." The ordeal aggravated his tuberculosis, however, and he died in 1900 at the age of 28.

Readers' Theater

Have students adapt "War Is Kind" for choral reading, using male and female solo voices and male and female choruses. Suggest that students analyze the poem carefully to determine which lines would be most effective for different qualities of voice. Several lines could be read by all voices. Encourage students to be attentive to the writer's ironic tone.

Swift blazing flag of the regiment,
Eagle with crest of red and gold,
These men were born to drill and die.
Point for them the virtue of slaughter,
Make plain to them the excellence of killing
And a field where a thousand corpses lie.

Mother whose heart hung humble as a button
On the bright splendid shroud of your son,
Do not weep.
War is kind.

From Stephen Crane, *War Is Kind*, 1899.

shroud: burial cloth

Paul Nash's painting, *We Are Making a New World,* captures the desolation in the aftermath of war. Notice how Nash makes the same use of irony in the title of his painting as Crane does in the title of his poem.

A Closer Look

1. According to Cleveland, how has the Provisional Government in Hawaii violated American principles?

2. In his poems Crane often uses irony—a method of expression in which the ordinary meaning of the words is the opposite of the thought in the speaker's mind. Explain Crane's use of irony in this poem.

3. CRITICAL THINKING Cleveland calls for a moral standard in foreign policy. Do you think that the United States has followed his advice? Explain.

Wrap-Up Activity

Thinking Ahead

To expand the lesson, have students respond to this question in their history journals. First, remind students that Cleveland withdrew the treaty to annex Hawaii, but that the Provisional Government remained in charge. Then, ask students to consider what course of action the United States should take next. Have them write one paragraph outlining a plan of action.

A Closer Look

Answers

1. The Provisional Government was not republican or constitutional in form and was not set up with the consent of the people.

2. Crane uses phrases such as "War is kind" and "Do not weep" to heighten the reader's sense of the horror and waste of war. He also mocks ideas of the heroism of war by describing the "battle-god's kingdom" as a "field where a thousand corpses lie."

3. Answers will vary, but students will probably recognize that the United States has supported a variety of governments, not all of them constitutional or republican in form.

Teaching the Citizenship Lab

In this feature students learn about the Insular Cases, including *DeLima* v. *Bidwell* and *Downes* v. *Bidwell* (both 1901). In those cases the Supreme Court answered the question of whether constitutional rights and guarantees apply to residents of acquired territories.

Before students read the feature, review the information about America's overseas empire on pages 382–383. Have students read the entire feature before assigning the Understanding Civic Issues questions and the Hands-On Citizenship activity. The Bonus Activity in this Teacher's Edition may be used as an alternative to, or in addition to, the Hands-On Citizenship. The Discussion questions in this Teacher's Edition may be used at appropriate points during students' reading or afterward.

Objectives

- ★ Explain the meaning of the question "Does the Constitution follow the flag?"
- ★ Summarize the Supreme Court's answer to that question as it developed in the Insular Cases, including *DeLima* v. *Bidwell* and *Downes* v. *Bidwell.*
- ★ Identify the relevance of the Court's position to the present day.

Supreme Court Cases: *DeLima* v. *Bidwell* and *Downes* v. *Bidwell*

Citizenship Lab

Does the Constitution Follow the Flag?

When the United States acquired territory in its early decades, most people assumed the territories eventually would gain statehood. But Americans of the early twentieth century believed territories like Puerto Rico and the Philippines might never become states. Thus, a difficult question arose: Did the constitutional rights and guarantees enjoyed by U.S. citizens apply to residents in the new territories? That is, did the Constitution follow the flag?

It took 14 Supreme Court decisions to answer the question. Because the cases had to do with islands, they are called the Insular Cases. Two of the best-known Insular Cases, *DeLima* v. *Bidwell* and *Downes* v. *Bidwell,* were decided on May 27, 1901.

Although Puerto Rico was about to gain parliamentary government under Spain, it instead submitted to U.S. rule. What point do you think the cartoonist was trying to make in this 1898 woodcut?

Two Different Decisions in One Day

The DeLima case came about because the New York port collector was charging tariffs on sugar shipments from Puerto Rico. Puerto Rican sugar producers were angry. Puerto Rico was under American control. Why should they have to pay tariffs, as if they were shipping goods from a foreign country? By a 5–4 vote, the Supreme Court agreed with them.

The Downes case also involved a tariff—on oranges, this time—charged by the New York port collector. In their lawsuit, Puerto Rican orange growers cited Article 1, Section 8, Clause 1 of the Constitution, which says in part that "all duties, imposts, and excises shall be uniform throughout the United States." Again the vote was 5–4, but this time it went against the orange growers.

How could the Court hand down such different decisions on the same day? For one thing, unlike the DeLima case, the Downes case raised the question of the constitutionality

History Footnote

In the election of 1900, voters rallied behind the Republicans' slogan—"Don't Haul Down the Flag"—and gave President William McKinley and his running mate, Theodore Roosevelt, a sweeping victory. Apparently, the Supreme Court got the message loud and clear, giving Congress and the President freedom to manage the nation's new position as a world power as they saw fit. Of course, not all the justices approved of imperialism. Justice Harlan was the most persistent and vocal of the dissenters. In contrast, Justice David J. Brewer often voted with Harlan but never actually wrote an opinion. His silence may have been due to the scolding that Republican newspapers had given him for anti-imperialist remarks he made during a speech in 1899.

As the Monroe Doctrine became more significant around the turn of the century, bringing about the need for Court rulings regarding new territories, several American cartoonists saw fit to flaunt American imperialistic aspirations. In this example, the European "chickens" in the background complain: "You're not the only rooster in South America!" Uncle Sam, represented as a rooster in the foreground, replies: "I was aware of that when I cooped you up."

of a specific law. That was the Foraker Act of 1900, in which Congress had established special tariffs on goods from Puerto Rico. Writing for the Court in both decisions, Associate Justice Henry B. Brown held that while Puerto Rico was no longer a foreign country, it was not part of the United States either. Thus, Article 1, Section 8, Clause 1 of the Constitution did not apply. Congress was within its rights in passing the Foraker Act.

Four justices, led by Edward D. White, concurred with the decision in the Downes case but disagreed with Brown's reasoning. For one thing, they disliked Brown's idea that only states, not territories, were part of the United States. Justice White proposed a new idea about territories: the incorporation theory. Under this theory, Congress had the power to distinguish among territories, incorporating some and leaving others unincorporated. Residents of incorporated territories would have full constitutional protection; residents of unincorporated territories would not.

Setting the Stage Activity

Interpreting a Question

To prepare for reading about the Insular Cases, have students do quick-writes telling what they think the question at the top of page 398 means and whether it is important today. Have students share their ideas and try to reach consensus. Later, they can assess the accuracy of their ideas.

Bonus Activity

Writing Editorials

To help students clarify the issues involved in the Downes case, ask them to imagine they are newspaper editors in 1901. Have students work alone or in pairs to write editorials responding to the opinions offered by justices Brown, White, and Harlan on the question of constitutional protection for residents of territories. (You may want to provide this interpretation of Brown's ideas: In stating that Puerto Rico was not part of the United States, he implied that the territory had little if any constitutional protection. By comparison, White's ideas were moderate.) Encourage students to write catchy headlines for their editorials.

Discussion

Checking Understanding

1. What does the question "Does the Constitution follow the flag?" mean? (Do the constitutional rights and guarantees enjoyed by U.S. citizens apply to residents of territories acquired by the United States?)

2. How did the incorporation theory answer that question? (It said that whether the Constitution follows the flag to a territory depends on what Congress decides about the territory's status: incorporated or unincorporated.)

Stimulating Critical Thinking

3. Do you agree or disagree with Justice Harlan's dissent in the Downes case? Explain. (Agree: if the U.S. acquires territories, it should live up to its ideals in its treatment of the people. Disagree: Constitution does not say how people in territories should be treated.)

4. Are there advantages to being a U.S. possession today, as opposed to being independent? Explain. (Yes: places that are vulnerable to attack or incapable of economic self-sufficiency might benefit. No: it is always best for people to govern themselves unless they are actually part of another nation, as the states are.)

Citizenship Footnote

The idea that the inhabitants of places like Puerto Rico and the Philippines were "fit" for neither independence nor U.S. citizenship was common in the early 1900s. In justifying his decision to annex the Philippines, President McKinley wrote: "[W]e could not leave them to themselves—they were unfit for self-government." Justice White predicted dire consequences if the Constitution were fully extended to every new territory. He said, the United States might discover an island with economic and strategic potential but "peopled with an uncivilized race." Extending constitutional protection to such a group might result in "grave detriment on the United States . . . from . . . the immediate bestowal of citizenship on those absolutely unfit to receive it."

Associate Justice John Marshall Harlan was one dissenter in the Downes case. "This nation," Harlan wrote, "is under the control of a written constitution, the supreme law of the land and the only source of the powers which our Government . . . may exert at any time or at any place. . . . The idea that this country may acquire territories anywhere upon the earth, by conquest or treaty, and hold them as mere colonies or provinces—the people inhabiting them to enjoy only such rights as Congress chooses to accord them—is wholly inconsistent with the spirit and genius as well as the words of the Constitution."

The Incorporation Theory Catches On

Harlan's eloquence failed to carry the day. Congress liked the incorporation theory and acted on it—for example, by making the Philippines an unincorporated territory in 1902. White's theory finally caught on with most of the Court in the 1904 case *Dorr* v. *United States.* In the Philippines, the defendant in a criminal trial had not been indicted by a grand jury, and the trial jury had not included 12 people. Had the defendant's constitutional rights been violated?

No, said the Court. If Congress chose to restrict the rights of accused

(Above left) John Marshall Harlan. (Above right) Members of the Philippine forces, led by Emilio Aguinaldo (seated in vest), that helped the United States drive Spain out of the Philippines in 1898. Although Aguinaldo expected the United States to recognize Filipino independence after Spain was driven out of the country, the United States refused to do so and instead made it an unincorporated territory in 1902. The Philippines finally gained independence on July 4, 1946.

Connections to Geography

Puerto Rico and the Northern Mariana Islands are the only U.S. possessions that are commonwealths, but the similarity ends there. Puerto Rico covers more than 3,500 square miles and has more than 3.5 million people. The Northern Marianas, which lie in the Pacific Ocean, cover about 185 square miles and have about 43,000 people. Although tourism is important in both economies, Puerto Rico also has hundreds of factories that make medicine, electronic equipment, and other goods.

Guam, with about 210 square miles of land and about 133,000 people, is the largest U.S. territory. The tiniest U.S. territories also are found in the Pacific. For example, Midway Island covers only about 2 square miles and has fewer than 500 people. The U.S. Navy has an air base there.

persons in an unincorporated territory like the Philippines, it could. Justice White's concurring opinion in the Downes case was cited as the precedent. This time, Justice Harlan was the only dissenter.

Status of Modern Territories —and One Former Territory

The Supreme Court's idea that the Constitution does not necessarily follow the flag has never been reversed. However, the idea no longer has the reach that it once had. The United States has no incorporated territories today. Residents of so-called "organized and unincorporated" territories—Guam and the Virgin Islands—are U.S. citizens and have local self-government. Other U.S. territories, including American Samoa, fall into different categories and are governed by executive branch officials rather than by Congress.

Puerto Rico has not been a U.S. territory for decades. But disagreements about the ideal relationship between Puerto Rico and the United States continue to make headlines. The statehood movement has much support in Puerto Rico. Some members of Congress also would like to end Puerto Rico's commonwealth status. Congress may soon ask Puerto Ricans to choose between statehood or sovereignty, either through a "free association" agreement with the United States or total independence. Thus, the question "Does the Constitution follow the flag?" would no longer apply to Puerto Rico.

Understanding Civic Issues

1. How were the DeLima and Downes cases similar? How did they differ?
2. What was the incorporation theory, and who first proposed it?
3. **Critical Thinking** Why do you suppose many Americans of a century ago could not envision statehood for places like Puerto Rico and the Philippines?
4. **Hands-On Citizenship** Imagine it is the year 2030, and the United States is in an expansionist mood. An American spacecraft has discovered humanlike beings on a previously unknown planet. They do not resist the occupying American forces, earning their planet the name *Pacifico*. As a member of Congress, you face the question of whether the Constitution will follow the flag to Pacifico.

- Decide what Pacifico's status should be: incorporated or unincorporated territory or something else. Recall what you've read here and on pages 382–383 about the kinds of territories.
- Prepare a speech defending your choice. You may want to cite opinions from this discussion or from the chapter.
- Deliver your speech to Congress (your classmates). After everyone has spoken, vote on the status of Pacifico.

Citizenship Lab Answers

1. Similar: involved tariffs charged on food from Puerto Rico; decided on the same day by a 5–4 vote. Different: Court voted for Puerto Rican growers in DeLima and against growers in Downes; Downes involved the constitutionality of the Foraker Act; Downes gave rise to the incorporation theory.

2. Justice White's theory: Congress could incorporate territories or leave them unincorporated. Only residents of incorporated territories would have full constitutional protection.

3. Possible answers: Prejudice made statehood for places with nonwhite populations seem unacceptable; the islands were too far away.

Teaching the Hands-On CITIZENSHIP

Make sure students understand that simply returning Pacifico to its former sovereign status is not an option.

The skill you are teaching in this activity is oral presentation. At the highest level of skill development, the following qualities should be present: all ideas are expressed in a way that provides evidence of knowledge and the presentation is well focused with a well-defined thesis. Of course, the presentation must be judged on how well students express their ideas, including eye contact, voice modulation, and speaking loud enough to be heard.

At·a·Glance **9**

World War I
1914–1920

Chapter Planning Guide

Section	Student Text	Teacher's Edition Activities
Opener and Story pp. 402–405	**Keys to History Time Line** **History Mystery** Beginning the Story with **Alvin C. York**	**Setting the Stage Activity** To Fight or Not to Fight?, p. 404
1 **The Roots of World War I** pp. 406–411	**Reading Maps** European Alliances in World War I, p. 408 **Hands-On History** Surviving life in a trench, p. 409 **Link to Technology** World War I Planes and Tanks, p. 410	**Warm-Up Activity** Charting WWI Weapons, p. 406 **Geography Question of the Day,** p. 406 **Section Activity** Creating a War Map, p. 408 **Bonus Activity** A Conversation in the Trenches, p. 410 **Wrap-Up Activity** Making a Concept Web, p. 411
2 **The United States Enters the War** pp. 412–420	**Point of View** What would you do if you were drafted?, p. 415 **Link to Art** *The Rope Dancer Accompanies Herself with Her Shadows,* p. 416 **Reading Maps** The Western Front 1918, p. 418 **World Link** Russia's civil war, p. 419 **Skill Lab** Analyzing Propaganda, p. 420	**Warm-Up Activity** Predicting War, p. 412 **Geography Question of the Day,** p. 412 **Section Activity** Diary Entries in the Trenches, p. 414 **Bonus Activity** Propagandizing, p. 417 **Wrap-Up Activity** Making Event Cards, p. 419
3 **The Search for Peace** pp. 421–425	**Reading Maps** Europe and the Middle East After World War I, p. 422 **Link to the Present** The United Nations, p. 423 **Geography Lab** The Great Migration, p. 425 **Link to Literature** *After the Dancing Days,* pp. 440–441	**Warm-Up Activity** Writing Terms for a Peace Treaty, p. 421 **Geography Question of the Day,** p. 421 **Section Activity** Press Interviews, p. 422 **Bonus Activity** Matching Nations with Former Empires, p. 423 **Wrap-Up Activity** Holding a Peace Conference, p. 424
Evaluation	☑ **Section 1 Review,** p. 411 ☑ **Section 2 Review,** p. 419 ☑ **Section 3 Review,** p. 424 ☑ **Chapter Survey,** pp. 430–431 **Alternative Assessment** Compiling a wartime scrapbook, p. 431	☑ **Answers to Section 1 Review,** p. 411 ☑ **Answers to Section 2 Review,** p. 419 ☑ **Answers to Section 3 Review,** p. 424 ☑ **Answers to Chapter Survey,** pp. 430–431 (Alternative Assessment guidelines are in the Take-Home Planner.)

Teacher's Resource Package

Chapter Summaries: English and Spanish, pp. 54–55

Chapter Resources Binder
Study Guide Summarizing Information, p. 81
Reinforcement Identifying Headlines, pp. 85–86

American Readings Life in the Trenches, pp. 41–42

Chapter Resources Binder
Study Guide Identifying Relationships, p. 82
Skills Development Analyzing Propaganda, pp. 87–88

American Readings Inside the *U-20,* p. 43; American Propaganda, p. 44

Using Historical Documents The Zimmermann Telegram, pp. 65–68

Chapter Resources Binder
Study Guide Identifying Main Ideas, p. 83

Geography Extensions Population Changes and the Work Force, pp. 23–24

Chapter and Unit Tests Chapter 9 Tests, Forms A and B, pp. 71–72

Take-Home Planner

Introducing the Chapter Activity Announcing a Declaration of War, p. 22

Chapter In-Depth Activity Rewriting History, p. 23

Reduced Views
Study Guide, p. 24
Reinforcement, p. 25
American Readings, p. 26

Unit 3 Answers, pp. 29–38

Reduced Views
Study Guide, p. 24
Skills Development, p. 25
American Readings, p. 26
Using Historical Documents, p. 27

Unit 3 Answers, pp. 29–38

Reduced Views
Study Guide, p. 24
Geography Extensions, p. 27

Unit 3 Answers, pp. 29–38

Reduced Views
Chapter Tests, p. 27

Unit 3 Answers, pp. 29–38

Alternative Assessment Guidelines for scoring the Chapter Survey activity, p. 23

Additional Resources

Wall Time Line

Unit 3 Activity

Transparency Package

Transparency 9-1 The Optimistic View—use with Section 2

Transparency 9-2 The Realistic View—use with Section 2

Transparency Activity Book

SelecTest Testing Software
Chapter 9 Test, Forms A and B

Vital Links

Videodisc

CD-ROM

WWI battlefield (see TE p. 410)
WWI submarine (see TE p. 413)
Women ambulance drivers (see TE p. 414)
Voice of WWI private (see TE p. 414)
Voice of Woodrow Wilson (see TE p. 415)
Antiwar demonstration (see TE p. 416)
WWI troops leaving for war (see TE p. 416)
"Over There" (see TE p. 416)
WWI soldiers with gas masks (see TE p. 418)
WWI soldiers returning home (see TE p. 430)
Voice of Norman Roberts (see TE p. 430)

9

Teaching Resources

Take-Home Planner 3
- Introducing Chapter Activity
- Chapter In-Depth Activity
- Alternative Assessment

Chapter Resources Binder
Geography Extensions
American Readings
Using Historical Documents
Transparency Activities
Wall Time Line Activities
Chapter Summaries
Chapter and Unit Tests
SelecTest Test File
Vital Links CD-ROM/Videodisc

Chapter Objectives

- ★ Explain how World War I began and why.
- ★ Describe how the United States helped the Allies win the war.
- ★ Describe the struggle over the peace treaty to end the war.

Chapter Overview

World War I was triggered in 1914 by the assassination of the Austrian Archduke Ferdinand, which led to war between Austria-Hungary and Serbia. Long-standing rivalries and military alliances among European countries soon drew most of Europe into war, pitting the Central Powers against the Allies. The opposing sides were locked in a stalemate for three years, with soldiers living

Time Line

Keys to History
Keys to History journal writing activity is on page 430 in the Chapter Survey.

Archduke Ferdinand assassinated This caused Austria-Hungary to declare war on Serbia, leading to World War I. (p. 406)

***Lusitania* sunk by German U-boat** The sinking of the British luxury liner shook the American commitment to neutrality and brought the United States closer to entering the war in Europe. (p. 412)

Looking Back Washington, in his Farewell Address of 1796, warned the nation against getting involved in European power struggles.

1914–1920

Chapter 9

World War I

Sections

1914
Archduke Ferdinand and wife assassinated in Sarajevo

1915
Lusitania sunk by German U-boat

1914

Looking Back

George Washington advises against foreign alliances
1796

and fighting from the trenches. Modern technologies such as tanks, submarines, and airplanes added to the war's destructiveness.

Americans at first were committed to neutrality. However, the sinking of the British luxury ship *Lusitania,* Germany's attempt to ally with Mexico, and other events drew the United States into the war in 1917. American troops were crucial in turning back the last German offensive in France and helping the Allies win the war in 1918.

The Treaty of Versailles gave independence to various national groups in Europe and set up a League of Nations, part of President Wilson's plan to ensure lasting peace. Other provisions punished Germany harshly, setting the stage for another war 20 years later. Wilson campaigned for passage of the Treaty of Versailles, but the Senate defeated it and made its own treaty with the Central Powers.

Teaching the *HISTORY*

Students will find the answer on p. 405. See Chapter Survey, p. 430, for additional questions.

Time Line

United States declares war on Germany American entry into the war brought desperately needed support to the Allies. (p. 413)

Wilson presents Fourteen Points President Wilson's plan to bring long-lasting peace to the world called for removing the causes of war, promoting human rights, and setting up a League of Nations. (p. 421)

Germany signs Armistice Germany and the other Central Powers signed a truce after an Allied offensive turned back the German advance into France. (p. 419)

Treaty of Versailles signed The treaty that ended World War I redrew the map of Europe and set up a League of Nations. It included terms to punish Germany. (p. 423)

Senate refuses to ratify Treaty of Versailles The Senate feared that the League of Nations would commit the United States to future wars on foreign soil. Without American support, the League had little chance of success. (p. 424)

World Link See p. 419.

Looking Ahead In 1941 the United States again became involved in a world war.

HISTORY

Mystery

Sgt. Alvin C. York received more military awards in World War I than any other American. Twice, however, York had tried to avoid going to war. Why?

1917
United States declares war on Germany

1918
Germany signs armistice

1918
Wilson presents Fourteen Points

1919
Treaty of Versailles signed

Hall of Mirrors, Versailles

1920
Senate refuses to ratify Treaty of Versailles

1917 — *1920*

World Link
Civil War in Russia
1918–1920

Looking Ahead

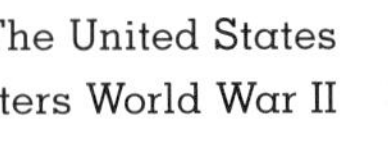

The United States enters World War II
1941

Beginning the Story

Alvin C. York

Alvin C. York was one of the American "doughboys" who served overseas in World War I. Prior to serving, York had struggled with the question of whether fighting in a war was right, because it went against his religious beliefs. He decided that world peace was a noble goal and went on to become the most decorated American soldier of World War I, receiving among other decorations the Congressional Medal of Honor.

Setting the Stage Activity

To Fight or Not to Fight?

To focus on Alvin York's dilemma, have small groups discuss under what circumstances, if any, they would be willing to go to war. Conclude by having groups share their responses with the class.

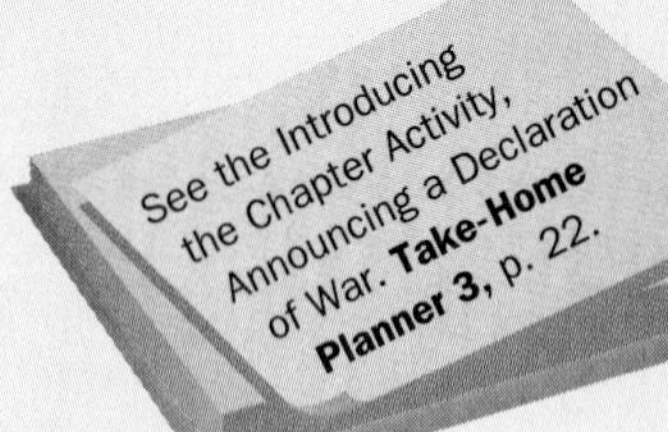

See the Introducing the Chapter Activity, Announcing a Declaration of War. **Take-Home Planner 3**, p. 22.

History Footnote

The Selective Service Act of May 18, 1917, required all men aged 21 to 30 to register for the draft. They were classified based on eligibility. Class I—eligible for immediate service—included able-bodied, unmarried men without dependents, unskilled workers, and workers in industries not considered essential. Husbands and fathers who had repeatedly failed to support their families were also in Class I. Classes II and III included married men with jobs useful to the war effort, such as skilled industrial and agricultural workers. Class IV consisted of married men who were the sole family provider, as well as heads of "necessary" businesses. All of the 2.8 million drafted came from Class I. Of these, 2 million were sent overseas, and about 1.4 million were involved in combat.

Beginning the Story with Alvin C. York

On the morning of October 8, 1918, American soldiers crouching in their trenches in France looked up to see an incredible sight. Two long lines of German soldiers emerged out of the woods and trudged toward the American lines. Leading this strange cavalcade was an American soldier named Alvin C. York.

"Well, York," his amazed commander said later, "I hear you have captured the whole German army."

"No, sir," York answered, "I have only one hundred and thirty-two." He did not add that he had also captured 35 German machine guns and left 32 Germans dead in the woods—all single-handedly. In recognition of his heroism, York would become the most decorated American soldier of World War I. At the end of his life, however, he credited his remarkable feat to God. "We know there are miracles, don't we?" York would say. "Well, this was one."

The First Miracle

The first miracle in York's life was that he was not in jail or dead when World War I began in 1914. Born in a one-room log cabin in the Cumberland Mountains of Tennessee, York had the restless blood of pioneers, like Daniel Boone and Davy Crockett, flowing through his veins. Even his mother admitted that her tall, lanky, red-haired son was "kind of a wild boy."

Then Alvin C. York fell in love with a churchgoing neighbor named Grace Williams. Through her he found the love of God. As York explained it:

> "Miss Gracie said that she wouldn't let me come a-courting until I'd quit my mean drinking, fighting, and card flipping. So you see, I was struck down by the power of love and the Great God Almighty all together."

York changed his wild ways and joined the Church of Christ in Christian Union.

History Bookshelf

Dank, Milton. *Khaki Wings.* Delacorte, 1980. A 17-year-old young man joins the Royal Flying Corps, serving first as a mechanic in France and then as a fighter pilot.

Also of interest:

Dolan, Edward F. *America in World War I.* The Millbrook Press, 1996.

Everett, Susanne. *World War I: An Illustrated History.* Rand McNally, 1980.

Frank, Rudolf. *No Hero for the Kaiser.* Lothrop, Lee & Shepard, 1986.

Hoobler, Dorothy and Thomas Hoobler. *The Trenches: Fighting on the Western Front in World War I.* G. P. Putnam's Sons, 1978.

Alvin C. York was one of millions of American soldiers sent to France during World War I. Troops on both sides dug trenches in the frozen ground to protect themselves from enemy fire.

"Thou Shalt Not Kill"

In 1917, at age 30, York received a letter that would change his life. The United States had joined the war in Europe and had sent him a notice to register for the draft. York considered himself as patriotic as any other American. However, he also believed in the Bible's commandment, "Thou shalt not kill." He later admitted, "I just didn't know what to do. I worried and worried. I couldn't think of anything else. My thoughts just wouldn't stay hitched."

On his draft registration form was the question, "Do you claim an exemption from the draft?" He wrote,"Yes. Don't want to fight."

"Blessed Are the Peacemakers"

York tried to be excused from military service because of his religious beliefs. However, because the government did not recognize his church—the Church of Christ in Christian Union—as a traditional pacifist faith, his appeals were denied.

When York learned that he was to be sent to fight on the front lines in France, he again asked to be excused from combat. He explained his religious beliefs to his commanding officer, Major George Edward Buxton. Convinced of York's sincerity, the major granted him a ten-day leave and sent him home to work out his inner conflict.

Back home York talked with his family and pastor. He went into the mountains to pray and think. He reread key passages in the Bible. One gave him special comfort. It said, "Blessed are the peacemakers."

Major Buxton had told York that Americans were going to war in Europe to bring peace to the world. "Was this a goal worth fighting, worth killing, worth dying for?" York asked himself. After much thought, he closed his Bible, looked up at his mother, and said, "I'm a-going."

Hands-On HISTORY Activity

Imagine that you are Alvin York's friend. It is the year 1917 and Alvin has just received his draft notice. He has written to you for advice. In his letter he explains that he is loyal to his country, yet knows that his religion is against fighting. Draft a response to Alvin telling him what you think he should do and why.

Discussion

Thinking Historically

1. What was the reason for the draft in 1917? (To raise an army of American soldiers to fight in World War I.)

2. What conflict did Alvin York experience when he received a notice to register for the draft? (He believed he was patriotic, but he did not want to fight because he also believed in the Bible's commandment "Thou shalt not kill.")

3. How did York resolve this conflict? (He decided that going to war in Europe would help bring peace to the world, and that this was a worthy goal. He found support for his decision in the Bible passage that says, "Blessed are the peacemakers.")

See the Chapter In-Depth Activity, Rewriting History, **Take-Home Planner 3,** p. 23.

Teaching the Hands-On HISTORY

If students are not sure what advice they want to give, suggest that they first make a two-column chart, listing the pros and cons of going to fight in the war.

For a journal writing activity on Alvin York, see student page 430.

Introducing the Section

Vocabulary

stalemate (p. 409) a deadlock

Warm-Up Activity

Charting WWI Weapons

To introduce the subject of modern warfare, have students list weapons and methods of fighting they think might have been used in a war taking place around 1914. Have them make their lists in a three-column chart under the headings *On Land, On Water,* and *In the Air.* As students read the section, they can make deletions and additions to their charts.

Geography Question of the Day

Write *World War* on the chalkboard. Ask students: What does this term mean to you? What do you think makes a war a "World War"? After they have read the chapter, have them recheck their answers to see if they apply to World War I.

Section Objectives

- ★ Describe the incident that started World War I and why.
- ★ Explain how the nations of Europe took sides in the war.
- ★ Identify the weapons and methods that were used in the war.
- ★ Describe the reaction of the United States to the war.

Teaching Resources

Take-Home Planner 3, pp. 20–26
Chapter Resources Binder
Study Guide, p. 81
Reinforcement, pp. 85–86
Skills Development
Geography Extensions
American Readings, pp. 41–42
Using Historical Documents
Transparency Activities
Chapter and Unit Tests

1. The Roots of World War I

Reading Guide

New Term **stalemate**

Section Focus **World War I begins in Europe**

1. **What incident started World War I and why?**
2. **How did the nations of Europe choose sides?**
3. **What weapons and methods were used in the war?**
4. **How did the United States react to the war?**

On June 28, 1914, Alvin York was enjoying life at home in the Tennessee mountains. Little did he—or his fellow Americans—suspect that an incident thousands of miles away was going to rock the world and forever change the direction of his country.

News of the incident reached Americans the next day. The *New York Times* announced the story with bold, front-page headlines:

> "Heir to Austria's Throne Is Slain with His Wife by a Bosnian Youth to Avenge Seizure of His Country"

Archduke Francis Ferdinand and his wife, Sophie, greet a well-wisher just one hour before their assassination.

The assassination of the Austrian Archduke Ferdinand and his wife, the Duchess of Hohenberg, in Sarajevo, the capital of the Balkan province of Bosnia, caused shock waves to roll through Europe. It caused little concern in the United States, though. Europe and its conflicts felt far removed from life at home.

Wilson's Neutrality Policy

Since the days of George Washington, the United States had tried to avoid involvement in European conflicts. President Woodrow Wilson sought to continue this policy.

On August 4, 1914, Wilson responded to the news of war in Europe by issuing a proclamation of neutrality. He urged Americans to be "impartial [not to take sides] in thought as well as in action." Wilson hoped that the United States could play the role of mediator to help bring peace to Europe.

European Rivalries

In the decades before 1914, Europe had been experiencing a period of industrial growth and prosperity.

History Footnote

While many Americans did not want the United States to get involved in the war in Europe, they still cared about who might win. In 1910 more than a third of the 92 million Americans were first- or second-generation immigrants. Of these, 8 million were German and 4 million were Irish, many of whom hated Britain for its centuries-old domination of Ireland. Members of both groups leaned toward the Central Powers.

Many other Americans sympathized with the Allied cause. The United States had many ties of culture and tradition with Britain. It also had historical ties with France, which had contributed to American political ideals and aided the American Revolution. Some Americans also saw Germany as a symbol of autocratic government and militarism.

As a result, the future looked brighter than it had for a long time.

Even so, European countries distrusted one another. With so many shared boundaries, each wanted to be armed for its own protection. Instead of bringing about the desired security, however, more weapons produced more fear. Feelings of nationalism added urgency to the race to build up arms and supplies.

The powder keg Friction between the nations of Europe was not new. The tiny countries of the Balkan Peninsula, for example, had feuded with one another for centuries over boundary lines. Matters there were so tense that the region was known as "the powder keg of Europe," just waiting to explode.

In truth, all of Europe was a powder keg. For 43 years the French had seethed with anger at Germany for annexing two of its richest provinces—Alsace and Lorraine—after the Franco-Prussian War of 1870–1871. Meanwhile, Italians resented Austrian control of their borderlands.

The powerful empires—Austria-Hungary, Russia, and the Ottoman Empire (including present-day Turkey)—added to the tension with their hunger for land. As you read in Chapter 8, the major powers of Europe had also raced to gobble up large chunks of Africa, Asia, and the Pacific.

The Alliances

Given these frictions, is it any wonder that the nations of Europe sought protection from their neighbors? Their solution was to form military alliances.

In 1871 Otto von Bismarck brought together 50 small, independent cities and states to form the large and powerful nation of Germany. Then "the Iron Chancellor," as Bismarck was known, sought allies to help protect Germany.

In 1882 Germany joined with Italy and Austria-Hungary to form the Triple Alliance. The members of the Alliance agreed to support each other in case of attack.

France, Russia, and Britain viewed the Triple Alliance with alarm. They felt that it upset the fragile balance of power among the nations of Europe. Thus, despite suspicions about one another, in 1907 they formed their own alliance known as the Triple Entente (ahn-TAHNT).

The two alliances maintained Europe's balance of power. They did nothing to defuse the European powder keg, however.

The Balkan Crisis

The powder keg exploded on June 28, 1914, when Archduke Ferdinand was assassinated by a 19-year-old Bosnian student. Austria-Hungary blamed the killing on the Serbian government. In late July it declared war on Serbia. Although none of the major powers wanted war, the very alliances they had made to maintain peace now forced them to take sides.

Russia sent troops to assist its ally, Serbia. Germany responded by declaring war on Russia on August 1 and on France, Russia's ally, two days later. German armies invaded Belgium in order to attack France. England entered the war on August 4 on the side of France and Russia.

Central Powers vs. Allies

Other countries were soon involved in the conflict. Russia's enemy, the Ottoman Empire, and Serbia's enemy Bulgaria sided with Austria-Hungary and Germany. These countries, which formed a large bloc in the center of Europe, became known as the Central Powers.

The forces against them—Britain, France, and Russia—were known as the Allies. Japan

Developing the Section

Discussion

Checking Understanding

1. How did President Wilson respond to the news of war in Europe and why? (Declared American neutrality, hoping United States could work with the warring nations to bring peace to Europe.)

2. Why had France resented Germany for 40 years before war broke out in 1914? (Germany had taken two of its richest provinces, Alsace and Lorraine, after the Franco-Prussian War of 1870.)

Stimulating Critical Thinking

3. Why do you think territory disputes are often a cause of war? (Territory may have key resources or be important to a nation's identity and history.)

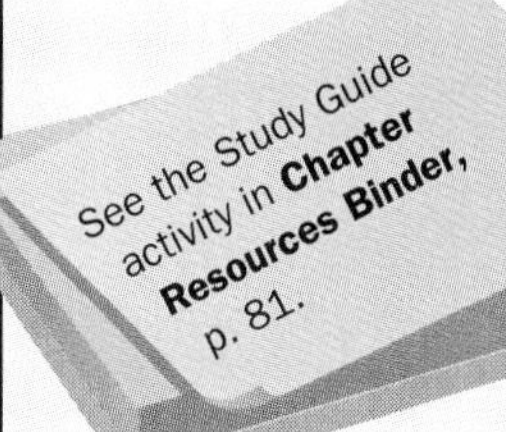

See the Study Guide activity in **Chapter Resources Binder,** p. 81.

Teaching the Reading Maps

Remind students that Germany's plan was to attack first on the western front through Belgium. After defeating France, Germany intended to turn east and invade Russia. **Answers to Reading Maps:** Western front: France, Belgium, Italy. Eastern: Russia, Romania, Serbia.

Section Activity

Creating a War Map

To link important facts and events from the section with particular places, have groups of students label an outline map of Europe in 1914. First have them draw the outline map on a large sheet of paper or poster board, marking each country, city, river, and province mentioned in the section. Then, for each location, they should write an explanation on a file card stating what happened there or why the place was significant. As a final step, have them arrange the cards in the white space around the map, and draw a line from each card to the appropriate point on the map.

Tips for Teaching

Students with Limited English

Directed reading lessons are a good way to help students with limited English understand textbook material. The following oral activity is most appropriate for those who have developed some ability in English.

To help students comprehend the two sides in World War I, give them typed copies of the "Central Powers vs. Allies" subsection (pp. 407–408) with key words and phrases deleted and replaced by blanks. As you read the passage aloud, students should read along and fill in the blanks with the missing words they hear.

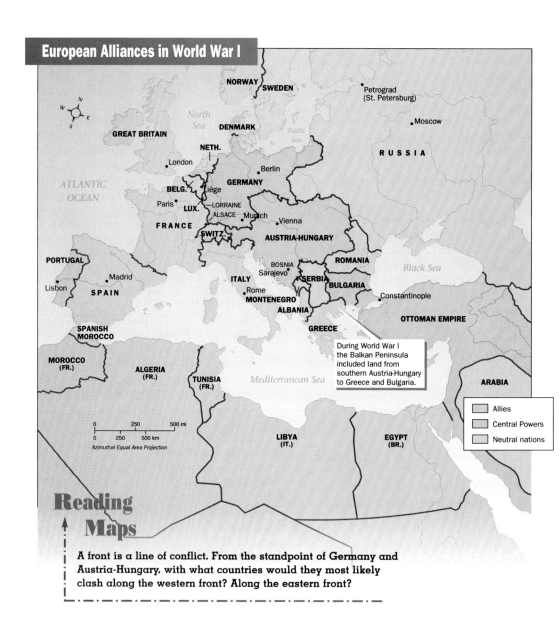

European Alliances in World War I

During World War I the Balkan Peninsula included land from southern Austria-Hungary to Greece and Bulgaria.

Allies
Central Powers
Neutral nations

0 250 500 mi
0 250 500 km
Azimuthal Equal Area Projection

Reading Maps

A front is a line of conflict. From the standpoint of Germany and Austria-Hungary, with what countries would they most likely clash along the western front? Along the eastern front?

joined the Allies to discourage German ambitions in the Pacific and Asia. Italy, hoping to gain territory from Austria-Hungary, joined the Allies in 1915. Eventually the Allies included 27 nations.

People on both sides expected a quick and easy victory, but some leaders knew better. "The lamps are going out all over Europe," warned Sir Edward Grey, Britain's foreign minister. "We shall not see them again in our lifetime."

At the time, people called this global conflict the Great War. Today it is known as World War I.

History Footnote

Later in the war, a trench defense typically consisted of three parallel trenches. At the front was the fire trench, the first line of defense against attack. Several hundred yards behind this trench was a support, or cover, trench. Soldiers in this trench provided reinforcements and a second line of defense if the front line broke. First-aid and cooking stations were often located here. A third, or reserve, trench was dug still farther to the rear in a safer area. Here men assembled before being sent into battle.

The three main trenches were connected by narrower, zigzagging trenches, some running for several miles. To keep from getting lost in the maze, soldiers added makeshift signs to the trenches. They often gave them names taken from familiar streets back home, such as Regent Street or the Champs Élysées.

Miracle on the Marne

In August 1914 Germany's plan was to attack first on the western front. It would roll through Belgium to crush France, then turn to the east and defeat Russia.

The plan worked well in the beginning, even though the Germans met unexpectedly stiff resistance from the outgunned and outnumbered Belgian army. The rapid German advance soon had French forces fleeing in disorder toward Paris. Confident of victory, the German commander in chief, Helmuth von Moltke, boasted that the war would be over in six weeks.

On September 6, however, just south of the Marne River and almost in sight of Paris, French and British forces finally overpowered the German troops and forced them to withdraw. The French called the victory "the Miracle on the Marne."

Stalemate on the Western Front

The German defeat on the Marne changed the character of the war. No longer was the conflict one of movement and maneuver. Instead, for three long years the opposing sides were stuck in a **stalemate**—deadlock—on the western front.

Trench warfare Soldiers on both sides of the stalemate dug trenches—long zigzag lines of ditches about 6 feet (1.8 m) deep and 3 feet (0.9 m) wide. Spaces dug into the sides of the trenches protected soldiers from enemy fire and provided room where they could eat and sleep.

Systems of trenches were barricaded with tangles of barbed wire. The stretch of ground between the opposing trenches was called "no man's land."

Hands-On HISTORY

Surviving life in a trench Describing the trenches he and fellow British soldiers dug during the war, Frank Richards wrote: "Little did we think when we were digging those trenches that we were digging our future homes for the next four years."

Activity With a group of five classmates, imagine living in a trench 6 feet deep by 3 feet wide by 20 feet long for a week. There is a lull in the fighting, but you must be alert. The enemy is less than 90 feet away, just across "no man's land." In your group of six, brainstorm answers to these questions:

1. If each of you could bring ten items into the trench—besides clothing and weapons—what would they be?
2. What are some activities you could do to pass the time in the trench?
3. What activities would not be a good idea? Why not?

Write down your ideas, and compare them with those of other groups in your class.

American soldiers in a trench

Discussion

Checking Understanding

1. Why is *stalemate* a good word to describe the conflict on the western front? (Instead of gaining or losing territory, each side was bogged down, unable to win a clear victory.)

Stimulating Critical Thinking

2. Why do you think Germany chose to invade France first rather than Russia? (It was a smaller country; its major city, Paris, was closer to Germany than was either Petrograd or Moscow; France was Germany's longtime rival.)

Teaching the Hands-On HISTORY

Before students begin, have them reread the "Trench warfare" passage to review the living conditions in the trenches. Also point out that beginning in 1915 soldiers in trenches had to wear gas masks to protect them from poison gas, a new weapon of war. After students make preliminary lists of items and activities, they should review the lists and cross out any items that would not have existed at the time of the war.

For firsthand accounts
of life in the trenches,
see American Readings,
pp. 41–42.

Teaching the

Link to Technology

Have students refer to the pictures, labels, and captions to answer these questions: What advantage would metal tracks have over wheels? (Would not sink into holes and get stuck; have a large gripping surface.) What other advantages would tanks have? (Made large guns mobile; offered good protection to operators.) What drawbacks did tanks have? (Traveled slowly; Mark IV had top speed of 4 mph. Tracks wore out quickly.)

Bonus Activity

A Conversation in the Trenches

To help students project themselves into a historical situation, have pairs write conversations between two soldiers in the trenches on the western front. One is experienced, the other is a new recruit. The dialogue should include responses to their living conditions as well as thoughts about combat. Ask some pairs to role-play their conversations.

Vital Links

WWI battlefield (Movie) Unit 4, Side 1, Search 26214, Play to 27270

See also Unit 4 Explore CD-ROM location 233.

History Footnote

The Spad fighter was developed by a French aircraft designer, Louis Bechereau. Production began in 1916. During the last part of the war, Spads were faster and stronger than any German airplanes. American flying ace Eddie Rickenbacker called the Spad "a racing car with wings."

The first true fighter plane, however, was designed for the Germans by Dutch designer Anthony Fokker. He solved one of the biggest problems with early fighter planes: how to mount the machine gun so it did not shoot off the propeller. In 1915 he invented a synchronizer gear that allowed a machine gun to fire straight ahead through the arc of the propeller. The highly maneuverable Fokker D-VII influenced aircraft design throughout the world and became the classic opponent of the Spad.

Link to Technology

World War I Planes and Tanks

Both in the air and on the ground, World War I was a different kind of war than had ever been fought before. For the first time planes were adapted to be fighting machines. On the ground the bloody stalemate of trench warfare called for an all-new weapon: the tank.

The Spad XIII was a favorite plane of Allied fliers. This fast plane had a top speed of 134 mph (214.4 km/hr) and was very durable. It was armed with two machine guns.

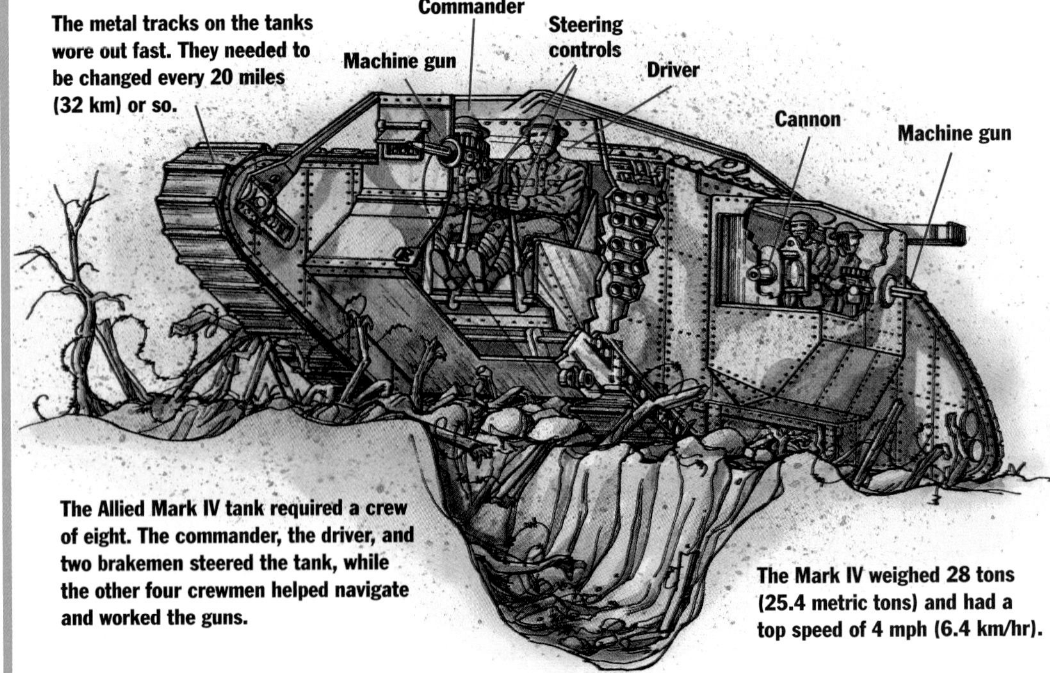

The metal tracks on the tanks wore out fast. They needed to be changed every 20 miles (32 km) or so.

The Allied Mark IV tank required a crew of eight. The commander, the driver, and two brakemen steered the tank, while the other four crewmen helped navigate and worked the guns.

The Mark IV weighed 28 tons (25.4 metric tons) and had a top speed of 4 mph (6.4 km/hr).

History Footnote

The mission of German U-boats was to destroy Allied ships carrying food and other supplies. By cutting off Britain's supplies, Germany hoped to force a surrender. In early 1917 the Germans seemed close to succeeding. U-boats roving the North Atlantic were destroying over 800,000 tons of cargo a month.

The British fought back, using warships to escort merchant vessels and sending hydroplanes to spot submarines, which could then be targeted with depth bombs (bombs that sink before exploding). In this way they destroyed many U-boats. These losses, along with the Allies' ability to produce more new ships after the United States entered the war, spelled the failure of the German submarine campaign.

Life in the trenches was horrible. The smell of dead bodies hung in the air. Rats and lice were constant companions. When it rained, soldiers stood and slept in mud. During attacks they had to dodge machine-gun fire. Otherwise, the days were long and tedious. One Allied soldier remembered:

> "There was no such thing as cooked food or hot tea at this stage of the War, and rations were very scarce: we were lucky if we got our four biscuits a man daily.
>
> One night there was an enemy attack which we beat off, and the next morning some corpses were to be seen lying just out in front of us. . . . We crawled out the next night and went through their packs, taking anything they had of value from them."

A dense network of trenches stretched for 400 miles (645 km) from Switzerland to the North Sea. Throughout 1915 and 1916 the Allies and Central Powers launched massive attacks against each other. Their gains never amounted to more than a few hundred yards, though, while losses amounted to hundreds of thousands of human casualties.

Modern Warfare

Progress in science and technology before 1914 made modern warfare increasingly destructive. Both sides unleashed new weapons and improved versions of familiar weapons. One new weapon was poison gas. Chlorine and mustard gases floated into the trenches, choking, blinding, and killing soldiers on both sides.

Tanks The British brought automotive technology to the battlefield when they introduced tanks in 1916. These heavily armored cars with tractor treads instead of wheels could travel over rough ground and through barbed wire. Tanks got bogged down in mud, though, and too few were used to make a difference in the outcome of the war.

German U-boats Far more effective and terrifying than tanks were the German submarines known as U-boats. These underwater craft could fire torpedoes into ships, destroying them without warning.

Airplanes To counter the U-boat threat, the Allies made good use of another recent invention—the airplane. Early in the war the Allies used airplanes to guard cargo ships and locate targets for artillery. Later, planes were equipped with machine guns.

The first use of aircraft as bombers was on August 6, 1914. A German zeppelin dropped 13 bombs on the Belgian city of Liège, killing 9 civilians. Now, observed a French writer,

> "the conquest of the air was truly complete. Men were going to die in the air as they had for centuries on the ground and on the seas, by killing each other."

For the next three years the war was fought mainly in the trenches. Americans looked on, listening to war reports but supporting Wilson's declaration of neutrality. As casualties continued to grow, however, remaining uninvolved became more and more difficult.

1. Section Review

1. Define **stalemate.**
2. Why, after many years of peace, did war break out in Europe?
3. What effects did developments in science and technology have on the way war was waged during World War I?
4. Critical Thinking Were the countries of Europe wise to form alliances? Why or why not?

Closing the Section

Wrap-Up Activity

Making a Concept Web

To underscore the political climate in Europe, have each student create a concept web with "The European Powder Keg, 1914" as the central idea. Branching from this, they should write factors contributing to the outbreak of war.

Section Review Answers

1. Definition: *stalemate* (409)

2. Mistrust, due to old boundary disputes, and nationalism caused European countries to build up arms and form alliances. Alliances helped keep peace but did not make nations feel secure. When Archduke Ferdinand was assassinated, the tense situation exploded. Austria-Hungary and Serbia went to war, and nations allied with them took sides.

3. Made warfare more destructive. Tanks traveled over rough ground and through barbed wire. Submarines could fire torpedoes without being seen. Airplanes bombed targets and guarded ships.

4. Yes: alliances offered protection and kept a country from being taken over. No: increased level of distrust among countries.

Introducing the Section

Vocabulary

propaganda (p. 412) the spreading of ideas or messages that promote one cause and hurt another

pacifists (p. 417) people who are against war under any circumstance

armistice (p. 419) truce

Warm-Up Activity

Predicting War

To prepare students to read about the American entry into the war, have them make a prediction. First remind them of President Wilson's position of neutrality when the war broke out. Then have them hypothesize some events that could cause the United States to change its position. They should write down their ideas so they can compare them with actual events as they read.

Geography Question of the Day

To help students understand the position of the Allied and Central Powers troops during the stalemate, ask them to write an explanation of how the map on p. 418 reflects the stalemate discussed on p. 409.

Section Objectives

- ★ Explain why the United States decided to join the Allies.
- ★ Describe how the war affected Americans in the armed forces and on the home front.
- ★ Explain why Germany finally admitted defeat.

Teaching Resources

Take-Home Planner 3, pp. 20–28
Chapter Resources Binder
Study Guide, p. 82
Reinforcement
Skills Development, pp. 87–88
Geography Extensions
American Readings, pp. 43–44
Using Historical Documents
Transparency Activities
Chapter and Unit Tests

2. The United States Enters the War

Reading Guide

New Terms **propaganda, pacifists, armistice**

Section Focus **How the United States helped the Allies win World War I**

1. Why did the United States decide to join the Allies?
2. How did the war affect Americans in the armed forces and on the home front?
3. Why did Germany finally admit defeat?

With the war raging in Europe, it became increasingly difficult for Americans not to take sides. Because this is a nation of immigrants, many Americans naturally felt some loyalty to the countries of their ancestors—as well as to the United States. Both the Central Powers and the Allies tried to take advantage of such loyalties as they competed to gain American support.

Propaganda

The Central Powers and the Allies flooded the nation with mail and telegraph messages accusing each other of killing civilians and violating international law. They used a new invention, the radio, to get their message out. The spread of ideas that help one cause and hurt another is called **propaganda.**

The Allies gained the upper hand in the propaganda battle after Britain cut the transatlantic cables linking the Central Powers to the United States, making telegraph communication impossible.

The *Lusitania*

American neutrality was severely shaken when word arrived that a German submarine had torpedoed the British passenger ship *Lusitania* on May 7, 1915. This tragic event took the lives of 1,198 people, including 128 American citizens.

Americans were outraged, and President Wilson lodged a strong protest with the German government. Although the *Lusitania* was in fact carrying arms and explosives to England, Germany apologized, offered to pay damages, and promised not to sink passenger vessels in the future.

Germany would not agree, however, to Wilson's demand that it stop submarine warfare. Using U-boats to cut off military supplies destined for the Allies was the Central Powers' chief chance for victory.

Building Defenses

After the sinking of the *Lusitania*, Wilson realized that the United States could not remain neutral much longer. At his urging, in 1916 Congress passed a series of measures designed to prepare the United States to defend itself from the Central Powers.

The National Defense Act doubled the size of the army, and the Naval Appropriations Bill provided money to build warships. The Council of National Defense was formed to direct and control the supply of the nation's industries and natural resources.

History Footnote

The British conducted a massive propaganda effort aimed at the United States. Between 1914 and 1917 the War Propaganda Bureau in London flooded the United States with pamphlets, books, speeches, and photographs publicizing the Allied cause. It sent literature to public libraries, YMCAs, colleges, and newspapers, and to a special list of 260,000 prominent Americans. Famous writers such as Arthur Conan Doyle (author of the Sherlock Holmes books) and J. M. Barrie (of *Peter Pan* fame) wrote or lectured for the Bureau. Propaganda releases were also carefully timed for the greatest effect. One report of German atrocities in Belgium, based partly on hearsay, was released five days after the sinking of the *Lusitania.*

The election of 1916 In his 1916 campaign for re-election, however, Wilson still preached neutrality. Running under the slogan, "He kept us out of war," he narrowly defeated his opponent, Charles Evans Hughes. Once re-elected, Wilson called on both sides to settle for "a peace without victory."

The End of Neutrality

Once again, forces beyond Wilson's control pushed the nation toward war. In January 1917 Germany's foreign minister, Arthur Zimmermann, sent a secret message to Mexico. He promised to help Mexico take back New Mexico, Arizona, and Texas in return for Mexican aid to Germany if the United States entered the war. The British intercepted and decoded the message.

Although Mexico quickly rejected the suggestion, the damage had been done. This violation of the 1823 Monroe Doctrine turned Americans even more against Germany. In March, when German U-boats sank five neutral ships, hopes for continued neutrality gave way to cries for revenge.

The Russian Revolution A final barrier keeping the United States from joining the Allies was lifted in March 1917. That month Russian revolutionaries overthrew their ruler, Czar Nicholas II, and replaced him with a democratic government. For many Americans, Russia was now an acceptable ally.

Declaring war With a heavy heart, President Wilson asked a special session of Congress to declare war on Germany. "The world," he vowed, "must be made safe for democracy." Congress issued the declaration on April 6, 1917.

The American entry into the war was crucial for the Allies. Their will to fight was almost gone. Units of the French army had rebelled, and Britain had lost an entire generation of its young men. The Allies desperately needed American supplies and support.

Americans in the Service

To raise a large army on short notice, Congress passed the Selective Service Act of May 18, 1917. The "draft" required men between the ages of 21 and 30 (later between 18 and 45) to register for military service. By war's end 4 million men were in the army, half of whom served overseas.

Doughboys The official name of the Yankee army was the American Expeditionary Force (AEF), but they were called "doughboys." Some say this name came from the cornmeal cakes they ate, others say it came from their youth and inexperience.

THE NAVY
NEEDS YOU!
DON'T READ
AMERICAN HISTORY—
MAKE IT!

Recruiting posters like this one inspired American men to volunteer for military service.

Developing the Section

Discussion

Checking Understanding

1. What was the *Lusitania* and what was it carrying? (British luxury ship carrying passengers and munitions.)

2. What did Germany's foreign minister offer Mexico? (Help in regaining New Mexico, Arizona, and Texas.)

Stimulating Critical Thinking

3. Why might Central Powers propaganda appeal to some Americans? Immigrant loyalty to countries of ancestors.)

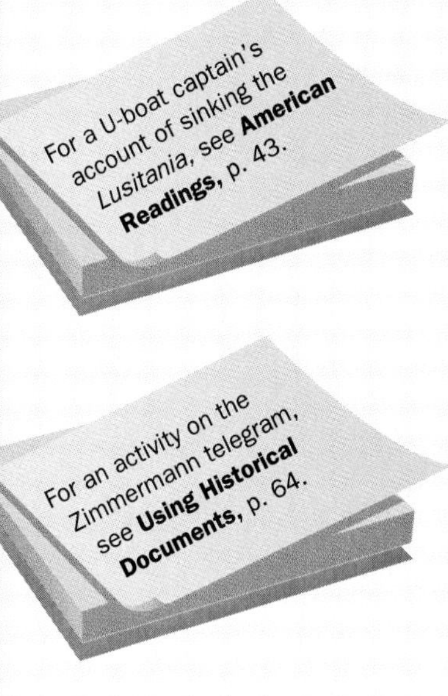

For a U-boat captain's account of sinking the Lusitania, see **American Readings**, p. 43.
For an activity on the Zimmermann telegram, see **Using Historical Documents**, p. 64.

Vital Links

WWI submarine (Movie) Unit 4, Side 1, Search 25012, Play to 26210

See also Unit 4 Explore CD-ROM location 218.

Connections to Music

The 369th Infantry Regiment was among the African American units that received the croix de guerre for bravery under fire. It was also famous for its regimental band, led by Lieutenant James Reese Europe, who had conducted dance orchestras in New York and been a Broadway musical director. The band played for French and American troops in camps and hospitals and for civilians. It is considered the first musical group to introduce jazz to European countries.

According to one story, French musicians found the jazz sounds so unusual that they thought the Americans' instruments made the difference. When they traded brasses and woodwinds with the Americans, they could not produce the same sounds, yet they found that the Americans played jazz just as easily on the French instruments.

Section Activity

Diary Entries in the Trenches

To help students understand the life of a soldier in the trenches, have them write series of diary entries from the point of view of an American soldier fighting on the western front. Have them include entries that reflect reactions to everyday life in the trenches. Ask students to share their entries with the class.

Vital Links

Women ambulance drivers (Picture) Unit 4, Side 1, Search 24420

See also Unit 4 Explore CD-ROM location 220.

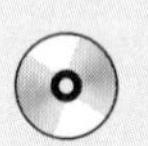

Voice of WWI private (First Person Account) Unit 4, Side 1, Search 22757, Play to 23679

See also Unit 4 Explore CD-ROM location 214.

The doughboys' commander was General Pershing, a hardened career army officer whom you read about in Chapter 8. Pershing worked to ensure that his soldiers were well trained before they saw any combat.

African Americans Some 360,000 African Americans joined the armed forces. African American leaders had encouraged young black men to enlist. They hoped that black patriotism would overcome racist prejudice in American society. As a columnist for the *Washington Bee* declared:

> "I am one of those who believe that the present war will settle forever the colored question in the United States. The black man will be recognized and be treated as a man and a brother."

Sadly, a society not yet ready for change dashed such hopes. Although three black regiments received France's highest military honor, the croix de guerre, most black soldiers were assigned to segregated units or to noncombat duty.

Native Americans Indians could not be drafted because they were not yet United States citizens. Even so, an impressive 17,213 Indians volunteered to fight, of whom 6,509 were enlisted. Their percentage was twice the national average. Those who served obtained citizenship.

Indian war heroes included Chauncey Eagle Horn, a Sioux, who was the first decorated soldier from South Dakota. The most brilliant record belongs to Private Joseph Oklahombi, a Choctaw. He received the croix de guerre for scrambling across 210 yards (192 m) of barbed wire, wrestling a machine gun from its crew, and then using it to capture 171 German soldiers.

Women Some 25,000 women contributed to the war effort by working for the armed services. Many served in the army and naval nurse corps or enlisted in the marines. Others were secretaries or telephone operators. Women served as doctors, dentists, decoders, librarians, interpreters, translators, and chauffeurs. They did almost everything except fight.

In response to African American demands that they be permitted to serve as combat troops, two all-black infantry divisions, the 92d and 93d, were formed and sent to France. The soldiers in this 1918 photograph were part of the 92d Division.

Connections to Economics

"If You Can't Enlist—Invest!" So said one poster urging American citizens to buy bonds. By doing so, people could help their country and reap a financial benefit for themselves. A liberty bond was a certificate of debt. An individual purchased a bond from the government. In return, the government promised to repay the purchase price of the bond—plus interest—at a future date.

See the Study Guide
activity in Chapter
Resources Binder,
p. 82.

Point of View

What would you do if you were drafted?

In 1917 when President Wilson and Congress decided to have a draft, many citizens opposed the war. One group, called the Fellowship of Reconciliation, felt that the United States should not get involved in other countries' wars. They wrote:

> "We are patriots who love our country and desire to serve her and those ideals for which she has stood . . . but we cannot believe that participation in war is the true way of service to America."

Other people, like Alvin York, were against the war because their religions opposed fighting for any reason. York explained his decision to join the army by saying:

> "I loved and trusted old Uncle Sam and I have always believed he did the right thing. But I . . . didn't want to go and kill. I believed in my Bible. And it distinctly said, 'Thou shalt not kill.' And yet old Uncle Sam wanted me. And he said he wanted me most awful bad."

How would you feel if you were drafted? Can you make a list of three reasons why you would or would not fight?

Financing the War

From the beginning it was clear that the American war effort was going to be costly. To help finance this unexpected expense, in October 1917 Congress passed the War Revenue Act, increasing income taxes.

The government also raised money by selling liberty bonds. Politicians and movie stars gave speeches urging people to buy bonds. Some 21 million Americans bought bonds—in effect, loaning money to the government. Through these measures, and by increasing taxes on corporations and on goods such as alcohol and tobacco, the government raised $10.8 billion.

As the war took men away from home, women stepped in to take over their jobs. This young woman is filling shells in a munitions factory.

"Use All Left-overs" Four years of war had laid waste to much of Europe. In addition to bullets and bombs, hunger and disease were killing thousands. The Liberty Loan Act of 1917 enabled the government to lend the Allies money to buy food and supplies from the United States.

President Wilson also set up an agency to make sure that there would be enough food for everyone, both at home and overseas. To head the Food Administration he chose Herbert Hoover, an engineer who had led relief efforts in Belgium. The Food Administration raised crop prices to encourage farmers to grow more, and it punished people who hoarded food.

Discussion

Checking Understanding

1. What was the purpose of the Liberty Loan Act of 1917? (To lend money to the Allies so they could buy food and supplies from the United States.)

Stimulating Critical Thinking

2. If you were an African American man in 1917, would you have been eager to enlist? (Yes: showing patriotic service and courage in combat might overcome white racism and lead to equal treatment. No: a government that did not give justice to African Americans had no right to expect them to fight in its armed forces.)

Teaching the Point of View

After students read the two points of view, ask them to condense into a single sentence each writer's attitude about war. (First: getting involved in war is not a good way to serve one's country. Second: war requires killing, and killing is wrong.) Point out that each statement is based on a different principle.

Vital Links

Voice of Woodrow Wilson (First Person Account) Unit 4, Side 1, Search 05960, Play to 06398

See also Unit 4 Explore CD-ROM location 28.

Teaching the

 **Link to Art**

Have students compare the painting to an example of another type of art popular at the time, Mary Cassatt's *The Letter* on page 386. Ask them to comment on the different style and approach of the Dada work (large areas of pure color; abstract lines and shapes offer only hints of subject matter). **Discussion Answer:** They were used to paintings that showed recognizable objects and scenes or told a story.

Vital Links

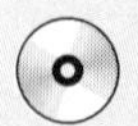

Antiwar demonstration (Picture) Unit 4, Side 1, Search 24455

See also Unit 4 Explore CD-ROM location 226.

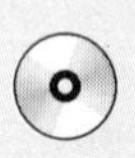

WWI troops leaving for war (Picture) Unit 4, Side 1, Search 24515

See also Unit 4 Explore CD-ROM location 235.

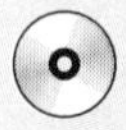

"Over There" (Song) Unit 4, Side 2, Search 09673, Play to 11832

See also Unit 4 Explore CD-ROM location 236.

Connections to Art

Dada artists responded to the war's destructiveness by rebelling against principles of established art. In their view the war, with its grotesque trench warfare, was mass suicide, and modern society was responsible. They could no longer identify with values of a culture they considered morally corrupt. Dada artists made works intended to bewilder or shock. Some made collages from unusual materials, such as newspaper clippings or pieces of trash. Others used the element of chance or accident in creating works. A prominent Dada artist, Marcel Duchamp, exhibited ordinary commercial products as art. The most famous of these "ready-mades" was a bicycle wheel mounted on a wooden stool. Another was a postcard of the *Mona Lisa* on whose face he had drawn a mustache and goatee.

Link to Art

The Rope Dancer Accompanies Herself with Her Shadows (1916)
Starting in 1916, a number of artists reacted to the war by making what they called "works of nonart." This movement was called Dada, a nonsense word that reflected the meaninglessness of the war to these artists. As artists left Europe to escape the war, they brought Dada to the United States. The painting above is by American artist Man Ray. **Discuss** Why do you think this style of art was shocking to Americans in the 1920s?

Hoover preferred voluntary efforts rather than government rules. His slogan, "Use All Left-overs," encouraged people to conserve food. Americans began observing "Wheatless Mondays and Wednesdays" and "Meatless Tuesdays." As a result, three times as much food could be shipped to the Allies.

Labor and the War Effort

The war also placed extraordinary demands on American industry. Almost overnight, factories began producing great quantities of tanks, airplanes, guns, and other war materials.

Connections to Economics

In exchange for labor union support, President Wilson made sure that business owners did not make excessive profits from war contracts at workers' expense. War profiteering had been a problem in previous wars. In addition some war opponents charged that big business sought financial gain from the war. While some business owners did become wealthy from war contracts, especially in the areas of new military technologies involving electronics and explosives, rigid formulas for the awarding of government contracts on the basis of costs firmly fixed the amount of profit most businesses could make. Meanwhile, the Wilson administration looked favorably on the practice of collective bargaining, which gave unions more freedom to negotiate for better wages, hours, and working conditions.

The dramatic increase in production would not have been possible without the dedication of factory workers. Samuel Gompers and other labor leaders pledged their support, and union members did the rest. During the war, union membership rose from 2.74 million in 1916 to 4.05 million in 1919.

More than 1 million women entered the work force, often taking the jobs of men who had joined the military. They drove trucks, delivered mail, and made ammunition.

The war also brought many more African Americans into the work force. Northern industries sent agents to the South, looking for workers. By 1917, responding to promises of good salaries and fair treatment, as many as half a million black workers had moved north to take factory jobs.

Silencing Opposition and Winning Support

Although most Americans threw themselves into the war effort, a few held back. Some people firmly believed that the nation should stay out of Europe's wars. Others were **pacifists**—people who are against war under any circumstance. Sergeant York was one of 20,000 pacifists to be drafted.

Afraid that opposition would hurt the war effort, Congress passed the Espionage Act in June 1917. The act set strict penalties for anyone who interfered with recruiting soldiers or made statements that might hinder the war effort.

The Sedition Act of May 16, 1918, made it illegal to utter disloyal statements about the Constitution, the government, the flag, or the armed forces. In 1919 the Supreme Court ruled that the government had the right to suspend free speech during wartime.

Winning support While the government was trying to silence opponents, it was also working to drum up support for the war. In May 1917 Wilson appointed newspaper editor George Creel to head the Committee on Public Information. His job was to "sell the war to America."

Creel's efforts had the unpleasant side effect of creating anti-German hysteria in the United States. Schools stopped teaching the German language. The governor of Iowa even banned speaking German on the telephone.

Over There

While the government was busy promoting the war effort in the United States, American troops began sailing for France. By June 1918 more than a million had arrived. As they stormed ashore, many sang the popular World War I song "Over There":

The day after Congress declared war, popular songwriter George M. Cohan wrote "Over There." The patriotic lyrics and catchy tune soon swept across the country.

Discussion

Checking Understanding

1. Who found new job opportunities as a result of the war's demands on industry? (Women and African Americans.)

Stimulating Critical Thinking

2. Do you think the government needed to use propaganda to win support for the war? Explain. (Yes: to combat Central Powers propaganda, foster unity, increase resources for war effort. No: created unnecessary hatred toward Germans; Americans were willing to fight anyway.)

For an example of American propaganda, see **American Readings,** p. 44.

Bonus Activity

Propagandizing

To help students understand the effectiveness of propaganda, have them sketch or describe posters with a slogan encouraging the American public to support the war. They should assume they work for the Committee on Public Information. Their boss has asked for ideas for a poster that will spur people to help the war effort. (Possible topics: buying liberty bonds, conserving food, taking jobs in factories.)

Teaching the Reading Maps

Have students describe the movements of German and Allied troops and the battles that occurred, using the names of cities, physical features, and movements shown on the map. (Example: The Germans advanced southwest from Reims to Belleau Wood, where they met American troops.) **Answers to Reading Maps:** To capture Paris, the capital of France, and take control of its government.

Teaching the World Link

Point out to students that although the Whites were supported by the Allies, they were poorly organized. When the Allies pulled out after World War I, the Whites were defeated by the Reds. Discuss reasons the Allies pulled out. For example they were exhausted from World War I and did not have the resources to support another war. Ask students if they think Russia's fate would have been different if the Allies had stayed and helped the Whites.

Vital Links

WWI soldiers with gas masks (Picture) Unit 4, Side 1, Search 24485

See also Unit 4 Explore CD-ROM location 228.

History Footnote

The anti-German feeling that swept across the nation permeated everyday life. Orchestras were barred from playing music by German composers such as Beethoven and Bach. German names for streets and parks were changed. In New Orleans, Berlin Street was renamed General Pershing Street (after the commander of the American Expeditionary Force). Even everyday words referring to something German were not tolerated. Sauerkraut was called "liberty cabbage," and German measles became "liberty measles." If a person dared to own a dachshund, he or she was smart to call it a "liberty pup." As brutal as it was silly, anti-German hysteria hurt German Americans, many of whom lost their jobs, victims of this new prejudice.

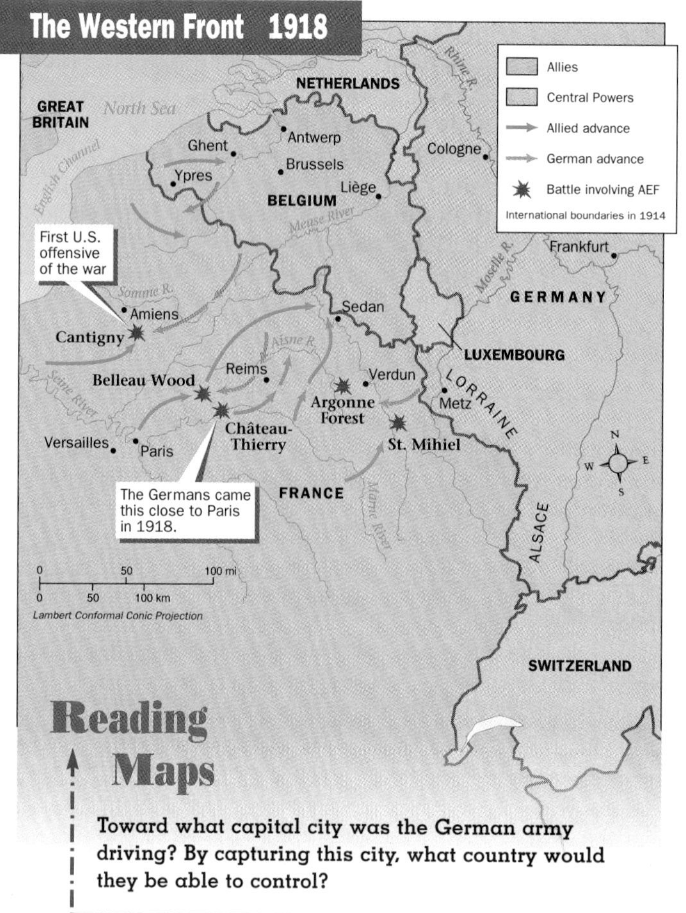

Reading Maps

Toward what capital city was the German army driving? By capturing this city, what country would they be able to control?

"Over there, over there,
Send the word, send the word over
there,
That the Yanks are coming, the Yanks
are coming,
The drums rum-tumming ev'rywhere."

The extreme patriotism of the American soldiers puzzled the Germans. After all, many of the doughboys had not even been born in the United States. Indeed, the troops reflected the ethnic makeup of the United States. Their letters home were written in dozens of different languages. Yet, as a German officer marveled, "These semi-Americans . . . feel themselves to be true-born sons of their country."

Last German Offensive

In the winter of 1917–1918, the Central Powers were gaining an advantage. First they crushed Italian troops on the southern front. Then, in Russia, the short-lived democratic government fell to a wing of the Communist Party called the Bolsheviks, led by Vladimir Lenin. In 1918 the Bolsheviks signed a peace agreement with Germany and pulled out of the war.

With Russia out of the way, Germany could focus on the western front. In the spring of 1918 the Germans launched a massive campaign to capture Paris. By the end of May, German troops were again at the Marne River, only 50 miles (81 km) from Paris. The Allied situation seemed desperate.

Belleau Wood The Americans of the AEF arrived just in time. Frenchmen too old to fight drove thousands of doughboys to the front lines in trucks, taxicabs, and cars. By June 1 American troops had reached Belleau (bel-LŌ) Wood, a square mile of forest between two hills.

For three weeks German and American armies fought each other over this small patch of blood-drenched soil, which had become a symbol far beyond its military importance. The Americans were determined

History Footnote
The armistice was an occasion for joyful celebration at home, but at the front many soldiers were too tired to cheer. Most of them were stunned by the utter quiet on the battlefield after the guns stopped. The weather was cold and bleak, the men cold, wet, and hungry. But the soldiers could now build fires to warm themselves and dry their shoes and socks. One soldier wrote, "It sure did seem strange. That night it was actually so quiet that I could not sleep."

They were not supposed to socialize with the enemy, but a lieutenant of one machine gun battalion in the 33d Division allowed two of his men (one was German-born) to cross no man's land to meet the Germans. The former combatants chatted pleasantly for a short time and exchanged souvenirs.

to capture it. The Germans were ordered to hold it at all costs.

On June 25, following an especially heavy day of fighting, United States Marines finally drove the Germans from Belleau Wood. This battle was a turning point for the Allied forces. As one American wrote home, "Folks, we have them on the run."

The AEF on the offensive Belleau Wood was the first Allied victory in which American troops played a part. Now General Pershing, acting under Allied commander Marshal Ferdinand Foch (FŌSH), launched a summer-long offensive campaign. In September half a million doughboys drove the Germans from the town of St. Mihiel (SAHN mee-YEL).

The next target was the Sedan railroad in northern France. For 47 days American forces fought their way through the heavily defended Argonne Forest toward Sedan. It was here that Alvin York made history by capturing 132 Germans.

The Armistice

Although the war ended before Sedan was taken, the doughboys had achieved their objective. "The American troops," Pershing later reported, "had cut the enemy's main line of communications, and nothing but surrender or an armistice could save his army from disaster."

The Central Powers saw that further resistance would be foolish. In November the Ottoman Empire, Bulgaria, and Austria-Hungary signed an **armistice**—a truce.

Finally Germany, its armies in full retreat on every front, admitted defeat. Delegates from Germany traveled to France, where they received the terms of the armistice from General Foch. On the morning of November 11, 1918, later known as Armistice Day, the Germans signed. Later that morning all firing ceased. World War I was over.

Russia's civil war Even as Lenin made peace with Germany, civil war was tearing Russia apart. Lenin's Communist forces, called Reds from the color of their flag, believed that property should be owned by society. Their opponents, the Whites, included landowners and others who stood to lose under communism.

Allied leaders wanted the Whites to win. The Allies were bitter about Russia's withdrawal from the war and desperately wanted Russia to rejoin the fight. Also, they were beginning to view communism as a potential world threat.

In the spring of 1918 Britain, France, and the United States began to send troops to support the Whites. For the most part they pulled out soon after World War I ended. The Reds defeated the Whites in 1920. Communism would hold Russia in its grip for the next 70 years.

2. Section Review

1. Define **propaganda, pacifists,** and **armistice.**
2. Describe three events that led the United States to declare war on Germany.
3. How did the United States raise money and conserve resources for the war?
4. How did American troops help the Allies defeat Germany?
5. Critical Thinking If you had been a member of Congress, would you have voted for the Espionage and Sedition acts? Explain your reasons.

Closing the Section

Wrap-Up Activity

Making Event Cards
To review World War I events, have pairs make at least five event cards. On one side should be an event such as the sinking of the *Lusitania*, and on the other its date and significance. Students can use these cards in two ways: to quiz each other by using them as flash cards, or by putting them on a desk with the events face up and asking another pair to put them in chronological order.

Section Review Answers

1. Definitions: *propaganda* (412), *pacifists* (417), *armistice* (419)
2. German submarine sank the *Lusitania;* Zimmermann telegram discovered; U-boats sank neutral ships; Russian Revolution led to democratic government, making Russia more acceptable as ally.
3. Increased income taxes and other taxes, sold liberty bonds. Set up Food Administration to monitor food production and distribution; promoted efforts to conserve food.
4. Fought on western front to turn the Germans back from France. A key victory occurred at Belleau Wood.
5. Yes: United States needs full support of its citizens to win the war. No: even in time of war, constitutional rights must be protected.

uses *bandwagon*. It suggests that true Americans buy liberty bonds. It uses *transference* to connect bonds with symbols of patriotism, liberty, and bravery: the flag, goddess-like woman, and brave soldiers. (b) Students may note that the posters use short, simple slogans and present strongly negative (in A) and positive (in B) images. (c) Accept opinions that take into account attitudes and concerns of the times.

For further application, have students do the Applying Skills activity in the Chapter Survey (p. 430).

If students need to review
the skill, use the Skills
Development trans-
parency and activity in
the **Chapter Resources**
Binder, pp. 87–88.

Introducing the Skill Lab

Point out that propaganda often appeals to emotions rather than to logic. Help students think of examples for each technique listed. You might also describe other techniques such as loaded words, false testimonials, and either-or thinking.

Skill Lab

Answers

1. (a) A German soldier (Kaiser Wilhelm) stands in the sea waving a bloody sword over bodies of women and children—probably American and European civilians drowned when ships like the *Lusitania* were sunk. (b) A woman who looks like a goddess of liberty leads eager American soldiers to battle.

2. (a) To encourage Americans to join the navy or support the navy and war effort generally. (b) To encourage Americans who are not in the military to buy liberty bonds, to provide money for the war.

3. (a) Poster A uses *card stacking* by not presenting the German view that submarine warfare is justified against ships carrying war materials through war zones. It uses *transference* to connect support of the navy to symbols of motherhood and innocent children. Poster B

(Answers continued in top margin)

Skill Lab

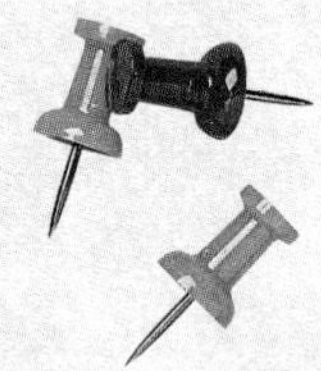

Skill Tips

Major propaganda techniques include:

- *Card stacking*—presenting only one side or part of a story.
- *Bandwagon*—playing on the desire to be part of a group and the fear of being left out.
- *Transference*—connecting a cause to a respected person, group, or symbol.

Thinking Critically

Analyzing Propaganda

The United States that declared war on Germany was ill-prepared to fight. The government needed everything: money, troops, weapons, supplies—and the support of the American people.

Question to Investigate

How did the United States government try to gain support for the war effort?

Procedure

To explore the Question to Investigate, you will analyze two posters circulated by the government during the war. The posters are examples of propaganda—efforts to promote or oppose a cause by appealing to emotions. Study A and B and do the following:

1 Identify the images.

a. Tell who the people are and what is happening in A.

b. Do the same for B.

2 Identify the purposes.

a. State the main purpose of A.

b. Do the same for B.

3 Identify and evaluate the propaganda techniques used.

a. List the techniques from the Skill Tips used in A and B.

b. Add your own ideas about the ways A and B attempt to achieve their purposes.

c. Tell whether you think A and B were effective in their time, and why or why not.

Sources to Use

A

B

ONLY THE NAVY CAN STOP THIS
FIGHT
OR
BUY BONDS
THIRD
LIBERTY LOAN

Section Objectives

- ★ Describe how the Allies differed in their ideas for a peace treaty.
- ★ Explain why the Senate rejected the Treaty of Versailles.
- ★ Explain how President Wilson tried to win support for the Treaty and why he failed.

Teaching Resources

Take-Home Planner 3, pp. 20–28
Chapter Resources Binder
Study Guide, p. 83
Reinforcement
Skills Development
Geography Extensions, pp. 23–24
American Readings
Using Historical Documents
Transparency Activities
Chapter and Unit Tests, pp. 71–74

3. The Search for Peace

Reading Guide

New Terms **self-determination, reparations**

Section Focus **The struggle over the peace treaty**

1. How did the Allies differ in their ideas for a peace treaty?
2. Why did the Senate reject the Treaty of Versailles?
3. How did Wilson try to win support for the Treaty and why did he fail?

When the war began, people thought it would last six weeks. Instead, it lasted more than four years. It was the largest and most costly war the world had ever known. More than 9 million people died, including 116,000 Americans. The financial cost was in the hundreds of billions of dollars.

President Wilson had entered the war reluctantly. Only when it seemed impossible for the United States to remain neutral did he agree to send troops to Europe. His dream was that World War I would serve to restore lasting peace and make the world safe for democracy. Instead, it set the stage for another, even more destructive war that would break out 20 years later.

Wilson's Fourteen Points

Even before the war officially ended, Wilson had developed a plan for a "just and durable peace." On January 8, 1918, he outlined this plan in his famous "Fourteen Points" speech before Congress.

The first five points of Wilson's plan were designed to remove the causes of war. He wanted to guarantee freedom of the seas, remove international tariff barriers, reduce the number of weapons, settle claims for colonies, and end secret treaties.

The next eight points promoted Wilson's belief in **self-determination**—the right of the people of a certain nation to decide how they want to be governed. To ensure self-determination, Wilson wanted to redraw the national boundaries of Europe.

The final point was the one most dear to Wilson's heart. He called for the formation of a League of Nations that would work to protect any nation that was attacked by another. In Wilson's mind, this league was the key to a lasting world peace.

The Paris Peace Conference

To promote his Fourteen Points, Wilson attended the Paris Peace Conference. He was the first American President to go overseas on a diplomatic mission.

Seventy representatives from 27 countries attended the conference, which opened on January 18, 1919. The key decisions, though, were made by the "Big Four": Britain's Prime Minister David Lloyd George, France's Premier Georges Clemenceau [kluh-mahn-SŌ], Italy's Premier Vittorio Orlando, and President Wilson of the United States.

The Allies agreed in principle to Wilson's Fourteen Points, but they brushed aside most of his suggestions as vague and impractical. Clemenceau remarked, "He bores me with his fourteen points. Why, God Almighty has only ten!"

Introducing the Section

Vocabulary

self-determination (p. 421) the right of the people of a certain nation to decide how they want to be governed

reparations (p. 423) payments for war damages

Warm-Up Activity

Writing Terms for a Peace Treaty

To get students thinking about the relationship of war and peace, have them assume that they will be delegates to the peace conference following the armistice. Their goal is to help write the terms of a treaty to provide for a lasting peace in Europe. Have them each write at least three terms they would include. As they read the section, they can see if their terms were discussed at the peace conference.

Geography Question of the Day

Ask students to locate Versailles on the map on p. 422. Have them write an explanation of why this would be a reasonable location for a World War I peace conference.

For a fictional account of a soldier's postwar trauma, see the Link to Literature on pages 440–441.

Developing the Section

Teaching the Reading Maps

Have students compare this map with the pre-war map on p. 408. Have them list nations formed from Austria-Hungary (Austria, Hungary, Czechoslovakia, parts of Poland, Romania, Yugoslavia) and western Russia (Finland, Estonia, Latvia, Lithuania, part of Poland). **Answer to Reading Maps:** Germany had to return Alsace and Lorraine to France; Austria-Hungary was divided into Czechoslovakia, Austria, Hungary, Yugoslavia, and Romania, and a part in the northeast was attached to Poland.

Section Activity

Press Interviews

To bring out differing American views on the Treaty of Versailles, have groups of five or six role-play *Meet the Press* shows. Two members will play the roles of Senator Henry Cabot Lodge and President Wilson. The others will be journalists interviewing them. Groups should prepare two or three questions to draw out the views of each man and then carry out the interviews.

Tips for Teaching

At-Risk Students

To help at-risk students understand new terms, link them with terms they know. For example, write *self-determination* and *reparations* on the chalkboard and write the base word below each term *(determine, repair)*. Point out the shared suffix *(-ation)* and its meaning (state of, condition of).

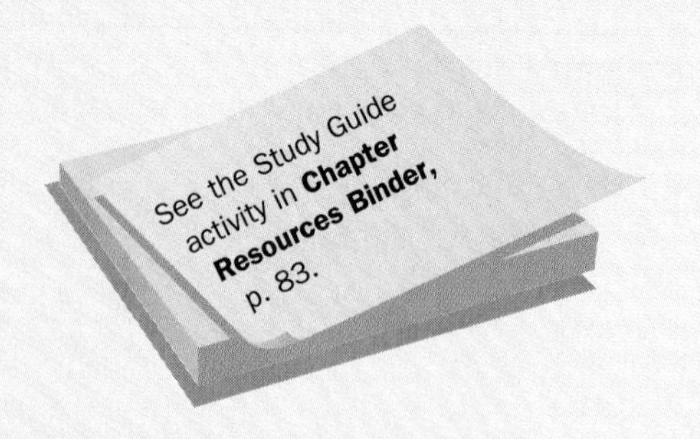

Europe and the Middle East After World War I

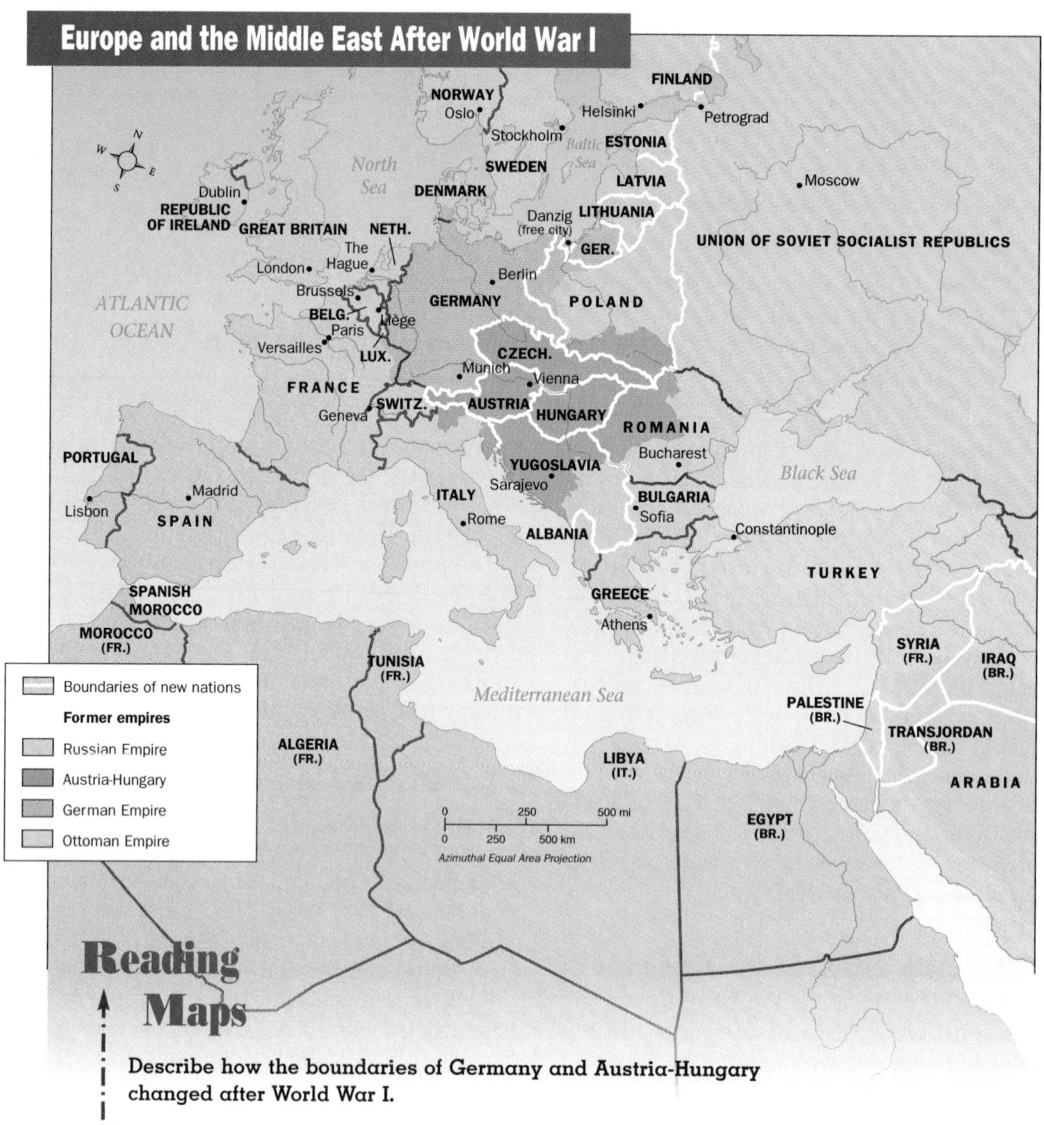

Reading Maps

Describe how the boundaries of Germany and Austria-Hungary changed after World War I.

The tone of the peace conference was clear from the start: The victorious Allies had soundly defeated the Central Powers and were determined to punish them, particularly Germany. David Lloyd George had just won re-election in Britain by promising to "Make Germany Pay."

The Treaty of Versailles

After four months of discussion, the delegates at the conference approved a treaty. Many provisions reflected Wilson's goals. The treaty set up a League of Nations and redrew the map of Europe (see map above).

History Footnote

When President Wilson delivered his Fourteen Points speech, he said of Germany, "We do not wish to injure her or block in any way her legitimate influence or power." However France was worried about its military security, and the other Allied countries represented at the peace conference had suffered much more than the United States had in the war. They wanted to be paid back for their sacrifices. Thus Wilson could not prevent the delegates from including harsh terms for Germany. When the German people learned of the treaty terms, they protested in the streets. A large crowd in Berlin unfurled a banner that said, "Only the Fourteen Points!"

However, Wilson could not prevent the other delegates from including harsh terms designed to punish Germany. The treaty stripped Germany of its armed forces and demanded $33 billion in **reparations**—payments for war damages. Worst of all, in the eyes of Germans, the treaty's "War Guilt Clause," required Germany to admit that it alone was responsible for the war.

German officials resented the terms, but there was little they could do. On June 28, 1919, in the elegant Hall of Mirrors of the Palace of Versailles (ver-SĪ), they signed the treaty. World War I was officially over.

Opposition Even at the time, people realized that the Versailles Treaty was too extreme to establish a lasting peace. Marshal Foch declared, "This is not peace. It is an armistice for twenty years."

Meanwhile, an Austrian army corporal named Adolf Hitler seethed with anger at the terms of the treaty. Twenty years later he was to lead Germany in a war of revenge that became World War II.

When President Wilson returned to the United States to get Senate approval for the treaty, he found that many Americans were unhappy with its terms. The strongest opposition was to the League of Nations.

Senator Henry Cabot Lodge of Massachusetts spoke for those who objected to the treaty. He argued that Article 10, which said that League members would act together against threats to peace, could commit the United States to future wars on foreign soil.

Wilson's defense Refusing to compromise yet realizing that the Senate's opposition would keep the United States out of the League of Nations, Wilson decided to take his ideals straight to the American people. He traveled by train on an 8,000-mile (12,900-km) tour. In just 22 days he delivered 40 speeches in 29 cities. This pace proved too much for the 63-year-old President.

Link to the Present

The United Nations History's largest gathering of leaders took place in New York City in October 1995 to celebrate the 50th anniversary of the United Nations (UN).

The United States is an active member of the UN, which rose from the ashes of the League of Nations in 1945. The UN resembles the League in some ways, but it has been more successful in settling disputes and halting aggression. For example, UN members expelled Iraqi invaders from Kuwait in 1991.

The UN also takes on more humanitarian responsibilities. Agencies like the United Nations International Children's Emergency Fund (UNICEF) and the World Health Organization (WHO) have gone a long way in easing problems like hunger, poverty, and disease.

On September 25, 1919, Wilson gave a speech in Colorado that reflected his heartfelt commitment to the League of Nations:

> "There is one thing that the American people always rise to . . . and this is the truth of justice and liberty and of peace. We have accepted that truth, and we are going to be led by it, and it is going to lead us . . . out into pastures of quietness and peace such as the world never dreamed of before."

Soon after he spoke these words, Wilson suffered a stroke that left him partially paralyzed. For the rest of his presidency, Wilson communicated only through his wife, Edith.

Discussion

Checking Understanding

1. Name three provisions of the Treaty of Versailles. (Set up League of Nations, reorganized map of Europe, punished Germany.)

Stimulating Critical Thinking

2. What do you think is a major lesson to be learned from World War I? (A punitive peace treaty can lead to future conflict.)

Teaching the

Link to the Present

Ask why a wide membership of nations is important for the UN to be effective in peace-keeping. (Gives UN more authority to try to settle disputes wherever they might arise.)

Bonus Activity

Matching Nations with Former Empires

To reinforce understanding of postwar boundaries, have four groups represent the pre-war empires. Have each group make signs with the names and outlines of new nations that emerged from its empire. Place the signs in a central place. Next, have the groups switch so that each now represents a different empire. Then have group representatives take turns collecting signs for the nations that emerged from that empire.

Closing the Section

Wrap-Up Activity

Holding a Peace Conference

To review issues and concerns of the countries trying to negotiate a peace treaty, have students hold a peace conference. Divide the class into four groups, each representing one of the Big Four nations. They should discuss possible terms, keeping in mind Wilson's Fourteen Points. Groups may accept, modify, or reject each point.

Section Review

Answers

1. Definitions: *self-determination* (421), *reparations* (423)

2. Allies adopted some of Wilson's ideas in principle, including self-determination and the League of Nations.

3. The Senate was afraid the treaty language might commit United States to future wars on foreign soil.

4. Yes: United States would have ratified treaty; League would have been more powerful with United States as member. No: important to stick to ideals, even against popular opinion.

To check understanding of "Why We Remember," assign Thinking Critically question 3 on student page 430.

History Footnote

When Woodrow Wilson was a widower of 16 months, he met and fell in love with Edith Grant, a charming and intelligent widow. After a whirlwind romance they were married in December 1915.

Edith was an essential aide to her husband as he continued to exercise the duties of President. After Wilson suffered a stroke in 1919, they went over important documents each day, and she wrote down his instructions about what to reply.

Although Edith Wilson was criticized for exercising undue influence, she said that she never made an important political decision during her husband's illness. She admitted, however, that at the height of the controversy over the Treaty of Versailles, she pleaded with the President to accept Senator Lodge's amendments to the Treaty.

Defeat of the Treaty

Twice an amended version of the Versailles Treaty came to a vote in the Senate. Both times Wilson refused to compromise. From his sickbed he instructed Senate Democrats to vote against it.

Wilson in 1919

If President Wilson had been willing to compromise, the Senate might have approved the treaty. Instead, in late November of 1919 the United States concluded a treaty of its own with the Central Powers.

Meanwhile in Geneva, Switzerland, the League of Nations began its peace-keeping efforts. Without American membership, however, it had little hope of success.

3. Section Review

1. Define **self-determination** and **reparations.**

2. What influence did Wilson's Fourteen Points have on the Treaty of Versailles?

3. Why did the United States Senate refuse to ratify the treaty?

4. Critical Thinking Do you think that Wilson should have compromised with the Senate on the Treaty of Versailles? Why or why not?

We remember World War I because it marked a sort of "coming of age" for Americans. When the United States declared war in 1917, Americans became involved in their first major overseas conflict. They took this step reluctantly but for the most honorable of reasons. President Wilson stated the nation's purpose in his address to Congress calling for war:

> "The world must be made safe for democracy. Its peace must be founded upon the trusted foundations of political liberty."

World War I taught Americans that being peacemakers is never easy, especially when war inflames old hatreds and creates new ones. It also revealed that not everyone shares our reverence for democracy and freedom. There was another lesson as well. World War I reminded us once more that our strength as a nation rests on the willingness of ordinary people like Alvin York to do extraordinary things in defense of our ideals. As the *New York Times* wrote at the time of York's death in 1964, "One likes to think that the United States was built and protected by such . . . simple and pure men."

Geography Footnote

The news of better pay, better jobs, and better treatment in the North spread fast. As one woman who moved to Chicago wrote in a letter to members of her church back home: "Hurry up and come to Chicago— it is wonderful."

Between 1910 and 1920 migrants swelled the African American populations in major northern cities: from 5,000 to 40,800 in Detroit, from 8,400 to 34,400 in Cleveland, from 44,000 to 109,400 in Chicago, and from 91,700 to 152,400 in New York City. Optimistic about their prospects, African Americans leaving the South by train often chalked slogans on the sides of the cars like "Bound for the Promised Land" and "Farewell—We're Good and Gone."

Geography Lab

The Great Migration

The effort to win the war reshaped our nation in ways that no one could have predicted. For example, people seeking jobs in war-related industries swelled the populations of northern cities. Many job seekers were African Americans from the South. They were recruited by agents from northern companies, who promised free transportation and other benefits as well as good wages.

Thus began a mass migration that would continue for decades. Use the quotations and the data in the table to understand the reasons for this migration and its effects.

Estimated African American Migration to (+) and from (–) Selected States 1910–1920

Alabama	–70,800
Georgia	–74,700
Illinois	+69,800
Louisiana	–51,200
Michigan	+38,700
Mississippi	–129,600
New York	+63,100
Ohio	+69,400
Pennsylvania	+82,500
South Carolina	–74,500

Source: *Historical Statistics of the United States*

Two Migrants' Stories

"The best wages I could make [in Georgia] was $1.25 or $1.50 a day. I went to work at a dye house at Newark, N.J., at $2.75 a day, with a rent-free room to live in. . . . The company paid my fare North."

"I should have been here [in Chicago] 20 years ago. I just begin to feel like a man. . . . My children are going to the same school with the whites and I don't have to umble [bow] to no one. I have registered— Will vote the next election and there isn't any 'yes sir' and 'no sir'—it's all yes and no and Sam and Bill."

Link to History

1. What reasons for moving to the North do you find in the quotations? What others can you think of?
2. Which state in the table lost the largest number of African Americans? Which state gained the largest number?
3. For each of the following states, tell whether it was likely to have experienced a gain or a loss in African American population between 1910 and 1920: Indiana, New Jersey, North Carolina, Virginia.
4. Name five cities that probably saw their African American populations grow rapidly between 1910 and 1920.
5. **Hands-On Geography** You are a northern company's agent, sent to a southern community in 1917. Make a poster or a brochure to persuade African Americans to apply for jobs at your company.

Teaching the Geography Lab

Have students make separate bar graphs of positive and negative migration. Have them speculate why Mississippi had the largest out-migration. (Living conditions for blacks were especially poor, black population was especially large compared with other states, or both.)

Link to History

Answers

1. Better wages, rent-free room, free transportation to North, unsegregated schools and better educational opportunities, ability to vote, sense of equality with whites, self-respect. Other reasons: better housing, desire to join family or friends, more varied jobs, avoid lynchings and other racial mistreatment.

2. Lost: Mississippi. Gained: Pennsylvania.

3. Gain: Indiana and New Jersey. Loss: North Carolina and Virginia.

4. Some answers: New York City, Chicago, Cleveland, Philadelphia, Detroit.

5. Posters or brochures should show understanding that target audience is a mix of tenant farmers and unskilled laborers attracted by promise of steady jobs, higher wages, and inexpensive housing.

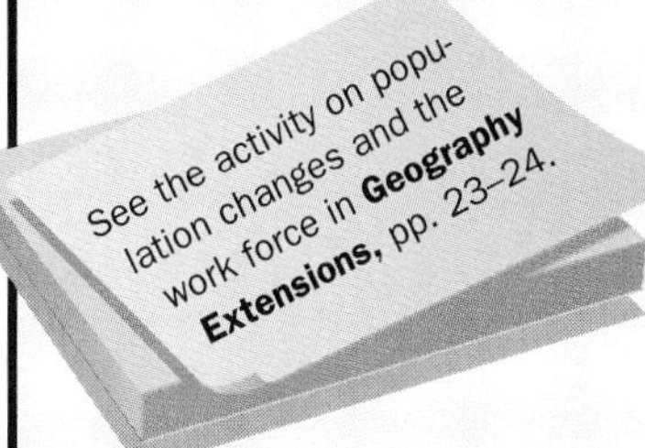

Picture Essay

Teaching the Picture Essay

In this feature, students will learn about American involvement in World War I through a series of pictures and captions. Picture essays not only enhance students' knowledge of history but also help students understand the value of different types of information sources. Visual learners especially will enjoy and benefit from the picture essay. The feature also will help students with limited English—who may be intimidated by lengthy written text—focus on important points about the war.

Have students study the entire feature before answering the Discussion questions or doing the Wrap-Up Activity. You may assign the Bonus Activity as an alternative to, or in addition to, the Wrap-Up Activity.

Warm-Up Activity

Getting into the Picture

To prepare students to study the feature, ask them to scan the pictures without reading the captions. Then have them choose a picture, imagine themselves as one of the persons shown, and give a short speech about what was going on and how they felt at the moment the picture was taken. Later, students can compare what they imagined with what they learned.

Essay Objectives

Use pictures and captions to trace events of World War I, with these emphases:

- ★ Explain how the U.S. government raised the army and the money needed to fight the war.
- ★ Identify roles played by women and African Americans in the war effort.
- ★ Summarize the contributions made, as well as the losses suffered, by American troops in the Meuse-Argonne offensive of 1918.

PICTURE ESSAY

World War I

NEW YORK JOURNAL
EIGHTH EDITION
House by a Vote of 373 to 50 Passes Joint Resolutio
WAR IS DECLARED BY U.S
Interned German Ships Seized by Customs Authoritie
VESSELS IN ALLIES REST PORT HERE TAKEN
BEFORE BIG DRIVE
"LOVE U.S. BUT CAN'T VOTE FOR WAR"—MISS RANKIN
CARRANZISTAS MISSING ON BORDER
AUSTRIA EAGER TO KEEP PEACE WITH U.S.
CZAR SUPPLIANT FOR PENSION TO DUMA

1. The headline from the *New York Journal* announced that the United States had declared war against Germany on Friday, April 6, 1917.

2 and 3. The United States was unprepared for war. To quickly increase the size of the American armed forces, Congress enacted a draft. Names were chosen at random from those registered. The Secretary of War, Newton Barker (2), draws from a bowl on June 27, 1918 the name of the first registered person to serve. Recruitment centers were set up across the country to encourage men to enlist voluntarily (3).

Connections to Art

Shortly after the United States declared war on Germany, George Creel, head of the Committee on Public Information, sent a telegram to the popular American artist Charles Dana Gibson. Creel proposed organizing a committee of volunteer artists to produce whatever artwork the government might need for the war effort. Gibson and hundreds of other artists responded enthusiastically. In the months that followed, they created more than 2,000 different war-related posters. With about 20 million copies in print, the posters became a common sight in American cities. The posters relied on forceful images and simple slogans to get their message across. Some images lived on long after World War I ended. The pointing Uncle Sam painted by James Montgomery Flagg (p. 403) is one example.

5

4

7

6

4 and 5. To help finance the war, posters (4) made the selling of Liberty bonds into a crusade. Bonds could be purchased on an installment plan or war savings stamps could be pasted in a book and redeemed for bonds. Although this poster addresses women, most savings stamps—more than a billion dollars' worth—were bought by schoolchildren. Also film stars such as Douglas Fairbanks (5) held rallies to encourage Americans to purchase bonds.

6 and 7. As part of the war effort, posters (6) asked Americans to eat less, to plant war gardens, and to can their own fruits and vegetables. Red Cross volunteers (7) show off some of the hundreds of pairs of socks they knitted for the armed forces.

Bonus Activity

Writing as a War Correspondent

To help students grasp the sacrifices and costs of World War I, have them imagine they are war correspondents for an American newspaper in 1918. They have been assigned to cover the Meuse-Argonne campaign. (In this final offensive of the war, which began in September 1918, American forces struggled through the Argonne Forest toward Sedan on the Meuse River.) Have students do library research and use what they learn to write an account of one of the 47 days of the campaign. Encourage students to be creative in the approach they take. For example, they might write an hour-by-hour account of one soldier's day as the soldier himself might write it. Or they might describe a battle from the viewpoint of an observer hiding high in the trees. Also encourage students to use details and imagery to make their accounts as vivid as possible. Ask volunteers to read their accounts aloud.

Wrap-Up Activity

Creating Collaborative Poems

To reinforce understanding of World War I and give students practice in interpreting visuals, ask small groups to create collaborative poems. Have the groups begin by holding discussions in which group members share the knowledge and impressions they have gained about World War I—on the battlefield and at home—through this picture essay. Next, group members should work on their own to write a line of poetry describing a sight or a feeling related to the war. When group members have completed their individual lines of poetry, they should work together to arrange the lines to form a collaborative poem. They may find they want to edit some of the lines to make the poem more cohesive. For example, they may decide to begin every line with a certain phrase, such as "War is. . . ." Ask each group to title its completed poem and post the poem where classmates can read it.

Connection to Economics

Demands for increased production, combined with the enlistment of many male workers in the military, created new job opportunities for women during the war. Besides riveting battleships, women learned to stitch wings for airplanes. They also loaded and unloaded ships, served as streetcar conductors, and repaired cars. For the most part, however, the economic advances made by women were short-lived. A government report issued in 1919 admitted that, contrary to orders given by the War Labor Board, many female workers had been paid less than male workers. After the war, most female industrial workers either gave up their jobs or were fired to make room for returning soldiers. By 1920 women made up a smaller percentage of the labor force than they had before the war.

8

9

Background. Women took pride in learning new job skills in mills and factories. The shipyard workers posed in front of their handiwork. The women carried hot rivets in cone-shaped holders and used tongs to insert the rivets into holes that had been drilled in two metal plates. Another worker hammered the open end of the rivets to meld the plates together. Note that the women wore slacks, which did not become popular generally until World War II.

8. American wounded and German prisoners stagger back from the front lines of the Meuse-Argonne. More Americans died in that campaign than in the rest of the war. The painting is by Harvey Dunn (1884–1952), one of the eight official artists with the American Expeditionary Force.

9. This shattered church in the ruins of the French town of Neuvilly furnished temporary shelter for the Americans wounded on the first

History Footnote

The 369th Infantry Regiment, from New York City's Harlem district, endured enemy fire for a record-breaking 191 days without losing a trench, retreating an inch, or surrendering a prisoner. It was for that performance that France awarded the Croix de Guerre to the entire unit. However, the experience of African American soldiers and sailors in World War I was often a frustrating one. The vast majority of the African American troops sent to France never saw combat; instead, they performed tasks like cooking and moving supplies. Even those African Americans who saw combat served in segregated units, usually under white officers. In addition, the U.S. military declared certain French cities and cafés off-limits to black soldiers.

10

11

12

day of the offensive in the Meuse-Argonne in September 1918. About 1,200,000 Americans fought in this battle and about one of every ten was killed or wounded.

10. Members of the 369th Infantry Regiment won high praise for their fighting in the Meuse-Argonne. These African Americans are shown here on the return voyage to the United States in 1919 after receiving the French Croix de Guerre (war cross) for bravery.

11. On November 7, 1918, in Washington, D.C., an Armistice Day crowd holds up copies of the special edition of the *Washington Times,* announcing the end of the war.

12. The Tomb of the Unknown Soldier of the United States is a symbol of all those who gave their life for our country. The first person to be buried in the tomb was an unidentified soldier who died in World War I. Every day crowds visit the tomb in Arlington Cemetery.

Discussion

Checking Understanding

1. How did government posters aid the war effort? (Encouraged Americans to buy bonds and to take action to ensure adequate food supplies. Students also may recall from the chapter that posters encouraged Americans to join the armed forces.)

2. Besides working for the armed services, how did women help win the war? (Worked as Red Cross volunteers, bought war bonds, grew and conserved food, took jobs in mills and factories.)

Stimulating Critical Thinking

3. Compare and contrast what Pictures 8 and 9 say about the costs of the Meuse-Argonne offensive. (Possible answer: Both pictures show wounded men. The painting portrays their suffering more dramatically through facial expressions, blood, and so on. Only the photo shows property destruction.)

4. What conclusions could you draw from Picture 10, even without its caption? (Possible answers: African Americans served in the armed forces but apparently in segregated units; the soldiers in the picture performed bravely, because they are wearing medals; the soldiers had difficult experiences, because they look so serious.)

Survey Answers

Reviewing Vocabulary

Definitions are found on these pages: *stalemate* (409), *propaganda* (412), *pacifists* (417), *armistice* (419), *self-determination* (421), *reparations* (423).

Reviewing Main Ideas

1. Most countries of Europe had joined one of two alliances. When Austria-Hungary declared war on Serbia after assassination of Archduke Ferdinand, other countries allied with each came to their aid.

2. Trenches were long ditches about six feet deep and three feet wide where soldiers lived during and between battles. They endured mud, rats, lice, the smell of dead bodies, danger, boredom, and poor rations.

3. German submarine torpedoed luxury ship *Lusitania*. Germany sent a secret message to Mexico, promising to help attack the southwestern United States if Mexico joined the Central Powers. German U-boats sank five neutral ships. Revolutionaries in Russia set up a democratic government.

4. Food Administration organized food production, distribution, and conservation. Factories began producing war materials. Women and African Americans took factory jobs.

5. Germans had advanced close to Paris. Allied victory at Belleau Wood marked beginning of the end for German forces.

6. It took land away from the empires of the Central Powers to create homelands for various national groups. It set up the League of Nations. It required Germany to pay reparations, reduce its military, and take sole responsibility for the war.

(Answers continued in top margin)

7. Senate Republicans objected to its terms, especially the League of Nations, fearing League membership would draw the United States into future foreign wars. Wilson refused to accept the Senate's amendments to the treaty.

Thinking Critically

1. Fits: war fought on two long fronts, death of civilians, widespread propaganda, economy switched to producing war materials, civilians conserved resources and helped finance war. Does not fit: no battle on American soil.

2. Possibilities: war might have ended sooner, with less destruction and milder treaty terms for Germany, which might have prevented World War II; a shorter war might have meant no revolution in Russia; earlier entry by the United States might

Chapter Survey

Reviewing Vocabulary

Define the following terms.

1. stalemate
2. propaganda
3. pacifists
4. armistice
5. self-determination
6. reparations

Reviewing Main Ideas

1. How did so many nations get drawn into World War I?
2. Describe the trenches and what life in them was like.
3. What events brought the United States into the war?
4. What were some ways that the United States quickly produced the huge amounts of supplies and weapons needed to fight the war?
5. Why was the Battle of Belleau Wood important?
6. Summarize the terms of the Versailles Treaty.
7. Why did the United States not sign the Versailles Treaty?

Thinking Critically

1. Analysis A total war, as defined in Chapter 2, is a war against armies and also against a people's resources and will to fight. How does World War I fit the definition of total war? Are there any ways it does not fit the definition? Explain your answer.
2. Synthesis Suppose the United States had entered the war two years earlier. How might the course of history have been different? Give three possibilities.
3. Why We Remember: Application What did President Wilson mean when he said, "The world must be made safe for democracy"? Were his Fourteen Points consistent with that statement? Why or why not?

Applying Skills

Analyzing propaganda Find an example of propaganda in a newspaper or magazine, on television or radio, or on a poster or billboard. Keeping in mind what you learned on page 420, write a paragraph describing the following:
- the words and images that make up the piece
- the apparent purpose of the piece
- the propaganda techniques used in the piece
- how effective you think the piece is and why

History Mystery

The choice to fight Answer the History Mystery on page 403. Do you think that Alvin York should have had to serve in the army? Why or why not?

Writing in Your History Journal

1. Keys to History (a) The time line on pages 402–403 has seven Keys to History. In your history journal, list each key and describe why the event is important to know about. (b) Choose any two events on the time line and explain in your journal how the events are related.
2. Alvin York In your journal, write your personal definition of the word *hero*. Then tell whether Alvin C. York fits your definition. Explain your answers.
3. Citizenship In trying to quiet opposition through the Espionage and Sedition acts, did the United States government go too far? How might Americans react to similar acts in a modern war? Explain your responses in your journal.

have failed to win American support, resulting in less success at raising an army and producing war materials, reducing American ability to help Allies.

3. He meant the Allies would defeat empires, making possible establishment of independent, self-determining democracies. Yes: Wilson's plan called for removing causes of war, protecting self-determination, and creating an organization to promote lasting peace. No: in redrawing European countries' borders, the Allies were assuming too much power and control over other countries.

Applying Skills

Answers should reflect understanding of the techniques of propaganda (p. 420) and ability to distinguish it from other forms of communication.

(Answers continued in side margin)

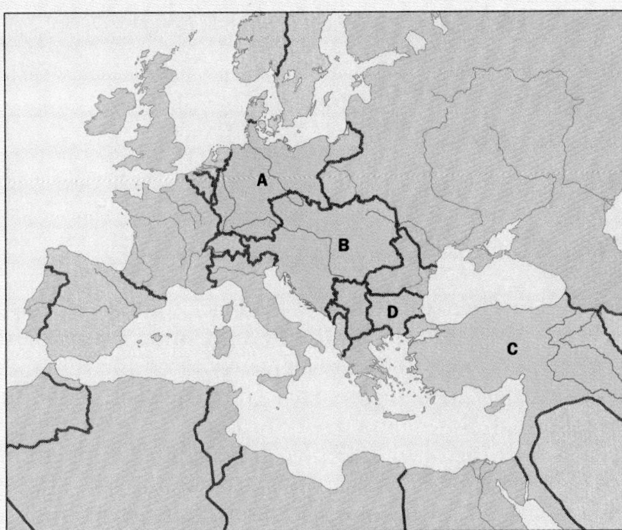

Reviewing Geography

1. Each letter on the map represents one of the Central Powers. Write the name of each.

2. Geographic Thinking Look at the map on pages R2–R3. How do you think the location of the United States relative to Europe affected the following:
- number of years the United States remained neutral
- impact of the war on Americans once the United States joined the Allies
- attitude of Senate Republicans toward the League of Nations

How might things have been different if the war had been centered in Canada?

Alternative Assessment

Compiling a wartime scrapbook With three classmates, put together a ten-page scrapbook of letters and other mementos that might have been compiled by an American family in World War I.

❶ Invent the family. Start by answering these questions:
- What ethnic or racial group do they belong to and where do they live?
- Who serves on the battlefront, and in what ways?
- How do other family members contribute to the war effort?

❷ Create materials for the scrapbook, such as articles, journal entries, and letters. Your materials should touch on major events in the chapter, including these:
- assassination of Archduke Ferdinand
- sinking of the *Lusitania*
- America's entry into the war
- the draft
- life on the home front
- trench warfare
- controversy over the Versailles Treaty

❸ Assemble the scrapbook.

Your work will be evaluated on the following criteria:
- it realistically portrays how ordinary Americans might have reacted to and been affected by World War I
- it contains materials that are clearly written and full of interesting details
- it shows imagination and creativity

History Mystery

Fighting in a war went against York's religious beliefs. Opinions will vary.

Writing in Your History Journal

1. (a) Explanations should be similar to the time line notes on teacher pages 402–403. (b) Accept explanations that are consistent with the chapter.

2. Definitions should be thoughtful and supported with examples of behavior. Students' opinions of York should refer to their definitions. They may admire his bravery, modesty, and the deep thought he gave to his decision to fight. Some students may say killing people is not a heroic trait.

3. Students might support punishment for acts that hinder the war effort but not for disloyal speech, saying that free speech is a right. They may feel Americans today would be less tolerant of such a law, citing stronger support for individual rights.

Reviewing Geography

1. (A) Germany, (B) Austria-Hungary, (C) Ottoman Empire, (D) Bulgaria.

2. Because United States was separated from the war by an ocean, it could stay neutral for a long time; no property damage or civilian casualties; Americans felt they should stay isolated from the League of Nations' problems. If the war had been centered in Canada, it might have joined more quickly, had civilian casualties and property destruction, and been more eager to join League of Nations.

Alternative Assessment

Teacher's Take-Home Planner 3, p. 23, includes suggestions and scoring rubrics for the Alternative Assessment activity.

Teaching the

Link to American Readings

In this feature students learn about the Great Migration of African Americans from the South to the cities of the North. The first reading includes letters to the editor of the *Chicago Defender*. Students will also examine some paintings from Jacob Lawrence's *The Migration of the Negro* series.

Before students begin the lesson, review African Americans (page 414). You may also choose to introduce students to Zora Neale Hurston (pages 450–451). Have students read the entire feature before assigning the A Closer Look questions. The Setting the Stage Activity and Bonus Activity may then be introduced according to the needs and interests of the students. The information contained in the Discussion questions and the Footnotes may be used throughout the lesson as appropriate. Readers' Theater is ideal for students who might find the readings somewhat difficult. Use the Wrap-Up Activity for students who would enjoy taking a step beyond the core lesson.

Literature Footnote

Zora Neale Hurston was one of the many African Americans who became part of the Great Migration. Unable to earn enough money as a maid and waitress to return to school after her mother died, Hurston moved to Boston. There she enrolled in a night school course that changed her life. The class proved instrumental in nudging her toward a career as a writer. As a fiction writer, Hurston became known for her lyrical language, her storytelling talent, and her celebration of southern black culture. She addressed issues of race and gender, often relating them to a search for freedom. Some of her works include: *Their Eyes Were Watching God* (1937), her best-known work; *Jonah's Gourd Vine* (1934); *Seraph on the Suwanee* (1948); *Dust Tracks on a Road* (1942), her autobiography; and short stories and plays.

Link to American Readings

READING 9A

Letters from the Great Migration

Between 1916 and 1920, approximately 500,000 black southerners migrated to the North. Nearly a million followed in the 1920s. During World War I, European immigration slowed and the war emergency intensified. To meet the demand for war materials, labor agents traveled to the South offering African Americans jobs, high wages, and free transportation in the North. African Americans also took their own initiative in seeking new opportunities. They responded to employment advertisements in the *Chicago Defender*, one of the most widely circulated African American newspapers in America. They also established migration networks, corresponding and sending information to family and friends. The first two letters reveal the energy and determination of southern blacks to improve their lives. In the third letter, a migrant describes the differences between life in the North and in the South.

Houston, Texas, April 29, 1917

Dear Sir: I am a constant reader of the "Chicago Defender" and in your last issue I saw a want ad that appealed to me. I am a Negro, age 37, and am an all round foundry man. I am a core maker by trade having had about 10 years experience at the business, and hold good references from several shops, in which I have been employed. I have worked at various shops and I have always been able to make good. It is hard for a black man to hold a job here, as prejudice is very strong. I have never been discharged on account of dissatisfaction with my work, but I have been "let out" on account of my color. I am a good brassmelter but i prefer core making as it is my trade. I have a family and am anxious to leave here, but have not the means, and as wages are not much here, it is very hard to save enough to get away with. If you know of any firms that are in need of a core maker and whom you think would send me transportation, I would be pleased to be put in touch with them and I assure you that effort would be appreciated. I am a core maker but I am willing to do any honest work. All I want is to get away from here. I am writing you and I believe you can and will help me. If any one will send transportation, I will arrange or agree to have it taken out of my salary untill full amount of fare is paid. I also know of several good fdry. men here who would leave in a minute, if there only was a way arranged for them to leave, and they are men whom I know personally to be experienced men. I hope

foundry: a factory where metal is cast

core: part of the mold that forms the interior of a hollow casting

Literature Footnote
Not all African Americans living in the cities of the North in the early twentieth century had the same, or even similar, experiences. An example is poet Paul Laurence Dunbar (1872–1906). Born in Dayton, Ohio, the son of former slaves, Dunbar was the only African American in his high school. Although he had dreams of becoming a lawyer, he could not afford college. The only job he could find was that of elevator operator. While working in Dayton, he wrote poems that he sometimes submitted to newspapers. His third volume of poetry, *Lyrics of Lowly Life*, brought him national recognition. Although he was applauded for his ability to express the lyrical qualities of African American life and dialect, he usually avoided racial issues in his writing. In addition to poetry, Dunbar wrote four novels.

that you will give this your immediate attention as I am anxious to get busy and be on my way. I am ready to start at any time, and would be pleased to hear something favorable.

New Orleans, La., June 10, 1917

Kind Sir: I read and hear daly of the great chance that a colored parson has in Chicago of making a living with all the priveleg that the whites have and it mak me the most ankious to want to go where I may be able to make a liveing for my self. When you read this you will think it bery strange that being only my self to support that it is so hard, but it is so. everything is gone up but the poor colerd peple wages. I have made sevle afford to leave and come to Chicago where I hear that times is good for us but owing to femail wekness has made it a perfect failure. I am a widow for 9 years. I have very pore learning altho it would not make much diffrent if I would be throughly edacated for I could not get any better work to do, such as house work, washing and ironing and all such work that are injering to a woman with femail wekness and they pay so little for so hard work that it is just enough to pay room rent and a little some thing to eat. I have found a very good remady that I really feeling to belive would cure me if I only could make enough money to keep up my madison and I dont think that I will ever be able to do that down hear for the time is getting worse evry day. I am going to ask if you peple hear could aid me in geting over her in Chicago and seeking out a position of some kind. I can also do plain sewing. Please good peple dont refuse to help me out in my trouble for I am in gret need of help God will bless you. I am going to do my very best after I get over here if God spair me to get work I will pay the expance back. Do try to do the best you can for me, with many thanks for so doing I will remain as ever,

Yours truly.

An African American family arrives in Chicago from the rural South, around 1920.

Setting the Stage Activity

Considering a Move

To help students understand the causes of the Great Migration, ask them to consider the reasons that people move from one place to another. Ask students why their own families left their old homes and moved to where they live today. If enough students respond, you may be able to point out certain patterns. For example, many people move for new jobs, for better living conditions, or for educational opportunities. Point out that the African Americans who moved from the South to the North were searching for the same things.

Bonus Activity

Illustrating Migration

To help students recognize the power of art and to understand how art can convey a message, have them make either a drawing or a poster, using the media of their choice, that encourages African Americans to move to the North from the South. Students should develop a plan before they begin. When they finish, hang the art in the classroom and discuss what makes each piece effective.

Discussion

Stimulating Critical Thinking

1. First, reread the letters to the editor of the *Chicago Defender*. Then determine what characteristics the writers have in common. (Students may point out several similarities. The writers have all had enough education to write a letter, but they have apparently not had the opportunity for education beyond grade school. They are looking for jobs with decent wages and want to live without fighting discrimination. The writer of the third letter has found the life he was seeking, but also misses his home in the South.)

2. The African Americans who came North were looking for a better life. No matter what situation they were leaving behind in the South, they wanted something better. Now picture yourself as a parent. What opportunities would you most like your children to have as they grow up? (Students' answers will vary, but might include: basic human rights such as freedom—political, religious, and social; a solid education; clean, crime-free areas in which to live; parks and other recreational facilities; quality housing.)

History Footnote

Jacob Lawrence's *Migration of the Negro* series is based on research and his family's recollections of their move to the North during the first big wave of the Great Migration between 1916 and 1919. According to Lawrence, "migration means movement. While I was painting, I thought about trains and people walking to the stations. I thought about field hands leaving their farms to become factory workers, and about the families that sometimes got left behind. The choices made were hard ones, so I wanted to show what made the people get on those northbound trains. I also wanted to show just what it cost to ride them. Uprooting yourself from one way of life to make your way in another involves conflict and struggle."

Philadelphia, Pa., Oct. 7, 1917

Dear Sir: I take this method of thanking you for yours early responding and the glorious effect of the treatment. Oh. I do feel so fine. Dr. the treatment reach me almost ready to move I am now housekeeping again I like it so much better than rooming. Well Dr. with the aid of God I am making very good I make $75 per month. I am carrying enough insurance to pay me $20 per week if I am not able to be on duty. I don't have to work hard. dont have to mister every little white boy comes along I havent heard a white man call a colored a nigger you no now—since I been in the state of Pa. I can ride in the electric street and steam cars any where I get a seat. I dont care to mix with white what I mean I am not crazy about being with white folks, but if I have to pay the same fare I have learn to want the same acomidation. and if you are first in a place here shoping you dont have to wait until the white folks get thro tradeing yet amid all this I shall ever love the good old South and I am praying that God may give every well wisher a chance to be a man regardless of his color, and if my going to the front would bring about such conditions I am ready any day—well Dr. I dont want to worry you but read between lines; and maybe you can see a little sense in my weak statement the kids are in school every day I have only two and I guess that all. Dr. when you find time I would be delighted to have a word from the good old home state. Wife join me in sending love you and yours.

I am your friend and patient. . . .

READING 9B

The Migration of the Negro Series

Born in 1917, American painter Jacob Lawrence is known for his series of paintings on African American historical figures and events. These narrative series consist of as many as sixty panels on a single topic or person. Some of his most famous works include the thirty-panel *Harriet Tubman* series, completed between 1939 and 1940, and *The Migration of the Negro* series. The sixty panels of *The Migration of the Negro* series, completed between 1940 and 1941, depict the mass migration of African Americans from the rural South to the urban industrial centers of the North. Three of the paintings from that series are shown on these pages.

Panel #46 from *The Migration of the Negro* series. What message do you think the artist meant to convey in this painting?

Readers' Theater

A group of three students might adapt the letters to the editor of the *Chicago Defender*. Students may read the letters as written, changing details, if necessary, to make them gender-appropriate. Students should attempt to pronounce the words as they are written to lend authenticity to the reading. Allow students time to rehearse their readings so that the dialect sounds natural.

Panel #1 from *The Migration of the Negro* series. Crowds of African Americans leave their southern homeland behind as they move toward the urban centers of the North. Chicago, New York, St. Louis, and other cities hold promises of jobs, homes, and some degree of relief from racial prejudice.

Panel #55 from *The Migration of the Negro* series shows one of the tragic results of crowded urban life. Many African Americans who moved to the North contracted tuberculosis, an often fatal disease. There was neither a vaccine to prevent this highly contagious lung disease nor a reliable cure.

A Closer Look

1. List some of the reasons that African Americans migrated from their homes in the South to unfamiliar northern cities.

2. Choose one of Jacob Lawrence's paintings. What does it say about the African American experience of migrating from the South to the North?

3. CRITICAL THINKING Consider the experience of the European immigrants that you have studied. How does their experience in the industrial urban cities compare to that of African Americans who moved to the North from the South? What are the similarities? What are the differences?

Wrap-Up Activity

Defining Migration

To extend the lesson and to help students think through the causes of migration, ask them to develop their own definition of *migration.* After studying these readings and art, how do they interpret the word? Students should put their interpretation, either a narrative or an illustration, in their history journals.

A Closer Look

Answers

1. African Americans moved to the North to find better jobs, housing, and education. They hoped to find more opportunities and to be relieved of racial prejudice. They wanted their children to have the opportunities that they had missed by living in the South.

2. Students' responses will vary. Students should support their interpretations with details from the paintings that relate to what they have learned about migration.

3. Students' responses might include some of the following points. Similarities: Both groups moved to seek better lives. Differences: Most European immigrants had to overcome a language barrier as well as adjust to new customs.

Teaching the Citizenship Lab

In this feature students learn about the Schenck case, one of the most important freedom-of-speech cases heard by the Supreme Court. The First Amendment issue raised by the case is whether freedom of speech is absolute. The Court decided that an individual's rights must be balanced against society's needs. The case established the "clear and present danger" doctrine.

Before students read the feature, review Silencing Opposition and Winning Support on page 417. Have students read the entire feature before assigning the Understanding Civic Issues questions and the Hands-On Citizenship activity. The Bonus Activity in this Teacher's Edition may be used as an alternative to, or in addition to, the Hands-On Citizenship. The Discussion questions in this Teacher's Edition may be used at appropriate points during students' reading or afterward.

Objectives

- ★ Understand that there were Americans opposed to WWI.
- ★ Know why Schenck was arrested and on what grounds he appealed his conviction.
- ★ Identify the "clear and present danger" doctrine.
- ★ Cite examples of issues today that may require the courts to redefine freedom of speech.

Supreme Court Case: *Schenck* v. *United States*

Citizenship Lab

Is Free Speech Limited During War Time?

In 1917 the United States was at war with Germany. Most Americans eagerly supported the war effort. Many volunteered to fight and most men cooperated with the Selective Service Act that required all men between the ages of 21 and 30 to register for the draft. Some groups, however, thought the war was wrong. To prevent these groups from sabotaging the war effort, Congress passed the Espionage and Sedition Acts.

The Espionage and Sedition Acts Outlawed Any Opposition to the War Effort

According to these laws, a person could be fined up to $10,000 and/or sentenced to 20 years in jail for interfering with the draft. Saying something disloyal or against the government was also a punishable offense. Six thousand people were arrested for violating the laws and 1,500 of them were convicted. The laws were so strict that a Bible class teacher, Rev. Clarence Waldron, was arrested for telling his class that "a Christian can take no part in the war." He was tried and sentenced to 15 years in jail.

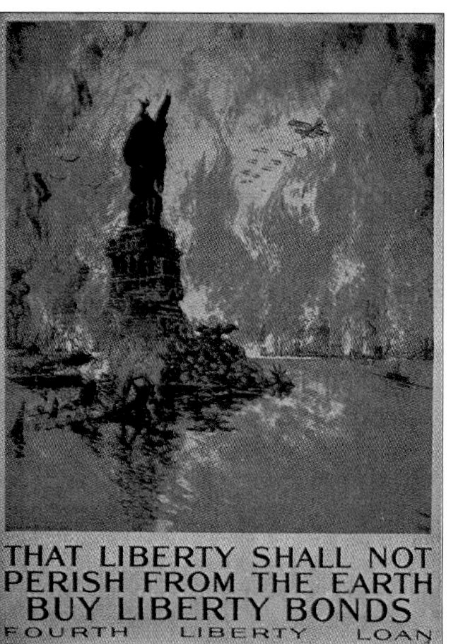
THAT LIBERTY SHALL NOT
PERISH FROM THE EARTH
BUY LIBERTY BONDS
FOURTH LIBERTY LOAN

Posters such as this one by Joseph Pennell moved many people to support the war effort.

Several political groups opposed America's involvement in the war. One of these groups was the Socialist party. The party's leader, Eugene Debs, was sentenced to ten years in prison for speaking out against the war. Charles T. Schenck was general secretary of the party. He believed the draft was not permitted by the Constitution. He sent out 15,000 pamphlets in which he wrote that anyone who agreed to be drafted

History Footnote

Oliver Wendell Holmes, Jr., was born in Boston in 1841, the son of a well-known writer. After graduating from Harvard University, he enlisted in the Union army during the Civil War. He fought at several battles and rose to the rank of captain. In July 1864, President Lincoln was visiting the troops. The Confederates chose this moment to attack. The 23-year-old Holmes is alleged to have shouted to the over six-foot-tall President, "Get down, you fool!" After the war Holmes studied law and later became a professor of law at Harvard. In 1902 he was appointed to the Supreme Court by Theodore Roosevelt. He held that position until his retirement in 1932.

was "little better than a convict." He urged young men to resist the draft. Schenck was arrested, prosecuted, and convicted of trying to cause disobedience in the armed services and of attempting to interfere with raising an army. His lawyers appealed his case to the Supreme Court. They argued that his First Amendment rights of free speech and press were violated.

What Did Schenck's Leaflet Say?

The leaflet had two printed sides. On the front side, it urged young men not to submit to "intimidation." It called on them to petition Congress to repeal the draft law. "Assert Your Rights" was the headline on the back side of the pamphlet. It stated that anyone who tried to stop

Antiwar protesters march in the May Day parade in 1916. At this time the war in Europe had been under way for 20 months and the entry of the United States was still opposed by most politicians.

Setting the Stage Activity

Discussing Important Issues

To prepare students for reading about the Schenck case, ask them to imagine that our country is at war. Some people believe the war is wrong and refuse to serve. If students were advising the President, what policy would they recommend regarding people who protest against the war and refuse to serve? Make sure that the discussion points out the conflict between the rights of the individual on one hand and the needs of society on the other hand.

Bonus Activity

Creating Charts

Have students develop a chart titled "The 5 Ws and H. " Column 1 should indicate the name of the feature. Columns 2–7 should be labeled: "Who", "What", "Where", "When", "Why", and "How".

Discussion

Checking Understanding

1. What did Justice Holmes mean when he said that freedom of speech is not absolute? (There are times and circumstances when rights must be curtailed. For example, a person should not be allowed to yell "fire" in a crowded move theater.)

2. What is the value of hearing speakers and opinions you disagree with or dislike? (Gaining knowledge from a wide variety of sources enables us to better make decisions regarding specific topics.)

Stimulating Critical Thinking

3. What is the danger of suppressing unpopular thought? (Ultimately, such suppression probably would lead to the development of a repressive government whose citizens would be fearful of speaking out at all because of possible penalties.)

Citizenship Footnote

In 1969 the Supreme Court heard a case involving freedom of expression for students. The case was *Tinker* v. *Des Moines Independent School District.* The Tinker family, along with several others, was opposed to the Vietnam War. To protest, the children wore black armbands to school. Because the children disobeyed a school policy by wearing the armbands, they were suspended from school. The Tinkers sued and the case eventually went to the Supreme Court.

The Court ruled in the Tinkers' favor. Justice Abe Fortas said: "First Amendment rights . . . are available to teachers and students. It can hardly be argued that either students or teachers shed their constitutional rights to freedom of speech or expression at the schoolhouse gate."

a citizen from speaking out against the draft was violating the Constitution. The leaflet also made the point that the government did not have the power to send soldiers to fight on foreign soil. It urged young men to do their "share to maintain, support and uphold the rights of the people of this country."

The Court Declares the "Clear and Present Danger Doctrine"

This case, *Schenck* v. *the United States*, was one of the first cases about freedom of speech. The Court had the difficult task of deciding how important the rights of individuals are compared to the security of the country. After hearing both sides, the Court ruled that in this case, the security of the country was more important than Schenck's freedom of speech.

Justice Oliver Wendall Holmes, Jr., wrote the unanimous decision. He pointed out that freedom of speech is not absolute. It does not give a person the right to shout "fire" in a crowded theater and cause a panic. Likewise, when the nation is at war, individual rights may have to be reduced.

In his decision, Justice Holmes declared a doctrine that has come to be known as the "clear and present danger doctrine." Justice Holmes wrote: "The character of every act depends on the circumstances in which it is done. . . . The question in every case is whether the words are used in such circumstances and are of such a nature as to create a *clear and present danger* that they will bring about the . . . evils that Congress has a right to prevent. . . . When a nation is at war, many things that might be said in time of peace are such a hindrance to its effort that their utterance will not be endured."

In other words, circumstances are different in times of peace and in times of war. If there is a clear and present danger that the words spoken or written will be put into action, and if the words will bring about an evil that Congress has a right to prevent, the words are not protected by the First Amendment. Holmes pointed out that the pamphlet was sent with the clear goal of convincing the men not to cooperate with the draft. This type of speech is not protected by the Constitution.

The Struggle to Define Freedom of Speech Today

There have been many court decisions involving free speech since the Schenck case in 1919. Recently, the Supreme Court has had to decide if the government may restrict the freedom of speech of people who demonstrate against abortions in front of clinics that perform them. In addition, the Court may have to rule regarding how the Internet is used. Some people have used the Internet to send hate messages or obscene images. They have argued

Connections to Science

Science teachers are sometimes caught in the conflict between scientific beliefs and religious beliefs. Ask students if they believe teachers should be allowed to express their own views or whether their freedom of expression should be limited to what the school officials prescribe. A famous case involving this issue was the Scopes trial in 1925. You may want to have students read ahead (page 463), and then discuss the case with them.

that this is protected by the Constitution even though many people object. Another potential case centers around whether the government is acting constitutionally if it restricts advertising of tobacco and alcoholic products. Supporters of restrictions argue that these products are a health danger and that much of the advertising is directed at young people. It will again be up to the Supreme Court to decide what limits if any should be imposed on freedom of speech.

"On the Internet, nobody knows you're a dog."

Do you agree with the cartoonist's viewpoint? Why?

Understanding Civic Issues

1. What is the important issue raised by the Schenck case?
2. How are people's rights limited by the Schenck case?
3. **Critical Thinking** Some people argue that freedom of speech means being able to say or write what is unpopular. They argue that if everyone agrees with you, you do not need protection to say what you want to say. What do you think about this argument? Do you agree that there must be limits on freedom of expression? Explain.
4. **Hands-On Citizenship** Imagine that your school has experienced some problems between students of different races and backgrounds. Assume you are given responsibility for running a class meeting to resolve some of the differences. Individually or with several classmates, make a list of guidelines for anyone who wants to speak. How long can any one person speak? Are there any words that speakers should not be allowed to say? How will you balance a person's right to express themselves with the need to maintain order and harmony? In what ways is your situation like the one in the Schenck case?

Citizenship Lab Answers

1. The key issue in the Schenck case is whether an individual's freedom of speech can be restricted if that speech threatens the security of the nation.

2. In the Schenck case, the Court declared the "clear and present danger" doctrine. If there is a clear and present danger that words spoken or written will be put into action, and if the words will bring about an evil that Congress has the right to prevent, the words are not protected by the First Amendment.

3. Answers will vary but should reflect the idea that people who express unpopular ideas or opinions should have a right to be heard or the result is a loss of freedom for all of us.

Teaching the Hands-On CITIZENSHIP

Assessing cooperative learning activities such as this one are sometimes a challenge. It may be helpful to create a form to help you evaluate each student's performance. Criteria for evaluating each individual might include the level of the student's communications skills and the quality of his or her interaction with other group members. You may also want to assess the groups as a whole. Criteria you may want to use include such things as the level of interaction and participation by all the members, whether time was used productively, and whether the opinions of all members were listened to and respected.

Literature Footnote

After the Dancing Days takes place in a small town near Kansas City. At the veteran's hospital where her father works, Annie befriends a young veteran returned from the battlefields of France. Horribly burned, he has withdrawn from the world. The story dramatizes the lasting effects of war and explores the meanings of patriotism and heroism, war and peace.

Teaching the Link to Literature

To make sure students understand this passage, ask them when the pictures in Annie's book about Europe were taken (some time before the war). Next, have them examine the last sentence. Ask what Annie is feeling (guilt for showing Andrew her books). Have them discuss what it is that Annie has "done" with her books and whether they think she is at fault.

Vital Links

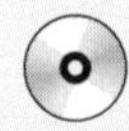

WWI soldiers returning home (Picture) Unit 4, Side 1, Search 24461

See also Unit 4 Explore CD-ROM location 240.

Voice of Norman Roberts (First Person Account) Unit 4, Side 1, Search 23683, Play to 24410

See also Unit 4 Explore CD-ROM location 215.

Link to Literature

After the Dancing Days by Margaret I. Rostkowski

In her novel *After the Dancing Days,* author Margaret I. Rostkowski tells the story of Annie, a 13-year-old girl living in Kansas after World War I. Annie visits a soldiers' hospital where she meets a young veteran, Andrew, who has been badly burned and disfigured by mustard gas. At first repulsed by Andrew's appearance, Annie later befriends him. In the following scene she shares with Andrew some books she has brought.

"What kind do you have today?"

For a moment, I didn't know what he meant. "What?" I finally said.

"Books. What kind of books?" He waved a bandaged hand at my bookbag.

"Oh, maps. I love to look at books of maps. And dream about traveling to all the places I see." My voice died away. I usually didn't talk about my love of maps, and I felt silly doing so now. Especially to this man.

"Let's see them."

"Really? They're just maps."

"I know." He sounded annoyed. "But it's something to do."

I pulled the books out of my bookbag, sliding the cookies and apples down into the bottom, and opened the world atlas.

But he was looking at the other book, *Europe in Pictures*.

"That one." He nudged it with the back of his hand.

I opened the heavy cover and balanced it between us on our knees. A spot of sun reflected off the glossy pages and made it hard to read. I lifted it a bit so the words were in shadow.

"A look at the wonders of Europe in photographs!" I read the subtitle and turned to the table of contents. As I ran my finger down the list of countries, he reached out with one bandaged hand and tapped clumsily on the section titled "France."

"I want . . ." his voice cracked and he swallowed, "to see that."

I paused, my hand covering the page in front of me. "France?" I stared at the page. When he didn't answer, I looked up at him.

I couldn't see his eyes under the shadow of his hat, only the red rippled skin around his nose and mouth. He nodded. So I found the page and opened the book to the section on France. Mounds of grapes lay on a table. A château arched gracefully across a river. People smiled. He motioned for me to turn the page. An ancient city circled with a high

World War I gas mask

Literature Footnote

Margaret I. Rostkowski uses family stories in her books. Her mother's uncles fought in World War I, and stories about them helped inspire *After the Dancing Days*. As a child she was an avid reader of historical fiction, and she majored in history in college. *After the Dancing Days* won many awards, including being named the 1986 Best Book for Young Adults by the American Library Association.

World War I ruins, September 1918

wall, a stone church with a steeple pointing into the sky, a palace of white marble.

"I don't remember any of that," he whispered. "Only mud. And burned trees."

I looked at the church and the people standing in the streets of the tiny village on the page before us.

"No people. The church was bombed out. I don't remember . . ."

I couldn't see the happy village. The page glared in the sun.

"There weren't any people. They all left before we got there. And no animals. They'd been eaten. The sergeant said the church was safest. But it'd been bombed. Blown apart. We slept in it anyway, what was left of it. I was afraid to sleep, afraid they'd come back."

He stopped and I slowly closed the book. I tried to imagine the church with the steeple gone.

Then he began again, that slow whisper.

"It had been farmland. When we got there, the barns were gone, fences down. Mud. Mud everywhere. And rats. I can still fell the rats running over my face at night."

I hugged the book to me.

"And then the gas . . ." He stopped and lifted both hands into the air.

I watched him, sick at what I had done with my books.

A Closer Look

1. Describe the two views of France: the one in Annie's book and the one in Andrew's memory.

2. What do we learn about Andrew in this scene? What do we learn about the war?

3. How do you think Annie's interaction with Andrew changes her? Cite examples from the passage to support your view.

Discussion

Stimulating Critical Thinking

1. Could soldiers today be affected the way Andrew was? Yes: modern wars have lasting psychological and physical effects on soldiers. No: soldiers today would not react as strongly because modern warfare has less direct fighting between soldiers.

2. Would you feel comfortable getting to know someone like Andrew? (Answers should show understanding of physical and psychological effects of war.)

A Closer Look

Answers

1. Annie's book: graceful chateau, grapes on a table, people smiling, ancient city with high wall, white stone church with a steeple. Andrew's memory: church bombed out, no people, no animals, ruined farmland, barns and fences destroyed, mud everywhere, rats.

2. Andrew was injured in the war (bandaged hand, burned skin around nose and mouth) and has terrible memories. War devastated the countryside.

3. Students may cite descriptive passages showing that Annie realizes the terrible destruction and shock the war caused by seeing its effects through Andrew's eyes. She feels compassion for Andrew, as expressed in the line, "I watched him, sick at what I had done with my books."

Unit Survey

Making Connections

Answers

1. Some examples: trust busting, regulating industries, conservation, income tax, Federal Reserve, obtaining Pacific and Caribbean islands and pursuing "Open Door policy," WWI mobilization effort.

2. Five of following: efforts to annex Hawaii, boundary dispute between Guiana and Venezuela, Cuban rebellion, Spanish-American War, Filipino uprising, governing new possessions, Boxer Rebellion, Russo-Japanese War, "Gentlemen's Agreement," Panama Canal treaty, crisis in Dominican Republic, "dollar diplomacy," Mexican Revolution, WWI entry, Versailles.

3. Examples of falling short of ideals: women could not vote, African Americans suffered discrimination and violence, Native Americans not citizens, United States had territories and protectorates whose residents were not allowed to govern themselves fully.

Teaching the Unit Project

Have students watch or read the news for ideas about projects. They might list several projects, then vote on one to address. Their goal should be specific.

Evaluation Criteria

The project can be evaluated according to the criteria listed below, using a scale for each: 4 = exemplary, 3 = good, 2 = adequate, 1 = poor.

(Continued in top margin)

Completing the task Project is planned carefully and carried out with tangible results.

Knowing content Planning and carrying out of project shows understanding of reform process.

Thinking critically Good judgment in choosing an appropriate issue and a project within their means.

Communicating ideas Project clearly outlines problem students want to solve.

Thinking It Over

Yes: millions of young people working for the good of the country could solve our problems. No: even with millions working for reform, it would be virtually impossible to have a problem-free country; different people have different ideas about what needs to be changed and thus might work at cross-purposes; people's efforts to solve a problem might result in a new problem.

Unit Survey

Making Connections

1. How did the role of the federal government in American life change during the era covered in this unit? Support your answer with examples.

2. The State Department handles the United States' relations with other countries. In 1892, a New York newspaper suggested abolishing it because it had so little work to do. Describe five events or situations between 1890 and 1920 that proved the newspaper wrong.

3. Agree or disagree with this statement: "Even while the United States fought to make the world safe for democracy, it failed to live up to its own democratic ideals." Explain your answer.

Linking History, Civics, and Language Arts

Working for Change in Your World

If they could observe American life today, Progressives might view it as a "good news/bad news" situation. The good news is that many of their goals have been accomplished. The bad news is that there are still problems confronting us. There is more good news, though: You can be the kind of citizen who helps solve problems.

Project Steps

Work with a group.

❶ Choose a problem to attack. Brainstorm answers to these questions:
- What problems do you see in your community, state, or country?
- Which of those problems do you care about most deeply?
- Which problem do you think you can do the most to solve?

❷ Begin researching the problem. What caused it? What laws or rules apply to it? Who are the people who could help solve it? The library is a good place to start. You can also get facts through observations and interviews.

❸ Decide exactly what you will try to do about the problem you have chosen. Write a brief statement of your goal. Be specific, concrete, and realistic.

❹ Write an action plan for achieving your goal. Here are some possibilities for activities to include in your plan:
- write letters to business managers and/or government officials
- write and circulate petitions
- make and hang posters
- make speeches at public meetings
- raise money
- organize boycotts
- organize peaceful demonstrations

❺ As you carry out your plan, make periodic progress reports to the class.

Thinking It Over Suppose that all Americans over age 12 spent three hours a week working for the reform of their choice. Could their combined efforts eventually produce a problem-free country? Explain your opinion.

Objectives

- ★ Define the term *classified records.*
- ★ Identify the kinds of information that historians can acquire from classified records.
- ★ Explain why scholars continually ask the government to declassify records.

How Do We Know?

Atomic bomb explosion

Scholar's Tool Kit

Classified Records

Have you ever seen a movie about international spies? Then you know that governments around the world keep secret certain information that might affect the safety of their countries. In the United States such information is called "classified" and is labeled according to the degree of secrecy. The main classifications are **Top Secret**, **Secret**, and **Confidential**. The United States began using these classifications in 1917.

Classified records are an important tool for historians. As a result, historians often put pressure on the government to "declassify" documents they think no longer need to be kept secret. Then scholars can study the documents to gain a more complete understanding of that time in history. This was the case with some important World War II documents.

The First Atomic Bomb

During World War II the government classified most of the documents that related to the war effort. Although historians have written many books about World War II, the inability to do research in classified files kept them from giving the complete story of certain key events and incidents. Slowly, over time, files have been declassified, each time enabling scholars to fill in some "blanks" in history.

Among the now-declassified files are ones concerning the development and testing of the first atomic bomb. This top-secret project had the code name "Manhattan Project." Many of its documents were

Introducing *How Do We Know?*

Classified Records

Explain that our government possesses information that could bring harm to the United States if it fell into the wrong hands. This includes information about weapons and military defenses and similar strategic data. In this feature, students learn how historians studying World War II have been helped by the declassification of documents relating to the development of the atomic bomb during the war.

Setting the Stage Activity

Listing Secrets

To prepare students to read about classified records, have them imagine that two nations are at war. Ask them to list five kinds of information that leaders of one nation might want to keep secret from leaders of the other. After they read their lists aloud, have the class discuss how each nation might keep the other from learning its secrets.

Critical Thinking

Answers

1. Students may mention military documents containing information about weapons development, locations of arsenals, planned movements of troops, and so on. Such documents could help an enemy gain military advantage in war.

2. Possibilities: there has been a planned explosion (planned because there was at least one witness prepared to draw it); the explosion was huge (because of the great height of the cloud).

3. The government waits until enough time has passed so the information can no longer bring harm to the United States. Another factor is the vast number of documents that must be reviewed.

Bonus Activity

Using Declassified Information

To help students grasp the importance of declassification, have pairs role-play a conversation between two historians who are working on a book about the first atomic explosion. The historians have just seen the Conant quotation and the drawings on these pages. They should discuss how the information will help them with their book and what questions the information raises that they would like to pursue.

History Footnote

Work on the Manhattan Project took place at several sites throughout the United States including Los Alamos, New Mexico, where the bombs were designed and built. The project was so secret that most of the thousands of Americans employed at the sites had no idea what the end product of their work would be. Even Roosevelt's Vice-Presidents were kept in the dark.

The culmination of the Manhattan Project—the explosion on July 16, 1945—was seen and felt for miles. An El Paso, Texas, newspaper quoted several accounts of the "accidental" blast. One man stated: "There was a tremendous white flash. This was followed by a great red glare, and high in the sky were three tremendous smoke rings. . . . They swirled and twisted as if being agitated by a great force."

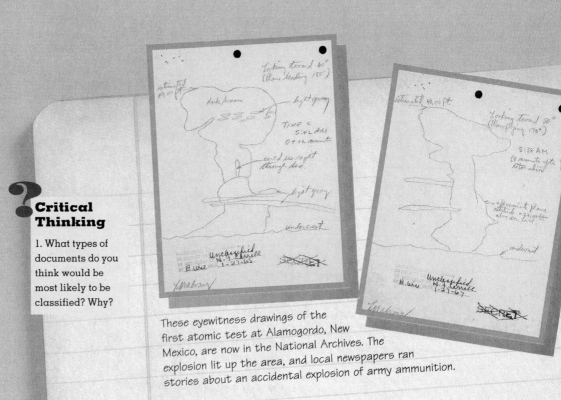

These eyewitness drawings of the first atomic test at Alamogordo, New Mexico, are now in the National Archives. The explosion lit up the area, and local newspapers ran stories about an accidental explosion of army ammunition.

Critical Thinking

1. What types of documents do you think would be most likely to be classified? Why?

declassified in the 1960s, giving scholars a window into this momentous event in history.

The Manhattan Project came about as a result of research by American and European scientists on the element uranium. The scientists discovered in the 1930s that uranium could be an important source of energy. They also suspected that uranium could be used as the basis for a bomb unlike any ever created.

When the brilliant scientist Albert Einstein warned President Franklin Roosevelt of the possibility of "extremely powerful bombs of a new type," Roosevelt knew he had to act. He brought together a group of scientists to organize research on nuclear weapons. This group was already at work when World War II broke out. Then the race was on to produce the first atomic bomb.

Critical Thinking

2. Imagine that you are a spy and that your country does not yet know about the testing of the bomb. What could you learn from these drawings?

The Story in Words and Pictures

The declassified documents from the Manhattan Project files are now in the National Archives. Among them are reports by James B. Conant,

Connections to Civics

The Freedom of Information Act (FOIA), passed in 1966 and amended in 1974, has gone a long way in making government records more accessible to the public. Under FOIA, anyone can submit a written request for copies of specific documents held by agencies of the executive branch. Although the agencies can choose to withhold certain documents—including records pertaining to national security—the effect of the law has been to encourage agencies to declassify and release some records in response to FOIA requests.

Declassification based on FOIA is a slow process. In contrast, President Clinton's 1994 order declassified about one-eighth of the secret documents held by the National Archives, including information on wartime spying and bombing activities.

a scientist who worked on the bomb. In one report Conant expressed the anxiety Manhattan scientists felt about creating nuclear weapons.

"I suppose everyone concerned with the project would feel greatly relieved and thoroughly delighted if something should develop to prove the impossibility of such an atomic explosion. Civilization would then, indeed, be fortunate—atomic energy for power a reality, for destruction an impossibility."

Conant's hope that atomic energy would have only peaceful uses ended on July 16, 1945. On that day the United States set off the first atomic explosion at a test site in New Mexico. The test was so secret that it was reported as an accident at a military arsenal. The drawings shown on page 444 are by one of the few eyewitnesses, and therefore have been of great interest to historians.

Once-classified information can be very important to scholars who study recent history. That is why scholars continually press the government to declassify records that are still kept from public view. In November 1994, as a part of the commemoration of the 50th anniversary of World War II, President Bill Clinton signed an executive order declassifying almost 21 million pages of documents from the war. The story these documents tell will become a part of the American history that students learn in the future.

Critical Thinking

3. Why do you think that the process of declassifying documents takes place slowly over time?

UNCLASSIFIED

Scholar at Work

Imagine that you are a scholar writing the history of World War II, and the Manhattan Project documents (such as the drawings shown on page 444) are still classified. Write a letter to a government official to persuade him or her that the files should be declassified. Explain why the papers are important and why historians should have access to them.

Discussion

Checking Understanding

1. **Why does our government maintain classified records?** (To protect the safety of the United States.)
2. **What was the Manhattan Project?** (Top-secret project to develop the atomic bomb, carried out by the United States during World War II.)
3. **What did the declassified documents from the Manhattan Project include?** (Reports by James B. Conant, a scientist who worked on the atomic bomb; eyewitness drawings of the first atomic explosion.)
4. **Why do historians want the government to declassify documents of the recent past?** (They want to gain a more complete understanding of historical events.)

Teaching the Scholar at Work

Suggest that before students begin their letters, they make a list of other types of documents, besides these drawings, that they, as scholars, would find useful in studying the Manhattan Project. Remind them that letters should be persuasive, factual, and polite.

Unit 4

Introducing the Unit

One-Man Caravan. Oklahomans on U.S. 99 San Joaquin Valley, California

This photograph by Dorothea Lange depicts a family—one of thousands—who headed west after dust storms drove them off their Great Plains farms. Many of the migrants ended up in California, where they took the only work available to them: harvesting other farmers' crops for very low wages. Their financial plight was one aspect of the economic crisis known as the Great Depression, which held the nation in its grip during the 1930s. Throughout this unit, students will learn about the challenges and changes that Americans faced in the years before, during, and after the Depression.

Teaching the Hands-On HISTORY

Have students work in pairs or small groups. The more they know about the Depression and Dust Bowl the more historically accurate their captions will be. On the other hand, less background knowledge may result in more imaginative, creative captions. If necessary, lead students to the realization that although their situation may be grim, the people in the photograph display dignity and a gritty determination to improve their lives.

Unit Overview

After World War I weary Americans faced labor and racial unrest at home. Cultural and social changes like the Harlem Renaissance and new freedoms for women also marked the 1920s. Fueled by auto production and advertising, the economy boomed.

The Great Depression began with the Stock Market Crash of 1929. Banks and businesses failed, and many Americans lost jobs, farms, and homes. President Roosevelt and Congress enacted New Deal programs to try to solve the nation's economic problems.

World War II began in 1939, but the United States did not enter the war until Japan attacked Pearl Harbor late in 1941. Men, women, and children then pitched in to aid the war effort. Germany surrendered in May 1945; Japan surrendered after the United States dropped two atomic bombs in August.

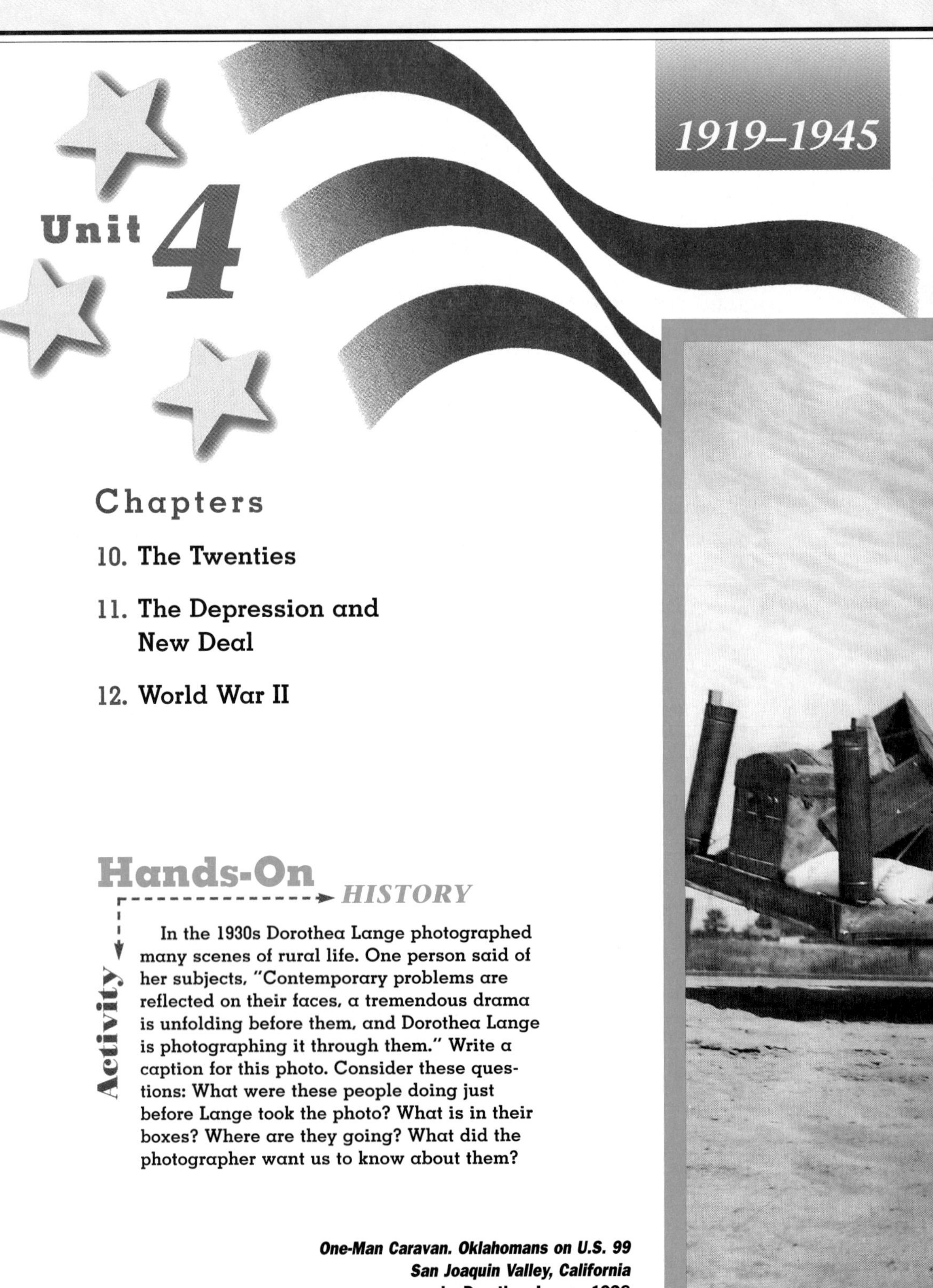

Unit 4

1919–1945

Chapters

Hands-On HISTORY

Activity

In the 1930s Dorothea Lange photographed many scenes of rural life. One person said of her subjects, "Contemporary problems are reflected on their faces, a tremendous drama is unfolding before them, and Dorothea Lange is photographing it through them." Write a caption for this photo. Consider these questions: What were these people doing just before Lange took the photo? What is in their boxes? Where are they going? What did the photographer want us to know about them?

***One-Man Caravan. Oklahomans on U.S. 99 San Joaquin Valley, California* by Dorothea Lange, 1938**

History Footnote

Dorothea Lange traveled through California, the South, and the Dust Bowl to capture the human impact of the Depression on film. When Lange saw people she wanted to photograph, she approached them without camera in hand. She introduced herself and struck up friendly conversations about the weather, the work that the people did, what their plans were, and so on. After a while, she asked if she might take some pictures. Most people said yes to this obviously empathetic woman who dressed so simply and walked with a limp. If there were children, Lange allowed them to examine and handle her camera before she began shooting. Out of respect for her subjects' privacy and dignity, Lange not only sought permission for every picture but also refused to shoot scenes of great emotional distress.

Trials at Home and Abroad

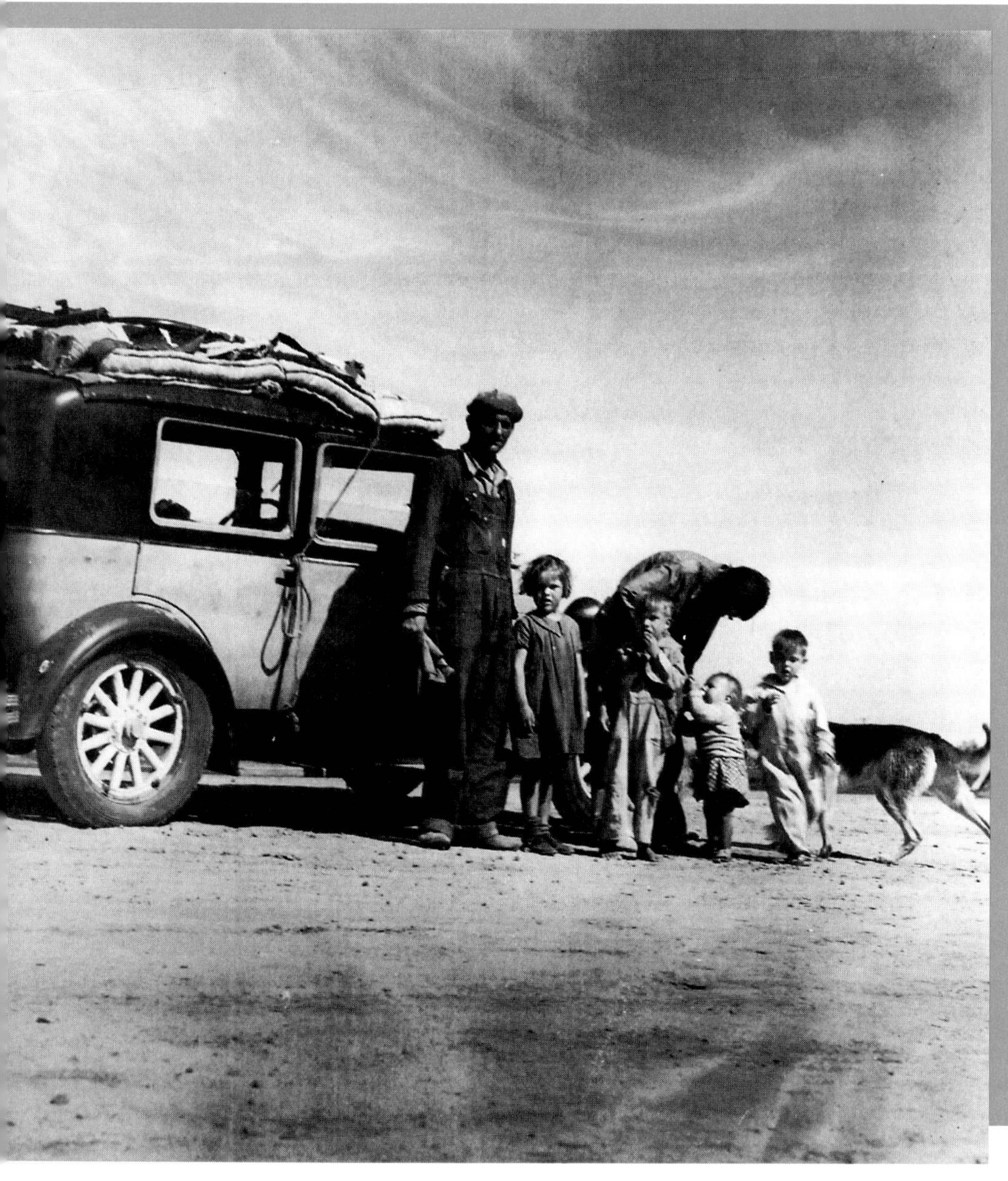

Discussion

Checking Understanding

1. What details suggest this is a rural family? (Clothing, especially the man's overalls; the fact that they are on a rural road.)

2. If someone said this family was on vacation, would you believe it? Explain. (No: they look too serious and have too many possessions with them.)

Stimulating Critical Thinking

3. How would you compare this family with families who headed west a century earlier? (All sought new lives and had courage to leave their homes for a strange land. However, most who headed west in the early 1800s probably went eagerly and with high hopes, whereas families like the one in the photo probably did not want to move, but felt that they had to.)

For an in-depth unit project on American popular music, see **Unit Interdisciplinary Projects**, pp. 25–42.

See the Unit 4 activity in **Wall Time Line Activities.**

At·a·Glance **10**

The Twenties
1919–1929

Chapter Planning Guide

Section	Student Text	Teacher's Edition Activities
Opener and Story pp. 448–451	**Keys to History Time Line** **History Mystery** Beginning the Story with **Zora Neale Hurston**	**Setting the Stage Activity** Imagining Travel Stories, p. 450
1 **From War to Peace** pp. 452–456	**World Link** Hitler tries to seize power, p. 456	**Warm-Up Activity** Connecting Unrest and Intolerance, p. 452 **Geography Question of the Day,** p. 452 **Section Activity** Creating Front Pages, p. 454 **Bonus Activity** Writing a Letter to Europe, p. 455 **Wrap-Up Activity** Speaking for Normalcy, p. 456
2 **The Jazz Age** pp. 457–464	**Link to Literature** The Poetry of Langston Hughes, pp. 474–475 **Link to Art** *Couple in Raccoon Coats,* p. 459 **Link to Technology** The Radio, p. 461 **Point of View** Was prohibiting the sale of alcohol a good idea?, p. 462 **Skill Lab** Recognizing Relevant Information, p. 464	**Warm-Up Activity** Labeling Our Age, p. 457 **Geography Question of the Day,** p. 457 **Section Activity** Creating a Roaring Twenties Mural, p. 458 **Bonus Activity** 1920s Conversations, p. 460 **Wrap-Up Activity** Writing Diary Entries, p. 463
3 **The Business Boom** pp. 465–471	**Reading Maps** First Transcontinental Auto Route—the Lincoln Highway, p. 466 **Link to the Present** Beyond the Model T, p. 467 **Hands-On History** Investing in stocks, p. 469 **Geography Lab** Why the Movies Moved to Hollywood, p. 471	**Warm-Up Activity** Inventing Slogans, p. 465 **Geography Question of the Day,** p. 465 **Section Activity** 1920s Interviews, p. 466 **Bonus Activity** Creating Advertisements, p. 468 **Wrap-Up Activity** Creating Concept Webs, p. 470
Evaluation	☑ **Section 1 Review,** p. 456 ☑ **Section 2 Review,** p. 463 ☑ **Section 3 Review,** p. 470 ☑ **Chapter Survey,** pp. 472–473 **Alternative Assessment** Planning a "decade-in-review" issue, p. 473	☑ **Answers to Section 1 Review,** p. 456 ☑ **Answers to Section 2 Review,** p. 463 ☑ **Answers to Section 3 Review,** p. 470 ☑ **Answers to Chapter Survey,** pp. 472–473 (Alternative Assessment guidelines are in the Take-Home Planner.)

Teacher's Resource Package

Chapter Summaries: English and Spanish, pp. 56–57

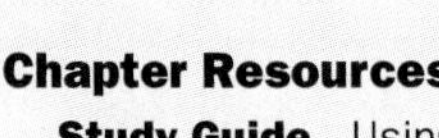

Chapter Resources Binder

Study Guide Using Visual Images to Preview, p. 89

Reinforcement Gathering Information, pp. 93–94

American Readings The Klan Through the Eyes of a Boy, pp. 45–46

Chapter Resources Binder

Study Guide Previewing Headings, p. 90

Skills Development Recognizing Relevant Information, pp. 95–96

American Readings "Drenched in Light," pp. 47–48

Using Historical Documents "The Big Specialist Reports His Findings" Political Cartoon, pp. 69–72

Chapter Resources Binder

Study Guide Identifying Causes and Effects, p. 91

Geography Extensions "The Automobile Capital of the World," pp. 25–26

Chapter and Unit Tests Chapter 10 Tests, Forms A and B, pp. 83–86

Take-Home Planner

Introducing the Chapter Activity Writing About the Lost Generation, p. 6

Chapter In-Depth Activity Harlem Renaissance Art Salon, p. 6

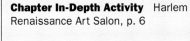

Reduced Views

Study Guide, p. 8

Reinforcement, p. 9

American Readings, p. 10

Unit 4 Answers, pp. 30–38

Reduced Views

Study Guide, p. 8

Skills Development, p. 9

American Readings, p. 10

Using Historical Documents, p. 11

Unit 4 Answers, pp. 30–38

Reduced Views

Study Guide, p. 8

Geography Extensions, p. 11

Unit 4 Answers, pp. 30–38

Reduced Views

Chapter Tests, p. 11

Unit 4 Answers, pp. 30–38

Alternative Assessment Guidelines for scoring the Chapter Survey activity, p. 7

Additional Resources

Wall Time Line

Unit 4 Activity

Transparency Package

Transparency 10–1 A Flapper—use with Section 2

Transparency 10–2 "Flaming Youth"—use with Section 2

Transparency Activity Book

SelecTest Testing Software

Chapter 10 Test, Forms A and B

Vital Links

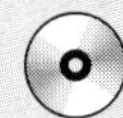

Videodisc

CD-ROM

Young Communist protestors (see TE p. 453)

Voice of Walter Lippmann (see TE p. 454)

Louis Armstrong (see TE p. 458)

Voice of Willie Smith (see TE p. 459)

Movie marquee (see TE p. 460)

Radio station (see TE p. 461)

"I Wish I Could Shimmy" (see TE p. 462)

Flappers (see TE p. 462)

Ford assembly line (see TE p. 467)

Oldsmobile advertisement (see TE p. 468)

10

Teaching Resources

Take-Home Planner 4
- Introducing Chapter Activity
- Chapter In-Depth Activity
- Alternative Assessment

Chapter Resources Binder
Geography Extensions
American Readings
Using Historical Documents
Transparency Activities
Wall Time Line Activities
Chapter Summaries
Chapter and Unit Tests
SelecTest Test File
Vital Links CD-ROM/Videodisc

Chapter Objectives

★ Explain how unrest gripped the nation after World War I.

★ Describe the cultural life of the United States during the 1920s.

★ Identify factors that contributed to the economic boom of the 1920s.

Chapter Overview

Americans faced postwar turmoil at home. Workers went on strike. There was also racial unrest. Prejudice against African Americans erupted in mob violence. Many Americans blamed foreign ideas—especially communism—and immigrants for the unrest. In this atmosphere of fear and nativism, Congress passed laws limiting immigration and the Ku Klux Klan spread.

Time Line

Keys to History

Keys to History journal writing activities are on page 472 in the Chapter Survey.

Red Scare begins Communists ("Reds") and immigrants were accused of causing labor unrest and bombings. (p. 453)

Prohibition begins The Eighteenth Amendment banned the manufacture, transport, and sale of liquor, making lawbreakers of many Americans. (pp. 462–463)

First radio broadcast Soon millions of Americans would turn to radio for entertainment and news. (p. 460)

Looking Back With the showing of the first motion picture, the seed was sown for the development of movies as popular entertainment.

1919–1929

Chapter 10

The Twenties

Sections

Beginning the Story with Zora Neale Hurston

1. From War to Peace
2. The Jazz Age
3. The Business Boom

Ben Shahn: *Bartolomeo Vanzetti and Nicola Sacco* from the Sacco-Vanzetti series of twenty-three paintings (1931–32)

1919
Red Scare begins

1920
Prohibition begins

1920
First radio station begins broadcasting

1919 1921

First motion picture
1895

The 1920s were also marked by cultural and social change as prosperity returned. African American writers, artists, and musicians flourished as part of the cultural movement known as the Harlem Renaissance. New ways of life evolved as Americans bought automobiles and moved to suburbs, women rebelled against old customs, and young people pursued fun at a breathless pace. Some Americans, alarmed by the rapid changes, tried to enforce old customs and values through Prohibition and other means.

The nation's economy boomed, thanks in part to the pro-business policies of Presidents Harding and Coolidge. The popularity of automobiles fueled the boom, as did high tariffs on goods from Europe, advertising, and the credit system. As stock prices skyrocketed in a frenzy of investing, signs pointed to economic trouble ahead.

HISTORY *Mystery*

On May 20, 1927, this young American was virtually unknown. Two days later, he was the idol of people throughout the world. Who was he, and why was he so admired?

1925
Scopes trial
Clarence Darrow and William Jennings Bryan

1927
Lindbergh completes transatlantic flight

1927
First "talking" motion picture

1924
Immigration Act of 1924

1923 | 1925 | 1927 | 1929

World Link
Hitler tries to seize power in Bavaria
1923

Looking Ahead
The New Deal begins
1933

Teaching the *HISTORY Mystery*

Students will find the answer on p. 460. See Chapter Survey, p. 472, for additional questions.

Time Line

Immigration Act of 1924 This law helped bring to an end the nation's history of nearly unlimited European immigration. (p. 455)

Scopes trial This Tennessee case brought nationwide attention to the debate over the teaching of evolution. (p. 463)

Lindbergh's flight Charles Lindbergh's solo flight across the Atlantic made him a hero and helped boost the airline industry. (p. 460)

First "talking" motion picture Movies became a national craze, with attendance at 100 million a week by 1930. (p. 460)

World Link See p. 456.

Looking Ahead With the nation in the depths of an economic depression, newly elected President Franklin Roosevelt implemented a program of recovery and relief.

Beginning the Story

Zora Neale Hurston

As a child in Eatonville, Florida, Zora Neale Hurston spent hours listening to adults swap tales at a local store. Thus began a love of storytelling that would make her a central literary figure in the Harlem Renaissance of the 1920s. First came years of wandering and working at low-paying jobs. Not until Hurston enrolled in a night class at age 26 did she begin to see herself as someone who might become a writer.

Setting the Stage Activity

Imagining Travel Stories

Remind students that many African Americans traveled during World War I, both in migrating to northern cities to find jobs and in fighting in Europe. Ask them to imagine what kinds of stories from faraway places these travelers might have told when returning home to a small town in the South. Have groups make lists of possible stories, the people who told them, and the places they journeyed to.

See the Introducing the Chapter Activity, Writing About the Lost Generation, **Take-Home Planner 4,** p. 6.

History Footnote

Zora Neale Hurston had only $1.50 and a stack of manuscripts to her name when she finally arrived in New York City in 1925. There the 34-year-old Hurston became known not only as a fine writer but also as a fascinating storyteller.

Recognizing the value of her heritage, Hurston traveled to Eatonville and other southern towns to collect tales, songs, and sayings. One result was *Mules and Men* (1935), the first popular book about black culture by an African American scholar.

In her work Hurston challenged the then-common assumption that African Americans lacked an identity and a voice. She also attacked the notion that black people had somehow been given a "dirty deal" by nature. "I saw no curse in being black," she wrote.

Beginning the Story with

Zora Neale Hurston

Zora Neale Hurston's mother used to say that someone put "travel dust" on the doorstep the day that Zora was born. That dust must have been powerful, for during her life Zora journeyed from Eatonville, Florida—where she was born sometime between 1891 and 1903—to Baltimore, New York City, Haiti, California, and back to Florida again. Wherever she traveled, Zora turned her restless mind to studies. She read everything she could, from anthropology to poetry to folktales. Zora's travels and studies inspired her to write seven books and more than 100 short stories, plays, and articles. Zora's special gift, though, was storytelling. Many of her best-loved stories are rooted in her memories of growing up in Eatonville.

Eatonville, Florida

"I was born in a Negro town," Zora Neale Hurston wrote on the first page of her autobiography. "Eatonville is, and was at the time of my birth, a pure Negro town. . . . [It was] the first attempt at organized self-government on the part of Negroes in America." Depending on who was asked in Eatonville, John and Lucy Hurston's seventh child was either sassy or spirited, shameless or bold. Looking back on her childhood years, Zora remembered:

> "Mama exhorted [urged] her children at every opportunity to 'jump at de sun.' We might not land on the sun, but at least we would get off the ground."

Zora's favorite place in Eatonville was Joe Clarke's store. Here, neighbors gathered to swap jokes, gossip, and stories. Best of all were the "lying"

History Bookshelf

Blocksma, Mary. *Ticket to the Twenties: A Time Traveler's Guide.* Little, Brown, 1993. In this lighthearted but informative book, students will learn what their lives might have been like in the 1920s. They will be immersed in the decade's fads, slang, entertainment and culture, innovations in medicine and travel, and more.

Also of interest:

Lyons, Mary E. *Sorrow's Kitchen: The Life and Folklore of Zora Neale Hurston.* Scribner's, 1990.

McKissack, Patricia, and Frederick McKissack, Jr. *Black Diamond: The Story of the Negro Baseball Leagues.* Scholastic, 1994.

Randolph, Blythe. *Charles Lindbergh.* Franklin Watts, 1990.

Discussion

Thinking Historically

1. Why do you think young Zora did not return to Eatonville after her mother died? (Did not want to face memories of mother; felt she would not be welcomed by father and stepmother; searching for a way to "jump at de sun.")

2. What might have been her future as a writer if she had not attended that night class? (Might have worked at jobs that did not use her talent; might have been inspired to be a writer by other experiences.)

Cab Calloway's band entertained jazz lovers in the Cotton Club in New York City's Harlem neighborhood. Hurston made Harlem her home in 1925.

sessions during which people competed to tell the tallest tales. The folktales told on Joe Clarke's porch inspired Zora to create her own stories.

When Zora was 9 death crept into town and took her mother, Lucy Hurston. "Mama died at sundown and changed a world," Zora wrote, "that is, the world that had been built out of her body and heart."

Zora's Wanderings

Zora lost her childhood when she lost her mother. "That hour began my wanderings," she later recalled. Her father remarried. His new wife, wanting nothing to do with stepchildren, sent Zora off to boarding school. When her father stopped paying for her schooling, Zora "was shifted from house to house of relatives and friends and found comfort nowhere."

For years Zora drifted. Money was scarce. She quit school and went to work, finding jobs as a maid or waitress. No matter how hard she worked, Zora never had enough money to return to school. "There is something about poverty that smells like death," she wrote of those dark years.

Zora's wanderings took her north to Baltimore. There, at the age of 26, she enrolled in a night-school class taught by a gifted teacher named Dwight O. W. Holmes. "He made the way clear," Zora wrote in her autobiography. "Something about his face killed the drabness and discouragement in me. I felt that things could be done."

One night, while the class was studying English poets, Zora saw something that would drive her on to college and to a new life in New York City. She saw herself not as a poor waitress, but as a woman who would dare to become a writer. "This was my world [the world of a writer]," she said to herself, "and I shall be in it, and surrounded by it, if it is the last thing I do on God's green dirt-ball."

Hands-On HISTORY

Activity

Imagine that you are to choose three images that would help illustrate a map of Zora Hurston's life (see page 300 for an example of a map with illustrations). Each image is to represent a different place where Zora lived. Write a description of each of the images that you would like to use, and write a two-sentence caption for each one.

Teaching the Hands-On HISTORY

To help students decide on three pictures, have them review the reading and write down the three places it describes—Eatonville (Joe Clarke's store), Baltimore (night school), and New York City. Explain that in New York she was part of the "Harlem Renaissance"—a cultural movement of writers, musicians, and artists that flourished in Harlem, where many blacks lived and gathered.

For a journal writing activity on Zora Neale Hurston, see student page 473.

Introducing the Section

Vocabulary

communism (p. 453) a system in which property is owned by society as a whole instead of by individuals

anarchism (p. 454) the idea that all forms of government are bad and should be done away with

Warm-Up Activity

Connecting Unrest and Intolerance

To prepare for reading about unrest and intolerance in the 1920s, divide the class into two groups. Have one brainstorm examples of modern American unrest and write them on the board or chart paper. Have the other do the same for intolerance. Have the groups compare lists, looking for similarities and cause-effect relationships.

Geography Question of the Day

Have students write brief predictions about immigration immediately after World War I. They should consider whether the numbers were likely to be high or low, where immigrants were likely to have come from, and why they might have found the United States appealing at the time.

Section Objectives

- ★ Describe the forms of unrest that gripped the United States after World War I.
- ★ Identify the groups and ideas that were blamed for the nation's troubles.
- ★ Explain how some political leaders and other Americans reacted against the unrest.

Teaching Resources

Take-Home Planner 4, pp. 4–11
Chapter Resources Binder
Study Guide, p. 89
Reinforcement, pp. 93–94
Skills Development
Geography Extensions
American Readings, pp. 45–46
Using Historical Documents
Transparency Activities
Chapter and Unit Tests

1. From War to Peace

Reading Guide

New Terms communism, anarchism

Section Focus The unrest that gripped the nation after World War I

1. **What forms of unrest gripped the United States after the war?**
2. **What people and ideas were blamed for the nation's troubles?**
3. **How did Americans respond to the unrest?**

Zora began to develop her gift for writing at Howard University just as World War I came to an end. It was a time when Americans were eager to shift their attention away from troubles overseas. They were weary of the storms of war—the death of young people, the stress of raising armies, and the daily news of battle victories and defeats.

Everyone, it seemed, craved rest. The nation retreated from world affairs, however, only to face turmoil at home.

Labor Unrest

During the war, American industry had focused on producing weapons and supplies. With the war over, pent-up demands for goods, and for better wages and working hours, were unleashed.

However, factories that had been producing war materials could not immediately change to making clothing, shoes, cars, and other goods that a peacetime population demanded. Prices for these scarce products rose. Meanwhile, returning soldiers, looking for places to live, drove up the cost of housing. By 1920 prices were twice as high as in 1914.

As rents and prices rose, however, workers' wages remained low. During the war American workers had not gone on strike so as not to hurt the war effort. It was now time, they believed, to push for higher wages and for workdays shorter than 12 hours.

Strikes spread In 1919 union leaders across the nation led workers out on strike. While early strikes succeeded, workers faced growing opposition as the year wore on.

When shipyard workers in Seattle walked off their jobs, other unions in the city showed support by striking, too. Seattle's mayor turned the public against the strikers by falsely claiming that their leaders were radicals—people calling for extreme, often violent, change. The strike failed.

In Pennsylvania and the Midwest, striking steelworkers called for an end to 12-hour workdays and 7-day workweeks. Steel mill owners ignored their demands. They also accused the strikers of being linked with radicals. Whether the accusations were true or not, political leaders and newspapers turned against the workers and sided with business leaders.

After four months the striking steelworkers gave up. This failure dealt a crushing blow to the union movement.

Racial Unrest

The tense mood of the nation was seen in racial violence as well. In 1919 white mobs terrorized black communities from Texas to

History Footnote
The American Communist movement began in 1919 in the form of two parties, the Communist Party of America and the Communist Labor Party. The two later merged into one group. As countries around the world experienced Communist uprisings and the United States was shaken by strikes, anonymous bombings, and labor unrest, people began to fear a world revolution.

Not everyone who went on strike was a Communist; many just wanted fair hours and pay. Nonetheless, people associated strikes with communism because Communists believed that the common working man should not be ruled by a small, rich ruling class. When the police in Boston went on strike in 1919, people feared the Communists were taking over.

Washington, D.C. Black tenant farmers in Arkansas were attacked for attempting to form a union. In Chicago a white mob stoned to death a black swimmer who had strayed into a "white section" of a beach on Lake Michigan. In the violence that followed, 38 people were killed.

Faced with such attacks, and thousands of lynchings since 1890, African Americans launched an anti-lynching campaign. In this campaign, the National Association for the Advancement of Colored People (NAACP) called on Congress to make lynching a federal crime. The Senate, however, refused.

Despite its failure in Congress, the NAACP continued to bring attention to the issue of lynchings. It won several victories in the 1920s, as when a court struck down an Oklahoma law denying blacks the right to vote.

The Red Scare

Alarmed by strikes and race riots, many Americans blamed foreign ideas—especially communism—as the source of the troubles. **Communism** is a system in which property is owned by society as a whole instead of by individuals. People pointed with fear to what was going on in Russia. There, in 1917, radical communists—called Bolsheviks or "Reds"—had taken over the government and seized all private property.

At the end of the war, Communist Parties were gaining support in other parts of Europe. Could the same thing happen in the United States? Rumors spread that unions were influenced by Reds. Old nativist feelings arose, too. Immigrants were accused of bringing dangerous ideas with them. Newspapers called it the "Red Scare."

Striking workers, like these on a Philadelphia street in 1919, often met with violent reactions by the police.

Developing the Section

Discussion

Checking Understanding

1. What happened when steelworkers went on strike? (Owners ignored demands, linked strikers with radicals. Political leaders and newspapers turned against them. Strikers gave up.)

2. How did the NAACP try to promote African American rights? (Anti-lynching campaign; got court to strike down Oklahoma law denying African Americans right to vote.)

Stimulating Critical Thinking

3. Why do you suppose many Americans quickly blamed foreigners and foreign ideas for the unrest? (Did not want to admit working conditions were bad and that many white Americans were racist; easier to blame outsiders than solve difficult problems.)

See the Study Guide activity in **Chapter Resources Binder**, p. 89.

Vital Links

Young Communist protestors (Picture) Unit 4, Side 1, Search 13041

See also Unit 4 Explore CD-ROM location 112.

Section Activity

Creating Front Pages

To explore postwar attitudes toward Communists and immigrants, have small groups act as newspaper staffs of the period. Half the groups should imagine their newspapers are strongly anti-Communist and anti-immigrant. The other groups should imagine their newspapers believe Communists and immigrants are unfairly blamed for the nation's troubles. Have each group create a front page for a 1920 issue, with headlines and articles that reflect their newspaper's view. Topics might include the Palmer raids, the upcoming Sacco-Vanzetti trial, the hiring of sales agents to expand the Ku Klux Klan's membership base, or the possibility of Congress passing a new immigration law. Conclude by having groups compare front pages.

Vital Links

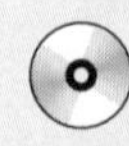

Voice of Walter Lippmann (First Person Account) Unit 5, Side 1, Search 06817, Play to 07572

See also Unit 5 Explore CD-ROM location 52.

Tips for Teaching

Students with Limited English

Graphs can help students understand key concepts. Point out that Congress passed laws in 1921, 1924, and 1929 limiting immigration. Then ask questions about the graph on p. 454: How many immigrants came from northern and western Europe in 1921? In 1922? From southern and eastern Europe? What was the biggest change? What might explain it?

See the Reinforcement activity in **Chapter Resources Binder,** pp. 93–94.

The Palmer raids The Red Scare gained force in April 1919 when the Post Office found bombs in nearly 40 packages addressed to American leaders. In June a bomb exploded at Attorney General A. Mitchell Palmer's home. On Palmer's orders, federal agents carried out raids on the homes and offices of suspected Communists.

The Palmer raids failed to turn up evidence linking these people to the bombs. Most people arrested were neither Communists nor foreigners. Still, over the next year nearly 6,000 people were imprisoned. Many were even deported to Europe.

Although some Americans protested that this treatment—of both citizens and aliens—was unconstitutional, the majority approved it. Support for Palmer's raids died down, however, when Communist revolutions did not break out in Europe and strikes dwindled at home. Still, the Red Scare had done much to encourage anti-immigrant feelings.

The Sacco-Vanzetti case During the heat of the Red Scare, the nation was rocked by news that seemed to prove the danger of immigrants and their ideas. In May 1920 two Italian immigrants, Nicola Sacco and Bartolomeo Vanzetti, were arrested and charged with robbing and murdering a paymaster and a payroll guard in Massachusetts.

The resulting case involved far more than robbery and murder. During the trial, the prosecutors attacked Sacco and Vanzetti for being foreign-born and for believing in **anarchism**—the idea that all forms of government are bad and should be done away with. The judge did nothing to stop the attacks. Although firm evidence linking the two men to the crime was lacking, the judge condemned them to death.

Protests poured in from around the world. The journalist Walter Lippman wrote:

> "The Sacco-Vanzetti case . . . is full of doubt. The fairness of the trial raises doubt. The evidence raises doubt. . . . No man, we submit, should be put to death where so much doubt exists."

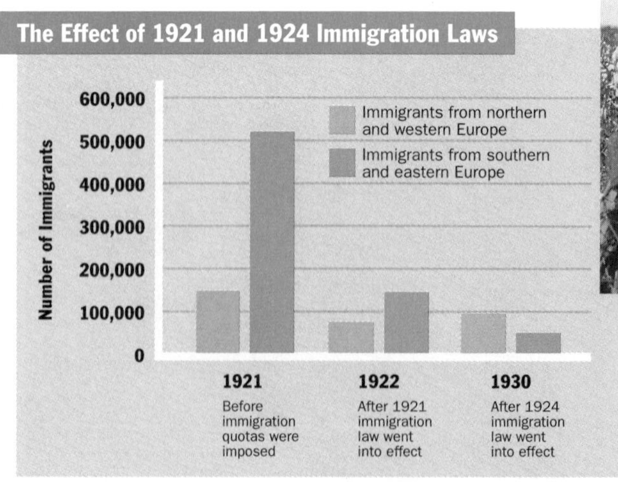

Demand for farmworkers in the fields of Texas and other southwestern states brought thousands of Mexican immigrants to the United States in the 1920s.

Connections to Civics

Our criminal justice system requires that prosecutors prove a defendant's guilt "beyond a reasonable doubt." If jurors have reasonable doubt, they are supposed to find the defendant "not guilty." Many historians and legal experts believe that the prosecution in the Sacco-Vanzetti case failed to prove the defendants' guilt beyond a reasonable doubt. For example, none of the robbery money was found in their possession. Also, Vanzetti had more than a dozen witnesses to support his alibi.

Vanzetti said, "I would not wish . . . to the most low and misfortunate creature of the earth . . . what I have had to suffer for things that I am not guilty of." In 1977 Governor Michael Dukakis of Massachusetts signed a proclamation recognizing the trial's flaws and clearing both men's names.

The Ku Klux Klan openly expressed its newfound strength in northern states, as in this Fourth of July parade in Long Branch, New Jersey.

All legal appeals failed, however. In 1927 the two were put to death in the electric chair. For years questions swirled around their trial. Political leaders, though, continued to blame immigrants for postwar troubles. Unrest would end, some argued, only if immigration were stopped.

Anti-Immigration Laws

In fact, efforts to limit immigration had begun early in the decade. In 1921 Congress passed an act limiting the number of immigrants from eastern and southern Europe—the Europeans most anxious to come to the United States.

In 1924 and 1929 Congress imposed even more restrictions on immigrants (see the chart on page 454). Thus, the nation's history of nearly unlimited European immigration came to an end. Meanwhile, most Asian immigration was still banned.

Anti-immigration laws, however, did not apply to people from the Americas. Nearly 500,000 people immigrated from Mexico in the 1920s, and 950,000 from Canada. Most Mexicans migrated to the Southwest, where their labors played a vital role in the growth of farmlands, railroads, and mines.

The Second Ku Klux Klan

As the anti-immigrant mood gripped the nation, an old organization took on new life. Leaders of the Ku Klux Klan, which had terrorized black southerners during Reconstruction, saw a chance to expand the Klan's strength beyond its base in the South.

In 1920 the Klan hired two sales agents to help achieve its goal. In a public campaign boosting "100 percent pure Americanism," they directed hatred against anyone who was not white and Protestant. White-hooded Klansmen and their wives now terrorized Catholics, Jews, Asians, and immigrants as well as African Americans.

By 1925 the Klan had as many as 5 million members. They helped elect five United States

Discussion

Checking Understanding

1. What were the Palmer raids? (Raids of homes and offices of suspected Communists on orders of Attorney General Palmer.)

2. How did anti-immigrant feelings affect the Sacco-Vanzetti case? (Convicted and executed partly because they were foreigners.)

Stimulating Critical Thinking

3. Did Sacco and Vanzetti deserve a fair trial under a system of government they did not believe in? (Yes: under Constitution, everyone has right to fair trial. No: those who want to destroy the government do not deserve its benefits.)

For a description of a Ku Klux Klan gathering, see **American Readings**, pp. 45–46.

Bonus Activity

Writing a Letter to Europe

To focus on immigrants' hardships, have students imagine being immigrants from eastern or southern Europe in the 1920s. Have them write letters to relatives back home, explaining why they should not come to the United States.

Teaching the World Link

Point out that while in prison Hitler wrote the first volume of *Mein Kampf* ("My Struggle"), which became the basis of Nazism. In it he discussed World War I, his desire for revenge, his racist ideology, and his plans for conquering Europe. Ask why, with the American postwar unrest and economic problems, no Hitler-like figure rose to power here. (Problems not as serious as in Germany, which was war-torn and ripe for a vengeful leader.)

Closing the Section

Wrap-Up Activity

Speaking for Normalcy

To review postwar issues, have students write brief campaign speeches for Harding, noting the nation's mood and problems, defining *normalcy,* and explaining how to achieve it. Ask some to read their speeches.

Section Review Answers

1. Definitions: *communism* (453), *anarchism* (454)

2. Rents and prices rose while wages stayed low.

3. Promoted "pure Americanism"; directed hatred against many groups.

4. Might worry about arrest and deportation due to being foreign and thus suspected of being a Communist.

History Footnote

Harding decided against campaigning on the road in 1920. Instead, he mimicked William McKinley's actions in 1896 by running a "front porch" campaign from his home in Ohio. He even had his front porch rebuilt to match McKinley's. Harding reflected the mood of the nation with statements like this one: "America's present need is not heroics but healing . . . not revolution but restoration." In contrast Cox and his running mate, Franklin D. Roosevelt, traveled extensively, speaking largely in favor of the League of Nations. In November, Harding won nearly 61 percent of the vote.

Voters were swayed in Harding's favor partly because of his appearance. One journalist remarked that Harding "looked more like a President than any President who ever lived."

World Link

Hitler tries to seize power Bankrupted by war, Germany faced economic chaos in the early 1920s. Industries struggled. Workers could not find jobs. As prices soared, the value of money plunged. Shoppers carried money in wheelbarrows. Housewives burned it for fuel.

Into this turmoil stepped a man named Adolf Hitler. A fiery speaker, he attracted followers by vowing to return Germany to its former greatness. Like leaders of the Ku Klux Klan, Hitler appealed to people who were looking for someone to blame for their problems. He created a private army that terrorized opponents of his Nazi Party.

In 1923 Hitler and his storm troopers tried to seize control of the government of the state of Bavaria. They failed, Hitler went to prison, and the Nazis were outlawed. Hitler was far from finished, though. Released from prison in 1924, he eventually led Germany into another world war (see Chapter 12).

senators and four state governors—in northern as well as southern states.

However, the Klan's increasing violence began to weaken its appeal. When a Klan leader was convicted of murder in 1925, membership began to drop. By 1930 the Klan had only 50,000 members.

The Election of 1920

Echoes of the Red Scare and anti-immigrant fears continued throughout the 1920s. They were at their height, however, in 1919 and 1920. These were the years, too, when President Wilson was urging Americans to support the League of Nations.

As the election of 1920 approached, voters wanted to put war and problems at home behind them. The Republicans nominated a handsome senator from Ohio, Warren G. Harding, who promised a "return to normalcy."

Harding opposed American involvement overseas. He called for pro-business policies such as lower taxes for the wealthy and higher tariffs on imports. As his running mate he chose Governor Calvin Coolidge of Massachusetts. Coolidge was known for his tough treatment of strikers in Boston. Harding easily defeated the Democratic candidate, James M. Cox.

Beginnings of the Boom

Although a recession struck the nation in 1921, by the next year factories were hiring workers to meet the soaring demand for goods. Harding's promise of prosperous times seemed on its way to fulfillment.

President Harding's promise of "normalcy," though, was not to be. Political and labor unrest might be fading, but American society was restless in other ways. For the United States, a period of unsettling social changes was about to unfold.

1. Section Review

1. Define **communism** and **anarchism.**

2. Why did American workers go on strike after World War I?

3. How did the Ku Klux Klan expand its appeal beyond southern states?

4. Critical Thinking As an immigrant to the United States after World War I, why might you have been worried by events during and after the Red Scare?

Section Objectives

- ★ Describe how African American politics and culture thrived in the 1920s.
- ★ Identify great changes that took place in American life during the Jazz Age.
- ★ Explain why some Americans resisted the social changes of the 1920s.

Teaching Resources

Take-Home Planner 4, pp. 4–11
Chapter Resources Binder
Study Guide, p. 90
Reinforcement
Skills Development, pp. 95–96
Geography Extensions
American Readings, pp. 47–48
Using Historical Documents
Transparency Activities
Chapter and Unit Tests

2. The Jazz Age

Reading Guide

New Terms **suburbs, Prohibition**

Section Focus **The cultural life of the United States during the 1920s**

1. How did African American politics and culture thrive in the 1920s?
2. What great changes took place in American life during the Jazz Age?
3. Why did some Americans resist the social changes of the 1920s?

The 1920s was a dizzying time. The nation was experiencing greater prosperity than ever before. With prosperity came change. People began to create new forms of music and literature. New fashions became the rage. The writer F. Scott Fitzgerald, whose novels and stories captured the spirit of the decade, called it the "Jazz Age." Others called it the "Roaring Twenties."

The 1920s was also a time of conflict. Some Americans, alarmed by rapid changes in values and behavior, struggled to hold on to more familiar ideas and ways of life.

The cafes and art galleries of Paris were magnets for artists and writers rebelling against American tastes and values after World War I.

The Lost Generation

The experience of fighting in Europe had opened up a new world to young Americans. For some, this new world was a troubling one. Many young writers looked back on the war as a monumental waste—a generation of youth killed in a useless war. They were also troubled by the contrast between the horrors of war and the period of prosperity that followed it.

Ezra Pound, an established writer, encouraged younger writers to "despise old forms and the old stuff, to rebel, break away and dare [to be different]." Gertrude Stein, an American poet in Paris, also inspired the young writers. Still, she understood their confusion, writing:

> "All of you young people who served in the war, you are the lost generation."

Two of the most successful Lost Generation writers were Ernest Hemingway and F. Scott Fitzgerald. In his novel *The Sun Also Rises*, Hemingway wrote about the lives of the expatriates—

Introducing the Section

Vocabulary

suburbs (p. 460) communities on the outskirts of cities

Prohibition (p. 462) banning the manufacture, transport, and sale of liquor

Warm-Up Activity

Labeling Our Age

To get students thinking about why certain periods are labeled as they are, point out that the 1920s were called the "Jazz Age" and the "Roaring Twenties." Ask what the words *jazz* and *roaring* bring to mind. Next, have pairs or small groups develop labels for our own age. Encourage them to base their labels on cultural and social life. Students may find it helpful to make "what's hot" lists first. Have pairs or groups compare labels.

Geography Question of the Day

Ask students to consider how their lives have been affected by cars, buses, and airplanes. Have them write a short paragraph or list of differences on what their lives would be like without these forms of transportation.

Section Activity

Creating a Roaring Twenties Mural

To focus on cultural contributions, have students create a mural titled "The Roaring Twenties: A Cultural Explosion." As a class they can determine size and general content. They might divide it into topical sections such as *Literature, Music,* and *Art;* or *Lost Generation, Harlem Renaissance,* and *Mass Entertainment.* Divide the class into groups to do the drawing or painting and lettering.

For poems by Langston Hughes, see the Link to Literature on pages 474–475.

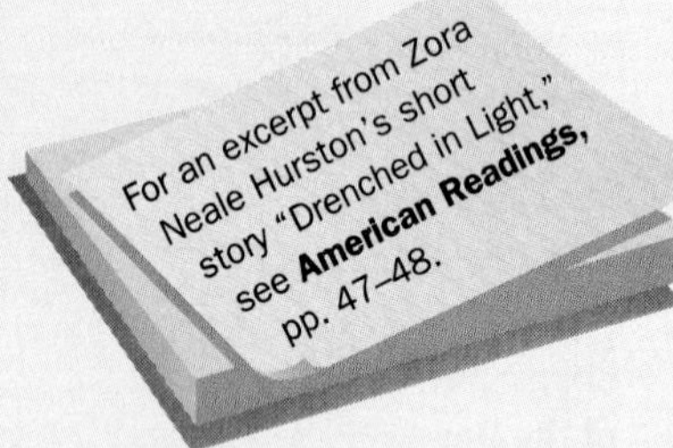

Vital Links

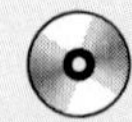

Louis Armstrong (Picture) Unit 4, Side 1, Search 43424

See also Unit 4 Explore CD-ROM location 373.

History Footnote

The first commercial motion-picture machine, the kinetoscope, was invented by Thomas Edison and his assistant, William Kennedy Laurie Dickson. It allowed one to view a short film through a peephole. Kinetoscope parlors opened in New York, London, and Paris in 1894. Jean and Auguste Lumière held the world's first public screening of projected motion pictures in Paris in 1895. One of their films showed a train arriving at a station. The audience cried in excitement and fear as the train moved toward them.

The first public screening of movies in the United States was in New York City in 1896. For several years moviemakers concentrated on re-creating news events rather than dramatizing original stories. *The Great Train Robbery,* produced in 1903, was the first to use modern film techniques to tell a story.

Americans who chose to live abroad. Fitzgerald did the same in *Tender Is the Night.* However, in earlier stories and novels, such as *This Side of Paradise,* he had portrayed the rebellious spirit of postwar youth at home.

Meanwhile, Sinclair Lewis was writing *Babbitt* and *Main Street.* In these novels Lewis criticized, as he saw it, the greed and lack of culture in small towns and small cities.

African Americans in the 1920s

African Americans, too, experienced the hopes and confusions of the postwar world. By 1930 the Great Migration had brought some 2 million black southerners to northern cities looking for factory jobs. There, a vibrant new African American culture took shape. It was to have a strong influence on American art and social life.

Marcus Garvey One aspect of the new culture was based on pride in African traditions. Thousands of African Americans were drawn to the ideas of Marcus Garvey, a Jamaican-born New Yorker. Garvey preached separation from white culture. African Americans, he said, should take pride in their African heritage. Instead of adopting white culture, they should set their own goals and build their own businesses.

Marcus Garvey wears his uniform in a 1922 parade.

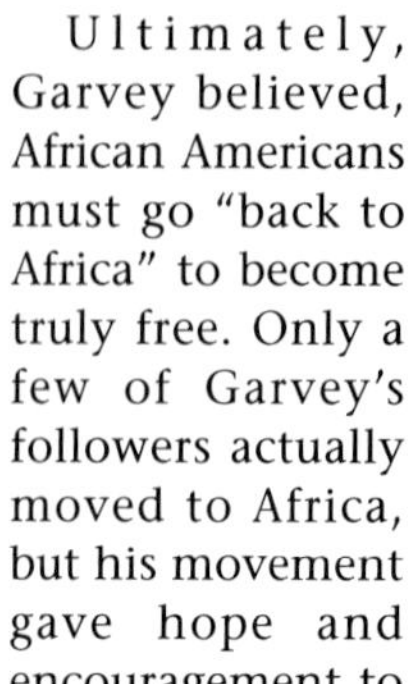

Ultimately, Garvey believed, African Americans must go "back to Africa" to become truly free. Only a few of Garvey's followers actually moved to Africa, but his movement gave hope and encouragement to many more. Although Garvey was jailed for mail fraud in 1925, his movement lasted for many years. Some of his ideas were revived in the 1960s.

Harlem Renaissance Garvey found a fertile field for his movement in the New York City neighborhood called Harlem. It was in Harlem that African American writers, musicians, and artists were finding ways to combine their traditions with the new opportunities of city life.

In fact, Harlem, where the black population more than doubled in the 1920s, gave birth to a flourishing new African American cultural movement. Known as the "Harlem Renaissance," this movement thrived in other American cities as well.

Black writers, in particular, wanted to reflect and strengthen the spirit of their people during the 1920s. Countee Cullen celebrated black culture in his poems. Another poet, Claude McKay, encouraged his African American readers to remain strong in the face of racial violence, for "the struggle is hard and long." James Weldon Johnson, too, hoped "to arouse and deepen the [African American] imagination."

Two writers stood out as central figures in the Harlem Renaissance: Zora Neale Hurston and Langston Hughes. Hurston uncovered the cultural roots of African Americans by exploring songs and tales of African and early American origin. She also published poems and novels. Hughes's poems ranged from powerful protests against racism to joyful celebrations of African American music and dance (see pages 474–475).

In fact, music was central to African American culture. Reaching back to African rhythms and songs, the blues and jazz began in New Orleans and the Mississippi Delta country of northwestern Mississippi.

Black southerners brought jazz north to Kansas City, Chicago, and Harlem. Both white and black music lovers flocked to

Tips for Teaching

Gifted Students

Gifted students benefit from collaborative activities that lead to authentic products. Have pairs or small groups choose a cultural work of the 1920s and create a new way of presenting it. They might set an existing poem to a new tune, create an original dance, write a play based on a short story or novel, and so on. Have them present their creations.

Link to Art

Couple in Raccoon Coats (1932) James Van Der Zee grew up in a family of artists and musicians. It came as no surprise, then, that from the day he received his first camera at the age of 14, he pursued the art of photography with passion. In his carefully composed and skillfully lighted portraits and his lively street scenes, Van Der Zee captured the spirit of Harlem in the 1920s and 1930s. **Discuss** What scenes from your life or your neighborhood would you most want to photograph and why?

nightclubs such as Harlem's Cotton Club to hear Joe "King" Oliver, Louis Armstrong, Duke Ellington, and other jazz greats. Armstrong went on to change jazz from primarily band music to a showcase for solo musicians.

The Roaring Twenties

The rhythms of jazz were well suited to the Roaring Twenties, a decade of change. To the journalist Lincoln Steffens, it appeared that

Discussion

Checking Understanding

1. What ideas did Marcus Garvey preach? (Separating from white culture, pride in African heritage, setting own goals, building own businesses, returning to Africa.)

2. Where did jazz begin, and how did it spread? (In New Orleans, northwestern Mississippi; spread to northern cities.)

Stimulating Critical Thinking

3. What effects do you think movies had on American life in the 1920s? (Helped people escape problems, helped create national culture and identity, gave unrealistic ideas about life.)

Teaching the

Link to Art

Have students tell what details in the photo reflect the 1920s and early 1930s. Point out that Van Der Zee was part of the Harlem Renaissance. His photos made everyday people look dignified and attractive.

Discussion Answers: Answers will depend on students' neighborhoods and sense of belonging there.

Vital Links

Voice of Willie Smith (First Person Account) Unit 4, Side 1, Search 42399, Play to 43360

See also Unit 4 Explore CD-ROM location 362.

Connections to Language Arts

Many terms that are standard English today were coined as slang during the 1920s, including *gate-crasher, blind date,* and *crush.* Following are additional slang terms from the decade that students may not have heard before: *all wet* (wrong); *applesauce* (nonsense); *big cheese* (important person); *cake eater* (ladies' man); *cat's meow* (wonderful); *copacetic* (very satisfactory); *dogs* (feet); *flat tire* (dull, boring person); *heebie-jeebies* (the jitters); *hotsy-totsy* (pleasing); *kisser* (mouth); *sheba* (attractive young woman); and *sheik* (attractive young man). That last term came from a movie called *The Sheik,* which starred Rudolph Valentino.

Bonus Activity

1920s Conversations

To focus on social and cultural changes that marked the 1920s, have pairs role-play conversations: between a flapper and her parents about her plans to go to a jazz club with her boyfriend; between two young rural African Americans about whether to go to Harlem to become writers; between a bar owner and a Prohibition supporter about whether the Eighteenth Amendment should be ratified; between two observers of the Scopes trial about whether evolution should be taught.

See the Study Guide activity in Chapter Resources Binder, p. 90.

Vital Links

Movie marquee (Picture) Unit 4, Side 1, Search 43382

See also Unit 4 Explore CD-ROM location 366.

"the whole world [was] dancing to American jazz." Indeed, jazz seemed to lead the way in what one fan described as "a blowing off of the lid." Americans were looking for ways to have fun.

Movies and radio Two new sources of entertainment captured the public in the 1920s: movies and radio. All classes of Americans flocked to grand, ornate movie "palaces." At first the films were silent. Then, in 1927 "talking pictures" arrived with *The Jazz Singer*, and the craze was on. By 1930 attendance was 100 million a week—almost one ticket for every American.

Radio turned into entertainment in 1920, when Frank Conrad sent out baseball scores and music to amateur radio operators from a wireless station in his garage. Discovering that he had attracted a national audience, Westinghouse officials set up the first radio station. Later that year, KDKA in Pittsburgh broadcast news of Harding's election. Two years later, more than 500 stations were broadcasting "every night, everywhere."

Heroes of the 1920s Jazz Age Americans were hungry for heroes. From baseball's George Herman "Babe" Ruth, to movie stars like Theda Bara and Rudolph Valentino, Americans made heroes of public figures.

For the first time, sports heroes included women. Babe Didrikson Zaharias competed in almost every sport, from basketball to golf. She eventually set Olympic records in track and field. Gertrude Ederle, meanwhile, broke all records when she swam across the English Channel in 1926.

The greatest hero of all, though, was a shy young pilot from Minnesota. On the drizzly morning of May 20, 1927, Charles A. Lindbergh strapped himself into his plane, *The Spirit of St. Louis*, and headed eastward from New York City. Thirty-four hours and 3,600 miles (5,790 km) later, he was greeted at a Paris airfield by 100,000 wildly cheering admirers waiting in the dark. He was the first person to fly solo across the Atlantic Ocean.

The world was seized by frenzy over the flight of the 25-year-old Lindbergh. Upon his return to the United States, he was given "the greatest welcome any man in history ever received." Soon after, Amelia Earhart became the first woman pilot to fly the Atlantic alone. Such flights boosted the infant airline industry. By 1930, 43 airlines operated in the United States.

New Ways of Living

In 1920, for the first time, a majority of Americans lived in urban rather than rural areas. Of those an increasing number were moving to the **suburbs**—communities on the outskirts of cities. Streetcar lines had first encouraged the growth of suburbs. Now automobiles did so as well.

The automobile age By 1921 automobiles were no longer "carriages of the rich." A family could buy a car for $400, half of what it had cost ten years earlier. Owning a car, advertisements promised, meant that "your freedom is complete." Farmers could enjoy the pleasures of the city, while city dwellers could escape to the country. A love affair blossomed between Americans, their cars, and the freedom of the road.

The lives of women For American women, the 1920s brought other freedoms as well. All women at last had the right to vote. Some women also had more free time as households installed electricity, telephones, and piped water. Electric washing machines, irons, and vacuum cleaners helped ease the tasks of daily life.

More women were working outside the home, too. With wider opportunities—and incomes of their own—young women, particularly, rebelled against old customs. They bobbed—cut short—their hair, threw away

History Footnote

When Italian inventor Guglielmo Marconi sent the first radio communication signals through the air in 1895, he could not have predicted the broadcasting boom that would soon take place. In 1920 there were 50,000 radios in American homes; by the end of 1927, 7.5 million radios had been sold. Unlike today, when music and talk shows dominate the airwaves, programs during the "Golden Age of Broadcasting" (roughly 1925–1950) also included comedies, mysteries, adventure dramas—and the first soap operas.

Radio became an important part of American politics in the 1928 presidential election. Because radio listeners would not sit still for long speeches, the average political speech that year was only 10 minutes long—setting the stage for the "sound bites" favored by politicians today.

Link to Technology

The Radio

Edwin Armstrong began development of the radio receiver while serving in World War I. By the 1920s he had perfected the technology, and soon millions of Americans had radios. Enthusiastic families crowded around "the magic box" to hear news and entertainment. The technology that Armstrong developed is the same basic design used in almost all radios today. The diagram below shows how radio transmitters and receivers work.

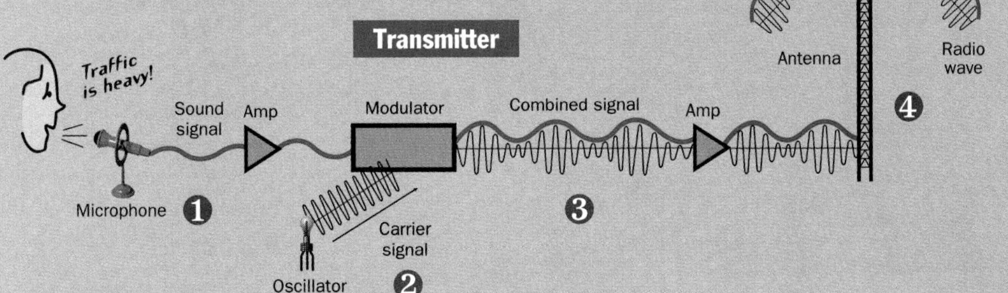

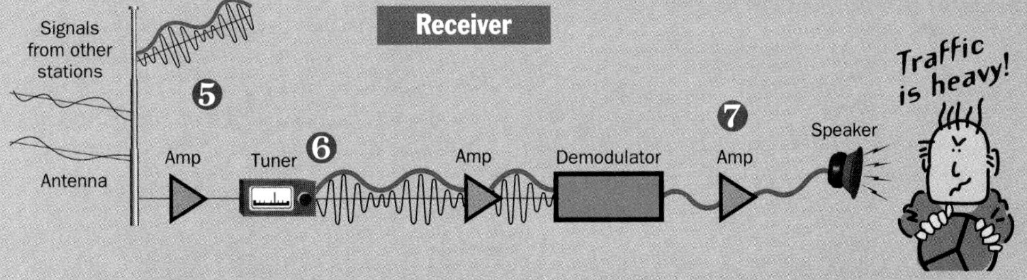

Edwin Armstrong displays his "portable" radio.

1. **At a radio station, a microphone converts sound to a sound signal.**
2. **An oscillator generates a second signal—the carrier signal—set to the frequency of the radio station.**
3. **A modulator combines the two signals, which are then amplified and sent to the antenna.**
4. **The movement of the combined signal in the antenna sends the wave into space.**
5. **On the receiver side, waves from many stations create signals in the antenna. The signals are amplified and fed into the tuner.**
6. **The listener chooses a station and the tuner selects that carrier signal.**
7. **The demodulator removes the carrier signal and the speaker broadcasts the sound.**

Discussion

Checking Understanding

1. Who were three heroes of the 1920s? ("Babe" Ruth, Theda Bara, Rudolph Valentino, Babe Didrikson Zaharias, Gertrude Ederle, Charles A. Lindbergh, Amelia Earhart.)

2. How did flappers look and act? (Short hair; short, sleeveless dresses; long, beaded necklaces; no corsets. Many worked; liked to dance; independent, assertive.)

Stimulating Critical Thinking

3. What dangers might Lindbergh have faced by flying alone? (No copilot in bad weather or other emergencies; no break to sleep, eat, or relax.)

Teaching the Link to Technology

After students read the introductory paragraph, guide them through the diagram. Read steps aloud as students follow along. Pause after each step and have volunteers restate it in their own words.

Vital Links

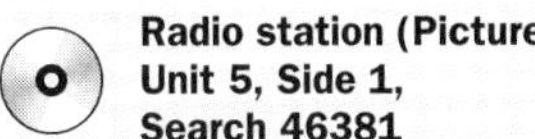

Radio station (Picture) Unit 5, Side 1, Search 46381

See also Unit 5 Explore CD-ROM location 288.

Teaching the

Point of View

Ask students the following questions: What do you think was the basic reason for the failure of Prohibition? (More people wanted to drink than did not.) What does Count von Luckner's last sentence imply? (Young people are naturally rebellious and thus will take up any practice denied to them precisely because it is denied.) Do you agree? Explain. (Accept all thoughtful responses.)

For an activity on a political cartoon about Prohibition, see **Using Historical Documents,** pp. 69–72.

Vital Links

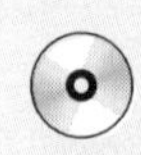

"I Wish I Could Shimmy" (Song) Unit 4, Side 2, Search 00001, Play to 02274

See also Unit 4 Explore CD-ROM location 393.

Flappers (Movie) Unit 4, Side 1, Search 43544, Play to 43899

See also Unit 4 Explore CD-ROM location 396.

History Footnote

Defiance of Prohibition was especially common in cities. In New York City alone, 15,000 bars closed, only to be replaced by about 32,000 speakeasies. Would-be drinkers gained entry by whispering a password at the door—that is, by "speaking easy." The liquor was brought in from Canada, Cuba, and offshore ships by bootleggers. This nickname came from smugglers of the late 1800s who hid liquor bottles in their boot legs when entering dry states.

Some people who did not have access to or money for bootleg liquor made their own so-called "bathtub gin." One popular song went like this: "Mother's in the kitchen washing out the jugs / Sister's in the pantry bottling the suds [beer] / Father's in the cellar mixing up the hops / Johnny's on the front porch watching for the cops."

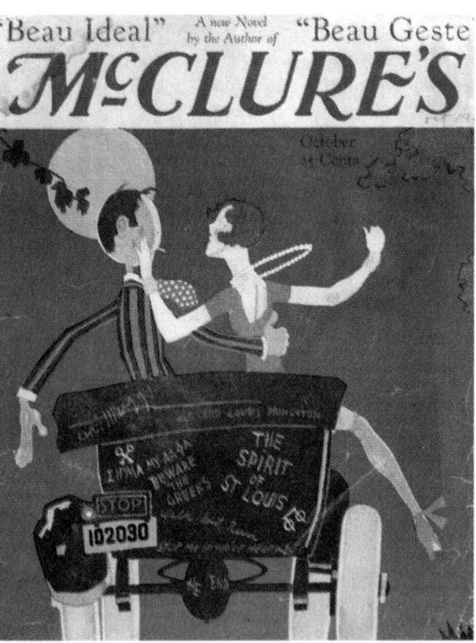

Magazines like *McClure's* spread the new spirit of American youth into even the smallest towns.

their corsets, and went out dancing in short, sleeveless dresses draped with long, beaded necklaces. Journalists called these independent, assertive young women "flappers."

"Flaming Youth" Young Americans created a new world in the 1920s. "The wildest of all generations" found it a thrilling time as they danced to music blaring from phonographs, crowded into movie houses, and took to the road in automobiles. *Flaming Youth*, the title of a 1923 novel, captured the spirit and passion of the time.

There was plenty of silliness, too. College students competed in goldfish-swallowing contests. A man called "Shipwreck" Kelly perched on a flagpole for 23 days, eating and drinking from a bucket raised from below. The idea caught on, and flagpole sitters cropped up everywhere.

In fact, American fads, fashions, music, and movies were spreading beyond the borders of the United States. The 1920s marked the beginning of the worldwide influence of American culture.

Reaction to the Jazz Age

Still, many Americans worried that society was changing too quickly. They reacted by trying to enforce old customs and values that they felt were being threatened.

Prohibition Progressives had long promoted **Prohibition**—banning the manufacture, transport, and sale of liquor—as a way to improve people's lives. By 1920 most states had passed some kind of Prohibition laws. In that year ratification of the Eighteenth Amendment made Prohibition law throughout the nation.

From the beginning, though, Prohibition was difficult to enforce. Many people who disagreed with the law willingly broke it. When saloons were closed down, people crowded into illegal clubs called speakeasies. Bootleggers, meanwhile, smuggled liquor into the United States. Criminal empires, run by gangsters like Al Capone, thrived from such activities.

Prohibition clearly was not working. In 1924 alone, $40 million worth of alcohol was smuggled in from Canada and the Caribbean islands. By the end of the decade, many Americans thought that Prohibition had done more harm than good. In 1933 the Twenty-First Amendment repealed it.

Point of View

Was prohibiting the sale of alcohol a good idea?

In 1927 a visitor to the United States, Count von Luckner, described the benefits of Prohibition for American workers:

Connections to Literature

Inherit the Wind, by Jerome Lawrence and Robert E. Lee, is a powerful, enduring play based on the Scopes trial. First staged on Broadway in 1955, it ran for three years. It was made into a movie starring Fredric March and Spencer Tracy in 1960 and has been adapted for television twice since.

In their introduction to the play, the playwrights state that it is neither history nor journalism. Although they spent over a year researching the Scopes trial, the play contains "only a handful of phrases" from the trial transcript. In the play, the teacher is Bert Cates and the lawyers are Matthew Harrison Brady and Henry Drummond. The stage directions describe the place as "A small town" and the time as "Not too long ago." The playwrights note, "It might have been yesterday. It could be tomorrow."

"The filthy saloons . . . in which the laborer once drank off half of his wages, have disappeared. Now he can instead buy his own car, and ride off for a weekend or a few days with his wife and children in the country or at the sea."

In the same report, however, Count von Luckner continued:

"A large part of the population has become accustomed to disregard and to violate the law without thinking. The worst is, that precisely as a consequence of the law, the taste for alcohol has spread ever more widely among the youth."

The dilemma described by Count von Luckner did not end with the repeal of Prohibition. To this day, Americans debate how best to protect citizens' well-being without interfering with personal freedom. 

Government agents smashed kegs of beer during the "noble experiment" of Prohibition.

The Scopes trial Another hot debate arose over ideas put forth by Charles Darwin, an English biologist. Darwin said that all living things, including humans, have gradually developed—or evolved—from simpler forms of life. Many Christians and Jews thought that Darwin's theory of evolution was dangerous because it raised questions about the Bible's story of creation.

In 1925 Tennessee banned teaching about evolution in its schools. To test the new law, town leaders in Dayton, Tennessee, encouraged a teacher named John Scopes to teach evolution in his class. If Scopes went to trial, they thought, it would bring fame and money to Dayton. They were right.

The Scopes trial drew nationwide attention. Reporters, souvenir vendors, and hordes of curiosity seekers descended on Dayton. In this carnival-like setting, William Jennings Bryan, the political leader and powerful speaker, represented those who opposed the teaching of evolution. Clarence Darrow, a famous lawyer, defended Scopes.

The judge ruled that Scopes was guilty because he had, in fact, broken the Tennessee law. Even so, many believed that Darrow had won because he had made Bryan sound foolish at the trial. The debate over teaching evolution continues to this day.

2. Section Review

1. Define **suburbs** and **Prohibition.**
2. What contributions did African Americans make to American culture and social life in the 1920s?
3. Describe at least three ways in which the lives of women changed in the 1920s.
4. **Critical Thinking** Could Prohibition have been successful? Explain your answer.

Closing the Section

Wrap-Up Activity

Writing Diary Entries

To review ways of life during the 1920s, ask students to imagine they were living then. Have them write diary entries for a typical day in their lives. Diary entries should include details from the section and reflect the student's gender, ethnic group, residence (city, suburb, rural area), and general views (conservative or liberal, and so on). Have students share their diary entries.

Section Review

Answers

1. Definitions: *suburbs* (460), *Prohibition* (462)
2. Literary works by writers like Countee Cullen, Claude McKay, James Weldon Johnson, Zora Neale Hurston, Langston Hughes; jazz by musicians like Joe "King" Oliver, Louis Armstrong, Duke Ellington.
3. Could vote; more free time because of household conveniences; worked outside home; rebelled against old customs; some changed hair and dress styles to become flappers.
4. Yes: promoters could have educated public about negative effects of alcohol and maybe won cooperation. No: too many wanted to drink; Prohibition spurred too much illegal activity.

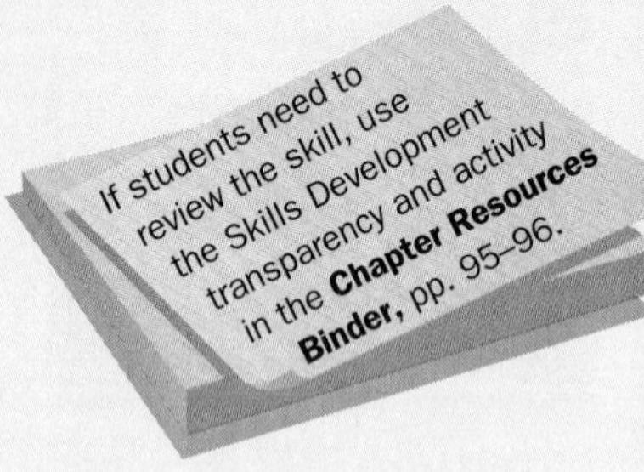

If students need to
review the skill, use
the Skills Development
transparency and activity
in the **Chapter Resources
Binder**, pp. 95–96.

Introducing the Skill Lab

Point out that our own era is often called the "Information Age." Every day of our lives, we are bombarded with huge amounts of information—more than we can possibly absorb. Thus, the ability to distinguish relevant information is crucial. Before students do the Procedure, be sure they understand what the terms *social, partly relevant,* and *irrelevant* mean.

Skill Lab

Answers

1. (a) Possible answer: the effects of cars on social life in the 1920s. (b) Possible answers: family relationships (husbands-wives, parents-children, siblings); relationships and activities between friends; community or recreational activities done in groups, such as at church; dating relationships and activities.

2. (a) A—irrelevant, B—relevant, C—relevant, D—relevant, E—partly relevant, F—irrelevant, G—relevant, H—irrelevant. (b) A—relevant to growth of car ownership; E—relevant to family communication; F and H—relevant to economic effects.

3. Answers should include information from sources B, C, D, E, and G and mention that cars were increasingly

(Answers continued in top margin)

used for leisure activities, especially by teens; that cars brought families together in some ways but also served as a source of disagreement between parents and teens; and that, for some, using cars for pleasure replaced attending church.

For further application, have students do the Applying Skills activity in the Chapter Survey (p. 472).

Skill Lab

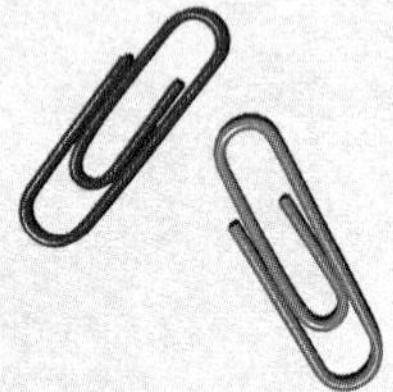

Thinking Critically

Recognizing Relevant Information

Americans of the 1920s knew that the car was reshaping their lives. Humorist Will Rogers expressed their feelings in this salute to Henry Ford: "It will take a hundred years to tell whether you have helped us or hurt us, but you certainly didn't leave us like you found us."

Question to Investigate

How did cars affect social life in the 1920s?

Procedure

To explore the question, you need **relevant information**—information that applies, relates, or is connected to the particular topic. Study the Skill Tips and do the following.

1 Identify the topic.
a. Use the Question to Investigate to come up with a phrase that names the topic.
b. What does "social life" mean? That is, what relationships or activities does it include? Give four examples of your own.

2 Examine each piece of information in the source to determine whether it is relevant to the topic you are investigating.
a. For each excerpt, **A** to **H**, tell whether it is relevant, partly relevant, or irrelevant to the topic.
b. For each excerpt that is either partly relevant or irrelevant, tell what other topic the information is actually relevant to.

3 Use what you have learned to answer the Question to Investigate.

Skill Tips

In general, these kinds of information may be relevant to a particular topic:

- definition of the topic
- explanation of the topic
- examples of the topic
- details about the topic
- evidence for or against the topic

Sources to Use

Below are excerpts from a report on life in a medium-sized American city: Muncie, Indiana, referred to as "Middletown."

A "At the close of 1923, there were 6,221 passenger cars in the city. . . . Of these 6,221 cars, 41 percent were Fords."

B "'I never feel as close to my family as when we are all together in the car,' said one business class mother."

C "The increase in surfaced roads and in closed cars is rapidly making the car a year-round tool for leisure-time as well as getting-a-living activities."

D "'What on earth *do* you want me to do? Just sit around home all evening!' retorted a popular high school girl of today when her father discouraged her going out motoring for the evening."

E "348 boys and 382 girls in the three upper years of the high school placed 'use of the automobile' fifth and fourth respectively in a list of twelve possible sources of disagreement between them and their parents."

F "A factory can [now] draw from workmen within a radius of forty-five miles."

G "A leading Middletown minister denounced 'automobilitis—the thing those people have who go off motoring on Sunday instead of going to church.'"

H "The automobile has apparently unsettled the habit of careful saving for some families. 'Part of the money we spend on the car would go to the bank, I suppose,' said more than one working class wife."

From Robert S. Lynd and Helen Merrell Lynd, *Middletown* (Harcourt, 1929)

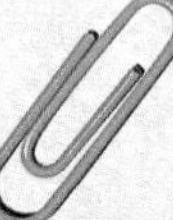

Section Objectives

- ★ Explain how the policies of Presidents Harding and Coolidge favored big business.
- ★ Describe the new products and methods for selling them that fueled the 1920s economy.
- ★ Identify signs that pointed to troubles ahead for the economy.

Teaching Resources

Take-Home Planner 4, pp. 4–11
Chapter Resources Binder
Study Guide, p. 91
Reinforcement
Skills Development
Geography Extensions, pp. 25–26
American Readings
Using Historical Documents
Transparency Activities
Chapter and Unit Tests, pp. 83–86

3. The Business Boom

Reading Guide

New Terms assembly line, credit

Section Focus The booming economy of the 1920s

1. How did the policies of Harding and Coolidge favor big business?
2. What new products and methods for selling them fueled the 1920s economy?
3. What signs pointed to troubles ahead for the economy?

As Zora Neale Hurston made her way north from Florida, she dreamed of a new life. She eventually moved to Harlem—the center of African American culture. There she found new opportunities. In fact, opportunity was in the dreams of most people in the 1920s. With President Warren G. Harding, they believed that if American business prospered, there would be opportunity for everyone.

A New Era for Business

As the economy rebounded from its slowdown in 1921, Harding's Secretary of the Treasury, Andrew W. Mellon, went to work. A wealthy banker, Mellon wanted to do everything possible to help business.

To protect American companies and their products, Mellon convinced Congress to raise tariffs on imports. As tariffs forced up prices on foreign goods, production soared at home. Congress also agreed to lower taxes for the wealthiest Americans. Mellon believed that if the rich paid less in taxes, they would use their extra money to build factories and put more people to work.

The economy would grow, too, as factory owners tried new systems for producing goods, invested in machinery, and switched to electric power from steam. Big business carried the nation into a boom—a period of extraordinary growth and prosperity.

Scandals Plague Harding

Harding, meanwhile, had chosen many of his friends from Ohio for jobs in his government. The "Ohio Gang," the public soon learned, had been accepting bribes and stealing money from federal agencies.

Teapot Dome The worst corruption involved Albert Fall, the Secretary of the Interior. He had control over two rich oil fields—one of them at Teapot Dome, Wyoming—that were set aside for the nation's navy. Fall leased the land to private oil companies, which gave him $400,000 in return. Convicted in the Teapot Dome scandal, Fall was the first cabinet member in the nation's history to go to prison.

Harding, depressed by the corruption and scandals, told a friend:

> "I have no trouble with my enemies . . . but my friends . . . they're the ones that keep me walking the floor nights!"

To escape from the attention given to his bribe-taking friends, Harding toured the West in 1923. On his way home he suffered a heart attack and died in San Francisco. On a Vermont farm in the early hours of August 3, Vice-President Calvin Coolidge was sworn in as President.

Introducing the Section

Vocabulary

assembly line (p. 467) a system in which the product moves from worker to worker, each of whom performs one task

credit (p. 468) a system in which a buyer takes home a product and then makes monthly payments until it is paid for

Warm-Up Activity

Inventing Slogans

To focus on what economic prosperity means, tell students that one 1920s slogan summed up prosperity as being "A Chicken in Every Pot, a Car in Every Garage." Ask students to write slogans that summarize what prosperity means to them. Have them share and compare slogans.

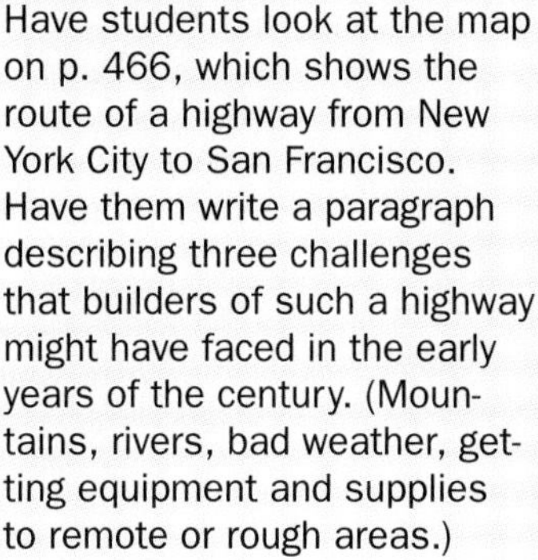

Geography Question of the Day

Have students look at the map on p. 466, which shows the route of a highway from New York City to San Francisco. Have them write a paragraph describing three challenges that builders of such a highway might have faced in the early years of the century. (Mountains, rivers, bad weather, getting equipment and supplies to remote or rough areas.)

Developing the Section

Teaching the Reading Maps

Explain that construction of the Lincoln Highway began in 1914. Ask why the highway was not built along a straight line. (Avoid major obstacles; go through cities where travelers could find gas, food, and lodging.)

Answer to Reading Maps: Trail followed easiest path; forests cleared; ground tramped down; and so on.

Section Activity

1920s Interviews

To focus on attitudes toward business in the 1920s, have groups of four act out "person in the street" interviews of the era. One member of each group will be a radio reporter. The others will take on roles like auto worker, labor union leader, homemaker, gas station owner, stockbroker, farmer, and banker. The interviewers begin by asking each person, "If the business of our country is business, is that a good thing or a bad thing?" Allow groups time to rehearse answers and follow-up questions before presenting the interviews.

History Footnote

Coolidge seldom wasted a word. Asked for his first thought upon becoming President, he said, "I thought I could swing it." Because of his calm and practical ways, his 1924 campaign slogan was "Keep Cool with Coolidge." Although he seldom smiled, Coolidge had a dry wit. When he presented his new wife with a pile of worn socks, she asked if he had married her to get his socks mended. Coolidge answered, "No, but I find it mighty handy." According to another story, a woman told Coolidge she had made a bet that she could get more than two words out of him. Coolidge answered, "You lose."

Coolidge conserved energy as well. He slept 11 hours a day and preferred sitting to walking. When he died, one Washingtonian jokingly asked, "How can they tell?"

Coolidge Takes Over

After the Harding scandals, Americans appreciated the soft-spoken Calvin Coolidge. Nicknamed "Silent Cal," he ran for election in his own right in 1924. The Democrats nominated John W. Davis. With the nation enjoying prosperity, "Silent Cal" easily won.

The boom continues Calvin Coolidge believed that the main job of government was to support business. "The business of the United States is business," he declared. Coolidge thought that government should do as little as possible. He appointed department heads who would not enforce government regulations on businesses. He also continued Harding's policy of lowering taxes on businesses and on wealthy Americans.

Between 1923 and 1929 industrial production grew by more than 30 percent. Early on, wages for many Americans went up as well. As wages rose, unions lost power. At the same time more people had more money to buy goods. The faith of Americans in big business reached new heights.

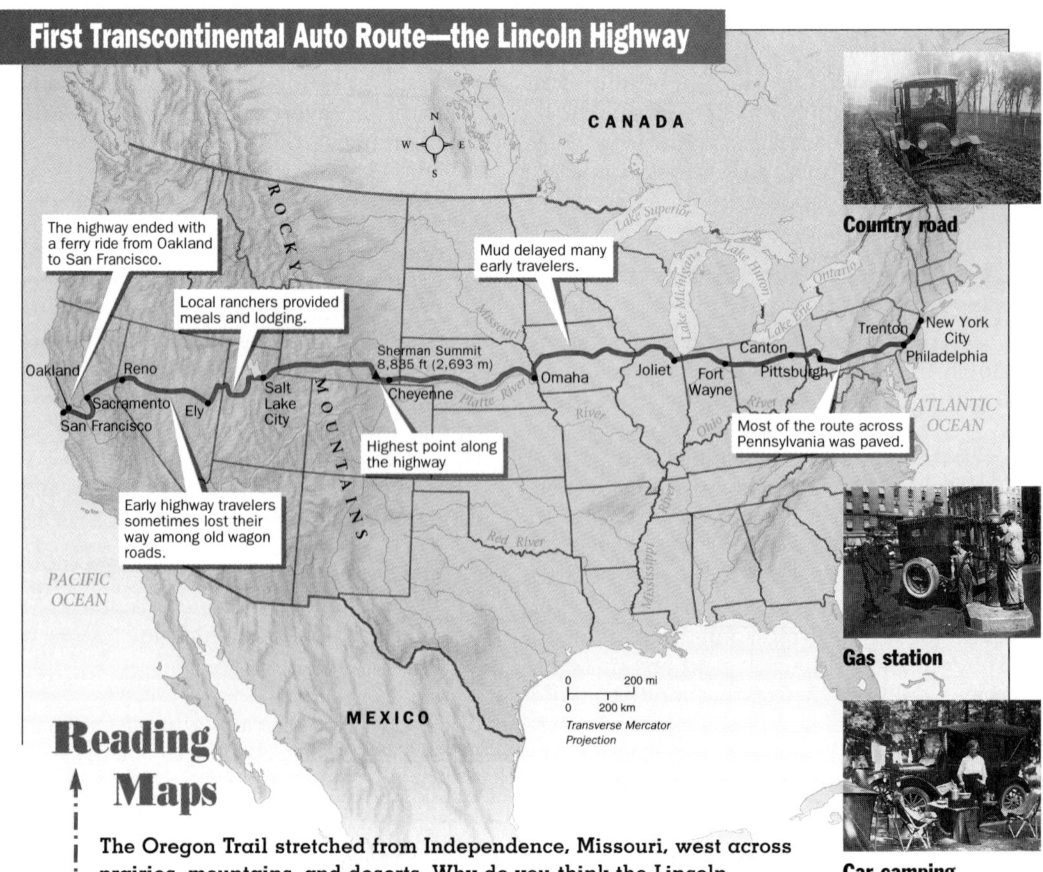

Reading Maps

The Oregon Trail stretched from Independence, Missouri, west across prairies, mountains, and deserts. Why do you think the Lincoln Highway sometimes followed a similar route?

History Footnote

In 1920 there were 8 million cars registered in the United States. By 1929 the number was 23 million. A farm woman summed up many Americans' passion for autos when she was asked why her family owned a car but not a bathtub. "You can't go to town in a bathtub," she answered.

For nearly two decades after its introduction in 1908, the most popular American car was Ford's plain-but-sturdy Model T, affectionately dubbed the "Tin Lizzie." Knowing a good thing when he had it, Ford made few changes in the car over the years. He might have built the Model T indefinitely, but challengers like General Motors began offering more comfortable cars with a wider variety of options. In response, Ford regretfully discontinued the Tin Lizzie and introduced the Model A.

The Automobile Boom

One of the greatest business successes of the 1920s was the automobile industry. Automobiles had been produced since the 1890s, but only the wealthy could afford them.

By the 1920s, however, automobile factories were using a less expensive production method. Developed by Henry Ford in 1913, the **assembly line** is a system in which the product moves from worker to worker, each of whom performs one task.

Demand for automobiles rose dramatically as the price dropped. Reporters were astonished by the throngs that gathered to view new models. When Ford introduced the Model A in 1928, mounted police were called in to control the crowds.

The popularity of automobiles helped fuel the economic boom. Industries essential to auto manufacturing, such as steel, glass, rubber, oil refining, and road construction, experienced rapid growth and created thousands of new jobs. Gas stations and tourist courts (motels)—unknown in horse-and-buggy days—lined the roadsides.

Link to the Present

Beyond the Model T "Of all the noises there is none worse, than a Model T Ford when it's in reverse." Americans were always making jokes about the Model T. They loved the car, though, for its price ($290 in 1924), speed (up to 45 miles/72 km per hour), and endurance. By the mid-1920s, however, many drivers had tired of its bone-rattling ride and lack of frills.

Today's cars have features undreamed of in the 1920s, from speeds of 120 miles an hour to computer-regulated engines. Carmakers also offer extras like air conditioning, sunroofs, and electrically operated windows and locks. Such features, of course, do not come cheap. New car prices range from $10,000 to $30,000 or more—far more than a Model T in 1921.

Workers on a Ford assembly line turned out the famous Model T for a price equal to just three months' pay for an average worker. Ford had hired the production expert Walter Flanders to redesign his factories. More than 1 million automobiles were built in 1916. Just four years later, 8 million came off the line.

Discussion

Checking Understanding

1. How did the automobile's popularity affect the economy? (Fueled growth of related industries such as steel making, oil refining, road construction, gas stations.)

Stimulating Critical Thinking

2. What might be an advantage of working on an assembly line? A disadvantage? (Advantages: comfortable knowing what is expected; not having to think about job. Disadvantages: boredom; carelessness that could lead to safety problems.)

Teaching the

Link to the Present

Have students list options today's cars offer, such as CD players, air bags, four-wheel drive, cruise control, and antilock brakes. Discuss whether these are worth their cost and whether Ford's philosophy that the best cars are simple and cheap should be adopted by modern car manufacturers.

Vital Links

Ford assembly line (Movie) Unit 4, Side 1, Search 16509, Play to 17455

See also Unit 4 Explore CD-ROM location 144.

Bonus Activity

Creating Advertisements

To focus on the style and content of 1920s advertising, have students create 1920s-style magazine ads for a product mentioned in this chapter. Ads should include artwork and copy. Before students begin, pass on the information in the History Footnote above. Also encourage them to study the pictures on pages 457, 459, 462, and 468 for ideas on how to portray any people they want to include. Have students post their completed ads and discuss how they resemble and differ from modern ads.

Vital Links

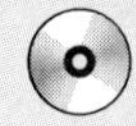

Oldsmobile advertisement (Picture) Unit 4, Side 1, Search 16503

See also Unit 4 Explore CD-ROM location 161.

History Footnote

The advertising business truly "came of age" in the 1920s. Showy billboards popped up along the new highways. Electric lights blazed brand names and slogans. Sponsors poured millions of dollars a year into loud, punchy radio commercials. Newspaper and magazine ads also adopted a bolder, "hard-sell" approach. Wordy black-and-white ads gave way to ads with large, colorful illustrations and simple, catchy slogans. Ads stressed low prices and high quality, made possible by advances in research and production. An ad for Atwater Kent radios boasted "prices which pass on to the public the savings achieved by scientific manufacture on a gigantic scale." Ads promoted credit buying too. By decade's end, 75 percent of cars and 50 percent of appliances were bought on credit.

New Ways to Sell

Now that American industries were producing more goods than ever before, they needed to sell them. To encourage consumers to buy their products, businesses turned to advertising and the credit system.

Companies bombarded Americans with advertisements on billboards, in newspapers, and on the radio. Ads were used to sell everything from cars to refrigerators. For example an advertisement for Dodge cars boasted:

> "America, when she starts, likes to start like a rocket, and here is a car that [does]."

Once they had decided to buy an exciting new product, Americans also had a new way to pay for it. Instead of paying cash, they could buy on **credit**—a system in which a buyer takes home a product and then makes monthly payments until it is paid for.

The credit system allowed many Americans to buy cars and other costly items that they could never have afforded before. Thus, credit buying helped fuel the business boom.

Hoover Wins

Republicans took credit for the nation's economic boom. Boasting that their pro-business policies had put "A Chicken in Every Pot, a Car in Every Garage," they promised even better times if Americans put another Republican in the White House.

President Coolidge decided against seeking re-election. The Republican banner passed to Herbert Hoover, a successful businessman. He had gained fame for setting up programs to feed the hungry in Europe after World War I. Hoover, like most Republicans in the 1920s, believed that government should play only a small role in the economy.

Al Smith, four-time governor of New York, became the Democratic candidate and the first Catholic to run for President. In a largely Protestant nation, Smith's Catholic background cost him votes among fearful Protestants. In any case, the voters gave the Republicans credit for the continuing prosperity. Herbert Hoover won by a landslide.

Taking office in March 1929, President Hoover confidently declared:

> "We in America are nearer to the final triumph over poverty than ever before in the history of the land."

Salespeople proudly display vacuum cleaners, washing machines, and other appliances now manufactured "on a gigantic scale."

The Soaring Stock Market

Public confidence that prosperity was here to stay was reflected in an increasing interest in the Stock Market. Before the war, only the wealthiest people could afford to buy stocks and thus share in the wealth created by business corporations. In the 1920s, however,

Connections to Economics

In the 1920s fortunes were created and lost in the stock market. The Fisher family earned $30 million to $50 million on $300 million invested for six weeks in 1928, but lost $200 million when the market crashed in 1929.

Average prices of stocks showed sharp changes at the end of the decade. In 1927 stock prices rose by 20 percent and almost doubled by 1929. In 1928 the price of a share of Radio Corporation of America rose from $85 to $420. Shares bought and then sold at these prices each yielded a $335 profit; 100 shares yielded $33,500.

When the stock market crashed, losses were as dramatic as the profits had been. The price of a share of Goldman Sachs Trading Corporation dropped from $60 to $35 in one day. A thousand shares lost $25,000 in a few hours.

Hands-On HISTORY

Investing in stocks If you have heard the phrase "playing the market," you might think that buying and selling stocks is a game or a gamble. Most people, however, make careful decisions when choosing a stock to buy.

A stock exchange floor today

Activity **Working with a classmate, you are to invest an imaginary sum of $1,000 in a company listed on the New York Stock Exchange.**

1 Choose a company in which to invest. Find out what products it makes or services it offers to people. Will there be demand for its products or services in the future?

2 On the day you "invest," find the price of the stock in the stock tables of a newspaper. Under the column labeled "Last," check how much one share will cost you.

3 Each day, look at the stock tables and record the last price of your stock. After one month, has your stock price gone up or down? Compare its value with the stocks of your classmates. Would you "sell" now or wait? Why?

stockbrokers—people who take orders to buy and sell stocks—developed an easy way for ordinary people to invest.

The new system was called "buying on margin." A buyer paid a small sum for shares of stock, with the stockbroker lending the rest of the money. Banks, in turn, loaned money to the stockbrokers. Now that they could buy on margin, people began to buy stocks as easily as they bought cars and refrigerators. By 1928 even bus drivers and elevator operators were "playing the market," expecting to get rich.

The frenzy of investing created a bull market—a period of rising stock prices—that many thought would go on forever. Cautious investors realized that the steady increase in stock prices could be dangerous. Even so, most people agreed with John Raskob, a business leader, who declared:

> "I am firm in my belief that anyone not only *can* be rich, but *ought* to be rich."

Signs of Trouble

Blinded by optimism and skyrocketing stock prices, few people could see that the economy was racing toward calamity. A careful observer, however, might have noticed signs warning of trouble.

In fact, a surprising number of Americans did not share in the prosperity. Farms, where 25 percent of Americans still lived, had been in a slump since early in the decade when crop prices had dropped.

Coal miners suffered, too, for oil was replacing coal as a major source of energy. Meanwhile, the textile industry suffered as women's fashions featured shorter dresses with less fabric. Unions, weakened by business and government hostility, had little power to help workers who had been laid off.

Declining demand Even though business profits climbed in the 1920s, business leaders held down workers' wages. This, in

Discussion

Checking Understanding

1. What led to Hoover's landslide victory? (Opponent was Catholic; voters gave Republicans credit for prosperity.)

Stimulating Critical Thinking

2. Has the credit system been good or bad for Americans? Explain. (Good: allows people to buy items they could not otherwise afford; sparks economy. Bad: encourages people to live beyond means; discourages saving.)

3. What is your reaction to John Raskob's statement on page 469? (Students may say it is unrealistic because uncontrollable factors can prevent people from becoming rich. Accept all thoughtful responses.)

Teaching the Hands-On HISTORY

Explain that information about companies can be found in newspapers, magazines, and business reference books at the library. Point out that many newspapers include tips on reading stock tables and that the "Last" price is the closing price for that day. In answering the final questions, students should consider the performance trend over the past month. For example, if a stock's price has risen steadily, they might wait until it goes higher before "selling."

Closing the Section

Wrap-Up Activity

Creating Concept Webs

To review the business boom, have groups make concept webs, labeled *A* and *B*. Each should have a center circle connected to outer circles by arrows, but in *A* the arrows point toward the center circle and in *B* they point away from the center circle. Each center should be labeled *1920s Business Boom.* Groups will use *A* to create a web showing causes of the boom and *B* to show effects. Some items may appear in both webs.

Section Review Answers

1. Definitions: *assembly line* (467), *credit* (468)

2. Policies of Harding and Coolidge, assembly line, popularity of automobiles, advertising, credit system, "buying on margin."

3. Failing farms, industry layoffs, low wages dampening demand for goods, inability of European nations to repay American bank loans.

4. Yes: "buying on margin" made it easy to invest; appeal of "getting rich quick." No: would have foreseen trouble and would not have wanted to take risk.

To check understanding of "Why We Remember," assign Thinking Critically question 3 on page 472.

History Footnote

The last years of Zora Neale Hurston's life were troubled ones. In 1950 a reporter discovered her working as a maid in Florida. The next year Hurston wrote to her literary agent that she was broke and "just inching along like a stepped-on worm." Although she still occasionally sold a magazine article and worked as a newspaper reporter, her writing days were mostly behind her. Hurston died in 1960 and was buried in an unmarked grave in a segregated cemetery in Fort Pierce, Florida. Friends and relatives took up a collection to pay for her funeral.

The 1970s brought renewed interest in Hurston's work. In 1973 Alice Walker, a future Pulitzer Prize winner, had a marker erected at Hurston's grave. It reads in part: "Zora Neale Hurston—A Genius of the South."

turn, led to a decline in demand for cars, homes, and appliances. After 1927, production slowed and more workers lost their jobs.

At the same time, Americans were buying fewer foreign goods. High tariffs had made them expensive. American banks suffered as European nations, unable to sell enough products, failed to pay back the money they had borrowed after World War I.

Failing farms, decreasing demand for goods, and risky bank loans all might have been warning signs that the economy was in trouble. At that time, though, the federal government did not watch such trends or business practices. As the Roaring Twenties drew to a close, few Americans could imagine the devastating events that lay ahead.

3. Section Review

1. Define **assembly line** and **credit.**
2. Describe three developments that helped business to prosper in the 1920s.
3. What factors were signs of economic troubles in the late 1920s?
4. Critical Thinking As an average American at the time, would you have invested in the stock market? Why or why not?

Why We Remember

The Twenties

Some years after the 1920s had become a mere memory, Zora Neale Hurston looked back on her life and wrote that she had "been in Sorrow's kitchen and licked out all the pots. Then I have stood on peaky mountains wrapped in rainbows." Indeed, many Americans spent the 1920s in Sorrow's kitchen. Immigrants lived in fear of Palmer's raids and the Ku Klux Klan. African Americans, weary of racism and the threat of lynch mobs, sought hope in Marcus Garvey's "back to Africa" movement. Farmers lost their farms and their futures, while other workers struggled just to survive.

Many Americans, however, also shared Zora's fond memories of the Jazz Age. Some had enjoyed the new culture created by movies, music, dance, and sports. Others had found expression as writers and musicians, or found new freedom in rebelling against traditional dress and customs. Many had enjoyed a prosperity beyond their wildest dreams. For all these Americans and more, the 1920s was a time wrapped in rainbows. Indeed, it seemed that the nation had never before reached peaks so high as it did in the 1920s. Even President Hoover believed that a "final triumph over poverty" was at hand. Yet as you will see in the next chapter, we also remember the 1920s as the decade that would end in Sorrow's kitchen.

Geography Footnote

The Spencer quotation is from an article in *Moving Picture World,* a trade periodical. The article described the varied scenery available to moviemakers in and near Los Angeles. Here are some additional excerpts: "Twenty miles to the west [of Los Angeles] lie the pleasure beaches with a score of high class beach resorts. . . ." "Within the same twenty-mile radius may be found some of the most beautiful country homes and gardens in the world. . . ." "A scenic mountain railway offers . . . a trip from roses to the snow line in forty minutes." The Chamber of Commerce promoted Los Angeles to early moviemakers with reminders like this: "Cold rain and slushy snow do not tend to the proper mental condition for the best creative work."

Geography Lab

Why the Movies Moved to Hollywood

One business that blossomed in the 1920s was the movie industry. The earliest movies were made in New York City and nearby New Jersey, where inventor Thomas Edison had his laboratory. In 1908, Edison's company joined others to form the Motion Picture Patents Company, which held patents on equipment and processes. The company tried to establish a monopoly in movie production, distribution, and exhibition. Independent movie producers fought the Patents Company and each other with lawsuits, spying, and dirty tricks.

Meanwhile, moviemakers discovered Hollywood, a sleepy suburb of Los Angeles. By 1920, 80 percent of the world's movies were made in or near Hollywood. Use the sources on this page to learn why.

Filming a western at Lone Pine, California, 1938

Richard V. Spencer, 1911

"Los Angeles and vicinity have acquired their reputation in the production of Western and Indian pictures. Here, of all places, is the ideal location for the production of such films. Here is found the necessary rolling country cut up by foothills, treacherous canyons and lofty mountain ranges in the background."

Fred J. Balshofer

"Los Angeles with its mild climate and sunshine beckoned as an escape both from the winter months of the East as well as the ever-present Patents Company detectives. . . . [Thus,] late in November, 1909, found our little company of players . . . departing for the West Coast."

Link to History

1. Sum up the appeal of the Los Angeles area to moviemakers, according to Richard Spencer.

2. Study the map on pages R6–R7. Why might the Los Angeles area seem like an attractive location to the owners of the New York Motion Picture Company?

3. In what way might Los Angeles's climate be an advantage in making movies?

4. Hands-On Geography Many modern movies include scenes shot "on location." Imagine that you work for your state's film office. Write a letter to the head of a Hollywood studio in which you offer reasons why your state would be the ideal location for the studio's next movie.

Teaching the Geography Lab

Have students recall what they know about the geography of New York City and Los Angeles to draw general contrasts between them (for example, on opposite coasts, New York has colder, wetter climate). Remind them that travel between the coasts was far more difficult in the early 1900s than it is today.

Link to History

Answers

1. Varied, interesting scenery appropriate for Western and Indian movies.

2. By relocating, the movie company could put more than 2,000 miles between itself and detectives from the Patents Company.

3. Mild temperatures and sunshine allow year-round outdoor moviemaking. Maps show Los Angeles is warm (more than 240 days a year without frost) and dry (less than 16 inches of precipitation a year).

4. Letters should stress the state's environmental advantages for specific moviemaking purposes: for example, snowy weather for stories set in cold climates, big-city streets for urban settings, wide-open spaces for battle scenes.

See the activity on why Detroit became the "automobile capital of the world" in **Geography Extensions**, pp. 25–26.

Survey Answers

Reviewing Vocabulary

Definitions are found on these pages: *communism* (453), *anarchism* (454), *suburbs* (460), *Prohibition* (462), *assembly line* (467), *credit* (468).

Reviewing Main Ideas

1. Economic conditions: scarcity drove up prices while wages remained low and workdays long. Union leaders and workers believed time had come to push for improvements and went on strike. Racial violence: lynchings and other mob violence against African Americans reflected and contributed to tension and suspicion.

2. Many Americans blamed foreign ideas, especially communism, for unrest. Anti-immigrant mood helped fuel Palmer raids, convictions of Sacco and Vanzetti, laws limiting immigration, revival of the Ku Klux Klan.

3. (a) Young Americans disillusioned by World War I. (b) An African American cultural movement that flourished in New York and other cities; any three: writers Countee Cullen, Claude McKay, James Weldon Johnson, Zora Neale Hurston, Langston Hughes; musicians Joe "King" Oliver, Louis Armstrong, Duke Ellington.

4. Any three: automobiles made it possible to travel more and live in suburbs. Airplanes allowed more distant travel. People enjoyed new entertainments provided by movies, radio, phonographs. Conveniences like telephones, running water, and electric washing machines, irons, and vacuum cleaners eased chores.

5. Prohibition, opposing teaching of evolution.

6. Harding: his Secretary of the Treasury convinced Congress to raise tariffs on imports and lower taxes on

(Answers continued in top margin)

the wealthy. Coolidge: appointed department heads who would not enforce regulations on businesses; pushed for lower taxes on businesses and the rich.

7. (a) Lower prices resulting from assembly-line production meant more people could buy automobiles. As auto industry grew, related industries did also. (b) Advertising convinced people to buy products like cars and refrigerators, boosting production and profits and creating jobs. (c) Credit allowed people to buy costly items, again boosting production and profits and creating jobs.

Thinking Critically

1. Agree: economic activities must be paramount because making money is a basic need; without a healthy economy, other concerns cannot be addressed. Disagree: most

Chapter Survey

Reviewing Vocabulary

Define the following terms.

1. communism
2. anarchism
3. suburbs
4. Prohibition
5. assembly line
6. credit

Reviewing Main Ideas

1. Explain how economic conditions and racial violence contributed to unrest after World War I.
2. Why were many Americans in an anti-immigrant mood in the 1920s, and what did they do about it?
3. (a) Who belonged to the "Lost Generation"? (b) What was the "Harlem Renaissance"? Name three people who were part of it and describe what they did.
4. Give three examples of how technology changed the everyday lives of Americans in the 1920s.
5. How did some people, worried by social changes occurring during the Jazz Age, try to maintain traditional customs?
6. In what ways did the Harding and Coolidge administrations support business?
7. What role did each of the following play in fueling the economic boom of the 1920s? (a) the automobile (b) advertising (c) credit

Thinking Critically

1. Evaluation Calvin Coolidge believed that "the business of the United States is business." Do you agree, or do you think our nation has other tasks more important than producing goods and services? Explain your answer.
2. Application It is March 1929 and President Hoover is taking office. What groups of Americans probably share his optimism about the future of the nation? What groups may feel more gloomy? Explain.
3. Why We Remember: Synthesis The 1920s has been called the Jazz Age and the Roaring Twenties. Make up your own label for the decade. Explain why you chose it.

Applying Skills

Recognizing relevant information Much as the automobile did in the 1920s, the computer is reshaping American life today. Look in newspapers or magazines for articles about the impact of computers. Recalling what you learned on page 464, read the articles to find five pieces of information on each of the following questions:

- How are computers affecting workers and businesses?
- How are computers changing communication between people outside of work?

Write answers to the questions based on the information that you find.

History Mystery

A famous flight Answer the History Mystery on page 449. Why did people throughout the world react with such wild enthusiasm to Lindbergh's flight? What consequences do you think it had for travel and future relations between the United States and other nations?

Writing in Your History Journal

1. Keys to History (a) The time line on pages 448–449 has seven Keys to History. In your journal, list each key and describe why it is important to know about. (b) Choose one event on the time line. Imagine that you are a teenager living at the time the event occurred. In your journal, write a letter to a friend giving your reactions to the event.

important "business" is living up to ideals of freedom, justice, equality; most important "business" is promoting a good quality of life through better health, safety, education.

2. Optimistic: rich individuals, bankers, business owners, stockbrokers, workers earning enough to buy cars and other goods, flappers. Gloomy: union leaders, farmers, immigrants, African Americans threatened by violence, workers in declining industries.

3. Best labels may indicate 1920s were not all prosperity. Accept all well-explained labels.

Applying Skills

Answers should reflect ability to distinguish between the two topics at hand and to locate relevant or partly relevant information in periodicals.

(Answers continued in side margin)

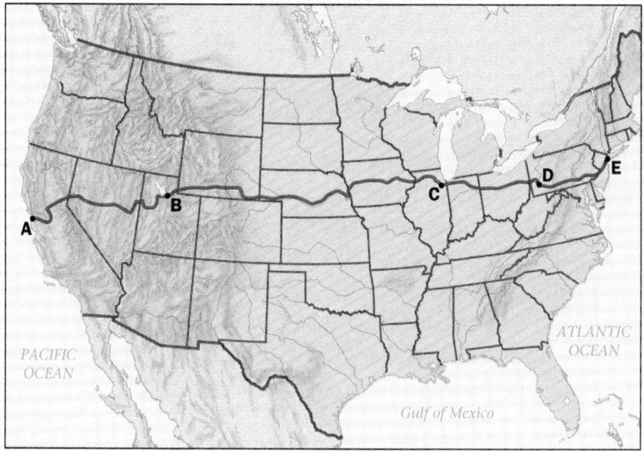

Reviewing Geography

1. The letters on the map represent cities along the Lincoln Highway. Write the name of each.

2. Geographic Thinking Name one effect that you think the automobile has had on each of the following:
- the natural environment
- the forms that cities, towns, and suburbs take
- people's ideas about the relative locations of places
- regional differences, such as in foods and customs

2. Zora Neale Hurston Sassy, spirited, shameless, bold: people of Eatonville used those words and others to describe young Zora. What other words would you apply to Zora? In your journal, list at least four and explain why you chose them.

3. Citizenship Many years after Prohibition ended, Americans still disagree about whether alcohol, tobacco, and other substances should be legal. How much should the government regulate or prohibit them? Or should the decision be left entirely to the individual? Why? Write your responses in your journal.

Alternative Assessment

Planning a "decade-in-review" issue Imagine that you and several classmates are the editors of a weekly magazine. It is July 1929 and you need to begin planning the special end-of-the-decade issue that will be published in December.

❶ Decide how to organize the issue. Although a year-by-year approach is possible, consider having sections of the magazine devoted to topics like entertainment, business, and sports, instead.

❷ Having planned the organization of the issue, think of a snappy title for each section. List the topics that each section will cover. This will be your table of contents.

❸ Create the cover and at least one section of the issue. Write text for the section and decide how you want to illustrate it. Arrange the text and images in a page layout.

Your work will be evaluated on the following criteria:
- it offers an accurate, thorough overview of events and people of the 1920s
- it is organized and written in a clear, logical, and interesting way
- its content and appearance capture the "flavor" of the 1920s

History Mystery

Lindbergh was first person to fly solo across the Atlantic. Enthusiasm may have resulted from appreciation for his bravery and skill or feelings that a new world was opening up. Probably hastened development of air travel and strengthened bonds between United States and distant nations.

Writing in Your History Journal

1. (a) Explanations should be similar to the time line notes on teacher pages 448–449. (b) Letters should reflect knowledge of the event and ability to imagine how someone of the time might view it.

2. Some possibilities: imaginative, articulate, ambitious, determined, restless. Accept evidence from the chapter or reasonable inferences.

3. Students favoring regulation/prohibition may say health and safety come first. Those against may say regulation/prohibition violates individual rights or may view antisubstance laws as unenforceable.

Reviewing Geography

1. (A) San Francisco, (B) Salt Lake City, (C) Joliet, (D) Pittsburgh, (E) New York City

2. Environment: pollution, changes in landscape for roads, motels. Cities, towns, suburbs: suburbs spread, expressways, decline in inner-city and small-town shopping areas. Relative locations: shrinkages in perceived distances. Regional: lessening of differences, customs and foods spread to new places.

Alternative Assessment

Teacher's Take-Home Planner 4, p. 7, includes suggestions and scoring rubrics for the Alternative Assessment activity.

Literature Footnote

Born in Joplin, Missouri, in 1902, Langston Hughes grew up in northern cities, where he found that only the lowest-paying jobs were open to African Americans. Writing in his spare time, he earned money by working as a dishwasher, janitor, porter, and busboy. At one point, determined to see the world, Hughes signed on as a cook's helper on a tramp steamer (a freighter without a regular route or schedule). The ship sailed to Africa, where Hughes discovered "the Africa I dreamed about—wild and lovely, the people dark and beautiful."

Through his long career and many travels, Hughes remembered the people and music of 1920s Harlem. He wrote, "I can still hear their laughter in my ears, hear the soft slow music, and feel the floor shaking as the dancers dance." Hughes died in 1967.

Teaching the Link to Literature

Remind students that Langston Hughes, like Zora Neale Hurston, was a central figure in the Harlem Renaissance. Hughes was an experimental writer, as can be seen in these poems featuring nontraditional rhythm and rhyme schemes. To add to students' enjoyment of the poems, have volunteers take turns reading them aloud. Caution them to speak in a natural voice and move ahead steadily until they come to punctuation that calls for pausing or stopping.

Link to Literature

The Poetry of Langston Hughes

No single writer of the Harlem Renaissance period was more prolific than Langston Hughes. Hughes first made his mark at age 19 with the poem "The Negro Speaks of Rivers." He went on to publish novels, plays, short stories, a newspaper column, essays, children's books, and two autobiographies. Born in Missouri, Hughes spent much of his adult life in Harlem. Although he traveled extensively and lived in Paris for a time, he found his greatest inspiration at home, where he found the ordinary people—"people up today and down tomorrow"—who filled his work.

I, Too, Sing America

I, too, sing America.
I am the darker brother.
They send me to eat in the kitchen
When company comes,
But I laugh,
And eat well,
And grow strong.

Tomorrow,
I'll be at the table
When company comes.
Nobody'll dare
Say to me,
"Eat in the kitchen,"
Then.

Besides,
They'll see how beautiful I am
And be ashamed—

I, too, am America.

Langston Hughes c. 1925 by Winold Reiss

Literature Footnote

From the beginning, Hughes's literary work addressed racial injustice honestly. For the most part, he wrote with ironic humor and sadness. However, he became somewhat more militant in his attitudes as he grew older.

Students who are interested in reading additional works by Hughes might look for the following titles at the library: *Selected Poems of Langston Hughes; Five Plays by Langston Hughes; Not Without Laughter*, a novel; or *The Ways of White Folks*, a collection of short stories. Students who would like to read more about Hughes's life might read his autobiography, *The Big Sea.*

Hughes was inspired by the vitality of Harlem life. This photo shows a Harlem street scene in the early 1930s.

Juke Box Love Song

I could take the Harlem night
and wrap around you,
Take the neon lights and make a crown,
Take the Lenox Avenue buses,
Taxis, subways,
And for your love song tone their rumble down.
Take Harlem's heartbeat,
Make a drumbeat,
Put it on a record, let it whirl,
And while we listen to it play,
Dance with you till day—
Dance with you, my sweet brown Harlem girl.

Lenox Avenue a street in the heart of Harlem

The Dream Keeper

Bring me all of your dreams,
You dreamer,
Bring me all of your
Heart melodies
That I may wrap them
In a blue cloud-cloth
Away from the too-rough fingers
Of the world.

A Closer Look

1. Who do you think "they" are in the poem "I, Too, Sing America"? Why do you think the narrator says they will be ashamed?
2. What is the narrator of "The Dream Keeper" saying about dreams?
3. Hughes's work was greatly influenced by the newly popular music forms of jazz and the blues. How do you think this influence is evident in these poems?

Discussion

Stimulating Critical Thinking

1. What impressions of Hughes do you get from the poems? (Possible answers: proud, optimistic but realistic, sensitive, appreciative of beauty and music.)

2. How do you suppose Hughes would feel about the position of African Americans in our nation today? (Possible answer: pleased about strides that have been made in gaining justice and equality but disappointed and perhaps angry about continued prejudice, discrimination, economic problems.)

A Closer Look

Answers

1. White Americans. They will be ashamed because they will realize how wrong they were to treat black people as inferiors.

2. Answers should include the idea that dreams are fragile and likely to be shattered when the dreamer confronts reality.

3. Like jazz, Hughes's poetry breaks traditional rules of form with unconventional rhythms, uneven and unrhymed lines. The serious, even sad, words of "I, Too, Sing America" could be lyrics of a blues song. All three poems make references to music, with "Juke Box Love Song" referring to the power of the music of Harlem.

Teaching the

Link to American Readings

In this feature students learn about the years following World War I from two very different perspectives: that of the Mexican migrant workers in California, and that of the young people who were squeezing all the fun and frivolity they could from the "Jazz Age." While some struggled to earn enough to feed their children, art, literature, and music flourished in other parts of the country.

Before students begin the lesson, review Anti-Immigration Laws (page 455) and The Jazz Age (pages 457–463). Have students read the entire feature before assigning the A Closer Look questions. The Setting the Stage Activity and Bonus Activity may then be introduced according to the needs and interests of the students. The information contained in the Discussion questions and the Footnotes may be used throughout the lesson as appropriate. Readers' Theater is ideal for students who might find the readings somewhat difficult. Use the Wrap-Up Activity for students who would enjoy taking a step beyond the core lesson.

Literature Footnote

Ernesto Galarza moved from Mexico to California when he was six years old. He fought for better working conditions for Mexican Americans by helping them form labor organizations, and later became a historian and civil rights leader. He also wrote several books addressing the problems of Mexican Americans. Galarza died in 1984.

Literature Footnote

Notable literature of the 1920s includes: Sherwood Anderson, *Poor White*; Eugene O'Neill, *Beyond the Horizon*; Willa Cather, *One of Ours*; Booth Tarkington, Alice Adams; Edith Wharton, *The Age of Innocence*; Theodore Dreiser, *An American Tragedy*; Ernest Hemingway, *In Our Time*; Gertrude Stein, *The Making of Americans*; Upton Sinclair, *Oil!*

Link to American Readings

READING 10A

Migrant Farm Labor in California

Born in Mexico, Ernesto Galarza moved to California with his family when he was a boy. Seasonal farm labor was in high demand in California, and Mexicans were employed by the thousands to perform the backbreaking work. Galarza describes the farm work he did while on summer vacation from high school.

Ernesto Galarza recalls his days as a migrant worker, around 1920

In the labor camps I shared the summertime of the lives of the barrio [neighborhood] people. They gathered from barrios of faraway places like Imperial Valley, Los Angeles, Phoenix, and San Antonio. Each family traveling on its own, they came in trucks piled with household goods or packed in their secondhand fotingos and cheuees [old cars]. The trucks and cars were ancient models, fresh out of a used-car lot, with license tags of many states. It was into these jalopies that much of the care and a good part of the family's earnings went. . . .

Our main street was usually an irrigation ditch, the water supply for cooking, drinking, laundering, and bathing. In the better camps there was a faucet or a hydrant, from which water was carried in buckets, pails and washtubs. If the camp belonged to a contractor, and it was used from year to year, there were permanent buildings—a shack for his office, the privies, weatherworn and sagging, and a few cabins made of secondhand lumber, patched and unpainted.

If the farmer provided housing himself, it was in tents pitched on the bare baked earth or on the rough ground of newly plowed land on the edge of a field. Those who arrived late for the work season camped under trees or raised lean-to's along a creek, roofing their trucks with canvas to make bedrooms. Such camps were always well away from the house of the ranchero, screened from the main road by an orchard or a grove of eucalyptus. I helped to pitch and take down such camps, on some spot that seemed lonely when we arrived, desolate when we left. . . .

Like all the others, I often went to work without knowing how much I was going to be paid. I was never hired by a rancher, but by a contractor or a straw boss [assistant foreman] who picked up crews in town and handled the payroll. The important questions that were in my mind—the wages per

lean-to: canvas or tarp pitched to create a one-sided tent

eucalyptus: tall, aromatic evergreen trees, common in California

Literature Footnote
The Harlem Renaissance is the name given to the explosion of African American music, art, and literature in the 1920s. During the Great Migration, many talented writers and musicians settled in the Harlem district of New York City. It was not long before Harlem developed a strong nucleus of artistic and literary talent. When W. E. B. Du Bois encouraged racial pride among African Americans, many black writers picked up and developed the theme, creating a truly new and unique American literature. Writers of the Harlem Renaissance include Arna Bontemps, Langston Hughes, Claude McKay, Countee Cullen, James Weldon Johnson, Zora Neale Hurston, and Jean Toomer.

hour or per lug box [crate], whether the beds would have mattresses and blankets, the price of meals, how often we would be paid—were never discussed, much less answered, beforehand. Once we were in camp, owing the employer for the ride to the job, having no means to get back to town except by walking and no money for the next meal, arguments over working conditions were settled in favor of the boss. I learned firsthand the chiseling techniques of the contractors and their pushers—how they knocked off two or three lugs of grapes from the daily record for each member of the crew, or the way they had of turning the face of the scales away from you when you weighed your work in.

There was never any doubt about the contractor and his power over us. He could fire a man and his family on the spot and make them wait days for their wages. A man could be forced to quit by assigning him regularly to the thinnest pickings in the field. The worst thing one could do was to ask for fresh water on the job, regardless of the heat of the day; instead of iced water, given freely, the crews were expected to buy sodas at twice the price in town, sold by the contractor himself. He usually had a pistol—to protect the payroll, so it was said. Through the ranchers for whom he worked, we were certain that he had connections with the Autoridades [authorities], for they never showed up in camp to settle wage disputes or listen to our complaints or to go for a doctor when one was needed. . . .

John Sloan's *Mother and Daughter*, painted in Santa Fe, New Mexico, in 1919, contrasts a young woman in modern clothes with an older woman in traditional black clothing. The new life in America did not always mesh well with the traditions and life the Mexicans had known in their homeland.

Setting the Stage Activity

Comparing Life-styles

To help students begin to understand the wide range of social and economic conditions in the United States in the 1920s, have them complete this exercise. Divide the class into two groups. Have one group list characteristics of the Mexican migrant workers' lifestyle. The second group should do the same for those who became the young people of the Jazz Age. When they have finished, ask volunteers to write items from their lists on the board. Discuss the differences between the two groups. What conclusions can they draw about life in the United States in the 1920s?

Bonus Activity

Mapping Immigration

To help students understand the patterns of immigration, have them locate on a map of the United States the areas where most Mexican immigrants settled. Emphasize that Mexicans were following existing patterns of migration established when California and the Southwest were Mexican provinces.

Discussion

Stimulating Critical Thinking

1. Why do you think Mexican migrant workers were locked into doing heavy farm labor for such meager pay? (They were poor, desperately needed the work for whatever it would pay, and did not have the training or education to do other jobs. Prejudice also was a factor. For example, white workers who did the same job were often paid more.)

2. Imagine that you are a migrant worker with a family who depends on you. Would you accept whatever work you could find regardless of the pay? Explain. (Students' responses will vary. Some might say that they would not risk the chance that their children might go hungry if they went on strike or did anything else that might risk their job. Others might say that unless people accept risk, a bad situation will never improve.)

3. If you were living in the Jazz Age, would you more likely be a cutting-edge flapper or sheik (the male counterpart to the stylish female flapper), or would you be more conservative? Explain. (Students' responses will reveal something of how they view themselves.)

Connections to Music

Bessie Smith was a famous blues and jazz singer of the 1920s and 1930s. In her late teens and early twenties, she traveled throughout the South performing in speakeasies and small theaters where she became popular with African Americans. In 1923 she made her first recording and became an instant success. Her records were usually available only in stores that catered to African American customers. However, as jazz become increasingly popular, whites began ordering her records. Smith's stardom was cut tragically short when she died in an automobile accident in 1937.

The only way to complain or protest was to leave, but now and then a camp would stand instead of run, and for a few hours or a few days work would slow down or stop. I saw it happen in a pear orchard in Yolo when pay rates were cut without notice to the crew. The contractor said the market for pears had dropped and the rancher could not afford to pay more. The fruit stayed on the trees, while we, a committee drafted by the camp, argued with the contractor first and then with the rancher. The talks gave them time to round up other pickers. A carload of police in plain clothes drove into the camp. We were lined up for our pay, taking whatever the contractor said was on his books. That afternoon we were ordered off the ranch.

Excerpt from *Barrio Boy* by Ernesto Galarza. Copyright © 1971 by University of Notre Dame Press. Reprinted by permission.

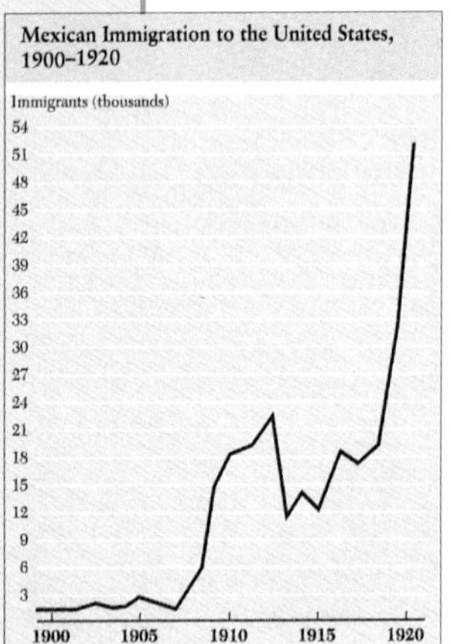

In the first two decades of the twentieth century, the number of Mexican immigrants arriving in the United States rose dramatically—from about one thousand in 1900 to nearly fifty-four thousand in 1920.

READING 10B

A Roaring Twenties Glossary

Dozens of new words and expressions sprang into existence during the Roaring Twenties. The terrifying and somber years of World War I were over. It seemed that everyone, especially young people, wanted to forget that time and to celebrate life. Dress changed, moral codes changed, and even language took on new life as fresh slang peppered conversations. A partial list of terms that were coined or popularized during the decade appears on the next page.

These flappers were representative of many young people of the Roaring Twenties.

Literature Footnote
If a single writer can be said to embody the Jazz Age, most would agree that it is F. Scott Fitzgerald. His works include: *This Side of Paradise* (1920), *The Beautiful and the Damned* (1922), *Tales of the Jazz Age* (1922), *The Great Gatsby* (1925), and *The Last Tycoon* (1941).

Readers' Theater
Ernesto Galarza's work might be adapted to a reading for several voices. Have students work together to determine logical places for a change in voice. Wherever there is a shift in thought, a new reader can step in. The script should be followed closely. Allow students to rehearse before presenting the reading.

Popular Slang, 1920s

APPLESAUCE: nonsense; same as *baloney*, *bunk*, *banana oil*, *hokum*, and *horsefeathers*.

BEE'S KNEES: a superb person or thing.

BERRIES: anything wonderful; similar to bee's knees.

CAT'S MEOW: anything wonderful.

DOGS: human feet.

FLAPPER: typical young girl of the Twenties, usually with bobbed hair, short skirt, and rolled stockings.

FLAT TIRE: boring person.

GIGGLE WATER: alcoholic drink.

HEEBIE-JEEBIES: the jitters.

HEP: wise.

JAKE: okay.

KISSER: the mouth or lips.

LINE: insincere flattery.

SPIFFY: elegantly fashionable.

STUCK ON: having a crush on.

SWANKY: ritzy.

This work captures the spirit of the Roaring Twenties. Artist John Held, Jr., was known for his reflections on contemporary society.

Use the glossary to translate the following paragraph that might have been written in the 1920s.

This "hep" young man and "spiffy flapper" thought the band they were dancing to was the "berries." After several numbers, however, she discovered that he was a "flat tire." He soon became aware of her feelings and got a good case of the "heebie-jeebies." Although he still thought she was the "bee's knees," he decided to give her a "line" and then retreat to a chair to rest his "dogs."

A Closer Look

1. Explain how employers maintained control over their immigrant workers.

2. Rewrite the "hep" young man and "spiffy flapper" paragraph using current slang to replace the slang from the 1920s.

3. CRITICAL THINKING Why were immigrant workers' attempts at labor organization unsuccessful? What safeguards have been created to prevent employers from taking advantage of their farm workers?

Wrap-Up Activity

Taking a Look at Slang
To demonstrate to students how language changes over time, have them list current slang terms and the definition for each. Then ask them to talk to their parents about slang that was popular in their teens. Have any terms stayed popular for more than one generation? Was their parents' slang more like that of the Jazz Age or more like their own?

A Closer Look
Answers
1. The employers cheated the workers when weighing the produce; they underpaid the workers; they would withhold water and charge for bottled drinks; they would make a worker quit by always assigning him or her to the thinnest part of the field; they would withhold wages.

2. Students' paragraphs will vary. You might ask volunteers to share their paragraphs with the class, or have them read them in small groups.

3. When workers tried to strike, there was no legal support; the employers just hired others. Today there are state and federal laws to protect workers, and unions intercede for their members.

Teaching the Citizenship Lab

In this feature students will learn about *Olmstead* v. *United States*. In this case the Supreme Court had to decide whether wiretapping constituted an illegal search and seizure, in violation of the Fourth Amendment.

Have students read the entire feature before assigning the Understanding Civic Issues questions and the Hands-On Citizenship activity. The Bonus Activity in this Teacher's Edition may be used as an alternative to, or in addition to, the Hands-On Citizenship. The Discussion questions in this Teacher's Edition may be used at appropriate points during students' reading or afterward.

Objectives

- ★ Understand that the right to privacy is only implied in the Constitution.
- ★ Identify and explain the exclusionary rule.
- ★ Understand the conflict between liberty and authority.
- ★ Cite examples of contemporary issues involving privacy.

Supreme Court Case: *Olmstead* v. *United States*

Citizenship Lab

Does the Constitution Protect the Right to Privacy?

There is no mention of the right to privacy anywhere in the Constitution. However, the Bill of Rights gives many signs that the framers were very concerned about privacy. They clearly wanted some areas of people's private lives to be free of governmental control. The First Amendment right to freedom of religion implies the right to exercise private and personal beliefs. The Fourth Amendment protects people's right to be secure "in their persons, houses, papers and effects." It also prohibits "unreasonable searches and seizures." Although the intent is generally clear, the Supreme Court has had a difficult time dealing with specifics. For example, what makes a search "unreasonable"? Does the Fourth Amendment protection extend to a telephone conversation in a public phone booth?

The Court Declares the Exclusionary Rule

The courts have had to deal with the important question of whether evidence that is unlawfully seized can be used in court. In 1914 the Supreme Court handed down a ruling that is still generally followed today. In *Weeks* v. *United States,* the Court developed what is known as the "exclusionary rule." It states that evidence acquired as a result of an illegal search cannot be used in court against the person from whom it was taken. Clearly, the Court was telling the police that as they enforce the laws, they too must obey them.

Does the Fourth Amendment Cover Wiretapping?

The development of electronic listening devices has raised new search and seizure questions. Probably the oldest and best-known form of electronic eavesdropping is wiretapping a telephone line. Today, there are a great variety of bugging devices. "Bugs" usually consist of a tiny radio transmitter, microphone, and amplifier. They are placed in a telephone receiver or "planted" anywhere in a room.

The Olmstead Case Was the First Wiretapping Decision

The first wiretapping case to be heard by the Supreme Court was in 1928. The case was *Olmstead* v. *United States*. The defendant was Roy Olmstead, a former police officer in Seattle, Washington. Olmstead

History Footnote

The conservatism of the Supreme Court in the 1920s reflected the alarm many Americans felt about the changes taking place in the nation. The Russian Revolution of 1917 bred fears in the United States of an overthrow of the government by communists. In the minds of many Americans, anyone who criticized the government or worked to improve working conditions through the union movement was considered a communist. Foreigners were especially suspect. Given this almost hysterical fear, it is not too surprising that the Court approved the use of wiretap evidence.

traded in his career in law enforcement to become a bootlegger. He and his partners made a lot of money—more than $2 million a year! But government agents learned about Olmstead's illegal activities. They began to listen in on his telephones. Over several months, they gathered information about his business. The police were careful not to trespass on Olmstead's property. But they nevertheless broke a Washington state law that made wiretapping illegal. On the basis of the evidence collected during the wiretapping, Olmstead was found guilty. He was convicted of violating the National Prohibition Act of 1919, which made it a federal offense to manufacture, transport, or sell alcoholic drinks. Olmstead was sentenced to four years in prison and fined $8,000.

Olmstead believed that his constitutional rights were violated. Eventually, the case was heard by the Supreme Court. In a landmark 5-4 decision, the Court decided against him. William Howard Taft, the Chief Justice and former President of the United States, wrote the opinion. Taft denied that the Fourth Amendment applied in Olmstead's case. "There was no searching," he wrote. "There was no seizure. The evidence was secured by the use of the sense of hearing and that only. There was no entry of the houses or offices of the defendants." Taft continued, the language of the Fourth Amendment "cannot be extended and expanded to include telephone wires reaching to the whole world from the defendant's house or office."

Some Justices Disagreed

Four justices disagreed with Chief Justice Taft. Justice Oliver Wendall Holmes pointed out that the evidence that was used to convict Olmstead had been unlawfully obtained. The federal officials knowingly broke the state law when they wiretapped Olmstead's phone. Holmes believed the Court was wrong for supporting police officers who broke the law. He said, "I think it a lesser evil that some criminals should escape than that the government should play an

What constitutes a "reasonable" search? The Court undoubtedly will wrestle with this question for many years to come.

Setting the Stage Activity

Discussing the Legality of Wiretapping

Ask students to consider the following scenario. A man is using a public phone to deal drugs. The police decide to bug the telephone. Ask students to discuss how they feel about this. Should the police have the right to wiretap? How would they feel if the phone booth was one they used regularly?

Bonus Activity

Discussing Privacy Issues

Divide the students into groups of three or four. Tell them that they are a group of citizens concerned about individual rights and freedoms. Ask them to consider the following: random drug tests, personality tests, and genetic testing. Are these tests a violation of one's privacy? Should people be forced to take them against their will? What dangers do you see in using such tests?

Discussion

Checking Understanding

1. What is the exclusionary rule? (Evidence acquired as a result of an illegal search cannot be used in court against the person from whom it was taken.)

2. What did the Katz decision establish? (It established that the Fourth Amendment applied wherever a person had "a reasonable expectation of privacy.")

Stimulating Critical Thinking

3. How can we combat rising crime if we do not allow the police to take advantage of technological inventions such as sophisticated listening devices? (Answers will vary but might include giving up some elements of individual privacy for the benefit of society.)

Citizenship Footnote

In *New Jersey* v. *T. L. O.* (1985), the Supreme Court considered the question of whether students are protected by the Fourth Amendment. The Court ruled that the Fourth Amendment's protection against "unreasonable search and seizure" extended to students. The Court qualified this, however, by ruling that school officials could conduct a search without a warrant as long as there were "reasonable grounds" to think that the search would yield evidence of a violation of the law or of school rules. In the majority opinion, Justice Byron White wrote, "It is evident that the school requires some easing of the restrictions to which searches by public authorities are ordinarily subject."

ignoble part." Justice Butler disagreed but for another reason. He noted that telephones are used to transmit "private and privileged" messages. For the sake of privacy, he argued, wiretapping should not be encouraged.

Justice Louis Brandeis agreed with Holmes, but went even further. He argued that the fourth and the fifth amendments should apply to this case. He pointed out that times change. New technologies for electronic surveillance will be developed that the framers of the Constitution could never have dreamed of. He asked, "Can it be that the Constitution affords no protection against such an intrusion of individual security?"

Brandeis denounced the government's action. "Experience should teach us to be most on our guard to protect liberty when the government's purposes are beneficent. Men born to freedom are naturally alert to repel invasion of their liberty by evil-minded rulers. The greatest dangers to liberty lurk in . . . men of zeal, well-meaning, but without understanding. Decency, security, and liberty alike demand that government officials shall be subjected to the same rules of conduct that are the commands to the citizen. Crime is contagious. If the government becomes a lawbreaker, it breeds contempt for law."

The Olmstead Decision Was Overruled in 1967

It was not until 1967 that the majority of the Court came to see wiretapping in the same way as justices Holmes, Butler, and Brandeis. The case was *Katz* v. *United States*. Katz was convicted of sending betting information across state lines. The evidence that convicted him was based on wiretaps placed outside a phone booth he was known to use. Justice Potter Stewart wrote the majority opinion. He wrote, "The Fourth Amendment protects people not places. What a person knowingly exposes to the public, even in his own home or office, is not the subject of Fourth Amendment protection. . . . But what he seeks to preserve as private, even in an area accessible to the public, may be constitutionally protected. . . . [Katz] did not shed his right [to privacy] simply because he made his calls from a place where he might be seen."

The Katz decision established that the Fourth Amendment applied wherever a person had "a reasonable

New technologies such as cell phones are tremendously useful. Yet they pose new threats to our privacy.

History Footnote

The United States experienced a huge growth in organized crime in the 1920s. No gangster was more notorious than Chicago's Al Capone. He built an empire on liquor, gambling, and "protection." By 1927 his holdings were worth more than $60 million. There were only 2,000 federal agents assigned to combat the growing crime problem. Agents such as Izzy Einstein and Moe Smith became famous for their inventiveness. They used many imaginative disguises to gain entrance to the speakeasies. In their careers they made more than 4,000 arrests and found more than 5 million bottles of liquor worth $15 million. But the task was overwhelming. Wiretapping was one way the authorities could fight back, and after the Olmstead decision, it was used extensively.

expectation of privacy," not just in a home or office. This phrase has become the critical test for what the Fourth Amendment protects. In the Katz decision, the Court ruled that the police could not listen in on telephone conversations without a warrant from the courts.

Privacy Issues Today

Privacy issues continue to be debated today. As Justice Brandeis had predicted during the Olmstead case, the framers of the Constitution never could have dreamed of the technologies we have available today. Although they provide us with incredible ways to make our lives easier, these technologies also provide many opportunities for invasions into our private lives. Most Americans are interested in preventing an abuse of governmental power. On the other hand, they want to make their communities, streets, and homes safe. Students and their parents are concerned with keeping drugs and guns out of schools. But does this justify the search of student lockers? Should students be forced to take drug tests if they are suspected of using drugs? Are people willing to allow the police to stop and search vehicles they suspect may be involved in illegal activities even if they are acting only on a hunch? The Supreme Court—and each individual citizen—must continue to weigh the balance between law and order on one side and individual privacy on the other.

Understanding Civic Issues

1. What two amendments in the Bill of Rights most directly imply the right to privacy?
2. On what grounds did Justice Brandeis disagree with the majority decision in the Olmstead decision?
3. **Critical Thinking** Do you think that Court restrictions on police searches interfere with law enforcement? Should the police be given more leeway in searching crime suspects? Would this result in less crime?
4. **Hands-On Citizenship** With several other students, investigate how technology affects our thinking about privacy. Your group might consider the following examples and issues:
   - caller ID
   - computer records of all the videotapes rented by a particular individual
   - the sale of consumers' names and addresses to marketing firms
   - the use of credit information without a person's knowledge
   - video surveillance in the workplace
   - the use of scanners to monitor cellular phone conversations

   Is there anything wrong with using this new technology? How has this technology changed our basic concept of privacy? Should limits be imposed on its use?

Citizenship Lab Answers

1. The two amendments that most directly imply the right to privacy are the first and fourth amendments.

2. Brandeis based his dissent on the fourth and fifth amendments. He said that times change and that the framers of the Constitution could not have anticipated all of them. He believed that it was just as important for the government to obey the law as it was for individuals to obey the law.

3. Answers will vary. Students should recognize that giving the police more power might result in less crime, but at the same time it might mean less freedom.

Teaching the Hands-On *CITIZENSHIP*

Teachers are often unsure of how to set up groups for discussions. Research shows that students learn best when they are teaching something to each other. As a result, it might be best to try to mix students of varying ability levels in each group. It may be that if all the most-able students were in the same group that they might get better results, but this success is usually at the expense of the less-able students.

At·a·Glance **11**

The Depression and New Deal
1929–1941

Chapter Planning Guide

Section	Student Text	Teacher's Edition Activities
Opener and Story pp. 484–487	**Keys to History Time Line** **History Mystery** Beginning the Story with **Franklin and Eleanor Roosevelt**	**Setting the Stage Activity** Wanted: Couple to Lead a Troubled Nation, p. 486
1 **The Great Depression** pp. 488–491	**World Link** The coffee crash, p. 489	**Warm-Up Activity** Writing Sketches, p. 488 **Geography Question of the Day,** p. 488 **Section Activity** Economic Problems Then and Now, p. 490 **Bonus Activity** Hooverville Skits, p. 490 **Wrap-Up Activity** Writing a Roosevelt Speech, p. 491
2 **The First New Deal** pp. 492–497	**Reading Maps** Examples of New Deal Projects, p. 494 **Hands-On History** Holding a fireside chat, p. 495 **Skill Lab** Comparing Historical Interpretations, p. 497	**Warm-Up Activity** Offering "New Deal" Solutions, p. 492 **Geography Question of the Day,** p. 492 **Section Activity** A Radio Panel Discussion, p. 494 **Bonus Activity** Creating Political Cartoons, p. 493 **Wrap-Up Activity** Letters to the Editor, p. 496
3 **The Second New Deal** pp. 498–505	**Point of View** Should public funds support the arts?, p. 498 **Link to the Present** Social Security in your life, p. 499 **Link to Art** *Years of Dust*, p. 501 **Reading Maps** The Dust Bowl, p. 502 **Geography Lab** Pacific Mountains and Valleys, p. 505	**Warm-Up Activity** Designing the Second New Deal, p. 498 **Geography Question of the Day,** p. 498 **Section Activity** Making Posters, p. 500 **Bonus Activity** A Migrant's Diary, p. 502 **Wrap-Up Activity** Competing Quizzes, p. 504
Evaluation	☑ **Section 1 Review,** p. 491 ☑ **Section 2 Review,** p. 496 ☑ **Section 3 Review,** p. 504 ☑ **Chapter Survey,** pp. 506–507 **Alternative Assessment** Creating a cause-effect graphic organizer, p. 507	☑ **Answers to Section 1 Review,** p. 491 ☑ **Answers to Section 2 Review,** p. 496 ☑ **Answers to Section 3 Review,** p. 504 ☑ **Answers to Chapter Survey,** pp. 506–507 (Alternative Assessment guidelines are in the Take-Home Planner.)

Teacher's Resource Package

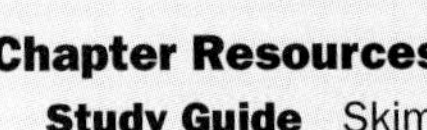

Chapter Summaries: English and Spanish, pp. 58–59

Chapter Resources Binder

Study Guide Skimming to Locate Information, p. 97

Reinforcement Summarizing Information, pp. 101–102

Chapter Resources Binder

Study Guide Reading for Details, p. 98

Skills Development Comparing Historical Interpretations, pp. 103–104

American Readings Letters of Desperation, pp. 49–50

Using Historical Documents Louis Kroll's Letter of Appeal to President Franklin D. Roosevelt, pp. 73–76

Chapter Resources Binder

Study Guide Using a Graphic Organizer, p. 99

Geography Extensions A View of California, pp. 27–28

American Readings A Sit-Down Striker, pp. 51–52

Chapter and Unit Tests Chapter 11 Tests, Forms A and B, pp. 87–90

Take-Home Planner

Introducing the Chapter Activity Connections to the Past, p. 14

Chapter In-Depth Activity Seeking Government Aid, p. 14

Reduced Views

Study Guide, p. 16

Reinforcement, p. 17

Unit 4 Answers, pp. 30–38

Reduced Views

Study Guide, p. 16

Skills Development, p. 17

American Readings, p. 18

Using Historical Documents, p. 19

Unit 4 Answers, pp. 30–38

Reduced Views

Study Guide, p. 16

Geography Extensions, p. 19

American Readings, p. 18

Unit 4 Answers, pp. 30–38

Reduced Views

Chapter Tests, p. 19

Unit 4 Answers, pp. 30–38

Alternative Assessment Guidelines for scoring the Chapter Survey activity, p. 15

Additional Resources

Wall Time Line

Unit 4 Activity

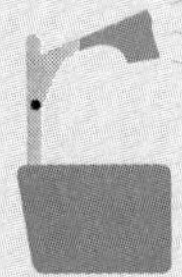

Transparency Package

Transparency 11-1 Map: Examples of New Deal Projects —use with Section 2

Transparency 11-2 A Federal Art Project—use with Section 2

Transparency Activity Book

SelecTest Testing Software

Chapter 11 Test, Forms A and B

Vital Links

Videodisc

CD-ROM

Bonus Army march (see TE p. 490)

Civilian Conservation Corps (see TE p. 493)

FDR speech on unemployment (see TE p. 495)

FDR speech on the poor (see TE p. 495)

Eleanor Roosevelt and Mary McLeod Bethune (see TE p. 500)

Oklahoma dust storm (see TE p. 502)

Migrant worker family (see TE p. 502)

Automobile factory (see TE p. 503)

General Motors strike settled (see TE p. 503)

11

Teaching Resources

- Take-Home Planner 4
  - Introducing Chapter Activity
  - Chapter In-Depth Activity
  - Alternative Assessment
- Chapter Resources Binder
- Geography Extensions
- American Readings
- Using Historical Documents
- Transparency Activities
- Wall Time Line Activities
- Chapter Summaries
- Chapter and Unit Tests
- SelecTest Test File
- Vital Links CD-ROM/Videodisc

Time Line

Keys to History

Keys to History journal writing activities are on page 506 in the Chapter Survey.

Stock Market Crash This event marked the beginning of the Depression. (p. 488)

Franklin Roosevelt promises a New Deal FDR began to put campaign promises into action. (p. 492)

The Hundred Days During FDR's first 100 days, Congress quickly enacted programs to ease the Depression. (pp. 492–493)

Tennessee Valley Authority Dam building helped develop an entire region. (pp. 493–494)

Indian Reorganization Act This law encouraged Indian tribal self-determination. (pp. 500–501)

Looking Back Veterans were scheduled to receive bonus payments in 1945.

World Link See p. 489.

Chapter Objectives

- ★ Identify the economic disasters that struck the United States in the 1920s and 1930s.
- ★ Summarize the early years of the New Deal.
- ★ Describe the last programs of the New Deal.

Chapter Overview

With the 1929 Stock Market Crash, the nation plunged into the Great Depression. A huge income gap, questionable business and banking practices, and overproduction had led to the crisis. Banks closed and millions lost jobs, farms, and homes. President Hoover hesitated to take action. Promising a "New Deal" for Americans, Franklin Roosevelt defeated Hoover in 1932.

1929–1941

Chapter 11 The Depression and New Deal

Sections

Beginning the Story with Franklin and Eleanor Roosevelt

1. The Great Depression
2. The First New Deal
3. The Second New Deal

Keys to History

BROOKLYN DAILY EAGLE
WALL ST. IN PANIC AS STOCKS CRASH
Attempt Made to Kill Italy's Crown Prince
Hollywood Fire Destroys Films Worth Millions
High Duty Group Gave $700,000 to Coolidge Drive
VANITY FAIR

1929 Stock Market Crash

1933 Franklin Roosevelt introduces New Deal bills

The Hundred Days

Tennessee Valley Authority

1934 Indian Reorganization Act

1929 1931 1933

Looking Back

WWI veterans promised a bonus **1924**

World Link

Brazil's coffee industry begins to collapse **1929**

President Roosevelt and Congress acted swiftly. Early New Deal programs such as the FDIC, AAA, NRA, and CCC helped bank depositors, farmers, business owners, and workers. To win support, Roosevelt held radio "fireside chats," while his wife, Eleanor, traveled the country, giving speeches and listening to the public. Critics charged that the New Deal gave the government too much power or did not do enough.

Responding to criticism, Roosevelt and Congress moved forward on a Second New Deal. The WPA employed millions on construction and cultural projects, the Wagner Act strengthened unions, and Social Security provided insurance for workers. Efforts to help women, African Americans, and Indians won support of those groups. However, the Depression was worsened by dust storms. It did not end until World War II.

HISTORY *Mystery*

In the 1930s thousands of families left their farms on the Great Plains, never to return. What caused this great migration?

1935
Works Progress Administration (WPA)

1935
Social Security Act

Wagner Act

1938
Congress of Industrial Organizations (CIO) founded

1935 1937 1939 1941

Looking Ahead

Roosevelt elected to his fourth term
1944

Teaching the *HISTORY Mystery*

Students will find the answer on pp. 501–503. See Chapter Survey, p. 506, for an additional question.

Time Line

Works Progress Administration Millions of Americans were put to work on construction and cultural projects. (p. 498)

Social Security Act About half the work force became eligible to receive unemployment, pensions, and other benefits. (p. 499)

Wagner Act Provisions of this law protected workers against unfair practices and strengthened the power of labor unions. (p. 499)

Organization of the CIO This association of industrial unions played a major role in the increased union activity of the 1930s. (p. 503)

Looking Ahead The only President to be elected to more than two terms, Roosevelt led the nation through the Depression and World War II.

Beginning the Story

Franklin and Eleanor Roosevelt

Wealthy, handsome, and charming, Franklin Roosevelt seemed to have it all. He and his wife, Eleanor, were the parents of five lively children. His political career was blossoming. Then in 1921 polio left him partially paralyzed. As he worked to regain physical strength, once-shy Eleanor kept his hopes of a political future alive through speeches, writings, and appearances. Their struggle strengthened them for the tasks that lay ahead as President and First Lady.

Setting the Stage Activity

Wanted: Couple to Lead a Troubled Nation

To focus on leadership qualities, have small groups write help-wanted ads for President and First Lady. Tell them that this pair will have to deal with a severe economic crisis that has left millions unemployed. Ads should list qualifications and personal qualities that the "First Couple" should possess. Conclude by having students share and compare ads.

See the Introducing the Chapter Activity, Connections to the Past, **Take-Home Planner 4,** p. 14.

History Footnote

Franklin Roosevelt was the adored only child of James Roosevelt, who died when Franklin was 18, and his wife, Sara Delano Roosevelt. His fifth cousin, Eleanor, was one of three children of Anna Hall and Elliott Roosevelt, brother of Theodore. Her mother and father had both died by the time she was 10 years old.

Franklin and Eleanor fell in love while Franklin was in college. Knowing his mother's jealous nature, Franklin told her nothing of his marriage plans until after the couple had become secretly engaged. Sara then tried to take Franklin's mind off Eleanor by getting him a job in London and taking him on a cruise. Neither scheme worked. Franklin and Eleanor married in 1905, with President Theodore Roosevelt giving his niece away.

Beginning the Story with

Franklin and Eleanor Roosevelt

On August 10, 1921, Franklin Roosevelt took three of his five children for a sailing lesson in the waters off Campobello Island, New Brunswick. On the way back to their summer house, they spotted a brushfire, dashed ashore, and beat it out with pine branches. Later, Franklin felt a bit shaky. Like his cousin Theodore Roosevelt, his remedy for feeling weak was more exercise. He challenged the children to race him to a pond for a swim before dinner.

Next morning, Franklin's head throbbed. As he walked to the bathroom to shave, his left leg crumpled beneath him. A day later, he could not sit up or stand without help. "I don't know what's the matter," he kept saying. He would soon learn that he had been struck down by polio—one of the most dreaded diseases of his day. He would never walk without help again.

"Will he ever be anything else?"

Until now, Franklin had seemed to be a man who had everything. Born to a wealthy family and gifted with good looks and charm, he had easily won the heart and hand of his distant cousin Eleanor. Those same gifts had served him well when he decided to make politics his career. Wealth and charm had no effect on polio, however. As the disease ran its devastating course, it left Franklin's lower body paralyzed and in pain. A family friend wrote:

> "He is only 39—both too old & too young for such a fell [cruel] germ to disable him. He's had a brilliant career as assistant [Secretary] of the Navy under [President] Wilson, & then a few brief weeks of . . . excitement when nominated by the Democrats for the Vice Presidency. Now he is a cripple—will he ever be anything else?"

History Bookshelf

Turner, Robyn Montana. *Dorothea Lange.* Little, Brown, 1994. Turner provides a lively account of a woman whose photographs of migrant farm workers and the urban poor helped shape the nation's understanding of the hardships faced in the Depression era. Many of Lange's most powerful photographs are included in this book.

Also of interest:

Feinberg, Barbara Silberdick. *Black Tuesday: The Stock Market Crash of 1929.* Millbrook Press, 1995.

Freedman, Russell. *Eleanor Roosevelt: A Life of Discovery.* Clarion, 1993.

Greenfield, Eloise, and Lessie Jones Little. *Childtimes: A Three-Generation Memoir.* Thomas Y. Crowell, 1979.

Stewart, Gail B. *The New Deal.* New Discovery, 1993.

That was a question that tormented Eleanor as she nursed her husband through his illness. She did everything she could to make his life as normal as possible. Still, Eleanor had grave doubts. "Do you really believe that Franklin still has a political future?" she asked Louis Howe, Roosevelt's closest political advisor. "I believe," Howe answered firmly, "that someday, Franklin will be President."

Leaning heavily on the arm of his son James, Franklin Roosevelt, with his wife Eleanor, arrives at the White House after his inauguration as President in 1933.

Patience and Persistence

The Roosevelts' lives were changed by Franklin's illness. Eleanor had always been extremely shy and lacking in self-confidence. Now, for her children's sake, she learned to swim, hike, camp, drive a car, and sail a boat. In the process, she became a more adventurous person.

Eleanor also saw that if Franklin was to have "a political future," she would have to help. "I had never done anything for a political organization before," she recalled, "nor had I ever made a speech in any sizable gathering." When bills began to pile up, she found ways to make money by giving speeches, writing magazine articles, and making guest appearances on the radio.

For the next few years, Franklin spent his energy working to regain his strength and some movement in his legs. His daughter Anna wrote:

> "It's a bit traumatic when you're fifteen . . . [to] see your father . . . struggling in heavy steel braces. And you see the sweat pouring down his face, and you hear him saying, 'I must get to the end of driveway today—all the way down the driveway.'"

As difficult as that time was, it was also, wrote Eleanor, "a blessing in disguise." Franklin's struggle, she believed, "gave him strength and courage he had not had before." It also forced him to "learn the greatest of all lessons—infinite patience and never-ending persistence." These hard lessons would serve Franklin Roosevelt well in the years ahead.

Hands-On HISTORY

Activity

Imagine that Franklin Roosevelt is not yet President, and an admirer has written to the Roosevelts asking for advice about how to overcome great personal misfortune. As either Eleanor or Franklin Roosevelt, write a brief reply. In your response, include three general guidelines for facing hard times.

Discussion

Thinking Historically

1. Was Franklin's illness a "blessing in disguise" for Eleanor? Explain. (Yes: made her more active and outgoing. No: gave her much more work to do.)

2. Why do you think Roosevelt concealed his disability? (People expected strong leaders; wanted people to feel confident in him; some were prejudiced against people with disabilities.)

3. Why might it be challenging for Eleanor to participate in politics? (Shy; had never done it before; women had only gained the right to vote in 1920 and had largely been kept out of politics.)

See the Chapter In-Depth Activity, Seeking Government Aid, **Take-Home Planner 4**, p. 14.

Teaching the Hands-On HISTORY

Point out that the Roosevelts were very different. She was shy; he was not. She was an idealist; he was a practical politician. Have students consider how each person's personality might affect what would be written.

For a journal writing activity on Franklin and Eleanor Roosevelt, see student page 506.

Introducing the Section

Vocabulary

durable goods (p. 489) goods meant to last

Warm-Up Activity

Writing Sketches

To prepare for reading about the Depression, have students imagine that the man in the picture on this page is their father. Ask them to write fictional sketches that answer these questions: Why did Dad have to sell the family car? How does the family feel about it? What might happen to the family next? Have students read their sketches aloud.

Geography Question of the Day

Ask students to imagine that an economic crisis has struck their community, causing many adults to lose their jobs. Have them list long-term effects on the community's physical appearance and population.

See the Study Guide activity in the Chapter Resources Binder, p. 97.

Section Objectives

- ★ Identify the causes of the Stock Market Crash and the Great Depression.
- ★ Describe how the Depression affected people's lives.
- ★ Summarize how the government responded to the Depression.

Teaching Resources

Take-Home Planner 4, pp. 12–19
Chapter Resources Binder
Study Guide, p. 97
Reinforcement, pp. 101–102
Skills Development
Geography Extensions
American Readings
Using Historical Documents
Transparency Activities
Chapter and Unit Tests

1. The Great Depression

Reading Guide

New Term durable goods

Section Focus The economic disasters that struck the United States in the 1920s and 1930s

1. What caused the Stock Market Crash and the Great Depression?
2. How did the Depression affect people's lives?
3. How did the government respond to the Depression?

Business began to slow in the fall of 1929. The value of stocks drifted down. The decline prompted some people to predict that the economic boom was coming to an end.

Worried investors rushed to sell stocks before the value dropped further. The more stocks they sold, the more the value of the stocks fell. Investors panicked as prices tumbled. To add to the troubles, stockbrokers demanded that people who had bought stocks on margin pay back their loans immediately.

Tuesday, October 29, 1929, was the worst day in Stock Market history. Thousands of frightened investors tried to sell stocks, but there were few buyers. The stocks sold for next to nothing. People who had put all their savings into stocks were ruined.

The Shaky Economy

The Stock Market Crash marked the beginning of the Great Depression, the worst economic crisis in United States history. Economists disagree about whether the Crash caused the Great Depression. Still, most blame basic problems in the economy.

One problem was the gap between the rich and everyone else. In 1929 just 5 percent of Americans earned 33 percent of the nation's personal income. After the Crash, the rich

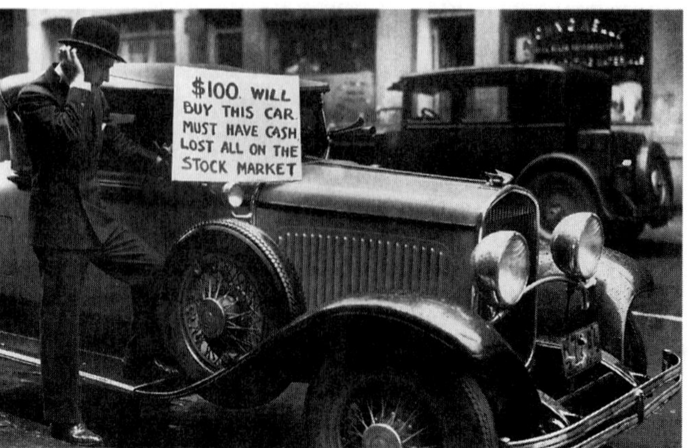

BUY THIS CAR
MUST HAVE CASH
LOST ALL ON THE

This man was lucky. When his stock became worthless, he put his shiny new car up for sale. Shortly after this picture was taken, he sold the car and repaid the money he had borrowed to buy the stocks.

History Footnote

The Depression was worldwide and predated 1929 in some places. Germany, Austria, Italy, and Poland had experienced widespread poverty since the end of World War I. After the Crash, United States bankers demanded repayment of loans they had made to other countries. Congress passed high tariffs to protect United States businesses. Other nations did the same to protect themselves. The resulting drop in trade only made matters worse. Prices for farm produce fell as tariffs made international trade unprofitable, and farmers everywhere suffered. Economic disaster led to political turmoil in some nations. Italy and Germany looked to dictators to lead them out of trouble. In Japan militarists argued that only imperialism could bring economic strength.

stopped spending, which hurt businesses that depended on them to buy and invest.

Another problem was poor business practices. For example, some large companies bought small companies just to take their profits. There was not enough money left in the small companies to help them through hard times.

A third problem was overproduction. Factories had been making **durable goods**—goods meant to last, like machinery and locomotives—faster than they could be sold. Now factories slowed production and laid off workers. People without jobs had less money to spend in stores, and stores had less money to buy goods from factories. So, more factories had to cut back on production.

Bank failures Banking practices were a problem, too. When customers deposited money, banks kept part of it in cash and invested the rest, sometimes in stocks. As the value of stocks fell, banks lost money.

When depositors saw a bank in trouble, they lost confidence in their own banks and withdrew their money. If a lot of people tried to withdraw money at once—a situation called a "run" on a bank—the bank might not have enough money on hand. Banks that could not pay all their depositors had to close down.

Unemployment

As banks and businesses failed, factory workers and clerks, salespeople and railroad engineers, miners and nurses lost their jobs. At the peak of the Great Depression, one worker out of four was unemployed.

People without work felt fear, shame, and despair. In 1936 a 12-year-old Chicago boy wrote to the Roosevelts:

"I want to tell you about my family. My father hasn't worked for 5 months. . . . We haven't paid 4 months rent, Everyday the landlord rings the door bell, we don't open the door for him. We are afraid that [we] will be put out, been put out before, and don't want to happen again. . . . My father he staying home. All the time he's crying because he can't find work. I talk him why are you crying daddy, and daddy said why shouldn't I cry when there is nothing in the house. I feel sorry for him. That night I couldn't sleep. The next morning I wrote this letter to you. . . . Please answer right away because we need it. [We] will starve Thank you."

The coffee crash The Depression struck other nations as well as the United States. Brazil's coffee industry was already troubled by overproduction. Then, during the Depression, the demand for coffee in the United States and other countries dropped. Coffee prices fell from 22¢ a pound in 1929 to 8¢ in 1931. Even so, millions of sacks of coffee sat in Brazilian warehouses. Brazil's government burned and dumped surplus coffee and destroyed some plantations, hoping to raise prices.

A popular American song of the time described Brazil's coffee crash:

"You can't get cherry soda
'Cause they've got to sell their quota,
And the way things are I guess they never will,
They've got a zillion tons of coffee in Brazil!"

Developing the Section

Discussion

Checking Understanding

1. How bad was the gap between the rich and the poor in 1929? (Very bad—5 percent were rich, earning 33 percent of nation's income.)

2. What happened when factories slowed production? (Workers were laid off and thus had less money to spend. Stores had less money to buy goods, so factories cut back further on production.)

Stimulating Critical Thinking

3. Why did unemployed people feel ashamed? (Had believed anyone willing to work could find a job; could not support families.)

Teaching the World Link

Explain that Brazilians had so much unsold coffee that a visitor to Brazil supposedly could get nothing else to drink. Ask students why they think the song was popular with Americans. (Took comfort in knowing that others suffered too; needed humor to keep going.)

See the Reinforcement activity in the Chapter Resources Binder, pp. 101–102.

Section Activity

Economic Problems Then and Now

To compare past and present economic problems, have students create a bulletin board. They should divide it into two sides, titled *The Depression* and *Today,* with four rows each titled *Unemployment, Homelessness, How People Help Themselves,* and *Government Response.* They may fill in the rows with data, photographs, drawings, news articles, poems, quotations, etc.

Bonus Activity

Hooverville Skits

To focus on Depression hardships, have groups present skits depicting an evening in a "Hooverville." Have each student write a brief character sketch for his or her role—a city person riding the rails, a member of a family that lost its farm, and so on. Characters can describe what has happened to them, offer their opinions of President Hoover, and discuss hopes.

Vital Links

Bonus Army march (Picture) Unit 5, Side 1, Search 13569

See also Unit 5 Explore CD-ROM location 92.

History Footnote

Although movie tickets in the 1930s were generally 25¢ for adults and 10¢ for children, many Americans had to scrimp and save to come up with the money. Desperate to escape life's realities for a few hours, they were willing to do so. In a nation of 127 million people, an average of 60 million to 75 million movie tickets were sold each week during the depths of the Depression.

Gangster films, musicals, and "screwball" comedies were among the most popular types of movies. Although many of the films churned out by Hollywood were highly forgettable, the 1930s are called "the golden age of movies" for classics such as *King Kong* (1932), *Snow White and the Seven Dwarfs* (1937), *The Wizard of Oz* (1939), and *Gone With the Wind* (1939).

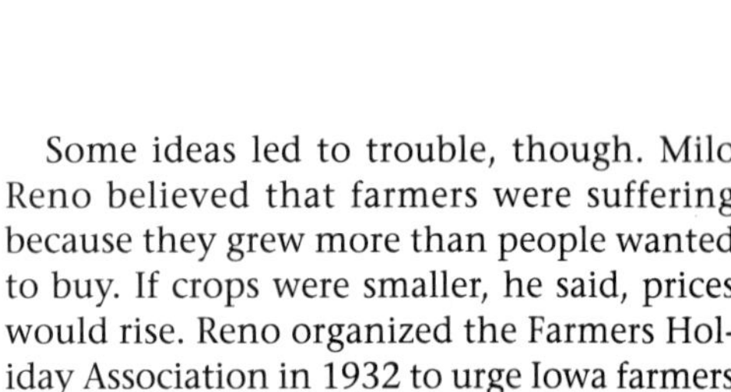

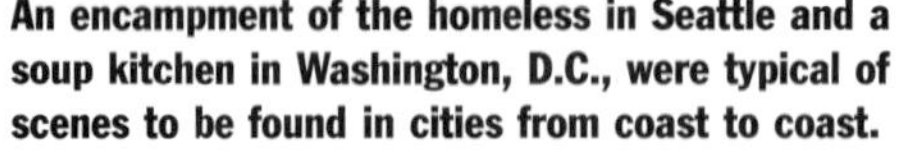

An encampment of the homeless in Seattle and a soup kitchen in Washington, D.C., were typical of scenes to be found in cities from coast to coast.

Looking for Help

Without work, many people were homeless and hungry. Communities tried to help, but they were not prepared for the numbers of people who needed help. When towns and cities set up soup kitchens, people lined up for blocks.

To get money to aid the poor, cities cut back other services. Some took money from teachers' salaries. Others just closed the schools. Still, local governments could not stop all the suffering.

People help themselves Some people found ways to help themselves and one another. For example, in the countryside people held "penny auctions." When a court ordered a sheriff to auction off farms to pay farmers' debts, friends and neighbors would frighten serious bidders away. Then they would bid just pennies. When the auctions were over, they would "sell" the farms back to their original owners for a few coins.

Some ideas led to trouble, though. Milo Reno believed that farmers were suffering because they grew more than people wanted to buy. If crops were smaller, he said, prices would rise. Reno organized the Farmers Holiday Association in 1932 to urge Iowa farmers to stop growing so much.

Holiday members set up roadblocks to stop other farmers from bringing their hogs and milk to market. Fights broke out. The governor had to call out the National Guard to open the roads.

People on the move Many homeless "rode the rails" looking for work. Too poor to buy tickets, they hopped onto freight trains and hid from railroad detectives. Single women disguised themselves as men to protect themselves.

Some families piled their things onto the family car or truck and took to the highway, looking for work. Many became migrant workers, moving from farm to farm, planting and harvesting crops with the seasons.

History Footnote
Two Bonus Army veterans were killed and dozens more were injured in Washington. Some veterans had brought their wives and children along, and they too were caught up in the violence. Franklin Roosevelt was not alone in his shocked and angry reaction. One newspaper said, "Routing men, women and children out of bed, drenching them with tear gas, ruthlessly burning their poor shelters and then driving cripples, babies, pregnant women up a steep hill at bayonet point. . . . Thus did the government persecute those hungry and ragged men it sent fourteen years ago into the trenches at the risk of death."

"Hoovervilles" Other homeless people huddled together in shacks made of cardboard, wooden boxes, and rusty old cars. They called their shantytowns "Hoovervilles," after President Hoover.

The President had not caused the Depression, but people blamed him. When people covered themselves with newspapers to keep warm, they called them "Hoover blankets." They turned their empty pockets inside out and called them "Hoover flags."

The Bonus Army As unemployment soared in 1932, World War I veterans looked to Washington for help. Congress had promised to pay them $1,000 bonuses in 1945. Instead, Texas Congressman Wright Patman proposed paying the bonuses immediately. When Hoover said the government did not have the money, nearly 20,000 veterans marched on Washington, D.C. Newspapers called them the "Bonus Army."

Hoover refused to meet with the veterans. He ordered General Douglas MacArthur to drive them out of Washington. MacArthur led the cavalry against the veterans' camp and burned it to the ground.

Franklin Roosevelt, who was then governor of New York, told a friend that he had once greatly admired Hoover. Now, he said, "there is nothing inside the man but jelly!"

Hoover Fights the Depression

Seeing that people were losing confidence in him, President Hoover tried to restore faith. "Recovery," he promised, "is just around the corner."

The President called on business and labor to cooperate. He asked business leaders to keep up jobs and wages. He asked labor leaders to stop demanding better wages and hours. To create jobs, he spent federal money on construction. To give people money to spend, he asked Congress to cut taxes.

Hoover hesitated to do more, however. He feared that if the government did too much, it would become too powerful. Worse, people might stop helping themselves.

The 1932 Election

As the 1932 election approached, Republicans nominated Hoover again. Their convention was a gloomy affair, though. They knew the public blamed them for hard times.

The Democrats were optimistic. They nominated Franklin Roosevelt. Warm and enthusiastic, Roosevelt believed that, unlike Hoover, he could inspire public confidence. He told cheering delegates:

> "Republican leaders . . . have failed in
> national vision, because in disaster
> they have held out no hope. . . .
> I pledge you, I pledge myself to
> a new deal for the American people."

Roosevelt said that he had no magic cures for the nation, but he would put the government to work to find solutions. Fifty-seven percent of the voters cast their ballots for Roosevelt and his "New Deal." He won the electoral votes of all but six states. Voters also gave the Democrats a majority in both houses of Congress.

1. Section Review

1. Define **durable goods.**
2. What were three economic conditions that contributed to the Depression?
3. What measures did Hoover take to fight the Depression? Why did he not do more?
4. **Critical Thinking** Explain the following statement: When a factory lays off a large part of its work force or shuts down entirely, an entire community can suffer.

Closing the Section

Wrap-Up Activity

Writing a Roosevelt Speech
To clarify how matters stood in 1932, have students imagine they are Roosevelt and write the rest of his speech to the convention delegates. Speeches should summarize key events up to this point and offer specific evaluations of Hoover's actions. Encourage students to try to capture Roosevelt's confidence. Conclude by having them present their speeches to the class.

Section Review Answers

1. Definition: *durable goods* (489)

2. Value of stocks fell, the Stock Market Crash, gap between the rich and others, poor business practices, overproduction, bank failures, unemployment.

3. Hoover promised recovery, asked business leaders to keep up jobs and wages, asked labor leaders to stop making demands, spent money on construction, and asked Congress to cut taxes. He did not do more because he feared the government would become too powerful and people would stop helping themselves.

4. Laid-off factory workers will have less money to spend. Storekeepers and service providers like doctors will then take in less money and may have to lay off employees. Children whose parents are out of work will suffer.

Introducing the Section

Vocabulary

pension (p. 496) retirement income

Warm-Up Activity

Offering "New Deal" Solutions

To prepare for reading about the New Deal, have pairs imagine themselves as Roosevelt's advisors. Each pair should write a proposal for a program to submit to Congress to help a particular group or solve a problem. Have pairs share their ideas and then read to see whether they resemble New Deal programs.

Geography Question of the Day

Tell students that one New Deal program sought to develop the economic life of a seven-state region centered on the Tennessee River Basin. Have them use the maps on pp. R4–R7 to list states likely to be affected. (Virginia, North Carolina, Georgia, Kentucky, Tennessee, Alabama, Mississippi.) Ask what kind of river project could serve so many states.

Section Objectives

- ★ Summarize the actions that Roosevelt and Congress took to fight the Depression.
- ★ Describe how Franklin and Eleanor Roosevelt won public support.
- ★ Identify critics of the New Deal and explain their criticisms.

Teaching Resources

Take-Home Planner 4, pp. 12–19
Chapter Resources Binder
Study Guide, p. 98
Reinforcement
Skills Development, pp. 103–104
Geography Extensions
American Readings, pp. 49–50
Using Historical Documents
Transparency Activities
Chapter and Unit Tests

2. The First New Deal

Reading Guide

New Term **pension**

Section Focus **The early years of the New Deal**

1. What actions did Roosevelt and Congress take to fight the Depression?
2. How did the Roosevelts win public support?
3. Who criticized the New Deal, and why?

By February 1933 the banking system had nearly collapsed. Over 5,000 banks had failed since the Crash, and more were failing each day. People began to think it was safer to keep their savings in a mattress than in a bank. Still, Franklin Roosevelt could do nothing until his inauguration.

March 4 was a chilly day. With his wife Eleanor beside him, Roosevelt stood before the Capitol Building. Placing his hand on a 300-year-old family Bible, he took the oath of office. Then in solemn tones he gave his first address as President. Radio networks broadcast his reassuring message across the nation:

> "This great nation will endure as it has endured, will revive and will prosper. So first of all, let me assert my firm belief that the only thing we have to fear is fear itself."

The First Hundred Days

To bring about the "New Deal" he had promised, the President and Congress acted swiftly during the first three months. Historians call this time "the Hundred Days." Because the Democrats controlled the presidency and the Senate and the House of Representatives, they were able to set New Deal programs in motion quickly.

Roosevelt's first act was to stop the run on banks. On March 6 he declared a bank holiday, ordering all banks to close. Once the government was sure a bank was sound, it could reopen.

To restore confidence in banks, Roosevelt and Congress created the Federal Deposit Insurance Corporation (FDIC). This agency would inspect banks and insure depositors' accounts. Now, Roosevelt promised, it was safer to "keep your money in a reopened bank than under the mattress."

Helping farmers During the Hundred Days the President and Congress also tackled problems in agriculture and industry. In May Congress passed the Agricultural Adjustment Act. The act created an agency—the Agricultural Adjustment Administration (AAA)—that would encourage farmers to grow less by paying them to farm fewer acres. The program's supporters expected that lower production would increase farm prices.

To help farmers who were struggling to pay their debts, another new agency, the Farm Credit Administration, provided low-cost farm loans. Home owners received similar help through the Home Owners' Loan Corporation.

Helping business and labor To help industry, Congress passed the National Industrial Recovery Act, which created the

History Footnote

The First New Deal created more programs than can be described in the section. They included the Federal Emergency Relief Administration (FERA), which channeled federal funds through state agencies that then provided cash and groceries to the neediest Americans; the Civil Works Administration (CWA), a one-year program that provided employment in small-scale public projects at federal expense; the Securities and Exchange Commission (SEC), which protected the public from investing in unsafe stocks; and the Federal Housing Administration (FHA), which insured bank loans for home construction and repair. The SEC and FHA, as well as the FDIC and TVA, are still in operation.

National Recovery Administration (NRA). Its goal was to help businesspeople earn reasonable profits while workers earned decent wages.

Promising not to prosecute businesses under antitrust laws, the NRA encouraged them to work together to draw up codes of fair competition. The codes set prices, production quotas, wages, and working conditions. Companies that joined the program displayed a blue eagle with the slogan "We Do Our Part."

FDR thought that if businesspeople were allowed to band together, workers should be, too. The National Industrial Recovery Act guaranteed workers the right to collective bargaining, the process by which unions and employers reach agreement on wages and working conditions. Employers who displayed the blue eagle agreed to minimum hourly wages and a maximum number of hours in the workday.

The National Industrial Recovery Act established another agency, the Public Works Administration (PWA). The PWA provided funds for construction projects—roads, dams, bridges, and warships. It helped businesses put people to work so that they would have money to spend.

Perhaps the most popular program of the first Hundred Days was the Civilian Conservation Corps (CCC). The CCC employed thousands of young men between the ages of 18 and 25. They were stationed in camps across the country, improving public lands by planting trees, clearing trails, and fighting forest fires.

The Tennessee Valley Authority

Most New Deal programs were intended to help the nation recover from the Depression. In May 1933, however, Roosevelt and Congress introduced a measure to help ward off future depressions. They created the Tennessee Valley Authority (TVA) to develop the economic life of an entire region.

The Tennessee Valley suffered from severe flooding. The area's topsoil was thin and its forests overlogged. The people of the valley

The young men of the CCC, like those in this reforestation camp, were known as "Roosevelt's Tree Army." They planted millions of trees from Canada to Texas. The NRA blue eagle was based on an Indian figure, the thunderbird.

Developing the Section

Discussion

Checking Understanding

1. Whom did the NRA try to help? (Business owners and workers.)

2. What did CCC workers do? (Improved public lands by planting trees, clearing trails, fighting forest fires.)

Stimulating Critical Thinking

3. Why might the AAA be more successful than the Farmers Holiday Association? (see p. 490) (AAA paid farmers for producing less, while the Holiday Association relied on voluntary action.)

Bonus Activity

Creating Political Cartoons

To help students evaluate the First New Deal, have them create political cartoons. Half should support the New Deal while half criticize it. An image students might use is "alphabet soup," a term used to refer to initials of New Deal programs.

Vital Links

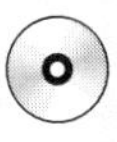

Civilian Conservation Corps (Movie) Unit 5, Side 1, Search 12525, Play to 13469

See also Unit 5 Explore CD-ROM location 75.

Teaching the Reading Maps

Ask students why Alaska and Hawaii are not shown on the map (not yet states). Point out that the map shows a small sampling of New Deal projects. **Answer to Reading Maps:** Statements should indicate understanding that some New Deal programs resulted in permanent contributions to the landscape, ranging from the practical to the artistic.

Section Activity

A Radio Panel Discussion

To focus on opposition to New Deal programs, have students act out a radio panel discussion. Assign roles: Eleanor Roosevelt, a Republican senator, Huey Long, Francis Townsend, Upton Sinclair, and a moderator. Assign the rest of the class to serve as farmers, factory workers, business owners, and elderly persons in the audience. Panelists should prepare statements promoting solutions to the Depression and criticizing other solutions. The audience should prepare probing questions to ask panelists.

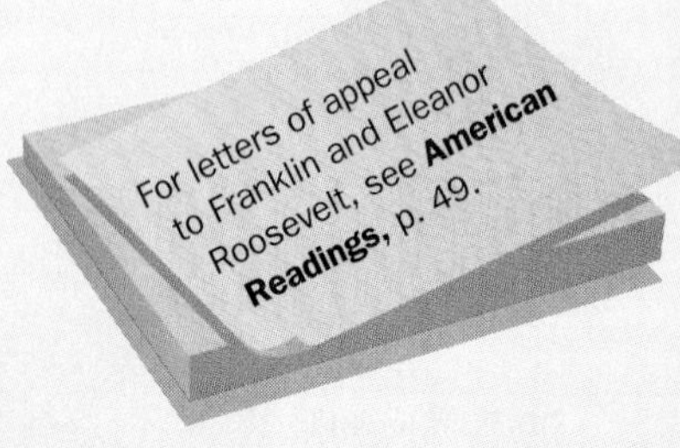

Tips for Teaching

Visual Learners

Visual learners can use the illustrations on p. 494 to strengthen understanding of effects of the New Deal. Have them find similarities and differences in the scales, styles, and purposes of the projects. They might also draw, paint, diagram, or make three-dimensional models of a project, based on what they see in the pictures.

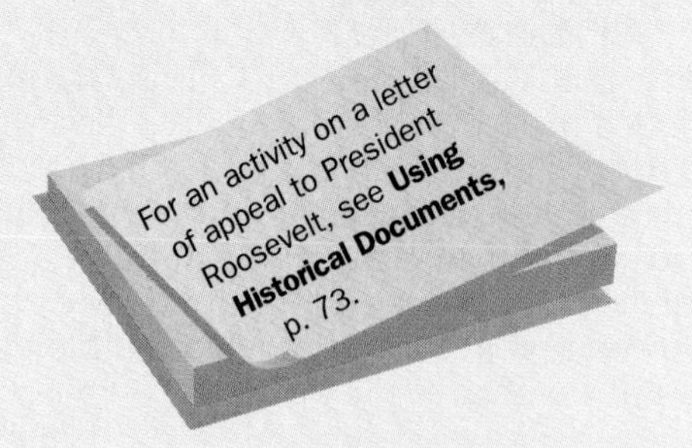

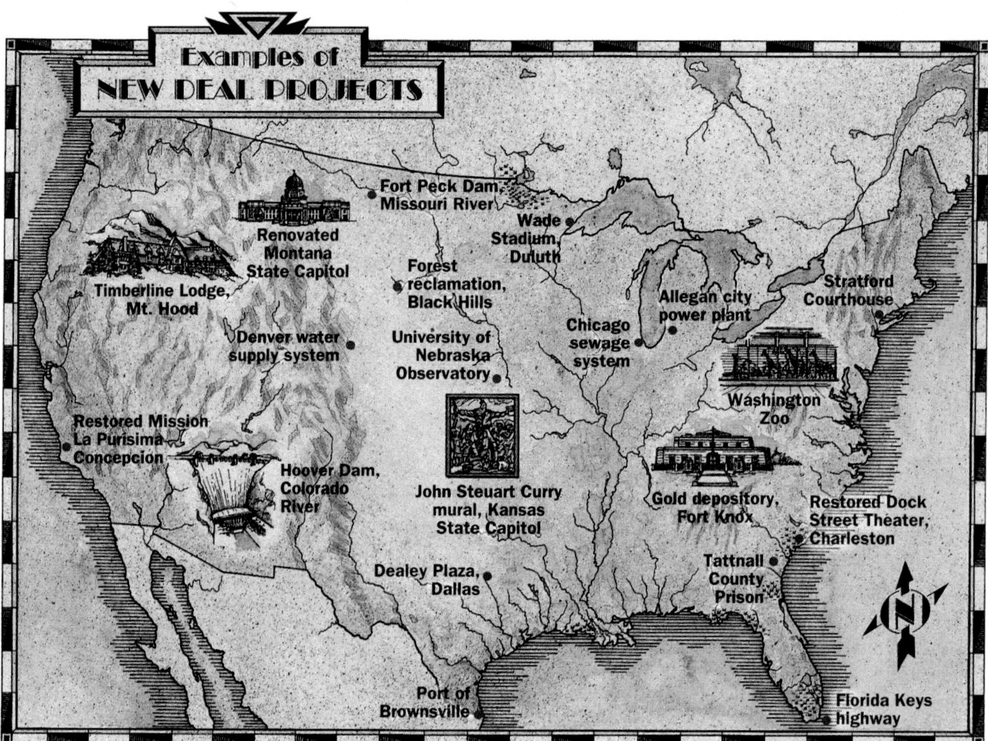

Reading Maps

Use the information on the map to help you write a statement about the lasting effects of New Deal projects.

had a hard time earning a living. In addition, like most rural areas at that time, in the Tennessee Valley few farms had electricity. Yet the Tennessee and other rivers could be made to supply plenty of waterpower for electricity.

The TVA planned to develop the entire area. Over the next 20 years they improved 5 existing dams and built 20 new ones. The TVA employed thousands of workers. The dams they built provided flood control and a reliable supply of water for irrigation, drinking, and recreation. The TVA also restored the region's soil and its forests. TVA power plants carried electricity to people in seven states.

Roosevelt Reaches Out

To inspire public confidence, Roosevelt explained programs like the TVA over the radio. He wanted to give his talks a personal touch. He imagined that he was speaking to a family in its living room, even though he was broadcasting to millions. Roosevelt called his talks "fireside chats." Listening to the fireside chats, many people grew to trust Roosevelt as they would a friend.

Roosevelt also wanted people to feel that he was strong enough to lead the nation out of the Depression. Polio had paralyzed him from the waist down, but he wore braces that

History Footnote

Actually, Roosevelt did not coin the term *fireside chat.* A CBS press release used the term before the President's radio speech of May 7, 1933. The press, the public, and eventually the President picked it up.

At least a dozen writers contributed to Roosevelt's speeches over the years, but the product always reflected the President's own character, convictions, and spirit. One writer remembered a time when Roosevelt asked him and two others to prepare drafts for an upcoming address. The President listened to the drafts and then "stretched himself on a couch and with his eyes on the ceiling dictated his own version . . . culling the best ideas that had been submitted and putting them in his own way." In addition, Roosevelt frequently ad libbed during his live radio broadcasts.

gave the impression that he could stand and walk. The back platform of his train car had a podium with a harness so that he could stand when he gave speeches.

Eleanor Roosevelt Although she was much shier than her husband, Mrs. Roosevelt also learned to demonstrate her strength and caring. She traveled thousands of miles every year, giving speeches, listening to the public, and inspecting conditions in coal mines and prisons and at dams.

Mrs. Roosevelt reached many people through her newspaper column, "My Day," in which she explained issues and also showed the human side of life in the White House. Many praised the First Lady's political role. Others condemned it. "Now we have a pair of Presidents," someone said. That was not true, but Franklin and Eleanor knew that in their own way they were a powerful team.

Critics of the New Deal

Despite the Roosevelts' popularity, not everyone supported the New Deal. Some critics charged that the government had given itself more power than the framers of the Constitution intended.

In Congress Southern Democrats sometimes joined forces with Republicans to block New Deal legislation, with all its agencies and regulations. They drew support from owners of small businesses who thought New Deal programs favored big business. At the same time, wealthy businesspeople and conservative politicians feared that the New Deal would give farmers and labor too much power. They formed the American Liberty League to work against it.

New ways to distribute wealth While some people blamed the government for exercising too much power, other critics

Hands-On HISTORY

Holding a fireside chat "My friends, I want to talk for a few minutes with the people of the United States about banking." That is how President Roosevelt began his first "fireside chat" on Sunday, March 12, 1933. In the years that followed, Roosevelt's radio broadcasts went a long way toward calming peoples' fears and winning support for the New Deal.

Activity Put yourself in the President's place. Write and present a two-minute chat.

1. Choose a New Deal program to talk about—one you have read about in this text or in another source.
2. Find out the purpose and main features of the program. Do library research if you need to.
3. Write a script. Explain how the program will help people. Aim for a friendly, reassuring tone.
4. Rehearse your chat, then read it aloud or make an audiotape and play it for the class. Afterward, ask the class what aspect of the chat inspired faith in the future.

A fireside chat, 1938

Discussion

Checking Understanding

1. What were the TVA's achievements? (Jobs created; dams for flood control, reliable supply of water and electric power; restored soil and forests.)

Stimulating Critical Thinking

2. Why do you suppose some did not like having "a pair of Presidents"? (Felt only elected officials should influence policy; disagreed with Eleanor's ideas; felt threatened by strong woman.)

Teaching the Hands-On HISTORY

To avoid many chats on one program, have groups write chats, with one member delivering each group's chat. Assign different programs to different groups or monitor choices and adjust as needed for variety.

Vital Links

FDR speech on unemployment (Movie) Unit 5, Side 1, Search 10142, Play to 10687

See also Unit 5 Explore CD-ROM location 68.

FDR speech on the poor (Movie) Unit 5, Side 1, Search 10691, Play to 11797

See also Unit 5 Explore CD-ROM location 69.

Closing the Section

Wrap-Up Activity

Letters to the Editor

To elicit students' own responses to the First New Deal, have them write letters to the *New York Times* responding to that newspaper's statement quoted on p. 496. Encourage students to put themselves in the shoes of individuals much like themselves in 1935. Have them explain why they agree or disagree with the newspaper's assessment of the President and his programs.

Section Review

Answers

1. Definition: *pension* (496)

2. Created the FDIC to inspect banks and insure depositors' accounts.

3. Answers will vary, depending on which program students choose. See pages 492, 493, and 494 for information. For example, the idea behind PWA was to put people to work so that they would have money to spend.

4. Their own situations had not been noticeably improved by New Deal programs; the crisis shook their faith in government and the economy, making them open to radical ideas.

History Footnote

Cocky, colorful Huey Long rose from farm boy to political powerhouse. Long favored catchy slogans like "Every man a king." He called himself "Kingfish" after a pompous radio character. However, Long was no buffoon. He built a powerful political machine in Louisiana, based on the support of the poor farmers who viewed him as their faithful friend. Elected to the U.S. Senate in 1930, only two years after being elected Louisiana's governor, Long refused to resign as governor until a hand-picked successor was elected to replace him in 1932.

Long, who supported Roosevelt at first, dreamed of replacing him. Long even wrote a book called *My First Days in the White House* (1935) in which he described such fantasies as offering "former" President Roosevelt a cabinet position.

"For gosh sakes, here comes Mrs. Roosevelt!" exclaims the astonished coal miner in this cartoon.

Drawing by Robt. Day; © 1933, 1961 The New Yorker Magazine, Inc.

said it did not go far enough. Their schemes attracted many of the desperately poor.

Senator Huey Long of Louisiana accused "Prince Franklin" of going along with the rich and powerful while neglecting the poor. Long gained followers with his "Share Our Wealth" plan. Under Long's plan, government would take surplus money from the wealthy and give everyone else land and an income. Even after an assassin gunned him down in 1935, Long's ideas lingered on.

Francis Townsend, a doctor from California, had another plan. He proposed that all citizens quit working at age 60 and receive a **pension**—retirement income—of $200 a month. To help the economy, people would be required to spend every penny of their pensions. Thousands of Townsend clubs sprang up to promote the plan.

Father Charles Coughlin, a Catholic priest, attracted millions to his weekly radio broadcasts from Detroit. He blamed bankers for the Depression. The government, he said, should take over the banks. People turned away from Coughlin, however, when he began to preach hatred of Jews. The Catholic Church ordered him to stop broadcasting.

Upton Sinclair, author of *The Jungle*, promoted socialism as a cure for the Depression. When he ran for governor of California in 1934, he proposed state-owned farms and factories. Farmers would trade their food for factory goods and vice versa, creating a barter system. Sinclair did not win the election, but nearly a million people voted for him.

Supreme Court Rulings

By the beginning of 1935, the New Deal seemed to be making a difference. Employment and production were up slightly. The *New York Times* said, "No President in so short a time has inspired so much hope."

Then in early 1935 a series of cases challenging New Deal programs began to reach the Supreme Court. In deciding the cases, the Court said that some programs stepped beyond the Constitution.

One case involved the NRA. The Court ruled that the National Industrial Recovery Act gave the executive and legislative branches too much power over the economy. Thus, the Court struck down one of the most important acts of the Hundred Days.

Roosevelt had once advised, "Take a method and try it. If it fails, try another. But above all, try something." It was time, Roosevelt saw, for him to try something new.

2. Section Review

1. Define **pension.**

2. How did Roosevelt restore confidence in banks?

3. Choose one of the following programs and explain how Roosevelt expected it to help the nation out of the Depression: AAA, NRA, PWA, CCC, and TVA.

4. Critical Thinking Why do you think people were attracted to the ideas of Long, Townsend, Coughlin, and Sinclair?

(*Answers continued from side margin*)
Might ask writers of source B: What are negative aspects of capitalism that the New Deal eliminated, and how did it do so? In what ways did Roosevelt show concern for the "forgotten man"? (c) Accept reasonable answers based on knowledge of the New Deal. Opinions should be supported with facts.

For further application, have students do the Applying Skills activity in the Chapter Survey (p. 506).

If students need to review the skill, use the Skills Development transparency and activity in the **Chapter Resources Binder**, pp. 103-104.

Skill Lab

Skill Tips

- An opinion that is stated as if it were a proven fact is still an opinion.
- Many historical questions have no "right" answer. Historical interpretations may differ and yet be reasonable.

Thinking Critically

Comparing Historical Interpretations

Soon after Roosevelt took office, a friend told him that if he succeeded in bringing the nation out of the Depression, he would go down in history as the greatest President. If he failed, however, he would be known as the worst. "If I fail," Roosevelt replied, "I shall be the last one."

Question to Investigate

Was the New Deal a success?

Procedure

In this Skill Lab, you will be comparing two historical interpretations.

1 Summarize the interpretations.
a. How does the writer of A view the New Deal? Explain.
b. How do the writers of B view the New Deal? Explain.

2 Identify how the writers support their interpretations.
a. What statements of fact, if any, does the writer of A offer? What opinions?
b. What statements of fact, if any, do the writers of B offer? What opinions?

3 Compare the interpretations.
a. In what ways do A and B disagree?
b. To investigate whether the New Deal was a success, what are two questions you might ask the writer of A? The writers of B?
c. Which interpretation do you think makes more sense? Explain.

Sources to Use

A "The New Deal failed to solve the problem of depression, it failed to extend equality and generally countenanced [allowed] racial discrimination and segregation. It failed generally to make business more responsible to the social welfare. . . . The New Deal assisted the middle and upper sectors [classes] of society . . . even at the cost of injuring the lower sectors."

From Barton J. Bernstein, *Towards a New Past: Dissenting Essays in American History* (1968)

B "[Roosevelt] purged American capitalism of some of its worst abuses so that it might be saved from itself. He may even have headed off a more radical swing to the left by what was mistakenly condemned as 'socialism.'. . .

"Roosevelt, like Jefferson, provided reform without a bloody revolution. . . . He was upbraided [scolded] by the left-wing radicals for not going far enough; by the right-wing radicals for going too far. . . . He was in fact Hamiltonian in his espousal [support] of big government, but Jeffersonian in his concern for the 'forgotten man.'"

From Thomas A. Bailey and David M. Kennedy, *The American Pageant* (D. C. Heath, 1991)

Introducing the Skill Lab

Remind students that writing about history involves interpreting the past. A *historical interpretation* offers an opinion about an event or person. It is usually supported by statements of fact and other opinions.

Skill Lab Answers

1. (a) Failure—lists several things the New Deal failed to accomplish. (b) Success—implies that the New Deal struck the right balance.

2. (a) All are opinions stated as if they were facts but not backed up with statistics or other factual information. (b) Two statements of fact: there was no bloody revolution; Roosevelt was scolded by various people. All other statements are opinions.

3. (a) They disagree in all ways; A has nothing good to say about the New Deal, while B has nothing bad to say. (b) Questions should seek concrete evidence to back up claims. Might ask writer of source A: What are examples of how the New Deal allowed racial discrimination and segregation? What specific aspects of the New Deal injured lower sectors of society, and how?

(Answers continued in top margin)

Introducing the Section

Warm-Up Activity

Designing the Second New Deal

To focus on problems after the Hundred Days, have groups review the First New Deal. Ask who might have been left out of these programs, or who still might need help. Have them suggest programs to help these people. They can compare their suggestions with the Second New Deal as they read.

Geography Question of the Day

Have students recall what they know about the Great Plains (see pp. 241–243 and 346). Ask them to write short paragraphs predicting what might happen to the Great Plains during an extended drought.

Teaching the

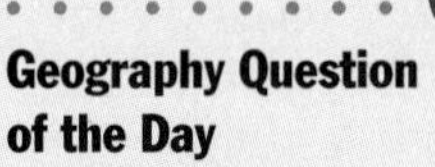

Point of View

Ask what Flanagan says plays could be about (tenements). What does she hope such plays would do? (Make people aware of the problem and move them to support better housing.) What does Dies argue that plays should not be about and why? (Should not show workers as heroes and the rich as villains because the rich pay taxes that support plays.) Ask whether public art should be regulated, and point out that this issue is hotly debated today.

Section Objectives

- ★ Describe the programs that Congress passed to expand the New Deal.
- ★ Identify groups of supporters that Roosevelt won for the Democratic Party.
- ★ Describe the problems besides economic ills that faced the nation in the 1930s.

Teaching Resources

Take-Home Planner 4, pp. 12–19
Chapter Resources Binder
Study Guide, p. 99
Reinforcement
Skills Development
Geography Extensions, pp. 27–28
American Readings, pp. 51–52
Using Historical Documents
Transparency Activities
Chapter and Unit Tests, pp. 87–90

3. The Second New Deal

Reading Guide

Section Focus **The last programs of the New Deal**

1. **What programs did Congress pass to expand the New Deal?**
2. **What supporters did Roosevelt win for the Democratic Party?**
3. **What problems besides economic ills faced the nation in the 1930s?**

The quick actions of the President and Congress during the Hundred Days gave Americans hope but did not cure the Depression. New Deal programs still did not reach many who needed help, so Roosevelt vowed to expand them. The Second New Deal—programs that became law after a new Congress met in 1935—included many people who had been left out of the earlier programs.

Broadening the New Deal

In 1935 the President recommended that the government spend more to put the jobless to work on projects of lasting value to the nation. To create the jobs, Congress voted to put more money into public works. Some money went to existing programs such as the CCC, and some to new programs such as the National Youth Administration, which provided jobs for young people.

Congress also created the Works Progress Administration (WPA), which was to employ millions. Many were put to work on construction projects such as schools, libraries, hospitals, roads, sewer systems, and airports.

The WPA gave a boost to culture, as well. It hired musicians to give music lessons and performances. Writers created state guidebooks, artists painted public murals, and actors brought theater to remote towns. WPA workers also collected the oral histories of men and women born into slavery before the Civil War.

Point of View

Should public funds support the arts?

One WPA effort, the Federal Theater Project, ran into opposition. Its director, Hallie Flanagan, hoped that drama could help solve social problems:

> "Could we, through the power of the theatre, spotlight the tenements and thus help in the plan to build decent houses for all people? Could we . . . carry music and plays to children in city parks, and art galleries to little towns? Were not happy people at work the greatest bulwark [defense] of democracy?"

Speaking for opponents of the project, Senator Martin Dies objected to using public money for political purposes:

> "Do you not also think that since the Federal Theater Project is an agency of the government and that all of our people support it through their tax money, . . . that no play should ever be produced which undertakes to portray the interests of one class [workers] to the disadvantage of another class [the wealthy]?"

Should government support the arts? That issue is as hotly debated today as it was during WPA times.

History Footnote

"They've got to eat just like other people." Harry Hopkins, WPA director, was referring to the writers, artists, musicians, and actors employed by the WPA's cultural programs. One such program, the Federal Art Project, produced 2,566 murals, 17,744 sculptures, 108,099 paintings, and 35,000 original posters between 1935 and 1943.

Such statistics meant little to most families in rural areas. It was another agency of the Second New Deal—the Rural Electrification Administration (REA)—that revolutionized their lives. The REA lent money to electric companies to put up power lines in farm areas. When the REA was established in 1935, about 10 percent of farm homes had electric service. By 1940 electricity was flowing to one-third of all farm homes, and by 1945, almost one-half.

The Wagner Act In July 1935 Congress passed the National Labor Relations Act. Known as the Wagner Act—after Senator Robert F. Wagner, who introduced it—it strengthened the power of labor unions.

The Wagner Act helped workers by outlawing unfair practices. Employers could no longer refuse to bargain with union representatives or prevent workers from joining unions. The act set up the National Labor Relations Board (NLRB) to oversee union elections and collective bargaining.

Social Security Probably the hardest battle of the Second New Deal was fought over the Social Security Act. Many people opposed such a plan because of its costs to business.

Roosevelt wanted everyone to be included, however. "I see no reason why every child, from the day he is born, shouldn't be a member of the social security system," he told Frances Perkins, Secretary of Labor and the first woman ever appointed to a President's cabinet.

Perkins knew that many people were against such a sweeping bill. In 1935 she drew up the first Social Security Act. The plan was a form of insurance. Employers and workers would pay taxes to create funds to cover unemployment benefits, old-age pensions, programs for the blind, and benefits for children of insured workers who died.

The bill covered only about half the work force. Farm and domestic workers were left out. Despite these limits, however, it gave millions of workers a sense of security.

Influencing the Court

Even as he was expanding the Second New Deal, Roosevelt worried about what the Supreme Court might do. In 1937 he introduced a plan that would let him add as many as six justices to the Court. That way he could create a Court sympathetic to his views.

Link to the Present

Social Security in your life You may think Social Security has no relevance to your life yet. However, you already have a Social Security number (SSN) if you are listed as a dependent on someone else's income-tax return. When you have a job, your employer will deduct a Federal Insurance Contribution Act (FICA) tax from your paycheck, match that amount, and send the money to the government to help pay for Social Security.

During your lifetime, the Internal Revenue Service and Social Security Administration will use your SSN to keep track of you. You will use your SSN when you open a savings account or apply for a credit card. Your SSN may serve as your driver's license number. No matter whether you move, get married, change careers, or change your name, your SSN will never change.

Presidents had changed the number of justices before, but members of Congress were outraged that Roosevelt would so openly try to force his will on another branch of government. Bitter debate followed, and in the end Congress rejected the plan.

Roosevelt Supporters

Roosevelt had said that he wanted "to improve the lot of the men and women whose voices have not always been heard." His determination to broaden the New Deal won him many supporters.

Developing the Section

Discussion

Checking Understanding

1. What are three types of WPA projects? (Schools, libraries, hospitals, roads, bridges, airports, music lessons/performances, guidebooks, murals, plays, oral histories.)

2. What were provisions of the Wagner Act? (Outlawed unfair labor practices; required employers to bargain and allow workers to join unions; set up NLRB to oversee union elections and collective bargaining.)

Stimulating Critical Thinking

3. Do you think Roosevelt should have been able to add new Supreme Court justices? Explain. (No: would have upset system of checks and balances. Yes: hard times called for new methods.)

Teaching the

Link to the Present

Point out that until fairly recently most people did not apply for SSNs until they got their first job or entered college. Starting in 1992 the IRS required parents to apply for SSNs for children 1 year old or older whom they wanted to claim as dependents. Roosevelt's idea that every baby should be part of the Social Security system is largely a reality. Ask how many students have memorized their SSNs.

Section Activity

Making Posters

To enhance understanding of New Deal programs and foster appreciation of the era's artistic works, have students create posters promoting a New Deal agency or project. Be sure they first study the Link to Art on p. 501. Posters should include written and visual material. Students who are not comfortable drawing or painting might create a collage of collected images or make an enlarged photocopy of a visual from the text and color it. Hang the completed posters around the room.

See the Study Guide activity in the **Chapter Resources Binder**, p. 99.

Vital Links

Eleanor Roosevelt and Mary McLeod Bethune (Picture) Unit 5, Side 1, Search 13617

See also Unit 5 Explore CD-ROM location 100.

History Footnote

In creating and managing the New Deal, President Roosevelt was aided by a set of highly capable cabinet members and other advisors. Frances Perkins, for example, had served with distinction as head of the New York State Industrial Board. With "faith and a dollar-and-a-half," educator Mary McLeod Bethune had founded a school for African American girls in Daytona Beach, Florida.

Dynamic Harry Hopkins—a former social worker like Frances Perkins—served in several capacities. Before heading the WPA, he directed the Federal Emergency Relief Administration and the Civil Works Administration. He would later become Secretary of Commerce and Roosevelt's most trusted wartime advisor.

On April 9, 1939, 75,000 people gathered at the Lincoln Memorial to hear Marian Anderson sing.

Women and the New Deal The Depression years were hard on working women. With jobs scarce, employers were likely to fire women and hire men in their place. Married women were in the greatest danger. Most states passed laws that barred them from government jobs. When the federal government was ordered not to hire more than one member of a family, it was the wives who usually gave up their jobs.

Throughout the 1930s Eleanor Roosevelt worked to improve opportunities for women. She and Mary Dewson, the head of the women's division of the Democratic Party, pressed hard for the appointment of women such as Frances Perkins to government posts.

When Mrs. Roosevelt learned that the CCC only employed young men, she encouraged her husband to establish the National Youth Administration to help both girls and boys. These efforts paid off in greater support by women for the President and the Democratic Party.

African Americans and the New Deal The Roosevelts also gained support from African Americans, who left "the party of Lincoln" and flocked to the Democratic Party. Roosevelt was not eager to challenge the powerful white southerners who dominated the Democratic Party in Congress. Yet under pressure from black leaders and from his wife, he moved quietly on behalf of African Americans.

In 1937, for example, Roosevelt appointed the first black federal judge, William Hastie. He also listened to a group of African American advisors, who spoke out against discrimination in New Deal programs.

One of Roosevelt's most influential African American advisors was Mary McLeod Bethune. As director of the Division of Negro Affairs in the National Youth Administration, she distributed funds to schools and training centers for African Americans. "Mrs. Bethune is a great woman," said the President. "She always comes here on behalf of others."

Eleanor Roosevelt set a powerful example in fighting racial prejudice. She made a point of ignoring rules of racial segregation. No African American leader had been invited to the White House during Hoover's term. In contrast, Mrs. Roosevelt arranged for Walter White of the NAACP to meet with President Roosevelt.

In 1939, Mrs. Roosevelt dropped her membership in the Daughters of the American Revolution because that organization refused to allow famed opera singer Marian Anderson to perform in its concert hall in Washington, D.C. Mrs. Roosevelt arranged for Anderson to sing instead at the Lincoln Memorial.

A New Deal for Indians Native Americans were also won over to the Democratic Party by New Deal policies. The poverty that afflicted other rural people hit Indians very hard. To help them fight the Depression, Roosevelt appointed John Collier to head Indian affairs.

Connections to Art

Ben Shahn was born in Lithuania and came to the United States in 1906, at the age of 8. As a teenager, he apprenticed in lithography, a printmaking technique. As a young adult, Shahn worked as a lithographer, studied fine art, and traveled in Europe and North Africa, where he painted mostly landscapes. After he returned to the United States in 1929, Shahn began exploring social and political themes in his art. He was especially interested in portraying victims of the government's abuse of power, and he soon attracted attention for a series of paintings about the Sacco-Vanzetti trial. (See the timeline image, p. 448, and pp. 454–455.) Shahn also produced powerful works on the themes of labor struggles, race relations, and atomic warfare.

Collier had long crusaded for Indian self-determination. In 1934 he championed through Congress the Indian Reorganization Act, which overturned the Dawes Act (page 235). The new law returned reservation lands to ownership by tribes instead of individuals. It gave tribes the right to form corporations and governments. It also guaranteed Indian women the right to vote in tribal elections.

Election of 1936

By 1936 Roosevelt had widespread support. The Democrats happily nominated him and Vice-President John Nance Garner to run again in 1936. Roosevelt vowed to continue the New Deal: "We are waging a great and successful war . . . for the survival of democracy."

The growing power of government and labor under the New Deal led Republicans to attack Roosevelt bitterly. They were worried by his popularity, though. They nominated Alfred M. Landon of Kansas. They hoped that his moderate views would attract New Deal supporters. Meanwhile, followers of Long, Townsend, and Coughlin formed their own party—the Union Party.

Roosevelt won 61 percent of the popular vote—an even greater victory than he had won in 1932. He had the electoral votes of every state except Maine and Vermont.

Dust Bowl

In the midst of hard times, the weather turned exceptionally bad. Floods, windstorms,

Link to Art

Years of Dust **(1936) Ben Shahn created this poster for the Resettlement Administration, later called the Farm Security Administration (FSA). This agency bought especially poor farms and helped the farmers start over on better land. From 1930 to 1946 Shahn worked for several government agencies, including the Federal Arts Project of the WPA. There, his first job was assisting famed Mexican muralist Diego Rivera. Shahn went on to create many murals and posters for the WPA and to photograph rural scenes for the FSA. Discuss Posters use art to get a message across. Why are pictures and the artistic arrangement of letters sometimes more effective than ordinary printed material for that purpose?**

YEARS OF DUST
DUST STORM
RESETTLEMENT ADMINISTRATION
Rescues Victims
Restores Land to Proper Use

Discussion

Checking Understanding

1. How did Eleanor Roosevelt improve conditions for women? (Pressed for government appointments of women; convinced Franklin to set up National Youth Administration for girls as well as boys.)

Stimulating Critical Thinking

2. If you could have voted in 1936, whom would you have voted for and why? (Answers will depend partly on views about how powerful the government should be.)

Teaching the

Link to Art

Tell students that Shahn is considered a "social-realist" painter and ask what they think that label might mean. Lead them to understand that in art "realism" does not necessarily mean that a drawing or painting looks like a photograph. Rather realist artists try to portray life as it is, without idealizing it or dressing it up. Shahn portrayed scenes that were not always pleasant in order to move people to social action.

Discussion Answer: Pictures and artistically arranged letters have greater visual and emotional impact and thus may make a stronger, more lasting impression. They can also be "read" faster.

Teaching the Reading Maps

Have students decide what the lighter yellow color depicts. (Places damaged but not as severely as darker area.) **Answers to Reading Maps:** Great Plains; Colorado, Kansas, Oklahoma, Texas, New Mexico.

Bonus Activity

A Migrant's Diary

To focus on effects of the dust storms, have students write three diary entries as members of an Oklahoma farm family. The first should describe a day in which a major dust storm damaged the farm. The second should describe a day during the trip to California. The third should describe a day working in another farmer's fields in California.

Vital Links

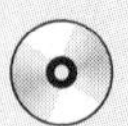

Oklahoma dust storm (Picture) Unit 5, Side 1, Search 11801

See also Unit 5 Explore CD-ROM location 70.

Migrant worker family (Picture) Unit 5, Side 1, Search 11813

See also Unit 5 Explore CD-ROM location 72.

History Footnote

The photograph on page 502 was taken by Dorothea Lange, one of the photographers hired by the Farm Security Administration (FSA) to record the effects of the Depression and drought on rural Americans. Lange had been a successful portrait photographer, but such work seemed trivial during hard times, and she began photographing victims of the Depression instead.

Lange followed the advice of FSA head Roy Stryker, who urged photographers to "look for the significant detail. The kinds of things that a scholar a hundred years from now is going to wonder about." However, there was more to the FSA effort than recording information for posterity. By making urban Americans aware of the plight of their rural cousins, FSA photos helped win support for federal aid to farm owners and workers.

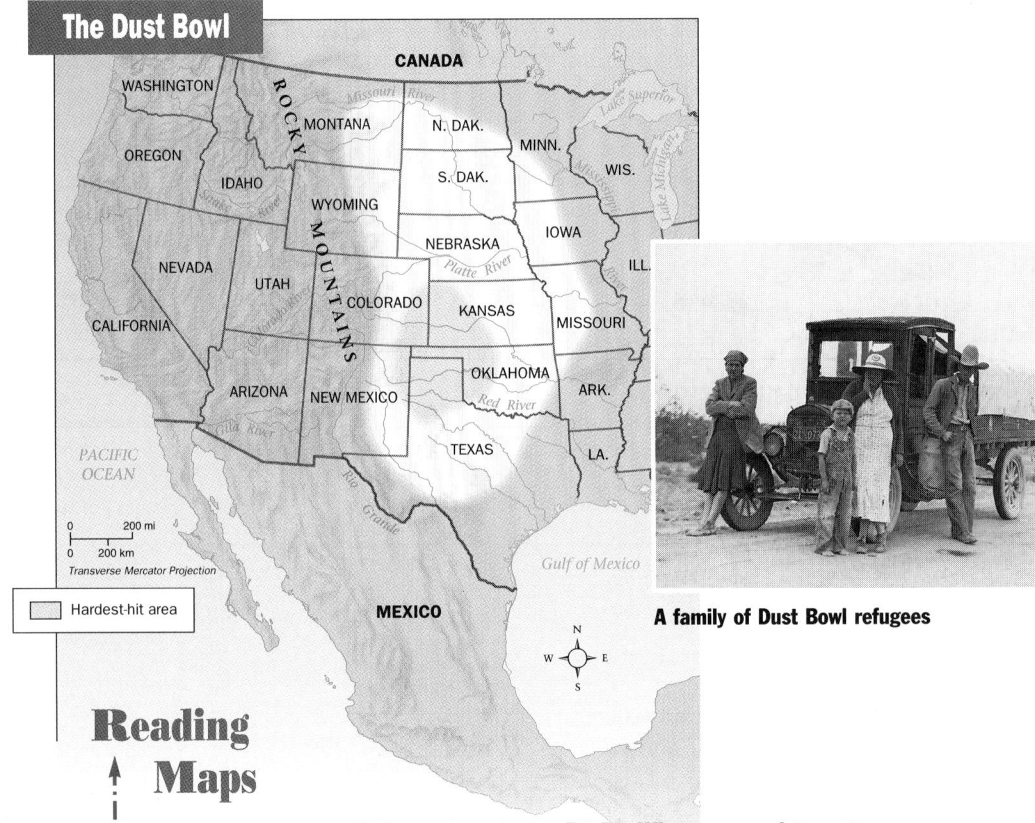

A family of Dust Bowl refugees

Reading Maps

Compare this map with the map on pages R4–R5. What geographic region was most affected by the dust storms? What states were hardest hit?

and blizzards destroyed property and lives. Drought added to the toll. Corn withered on the stalk, and grassfires raced across the Great Plains.

Then came the dust. Years of overgrazing and overplowing had killed off the grass that held plains soil. Windstorms carried the dry, dead earth into the sky. One of the first storms struck South Dakota in November 1933. The sky was dark at noon, and people gagged on the dirt.

The drought continued. Without grass and water, cattle died, their lungs full of dust. In May 1934, 12 million pounds of plains soil fell on Chicago. Kansas and Nebraska soil rained down on Boston, New York City, and Washington, D.C., and onto ships hundreds of miles out in the Atlantic.

Throughout the 1930s, the windstorms carried away the hopes of thousands of farmers along with the topsoil necessary for their crops. One Kansas woman described the storms:

> "When we opened the door, swirling whirlwinds of soil beat against us unmercifully. The dust seeped into

Connections to Literature

Writer John Steinbeck turned the suffering he witnessed during the Depression into memorable works of fiction—most notably *The Grapes of Wrath* (1939), for which he won the Pulitzer Prize. The novel tells the story of the Joad family, driven off their Oklahoma land by dust storms and the Depression. The Joads seek opportunity as farmworkers in California. They encounter exploitation and violence instead. The novel was made into an Oscar-winning movie starring Henry Fonda in 1940.

Steinbeck was born in Salinas, California, the setting of many of his stories. As a struggling young writer, he was briefly employed by the WPA to perform an unusual task: taking a census of all the dogs on the Monterey Peninsula.

Discussion

Checking Understanding

1. What were the causes of the Dust Bowl? (Drought, overgrazing, overplowing.)

2. Why did auto workers strike in 1936? (They wanted automobile manufacturers to recognize and negotiate with their union.)

Stimulating Critical Thinking

3. If auto workers had gone out on strike, rather than sitting down in the plant, would they have been as effective? (Probably not, because manufacturers could have replaced them with new workers.)

For an account of a department store sit-down strike, see **American Readings**, pp. 51–52.

cupboards and closets. It turned everyone's hair gray and stiff. We ground dirt between our teeth.”

Farm families piled their belongings onto old trucks, turned their backs on the area they called “the Dust Bowl,” and drove off, never to return. Most headed west, especially to California. Many Dust Bowl refugees were taunted with the name “Okies,” because so many came from Oklahoma. Without money, they wandered the highways seeking work harvesting crops.

With more farmworkers than jobs in the West and Southwest, competition was keen. One result was that thousands of Mexican citizens, welcomed as farmworkers when the economy boomed in the 1920s, were forced to return to Mexico in the 1930s.

The dust storms could be blamed on drought, but careless farming and ranching practices had played a part. The Dust Bowl tragedy led the federal government to look at farming methods closely. Roosevelt ordered the CCC to plant a belt of trees from Mexico to Canada to break the wind. Congress passed the Taylor Grazing Act in 1934 to regulate grazing on federal lands.

Sit-Down Strikes

During Roosevelt's second term in office, labor continued to gain strength. Protected by the Wagner Act, unions were on the rise.

In 1936 the United Auto Workers demanded that automakers recognize their union. The union was part of a group of industrial unions that were in the process of splitting off from the American Federation of Labor (AFL). The group—the Congress of Industrial Organizations (CIO)—became independent of the AFL in 1938.

When General Motors announced that it would not negotiate with a union, the workers of Chevrolet No. 1 Factory in Flint, Michigan, decided to act. They sat down at their posts and refused to move until General Motors accepted their union.

Workers in other plants quickly did the same. The autoworkers had invented a new kind of strike—the sit-down strike. As long as they stayed where they were, automakers could not get factories running again.

The strike began late in December and lasted into February. General Motors managers turned off the heat, but the workers stayed put. Friends and families slipped food and clothing past the company guards.

When negotiations stalled, Roosevelt intervened. General Motors finally agreed to recognize the union. Soon, workers in other industries were using the sit-down strike to gain recognition for their unions.

The End of the New Deal

Many thought that the nation was on the road to recovery in 1937. Congress cut back employment programs, and after years of spending more than the government took in, Roosevelt talked of balancing the budget.

Suddenly, the economy took a turn for the worse. Factories shut down once more, and workers returned to unemployment lines.

What had happened? Nobody knew for sure. Some blamed the cuts in employment programs or the costs of the new Social Security program. Roosevelt turned again to relief efforts, and after about a year the economy seemed to improve.

Nevertheless, public confidence in the New Deal began to waver. Some people still believed the government was spending too little. Others, though, heeded Republican arguments that the government should cut spending and lower taxes.

In the congressional election of 1938, Republicans gained 81 seats in the House of Representatives and 8 in the Senate. Republicans used their new power to block further

Vital Links

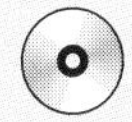
Automobile factory (Picture) Unit 5, Side 1, Search 27474

See also Unit 5 Explore CD-ROM location 115.

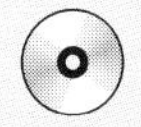
General Motors strike settled (Picture) Unit 5, Side 1, Search 27486

See also Unit 5 Explore CD-ROM location 117.

Closing the Section

Wrap-Up Activity

Competing Quizzes

To review the Second New Deal, have small groups create quizzes. Divide each group into two teams. One develops five questions about pp. 498–500. The other develops five about the remaining pages. The two teams then quiz each other.

Section Review Answers

1. Employers and workers pay taxes for unemployment benefit funds, pensions, programs for blind, and benefits for children of deceased workers.

2. Roosevelt appointed first black federal judge, listened to African American advisors. Eleanor Roosevelt defied segregation, invited Walter White to the White House, dropped DAR membership, arranged for Marian Anderson to sing at Lincoln Memorial.

3. Overgrazing and overplowing killed grass that held soil. Farmers headed west to seek work, becoming poor migrant farmworkers; many Mexican farmworkers forced out.

4. For: unions best hope for fair treatment; workers have right to organize to protect interests. Against: businesses should be able to choose whether to deal with unions; government should stay out of business affairs.

To check understanding of "Why We Remember," assign Thinking Critically question 3 on student page 506.

Tips for Teaching

Auditory Learners

Auditory learners can benefit from listening to true stories of people who lived through the Depression. Obtain a copy of *Hard Times: An Oral History of the Great Depression in America* by Studs Terkel (Pantheon, 1986) and read aloud or have students read aloud from it. They may want to record interviews with relatives, friends, or neighbors about the Depression and share the recordings. Questions might include: How old were you when the Depression started? How did it affect your family? What New Deal programs did your family or neighbors take part in? What did you think of Roosevelt and the New Deal?

New Deal measures. Faced with growing opposition, Roosevelt put his energy into supporting existing programs instead of introducing new measures.

By the end of the 1930s, Roosevelt's attention turned to troubles in Europe and Asia. The world was being drawn into another war. No one would ever know if the New Deal had rescued the United States from the Depression, but with the outbreak of World War II, the Depression finally came to an end.

3. Section Review

1. What were the provisions of the first Social Security Act?
2. Why did many African Americans turn to the Democratic Party during the Depression?
3. How had people's actions led to the Dust Bowl? What were some of its effects?
4. Critical Thinking Give two arguments for the Wagner Act and two against it.

Why We Remember

The Depression and New Deal

When Franklin Roosevelt ran for President in the darkest days of the Great Depression, the nation's problems seemed overwhelming. Roosevelt, however, was not overwhelmed. He had been strengthened by his experience with polio. "Once I spent two years lying in bed, trying to move my big toe," he said. "That was the hardest job I ever had to do. After that, anything else was easy." In fact, ending the Depression was not easy, though. As Roosevelt himself admitted in his second inaugural address in 1937, "I see one-third of a nation ill-housed, ill-clad, ill-nourished."

Today we remember the Great Depression not only because of the suffering of that one-third of a nation—and not only because of the Roosevelts' efforts to end that suffering. We remember the Great Depression for another reason as well. It was in these dark years of hunger, homelessness, and human misery that many Americans changed their views of the role of government.

Before the Depression, most Americans probably agreed with Thomas Jefferson that the best government was that which governs least. Franklin Roosevelt, however, put forth a different view of government. In his view, one of the duties of government was "caring for those of its citizens who find themselves . . . unable to obtain even the necessities of mere existence without the aid of others." "That responsibility," Roosevelt asserted, "is recognized by every civilized nation." After the Great Depression, it was also recognized by Americans.

Geography Footnote

Not all migrant workers were driven to California by the effects of the Dust Bowl. Cesar Chavez's family had owned a farm near Yuma, Arizona, that originally covered 80 acres and produced enough cattle, grain, vegetables, and watermelons to support a large extended family. During the hard times of the 1930s, a series of financial setbacks, rather than dust storms, reduced the Chavez holdings and eventually eliminated them. The family headed to California in 1937, when Cesar was 10. As an adult, he organized California farmworkers to gain better wages and working conditions. He established a union that grew and merged with other unions to become the United Farm Workers of America. Students will read more about Chavez in Chapter 14.

Geography Lab

Pacific Mountains and Valleys

Dust Bowl migrants heading west had little idea of what they would find. What they discovered in the region we call the Pacific Mountains and Valleys were scenes of stunning beauty and great variety. More importantly, they found miles and miles of some of the richest agricultural land on earth. Use the quotation and the photographs on this page to form a mental image of the Pacific Mountains and Valleys.

Cesar Chavez

"When we moved to California, we would work after school. . . . 'Following the crops,' we missed much school. Trying to get enough money to stay alive the following winter, the whole family picking apricots, walnuts, prunes. We were pretty new, we had never been migratory workers."

Cascade Mountains, Washington

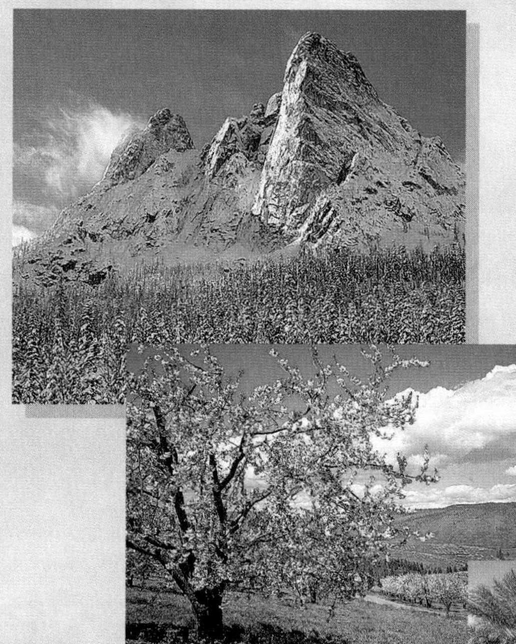

Cherry orchard, Oregon

Date palms and bell peppers, California

Developing a Mental Map

Use the maps on pages R4–R7 to help answer the questions.

1. Which states are partially within the Pacific Mountains and Valleys region? Which state is completely within the region?
2. Name two mountain ranges that lie in the region.
3. How do the photographs confirm what you see on the map on pages R4–R5?
4. Describe one area within the region where you would expect to find a concentration of farming, and tell why.
5. **Hands-On Geography** Imagine that you are a member of a family that has fled the Dust Bowl. You come upon one of the scenes pictured on this page. Write a poem that describes your reaction to it.

Teaching the Geography Lab

Before students read the lab, have them study the photographs to draw preliminary conclusions about differences between the Pacific Mountains and Valleys and the Great Plains (see p. 346). (Differences: greater variety of conditions and crops in Pacific area; more rugged mountains in Pacific region; Great Plains more level.)

Developing a Mental Map

Answers

1. Partially covered: Alaska, Washington, Oregon, California. Completely covered: Hawaii.

2. Any two: Sierra Nevada, Coast Ranges, Cascade Range, Alaska Range.

3. They show that the region has a wide range of elevations and landforms, from low, level land along coasts and in the Central Valley and Columbia River valley to high mountains.

4. Possible answers: Central Valley, because it is a low, level area with rivers for irrigation; Columbia River valley, for same reasons.

5. The most effective poems (which need not rhyme) will show ability to imagine how someone from the flat, devastated Dust Bowl might be affected by the sight of mountains or healthy crops.

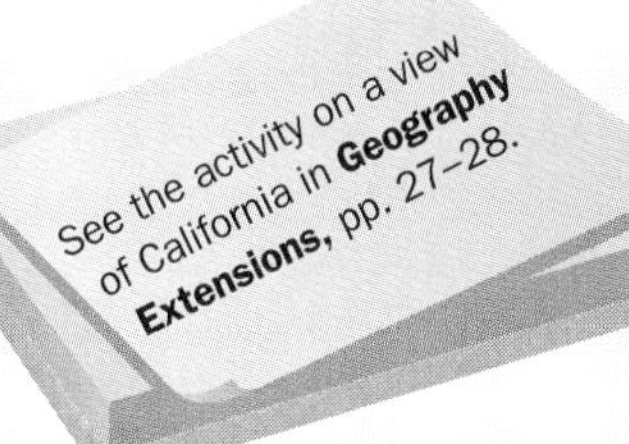

See the activity on a view of California in **Geography Extensions**, pp. 27–28.

Survey Answers

Reviewing Vocabulary

Definitions are found on these pages: *durable goods* (489), *pension* (496).

Reviewing Main Ideas

1. Any two: income gap between the rich and everyone else, poor business practices, overproduction, poor banking practices.

2. Many depositors lost savings, workers lost jobs, farmers lost farms. They faced homelessness and starvation and felt fear, shame, and despair. Some took to railways and highways seeking work. Some lived in shantytowns.

3. (a) AAA tried to raise farm prices by lowering production; paid farmers to farm fewer acres. (b) NRA tried to help businesspeople earn reasonable profits and workers earn decent wages; encouraged businesses to draw up codes setting prices, production quotas, wages, and working conditions. (c) PWA tried to help workers have money to spend, which would help businesses; funded construction projects that employed workers. (d) TVA tried to develop the economic life of Tennessee River valley; built and improved dams, restored soil and forests.

4. That it gave the government too much power, favored big business, or that it favored farmers and labor, did not go far enough to help the poor.

5. Any two: National Youth Administration provided jobs for young people; Works Progress Administration hired workers for construction and cultural projects; Wagner Act outlawed unfair labor practices and empowered unions; Social Security Act established taxes to create funds for unemployment and other benefits.

(Answers continued in top margin)

6. (a) Eleanor pressed for appointments of women to government posts and encouraged establishment of National Youth Administration. (b) Franklin appointed first black federal judge, listened to African American advisors; Eleanor publicly defied segregation. (c) Franklin appointed John Collier to head Indian affairs; Collier championed Indian Reorganization Act.

7. Workers stop working, sit down at their posts, refuse to move. First such strike occurred in 1936 after General Motors said it would not negotiate with a union. Roosevelt intervened; General Motors recognized the union; other sit-down strikes occurred.

Chapter Survey

Reviewing Vocabulary

Define the following terms.
1. durable goods
2. pension

Reviewing Main Ideas

1. Describe two problems in the economy that contributed to the Great Depression.
2. How did the Depression change Americans' lives?
3. What were the purpose and the methods of each of the following? (a) AAA (b) NRA (c) PWA (d) TVA
4. What criticisms of the New Deal did its opponents offer?
5. Name and describe two programs set up under the Second New Deal.
6. How did the Roosevelts gain the support of each group? (a) women (b) African Americans (c) Indians
7. What is a sit-down strike, how did the first such strike come about, and what were the results?

Thinking Critically

1. Application Why do you suppose President Roosevelt thought it so important to inspire hope and confidence in the American people?
2. Analysis Imagine that you are the owner of a large company in the 1930s. You claim that Roosevelt has abandoned people like you to help others who are suffering. How do you support the claim?
3. Why We Remember: Synthesis In what ways does the New Deal live on in the United States today?

Applying Skills

Comparing historical interpretations Think of a controversial government program of today. Write brief "historical interpretations" that reflect two different ways the program might be viewed by historians of the future. Exchange interpretations with a classmate. Recalling page 497, write a paragraph in which you do the following:
1. Summarize the two interpretations written by your classmate.
2. Identify how the interpretations are supported.
3. Evaluate the interpretations. Are they thorough? Are they persuasive? Explain.

History Mystery

Answer the History Mystery on page 485. More than 150,000 migrants ended up on the West Coast in just a few years. With so many people seeking work, what problems were these refugees likely to have?

Writing in Your History Journal

1. Keys to History (a) The time line on pages 484–485 has nine Keys to History. In your journal, list each key and describe why it is important to know about. (b) Choose three events from the chapter to add to the time line. Write the events and their dates in your journal, and tell why you think each event should be added.
2. Franklin and Eleanor Roosevelt Reread the letter that the Chicago boy wrote to the Roosevelts in 1936 (page 489). Imagine that you are either the President or Eleanor Roosevelt. In your journal, write a reply to the boy.
3. Citizenship Today, as in the 1930s, Americans disagree about the best role for the First Lady. In your journal, describe what you think the First

Thinking Critically

1. Possible answers: American people needed hope and confidence to make it through hard times; people with money might invest and spend more if confident and hopeful.

2. Students might point to relative scarcity of New Deal programs designed to help big business compared with programs geared to farmers, workers, and the unemployed. Also could point to intervention in the General Motors strike.

3. Possible answers: Continued involvement of government in the economy and debate over that involvement. Widespread belief that government must provide "safety net" for the very poor. Continued existence of such programs as FDIC and Social Security. Still-standing construction and art projects.

(Answers continued in side margin)

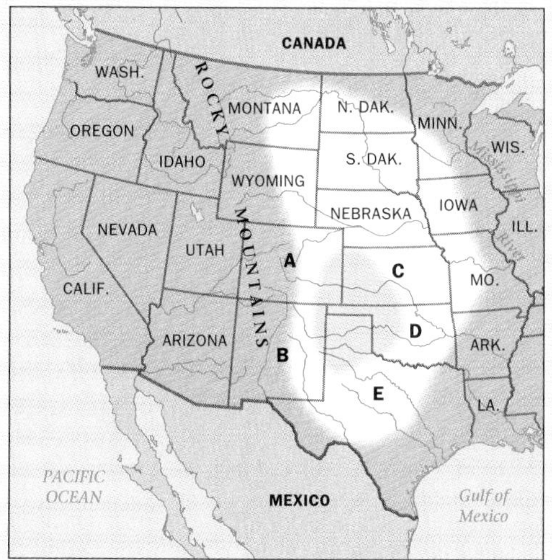

Reviewing Geography

1. Each letter on the map represents one of the Dust Bowl states. Write the name of each state.

2. Geographic Thinking How people view a place is influenced by their culture. The way people think about a particular environment may differ from one group to another and from one time to another. How might each of the following have described the Great Plains? a Plains Indian of the 1500s, a Spanish explorer of the 1600s, an American explorer of the 1820s, a farmer of the 1880s, a farmer of the 1930s

Lady's role should be, and why. Also tell which First Lady—past or present—has come closest to fulfilling the role as you see it. Explain your answer.

Alternative Assessment

Creating a cause-effect graphic organizer You have been asked to teach a group of younger students about the 1930s. You decide that the best way is to use a graphic organizer. A graphic organizer is made up of symbols such as circles, squares, graphs, and arrows, as well as pictures and words. The elements are arranged to show relationships.

With several classmates, create a graphic organizer showing causes and effects involved in the Great Depression and the New Deal.

❶ Brainstorm events and situations relating to the Great Depression and New Deal. Write each event or situation on a note card as it is mentioned.

❷ Create a "rough draft" of your graphic organizer by arranging the note cards on mural paper, bulletin board, or other surface. Your arrangement should show some or all or the following kinds of cause-effect relationships:

- single cause/single effect
- multiple causes/single effect
- single cause/multiple effects
- chain reaction—one or more causes lead to one or more effects, which in turn cause one or more effects, and so on

❸ Create a "final draft" of your graphic organizer. You might rewrite the note-card items in large, neat print; use lengths of yarn or draw arrows to show relationships; and include artwork.

Your work will be evaluated on the following criteria:

- it presents cause-effect relationships among events and situations of the 1930s thoroughly and accurately
- it is clear and easy to follow
- it has visual appeal

Applying Skills

Paragraphs should reflect understanding of how historical interpretations can be supported by facts and opinions, and how interpretations can vary.

History Mystery

Information on the migration can be found on pages 501–503. Problems likely included difficulty finding work, resulting low pay, poor housing and food, lack of public services, hostility from residents.

Writing in Your History Journal

1. (a) Descriptions should be similar to the time-line notes on teacher pages 484–485. (b) Additions should be accurately described, dated, and justified.

2. Letters may offer concern for the family's plight, descriptions of how the New Deal aims to help, and perhaps specific suggestions (for example, father might apply for a WPA job). Best letters will reflect the personality of Eleanor or Franklin.

3. Preferences should be reasonably supported.

Reviewing Geography

1. (A) Colorado (B) New Mexico (C) Kansas (D) Oklahoma (E) Texas

2. Possible answers: Plains Indian—grasslands provide food for buffalo; Spanish explorer—no gold; American explorer—no good for farming; 1880s farmer—crops grow during years of abundant moisture, fail in drought; 1930s farmer—plains are no longer good for farming, wind is blowing topsoil away.

Alternative Assessment

Teacher's Take-Home Planner 4, p. 15, includes suggestions and scoring rubrics for the Alternative Assessment activity.

Teaching the

Link to American Readings

In this feature students learn about the Dust Bowl and its victims, some of the hardest-hit Americans of the Great Depression. They will learn how, in spite of the odds against them, these people persevered. They will also take a look at the entertainment of the Depression years and learn how Americans used movies and radio to escape for a short time from the grim reality of their lives.

Before students begin the lesson, review Dust Bowl (pages 501–503). Have students read the entire feature before assigning the A Closer Look questions. The Setting the Stage Activity and Bonus Activity may then be introduced according to the needs and interests of the students. The information contained in the Discussion questions and the Footnotes may be used throughout the lesson as appropriate. Readers' Theater is ideal for students who might find the readings somewhat difficult. Use the Wrap-Up Activity for students who would enjoy taking a step beyond the core lesson.

Connections to Economics

World War I had created a high demand for American wheat. Farmers set out to meet that demand by employing new farm machinery, including tractors, plows, and threshers. During the 1920s agricultural production soared by 300 percent, and more than 5 million acres of natural vegetation on the southern plains were plowed. This overproduction had two devastating consequences. First, it caused a glut on the market and sent prices plummeting. Second, when drought and high winds hit the plains, there was not enough natural vegetation left to hold down the topsoil. Dramatic dust storms turned the Great Plains into sand dunes, and windstorms created the Dust Bowl, carrying topsoil as far east as New England.

Link to American Readings

READING 11A

Out of the Dust Bowl

Tenant and small farmers, who barely earned a living in the best of years, were hit the hardest by the Dust Bowl. Thousands of farmers migrated to California, where they hoped to start a new life. Former Superintendent of Kern County (California) Schools, Leo Hart, recalls his work with the migrant children.

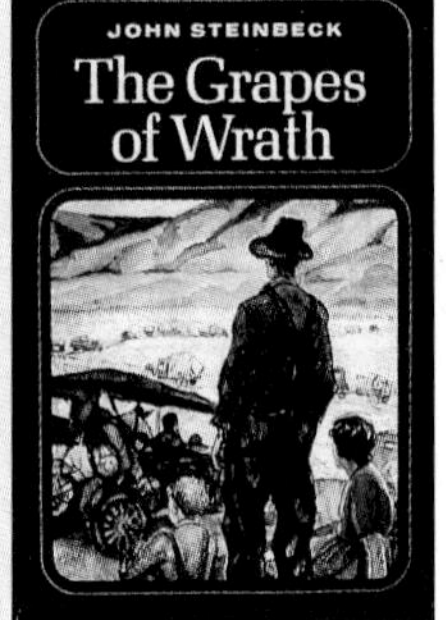

In 1939 John Steinbeck wrote *The Grapes of Wrath*, the story of migrant farmers who moved to California during the Great Depression.

The experiences of Leo Hart and his migrant schoolchildren, 1940–1944

Nineteen thirty-nine was a hard year for the Dust Bowlers. Drought still gripped the Central Plains and the Southwest, and Route 66, bearing weary migrants from Oklahoma, Texas and Arkansas to Kern County, was still crowded with people wearing baggy overalls, tattered dresses and the look of down-and-out poverty. They called themselves "Okies." Most believed there was work in California, so they joined the caravan of Model A's and ramshackle buses and headed for the Great San Joaquin, the rich agricultural valley where, they heard, pickers were needed.

By 1940, some 180,000 migrants had settled in the rural areas of the San Joaquin Valley, and Kern County experienced its greatest population explosion. . . . All the kids looked undernourished and in need of medical attention. They spoke a different language, they possessed a different culture, they lacked skills in hygiene and in "manners, morals and etiquette," Hart recollects.

With little or no formal education, the children of the Dust Bowl crowded into Kern County's schools: The results were predictable. Teachers and taxpayers believed the newcomers were "uneducable," and their appearance offensive. Swiftly, the children were either banned from the public schools or forced to sit on the floor in the back of crowded classrooms, humiliated. . . .

Hart decided the Dust Bowl children should have their own school. Accordingly, he persuaded the Arvin-Lamont School Board to declare an "emergency" and to give him permission to build a school adjacent to Arvin Federal Camp [camp for migrant workers].

adjacent: next to

. . . In 1940 Hart leased a 10-acre site from the federal government for $10 and established Arvin Federal Emergency School, which started with no grass, no sidewalks, no playground equipment, no toilets, no water, no books, no teachers. It started, Hart remembers, with two condemned buildings and "50 poorly clad, undernourished and skeptical youngsters."

Literature Footnote

Although author John Steinbeck did not intend it to be such, *The Grapes of Wrath* has been adopted by Americans as a vivid historical documentary of the Great Depression. It has come to represent the poverty, injustice, and anger generated by the Depression. Steinbeck believed that the Depression had revealed the shallowness of the American dream of individualism and wealth. He wrote *The Grapes of Wrath* both to express his outrage at social injustice in this country and to show that there is still hope to go beyond that—to become something more than we are as individuals and as a nation. In 1940 the movie version of *The Grapes of Wrath* was released. Directed by John Ford with a cast that includes Henry Fonda, Jane Darwell, and John Carradine, the film closely follows Steinbeck's work.

Hart said his goal was to provide the unwanted children "with educational experiences in a broader and richer curriculum than were present in most schools." He did that and more. Before the school opened in September 1940, Hart visited several colleges and universities in California and sought out "the best teachers . . . teachers whose attitudes indicated that they were really interested in this type of student and wanted to help in the program."

Then Hart became a beggar, a borrower, a scrounger of wood and nails, of books and paper, of whatever he could lay his hands on that might be of some use. "I became a panhandler," he remembers.

He stumped the county for donations of supplies and materials. . . .

From the National Youth Authority, he secured 25,000 bricks. From the Sears Roebuck Foundation, an assortment of sheep, pigs, and cows. From local nurseries, plants and vegetables. From local ranchers, farm machinery. In September 1940, on a barren stretch of land marked by piles of bricks and boards and boxes of odds and ends, Hart met with his faculty, introduced them to the students and told them all to get to work.

They did. Brick by brick, board by board, the children of the Dust Bowl, along with Hart and his staff, built Arvin Federal Emergency School. . . .

The girls needed a home economics building. No problem. An old railroad car was located and moved to the school, where the boys added plumbing, wired the boxcar and remodeled its interior. They learned carpentry, plastering and masonry, built pens for livestock, dug a basement to store slaughtered cattle, plowed fields for raising school-grown vegetables. They made the school self-sufficient.

"The longer we ran the school," Hart said, "the longer the people stayed. The greater portion of them stayed there and would stay the year round and work so that their kids could stay in this school." . . .

Altogether, from 1940 to 1944 about 300 migrant children attended Hart's handmade school. . . . Arvin Federal became known statewide for its lack of truancy and disciplinary problems. "We left everything lying around," Hart recalls, "and no one ever stole a thing."

truancy: skipping school

Some of Leo Hart's eighth-graders are learning about aircraft mechanics in an old warplane-turned-classroom.

Setting the Stage
Activity

Reacting to the Dust Bowl

To help students understand the victims of the Dust Bowl, have them put themselves in the place of the children in the first reading. Have students imagine that their family has suddenly lost all of its financial resources and is being forced to move. They will attend a school in a strange place where they are not wanted, and where they are ridiculed for the way they dress and speak. Give students five to ten minutes to respond in their journals to the scenario. Then ask volunteers to read their journal entries to the class. Discuss the various responses.

Bonus Activity

Creating a Curriculum

Have students work in small groups to create their own curriculum for a school, one that shares the philosophy expressed by Leo Hart in the first reading and that attempts to reach the same goals. Encourage students to emphasize jobs and activities that are especially appropriate to their own lives.

Discussion

Stimulating Critical Thinking

1. Consider how you might feel if you, like Hart's schoolchildren, had a part in building and maintaining your school. Would you feel differently about it than you do now? Explain. (Students might respond that because they had invested their own time and energy, they would be more likely to respect the facilities.)

2. When Leo Hart was faced with the problem of educating migrant children, he commented, "The big problem . . . was to find out what to do for these children to get them adjusted into society and to take their rightful place." Do you agree or disagree that it is the duty of the public school system to do all this? Explain. (Answers will vary. Some might say that it is the duty of the school system to educate students in all respects; others might say that it is the duty of parents to help their children adjust to society.)

3. Which movies from the list in the second reading have you seen? Which did you like best? Why? (Answers will vary. Students should support their answers with specific details.)

Literature Footnote

Billie Holiday (1915–1959) is considered to be one of the greatest jazz-blues artists of all time. Born in Baltimore, Holiday lived in poverty until she moved to New York City and began singing in Harlem nightclubs in the late 1920s. Starting in 1935 Holiday sang with orchestras such as those of Count Basie and Artie Shaw. She made numerous recordings with saxophonist Lester Young and pianist Teddy Wilson. Although she continued to sing throughout the 1940s and 1950s, Holiday's long-term heroin addiction took its toll. She died while under arrest for possession of illegal drugs. Although she rarely sang traditional blues, Holiday had an uncanny ability to transform popular songs into something all her own. Her autobiography, *Lady Sings the Blues*, (1956) was made into a movie in 1972.

READING 11B

Diversions: Moving from Reality to Fantasy

The 1930s was a decade of economic and social depression. Poverty ate away at those who had been comfortable with their lifestyles. It even threatened those who had known only luxury their whole lives. Hunger was always ready to claim another victim. What did people do to escape from these very real problems? Adults and children alike could spend an entire afternoon in a movie theater for a dime—an investment that brought guaranteed returns, a brief reprieve from the harsh realities of life. It is not surprising then that the most popular movies were fantasies, stories of good triumphing over evil, and anything else that enabled the people of the day to "get away." Other diversions, such as comics and radio, followed suit.

Some of the most popular movies, 1930s

Dinner at Eight
Mutiny on the Bounty
Blonde Venus
Lives of a Bengal Lancer
The Private Lives of Elizabeth and Essex
Rose Marie
Carefree
Born to Dance
Flirtation Walk
Gold Diggers of 1933
Little Caesar
A Day at the Races
My Little Chickadee
Gone with the Wind
King Kong
Stage Coach
The Wizard of Oz
You Can't Take It with You
Snow White and the Seven Dwarfs
Public Enemy

Films such as *King Kong* (below left) and *The Wizard of Oz* (below right) pulled Americans toward fantasy and away from the real horrors of everyday life.

Connections to Music

Glen Miller (1904–1944) was a jazz band-leader, arranger, and trombone player. He led the most popular dance band of the late 1930s and early 1940s. In 1939 he was frequently heard on the radio and in that same year, several of his songs became hits, including "Sunrise Serenade," "Moonlight Serenade," and "In the Mood."

Readers' Theater

Because the only person quoted in the first reading is Leo Hart, suggest that students create some specific characters in addition to a number of narrators. They should then develop some specific dialogue for each character. They might introduce a student, a parent, and a teacher, for example. Allow plenty of time for writing and rehearsing.

Wrap-Up Activity

Outlining a Movie Script

To extend the lesson, ask students to imagine that they are screenwriters in the 1930s. Have them write the outline for a movie that they think would be a big hit. Remind students that they are writing for people who want to escape from the realities of the Depression. Ask volunteers to share their outlines with the class.

The Comics, 1930s

The "funny pages" of the newspapers still had comic strips such as *Blondie* and sports strips such as *Joe Palooka* that were popular in the 1920s. However, in the 1930s new heroes such as Flash Gordon, Buck Rogers, and Prince Valiant began appearing in adventure strips. Dick Tracy fought crime, and Lil' Abner provided social satire. Little Orphan Annie, another carry-over from the 1920s, continued to battle evil and promote the "American Way."

Radio, 1930

Having a radio became essential in the 1930s. It carried the voice of Roosevelt, the comedy of Amos & Andy, the continuing saga of "One Man's Family," and the cops of "Gang-busters." There were comedians Jack Benny and Fred Allen, singers Kate Smith and Bing Crosby, and imaginary heroes such as Jack Armstrong, the "all-American boy." In the world of popular music, this was the Age of Swing. Big Bands became popular under band leaders such as Duke Ellington, Benny Goodman, Tommy and Jimmy Dorsey, Count Basie, and Glenn Miller. Singers such as Helen O'Connell, Billie Holiday, Bing Crosby, and Ella Fitzgerald set the style.

Toys and Games, 1930s

Toys and games often reflected Depression-era themes. The game of Monopoly gave those who felt powerless a sense of being in control—of being millionaires. Shirley Temple dolls, modeled after the star child actress, were highly prized. Other toys were reminiscent of heroic cowboy characters such as long-time movie star Tom Mix.

(Above Right) Little Orphan Annie, a popular comic strip character in the 1930s, appeared both in the "funnies" and in books. (Right) A model of innocence, talent, and sweet intelligence, child actor Shirley Temple inspired the creation of a doll that was popular in the 1930s.

A Closer Look

1. How did Leo Hart carry out his plan for educating the migrant children?
2. What common theme runs throughout the popular entertainment features of the 1930s? Why was the theme so successful at this time in American history?
3. **Critical Thinking** How did Hart's plan for a "broader and richer curriculum" help the migrant children? Do you think his concept is valid today? Explain.

A Closer Look

Answers

1. Hart leased a ten-acre site from the government for ten dollars; he sought out the best teachers—those who would be committed to his plan; he begged, borrowed, and scrounged everything from building materials to school supplies; he asked students to help build their school. They did so and the school became virtually self-sufficient.

2. Fantasy and escape were popular themes because they helped people forget the Depression.

3. The children learned skills they needed in real life as well as traditional "book learning." Many will agree that practical training, such as computer skills, is essential.

Teaching the
Citizenship Lab

This feature focuses on the issues of the separation of powers and the government's role in regulating business through the Commerce clause.

Have students read the entire feature before assigning the Understanding Civic Issues questions and the Hands-On Citizenship activity. The Bonus Activity in this Teacher's Edition may be used as an alternative to, or in addition to, the Hands-On Citizenship. The Discussion questions in this Teacher's Edition may be used at appropriate points during students' reading or afterward.

Objectives

- ★ Compare ideas about the role of the federal government in the nation's economy.
- ★ Understand the primary responsibilities of each branch of government and the ways in which each branch shares powers.
- ★ Focus on one of the ways that public policies are formed and implemented.
- ★ Recognize some basic, contemporary issues related to economic rights.

Supreme Court Case: *Schechter* v. *United States*

Citizenship Lab

What Powers Does the Federal Government Have to Regulate Business?

Joseph Schechter and his three brothers ran a poultry business in New York City. They bought live chickens from shippers, had them slaughtered, and then sold them to local butchers. In 1934 they were charged with the following crimes: selling a sick chicken, allowing some customers to select particular chickens, requiring employees to work more than forty hours per week, and failing to pay the minimum wage. The Schechters were convicted. They appealed their case all the way to the Supreme Court.

Why the Schechter Case Was Controversial

No one, not even the Schechters themselves, would have argued that it should be legal to sell a sick chicken, if the seller knew the chicken was sick. They appealed their case on the grounds that the laws themselves were not made legally. The violations that the Schechters had been charged with were part of the Live Poultry Code. This code had been established by the National Recovery Administration (NRA), a major New Deal agency, in 1933. The code had been approved by the President himself. That, according to the Schechters, made the laws invalid.

The Court Strikes Down the NRA

The Supreme Court chamber was packed on May 27, 1935. The atmosphere in the courtroom was tense. Chief Justice Charles Evans Hughes read the verdict in the Schechter case with noted force. The decision was unanimous. The Supreme Court declared the NRA, and the codes made under it (including the Live Poultry Code), unconstitutional.

A woman from San Antonio, Texas, prepares a quilt decorated with the NRA logo. To many people, the NRA symbol came to represent patriotism and loyalty in a time of duress.

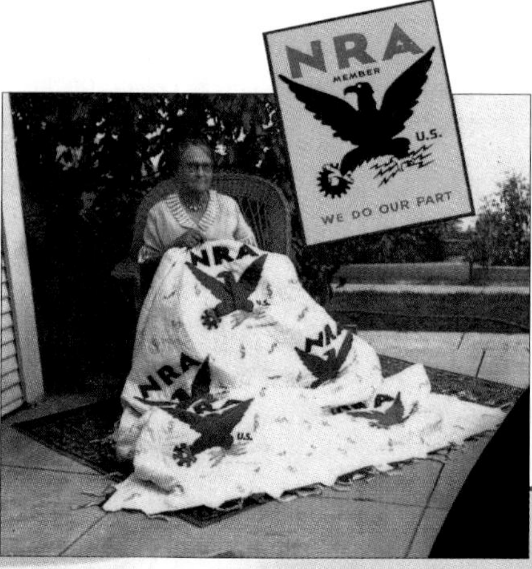

History Footnote

The National Recovery Administration (NRA) was the administrative arm of the National Industrial Recovery Act. Its purpose was to establish codes to regulate business and aid economic recovery from the Depression. During its two years of operation, the NRA passed almost 800 different codes. These codes dealt with a number of issues that, at the time, were controversial: unfair trade practices, minimum wages, maximum working hours, and the right of workers to join unions. Businesses that subscribed to the codes could display a Blue Eagle emblem, an emblem that many business owners were proud of. After the NRA was struck down by the Supreme Court, some business owners continued to adhere to the codes. Some codes provided the basis for subsequent legislation.

Their reasoning was that, with the NRA, Congress had illegally passed its legislative duties over to the executive branch. According to the Constitution, the job of the executive branch, headed by the President, is to enforce the laws, not to make them. The Court declared that, with the NRA, Congress had given the President too much power and had not provided sufficient guidelines on how to use the power. Justice Benjamin Cardozo wrote a descriptive, concurring opinion for the Schechter case. He declared that the power Congress granted the President through the NRA "was not canalized within banks that kept it from overflowing. It is unconfined and vagrant [not careful]."

The Court went further. It referred to part of the Constitution known as the Commerce clause. The Commerce clause states that Congress has the power to regulate commerce among the states. In *Schechter* v. *United States*, the justices interpreted this clause very narrowly. They argued that the Schechters' poultry business was purely local in character. Therefore, Congress had no power to set a minimum wage or to limit working hours. The Schechters were cleared on all counts.

Political cartoonists of the day were both sympathetic and critical of the Supreme Court in its handling of the NRA. How do you think the creator of this cartoon felt about the Court's decision in the Schechter case?

Changing Interpretations of the Commerce Clause

The Schechter case has never been overturned. However, shortly after this ruling, the Supreme Court began interpreting the Commerce clause much more broadly. For example, in 1938 Congress passed the Fair Labor Standards Act. This act limited the workweek to 40 hours and set minimum wages. It also prohibited the shipment of goods made without compliance with the act's rules against child labor. In 1941 the Court upheld the Fair Labor Standards Act. The majority of justices reasoned that the power this act granted the President was clearly limited; the act gave precise guidelines for setting minimum wages in different industries. The Court was comfortable with this more limited delegation of power. By upholding Fair Labor Standards Act, the Court took a broader view of the Commerce clause and of Congress's powers to regulate business.

Setting the Stage
Activity

Thinking About the Different Branches of the Government

Review with students the three branches of the government. With the class, make a chart that lists government bodies that are part of each branch and defines the powers of each branch. Ask students to talk about the benefits of having a government with three branches.

Bonus Activity

Summarizing the Decision

Ask students to imagine they are Chief Justice Hughes announcing the verdict in the Schechter case. Have them write down what they would say to the people in the courtroom, including a brief summary of the reasoning behind the verdict. Let volunteers read their announcements aloud to the class.

Discussion

Checking Understanding

1. Who approved the legal code that the Schechters violated and on what legal grounds did the Schechters raise objections to the code? (The President approved the legal code. The Schechters raised the objection that the Constitution did not give the President the power to legislate.)

2. Why did the Supreme Court strike down the NRA but not the Fair Labor Standards Act? (The Court felt that the powers granted the Executive Branch through the NRA were too broad, but that the powers granted by the Fair Labor Standards Act were more limited by precise guidelines.)

Stimulating Critical Thinking

3. Do you think the federal regulation of business is good or bad for our country? (Students might give examples relating to unfair competition, environmental protection, consumer safety, foreign commerce, preservation of historic sites, etc.) Accept students' assessments of these regulations that are based on clear and logical reasoning.)

Civics Footnote

During the New Deal era, the Court was criticized by many FDR supporters for striking down popular legislation. However, Justice Owen Roberts maintained that the Court was simply performing its duty of analyzing laws according to the Constitution. To combat the conservativeness of the Court, in 1936, FDR introduced a plan to appoint more justices. Many people were outraged. They thought FDR was trying to blur the separation of powers for political ends. The Court, at the same time, started broadening its interpretations of the Constitution and upholding more New Deal legislation. FDR eventually dropped his plan for more justices. This era exemplifies the complex interplay between politics and constitutional principles that determines how our government runs.

Regulation of Business Today

Many people take Congress's setting of a national minimum wage as a given in the country's economic life. However, every time the issue of raising the minimum wage comes up, it is fiercely debated. And there are people who would very much like to abolish the minimum wage. They argue that the minimum wage restricts business owners too much. On the other hand, there are people who would like to see a maximum wage set as well as a minimum wage. Another issue often debated is the extent to which the federal government has the right to regulate business to protect the environment. Clearly, the federal government's right to regulate business, in general and specific terms, will be debated far into the future.

(Above) Shortly after the Schechter decision, and largely as a result of the passage of the Wagner Act in 1935, union membership and power rose greatly. Here laundry workers, who typically earned very low wages, strike in front of their Brooklyn, New York, workplace. In 1937 the United Laundry workers enrolled nearly 14,000 new members.

(Right) To what extent do you think the federal government has a right to regulate business in an effort to protect the environment?

Connections to Economics

Many of the economic issues brought up during the New Deal era are still controversial today. Although U.S. laws against child labor are generally enforced in our country, many other countries have no such laws. Some Americans are pushing for U.S. companies to adopt standards barring the import or sale of products made anywhere in the world with the use of child labor. Such standards would especially affect the importation of rugs, textiles, toys, and clothing. The right of workers to join unions and the right of union workers to strike (rights largely consolidated during the years of the New Deal) are also, at times, under dispute today. These issues continue to shape our economy and our history.

Understanding Civic Issues

1. Why and under what laws were the Schechters brought to trial?
2. For what two main reasons did the Supreme Court strike down the NRA?
3. **Critical Thinking** What are the pros and the cons of a federally mandated minimum wage? List three of each. Then decide whether the pros outweigh the cons or vice versa, and give a reason for your answer.
4. **Hands-On Citizenship** Your class has been appointed to form a commission to answer the following question: Under what circumstances should Congress make laws regulating businesses?

- List different businesses and decide among your class, who will research laws about which businesses. Some examples of businesses might include building, mining, garments (clothing), retail stores, food processing, restaurants, health care, car manufacturing, and sports franchises.
- Use magazines, newspapers, and on-line sources to find out about laws regulating the particular business you chose. Make a chart listing some of the laws and indicating their general purposes. Some purposes might include: safety of workers, safety of consumers, safety of the environment, protection against unfair competition.
- Share your chart with your class. Compare the purposes for the different laws regulating businesses. Together, write up a class list of guidelines for Congress as it makes such laws.

Citizenship Lab Answers

1. They violated various parts of the Live Poultry Code.

2. The Court said Congress illegally passed its duties to the Executive Branch and it had no power to regulate working hours and wages.

3. Pros: employers not being able to take unfair advantage of unskilled labor; all people having a chance to make enough money to live on; periodic review of wage rates against inflation. Cons: reducing competition in the labor market; reduction of competition among businesses that cannot survive if minimum wages must be paid; increase of federal laws that have to be enforced.

Teaching the Hands-On Citizenship

This lesson affords an excellent opportunity to introduce students to the resources available on the Internet. The following are a list of websites that might prove useful:

The Federal Web Locator: http//www.law.vill.edu/fedagency/fedweb.new.html

GPO (Government Printing Office): http//www.access.gpo.gov/su_docs/index.html

Library of Congress Congressional Server: http//thomas.loc.gov/

The White House http//www.whitehouse.gov/

At·a·Glance 12

World War II
1930–1945

Chapter Planning Guide

Section	Student Text	Teacher's Edition Activities
Opener and Story pp. 516–519	**Keys to History Time Line** **History Mystery** Beginning the Story with **Benjamin O. Davis, Jr.**	**Setting the Stage Activity** Writing Letters Home, p. 518
1 **Threats to World Peace** pp. 520–523	**Link to Art** *Hitler Youth, Moravia,* p. 522 **World Link** The Abraham Lincoln Brigade, p. 523	**Warm-Up Activity** Describing Germany's Mood, p. 520 **Geography Question of the Day,** p. 520 **Section Activity** Debating Responses to Fascism, p. 521 **Bonus Activity** Role-Playing a Family's Conflict, p. 522 **Wrap-Up Activity** Making a Time Line, p. 523
2 **World War II Begins** pp. 524–528	**Point of View** Should the United States have aided Great Britain?, p. 525 **Reading Maps** Aggression in Europe by 1940, p. 526 **Skill Lab** Identifying Gaps in Information, p. 528	**Warm-Up Activity** Writing a War Scenario, p. 524 **Geography Question of the Day,** p. 524 **Section Activity** Working as a War Correspondent, p. 526 **Bonus Activity** Advising Roosevelt, p. 526 **Wrap-Up Activity** Writing Headlines, p. 527
3 **The Early War Effort** pp. 529–533	**Hands-On History** Creating your own code, p. 531 **Reading Maps** Aggression in Asia 1931–1942, p. 533	**Warm-Up Activity** Coping with Wartime Shortages, p. 529 **Geography Question of the Day,** p. 529 **Section Activity** Home Front Eyewitness Accounts, p. 530 **Bonus Activity** Making Posters for the War Effort, p. 532 **Wrap-Up Activity** Charting Effects of the War, p. 533
4 **Winning the War** pp. 534–539	**Reading Maps** War in Europe and North Africa 1942–1945, p. 535 **Link to the Present** Remembering the Holocaust, p. 537 **Geography Lab** Tracing Events Over Time and Space, p. 539	**Warm-Up Activity** Deciding Whether to Fight On, p. 534 **Geography Question of the Day,** p. 534 **Section Activity** Speaking as Truman, p. 536 **Bonus Activity** Writing War Poems, p. 536 **Wrap-Up Activity** A V-J Day Letter, p. 538
Evaluation	**Section 1 Review,** p. 523 **Section 2 Review,** p. 527 **Section 3 Review,** p. 533 **Section 4 Review,** p. 538 **Chapter Survey,** pp. 544–545 **Alternative Assessment** Covering the war for radio, p. 545	**Answers to Section 1 Review,** p. 523 **Answers to Section 2 Review,** p. 527 **Answers to Section 3 Review,** p. 533 **Answers to Section 4 Review,** p. 538 **Answers to Chapter Survey,** pp. 544–545 (Alternative Assessment guidelines are in the Take-Home Planner.)

Teacher's Resource Package

Chapter Summaries: English and Spanish, pp. 60–61

Chapter Resources Binder

Study Guide Organizing Information, p. 105

Chapter Resources Binder

Study Guide Making and Reading a Time Line, p. 106

Skills Development Identifying Gaps in Information, pp. 111–112

American Readings Remembering Pearl Harbor, p. 53

Using Historical Documents Franklin Roosevelt's "Day of Infamy" Speech, pp. 77–85

Chapter Resources Binder

Study Guide Previewing Headings, p. 107

Reinforcement Distinguishing Relationships, pp. 109–110

American Readings On the Other Side, pp. 54–55

Chapter Resources Binder

Study Guide Webbing, p. 108

Geography Extensions Making a War Map, pp. 29–30

American Readings Wartime Logs, p. 56

Chapter and Unit Tests Chapter 12 Tests, Forms A and B, pp. 91–94

Take-Home Planner

Introducing the Chapter Activity Mapping World War II, p. 22

Chapter In-Depth Activity Points of View About the War, p. 22

Reduced Views

Study Guide, p. 24

Unit 4 Answers, pp. 30–38

Reduced Views

Study Guide, p. 24

Skills Development, p. 25

American Readings, p. 26

Using Historical Documents, p. 27

Unit 4 Answers, pp. 30–38

Reduced Views

Study Guide, p. 24

Reinforcement, p. 25

American Readings, p. 26

Unit 4 Answers, pp. 30–38

Reduced Views

Study Guide, p. 24

Geography Extensions, p. 27

American Readings, p. 26

Unit 4 Answers, pp. 30–38

Reduced Views

Chapter Tests, p. 27

Unit 4 Answers, pp. 30–38

Alternative Assessment Guidelines for scoring the Chapter Survey activity, p. 23

Additional Resources

Wall Time Line

Unit 4 Activity

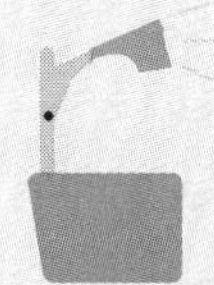
Transparency Package

Transparency 12-1 Working Women—use with Section 3

Transparency 12-2 The Home Front—use with Section 3

Transparency Activity Book

SelecTest Testing Software

Chapter 12 Test, Forms A and B

Vital Links

Videodisc

CD-ROM

Mussolini addressing troops (see TE p. 521)

Adolf Hitler (see TE p. 522)

Churchill on the Battle of Britain (see TE p. 525)

Roosevelt on Pearl Harbor (see TE p. 527)

Japanese American GIs (see TE p. 530)

"Praise the Lord and Pass the Ammunition" (see TE p. 532)

Eisenhower on D-Day (see TE p. 535)

Truman on the atomic bomb (see TE p. 536)

Margaret Bourke-White on Buchenwald (see TE p. 537)

12

Teaching Resources

Take-Home Planner 4
- Introducing Chapter Activity
- Chapter In-Depth Activity
- Alternative Assessment

Chapter Resources Binder
Geography Extensions
American Readings
Using Historical Documents
Transparency Activities
Wall Time Line Activities
Chapter Summaries
Chapter and Unit Tests
SelecTest Test File
Vital Links CD-ROM/Videodisc

Chapter Objectives

★ Explain how Japanese expansionism and the rise of fascist dictatorships in Italy and Germany threatened world peace.
★ Identify the events that led to the entry of the United States into World War II.
★ Summarize the struggles and successes on the American home front and in the early years of the war in the Pacific.
★ Describe how the Allies defeated the Axis powers.

Chapter Overview

In the 1920s and 1930s, the United States followed a policy of isolationism while trying to maintain world peace through international agreements. However, Japan, Italy, and Germany built up armies and weapons and began invading other countries.

In 1939 and 1940 Germany conquered several nations, including France, and launched air attacks on Britain. The United

Time Line

Keys to History

Keys to History journal writing activities are on p. 544 in the Chapter Survey.

Hitler becomes German chancellor Hitler soon gained total control of the country and led it on a path of aggression in Europe. (p. 521)

Crystal Night attack The Nazis' organized attack on German Jews resulted in hundreds dead and thousands sent to work camps. (pp. 521–522)

Looking Back The treaty that ended World War I demanded $32 billion in reparations from Germany and helped push that country into economic and political turmoil.

World Link See p. 523.

1930–1945

Chapter 12 World War II

Sections

Beginning the Story with Benjamin O. Davis, Jr.
1. Threats to World Peace
2. World War II Begins
3. The Early War Effort
4. Winning the War

Keys to History

1933 January
Hitler becomes chancellor of Germany

1938 November
Crystal Night attack on Jews in Germany

1933
1938

Looking Back
Germany signs Treaty of Versailles
1919

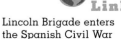

Lincoln Brigade enters the Spanish Civil War
1937

States began providing weapons and other aid to Britain. Relations with Japan became increasingly strained, and in December 1941 Japanese planes bombed Pearl Harbor.

Americans at home helped the war effort by conserving resources and manufacturing war materials. Reacting to anti-Japanese feelings, the federal government put thousands of Japanese Americans in internment camps. The Japanese advance in the Pacific was halted by the 1942 Battle of Midway.

The Allies defeated the Germans in North Africa and invaded Italy, while the Soviets repelled the Germans at Stalingrad. In June 1944 the Allies invaded France. The war in Europe ended in May 1945, but Japan fought on until the United States dropped two atomic bombs in August. The war in which millions of people had died—including 6 million Jewish civilians—was over.

HISTORY Mystery

In 1940 and 1941 thousands of people slept in the subways of London. Who were these people and why were they sleeping there instead of in their homes?

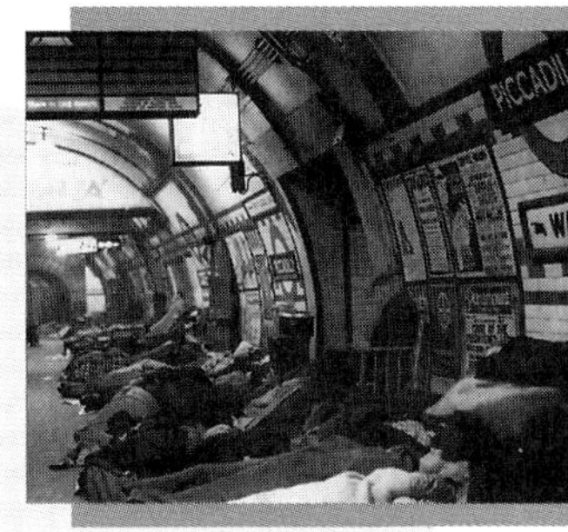

1942 February Japanese American internment begins

1941 December Pearl Harbor

1944 June D-Day

General Dwight D. Eisenhower

1945 May V-E Day

1945 August U.S. drops atomic bombs on Hiroshima and Nagasaki

1941 1943 1945

Looking Ahead

United States and Soviet Union sign first SALT agreement to control arms race

1972

Teaching the HISTORY Mystery

Students will find the answer on p. 524. See Chapter Survey, p. 544, for an additional question.

Time Line

Pearl Harbor Japan's attack on the American naval base brought the United States into World War II. (p. 527)

Japanese internment Reacting to a wave of anti-Japanese hysteria, the United States government removed 110,000 Japanese Americans from their homes and put them in isolated camps. (p. 531)

D-Day The Allies successfully invaded France and began to drive German forces back to Germany. (p. 534)

V-E Day Germany surrendered, ending the war in Europe. (p. 536)

Atomic bombs dropped The United States used its new weapon for the first time. After a second bomb was dropped on Nagasaki, Japan surrendered, ending World War II. (pp. 536–537)

Looking Ahead After nearly 30 years of Cold War tensions, the leading world powers agreed to limit their nuclear weapons.

Beginning the Story

Benjamin O. Davis, Jr.

Benjamin O. Davis, Jr., entered the United States Military Academy at West Point in 1932. He endured four years of silence from the white cadets, who resented the presence of an African American in their midst. Davis's desire to be a pilot was denied until 1941, when a flight-training school for African Americans was set up at Tuskegee Army Air Field in Alabama. But the Tuskegee airmen received no combat assignment until Eleanor Roosevelt stepped in. In 1943, under Davis's command, the airmen flew into combat in North Africa.

Setting the Stage Activity

Writing Letters Home

To help students understand what Benjamin Davis went through at West Point, ask them to imagine attending a summer camp. For some reason, none of the other campers will talk to them. Have students write letters home in which they describe this "silent treatment" and their reactions. Volunteers might share letters with the class.

See the Introducing the Chapter Activity, Mapping World War II, **Take-Home Planner 4**, p. 22.

History Footnote

When the Tuskegee Army Air Field (TAAF) flight school was created, hundreds of applications poured in. The men accepted for the program were an outstanding group. Their military-aptitude test scores were so high that white officers made them take the tests again because they suspected cheating. That kind of thinking dogged the airmen during their entire time at TAAF.

Eventually the 99th Squadron became part of the 332nd, a larger all-black unit. Altogether, African American pilots flew 1,578 missions and were among the most highly decorated pilots of the war. They destroyed or damaged hundreds of enemy planes and never lost a bomber under their protection. A 1995 television movie, *The Tuskegee Airmen,* dramatized their struggle and achievements.

Beginning the Story with Benjamin O. Davis, Jr.

In 1944, Brigadier General Benjamin O. Davis, Sr., a career soldier who had joined the U.S. Army in 1899, pinned the Distinguished Flying Cross on his son. For both father and son, it was a proud and emotional moment.

Benjamin O. Davis, Jr., had known he wanted to fly since he was 13 years old. That year his father took him to see barnstormers—pilots who thrilled audiences with breathtaking aerial stunts. To Benjamin's surprise, his father bought him a ride. "I cannot explain my father's motives in buying me an airplane ride," Benjamin later wrote. "He was not a frivolous spender, and $5 was a considerable sum in 1926. I can only guess that he was looking far into the future . . . and realized . . . that I would benefit from the experience."

It was a wonderful ambition, but not for an African American at that time. "The harsh reality was," Benjamin soon realized, "that there was no way for a black man to become a professional pilot." His only hope, Benjamin decided, was to follow his father into the army and apply for pilot training. The first step was to win an appointment to the elite United States Military Academy at West Point.

The "Silencing"

Weeks after arriving at West Point in 1932, Benjamin realized that being the only African American at West Point would be a severe test of his character and courage.

> "Certain cadets . . . enforce[d] an old West Point tradition—'silencing.' . . . I was to be silenced solely because cadets did not want blacks at West Point. . . . What they did not realize was that I was stubborn enough to put up with their treatment to reach the goal I had come to attain."

History Bookshelf

Colman, Penny. *Rosie the Riveter.* Crown, 1995. Colman introduces the nation's unsung female heroes: the millions of women who joined the industrial work force during World War II. Through photographs and interviews Colman lets the women tell their own stories of how this era changed their lives.

Also of interest:

Frank, Anne. *The Diary of a Young Girl.* Doubleday, 1967.

Mauldin, Bill. *Bill Mauldin's Army: Bill Mauldin's Greatest World War II Cartoons.* Presidio Press, 1983.

Stanley, Jerry. *I Am an American: A True Story of Japanese Internment.* Crown, 1994.

Aviation cadets study a map at the Tuskegee Army Air Field training school in Tuskegee, Alabama. In March 1942 the first class of African American pilots completed their training. Benjamin Davis was one of the five graduates.

For the next four years, Davis lived in silence. He bunked alone in a big room designed for two. He ate meals, trained, and went to classes without speaking to another cadet.

In 1936, Davis faced graduation with bittersweet feelings. "I was extremely proud that I had withstood the forces that opposed me so actively . . . and that I would be the first black in the 20th century to graduate from West Point." However, his application to become a pilot was turned down. Disappointed, Davis accepted a position as an officer in the infantry.

The "Experiment"

While Davis was beginning his military career, African American leaders were pressuring President Roosevelt to open up opportunities for African Americans in the armed forces. In 1941, with war on the horizon, the army agreed to an "experiment." It set up a flight-training school at Tuskegee Army Air Field (TAAF) in Alabama, with the goal of creating a black flying unit. In the first group of 13 African American volunteers, 5 completed the rigorous training. One was Benjamin Davis.

Even after enough pilots had been trained to form the 99th Fighter Squadron, the Tuskegee airmen were passed over for combat assignments until the day Eleanor Roosevelt visited the base in 1943. Against the advice of her staff, the First Lady took a test flight with one of the black airmen. After this well-publicized vote of confidence, the 99th, under the command of Lieutenant Colonel Benjamin Davis, was ordered into combat in North Africa. "As we said our goodbyes," wrote Davis,

> "we pushed far back and away the ugliness that we had endured. . . . We did not regret leaving TAAF. We knew that there were many decent human beings elsewhere in the world, and we looked forward to associating with them."

Hands-On HISTORY

Activity

Benjamin Davis endured the years of "silencing" at West Point because his dream of graduating was so important to him. Think about an important dream of yours. It could involve creating something, winning a competition, or traveling somewhere. Write about this dream and describe some of the hardships or obstacles you might have to overcome to make it come true.

Discussion

Thinking Historically

1. What qualities did Davis show at West Point that probably served him well in combat? (Courage, perseverance, self-reliance.)

2. How do you suppose Davis's fellow cadets felt when he graduated? (Amazed, angry, admiring.)

3. What does Davis's statement about leaving TAAF tell you? (He was bitter about how the Army had treated the Tuskegee airmen and perhaps bitter about how African Americans were treated in general.)

See the Chapter In-Depth Activity, Points of View About the War, **Take-Home Planner 4,** p. 22.

Teaching the Hands-On HISTORY

Encourage students to write about dreams that might come true. Also remind them that obstacles can come from outside, as in Davis's case, or from within. A person may have to overcome lack of knowledge, skills, experience, or courage.

For a journal writing activity on Benjamin O. Davis, Jr., see student page 544.

Introducing the Section

Vocabulary

arms race (p. 520) competition between countries for more and better weapons

isolationism (p. 520) policy of staying out of foreign affairs

dictator (p. 521) a person with complete control of a government

fascism (p. 521) a political system that appeals to racism and nationalism and is ruled by a dictator and a single political party

totalitarian state (p. 521) a government with total control over the lives of its citizens

appeasement (p. 523) giving in to another nation's demands just to keep peace

Warm-Up Activity

Describing Germany's Mood

To focus on circumstances leading to Hitler's rise, have students imagine themselves as Germans in the 1920s and early 1930s. Have them write paragraphs describing resentments over the Treaty of Versailles and the economic depression.

Geography Question of the Day

Have students use the map on pp. R2–R3 to infer why Japan might want to gain territory. (Small island nation—needed more resources and living space.)

Section Objectives

★ Explain how the United States tried to maintain world peace in the 1920s and 1930s.

★ Identify events in Japan, Italy, and Germany that threatened world peace.

★ Describe how Americans differed in their responses to the rise of fascism.

Teaching Resources

Take-Home Planner 4, pp. 20–29

Chapter Resources Binder

- **Study Guide, p. 105**
- Reinforcement
- Skills Development

Geography Extensions
American Readings
Using Historical Documents
Transparency Activities
Chapter and Unit Tests

1. Threats to World Peace

Reading Guide

New Terms **arms race, isolationism, dictator, fascism, totalitarian state, appeasement**

Section Focus **How Japanese expansionism and the rise of fascist dictatorships threatened world peace**

1. How did the United States try to maintain world peace?
2. What events in Japan, Italy, and Germany threatened world peace?
3. How did Americans differ in their response to the rise of fascism?

When Benjamin Davis entered West Point in 1932, the horrors of World War I were still fresh in everyone's memory. In spite of Woodrow Wilson's hopes, however, it had not been a "war to end all wars." In fact, no sooner had the peace treaties been signed than an **arms race**—a competition between countries for more and better weapons—began to sow the seeds of future conflict.

Efforts to Keep Peace

President Warren Harding, who followed Wilson, worked to end the arms race. In 1921 he invited delegates from Europe and Japan to the Washington Naval Conference. There they agreed to limit the production of warships. They also agreed not to attack one another's possessions in the Pacific and to respect China's independence.

Another treaty designed to maintain peace was the 1928 Kellogg-Briand Pact. In this treaty 62 nations agreed to stay out of war except in cases of self-defense. Unfortunately, this treaty was impossible to enforce. As one senator said, it was a "worthless, but perfectly harmless treaty."

The United States also tried to stay out of war by adopting a policy of **isolationism,** which means staying out of foreign affairs. With the onset of the Depression, Americans felt that the government should work on problems at home instead of abroad.

A Good Neighbor

The exception to isolationist policy was Latin America. There the United States had continued to intervene to protect American business interests. President Hoover took a new approach, however, when he announced that the United States wanted to be "a good neighbor." President Roosevelt continued Hoover's Good Neighbor policy. In 1934 he called home the last American troops from Latin American soil.

The Rise of Dictators

The efforts to promote peace failed in Japan, Italy, and Germany. These countries continued to build up armies and weapons, even though all three had taken part in the Washington Naval Conference.

Japan Japan's goal was expansion. An island nation, it needed space for its growing population. It also needed raw materials—coal, oil, rubber—for its booming industries. In 1931 Japan's military leaders, who had

History Footnote

Benito Mussolini had grand dreams of building a new Roman Empire. He named his political movement *fascism* after the Latin *fasces:* bundles of wooden rods tied around an ax handle, symbolizing the authority of officials in ancient Rome. In public, Mussolini played the part of bully to the hilt—strutting about, jutting his jaw, and clenching his fists. His followers called him *Il Duce,* which means "the leader" in Italian. Hitler looked up to Mussolini at first. He copied elements of Italian fascism and became known as *Führer,* which means "leader" in German. Mussolini was contemptuous of Hitler, calling him a "mad little clown." However, by the time World War II started, Mussolini was a puppet in the hands of his more powerful partner.

taken control of the government, invaded Manchuria in northern China. During the next six years, Japanese armies continued to move through China as well as other parts of the Pacific in order to develop industries.

Italy Even more threatening were events in Europe. Weakened by strikes and riots after World War I, Italy fell under the influence of a dictator named Benito Mussolini. A **dictator** is a person with complete control of a government.

Mussolini organized a government based on fascism. **Fascism** is a political system based on racism and nationalism and ruled by a dictator and a single political party. In 1922 Mussolini seized control of Italy.

Germany In Germany, too, hard times led to fascism. Here the guiding hand belonged to another dictator named Adolf Hitler. Hitler led the National Socialist German Workers' Party—the Nazis—to power by promising Germans that he could rebuild their fallen country. By 1933 the Nazis were the largest party in Germany, and Germany's president made Hitler chancellor.

In 1934, when the president died, Hitler took control. He turned Germany into a **totalitarian state,** a government with total control over the lives of its citizens. Under Hitler, the Nazis controlled schools, newspapers, and radio stations. No one was allowed to criticize the government. Hitler began his reign by building up his armed forces.

Hitler united Germans by telling them that they belonged to a "master race." He played on anti-Semitic feelings by saying that Jews were the Germans' main enemy. Beginning in 1935 Hitler passed laws that stripped Jews of their citizenship, barred them from many types of work, and forbade them from using public facilities. To set them apart, Hitler forced every Jew to wear a yellow Star of David.

Tens of thousands of Jews fled Nazi Germany during this period. In the fall of 1938, though, new German laws made it almost impossible for them to leave. Hitler's troops began rounding up Jews and sending them to concentration camps to work as slave laborers.

On November 9–10, 1938, the Nazis carried out an organized attack on Jews throughout

Nazi storm troopers in Warsaw, Poland, herd a group of terrified Jewish citizens from their homes. Photographs such as this one were later used in court as evidence of Nazi brutality and terrorism.

Developing the Section

Discussion

Checking Understanding

1. What was life in Nazi Germany like? (Government controlled schools, media; no free speech; Jews persecuted.)

Stimulating Critical Thinking

2. Besides anti-Semitism, why do you think Hitler persecuted Jews? (Scapegoats for Germany's problems; united other Germans to have "inferior enemies.")

Section Activity

Debating Responses to Fascism

To focus on responses to fascism, have groups debate isolationism versus opposition. Half of each group takes isolationist views while the other half take views of people like the Lincoln Brigade. (See the World Link on p. 523.) They should try to think like people of the 1930s.

Vital Links

Mussolini addressing troops (Picture) Unit 5, Side 1, Search 39623

See also Unit 5 Explore CD-ROM location 222.

Connections to Art

Margaret Bourke-White was one of dozens of American photographers who covered events preceding and during World War II. Like Bourke-White, many worked at one time or another for *Life,* a much-imitated picture magazine founded in 1936. In fact, *Life* sent more photographers and artists to cover the war than all American newspapers combined. Combat photographers and artists had to be brave. They worked on the front lines of battle because, as one of them said, "If your pictures are no good, you aren't close enough." Although none of *Life*'s photographers were killed during the war, five were wounded, two flew on planes that were shot down, two sailed on ships that were torpedoed, and a dozen found themselves overboard during sea maneuvers.

Teaching the

Link to Art

Have students imagine seeing this photo in a magazine in the 1930s. As young Americans, would they have found it unsettling? If they were isolationists might it make them question their position? Why? **Discussion Answer:** He wanted to unite Germans of all ages to fight for the Nazi cause.

Bonus Activity

Role-Playing a Family's Conflict

To focus on the situation of German Jews, have groups role-play a German Jewish family discussion in 1936. Roles include parents, two children, and relatives such as grandparents. They should discuss whether to flee or to stay and hope the situation improves or does not worsen. Have the class discuss which role-plays were most authentic.

Vital Links

Adolf Hitler (Movie) Unit 5, Side 1, Search 27582, Play to 27975

See also Unit 5 Explore CD-ROM location 134.

Link to Art

Hitler Youth, Moravia (1938) In World War II new magazines, such as *Look* and *LIFE,* sent photographers to Europe and the Pacific to document the events of the war. The work of these photographers, who called themselves photojournalists, shaped how Americans viewed the war. Margaret Bourke-White, a talented photojournalist, took some of the war's most memorable pictures. In the photograph at right, taken in Czechoslovakia, she captured German boys training to be Nazi storm troopers. **Discuss** What does this image tell you about Hitler's goals for Germany?

Germany. This tragic event is called Crystal Night for the shattered windows of more than 200 synagogues and 7,000 shops and homes. Nearly a hundred Jews were killed and thousands sent to work camps.

The Axis powers In 1936 Germany and Italy formed an alliance. Mussolini described the ties between their capitals, Rome and Berlin, as the "axis" around which Europe would revolve. The alliance became known as the Axis powers. In September 1940 Japan joined the Axis. The three countries agreed to support each other if the United States attacked any one of them.

Roosevelt and Isolationism

Many Americans were worried by the actions of Japan, Germany, and Italy. However, many were still disillusioned by the results of World War I. As the celebrated hero Alvin York said, "I can't see we did any good. There's as much trouble now as there was then, when we went over there."

It was clear to Roosevelt and to Congress that most Americans did not wish to be involved in Europe or Asia. To ensure that the United States maintained its isolationism, Congress passed a series of neutrality acts. The first act, passed in 1935, banned the sale of weapons to any country engaged in war. Its purpose was to discourage the United States from taking sides in a conflict.

The strength of isolationist feeling presented President Roosevelt with a challenge. He saw another world war coming, yet he feared losing public support if he began to build up the nation's military forces.

The Axis powers did not give Roosevelt much time. By early 1936, Italy had invaded the African nation of Ethiopia, and German armed forces were threatening France.

History Footnote

Ernest Hemingway, who covered the Spanish Civil War as a correspondent, based one of his most highly acclaimed novels—*For Whom the Bell Tolls* (1940)—on what he observed. His fictional hero, Robert Jordan, was modeled on Robert Merriman, a commander of the Lincolns who was killed in battle.

Although Hemingway and some other Americans admired the Lincolns, those who returned to the United States encountered much suspicion and harassment. United States customs officials seized their passports for violations of the Neutrality Acts. Some ex-Lincolns encountered discrimination in the workplace. In later years the United States military hesitated to allow ex-Lincolns to serve in World War II, giving them what it considered a negative classification: PAF, or "Premature Anti-Fascists."

The Spanish Civil War

Germany and Italy followed these successes by intervening in a civil war that broke out in Spain in 1936. Mussolini and Hitler supported Francisco Franco, a fascist determined to overthrow the democratic government of the Spanish Republic.

Many European leaders realized that the Spanish Civil War was a dress rehearsal for a coming world war, but they did not want to get involved. Finally Russia (renamed the Soviet Union by the Bolsheviks in 1922) sent supplies to the anti-Franco forces. Then 3,000 American volunteers formed the Abraham Lincoln Brigade to help fight Franco. It was a lost cause, however. In 1939 a victorious Franco set up a fascist dictatorship in Spain.

The Third Reich

Meanwhile, Hitler was proceeding with his plan to build a great German empire that he called the Third Reich. One of his goals was to rule over all German-speaking people. In March 1938 he annexed Austria. Then he demanded that Czechoslovakia give him the Sudetenland, home to some 3 million people of German ancestry.

Hoping to avoid war, and willing to believe that Hitler would soon be satisfied, Great Britain and France signed the fateful Munich Agreement in the fall of 1938. The agreement forced the Czech government to surrender the Sudetenland to Germany. In return, Hitler promised to make no more territorial demands on Europe.

Many felt that **appeasement**—giving in to another nation's demands just to keep peace—was cowardly. Rising in Parliament, Winston Churchill, the future British prime minister, declared:

> "All is over. Silent, mournful, abandoned, broken Czechoslovakia recedes into the darkness."

The Abraham Lincoln Brigade They were writers, teachers, students, farmhands, mechanics, and clerks. They included African Americans, American Indians, and Americans of various European ancestries. They were the men and women volunteers of the Abraham Lincoln Brigade. They all fought in the Spanish Civil War because they believed that isolationism was the wrong response to fascism.

These idealistic Americans bought their own tents, canteens, and mess kits from army surplus stores before they sailed for Europe. The first group arrived in Spain in January 1937. Over the next 21 months, nearly one-third of "the Lincolns" lost their lives fighting for the doomed Republican, or Loyalist, cause. As the surviving Lincolns prepared to leave Spain, a grateful Loyalist leader told them, "You can go proudly. You are history. You are legend."

1. Section Review

1. Define **arms race, isolationism, dictator, fascism, totalitarian state,** and **appeasement.**
2. What are three ways the United States tried to avoid getting involved in the war?
3. How did Hitler gain power and support?
4. **Critical Thinking** Could the United States have prevented the rise of fascism in Europe? Explain your answer.

Teaching the

Explain that the Lincolns withdrew by order of Spain's Republican leaders, who hoped for a withdrawal of Franco's allies. Have students explain whether they would fight for a cause in another country.

Closing the Section

Wrap-Up Activity

Making a Time Line

To summarize threats to world peace in the 1920s and 1930s, have groups create time lines with titles such as "Stepping Stones to War." They should include relevant events and years from the section, illustrating some or all events with photocopies or drawings.

Section Review Answers

1. Definitions: *arms race* (520), *isolationism* (520), *dictator* (521), *fascism* (521), *totalitarian state* (521), *appeasement* (523)

2. Any three: Washington Naval Conference, Kellogg-Briand Pact, isolationism, Good Neighbor Policy, Neutrality Acts.

3. Promised to rebuild Germany; created totalitarian state; built up army; persecuted Jews.

4. Yes: by cutting off diplomatic ties or trade. No: events made some countries ripe for fascism.

Introducing the Section

Warm-Up Activity

Writing a War Scenario

To prepare for reading about how the United States was drawn into the war, have students imagine that a war involving many other countries is going on today. Have them write brief, realistic scenarios describing an event that would pull the United States into such a war. Have volunteers read scenarios aloud. Discuss similarities and differences among them.

Geography Question of the Day

Have students refer to the maps on pp. 422 and R2–R3 to list countries they would expect Germany and Japan to invade, explaining why. As they read the section, have them revise their lists to make them accurate.

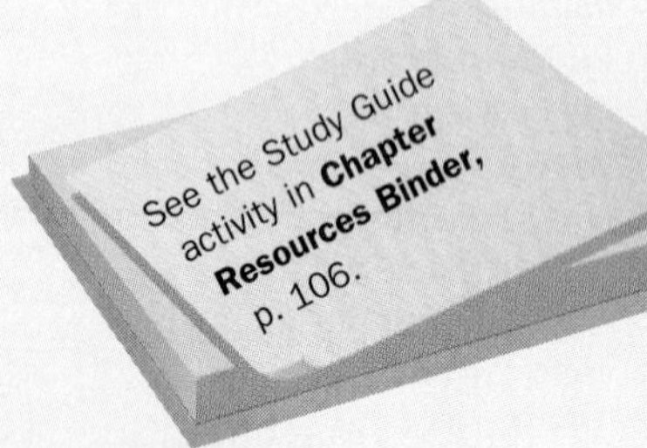
See the Study Guide
activity in **Chapter
Resources Binder**,
p. 106.

Section Objectives

- ★ Explain why Germany was successful in the early years of the war.
- ★ Describe ways in which the United States aided Great Britain.
- ★ Summarize the events that led to the Japanese bombing of Pearl Harbor.

Teaching Resources

Take-Home Planner 4, pp. 20–29
Chapter Resources Binder
Study Guide, p. 106
Reinforcement
Skills Development, pp. 111–112
Geography Extensions
American Readings, p. 53
Using Historical Documents, pp. 77–85
Transparency Activities
Chapter and Unit Tests

2. World War II Begins

Reading Guide

Section Focus **Events that led to the United States entering the war**

1. **Why was Germany successful in the early years of the war?**
2. **How did the United States aid Great Britain?**
3. **What events led to the bombing of Pearl Harbor?**

Churchill's prediction was correct. In the spring of 1939, Hitler's troops took over the entire Czech nation. Then Hitler signed a peace treaty with Joseph Stalin, the Soviet leader. In truth, their treaty was mainly a secret agreement to invade Poland and divide it between them.

On September 1, 1939, Hitler shocked the world by invading Poland. The invasion was such a surprise and so powerful that it was known as a *blitzkrieg,* or lightning war. Realizing at last that the appeasement policy had failed, Great Britain and France declared war on Germany two days later. Within two weeks, the Soviet Union had struck Poland from the east. World War II had begun.

German Triumphs

At first, Germany seemed invincible. By the end of September, with all Polish resistance crushed, Hitler shifted his attention to western Europe.

In April 1940 German armies captured Denmark and Norway. A month later German armored vehicles sliced through the Netherlands and Belgium and swept into France. Within days German troops reached the English Channel, trapping more than 340,000 French, British, and Belgian soldiers in the French port city of Dunkirk.

Although heroic efforts by the British rescued some 338,000 of the stranded soldiers, it was a crushing defeat for the Allies. France surrendered on June 22, 1940, and the German flag fluttered above Paris.

The Battle of Britain

Now Great Britain was fighting Germany alone. In 1940 Hitler launched a series of air attacks in preparation for an invasion. This "blitz" left airfields, ports, and cities in smoldering ruins. Few thought the island nation stood a chance. British prime minister Winston Churchill, though, was confident. Speaking for the British people, he promised:

> "We shall fight on the beaches, we shall
> fight in the fields and in the streets,
> we shall never surrender."

Indeed, the British spirit never broke. City children were sent to live in the country. By night Londoners used subway stations as air-raid shelters. By day they cleared the wreckage, buried the dead, and tried to carry on. It was, as Churchill rightly said, their "finest hour."

The Royal Air Force was badly outnumbered by the German Luftwaffe, but the British had developed radar, which helped them locate and shoot down German planes. By the spring of 1940, Britain had used up almost all its resources fighting off the German attacks. Despite months of bombing, though, Hitler still had not been able to clear the English Channel for an invasion.

History Footnote

The evacuation of Allied soldiers from France came to be called "the miracle of Dunkirk." One reason is that German troops and tanks had been only a few miles from Dunkirk when Hitler ordered them to halt. Hermann Göring, head of the Luftwaffe, had assured him that the air force could destroy the troops at Dunkirk. It took three days before Hitler allowed the German army to advance.

Another aspect of the "miracle" is that it was carried out by civilians as well as navy personnel. All along England's southern coast, fishermen, yachtsmen, retired sailors, and others answered the call for help. Braving high waves and German bombs, they shuttled vessels of every shape and size—including motorboats, trawlers, and yachts—back and forth across the channel to save the soldiers at Dunkirk.

Surveying a bombed building outside London, Winston Churchill shook his fist and shouted, "We shall let them have it back!" Churchill's courage inspired the British people. Hitler had boasted that his troops would take over London within three months, yet by late 1940 Germany had given up its plans to invade Britain.

Aid for Britain

Americans were shocked and outraged by Germany's attacks on England. At this point, wrote one editor, "What the majority of the American people want is to be as unneutral as possible without getting into war."

Roosevelt felt obliged to help England. At his request, in 1939 Congress passed another neutrality act. This act allowed Americans to sell weapons to countries at war. The United States Navy immediately started selling its older planes to Britain.

Roosevelt also knew that the time had come to begin preparing for war. At his urging, Congress voted to expand and modernize the nation's armed forces. In September 1940 Congress passed the first peacetime draft in American history. By October it had voted $17 billion for defense spending. This was equal to American military spending in all of World War I.

In answer to isolationist critics, Roosevelt claimed that aid to Britain and stronger defenses would help keep the United States out of the war. He called on Americans to produce more war goods "to keep war away

Point of View

Should the United States have aided Great Britain?

Defending itself against Germany was crushing Britain. It could no longer afford to buy or make ships and weapons. At his wit's end, Winston Churchill appealed to President Roosevelt "to supply the additional shipping capacity so urgently needed, as well as the crucial weapons of war."

Roosevelt wanted to help. He thought of a way to provide war supplies to Britain without asking for payment. The United States would lend arms and supplies to the British, who would return or replace them after the war. At a press conference in December, 1940 he explained his proposal, which he called "Lend-Lease," in simple, everyday terms:

> "Suppose my neighbor's home catches on fire. If he can take my garden hose and connect it up with his hydrant, I may help to put out his fire. Now I don't say to him, 'Neighbor, my garden hose cost me $15.' I don't want $15—I want my garden hose back after the fire is over."

Developing the Section

Discussion

Checking Understanding

1. What were Germany's early war successes? (Conquests of Poland, Denmark, Norway, Netherlands, Belgium, France; damage to Britain.)

2. How would producing war goods "keep war away" from the United States? (Would give Britain what it needed to fight Germany so the United States would not have to.)

Stimulating Critical Thinking

3. How could Roosevelt justify his "foreign wars" statement when he felt sure war was coming? (Believed that when the United States entered the war, it would be because the war had directly affected the nation and thus was no longer "foreign.")

Teaching the Point of View

Ask students which seems more accurate: comparing war supplies to a garden hose or to gum. Also ask why they think Lend-Lease passed. (Many legislators were sympathetic to Britain.)

Vital Links

Churchill on the Battle of Britain (Movie) Unit 5, Side 1, Search 32867, Play to 33856

See also Unit 5 Explore CD-ROM location 174.

Teaching the Reading Maps

To focus on the extent of aggression, have students compare this map with the map on page R3. **Answer to Reading Maps:** Those who see situation as alarming but not hopeless may favor sending aid or troops.

Section Activity

Working as a War Correspondent

To explore effects of the "blitz," have students imagine being American journalists at the scene shown on p. 525. Have them write articles, including quotes from people interviewed and "human interest" details. They should try to get readers to agree with their views.

Bonus Activity

Advising Roosevelt

To clarify opinions about American policy before Pearl Harbor, have small groups role-play advisors to Roosevelt in November 1941. Have them discuss how the nation should respond to events in Europe and Asia. A group representative can report conclusions.

Tips for Teaching

At-Risk Students

At-risk students may dislike writing and prefer group over individual work. To help them succeed, adapt activities so they work with partners who enjoy writing. They can contribute ideas and phrases without having to write. Another possibility is to have them create non-written products, such as tape recordings.

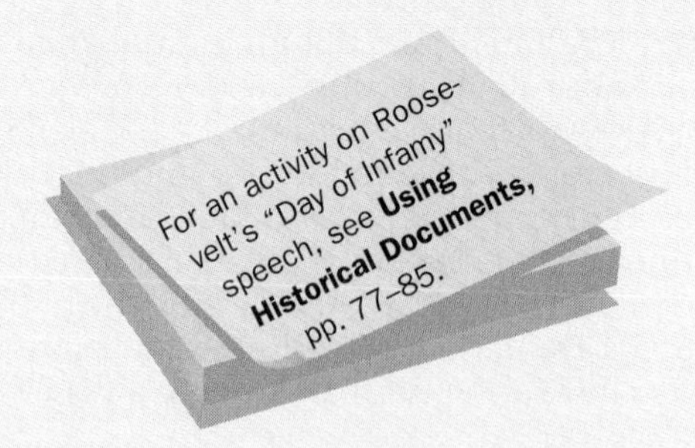

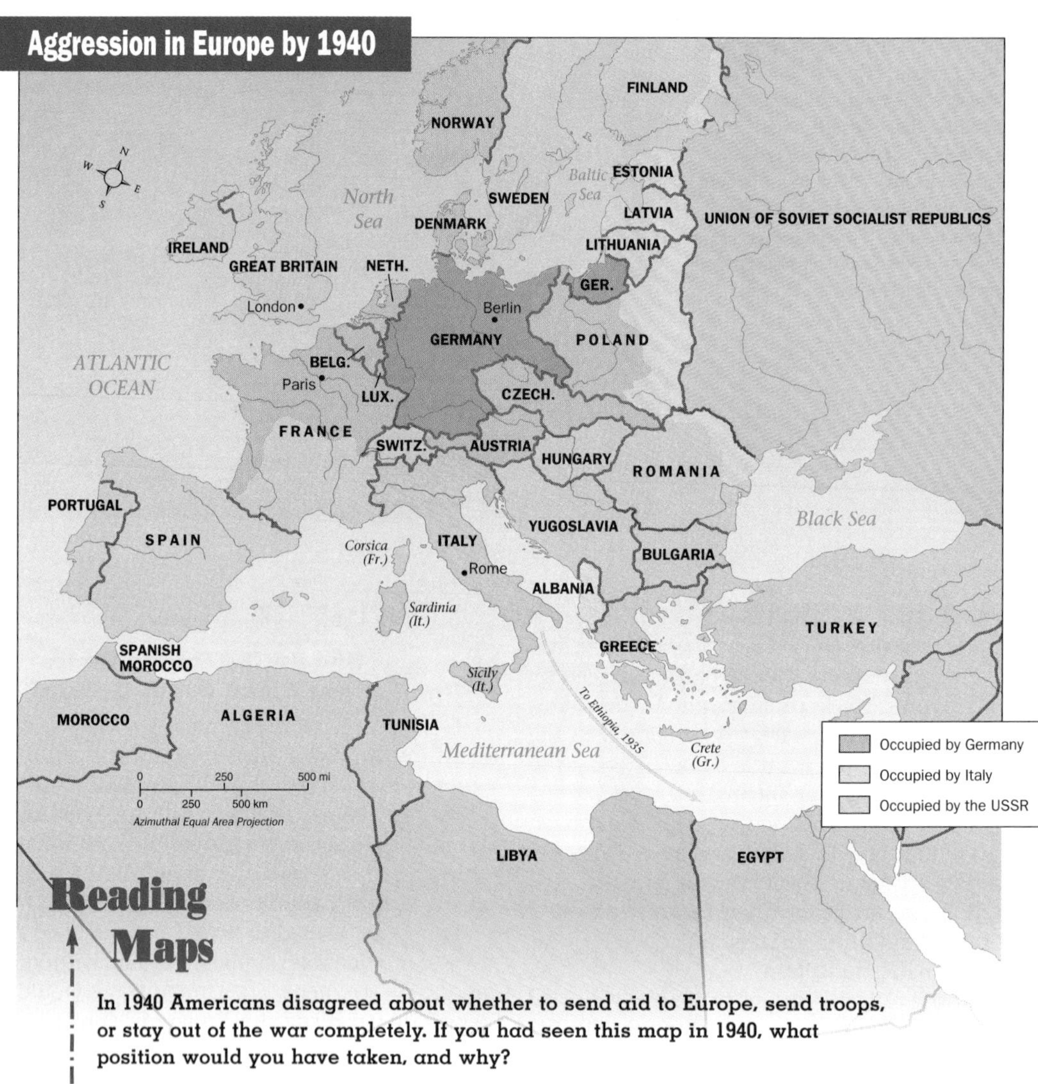

Reading Maps

In 1940 Americans disagreed about whether to send aid to Europe, send troops, or stay out of the war completely. If you had seen this map in 1940, what position would you have taken, and why?

Isolationists feared that Roosevelt's scheme would drag the United States into the war. If that happened, they argued, we would need those supplies. One senator opposed Lend-Lease with this example: "Lending war equipment is a good deal like lending chewing gum. You don't want it back."

In spite of isolationist opposition, the Lend-Lease bill passed. Soon the United States was sending supplies to Britain.

When Roosevelt ran for an unprecedented third term in 1940, he promised voters, "Your boys are not going to be sent into any foreign wars." He won re-election easily.

History Footnote

In July 1941, after Japan completed its takeover of Indochina, Roosevelt froze Japanese assets in the United States. In Tokyo, militarists like General Hideki Tojo argued with civilian leaders about whether to attack the United States. As negotiations between the two nations dragged on, Japanese "doves" became increasingly downhearted. On October 16 Japan's civilian premier resigned along with his cabinet. The "war hawk" Tojo became premier, and the stage was set for the attack on Pearl Harbor.

For Americans' accounts of first hearing about Pearl Harbor, see **American Readings**, p. 53.

The Atlantic Charter

By now, most Americans were preparing themselves mentally for war. This time, when asked his opinion, Alvin York said, "Hitler and Mussolini jes' need a good whuppin', an' it looks like Uncle Sam is gonna have to do it."

In early 1941 military cooperation between Britain and the United States began. The United States Navy sent ships far into the North Atlantic to report to the British on the presence of German U-boats. In April, American troops occupied Greenland and soon replaced British soldiers in Iceland.

In August 1941 Churchill and Roosevelt met to draw up a statement of Allied goals called the Atlantic Charter. They pledged not to seek territory but to support the right of all peoples to choose their own governments and to enjoy the "Four Freedoms"—freedom of speech, freedom of religion, freedom from want, and freedom from fear.

Japan in Southeast Asia

Meanwhile, Japan's leaders were becoming much more aggressive. They seized resource-rich French Indochina and laid plans to conquer the rest of Southeast Asia. To "slow Japan up," Roosevelt declared an embargo on exports to Japan. He also fortified bases in Guam and the Philippines and increased aid to China.

Relations between Japan and the United States became increasingly strained. Japan demanded that the United States cut off aid to China and end the embargo. The United States asked Japan to leave the Axis powers and to withdraw from China and French Indochina. Neither side would give in.

The Japanese made one last offer on November 20. The United States made a counteroffer on November 26. Neither nation agreed to the other's terms. Meanwhile, a Japanese fleet was steaming secretly toward Hawaii.

The battleships *West Virginia* and *Tennessee* were set aflame in the Japanese attack on Pearl Harbor.

Pearl Harbor

President Roosevelt called December 7, 1941, a "day that shall live in infamy." That morning some 360 Japanese bombers filled the sky in a surprise attack on Pearl Harbor, Hawaii. The attack killed 2,403 American military personnel and civilians and sank several American battleships and destroyers. The next day Congress declared that a state of war existed with Japan.

On December 11 Germany and Italy, the other Axis powers, declared war on the United States. What had started in Poland on September 1, 1939, had become a global war.

2. Section Review

1. What were the main reasons for Germany's early military successes?
2. Summarize the arguments for and against Roosevelt's Lend-Lease proposal.
3. Critical Thinking Do you think the United States should have imposed its embargo on Japan? Why or why not?

Vital Links

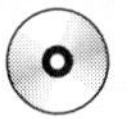

Roosevelt on Pearl Harbor (Movie) Unit 5, Side 1, Search 29603, Play to 30504

See also Unit 5 Explore CD-ROM location 144.

Closing the Section

Wrap-Up Activity

Writing Headlines

To review major events, have students write newspaper headlines (main head and subhead) for each of these dates: September 1, 1939; June 22, 1940; and December 7, 1941. Then ask them to choose two additional events described in the section and write similar headlines for each. After they read their headlines aloud, discuss what makes a good headline.

Section Review Answers

1. Misleading Britain and France about plans for Czechoslovakia, treaty with Soviets, *blitzkrieg.*
2. For: defeat of Britain would bring war closer to United States; obligated to help ally. Against: would pull United States into war; United States might need supplies it sent to Britain.
3. Yes: punish aggression. No: too severe, invited retaliation.

they lack complete information about why no one warned Pearl Harbor of the possibility of attack. (b) Secondary sources such as books about the war written afterward; primary sources such as military and diplomatic documents. (c) Probably not: Roosevelt and many others of the time are dead; those still alive may not tell all they know; documents and other evidence may be lost. Accept reasonable answers.

For further application, have students do the Applying Skills activity in the Chapter Survey (p. 544).

If students need to review the skill, use the Skills Development transparency and activity in the **Chapter Resources Binder**, pp. 111–112.

Introducing the Skill Lab

Mention a recent front-page news event, asking students whether reporters who covered the event likely learned every detail about it. Point out that information gaps are even more of a problem when dealing with long-past events. For example, despite thousands of available resources, historians still have questions about World War II that may never be answered. Before students read source B, note that Pearl Harbor is on Oahu.

Skill Lab

Answers

1. (a) If no United States officials knew about the plans, that explains why the United States was unprepared. If some knew anything about the plans, the Question to Investigate must be explored further. (b) One possibility: If United States officials did know about the plans, why did they not warn Pearl Harbor?

2. (b) Charts should include information from all four sources, such as the following: *What Was Known*—Rumors that Japan would attack Pearl Harbor if a break took place. *Who Knew*—Joseph Grew; officials who received his warning.

3. (a) Among other possibilities, students should realize

(Answers continued in top margin)

Skill Lab

Skill Tips

- Questions of "why" and "how" pose the greatest challenges to historians.
- Information gaps often occur because witnesses have died, no written records were kept, or written records were lost.

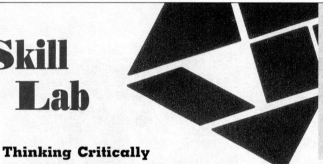

Thinking Critically

Identifying Gaps in Information

On the night of December 7, 1941, a grim President Roosevelt invited congressional leaders to the White House. After hearing about the attack on Pearl Harbor, Senator Tom Connally of Texas exploded. "How did it happen that our warships were caught like tame ducks?" he shouted. "Where were our patrols? They knew these negotiations were going on." The President replied, "I don't know, Tom. I just don't know."

Question to Investigate

Why was the United States unprepared for an attack on Pearl Harbor?

Procedure

Historians often lack complete information. Try identifying gaps in information about events before the Pearl Harbor attack.

1 Identify the information you seek.
a. Why might you want to learn who knew what about the Japanese plans?
b. Tell what else might be useful to learn.

2 Determine what information you have.
a. Make a chart with the headings *What Was Known About Japanese Plans* and *Who Knew.*
b. Fill in the chart with information you know, based on reading A through D.

3 Identify gaps in the information.
a. List the information you are missing.
b. Name two types of sources you might check to try to find that information.
c. Can the Question to Investigate ever be answered? Explain.

Sources to Use

A In January 1941 Ambassador to Japan Joseph Grew warned: "There is a lot of talk around town to the effect that the Japanese, in case of a break with the United States, are planning to go all out in a surprise mass attack on Pearl Harbor."

B "The island of Oahu, due to its fortifications, its garrison and its physical characteristics, is believed to be the strongest in the world. . . . A major attack . . . is considered impracticable."
Army Chief of Staff George Marshall in a May 1941 memo to President Roosevelt

C On November 27, 1941, the War Department sent a warning to commanders in Hawaii that a Japanese attack was expected within days, probably against the Philippines or another target in Southeast Asia. It did not mention Pearl Harbor.

D Three days before the attack, American military officials picked up a coded radio broadcast to Japanese embassies: "Higashi no kazeme" (East winds, rain). It meant that Japan was going to break diplomatic relations with the United States. Hawaii was not informed.

Section Objectives

- ★ Describe ways Americans at home contributed to the war effort.
- ★ Identify reasons President Roosevelt ordered the internment of Japanese Americans.
- ★ Explain why the Battle of Midway was a turning point in the war.

Teaching Resources

Take-Home Planner 4, pp. 20–29
Chapter Resources Binder
Study Guide, p. 107
Reinforcement
Skills Development
Geography Extensions
American Readings, pp. 54–55
Using Historical Documents
Transparency Activities, pp. 43–44
Chapter and Unit Tests

3. The Early War Effort

Reading Guide

New Term rationing

Section Focus Early struggles and successes on the home front and in the Pacific

1. How did Americans at home contribute to the war effort?
2. Why did Roosevelt order the internment of Japanese Americans?
3. Why was the Battle of Midway a turning point in the war?

The war affected every American family. In a fireside chat shortly after Pearl Harbor, President Roosevelt put it bluntly:

> "We are now in this war. We are all in it—all the way. Every single man, woman, and child is a partner."

Rationing and Producing

To provide American and Allied forces with food, clothing, and war equipment, everyone had an important part to play. One way to conserve resources was by **rationing**—limiting the amount of scarce goods people could buy. Basic foods such as butter, sugar, coffee, and meat were rationed. So were crucial items such as shoes and gasoline. Rationing made life on the home front inconvenient, but most people were glad to help.

The War Production Board To help American industry do its part in the war effort, Roosevelt set up the War Production Board (WPB). The WPB's job was to supervise the changeover from producing goods for peacetime use to producing war materials such as planes, ships, and tanks. The WPB also set high goals for production. Under its guidance, output nearly doubled.

In 1942 alone the WPB directed the spending of $47 billion. Production of airplanes increased from 19,000 a year in 1941 to 95,000 in 1944. Ship tonnage rose from 237,000 in 1939 to 10 million in 1943. The industrialist Henry J. Kaiser, who had never built a ship before, cut the average time it took to build a "Liberty" ship from 355 days in 1941 to 56 days at the end of 1942.

After Mexico declared war on the Axis in 1942, the Mexican government sent 375,000 temporary farm workers to the United States to help grow and harvest crops. Farm production increased by 25 percent.

Workers on the Move

The increase in production meant more jobs—a big change from the Great Depression. By 1943 unemployment had all but disappeared and workers enjoyed real benefits: good wages, paid vacations, extra pay for overtime work, and—in some cases—paid health insurance.

People migrated from rural to urban areas for better jobs. New defense industries, especially in the North and West, attracted thousands of workers. California's population, for example, more than doubled in the 1940s. As men left for the military, more and more women stepped into the jobs they left behind.

Introducing the Section

Vocabulary

rationing (p. 529) limiting the amount of scarce goods people could buy

Warm-Up Activity

Coping with Wartime Shortages

To prepare for reading about the home front, write the following on the chalkboard: *sugar, meat, shoes, gasoline.* Divide the class into four groups, assign one item to each group, and have each group list ways they would be affected if that item were limited for several years. Post the lists and invite ideas about how people might have coped with wartime shortages.

Geography Question of the Day

Write the following scenario on the chalkboard: *Our nation has entered a huge war. Suddenly factories are busy making war materials, and the armed forces are growing.* Have students write paragraphs predicting how this scenario would affect internal migration.

See the Study Guide activity in **Chapter Resources Binder**, p. 107.

Developing the Section

Section **Activity**

Home Front Eyewitness Accounts

To focus on everyday life during the war, have students imagine living in the United States in 1943. Have them decide where they are (anywhere from an industrial city to an internment camp) and write an eyewitness account of daily life. They might imagine meeting a teenager who guides them through workplaces, stores, homes, and so on. Conclude by sharing accounts.

For a young Japanese girl's account of life in Japan during and after the war, see **American Readings**, pp. 54–55.

Point out that it was not until 1948 that segregation was outlawed in the armed forces.

Vital Links

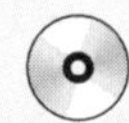

Japanese American GIs (Picture) Unit 5, Side 1, Search 32813

See also Unit 5 Explore CD-ROM location 160.

History Footnote

The first female defense workers were mostly women who had been employed in other jobs or had recently graduated from high school. However the need to meet production quotas soon led the government to encourage homemakers to enter defense industries with slogans like these: "If you've used an electric mixer, . . . you can learn to run a drill press." About 6 million women joined the work force during the war. In the aviation industry alone, the percentage of female employees skyrocketed from 1 percent in 1941 to 65 percent in 1943.

Despite the popular image of "Rosie the Riveter," wartime women did not only manufacture planes, ships, tanks, and weapons. They also replaced men as meat packers, plumbers, trash collectors, truck drivers, crane operators, and so on.

Resentment of newcomers This huge migration put great strains on American society. Longtime residents complained that newcomers competed for scarce housing. In many cities the resentment of newcomers—especially those of different races or religious backgrounds—led to racism and violence. In 1943 alone there were more than 200 incidents of racial violence.

Zoot suit riots In Los Angeles, men wearing "zoot suits," a popular Mexican American clothing style, were attacked on the streets. The media blamed the "zoot suit riots" on Mexican Americans. However, Eleanor Roosevelt noted in her newspaper column that the violence was an example of "longstanding discrimination against the Mexicans in the Southwest."

Challenging discrimination In 1941 A. Philip Randolph called for a march on Washington to protest the exclusion of African Americans from defense industries. To head off the march, Roosevelt agreed to issue Executive Order 8802, banning discrimination in defense industries and government jobs. To enforce the order, he set up the Fair Employment Practices Committee (FEPC) to investigate charges of discrimination.

The FEPC—and the growing need for workers—opened many jobs that had previously been closed by racism. By the end of 1944, some 2 million African Americans were working in war plants.

Diversity in the Military

As in World War I, Americans of all backgrounds joined the armed services. Half a million Hispanics served, as did 25,000 American Indians and 900,000 African Americans. In 1940 Congress passed a bill prohibiting discrimination in the draft on the basis of race or color.

Despite this bill, nonwhites still faced racial prejudice in the military. For example, although African Americans enlisted in all branches of the armed forces, most of them, like the pilots who trained and fought with Benjamin Davis, had to serve in all-black units. Most, too, still served in support positions rather than on the battlefield.

Navajo code talkers One group of American Indians who gained fame in the armed forces were the 420 Navajo marine "code talkers." They helped maintain the security of communications during the war by sending orders in the Navajo language—a "code" that the enemy never broke.

Female workers, like these welders, moved into jobs traditionally held by men. By the end of the war, a third of the work force were women.

Women in the military Women were not drafted, but 350,000 volunteered for military service. These women worked mostly as clerks or administrators, but some were map makers, electricians,

Connections to Language Arts

Most of the non-Navajos who knew the Navajo language were anthropologists or missionaries. A missionary's son who had lived among the Navajos persuaded the Marines to try a Navajo-based code.

The first Navajos recruited as code talkers were given the job of devising the code. This was more difficult than it seems. The code had to include military terms that had no Navajo equivalents. For example, *corps* became *din-neh-ih,* which means "clan" in Navajo. Also, the code had to be complex enough so that no civilian Navajo speaker could decipher it for the Japanese. Thus many English words were spelled out during transmission, using an "alphabet" of Navajo words. For example, the Navajo word for *zinc—besh-do-gliz—*was used in place of the letter *z.*

Discussion

Checking Understanding

1. What opened up defense-industry jobs to African Americans? (Executive Order 8802 banning discrimination in defense industries; the FEPC; need for workers.)

2. How did women help the war effort? (Factory work; noncombat roles in military.)

Stimulating Critical Thinking

3. Could an order like Executive Order 9066 be issued in a national emergency today? Explain. (Probably not—groups more aware of rights; politically hard to justify.)

Hands-On HISTORY

Creating your own code Specialists on each side of the war tried to "break" (decipher) one another's codes. Often they succeeded. However, the Japanese never broke the code used by the Navajo code talkers in the Pacific.

The Navajo code was so successful because at the time, the language had no written alphabet. Also, a word can have more than one meaning depending on the speaker's tone. The language is so complex and so unlike most European and Asian languages that in the 1940s only 28 non-Navajos understood it.

A Navajo code talker

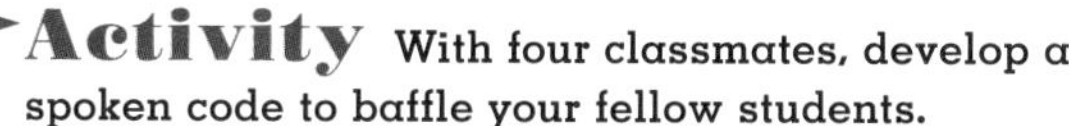

Activity **With four classmates, develop a spoken code to baffle your fellow students.**

1 Discuss familiar codes like "pig latin." Consider what makes them work: for example, simple rules that can change any English word into a new word.

2 Once you have an idea for your own code, practice until you can speak it naturally and rapidly.

3 Carry on a conversation in front of the rest of the class. Can anyone break your code?

Teaching the Hands-On HISTORY

Review rules of pig latin: If the word begins with a consonant, move the consonant to the end and add *ay.* If it begins with a vowel, add *way* to the end of the word. To spark creativity, students might refer to sources like these: *The Cat's Elbow and Other Secret Languages* by Alvin Schwartz (Farrar Straus Giroux, 1982); *How to Keep a Secret: Writing and Talking in Code* by Elizabeth James and Carol Barkin (Lothrop, Lee & Shepard, 1978); and *Loads of Codes and Secret Ciphers* by Paul B. Janeczko (Macmillan, 1984).

mechanics, parachute riggers, or welders. As in World War I, women did almost everything but fight.

Japanese Americans

The attack on Pearl Harbor set off a wave of anti-Japanese hysteria. Americans feared that Japanese submarines would blow up military installations, torpedo ships, or shell cities along the West Coast. Some people took this hysteria one step further. They began to distrust their Japanese American neighbors, wondering whether they might be spies working for Japan.

The intense anti-Japanese fears led President Roosevelt to issue Executive Order 9066 in February 1942. The order, which authorized the Secretary of War to remove civilians from military areas, was used as the excuse to remove 110,000 Japanese Americans from their homes in Pacific Coast states.

Many of those forced to move were *nisei*—children born in the United States to Japanese parents. By law they were American citizens. Emotions overruled common sense, though, and nisei as well as foreign-born Japanese were removed to camps in isolated areas. The fears were groundless, however. There was not a single documented case of disloyalty by a Japanese American.

One Japanese American who was forced to leave was Kisaye Sato, who recalled bitterly:

> "We only had 48 hours to get out of our homes. They came in truckloads to buy our things. We had to get rid of our furniture and appliances for whatever the people would pay. They took terrible advantage of us."

Nevertheless, some 17,600 Japanese Americans showed their loyalty by joining the armed services. Many of them fought in

Tips for Teaching

Kinesthetic Learners

Kinesthetic learners often find it easier to understand maps through tactile experiences. Provide enlarged photocopies of the map on page 533, or have students redraw it at enlarged size. Have them use objects such as small banners on straight pins to show troop movements, battles, and territory gained.

Teaching the Reading Maps

Have students brainstorm ideas for a chart with the headings *Advantages of Sea War* and *Disadvantages of Sea War.* (One advantage: ships can transport troops quickly. One disadvantage: few places for rest and supplies.) **Answer to Reading Maps:** By mid-1940 France and the Netherlands had been conquered and thus could not defend colonies; Britain was busy fighting Germany so could devote little effort to defending colonies.

Bonus Activity

Making Posters for the War Effort

To help students appreciate civilian contributions, have them create colorful posters urging Americans to support the war effort in specific ways. Have them consider ways to conserve gasoline, reduce the amount of food needed, save cloth, and raise money. If possible, provide source materials on home-front efforts.

Vital Links

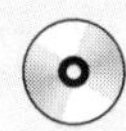

"Praise the Lord and Pass the Ammunition" (Song) Unit 5, Side 2, Search 04415, Play to 07164

See also Unit 5 Explore CD-ROM location 164.

Japanese Americans arrive at their new home—a relocation camp in Wyoming. Of the 110,000 Americans of Japanese descent forced to relocate, most remained in camps for more than three years.

North Africa, Italy, and France with the 442d Regimental Combat Team and the 100th Infantry Battalion. These units, made up entirely of Japanese Americans, won thousands of military awards and medals. Two much-decorated nisei war veterans—Daniel K. Inouye and Spark Matsunaga—were later elected to the United States Senate from the state of Hawaii.

In 1988, 46 years after the internment order, Congress responded to pressure from former internees and their children by passing a bill formally apologizing for the treatment of Japanese American citizens. Each of the estimated 60,000 survivors of the internment camps was to be given $20,000 in recognition of the human rights violations they suffered during World War II.

Japan's Conquests

During the months after Pearl Harbor, Japan seemed as unstoppable as Hitler's forces in Europe. Japanese fighter planes attacked the Philippines, destroying more than half the American planes on the ground at airstrips. Despite valiant efforts, American and Filipino soldiers were forced to surrender. Vowing, "I shall return," their commander, General Douglas MacArthur, retreated to Australia.

In the next three months, Japan won victory after victory, advancing into Thailand and Burma on the way toward Australia. Within four months Japan had conquered most of Southeast Asia as well as parts of the Pacific. As the Allies witnessed Japan's string of conquests, they began to feel desperate.

Stopping the Japanese Finally, in early May 1942 American and Australian fleets succeeded in stopping Japan's advance. In the Battle of the Coral Sea, the Allies intercepted the Japanese fleet as it attempted to take more territory.

This battle was fought entirely by carrier-based planes. For the first time there was no ship-to-ship contact—only plane against plane and plane against ship. The Allies prevented Japanese troops from landing at Port Moresby in southern New Guinea and spared Australia from invasion.

The Battle of Midway

In early June 1942 Japan suffered an even worse defeat in the Battle of Midway. The Japanese had planned to take the small Pacific island and use it to launch another attack on nearby Pearl Harbor—which was still the home of the American Pacific Fleet. Learning of the planned attack when code breakers cracked the Japanese naval code, American admirals raced their ships toward Midway Island.

History Footnote

Ordered to abandon the Philippines in March 1942, MacArthur left behind thousands of American and Filipino troops on Bataan Peninsula. For weeks, they held off the Japanese while surviving on the flesh of pack mules, monkeys, and reptiles. They finally surrendered on April 9.

In what became known as the Bataan Death March, the Japanese forced 75,000 captured soldiers—including 12,000 Americans—to walk 65 miles under a burning sun to prison camps. Between 7,000 and 10,000 prisoners died along the way, partly because of the treatment by Japanese guards. The prisoners were allowed little rest, food, or water. Those too weak to continue were clubbed, shot, or buried alive—sometimes by other prisoners forced to do the job at bayonet point.

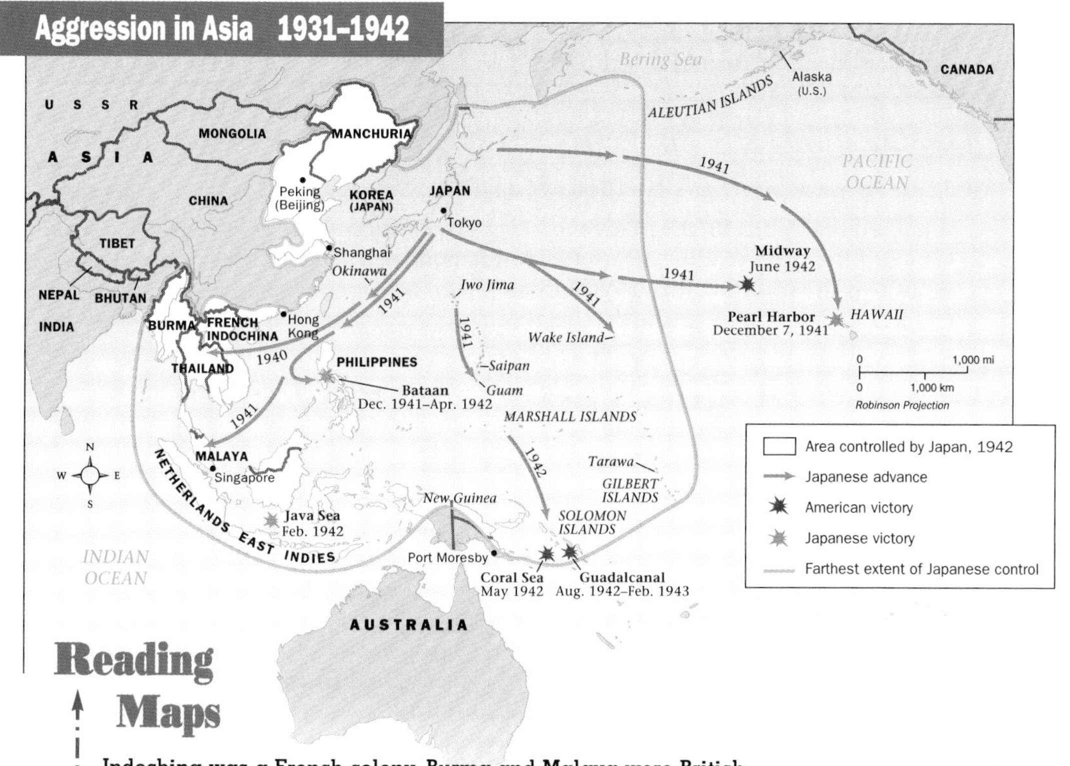

Reading Maps

Indochina was a French colony, Burma and Malaya were British colonies, and the East Indies was a Dutch colony. How do you think events in Europe in the 1940s might have helped Japan expand its empire in Asia?

Planes from Japanese carriers attacked the island, but American antiaircraft fire brought many of them down. Arriving just in time, American carriers launched their own planes against the Japanese fleet. Although Japanese fighter planes and ships' guns shot down many of them, American dive-bombers scored direct hits on three of the four carriers, causing heavy losses.

The Battle of Midway was a turning point in the war. After this defeat the Japanese no longer controlled the Pacific. Gradually, the Allied forces began to drive them back to their home islands.

3. Section Review

1. Define **rationing.**
2. Describe at least three ways that the lives of Americans on the home front were changed by the war.
3. Why was it essential that the Allies stop Japan's advance at Midway?
4. Critical Thinking If you had been a young nisei man whose family was in an internment camp, would you have volunteered to fight in the war? Why or why not?

Closing the Section

Wrap-Up Activity

Charting Effects of the War

Have small groups create charts showing effects of the war on certain groups. At the top of the chart, have them write the headings *Home Front* and *Military.* At the left, they should write *African Americans, Native Americans, Japanese Americans,* and *Women.* Have them brainstorm what to include in each category. Charts should describe each group's roles and how the war affected each group.

Section Review Answers

1. Definition: *rationing* (529)

2. Rationing, more employment, jobs in war plants for women and African Americans, migrations to urban areas, race riots, internment of Japanese Americans.

3. To keep Japan from controlling Pacific, and to prevent second attack on Pearl Harbor.

4. Yes: a way to get out of the camp and gain benefits for family; would prove loyalty to United States. No: nation did not deserve help from imprisoned citizens; would be too resentful.

Introducing the Section

Warm-Up Activity

Deciding Whether to Fight On

To prepare for reading about the Allied victory and Axis defeat, have small groups imagine living in a nation facing almost certain defeat in a long, grueling war. Have them decide whether they would surrender before being overrun by the enemy. Each group should list at least three reasons for its decision. Conclude by having the groups compare decisions and reasons.

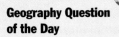

Geography Question of the Day

After explaining that the Soviet Union joined the Allies in 1941, have pairs use the map on p. 526 to plan Allied strategy for defeating Germany. They should place tracing paper over the map and indicate jumping-off points for movements across water and land toward Germany and its occupied territory. They can later compare their plans with the map on p. 535.

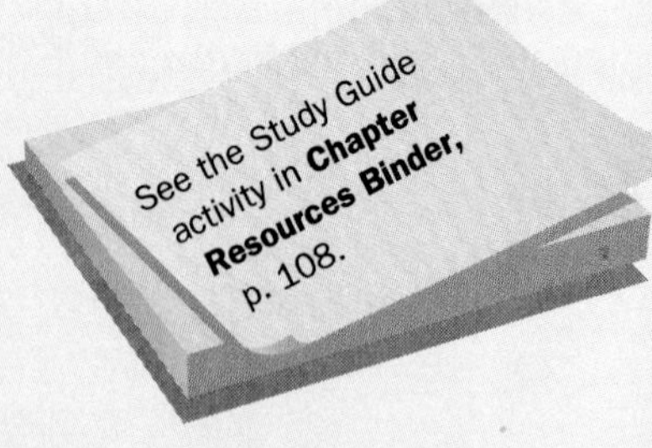

See the Study Guide activity in **Chapter Resources Binder,** p. 108.

Section Objectives

- ★ Describe the strategies the Big Three used to win victory in Europe.
- ★ Explain why the United States dropped the atomic bomb on Japan.
- ★ Summarize the human cost of World War II.

Teaching Resources

Take-Home Planner 4, pp. 20–29
Chapter Resources Binder
Study Guide, p. 108
Reinforcement
Skills Development
Geography Extensions, pp. 29–30
American Readings, p. 56
Using Historical Documents
Transparency Activities
Chapter and Unit Tests, pp. 91–94

4. Winning the War

Reading Guide

Section Focus **How the Allies defeated the Axis powers**

1. **What strategies did the Big Three use to win victory in Europe?**
2. **Why did the United States drop the atomic bomb on Japan?**
3. **What was the human cost of World War II?**

While American forces clashed with the Japanese in the Pacific, Hitler continued his campaign to conquer Europe. On June 22, 1941, he launched a surprise attack on his ally the Soviet Union. Betrayed by Hitler, Stalin joined the Allied effort.

Stalin, Roosevelt, and Churchill became known as the "Big Three." Together they planned strategies to defeat the Axis. Germany posed a more immediate threat than Japan, so they concentrated on defeating it first.

Early Allied Victories

In the fall of 1942 American and British troops invaded North Africa. Led by the American general Dwight David Eisenhower, their goal was to drive out the German Afrika Korps. Its commander, General Erwin Rommel, was called "the Desert Fox" because of his brilliant desert-warfare tactics.

It was in North Africa that Ben Davis and his pilots from Tuskegee first went into combat. They were to provide air cover on bombing missions. When one of the pilots shot down a German plane—the first aerial victory by an African American pilot—General Eisenhower personally came to the air base to offer his congratulations.

In the spring of 1943, after six months of bitter fighting, the Allies finally forced Rommel's Afrika Korps to surrender. With this defeat, the Axis lost control of Africa as a military gateway to southern Europe.

Stalingrad Meanwhile, in the Soviet Union the German attack had stalled, thanks to a long, brutal winter and the courage of the Soviet people. In September 1942 the Germans had launched an attack on the city of Stalingrad, but the Soviets had struck back with everything they had. The Soviet victory on February 2, 1943, put an end to Germany's eastward advance.

Italy's defeat From North Africa the Allies now mounted a successful invasion of Italy. King Victor Emmanuel III dismissed Mussolini from office, and on September 8, 1943, the new government surrendered. Although the Allies liberated Rome in June 1944, they faced months of fierce fighting before the German forces in Italy finally surrendered in May 1945.

D-Day

In November 1943 the Big Three met at Tehran, Iran, and agreed to an Allied invasion of France. "Operation Overlord" was to be planned and staged in Great Britain.

Although Hitler was expecting an invasion, the Allies succeeded in keeping secret the fact that they would be landing on the beaches of France's Normandy coast (see map, page 535). Despite foul weather, on June 5, 1944, General Eisenhower made the call: "O.K. We'll go." The next day the invasion, known as D-Day, began.

History Footnote

The Soviet Union suffered the highest number of casualties in the war: about 6 million members of the military died, while an additional 14 million were wounded. Incredibly, about 10 million civilians also died—about 1 million of them in the 872-day siege of Leningrad (now St. Petersburg). With supply lines almost completely cut off, Leningrad's people suffered horribly from lack of heat and food. They ate their pets, and then hair oil, petroleum jelly, and "soup" made from furniture and wallpaper glue.

War in Europe and North Africa 1942–1945

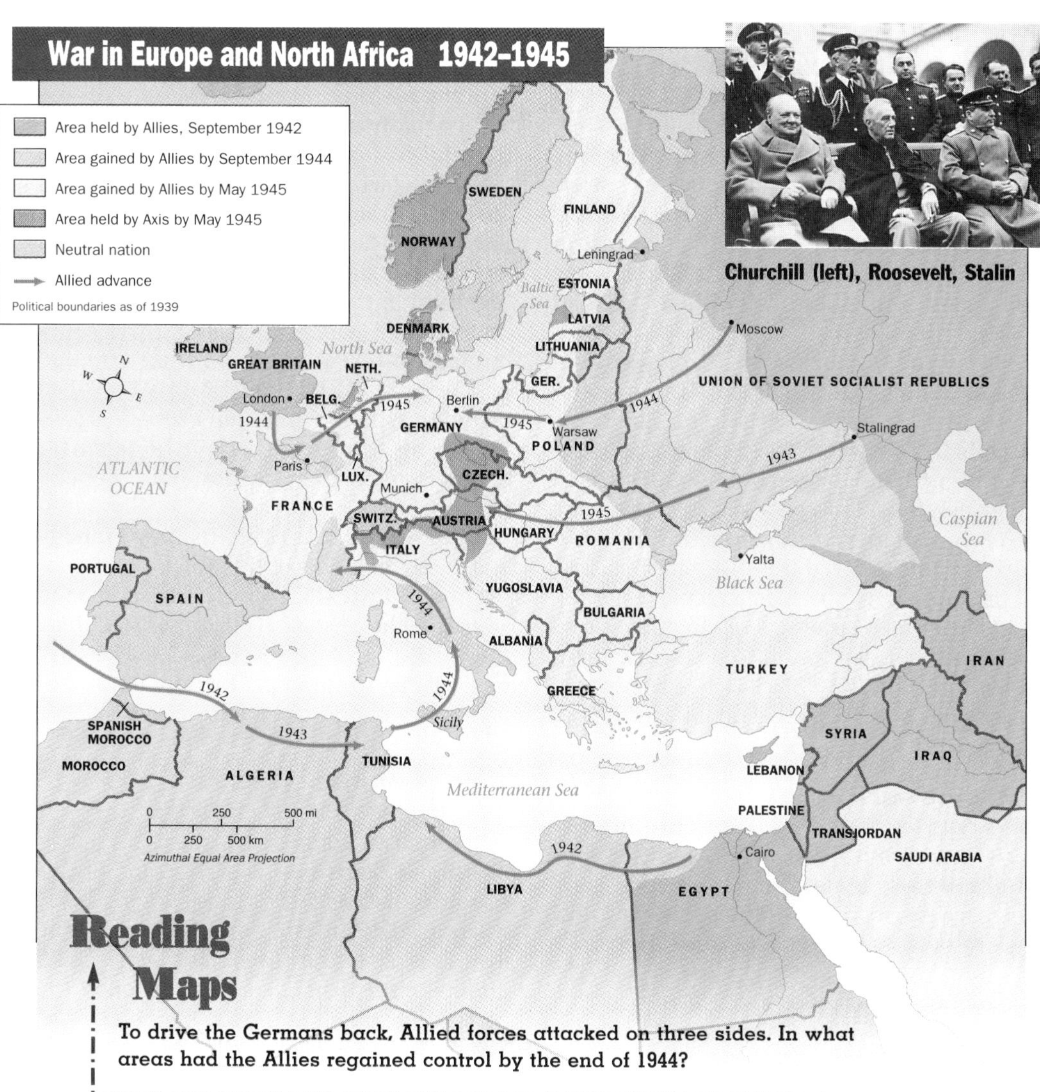

Churchill (left), Roosevelt, Stalin

Reading Maps

To drive the Germans back, Allied forces attacked on three sides. In what areas had the Allies regained control by the end of 1944?

Within a month 1 million troops had stormed ashore. The Germans fought back fiercely, but in late July the Allies broke through German lines. In August another Allied force landed on France's southern coast and advanced northward. On August 25, 1944, the French flag once again waved over Paris.

The election of 1944 While the Allies were driving the Germans out of western Europe, Roosevelt ran for a fourth term. His running mate was Senator Harry S Truman of Missouri. Although Roosevelt's health was failing, he felt it would be a mistake for the nation to change leaders during the war. The Roosevelt-Truman ticket won easily.

Developing the Section

Discussion

Checking Understanding

1. What happened on D-Day? (Allies landed on Normandy coast and began fighting Germans there.)

Stimulating Critical Thinking

2. What Americans might disagree with the decision to defeat Germany first? Why? (West Coast, fearing invasion; families of military in Pacific, fearing for relatives; internees—would be freed if Japan defeated.)

Teaching the Reading Maps

Ask how existence of neutral nations affected strategy. (Could not march through them.) **Answer to Reading Maps:** North Africa; Italy; northern and south-central France; western Soviet Union; eastern Estonia, Latvia, Lithuania, Poland, Romania.

Vital Links

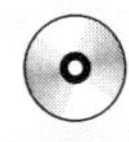

Eisenhower on D-Day (Movie) Unit 5, Side 1, Search 34712, Play to 35332

See also Unit 5 Explore CD-ROM location 186.

Section Activity

Speaking as Truman

To focus on what led to the Allied victory, have pairs or small groups write speeches that Truman might have given on V-J Day. Speeches should highlight Allied achievements while reflecting on the tragic costs of the war. Ask a representative of each pair or group to present its speech to the class. Discuss differences in emphasis or tone in the speeches.

Bonus Activity

Writing War Poems

To solicit opinions about the war, have students write poems about a wartime event that has touched their emotions. Possibilities include D-Day, Roosevelt's death, war in the Pacific, the atomic bomb, or the Holocaust. Remind them that poems need not rhyme. Volunteers might share poems with the class.

Vital Links

Truman on the atomic bomb (Movie) Unit 5, Side 1, Search 37683, Play to 38503

See also Unit 5 Explore CD-ROM location 199.

History Footnote

Even as 1944 drew to a close, Hitler was not ready to give up. In December he ordered his weary generals and soldiers to launch a surprise attack against the Americans in the Ardennes forest of Belgium and Luxembourg. The ensuing battle, fought in bitter cold and snow, became known as the Battle of the Bulge because the Germans managed to break through the Allied front and advance about 60 miles into Belgium, creating a "bulge" in American lines before they were stopped. The Americans' gritty determination in this last major European battle was exemplified by General Anthony McAuliffe. When the Germans demanded that McAuliffe's division surrender, he contemptuously answered, "Nuts!" American casualties numbered 77,000, but the battle had no effect on the outcome of the war.

Germany Retreats

By September 1944 German forces were retreating on all fronts. As the Allies pressed forward through western Europe, the Soviets launched an attack that pushed the Germans back along an 800-mile (1,287-km) front in eastern Europe. As the war in Europe drew to a close, Allied bombers filled the skies over Germany.

With the bombers flew black guardian angels. In March 1945 alone, African American airmen flew 50 missions. The most notable strike was a 1,600-mile (2,580-km) round-trip bombing run over Berlin in which they destroyed three jets—a type of plane the Germans had just developed. Benjamin Davis's unit received the Distinguished Unit Citation for this spectacular achievement.

When Allied armies closed in on Berlin in late April, Hitler committed suicide. Eight days later, on May 8, 1945, Germany surrendered. May 8 is still known as V-E Day, for Victory in Europe.

Roosevelt's death Franklin Roosevelt did not live to see V-E Day. On April 12, 1945, worn out by ill health and the pressures of the job, he died of a cerebral hemorrhage. The burdens of the presidency now rested on the shoulders of Harry Truman.

Japan Fights On

While the nation mourned the loss of a great leader, the Allies turned their attention to Japan. In successful but bloody assaults, they had already recaptured the South Pacific island clusters of the Solomons, Gilberts, Carolines, and Marianas.

These victories permitted General MacArthur to make good on his vow to return. On October 20, 1944, he waded ashore on the Philippine island of Leyte.

As American forces closed in, Japanese pilots resorted to the desperate tactic of deliberately crashing their planes into American ships. These *kamikaze* ("divine wind") pilots sank 34 Allied ships, but at the frightful cost of 5,000 Japanese lives.

Suicide tactics did not stop the American advance toward Japan, but every inch was bitterly contested. The island of Iwo Jima fell after bloody hand-to-hand fighting that left one-third of the American force either dead or wounded. On April 1, 1945, the Allies landed on Okinawa. More than 100,000 Japanese and 11,000 Americans were killed before the island fell on June 22.

Now all that remained of the Japanese empire was the island nation itself. Because Japan refused to surrender, the Allies faced the prospect of launching the most bloody and costly invasion of the war.

On July 17, 1945, Truman, Churchill, and Stalin met in Potsdam, Germany. From there they issued a strangely worded message. They urged Japan to surrender before August 3 or face "prompt and utter destruction."

The Atomic Bomb

"Prompt and utter destruction" was not an idle threat. Since 1941 American and British scientists had been secretly developing a new weapon—the atomic bomb. Japan let the deadline pass, and three days later a B-29 bomber called the *Enola Gay* dropped the first atomic bomb on the city of Hiroshima. The blast, and the devastating firestorm that followed, killed 66,000, injured another 70,000, and totally destroyed the city.

One woman described the experience:

> "I felt I had lost all the bones in my body. . . . I passed out. By the time I woke up, black rain was falling. I thought I was blind, but I got my eyes open, and I saw a beautiful blue sky and a dead city. Nobody is standing up. Nobody is walking around."

History Footnote

President Franklin Roosevelt died a peaceful death and was eulogized by the people whom he had led for so long. A reporter for *Life* magazine wrote, "This gallant, fearless man, who could not stand on his own feet without help, bestrode his country like a giant through great and changeful years." The deaths of the major Axis leaders were quite different. Benito Mussolini was shot by Italians opposed to fascism on April 28, 1945. His body was strung up by the feet in front of a gas station for all to see. Adolf Hitler and his new wife killed themselves on April 30. Aides burned the bodies rather than have the Allies find them. Hideki Tojo was arrested after Japan's surrender. He tried but failed to kill himself. Convicted as a war criminal, he was hanged on December 23, 1948.

Three days later a second atomic bomb was dropped on the city of Nagasaki.

Although later criticized for a decision that brought death to so many innocent civilians, Truman never regretted it. He believed that invading Japan would have meant the loss of many more American lives in the long run. "I regarded the bomb as a military weapon," Truman said, "and never had any doubt that it should be used."

V-J Day On August 15, 1945—V-J Day—Japan surrendered. Joyful Americans took to the streets. Strangers embraced one another. In New York City, a soldier walked up to a group of strangers with a look of shocked disbelief on his face: "I'm alive. I'm alive. The war's over—and I'm alive."

The Human Cost

The most deadly conflict in world history had finally come to an end. Nearly 20 million soldiers and twice as many civilians died. Property losses totaled trillions of dollars. Simple statistics, however, cannot give a real sense of the human cost of the war. Across the globe homes were destroyed and families scattered. Millions were homeless and near starvation.

On May 7, 1945, American soldiers came upon these starving Holocaust survivors in a Nazi concentration camp in Austria.

Link to the Present

Remembering the Holocaust Each visitor who enters the United States Holocaust Memorial Museum in Washington, D.C., receives an identification card picturing a Holocaust victim. The visitor can use this card to follow the victim's story through a series of computer stations. Visitors can also walk through a railroad car like the ones that brought prisoners to Nazi death camps. They can stand in a barracks like the ones where prisoners slept, and view piles of shoes and other belongings taken from the dead.

The Holocaust Museum, which opened in 1993, is dedicated to keeping alive the memory of the 11 million people—6 million of them Jews—who died in the Holocaust. The museum's message is summed up by the buttons offered for sale to visitors—buttons that say "Remember" and "Never Again."

The Holocaust Only with Germany's defeat were some of the worst horror stories of the war fully revealed. Many of the civilians who died in Europe had been deliberately killed by Hitler in a Nazi extermination policy now known as the Holocaust.

As the Allies marched through Germany and Poland at the end of the war, they came upon Hitler's concentration camps. With

Discussion

Checking Understanding

1. How did the Japanese show determination in the war's final year? (Kamikaze attacks, hand-to-hand fighting, refusal to surrender after first atomic bomb dropped.)

Stimulating Critical Thinking

2. Do you think a world war could happen again? Explain. (Yes: nuclear conflict could escalate quickly. No: UN and global interdependence would deter large war.)

Teaching the

Link to the Present

Point out that those who deny the Holocaust are typically anti-Semites belonging to neo-Nazi groups. Such denial fails in the face of survivors' accounts, gas chamber blueprints, Nuremberg testimony by Nazis, Nazi documents, and Allied photos and movie footage of concentration camps.

Vital Links

Margaret Bourke-White on Buchenwald (First Person Account) Unit 5, Side 1, Search 28422, Play to 28976

See also Unit 5 Explore CD-ROM location 139.

Closing the Section

Wrap-Up Activity

A V-J Day Letter

To review events that led to the war's end, have students imagine being the American soldier whose reaction to V-J Day is quoted on page 537. On this day he wants to prepare a letter for his future children and grandchildren to read. Have students write the letter, describing how the Allies won and elaborating on their feelings about the end of the conflict.

Section Review Answers

1. Formation of the Big Three, successful invasions of North Africa and Italy, Soviet victory at Stalingrad, successful invasion at Normandy (D-Day), depletion of German resources, bombing of Germany.

2. For: many American lives saved; Japan would never have surrendered otherwise. Against: too many civilians killed; Japan might have surrendered if given more information about the bomb.

3. It is an important part of history. People need to know so it will not happen again.

To check understanding of "Why We Remember," assign Thinking Critically question 3 on student page 544.

History Footnote

People ask why so little was done to save the Jews. The tragic fact is that other nations were not aware of the extreme horrors being committed, and during the period when Jews could flee Germany many nations refused to accept refugees, especially Jewish ones. For example, a ship called the *St. Louis* left Germany in 1939 with 930 Jewish refugees aboard. Cuba turned it away; so did the United States. The ship was forced to return to Europe. Many of its passengers died in concentration camps.

The United States did take in about 105,000 refugees between 1933 and 1940—far more than any other country. However, this was only a fraction of the number who wanted to come. Afraid of stirring up anti-Semitism, Roosevelt failed to press Congress to relax immigration restrictions on Jews.

horror they realized that more than 11 million people had been murdered by Nazis because they belonged to one of the many groups—including Jews, Gypsies, and the mentally and physically handicapped—that Hitler regarded as inferior to the "master race."

In 1945 and 1946 the Allies held war crimes trials in Nuremberg, Germany. The Nuremberg Trials found thousands of Nazis guilty of war crimes and sentenced 12 Nazi leaders to death.

4. Section Review

1. Describe the major events that led to V-E Day.

2. Give a strong argument for and a strong argument against dropping atomic bombs on Japan.

3. Critical Thinking Why do you think it is important to study the Holocaust? Explain your answer.

Why We Remember

World War II

It was over. After 2,194 days of death and destruction, the most devastating war in history was over. There had never been a conflict like this before. It was fought by more men—some 70 million—using more machines and more destructive weapons over more of the globe than any past war. The cost in human lives was staggering. Nearly 20 million soldiers died on battlefields. More than twice as many civilians lost their lives. The financial costs were just as unimaginable. A trillion dollars had been spent fighting the war worldwide. The amount of property damage was at least twice that figure.

These numbers are reason enough to remember World War II, but there are others equally as important. We remember this war to honor its heroes. Many, like Benjamin Davis, were soldiers who risked their lives in battle. Others were civilians who made huge sacrifices for their countries. All deserve our admiration and gratitude.

We remember this war for its horrors, too. This was the conflict that left us with images of living skeletons in German concentration camps and mushroom clouds rising over Japanese cities. This was the war that showed us that for all our progress in science, technology, and culture, human hate could still create a holocaust. This was the war that gave the world nuclear weapons that would soon be capable of destroying all life on earth.

We remember this war as well for its legacy of hope. For in this terrible conflict, the organized forces of freedom proved stronger than those of fascism. Democracy triumphed over dictatorship. It was far from a total victory, as the coming years would show. Still, the democratic ideals Americans held most dear had survived and, it was hoped, would never be tested in this way again.

Geography Footnote

The Allies paired their "island hopping" strategy with a strategy they called "leapfrogging." Leapfrogging involved bypassing islands that were Japanese strongholds and concentrating instead on invading islands over which the Japanese hold was weaker. Leapfrogging saved the Allies lives and time. Still, the struggle to take islands was extremely difficult, partly due to environmental reasons. One Marine described the island campaign this way: "Always the rain and the mud, torrid heat and teeming insect life, the stink of rotten jungle and rotting dead; malaria burning the body and fungus infection eating away the feet, and no hot chow for weeks."

Geography Lab

Tracing Events Over Time and Space

After the battle on Iwo Jima, one marine muttered, "I hope to God that we don't have to go on any more of those screwy islands." He had reason to be weary. Beginning in 1942, Allied forces had been following a strategy called "island hopping." They attacked certain Pacific islands held by Japan and then used those islands as bases from which to attack other islands. In all, the Allies launched more than 100 island invasions as they gradually closed in on Japan.

The map shows highlights of the campaigns of General Douglas MacArthur and Admiral Chester Nimitz. Use the map to trace the Allied path to victory in the Pacific.

Using Map Skills

1. Proceeding from Hawaii, where did Nimitz's forces strike first?
2. List in chronological order the battles in which Nimitz's forces took part.
3. Where did Nimitz's and MacArthur's forces first join? What was their joint objective after that?
4. MacArthur left the Philippines in January 1942. How long did it take him to return?
5. **Hands-On Geography** Imagine that atomic bombs had not been dropped. Trace the map on this page. Add movements and battles that might have taken place after Okinawa. Where and when would the war have ended?

War in the Pacific and Asia 1942–1945

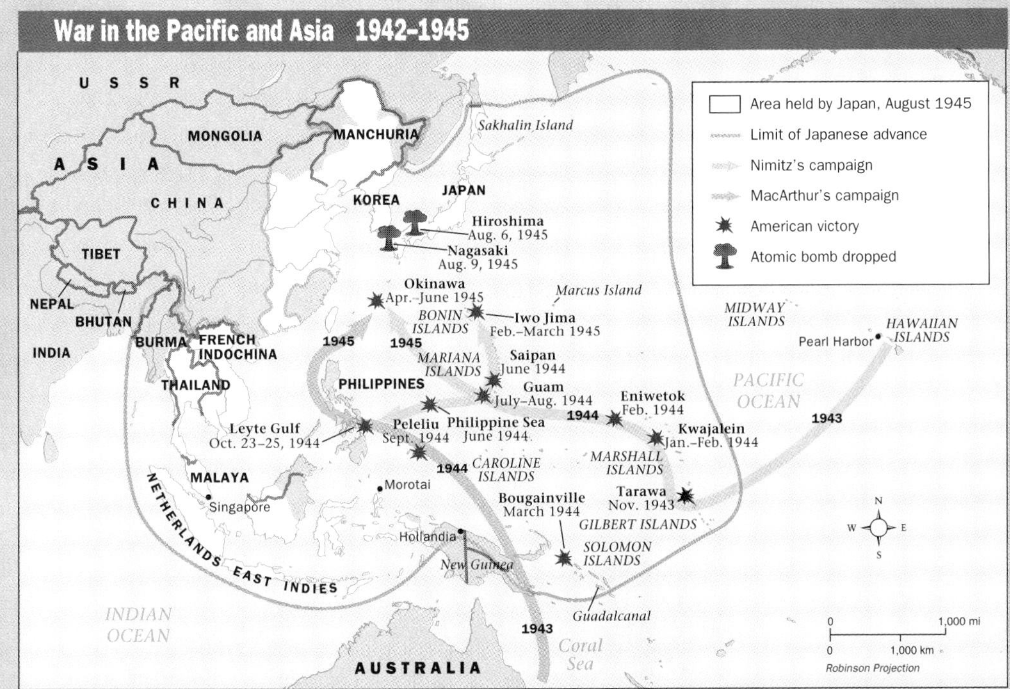

Teaching the Geography Lab

Explain that all battles shown on the map were Allied victories. When one island was taken, the Allies moved on to the next. To help students analyze the map, ask interpretation questions, such as having them identify the two places in the Marshall Islands that Nimitz's forces had taken by March 1944. (Kwajalein in January–February, Eniwetok in February.)

Using Map Skills

Answers

1. Tarawa

2. Tarawa, Kwajalein, Eniwetok, Philippine Sea, Saipan (or Saipan, Philippine Sea), Guam, Peleliu, Leyte Gulf, Iwo Jima, Okinawa.

3. Leyte Gulf, October 1944; Okinawa.

4. About two and a half years.

5. Maps and answers will be speculative but should be based on facts and reasonable inferences. For example, maps should show a series of battles, because the Japanese probably would not have yielded any soil without a fight.

See the activity on making a war map in **Geography Extensions**, pp. 29–30.

Picture Essay

Teaching the Picture Essay

In this feature, students will learn about American involvement in World War II through a series of pictures and captions. Picture essays not only enhance students' knowledge of history but also help students understand the value of different types of information sources. Visual learners especially will enjoy and benefit from the picture essay. The feature also will help students with limited English—who may be intimidated by lengthy written text—focus on important points about the war.

Have students study the entire feature before answering the Discussion questions or doing the Wrap-Up Activity. You may assign the Bonus Activity as an alternative to, or in addition to, the Wrap-Up Activity.

Warm-Up Activity

Looking for Answers

To prepare students to study the feature, have them write questions they have about World War II that might be answered by photographs from the era. For example, they might write, "How did teens help the war effort?" Suggest that students study the picture essay to see whether any of their questions are answered. If not, where else might they seek answers?

Essay Objectives

Use pictures and captions to trace events of World War II, with these emphases:

- ★ Explain how American civilians, including women and young people, helped the war effort on the home front.
- ★ Describe activities of American armed forces, including African Americans, in Europe.
- ★ Identify key events in American involvement in the war in the Pacific.

PICTURE ESSAY

World War II

On the Home Front

1

Background. During the war, a growing number of women not only joined the armed services, but also helped out in the labor force at home by filling jobs normally held by men. Above background, women assemble nose cones for America's fighting planes at the Douglas aircraft plant in Long Beach, California.

1 and 2. Almost every community in America organized paper and scrap drives to collect used paper, rubber, and metal to be reprocessed for the war effort. Civilians in Butte, Montana, fill trucks with scrap (1). These two students ruled for an hour over their fellow students at

History Footnote

"Don't you know there's a war on?" With that good-natured question, Americans on the home front reminded one another that their efforts were crucial to victory. Here is a partial list of how civilians contributed to the war effort:

- Used public transportation, drove their cars more slowly, and organized car pools to conserve gasoline.
- Collected waste fats from cooking; the fats were then recycled to make explosives.
- Turned in nylon and silk stockings to be used to make powder bags for naval guns.
- Bought books that had been printed in small type to save paper.
- Took jobs on farms to help raise food.
- Rolled bandages for soldiers.
- Used coffee grounds to brew second pots and ate horsemeat burgers instead of beef.

a Hammond, Indiana, high school where 50,000 pounds of waste paper was collected on January 17, 1944 (2).

3. Posters such as this one helped recruit women for a variety of work.

4. During and immediately after the war, Americans used ration stamps to buy scarce consumer goods such as food items, shoes, tires, and gasoline.

5. Many homes displayed flags that showed blue stars for family members serving in the war and gold stars for people killed in action.

Bonus Activity

Collecting Oral Histories of the War

To help students gain better understanding of the World War II experience, have them interview people who served in the armed forces during the war. Begin with a discussion of the term *oral history* (personal recollections or stories passed by word of mouth). Solicit students' ideas about the value of such recollections in understanding historical events. Then have students brainstorm a list of possible questions to ask World War II veterans and assign them the task of getting answers to those questions from actual veterans. (If students do not know any veterans, they might contact local veterans' organizations for help in locating men and women willing to talk about their experiences.) Instruct students to take careful notes or record their interviews on audiotape or videotape. Later invite them to share the results of their interviews in some way: for example, by reading their notes aloud, playing their tapes, writing reports and binding them into a class book, and so on.

Wrap-Up Activity

Thanking Those Who Won the War

To reinforce understanding of World War II and give students practice in interpreting visuals, have students "toast" the people pictured on these pages for their role in winning the war. Each student should choose a person from one of the photographs and prepare a short speech recognizing, and expressing gratitude for, that person's efforts in achieving victory. For added realism, encourage students to invent a name and a short biography of their chosen person and to include that information in the speech. Ask volunteers to deliver their speeches before the rest of the class.

History Footnote

In the early morning of June 5, 1944, the commanders of Operation Overlord, based in southern Britain, gathered to hear the weather forecast. On the basis of it, General Eisenhower would decide whether to launch the Allied invasion of Normandy. A fleet of 4,500 ships carrying 170,000 men was ready. More than 10,000 airplanes stood waiting on runways. A fierce storm raged, but the weather forecaster predicted that the next day would bring a short break in the rain. Postponing the invasion would mean waiting another month until first light and low tides would again coincide. However, a miscalculation could mean huge casualties and even defeat. Eisenhower took the chance, and the D-Day invasion was launched. The Germans were caught by surprise.

In Europe

8

7

7. African American pilots and support staff plot targets and formulate strategies during the campaign to liberate Italy from the Nazis.

8. American reinforcements, ready for their shot at the Germans in Normandy, jump from a Coast Guard landing barge into the surf on the French coast. They are going in to reinforce and replace the fighting units that secured the Normandy beachhead.

History Footnote

Japan's kamikaze pilots were named for the "divine wind," a typhoon that had saved Japan from invasion in 1281 by destroying the fleet of Kublai Khan. Pilots volunteered for kamikaze missions because they considered it a privilege to die for their cause. One pilot said this before carrying out his mission: "I am nothing but a particle of iron attracted by a magnet—the American aircraft carrier." Americans had difficulty understanding that point of view. U.S. Vice Admiral Charles R. Brown, who witnessed many kamikaze attacks, recalled: "There was a hypnotic fascination to a sight so alien to our Western philosophy. We watched each plunging kamikaze with the detached horror of one witnessing a terrible spectacle . . . . And dominating it all was a strange mixture of respect and pity."

In the Pacific

10

11

Background. Japan's suicide air corps, known as the kamikazes, wreaked havoc on American ships toward the end of the war. The U.S.S. *Bunker Hill* was hit by two suicide planes within thirty minutes on May 11, 1945.

10. On August 14, 1945, residents of New York City's "Little Italy" in Manhattan greet the news of the Japanese acceptance of the Allied surrender terms with waving flags and a rain of paper.

11. The memory of the Japanese surprise attack on the American naval base at Pearl Harbor on December 7, 1941, lives on today at the Battleship *Arizona* Memorial. The memorial is positioned directly above the sunken remains of the *Arizona*.

Discussion

Checking Understanding

1. What was one role played by African Americans in the war in Europe? (Served as fighter pilots; served as support staffers to fighter pilots.)

2. What desperate action did the Japanese take toward the end of the war in the Pacific? (Kamikaze pilots crashed their planes into American ships to try to damage them and injure or kill the men on board.)

Stimulating Critical Thinking

3. As a teenager in World War II, how might you have contributed to the war effort? (Might have collected paper and scrap, conserved food and other scarce consumer goods, taken on additional responsibility in the family when parents or other family members entered the armed services or took jobs in war industries.)

4. At the war's end, how might the emotions of a family with a gold star in their window compare with the emotions reflected in Picture 10? (Possible answer: although the gold-star family was probably relieved that the war was over, they may not have had the same feelings of jubilation and triumph as the people in Picture 10, because of the loss of a loved one in the war.)

Survey Answers

Reviewing Vocabulary

Definitions are found on these pages: *arms race* (520), *isolationism* (520), *dictator* (521), *fascism* (521), *totalitarian state* (521), *appeasement* (523), *rationing* (529).

Reviewing Main Ideas

1. (a) Built up army and weapons; invaded Manchuria, other parts of China and the Pacific. (b) Built up army and weapons; allied with Germany; invaded Ethiopia; intervened in Spanish Civil War. (c) Built up army and weapons; persecuted Jews; allied with Italy; intervened in Spanish Civil War; annexed Austria; demanded Sudetenland.

2. (a) Roosevelt and other Americans were outraged by Germany's bomb attacks on Britain. (b) United States sold older planes to Britain, provided war supplies through Lend-Lease, sent ships to report U-boats, sent troops to Greenland and Iceland, helped draw up Atlantic Charter.

3. Japan seized French Indochina. Roosevelt embargoed exports to Japan, fortified bases in Pacific, increased aid to China. Japan demanded end to embargo and aid to China; United States asked Japan to leave Axis and withdraw from China and French Indochina.

4. (a) Worked in war plants; served in military. (b) Served in military, with accomplishments of Navajo code talkers especially noteworthy. (c) Worked in war plants; served in military in noncombat roles.

5. It authorized removal of civilians from military areas. Roosevelt issued it in response to anti-Japanese hysteria. It resulted in the internment of 110,000 Japanese Americans.

(Answers continued in top margin)

6. Defeated Germans in North Africa, at Stalingrad, and in Italy; invaded France and liberated Paris; pressed toward Germany from east and west; bombed Germany.

7. Atomic bombs dropped on Hiroshima and Nagasaki.

Thinking Critically

1. The reasons were somewhat different: Japan sought living space and raw materials. Germany sought to rebuild and assert itself after losses in World War I; also had racist motives.

2. Possible answers: world's Jewish population might be reduced even more severely. Japan might be the dominant military, political, economic power in Asia. Europe might be dominated by Germany—or Germany and Soviet Union might have fought for

Chapter Survey

Reviewing Vocabulary

Define the following terms.

1. arms race
2. isolationism
3. dictator
4. fascism
5. totalitarian state
6. appeasement
7. rationing

Reviewing Main Ideas

1. Explain how each country threatened world peace in the 1930s. (a) Japan (b) Italy (c) Germany
2. (a) Why did the United States decide to aid Britain in the war? (b) What forms did the aid and cooperation take?
3. Describe the events that led up to the Japanese attack on Pearl Harbor.
4. How did each group contribute to the war effort? (a) African Americans (b) Native Americans (c) women
5. What was Executive Order 9066, why did Roosevelt issue it, and what result did it have?
6. Summarize how the forces led by the "Big Three" defeated Italy and Germany.
7. What caused Japan to surrender?

Thinking Critically

1. Analysis Both Germany and Japan gobbled up territory as fast as they could. Were their reasons exactly the same, or were they somewhat different? Explain your answer.
2. Synthesis Suppose the Axis, rather than the Allies, had won World War II. In what major ways might the world be different today? Give three possibilities.
3. Why We Remember: Evaluation World War II is sometimes referred to by Americans as "the good war." Why do you suppose that label has stuck? Do you think it is an appropriate label, or not? Explain your answer.

Applying Skills

Identifying gaps in information Think about an event of World War II, besides the attack on Pearl Harbor, about which you might ask a "how" or "why" question. Write the question. (Example: "How could the Holocaust happen without the entire world knowing?") Then, recalling what you learned in the Skill Lab on page 528, do the following:
1. Describe the types of information you need to answer the question.
2. Summarize the relevant information presented in this textbook.
3. State one gap in that information.
4. Name two types of sources you might consult to try to fill the gap.

History Mystery

The Battle of Britain Answer the History Mystery on page 517. What do the people sleeping in the subways tell you about the war effort in London?

Writing in Your History Journal

1. Keys to History (a) The time line on pages 516–517 has seven Keys to History. In your journal, describe why each one is important to know about. (b) Choose two events on the time line. In your journal, explain how they are related.
2. Benjamin Davis Imagine that you are Benjamin Davis, invited to speak to the West Point graduation class of 1946. In your journal, write the introduction to a speech that he might have given.
3. Citizenship Imagine that you are a Japanese American living in 1942. Write a letter to President Roosevelt urging him to reconsider Executive

dominance. United States might be under German or Japanese control.

3. Possible answers: the war was a clear-cut conflict between good and evil; millions behaved heroically; the war taught important lessons about dictators and racism. Opinions may vary: some may feel that no war can be "good" or that the horrible cost of this war makes a "good" label inappropriate.

Applying Skills

Students should show ability to apply the Procedure substeps on page 528 to whatever questions they write.

History Mystery

The people were London civilians using the stations as air-raid shelters during the blitz. Possible answers to the second question:
(Answers continued in top margin)

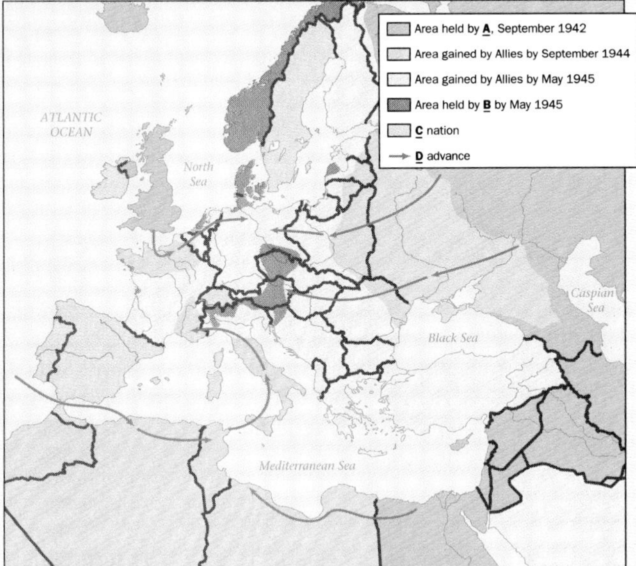

Reviewing Geography

1. Each letter in the map legend stands for a missing word. Write the word.

2. Geographic Thinking The word "theater" is sometimes used to refer to a major place of action during a war. How do you suppose geography challenged the fighting forces in the three major theaters of World War II: Europe, North Africa, and the Pacific? How do you suppose geography aided the fighting forces in each theater? Consider such things as distance, climate, vegetation, bodies of water, and landforms.

Order 9066. Give as many sound, logical arguments as you can.

Alternative Assessment

Covering the war for radio "This . . . is London." With those words, American correspondent Edward R. Murrow opened his nightly radio broadcast during the blitz. Murrow often spoke from a rooftop as bombs exploded, sirens screamed, and antiaircraft guns boomed. His broadcasts made the war powerfully real to listeners across the United States.

With a partner, act the roles of correspondents before and during the war.

❶ Choose four events or situations from the chapter to cover: one from each section of the chapter.

❷ Write a brief radio broadcast about each of these events or situations. Include background information you think your listeners may need. Provide colorful details to help your listeners "see" what you are describing.

❸ Plan how to present your four broadcasts. You might take turns speaking in each broadcast, or each cover two "stories." If you plan to include interviews with "eyewitnesses," one of you can be the correspondent while the other acts as the interviewee.

❹ Present your broadcasts to the class.

Your work will be evaluated on the following criteria:

• you report historical events and situations accurately
• your descriptions are lively, specific, and vivid
• your broadcasts capture and hold your audience's imagination

War effort was highly organized; Londoners cooperated to keep safe; Londoners were determined to wait out the bombing.

Writing in Your History Journal

1. (a) Descriptions should be similar to the time-line notes on teacher pages 516–517. (b) Explanations should reflect cause-effect or other connections as described or implied in the chapter.

2. Introductions should reflect Davis's belief that some goals are worth suffering for if necessary. Students may also choose to include statements condemning racism.

3. Letters might include such points as these: Evacuation and internment of citizens violate the Constitution; there is no evidence of Japanese American disloyalty; there is no reason beyond racism to intern Japanese Americans and not Italian or German Americans; people of the future will view the action unfavorably.

Reviewing Geography

1. (A) Allies (B) Axis
(C) Neutral (D) Allied

2. Europe: discomfort due to cold, snowy weather in places like the Soviet Union; hindrances to movement presented by mountains in Italy and southern France. On the other hand, the English Channel helped keep Britain from being invaded, and the relatively short distances in Europe probably aided communication and movement. North Africa: hot, dry climate and sand; lack of water. Pacific islands: hot, wet climate and thick vegetation; distance between islands.

Alternative Assessment

Teacher's Take-Home Planner 4, p. 23, includes suggestions and scoring rubrics for the Alternative Assessment activity.

Teaching the

Link to American Readings

In this feature students learn about World War II from three different perspectives: from the American soldier crouching in cold, wet crevices in the Italian mountains; from those at home whose days began and ended with waiting for news of loved ones at war; and finally, from rulers of two countries—the victor and the defeated—on the use of the atomic bomb.

Before students begin the lesson, review Italy's Defeat (page 534), The Atomic Bomb (pages 536–537), and Rationing and Producing (page 529). Have students read the entire feature before assigning the A Closer Look questions. The Setting the Stage Activity and Bonus Activity may then be introduced according to the needs and interests of the students. The information contained in the Discussion questions and the Footnotes may be used throughout the lesson as appropriate. Readers' Theater is ideal for students who might find the readings somewhat difficult. Use the Wrap-Up Activity for students who would enjoy taking a step beyond the core lesson.

Literature Footnote

Ernest Hemingway (1899–1961) wrote about war on the Italian front in his novel, *A Farewell to Arms*. Although his war was World War I, not much had changed for the soldier between the two wars. The cold, snow, mud, disease, and death were still there. Hemingway's main character has this to say about war: "I was always embarrassed by the words sacred, glorious and sacrifice. . . . We had heard them, sometimes standing in the rain almost out of earshot, so that only the shouted words came through, and had read them, on proclamations that were slapped up by billposters over other proclamations, now for a long time, and I had seen nothing sacred, and the things that were glorious had no glory and the sacrifices were like the stockyards at Chicago if nothing was done with the meat except to bury it. "

Link to American Readings

READING 12A

The Mountain War

The Allied Forces liberated Naples, Italy, on October 1, 1943. Although Rome was only 100 miles away, it took 8 more months of fierce combat before the Allies occupied the capital city. In his book *Brave Men*, Pulitzer Prize-winning journalist Ernie Pyle described why the progress of the war in Italy was so slow. Pyle was killed by Japanese machine-gun fire in 1945 while covering the war in the Pacific.

Ernie Pyle describes the Italian campaign, 1943

Our troops were living in almost inconceivable misery. The fertile black valleys were knee-deep in mud. Thousands of the men had not been dry for weeks. Other thousands lay at night in the high mountains with the temperatures below freezing and the thin snow sifting over them. They dug into the stone and slept in little chasms and behind rocks and in half-caves. They lived like men of pre-historic times, and a club would have become them more than a machine gun. How they survived the dreadful winter at all was beyond us who had the opportunity of drier beds in the warmer valleys. . . .

chasm: deep crack in the earth's surface

You've heard of trench mouth and athlete's foot, but still another occupational disease of warfare sprang up on both sides in the Italian war. It was called "trench foot," and was well known in the last war. . . .

Trench foot comes from a man's feet being wet and cold for long periods and from not taking off his shoes often enough. In the mountains the soldiers sometimes went for two weeks or longer without ever having their shoes off or being able to get their feet dry. The tissues gradually seem to go dead, and sores break out. It is almost the same as circulation stopping and the flesh dying. In extreme cases gangrene occurs. We had cases where amputation was necessary. And in others soldiers couldn't walk again for six months or more. . . .

gangrene: decay of tissue when blood supply is obstructed, often requires amputation of limb to prevent death

Sometimes the men let trench foot go so long without complaining that they were finally unable to walk and had to be taken down the mountain in litters. Others got down under their own power, agonizingly. One boy was a day and a half getting down the mountain on what would normally be a two-hour descent. He arrived at the bottom barefooted, carrying his shoes in his hand, feet bleeding. He was in a kind of a daze from the pain.

The fighting on the mountaintop almost reached the caveman stage sometimes. Americans and Germans were frequently so close that they actually

History Footnote

Civilians served in many capacities during World War II, providing everything from medical care to entertainment. One of the most famous people to entertain troops was the bandleader Glen Miller. Although too old to be drafted, Miller felt a moral obligation to serve his country in wartime. After joining the Army Air Forces, he put together a special Air Forces band, pirating drafted musicians from all over the country. The band played for troop shows, for marching cadets, and on a radio recruiting program. In June 1944 Miller received permission to perform overseas. After six months in England, the band was allowed to go to Paris. On December 15, 1944, Miller boarded a small Air Force plane in bad weather to make arrangements for his tour. His plane disappeared without a trace.

threw rocks at each other. Many more hand grenades were used than in any other phase of the Mediterranean war. And you have to be pretty close when you throw hand grenades.

Rocks played a big part in the mountain war. Men hid behind rocks, threw rocks, slept in rock crevices, and even were killed by flying rocks.

When an artillery shell bursts on a loose rock surface, rock fragments are thrown for many yards. In one battalion fifteen percent of the casualties were from flying rocks. Also, now and then an artillery burst from a steep hillside would loosen big boulders which went leaping and bounding down the mountainside for thousands of yards. The boys said such a rock sounded like a windstorm coming down the mountainside.

When soldiers came down the mountain out of battle they were dirty, grimy, unshaven and weary. They looked ten years older than they were. They didn't smile much. But the human body and mind recover rapidly. After a couple of days down below they began to pick up. It was a sight to see a bunch of combat soldiers after they had shaved and washed up. As one said, "We all look sick after we've cleaned up, we're so white."

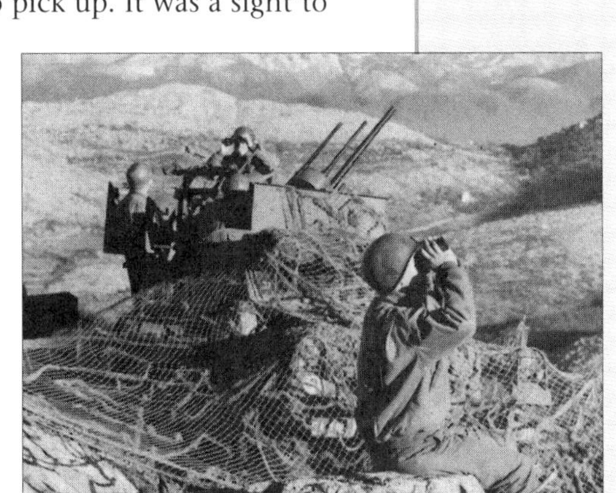

An American anti-aircraft battalion searches for enemy planes in the skies over the Italian front.

READING 12B

Hasten the Homecoming

Norman Rockwell was one of the most popular artists in the United States before, during, and after World War II. When he was 16 years old, Rockwell went to work for *Boys' Life* magazine. Three years later he became the art director for the monthly publication.

In 1916, when he was only 22, Rockwell sold his first illustration to *The Saturday Evening Post* magazine. He continued to illustrate *Post* covers, about 10 each year, until the magazine ceased weekly publication in 1969. He also illustrated classic books such as *The Adventures of Tom Sawyer* and *The Adventures of Huckleberry Finn.*

Setting the Stage Activity

Considering the Costs

To help students understand that war is more—or far less—than honor, glory, and uniforms, have them complete this exercise. Ask students to write in their history journals about the most miserable day or night they have spent in terms of physical discomfort. They should describe their discomfort and how they felt, both physically and emotionally. Ask volunteers to share their ideas. Then remind students that the first reading deals with just this aspect of war—the cold, the wet, the waiting, the hiding, the fear, the boredom.

Bonus Activity

Recognizing Rockwell's Appeal

To help students understand why Norman Rockwell was so popular, have them look for details in his poster that focus on the warmth and humor expressed in the faces and poses of the various figures. Have students make their own posters that ask citizens to support the war effort. How will they touch the emotions of the average American?

Discussion

Stimulating Critical Thinking

1. In your opinion, how important is it that people back home receive detailed descriptions of what it is like to fight or to be at a war front? (Opinions will vary. Most students will feel it is necessary to get detailed descriptions in order for people back home to understand what the soldiers are going through and to keep up everyone's morale. Without news from the front, the war becomes only a vague idea rather than a reality that requires an end.)

2. Truman believed that the only way to end the war was to use the atomic bomb on an enemy target. Sakomizu agreed that nothing less would have allowed the Japanese army to accept defeat. Now look ahead to the future. What decisions do you think the nations of the world will have to make concerning global peace? (Many students will agree that, based on the experience of World War II, the potential for destroying the Earth in the course of a nuclear war is very real. Learning to live in peace may be the only route to global survival.)

History Footnote

For every son or daughter serving in the armed forces, the parents received a blue star, which was proudly displayed in a prominent window of their home. Parents who lost their sons or daughters were given gold stars to display. People used the term "a gold-star mother" or "double gold-star father" to describe others or themselves affectionately and patriotically.

Literature Footnote

A former war correspondent, John Hersey (1914–1993) is probably best known for his book *Hiroshima*, which chronicles the lives of several residents of the city from just before the bomb was dropped until long after. Japanese writer Kenzaburo Oe, a writer best known for his powerful accounts of the bombing of Hiroshima, won the Nobel Prize for Literature in 1994.

Most Rockwell paintings were of small-town and rural America. They told clear stories of "middle America" in painstakingly realistic detail. The Rockwell painting used on the Victory Bond poster at left was originally a *Saturday Evening Post* cover. The purchase of Victory Bonds was a way for every American to support the war effort. Rockwell's illustration encouraged this patriotic investment.

How does Rockwell subtly show the patriotism of the people in this neighborhood?

READING 12C

The Atomic Bomb

The atomic bomb dropped on Hiroshima, Japan, in August, 1945, was the single most destructive weapon of the war. Whether measured in terms of lives lost, property damaged, human suffering, or long-term ill effects, that bomb surpassed any other. Undeniably, it changed the course of the war, and ultimately the course of history.

The following excerpts are two different perspectives on the use of the atomic bomb. The first is a statement by Hisatune Sakomizu, secretary to the Japanese cabinet during the summer of 1945. The second is a well-known excerpt from U.S. President Harry S Truman's memoirs concerning his decision to use the bomb against the Japanese.

Hisatune Sakomizu, a Japanese government official, on U.S. use of the atomic bomb

pretext: false reason

At the time the [Japanese] Army felt it would be a great shame for them if they were to surrender unconditionally as a military force, even if it was not a national surrender. They felt it was impossible. Therefore it was necessary to work out a suitable pretext which would make the Army feel they could not do anything else but just follow it. That's why we asked for the decision of the Emperor. The A-Bomb provided an excellent help, because the A-Bomb sacrificed many people other than Japanese military men. This provided us with an excuse that America would not refrain from doing such evils, that therefore there would be no other choice but to cease the war to save many innocent Japanese citizens. If the A-Bomb had not been dropped we would have had great difficulty to find a good reason to end the war.

History Footnote

The design and construction of the first nuclear weapons was directed by Dr. Robert Oppenheimer. In a *Time* article Oppenheimer said, "In some sort of crude sense, which no vulgarity, no humor, no overstatement can quite extinguish, the physicists have known sin; and this is a knowledge which they cannot lose."

Readers' Theater

Students might adapt the Pyle reading. Several students can alternate as the speaker. Have them study the excerpt to find logical breaks or shifts in thought. A new reader may step in at each natural break. Readers should assume the tone of one who has experienced the Italian mountains firsthand. Allow enough time for students to rehearse.

Harry S Truman on his decision to drop the atomic bomb on Japan

"I was there. I did it. I would do it again."

My own knowledge of these [atomic] developments had come about only after I became President, when Secretary Stimson had given me the full story. He had told me at that time that the project was nearing completion, and that a bomb could be expected within another four months. It was at his suggestion, too, that I had then set up a committee of top men and had asked them to study with great care the implications the new weapon might have for us. . . .

implications: consequences

It was their recommendation that the bomb be used against the enemy as soon as it could be done. They recommended further that it should be used without specific warning. . . . I had realized, of course, that an atomic bomb explosion would inflict damage and casualties beyond imagination. On the other hand, the scientific advisors of the committee reported, "We can propose no technical demonstration likely to bring an end to the war; we see no acceptable alternative to direct military use." It was their conclusion that no technical demonstration they might propose, such as over a deserted island, would be likely to bring the war to an end. It had to be used against an enemy target.

The final decision of where and when to use the atomic bomb was up to me. Let there be no mistake about it. I regarded the bomb as a military weapon, and never had any doubt that it should be used.

Top: The remains of a wristwatch found in the rubble in Hiroshima record the terrifying beginning of the nuclear age. Right: Survivors of the atomic blast wait to receive first aid.

A Closer Look

1. Describe the hardships suffered by American troops during the Italian campaign.

2. How does Pyle's soldier differ from the one in Rockwell's illustration? Which do you think interested the American public more? Why?

3. CRITICAL THINKING Sakomizu's reaction to the use of the atomic bomb may be unexpected from a Japanese official. Truman's blunt statements, like Sakomizu's, might seem to be without compassion. Carefully consider the comments and reasons presented by each man. Then state why you agree or disagree with each. What would you have done in Truman's place?

Wrap-Up Activity

Responding to a Blast That Changed the World

To extend the lesson, have students respond in their journals to this statement: "I am become Death, the shatterer of worlds." Explain that these words from the *Song of God*, a sacred Hindu text, came to Robert Oppenheimer's mind as he watched the explosion of the first atomic bomb at Los Alamos, New Mexico.

A Closer Look

Answers

1. The troops waded through knee-deep mud, slept in caves and crevices, suffered the cold and wet, were crippled by trench foot, fought hand-to-hand, and dodged rock splinters as well as bullets.

2. Pyle's soldier was real; Rockwell's was idealized. Many students will agree that the idealized soldier is the one those back home wanted to believe in.

3. Some students will agree with Truman; there was no way to convince the Japanese other than to use the atomic bomb. Others might say that there is no justification for atomic warfare. Students should support their opinions with facts.

Teaching the

Citizenship Lab

The issues of due process (U.S. Constitution, Fifth Amendment) and of balancing the security needs of the nation with individual liberties are the focus of this citizenship lab.

Before students read the feature, review Japanese Americans on pages 531–532. Have students read the entire feature before assigning the Understanding Civic Issues questions and the Hands-On Citizenship activity. The Bonus Activity in this Teacher's Edition may be used as an alternative to, or in addition to, the Hands-On Citizenship. The Discussion questions in this Teacher's Edition may be used at appropriate points during students' reading or afterward.

Objectives

- ★ Understand the importance of the Constitution's due process clause to limit the powers of government and safeguard the rights of individuals.
- ★ Realize that justice, equality, and diversity are fundamental to American public life.
- ★ Examine the conflict about minority civil rights that occurred during World War II, when the Japanese were sent to internment camps.

Supreme Court Case: *Korematsu* v. *United States*

Citizenship Lab

Can a Citizen's Rights Be Denied on the Basis of Race?

In the months after the bombing of Pearl Harbor, Japanese submarines cruised along the U.S. Pacific coast. They sank a ship near Seattle. The Japanese shelled the cities of Santa Barbara, California, and Seaside, Oregon. The war seemed to be advancing rapidly—not only on distant Pacific islands, but to our very shores. In this climate of fear, the U.S. military ordered all people of Japanese ancestry, resident aliens and citizens alike, to leave the Pacific coast.

One Person's Story

Fred Korematsu, a Japanese American citizen and native of California, was 23 when the evacuation was ordered. Engaged to an Italian girl, Korematsu decided to disobey the order. He had an operation on his face so he would look Caucasian and he changed his name. A fugitive in his hometown of Oakland, Korematsu held out for only a month. He caved in to the pressures and loneliness of his secret life and turned himself in to the police on May 30, 1942.

Korematsu was convicted of disobeying the evacuation order, which applied to him because of

A wind storm sweeps through Manzanar Relocation Center in California.

History Footnote

During his trial, Fred Korematsu presented evidence that he was a loyal U.S. citizen. He explained that, at a younger age, he had tried to enlist in the Army, but was rejected because of a stomach ulcer. He had been a welder, working on Navy ships, until he was fired because of his ancestry. He swore his loyalty to the United States and stated his continued willingness to join the Army. Despite his testimony, he was convicted of disobeying a law that denied him his liberty not because of anything he had done but because of his Japanese heritage. Even after the two-year appeals process, during which Korematsu was held without bail, he continued to face the consequences of his conviction. His choice of jobs was severely limited because of his criminal record.

his Japanese ancestry. Like other Japanese Americans, he was sent to an internment camp. Korematsu appealed the court's decision, taking it up to the U.S. Supreme Court.

The Court Upholds Korematsu's "Crime"

The case *Korematsu* v. *United States* was heard in December 1944. The justices were well aware that laws restricting the rights of people solely on the basis of their race must be examined very closely. Nevertheless, the Court ruled against Korematsu. Justice Hugo Black wrote the majority opinion, stating:

"No question was raised as to petitioner's [Korematsu's] loyalty to the United States. . . . [Korematsu was evacuated from his home] because the properly constituted [legal] military authorities feared an invasion of our West Coast . . . , because they decided that the military urgency of the situation demanded that all citizens of Japanese ancestry be segregated from the West Coast."

Three of the justices strongly disagreed. Justice Owen Roberts argued that Korematsu's constitutional rights had been violated when he was forced from his home "solely because of his ancestry, without evidence or inquiry concerning his loyalty and good disposition toward the United States." Justice Frank Murphy went further, calling the Court's decision "legalization of racism." Justice Robert Jackson spelled out the legal dangers of the decision:

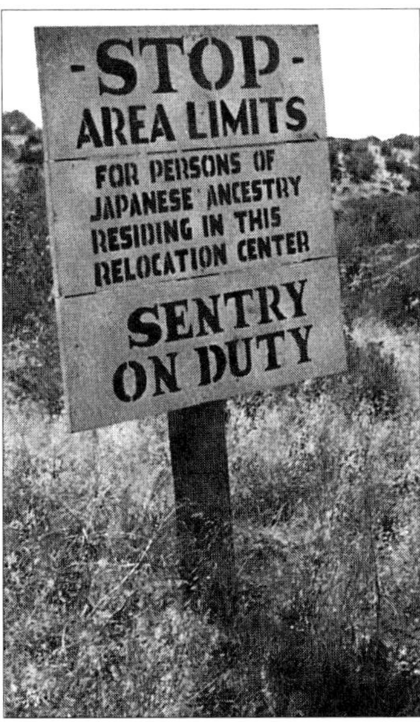

A sign warns Japanese Americans to stay within the camp's boundaries.

"Much is said of the danger to liberty from the Army program for deporting and detaining these citizens of Japanese extraction [ancestry]. But a judicial construction of the due process clause that will sustain [uphold] this order is a far more subtle blow to liberty than the promulgation [carrying out] of the order itself."

Jackson referred to the due process clause of the Fifth Amendment to the Constitution: "No person shall . . . be deprived of life, liberty, or property, without due process of law." Due process includes the right to a fair trial. By his statement, Jackson implied that Fred Korematsu should have had a trial in which

Setting the Stage Activity

Thinking About Discrimination

Ask students to imagine that signs have been posted in their neighborhood ordering all people of their ethnic background to prepare to give up their homes within a few weeks. The signs indicate that the people will be moved to a new location far away. The only reason given for this evacuation is that the people with this background pose a threat to the country. Have students write a journal entry describing their reaction to the order.

Bonus Activity

Exploring Due Process Issues

Ask students to look for contemporary examples in which due process may be in danger. Students can look in newspaper or magazine editorials, listen to radio broadcasts, or read news analyses. Examples might include issues related to: the rights of gay people serving in the military, threats to individuals or groups of people from hate groups, threats to individuals from government agencies running secret investigations. Ask volunteers to outline how their issues may involve a violation of the due process clause.

Discussion

Checking Understanding

1. What was Fred Korematsu's crime? (He disobeyed the order the Army issued forcing all people of Japanese descent on the West Coast to leave their homes by a certain date.)

Stimulating Critical Thinking

2. If you had been a justice on the Supreme Court during the Korematsu case, how would you have ruled in this case? Explain your answer. (Many students will probably say they would rule to overturn the conviction, because the government denied Korematsu and other Japanese American citizens their rights without giving them a chance to prove their loyalty to the U.S. Some students may say they would uphold the conviction because of the importance of national security during wartime. Accept any answer that students explain logically.)

3. The Korematsu case is discussed in *Black Mondays: Worst Decisions of the Supreme Court* by Joel D. Joseph. Do you think this case belongs in this collection? Explain your answer. (Most students will probably say yes, because of its validation of the principle of racial discrimination, which most students will consider a continuing danger.)

Civics History

German and Italian aliens living on American soil during World War II were not treated as harshly as Japanese Americans or Japanese aliens living in the United States. On December 8, 1941, President Roosevelt issued an executive order concerning Italian, German, and Japanese enemy aliens. In addition to suspending naturalization proceedings for members of these three groups, it required them to register, restricted their mobility, and prohibited them from owning items such as cameras and shortwave radios that might be used for sabotage. In practice, however, the government was anything but even-handed. Racial attitudes at the time greatly influenced how public policy was applied; Germans and Italians were treated fairly, but Japanese suffered great injustices.

he could prove his loyalty to his country. Without such a trial, the government violated the Constitution. According to Jackson, the government had deprived Korematsu and other Japanese Americans of their liberty (forcing them to go to the camps) without due process.

(Above) Mine Okubo was an artist who was interned at Camp Topaz in central Utah. She made a series of drawings depicting camp life. In this illustration, Japanese Americans are detained near San Francisco.

(Opposite) Today, many Japanese Americans make a yearly pilgrimage to the site of the Manzanar Relocation Center.

Is Due Process Still in Danger?

Over time, public opinion about the Korematsu case has shifted to the side of the dissenting judges. A congressional report released in early 1983 censured the detention of Japanese Americans. The report called it a shameful example of race prejudice, war hysteria, and a failure of political leadership. In a trial later that year, lawyers showed that the government knowingly presented false evidence in the Korematsu case. At the time of the exclusion order, the FBI reported there was no identifiable threat of Japanese Americans acting as spies. On that basis, Judge Marilyn Patel overturned Korematsu's conviction in federal court.

But the Supreme Court decision still stands. The Court refused to reverse the case in 1988. That the decision still has legal force is cause for concern for many. As Justice Jackson stated "the Court has validated the principle of racial discrimination . . . [which] then lies about like a loaded weapon." This weapon might be pointed at any identifiable group of people, forcing them to give up constitutional rights.

America will always be a nation of diverse peoples. Therefore, both in times of war and of peace, Americans have a duty to be aware of issues of racial discrimination and to balance the security needs of the country with the individual rights of each citizen.

Connection to Literature

Japanese Americans have shared their experiences during the war years through publishing autobiographies, journals, and diaries. One vivid autobiographical account is *The Invisible Thread* by Yashiko Uchida. In the following passage, Uchida describes the irrational fear and mistrust cast toward Japanese Americans after Pearl Harbor:

"Strange ideas seemed to be erupting in the minds of many Americans. I was astonished when a white friend of many years [referring to Pearl Harbor] asked, 'Didn't you have any idea it was going to happen?'

I was hurt that she had asked. Her question implied that we somehow knew of Japan's war plans simply because we were Americans of Japanese ancestry. It was a ridiculous assumption."

Understanding Civic Issues

1. In 1942, why did the Army view Japanese Americans living on the West Coast as a threat to the nation's security?
2. According to Justice Jackson, why was the Supreme Court's ruling in the Korematsu case a threat to individual rights?
3. **Critical Thinking** If you were a military commander, how would you decide whether to order a group of people to leave their homes. List the different circumstances under which you think such an order would be justified.
4. **Hands-On Citizenship** Imagine you and two classmates were members of one of the internment camps. You have decided to pool your money and use it to help middle-school students learn about the camps and the injustices done to the Japanese American people during World War II.
   - Decide what is the best way to educate young people about the issue. You might consider producing a movie or play, making a museum exhibit, publishing a political comic book, recording a song, putting on a concert, or any other ideas.
   - Write up a proposal for your idea. Include as many details as possible, such as outlines, pictures, scripts, floor plans, or tapes.
   - Share your proposals. As a class, pick out the three best proposals and discuss what makes each a good way to educate young people about this issue in history.

Citizenship Lab Answers

1. It thought Japanese Americans might aid the Japanese military in an invasion of the West Coast.

2. Jackson considered the ruling a legalization of racism, which would lead to possible curtailment of rights based solely on race.

3. Possible answers: if the people were in danger due to threat of war; if the people were in danger due to threat from other citizens; if the people were a proven danger to the country.

Teaching the Hands-On Citizenship

This activity is a valuable tool to get students to think about what is important in history. It is also a good way of having students evaluate and compare the impact of various kinds of presentations on them. Ask students who chose to produce a film why it would be more effective in educating young people than other options. Do the same for students who chose the other options. Explore the advantages and disadvantages of each form of presentation. Ask students to give examples of movies, songs, exhibits, etc., that have changed the way they feel about something.

Unit Survey

Making Connections

Answers

1. 1920s: labor and racial unrest; Red Scare; anti-immigration laws; Ku Klux Klan. 1930s: New Deal critics; hostility to Dust Bowl migrants. 1940s: discrimination, violence against Mexican Americans and African Americans; anti-Japanese hysteria.

2. Period fits idea well. 1920s: withdrawal from other nations' problems; focus on prosperity. 1930s: New Deal. 1940s: isolationism followed by war.

3. Agree: tackled problems head-on; inspired hope; kept nation intact. Disagree: expanded government too much; did not end Depression; Executive Order 9066.

Teaching the Unit Project

Provide board-game samples to spark thinking. Note ways people supported the war effort: to save cloth they bought clothing with short hemlines and no pleats, frills, cuffs, or pockets; collected scrap paper, rags, metal, and rubber for war production; gave blood; bought war bonds; grew own food.

Evaluation Criteria

The project can be evaluated according to the criteria listed below, using a scale for each: 4 = exemplary, 3 = good, 2 = adequate, 1 = poor.

Completing the task Game includes all rules and materials needed.

(Continued in top margin)

Knowing content Game includes accurate facts about home front.

Thinking critically Students show good judgment in planning an enjoyable game that provides information about the home front.

Communicating ideas Game rules are clear. Playing materials are attractive.

Thinking It Over

Students may say it is good advice because it encourages saving money and recycling. Students should realize that some Americans today must follow the advice for economic reasons or are willing to follow it because they want a simple life or want to help the environment. However, students may feel that waste and preference for new things are more typical of modern America.

Unit Survey

Making Connections

Review

1. Give one example from each decade to support this statement: Overwhelmed by the rapid changes of the 1920s, 1930s, and 1940s, many Americans reacted to certain ideas and groups of people with distrust and anger.

2. One historian says that United States history runs in cycles, with times of "private interest" (when efforts by businesses and individuals are strong) and times of "public purpose" (when government and the nation as a whole tackle problems). How well does the period covered in this unit fit that idea?

3. The United States under Franklin D. Roosevelt faced hard times. Many historians regard Roosevelt as second only to Abraham Lincoln in dealing with a national crisis. Do you agree or disagree? Support your answer with examples.

Linking History, Art, and Language Arts

Project

A Game About the Home Front

Pitching in for victory was a matter of pride and patriotism during World War II. You have read about rationing and working in war industries. Find out more (and have some fun) by creating a board game about life on the home front.

Project Steps

Work with a partner or a small group.

❶ Do research to learn how ordinary Americans supported the war effort. If possible, interview older relatives. Use the library too. You may discover wartime magazines, cookbooks, or pamphlets about rationing and other topics.

❷ Develop a format and rules for your game. You can use an existing game as a model. Your game must teach or ask questions about the home front.

• You might have "chance" cards like *Bake a birthday cake without sugar—Advance 2 spaces* and *Drive the car when you could have walked—Go back 4 spaces.*

• You might have "trivia question" cards like *Why did some Americans stare at the sky through binoculars?* (acting as volunteer enemy-aircraft spotters) and *What did the Portland (Oregon) Zoo and the Cook County (Illinois) jail yard have in common?* (sites of victory gardens).

❸ Make the game.

• Use markers and poster board to create an attractive game board.

• Make tokens out of materials like clay or paper. Your tokens might look like ration stamps, for example.

• Make game cards by writing questions or information on slips of colored paper.

• Write the rules of the game. Make them thorough but easy to follow.

❹ Play the game with classmates, friends, or family members.

Thinking It Over One wartime saying went, "Use it up, wear it out, make it do, or do without." Is that good advice for peacetime, too? Are modern Americans willing to live by that advice? Explain.

Objectives

- ★ Describe the tools and methods used by family historians.
- ★ Explain how historical events influence a family's history.
- ★ Discuss how family histories fit into the broader history of the nation.

How Do We Know?

The Erminio Viola family. (Joseph is the baby.)

Scholar's Tool Kit

Family Histories

More than a century ago the writer Herman Melville noted, "America has been settled by people of all nations. . . . We are not a nation so much as a world." Melville was right. As you have learned, beginning in Chapter 1 of this book, everyone in America originally came from someplace else. Even Indians, the first Americans, came from elsewhere thousands of years ago. The stories of where Americans came from are valuable to scholars who use those stories to add flesh to the bare bones of historic events. The stories are one of the building blocks of American history.

Collecting Family Stories

In its simplest form a family history is a list of births, marriages, and deaths, also known as a genealogy. In its most complete form, a family history consists of biographies—life stories—of each person. Many families take great pride in the stories of their ancestors and keep written records or taped interviews with older family members.

In researching history, scholars sometimes interview people about their family histories. Family stories are especially important to scholars studying immigration history, a field of research very popular today. Scholars want to know why immigrants left their homelands and how they adapted to their new homes.

Until recently, scholars assumed that most immigrants stayed in the United States after they got here. Now, however, they are learning

Introducing How Do We Know?

Family Histories

Ask students to define *family history.* Explain that scholars research family histories to find out more about how historical events affect people's lives and to learn more about their own ancestors. In this feature students learn how American family histories can shed light on our knowledge of immigration. For many years, scholars believed that most immigrants stayed in the United States permanently. By studying family histories, however, they have learned that many immigrants returned to their native lands.

Setting the Stage Activity

Asking Historical Questions

To help prepare students to explore their own family histories, have them write five questions about their families' past that could be answered by family members or family records such as photographs, documents, and letters. Invite volunteers to share their questions. Then encourage students to add to their lists if these questions spark other ideas.

Critical Thinking

Answers

1. They may have assumed that everyone who came to the United States had equally good fortune or was equally impressed by what they found here and therefore stayed. Also, historians would be likely to focus on individuals who stayed long enough to make long-lasting contributions to the United States.

2. The development of coal mines in Pennsylvania in the late 1800s provided a place of employment for Erminio Viola. His son Joseph found jobs building the subway in New York and the elevated train in Chicago. Because of the Great Depression in Italy, his boss had taken a job in Chicago; when his daughter visited, she met Joseph and they married.

3. Answers may focus on an individual or the family as a whole. Some possibilities are a family achievement or success that is a source of pride, or an experience that helped to shape the family.

Bonus Activity

Analyzing a Historical Source

To give students practice in analyzing a historical document, have them study the passport shown on p. 556. Then ask: What can you learn about Maria Incollingo from the document? Have pairs write a brief description of her, using only this written record.

History Footnote

Newly arrived immigrants to the United States invariably faced difficult times at first. They had to adjust to new foods and new surroundings. Finding employment and housing could be an overwhelming challenge. If the hardships proved too great or the longing for home was strong enough, immigrants returned to their countries of origin. Homesickness affected successful immigrants as well, as shown in this excerpt from a poem by a person who came to this country several generations ago:

> For many a man has gone to America;
> but many a man has come disappointed away
> But even should you find gold as abundant as the sands of the sea, one thing
> you will never find—a fatherland.

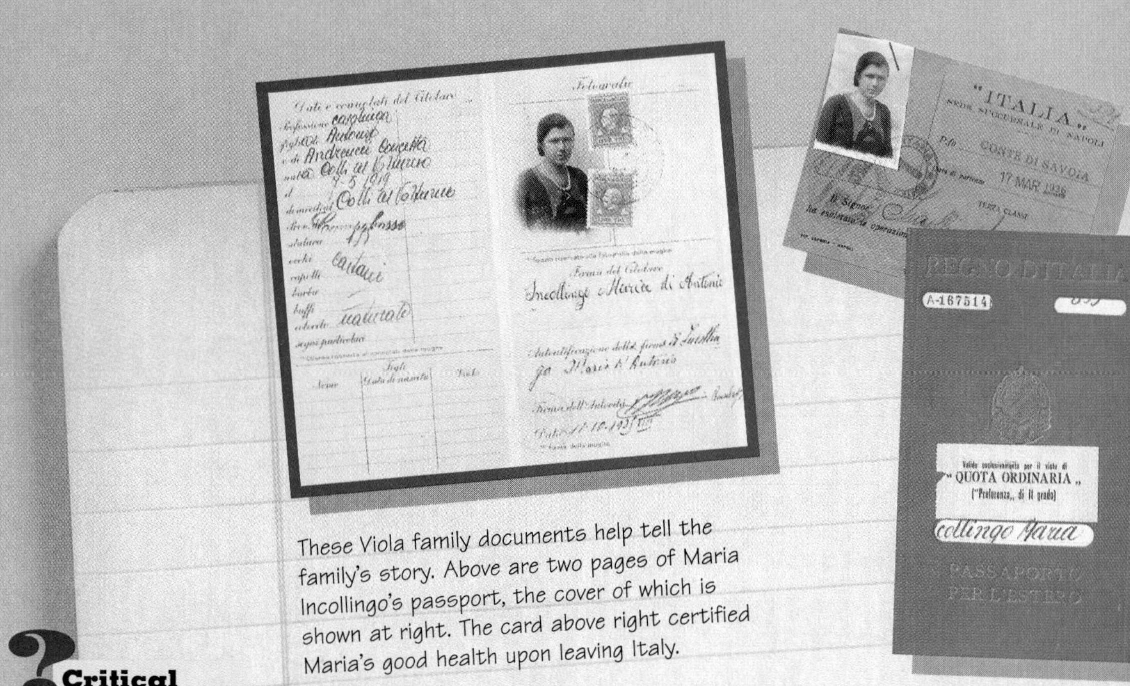

These Viola family documents help tell the family's story. Above are two pages of Maria Incollingo's passport, the cover of which is shown at right. The card above right certified Maria's good health upon leaving Italy.

Critical Thinking

1. Why do you think that American historians might have overlooked the study of immigrants who returned to their native lands?

that a surprising number of immigrants later chose to return to their native lands. Indeed, many of the returned immigrants had come to earn money and had never intended to stay. Others returned because they were unhappy or discouraged.

The Author's Story

One immigrant who returned to his homeland was Erminio Viola, my grandfather. In the 1890s he came to the United States from the Tyrol region of Austria, leaving his wife and three young children behind. He found a job in a Pennsylvania coal mine, but lost a leg in a mining accident soon after his arrival. Nonetheless, he liked America well enough to send for his family. The family had been in the United States only a short time, however, when Erminio's wife, Louisa, became ill. Having lived in the Dolomite Mountains all their lives, the family thought her illness was due to the change in altitude, so they returned to their village.

Critical Thinking

2. In what ways did historical events affect the Viola family history?

While in the United States, Erminio and Louisa had had a son, Joseph. After World War I, at age 17, Joseph chose to return to the United States upon completing his apprenticeship as a cabinetmaker.

Although Joseph arrived in New York penniless and unable to speak English, he immediately found a job helping build the New York City

Connections to Civics

Family historians researching immigrant ancestors often turn to ships' passenger lists. Captains were required to make a list of all passengers leaving a foreign port and entering a U.S. port. Between 1820 and the 1880s these reports were filed with the United States Customs Service. Later they were filed with the Bureau of Immigration. Many passenger lists for vessels arriving at major ports such as Boston, Detroit, New Orleans, and San Francisco can be found in the National Archives in Washington, D.C. Other items in the National Archives that are of interest to family historians include military service and pension records, naturalization records, passports, homestead records, and census lists.

subway. When the project was completed, he went to Chicago to help construct that city's elevated train. His boss was Antonio Incollingo, a contractor from Italy. At the time, Italy was suffering through the Great Depression. Benito Mussolini, dictator of Italy, encouraged workers like Antonio to find jobs abroad and send money home to bolster the country's sagging economy.

Antonio's 16-year-old daughter Maria (Mary) came to visit her father in Chicago. She wanted to see the United States before marrying a young man waiting for her at their village near Rome.

Mary immediately fell in love with the new land and did not want to go back. Upon meeting Joseph, who was 11 years older, she asked him to marry her so she could stay in the United States. The marriage took place a few weeks later and lasted until Mary's death more than 50 years later. They had two children: my sister, Mary Lou, and me.

For Joseph and Mary, the United States turned out to be the promised land. They had no regrets about staying, even though their families were in Europe. Joseph never once returned to his Tyrolean village, which is now part of Italy. Mary, however, missed her family very much. Over the years she made several trips to Italy to visit her brother and sisters.

Critical Thinking

3. If you were to tell your children one important thing about your family, what would it be? Why?

Scholar at Work

Every family has a history. Interview your parents or other family members and record what you learn. Find out if your family has kept any written records, and use them to add to your family history. Then, think of a way to present your family history to the class. You might want to make a poster with your family tree; tell a story of an interesting family member; make a videotape or audiotape of an interview; or bring in old photographs, letters, or other historical documents. Present your history to the class.

Discussion

Checking Understanding

1. Why did many immigrants choose to return to their homelands? (Many had come to earn money and returned once they achieved their goal; others were unhappy or discouraged.)

2. Why did Erminio and Louisa Viola return to their homeland? (They thought returning to a higher altitude in the Austrian mountains would improve Louisa's health.)

3. What did Mussolini hope immigrants would do with money they earned in the United States? (Send it home to help Italy's economy during the Depression.)

4. How did Mary Viola deal with homesickness for her family in Italy? (Made several trips over the years to Italy to visit her brother and sisters.)

Teaching the Scholar at Work

Students might look for connections between their family histories and the history of the United States. For example, they might ask how their relatives' lives were affected by events such as immigration laws, changes in technology, or wars and other conflicts. To help them place family events in time, suggest that they include birth, marriage, and death dates as part of their histories—in notations to photographs, on a family tree, or on a time line.

Unit 5

Introducing the Unit

The Hubble Space Telescope

The Hubble space telescope, a permanent observatory in space, is a joint program of the European Space Agency (ESA) and the National Aeronautics and Space Administration (NASA). It is one of the latest developments in a national space program established by Congress in 1961. The program was a response to the Soviet launching of the first space satellite. In this unit students will learn that competition in space was just one aspect of the Cold War competition between the United States and the Soviet Union. The post–Cold War era has been marked by cooperative Russian-American space missions and other joint efforts like the Hubble space telescope.

Teaching the Hands-On HISTORY

Before students begin to write, have them make a few notes about what Columbus would be able to observe as he looked at earth from space. For example, what would he learn about the landmasses? About the shape of the planet? About the location of oceans? They might look at a globe to simulate viewing earth from space. Have them refer to their notes as they write.

Unit Overview

After World War II, Communist and non-Communist nations struggled for influence in the world. The Cold War drew the United States into military conflicts in Korea and Vietnam and led to an arms race with the Soviet Union. It ended with the collapse of the Soviet Union in 1991.

The Cold War era at home was a time of prosperity, but many people remained poor. Great Society programs of the 1960s tried to end poverty and racial injustice. Still, many groups had to struggle for equal rights. Richard Nixon's presidency was marred by the Watergate scandal.

The post–Cold War era presents new challenges. Americans are addressing the role of government, the "new world order," environmental problems, an increasingly diverse population, and a global economy.

Unit 5

1945–Present

Chapters

Hands-On HISTORY

Activity

The Hubble space telescope, launched in 1990, is an astronomical observatory in space. This photo shows astronaut Storey Musgrave (lower right) servicing the telescope. Imagine that you are Christopher Columbus standing on the Hubble telescope. Five hundred years after your explorations, you now have a full view of the earth for the first time. In your journal reflect on how this view might have affected your plans for your voyage.

Hubble space telescope, Johnson Space Center, NASA photo, 1993

History Footnote

The Hubble space telescope was deployed by the crew of the space shuttle *Discovery*. Powered by two solar panels, the roughly cylindrical telescope measures about 13 meters by 4 meters. Its instruments produce much clearer images of astronomical objects than can ground-based telescopes. The telescope requires service missions every three years to keep it in good repair.

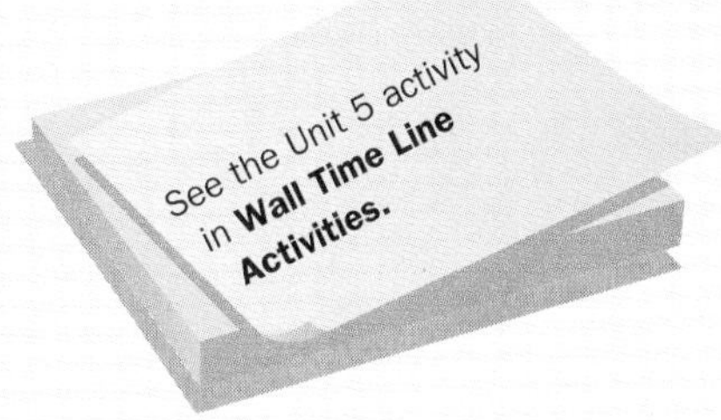

See the Unit 5 activity
in **Wall Time Line Activities.**

Power and Responsibilities

Discussion

Checking Understanding

1. The Hubble instruments are solar powered. Where can you see the solar panels in the photo? (Center, top.)

2. What color does earth appear to be from space, and why? (Blue; oceans cover most of its surface.)

Stimulating Critical Thinking

3. If you were an astronaut assigned to repair the Hubble telescope, what training and knowledge would you need? (Knowledge of the telescope's parts and how they work together; knowledge of astronomy; training in operating a spacecraft and working in space.)

4. If you were the head of NASA, would you have supported development of the Hubble space telescope? Why or why not? (Yes: pictures could be very useful to astronomers and earth scientists. No: other programs, such as the space shuttle or improving communications satellites, are more important because they may have more of an effect on everyday lives.)

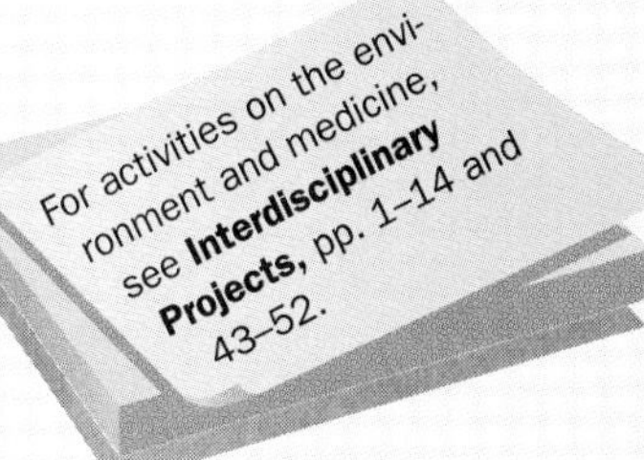

For activities on the environment and medicine, see **Interdisciplinary Projects,** pp. 1–14 and 43–52.

At·a·Glance 13

The Cold War Era
1945–1991

Chapter Planning Guide

Section	Student Text	Teacher's Edition Activities
Opener and Story pp. 560–563	**Keys to History Time Line** **History Mystery** Beginning the Story with **Harry S Truman**	**Setting the Stage Activity** From Vice-President to President, p. 562
1 **The Start of the Cold War** pp. 564–571	**World Link** The birth of Israel, p. 565 **Reading Maps** Europe 1955, p. 567 **Reading Maps** The Korean War 1950–1953, p. 568 **Geography Lab** Reading a Polar Map, p. 571	**Warm-Up Activity** Guessing the Meaning of "Cold War," p. 564 **Geography Question of the Day,** p. 564 **Section Activity** Designing a Propaganda Campaign, p. 566 **Bonus Activity** Writing a Foreign Policy Memo, p. 568 **Wrap-Up Activity** Identifying Cold War Hot Spots, p. 570
2 **The War in Vietnam** pp. 572–577	**Reading Maps** The Vietnam War 1954–1975, p. 573 **Link to Art** The Vietnam Veterans Memorial, p. 576 **Point of View** What are the lessons of Vietnam?, p. 577	**Warm-Up Activity** Impressions of the Vietnam War, p. 572 **Geography Question of the Day,** p. 572 **Section Activity** Planning a Photo-essay, p. 574 **Bonus Activity** Writing a War Zone Letter, p. 575 **Wrap-Up Activity** Creating a Time Line, p. 577
3 **The End of the Cold War** pp. 582–587	**Link to the Present** China's military power, p. 583 **Hands-On History** Planning a Cold War museum, p. 585 **Skill Lab** Asking Historical Questions, p. 587	**Warm-Up Activity** Making a Prediction, p. 582 **Geography Question of the Day,** p. 582 **Section Activity** Role-Playing a TV Interview, p. 584 **Bonus Activity** Writing Newspaper Headlines, p. 584 **Wrap-Up Activity** Compiling a "Who's Who," p. 586
Evaluation	**Section 1 Review,** p. 570 **Section 2 Review,** p. 577 **Section 3 Review,** p. 586 **Chapter Survey,** pp. 588–589 **Alternative Assessment** Recalling Cold War presidencies, p. 589	**Answers to Section 1 Review,** p. 570 **Answers to Section 2 Review,** p. 577 **Answers to Section 3 Review,** p. 586 **Answers to Chapter Survey,** pp. 588–589 (Alternative Assessment guidelines are in the Take-Home Planner.)

Teacher's Resource Package

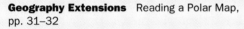

Chapter Summaries: English and Spanish, pp. 62–63

Chapter Resources Binder

Study Guide Supplying Supporting Evidence, p. 113

Geography Extensions Reading a Polar Map, pp. 31–32

American Readings Unsent Letter from President Truman, p. 57

Chapter Resources Binder

Study Guide Using Visual Images to Preview, p. 114

Reinforcement Writing Newspaper Accounts, pp. 117–118

American Readings Fighting in Vietnam, pp. 58–59

Chapter Resources Binder

Study Guide Relating Cause and Effect, p. 115

Skills Development Asking Historical Questions, pp. 119–120

American Readings The Fall of the Berlin Wall, p. 60

Using Historical Documents Ronald Reagan's "Evil Empire" Speech, pp. 86–91

Chapter and Unit Tests Chapter 13 Tests, Forms A and B, pp. 103–106

Take-Home Planner

Introducing the Chapter Activity Advising the President, p. 6

Chapter In-Depth Activity Mapping Change, p. 6

Reduced Views

Study Guide, p. 8

Geography Extensions, p. 11

American Readings, p. 10

Unit 5 Answers, pp. 31–38

Reduced Views

Study Guide, p. 8

Reinforcement, p. 9

American Readings, p. 10

Unit 5 Answers, pp. 31–38

Reduced Views

Study Guide, p. 8

Skills Development, p. 9

American Readings, p. 10

Using Historical Documents, p. 11

Unit 5 Answers, pp. 31–38

Reduced Views

Chapter Tests, p. 11

Unit 5 Answers, pp. 31–38

Alternative Assessment Guidelines for scoring the Chapter Survey activity, p. 7

Additional Resources

Wall Time Line

Unit 5 Activity

Transparency Package

Transparency 13-1 The Vietnam Veterans Memorial—use with Section 2

Transparency 13-2 Offerings at the Vietnam Wall—use with Section 2

Transparency Activity Book

SelecTest Testing Software

Chapter 13 Test, Forms A and B

Vital Links

Videodisc

CD-ROM

Maoist China (see TE p. 566)

Korean War (see TE p. 568)

The Cuban missile crisis (see TE p. 569)

Marine fighter-bomber (see TE p. 573)

Lieutenant Philip Caputo (see TE p. 574)

"Blowin' in the Wind" (see TE p. 574)

President Nixon on peace (see TE p. 576)

Vietnam Veterans Memorial (see TE p. 576)

Signing nuclear arms treaty (see TE p. 583)

President Reagan on foreign policy (see TE p. 584)

Berlin Wall (see TE p. 585)

13

Teaching Resources

Take-Home Planner 5
- Introducing Chapter Activity
- Chapter In-Depth Activity
- Alternative Assessment

Chapter Resources Binder
Geography Extensions
American Readings
Using Historical Documents
Transparency Activities
Wall Time Line Activities
Chapter Summaries
Chapter and Unit Tests
SelecTest Test File
Vital Links CD-ROM/Videodisc

Discussion

Keys to History

Keys to History journal writing activity is on p. 588 in the Chapter Survey.

United Nations founded This body replaced the League of Nations. (p. 564)

Marshall Plan begins This American economic aid made possible Western Europe's postwar recovery and stopped the spread of communism there. (p. 565)

Communists come to power in China Led by Mao Zedong, Communist rebels drove away the ruling Nationalists. (p. 566)

Korean War Truman sent American troops to aid South Korea when it was invaded by Communist North Korea. (p. 567)

Looking Back The Soviet Union emerged after a revolution overthrew Russia's czar.

World Link See p. 565.

Chapter Objectives

- ★ Explain how the American-Soviet relationship changed after World War II.
- ★ List the causes and effects of American involvement in Vietnam.
- ★ Describe how the Cold War came to an end.

Chapter Overview

After World War II the United States adopted a policy of blocking Communist expansion. It contained communism in Europe through economic aid. It became involved in a war between Communists and non-Communists in Korea. During the Cuban missile crisis of 1962, Cold War tensions nearly led to a nuclear war between the United States and the Soviet Union.

1945–1991

Chapter 13 The Cold War Era

Sections

Beginning the Story with Harry S Truman

1. The Start of the Cold War
2. The War in Vietnam
3. The End of the Cold War

Keys to History

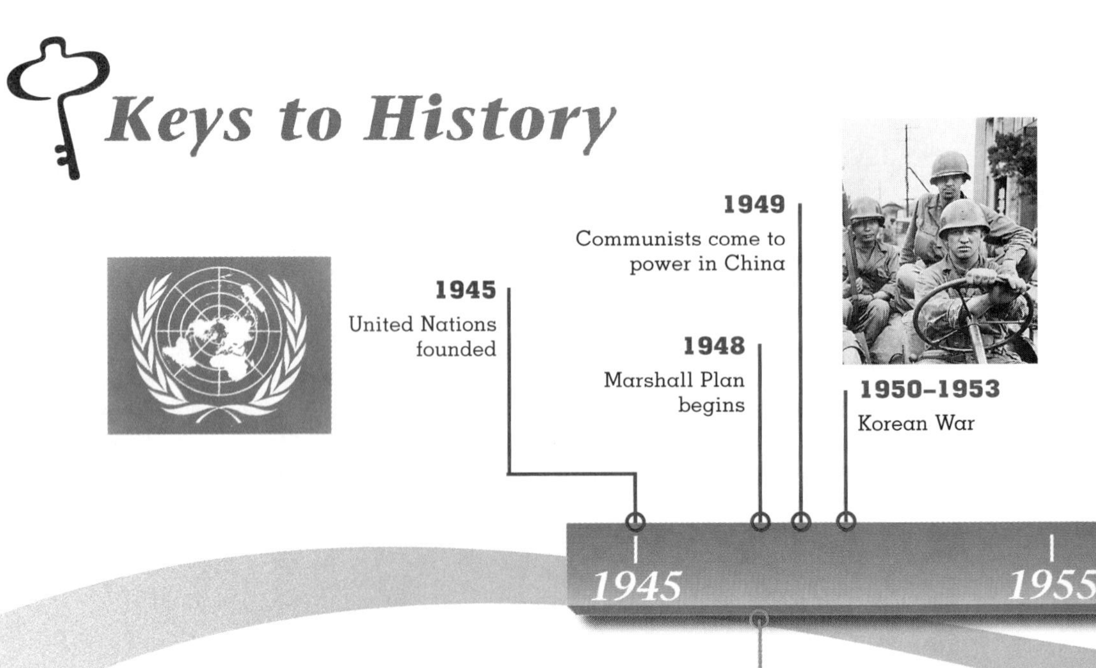

To save South Vietnam from communism and prevent Communist expansion in Southeast Asia, the United States became involved in the war in Vietnam. By 1965 American forces were fighting Viet Cong guerrillas on the ground and bombing North Vietnam. As the war dragged on, a strong antiwar movement developed at home. The war cost many American lives and shook Americans' confidence in their government.

Nixon improved relations with China and the Soviet Union by visiting Communist China and signing the first strategic arms agreement with the Soviet Union. Carter tried to expand détente and emphasized human rights. Late in Reagan's presidency, Cold War tensions thawed as the Soviet Union made democratic reforms. These reforms led to a call for democracy in Eastern Europe and the breakup of the Soviet Union.

HISTORY *Mystery*

This small ball of steel, called *Sputnik*, weighed a mere 184 pounds (83 kg). Why did it strike fear into the hearts of Americans?

1962
Cuban missile crisis

1965–1973
American troops fight in Vietnam War

1972
President Nixon visits China

1991
Soviet Union collapses

1965 1975 1991

Looking Ahead

American and Russian peacekeepers sent to Bosnia
1995

Teaching the *HISTORY Mystery*

Students will find the answer on p. 569. See Chapter Survey, p. 588, for additional information and questions.

Time Line

Cuban missile crisis The incident brought the world to the brink of a nuclear war. (p. 570)

American troops fight in the Vietnam War The United States tried unsuccessfully to save South Vietnam from communism. (pp. 572–577)

President Nixon visits China The visit opened the door to United States relations with Communist China. (pp. 582–583)

Soviet Union collapses The 15 Soviet republics declared their independence, marking the end of the Cold War. (p. 585)

Looking Ahead In 1995 the United Nations sent an international force of peacekeepers to war-torn Bosnia.

Beginning the Story

Harry S Truman

Harry Truman was given a middle initial but no middle name. That way the "S" could stand for both grandfathers. Growing up, he never imagined being in politics. However, after his clothing store failed during the recession, he ran for county judge. An influential Democrat thought Truman's farm background, World War I record, determination, and charming personality could get him elected. He was right. He went on to be a senator and then Vice-President. He was sworn in as President having been Vice-President for only 83 days. He was the first President to lead the United States during the Cold War years.

Setting the Stage Activity

From Vice-President to President

To help students think about how citizens feel when a Vice-President suddenly becomes President, present this hypothetical situation. They have just heard that the President has died in a car accident. Have them write paragraphs describing how they feel about suddenly having a new leader.

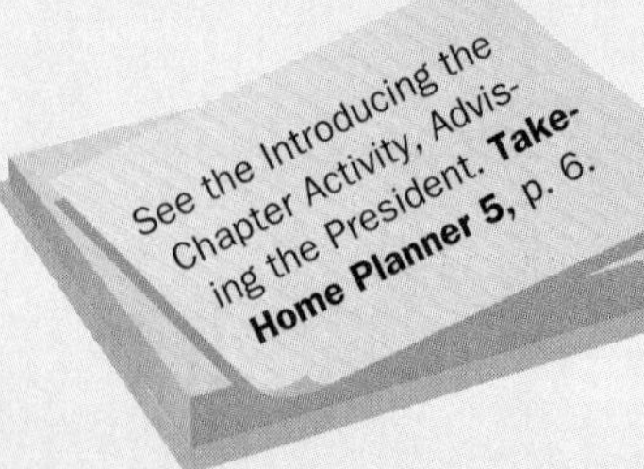

See the Introducing the Chapter Activity, Advising the President. **Take-Home Planner 5,** p. 6.

History Footnote

Truman believed that a good President had to be decisive, as shown by his motto, "The buck stops here." He also quoted Mark Twain: "Always do right. This will gratify some people and astonish the rest." Truman believed that a President had to accept that some of his decisions would be controversial. "If you can't stand the heat," he was fond of saying, "stay out of the kitchen."

Beginning the Story with

Harry S Truman

On April 12, 1945, Vice-President Harry S Truman received a message to call the White House. "Please come over right away," said a voice choking with emotion. Truman later recalled:

> "I reached the White House about 5:25 P.M. and was immediately taken in the elevator to the second floor and ushered into Mrs. Roosevelt's study. . . . I knew at once that something unusual had taken place. Mrs. Roosevelt seemed calm in her characteristic, graceful dignity. She stepped forward and placed her arm gently around my shoulder. 'Harry,' she said quietly, 'the President is dead.' For a moment I could not bring myself to speak. . . . 'Is there anything I can do for you?' I asked at last. I shall never forget her deeply understanding reply. 'Is there anything *we* can do for *you*?' she asked. 'For you are the one in trouble now.'"

The Man from Missouri

Born on a Missouri farm in 1884, Truman had not grown up wanting to be President, or even a politician. After serving in World War I, he and his pal Eddie Jacobson opened a men's clothing store in Kansas City, Missouri. In 1922, however, the firm of Truman & Jacobson failed, leaving Truman deeply in debt and with a family to support.

Only then, at the age of 38, did Truman try his luck at politics. When he told a friend he was planning to run for a county office, the response was, "I think you're crazy." Truman replied, "I got to eat." He was elected a county judge in 1926 and won a second term four years later.

In 1934 Truman was chosen by the Kansas City Democratic machine to run for the Senate. However, even his most powerful backer admitted, "I don't feel that Harry Truman has a chance." To almost everyone's surprise,

History Bookshelf

Hahn, Mary Downing. *December Stillness.* A teenage girl struggles to understand the effect of the Vietnam War on men of her father's generation. Clarion Books, 1988.

Also of interest:

Edelman, Bernard, ed. *Dear America: Letters Home from Vietnam.* Norton, 1985.

Emerson, Zack. *Welcome to Vietnam.* Scholastic, 1991.

Foster, Leila. *The Story of the Cold War.* Children's Press, 1990.

Hoobler, Dorothy and Thomas Hoobler. *Vietnam: Why We Fought: An Illustrated History.* Knopf, 1990.

Meltzer, Milton, ed. *The American Promise: Voices of a Changing Nation, 1945–Present.* Bantam Books, 1990.

Myers, Walter Dean. *Fallen Angels.* Scholastic, 1988.

Truman turned out to be a rousing campaigner and won the election. As he went off to Washington, the man from Missouri described himself modestly as "a humble member of the next Senate, green as grass and ignorant as a fool about practically everything worth knowing."

"Good Luck, Mr. President"

When President Roosevelt decided to run for a fourth term in 1944, his advisors talked about possible candidates for Vice-President. Truman's name came up again and again. His record in the Senate was good. He was acceptable to labor unions. He had a reputation for honesty. One advisor recalled, "Truman was the man who would hurt him [Roosevelt] least."

Truman was not so sure he wanted the job. Roosevelt was in poor health, and many believed he would not live out another term. Asked by a journalist about the possibility of becoming President, Truman replied:

Truman had a reputation for being down-to-earth and energetic. "Being a President is like riding a tiger," he wrote. "I never felt that I could let up for a single moment."

> "Do you remember your American history well enough to recall what happened to most Vice-Presidents who succeeded to the Presidency? Usually they were ridiculed in office, had their hearts broken, lost any vestige [trace] of respect they had before. I don't want that to happen to me."

When Truman suddenly did have to take office as President, the challenges ahead must have seemed overwhelming. Talking with reporters the day after he was sworn in, Truman said:

> "Boys, if you ever pray, pray for me now. I don't know whether you fellows ever had a load of hay fall on you, but when they told me yesterday what had happened, I felt like the moon and stars, and all the planets had fallen on me."

One of the reporters called out, "Good luck, Mr. President." Truman turned to him and replied, "I wish you didn't have to call me that."

Hands-On HISTORY Activity

Imagine that you are Harry Truman after receiving the news that President Roosevelt has died. Write a diary entry expressing your thoughts about the responsibilities of becoming President. Comment on challenges you will face and tell in what ways you think you are suited or unsuited to be President.

Discussion

Thinking Historically

1. Why was Truman selected to run for Vice-President in 1944? (Reputation for honesty and a good record in the Senate; acceptable to labor unions.)

2. Why did Truman have doubts about becoming President? (Most Vice-Presidents who succeeded to the presidency suffered ridicule, disappointment, and lack of respect. Felt burdened by the problems he would have to face.)

3. Do you think Truman was well prepared to be President? Why or why not? (Yes: almost 20 years of political experience, most at the national level. No: never envisioned self as President and thus was not prepared mentally.)

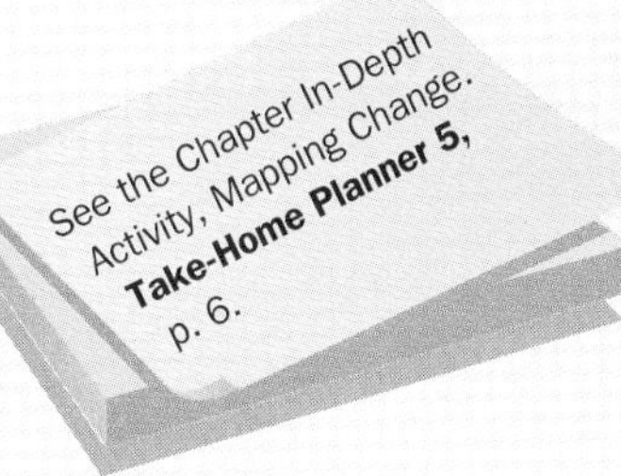

See the Chapter In-Depth Activity, Mapping Change, **Take-Home Planner 5,** p. 6.

Teaching the Hands-On HISTORY

Before students begin their diary entries, ask them to think about Truman's life and character before he entered politics. They might review historical events to consider problems he would be inheriting.

For a journal writing activity on Harry Truman, see student page 588.

Introducing the Section

Vocabulary

Cold War (p. 564) the struggle for power between Communist and non-Communist nations between 1945 and 1991

containment (p. 565) Truman's policy of blocking Communist expansion

Warm-Up Activity

Guessing the Meaning of "Cold War"

To introduce the topic of the Cold War, write the term on the chalkboard and ask what it might mean. Have students brainstorm a list of words and phrases that might describe a "cold war."

Geography Question of the Day

To help students see that the Cold War was global, have them color in on a world outline map (see **Geography Extensions**) these locations discussed in the section: Greece, Turkey, West Berlin, France, Italy, mainland China, Korea, Hungary, Iran, Lebanon, Jordan, and Cuba. They should refer to the map on pp. R2–R3 for names of countries.

See the Study Guide activity in Chapter Resources Binder, p. 113.

Section Objectives

- ★ Describe how the United States contained communism in Europe.
- ★ Explain why the Cold War spread to Asia and the Middle East.
- ★ Describe the Cold War conflicts that arose over Cuba.

Teaching Resources

Take-Home Planner 5, pp. 4–11
Chapter Resources Binder
Study Guide, p. 113
Reinforcement
Skills Development
Geography Extensions, pp. 31–32
American Readings, p. 57
Using Historical Documents
Transparency Activities
Chapter and Unit Tests

1. The Start of the Cold War

Reading Guide

New Terms Cold War, containment

Section Focus The change in American-Soviet relations after World War II

1. How did the United States contain communism in Europe?
2. Why did the Cold War spread to Asia and the Middle East?
3. What Cold War conflicts arose over Cuba?

During Harry Truman's first months in office, World War II was finally coming to an end. However, the seeds of new conflicts were already planted. The United States and Britain believed the Soviet Union was committed to spreading communism throughout the world. They were determined to prevent that from happening.

The struggle for power between Communist and non-Communist nations came to be called the **Cold War.** Although it was more a war of threats and propaganda than of guns and bullets, the Cold War was to keep the world in a state of fear and hostility from 1945 until 1991.

To tell the whole story of the Cold War, this chapter focuses on events that took place outside of the United States. Chapter 14 tells what was happening at home, including events influenced by the Cold War.

The United Nations

Before his death, President Roosevelt had committed himself to efforts to prevent future wars. At a meeting at Yalta in early 1945 he, Churchill, and Stalin had agreed on the need for a new international body to replace the failed League of Nations.

In April delegates from 50 nations met in San Francisco to draw up a charter for the United Nations (UN). This time, American support was strong. The Senate voted 89 to 2 to approve joining the UN.

The UN has two main parts: the General Assembly and the Security Council. Every member nation sends representatives to the General Assembly. As at a great town meeting, they debate world issues.

The Security Council is responsible for peace-keeping. Each of its five permanent members—the United States, Great Britain, France, China, and the Soviet Union (the seat now held by Russia)—has the right to veto a decision to use UN military force.

The "Iron Curtain"

Cold War tensions cast a shadow over the UN. Stalin soon seized control of Eastern Europe to give the Soviet Union a buffer against attacks in future wars. The nations of Eastern Europe became totalitarian states whose citizens were denied freedom of speech and even freedom to travel.

As the Soviet Union tightened its grip on the nations of Eastern Europe, Churchill warned that "an iron curtain has descended across the continent." For decades that "Iron Curtain" was to divide the democratic nations of "the West" from the Communist nations of "the East."

Tips for Teaching

Auditory Learners

To help students process text, give them a chance to read in several ways. Read aloud the first paragraph of a subsection as they follow in their texts. Next have them take turns reading sentences aloud for a paragraph or two. Then have them read a paragraph silently. Have pairs finish the selection by reading aloud to each other.

Containing Communism in Europe

Truman shared Churchill's view that the Soviet Union, having created a Communist empire in Eastern Europe, was eager to expand its power. He saw Soviet threats to Greece and Turkey. Greece was struggling to put down a Communist revolt, and Stalin was demanding land and naval bases from Turkey.

Truman wasted no time. At his urging, in 1947 Congress gave $400 million to Greece and Turkey to help them protect themselves. In what became known as the Truman Doctrine, the President declared that the United States would "support free peoples" to resist Communist takeovers.

Truman's policy of blocking Communist expansion was known as **containment.** To carry out the policy, Congress passed the National Security Act of 1947. The act created the Department of Defense, the National Security Council (NSC) to advise the President, and the Central Intelligence Agency (CIA) to spy on other nations.

To Truman, though, the strongest Cold War weapon was economic aid. He declared:

> "The seeds of totalitarian regimes are nurtured by misery and want. They spread and grow in the evil soil of poverty and strife. They reach their full growth when the hope of a people for a better life has died. We must keep that hope alive."

The Marshall Plan It was clear that hope was dying in Western Europe, where the economy had been shattered by the war. Desperate, starving Europeans might be attracted to the false promises of communism, just as their parents had been to fascism and Nazism. In fact, Communist parties were gaining strength in France and Italy.

The United States responded with a bold and generous program announced by Secretary of State George C. Marshall in June 1947. Under the Marshall Plan, Western Europe received $13 billion in American aid from 1948 through 1951. The aid made it possible to rebuild cities, repair railroads, and regain economic prosperity. An outstanding success, the Marshall Plan is credited with saving France and Italy from communism.

The Berlin airlift At the Yalta Conference, the Big Three had agreed to divide Germany into four zones, managed separately by American, British, French, and Soviet

The birth of Israel The UN faced its first major challenge in Palestine. Although it was the Jewish homeland in ancient times, Palestine had been home to Arab peoples since the 600s. In 1922 the League of Nations approved placing Palestine under British control. Jewish refugees from Europe poured into Palestine in the 1930s. Many hoped to create an independent Jewish state, an idea the Arab majority opposed. Tensions grew, and eventually Britain asked the UN to step in.

Moved by sympathy for Holocaust victims, the UN voted in 1947 to divide Palestine into Jewish and Arab states. After Jews proclaimed the state of Israel in May 1948, Arab nations sent troops to help the Palestinian Arabs fight the Israelis. The Soviet Union took the Arab side. While supporting Israel, the United States tried to avoid offending the Arab states, which held most of the world's oil reserves. The Arab-Israeli conflict would continue to be tied to the Cold War.

Developing the Section

Discussion

Checking Understanding

1. What is the Security Council? (UN peacekeeping body with five permanent members: United States, Britain, France, China, and Russia.)

2. What was the purpose of the CIA and when was it established? (To spy on other nations; by National Security Act of 1947.)

Stimulating Critical Thinking

3. If you were a member of Congress while Truman was President, would you favor containment? Why or why not? (Yes: to prevent another world war. No: countries should be able to choose own types of government; cannot afford so much aid to other countries.)

Teaching the

Explain that Zionism, a movement to set up a Jewish homeland in Palestine, had been gaining support before World War II. Jews consider Palestine their homeland, and as early as the 1500s some Jewish leaders urged a return to Palestine. In 1897 Austrian journalist Theodore Herzl convened the first Zionist Congress at Basel, Switzerland. They drew up a program to secure by law a Jewish state in Palestine.

Section Activity

Designing a Propaganda Campaign

To emphasize the role of propaganda, have students design Cold War propaganda campaigns. Divide the class into small groups, each reflecting the foreign policy of one administration: Truman's, Eisenhower's, or Kennedy's. Have groups assign each member one form of communication (such as posters, editorials, radio spots, bumper stickers, games, or films). Groups should brainstorm messages and goals of the campaign, draw up designs for their ideas, and include brief plans for how their propaganda will be distributed. Conclude by having groups present their campaigns to the class.

Vital Links

Maoist China (Picture)
Unit 5, Side 1,
Search 39683

See also Unit 5 Explore CD-ROM location 232.

History Footnote

The planners of the Berlin airlift calculated that keeping two and half million Berliners alive would take a minimum of 4,000 tons of food and other necessities a day—or one cargo-plane landing about every three minutes around the clock. To run the city normally would take 8,000 tons of food, fuel, medicine, and clothing. In the beginning the task seemed impossible. The American and British pilots who flew in "Operation Vittles," as they called it, delivered just 1,150 tons a day in its early months. By winter, with three airfields, some larger planes, and additional French pilots, Berlin was receiving 4,500 tons daily. By early spring 8,000 tons a day were being landed, and Soviet leaders realized the blockade was a failure. The airlift had succeeded.

To overcome the Soviet blockade, the Allies flew supplies to West Berlin. During the 318-day airlift, a plane landed every three minutes.

forces. Germany's capital of Berlin, deep within the Soviet zone, was also divided.

In June 1948 Stalin ordered a blockade of West Berlin, hoping to force out the western allies by cutting off their supplies. They responded with the massive "Berlin airlift." Huge cargo planes flew tons of food, medicine, and other supplies to West Berlin. In May 1949 the Soviets finally gave up the blockade. The West had won a dramatic Cold War victory.

Meanwhile, the three western zones of Germany were merged into the independent West German Federal Republic. The Soviets organized their zone into the East German Democratic Republic. The once powerful German nation had been split in two, with East Germany disappearing behind the Iron Curtain.

NATO In the election of 1948, Truman was returned to office. The next spring the United States helped form the North Atlantic Treaty Organization (NATO), a military alliance to guard against a Soviet attack. NATO counted on the threat of the atomic bomb to keep the Soviets from attacking the West. The Soviets, it was believed, would need ten years to develop nuclear weapons. In September 1949, however, Truman received shocking news of a Soviet nuclear test. One nuclear scientist noted:

> "There is only one thing worse than one nation having the atomic bomb—that's two nations having it."

What followed was a terrifying arms race. Truman approved plans to build an even more powerful nuclear weapon, the hydrogen bomb, and Congress voted $1 billion to arm NATO.

Fearful of NATO, in 1955 the Soviet Union formed the Warsaw Pact, an alliance of all the Communist countries in Eastern Europe except Yugoslavia. Once again Europe was divided into armed camps ready for war.

Communist Victory in China

Adding to western worries was the Communist takeover of China in 1949. Led by Mao Zedong (mow dzuh-doong), Communist rebels had won a bitter civil war with the ruling Nationalists, who retreated to the island of Formosa (now called Taiwan).

During China's civil war some advisors had urged Truman to give the Nationalists more aid and even to send troops. Truman, though, saw the Nationalist cause as almost hopeless. He preferred to focus on containing communism in Europe. Still, the United States refused to recognize the government of Communist China. With American support, the Nationalists kept China's seat on the UN Security Council.

History Footnote

Maintaining a balance of power was central to the arms race. News that the Soviets had exploded an atomic bomb sent shock waves through the United States. Defense experts said if the Soviet Union dropped an A-bomb on the United States, 10 million to 15 million people could die in one day. The Soviets had broken the American monopoly on nuclear weapons. Also, their non-nuclear forces far outnumbered those of the United States. In 1950 they had 3 times more combat airplanes, 4 times more troops, and 30 times more tanks.

Although most scientists opposed building an even more devastating weapon, American leaders worried that the Soviets might develop a hydrogen bomb first. Therefore, on January 31, 1950, Truman announced that the United States would develop an H-bomb.

Discussion

Checking Understanding

1. What was NATO's purpose? (Guard against Soviet attack.)

2. How did the United States respond to the Communist takeover of China? (Did not recognize the Communist government, supported Nationalist seat on Security Council.)

Stimulating Critical Thinking

3. Why do you think the blockade of Berlin did not lead to war between the East and the West? (Neither had recovered from World War II; did not want the destruction of another war; airlift made war unnecessary.)

Reading Maps

During the Cold War, people spoke of an "iron curtain" dividing Europe into the East and the West. What nations were on each side of this imaginary curtain?

Teaching the Reading Maps

To focus on the division of Europe into Communist and non-Communist blocs, have students trace with their fingers, from north to south, the borders that represent the Iron Curtain. **Answers to Reading Maps:** East: East Germany, Poland, Czechoslovakia, Hungary, Romania, Bulgaria, Albania, the Union of Soviet Socialist Republics. West: Great Britain, Denmark, Norway, Sweden, Finland, Iceland, Ireland, West Germany, France, Belgium, Netherlands, Luxembourg, Switzerland, Austria, Italy, Greece, Turkey, Spain, Portugal.

The Korean War

Meanwhile, to the south of China, trouble was brewing in Korea. Ruled by Japan during World War II, Korea had been divided after the war. Soviet troops occupied North Korea, and American troops occupied South Korea. After setting up governments, the Soviet Union and the United States withdrew their forces.

In June 1950 the North Korean army suddenly invaded South Korea. Truman quickly asked the Security Council to send a UN force to South Korea. The Soviet delegate was not present at the UN debate and so failed to veto the proposal.

Teaching the

Reading Maps

Have students describe each phase in a sentence. (Example: In September 1950, Communists advanced near Korea's southern tip.) **Answer to Reading Maps:** Some answers: How far did Communists invade the South? How far did UN forces push them back? By July 1953, who controlled what territory?

Bonus Activity

Writing a Foreign Policy Memo

To assess Cold War developments, have students imagine being Secretary of State in 1953. Have them write a memo recommending a policy for dealing with communism.

Vital Links

Korean War (Movie)
Unit 5, Side 1, Search 39719, Play to 40469

See also Unit 5 Explore CD-ROM location 238.

Connections to Science

Sputnik I was an aluminum sphere 23 inches in diameter weighing 184 pounds. It orbited between 141 and 588 miles above the earth, completing an orbit in 96.2 minutes. Inside the sphere were instruments that radioed data about cosmic rays, meteoroids, and the density and temperature of the upper atmosphere. These transmissions continued for 21 days. After 57 days the satellite reentered the atmosphere and was destroyed by frictional heat.

Sputnik II, launched in the same year, weighed over 1,000 pounds, and its orbit was even higher. It carried a small dog named Laika and transmitted the first biomedical measurements in space. *Sputnik II* stayed aloft for 162 days.

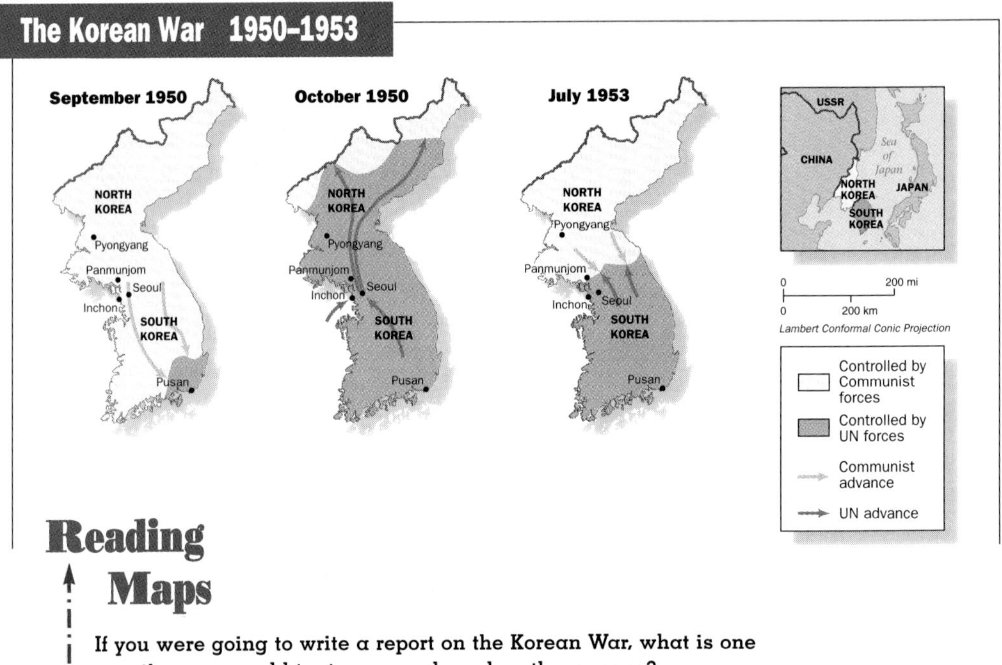

Reading Maps

If you were going to write a report on the Korean War, what is one question you would try to answer based on these maps?

Troops from 16 nations made up the UN force in Korea—with the vast majority of them Americans. The UN commander, General Douglas MacArthur, found himself in a desperate situation as his troops were pushed far to the south. He boldly launched a surprise counterattack by landing at Inchon, deep behind enemy lines. Soon the North's army was in full retreat.

MacArthur pressed on into North Korea. By November UN forces were nearing the Chinese border. Suddenly, what MacArthur called a "bottomless well" of Chinese soldiers swept down to help the North Koreans push the UN forces back into South Korea.

A stunned MacArthur asked to have "thirty to fifty atomic bombs" dropped on military targets in China. Afraid of starting a third world war, Truman refused. When MacArthur criticized him publicly, the President fired the general.

Eventually peace talks ended the war in 1953, leaving Korea still divided. Communist aggression had been stopped, but the war had cost the lives of about 33,000 Americans. The United States had demonstrated that it would stand by its policy of containment.

Foreign Policy Under Eisenhower

Foreign policy took a dramatic turn after Dwight D. Eisenhower was elected President in 1952. While Truman had declared, "*I* make foreign policy," Eisenhower gave much of that responsibility to his Secretary of State, John Foster Dulles. Dulles wanted to move beyond containment. His goal was to free people from Communist rule.

Dulles declared that the United States would go to "the brink of war" to stop the spread of communism. It would even use

History Footnote

The September 15, 1961, issue of *Life* magazine displayed a civilian in a fallout suit (on sale for $21.95) with the headline "How You Can Survive Fallout." The issue included directions for building a fallout shelter. A typical one was a small underground room, about 8 feet by 10 feet, built of concrete, wood, or sandbags. Some people built shelters in their backyards; others in their basements. Ready-made bomb shelters were also sold. The Mark I Kidde Kokoon, for example, came with everything a family of five might need to live underground for three to five days, including canned food and water, a chemical toilet, five bunks with mattresses and blankets, a gasoline-driven generator and gasoline, a radiation detector, a three-way portable radio, and a pick and shovel for digging out after the blast.

nuclear weapons—"massive retaliation"—if necessary. Dulles's critics called his approach "brinkmanship." Dulles also encouraged secret CIA efforts to overthrow governments considered unfriendly to the United States.

Revolution in Hungary Cold War tensions relaxed for awhile when Nikita Khrushchev (nuh-KEE-tuh kroosh-CHAWF) emerged as the Soviet leader after Stalin's death in 1953. Khrushchev proposed "peaceful coexistence" with the West. Western leaders were encouraged when he granted limited self-rule to Poland.

Inspired by events in Poland, rebels in Hungary tried to break free of Soviet control in 1956. As Khrushchev crushed the rebellion with tanks and troops, Dulles's earlier threats proved hollow. The United States was unwilling to go to war over Hungary.

***Sputnik* and the arms race** As Dulles and Eisenhower backed away from threats of massive retaliation, Khrushchev grew bolder. In 1957 the Soviets alarmed the West by launching the first satellite, *Sputnik I*. Americans feared that if the Soviets could send satellites into space, they could also launch intercontinental ballistic missiles (ICBMs) to destroy American cities.

Convinced that the Soviets had surged ahead in the arms race, the United States rushed to build more, and more powerful, nuclear weapons. The threat seemed so real that schoolchildren were taught to duck under their desks in case of a nuclear missile attack. Many families built bomb shelters in their backyards.

The Middle East and Latin America Meanwhile, the Cold War had spread to the Middle East. Both the Soviet Union and the United States sought allies in that oil-rich region. When Iran's leaders acted friendly toward the Soviets, CIA agents helped the Shah of Iran regain control of the government in 1953.

Hungarian rebels, like this woman in Budapest, fought for independence in 1956. Soviet troops and tanks crushed the revolt, killing thousands.

In 1957 Congress approved what became known as the Eisenhower Doctrine—a plan to help Middle Eastern nations resist Communist takeovers. When Lebanon and Jordan asked for aid in 1958, the United States and Britain quickly sent troops.

Eisenhower and Dulles also saw threats in Latin America. In 1954 CIA-backed rebels overthrew Guatemala's pro-Communist government. The United States also sent arms to Honduras and Nicaragua to prevent Communists from coming to power.

Conflict Over Cuba

The threat of communism came closest to home on the island of Cuba. There, in January 1959, a young revolutionary named Fidel Castro forced the military dictator, Fulgencio Batista, to flee the country.

Discussion

Checking Understanding

1. Why did some critics call the foreign policy shaped by John Foster Dulles "brinkmanship"? (He declared the United States would go to "the brink of war"—and even use nuclear weapons—to stop the spread of communism.)

Stimulating Critical Thinking

2. If you were an advisor to Eisenhower, would you support CIA efforts to overthrow Communist governments? Why or why not? (Yes: communism seems a serious threat to freedom. No: United States should not intervene in internal affairs of other countries.)

3. How might an arms race be harmful to rival countries? (Economy might be hurt because money and resources are used to build weapons rather than saleable products. The threat of war would hang over the countries.)

Vital Links

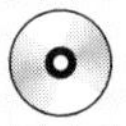

The Cuban missile crisis (Map) Unit 5, Side 1, Search 06107

See also Unit 5 Explore CD-ROM location 39.

Closing the Section

Wrap-Up Activity

Identifying Cold War Hot Spots

To help summarize the section, have students create a "hot spots" chart to describe the major Cold War conflicts from 1947 to 1962. Suggest that they place location names across the top of their chart and use these side headings: *Dates, United States President, How conflict began, Outcome.*

Section Review

Answers

1. Definitions: *Cold War* (564), *containment* (565)

2. Marshall Plan kept the Communists from gaining strength in France and Italy. Berlin airlift forced Soviets to end blockade.

3. Asia: China's civil war, Korean War. Middle East: CIA agents helped Shah of Iran regain control from Communists; under Eisenhower Doctrine, United States sent troops to Lebanon and Jordan.

4. After Soviets placed nuclear missiles in Cuba, Kennedy ordered navy to blockade Cuba and demanded removal of the missiles. The Soviets backed down.

5. No: Soviet Union's decision to control Eastern Europe was a shocking development and implied desire to expand power. Yes: better communications and more peace talks might have made Cold War unnecessary.

History Footnote

When the United States learned on October 14 that Cuba had Soviet medium-range missiles—capable of hitting Washington, D.C., Mexico, or Central America within minutes—and that sites for more advanced missiles were being built, President Kennedy faced a grave decision. After wrestling with many choices, he decided on a naval blockade. Letters revealing this course of action were sent to 43 allied nations, to all Latin American nations, and to Khrushchev. On October 22 Kennedy delivered a televised message to the nation in which he laid out a seven-step course of action. He stated in his speech, "The path we have chosen for the present is full of hazards, as all paths are; but it is the one most consistent with our character and courage as a nation and our commitments around the world."

During the 1950s and early 1960s, schools held "duck and cover" drills to prepare for possible Soviet nuclear attacks. Another reflection of Cold War fears is this American film poster, which portrays Communist leaders as villains.

Castro later allied Cuba with the Soviet Union and threatened to spread communism in Latin America. In response, Eisenhower approved a CIA plot to train anti-Castro rebels to invade Cuba and overthrow Castro.

The Bay of Pigs invasion When John F. Kennedy became President in 1961, he approved the CIA's invasion plan. On April 17 nearly 1,500 Cuban rebels landed at Cochinos Bay (the Bay of Pigs), where they hoped to find support among the Cuban people. Instead, most of the invaders were quickly killed or captured.

Within weeks of the Bay of Pigs disaster, Khrushchev tested the new President by demanding that the western powers leave Berlin. Kennedy stood firm, however, and Khrushchev had to back down. The Soviet Union then built a concrete wall to stop people escaping from East to West Berlin. The Berlin Wall became a bitter symbol of the Cold War.

The Cuban missile crisis In October 1962 Kennedy faced still another test—one that brought the world to the brink of nuclear war. Spy planes flying over Cuba had photographed secret Soviet-built nuclear missile sites. Kennedy ordered the navy to blockade weapons shipments to Cuba and demanded that Khrushchev remove the missiles from the island.

As Soviet cargo ships loaded with more missiles approached the American warships, the world held its breath. At the last minute, Khrushchev ordered them to turn back. Over the next few weeks, the Soviets removed their missiles from Cuba, and the United States lifted its blockade. Sobered by how close they had come to war, Khrushchev and Kennedy set up a telephone "hot line" to help avoid future crises.

1. Section Review

1. Define **Cold War** and **containment.**
2. How did American aid help contain communism in Europe?
3. What Cold War conflicts arose in Asia and the Middle East?
4. What was the Cuban missile crisis?
5. Critical Thinking Could the Cold War have been avoided? Explain.

Geography Footnote

In addition to radar, NORAD uses sonar, laser beams, high-tech optical devices, and magnetic, thermal, chemical, and acoustical sensors. All of these detection devices—which may be located on the ground, on the sea, on airplanes, or on space satellites—work together as a defense system.

The most important component of NORAD is the Ballistic Missile Early Warning System. This radar network can detect a missile as far away as 3,000 miles and provide a 15-minute warning of an attack on North America.

Geography Lab

Reading a Polar Map

In August 1957 the Soviet Union successfully tested the first intercontinental ballistic missile (ICBM). Suddenly, Americans faced the possibility of a long-range nuclear missile attack.

Americans looking for comfort may have found some in maps like the one on pages R2–R3. The Soviet Union looked so very far away. Maps centered on the North Pole, however, gave reason to be concerned.

An American ICBM

The Northern Hemisphere

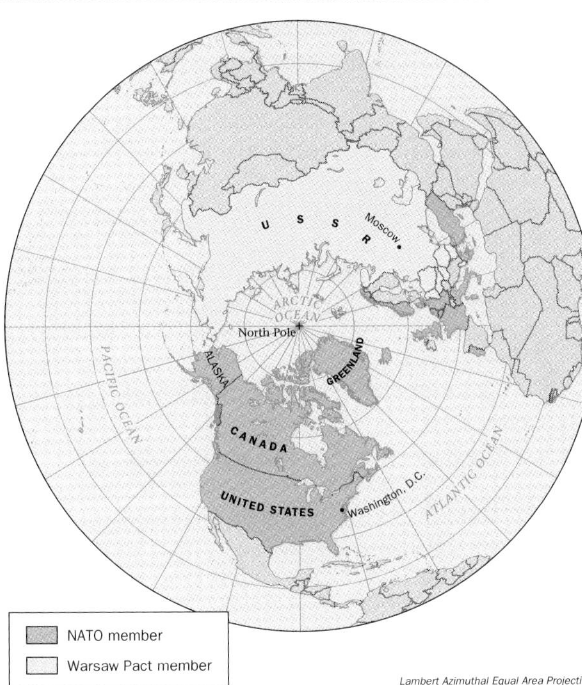

Using Map Skills

1. Using the map on pages R2–R3, describe the most direct air route between Moscow and Washington, D.C.
2. Using the polar map on this page, describe the most direct route between Moscow and Washington. Is it the same?
3. Use a globe to measure the actual distance between Moscow and Washington. Which is the most accurate route—the route you chose using the map on pages R2–R3 or the polar map on this page?
4. Would Moscow necessarily be the best place for Soviet missile bases? Explain.
5. **Hands-On Geography** The North American Air Defense System (NORAD) was set up in 1957, with radar stations in Canada, Greenland, and Alaska to detect missiles and aircraft. As a NORAD planner, make a speech in Congress explaining the radar locations.

Teaching the Geography Lab

Have students review the lab on understanding a map's point of view (p. 376). Then ask how a polar map differs in point of view from maps with other perspectives. (It looks down on either pole, unlike maps that center on other parts of the earth such as the equator.)

Using Map Skills

Answers

1. Across northern Europe and Atlantic Ocean.

2. Across Finland, Norway, Sweden, Greenland, eastern Canada. Not the same.

3. The route using the polar map. (Students might use a string or a cloth tape measure.)

4. No: it is the capital and a large population center. Since in a war an enemy would be likely to target missile bases, an attack on such a city would be devastating to the country.

5. Speeches will vary but should emphasize that NORAD stations are located along the likely path of missiles sent from the Soviet Union and are as close as possible to the Soviet Union.

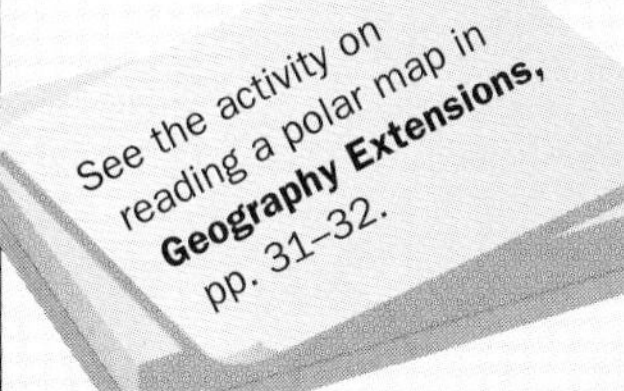

571

Introducing the Section

Warm-Up Activity

Impressions of the Vietnam War

To get students thinking about the Vietnam War, ask what they know about the war or what impressions they have of it. Some sources of prior knowledge are adults they know, books, movies, and visits to memorials. Create a web on the chalkboard to record words, images, and ideas they offer. Tell students that they will have a chance to compare their impressions with the facts as they read the section.

Geography Question of the Day

Have students locate Vietnam on the map on pp. R2–R3. Ask them to notice what other countries in both hemispheres are located at the same latitude. From this, have them write a short paragraph describing the landscape and climate they would expect to find in Vietnam.

See the Study Guide activity in **Chapter Resources Binder**, p. 114.

Section Objectives

- ★ Explain what led to American intervention in Vietnam.
- ★ Describe how the Vietnam War was different from other wars.
- ★ Identify several effects of the Vietnam War.

Teaching Resources

Take-Home Planner 5, pp. 4–11
Chapter Resources Binder
Study Guide, p. 114
Reinforcement, pp. 117–118
Skills Development
Geography Extensions
American Readings, pp. 58–59
Using Historical Documents
Transparency Activities, pp. 44–45
Chapter and Unit Tests

2. The War in Vietnam

Reading Guide

Section Focus The causes and effects of American involvement in Vietnam

1. **What led to American intervention in Vietnam?**
2. **How was the Vietnam War different from other American wars?**
3. **What were some effects of the Vietnam War?**

With the end of the Cuban missile crisis, the nation breathed a sigh of relief. Meanwhile, however, the United States was gradually being drawn into a war in far-off Southeast Asia. When Kennedy took office in 1961, few Americans had heard of the tiny country of Vietnam. Soon, though, it would be a household word.

When informing Kennedy of the conflict brewing in Vietnam, Eisenhower had said, "This is one of the problems I'm leaving you that I'm not happy about. We may have to fight." In fact, the United States did eventually go to war in Vietnam—the longest and most unpopular war in the nation's history.

A Divided Country

The conflict was rooted in a struggle by the Vietnamese to free themselves from French colonial rule after World War I. The leader of that effort, Ho Chi Minh, had asked for American help, but the United States remained loyal to France, its World War I ally. Also, Americans were suspicious of Ho because his followers, called Vietminh, included Communists. Ho soon became a Communist and received Soviet aid.

The Vietminh stepped up their struggle after World War II. Despite millions of dollars in American aid, the French finally gave up in 1954. A peace treaty signed that year in Geneva, Switzerland, divided Vietnam in half. A Communist Vietminh government ruled the North, and a pro-Western government ruled the South.

The treaty did not bring peace, though, for Ho was determined to unify the country. He sent arms to help South Vietnamese guerrillas, called the Viet Cong, to overthrow their new government. The stage was set for a major Cold War conflict.

The "domino theory" Eisenhower was determined to save South Vietnam from communism. In 1954 he compared the situation to playing with dominos:

> "You have a row of dominos set up, and you knock over the first one, and what will happen to the last one is the certainty that it will go over very quickly."

American policymakers believed that the fall of South Vietnam would lead to Communist control of all of Southeast Asia. To prevent that from happening, Eisenhower sent more aid and military advisors.

Growing Involvement

Sharing Eisenhower's concern, Kennedy expanded the aid and sent many more military advisors. By the end of 1962, more than 12,000 American advisors were in South Vietnam. Their efforts, however, were hampered by the fact that the corrupt government had little support among the people.

Tips for Teaching

Kinesthetic Learners

To help kinesthetic learners understand the "domino theory," bring dominos to class. If they are not available, use books or have students bring in empty cereal boxes. Have them line up the objects so when one is touched, the next falls, and so on. Ask how this reveals why the domino theory created fear in Americans.

With the tragic assassination of Kennedy in November 1963, Lyndon Johnson became President. When Johnson learned how bad the situation in Vietnam was, he said he felt like a fish that had "grabbed a big juicy worm with a right sharp hook in the middle of it."

Johnson faced a difficult decision: Should he use American force to win the war for South Vietnam or withdraw completely? Unwilling to withdraw, he secretly ordered raids against Communist bases in neighboring Laos. He hesitated, though, to send troops unless he could get support from Congress. That support would come only if American forces were attacked.

The Gulf of Tonkin Resolution On August 2, 1964, an American navy destroyer reported being fired upon by North Vietnamese torpedo boats in the Gulf of Tonkin. Two days later, another attack was reported. Johnson saw his opportunity.

Claiming that the attacks were unprovoked, the President argued that the conflict was no longer a civil war. At his request, on August 5 Congress passed the Gulf of Tonkin Resolution. It gave him the power to enlarge the American role in the fighting. It was not a declaration of war, but it did give the President the power to take any military actions he felt were necessary in Vietnam.

Much later it was revealed that neither of the attacks in the Gulf of Tonkin had been confirmed. The public also learned that the American warships had been there to protect South Vietnamese gunboats that were attacking North Vietnam.

An escalating American role Slowly but surely the United States was drawn deeper into the war. At first it had sent only advisors. Now its planes made massive bombing raids on North Vietnamese factories and military bases. Johnson hoped the raids would break the enemy's will to fight.

Instead, North Vietnam sent Chinese and Soviet weapons to the Viet Cong along a route called the Ho Chi Minh Trail. Troops from the North Vietnamese Army (NVA) soon began pouring south in order to help the Viet Cong.

In response, Johnson decided to use American ground troops. In early 1965, 3,500 marines landed. Within three years the number of American troops had escalated to more than 500,000.

The Vietnam War 1954–1975

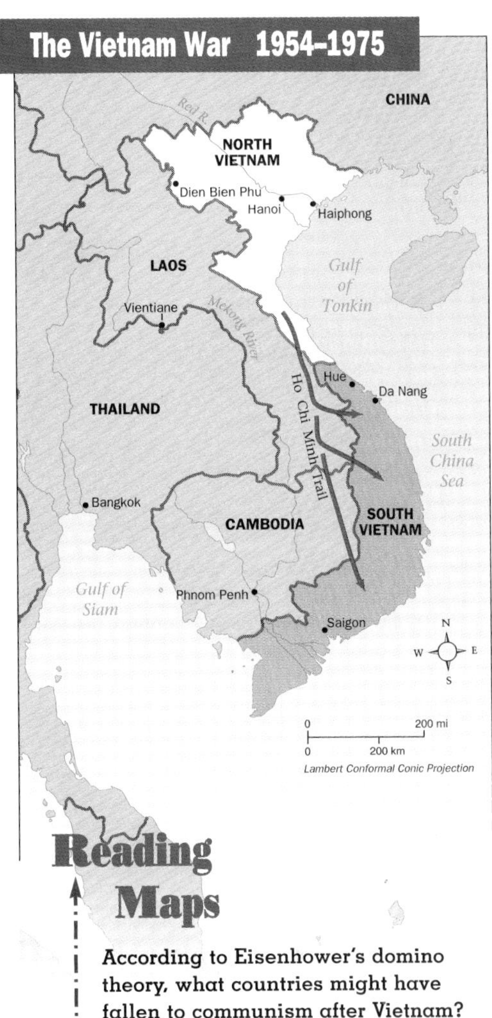

Reading Maps

According to Eisenhower's domino theory, what countries might have fallen to communism after Vietnam?

Developing the Section

Discussion

Checking Understanding

1. What was the "domino theory" and why was it important? (According to the theory, if South Vietnam fell to Communists nearby nations would too. Used to justify American involvement.)

Stimulating Critical Thinking

2. Why do you think the United States did not declare war on North Vietnam? (To avoid war with North Vietnam's allies, the Soviet Union and China.)

Teaching the Reading Maps

Have students find the Gulf of Tonkin and Ho Chi Minh Trail and explain their importance. Ask what nations border the Gulf of Tonkin and through which ones the Ho Chi Minh Trail passes. (North Vietnam, China; North Vietnam, Laos, Cambodia, South Vietnam) **Answer to Reading Maps:** Laos, Thailand, Cambodia.

Vital Links

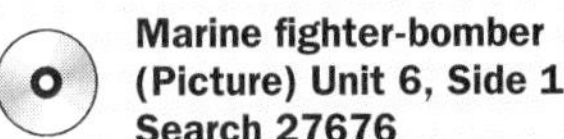

Marine fighter-bomber (Picture) Unit 6, Side 1, Search 27676

See also Unit 6 Explore CD-ROM location 190.

Section Activity

Planning a Photo-Essay

To focus on the war's events and impact, have pairs of students assume they have access to a large file of photographs from the Vietnam era. They have been asked to select eight for a photo-essay on the war to appear in a national student news magazine. Remind them that in a photo-essay pictures convey most of the information and are often selected to stir a strong emotional response. Ask the pairs to prepare a numbered list in which they describe each photo and state why it is included. Conclude by having pairs trade lists for evaluation and comment.

Vital Links

Lieutenant Philip Caputo (First Person Account) Unit 6, Side 1, Search 26780, Play to 27558

See also Unit 6 Explore CD-ROM location 168.

"Blowin' in the Wind" (Song) Unit 6, Side 2, Search 02402, Play to 05072

See also Unit 6 Explore CD-ROM location 69.

History Footnote

In late 1960 the Vietminh and other groups formed the National Liberation Front (NLF), or Viet Cong. The Viet Cong organized guerrilla units as well as village militia. It also functioned almost as an alternative government, arranging for self-defense in the villages, establishing schools, and supporting local irrigation projects. Many peasants who did not take part in combat supported the Viet Cong by furnishing military information, food, medical services, and homemade weapons.

For firsthand accounts of the fighting in Vietnam, see **American Readings,** pp. 58–59.

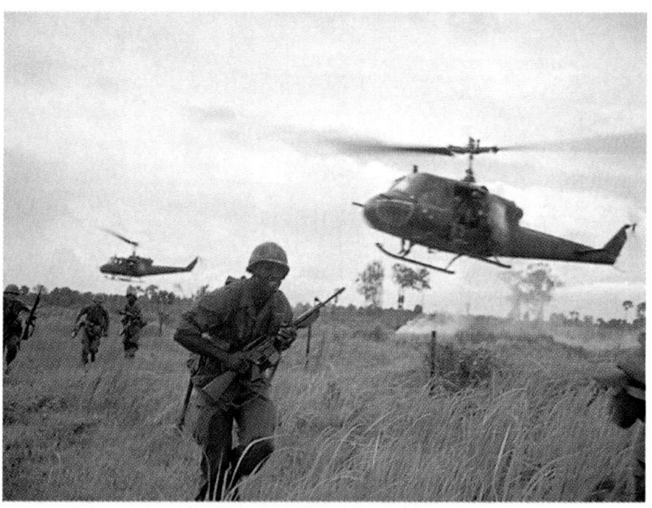

Helicopters played a key role in the war, carrying troops to remote sites for "search and destroy" missions. Despite their high-tech weapons, American forces could not break the Viet Cong's will to fight.

American troops now conducted missions independent of the South Vietnamese Army. Helicopters whisked troops to likely hideaways in the jungle with orders to "search for and destroy" Viet Cong guerrillas, supplies, and bases. As the American role increased, so did North Vietnam's support of the Viet Cong. American casualties rose at an alarming rate. In 1965 there were 2,500 killed, wounded, or missing. A year later the total had risen to more than 10,000.

A Different Kind of War

Both in Vietnam and at home this war was different from any other the United States had fought. It was hard to identify the enemy. The Viet Cong wore no uniforms. They fought at night, often from ambush, then returned to their villages and farmed by day. No matter how much damage American planes and troops did, the Viet Cong kept fighting.

At home, meanwhile, an antiwar movement grew that was stronger than during any previous American war. At first most protests could be heard on college campuses. As the war casualties mounted, however, the movement expanded. Many young men refused to be drafted. Some burned their draft cards, a few went to jail, and thousands fled to Canada and Britain.

Adding to the rising discontent was disgust with the corrupt leaders of the South Vietnamese government. Meanwhile, television coverage was for the first time bringing shocking video images of war into American homes.

Hawks vs. doves Antiwar rallies sometimes drew more than 100,000 protestors. The war divided the American public. Those who wanted the United States to withdraw were called "doves," for the traditional symbol of peace. Those in favor of continuing to fight were called "hawks."

Through 1967 most Americans were still hawks. To withdraw and admit defeat seemed shameful. It would send a signal that the United States no longer stood by its commitment to defend against Communist takeovers. Anyway, since the United States was the world's most powerful nation, most Americans remained confident of victory.

The Tet Offensive

That confidence was shattered on January 30, 1968, the first day of Tet—the Vietnamese New Year. Usually soldiers declared a cease-fire on the eve of Tet. This time, however,

Connections to Geography

Vietnam's land and climate made fighting even more treacherous for the American ground troops. In this tropical country, temperatures above 100°F are common. The humidity is high all year, and monsoons, or strong winds, bring frequent tropical storms called typhoons. The land is a combination of rugged, forested mountain ranges, dense rain forests, and lush coastal plains. Soldiers drenched in perspiration from the suffocating heat often had to carry 50–70 pounds of equipment while climbing mountains, crawling along muddy trails, wading through flooded rice fields, and creeping through jungles of sharp grasses, wild animals, mosquitoes, leeches, and hidden mines—with no way to distinguish Vietnamese friends from Vietnamese foes.

84,000 Viet Cong and NVA soldiers attacked military bases and cities in South Vietnam, including the capital, Saigon.

The "Tet Offensive" came as a complete surprise. Although most of the cities were later recaptured, the damage had been done. American casualties were high and morale plummeted.

The Tet Offensive was the war's turning point. The American public lost faith, having been told too many times that victory was just around the corner. In a poll taken after Tet, approval of Johnson's handling of the war reached a low of 26 percent. In March he announced he would not run for re-election.

The Election of 1968

The war was a major election issue in 1968. The leading candidates for the Democratic nomination were Senators Eugene McCarthy and Robert Kennedy and Vice-President Hubert Humphrey. Both McCarthy and Kennedy were doves, while Humphrey supported Johnson's policies. Kennedy fell victim to an assassin's bullet on June 6. Soon afterward, at a convention in Chicago that was disrupted by antiwar riots, Humphrey won the party's nomination.

The Republicans nominated former Vice-President Richard Nixon. He pledged to end the war and restore "law and order" by cracking down on violent antiwar protests. A third-party candidate, hawkish Alabama governor George Wallace, also ran. Appealing to conservative voters, Nixon won a narrow victory.

"Vietnamizing" the War

Promising "peace with honor," Nixon announced a strategy called "Vietnamization." The United States would build up and equip the South Vietnamese Army so that it could carry on the struggle alone. As Vietnamization took place, American forces would be gradually withdrawn.

Into Cambodia and Laos By the end of 1969 American forces in South Vietnam had been reduced to fewer than 400,000. Their orders were to remain on the defensive unless attacked. Meanwhile, Nixon secretly ordered bombings of Communist bases in Cambodia. When these attacks failed to lead to peace talks, he sent troops into Cambodia and Laos to destroy Viet Cong bases and supply depots.

News of these secret operations leaked out, causing a firestorm of public outrage. The worst incident was at Kent State University in Ohio, where nervous National Guardsmen killed four student protestors.

Demonstrations against the Vietnam War sometimes led to violent confrontations. During this 1967 antiwar rally in Washington, D.C., military police clashed with protestors.

Discussion

Checking Understanding

1. What was the "Vietnamization" strategy? (United States would give aid to enable the South Vietnamese Army to fight on its own.)

2. Why was the Tet Offensive of 1968 important? (This successful surprise attack caused many American deaths and demoralized the American public; it was the turning point in the war.)

Stimulating Critical Thinking

3. Do you think Nixon's plan to "Vietnamize" the war was a good idea? Why or why not? (Yes: allowed United States to withdraw in a dignified way. No: decision should have been made sooner; impossible for South Vietnamese to win without American troops.)

Bonus Activity

Writing a War Zone Letter

To highlight the nature of the fighting and the controversy surrounding the war, have students imagine serving as soldiers in Vietnam. They should write letters to friends or relatives back home describing their experiences and their attitude toward the war. Before assigning this activity, read aloud the Connections to Geography on this page. Have volunteers read their letters to the class.

Teaching the Link to Art

Ask students to describe the physical appearance of the memorial. If any have visited the memorial, ask them to describe their impressions. **Discussion Answer:** The memorial is much longer than it is tall, so visitors must take time to absorb it as they walk along it. As you walk along the wall, you descend below ground level. The wall gives a sense of a safe outdoor room, but the downward movement into the earth, as well as the thousands of names, reminds the visitors of the dead.

Vital Links

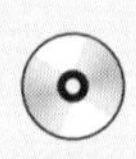

President Nixon on peace (First Person Account) Unit 6, Side 1, Search 27700, Play to 28732

See also Unit 6 Explore CD-ROM location 194.

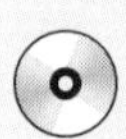

Vietnam Veterans Memorial (Picture) Unit 6, Side 1, Search 28742

See also Unit 6 Explore CD-ROM location 196.

Connections to Art

According to Maya Lin, the purpose of the Vietnam Veterans Memorial was "to help the veterans coming back, to help their families, to talk to people 100 years from now who will know nothing about that war and nobody on that wall." She believed that putting up something heroic would not help them. Instead she wanted to focus on the individual lives lost in order to help people overcome the pain of that loss. Lin purposely did not do research on the history and politics of the war, but she did spend several months delving into the meaning of a memorial. Her idea for the Vietnam Veterans Memorial came out of a class at Yale University on funereal architecture. In particular, she had been impressed by the World War I memorials in Europe, which were the first to focus on the average foot soldier.

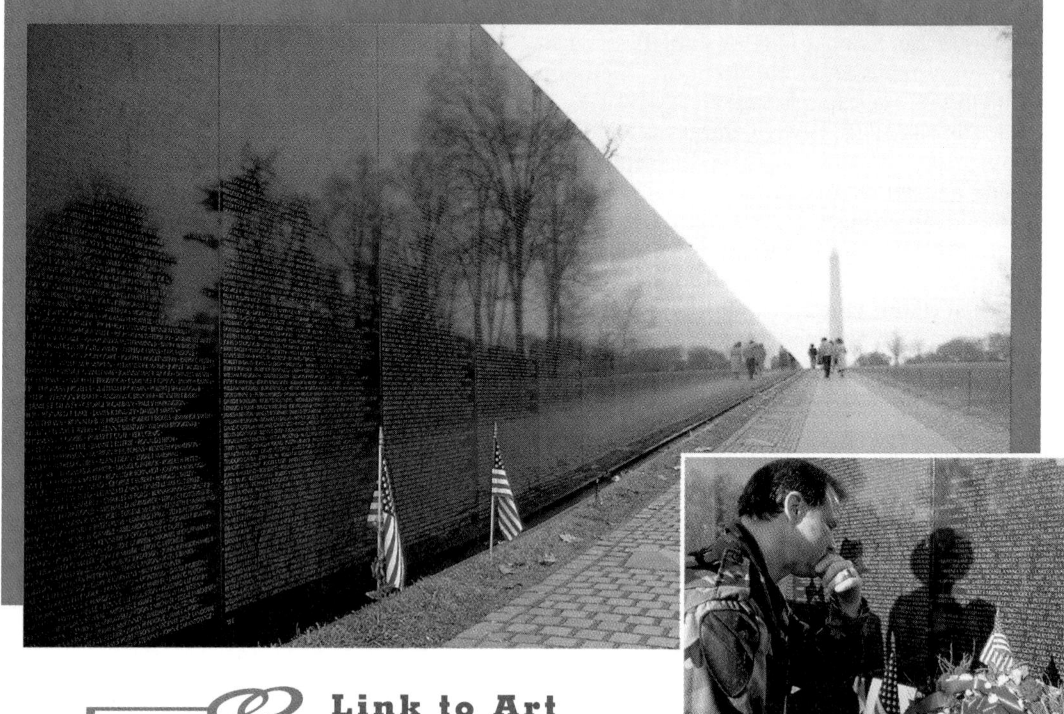

Link to Art

The Vietnam Veterans Memorial (1982) This memorial, which stands in Washington, D.C., is a 500-foot-long (150 m) V-shaped wall that rises out of the ground, angles up to a height of 10 feet (3 m), and slopes back into the earth. Carved on its black granite surface are the names of the Americans who were killed or are missing in the Vietnam War. The artist, 21-year-old Maya Lin, described her goal for the memorial: "I wanted something horizontal that took you in, that made you feel safe within the park, yet at the same time reminding you of the dead. So I just imagined opening up the earth." **Discuss** How do you think the memorial reflects the artist's goal?

President Nixon defended his actions by warning that "totalitarianism" would threaten all free nations if the United States acted like a "pitiful, helpless giant."

Like the Presidents before him, Nixon had a tiger by the tail and did not know how to let go. Even as he withdrew troops, he increased the bombing of North Vietnam and blockaded its coast. Nothing, however, weakened the Communists' will to fight.

The end of the war On December 30, 1972, the United States abruptly halted its air attacks. Two weeks later, Nixon declared that so much progress had been made in secret peace talks that he was ordering an end to

History Footnote

James Quay, a conscientious objector, took away another lesson from the Vietnam War. Pointing out that the Vietnamese were being killed in the name of freedom for Vietnam (sometimes whole villages were destroyed in response to attacks by guerrilla bands), he said, "I came to feel that the destruction America was causing was incompatible with any proper American objective in Vietnam." He became morally opposed to the war. Like other young men who applied for exemption from combat based on "CO" status, he had to explain his beliefs to the draft board in his town. When the draft board accepted his claim, Quay volunteered for two years of alternative service and was assigned to work as a social services counselor in Harlem.

American fighting. On January 27, 1973, representatives of the United States, South Vietnam, North Vietnam, and the Viet Cong signed a peace agreement in Paris.

By the end of March, the last American soldiers had come home, though the situation remained unsettled. When the government of South Vietnam broke its pledge to cooperate with the Viet Cong in organizing elections, the NVA launched a final attack. In April 1975, the South Vietnamese government surrendered, leaving the Communists in control of all of Vietnam.

Costs of the War

The war cost the lives of more than 58,000 Americans. Hundreds of thousands of others suffered permanent physical or mental damage. For many of the survivors, war memories were an unending nightmare. One veteran commented:

> "Sometimes I wish I could've just went ahead and died with my friends. I used to say, 'I'm only dreaming. I'll wake up some day.'"

Another great cost of the war was its effect on the attitude of Americans toward their government. Many people were shaken by the failure of the rich and powerful United States to defeat a poor and tiny nation. Also, the knowledge that government officials had lied about many aspects of the war undermined the public's faith in their leaders.

Vietnam, too, was badly scarred by the war, with as many as 2 million killed, millions wounded, and millions left homeless. Suffering continued as the Communist victors dealt harshly with their former South Vietnamese enemies. Interestingly, though, despite the domino theory, North Vietnam's victory did not result in a Communist takeover of Southeast Asia.

Point of View

What are the lessons of Vietnam?

A junior high school teacher in Oklahoma asked key supporters and opponents of the war: "What should we tell our children about Vietnam?" Here are some responses:

> "No American must ever be called upon to sacrifice his life for a cause that is poorly understood, blurred, or deceptively explained."
>
> Marvin Kalb, television news correspondent

> "We were in Vietnam for the same reason we had been in Korea: to stop the spread of communism. . . . The mistake we made was not to allow the military people unlimited authority to win."
>
> Carl Albert, House Majority Leader, 1962–1971

> "The United States should not intervene in other countries with military forces unless that country is a serious threat to our own security."
>
> J. William Fulbright, U.S. Senator, 1945–1975

One lesson most Americans could agree on was that fighting a war requires the support of the American people. In 1973 Congress passed the War Powers Act, forbidding troops to be sent into combat for more than 90 days without the approval of Congress.

2. Section Review

1. Why did the United States go to war in Vietnam?
2. How did the Vietnam War differ from other American wars?
3. What were the costs of the war?
4. Critical Thinking Was the United States right to fight in Vietnam? Explain.

Teaching the Point of View

Ask three volunteers to read each point of view aloud from a different corner of the room. Have other students join the spokesperson they agree with most. Ask each group to explain its point of view.

Closing the Section

Wrap-Up Activity

Creating a Time Line

Have groups create an illustrated Vietnam War time line for 1954–1975. They should record foreign events above the line and domestic events below, with brief labels describing the importance of each event.

Section Review Answers

1. To prevent Communist takeover of South Vietnam and all Southeast Asia.

2. Enemy hard to identify; antiwar demonstrations widespread; many refused to be drafted; first war covered on television.

3. Over 58,000 Americans died, 1,200 were missing, and many suffered physical and mental damage. Americans lost confidence in their government. Millions of Vietnamese killed, wounded, or left homeless.

4. Answers should show awareness of causes and effects of involvement.

Picture Essay

Teaching the Picture Essay

In this feature, students will learn about American involvement in the Vietnam War through a series of pictures and captions. Picture essays not only enhance students' knowledge of history but also help students understand the value of different types of information sources. Visual learners especially will enjoy and benefit from the picture essay. The feature also will help students with limited English—who may be intimidated by lengthy written text—focus on important points about the war.

Have students study the entire feature before answering the Discussion questions or doing the Wrap-Up Activity. You may assign the Bonus Activity as an alternative to, or in addition to, the Wrap-Up Activity.

Warm-Up Activity

Previewing Pictures

To prepare students to study the feature, have them scan the pictures without reading the captions. Ask which photo they find most intriguing or puzzling. Invite speculation about the setting, the people's identities, and the meaning of the action pictured. Write all ideas on the chalkboard. Later students can compare these ideas with what they learned in the feature.

Essay Objectives

Use pictures and captions to trace events of the Vietnam War, with these emphases:

- ★ Identify challenges faced by American soldiers in Vietnam.
- ★ Describe how South Vietnamese civilians were affected by the war.
- ★ Explain how the war affected the American public and how people made their different opinions about the war known.

PICTURE ESSAY

Vietnam War

1 2

1. With a column of tanks closely behind them, a South Vietnamese family is forced to quickly move their oxcart out of the way. The tanks of the U.S. 173rd Airborne Division were on the move to support the South Vietnam government in its battle against Communist North Vietnam in 1966.

2. Despite his own injuries, an American marine reaches out to help his wounded buddy. Some ten thousand GI's lost at least one limb in Vietnam as a result of ambushes, mines, and booby traps.

3. By mid-1967, fighting in Vietnam had escalated greatly with more than 400,000 Americans involved. Even though the United States

Connections to Art

The Vietnam War was the most photographed war in history, partly because both civilian and military photographers were allowed to train their cameras on every aspect of the war without hindrance from U.S. military officials. Army Sergeant Ronald L. Haeberle became one of the most famous war photographers. He was with a unit of American soldiers who killed more than 200 Vietnamese civilians in the village of My Lai in March 1968. Haeberle turned in most of his pictures to his superiors but secretly held on to one roll of color slides. Nearly two years later, as the My Lai massacre was coming to light, Haeberle published the slides. These portraits of civilian terror and military brutality helped to convict Lieutenant William L. Calley, Jr., the My Lai operation's commander, of murder.

Bonus Activity

Collecting Memories of the War

To help students gain better understanding of the Vietnam War experience, ask each student to interview a parent or other adult about his or her memories of the war. The adults may be Vietnam veterans, people who had family members or friends who served in Vietnam, people who took part in prowar or antiwar activities, or people with vivid memories of observing the war on television. Before students conduct their interviews, have them brainstorm lists of possible questions to ask. Instruct students to take careful notes or record their interviews on audiotape or videotape. Later have students share the results of their interviews by reading their notes aloud, playing their tapes, writing reports and binding them into a class book, and so on. If students did the Bonus Activity on page 541 of this Teacher's Edition, they might create a combination product, such as a bulletin-board display of interview reports with a title such as "Different Wars, Different Memories."

3

4

5

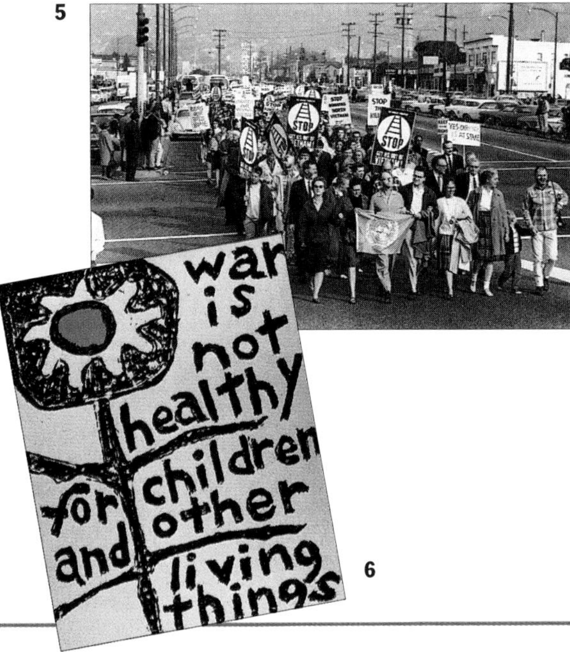

6

had the best artillery, it was unprepared for the ground fighting in Vietnam's dense jungles, which included avoiding pongee sticks placed in the beds of streams by the Viet Cong. These sticks were sharp-tipped slivers of wood, usually bamboo. They were imbedded, sharp tips upward and usually daubed with some poisonous substance, and left for the unwary soldier.

4, 5, and 6. The war divided Americans. Many Americans strongly supported U.S. policies in Vietnam and believed the war against communism had to be won (top). Others were vehemently opposed because they felt that the American involvement was unnecessary and immoral. Antiwar demonstrators protested in marches (center) and with posters (bottom).

Wrap-Up Activity

Writing About the Fall of South Vietnam

To reinforce understanding of the Vietnam War and give students practice in interpreting visuals, ask students to write journal entries about the fall of South Vietnam. Students should imagine they are one of the following persons living in April 1975: a South Vietnamese civilian, an American soldier who has returned home from serving in Vietnam, an American civilian who was a "hawk" during the war, or an American civilian who was a "dove" during the war. Students should derive clues about how their chosen person might have been affected by South Vietnam's fall from the appropriate photographs and captions in this picture essay as well as from what they have learned previously. Invite students to read their completed journal entries aloud.

History Footnote

The incident at Kent State University occurred on May 4, 1970. In response to student demonstrations Ohio's governor had called in the National Guard. Carrying loaded rifles and wearing gas masks, the Guardsmen tried to disperse a crowd of angry protesters. As the students fell back, some threw rocks and empty tear-gas canisters at the troops. The soldiers knelt and aimed their rifles at the students as if to warn them to stop. Then the soldiers stood up and retreated to the top of a nearby hill. Suddenly, they turned and began firing at the students below. Two of the four students killed were demonstrators; the other two were innocent bystanders who had been passing by on their way to class. Nine students were wounded.

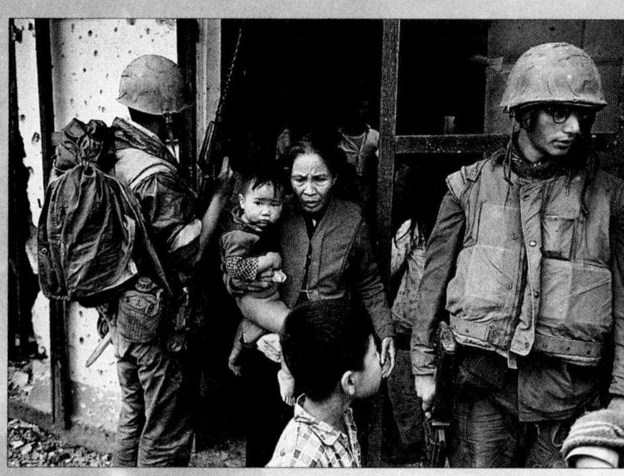

7

8

Background and 7. More than one hundred towns and military bases were simultaneously attacked by the Viet Cong and NVA soldiers during the Tet Offensive of 1968. A rocket explodes at Khe Sanh, an American base. Civilians are being rounded up by American marines (top) in Hue.

8. A young woman kneels beside the body of Jeffrey Miller, one of the four students killed by guardsmen at Kent State University in 1970. The shootings triggered massive demonstrations and protests across the nation.

9. Beginning in March 1975, a major offensive from North Vietnam swept through South Vietnam. Fleeing the advancing Communist

History Footnote

Even while they were in Vietnam, American soldiers knew that many people back home did not support their efforts. The soldiers themselves often wondered if their presence in Vietnam was a mistake. One said, "That's what really bothers me about this war. Sometimes I feel like one of the bad guys." That feeling continued when the soldiers returned home. Vietnam veterans did not receive the kind of hero's welcome that veterans of earlier wars did. There were no joyful parades or ringing speeches. At best, the veterans were ignored; at worst, they were denounced for being willing to serve in the war. Gradually, however, attitudes changed. The Vietnam Veterans Memorial is just one indication of Americans' desire to honor the sacrifices made by all the men and women who served in Vietnam.

9

10

11

forces, South Vietnamese refugees left their homes with only the belongings they could carry or pile on available trucks.

10. Without U.S. support, South Vietnam fell to the North in April 1975. Just before the surrender, the United States officials in Saigon were busy evacuating American civilians and Vietnamese who had worked closely with them. Anxiously some of them push to board an evacuation flight from the roof of the U.S. embassy. Helicopters took the people to American ships waiting offshore.

11. In 1993 a statue of three service women, commemorating their role in the Vietnam War, was added to the Vietnam Veterans Memorial in Washington, D.C.

Discussion

Checking Understanding

1. Besides enemy soldiers with guns, what were some dangers that American soldiers faced in Vietnam? (Mines, booby traps, other potentially deadly hazards like pongee sticks.)

2. What were some disruptions that South Vietnamese civilians encountered during the war? (The presence of soldiers and equipment all around them, soldiers forcing them from their homes, the need to escape when their country fell.)

Stimulating Critical Thinking

3. What major difference between the Vietnam War and World Wars I and II can you infer from Picture 2? (African American soldiers served alongside white soldiers rather than in segregated units.)

4. Compare and contrast Picture 6 with posters you have seen from World Wars I and II. (Possible answer: This poster is similar to earlier ones in having a single large image and a fairly simple slogan. However, posters from the earlier wars were produced by the government and called for action to help the war effort. This poster simply states an opinion—and it is an opinion contrary to government policy.)

Introducing the Section

Vocabulary

détente (p. 582) a relaxing of tensions between nations

strategic arms (p. 583) weapons designed to strike at an enemy's military bases and industrial centers

Warm-Up Activity

Making a Prediction

To prepare for studying the end of the Cold War, ask students to imagine making predictions in 1970 about future Soviet-American relations. Have them write paragraphs explaining whether they see any hope for an end to the Cold War. Conclude by having them share and discuss their predictions.

Geography Question of the Day

To remind students that physical features on the landscape can have both geographic and symbolic significance, ask them to write a short description of how the Berlin Wall (see p. 570) might have affected people both physically and mentally.

See the Study Guide activity in Chapter Resources Binder, p. 115.

Section Objectives

★ Describe how Richard Nixon improved relations with China and the Soviet Union.

★ Explain the actions taken by Jimmy Carter and Ronald Reagan to deal with the Cold War.

★ Identify the reasons for the collapse of communism in Eastern Europe and the Soviet Union.

Teaching Resources

Take-Home Planner 5, pp. 4–11
Chapter Resources Binder
Study Guide, p. 115
Reinforcement
Skills Development, pp. 119–120
Geography Extensions
American Readings, p. 60
Using Historical Documents, pp. 86–91
Transparency Activities
Chapter and Unit Tests, pp. 103–106

3. The End of the Cold War

Reading Guide

New Terms détente, strategic arms

Section Focus How the Cold War came to an end

1. **How did Richard Nixon improve relations with China and the Soviet Union?**
2. **What actions did Jimmy Carter and Ronald Reagan take to deal with the Cold War?**
3. **What led to the collapse of communism in Eastern Europe and the Soviet Union?**

Early in his career, President Nixon had carved out a reputation as a fierce foe of communism. As he struggled to end the war in Vietnam, however, he realized that he needed the help of China and the Soviet Union in order to bring North Vietnam to the peace table.

Looking beyond Vietnam, Nixon saw that the United States could not afford to remain bitter enemies with the two most powerful Communist nations. With his chief foreign policy advisor, Henry Kissinger, Nixon began a bold new policy of **détente** (day-TAHNT)—a relaxing of tensions between nations.

Nixon Visits China

Taking the first step in détente, Nixon convinced the UN to accept Communist China as a member:

> "We simply cannot afford to leave China forever outside the family of nations. There is no place on this small planet for a billion of its potentially most able people to live in angry isolation."

In 1971 China replaced Taiwan on the Security Council.

Meanwhile, Nixon saw an opportunity in the growing conflict between the Soviet Union and China over territory and power. He decided to take advantage of this rift by playing off one Communist power against the other.

In February 1972, in a dramatic move, President Nixon traveled to Communist China to meet with its leaders. For more than

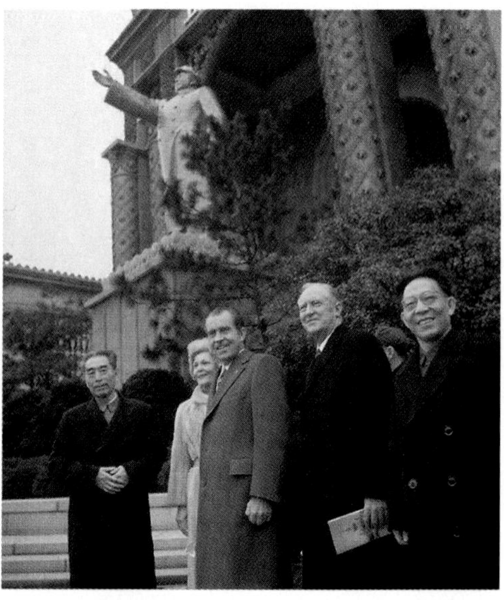

In 1972 President Nixon met with China's Premier Chou En-Lai (left) in Beijing. The historic visit paved the way for diplomatic relations with China.

History Footnote

SALT negotiations were first proposed by President Johnson in 1967. The talks were agreed upon by both the Soviet Union and the United States in 1968, and meetings began in 1969. They took place in Helsinki, Finland; Vienna, Austria; and Geneva, Switzerland, and were completed in 1972 when Nixon and Brezhnev signed the agreements at a summit in Moscow. The SALT I agreements included the Treaty on Anti-Ballistic Missile (ABM) Systems and the Interim Agreement and Protocol on Limitation of Strategic Offensive Weapons. The ABM treaty limited each nation's defenses to one ABM launching site and 100 interceptor missiles. The Interim Agreement froze the number of each nation's offensive weapons—intercontinental ballistic missiles and submarine-launched ballistic missiles—for five years.

20 years the United States had refused all contact with Communist China. Now, as Nixon said, he had "opened the door for travel, . . . for trade."

The Soviet Union and SALT

Just three months later Nixon made his next move, a visit to the Soviet Union. Soviet leader Leonid Brezhnev (LAY-uh-NEED BREZH-nef), alarmed by Nixon's China visit, agreed to more cooperative relations with the United States.

Most importantly, Nixon and Brezhnev took steps to slow the arms race. They signed the first Strategic Arms Limitation Treaty (SALT I), agreeing to build fewer nuclear missiles. **Strategic arms** are weapons designed to strike at an enemy's military bases and industrial centers. The two leaders also agreed to limit antiballistic missile (ABM) systems—weapons designed to shoot down incoming missiles.

Conflict in the Middle East

Nixon's trips to China and the Soviet Union helped him win re-election in 1972, in a landslide victory over Democratic Senator George McGovern. During his second term, however, détente was threatened by conflict in the Middle East.

On October 6, 1973, Egypt and Syria attacked Israel on the Jewish holy day Yom Kippur. The Yom Kippur War was part of a long-running conflict. Arab nations in the Middle East were determined to destroy Israel and return control of the land to the Palestinians. (See the World Link on the birth of Israel, page 565.) The Israelis were determined to protect their new nation as a homeland for Jews.

When Nixon learned that the Soviets were supplying Egypt and Syria with weapons and advisors, he airlifted helicopters, tanks, and other weapons to Israel. The war ended with a UN-arranged cease-fire on October 25.

The oil embargo The United States paid a stiff penalty for supporting Israel. Arab nations halted oil shipments to the United States and its allies, causing a severe energy shortage that winter. Long lines at gas stations showed how much Americans depended on "black gold" from the Middle East. Policymakers now had to balance the nation's commitment to Israel against its need for oil and its fear of Soviet influence in the Middle East.

Link to the Present

China's military power Relations with China have thawed since President Nixon's visit. Still, they are far from warm. China's growing military power is one cause of the tension.

China has more than 400 nuclear warheads. Despite international protests, it continues to develop longer-range, more accurate missiles. China has also violated international agreements by selling missiles to other countries.

Selling missiles is a way to make money. In addition, the Chinese may believe that a nuclear threat will help them extend their influence in Asia. For example, China regards Taiwan as its territory and expects official reunification in the near future. In 1996 China carried out missile launches and other military exercises near Taiwan to discourage pro-independence feelings among the island's people.

Developing the Section

Discussion

Checking Understanding

1. How did relations with the Soviet Union improve under Nixon? (SALT I limit on missiles and ABM systems.)

Stimulating Critical Thinking

2. How do you think the oil embargo affected average citizens? (Fewer trips; car pools; inconvenience.)

Teaching the

Link to the Present

Ask students if they think China's military power represents a threat today. Have them find Taiwan on the map on p. R3. Ask why China might want this island. As background, note these facts about China: the United States is an important trade partner; China is still modernizing, and most of its population farms for a living; most of China's Communist leaders are very old; many young people in China are interested in Western culture and ideas.

Vital Links

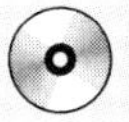

Signing nuclear arms treaty (Picture) Unit 6, Side 1, Search 32679

See also Unit 6 Explore CD-ROM location 255.

Section Activity

Role-Playing a TV Interview

To focus on attitudes regarding the end of the Cold War, have groups of three role-play an interview in 1991. Roles include a reporter, a world leader (such as Nixon, Carter, Gorbachev, or Reagan), and a common citizen—German, Russian, or American. Have groups practice and then present their interviews.

Bonus Activity

Writing Newspaper Headlines

To highlight key events of the late Cold War period, have students create newspaper headlines from the period between 1971 and 1991. They should write at least six. Remind them that most headlines include a subject and verb but are worded concisely. Some may wish to include subtitles.

Vital Links

President Reagan on foreign policy (Movie) Unit 6, Side 2, Search 18840, Play to 19876

See also Unit 6 Explore CD-ROM location 152.

History Footnote

Mikhail Gorbachev made two significant changes in his country—*perestroika,* a total restructuring to revive the economy, and *glasnost,* a policy of openness to encourage free expression. Under *glasnost* Soviet citizens could speak more freely about their society's problems. Books by certain authors were no longer banned. Many secrets about the nation's history, especially under Stalin and Brezhnev, were made public. People could listen to radio broadcasts from the West.

Under *perestroika* Gorbachev introduced economic reforms. Instead of having the government set prices for products, prices began to be based on the actual cost of producing them. Instead of having the government plan industrial production by itself, local factories were given more control over decisions.

Carter and Human Rights

The election of Jimmy Carter in 1976 brought a Democratic administration back to the White House. A former governor of Georgia, Carter declared that human rights—rather than rigid opposition to communism—would be the "soul of our foreign policy." He cut off aid to some dictators who abused human rights, even though some were anti-Communist.

Meanwhile, Carter took steps to expand détente. In 1979 he announced that the United States would recognize Communist China, rather than Nationalist Taiwan, as China's rightful government. That same year he and Soviet leader Brezhnev signed a new strategic arms treaty—SALT II.

Later that year, though, détente received a blow when Soviet troops invaded neighboring Afghanistan to put down a rebellion. Carter denounced the invasion, cut off most trade with the Soviet Union, and refused to let the United States take part in the 1980 Olympics in Moscow. His reaction killed SALT II and ended détente.

Reagan and the "Evil Empire"

In the election of 1980, Ronald Reagan won a resounding victory over Carter. A former governor of California, he was known for his tough stance against communism. In a speech he warned that the Soviet Union was an "evil empire" bent on world domination. As you will read in Chapter 15, he stepped up efforts to support anti-Communist leaders, especially in Latin America.

Reagan believed in dealing with the Soviets from a position of strength. During his first three years in office, he got Congress to increase defense spending by 44 percent. He also approved research on a plan to use lasers to destroy incoming missiles.

Changes in the Soviet Union Reagan easily won a second term in 1984. He then softened his anti-Soviet attitude, in part because of changes in the Soviet Union after Mikhail Gorbachev (mih-kĪL gōr-bah-CHAWF) became the Soviet leader in 1985.

Gorbachev recognized that the Soviet economy was on the brink of collapse and the people were losing faith in the government. His response was to allow them more freedom of speech and of the press. He also introduced limited free enterprise, allowing private citizens to own businesses.

To succeed in saving the economy, however, Gorbachev knew that he would have to reduce military spending. The arms race and the war in Afghanistan had become costly burdens.

The United States welcomed Gorbachev's new policies. Almost immediately Cold War tensions began to thaw. In December 1987 Reagan and Gorbachev agreed to get rid of all Soviet and American short- and intermediate-range missiles. The Intermediate Nuclear Force (INF) Treaty was the first Cold War agreement to destroy nuclear weapons.

President Reagan met with Soviet leader Mikhail Gorbachev to discuss how to slow the arms race.

History Footnote

The Berlin Wall was about 28 miles long, made of concrete blocks, and topped with barbed wire. Guards, watchtowers, alarms, guard dogs, mines, and trenches made it very difficult to escape from East Berlin to West Berlin. Nonetheless about 5,000 East Germans managed to cross the barrier safely. Another 5,000 were captured, and 191 more were killed while trying to cross.

For an activity on
Reagan's "Evil Empire"
speech, see Using
Historical Documents,
pp. 86–91.

Hands-On HISTORY

Planning a Cold War museum With each year, memories of the Cold War fade. You likely remember little about it; your children will have no memory of it.

Activity With a group, plan a museum to give future generations an overview of the Cold War. Each room should illustrate a major theme.

1. Decide on the themes to illustrate, such as The Arms Race, Conflict in Eastern Europe, and War in Vietnam. Choose at least five themes.
2. Briefly describe the items to display in each theme room. You do not have to find or make the items, so you can include almost anything. A model of *Sputnik*, photographs of the Berlin Wall, a diorama of a bomb shelter, and plaques with quotations from President Truman are just a few possibilities.
3. Consider how to arrange the displays. Your arrangement should help visitors understand both the sequence of Cold War events and the cause-effect relationships between events.
4. Draw a floor plan of your museum. Label the theme rooms, and show and label the displays.

The Berlin Wall, 1989

The Fall of the Iron Curtain

Gorbachev's policies encouraged people in Eastern European nations to call for democracy and greater economic opportunity. In 1989 Poland became the first to form a non-Communist government. Others soon followed, as demonstrators took to the streets in Czechoslovakia, Hungary, and East Germany to protest Communist rule.

In November 1989 German students and workers attacked the Berlin Wall with crowbars and sledgehammers. Eleven months after that hated symbol of the Cold War was torn down, East and West Germany were united as a democratic nation. The Iron Curtain was no more.

The collapse of communism in Eastern Europe was soon followed by the stunning breakup of the Soviet Union itself. Nationalistic feelings, long held down by Communist rule, erupted among the diverse peoples of the 15 Soviet republics. Gorbachev's efforts to save the Soviet Union had unleashed a tiger that could no longer be caged.

In August 1991 Communist officials tried to turn back the clock. They arrested Gorbachev, but their attempt to seize the government failed after thousands of angry demonstrators rallied against them.

The attempted takeover sped the breakup of the Soviet Union. By the end of the year all 15 republics had declared independence, leaving what one observer called "the Soviet Disunion." Almost overnight, the totalitarian system that since World War II had challenged the United States for world leadership had collapsed. The Cold War had come to an end.

Discussion

Checking Understanding

1. What was Reagan's attitude toward the Soviet Union? (Tough stand against communism in first term; softened stance during second because of changes in Soviet Union.)

Stimulating Critical Thinking

2. Why do you think the Soviet government did not try to reestablish its empire in Eastern Europe? (Soviet Union was economically weak.)

Teaching the Hands-On HISTORY

Offer additional suggestions for exhibit items and formats such as artifacts, documents, maps, audio recordings, video clips, and multimedia. Students might share ideas from museum exhibits they have seen.

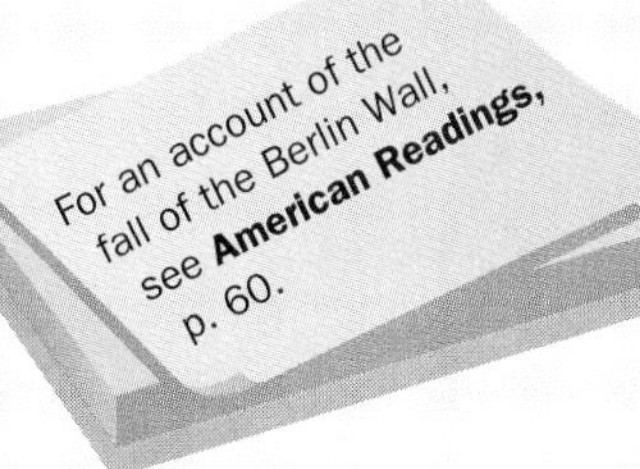

For an account of the
fall of the Berlin Wall,
see American Readings,
p. 60.

Vital Links

Berlin Wall (Movie)
Unit 6, Side 2, Search
14263, Play to 15288

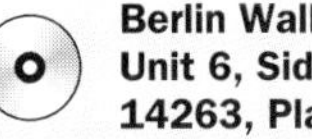

See also Unit 6 Explore CD-ROM location 261.

Closing the Section

Wrap-Up Activity

Compiling a "Who's Who"

To focus on contributions of American and Soviet leaders in the final years of the Cold War, have students create a "Who's Who" of key figures. Entries should identify each leader, his time in office, and the effects of his policies on the Cold War.

Section Review Answers

1. Definitions: *détente* (582), *strategic arms* (583)

2. Visited leaders of Communist China; arms reduction agreements with Soviet leader Brezhnev.

3. Carter: declared foreign policy would defend human rights rather than rigidly oppose communism; tried to expand détente. Reagan: hard line against Soviets at first; later softened position.

4. Gorbachev allowed greater freedom and some free enterprise, which led Eastern Europeans to demand democracy and greater economic opportunity.

5. Yes: with some Communist nations and Middle East tensions, Cold War is always a threat. No: arms race has stopped; world leaders more open to communication; communism no longer threatening.

To check understanding of "Why We Remember," assign Thinking Critically question 3 on student page 588.

History Footnote

Despite their new freedom, it will take time for Eastern Europe and the Eurasian republics to recover from decades of living under the rigid control of the Soviet system. These nations face many problems. Since the environment was not a priority in Communist nations, pollution is widespread. Inefficient businesses, once propped up by the Communist government, have closed, leaving many people unemployed for the first time in their lives. Prices, once closely controlled by the government, have risen sharply, and food shortages continue to be a problem. Meanwhile, ethnic wars have erupted in several countries, notably the former Yugoslavia and Azerbaijan.

Truman's prediction In his farewell speech at the end of his second term in January 1953, President Truman had predicted that the West would win the Cold War:

> "As the free world grows stronger, more unified, more attractive to men on both sides of the Iron Curtain—and as the Soviet hopes for easy expansion are blocked—then there will have to come a time of change in the Soviet world. . . . I have a deep and abiding faith in the destiny of free men."

Truman's remarkable prediction proved to be correct. His policy of blocking the spread of communism gave communism time to destroy itself.

3. Section Review

1. Define **détente** and **strategic arms.**

2. How did President Nixon pursue his policy of détente?

3. How did the policies of Presidents Carter and Reagan differ?

4. What led to the collapse of communism in Eastern Europe?

5. Critical Thinking Do you think the Cold War could ever start again? Explain.

Why We Remember

The Cold War Era

Years after leaving office, Harry Truman sat down at his desk in Independence, Missouri, to write his memoirs. "During the years I was President," he began in his preface, "the one purpose that dominated me in everything I thought and did was to prevent a third world war." Those same words could have been written by each of the Cold War era Presidents.

In 1945 the United States faced a historic choice. Would it retreat into isolationism as it had after World War I? Or would it help create a better world out of the chaos of war? Americans chose to play an active role, helping to protect basic human rights and freedoms around the world.

This was not an easy choice. The Cold War was one of the most frightening times in our history. After World War II, the thought of another global conflict was alarming. Even more terrifying was the knowledge that a war fought with nuclear weapons might mean the end of all life on earth.

No one knew that the Cold War struggle against communism would drag on for more than 40 years. No one knew that it would take Americans into distant conflicts or lead to a costly arms race. Americans did know, however, that they were willing to pay the price to preserve freedom. Victory in the Cold War was victory for freedom-loving people everywhere.

(Answers continued from side margin)
What did the Soviets do to make the United States suspicious? Did the United States do anything to anger the Soviets that Mrs. Roosevelt does not mention? Is Khrushchev's reply relevant to the question of who started the Cold War?
4. (a) Answers depend on questions. (b) The rest of Mee's article and relevant material in Mrs. Roosevelt's book; other historians' descriptions of the Cold War's origins; primary sources—such as memoirs, letters, and speeches by Franklin Roosevelt, Truman, and Molotov.

For further application, have students do the Applying Skills activity in the Chapter Survey (p. 588).

If students need to review the skill, use the Skills Development transparency and activity in the **Chapter Resources Binder**, pp. 119–120.

Skill Lab

Using Information

Asking Historical Questions

The Cold War is over. The West won. Yet there is still much controversy over the long conflict between Communist and non-Communist countries. Historians cannot even agree as to which side fired the first "shot."

Question to Investigate

Who started the Cold War?

Procedure

Imagine that you are a historian trying to answer that question. Begin your research by asking historical questions about sources A and B. Those questions will give you a direction for additional research.

1 State your immediate goal.

2 Identify the information.
a. Read sources A and B carefully.
b. Make a column for each source. List what each source says or implies about the actions and attitudes of the two sides at the start of the Cold War.

3 Identify questions to ask.
a. Read the Skill Tips for ideas.
b. List four questions for each source.

4 Decide how to get the answers.
a. Write the answers you know.
b. Describe three ways you might get more information.

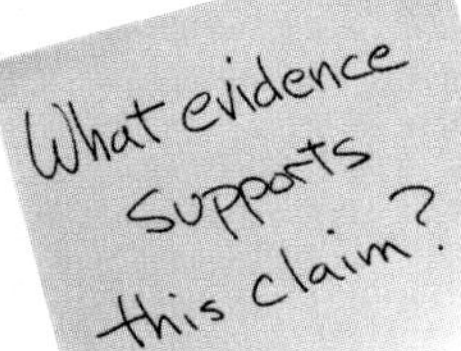
What evidence supports this claim?

Skill Tips

See the Skill Tips on page 119. You might also ask:
- Where did the writer get the information?
- What was the writer's purpose?
- What information is relevant?
- What gaps, if any, are there in the information?

Sources to Use

A "[On April 13, 1945] Truman received [Soviet foreign minister] Molotov in the Oval Office and, as Truman recalled it, chewed him out 'bluntly' for the way the Russians were behaving in Poland. Molotov was stunned. He had never, he told Truman, 'been talked to like that in my life.' 'Carry out your agreements,' Truman responded, 'and you *won't* get talked to like that.'

"That's a good way to talk, if you want to start an argument."

From "A Good Way to Pick a Fight," by Charles L. Mee, Jr., in *American Heritage*, August 1977

B "I told him [Khrushchev] that after World War II we had not been suspicious of Russia. I knew that my husband had hoped we would be able to come to an understanding. 'But then,' I went on, 'we found the Russians did not strictly keep agreements made at Yalta and we became more and more suspicious.'

"'Communism will win in the whole world,' he told me. 'This is scientifically based on the writings of Karl Marx, Engels and Lenin.' He went on to assure me blandly: 'We are against any military attempt to introduce communism or socialism into any country.'"

From Eleanor Roosevelt's description of her 1957 meeting with Khrushchev, in *The Autobiography of Eleanor Roosevelt* (New York: Harper, 1961)

Introducing the Skill Lab

Point out that asking questions can help in evaluating accuracy and completeness of an account. Review the Skill Tips and ask why written accounts often disagree.

Skill Lab Answers

1. Example: to compare what the two sources say about who started the Cold War.
2. Source A: Russians taking actions in Poland that United States did not like; Molotov took offense at Truman's criticism. Source B: Russians did not keep Yalta agreements, so the United States became suspicious; Khrushchev said communism will take over world and that the Soviet Union is against forcing communism or socialism on any country.
3. Source A: What did the Soviets do in Poland? Did Molotov recount the conversation in the same way? Is this account complete? Did Soviet leaders ever act this way toward American leaders? What was Charles Mee's purpose in writing? Source B: Was Eleanor Roosevelt trying to explain the start of the Cold War, or did she have another purpose? Did she hear leaders say they were not suspicious of the Soviet Union or is that her interpretation?
(Answers continued in top margin)

Survey Answers

Reviewing Vocabulary

Definitions are found on these pages: *Cold War* (564), *containment* (565), *détente* (582), *strategic arms* (583).

Reviewing Main Ideas

1. Gave $400 million to Greece and Turkey for defense; sent $13 billion to Western Europe under the Marshall Plan; airlifted food and supplies to West Berlin during Stalin's blockade; joined NATO.

2. (a) Communists won a civil war against ruling Nationalists. (b) Communist North Korea invaded non-Communist South Korea. (c) In Iran the Soviet Union and the United States competed for influence. Lebanon and Jordan asked the United States and Britain for aid in resisting Communist revolts.

3. Kennedy ordered a blockade of military shipments to Cuba. Khrushchev sent more Soviet ships toward Cuba loaded with missiles. Khrushchev finally ordered ships back, and Kennedy lifted blockade.

4. United States gave financial aid to French rulers in Vietnam. Eisenhower sent economic aid and military advisors to resist Communist-backed rebels. Kennedy expanded aid and sent more advisors. Johnson ordered bombing raids on North Vietnam and sent the first American ground troops. Nixon ordered bombings in Cambodia and sent troops to Cambodia and Laos.

5. About 58,000 soldiers were killed, 1,200 were missing, and many more were wounded physically or mentally. People lost faith in the government.

6. (a) Got the Soviets to be more cooperative by opening

(Answers continued in top margin)

ties with their Communist rival China; signed SALT I. (b) Signed SALT II; expanded détente and emphasized defense of human rights; responded to Soviet invasion of Afghanistan with trade ban. (c) Increased defense spending; later softened anti-Soviet stance; signed the INF treaty.

7. Gorbachev granted more economic and political freedoms to help rescue the failing Soviet economy. These changes unintentionally inspired Eastern Europeans to demand freedom and form non-Communist governments, and led the Soviet republics to declare independence.

Thinking Critically

1. Hungary was much closer to the Soviet Union, so the risk of direct conflict was greater; wanted to avoid a war in Europe.

Chapter Survey

Reviewing Vocabulary

Define the following terms.

1. Cold War
2. containment
3. détente
4. strategic arms

Reviewing Main Ideas

1. Give three examples of how the United States contained communism in Europe.
2. Describe Cold War conflicts that arose in each of the following places. (a) China (b) Korea (c) the Middle East
3. How did conflict over Cuba almost lead to nuclear disaster?
4. Summarize the steps by which the United States became more and more involved in the war in Vietnam.
5. Describe two effects of the Vietnam War on the United States and its people.
6. Tell how each of the following Presidents handled relations with the Soviet Union. (a) Richard Nixon (b) Jimmy Carter (c) Ronald Reagan
7. Trace the events that led to the collapse of communism in Eastern Europe and the Soviet Union.

Thinking Critically

1. Analysis Why do you think that the United States was willing to intervene in Korea and Vietnam, but did not intervene during the revolt in Hungary?
2. Evaluation Do you think that the domino theory was reasonable? Why or why not?
3. Why We Remember: Synthesis It is widely agreed that the Cold War ended in victory for the West and for the forces of freedom and democracy. But was the victory a total one? Use what you have learned in this chapter and what you already know about current world events to answer the question.

Applying Skills

Asking historical questions You know that asking questions is useful when studying events of the past, like the Cold War. Asking questions is equally useful when learning about events of today.

Read or listen to two different accounts of a recent event at your school, in your community, or in our nation. Your goal is to compare what the accounts say about the causes of the event. Use what you learned on page 587 to do the following:

1. Summarize the information that each source gives about the causes of the event.
2. List three questions about each source.
3. Write the answers you already know.
4. Name two ways that you might get more information.

History Mystery

Sputnik Answer the History Mystery on page 561. The news of the Soviet launching of *Sputnik* sparked a strong effort to improve science and mathematics education in schools throughout the United States. Why do you think this happened?

Writing in Your History Journal

1. Keys to History (a) The time line on pages 560–561 has eight Keys to History. In your journal, describe why each one is important to know about. (b) Decide on a category of additional events for the time line, such as Middle East Events, Growing Involvement in Vietnam, or Defrosting the Cold War. Write the appropriate events and dates in your journal, explaining why you think the events should be added.

2. Harry Truman *Although unprepared to be President, Harry Truman rose to the occasion*

2. Yes: success would inspire further takeovers in nearby countries. No: North Vietnam's victory over the South did not lead to more Communist takeovers in Southeast Asia.

3. Victory was not total. Communism is still a political force within China, Russia, Cuba, Vietnam, North Korea, and other nations, but communism seems unlikely to expand or threaten world peace.

Applying Skills

Answers should show an understanding of the kinds of questions students should ask, such as those listed in the Skill Tips on p. 837.

History Mystery

Sputnik, the first space satellite, was launched by the Soviet Union. Americans feared that greater Soviet scientific knowledge and

(Answers continued in side margin)

research could make the Soviet Union strong enough to defeat the United States. The way to keep up with the Soviets was to improve the education of American youth, who would be future scientists.

Writing in Your History Journal

1. (a) Explanations should be similar to the time line notes on teacher pages 560–561. (b) Events and dates should be accurate. Explanations should refer to Cold War attitudes and actions of the countries involved.

2. Agree: success of Truman Doctrine; decision to drop atomic bombs on Japan; refusal to drop atomic bombs on China; firing of MacArthur. Disagree: students will explain why they disagree with some of his decisions.

3. Responses should show understanding of issues involved and the price of "going public" with views. Students may say that their feelings would have changed as the war dragged on.

Reviewing Geography

1. (A) East Germany, (B) Poland, (C) Czechoslovakia, (D) Hungary, (E) Romania, (F) Bulgaria, (G) Albania.

2. A Communist Korea would give China a friendly neighbor. Since Hungary borders the Soviet Union, it was a key part of the Soviet buffer against Western Europe. Guatemala was in the Western Hemisphere, where the United States had always protected its interests. West Berlin was an anti-Communist thorn within the eastern bloc. Cuba is close to Florida, so having enemy missiles there made Americans feel unsafe.

Alternative Assessment

Teacher's Take-Home Planner 5, p. 7, includes suggestions and scoring rubrics for the Alternative Assessment activity.

Reviewing Geography

1. Each letter stands for a Warsaw Pact member in Eastern Europe. Write the name of each country.

2. Geographic Thinking Tell how you think location influenced the decision in each of these Cold War situations:
- China's intervention in the Korean War
- The Soviet Union's response to the Hungarian revolt
- U.S. support of the overthrow of Guatemala's government
- The Soviet Union's demand that western powers leave Berlin
- U.S. insistence that Soviet missiles be removed from Cuba

admirably. Do you agree? Explain. Write your responses in your journal.

3. Thinking Historically Suppose you had been a teenager during the Vietnam War. In your journal, tell whether you would have been a hawk or a dove and whether you would have made your feelings known in a public way. Explain why.

Alternative Assessment

Citizenship: Recalling Cold War presidencies Imagine that you and six classmates are Presidents Truman, Eisenhower, Kennedy, Johnson, Nixon, Carter, and Reagan. Prepare individual presentations that answer the following questions. You may include visual aids.

❶ What actions did you take in the Cold War? (Depending on the President, these might include sending troops into battle.)

❷ What was your attitude toward the Soviet Union and communism?

❸ Do you think that your actions helped the West win the Cold War? Explain.

❹ If you had it to do over again, would you do anything differently? Explain.

Your work will be evaluated on the following criteria:
- you present the actions accurately
- you reflect the President's point of view based on what you know about him from reading the chapter
- you make the President seem real

Teaching the

Link to American Readings

In this feature students learn about the Cold War from three viewpoints: that of political scientist Hans Morgenthau, historians Gabriel and Joyce Kolko, and historian Thomas Paterson. They will also learn how technology entered into the Cold War, specifically the Soviet launch of *Sputnik*, and how it affected American efforts to develop a space program.

Before students begin the lesson, review The Start of the Cold War (pages 564–570). Have students read the entire feature before assigning the A Closer Look questions. The Setting the Stage Activity and Bonus Activity may then be introduced according to the needs and interests of the students. The information contained in the Discussion questions and the Footnotes may be used throughout the lesson as appropriate. Readers' Theater is ideal for students who might find the readings somewhat difficult. Use the Wrap-Up Activity for students who would enjoy taking a step beyond the core lesson.

History Footnote

The scholarly debate over the origins of the Cold War has followed the course of the Cold War itself. During the 1950s, when tensions were at their height, historians tended to blame the conflict on Soviet aggression. Soviet behavior was viewed as similar to the plans for world domination followed by Germany and Japan before World War II. Over the next decade, doubt and dissent over America's foreign policy rose with the escalation of the Vietnam War. As détente improved Soviet-American relations in the 1970s and 1980s, historians took a more complex view of the origins of the Cold War. They tried to understand the Cold War in a broader historical context, pointing to other possible causes such as power vacuums and the development of the atomic bomb.

Link to American Readings

READING 13A

The Origins of the Cold War

Historians and political scientists disagree on the origins and causes of the Cold War. Some have blamed its emergence on an expansionist Soviet Union that was committed to world domination. Others accused the Americans of pr voking the conflict with their efforts to shape the postwar world. In the following excerpts, four authors present their views on the causes of the Cold Wa

Political scientist Hans J. Morgenthau

Morgenthau was one of the first to write about the origins of the Cold War. He believ that after World War II the Soviet Union no longer wished to remain allied with the United States. Instead, the Soviets wanted to expand their territory as much as possib Thus the United States was forced to seek alliances such as NATO and to adopt the policy of containment. His arguments follow.

containment: U.S. post-World War II policy of limiting the political and economic expansion of the Soviet Union

The Cold War, in terms both of its historic origins and its main issues, has been a contest over the peace settlement ending the Second World War. The United States postulated [took for granted] as the basis of such a settlement th continuing unity in interests and policies of the victorious allies, a unity whic would have made obsolete the arrangements, such as alliances and spheres of influence, by which nations have traditionally tried to protect their separate interests. The Soviet Union and, less consistently, Great Britain assumed that t conflict between the Axis and the Allies was bound to be superseded [replaced] by other conflicts of interests and that the main function of the peace settlement, as of the war itself, was to promote the distinct interests of the different nations concerned.

Stalin, in particular, saw in the war the great opportunity for Russia to attai her traditional objectives in Eastern Europe and the Balkans, and as much beyond them as was obtainable. For Stalin, the peace settlement was to have two functions: to ratify, in an agreement on worldwide spheres of influence, the distribution of military power established at the end of the Second World War; and to create opportunities for further Russian expansion.

ratify: approve or confirm

The incompatibility of these conceptions of the postwar world led, first of all and virtually at the moment it was signed, to the breakdown of the Yalta Agreement, which both sides interpreted in terms of these conceptions, and, second, to the development of that breakdown into the Cold War.

Excerpt from "The Revolution in U.S. Foreign Policy" by Hans J. Morgenthau, *Commentary*, February 1957. Reprinted by permission of Mathew Morgenthau.

Literature Footnote

John Le Carré (1931–), a writer of spy novels that realistically portray international espionage, gained his expertise first-hand—he worked for the British foreign service. The underworld enveloping the British secret service became the milieu for Le Carré's work. His first novel, *Call for the Dead* (1961), introduced his feature character, George Smiley, a wise, aging British intelligence agent who also appears in later novels. Other works include *The Spy Who Came in From the Cold* (1963), *The Looking Glass War* (1965), *A Perfect Spy*, (1986), and *Our Game* (1995). Le Carré's trilogy, *Tinker, Tailor, Soldier, Spy* (1974), *The Honourable Schoolboy* (1977), and *Smiley's People* (1980) pits Smiley against a secret-service agent from the Soviet Union.

Historians Gabriel and Joyce Kolko

The Kolkos rejected the nationalist viewpoint. They argued instead that economic considerations lay at the root of American foreign policy. According to the Kolkos, the American-Soviet conflict was secondary to America's goal of controlling world markets. Their comments follow.

Surrounded by this vast upheaval [World War II], the United States found itself immeasurably enriched and, without rival, the strongest nation on the globe. It emerged from the war self-conscious of its new strength and confident of its ability to direct world reconstruction along lines compatible with its goals. And these objectives, carefully formulated [stated] during the war, were deceptively simple: Essentially, the United States' aim was to restructure the world so that American business could trade, operate, and profit without restrictions everywhere. . . . American business could operate only in a world composed of politically reliable and stable capitalist nations, and with free access to essential raw materials. . . .

Washington neither feared nor suspected that the world was irrevocably in transition, decentralized, unpredictable, and beyond the control of any nation—and especially its own mastery. But, in the short run, American leaders had to consider whether the Left [in the Kolkos' view: anti-American forces] had the will and capacity to act and take power—and how to respond in the event it did. At the same time they had to confront the question of the future of the USSR, a prospect that the deepening wartime diplomatic crisis between Russia and the West had left enshrouded in dark pessimism. The Left and Russia usually appeared as synonymous in America's litany [repeated words], as Washington often assigned the Kremlin powers in the world that must have surprised the quite circumspect [cautious] rulers of that war-devastated country. For the USSR's very existence was a reminder of the profound weakening of European capitalism and the traditional order [governments] after World War I, and potentially a catalyst for undermining capitalism in the future. . . . [It] was often politically convenient for America's leaders to fix the blame for capitalism's failures on the cautious men in the Kremlin.

catalyst: person or thing that acts to bring about a result

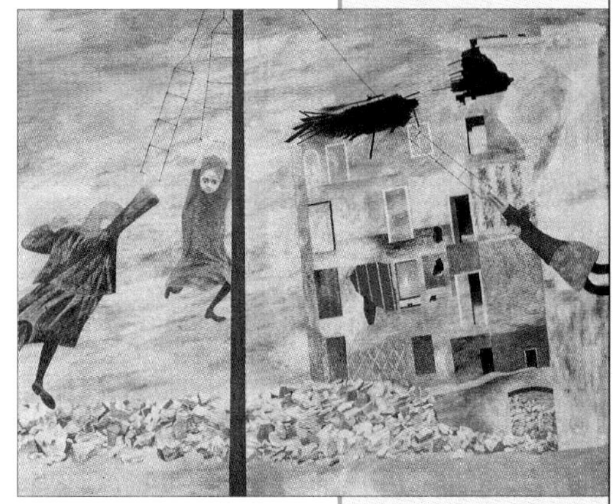

***Liberation*, 1945, by Ben Shahn. To Ben Shahn, art was "one of the last remaining outposts of free speech." His work expressed his social consciousness. Study this painting. What is ironic about its title? Who is liberated? What does liberation bring to them? What should it mean to them?**

Setting the Stage Activity

Defining Nationalism

To help students understand the origins of the Cold War, first write this definition on the chalkboard: "the policy or doctrine of asserting the interests of one's own nation, viewed as separate from the interests of other nations or the common interests of all other nations."

Challenge students to name events in American history that show this policy at work. Lead them to mention territorial conflicts (Revolutionary War) and economic ventures (building of the Panama Canal). Tell students that the Cold War was about nations competing for territorial and economic control on a global scale.

Bonus Activity

Making a Time Line

To help students recognize how *Sputnik* sparked the space race between the United States and the Soviet Union, have them work in groups to create a time line of American space ventures, assigning one decade to each group. Discuss how competition was a major factor in motivating the exploration of space.

Discussion

Stimulating Critical Thinking

1. You have read experts' opinions on the causes of the Cold War: nationalism, economic factors, or a combination of the two. What do you think about the political systems of the Soviet Union and the United States? Do you think there might have been problems caused by a communist government trying to communicate and work with a democratic country? Explain. (Students should recognize that there were bound to be difficulties in communication and misunderstandings because of the very different political ideologies of the two countries. These factors intensified the struggle created by nationalism and/or the desire for economic control.)

2. Do you think that the American space program would be as advanced as it is today if the Soviet Union had not launched *Sputnik* when it did? Explain. (Most students will agree that it was the American desire to lead the world in science, nuclear development, and space exploration that spurred them to action when the Soviets launched the first satellite.)

History Footnote
On the night of October 4, 1957, millions of people all over the world watched a point of light move across the night sky. It was *Sputnik I*, the first artificial satellite, launched by the Russians. It went around the world once every hour or so. By radio one could listen to the signals it gave out: *ping, ping, ping*. One man remembers, "I got up about two in the morning because that was when the satellite could be seen best. I stepped into the back yard and waited. Then I saw this little light. I could hear murmurs on all sides so I knew that my neighbors were all out watching too. I was sorry that the Russians had beaten us. But I couldn't help but feel a lump in my throat. To think what wonders humankind is capable of. Once again a bold and brilliant step had been taken in the exploration of our universe."

Historian Thomas G. Paterson

Paterson did not share the Kolkos' view that postwar American foreign policy was determined solely by economic factors. Instead, he believed that the Cold War had many causes. Although he recognized the Soviet Union's expansionist policies, he argued that the United States also shared much of the blame for the start of the Cold War.

It is obvious that the reconstruction crisis and diplomatic use of American economic power cannot alone explain the origins of the Cold War. Important factors were the long-standing Soviet anti-capitalist and American anti-Communist sentiments dating from 1917, the troubled relations before and after diplomatic recognition of the Soviet Union in 1933, and the strained alliance between the two in World War II. In 1945 and after, Soviet expansion into eastern Europe and rude diplomatic conduct aroused understandable hostility in Washington. Yet . . . United States diplomatic maneuvers helped trigger some reprehensible Soviet actions, and United States diplomats exaggerated the impact of many others. Because the United States was maneuvering from an uncommonly powerful position and on a global scale, its foreign policy often was haughty, expansionist, and uncompromising. Washington attempted to exploit Europe's weaknesses for its advantage and must share a substantial responsibility for the division of the world into competing blocs. This is not to ignore or excuse the Soviet grip on eastern Europe, but . . . Soviet policy was flexible in the immediate postwar years. Use of economic power as a weapon served to encourage further Soviet intrusions and thereby reduced the independence of the eastern European nations.

Excerpts from *Soviet-American Confrontation: Postwar Reconstruction and the Origins of the Cold War* by Thomas G. Paterson, pp. 260-261. Baltimore, Maryland: The Johns Hopkins University Press, 1973.

The Cold War began to heat up in 1949 when Americans learned that the Soviet Union had acquired nuclear technology.

READING 13B

The Cold War Embraces Technology

The post-World War II United States was a strong, prosperous nation with ample authority in the free world. Even when the Soviet Union developed nuclear weapons, Americans knew that they had developed the technology first, and assumed that theirs

Readers' Theater

The first reading will adapt well to interpretation as a panel discussion. Have one student play the part of Morgenthau, another might be either Gabriel or Joyce Kolko, and a third, Paterson. A fourth student might be the discussion moderator/narrator. Have all students in the group work together to write a script based on the readings. They should consider having the moderator ask a question, and then have each panel member address that question based on the philosophy of their character. Allow at least one work session to plan and prepare the script, and another to rehearse the presentation. At that point, they might find that the script needs some adjustment. By the end of the presentation, the philosophy of each panel member should be clear to the audience.

was superior. However, Americans' confidence in their technological, and therefore political, superiority was soon shaken.

Although U.S. government and military leaders predicted that satellites would be in orbit by 1957, there were delays. Americans were shocked and their confidence plummeted when the Soviets launched their *Sputnik* satellite in that same year, effectively triggering a space race and escalating the arms race.

It became apparent the United States could not take its position in world politics for granted. Neither could it underestimate the ability of Soviet scientists. Although the Americans did succeed in sending a satellite into space in 1958, it was not until the space program of the 1960s that American confidence was restored.

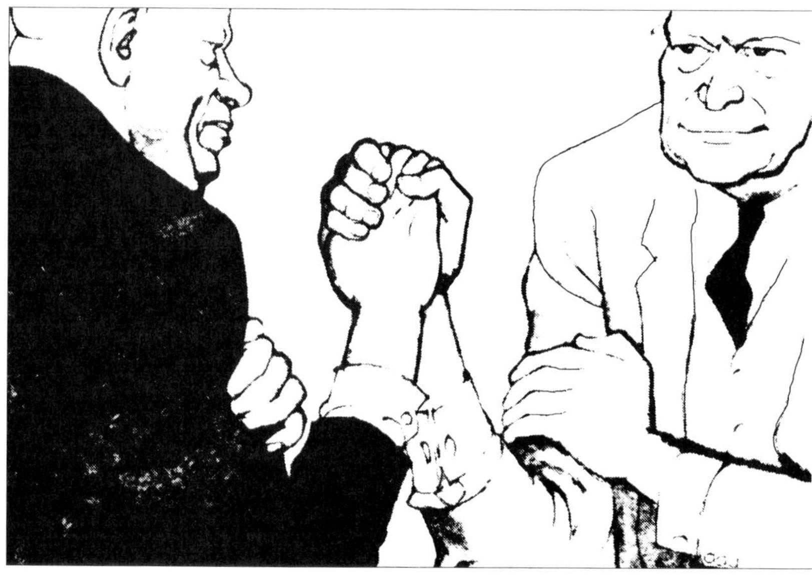

Titled "Handshake," this political cartoon portrays diplomatic relations between Soviet Premier Khrushchev and U.S. President Eisenhower as an arm-wrestling match.

A Closer Look

1. Summarize the theories on the origin of the Cold War for each of these experts: Morgenthau, the Kolkos, and Paterson.

2. How did Soviet advances in technology intensify the Cold War?

3. CRITICAL THINKING Consider the arguments and evidence presented in these readings. With whom do you think the greatest responsibility for the Cold War lies? Support your response with facts from the readings.

Wrap-Up Activity

Considering Alternative Theories

To extend the lesson and to help students understand that there might be several interpretations of a single historical event, have them respond to this quote in their history journals. "What has kept the world safe from the bomb since 1945 has not been deterrence, in the sense of fear of specific weapons, so much as it's been memory. The memory of what happened at Hiroshima." —*John Hersey*, novelist and journalist.

A Closer Look

Answers

1. Morgenthau believes that the Soviet Union did not want to remain allied with the United States but wanted to expand its own territory as much as possible. The Kolkos believe economic concerns were the cause of the Cold War. Paterson believes there were many causes: economic, political, and nationalistic.

2. The launch of *Sputnik* triggered a space race.

3. Students might reasonably agree with any of the theories. It is important that they support their opinions with at least three concrete details.

Teaching the
Citizenship Lab

In this feature students learn about *New York Times* v. *United States* (1971). In this landmark case, the Supreme Court ruled that newspapers could publish classified materials they had obtained, despite the government's claim that such publication would endanger national security.

Before students read the feature, review the information about classified records on pages 443–445. Have students read the entire feature before assigning the Understanding Civic Issues questions and the Hands-On Citizenship activity. The Bonus Activity in this Teacher's Edition may be used as an alternative to, or in addition to, the Hands-On Citizenship. The Discussion questions in this Teacher's Edition may be used at appropriate points during students' reading or afterward.

Objectives

- ★ Describe the government's efforts to stop the *New York Times* and the *Washington Post* from publishing the documents known as the Pentagon Papers.
- ★ Identify the arguments made by lawyers for the government and the newspapers.
- ★ Summarize the Supreme Court's ruling on the constitutional guarantee of freedom of the press in *New York Times* v. *United States.*

Supreme Court Case: *New York Times* v. *United States*

Citizenship Lab

Is Freedom of the Press Absolute?

Americans' awareness that their leaders had misled them about the Vietnam War was heightened on June 13, 1971. That day, the *New York Times* published the first in a series of articles about a secret Defense Department study of U.S. involvement in Vietnam. A former Defense Department employee had "leaked" the study to the newspaper. The newspaper's editors knew that publication of the so-called Pentagon Papers would anger government officials. They did not know that it would lead to a landmark Supreme Court decision on freedom of the press.

Background of the Pentagon Papers

The Defense Department study had been ordered by Robert McNamara, President Johnson's secretary of defense. Completed in early 1969, it consisted of 7,000 pages and was classified as top secret. Only 15 copies were made.

Daniel Ellsberg had helped write the study. Once a supporter of U.S. involvement in Vietnam, he was becoming increasingly disillusioned. Reading the completed study did not help. For example, the report showed President Johnson had planned to send combat forces to Vietnam while promising Americans he would not do so.

Ellsberg decided the study should be made public. He thought it would enrage Americans and put pressure on President Nixon to end the war quickly. In March 1971 Ellsberg gave a copy of the study to a *New York Times* reporter.

The Government Goes to Court

The newspaper's publisher and editors took three months to decide to publish the documents. But once the first installment appeared in print, events moved quickly. At Nixon's direction, the government went to the U.S. district court in New York on Tuesday, June 15, and asked it to order the *Times* to stop publishing the documents. The judge agreed to hear the case that Friday. In the meantime, he issued a temporary restraining order against the *Times.*

Ellsberg now gave another copy of the Pentagon Papers to the *Washington Post,* which began publishing them on Friday. The government went to the U.S. district court in Washington, D.C., to try to stop the *Post.* When both district courts ruled against the government, it turned to

History Footnote

The Defense Department study of the Vietnam War was so secret that even President Lyndon Johnson knew nothing about it. President Nixon also was unaware of the study until the *New York Times* began publishing it. When that happened, Nixon's first reaction was to do nothing. The study, completed before Nixon had become President, reflected badly on the Kennedy and Johnson administrations but said nothing about his own administration's role in the war. However, Nixon's advisors—particularly Henry Kissinger—persuaded him to take a different tack. They realized that publication of the Pentagon Papers would add fuel to the ongoing debate over the war and might encourage future "leaks" of classified documents that could be damaging to Nixon or to future Presidents.

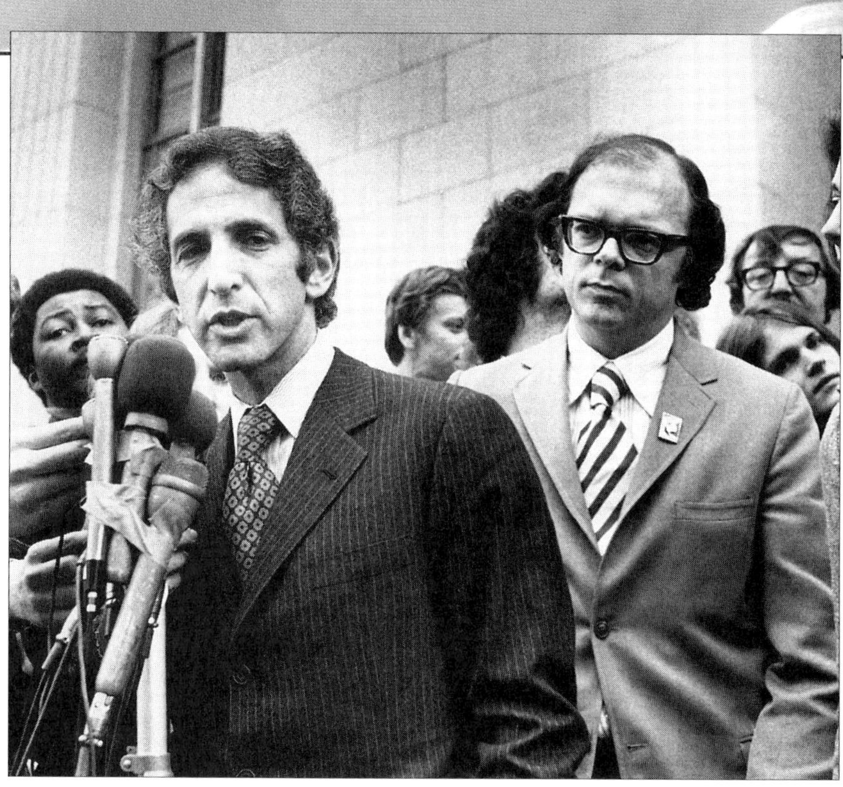

Pentagon Papers defendants Daniel Ellsberg (left) and Anthony Russo (right) talk with reporters after the opening session of their trial.

the appropriate courts of appeals. In the *Times* case, the appeals court returned the case to the lower court for more hearings. In the *Post* case, the appeals court upheld the lower court's decision. It was now June 23. The government and the *Times* appealed to the Supreme Court to settle the conflict.

The Supreme Court Acts

The Supreme Court usually takes months to decide a case. But the Pentagon Papers cases came up just before the summer recess. Putting the cases off until autumn seemed unwise. The justices agreed to hear the cases, consolidated under the name *New York Times* v. *United States,* right away.

Oral arguments took place on June 26, 1971. Government lawyers said what they had said all along: publication of the Pentagon Papers endangered national security. The enemy would learn U.S. secrets. More American soldiers would die. The peace process would be harmed.

The newspapers' lawyers focused on the part of the First Amendment that reads: "Congress shall make

Setting the Stage Activity

Rating the Press

To prepare for reading about freedom of the press, ask small groups to consider whether today's journalists go too far, not far enough, or just far enough in their efforts to "get the story." Groups should list examples from their own newspaper reading or television-news viewing to support their opinions.

Bonus Activity

Seeing the Government's Side

To help students understand the government's actions in this case, have small groups act out a meeting of President Nixon's advisors and government lawyers. They should imagine that the first Pentagon Papers have just been published in the *New York Times*. What are their reactions to seeing secret documents about the war in print? What ideas do they have for steps the government should take? Encourage students to make their acted-out meetings as realistic as possible, with participants brainstorming ideas for action, considering possible consequences of various actions, arguing pros and cons, and so on.

Discussion

Checking Understanding

1. How did the two Pentagon Papers cases make their way to the Supreme Court? (The government went to district courts in New York and Washington, D.C., to stop the newspapers from publishing. Both courts ruled against the government, which appealed. When the appeals courts reached different decisions, the government and the *Times* asked the Supreme Court to settle the conflict.)

2. What did the Court say in its unsigned opinion? (The government had not made a strong enough case for prior restraint.)

Stimulating Critical Thinking

3. Was Daniel Ellsberg right to "leak" classified material, and were the newspapers right to use it? Explain. (Answers will vary. One possibility: Ellsberg was wrong to take secret material that belonged to the government, but once the newspapers possessed it, they had a duty to publish it.)

4. Can you think of a case in which prior restraint would be justified? If so, describe it. If not, tell why not. (One possible case: In time of war, a newspaper publishes details of planned troop movements.)

Citizenship Footnote

Only Associate Justice William O. Douglas agreed with Justice Black's absolutist view of the First Amendment. Although the details of their positions varied, the other majority justices believed prior restraint might be allowable in extreme situations. The three dissenting justices took a similar view. But, they wrote, they had been forced to hear the case so hastily that they could not make an informed judgment about whether this situation qualified as extreme.

Chief Justice Warren E. Burger was one of the dissenters. In his opinion Burger suggested that the *New York Times* could have told the government it had the secret documents and tried to reach an agreement about which parts of the documents it could safely publish.

no law . . . abridging the freedom . . . of the press. . . ." Legal experts agree that in writing those words, the framers were referring to *prior restraint,* or action taken by a government to prevent material from being published. Another word for *prior restraint* is *censorship.* The newspapers' lawyers said that in times of national emergency, prior restraint might be justified, but this was not such a time.

Four days later, the Court ruled 6–3 for the newspapers. In an unsigned opinion, the Court said the government had to make a very strong case for prior restraint, and it had not. Separate opinions by the nine justices followed.

The opinion written by Associate Justice Hugo L. Black left no room for compromise. Black viewed even the temporary restraining order against the *Times* as a "flagrant, indefensible . . . violation of the First Amendment." He wrote: "[F]or the first time . . . since the founding of the Republic, the federal courts are asked to hold that the First Amendment does not mean what it says, but rather means that the Government can halt the publication of current news of vital importance to the people of this country. . . . Both the history and language of the First Amendment support the view that the press must be left free to publish news, whatever the source, without censorship. . . ."

Segments of the Pentagon Papers that appeared in the *New York Times*.

The New York Times

KEY TEXTS FROM PENTAGON'S VIETNAM STUDY

Rusk Cable to Embassy in Laos On Search and Rescue Flights

The New York Times

Vietnam Archive: Pentagon Study Traces 3 Decades of Growing U.S. Involvement

"All the News That's Fit to Print"

The New York Times

PRESIDENT ORDERS DRIVE TO PROVIDE JOBS TO VETERANS

Vietnam Archive: A Consensus to Bomb Developed Before '64 Election, Study Says

"All the News That's Fit to Print"

The New York Times

LATE CITY EDITION

MAYOR'S BUDGET OF $8.8-BILLIONS AVOIDS LAYOFFS

COURT SAYS CITIES MAY CLOSE POOLS TO BAR RACIAL MIX

MITCHELL SEEKS TO HALT SERIES ON VIETNAM BUT TIMES REFUSES

Vietnam Archive: Study Tells How Johnson Secretly Opened Way to Ground Combat

COURT STEP LIKELY

Return of Documents Asked in Telegram To Publisher

ATTRITION ON JOBS

Losses Put at 14,320 And 5,013 Vacancies Due to Go Unfilled

History Footnote

The idea behind the formation of the White House "plumbers" unit was not only to "plug" further "leaks" of secret information but also to discredit Nixon's enemies. One of the plumbers' covert missions was a break-in at the offices of Daniel Ellsberg's psychiatrist in September 1971. The purpose of the break-in was to find information damaging to Ellsberg, who was being prosecuted by the government on espionage and theft charges related to the Pentagon Papers. When the administration's involvement in the break-in later came to light, the judge in the Ellsberg case declared a mistrial and dismissed the charges against him. In the meantime, the White House plumbers had conducted yet another break-in: at the offices of the Democratic National Committee in the Watergate complex.

Hugo Black

The Aftermath

The *Times* and the *Post* resumed publishing the Pentagon Papers. The government chose not to file charges against them for breaking national security laws. However, the Nixon administration became determined to prevent further "leaks." A secret unit called the "plumbers" was set up, leading eventually to the Watergate break-in and the crisis that followed. (See Chapter 14.)

In addition, the Court's decision in the Pentagon Papers case changed the relationship between the press and the government. Modern journalists are more likely to challenge what officials say and do than they were before 1971. Some Americans find this aggressive approach distasteful. Others applaud it as a vital part of a healthy democracy.

Understanding Civic Issues

1. What were the Pentagon Papers, and why did Ellsberg "leak" them?
2. What arguments did each side make before the Supreme Court?
3. **Critical Thinking** Carefully read the words of the First Amendment relating to freedom of the press (page R59). Do you interpret them the same way that Justice Black did, or not? Explain.
4. **Hands-On Citizenship** You and two classmates are the editors of a big-city newspaper. Someone has leaked top-secret material about an American terrorist group to you. You have not published the material, but the government has learned of the leak. You receive a call from the attorney general warning you not to publish.

- In your group, discuss your options. You could publish. You could not publish and either keep the material or return it to the government. What other option can you think of?
- Discuss the pros and cons of each option. Consider how the American people, the government, and your newspaper might be affected.
- Decide what to do. Appoint a spokesperson to share your decision and your reasons with the class.

Citizenship Lab Answers

1. A top-secret Defense Department study of U.S. involvement in Vietnam; Ellsberg thought the contents would pressure President Nixon to end the war.
2. Government: publication endangers national security. Newspapers: First Amendment prohibits prior restraint (censorship).
3. Some students may disagree with Black's broad interpretation because the amendment specifically refers to Congress. Others may say it is unreasonable to think the amendment was designed to allow the President to abridge fundamental rights, even though Congress cannot.

Teaching the Hands-On CITIZENSHIP

Moral dilemmas such as the one posed in this activity are interesting and challenging to students. What's more, they help us teach character. Walter Parker and John Jarolimek, in *Social Studies in Elementary Education,* say: "At the heart of any character education program are the moral values that children are expected to develop and that teachers are expected to encourage and model. . . . These are drawn from the values that underpin the 'rule book' of our society, the Constitution of the United States."

At·a·Glance **14**

The Postwar Years at Home
1945–1974

Chapter Planning Guide

Section	Student Text	Teacher's Edition Activities
Opener and Story pp. 598–601	**Keys to History Time Line** **History Mystery** Beginning the Story with **Martin Luther King, Jr.**	**Setting the Stage Activity** Living in a Segregated Society, p. 600
1 **Adjusting to Peace** pp. 602–606	**Reading Maps** Interstate Highways 1967, p. 604 **Link to the Present** Television then and now, p. 605 **Geography Lab** The Growth of Suburbs, p. 606	**Warm-Up Activity** Thinking About Prosperity, p. 602 **Geography Question of the Day,** p. 602 **Section Activity** Assembling a Scrapbook, p. 603 **Bonus Activity** Creating Political Cartoons, p. 604 **Wrap-Up Activity** Writing Definitions, p. 605
2 **A Spirit of Change** pp. 607–610	**Hands-On History** Collecting memories of Kennedy's assassination, p. 608 **Link to Art** *Signs,* p. 610	**Warm-Up Activity** Creating Images of Domestic Programs, p. 607 **Geography Question of the Day,** p. 607 **Section Activity** A New Frontier/Great Society Display, p. 608 **Bonus Activity** Writing a Song or Poem, p. 609 **Wrap-Up Activity** Asking Kennedy and Johnson, p. 610
3 **Fighting for Equal Rights** pp. 611–617	**World Link** Gandhi and nonviolence, p. 613 **Point of View** Were the demonstrations in Birmingham necessary?, p. 613	**Warm-Up Activity** Defining Equality, p. 611 **Geography Question of the Day,** p. 611 **Section Activity** A TV Talk Show, p. 612 **Bonus Activity** Singing Civil Rights Songs, p. 616 **Wrap-Up Activity** Comparing Two Leaders, p. 617
4 **The Nixon Years** pp. 622–627	**Link to Technology** *Skylab,* p. 623 **Skill Lab** Synthesizing Information, p. 627	**Warm-Up Activity** Debating a President's Right to Resign, p. 622 **Geography Question of the Day,** p. 622 **Section Activity** Assessing the Watergate Legacy, p. 624 **Bonus Activity** Taking a Position, p. 624 **Wrap-Up Activity** Evaluating Nixon, p. 626
Evaluation	**Section 1 Review,** p. 605 **Section 2 Review,** p. 610 **Section 3 Review,** p. 617 **Section 4 Review,** p. 626 **Chapter Survey,** pp. 628–629 **Alternative Assessment** Writing editorials, p. 629	**Answers to Section 1 Review,** p. 605 **Answers to Section 2 Review,** p. 610 **Answers to Section 3 Review,** p. 617 **Answers to Section 4 Review,** p. 626 **Answers to Chapter Survey,** pp. 628–629 (Alternative Assessment guidelines are in the Take-Home Planner.)

Teacher's Resource Package

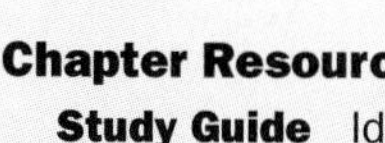

Chapter Summaries: English and Spanish, pp. 64–65

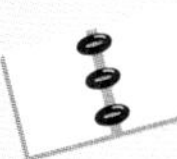

Chapter Resources Binder

Study Guide Identifying Main Ideas, p. 121

Geography Extensions The Changing Town, pp. 33–34

Chapter Resources Binder

Study Guide Using Questions to Guide Readings, p. 122

Reinforcement Organizing Information, pp. 125–126

Chapter Resources Binder

Study Guide Completing a Graphic Organizer, p. 123

American Readings Going to School in the South, pp. 61–62; Civil Rights Songs, p. 63; Joining the United Farm Workers, p. 64

Chapter Resources Binder

Study Guide Telling *Who, What, When,* and *Where*, p. 124

Skills Development Synthesizing Information, pp. 127–128

Using Historical Documents President Richard Nixon's Letter of Resignation, pp. 92–95

Chapter and Unit Tests Chapter 14 Tests, Forms A and B, pp. 107–110

Take-Home Planner

Introducing the Chapter Activity Understanding McCarthyism, p. 14

Chapter In-Depth Activity Writing a Protest Song, p. 14

Reduced Views

Study Guide, p. 16

Geography Extensions, p. 19

Unit 5 Answers, pp. 31–38

Reduced Views

Study Guide, p. 16

Reinforcement, p. 17

Unit 5 Answers, pp. 31–38

Reduced Views

Study Guide, p. 16

American Readings, p. 18

Unit 5 Answers, pp. 31–38

Reduced Views

Study Guide, p. 16

Skills Development, p. 17

Using Historical Documents, p. 19

Unit 5 Answers, pp. 31–38

Reduced Views

Chapter Tests, p. 19

Unit 5 Answers, pp. 31–38

Alternative Assessment Guidelines for scoring the Chapter Survey activity, p. 15

Additional Resources

Wall Time Line

Unit 5 Activity

Transparency Package

Transparency 14-1 An Artist's View of the Sixties—use with Section 2

Transparency 14-2 The Spirit of the Sixties—use with Section 2

Transparency Activity Book

SelecTest Testing Software

Chapter 14 Test, Forms A and B

Videodisc

CD-ROM

"Rock Around the Clock" (see TE p. 604)

"The Twist" (see TE p. 604)

Kennedy on the space program (see TE p. 608)

Johnson on the Great Society (see TE p.609)

"Sister Rosa" (see TE p. 612)

Little Rock students (see TE p. 612)

"Keep On a-Travelin' On" (see TE p. 614)

Martin Luther King, Jr. (see TE p. 614)

Watts riots (see TE p. 615)

L.A. riots, 1992 (see TE p. 615)

Voice of housewife (see TE p. 616)

Voice of Mary Crow Dog (see TE p. 616)

Earth Day banner (see TE p. 624)

14

Teaching Resources

Take-Home Planner 5
- Introducing Chapter Activity
- Chapter In-Depth Activity
- Alternative Assessment

Chapter Resources Binder
Geography Extensions
American Readings
Using Historical Documents
Transparency Activities
Wall Time Line Activities
Chapter Summaries
Chapter and Unit Tests
SelecTest Test File
Vital Links CD-ROM/Videodisc

Time Line

Keys to History

Keys to History journal writing activity is on p. 628 in the Chapter Survey.

Senator Joseph McCarthy The Wisconsin senator's charges increased Americans' fears of a Communist overthrow of the government. (p. 603)

School segregation outlawed The Supreme Court ruled unanimously that separate schools for black and white students were unconstitutional. (p. 611)

Montgomery bus boycott Protests by black citizens led by Martin Luther King, Jr., helped lead to the integration of the city's bus lines. (p. 612)

Looking Back Americans' fear of communism after the Russian Revolution of 1917 led to arrests of suspected Communists.

World Link See p. 613.

Chapter Objectives

- ★ Identify the challenges Americans faced at home following the end of World War II.
- ★ Explain the new domestic goals set by John Kennedy and Lyndon Johnson.
- ★ Discuss the struggles to gain justice and equal rights.
- ★ Describe the Nixon presidency and the scandal that ended it.

Chapter Overview

After World War II the economy boomed. Along with the increase in demand for goods, there was a steep rise in the birth rate, known as "the baby boom." Meanwhile, fear of communism, fanned by Senator Joseph McCarthy, led to a hunt for traitors. Prosperity continued throughout Dwight D. Eisenhower's presidency. However more than a fifth of the population lived in poverty.

1945–1974

Chapter 14

The Postwar Years at Home

Sections

Keys to History

1950–1954
Senator Joseph McCarthy spreads fear and distrust

1954
Supreme Court rules school segregation unconstitutional
NAACP lawyers celebrate Court's decision

1955
Montgomery bus boycott
Rosa Parks rides an integrated bus

1945 — 1955

Looking Back
The "Red Scare"
1919

World Link
Gandhi wins struggle for India's independence
1947

A spirit of change swept the nation in the 1960s, as Presidents John F. Kennedy and Lyndon B. Johnson sought to fight poverty, provide health care, and end discrimination. However, Johnson's policy in Vietnam limited the success of his domestic programs.

African Americans struggled for equal rights. The civil rights movement they created removed the legal basis for segregation and protected voting rights. The Civil Rights Act of 1964 banned discrimination on the basis of race, religion, gender, or nationality. Through court challenges as well as protests, women, Hispanics, and American Indians also made strides toward equality.

Under President Richard Nixon, the nation faced economic and environmental problems. The Watergate scandal led to Nixon's resignation, yet showed the strength of our Constitution.

HISTORY *Mystery*

This young girl lived within 7 blocks of an elementary school. Why did she have to take a bus 21 blocks to another school?

1963
President Kennedy assassinated

1964–1965
Civil rights acts

1965
President Johnson announces Great Society program

Cartoon of President Johnson

1968
Martin Luther King, Jr., assassinated

1974
Watergate scandal leads President Nixon to resign

Marine removes portrait of Nixon

1965

1975

Looking Ahead

First woman appointed to Supreme Court

1981

Teaching the HISTORY *Mystery*

Students will find the answer on p. 611. See Chapter Survey, p. 628, for additional information and questions.

Time Line

President Kennedy assassinated The murder of the young President shocked the nation. (p. 608)

Civil rights acts Under President Johnson's leadership, Congress passed the first significant civil rights legislation since Reconstruction, banning many kinds of discrimination and protecting voting rights. (p. 614)

President Johnson announces Great Society Under President Johnson's leadership, Congress established antipoverty programs and improved health care, education, and housing for millions of Americans. (pp. 609–610)

Martin Luther King assassinated The black leader's murder set off an outpouring of grief among Americans of all races. (pp. 615–616)

President Nixon resigns Congress traced the trail of the Watergate scandal to the White House, and President Nixon resigned rather than face impeachment. (p. 625)

Looking Ahead Sandra Day O'Connor became the first woman to sit on the Supreme Court.

Beginning the Story

Martin Luther King, Jr.

Growing up in a climate of rigidly enforced segregation shaped the character of the young Martin Luther King, Jr. His experience of the pain of segregation and his religious training and beliefs led him to advocate nonviolent resistance to injustice. Until his death in 1968, he was one of the leading campaigners in the struggle for equal justice for all Americans.

Setting the Stage Activity

Living in a Segregated Society

To help students understand the climate in the South during the period of King's childhood, have them imagine living in a society where left-handed people are denied many basic rights and privileges. Ask them to help you make a list of common rights, such as riding on a bus, using a drinking fountain or restroom, and eating in a restaurant. Have right-handed and left-handed students write about how they feel living in such an imaginary society. Ask a left-handed student and a right-handed student to read their writings aloud.

See the Introducing the Chapter Activity, Understanding McCarthyism, **Take-Home Planner 5,** p. 14.

History Footnote

King suffered when his own children were victims of prejudice. In his "Letter from Birmingham Jail" (see pp. 613–614), he described the difficulty of explaining "to your six-year-old daughter why she can't go to the public amusement park that has just been advertised on television, and see tears welling up in her little eyes when she is told that 'Funtown' is closed to colored children."

Beginning the Story with

Martin Luther King, Jr.

Young Martin Luther King, Jr., was confused. "M. L.," as he was called, always played with the two boys who lived across the street from his Atlanta home. When they began school, M. L. went to a different school than his friends. At the end of the first day, when he ran over to their house to compare notes, their mother said they could not play with him anymore. "Why not?" he asked. Her only answer was that "they were white and I was colored." M. L. ran home in tears. He later recalled that his mother

> "tried to explain the divided system of the South—the segregated schools, restaurants, theaters, housing; the white and colored signs on drinking fountains, waiting rooms, lavatories—as a social condition rather than a natural order. Then she said . . . 'You are as good as anyone.'"

"A Sense of Somebodiness"

Sometimes it was hard for M. L. to feel "as good as anyone." Outside of the close circle of family, friends, and the Ebenezer Baptist Church led by his father, the Reverend Martin Luther King, Sr., it was impossible to ignore the stings of segregation. M. L. would never forget a trip with his father to an Atlanta shoe store. When the two sat down in empty seats at the front of the store, a clerk said politely, "I'll be happy to wait on you if you'll just move to those seats in the rear." Mr. King responded, "We'll either buy shoes sitting here or we won't buy shoes at all." As they walked out, M. L. heard his father mutter, "I don't care how long I have to live with this system, I will never accept it." Nor would his son. King later wrote:

History Bookshelf

Myers, Walter Dean. *Now Is Your Time! The African-American Struggle for Freedom.* HarperCollins, 1991. This readable account by a popular author for young readers traces the events of the civil rights movement and the history of African Americans.

Also of interest:

Hale, Janet Campbell. *The Owl's Song.* HarperCollins, 1995.

Hamilton, Virginia. *M. C. Higgins the Great.* Simon & Schuster, 1987.

Merriam, Eve, ed. *Growing Up Female in America.* Beacon, 1987.

Moore, Yvette. *Freedom Songs.* Puffin, 1992.

Witherspoon, W. R. *Martin Luther King, Jr.: To the Mountaintop.* Doubleday, 1985.

"My mother taught me that I should feel a sense of somebodiness. On the other hand, I had to go out and face the system, which stared me in the face every day, saying, 'You are less than.' 'You are not equal to.' So this was a real tension within."

"The Best Jitterbug"

Most of the time, M. L. kept this tension hidden. He was a bright child who loved to read. At the age of 8 he had a newspaper route, and by 13 he was the youngest assistant manager of a delivery station for the *Atlanta Journal.*

As a teenager, M. L.'s friends nicknamed him "Tweed" because he spent most of his money on stylish tweed suits. His other street name was "Will Shoot." Whenever he got his hands on the basketball, he was sure to shoot rather than pass. He also loved to dance. According to his brother, he was "the best jitterbug in town."

Martin Luther King, Jr., became a leader of the struggle against racial injustice. Here, he and his wife, Coretta, lead a march for voting rights.

M. L. could also be just about the best student. He skipped two years of high school, graduating at the age of 15. When he was 14, M. L. entered a statewide speech contest in Dublin, Georgia. Accompanied by his teacher, Mrs. Bradley, M. L. made the trip, delivered his speech, and won first prize. On the way home, though, his joy at winning turned to rage. He later wrote:

"Some white passengers boarded the bus, and the white driver ordered us to give the whites our seats. We didn't move quickly enough to suit him, so he began cursing us. . . . Mrs. Bradley finally urged me up, saying we had to obey the law. And so we stood in the aisle for the 90 miles to Atlanta. . . . It was the angriest I have ever been in my life."

M. L. had grown up with the commandment of Jesus to "love your enemy." On this night, though, it was hard for him to hate the sin but not the sinner. It was easy for him to believe that "the only way we could solve our problem of segregation was an armed revolt." Only after King became a minister would he find a different way to fight injustice.

Hands-On HISTORY — Activity

Imagine that you were traveling with Martin Luther King, Jr., on the way home from the speech contest. Create a dialogue between yourself and King about whether you should give up your bus seats.

Discussion

Thinking Historically

1. What traits do you see in King that help explain how he became a crusader for justice? (He was very intelligent, an excellent speaker, and a hard worker. He refused to accept segregation.)

2. How did King's parents help shape his attitudes toward segregation? (Taught him he was as good as anyone, never to accept segregation, and to feel a sense of "somebodiness.")

3. Why do you think it was hard for young African Americans like King to feel they were as good as anyone? (Society in many ways insisted they be treated as if they were not equal.)

See the Chapter In-Depth Activity, Writing a Protest Song, **Take-Home Planner 5,** p. 14.

Teaching the Hands-On HISTORY

To help students create their dialogues, have them list some words that might describe King's thoughts and feelings at the time of the bus incident. Have them consider possible results of giving up and not giving up their seats, and whether they would be willing to suffer the consequences of their decisions.

Introducing the Section

Vocabulary

closed shop (p. 602) a workplace in which only union members can be hired

Warm-Up Activity

Thinking About Prosperity

To focus on the meaning of prosperity, have students list things that characterize life in affluent nations and life in poor nations. As they read the section, have them note ways Americans became more prosperous in the postwar period.

Geography Question of the Day

Write names of the following states on the chalkboard: Alaska, Arizona, California, Colorado, Florida, Nevada, Texas, and Utah. Tell students the populations of these states grew the fastest from 1950 to 1980. Have them list qualities of these states and possible reasons why they grew the most.

See the Study Guide
activity in **Chapter Resources Binder,**
p. 121.

Section Objectives

- ★ Explain how the change from war to peace affected the nation's economy.
- ★ Discuss why fear of communism swept the country.
- ★ Identify ways prosperity affected Americans in the 1950s.

Teaching Resources

Take-Home Planner 5, pp. 12–19
Chapter Resources Binder
Study Guide, p. 121
Reinforcement
Skills Development
Geography Extensions, pp. 33–34
American Readings
Using Historical Documents
Transparency Activities
Chapter and Unit Tests

1. Adjusting to Peace

Reading Guide

New Term **closed shop**

Section Focus **The challenges Americans faced at home after World War II**

1. **How did the change from war to peace affect the nation's economy?**
2. **Why did fear of communism sweep the country?**
3. **How did prosperity affect Americans in the 1950s?**

When World War II ended in 1945, Martin Luther King, Jr., was studying to be a minister at Morehouse College. During the next few years that quiet campus would be flooded with returning war veterans.

For civilians as well as veterans, the first years after the war brought both uncertainty and opportunity. Fears stemming from the Cold War haunted Americans. So did hopes for a better life after a decade and a half of depression and war.

"The Great Boom"

Wartime production had lifted the United States out of the Great Depression. Now the nation rose to new heights of prosperity. "The Great American Boom is on," *Fortune* magazine declared in 1946.

People were eager to use their wartime wages to buy goods they had not been able to get during the war. In addition, the GI Bill, passed in 1944, gave veterans money to spend on businesses, homes, and schooling.

Labor on strike Although industries increased production, there were still shortages of many goods. The prices of scarce items, such as meat, skyrocketed. Workers pressed hard for wage increases to keep pace with rising prices. When employers refused, a wave of strikes swept the nation.

Although President Truman supported labor, he feared that wage increases would lead to even higher prices. In April 1946 he ended a United Mine Workers' strike by seizing the mines. A month later he forced striking railroad workers back to work.

In 1947 Congress passed the Taft-Hartley Act to curb the power of unions. The act banned the **closed shop**—a workplace in which only union members can be hired. It also gave the President the power to delay a strike by declaring a "cooling off" period.

Truman's Second Term

By the presidential election of 1948, the Democratic Party was divided over Truman's policies at home and abroad. Polls predicted a sure win for the Republican candidate, Governor Thomas Dewey of New York. Truman campaigned tirelessly, however, and pulled out a surprise victory.

The Fair Deal In 1949 Truman submitted to Congress his "Fair Deal" plan. His goal was to give all Americans a share in the nation's economic opportunities.

Under Truman, Congress extended the Social Security program to more Americans. It also provided funds for low-income housing. However, southern Democrats joined with Republicans to block many of Truman's proposals, including health insurance.

History Footnote

The Serviceman's Readjustment Act of 1944, known as the GI Bill, profoundly influenced the lives of an entire generation of Americans. The term *GI,* the universal nickname for an American soldier, comes from the words "government issue" or "general issue," which were stamped on all equipment issued to soldiers. More than 2 million veterans of World War II each received about $1,400 a year to attend college, graduate school, or technical school. By the late 1940s veterans made up about half of all male college students. Millions of others received on-the-job training and education below the college level. Among these veterans were many who would never have been able to further their education without the GI Bill. Their numbers included 60,000 women and 70,000 African Americans.

The Hunt for Communists

There was one thing, though, on which many Americans could agree. They feared that Communists and people sympathetic to communism were trying to overthrow the government.

"Spy fever" gripped the nation, and the hunt for traitors was on. Government workers suspected of disloyalty lost their jobs. Congress searched for Communists in the movie industry. Writers, actors, and directors who refused to answer questions about their political beliefs were "blacklisted." Major studios would not hire them, even when there was no proof of their disloyalty.

When the Soviet Union exploded its first atomic bomb in 1949, many people thought that spies must have given American atomic secrets to the Soviets. In 1953 Julius and Ethel Rosenberg, former members of the Communist Party, were convicted of being atomic spies and put to death.

Joseph McCarthy Senator Joseph R. McCarthy of Wisconsin fanned Americans' fear of communism to gain fame and power. In 1950 he claimed that 205 State Department employees were Communists.

A special committee, led by Senator Millard Tydings of Maryland, investigated and declared the charges a "fraud and a hoax." In response, McCarthy spread false charges that Tydings was pro-Communist. As a result, Tydings lost his 1950 campaign for re-election.

Aware of McCarthy's power to destroy careers, few people were brave enough to oppose him and his scare tactics. In fact, many businesses, schools, and unions joined the hunt for traitors. They required employees to sign "loyalty oaths," and fired them if they refused.

One brave opponent did come forward, however. Senator Margaret Chase Smith of Maine was outraged that people were "afraid to speak their minds lest they be politically smeared as Communists." She declared, "Freedom of speech is not what it used to be in America."

Finally, in 1954 McCarthy went too far. That year 20 million television viewers saw him make false charges against the United States Army. The Senate voted to condemn McCarthy for his conduct. His power gone, McCarthy sank from public view.

President Eisenhower

As the presidential election of 1952 drew near, fear of communism was still strong, and the Korean War was dragging on. Hoping that the voters would welcome a change,

Senator Joseph McCarthy fell from power when his charges of Communist influence in the United States Army proved false. Margaret Chase Smith was one of the first senators to oppose McCarthy's scare tactics.

Developing the Section

Discussion

Checking Understanding

1. What did the Taft-Hartley Act do? (Banned the closed shop and gave the President the power to delay a strike by declaring a cooling-off period.)

2. What was the goal of the Fair Deal plan? (To give all Americans a share in the nation's economic opportunities.)

Stimulating Critical Thinking

3. Do you believe that the threat of communism in the postwar years justified "blacklists" and ignoring individual rights? Explain. (Yes: could not risk end of democracy. No: Constitution guarantees freedoms; people innocent unless proven guilty.)

Section Activity

Assembling a Scrapbook

To help students understand American life from 1945 to 1960, have the class make a "scrapbook," creating illustrations, ads, headlines, and other elements portraying life of the period. Have them consider world and domestic politics, popular culture, science, and education. They may organize it chronologically or by subject.

Teaching the

Reading Maps

Ask why places shown with heavy traffic were chosen as focuses of highways. (Population, government, and manufacturing centers; central location.) **Answer to Reading Maps:** Boston, New York City, Philadelphia, Washington, D.C., Richmond; Cleveland, Detroit, Indianapolis, Cincinnati, Chicago; Los Angeles, San Francisco, San Diego

Bonus Activity

Creating Political Cartoons

To focus on postwar challenges, have pairs create political cartoons for two topics presented in the section. Some possibilities are McCarthy, the baby boom, suburban growth, and poverty. Have pairs share their cartoons with the class.

Vital Links

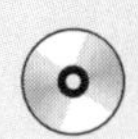

"Rock Around the Clock" (Song) Unit 5, Side 2, Search 18541, Play to 21201

See also Unit 5 Explore CD-ROM location 383.

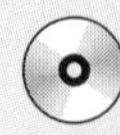

"The Twist" (Song) Unit 6, Side 2, Search 00001, Play to 02398

See also Unit 6 Explore CD-ROM location 68.

History Footnote

The interstate highway system became the nation's most expensive public works program ever, costing $76 billion by the time more than 41,000 miles of road had been built. Among the stated purposes were national defense and improved mail service. However several other consequences also resulted from the program. Highways meant the death of the railroads in most of the nation. No longer was the train station at the heart of a city's transportation network. Highways brought about the tremendous growth of the trucking and automobile industries. Billion-dollar industries grew up around the interstates: food services, gas stations, and motels. The interstates also profoundly changed American cities. The new roads allowed families to move to far-flung suburbs and doomed many inner-city areas to decay.

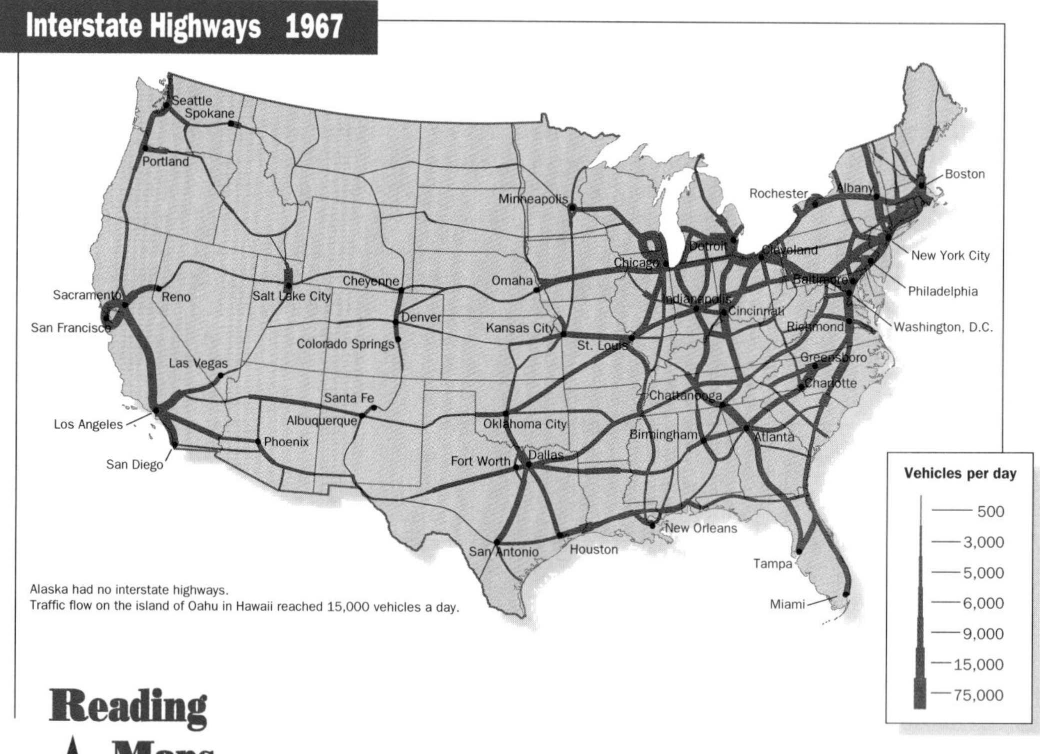

Reading Maps

In each of the following areas list three cities that are in the center of heavy traffic flow: East Coast, Midwest, West Coast.

the Republicans nominated General Dwight ("Ike") Eisenhower.

A war hero, Ike was widely admired. He defeated the Democratic candidate, Adlai E. Stevenson, in 1952 and again in 1956. For the first time since 1933, a Republican occupied the White House.

Eisenhower's goals President Eisenhower believed that the federal government should play a smaller role in the economy. He called for cutting spending, though not for ending programs that helped people. In fact, he increased the number of people who could receive Social Security benefits.

Perhaps Eisenhower's greatest achievement was the Interstate Highway Act of 1956. It provided funds for a vast system of freeways to link all parts of the United States (see map above). The act had far-reaching results. Increasingly, Americans used highways instead of railroads for traveling and for transporting goods.

The Prosperous 1950s

As Europe and Asia struggled to recover from World War II, prosperity continued in the United States. One reason was the many

Connections to Economics

The most influential home builder of the 1950s was William Levitt, who foresaw the tremendous need for houses during the post-war boom and met the demand in a new way. Levitt used the assembly line techniques of automaker Henry Ford to build thousands of identical houses, each with four rooms and a bathroom. Using mass-produced parts, Levitt's workers each specialized in just one task: one crew laid the floors, another crew put up walls, while another laid tiles. Levitt even had painters who painted only red and others who painted only white. Levitt's houses were astonishingly popular. In March 1949, he sold 1,400 houses in a single day. His developments became known as Levittowns. The first Levittown was built on New York's Long Island.

Teaching the

Link to the Present

Have students compare TV in 1953 with TV today. They should note effects on people's lives, advances in technology, and choices of programs and channels.

jobs created in industries producing weapons for the Cold War arms race. Another reason was that productivity was increasing. The use of new technology and more efficient machines made workers more productive. Between 1945 and 1960, for example, the time needed to make a car was cut in half.

A third reason for continued prosperity was increasing demand for housing, cars, and consumer goods. Car production soared from 2 million in 1946 to 8 million in 1955. There was also great demand for televisions, which had been developed during the war. Between 1946 and 1960, the number of TV sets soared from 7,000 to 50 million.

With this steady increase in demand for goods came a steep rise in the birth rate, called the "baby boom." Families with four or five children became common. Meanwhile, people were living longer, thanks to advances in medicine such as the discovery of penicillin and a vaccine against polio.

Suburban growth The baby boom created a great demand for better housing. Instead of renting city apartments, families wanted homes of their own in the suburbs. GI loans made buying houses affordable. Cars and good roads made it easy to commute longer distances to work.

During the 1950s the number of Americans living in suburbs grew by 50 percent. Developers met the demand for suburban housing by buying cheap land outside cities. There they built row upon row of mass-produced homes, known as tract houses.

The problem of poverty Unfortunately, some Americans did not share in the prosperity of the 1950s. By 1960 more than one-fifth of the population, including unskilled workers, migrant farmworkers, and the aged, lived in poverty.

Rural areas suffered some of the greatest poverty, but most of the poor were trapped in big-city slums. As families and industries moved to the suburbs, cities lost important tax money. City schools and other services declined. Crime rose. More and more, the people who stayed in the cities were those who could not afford to move.

Link to the Present

Television then and now It is a Sunday evening in 1953, and a family sits down to watch TV. Neighbors who do not yet have TV sets drop by to watch, too. They crowd around the black-and-white screen, which is barely more than a foot (30 cm) wide. At 8 o'clock, there is a choice of three programs.

Today, about 98 percent of American households have at least one TV set. Programs appear in color on screens that may be 4 feet (120 cm) wide or larger. Many families subscribe to cable TV systems or have satellite dishes that allow them to receive 50, 100, 200, or more channels.

1. Section Review

1. Define **closed shop.**
2. Why did workers strike after the war?
3. Describe at least two ways that the United States changed in the 1950s.
4. **Critical Thinking** As a senator, would you have voted to condemn McCarthy for his conduct? Why or why not?

Closing the Section

Wrap-Up Activity

Writing Definitions

To review the main topics, have groups create definitions for *"Great Boom," Fair Deal, McCarthyism, prosperity,* and *baby boom.* After each group presents its definitions to the class, have the class find examples of what could be considered McCarthyism today and discuss how they fit the definition.

Section Review Answers

1. Definition: *closed shop* (602)

2. Wage increases did not keep pace with rising prices.

3. Start of interstate highway system; increased productivity due to more efficient technology; increased demand for housing, cars, and consumer goods; longer life expectancies; steep rise in birth rate; growth of suburbs.

4. Yes: resorted to scare tactics for personal motives, denied people constitutional rights, made unfounded charges. No: possible threat to national security outweighed rights of accused Communists.

Teaching the Geography Lab

Have students compare the direction of movement of people in the St. Louis area with that in your town or city. Ask them for explanations.

Link to History

Answers

1. Interstate and other highways, such as I-70, I-44, and I-64.

2. Many people live in one suburb and work in another, or live in one suburb and seek shopping, cultural, and recreational activities in other suburbs, rather than in downtown St. Louis.

3. Possible answers: desire for new housing and more space, the feeling that suburbs are safer and cleaner than cities, the wish to be near workplaces that had moved out of the central cities, and the desire to live among people with the same socioeconomic and ethnic backgrounds.

4. Students who prefer suburbs may highlight suburbs' newer homes, larger lots, uncrowded streets, and cleanliness as opposed to cities' older buildings, dirt, crime, and crowding. Students who prefer cities may show cities' cultural and recreational activities, public transportation, and sense of history and diversity as opposed to suburbs' isolation, lack of diversity, and long commutes.

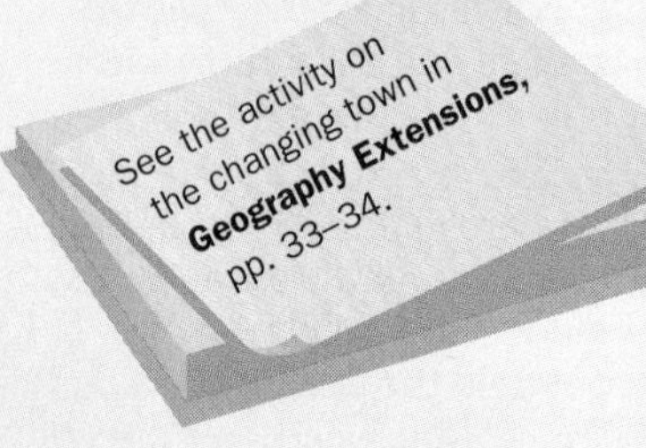

Geography Footnote

In contrast to most of our nation's major urban areas, St. Louis cannot expand its boundaries into the surrounding areas. The city of St. Louis is surrounded by St. Louis County, a separate administrative area that includes the suburbs shown on the map, as well as bordering the Illinois state line. This division was created in 1876 when St. Louis withdrew from St. Louis County and became an independent city. As a result, the city remains 61 square miles. The surrounding county has blocked efforts to expand its borders or to rejoin the county. The population, wealth, manufacturing base, and commercial strength of the city itself have eroded, while those of the county around it have grown. The city of St. Louis proper is ranked 34th in population among United States cities, but the metropolitan area is the 17th largest.

Geography Lab

The Growth of Suburbs

In St. Louis, as in many cities, the suburban boom of the 1950s led to urban "bust." Between 1950 and 1960, the population of St. Louis dropped from 856,800 to 750,000. People were moving to suburbs, which sprouted outside the central city, filling in the spaces between older, once separate communities.

Today the city of St. Louis has about 396,700 people. However, the St. Louis metropolitan area—which includes surrounding communities in Missouri and Illinois—has a population of nearly 2.5 million. Study the map and answer the questions.

By the 1970s extensive freeway networks connected cities and suburbs.

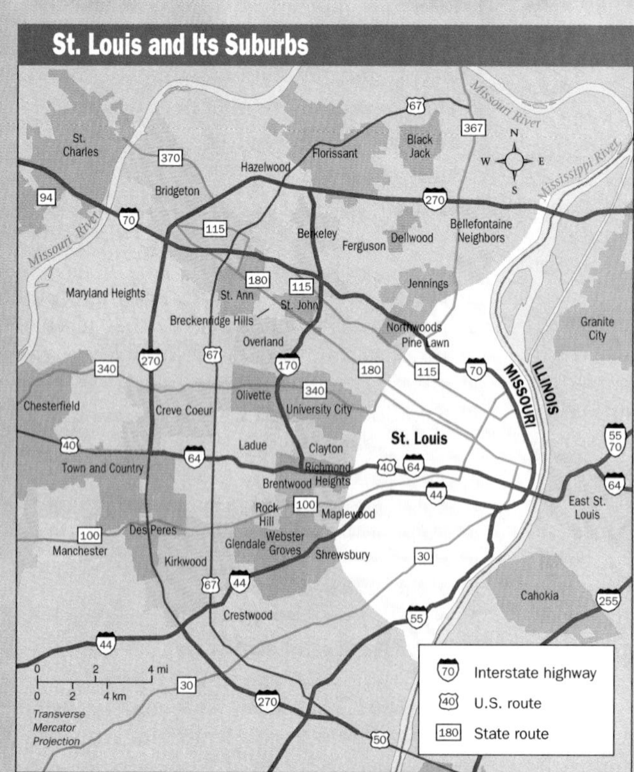

Link to History

1. What makes it possible for people to live in places like Bridgeton and Webster Groves and yet work in downtown St. Louis?

2. You can see that some highways, like Interstate 170, do not go into St. Louis. What inferences about people's jobs and ways of life do you draw from that?

3. Affordable housing was one reason people began moving out of central cities in the 1950s. Name two other reasons that occur to you.

4. **Hands-On Geography** Which suits you better: suburban or city life? Make a collage of pictures and headlines from newspapers and magazines to show why you feel as you do.

Section Objectives

- ★ Identify the "New Frontier" programs proposed by President Kennedy.
- ★ Discuss how President Johnson pursued his vision of the Great Society.
- ★ Explain what destroyed Johnson's Great Society plans.

Teaching Resources

Take-Home Planner 5, pp. 12–19
Chapter Resources Binder
Study Guide, p. 122
Reinforcement, pp. 125–126
Skills Development
Geography Extensions
American Readings
Using Historical Documents
Transparency Activities, pp. 47–48
Chapter and Unit Tests

2. A Spirit of Change

Reading Guide

New Term **civil rights**

Section Focus **The new domestic goals set by John Kennedy and Lyndon Johnson**

1. What "New Frontier" programs did Kennedy propose?
2. How did Johnson pursue his vision of the Great Society?
3. What destroyed Johnson's Great Society plans?

"America is today the strongest, the most influential, and most productive nation in the world." So said President Eisenhower as he prepared to leave office in 1960.

The Presidents who followed Eisenhower faced a two-part challenge. Could they continue to use the nation's strength and wealth to contain communism and protect democracy abroad, and still take care of Americans at home?

The Election of 1960

The presidential election of 1960 focused on that question. The Republicans nominated Vice-President Richard M. Nixon, who promised he would continue Eisenhower's policies.

The Democratic candidate, Senator John F. Kennedy of Massachusetts, faced an uphill battle. Only 43 years old, he was less well known than Nixon. He was also a Catholic, and Americans had never elected a Catholic to the presidency.

This was the first campaign in which television played an important part. In a televised debate, 70 million viewers saw Nixon, weak from a recent illness, looking tired and tense. In contrast, Kennedy, healthy and tanned, looked relaxed and confident. Many historians believe that the debate made the difference, ensuring Kennedy's narrow victory.

Kennedy's "New Frontier"

Filled with idealism and energy, Kennedy immediately set about his goal of "getting the country moving again." He called his program the "New Frontier."

Faced with a recession that had begun in 1960, Kennedy persuaded Congress to pass legislation to create new industries and retrain unemployed workers. He also called for a tax cut to help business.

One of Kennedy's most successful programs still exists—the Peace Corps. Since 1961 thousands of Americans have volunteered for two-year stints in Asia, Africa, and Latin America. They offer their skills as engineers, teachers, and farmers, for example, to help people help themselves.

In 1961 Congress also approved $20 billion for a space program that Kennedy promised would "put a man on the moon" by 1970. The program quickly bore fruit. Within a year, John H. Glenn, Jr., became the first American to orbit the earth.

Poverty Kennedy had less success in attacking problems of poverty and inequality. He had been deeply moved by a book called *The Other America,* by Michael Harrington, who warned: "[The poor] are hungry. . . . They are without adequate housing and education and medical care."

Introducing the Section

Vocabulary

civil rights (p. 608) the rights guaranteed to all Americans by the Constitution

Warm-Up Activity

Creating Images of Domestic Programs

To focus on domestic goals of the 1960s, write *New Frontier* and *Great Society* on the chalkboard. Have small groups list images these names bring to mind and types of legislation they might involve. Have groups compare lists and refer to them as they read the section.

Geography Question of the Day

Tell students that John Kennedy was from Massachusetts, while Lyndon Johnson was a Texan. Have them write paragraphs explaining why such a combination would have been a strong ticket in the presidential election of 1960.

Vital Links

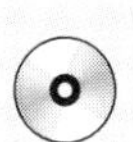

Kennedy on the space program (First Person Account) Unit 6, Side 2, Search 09916, Play to 11121

See also Unit 6 Explore CD-ROM location 357.

History Footnote

The funeral of President John Kennedy on Monday, November 25, was a moving pageant, filled with many traditional and symbolic elements. Many of the same elements had been used 98 years earlier in the funeral of Abraham Lincoln. The drum that accompanied the funeral procession was padded so that it made a mournful sound. Behind the casket was the traditional riderless black horse, with a pair of boots reversed in the stirrups and a silver sword hanging in its scabbard. The flag-draped casket was set on a caisson (two-wheeled wagon) pulled by six white horses. Military taps were played at the graveside, and the President's widow lit the eternal flame.

Developing the Section

Section Activity

A New Frontier/ Great Society Display

To focus on the Kennedy-Johnson legacy, have students create a display titled "New Frontier and Great Society: Where Are They Now?" Have them identify each achievement, illustrate it, and provide an update on its impact today. For example, the space program might be illustrated by a rocket, followed by an update giving milestones up to the present.

See the Study Guide activity in **Chapter Resources Binder,** p. 122.

Teaching the Hands-On HISTORY

To help students brainstorm, suggest some questions such as "Where were you and what were you doing when you learned of the assassination?," "What was your first reaction?," "How did others around you react?," and "What other things do you remember about it?"

To get at the causes of poverty, Kennedy proposed more federal aid to improve schools and city housing. He also asked for laws providing health insurance for the aged. Congress refused to act. As you will read in Section 3, Congress also refused to pass a bill to enforce African Americans' **civil rights**—the rights guaranteed to all Americans by the Constitution.

Kennedy's Assassination

Looking ahead to a second term, Kennedy hoped to have more success with his programs to fight poverty and protect civil rights. He never got the chance.

In Dallas, Texas, on November 22, 1963, Kennedy and his wife, Jacqueline, were riding in an open car past cheering crowds when rifle shots rang out. The President slumped forward. Struck in the neck and the head, he died quickly.

That day Dallas police arrested a young man named Lee Harvey Oswald and charged him with the President's assassination. Two days later, while police were moving him to another jail, Oswald himself was shot dead by a man named Jack Ruby.

In 1964 an investigation by the Warren Commission, headed by Chief Justice Earl Warren, concluded that Oswald had acted alone. Still, many people were sure that Oswald was part of a group that had planned the assassination. Although the evidence was examined again in the 1970s, the motive for the murder remains a mystery.

Hands-On HISTORY

Collecting memories of Kennedy's assassination A woman who was a teenager when John F. Kennedy was assassinated remembers it this way: "I was in English class when the public address system suddenly came on, but it was not the principal talking. It was a radio broadcast, a very confused one. It took us a few minutes to realize what was being said—that President Kennedy had been shot. My teacher started crying. I felt frozen, numb."

This frame from a home movie shows Kennedy being struck by the first bullet.

Activity Interview an adult who remembers the assassination of President Kennedy.

1. Ask the person for permission to do the interview and to share the results with your class.
2. Before the interview, write a list of questions. Plan to ask for personal recollections of the assassination.
3. Conduct the interview. Tape it or make detailed notes. If the person says something you want to hear more about, ask follow-up questions.
4. Report on the interview. Play the tape or quote the questions and answers. Include your observations about the person's reactions.

History Footnote

The Head Start program, created in 1965 as part of Lyndon Johnson's Great Society, was an important milestone in the federal government's campaign to remedy the problems of disadvantaged preschoolers. Both Head Start and the Title I programs of the Elementary and Secondary Education Act of 1965 that targeted grade-school children were based on the same theory. Educators felt that remedial programs were most effective when applied early in the lives of youngsters, before the effects of cultural, economic, and social disadvantages became too great to overcome. The lessons of Head Start have since been applied to other target groups. These include students with limited English proficiency (the Bilingual Education Act of 1967) and disabled children (the Education for All Handicapped Children Act of 1975).

Americans were stunned by Kennedy's death. They had taken to their hearts their handsome young President, his glamorous wife, and two young children. The nation was plunged into mourning.

Johnson's "Great Society"

Two hours after Kennedy's death, Vice-President Lyndon B. Johnson was sworn in as President. Americans, Johnson later recalled, "were like a bunch of cattle caught in the swamp, . . . circling 'round and 'round." As a Texan who had grown up in cattle country, he knew that

> "there is but one way to get the cattle out of the swamp. And that is for the man on the horse to take the lead."

President Johnson was prepared to be that man. He had served in Congress for 23 years. A tireless worker and brilliant political deal maker, he was able to turn Kennedy's vision, as well as his own, into law.

Civil rights Although Johnson was a southerner, he was deeply committed to the cause of civil rights. "I never had any bigotry in me," he explained. "My daddy wouldn't let me. He was a strong anti-Klansman."

As you will read in Section 3, under Johnson's leadership, Congress passed the first significant civil rights laws since Reconstruction. President Johnson also appointed the first black Supreme Court justice—NAACP lawyer Thurgood Marshall—and the first black cabinet member—economist Robert C. Weaver.

The war on poverty Johnson also shared Kennedy's desire to end poverty. As a teacher in Cotulla, Texas, he had known students who were too poor even to bring lunch to school. Early in 1964 Johnson called for a "war on poverty." He told Congress:

First Lady Jacqueline Kennedy, still in her blood-stained clothes, looks on as Lyndon Johnson takes the oath of office aboard Air Force One at the Dallas airport.

> "Many Americans live on the outskirts of hope, some because of their poverty and some because of their color, and all too many because of both."

That year Congress passed the Economic Opportunity Act, providing almost $1 billion for antipoverty programs. One program offered job training for unemployed young people in inner cities. Another sent volunteers into cities to teach reading and job skills. A third, the Head Start program, helped preschoolers learn the skills they would need in school.

Johnson hoped that these programs would help Americans to create a "Great Society." This new society, he said, "rests on abundance and liberty for all. It demands an end to poverty and racial injustice."

The 1964 election In the election of 1964 the Republican candidate, Senator Barry Goldwater of Arizona, attacked the Great Society programs as unnecessary and wasteful. He also criticized Johnson for not taking a tougher stand in the Cold War.

Discussion

Checking Understanding

1. How did Johnson's life affect his commitment to fight poverty and injustice? (Father instilled a hatred for bigotry; as young teacher, saw evils of poverty.)

Stimulating Critical Thinking

2. Compare the Great Society and New Deal programs. (Reflected belief that government should help citizens; New Deal focused on helping farmers and workers; Great Society dealt more with civil rights, poverty, health, education.)

Bonus Activity

Writing a Song or Poem

To explore emotions of the 1960s, have students write folk songs or poems from the point of view of a teenager then. They may focus on one issue or on the times in general. Ask students to share their writings with the class.

Vital Links

Johnson on the Great Society (First Person Account) Unit 6, Side 1, Search 24764, Play to 25962

See also Unit 6 Explore CD-ROM location 139.

Connections to Art

Robert Rauschenberg is considered one of the fathers of the most famous art style to emerge in the 1960s—pop art. Rauschenberg's decision to include popular images and well-known faces and objects in his collages helped pave the way to the art of such figures as Andy Warhol—who re-created Coke bottles, Brillo boxes, and Campbell's soup cans as art objects—and Roy Lichtenstein, who painted large comic book scenes. Pop artists chose as their subjects the everyday material of life in the 1960s. They reflected the interest in celebrities, advertising, and consumer products. As the 1960s grew more turbulent, pop art became a mirror of society.

Teaching the

Link to Art

Ask why a collage is a good way to represent the 1960s. Have students identify images and name others the artist might have used. **Discussion Answers:** To mirror era; content and arrangement reflect turmoil and tragedy.

Closing the Section

Wrap-Up Activity

Asking Kennedy and Johnson

Have pairs write three questions they would have asked each President about his goals and accomplishments, and answers they think each would have given. Then discuss as a class.

Section Review Answers

1. Definition: *civil rights* (608)

2. Job training for unemployed youth, sending volunteers to cities to teach reading and job skills, Head Start, Medicare, Medicaid.

3. Took money needed for Great Society programs.

4. Yes: Kennedy expanded spending with Peace Corps, federal aid for education and housing, civil rights, and space program. No: both wanted to keep nation strong and help citizens by increasing benefits.

Link to Art

Signs **(1970) As an art student, Robert Rauschenberg studied photography. Later he began to use collage (kuh-LAHZH), a method of creating a work of art by gluing pictures and other materials onto paper or canvas.**

In *Signs,* Rauschenberg made a collage of the 1960s out of newspaper and magazine photographs of memorable people and events of that time. Discuss Why might Rauschenberg have chosen these images? What do you think he wants you to think about the 1960s?

The conservative Goldwater did not appeal to all Republicans. Many moderates voted instead for Johnson. On election day, Johnson swept to victory with more than 61 percent of the votes.

Expanding the Great Society Now Johnson pressed successfully for more Great Society legislation. A flood of bills poured through Congress in 1965. The Elementary and Secondary School Act granted more than $1 billion to education. In health care, Congress established the Medicare program for the aged and the Medicaid program to help the needy and the disabled.

Congress also created the Department of Housing and Urban Development (HUD). Headed by Secretary Robert Weaver, HUD made housing available to low-income families and helped local and state governments with urban problems.

The Great Society stalls At the same time that he was building his Great Society, however, President Johnson was pouring money into the war in Vietnam. As the cost of the war skyrocketed, funds for programs at home dried up. "The Great Society has been shot down on the battlefields of Vietnam," said Martin Luther King, Jr., sadly.

As you read in Chapter 13, President Johnson's hopes for re-election in 1968 were shot down as well. Nonetheless, he left a strong legacy. Under his leadership, Congress took its first steps against racial discrimination and the poverty that it had created.

2. Section Review

1. Define **civil rights.**
2. Describe two programs set up as part of President Johnson's war on poverty.
3. How did the Vietnam War affect Johnson's plans for the Great Society?
4. Critical Thinking Do you think that President Kennedy succeeded in leading the nation in a direction different from that of President Eisenhower? Explain.

Section Objectives

- ★ Discuss how African Americans broke down legal barriers to equality.
- ★ Explain how the African American struggle for equality became a mass movement.
- ★ Identify changes that women, Hispanics, and American Indians brought about.

Teaching Resources

Take-Home Planner 5, pp. 12–19
Chapter Resources Binder
Study Guide, p. 123
Reinforcement
Skills Development
Geography Extensions
American Readings, pp. 61–64
Using Historical Documents
Transparency Activities
Chapter and Unit Tests

Introducing the Section

Vocabulary

integration (p. 611) the process of ending segregation

Warm-Up Activity

Defining Equality

Ask students to write several different meanings of the term *equality* and give examples of each use. Then have them write a definition concerning human relationships. Have them save their definitions to compare with Thurgood Marshall's on page 611.

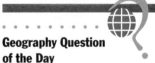

3. Fighting for Equal Rights

Reading Guide

New Term integration

Section Focus Struggles to achieve justice and equal rights in the 1950s–1970s

1. **How did African Americans break down legal barriers to equality?**
2. **How did the African American struggle for equality become a mass movement?**
3. **What changes did women, Hispanics, and American Indians bring about?**

Soon after World War II, when an African American veteran named Medgar Evers tried to vote, he was driven away from his polling place at gunpoint. A Mexican American veteran, Macario García, was refused service in a restaurant.

Before the war, such treatment was common. Now, however, thousands of veterans like Evers and García were no longer willing to accept discrimination. They had fought for democracy around the world, and now they wanted equal rights and opportunities at home.

Taking Court Action

Like many African American veterans, Medgar Evers joined the NAACP. Since its birth in 1909 (see page 352) it had dedicated itself to protecting African Americans' civil rights. The NAACP pressed for laws enforcing those rights, and its lawyers went to court again and again to obtain equal opportunities for black Americans.

However, Jim Crow laws continued to impose segregation in the South. To attack it, the NAACP had to convince the Supreme Court to move away from *Plessy* v. *Ferguson*, which had ruled that segregation laws were constitutional as long as facilities for both races were roughly equal (see pages 198–200).

Brown* v. *Board of Education In 1952 the Court agreed to review the "separate but equal" rule in the case *Brown* v. *Board of Education*. The case had been filed by Oliver Brown. He had sued the Topeka, Kansas, school board because his 8-year-old daughter, Linda, was forced to go 21 blocks by bus to a black school when there was a white school only 7 blocks from her home.

In court, NAACP lawyer Thurgood Marshall argued that segregated schools could never be equal. The fact of being segregated, he claimed, made children feel inferior no matter how good the school might be. Asked what he meant by *equal*, Marshall replied,

> "Equal means getting the same thing, at the same time, and in the same place."

In 1954 Chief Justice Earl Warren delivered the Court's unanimous decision: Segregated schools were unequal and thus unconstitutional. By destroying the legal basis for segregation, this historic decision reopened the road to equality.

Conflict at Little Rock After the *Brown* ruling, many white southern leaders called for resistance to **integration**—the process of ending segregation. In 1957 a federal court ordered the integration of a high school in

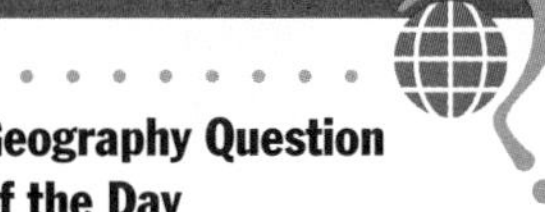

Geography Question of the Day

Have students look at the map on pp. R6–R7. Have them find the following locations that played an important part in the civil rights struggle: Little Rock, Arkansas; Montgomery and Birmingham, Alabama; Los Angeles, California; Memphis, Tennessee; and Washington, D.C. Have them write the name of each place on a sheet of paper and, as they read the section, write a sentence about why the location is significant.

For an account of going to segregated schools in the South, see **American Readings**, pp. 61–62.

Developing the Section

Section Activity

A TV Talk Show

To review civil rights issues, have small groups present TV talk shows with Martin Luther King, Jr., Malcolm X, Cesar Chavez, Betty Friedan, and Wilma Mankiller. Have them write the moderator's questions, panelists' responses, and comments panelists might make to each other. Sample questions might be "What have you tried to accomplish in your life?," "What is the best way to call attention to your cause?," "What is your greatest achievement?," and "What is your greatest failure?" Groups may present their talk shows to the class.

Vital Links

"Sister Rosa" (Song) Unit 6, Side 1, Search 51260, Play to 53958

See also Unit 6 Explore CD-ROM location 66.

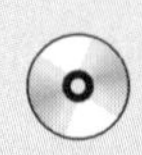

Little Rock students (Movie) Unit 5, Side 1, Search 44429, Play to 44992

See also Unit 5 Explore CD-ROM location 270.

History Footnote

Montgomery, Alabama, is home to the Civil Rights Memorial, created to honor those killed in the struggle for justice. The memorial was the idea of Morris Dees, a white Montgomery lawyer and civil rights crusader who cofounded the Southern Poverty Law Center, where the memorial is located. Designed by Maya Lin, architect of the Vietnam Veterans Memorial, it was dedicated in 1989. It includes a paraphrase of a verse from the Book of Amos that was a favorite of Martin Luther King, Jr.: "until justice rolls down like waters and righteousness like a mighty stream." This quote is carved into a nine-foot-high wall of black granite. Nearby stands a round granite "table," on which are carved the movement's milestones and the names of 40 people killed between 1954 and 1968. Water flows over the wall and table.

Little Rock, Arkansas. Nine black students enrolled, but shouting, spitting white mobs kept them from entering the school.

Finally President Eisenhower sent troops to Little Rock to protect the students. Even so, recalled one of the students, "Every day something more horrible happened."

Bit by bit, though, brave black students, supported by NAACP lawyers, insisted on their right to attend integrated schools and colleges. Lawyers attacked other segregation laws, too. In case after case, the Court struck down segregation in public facilities such as parks and beaches.

Taking Direct Action

While lawyers worked through the courts, black citizens were organizing to take direct action against segregation. This growing civil rights movement made news in 1955 when Rosa Parks was arrested in Montgomery, Alabama, for refusing to give up her seat on a city bus to a white man.

As 15-year-old Elizabeth Eckford tried to enter Little Rock's Central High School, an angry mob screamed, "Get her! Lynch her!" Arkansas National Guardsmen turned her away at the door.

The Montgomery bus boycott The day after Parks's arrest, black citizens of Montgomery called a mass meeting. Led by Martin Luther King, Jr., they voted to boycott all city buses.

The city fought back, jailing many of the boycott leaders. White segregationists turned to violence. They bombed four churches and King's home.

In response, King preached the power of nonviolent resistance. "The only weapon that we have in our hands is the weapon of protest," he said. The peaceful boycott continued until in 1956 the Supreme Court outlawed segregation on local bus lines.

Student sit-ins King's belief in nonviolent protest inspired thousands to challenge discrimination with direct action. Students took a leading role, confronting segregation wherever it occurred.

On February 1, 1960, four black college students sat down at a whites-only Woolworth's lunch counter in Greensboro, North Carolina. When the waitress refused to serve them, they sat there until the store closed. Joined by other students, they returned day after day.

Sit-ins quickly spread through the South. In April student leaders of the movement formed the Student Nonviolent Coordinating Committee (SNCC) to coordinate the sit-in effort.

In the next year, 70,000 people, mostly black, but some white, took part in demonstrations in 100 cities. More than 3,600 were jailed. By the end of 1960, however, lunch counters in Greensboro and many other southern towns were open to African Americans.

Connections to Civics

As a result of legislation such as the 1965 Voting Rights Act and voter registration drives by numerous groups over several decades, African Americans now hold thousands of local, state, and national offices across the country. Among the best-known black elected officials of the past several decades is Andrew Young, a close associate of Martin Luther King, Jr. Young served in Congress as a representative from Georgia from 1973–1977 and was mayor of Atlanta from 1982–1989. Richard Arlington was elected mayor of Birmingham, a city scarred by civil rights violence, in 1979.

Sit-in protestors bravely practiced nonviolent resistance as angry whites shouted abuse and smeared them with catsup, mustard, and sugar.

Freedom Riders A "sit-in on wheels" was equally successful. In May 1961 the Congress of Racial Equality (CORE), founded by James Farmer in 1942, sent a group of black and white "Freedom Riders" to ride interstate buses through the South.

Two buses left Washington, D.C., for New Orleans. They never got there. In Alabama mobs beat the riders and burned one of the buses. New riders arrived and were also attacked. The Freedom Riders won, though. President Kennedy ordered the integration of all buses, trains, and terminals.

Crisis in Birmingham

Nonviolence was met with violence again in Birmingham, Alabama, in April 1963. There King had launched peaceful demonstrations against discrimination in stores, restaurants, and workplaces. Birmingham police chief Eugene "Bull" Connor ordered fire hoses and police dogs turned on the protestors. Televised images of the police attacks helped turn public opinion against segregation.

Gandhi and nonviolence India offered dramatic proof of what nonviolence could achieve. There, Mohandas K. Gandhi used nonviolent resistance to force Britain to grant independence to India.

A lawyer, Gandhi became a leader of the independence movement about 1920. He and his followers refused to buy British goods. They stopped trains by lying down on the tracks. They sat in front of government buildings, forcing officials to climb over them. Gandhi was arrested many times, but India finally won its independence in 1947.

Howard Thurman, an African American teacher and minister, traveled to India in 1935 to learn about Gandhi's philosophy of nonviolence. Thurman later passed the philosophy on to his university students, who included James Farmer and Martin Luther King, Jr.

Point of View

Were the demonstrations in Birmingham necessary?

During the demonstrations Martin Luther King, Jr., was arrested. While he was in jail, a group of white Birmingham ministers criticized the demonstrations as "unwise and untimely." In a letter to the ministers, King defended the need for resistance. He wrote:

"Injustice must be exposed . . . to the light of human conscience and the air of national opinion before it can be cured."

Discussion

Checking Understanding

1. What was the cause of the Montgomery bus boycott? (Rosa Parks, a black woman, was arrested for refusing to give up her seat to a white man, as the law required.)

2. What were the Freedom Riders trying to accomplish? (The integration of buses, trains, and terminals.)

Stimulating Critical Thinking

3. Do you agree with King that peaceful protest was the only weapon opponents of segregation had? Explain. (Yes: armed resistance would have been suicidal; peaceful resistance sways public opinion favorably, showing unjust ways of police and officials. No: rioting or other more violent methods might have brought change as well.)

Teaching the World Link

Explain that at the time of independence, India had two main religious groups: the majority Hindus and the minority Muslims. Violent conflict led to the creation of two nations, Hindu-majority India and almost entirely Muslim Pakistan. After independence, India still retained a large Muslim minority. Although Gandhi's nonviolent campaign did achieve independence from Britain, it could not prevent the religious conflict, and Gandhi himself was murdered by a Hindu who opposed Gandhi's call for reconciliation.

Teaching the Point of View

After students read King's reply to the ministers, point out that these ministers were liberals and moderates who had denounced segregation. They and others who criticized King's actions thought that the city of Birmingham was making progress in race relations, even if this progress was slow, and that the protests were upsetting, extreme actions. You may also wish to tell students that King had a friend, Clarence Jones, who smuggled newspapers to him while he was in jail. It was in one of these newspapers that he read the ministers' letter, and he began to write his famous reply in the blank spaces between its columns.

Vital Links

"Keep On a-Travelin' On" (Song) Unit 6, Side 2, Search 05076, Play to 07468

See also Unit 6 Explore CD-ROM location 58.

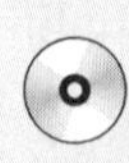
Martin Luther King, Jr. (Movie) Unit 6, Side 2, Search 08738, Play to 09912

See also Unit 6 Explore CD-ROM location 48.

Tips for Teaching

Auditory Learners

Auditory learners respond well to recordings. Have them listen to key civil rights speeches, noting techniques and images that make them striking. For instance, they might note use of repetition in King's "I Have a Dream" speech and striking phrases such as "the content of their character."

For lyrics from some civil rights songs, see **American Readings**, p. 63.

As for timeliness, King continued:

> "I have never yet engaged in a direct action movement that was 'well-timed,' according to the timetable of those who have not suffered unduly from the disease of segregation. For years now I have heard the word 'Wait!' . . . This 'wait' has almost always meant 'never.'"

Protestors often face questions about whether and when to take action to call attention to their cause. King's "Letter from Birmingham Jail" has become famous as a defense of nonviolent action and the goals of the civil rights movement.

Enforcing Civil Rights

In June 1963 President Kennedy gave his strong support to the struggle for civil rights. He asked Congress to pass a civil rights bill to provide "the equality of treatment which we would want ourselves."

Police in Birmingham who used fire hoses to break up a civil rights demonstration were fighting "a fire that won't go out."

March on Washington To show their support for Kennedy's civil rights bill, more than 200,000 people took part in a march on Washington, D.C., on August 28. In a famous speech, King captured the idealism of the marchers:

> "I have a dream that one day this nation will rise up and live out the true meaning of its creed . . . 'that all men are created equal.'"

The Civil Rights Act of 1964 After Kennedy's death, Lyndon Johnson pushed the Civil Rights Act of 1964 through Congress. It banned discrimination in public places such as restaurants. It also banned discrimination in hiring on the basis of race, religion, gender, or nationality. It halted federal aid to segregated institutions. This act placed the federal government squarely on the side of the fight for equality.

Voting rights Civil rights leaders knew that the best way to gain and protect the rights of African Americans was through the ballot box. Thus in the summer of 1964 they launched a campaign to register black voters. Hundreds of volunteers, black and white, risked their lives to help.

Early in 1965 King led a march from Selma, Alabama, to Montgomery, the state capital, to demand voting rights. On the way, police attacked the marchers. Shocked by television pictures of "Bloody Sunday," the public demanded that Congress act.

In response, Congress passed the Voting Rights Act of 1965. Where African

History Footnote

Malcolm X was born Malcolm Little in Omaha, Nebraska, in 1925. His family moved to Michigan, where his father, a Baptist minister and follower of black nationalist Marcus Garvey, was murdered. His mother suffered a nervous breakdown and was placed in a mental institution. Malcolm was sent first to a foster home and then to a reform school. As a teenager he moved to Boston, where he was sent to jail for burglary. In jail he came into contact with the Nation of Islam and became a member of the group. He was released in 1952, and by 1960 was the group's leading spokesperson and an advocate of racial separation. In 1964, however, he made a pilgrimage to Mecca, Saudi Arabia. There he saw Muslims of many colors gathering together as equals. As a result of his pilgrimage, he moved away from black separatism.

Americans had not been able to register, it allowed federal officials to register them. It also banned literacy tests as a voting requirement. The new law, and the Twenty-fourth Amendment banning poll taxes, opened voting booths to black southerners. By 1968, 60 percent were registered, compared with only 20 percent in 1952.

The Movement Splinters

Black southerners rejoiced over the freedoms they were winning for themselves. In northern cities, however, racial discrimination was based on customs rather than on laws that could be challenged in court. Thus there was little improvement in the lives of black northerners, who faced unemployment and decaying housing and schools.

Frustrated, many African Americans in the North turned to Malcolm X. A minister of the Nation of Islam (the Black Muslims), Malcolm X rejected King's call for nonviolence. He told black Americans to fight back. Like Marcus Garvey, he also urged them to start their own businesses, govern their own communities, and take pride in their African heritage.

Bitter disagreements led Malcolm X to quit the Nation of Islam in 1964. A year later three Black Muslims gunned him down.

Malcolm X's ideas lived on, though. They had a powerful influence on a number of young black leaders. One was Stokely Carmichael, who condemned white America as racist and called for "black power."

Most people thought black power meant working together to build black economic and political power. A few, though, took it as a call to armed revolt against white society.

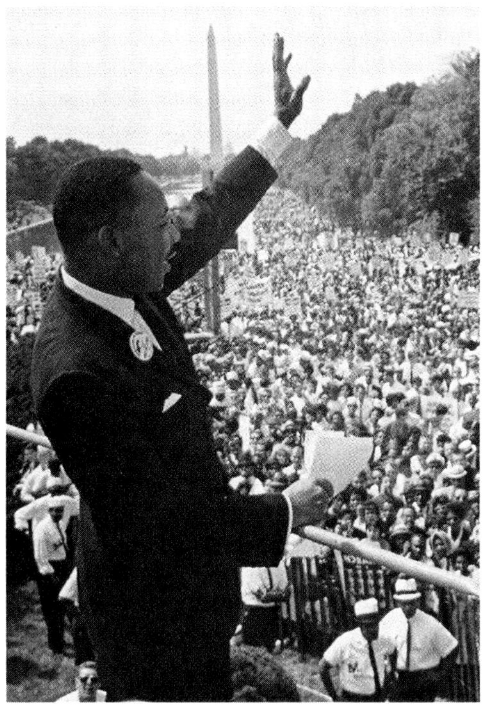

Civil rights marchers of all races and from all parts of the nation took part in the 1963 March on Washington. Martin Luther King, Jr., summed up their hopes in his "I Have a Dream" speech.

Urban violence Before he died, Malcolm X warned Americans that they were sitting on a "racial powder keg." The keg exploded in August 1965 in Watts, a black neighborhood in Los Angeles. Rumors of police brutality set off a riot that lasted 6 days and claimed 34 lives. During the next three years, almost every major American city was torn by riots.

President Johnson set up the Kerner Commission to investigate the violence. In 1968 the commission reported its findings. One of the basic causes of the riots, it said, was "discrimination in employment and education" and "segregated housing and schools."

King, too, was concerned about the related problems of racism and poverty. In April 1968 he went to Memphis, Tennessee, to support a strike of sanitation workers. While standing on a balcony outside his hotel room, he was shot by a white segregationist.

Discussion

Checking Understanding

1. What did the Civil Rights Act of 1964 do? (Banned discrimination in public places and hiring practices, halted federal aid to segregated institutions.)

2. What did the Voting Rights Act of 1965 do? (Banned literacy tests, allowed federal officials to register black voters.)

Stimulating Critical Thinking

3. Do you agree with Malcolm X that black Americans needed to fight back? (Yes: needed to show strength and power. No: need to use legal means to change laws; violence invites retaliation.)

Vital Links

Watts riots (Picture) Unit 6, Side 1, Search 06888

See also Unit 6 Explore CD-ROM location 61.

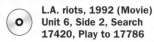

L.A. riots, 1992 (Movie) Unit 6, Side 2, Search 17420, Play to 17786

See also Unit 6 Explore CD-ROM location 291.

Bonus Activity

Singing Civil Rights Songs

To help students understand the role that music played in the civil rights movement, have them learn several "freedom songs." Well-known songs frequently collected in songbooks include "Go Down, Moses," "Oh, Freedom," "If I Had a Hammer," "We Shall Not Be Moved," "This Little Light of Mine," and "We Shall Overcome." Have students obtain recordings and report on the backgrounds of various songs. If possible, have student musicians learn several songs and lead the class in singing them. Conclude by having the class discuss how music contributed to the success of the civil rights movement.

Vital Links

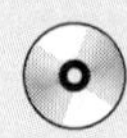

Voice of housewife (First Person Account) Unit 6, Side 1, Search 09579, Play to 10298

See also Unit 6 Explore CD-ROM location 90.

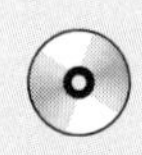

Voice of Mary Crow Dog (First Person Account) Unit 6, Side 1, Search 07586, Play to 08456

See also Unit 6 Explore CD-ROM location 74.

Connections to Economics

A dispute between the United Farm Workers, the union founded by Cesar Chavez and Dolores Huerta in 1962, and a large California lettuce grower, Red Coach, began in 1978 and included lawsuits, a boycott, and a lengthy strike. The dispute lasted until 1996. By then both Chavez and the Red Coach president had died, but their successors were able to reach an agreement that satisfied both sides. The settlement raised wages, created various health and pension benefits, and included a no-strike pledge.

For memories of a migrant farm worker, see **American Readings**, p. 64.

King's death set off riots in more than 60 cities and an outpouring of grief among Americans of all races.

Gains of the movement Although the struggle for equality and economic opportunity was far from over, the civil rights movement had accomplished a great deal. It had removed the legal basis for segregation. By protecting voting rights it also offered African Americans the keys to political power.

For the first time since Reconstruction, black southerners were elected to political offices. Birmingham, the city where "Bull" Connor had unleashed his police dogs, elected its first black mayor in 1979.

The Women's Movement

Women who took part in the civil rights movement were inspired to take action to gain equality for themselves. In 1960 most working women could find jobs only in low-paying clerical, sales, or food services positions. Even when they did the same jobs as men, they earned less money.

Although the 1964 Civil Rights Act banned job discrimination against women, employment practices were slow to change. "I've suffered more discrimination as a woman," reported Congresswoman Shirley Chisholm, "than as a black."

In 1966 author Betty Friedan helped found the National Organization for Women (NOW). NOW worked with other women's groups to win passage of laws requiring equal pay for equal work.

In 1972 Congress responded by passing the Equal Rights Amendment (ERA) to the Constitution. It would have banned all discrimination on the basis of gender. The ERA failed ratification, though. Opponents argued that it would take away important legal protections for women and make them subject to the draft.

Despite this setback, the women's movement opened new opportunities—in business, government, the armed forces, and sports. By the late 1970s, it was no longer surprising to see women working as coal miners, police officers, doctors, television newscasters, and astronauts.

Hispanics Organize

Since the 1920s Americans of Mexican, Puerto Rican, Cuban, and Central and South American heritage had fought discrimination and encouraged cultural pride through organizations such as the League of United Latin American Citizens (LULAC). The civil rights movement inspired them to new efforts.

For example, in the 1960s Mexican Americans, the largest group of Hispanics, began to organize to demand their rights and fight discrimination. Many Mexican Americans were farmworkers who had none of the rights and protections of factory workers. Their leader, Cesar Chavez, believed that a union was the only way they could win fair treatment from landowners.

In 1962 Chavez, with his wife, Helen, and Dolores Huerta, a teacher, formed the United Farm Workers (UFW) in California. They launched strikes and boycotts to gain better wages and working conditions. Like King, Chavez was committed to a "totally nonviolent struggle for justice." In 1970 the UFW finally won a great victory—the right to bargain for workers in talks with California grape growers.

Meanwhile, in the cities young Mexican Americans launched the *Chicano* (chee-KAH-noh) movement. Their goal was to gain political power, equal opportunities in business and education, and respect for their Mexican heritage. In Miami, with its large Cuban American population, and other cities, Hispanics increasingly won elective office and made their voices heard in schools and the workplace.

History Footnote

Since 1820, the Cherokee Nation has been ruled by a government modeled after the U.S. government, with a legislature and an elected chief. In 1985 Wilma Mankiller was elected chief of the Cherokee Nation, headquartered in Tahlequah, Oklahoma. As chief, Mankiller administered a $76 million budget, supervised 1,200 employees, and created health care, educational, and social service programs for the 156,000 people of the Cherokee Nation. She faced many challenges including high unemployment, poor educational opportunities, and numerous health-care problems. For ten years, Mankiller helped organize new businesses, schools, and construction projects, as well as lobbying efforts in Washington, D.C. She said being chief is like "being president of a tiny country, a CEO, and a social worker."

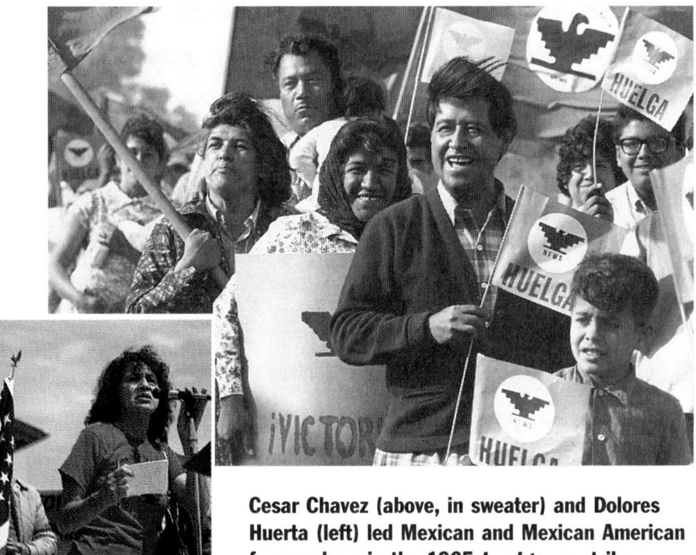

Cesar Chavez (above, in sweater) and Dolores Huerta (left) led Mexican and Mexican American farmworkers in the 1965 *huelga*, or strike, against California grape growers.

Indians Seek Recognition

In the 1960s and 1970s American Indians also learned to make the public aware of their need for respect and for better educational and economic opportunities. A central issue was gaining the right to manage their own affairs.

For Indians, World War II had unleashed forces of change that continue to this day. The armed forces and wartime jobs brought Indians off their reservations. After the war Indians continued to move from reservations to urban areas. Still, few Indians could break out of the cycle of discrimination and poverty.

Drawing on the lessons of the civil rights movement, Indian activists found ways to call public attention to their problems. In 1969 a group of Indians took over Alcatraz Island in San Francisco Bay. In 1972 leaders of the American Indian Movement (AIM) took over the offices of the Bureau of Indian Affairs in Washington, D.C. A year later AIM members occupied Wounded Knee, South Dakota.

Self-determination Indian actions caught the attention of President Nixon, who called for a government policy of self-determination. In 1975 Congress passed the Indian Self-Determination and Energy Act. It was a major step in giving tribes control over the government programs that affected them.

Indians also defended their rights in court. In Alaska, Maine, and Massachusetts they won payment for lands taken by the federal government. They regained old rights to fish and cut timber. Many western tribes also gained control of valuable mineral deposits discovered beneath their lands.

Despite ongoing problems—on reservations and in cities—Indian faith in the future remains strong. In 1990 Cherokee chief Wilma Mankiller predicted that "500 years from now there will still be strong tribal communities . . . where ancient languages, ceremonies, and songs will be heard."

3. Section Review

1. Define **integration.**
2. Explain the reasoning behind the Supreme Court decision in the *Brown* case.
3. Describe two methods that were used for promoting integration in the South. How successful were these methods?
4. Name at least one issue that concerned each group: women, Hispanic Americans, and American Indians.
5. **Critical Thinking** Imagine that Cesar Chavez asked you, as a farmworker, to join his union even though it could cost your job. How would you respond? Why?

Closing the Section

Wrap-Up Activity

Comparing Two Leaders

To compare Martin Luther King, Jr., and Malcolm X, have students create two profiles. Under a photo or illustration of each leader, have them list their beliefs, religions, biographical details, important milestones, and well-known quotations. Conclude by discussing the comparisons.

Section Review

Answers

1. Definition: *integration* (611)

2. Because they were separate, segregated schools were unequal and therefore unconstitutional.

3. Legal challenges against Jim Crow laws, protest marches, boycotts, sit-ins, Freedom Rides, federal court orders for school integration, Civil Rights Act of 1964. These methods removed the legal basis for segregation.

4. Women: equal pay for equal work, gender discrimination, ERA. Hispanics: discrimination, respect for heritage, fair treatment for farmworkers, political power, equal opportunities in business and education. Indians: respect for their traditions, better educational and economic opportunities, self-determination, payment for lands, control of natural resources on Indian lands.

5. Yes: I'm tired of low wages and poor working conditions. No: I will not be able to find a new job.

Picture Essay

Teaching the Picture Essay

In this feature, students will learn about the civil rights movement through a series of pictures and captions. Picture essays not only enhance students' knowledge of history but also help students understand the value of different types of information sources. Visual learners especially will enjoy and benefit from the picture essay. The feature also will help students with limited English—who may be intimidated by lengthy written text—focus on important points about the movement.

Have students study the entire feature before answering the Discussion questions or doing the Wrap-Up Activity. You may assign the Bonus Activity as an alternative to, or in addition to, the Wrap-Up Activity.

Warm-Up Activity

Listing Picture Ideas

To prepare students to study the feature, have small groups review pages 611–616 and list ideas for six more photographs on the black civil rights movement that the editors could have included. The photos can be ones that students have seen or ones that they imagine might exist. Have students look to see how many of their ideas are in the picture essay.

Essay Objectives

Use pictures and captions to trace the civil rights movement, with these emphases:

★ Identify some contributions made by African Americans in the fields of music, government, and sports through the 1940s.

★ Describe struggles and gains in the fight against segregation in the 1950s.

★ Summarize the background and results of the Voting Rights Act of 1965.

PICTURE ESSAY

The Civil Rights Movement

1

2

3

1. Leaders of the Niagara Movement pose in 1905 before the falls that gave their movement its name. The group led by W. E. B. Du Bois, middle row, second from the right, met to draw up demands for full civil rights and an end to segregation. Five years later this movement gave birth to the National Association for the Advancement of Colored People (NAACP).

2. In the 1920s, African Americans migrating northward brought a significant contribution to American music—the spread of jazz. Jazz performers enjoyed popularity around the world. Among the many great jazz performers was the vocalist Bessie Smith, who won the title "Empress of the Blues." A series of recordings she made from 1923 to 1933 rank among the best in jazz. Louis Armstrong, Fletcher Henderson, Joe Smith, and James P. Johnson were a few of the jazz musicians who played on her records.

3. Presidents Calvin Coolidge, Herbert Hoover, Franklin D. Roosevelt, and Harry S Truman appointed Mary McLeod Bethune, an African American educator, to various government posts. From 1935 to 1944, she served as Roosevelt's Special Advisor on Minority Affairs. Bethune also served, from 1936 to 1944, as director of the Division of Negro Affairs of the National Youth Administration. When she took this office, she became the first black woman to head a federal agency.

History Footnote

The troops sent to Little Rock by President Eisenhower stayed through the school year. For Melba Pattillo Beals, one of the "Little Rock Nine," it was a year of mixed emotions: "There was a feeling of pride and hope that yes, this is the United States; yes, there is a reason I salute the flag; and it's going to be okay. . . . The troops did not, however, mean the end of harassment. . . . I worried about . . . which part of the hall to walk in that's the safest. Who's going to hit me with what? Is it going to be hot soup today?"

Not all the white people of Little Rock were cruel to the African American students. Student Elizabeth Eckford (pictured on p. 612) recalled some gestures of support from white adults.

5

4

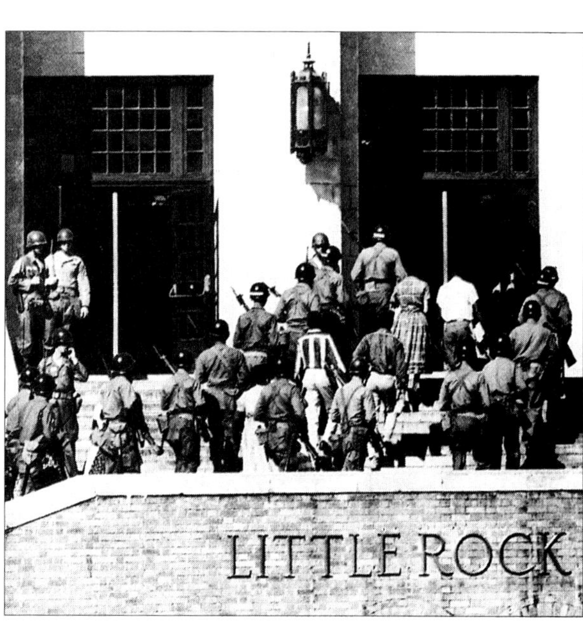

6

4. Other African Americans made important breakthroughs for equal rights in the 1940s. In the field of sports, Jackie Robinson became the first African American to play major league baseball when he joined the Brooklyn Dodgers in 1947. An exceptional hitter and fielder, he was elected to the National Baseball Hall of Fame in 1962. Although he faced taunts, challenges, and insults from whites, in time his courage and skill won acceptance for him and other black athletes.

5. By the 1950s, a strong civil rights movement had developed. Ending segregation in public schools became one of its primary targets. In 1954 the Supreme Court agreed to hear the case of *Brown* v. *Board of Education of Topeka* (Kansas). The case involved Linda Brown, an eight-year-old African American girl. She was required to attend an all-black school 21 blocks from her home, even though there was an all-white school only a few blocks away. With help from the NAACP, Linda's father sued the Topeka Board of Education so that his daughter could attend the nearby all-white school. On May 17, 1954, the Supreme Court ruled unanimously to ban segregation in public schools.

6. Despite the Brown decision, African Americans had to overcome continued opposition to integration of the public schools. Some states resisted orders of the federal government to desegregate. In September 1957 Arkansas Governor Orval Faubus called out the Arkansas National Guard to prevent the integration of Central High School in Little Rock. President Eisenhower finally had to send federal troops (shown above) to escort nine African American students to classes to ensure their safety.

Bonus Activity

Creating an Exhibit

To help students gain deeper understanding of the struggles and achievements of the civil rights movement, have the class create a museum exhibit about the movement. As a first step, students should brainstorm a "wish list" of items to put in the exhibit. Possibilities include photographs or drawings of people or events, newspaper headlines or articles, and recordings or sheet music of songs such as "We Shall Overcome." Besides deriving ideas and information from the textbook, students will need to do library research, both to obtain items such as photos and to gather information for creating items such as drawings. Students' families also may have things to contribute, including recollections of the civil rights movement that students could capture in writing or on tape. Once students have gathered their items, they should arrange them in a logical way and create labels or captions for them. If possible, invite other classes and families to view the exhibit.

Wrap-Up Activity

Role-Playing Interviews

To reinforce understanding of the civil rights movement and give students practice in interpreting visuals, have pairs of students role play an imaginary interview with one of the persons pictured. (If students did the Section Activity on page 612 of this Teacher's Edition, you may want to discourage interviews with Martin Luther King, Jr.) Pairs should prepare for their role plays by studying the picture of their chosen person as well as its caption. If the person is one who is identified, students should list anything else they know about him or her. As a next step, pairs should list questions they would like to ask the person if they could. They also should list answers that the person might give. Suggest that students rehearse their role plays at least once before presenting them to the rest of the class.

History Footnote

At the time of her arrest, Rosa Parks had been secretary of the Montgomery chapter of the NAACP for over a decade. However, when she refused to give up her bus seat, she did it on her own, without any inkling that her action would be a flash point in the civil rights movement.

A one-day bus boycott was set for Monday, December 5, 1955, the day of Parks's trial. The Women's Political Council, a group of black professional women, did the planning. The council's president, Jo Ann Gibson Robinson, distributed 35,000 leaflets announcing the boycott. On Monday morning, signs at bus stops read, "People, don't ride the bus today. Don't ride it for freedom." One day turned into 382 days, during which thousands of boycotters walked, bicycled, and used car pools.

7

8

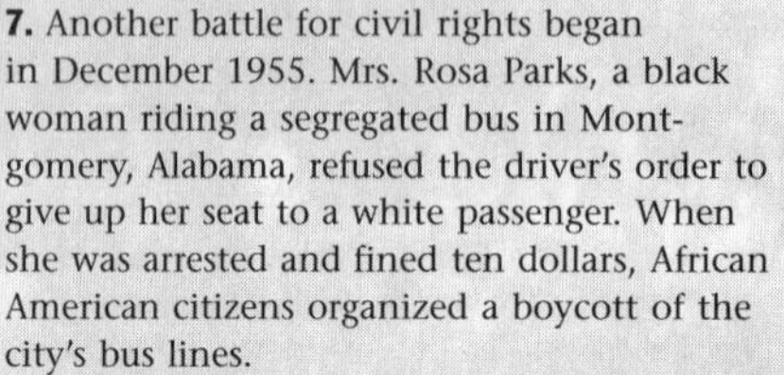

7. Another battle for civil rights began in December 1955. Mrs. Rosa Parks, a black woman riding a segregated bus in Montgomery, Alabama, refused the driver's order to give up her seat to a white passenger. When she was arrested and fined ten dollars, African American citizens organized a boycott of the city's bus lines.

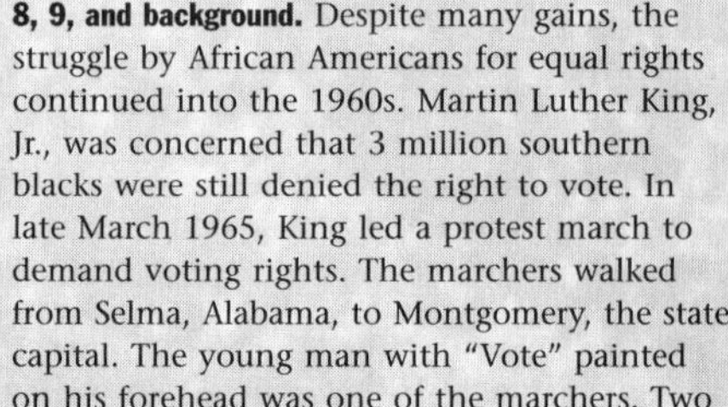

8, 9, and background. Despite many gains, the struggle by African Americans for equal rights continued into the 1960s. Martin Luther King, Jr., was concerned that 3 million southern blacks were still denied the right to vote. In late March 1965, King led a protest march to demand voting rights. The marchers walked from Selma, Alabama, to Montgomery, the state capital. The young man with "Vote" painted on his forehead was one of the marchers. Two

History Footnote

On March 7, 1965, about 600 protesters left Selma for Montgomery to demand voting rights. On620 the outskirts of Selma, the marchers were confronted by members of the Alabama highway patrol, who were under orders by Governor George Wallace to stop the march. One of the marchers, the Baptist minister and civil rights leader John Lewis, recalled the confrontation this way: "The troopers came toward us with billy clubs, tear gas, and bullwhips, trampling us with horses. . . . I saw people rolling, heard people screaming and hollering. We couldn't go forward. We couldn't go to the side, to the left or to the right, because we would have been going into the Alabama River, so we were beaten back down the streets of Selma." Lewis suffered a fractured skull in the attack.

9

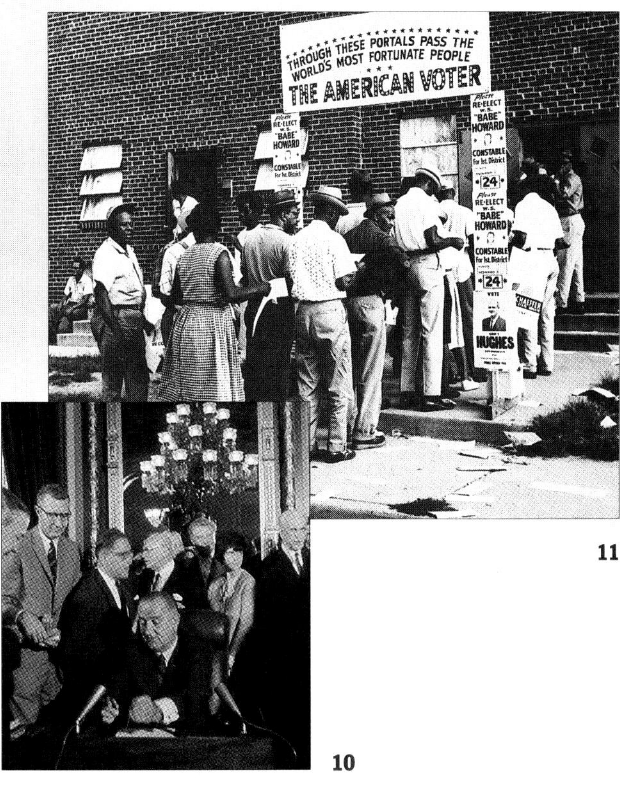

11

10

weeks earlier, on March 7, voting-rights marchers had tried to walk from Selma to Montgomery but had been attacked by state troopers.

10. The shocking events in Selma forced President Johnson to act. On March 15, in an address to Congress, he called for a tough new voting rights bill. Five months later, Congress passed the Voting Rights Act of 1965. Above, President Johnson signs the bill. This new law provided for direct federal intervention to guarantee registration. By this act, African Americans were finally included in the democratic process in the way intended by emancipation a century earlier.

11. After the Voting Rights Act was passed, the number of registered African American voters rose significantly. Here, black men and women are lining up to vote in Memphis.

Discussion

Checking Understanding

1. What breakthrough for equal rights did Jackie Robinson make? (Became the first African American player in major league baseball; his skill and courage opened the door for other black athletes.)

2. Why didn't the Brown decision result in immediate integration of public schools? (Some states, like Arkansas, actively resisted the federal government's order to desegregate their schools.)

Stimulating Critical Thinking

3. What do Pictures 8 and 9 tell you about the emotions of the voting-rights marchers? Explain. (Through the facial expressions and postures shown, the photos tell us that the marchers were serious, determined, and perhaps somewhat concerned about what might happen during the march.)

4. What do you suppose the people in Picture 11 thought of the message above them? (Possible answer: they probably agreed with the message in that they cherished their hard-won right to vote, but they also may have had some negative feelings about it because they had been denied membership among the "fortunate" for so long.)

Introducing the Section

Warm-Up Activity

Debating a President's Right to Resign

To prepare students to read about Richard Nixon and the Watergate scandal, have the class debate the following question: Should a President be allowed to resign to prevent being impeached? Have them refer to the impeachment of Andrew Johnson on page 189.

Geography Question of the Day

Ask students to think of different kinds of environmental pollution (air, water, soil). Then have them list a location in your state that suffers from one of these kinds of pollution and explain what geographical factors might contribute to the place's endangered environment. For example, a lake may be polluted because a large factory is located upstream on a tributary that empties into the lake.

See the Study Guide activity in **Chapter Resources Binder**, p. 124.

Section Objectives

- ★ Explain the challenges President Nixon faced at home.
- ★ Identify the events that led to the Watergate scandal.
- ★ Explain why the Watergate scandal was a serious constitutional crisis.

Teaching Resources

Take-Home Planner 5, pp. 12–19
Chapter Resources Binder
Study Guide, p. 124
Reinforcement
Skills Development, pp. 127–128
Geography Extensions
American Readings
Using Historical Documents, pp. 92–95
Transparency Activities
Chapter and Unit Tests, pp. 107–110

4. The Nixon Years

Reading Guide

Section Focus **Richard Nixon's presidency and the scandal that ended it**

1. **What challenges did President Nixon face at home?**
2. **What events led to the Watergate scandal?**
3. **Why was the Watergate scandal a serious constitutional crisis?**

As he entered the White House in 1969, President Richard Nixon faced a nation deeply divided over the Vietnam War and struggles for equality. In his inaugural address, he called for calm. "We cannot learn from one another until we stop shouting at one another," he said. The government, he promised, "will strive to listen in new ways."

Nixon's Goals

Like Eisenhower, President Nixon thought that the federal government should play a smaller role in the economy. He called for returning power to the states over such matters as education and public health. He also backed away from using federal power to enforce integration. He tried to block renewal of the Voting Rights Act and delay court orders to integrate schools.

In some areas, though, Nixon willingly used federal power. When unemployment rose in 1969, he used federal money to build the economy. To stop soaring inflation in 1971 he placed a 90-day freeze on all wages and prices. To help states pay for social programs, he provided matching federal funds.

Space successes On July 20, 1969, American astronauts Neil A. Armstrong and Edwin E. Aldrin, Jr., landed a spacecraft on the moon. The United States had fulfilled President Kennedy's dream of putting a man on the moon by the end of the decade.

With Nixon's support, the United States took another major leap into space four years later. May 14, 1973, saw the launch of *Skylab,* the first American orbiting space station. Later two more Skylab missions were sent into orbit with researchers photographing the earth and conducting scientific experiments.

Nixon also started a program to develop a space shuttle, a reusable spacecraft that blasted off like a rocket and landed like an airplane. The first space shuttle, *Columbia,* lifted off in 1981.

Environmental Problems

During the 1970s, Americans were becoming more and more concerned about the effects of technology on the environment. Factories and cars were spewing poisons into the air. Industrial wastes, city sewage, and farm pesticides were killing fish and wildlife.

Biologist Rachel Carson had sounded an early warning about the danger of pollution. In her 1962 book *Silent Spring,* Carson declared, "The question is whether any civilization can wage [such] relentless war on life without destroying itself." Her writing helped to spark an environmental movement.

Under pressure from environmentalists, Congress passed a number of laws, such as the Clean Air Act of 1963 and the Water Quality Act of 1965, to fight air pollution and

Connections to Science

Marine biologist Rachel Carson, a leader of the movement to protect the environment, was also the person most responsible for the ban on the use of the pesticide DDT (dichlorodiphenyltrichloroethane). A nerve poison, DDT was one of the most effective pesticides in the worldwide battle against disease-carrying insects. However, in *Silent Spring,* Carson claimed that DDT entered the food chain and concentrated in higher animals. Among its damaging effects were reproductive problems, such as thin eggshells in some birds including the bald eagle, the national bird. Further testing revealed Carson's charges to be substantially true, and in 1973 DDT was banned in the United States except for emergencies. Other nations have also banned or drastically cut back on the use of this dangerous chemical.

Link to Technology

Skylab

Launched on May 14, 1973, *Skylab* was the United States' first manned orbiting laboratory. Three crews carried out missions on board the space station, gathering information about the earth and its resources, the sun and stars, and the effects of weightlessness on humans. Their findings have been essential in planning future space exploration.

The Apollo telescope mount had special instruments for studying the sun.

Solar panels

This solar panel ripped off soon after launch. The remaining panels powered the lab.

Apollo telescope mount

Apollo spacecraft

An Apollo spacecraft ferried each three-member crew to *Skylab*, and connected to a docking port. The crew entered the lab through the air lock module.

Docking ports

Living quarter

Laboratory

Air lock module

Astronauts slept in a vertical position in special sleeping bags attached to the wall.

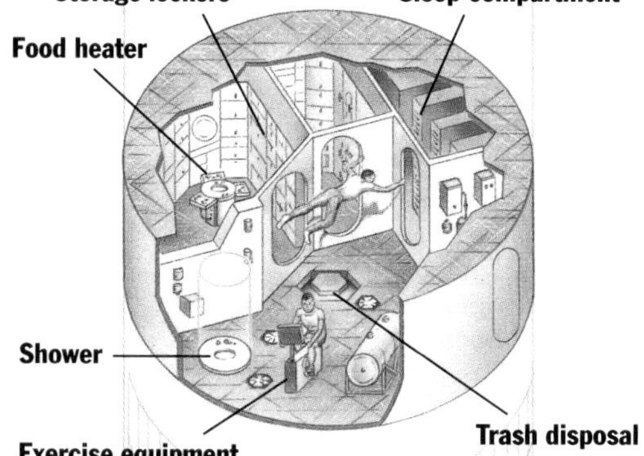

The shower was fully enclosed, and the wastewater was sucked into a storage tank.

Astronauts used exercise equipment to stay in shape and to study whether human fitness is affected by a long stay in space.

Developing the Section

Discussion

Checking Understanding

1. In what ways did Nixon try to limit federal power? (Called for giving states more power over education and public health; tried to limit federal enforcement of integration.) What were some ways he used federal power? (Wage and price freeze; matching funds for states; support for space program.)

2. Why was July 20, 1969, a historic day? (Two American astronauts landed on the moon.)

Stimulating Critical Thinking

3. The space program in the 1960s and 1970s was very expensive. Do you think this money was well spent? Explain. (Yes: space exploration and the "spin-off" technologies are important for future survival. No: more important to address problems of poverty, poor housing and health care, and pollution.)

Teaching the

Link to Technology

Ask students to name ordinary activities that would cause problems for people living in a space station. Have them study the illustration and text to find out how the designers of the space station solved these problems. Then ask them to discuss whether they would like to take a long trip in space and how they might prepare for it.

Section Activity

Assessing the Watergate Legacy

To evaluate the legacy of Watergate, have small groups write newspaper articles on the following three subjects: how Watergate increased mistrust of politicians and government, how it reaffirmed the Constitution's ability to weather a serious threat, and how trust in elected officials might be restored. Have the class make a newspaper with one page for each subject's articles.

Bonus Activity

Taking a Position

To analyze the importance of environmental protection, have small groups discuss the following statement: *Strict environmental regulations are bad.* Then ask a spokesperson from each group to summarize the outcome of their discussion.

Vital Links

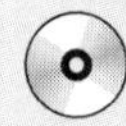

Earth Day banner (Picture) Unit 6, Side 1, Search 22972

See also Unit 6 Explore CD-ROM location 109.

History Footnote

The early 1970s were important years for the environment. The first Earth Day was celebrated on April 22, 1970, and Congress passed the Clean Water Act. Disgusted by widely distributed photos of the Cuyahoga River ablaze, tons of raw sewage gushing into San Francisco Bay, and other environmental problems, Americans demanded that the nation's water supply be protected. Since the passage of the Clean Water Act in 1972, the percentage of people served by wastewater treatment facilities has doubled, the release of untreated organic wastes has been halved, and the release of toxic organic pollutants and metals has been cut by 99 percent. The act was a major success in the battle for a clean environment.

The Cuyahoga River in Cleveland, Ohio, was heavily polluted with oil, grease, and debris. Americans learned how dangerous pollution could be when the river caught fire in 1969.

clean up the nation's lakes and rivers. In 1970 President Nixon created the Environmental Protection Agency to carry out federal programs to combat pollution. On the first "Earth Day," April 22, 1970, millions of Americans took part in teach-ins, protests, and cleanup projects to "save the earth."

The Election of 1972

As the 1972 election approached, the Republican Party nominated Nixon for a second term. As you read in Chapter 13, his trips to China and the Soviet Union had sent his popularity soaring.

A curious event occurred early in the election campaign. At 2:00 A.M. on June 17, five burglars were arrested in a Washington, D.C., office complex called Watergate. They had broken into the offices of the Democratic National Committee. They carried cameras and listening devices, or "bugs," for telephones.

Nixon assured the nation that "no one in this administration is involved in this very bizarre incident." By election day it seemed to have been forgotten. Nixon was easily re-elected with 47 million votes to 29 million for the Democrat, George McGovern.

The Watergate Scandal

Early in 1973 the Watergate burglars were tried and convicted. After the trial, one of them charged that high officials had been involved in the break-in. This information led to an investigation by a Senate Committee headed by North Carolina Senator Sam Ervin, Jr.

Tips for Teaching

Gifted Students

Gifted students often benefit from reading primary sources. Using transcripts of the White House Watergate tapes or the Senate Watergate hearings, small groups can act out important Watergate episodes. Tell them to focus on key figures such as John Dean, Bob Haldeman, John Ehrlichman, or Senator Sam Ervin.

Discussion

Checking Understanding

1. What was Earth Day? (A day for activities to call attention to environmental problems and solutions.)

2. Why did burglars break into the headquarters of the Democratic National Committee? (To plant bugs and cameras to gain Democratic campaign information illegally.)

3. What misdeeds was Nixon accused of? (Covering up Watergate scandal by blocking FBI investigation and paying "hush money" to burglars, illegally tapping phones, accepting illegal campaign contributions.)

Stimulating Critical Thinking

4. Did Nixon deserve to be impeached? Explain. (Yes: lied, accepted bribes, tried to cover up illegal actions, brought disgrace to the office. No: some Presidents have committed similar or worse misdeeds without being impeached.)

I AM
A CROOK
NOT
©1974 HERBLOCK

This cartoon was published after the release of Nixon's tapes of his Watergate conversations. Nixon had promised, "I am not a crook."

From May to July 1973, Americans watched the televised Senate hearings with dismay. Witnesses told that the burglars had been hired by the Committee to Reelect the President (CREEP) and that Nixon had tried to "cover up" the Watergate scandal. He had blocked an FBI investigation and approved payments of "hush money" to the burglars.

During the hearings, one witness revealed that many of Nixon's conversations about Watergate had been taped. The committee asked the President for the tapes, and Nixon spent the next year fighting a legal battle to prevent the release of any of the tapes.

Meanwhile the Senate committee uncovered other wrongdoings. CREEP officials had accepted illegal campaign contributions. Nixon had allowed White House employees to use illegal phone taps to stop "leaks" of secret information to the press.

Nixon resigns On July 24, 1974, the Supreme Court ruled that the President had to release the tapes of his Watergate conversations. The tapes revealed that Nixon had been involved in the cover-up from the start.

A week later, members of the House Judiciary Committee charged Nixon with blocking the Watergate investigation, misusing his power, and illegally withholding evidence from Congress. They recommended that Nixon be impeached.

It seemed certain that the House would vote for impeachment. Rather than face a trial in the Senate, President Nixon submitted his resignation on August 9, 1974.

As Nixon stepped down, Vice-President Gerald Ford of Michigan assumed office. Ford was the first non-elected President. Nixon's Vice-President, Spiro Agnew, had resigned in 1973 when it became known that he had accepted bribes. With Congress's approval Nixon had then named Ford, the House Republican leader, to replace Agnew.

Having resigned rather than face impeachment, Nixon put on a bold face as he boarded a helicopter to leave the White House.

For an activity on Nixon's letter of resignation, see **Using Historical Documents**, pp. 92–95.

Refer students to pages R38 and R40 for information on the impeachment process.

Closing the Section

Wrap-Up Activity

Evaluating Nixon

To evaluate Nixon's presidency ask students to draw a balance scale. On one side, have them write Nixon's positive accomplishments. (Have them review pages 582–583 also.) On the other side, have them list his negatives and failures. Ask them to show the scale weighted to one side or the other, based on their overall evaluation of Nixon.

Section Review Answers

1. Used federal money to build economy and fight unemployment, placed freeze on wages and prices to fight inflation, and provided matching federal funds to states for social programs.

2. Congress learned from one convicted burglar that high officials had been involved in the break-in.

3. Nixon was the spider, caught in web created by efforts to cover up break-in.

To check understanding of "Why We Remember," assign Thinking Critically question 3 on student page 628.

History Footnote

Two of the best-known figures to emerge from the Watergate scandal were *Washington Post* reporters Carl Bernstein and Bob Woodward. More than any other journalists, they helped break open the Watergate case. Originally assigned to cover the burglary attempt at Democratic headquarters, Woodward and Bernstein followed the case from its small beginnings all the way to its end—President Nixon's resignation. Over a period of two years, they painstakingly talked with hundreds of sources, dug out details of the cover-up, and traced the trail of illegal activities to the White House. Along the way Woodward and Bernstein won the Pulitzer Prize for their newspaper, wrote two best-selling books, and were portrayed by Robert Redford and Dustin Hoffman in the movie *All the President's Men.*

"Our Constitution works" The Watergate scandal taught Americans a painful lesson about the dangers of presidential power. When a 1974 poll asked people how much faith they had in the executive branch of government, 43 percent replied, "Hardly any."

On the other hand, the scandal proved that the Constitution's system of checks and balances is still our best protection against abuses of power. "Our national nightmare is over," President Ford assured Americans, "Our Constitution works."

4. Section Review

1. How did Nixon respond to economic problems?
2. What led Congress to investigate the Watergate burglary?
3. Critical Thinking Describing the Watergate scandal, a political leader said that in the end "the spider got caught in his web." Who was the spider, and what was the web?

Why We Remember

The Postwar Years at Home

The postwar decades were a time of dizzying change in American life. These were the years of the baby boom and the migration of young families from cities to suburbs. This was the time when TV sets arrived in most American living rooms. This was the era when ordinary people became concerned about protecting the environment, a President declared war on poverty, and American astronauts landed on the moon.

Just as important, this was a time when Americans' commitment to the Constitution and their ideals of liberty and equality were tested again and again. The first great test came in the early 1950s, when the accusations of Senator Joseph McCarthy threatened our right to express our beliefs freely. The second great test came in the 1950s and 1960s, when African Americans set out to destroy the terrible injustice of racial discrimination and segregation. Yet another test came in the 1970s, when President Nixon used his power to deceive the public.

The nation and the Constitution survived these challenges. At the same time, Americans were reminded again of a truth that is all too easily forgotten. As Martin Luther King, Jr., reminded us, "Injustice anywhere is a threat to justice everywhere. . . . Whatever affects one directly affects all indirectly."

(Answers continued from side margin)
events clustered around a main item and connected by lines, a flowchart, or a collage. (b) Well-designed layouts will show quickly and clearly the events of the President's administration, as well as the relationships between the events.

For further application, have students do the Applying Skills activity in the Chapter Survey (p. 628).

If students need to review the skill, use the Skills Development transparency and activity in the **Chapter Resources Binder,** pp. 127–128.

Skill Lab

Using Information

Synthesizing Information

As you know, the time spans of Chapters 13 and 14 overlap. Certain names—especially those of Presidents—pop up in both chapters. Suppose you want to show key events during one President's administration. How might you approach the task?

Skill Tips

When synthesizing, examine the pieces of information to look for:

- order of importance
- ways to group pieces of information to show similarities and differences, time order, and cause-effect connections

Question to Investigate

What were the key events of one postwar President's administration?

Procedure

When you synthesize, you put together information to create a written, oral, or visual product. Here you will create a layout for a group of pictures.

1 Collect relevant information.
a. Choose one of these Presidents: Truman, Eisenhower, Kennedy, Johnson, or Nixon.
b. Choose six major events from Chapters 13 and 14 having to do with this President.

2 Identify connections between the pieces of information.
a. For each event, imagine a picture and then write a description and caption for it.
b. Identify the sequence of events and whether each event occurred inside or outside of the country. Decide which two events were most important.

3 Create a product to show the connections between the pieces of information.
a. Sketch possible layouts for the group of pictures. Try varying the sizes and placement of the pictures.
b. Sketch a final layout that you think would best show highlights of this President's administration. Include captions and descriptions of the pictures. See the partial sample below for President Franklin D. Roosevelt.

Source to Use

Damaged battleships at Pearl Harbor

The attack on Pearl Harbor on December 7, 1941, brought the United States into World War II.

Troops landing in Normandy

On D-Day, June 6, 1944, Allied troops landed in Normandy to begin freeing France from Nazi rule.

Introducing the Skill Lab

Explain that synthesizing information is a skill used every day. In this Skill Lab, students synthesize information about one President, analyze the importance of the information, and present it in an interesting way. Have them examine the sample layout. Then have them follow the procedure steps. Remind students that they should look for connections between foreign and domestic events—for example, the fact that the Cold War helped lead to McCarthyism or that the Vietnam War affected Johnson's Great Society plans.

Skill Lab Answers

1. (a) Choices will vary. (b) Students should choose both domestic and international events from both chapters, paying attention to the first Skill Tip.
2. (a) Make sure students understand that the pictures do not have to be ones they have seen or know exist. Picture descriptions should be brief fragments, while captions should be one sentence conveying the importance of the event. (b) Encourage students to look for connections between events.
3. (a) Possible layouts include a straight line or chain of causes, a web of

(Answers continued in top margin)

Survey Answers

Reviewing Vocabulary

Definitions are found on these pages: *closed shop* (602), *civil rights* (608), *integration* (611).

Reviewing Main Ideas

1. Government workers fired, members of movie industry blacklisted, suspected spies convicted and executed, officeholders not re-elected, employees fired if did not sign loyalty oaths.

2. Causes: growing defense industry; increasing productivity due to new technology; increasing demand for housing, cars, consumer goods. Effects: growth of suburbs, exodus from cities, poor trapped in city slums.

3. (a) Persuaded Congress to pass laws to create new industries and retrain workers, created Peace Corps, and persuaded Congress to fund space program. (b) Congress ignored requests for health insurance for aged, federal aid for schools and city housing, and civil rights bill.

4. Economic Opportunity Act, Elementary and Secondary School Act, Medicare and Medicaid, new Department of Housing and Urban Development.

5. (a) In *Brown,* attacked legal basis for segregation, insisted on black students' right to attend integrated schools, and attacked segregation in public facilities. (b) Organized protests, boycotts, Freedom Rides, sit-ins, marches, and voter registration drives. (c) Civil Rights Act of 1964, Voting Rights Act of 1965, Twenty-Fourth Amendment.

6. (a) Laws requiring equal pay for equal work; greater job opportunities. (b) UFW bargaining rights and better conditions for farmworkers; political power. (c) Greater self-determination, control

(Answers continued in top margin)

of natural resources on Indian lands, and payment for lands seized.

7. Convicted burglar's charge that high officials involved in break-in led to Senate investigation. Evidence showed Nixon tried to cover up scandal. Facing likely impeachment, he resigned.

Thinking Critically

1. Truman: decisive, forced ironworkers back to work, willing to use federal funds to achieve Fair Deal goals, called for new health insurance program. Eisenhower: wanted smaller federal role in economy, cut federal spending but supported Interstate Highway Act. Kennedy: idealistic and energetic, started Peace Corps, supported active role for government to end recession, promoted integration. Johnson: energetic and skilled at working with Congress, supported

Chapter Survey

Reviewing Vocabulary

Define the following terms.

1. closed shop
2. civil rights
3. integration

Reviewing Main Ideas

1. What happened to people who were suspected of having Communist sympathies after World War II? Give three examples.
2. What were the main causes and effects of American prosperity in the 1950s?
3. (a) In what ways was President Kennedy successful in putting into effect his "New Frontier" plans? (b) In what ways was he unsuccessful?
4. Describe three ways that President Johnson and Congress tried to end poverty.
5. Give an example of how each helped to break down barriers to equality for African Americans. (a) the NAACP (b) students and other ordinary Americans (c) Congress
6. Summarize the gains made by each group as of the mid-1970s. (a) women (b) Hispanics (c) American Indians
7. How did the Watergate burglary lead to the resignation of President Nixon? Describe the chain of events.

Thinking Critically

1. Application Choose two Presidents discussed in this chapter and compare their styles of leadership. Give examples from the text to support your views.
2. Analysis African Americans had been working to gain full citizenship since Reconstruction. Why were they able to accomplish so much in the 1950s and 1960s?
3. Why We Remember: Evaluation Many Americans look back on the 1950s as a wonderful "golden era." They view the 1960s and early 1970s as troubled, unpleasant years. Do you think these views of the United States in the postwar years are realistic, or not? Explain.

Applying Skills

Synthesizing information Apply what you learned on page 627 to create a collage of key events in your life:
1. Collect information. List key events that you remember. Talk to relatives about events that occurred when you were very young. List them.
2. Develop items for your collage. If possible use photographs and artifacts, such as souvenirs and awards, to portray the events you have listed, or write descriptions of the items on index cards. Write captions, too.
3. Arrange the items to show connections. For example, you might group items representing events from a particular year or events that relate to a sport or other special interest.

History Mystery

A young girl goes to school Answer the History Mystery on page 599. Segregated schools in many northern and western states as well as in the South were not "separate but equal." States that had segregated school systems spent far more on the education of white students than of black students. How might this situation affect the views of black students? Of white students?

Writing in Your History Journal

1. Keys to History (a) The time line on pages 598–599 has eight Keys to History. In your journal, describe why each one is important to know about. (b) Choose the event from the time line that you think has had the greatest influence on life in the United States today. Explain your choice in your journal.

active role for government, got Congress to set up "Great Society" programs and pass Civil Rights Act of 1964 and Voting Rights Act of 1965. Nixon: promoted less active role for government, did not support federal enforcement of school integration, resigned in face of probable impeachment.

2. Black soldiers fought for democracy overseas and wanted equal rights and opportunities at home; NAACP work to destroy legal basis for segregation; growth of civil rights movement based on nonviolent resistance; strong leaders such as Malcolm X and Martin Luther King, Jr.; support of Kennedy and Johnson; TV coverage of police attacks helped turn public against segregation.

3. 1950s were prosperous for many, but one-fifth lived in poverty, including many

(Answers continued in side margin)

African Americans, Hispanics, and American Indians who faced discrimination. Fear of communism spread, and suspected Communists were hounded and lost jobs. Although 1960s and 1970s were troubled, African Americans broke down legal barriers to equality; women, Hispanics, and Indians made gains; Americans dealt with environmental problems; success in space.

Applying Skills

Collages should reflect ability to apply Procedure steps and Skill Tips on page 627 to a personal situation.

History Mystery

Because of segregation, Linda Brown had to go to a black school. Segregation made black students feel inferior and white students superior. It angered black students, spurring them to seek change.

Writing in Your History Journal

1. (a) Explanations should be similar to the time line notes on teacher pages 598–599. (b) Entry should reflect understanding of event's importance.

2. Replies should show understanding of his belief in Christianity and nonviolent resistance.

3. Students may argue that unjust laws should not be obeyed. They should recognize no one is above the law.

Reviewing Geography

1. (A) Detroit, (B) Richmond, (C) Indianapolis, (D) Dallas, (E) Salt Lake City, (F) Seattle

2. Rapid growth of auto industry, suburbs, motel and food service industries, and vacation resorts; decline of public transportation.

Alternative Assessment

Teacher's Take-Home Planner 5, p. 15, includes suggestions and scoring rubrics for the Alternative Assessment activity.

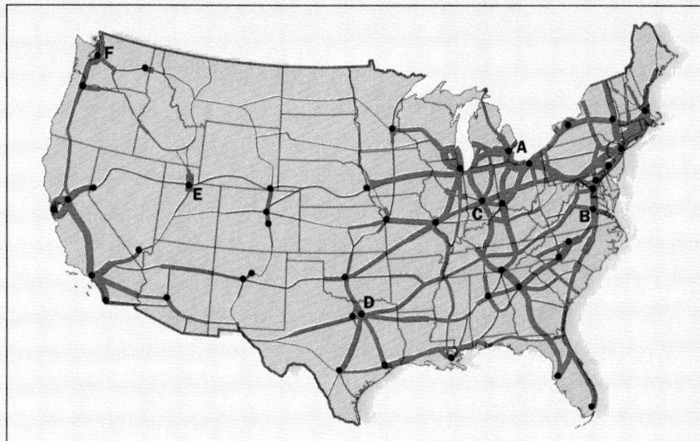

Reviewing Geography

1. Each letter on the map represents a city that lies on the interstate highway system. For each letter, write the name of the city.

2. Geographic Thinking In Chapter 10, you thought about the far-reaching effects of the automobile. Now think about how interstate highways further transformed our way of life. List at least three effects. Consider, for example, effects on the tourist industry.

2. Martin Luther King, Jr. The year is 1963, and a student has written to King expressing anger about the continuing injustices suffered by African Americans. "Nonviolence has had its chance," the teenager writes. "From now on, we have to fight fire with fire." In your journal, write a reply that King might have written.

3. Citizenship Various people you read about in this chapter, from Rosa Parks to Richard Nixon, broke the law and believed they were justified in doing so. When, if ever, is breaking the law justified? Does it matter who is doing the lawbreaking and why they are doing it? Write your responses in your journal.

Alternative Assessment

Writing editorials Imagine that you and a partner are editors of your community's newspaper during the years between 1950 and 1974. Work together to write five editorials, on these topics:

❶ whether Senator McCarthy is doing the right thing in his hunt for Communists

❷ whether President Kennedy's proposed civil rights bill should be enacted

❸ whether President Johnson's efforts to create the Great Society are good policy

❹ whether President Nixon should be impeached

❺ another issue of your choice from the chapter

Your work will be evaluated on the following criteria:

- you provide accurate information to help readers understand the pros and cons of the issue and to support your opinions
- you offer opinions that are realistic for people in your community during the era in question
- you write in a way that is persuasive and to the point

Teaching the

Link to American Readings

In this feature students learn about law and justice as they were interpreted by two well-known public figures: Dr. Martin Luther King, Jr., and Richard Nixon. Students will discover that law and justice each have more than one definition. They will also be asked to define the terms according to their own experience and philosophies.

Before students begin the lesson, review Fighting for Equal Rights (pages 611–617) and The Watergate Scandal (pages 620–622). Have students read the entire feature before assigning the A Closer Look questions. The Setting the Stage Activity and Bonus Activity may then be introduced according to the needs and interests of the students. The information contained in the Discussion questions and the Footnotes may be used throughout the lesson as appropriate. Readers' Theater is ideal for students who might find the readings somewhat difficult. Use the Wrap-Up Activity for students who would enjoy taking a step beyond the core lesson.

History Footnote

On April 3, 1963, the Southern Christian Leadership Conference (SCLC) launched Project C, a plan designed to raise national awareness of Birmingham, Alabama's race problems through nonviolent demonstrations. Initially, the campaign failed to produce headlines. Stores handled sit-ins simply by closing their lunch counters instead of calling the police, and the city's African Americans were hesitant to march and go to jail because they feared that they would lose their jobs. In mid-April, veteran SCLC organizer James Bevel approached the city's African American high-school students and recruited them to march in place of their working parents. The plan succeeded, and the demonstrations that shocked the nation in early May were largely led by the area's teenagers.

Link to American Readings

READING 14A

Letter from Birmingham Jail

During the Birmingham civil rights demonstrations in 1963, Martin Luther King, Jr., was arrested for violating an Alabama state court order temporarily prohibiting public demonstrations without a permit. Eight white ministers then published an attack on King in a Birmingham newspaper, accusing him of being a troublemaker and a communist. While jailed in solitary confinement, King answered his accusers in his famous "Letter from Birmingham Jail."

Central to King's strategy of civil disobedience was a willingness to accept "the penalty of imprisonment in order to arouse the conscience of the community over its injustice."

An essay by Martin Luther King, Jr., 1963

We know through painful experience that freedom is never voluntarily given by the oppressor; it must be demanded by the oppressed. . . . For years now I have heard the word "Wait!" It rings in the ear of every Negro [black] with piercing familiarity. This "Wait" has almost always meant "Never." We must come to see, with one of our distinguished jurists, that "justice too long delayed is justice denied."

. . . Perhaps it is easy for those who have never felt the stinging darts of segregation to say, "Wait." But when you have seen vicious mobs lynch your mothers and fathers at will and drown your sisters and brothers at whim; when you have seen hate-filled policemen curse, kick and even kill your black brothers and sisters; when you see the vast majority of your twenty million Negro brothers smothering in an airtight cage of poverty in the midst of an affluent society; . . . then you will understand why we find it difficult to wait. There comes a time when the cup of endurance runs over, and men are no longer willing to be plunged into the abyss of despair. I hope, sirs, you can understand our legitimate and unavoidable impatience.

You express a great deal of anxiety over our willingness to break laws. This is certainly a legitimate concern. Since we so diligently urge people to obey the Supreme Court's decision of 1954 outlawing segregation in the public schools, at first glance it may seem rather paradoxical for us consciously to break laws. . . . There are two types of laws: just and unjust. I would be the first to advocate obeying just laws. One has not only a legal but a moral responsibility to obey just laws. Conversely, one has a moral responsibility

paradoxical: contrary

Literature Footnote

The global movement of ideas can unleash powerful forces. In 1846 the American writer Henry David Thoreau refused to pay a poll tax in protest against the Mexican War. As punishment, he spent a night in jail. In 1849 he wrote an influential essay called "Civil Disobedience" in which he said that people should refuse to obey government laws that they considered unjust. Thoreau's essay influenced the great Indian nationalist leader Mohandas K. Gandhi, who organized massive nonviolent demonstrations against British rule in the 1920s and 1930s. Gandhi's ultimate success in using the principles of passive disobedience inspired Dr. Martin Luther King, Jr., to fight against segregation using similar strategies.

to disobey unjust laws. I would agree with St. Augustine that "an unjust law is no law at all."

. . . A just law is a man-made code that squares with the moral law or the law of God. An unjust law is a code that is out of harmony with the moral law. . . . Any law that degrades human personality is unjust. All segregation statutes are unjust because segregation distorts the soul and damages the personality. It gives the segregator a false sense of superiority and the segregated a false sense of inferiority. . . . Thus it is that I can urge men to obey the 1954 decision of the Supreme Court, for it is morally right; and I can urge them to disobey segregation ordinances, for they are morally wrong.

Media coverage of police violence in the 1963 civil rights demonstrations in Birmingham triggered a national outcry against segregation.

Saint Augustine: early Christian theologian

Let us consider a more concrete example of just and unjust laws. An unjust law is a code that a numerical or power majority group compels a minority group to obey but does not make binding on itself. This is difference made legal. By the same token, a just law is a code that a majority compels a minority to follow and that is willing to follow itself. This is sameness made legal.

Let me give another explanation. A law is unjust if it is inflicted on a minority that, as a result of being denied the right to vote, had no part in enacting or devising the law. Who can say that the legislature of Alabama which set up that state's segregation laws was democratically elected? Throughout Alabama all sorts of devious methods are used to prevent Negroes from becoming registered voters, and there are some counties in which, even though Negroes constitute a majority of the population, not a single Negro is registered. Can any law enacted under such circumstances be considered democratically structured?

Sometimes a law is just on its face and unjust in its application. For instance, I have been arrested on a charge of parading without a permit. Now, there is nothing wrong in having an ordinance which requires a permit for a parade. But such an ordinance becomes unjust when it is used to maintain segregation and to deny citizens the First Amendment privilege of peaceful assembly and protest.

I hope you are able to see the distinction I am trying to point out. In no sense do I advocate evading or defying the law, as would the rabid segregationist. That would lead to anarchy. One who breaks an unjust law must do so openly, lovingly, and with a willingness to accept the penalty. I submit that an individual who breaks a law that conscience tells him is unjust, and who willingly accepts the penalty of imprisonment in order to arouse the conscience of the community over its injustice, is in reality expressing the highest respect for law.

Setting the Stage Activity

Rating Leaders

To help students learn how to make judgments about what makes a good leader, and to help them understand that being a leader does not exempt one from accountability, have them complete this exercise. First ask for volunteers to suggest qualities that make a good leader. Write these suggestions on the chalkboard. Then draw two columns next to each point. Write "King" above one column and "Nixon" above the other. Next, ask students to rate each leader on a scale of 1 to 5 for each quality. Discuss which leader totals the most points and why.

Bonus Activity

Addressing Personal Convictions

To help students sort through their own ideas concerning issues of law and justice, have them complete this exercise. Ask students to compose a list of personal convictions dealing with how they think people should treat each other. Have students consider a variety of situations. Allow time for small group discussion of their lists.

Discussion

Stimulating Critical Thinking

1. In 1988 *Parents* magazine conducted a nationwide public opinion poll to determine the current state of race relations in America. Only one-quarter of those polled gave race relations a "good" rating. What rating would you give race relations in the nation now? How would you rate your city or town? What might be done to improve situations that have a "poor" rating? (Students' responses will depend on where they live and how they interpret their own experience. Encourage students to try to examine the nation as a whole as objectively as possible. It may be more difficult for them to be objective about their own experiences.)

2. King stated that one who breaks an unjust law must be willing to accept the punishment for doing so. Do you agree or disagree? Explain. (Students who agree might suggest that it is important to show respect for the law and to accept the penalty for breaking it, thus increasing the likelihood of change. Others might be unwilling to accept imprisonment; doing so would not necessarily bring about change.)

Literature Footnote

Bob Woodward and Carl Bernstein were two relatively unknown city-beat reporters for the *Washington Post* when the Watergate break-in occurred. Their determination to reveal the truth about the burglary eventually led to the resignation of President Nixon. However, they had help with their investigation. Disgruntled members of the Nixon White House became reliable sources of information. One source, whom the reporters called "Deep Throat," provided amazing and detailed information on the most secret inner workings of the Oval Office. The nickname was chosen to protect the person's identity, and although there has been much speculation on who Deep Throat was, the identity of the informant has yet to be revealed.

READING 14B

The Web of Watergate

Watergate was an office and apartment complex in Washington, D.C., where, in 1972, five burglars were arrested for breaking into the offices of the Democratic National Committee. Over the next two years, the term Watergate came to represent a vast, complex web of illegal activities and cover-ups that implicated a number of people in influential places—including President Richard Nixon. Hints of the scandal were first exposed in stories written by *Washington Post* reporters Carl Bernstein and Bob Woodward. Later they detailed their investigation in *All the President's Men*, a book that was later made into a movie. In the following article, Bernstein and Woodward discuss Watergate.

An article by Carl Bernstein and Bob Woodward, 1974

The morning after the arrest of five men inside the Watergate, a front-page story in *The Washington Post* noted: "There was no immediate explanation as to why the five suspects would want to bug the Democratic National Committee offices, or whether or not they were working for any other individuals or organizations." . . .

Unlike the rest of the nation that day, the President and his men then knew the real meaning of Watergate was not merely a "third-rate burglary," as Ronald L. Ziegler, the White House press secretary, had described it. Watergate—a term that would be hammered into the American consciousness and the soul of Richard Nixon's presidency for the next two years—represented something far more serious. To the President and his men, Watergate meant the potential exposure of the crimes of the Nixon administration— "The White House horrors," as John Mitchell would later derisively [scornfully] call them. . . .

It was the President who took the irrevocable [not changeable] step, six days after the break-in, of ordering his aides to insure that the FBI or the American people never learn what lay underneath: the wiretapping, burglaries, cover-ups, lies, money-laundering, secret funds, enemies' lists, dirty tricks, "plumbers," physical surveillance, forged cables, attempted character assassinations, IRS [Internal Revenue Service] audits . . . a veritable catalogue of illegal activities and abuses conceived and directed by the President and his men.

As the President himself was forced to gradually reveal, he was the man behind the web of Watergate. It was his passion for secrecy that made the demise [death] of his presidency inevitable. Similarly, it was his response to the threat of discovery that set in motion those forces which finally destroyed him.

The longer the cover-up went on—the more intensely that investigators, lawyers, grand jurors, reporters, and congressional committees pursued the larger meaning of Watergate—the more they found. And, as the cover-up

Literature Footnote

Henry David Thoreau, in *On the Duty of Civil Disobedience*, said "There will never be a really free and enlightened State until the State comes to recognize the individual as a higher and independent power . . . and treats him accordingly. . . a State at last which can afford to be just to all men, and to treat the individual with respect. . . .

Readers' Theater

King's letter can be presented with multiple voices. Students should follow the script as printed. Have them change voices whenever there is a logical break in thought. Students should practice reading for emphasis—pauses and inflection should be planned to lend meaning and to strengthen the emotional appeal of the message.

spun out in its myriad [many] directions, the web grew; each misdeed in turn required its own cover-up.

In the end, it was finally possible to trace the repeated miscalculations which Richard Nixon had woven. There was no grand plan—for the illegal activities or for the attempts to hide them. But the single unraveling strand was the character, ideology and insecurity of Richard M. Nixon.

He totally failed to perceive the goodwill extended to any President by the people, the bureaucracy, the military, the press, his political party, Congress and the institutions of justice. Instead of using them as allies—in the tradition of his predecessors—he assumed their enmity [hostility]. In the process, he eroded their ability to help him. . . .

As the tapes demonstrate, Mr. Nixon came to the White House full of suspicions and phobias [fears]. . . . Members of Congress, where he had served for 6 years, were . . . to be loathed and manipulated; the IRS was a tool of the Democrats, to be turned into an instrument of retribution; the FBI was inept and, worse, unwilling to break the law in pursuing the enemies, real or imagined, of the White House; the nation's newspapers, which overwhelmingly supported his re-election, were after Nixon; the bureaucracy, those nameless, faceless and hidebound civil servants, were Kennedyites, or, little better, paper-pushing remnants of the Great Society; the Republican Party was committed not to Richard Nixon but to some vague ideals that drained off money and energy from the President's own electoral ambitions.

retribution: punishment

Kennedyites: followers or supporters of John F. Kennedy

The President's men, as revealed on the tapes, shared the fearsome vision of their leader. . . . Willingly, even enthusiastically, they outdid each other with plans to [destroy] the White House enemies, to supplant the security functions of the FBI with a squad of White House vigilantes, to undermine the electoral process through disruption of the opposition party's primaries, to "fix" mock elections in high schools, to smear the reputations of politicians and public servants of both parties and—finally—to undermine the administration of justice.

Excerpt abridged from "A Passion for the Covert: The Response to the Threat of Discovery" by Carl Bernstein and Bob Woodward from *The Fall of a President*.

This cartoon, captioned 'I AM THE LAW!', mocked Nixon's misuse of power while President.

A Closer Look

1. What does King mean when he says that "justice too long delayed is justice denied"?

2. For what crimes was Nixon responsible?

3. CRITICAL THINKING Contrast King's definitions of just and unjust laws to Nixon's interpretation of the law.

Wrap-Up Activity

Writing About Law and Justice

To extend the lesson and to help students solidify their own philosophy about law and justice, have them respond to these questions in their history journals.

1. What are just and unjust laws? Define these terms in your own words.
2. Should anyone be—as Nixon claimed to be—beyond the jurisdiction of all laws? Explain.

A Closer Look

Answers

1. King claims that blacks have been denied justice for more than 340 years. He says that if justice is delayed indefinitely, the delay becomes denial—the rights are never granted.

2. Nixon was responsible for ordering or condoning wiretapping, burglaries, cover-ups, lies, money-laundering, secret funds, unethical behavior of many varieties, IRS audits, and other crimes.

3. According to King, a just law is one that meshes with God's law; it is moral. An unjust law is out of harmony with the moral law. Nixon believed that as President he was not bound by any laws. He believed he was above the law.

Teaching the

Citizenship Lab

In this feature students learn about the Gideon and Miranda decisions. By reading about these landmark cases, students will gain an appreciation of why the rights of all defendants must be respected. They will also gain insights into the difficulty of interpreting the law.

Have students read the entire feature before assigning the Understanding Civic Issues questions and the Hands-On Citizenship activity. The Bonus Activity in this Teacher's Edition may be used as an alternative to, or in addition to, the Hands-On Citizenship. The Discussion questions in this Teacher's Edition may be used at appropriate points during students' reading or afterward.

Objectives

- ★ Understand that the framers of the Constitution were very concerned about the rights of the accused.
- ★ Identify the constitutional issue raised by the Gideon decision.
- ★ Explain the significance of the Miranda decision.
- ★ Recognize that the Supreme Court is constantly modifying its earlier decisions.

Supreme Court Cases: *Gideon* v. *Wainright* and *Miranda* v. *Arizona*

Citizenship Lab

What Are the Rights of the Accused?

The framers of the Constitution were very concerned about the rights of accused individuals. Five of the ten amendments that make up the Bill of Rights limit or prohibit the use of governmental power in dealing with persons accused of crimes.

Six ideas that have developed through American history are the basis of the rights of the accused:

• **Protection of the innocent.** A person suspected of committing a crime is innocent until proven guilty.

• **Fair trials.** No one's life or liberty should be taken without "due process of law." No one should be convicted without having a chance to have his or her story heard.

• **Democratic process.** Juries are democratically chosen. Trials are conducted openly and the public is aware of criminal proceedings.

• **Limited governmental power.** Unreasonable searches and seizures are forbidden.

• **Human dignity.** No one shall be subjected to cruel, brutal, unusual, or undeserved treatment. People cannot be forced to be witnesses against themselves.

• **Privacy.** Every individual has the right to privacy. Unreasonable searches and seizures and forced confessions would violate this right.

With few exceptions, there is little controversy or disagreement about these ideas. However, there is much controversy about how they apply in specific cases.

The Warren Court Upheld Defendants' Rights

Earl Warren was chief justice of the Supreme Court from 1953 to 1969. Under Warren's leadership, the Court boldly moved in many new directions to protect the rights of individuals. Among the most important actions of the Court in the area of the rights of the accused were the following cases.

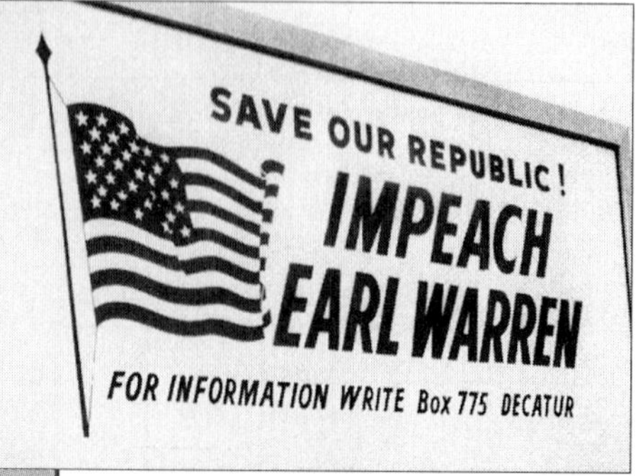

SAVE OUR REPUBLIC!
IMPEACH
EARL WARREN
FOR INFORMATION WRITE Box 775 DECATUR

The liberal political activism of the Supreme Court during the 1960s drew praise from some groups but harsh criticism and demands for the impeachment of Earl Warren from others.

History Footnote

Earl Warren spent much of his life in public service. He held various offices in local government and was elected district attorney of Alameda County, California, three times. In 1938 he was elected attorney general of California and in 1942, governor. He was reelected in 1946 and 1950. Because he was popular with Democrats as well as Republicans, he was selected as the Republican vice-presidential candidate in 1948. The presidential candidate was Thomas Dewey. Although Dewey was the overwhelming favorite over the Democratic candidate, he lost in one of the biggest political upsets of all time. President Truman won reelection. Had Dewey won, it is unlikely Warren would ever have been appointed to the Supreme Court.

***Gideon* v. *Wainwright*.** The defendant, Clarence Earl Gideon, was charged with burglarizing a pool hall. Because he couldn't afford a lawyer, he asked the court to appoint one to act in his defense. The Florida state judge denied his request, explaining that under Florida law the only time the court can appoint an attorney is when the defendant is charged with a capital crime. Gideon then decided to defend himself at his trial. He was convicted and sent to jail for five years.

While in prison, Gideon carefully prepared a petition asking higher courts to overturn his conviction because he was refused his constitutional right to counsel. The case was heard by the Supreme Court in 1963. The Court voted unanimously to reverse Gideon's conviction. Justice Hugo L. Black wrote the opinion. He said the right-to-counsel provision of the Sixth Amendment is "fundamental and essential to a fair trial" in both federal and state courts. As a result of this decision, all persons charged in criminal cases in state courts now have the right to be defended by a lawyer.

Clarence Earl Gideon and his handwritten petition to the Supreme Court.

***Miranda* v. *Arizona*.** Ernesto Miranda was arrested in 1963 for kidnapping an 18-year-old woman near Phoenix. He was questioned for two hours by the police, and then confessed. His signed confession was used as evidence against him in court. He was found guilty and sentenced to prison for a minimum of 20 years.

Miranda, however, claimed that the evidence used in the trial was illegally obtained. He said the police never informed him of his Fifth Amendment right to remain silent or his Sixth Amendment right to counsel. His lawyers appealed his conviction and in 1966 the Supreme Court agreed to hear his case. In a 5-4 vote, they decided to overturn Miranda's conviction.

Chief Justice Warren, writing for the majority, declared that this case raised "questions which go to the roots of our concepts of American jurisprudence." These questions, he continued, involved "the constraints society must observe consistent with the federal Constitution in prosecuting individuals for crime." Warren said the police must inform suspects of their right to stop the questioning at any time, to remain silent, and to have a lawyer present during questioning. If they cannot afford a

Setting the Stage Activity

Analyzing Police Procedures

A day or two before teaching this lesson, have students watch a television show about police work. Instruct students to watch the procedures followed by the police carefully and to take notes. Ask: Do you think the police acted in a reasonable manner? Were the suspects informed of their rights? If so, did this hinder the investigation? Would it be better if the accused had fewer rights?

Bonus Activity

Making Charts

Break the class into small groups. Give each group a large sheet of paper or posterboard. Have each group make a chart outlining the rights Americans have when they are accused of crimes. To help them get organized, have them divide their papers into four columns labeled: Fourth Amendment, Fifth Amendment, Sixth Amendment, and Eighth Amendment.

Checking Understanding

1. Wealthy defendants often hire experts such as psychiatrists to help them prove their innocence. Is it fair that states are not required to provide such experts to poor defendants like Gideon and Miranda? (Answers will vary. On one hand, one could argue that it is unfair. Rich defendants can hire a team of lawyers and all the experts they can find to win their case while poor defendants are often represented by an overworked public defender and must depend on prosecution witnesses to make their case. On the other hand, it would probably cost an incredible amount of money to the taxpayers if they had to pay for whatever expert witnesses the defense asked for.)

Stimulating Critical Thinking

2. Have recent Court decisions such as *Illinois* v. *Perkins* and *Arizona* v. *Fulminante* made the job of the police even more difficult? (Answers will vary. Some students may argue that these decisions have enabled guilty defendants to avoid punishment. Other students may argue that to safeguard the rights of all Americans, we must make sure that all persons accused of a crime are informed of their rights.)

Citizenship Footnote

The framers of the Constitution knew from their recent history as colonies of Great Britain that governments often use their power to enforce the law in ways that violate the basic rights of citizens. Sometimes the innocent are punished and the law is applied unjustly or unfairly. It was for this reason that the Bill of Rights was added to the Constitution. The framers believed that putting specific limitations on the government's power would help prevent future violations.

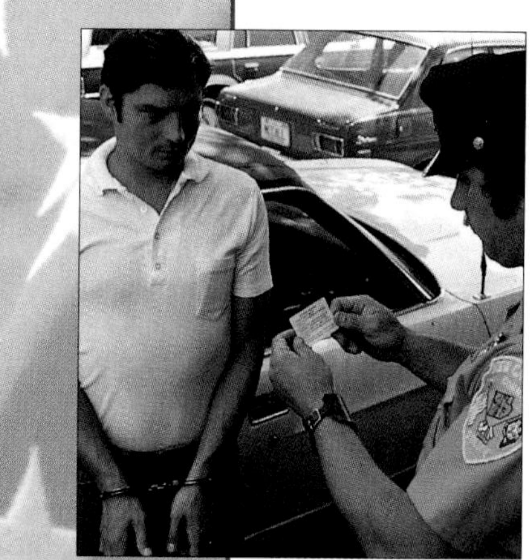

(Top Left) An officer may arrest you with a warrant issued by a judge who has received evidence that you have committed a crime. But you may also be arrested without a warrant if an officer has "probable cause," or sufficient reason, to believe that you have committed or are committing a crime. His or her good reason must be based on evidence, but that evidence may be less than would be needed to prove you were guilty beyond a reasonable doubt.

(Bottom Left) The Supreme Court has ruled that "lawyers are necessities, not luxuries."

lawyer, the police must tell suspects that a lawyer will be appointed for them free of charge. Finally, the police must warn suspects that anything they say can be used against them in a trial. Today, these rights are commonly referred to as Miranda rights.

The four justices who disagreed with the majority were worried about the far-reaching implications of the decision. Justice Byron White wrote: "There is, in my view, every reason to believe that a good many defendants who otherwise would have been convicted . . . will now . . . either not be tried at all or will be acquitted if the State's evidence, minus the confession, is put to the test of litigation." Justice John Marshall Harlan said the Court "is taking a big risk with society's welfare in imposing its new rules" for police procedure in dealing with persons accused of committing crimes.

Recent Court Decisions Have Retreated from Earlier Actions

Since the Miranda decision was issued, the Court has considered many other cases involving the rights of the accused. Key issues have been whether the defendant was in custody and whether police were interrogating the suspect. According to recent decisions, if the suspect is not in custody or being questioned, the Miranda warnings are unnecessary. However, questioning does not have to be formal to be covered by the Miranda decision.

In 1990, in *Illinois* v. *Perkins,* the Supreme Court upheld a jailed suspect's confession even though he had not been informed of his rights. The suspect had bragged to his cellmate that he had committed the alleged murder. He did not know that the cellmate was a police officer posing as an inmate. The Court said that the Miranda decision forbids "coercion," but not "strategic deception." In this instance, taking advantage of the suspect's misplaced trust was not unconstitutional.

A 1991 case, *Arizona* v. *Fulminante,* also dealt with the rights of accused persons. Fulminante's confession to a fellow inmate who was an FBI

Connections to Literature

The book *Gideon's Trumpet*, by Anthony Lewis, is a very readable, interesting account of the facts surrounding the *Gideon* v. *Wainwright* decision. The book describes the hard-luck story of Clarence Earl Gideon and how this alcoholic, small-time thief was responsible for one of the most important Supreme Court decisions of this century. Although the book focuses on Gideon's case, it also serves as a primer on how the Supreme Court operates. The book was made into a film and is now available on video. It starred Henry Fonda as Gideon and Jose Ferrer as the noted lawyer, Abe Fortas, who represented Gideon before the Supreme Court.

informer was thrown out by the Court. The confession was given in return for the promise of protection from other prisoners. This the Court believed was coercion. But at the same time, the Court reversed itself by ruling that involuntary confessions need not always result in a new trial on appeal. The Court held that such confessions can be "harmless error" if the appeals court finds that the jury would have convicted the defendant anyway.

Trying to Find a Balance Between Individual Rights and Public Safety

Many people criticize the Court for being too concerned about the rights of the accused. They believe that the Court's actions have put criminals back on the street and that the rights of victims of crime are often overlooked. They want the courts to get tougher on criminals even if it means the loss of some rights. This, some believe, is a small price to pay for ridding the streets of crime. Others, however, believe that our liberty is one of the greatest privileges Americans enjoy. To preserve all our rights, there must be limits on police powers. Otherwise, they would be able to force confessions out of people—including the innocent. Some guilty persons may occasionally be allowed to go free, but preserving our individual rights is more important. The debate will doubtless continue.

Understanding Civic Issues

1. What rights do accused persons have according to the Constitution?
2. After the Miranda decision, the police must inform accused suspects of their rights. What specific rights are included in the Miranda warnings?
3. **Critical Thinking** Do you agree with the majority or the minority in the Miranda case? Has the Court gone too far in protecting the rights of the accused?
4. **Hands-On Citizenship** Imagine that you are told that all of your rights as an accused person except for one will be taken away from you. Listed below are your rights:
   - right to a fair trial
   - right to be judged by a jury of your peers
   - right to an open and public trial
   - protection from unreasonable searches and seizures
   - right to remain silent
   - right to an attorney

   With two other classmates, decide which right is most important. Which right would you never want to lose?

   Present your explanation to the rest of the class. Why was the right you retained the most important?

   Review the issues raised in the last paragraph. Where does your group stand on the issue of the rights of the accused versus the need for society to protect itself from criminal activity? How can a balance be achieved?

Citizenship Lab Answers

1. The Constitution guarantees accused persons many rights. Among these are protection against unreasonable search and seizure and against being forced to testify against themselves. Accused persons are guaranteed due process, a speedy and public trial, the right to have a lawyer, and a reasonable bail. People found guilty of crimes shall not be punished in cruel and unusual ways.

2. The right to remain silent and the right to have a lawyer present during questioning; police must inform suspects of their rights to remain silent and must warn suspects that anything they say can be used against them in a trial.

3. Answers will vary. Students who agree will point out that every person is entitled to know their rights; students who disagree will argue that informing accused persons of their rights probably results in some guilty suspects going free.

Teaching the Hands-On Citizenship

In this activity, you should not be looking for a particular answer, but rather at the reasoning skills the students exhibit. At the highest level of reasoning skills, students should be able to identify and logically organize all relevant information: they should use critical thinking skills to analyze, evaluate, and synthesize the information and they should reach informed conclusions based on the information they present.

At·a·Glance 15

New Roles in a Changing World
1974–Present

Chapter Planning Guide

Section	Student Text	Teacher's Edition Activities
Opener and Story pp. 638–641	**Keys to History Time Line** **History Mystery** Beginning the Story with **Jaime Escalante**	**Setting the Stage Activity** Profiling the Ideal Teacher, p. 640
1 **The Nation After Vietnam and Watergate** pp. 642–647	**Point of View** Should President Nixon have been pardoned?, p. 642 **Link to the Present** New role for an ex-President, p. 644 **World Link** Democracy in the Philippines, p. 646	**Warm-Up Activity** Advising Ford, p. 642 **Geography Question of the Day,** p. 642 **Section Activity** A Presidential Conversation, p. 644 **Bonus Activity** Letters About Terrorism, p. 646 **Wrap-Up Activity** Creating Political Cartoons, p. 647
2 **The Post–Cold War Era Begins** pp. 648–655	**Hands-On History** Balancing the budget, p. 649 **Reading Maps** Some Trouble Spots of the 1990s, p. 650 **Geography Lab** The Interior Highlands, p. 655	**Warm-Up Activity** Solving Budget Woes, p. 648 **Geography Question of the Day,** p. 648 **Section Activity** Acting Out Radio Talk Shows, p. 650 **Bonus Activity** Grading Presidents, p. 651 **Wrap-Up Activity** Planning a Campaign, p. 652
3 **New Challenges and Hopes** pp. 656–663	**Reading Maps** Examples of Environmental Protection, p. 658 **Link to Art** *El Lenguaje Mudo del Alma (The Silent Language of the Soul),* p. 661 **Skill Lab** Taking Action, p. 663	**Warm-Up Activity** Charting Changes, p. 656 **Geography Question of the Day,** p. 656 **Section Activity** Designing a Neighborhood, p. 660 **Bonus Activity** Proposing Solutions, p. 658 **Wrap-Up Activity** Causes for Concern, Reasons to Hope, p. 662
Evaluation	**Section 1 Review,** p. 647 **Section 2 Review,** p. 652 **Section 3 Review,** p. 662 **Chapter Survey,** pp. 664–665 **Alternative Assessment** Acting out political discussions, p. 665	**Answers to Section 1 Review,** p. 647 **Answers to Section 2 Review,** p. 652 **Answers to Section 3 Review,** p. 662 **Answers to Chapter Survey,** pp. 664–665 (Alternative Assessment guidelines are in the Take-Home Planner.)

Teacher's Resource Package

Chapter Summaries: English and Spanish, pp. 66–67

Chapter Resources Binder
Study Guide Skimming to Locate Information, p. 129
Reinforcement Determining Cause and Effect, pp. 133–134

American Readings Thoughts on Patriotism, p. 65

Chapter Resources Binder
Study Guide Using a Graphic Organizer, p. 130

Geography Extensions Exploring the Interior Highlands, pp. 35–36

Using Historical Documents The Gulf War Resolution, pp. 96–100

Chapter Resources Binder
Study Guide Using Questions to Guide Reading, p. 131
Skills Development Taking Action, pp. 135–136

American Readings The Joy Luck Club, p. 66; Computer Commuters, p. 67; Life Lessons, p. 68

Chapter and Unit Tests Chapter 15 Tests, Forms A and B, pp. 111–114

Take-Home Planner

Introducing the Chapter Activity
A President by Design, p. 22

Chapter In-Depth Activity Conducting a Survey, p. 22

Reduced Views
Study Guide, p. 24
Reinforcement, p. 25
American Readings, p. 26

Unit 10 Answers, pp. 31–38

Reduced Views
Study Guide, p. 24
Geography Extensions, p. 27
Using Historical Documents, p. 27

Unit 5 Answers, pp. 31–38

Reduced Views
Study Guide, p. 24
Skills Development, p. 25
American Readings, p. 26

Unit 5 Answers, pp. 31–38

Reduced Views
Chapter Tests, p. 27

Unit 5 Answers, pp. 31–38

Alternative Assessment Guidelines for scoring the Chapter Survey activity, p. 23

Additional Resources

Wall Time Line

Unit 5 Activity

Transparency Package

Transparency 15-1 Changes in Population and Households—use with Section 3

Transparency 15-2 The Changing Home—use with Section 3

Transparency Activity Book

SelecTest Testing Software
Chapter 15 Test, Forms A and B

Vital Links

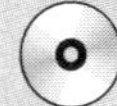

Videodisc

CD-ROM

Gas line (see TE p. 643)
Carter on Camp David (see TE p. 644)
Voice of hostage Bill Belk (see TE p. 645)
Senator on Iran-Contra (see TE p. 646)
Gulf War (see TE p. 649)
Haitian refugees (see TE p. 650)
Senior rally for health care (see TE p. 657)
Boycott to protest Styrofoam (see TE p. 657)
Beach cleanup (see TE p. 658)
Robotics (see TE p. 659)
Citizenship ceremony (see TE p. 660)
League of Women Voters (see TE p. 660)

15

Teaching Resources

Take-Home Planner 5
- Introducing Chapter Activity
- Chapter In-Depth Activity
- Alternative Assessment

Chapter Resources Binder
Geography Extensions
American Readings
Using Historical Documents
Transparency Activities
Wall Time Line Activities
Chapter Summaries
Chapter and Unit Tests
SelecTest Test File
Vital Links CD-ROM/Videodisc

Chapter Objectives

- ★ Explain how the nation recovered from the Vietnam War and the Watergate scandal.
- ★ Identify the post–Cold War challenges at home and abroad.
- ★ Describe the challenges that lie ahead as American society and democracy move into a new century.

Chapter Overview

Presidents following Nixon tried to respond to the "crisis of confidence." Ford granted Nixon a full pardon. Carter got Egypt and Israel to sign a peace agreement at Camp David. However he could not curb inflation or gain release of hostages in Iran. Reagan tried to shrink the size of government, except defense spending. Despite Iran-Contra, he remained popular.

Time Line

Keys to History

Keys to History journal writing activities are on p. 664 in the Chapter Survey.

Ford pardons Nixon The former President was spared a trial for Watergate-related crimes, but Americans disagreed about whether the pardon was a good idea. (p. 642)

Camp David Accords This agreement between Israel and Egypt gave the world hope for peace in the Middle East. (p. 644)

Iranian militants seize American hostages President Carter's handling of the crisis undermined Americans' confidence in him and helped Ronald Reagan win the presidency. (pp. 644–645)

Looking Back Watergate shook Americans' faith in their political system and leaders.

1974–Present

Chapter 15 New Roles in a Changing World

Sections

Beginning the Story with Jaime Escalante

1. The Nation After Vietnam and Watergate
2. The Post–Cold War Era Begins
3. New Challenges and Hopes

1974
President Ford pardons Nixon for possible Watergate crimes

1978
Camp David Accords
Carter, Begin, and Sadat negotiate a peace

1979
Iranian militants seize American hostages in Tehran

1970 | 1980

Looking Back

Watergate scandal
1972–1974

Under Bush, the first post–Cold War President, the United States led an international coalition against Iraqi invaders in Kuwait. Bush also supported sending United Nations troops to Somalia and Bosnia. His presidency was beset by domestic problems, such as the federal deficit. Bush was succeeded by Clinton, whose achievements included NAFTA and restoration of democracy in Haiti. Although deadlocked with Congress on health care and the budget, Clinton was re-elected in 1996.

As the nation moves into a new century, its population is becoming older and more ethnically and racially diverse. New environmental issues demand attention. Advances in technology have created an "information economy." Most important, Americans face the challenge of keeping ideals of community and democracy alive.

HISTORY *Mystery*

His occupations include nuclear engineering, politics, carpentry, poetry, and peanut farming. Who is he, and why do we remember him?

1981
First woman appointed to Supreme Court
Sandra Day O'Connor

1990
Americans with Disabilities Act

1991
American-led coalition fights Iraq in Persian Gulf War
Oil fields set afire during the war

1993
North American Free Trade Agreement (NAFTA) approved

1990 — Present

World Link
Democracy triumphs in the Philippines
1986

Looking Ahead

Your generation embraces the opportunities and challenges facing the United States

Teaching the HISTORY *Mystery*

Students will find the answer on p. 644. See Chapter Survey, p. 664, for additional questions.

Time Line

First woman appointed to Supreme Court President Reagan appointed Sandra Day O'Connor to the Supreme Court in 1981. (p. 645)

Americans with Disabilities Act This law made daily activities and equal employment opportunities possible for disabled Americans. (p. 648)

Troops sent to Persian Gulf President Bush's idea that nations could cooperate to oppose aggression proved successful when Iraqi invaders were pushed out of Kuwait. (p. 649)

NAFTA approved Under President Clinton, Congress passed this trade agreement between the United States, Mexico, and Canada. (p. 651)

World Link See p. 646.

Looking Ahead The dreams of equality, opportunity, freedom, and respect for individual rights provide a solid foundation for the future.

Beginning the Story

Jaime Escalante

An immigrant from Bolivia, Escalante gained national attention for preparing high school students in a mostly poor and Hispanic area of Los Angeles to pass a college-level calculus exam. He represents a new wave of Hispanic immigrants in the 1960s and 1970s that has contributed to the nation's growing diversity. His efforts highlight the importance of high educational standards to prepare students for the competitive atmosphere of a rapidly changing economy.

Setting the Stage Activity

Profiling the Ideal Teacher

To prepare students for reading about Jaime Escalante, ask them to imagine being on a board of education. They seek a teacher to replace one who found the condition of the local high school depressing and had trouble "reaching" students. Ask groups to write a profile of the ideal candidate. They should consider personal qualities, teaching philosophy, and attitude toward teens.

See the Introducing the Chapter Activity, A President by Design, **Take-Home Planner 5**, p. 22.

History Footnote

Jaime Escalante began teaching at Garfield in 1974. He had to battle administrators for better textbooks and more challenging math courses. He also struggled to win over his students. He challenged, intrigued, and teased them—even provoked them to anger. The respect they felt for him was shown in the nickname they gave him: *Kimo* is based on *Kemo Sabe,* the nickname given to the fictional Lone Ranger by his faithful companion Tonto.

The incident of the Advanced Placement calculus exam drew national attention. A movie, *Stand and Deliver,* retold Escalante's story, and a biographer dubbed him "the best teacher in America." Escalante also starred in a public TV series on math, science, and careers.

Beginning the Story with

Jaime Escalante

On May 19, 1982, 18 high-school seniors filed into Room 411 of Garfield High School in a mostly poor and Hispanic area of east Los Angeles. Many had had trouble sleeping the night before. Some had broken down and cried with nervousness as they prepared to take a grueling college examination in calculus. Jaime Escalante (HĪ-mee es-kuh-LAHN-tay), their calculus teacher, paced nervously in a nearby classroom. After three hours, his students finally emerged from Room 411, tired but happy. On seeing their teacher, one student exclaimed, "Kimo! That was a piece of cake."

Escalante's students passed the exam with flying colors. Their joy turned to dismay, however, when 14 of the 18 were accused of cheating because their answers to one question looked suspiciously similar. Escalante was outraged at the accusation. He had known that his drill-like approach to teaching would result in similar student responses to questions. "I stand behind my kids," he said. "I believe in my students."

The Move to California

Growing up in La Paz, Bolivia, Jaime had no idea that he would become a teacher. When he reached his teen years, however, he found that he had a talent for math and science. He decided to become a physics teacher. Soon Jaime earned enough to support his wife and small son.

In 1963 Jaime and his wife left Bolivia for the United States, where they hoped to find more opportunities for their son. Upon arrival in Los Angeles, the Escalantes received a rude shock. Jaime's education in Bolivia did not qualify him to teach in California. He would have to go to college again. This time he would do so in a new language—English.

Jaime found a job mopping the floors at a restaurant while he went back to college. When he finished, he was hired to teach math at Garfield High School. The school's crumbling buildings and graffiti-covered walls depressed

History Bookshelf

White, Ryan. *Ryan White: My Own Story.* Dial, 1991. Ryan White's story of his experiences as a young person with AIDS helps put a human face on the epidemic. The book also includes easily accessible facts about the illness.

Also of interest:

Landau, Elaine. *Bill Clinton.* Franklin Watts, 1993.

Lewis, Barbara. *Kids with Courage: True Stories About Young People Making a Difference.* Free Spirit, 1992.

Palacios, Argentina. *Standing Tall: The Stories of Ten Hispanic Americans.* Scholastic, 1994.

Takaki, Ronald T. *Strangers at the Gate Again: Asian American Immigration After 1965.* Chelsea House, 1995.

Jaime Escalante works with students at Hiram Johnson High School in Sacramento, California, where he moved after many years of teaching in Los Angeles.

him so much that he planned to quit after his first year. As he came to know his students, however, he became determined to help them succeed by teaching them to believe in themselves. What better way, he thought, than by having them master calculus for the college placement exams?

"We can do it"

When Escalante announced plans to teach a college-level calculus class at Garfield High, few believed he would succeed. Garfield students could not handle college-level math, critics claimed. To start his class, Escalante recruited students from basic math classes much like a coach recruits top athletes for the big league. He enforced strict discipline in his classroom. He also used unusual but effective teaching methods. For example, to help students master difficult mathematical ideas he explained them by using terms from sports and even soap operas.

As the exam approached, Escalante set up after-school cram sessions. Day after day he drilled his students mercilessly. They developed a team spirit and a belief that they could succeed. Imagine, then, how shocked they were by the accusation that they had cheated. When offered a chance to retake the test, 12 of the 14 students decided to do so. As one student explained:

> "I want to . . . show Escalante that what he taught me I didn't forget, and that I really appreciate all the time he put in . . . and to prove to . . . ourselves that we can do it again."

They could and they did. On their second try, all 12 students again passed the exam. Jaime Escalante smiled at the results. He had known all along that his students would succeed.

Source: *Escalante: The Best Teacher in America* by Jay Matthews, Harcourt Brace, 1982.

Hands-On HISTORY

Activity

Many people did not believe that high-school students in east Los Angeles could succeed in a college-level math class. Jaime Escalante proved them wrong. Imagine that you are Escalante and you have just come home from your first day of teaching the class described above. Write in your diary how you felt standing in front of the class and teaching. What hopes, and what worries, might you have for the students?

Discussion

Thinking Historically

1. Why do you think Escalante returned to college in California? (Loved teaching, wanted to prove he could succeed at his old career in a new country.)

2. What does Escalante's decision to teach at a "difficult" school tell you about him? (Likes challenges, prefers working with students who really need his help.)

3. Would you like to be one of Escalante's students? Explain. (Yes: challenging, learn a lot. No: drill would get dull, too much work.)

See the Chapter In-Depth Activity, Conducting a Survey, **Take-Home Planner 5**, p. 23.

Teaching the Hands-On HISTORY

Before students write, have them visualize that first day of class. For example, did Escalante dive into the subject matter or spend time getting acquainted with the class? Were students attentive or jumpy? Did the period drag or go quickly?

For a journal writing activity on Jaime Escalante, see student page 664.

Introducing the Section

Warm-Up Activity

Advising Ford

To prepare for studying the period following Nixon's resignation, have students imagine they are Ford's advisors as he steps into the presidency. Ask them to list three actions the new President might take to restore confidence in the government and help Americans recover from Watergate. Conclude by having them compare lists.

Geography Question of the Day

Give students copies of an outline map of the world (see **Geography Extensions**). Write the following on the board: Iran, Panama, Israel, Egypt, Grenada, Nicaragua, Lebanon. Tell them that much of American foreign policy in the 1970s and 1980s focused on these nations. Have them shade and label as many as they can without consulting another source. Then have them use the map on pp. R2–R3 to locate any they did not know. Have them save their maps for use on the Geography Question of the Day on teacher p. 648.

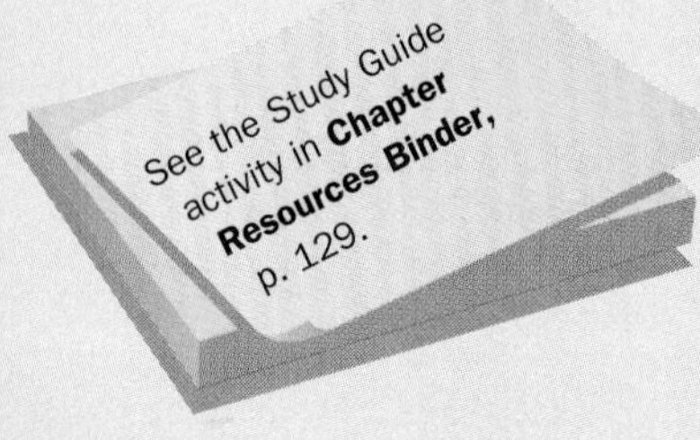

See the Study Guide activity in **Chapter Resources Binder**, p. 129.

Section Objectives

- ★ Explain how Presidents Ford and Carter tried to restore the confidence of Americans in their government.
- ★ Identify the successes and failures of President Carter's foreign policy.
- ★ Describe how President Reagan tried to change the role of the federal government.

Teaching Resources

Take-Home Planner 5, pp. 20–30
Chapter Resources Binder
Study Guide, p. 129
Reinforcement, pp. 133–134
Skills Development
Geography Extensions
American Readings, p. 65
Using Historical Documents
Transparency Activities
Chapter and Unit Tests

1. The Nation After Vietnam and Watergate

Reading Guide

Section Focus **The nation as it recovered from Vietnam and Watergate**

1. **How did Presidents Ford and Carter try to restore the confidence of Americans in their government?**
2. **What were the successes and failures of President Carter's foreign policy?**
3. **How did President Reagan try to change the role of the federal government?**

The Vietnam War and the Watergate affair shook the faith of Americans in their nation's political system and leaders. The three Presidents who followed Nixon—Gerald Ford, Jimmy Carter, and Ronald Reagan—each made his own effort to respond to this "crisis of confidence" and to heal the wounds caused by war and scandal.

Ford: Healing the Wounds

Confidence in the nation's leaders would not be easy to restore, however. A 1975 survey showed that 83 percent of Americans still believed that "the people running this country . . . don't tell us the truth."

President Ford moved quickly in late 1974 to grant former President Nixon "a full, free and absolute pardon" for all crimes that he may have committed as President. Ford's pardon meant that Nixon would never be put on trial. The new President hoped that the pardon would help "heal the wounds" left by the Watergate scandal.

Many Americans disapproved. It was unfair, they argued, to pardon Nixon when his top aides had gone to prison for Watergate-related crimes. The pardon left "a sour smell" in the nation's capital, reported a newspaper.

Point of View

Should President Nixon have been pardoned?

Some called it an act of "compassion" when President Ford pardoned former President Nixon of any possible wrongdoing against the nation. Ford believed that "Richard Nixon and his loved ones . . . [had] suffered enough," and the nation needed to put the Watergate issue to rest. Ford said he was concerned about the "future of this great country. . . . I cannot prolong the bad dreams that continue to reopen [the nation's wounds]."

Harvard law professor Raoul Berger disagreed. The pardoning of Nixon, he argued, would "breed disrespect for the law [and encourage future Presidents] to feel that Presidents are untouchable." Senator Floyd Haskell of Colorado feared that the pardon would only

> "confirm what too many Americans already believe: that there is one set of laws for the rich and powerful, another for everyone else."

Some Americans still think it would have been better to seek the truth about Watergate,

History Footnote

After his resignation former President Nixon retreated in disgrace to his California home. In 1977 he told an interviewer, "My political life is over." However, the next year he began making carefully selected public appearances. He published his memoirs and eight other nonfiction books. Presidents Reagan, Bush, and Clinton all called him for advice on international strategy. He traveled to other nations, including China and the Soviet Union, and came to be considered an elder statesman. One news magazine said, "Richard Nixon failed more spectacularly than any other U.S. President, yet by sheer endurance he rebuilt his standing as the most important figure of the postwar era."

even if it meant putting Nixon on trial. Others respect Ford for sparing Nixon—and the nation—that painful process.

Carter: Washington Outsider

Distrust of political leaders continued to dominate the thoughts of voters in the 1976 presidential election. The Democrats nominated Jimmy Carter, a nuclear engineer, peanut farmer, and former governor of Georgia. Carter ran as a Washington outsider—someone unconnected to national politics or the Watergate scandal. He won by a narrow margin over Gerald Ford.

Carter's approach to politics seemed like a breath of fresh air. When he traveled, for example, he stayed in the homes of ordinary people. The nation's leaders could not understand people's concerns, he said, if they lived "like royalty here in Washington."

Rising prices and energy problems As President, Carter convinced Congress to decrease military spending and to lower taxes on businesses and on personal incomes. Inflation, however, had plagued the nation since the late 1960s. Fueled by high oil prices, the prices of goods were soaring. American workers worried as their paychecks bought fewer and fewer goods.

Carter believed that high energy costs were at the root of inflation. If people used less oil, he argued, prices of all goods would drop. In 1977 Carter proposed an energy program that encouraged conservation and use of alternative energy sources, such as solar power. The public, however, failed to support him, and the energy program stalled in Congress.

Then, in January 1979 Muslim revolutionaries in oil-rich Iran overthrew their ruler, the Shah. Soon, Iran's vast flow of oil slowed to a trickle. The entire world now faced an oil shortage. Other oil-producing nations raised their prices.

As they had in 1973, American drivers lined up for hours to buy expensive gasoline. Heating oil costs also rose. In the face of this crisis, Congress finally passed part of Carter's energy program. Americans cut back their use of fuel, too, and the shortage eased.

New Policy Overseas

You read in Chapter 13 that Carter's foreign policy goal was to encourage nations to protect their citizens' human rights. Carter kept this goal in mind as he faced a controversy over the future of the Panama Canal.

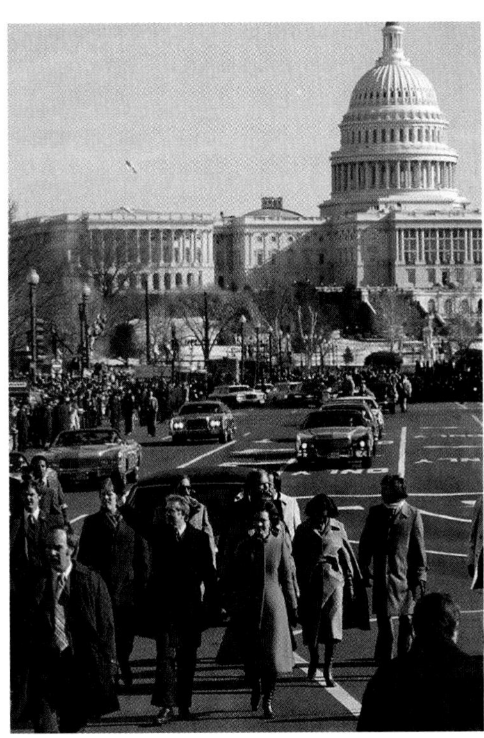

By walking in his inaugural parade rather than riding in a limousine, Carter set a new tone for the American presidency on the first day he took office.

Developing the Section

Discussion

Checking Understanding

1. What caused the energy crisis of 1979? (Muslim revolutionaries took control of Iran and slowed its oil exports to a trickle.)

Stimulating Critical Thinking

2. Are most of today's political leaders honest with the public? Explain. (Yes: they try to be honest because the press usually exposes lies. No: most would lie to avoid losing an election. Some information must be kept secret for security reasons.)

Teaching the Point of View

Tell students that during the 1973 Senate hearing to approve Ford as Vice-President, he was asked if he would pardon Nixon if given the chance. He replied, "I do not think the American public would stand for it." Later he changed his mind. Ask if they think the public did stand for it. Discuss whether they agree with Raoul Berger and Senator Haskell.

Vital Links

Gas line (Picture) Unit 6, Side 1, Search 29347

See also Unit 6 Explore CD-ROM location 224.

History Footnote

In signing the Camp David Accords, Israel agreed to withdraw from Egypt's Sinai Peninsula, which Israel had seized in 1967. Egypt and Israel signed a peace treaty in 1979, and Israel completed withdrawal from the Sinai in 1982. The Accords also set up diplomatic relations between Israel and Egypt. Egypt became the first Arab nation to officially recognize Israel.

Sadat and Begin won the 1978 Nobel Peace Prize. However, Sadat's peacemaking efforts cost him dearly. Other Arab leaders rejected the peace treaty, criticized Sadat for negotiating independently with Israel, and expelled Egypt from the Arab League. In Egypt, Islamic fundamentalists fanned the flames of discontent aroused by Sadat's policies and the nation's economic woes. A militant group assassinated Sadat in 1981.

Teaching the

Link to the Present

Point out that Carter also has written books of nonfiction and poetry, monitored elections in developing nations, and sponsored conferences on issues. He has been nominated for the Nobel Peace Prize. Ask why qualities listed by the newspaper might "hobble" a President. (With so many issues and problems, Presidents need to focus on the "big picture" rather than details. To be effective, they have to "play politics.")

Section Activity

A Presidential Conversation

To focus on beliefs and policies of Ford, Carter, and Reagan, have groups of three role-play a conversation between them after Nixon's funeral in 1994. What will they say about him, the 1976 and 1980 elections, their presidencies, and their hopes for the nation? Have groups present their role-plays.

Vital Links

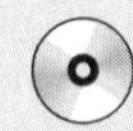

Carter on Camp David (First Person Account) Unit 6, Side 1, Search 29401, Play to 30225

See also Unit 6 Explore CD-ROM location 233.

Link to the Present

New role for an ex-President Since leaving office, Jimmy Carter has devoted his life to causes in which he believes. Helping the poor is one. For example, Carter works as a carpenter with Habitat for Humanity, a group that builds homes for the poor. He has also launched the Atlanta Project, which tries to help neighborhoods solve problems—including crime and unemployment.

Helping bring peace to nations in turmoil is another of Carter's goals. He helped end military rule in Haiti (see page 651) and brought warring parties in both Bosnia and Sudan together for negotiations.

Many people agree with these observations of a newspaper: "Attention to detail. A distaste for politics. Above all, a commitment to doing the right thing. The qualities that hobbled [handicapped] Jimmy Carter in the White House seem to be making him a great ex-President."

Panama Canal Treaty The people of Panama had long resented American control of the Panama Canal. They thought the canal should belong to Panama. Carter agreed. In 1977 he signed a treaty that would return the canal to Panama by 2000. The treaty ran into stiff opposition among Americans. Many did not want the United States to give up control of the canal. Even so, the Senate ratified the treaty in early 1978.

Middle East peace While many Americans opposed the Panama Canal Treaty, most supported Carter's efforts to promote peace in the Middle East. There, the hostility between Israel and the Arab nations around it continued to simmer.

In 1978, in an effort to break the cycle of violence, Carter invited Egypt's Anwar al-Sadat (sah-DAHT) and Israel's Menachem Begin (BAY-gin) to a meeting at Camp David in Maryland. Upon arrival, the two refused to speak to one another. A frustrated Sadat prepared to pack up and return home.

Carter convinced Sadat to stay and steered the two men through days of difficult negotiations. On September 17, 1978, the leaders of Israel and Egypt signed a peace agreement called the Camp David Accords. Weary but triumphant, Carter declared, "This is one of those rare, bright moments of history."

The hostage crisis All too soon, however, Carter faced a new crisis. The Shah, who had fled Iran during the revolution, came to the United States for medical treatment.

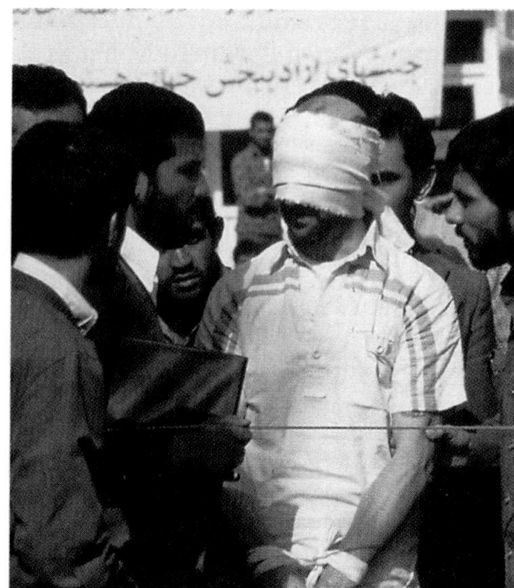

For 444 days American hostages were held captive by Iranian revolutionaries who blamed the United States for having supported the former Shah of Iran.

History Footnote

For a dozen years Justice Sandra Day O'Connor was the only woman on the Supreme Court. Then, the retirement of Justice Byron White in 1993 provided President Bill Clinton with the opportunity to nominate a justice. Clinton wanted to counterbalance O'Connor and the other conservative appointments made by Presidents Reagan and Bush. He also wanted to live up to his campaign pledge to seek diversity in his appointments. He appointed Ruth Bader Ginsburg, a judge and former lawyer who had successfully argued cases involving women's rights before the Supreme Court. Ginsburg, who is considered a moderate, became the first Supreme Court justice appointed by a Democrat since Thurgood Marshall was appointed by President Lyndon Johnson in 1967.

Outraged Iranians demanded that the United States return him to Iran to face trial. Carter refused, and young Iranians stormed the American embassy in Tehran, taking 66 Americans hostage.

Carter first tried to negotiate the release of the hostages. Then he sent military aircraft to rescue them. Both efforts failed. Meanwhile, night after night, Americans watched the blindfolded hostages paraded before television cameras as Iranians chanted, "Death to Carter, death to the Shah."

Carter's handling of the hostage crisis undermined public confidence in his presidency. The tragic events in Iran haunted the President all the way to election day.

The Election of 1980

As the 1980 election approached, the Republicans nominated Ronald Reagan, a former actor who had been governor of California. While Carter talked of the need to make sacrifices and "hard choices," Reagan radiated optimism about the future. "There's nothing the American people cannot do when we try," he declared.

One week before the election, Reagan asked Americans, "Are you better off than you were four years ago?" With inflation climbing and Americans held hostage in Iran, voters answered "No." Reagan won with 51 percent of the vote. Just hours after Carter stepped down as President, Iranian guards freed the American hostages.

The Reagan "Revolution"

In 1981 Ronald Reagan took office, declaring that it was "morning in America." He set forth ideas that some called "revolutionary." Others called them a return to the conservative politics of the 1950s.

In any case, Reagan's style was immensely popular. People enjoyed the smiling, easy-

Ronald Reagan's personal style and political skills re-established the power of the presidency in a way not seen since Lyndon Johnson and Franklin Roosevelt.

going manner of this energetic 69-year-old. They also approved when Reagan made history by appointing Sandra Day O'Connor to the Supreme Court in 1981. She was the first woman to sit on the nation's highest court.

"Government is the problem" Ever since Franklin Roosevelt, Reagan claimed, Americans had depended too much on the federal government. As a result, it had grown too large. Now, Reagan declared, "Government is not the solution to our problem; government *is* the problem." It was time, he said, for Americans to put their faith in American business rather than in the government.

In his effort to shrink the size of government, Reagan pushed for cuts in welfare programs, education, and public transportation. The budgets of government agencies such as the Environmental Protection Agency and Equal Employment Opportunity Commission were slashed. Such actions slowed government efforts to enforce antipollution and antidiscrimination regulations.

Reaganomics Following the tradition of Republicans in the 1920s, Reagan believed that the best way to ensure prosperity was to lower taxes on the wealthy and on businesses. This policy would make more money available to businesses to expand and hire more workers. The benefits of tax cuts would

Discussion

Checking Understanding

1. Why were Iranians angry at Carter? (He refused their demand to return the Shah to Iran.)

2. What did Reagan mean by stating "government is the problem"? (Federal government tries to do too much and spends too much.)

Stimulating Critical Thinking

3. Whom would you have voted for in 1980—Carter or Reagan? Explain. (Carter: did as well as anyone could have with the hostage crisis; had good qualities and ideas. Reagan: nation needed his positive attitude and willingness to shrink the government.)

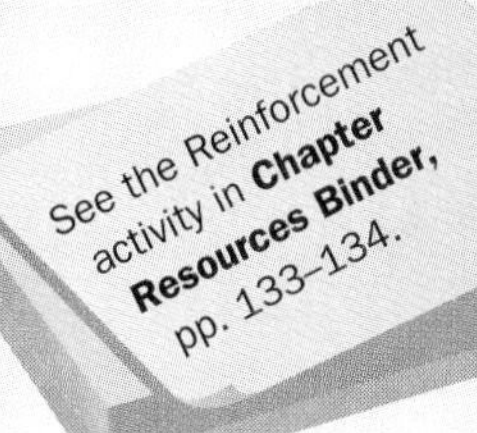

See the Reinforcement activity in **Chapter Resources Binder**, pp. 133–134.

Vital Links

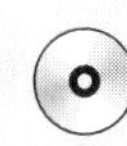

Voice of hostage Bill Belk (First Person Account) Unit 6, Side 1, Search 30241, Play to 31105

See also Unit 6 Explore CD-ROM location 236.

Teaching the World Link

Remind students that the United States took control of the Philippines after the Spanish-American War and that the Philippines gained independence in 1946. (See Chapter 8.) Note that Marcos became president in 1965. His long rule included nearly a decade of martial law. Aquino inherited serious economic problems, and the military tried to overthrow her. She did not run for re-election in 1992. Marcos died in exile in 1989.

Bonus Activity

Letters About Terrorism

To focus on issues involved in a hostage crisis, have pairs role-play President Reagan and an American hostage in a foreign country. Ask the "hostages" to write letters to Reagan describing their situation and feelings, and suggesting what should be done. Have "Presidents" write responses as they think Reagan would have.

Vital Links

Senator on Iran-Contra (First Person Account) Unit 6, Side 1, Search 28874, Play to 29325

See also Unit 6 Explore CD-ROM location 220.

History Footnote

Ronald Reagan had been President only a few weeks when a man named John W. Hinckley, Jr., tried to assassinate him. Reagan and three others, including White House Press Secretary James S. Brady, were shot. Reagan handled the situation with a sense of humor. Entering the operating room, he said to the surgeons, "Please tell me you're Republicans." When an aide later tried to assure him that the government was still running normally, Reagan joked, "What makes you think I'd be happy about that?" Reagan's likable personality and sense of humor helped him remain popular. For example, many Americans wondered why he was not impeached due to the Iran-Contra scandal. Some called him "the Teflon President" because, with his public appeal, no criticism seemed to stick to him.

World Link

Democracy in the Philippines "Today the Filipino people celebrate the triumph of democracy, and the world celebrates with them," said President Reagan in 1986. The world was celebrating the fall of the Filipino dictator Ferdinand Marcos, a one-time friend of the United States.

The end of his rule had been in sight for several years. In 1983 Marcos was suspected of involvement in the killing of Benigno S. Aquino, Jr., his chief critic. The Filipino people grew disgusted with Marcos and forced him to hold elections on February 7, 1986.

Corazon Aquino, widow of the slain leader, ran against Marcos. Despite evidence that Aquino had won, Marcos declared himself the winner. Filipinos took to the streets, forming human barricades against the tanks that Marcos sent to push them back. The last straw came when Reagan withdrew support. Marcos fled to Hawaii, and Aquino became President.

thus "trickle down" from the wealthiest Americans to the poorest. This theory came to be known as "Reaganomics."

In 1981 Congress passed the largest income tax cut in the nation's history. At the same time, prices—including oil prices—were falling. By 1983 a business and construction boom was underway.

The Election of 1984

Reagan's critics claimed that his tax and budget cuts hurt the poor and the elderly as well as the environment. Polls showed, however, that the majority of Americans felt that the President was doing a good job.

In the 1984 election Reagan faced Walter Mondale, who had served as Vice-President under Carter. Mondale chose Geraldine Ferraro as his running mate. She was the first woman to run on the presidential ticket of a major political party.

During his campaign, Mondale warned voters that Reagan's tax cuts were driving the national deficit to its highest levels ever. However, Reagan easily won re-election. As one supporter said, "Reagan is a symbol to a generation happy with itself."

Reagan's Foreign Policy

Foreign policy dominated Reagan's second term. A staunch anti-Communist, the President promised that he would help the United States "stand tall in the world again" by fighting communism abroad. Even though he cut spending on domestic programs, he increased the military budget to record levels.

Grenada When a pro-Communist group took control of the government on the tiny Caribbean island of Grenada in 1983, Reagan ordered American troops to invade and drive them out. Critics at home and abroad denounced American interference in Grenada's affairs. Still, the quick success of the mission there heartened people distressed by American failures in Vietnam.

Nicaragua While the invasion of Grenada went smoothly, Reagan's policy toward Nicaragua hit serious snags. In 1979 rebels—called Sandinistas—in that Central American nation overthrew a brutal dictatorship that had ruled for 43 years. The Sandinista government sought to create an

History Footnote

In the spring and summer of 1987, a congressional committee held televised hearings on the Iran-Contra scandal. The key witness was Marine Lieutenant Colonel Oliver North, assistant to Reagan's national security advisor and mastermind of the shadowy group that had arranged the secret deals with Iran and the contras. North called the diversion of funds from Iran to Nicaragua a "neat idea" and admitted lying to Congress and destroying important documents. He said he did it in the name of patriotism and democracy. After a few years in the courts, the case against North was dismissed in 1991. North ran for the U.S. Senate from Virginia in 1994 but was defeated.

For Senator George Mitchell's statements to Oliver North on patriotism, see **American Readings**, p. 65.

HIGGINS
C'mon, boys... Somebody had to be driving.
IRAN
CONGRESS

Neither Reagan nor his political advisors wanted to admit responsibility for the arms-for-hostages deal with the government of Iran.

economy that combined elements of both communism and capitalism.

Reagan feared that the Soviet Union was trying to gain a foothold in Central America by supporting the Sandinistas. He urged Congress to give arms to anti-Sandinista rebels known as "contras." Congress opposed arming the contras. Instead, it passed the Boland Amendment, which banned all American aid to the contras.

Civil war in Lebanon Reagan's foreign policy also stumbled in the Middle East. In the 1970s conflict between Christians and Muslims in Lebanon had erupted into civil war. Reagan sent American troops to help as part of a United Nations peace-keeping force. In October 1983 a truck bomb explosion killed 241 American marines. Americans reacted with horror, and Reagan withdrew the remaining troops from Lebanon.

As the conflict dragged on, terrorists sympathetic to Iran kidnapped six Americans and held them hostage. Reagan refused to negotiate for the release of the hostages, declaring, "America will never make concessions to terrorists—to do so would only invite more terrorism." Behind the scenes, however, his aides were following a different policy.

The Iran-Contra Scandal

In November 1986 Americans learned that Oliver North and other aides to Reagan had been secretly selling weapons to Iran. By doing so, they hoped to gain the release of the hostages in Lebanon. The money from the sales, in turn, was used to buy arms for the contras in Nicaragua. The dealings broke Reagan's ban on negotiating with terrorists and violated the Boland Amendment.

Americans were stunned. Did the President know about the secret dealings? If so, could he be impeached for breaking the law? Reagan denied any knowledge of this illegal use of funds. The Iran-Contra scandal threw a shadow over Reagan's last years as President. Still, he left office in 1989 as one of the nation's most popular Presidents.

1. Section Review

1. Give three reasons why people objected to Ford's pardon of Nixon.
2. How did Carter handle conflicts in Panama, the Middle East, and Iran? What was the result in each case?
3. Critical Thinking If Reagan had looked back to the policies of past Presidents for inspiration, which decade do you think he would have most admired: the 1920s or the 1930s? Give reasons for your choice.

Closing the Section

Wrap-Up Activity

Creating Political Cartoons

To reinforce understanding of issues dominating the 1970s and 1980s, have pairs or small groups create political cartoons on issues of their choice. The cartoon on this page may serve as inspiration. Post completed cartoons in the classroom.

Section Review Answers

1. Any three: unfair to pardon Nixon when his top aides had gone to prison; encouraged disrespect for the law; confirmed belief of many that the law does not apply equally; better to seek the truth.

2. Signed treaty to return Panama Canal to Panama by year 2000; steered Sadat and Begin through negotiations resulting in Camp David Accords; failed to secure release of American hostages in Iran.

3. The 1920s, when Presidents Harding and Coolidge pursued policies that favored business and the wealthy and kept government involvement to a minimum.

Introducing the Section

Vocabulary

deficit (p. 648) the amount by which the government's spending is greater than its income

Warm-Up Activity

Solving Budget Woes

To prepare for learning about the budget deficit, have small groups consider this scenario: A family of four, in which both parents have jobs, finds it spent $5,000 more last year than it took in. Have the groups brainstorm ways for the family to avoid this situation in the future. Bring the groups together to compare ideas.

Geography Question of the Day

Have students take out the outline maps they saved from the Geography Question of the Day on p. 642. Have them shade and label Iraq, Kuwait, Somalia, Haiti, and Bosnia. Explain that these nations held key roles in United States foreign policy during the 1990s.

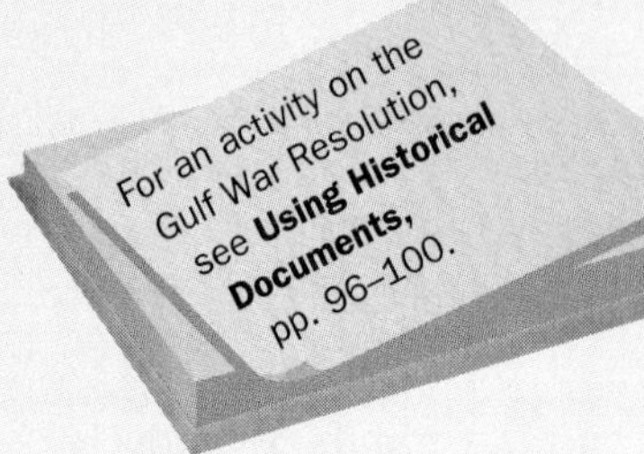
For an activity on the Gulf War Resolution, see **Using Historical Documents,** pp. 96–100.

Section Objectives

★ Identify the policies of President Bush at home and abroad.
★ Describe President Clinton's accomplishments and setbacks.

Teaching Resources

Take-Home Planner 5, pp. 20–30
Chapter Resources Binder
Study Guide, p. 130
Reinforcement
Skills Development
Geography Extensions, pp. 35–36
American Readings
Using Historical Documents, pp. 96–100
Transparency Activities
Chapter and Unit Tests

2. The Post–Cold War Era Begins

Reading Guide

New Term **deficit**

Section Focus **Post–Cold War challenges at home and abroad**

1. **What were the policies of President Bush both at home and abroad?**
2. **What were President Clinton's accomplishments and setbacks?**

As the 1980s drew to a close, so did the Cold War. You read in Chapter 13 that by 1989 a mostly peaceful "velvet revolution" was sweeping across Eastern Europe, ending decades of Communist rule. The next President faced a new world overseas as well as the legacy of Reagan's presidency at home.

Bush's Presidency

Republicans nominated George Bush, Ronald Reagan's Vice-President, to run for President in 1988. To "stay the course" set by Reagan, Bush promised to take a conservative approach to government. However, he also tried to calm the fears raised by Reagan's cuts in programs such as environmental protection and education. Bush called for more modest cuts in government spending.

Democrats, meanwhile, chose Michael Dukakis, the governor of Massachusetts, to oppose Bush. He promised to increase aid for schools and health care by raising taxes for the wealthy. Bush easily won the election.

As President, George Bush sought ways to make his campaign promises a reality. A Democratic Congress was eager to cooperate in Bush's goal of a "kinder, gentler nation."

To further that goal, Congress passed the Americans with Disabilities Act in 1990. This act was designed to make daily activities—such as entering buildings and crossing streets—possible for disabled Americans. It made it illegal, too, to discriminate against a disabled person who applied for a job.

Next, Congress updated laws protecting the environment. For example, the Clean Air Act of 1990 set tighter standards to control pollution by factories and automobiles. Bush called it "the most significant air pollution legislation in our nation's history."

The AIDS crisis In 1981 a frightening disease—acquired immunodeficiency syndrome (AIDS)—was identified among Americans. It is a disease that destroys the human body's protection against infection. The Ryan White Act was passed in 1990 to help provide services—such as medical care and housing—to the hundreds of thousands of Americans living with AIDS.

Budget problems The greatest challenge facing Bush was the federal deficit. The **deficit** is the amount by which the government's spending is greater than its income. To reduce the deficit, the government must cut spending, raise taxes, or do both.

During Reagan's presidency, government spending—especially on defense—had skyrocketed. Even so, in the 1988 campaign Bush had promised: "Read my lips, no new taxes." In 1990, however, he faced a deficit much larger than expected. That year, Bush broke his "no new taxes" pledge. He struck a bargain with Congress to trim $500 billion from the deficit by cutting spending and raising taxes.

History Footnote

The Ryan White Act was named for a courageous teenager who became a symbol of the struggle against AIDS. When Ryan was 13, doctors found that he had contracted AIDS from a contaminated blood transfusion. Mistakenly fearing that their children could get AIDS from him, neighbors demanded that Ryan be barred from school. Ryan and his family were taunted and ostracized. Ryan won his legal battle to attend school. Publicity about his case made Ryan a household name, and he found himself serving as a national spokesperson for AIDS patients. He testified before congressional committees and appeared on talk shows. Rock stars and other celebrities befriended him. Through it all, Ryan tried to remain a "regular kid." He died from complications of AIDS in April 1990. He was 18 years old.

A Post-Cold War President

With the end of Soviet communism, Bush called for a "New World Order." It would, he said, be a world in which nations worked together to prevent small crises from turning into world wars.

The Persian Gulf War The first test of Bush's idea of a New World Order came in the Middle East. In August 1990 the President of Iraq—Saddam Hussein—ordered his army to invade neighboring Kuwait, a small oil-rich nation on the Persian Gulf. Hussein claimed that it belonged to Iraq.

Bush saw the invasion as a threat to peace and to the world's supply of oil—a resource too vital "to be dominated by one so ruthless." When other pressures failed, the United Nations—including Russia—voted to free Kuwait by force. In January 1991 an American-led coalition of 28 nations struck Iraqi forces in Kuwait and Iraq. Six weeks later, the war was over. Bush's popularity soared.

Somalia Bush's New World Order was put to the test again in the African nation of Somalia. A civil war had left up to 2 million Somalis on the brink of starvation. Americans were horrified by TV images of people so thin they resembled skeletons.

In December 1992 Bush sent 28,000 troops to Somalia. Their mission was not to fight a war, but to protect relief workers who were bringing food to the people. The task proved more difficult than anyone had imagined. While the troops did help save many people from starving, they were unable to restore a stable government in Somalia. The American troops finally withdrew in March 1994.

Hands-On HISTORY

Balancing the budget Between October 1, 1994, and September 30, 1995, the federal government took in $1,420 billion. Unfortunately, it spent $1,578 billion. Where did the money go? The table tells you.

Activity Maybe you can succeed where the government has not. Working with two classmates, try to balance the federal budget.

1. Go through the table and decide which types of spending to cut and by how much. If cuts do not total $158 billion, then decide what taxes you will raise. As you plan your cuts and taxes, consider who will be affected by them and what the results might be.
2. Be prepared to defend your cuts or taxes. What criticisms might you hear? How will you respond to them?
3. Present your ideas to your classmates. Can they live with your proposals? If not, what do they suggest?

Federal Spending 1995 (in billions of dollars)

Social Security	336
Health, education	328
Defense	272
Interest on the debt	232
Welfare, housing	220
Other*	110
Environment, space, science	41
Transportation	39
Total	1,578

*Includes agriculture, energy, foreign affairs, justice, veterans' benefits

Source: *World Book Yearbook 1996*

Developing the Section

Discussion

Checking Understanding

1. Describe a law intended to create a "kinder, gentler nation." (Americans with Disabilities Act, Ryan White Act.)

Stimulating Critical Thinking

2. Should a candidate for President ever make a promise about taxes? Explain. (Yes: if sure Congress will support promise, perhaps after public pressure. No: cannot be sure of having the needed votes in Congress.)

Teaching the Hands-On HISTORY

Point out that the 1995 budget year ran from 10/1/94 to 9/30/95. Point out that "Health, education" includes Medicare, Medicaid, medical research, and food inspection. "Welfare, housing" includes public housing, food stamps, and unemployment compensation. Have students look for articles or interview adults for ideas on balancing the budget.

Vital Links

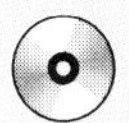
Gulf War (Movie)
Unit 6, Side 2, Search 15292, Play to 16353

See also Unit 6 Explore CD-ROM location 248.

Teaching the

Reading Maps

Have students locate the four trouble spots and the Persian Gulf. Ask why Saudi Arabia invited foreign troops in. (Concerned that Iraq might attack it next.) **Answers to Reading Maps:** Dependence on oil supplies can influence decision to intervene in region. Oman, United Arab Emirates (U.A.E.), Qatar, Bahrain, Saudi Arabia, Kuwait, Iraq, Iran.

Section Activity

Acting Out Radio Talk Shows

To assess the Bush and Clinton presidencies, have small groups role-play pre-election talk shows in 1992 and 1996. Assign two groups for each year. Each group has a host to guide the discussion. Other members role-play the audience calling in with opinions on how well the President handled issues. Some should respond to previous calls to build on the discussion. After groups rehearse, they can present their shows.

Vital Links

Haitian refugees (Picture)
Unit 6, Side 1,
Search 09525

See also Unit 6 Explore CD-ROM location 81.

History Footnote

President Bush also took decisive action in Panama, a nation unofficially controlled by General Manuel Antonio Noriega since 1983. In 1988 a U.S. federal grand jury indicted Noriega on charges that included drug dealing in the United States. However Noriega remained in Panama, where a presidential election was held in May 1989. The winner appeared to be Guillermo Endara, but Noriega simply declared the election invalid and continued to rule. Fearing that Noriega might block American access to the Panama Canal, President Bush sent troops to Panama in late 1989 to overthrow Noriega and bring him to the United States for trial. He surrendered to United States officials in January 1990 and was convicted in 1992.

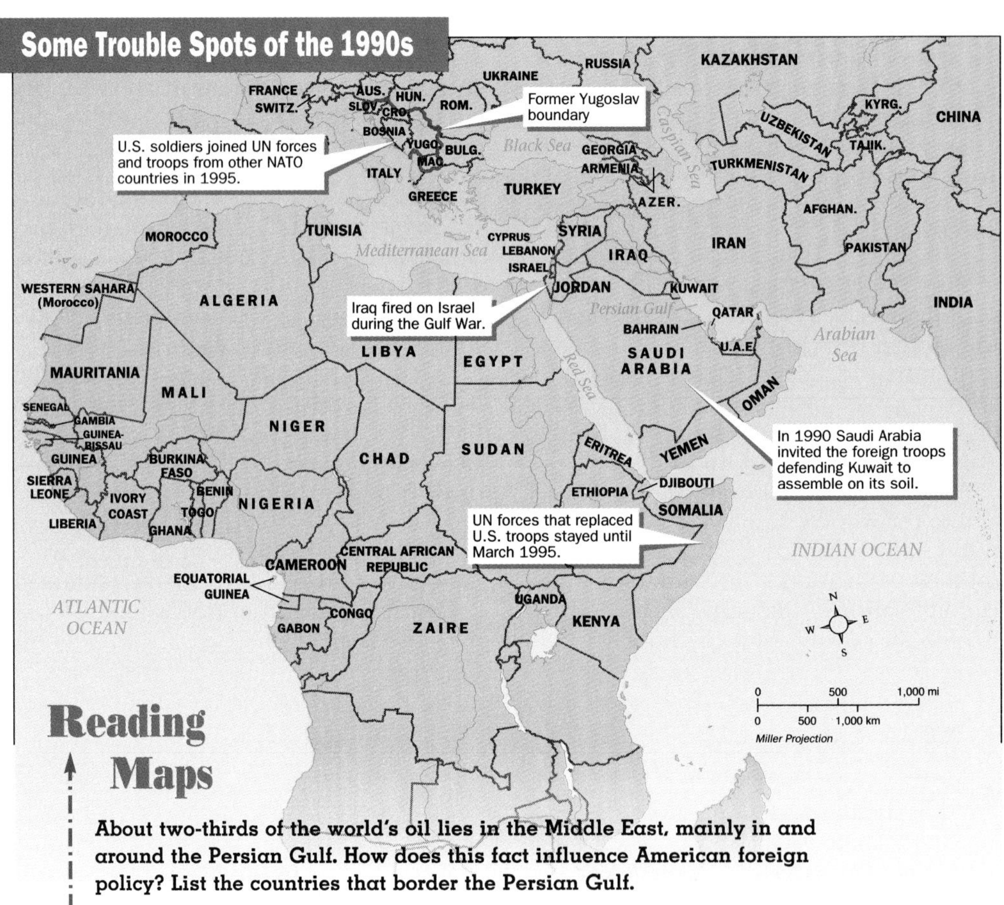

Reading Maps

About two-thirds of the world's oil lies in the Middle East, mainly in and around the Persian Gulf. How does this fact influence American foreign policy? List the countries that border the Persian Gulf.

Troubles for Bush

With American successes in Somalia and the Persian Gulf fresh in voters' minds, Bush's re-election in 1992 seemed certain. Problems at home, however, haunted the President.

As you read on page 648, the growing federal deficit plagued the nation. Meanwhile, a banking crisis erupted. Certain banks, called savings and loan associations (S&Ls), had made risky loans. Now they faced collapse. To protect people who had money in the shaky banks, the government paid out $100 billion, further adding to the deficit.

Even worse, by 1991 the nation had fallen into a recession. The number of people without jobs rose sharply. Many Americans now felt the effects of Reagan-era cutbacks in government programs. For example, a shortage of housing for the poor increased the number of homeless Americans. So did the policy of closing large institutions for the mentally ill.

Clinton Takes Over

Public dissatisfaction with President Bush presented Democrats with an opportunity to take the White House for the first time since

History Footnote

President Clinton took a strong interest in achieving peace in the Middle East. In September 1993, he hosted a historic meeting between longtime enemies Yitzhak Rabin, Israel's prime minister, and Yasser Arafat, head of the Palestine Liberation Organization, or PLO, which was founded in 1964 to establish an Arab state in Palestine. With Clinton looking on, Rabin and Arafat shook hands on a pact that included steps for ending their conflict. In November 1995, as Israel and the PLO worked to carry out those steps, Rabin was assassinated by an Israeli opposed to the peace process. In May 1996, Benjamin Netanyahu was elected as Israel's prime minister. He took a harder line on Arab-Israeli issues than Rabin had, casting doubt on the future of the peace process.

1980. They nominated Bill Clinton, the governor of Arkansas, who promised change and talked of putting "people first."

Meanwhile, Ross Perot, a wealthy Texas businessman, entered the race as a third-party candidate. He pushed for a balanced federal budget. With votes split three ways, Clinton was elected President by less than half the voters. He began his presidency promising to create jobs, cut the deficit, and provide health care for all Americans.

Health-care reform Clinton's first priority was health care. In 1992 the United States had spent more on health care than on education and defense combined. Even so, millions of people could not afford medical treatment. To solve the problem, the President appointed a commission led by his wife, Hillary Rodham Clinton, a lawyer.

The commission proposed a complex program that made major changes in the nation's health-care system. Such fierce controversy erupted around the proposal, however, that Congress failed to pass it.

Successful legislation Clinton was more successful at convincing Congress to pass the Family and Medical Leave Act in 1993. This popular law required large businesses to give an employee up to 12 weeks unpaid leave for such urgent situations as an illness or the birth of a child.

Clinton also pushed an anticrime bill through Congress. It provided funds to help states build more jails and hire more police. The act also toughened penalties for some crimes and banned sales of military-style weapons.

Trade agreements As part of his promise to improve trade and create jobs, Clinton got Congress to approve two trade agreements. In 1993 the North American Free Trade Agreement (NAFTA) ended many trade barriers between the United States, Mexico, and Canada.

Critics charged that Americans would lose jobs to lower-paid workers in Mexico. Clinton, though, argued that NAFTA would create jobs by making it easier for Mexicans and Canadians to buy American goods.

In 1994 more than 100 nations ratified a General Agreement on Tariffs and Trade (GATT). It called for lower tariffs and a World Trade Organization to help bring down barriers to trade.

Clinton's Policy Overseas

During the 1992 campaign, Clinton had made clear that he wanted to focus on problems at home. However, events overseas soon demanded his attention.

Haiti One of Clinton's first challenges came in the Caribbean nation of Haiti. Ruled by brutal military dictators for years, Haiti finally held free elections in 1991. Eight months later, the military overthrew the new President, Jean-Bertrand Aristide. To force the military from power and restore Aristide to office, Clinton imposed a blockade of Haiti. He warned the military leaders to leave or face American troops.

As troops prepared to invade, Clinton sent former President Carter to make a final appeal to Haiti's military to give up power. Carter succeeded. The military leaders agreed to step down, and American troops oversaw the return of President Aristide. Restoring democracy in Haiti was a victory for both Clinton and the Haitian people.

Bosnia Clinton's next challenge came in Europe. In 1991 the Communist nation of Yugoslavia had splintered into five republics—including Bosnia, Croatia, and Yugoslavia. Bosnia was home to Serbs, Muslims, and Croats. Having lived side by side in the same villages for centuries, most Bosnians hoped to continue to do so in their young republic.

Discussion

Checking Understanding

1. Why did Bush lose the 1992 election? (Economic problems such as the federal deficit, savings and loans crisis, and recession. Clinton promised change. Perot's candidacy caused a three-way split in vote.)

Stimulating Critical Thinking

2. Is a vote for a third-party candidate "wasted"? Why or why not? (Yes: third-party candidates have never won. No: strong third-party showing can pressure Democratic and Republican leaders to address issues.)

3. What main goal should drive American foreign policy? Explain. (Some goals: promoting human rights, democracy; national security; keeping peace.)

Bonus Activity

Grading Presidents

To encourage thoughtful judgments of presidential policies, have students fill out report cards for Bush and Clinton. They might create their own categories for grading each President, or the class might settle on categories for everyone to use. ("Lived up to promises" is one possibility.) Have students discuss their completed report cards.

Tips for Teaching

Gifted Students

Gifted students benefit from creating products. Have small groups edit and expand Section 2 to bring readers up to date on events and issues, such as the federal deficit. They should include a revised Reading Guide, subheads, Section Review questions, and new graphics as needed.

Closing the Section

Wrap-Up Activity

Planning a Campaign

To reinforce understanding of the political situation in 1996, have pairs or small groups outline 1996 campaign plans for Clinton and Dole. Each campaign plan should include achievements for candidates to play up, setbacks for candidates to play down, and points to use against the opposing candidate and party.

Section Review Answers

1. Definition: *deficit* (648)

2. In the Middle East, where Iraq had invaded Kuwait, Bush successfully led an international coalition against Iraq. He sent troops to Somalia, which had been devastated by civil war. The troops protected relief workers but were unable to restore a stable government.

3. Yes: world's leading power has duty to take lead in trying to preserve order. No: nations must solve own problems; United States would resent intervention in its domestic affairs. Americans should not have to die for faraway causes that do not directly affect the United States.

Before the 1996 election, President Clinton faced a Republican Congress led by his rival, Bob Dole (right), and Newt Gingrich (left).

Tragically, however, age-old rivalries, inflamed by Serb leaders greedy for power, unleashed a cruel war. In 1992 Bosnian Serb forces began a brutal policy of "ethnic cleansing"—driving Muslims and Croats out of Bosnia by slaughtering men, women, and children and destroying their farms and towns. European leaders and President Bush backed away from the conflict. Peacemaking efforts by the United Nations failed, too.

In 1995 the tide of war turned against the Serb forces. It was then that they bowed to pressure from Clinton to end the war. Leaders of Bosnia's Muslims, Croats, and Serbs signed a peace agreement in Dayton, Ohio. To enforce it, Clinton sent 20,000 troops to Bosnia.

A Republican Congress

In November 1994 Clinton's presidency suffered a blow when voters elected Republican majorities in both houses of Congress. Confident that their victory meant public approval for drastic change, Republicans pushed to get rid of federal programs and powers—many dating from Franklin Roosevelt's New Deal.

Above all, Republicans wanted to reduce the deficit by balancing the budget. Early in 1995 they proposed deep cuts in social programs, including school lunches, college loans, and health care for poor and elderly Americans. At the same time, however, they proposed lowering taxes.

Clinton, too, wanted to balance the budget. However, he argued that the Republican plan would hurt the needy, while wealthy Americans benefited from lower taxes. Congress and the President came to a stalemate, both looking for a boost in the 1996 election.

The Election of 1996

Republican hopes that they could unseat Clinton in 1996 were dashed. As the deficit began to shrink and the economy gained strength, voters gave Clinton the credit. He and Vice-President Albert Gore won 31 states to only 19 for Republicans Robert Dole and Jack Kemp.

In spite of Clinton's victory, the Republicans kept majorities in both houses of Congress. It seemed that the public preferred to maintain a balance of power, forcing President and Congress to compromise.

2. Section Review

1. Define **deficit.**

2. How did Bush pursue a New World Order in the Middle East and Somalia?

3. Critical Thinking Should the United States get involved in civil wars, such as in Bosnia? Explain your answer.

Essay Objectives

Use pictures and captions to trace events of President Bill Clinton's second term in office, with these emphases:

- ★ Explain the significance of Clinton's choice for Secretary of State.
- ★ Identify major goals of Clinton's second term and describe some ways the President has sought to achieve those goals.

PICTURE ESSAY

Clinton's Second Term

1

2

1. Bill Clinton's wife Hillary and daughter Chelsea watch as Chief Justice William H. Rehnquist administers the oath to the reelected President at his inauguration on January 20, 1997.

2. Madeleine Albright was Clinton's choice for Secretary of State. She was the first Cabinet member in Clinton's second term approved by the Senate and the first woman to ever fill this post.

Picture Essay

Teaching the Picture Essay

In this feature, students will learn about President Bill Clinton's second term through a series of pictures and captions. Have students study the entire feature before doing the Bonus Activity or answering the Discussion questions.

Bonus Activity

Planning a TV Documentary

To deepen students' understanding of the Clinton presidency, have groups plan a one-hour television documentary about it. Students will need to visit the library and/or do at-home electronic research (for example, by accessing the White House web site on the Internet) to make their documentary as up-to-the-minute as possible. As a first step, students should decide whether the documentary's organization will be chronological, thematic, or a combination. Students should then prepare an outline of the documentary, including time allotments for each segment. Finally, students should write a script for one five-minute segment, including the narrator's and commentators' remarks, lists of images to appear on the screen, and suggestions for background music.

Discussion

Checking Understanding

1. What was significant about President Clinton's nomination of Madeleine Albright? (She was the first Cabinet member in Clinton's second term to be approved by the Senate; more importantly, she was the first woman ever to fill the post of Secretary of State.)

2. Name one of Clinton's goals for his second term. (Any of the following: to help make American schools the best in the world, to fight juvenile crime, to fight juvenile drug use.)

Stimulating Critical Thinking

3. Based on their facial expressions, how do you suppose the DARE members felt when they had their picture taken with the President? (Possible answers: excited, happy, proud, nervous.)

4. Suppose you were asked to speak to a gathering like the one shown in Picture 4. What is one solution to the problem of juvenile crime that you would suggest? (Accept all thoughtful answers. Possibilities that students might mention include community-sponsored programs to give students something meaningful to do after school; tougher penalties for juvenile crime.)

History Footnote

President Clinton promoted volunteerism as a key component in solving many of the nation's problems. In the spring of 1997, the Clinton administration sponsored the Presidents' Summit for America's Future, a three-day conference aimed at mobilizing citizen and corporate volunteers to improve the lives of 2 million American children. Former Presidents Gerald Ford, Jimmy Carter, and George Bush joined Clinton at the conference, which was chaired by retired General Colin Powell. At the end of the conference, Powell announced he would lead a three-year follow-up program—called America's Promise, the Alliance for Youth—to provide at-risk children with mentors, safe places to go after school, health care, job skills, and opportunities to perform community service.

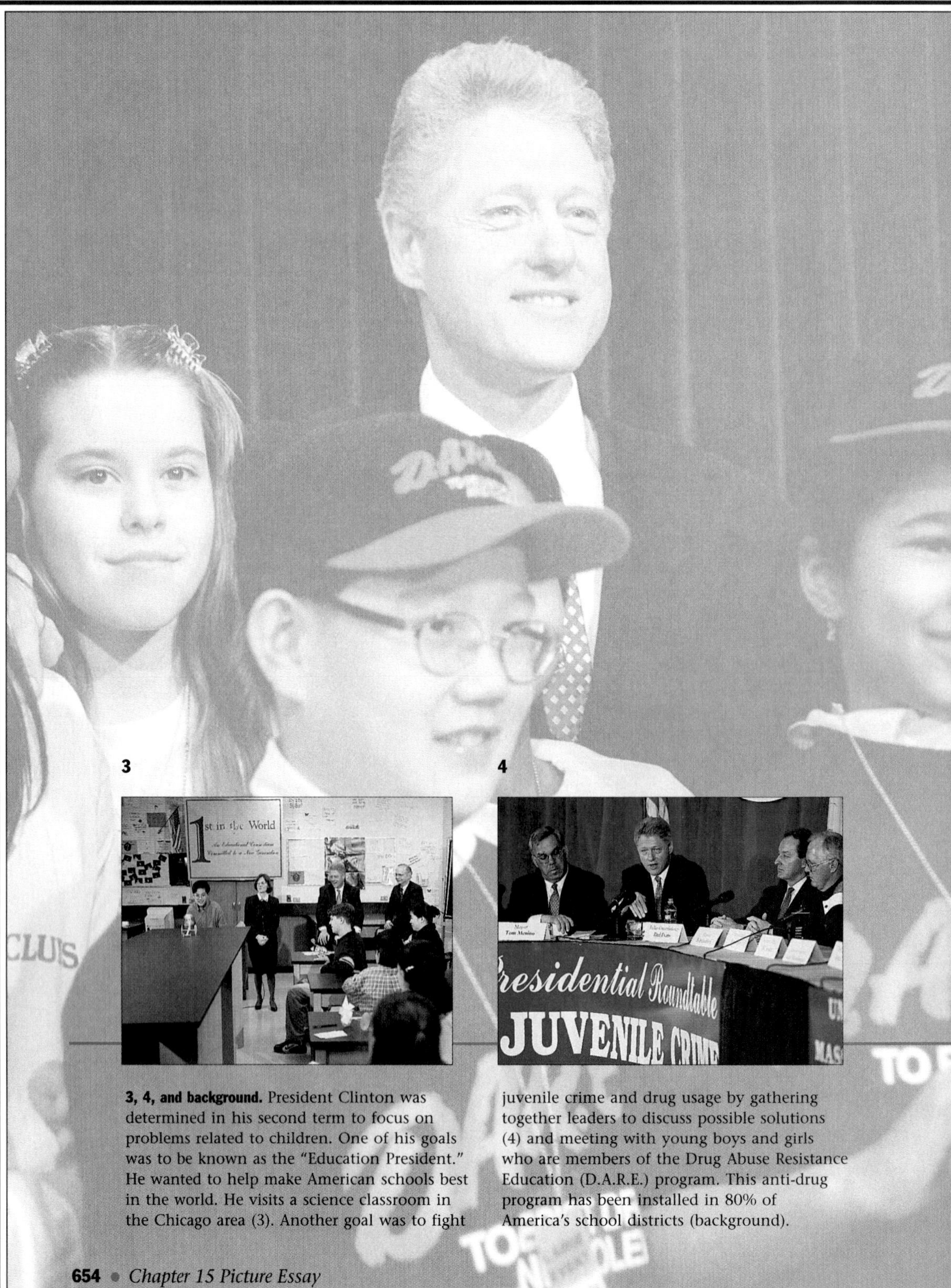

3, 4, and background. President Clinton was determined in his second term to focus on problems related to children. One of his goals was to be known as the "Education President." He wanted to help make American schools best in the world. He visits a science classroom in the Chicago area (3). Another goal was to fight juvenile crime and drug usage by gathering together leaders to discuss possible solutions (4) and meeting with young boys and girls who are members of the Drug Abuse Resistance Education (D.A.R.E.) program. This anti-drug program has been installed in 80% of America's school districts (background).

Geography Footnote

Congress passed the original Wild and Scenic Rivers Act in 1968. Under this law, Congress or the Secretary of the Interior can designate a particular stream or river as a "national wild and scenic river." This status prohibits dams, canals, and other potentially damaging water projects from being built along the waterway. Since 1968 the National Wild and Scenic Rivers System has grown from 12 protected waterways to more than 200, including those added by the 1992 Arkansas Act. No system like it exists in any other nation, although Canada, Costa Rica, and some other nations do have legal protection for some rivers. One author has called the protected American rivers "stretched-out green reserves overflowing with life, potential, and promise."

Geography Lab

The Interior Highlands

Americans thought a great deal about the environment in the early 1990s. One result of their concern was the Arkansas Wild and Scenic Rivers Act of 1992. The law added about 200 miles of streams to the National Wild and Scenic Rivers System, guaranteeing that they will be preserved in their natural state for future generations to enjoy.

Several rivers covered by the act flow through the region known as the Interior Highlands. The crystal-clear waters, abundant fish, and wooded, often rugged banks of these rivers attract thousands of tourists each year. Use the photographs to form an image of the region.

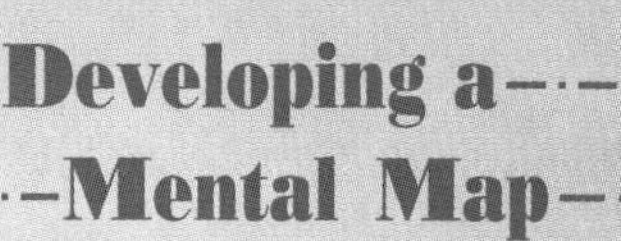

Refer to the maps on pages R4–R7.

1. What three states are partially covered by the Interior Highlands?
2. What major rivers flow through the region?
3. Judging from the photographs, what is the terrain like in the Interior Highlands? What is the highest elevation range in the region, and where is it located?
4. According to the map on page R8, what kinds of vegetation grow naturally in the region?
5. **Hands-On Geography** Imagine that you are putting together a travel brochure about the Interior Highlands. Using the photos on this page as inspiration, write several paragraphs that will persuade tourists to visit the region. Include the kinds of activities visitors might expect to enjoy.

Mountain overlook, Petit Jean State Park, Arkansas. Canoeing on the Buffalo National River, Arkansas (above). Waterfalls near the Buffalo River (right).

Teaching the Geography Lab

Have students use the maps on pp. P4–P5 and R4–R5 to name a mountain range and plateau in the Interior Highlands. (Ouachita Mountains, Ozark Plateau.) Point out that the Ozark Plateau (also called the Ozark Mountains) consists mostly of hills and low mountains. The only level land is in river valleys. The Ouachita Mountains are a series of ridges and valleys. The region has abundant caves and mineral springs.

Developing a Mental Map

Answers

1. Missouri, Arkansas, Oklahoma.

2. Mississippi, Missouri, Red, and Arkansas Rivers.

3. Somewhat hilly and rugged. Highest is 1,640 to 3,280 feet, north of Arkansas River in northwestern Arkansas.

4. Broadleaf, needleleaf, and mixed needleleaf and broadleaf forests.

5. Paragraphs should describe unspoiled wilderness. Some activities are camping, swimming, fishing, boating, hiking, nature photography, and bathing in hot or mineral springs.

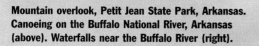

See the activity on the
Interior Highlands in
Geography Extensions,
pp. 35–36.

Introducing the Section

Vocabulary

Internet (p. 659) a web of computer networks linked through telephone lines

Warm-Up Activity

Charting Changes

To prepare for reading about recent changes in American society, have students chart changes they know about. Write these column headings on the board: *Life When Our Parents Were Young* and *Life Today.* Row headings might include *School, Home,* and *Recreation.* Have students brainstorm items to add to the chart. To stimulate thinking, ask whether they think their parents' schools had computers, whether their parents could watch videos at home, and so on.

Geography Question of the Day

Ask students to write paragraphs describing a local environmental problem. Have them explain whether the problem is related to the geography of your area (for example, smog being trapped in a valley).

See the Study Guide activity in Chapter Resources Binder, p. 131.

Section Objectives

- ★ Describe how the American population is changing.
- ★ Identify the challenges that the environment and a new economy present to the nation.
- ★ Predict how democracy will fare as the American way of life continues to change.

Teaching Resources

Take-Home Planner 10, pp. 20–30
Chapter Resources Binder
Study Guide, p. 131
Reinforcement
Skills Development, pp. 135–136
Geography Extensions
American Readings, pp. 65–68
Using Historical Documents
Transparency Activities, pp. 49–50
Chapter and Unit Tests, pp. 111–114

3. New Challenges and Hopes

Reading Guide

New Term **Internet**

Section Focus **American society and democracy move into a new century**

1. **How is the American population changing?**
2. **What new challenges do the environment and the economy present?**
3. **How will democracy fare as the American way of life continues to change?**

The United States is a nation that has learned to expect and welcome change. As a new century unfolds, we can be certain that how we live and work will continue to change—sometimes for the better, and sometimes in ways that concern and challenge us.

A Changing Population

In recent years, the American population has become increasingly diverse. It is also older and better educated than at any other time in its history.

Recent immigration The growing diversity of Americans is largely the result of a new wave of immigrants from Asia and Latin America. Like earlier immigrants, these recent arrivals hope to find freedom and opportunity in their new home.

Jaime Escalante was among the 1 million Hispanic immigrants who came to the United States in the 1960s. Just 18 months after his arrival, the 1965 Immigration and Nationality Act opened the doors to more immigrants—including Asians, who had been excluded for decades.

The 1965 law ended policies followed since the 1920s. It doubled the number of immigrants legally admitted—to 290,000 a year. It also set quotas by hemisphere instead of by nation. In 1995 the limit was set at 675,000 immigrants each year.

During the 1980s the nation's Asian population more than doubled. The Hispanic population increased by 53 percent. By the year 2050 almost one-half of the nation is expected to claim Asian, African, Hispanic, or Native American ancestry.

The new diversity affects the nation's schools and neighborhoods. Students in Los Angeles, for example, speak 86 languages. This poses challenges for teachers trying to help students succeed in their new country. Meanwhile, recent immigrants are bringing new life to city neighborhoods that had been losing population since the 1950s.

Changing households As the face of the nation has changed, so has the American household. Perhaps the greatest change has been the increasing number of single-parent households. One in four children born in the 1990s is being raised by a single parent. Meanwhile, people are marrying later and some are choosing not to have children.

An aging nation The nation is also seeing a growing number of people over the age of 55. Improved diets and health care help people live longer. During the 1980s the number of Americans in their eighties doubled. This "graying of America" will increase as the baby-boom generation ages. It will also put greater demands on the Social Security and health-care systems.

Tips for Teaching

Students With Limited English

Making oral presentations on familiar topics is a good way to practice English. Ask students to give a short talk about their experiences here or life in their family's country of origin. They should include specifics to help listeners visualize places, people, customs, events, and experiences.

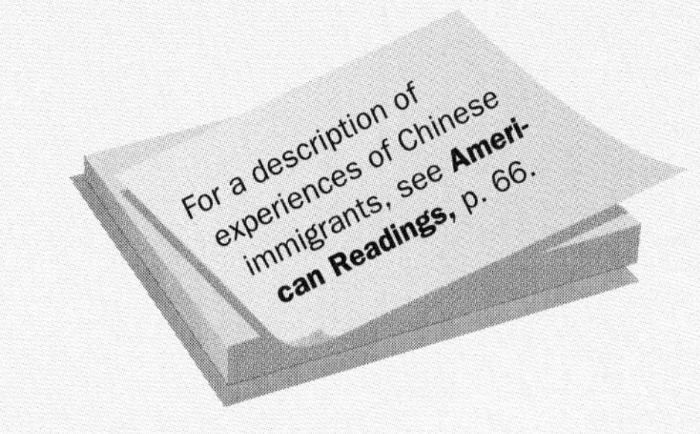

For a description of experiences of Chinese immigrants, see **American Readings**, p. 66.

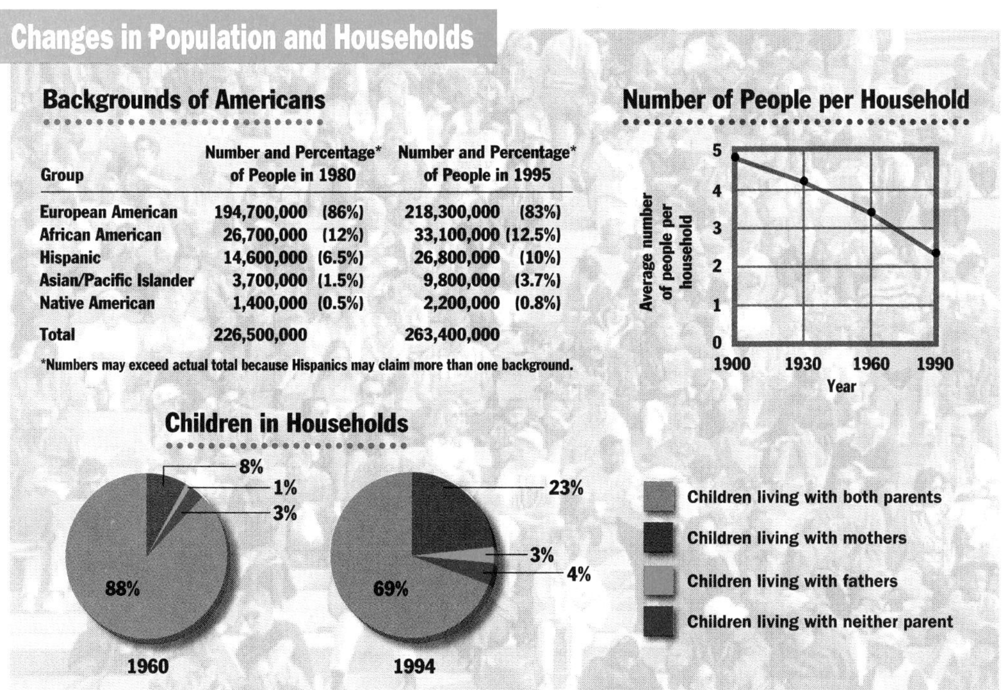

Changes in Population and Households

Backgrounds of Americans

Group	Number and Percentage* of People in 1980	Number and Percentage* of People in 1995
European American	194,700,000 (86%)	218,300,000 (83%)
African American	26,700,000 (12%)	33,100,000 (12.5%)
Hispanic	14,600,000 (6.5%)	26,800,000 (10%)
Asian/Pacific Islander	3,700,000 (1.5%)	9,800,000 (3.7%)
Native American	1,400,000 (0.5%)	2,200,000 (0.8%)
Total	226,500,000	263,400,000

*Numbers may exceed actual total because Hispanics may claim more than one background.

Source: United States Census Bureau

A Changing Environment

In recent decades Americans have been increasingly concerned about the environment. Information about the dangers of toxic substances flowing from smokestacks, car exhausts, and sewer pipes has helped launch a popular environmental movement.

Starting in the 1960s, Congress responded by passing laws to reduce pollution and clean up the nation's water and air. Although pollution remains a problem, environmentalists can point to major improvements in air quality. Lakes and rivers are cleaner, as well. For example, only 20 years after being labeled a "dying sinkhole," Lake Erie is again home to large numbers of fish.

Americans at home and at work are helping to reduce waste by recycling bottles, cans, and paper. In 1995 more than one-fifth of the nation's garbage was made into new products—a rate that doubters had claimed "could not be achieved."

Threats to the atmosphere Meanwhile, other environmental issues have emerged. Some scientists fear that global warming—a rise in the earth's surface temperature—will melt the polar ice caps, raising sea levels and flooding coastal regions. They urge people to cut back on the use of wood, coal, and oil for fuel. However, other scientists say that the danger of global warming is exaggerated.

Destruction of the ozone layer troubles many scientists. The ozone layer—a protective blanket of gases in the atmosphere—screens out harmful rays from the sun. The cause of this destruction is thought to be chlorofluorocarbons—chemicals used in refrigerators, air conditioners, and spray cans. Some people find hope in the swift

Developing the Section

Discussion

Checking Understanding

1. What is the "graying of America" and why is it occurring? (Growing number of people over 55, due to improved diets and health care.)

Stimulating Critical Thinking

2. Should there be stricter limits on immigration? Explain. (Yes: not enough jobs; overcrowding; heavy demands on welfare system. No: we are a nation of immigrants; immigrants contribute more to the economy than they use in government services.)

Vital Links

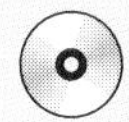

Senior rally for health care (Picture) Unit 6, Side 1, Search 26726

See also Unit 6 Explore CD-ROM location 159.

Boycott to protest Styrofoam (Picture) Unit 6, Side 1, Search 22996

See also Unit 6 Explore CD-ROM location 113.

Teaching the Reading Maps

Have students list states where the activities shown took place. They can refer to the map on pp. R6–R7. Discuss each activity, asking for ideas about others that could be added to the map. **Answer to Reading Maps:** Loss of natural habitats, threats to wildlife, water pollution, solid-waste buildup.

Bonus Activity

Proposing Solutions

To focus on challenges, have students propose solutions to national problems. Have them use information in the section as a jumping-off point for brainstorming a list of problems. Then divide the class into small groups, assigning each a problem and telling them to imagine being given a billion dollars to help solve it. Ask them to write a proposal describing what the problem is, how they plan to use the money, and how their solution will benefit society. Have groups present their proposals.

Vital Links

Beach cleanup (Picture)
Unit 6, Side 1,
Search 22990

See also Unit 6 Explore CD-ROM location 112.

Connections to Science

When spring comes to Antarctica each September, a temporary thinning occurs in the ozone layer there. This so-called "hole" in the ozone layer worsened nearly every year between the late 1970s and the mid-1990s. As chlorofluorocarbons (CFCs) are phased out, scientists believe the hole will stabilize and eventually diminish. In addition to CFCs, which contain chlorine, scientists blame ozone destruction on substances containing bromine. In fact bromine is 50 times more destructive to ozone than chlorine is. In response to concerns about bromine, the world's industrial nations agreed in 1995 to end their use of the pesticide methyl bromide by the year 2010.

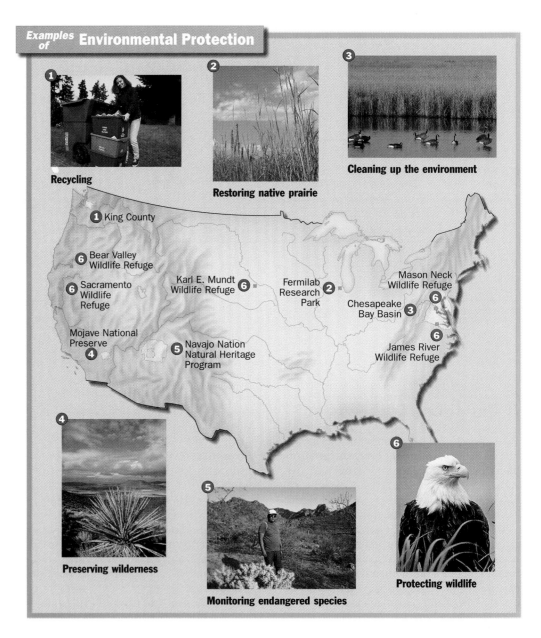

Examples of Environmental Protection

1 Recycling

2 Restoring native prairie

3 Cleaning up the environment

1 King County
6 Bear Valley Wildlife Refuge
6 Sacramento Wildlife Refuge
Karl E. Mundt Wildlife Refuge 6
Fermilab Research Park 2
Mason Neck Wildlife Refuge 6
Chesapeake Bay Basin 3
6 James River Wildlife Refuge
Mojave National Preserve 4
5 Navajo Nation Natural Heritage Program

4 Preserving wilderness

5 Monitoring endangered species

6 Protecting wildlife

Reading Maps

Judging from the examples shown on the map, what are some different kinds of environmental problems that Americans have tried to solve in recent years?

Connections to Economics

According to one survey in the mid-1990s, 45 percent of Americans worried "a lot" about the state of the economy, 43 percent worried "a little," and the rest worried "not at all." People were less concerned about their own ability to keep up with their bills: 30 percent worried a lot, 32 percent worried a little, and the rest did not worry. When they thought about trying to save money, however, Americans tensed up again: 41 percent worried a lot about saving for the future. There was good reason: Americans were saving only 4.6 percent of their disposable (after-tax) household income. By comparison, Canadians saved 10.6 percent of their disposable income, while Japanese families put 14.6 percent into savings.

reaction of the world's nations, 93 of which agreed to ban such chemicals by 1996.

A Changing Economy

Since the 1980s new technologies have radically changed people's lives and ways of working. The most striking example is computer technology. Computers were first developed at the end of World War II. Big, bulky, and expensive, the early computers were available only to the military, and to corporations and universities.

Today, improved technology has made computers smaller and less expensive but increasingly powerful. They have become such an essential part of personal and working lives that it is difficult to imagine how people ever lived without them. They are capable of assisting with an amazing range of tasks—from surgery to creating artwork to tracking the earth's climate.

The information revolution The use of computers has created an "information revolution." One CD-ROM can provide as much information as an entire encyclopedia, to say nothing of pictures and sounds.

Through the **Internet**—a web of computer networks linked through telephone lines—people can find information provided by government agencies, libraries, and businesses. The Internet also helps people around the world communicate quickly and at little cost.

Effects on the economy As information flows more easily, the American economy is changing dramatically. Increasingly, jobs are in the service and information industries rather than in manufacturing. At the same time, workers can no longer count on the security of a long-term job.

In earlier times, most Americans expected to spend their whole careers working for one company. In the 1970s, however, many factory jobs disappeared as businesses moved overseas and hired lower-paid workers. New technologies, too, allowed factories to produce more goods with fewer workers. As a result, American factory workers felt less and less secure about their futures.

In the 1980s and 1990s job insecurity spread to other workers, as well. In almost every industry—even in computer-related ones—employers were cutting their work forces in an effort to reduce costs. More confusing still, such job losses occurred in good as well as bad times. Many workers felt betrayed. Dan Skowron, a worker in the Midwest, observed: "My eyes are much more open, now. You can't assume any job will last forever."

The income gap Meanwhile, the income gap between the wealthy and the rest of the population has been growing. The average annual income of the wealthiest 10 percent of American households increased from $68,805 in 1973 to $76,436 in 1993. During the same period, the average income for the lower half of American households decreased from $30,580 to $27,148.

In the 1990s millions of new jobs have been created. People who thrive in this new economy will be educated service and information workers who have the skill to put ideas and information to work to create something of value. Meanwhile, less-educated workers wonder how they will make a living in the new information economy.

The Future of American Democracy

As Americans face major changes in the environment, economy, and technology, they also continue to dream of new opportunities—just as their parents and grandparents did. At the same time, many wonder what effect such changes are having on society. They raise the pressing question: What is the future of American democracy?

Discussion

Checking Understanding

1. Why can Americans no longer count on the security of a long-term job? (Many companies are moving jobs overseas to lower-wage workers; technological advances mean many products can be made with fewer workers; many employers try to reduce costs by laying off workers.)

Stimulating Critical Thinking

2. How might the "information revolution" be opened to people who cannot afford computers and other specialized equipment? (Possibility of accessing Internet through cable TV rather than computers and modems.)

For a prediction on the impact of telecommuting, see **American Readings**, p. 67.

Vital Links

Robotics (Movie) Unit 6, Side 2, Search 20921, Play to 21560

See also Unit 6 Explore CD-ROM location 382.

Section Activity

Designing a Neighborhood

To focus on the idea of community, have groups design neighborhoods that encourage face-to-face interaction and reduce reliance on cars. Each group can either design a new neighborhood or redesign an existing one. Neighborhoods should not be purely residential. The ideas on p. 661 might spark students' thinking. Have groups display and explain completed designs, which should take the form of street maps with labeled buildings, parks, and so on.

Vital Links

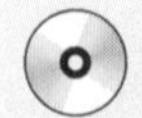

Citizenship ceremony (Picture) Unit 6, Side 1, Search 09537

See also Unit 6 Explore CD-ROM location 83.

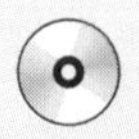

League of Women Voters (Picture) Unit 6, Side 1, Search 23961

See also Unit 6 Explore CD-ROM location 128.

History Footnote

Alexis de Tocqueville was a French historian and political philosopher who wrote a famous two-volume book called *Democracy in America* (1835, 1840). He based it on a nine-month visit to the United States, during which he interviewed Americans—from President Andrew Jackson to ordinary citizens—and took detailed notes about what he heard and saw. More than a century and a half later, Tocqueville is still quoted by journalists and historians struggling to understand and shed light on our complex nation. His observations about American politics, lifestyles, and attitudes were remarkably insightful, and many still apply. For example, he wrote, "I know of no [other] country . . . where the love of money has taken a stronger hold on the affections of men."

Are Americans willing to perform the duties and take the responsibilities necessary for democracy to succeed in a changing world?

Citizens' rights and duties As citizens of the United States, Americans have the right to vote, to have a fair trial, and to express their opinions. These and other rights are based on ideals—freedom, equality, and justice—that Americans share and that are protected by the Constitution.

Americans have certain duties, as well. These duties range from serving on a jury to attending school, paying taxes, and obeying laws.

Citizens' responsibilities Unlike a citizen's duties, a citizen's responsibilities are voluntary. The most basic one is to work for the common good—to contribute to the well-being of society as a whole. This responsibility includes working to make communities, states, and the nation better places for everyone to live.

There are many ways in which individuals can work for the common good. They can vote, hold public office, write letters to elected officials, or attend school board meetings. They can form or join organizations that seek to solve problems—from protecting the environment to creating new jobs.

Communities in a democracy The tradition of participation in community organizations reaches far back into the nation's history. Thomas Jefferson believed that the willingness of citizens to join together in the task of building a community was at the heart of democracy.

In the 1830s a French writer, Alexis de Tocqueville, noted with approval the number of community organizations he saw while touring the United States. A hundred years later a national women's association concluded:

> "Participation is the life of democracy. Without it, democracy dies."

Threats to democracy Since Tocqueville's visit, new technologies—including the automobile, television, and the computer—are changing how Americans interact with one another. Some fear that such technologies, which encourage Americans to lead lives increasingly separate from one another, are a threat to democracy.

People come together in revived public places like Quincy Market in Boston, where they can stroll, shop, eat, and find entertainment.

A person can now work or watch a movie at home, get money from an automated teller machine, and pick up a meal at a drive-through restaurant—all without talking to anyone else. Is this new way of life replacing an older one in which work and social life involved communicating with strangers as well as with friends?

Many worry, too, that the demands of modern life leave little time for participating in community organizations. Commuting to work, driving children to

Connections to Civics

In the mid-1990s, Robert D. Putnam of Harvard University wrote about a steep decline in "civic engagement and social trust." He noted that since the 1970s membership in civic associations had decreased by 25 to 60 percent and that group political participation (such as attending rallies) was down by almost as much. Putnam also observed that while 58 percent of Americans in 1960 agreed that "most people can be trusted," only 35 percent felt that way in 1994.

Putnam noted that such declines occurred mostly among people raised after World War II. He jokingly wondered if they had been struck by a "mysterious 'anti-civic' x-ray." In reality, he decided, the problem is television, which "narrows the gap between us and Bosnia, but widens the distance between us and our neighbors."

Link to Art

El Lenguaje Mudo del Alma (The Silent Language of the Soul) (1990) Painting a mural on the outside of a building is a form of community art. Such a mural often becomes a well-loved part of the neighborhood—especially if it reflects the activities or culture of the people who live there. An example is the mural that artists Juana Alicia and Susan Cervantes painted around the entrance to Cesar Chavez School in San Francisco. Neighbors enjoy seeing the images of children using sign language to express their thoughts and feelings. **Discuss** Choose a building in your neighborhood on which you would like to paint a public mural. What would be the purpose of your mural? Describe the scene—including the colors and images—that you would want to depict.

school, shopping in huge malls, and keeping up with friends in far-flung suburbs consumes most hours in a day.

Finally, there is concern that Americans are losing faith in the political system. Public distrust of government, spurred by the painful years of the Vietnam War and the Watergate scandal, remains high. At the same time, the percentage of Americans who vote in elections has been dropping.

New signs of community Despite these signs that people are losing their sense of community, there is also evidence that Americans are making great efforts to come together. For example, public places—such as baseball parks, tree-lined waterfronts, churches, cafés, and health clubs—are growing in popularity.

Today's public places bring together people of different backgrounds and classes. Revived farmers' markets and downtown main streets, as well as malls that include libraries and museums, thrive throughout the nation. A 1996 study revealed that most people would like to live in areas where they can walk to traditional town centers.

Meanwhile, as a *Chicago Tribune* writer observed, Americans continue to feel an "optimism that makes them determined to keep their neighborhood [a good place to live]." Mary Ann Smith helped her Chicago neighborhood clean up a crime-ridden housing complex. Afterward, she concluded:

> "We've found [that] every problem is also an opportunity to make people feel powerful."

Discussion

Checking Understanding

1. What is a citizen's most basic responsibility in a democracy? (To work for the common good.)

Stimulating Critical Thinking

2. How might computers and the Internet aid democracy? (By allowing people separated by great distances to share ideas about politics and freedom.)

3. Abraham Lincoln declared that a democracy must be "of the people," not just "for the people." What do you think he meant? (All citizens must take responsibilities and fulfill certain duties.)

For an excerpt from
Marian Wright Edelman's
"life lessons" for youth,
see American Readings,
p. 68.

Teaching the

Link to Art

Ask students to describe how the mural makes them feel and tell whether they would like to see it every day as they enter school. **Discussion Answer:** Locations and descriptions will vary. Students may describe murals to beautify the neighborhood, make people feel good about themselves, pay tribute to individual accomplishments, encourage neighbors to work together for a common cause, and so on.

Closing the Section

Wrap-Up Activity

Causes for Concern, Reasons to Hope

To review and evaluate challenges to American society and democracy, have students work in groups to compile two lists titled *Causes for Concern* and *Reasons to Hope.* Have them pull items from the section and put them in the appropriate list. Conclude by discussing whether reasons to hope outweigh causes for concern.

Section Review Answers

1. Definition: *Internet* (659)

2. Air over most cities is cleaner. Lakes and rivers are cleaner. One-fifth of all garbage is recycled. Many wild plant and animal populations, including endangered species, have been preserved and restored.

3. Suggestions will vary, such as giving rewards for voting, holding Internet "town meetings," and requiring city planners to design community-oriented neighborhoods.

To check understanding of "Why We Remember," assign Thinking Critically question 3 on student page 664.

Connections to Geography

In 1995 a weekly news magazine published an article that explored ways to create the sociable, walkable neighborhoods that Americans say they want. The list of ideas included the following: Make lot sizes smaller and streets narrower. Mix single-family houses, apartment buildings, and small shops and businesses like corner groceries, dry cleaners, and drugstores within a few blocks of one another. Reduce dependence on cars by creating pockets of housing within short distances of bus or train stops. Shrink the size of parking lots, and put them behind buildings rather than around or in front of them. Create a public green space in the center of the neighborhood to serve not only as a geographical reference point but also as a focus of community life.

The confidence that individuals have the power to improve their communities is essential to life in a democracy. Other ways in which people are exercising that power include writing letters to newspapers, calling in to radio talk shows, and participating in chatlines on the Internet.

The renewed yearning for a sense of community in which all people are valued and respected is an important step toward maintaining a democratic society where freedom and opportunity thrive. Indeed, the success of democracy in the United States will always depend upon citizens who are willing to vote, to help out their neighbors, and to respect their fellow citizens.

3. Section Review

1. Define **Internet.**

2. In what ways has the American environment improved in the past 20 years?

3. Critical Thinking To encourage people to participate more in their communities and government, what three changes would you make in American society?

Why We Remember

New Roles in a Changing World

The last decades of the twentieth century have been filled with wonders and worries. For some, the most amazing wonders have been advances in technology and in preserving the environment. Others have been heartened by the end of the Cold War and the spread of democracy. For many, the wonders have been more personal—such as the success of Jaime Escalante's Garfield High students in passing the college placement exam for calculus.

However, our rapidly changing world has brought new worries as well. With a new century dawning, Americans have concerns ranging from AIDS and the income gap to the federal deficit and global warming. As the only remaining superpower, the United States struggles to decide what role to play in the world. Meanwhile, workers seeking a place in the new "information economy" worry that dreams of a better life might be slipping away.

Since all people are "explorers" into a new century, no one knows just what to expect. Still, the past can serve as a guide. History reminds Americans that they live in a nation founded on dreams—dreams of equality, opportunity, freedom, and respect for the rights of the individual. These are dreams that Americans will cherish as they journey into that unknown land that is the future.

(*Answers continued from side margin*)
teacher for drawing supplies, making and putting up anti-litter posters, and planning a contest with prizes for picking up the most litter.

4. Presentations should be thorough and clear and should address the question of how students would approach the task differently next time.

For further application, have students do the Applying Skills activity in the Chapter Survey (p. 664).

If students need to review the skill, use the Skills Development transparency and activity in the **Chapter Resources Binder**, pp. 135–136.

Skill Lab

Using Information

Taking Action

Skill Tips

- Set an achievable goal, and state it clearly and specifically.
- Keep the number of tasks reasonable.
- Divide the tasks fairly. Do not expect one or two people to do all the work.

Like many people, you may find it frustrating to hear about global environmental problems. After all, what can you do about the ozone layer? Actually, every person can take small steps to help solve environmental problems, especially local ones. As the saying goes, "Think globally, act locally."

Question to Investigate

How can we help solve local environmental problems?

Procedure

In the following steps, you and a group of classmates will deal with an environmental problem in your school or community.

1 State your goal.
a. Choose a local environmental problem.
b. State what you want to accomplish.

2 Identify resources (what will help you) and obstacles (what you have to overcome).
a. List people to approach for suggestions or other help. List other resources.
b. List problems that may stand in your way.

3 Identify what to do to achieve your goal.
a. List all tasks that need to be done, including those that involve using resources and overcoming obstacles.
b. Assign group members to the tasks.
c. Set a deadline for completing each task.

4 Carry out your plan.
a. Meet regularly to discuss progress.
b. If something does not work, change parts of your plan.
c. Give a presentation to classmates in which you answer the Question to Investigate based on your experience with carrying out your action plan.

Source to Use

Below is a sample of part of an action plan:

Goal
To make our school a litter-free zone
Resources
• Library (newspaper articles on last year's park cleanup project)
•
•
Obstacles
• Lack of time in school day for project
•
•
Tasks
• Do library research to get more ideas.
• Ask principal's permission to put up anti-litter posters.
•
•

Introducing the Skill Lab

In the process of familiarizing students with the basic steps of an action plan, this lab also increases their awareness of environmental problems. As a class, compile a list of local environmental problems. (Before the discussion, students might research ideas.) Have students vote on one problem to work on as a class, or divide the class into groups and let each group choose a problem.

Skill Lab

Answers

1. (a) Problems should be ones that exist at the school or neighborhood level and can be solved, or partially solved, through student efforts. Making the school a litter-free zone is just one possibility. (b) Statements should be concise, like the goal in the sample.

2. (a) For a litter-free-school project, resources might include the principal (for permission to put up posters and so on) and the art teacher (for drawing supplies). (b) For a litter-free-school project, student resistance to helping clean up litter might be one obstacle.

3. Tasks for a litter-free-school project might include asking the principal for permission to spend part of lunch period on the project, asking the art

(*Answers continued in top margin*)

Survey Answers

Reviewing Vocabulary

Definitions are found on these pages: *deficit* (648), *Internet* (659).

Reviewing Main Ideas

1. He felt that Nixon had suffered enough. He hoped the pardon would allow the wounds left by Watergate to heal more quickly.

2. Americans saw Carter as a Washington outsider—someone unconnected to national politics and the Watergate scandal. They also liked the way he stayed in touch with ordinary people.

3. (a) Pushed for spending cuts on welfare, education, public transportation, and other programs; pushed for tax cuts for wealthy people and businesses. (b) Increased military budget; sent troops to Grenada to drive out pro-Communists; tried to get Congress to arm contras in Nicaragua; sent troops to Lebanon; vowed not to negotiate with terrorists.

4. Persian Gulf War—led coalition of 28 nations to strike at Iraqi invaders of Kuwait. Civil war in Somalia—sent troops to protect relief workers.

5. (a) Family Medical Leave Act, anti-crime bill, NAFTA, GATT. (b) Health-care reform, balancing the budget.

6. (a) More diverse; single-parent, single-person, and childless households have increased; number of people over age 55 has increased. (b) Air and water pollution have decreased; recycling has increased; global warming has emerged as a potential threat; ozone layer has been partly destroyed. (c) Jobs in service and information industries have increased; factory jobs have decreased; many workers have lost jobs; income gap

(Answers continued in top margin)

between the wealthy and other people has grown.

7. They are concerned that democracy may suffer because citizen participation and feelings of community seem to be on the decline. There is also concern that many are losing faith in the political system and that voter turnout is declining.

Thinking Critically

1. Yes: pardon spared the nation pain, time, effort, and money. No: truth should always be sought. Pardon encouraged those involved in Iran-Contra and may encourage future misbehavior at high levels.

2. Carter: Although he played an important role in Camp David Accords, public lost confidence when he failed to solve the Iranian

Chapter Survey

Reviewing Vocabulary

Define the following terms.

1. deficit

2. Internet

Reviewing Main Ideas

1. Why did President Ford pardon former President Nixon?

2. Why did President Carter's image and style of leadership appeal to the American people at the time of his election?

3. (a) How did President Reagan try to shrink the government and boost prosperity? (b) How did he try to improve the image of the United States in the world?

4. Describe two events overseas and how President Bush responded to the challenge that they presented.

5. Give specific examples for each of the following: (a) President Clinton and Congress worked together to solve problems and achieve goals. (b) President Clinton and Congress clashed.

6. Describe one way that each of the following has changed since the 1960s: (a) the American population (b) the environment (c) the economy

7. What concerns do some people have for the future of American democracy?

Thinking Critically

1. Evaluation Do you think President Ford did the right thing in pardoning former President Nixon? Explain.

2. Analysis What effect did events in the Middle East have on the presidencies of Carter, Reagan, and Bush?

3. Why We Remember: Synthesis What do you think is the greatest challenge that Americans face today? Describe what you, as an individual, would want to do to help meet that challenge.

Applying Skills

Taking action We Americans have long been known for our active efforts to improve our nation and ourselves. What change for the better would you like to make in your own life? Maybe you would like to spend more time with friends, improve your grades in school, or increase your skill at playing basketball, singing, or creating computer art. Apply what you learned on page 663 to develop an action plan for making the desired improvement.

1. State your goal.

2. Identify resources that will help you and obstacles to be overcome.

3. Identify what you will do to achieve your goal.

4. Carry out your plan.

History Mystery

Answer the History Mystery on page 639. Which of the former President's occupations would you find most interesting? Which would be most helpful to American society today?

Writing in Your History Journal

1. Keys to History (a) The time line on pages 638–639 has seven Keys to History. In your journal, describe why each one is important to know about. (b) Choose a key event and imagine that you are a television reporter assigned to cover it. In your journal, write what you will say in tonight's broadcast. Include background information and predict possible consequences of the event.

2. Jaime Escalante Is Jaime Escalante typical of the immigrants who have come to the United States over the past two centuries, or is he markedly different? Explain your response in your journal.

hostage crisis. Reagan: Middle East events shadowing his presidency included the killing of 241 American marines in Lebanon, and the sale of weapons to Iran to try to gain release of hostages in Lebanon. Bush: Handling of the Iraqi invasion of Kuwait brought popularity, but not enough for re-election.

3. Answers may reflect concerns mentioned in the chapter such as the environment, budget deficit, AIDS, technological change, immigration and diversity, community, economic change, Middle East, future of democracy. Ideas for meeting the challenges should be realistic.

Applying Skills

Students should show ability to apply the Procedure steps and the first two Skill Tips on page 663 to a personal situation.

(Answers continued in side margin)

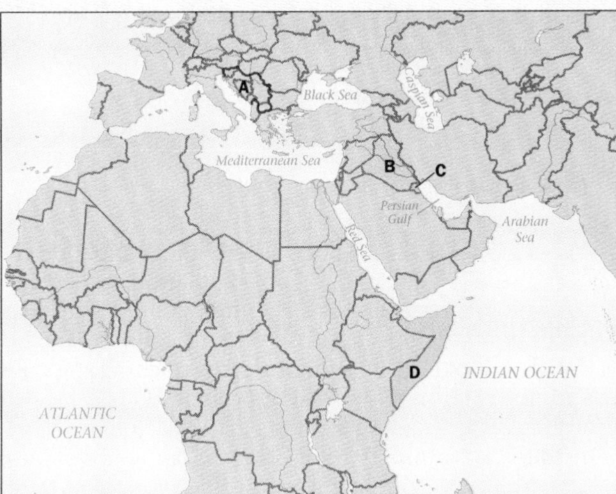

Reviewing Geography

1. Each letter represents a country that was a "hot spot" in the 1980s or 1990s. Write the name of each country.

2. Geographic Thinking Suppose you were asked to update the "hot spots" map to reflect world events today. What additions to and subtractions from the map would you make? Explain. Now try to imagine the world 20 years from now. Where do you think the hottest spot will be? (You can name a continent or other region rather than a country.) Explain.

3. Citizenship The United States is a nation made up of increasingly diverse groups of people. What advantages and disadvantages do you see in this diversity? What beliefs, experiences, or characteristics do you think unify all Americans despite their diversity? Write your responses in your journal.

Alternative Assessment

Acting out political discussions With a partner, prepare and act out discussions between two friends—one a Republican and the other a Democrat—in each of these presidential election years: 1976, 1980, 1988, and 1992. You will act out four 10-minute discussions.

❶ Choose roles. You might make the "characters" more realistic by assigning names and ages, ethnic backgrounds, places of residence, occupations, and so forth. Keep the same roles for all four discussions.

❷ Write scripts for the discussions. In each case, the characters should discuss their positions on current issues as well as the records and qualifications of the two presidential candidates. You might need to do further research on the presidential candidates by looking at magazine or newspaper articles of the times.

❸ Present the discussions to the class.

Your work will be evaluated on the following criteria:

- your scripts accurately present the events and issues of each time period
- you offer opinions in a way that is lively yet clear, logical, and reasonable
- you stay "in character" as a Republican or Democrat of each time period

History Mystery

Information on Jimmy Carter can be found on pp. 643–645. Carter is remembered chiefly for serving as President from 1977 to 1981. Ideas on which occupation is most interesting and which is most useful to society will vary.

Writing in Your History Journal

1. (a) Descriptions should be similar to the time line notes on teacher pp. 638–639. (b) Broadcast notes should reflect information in the text and show ability to imagine the scene of an event and predict realistic consequences.

2. Students may conclude that in his determination, high hopes, and willingness to work hard, Escalante is typical of immigrants. However, they may decide that his ability to inspire sets him apart from most people, regardless of nationality and ethnic background.

3. One advantage is that it makes the nation culturally richer; a disadvantage is that conflicts may arise between groups. Some unifying factors are shared belief in democracy, belief in individual rights, and determination to succeed.

Reviewing Geography

1. (A) Bosnia (B) Iraq (C) Kuwait (D) Somalia

2. Answers to the first question should reflect current events. Answers to the second question should involve reasonable inferences. For example, because the Middle East is a major source of oil and is characterized by deep religious, cultural, and political rifts, students might reasonably predict that it will be the hottest spot 20 years from now.

Alternative Assessment

Teacher's Take-Home Planner 5, p. 23, includes suggestions and scoring rubrics for the Alternative Assessment activity.

Teaching the

Link to American Readings

In this feature students learn about America's give and take with other countries of the world—the giving of experience in aiding other countries to write constitutions, and the taking in of immigrants who have chosen to make the United States their home. Many people of the world envy our society, evidenced by the contemporary immigrants, and others admire our Constitution. Students will learn about those immigrants and that unexpected export, our Constitution.

Before students begin the lesson, review A Changing Population (page 654). Have students read the entire feature before assigning the A Closer Look questions. The Setting the Stage Activity and Bonus Activity may then be introduced according to the needs and interests of the students. The information contained in the Discussion questions and the Footnotes may be used throughout the lesson as appropriate. Readers' Theater is ideal for students who might find the readings somewhat difficult. Use the Wrap-Up Activity for students who would enjoy taking a step beyond the core lesson.

Literature Footnote

Since passage of the Immigration Reform Law in 1965, there has been a big change in immigration patterns to the United States. To distinguish the new immigration of the early twentieth century, many people refer to this latest group as "recent immigrants." The recent immigrants come primarily from three areas: Asia (including Vietnam, Thailand, Cambodia, Laos, the Philippines, Korea, and India), Mexico, and Central America. These new Americans have brought a rich cultural heritage with them, including literature.

Some authors of note who write about the ethnic experience in America include Nguyên Qúi Dú'c, Sandra Cisneros, Martin Espada, Cathy Song, Ana Castillo, Barbara Kingsolver, Amy Tan, and Sherman Alexie.

Link to American Readings

The Quintero family

READING 15A

At Home in the United States

For more than twenty years, immigration has been a major political and social issue in this country. The U.S. Congress took one important step in opening the doors for immigrants who wanted to become U.S. citizens when it revised the immigration laws in 1986. The new laws included an "amnesty provision" that offered American citizenship to illegal aliens who could prove that they had lived in the United States since 1982. The selection that follows is about one family of Mexican Americans for whom the amnesty provision meant a new life.

The story of the Quintero family, 1987

. . . "I am an immigration officer. And I would like to see your papers."

Like most of the other 6 million to 7 million foreign-born people residing illegally in the U.S., Javier and Juana Quintero lived in daily dread of a moment such as this. In the seven years since they left Mexico, they had achieved a prosperity almost unimaginable back home. Javier, solid and easygoing, ran a carpet-laying business in the Phoenix suburb of Mesa, earning as much as $30,000 a year, more than seven times as much as the average Mexican wage earner. Soft-spoken, efficient Juana was raising their three children—Beatriz, 7, Monica, 5, and the infant Rogelio, all U.S. citizens by birth—in a three-bedroom house with new furniture, a washing-machine and central air conditioning. Now, suddenly, all that was in serious jeopardy. "I thought, 'This is the end of our life here,' " recalls Javier. "I was afraid we were going to lose everything."

jeopardy: great danger

Had they been caught a few months earlier, that might have been the case. But by a twist of timing that will remain forever sweet, the day before the undercover officer caught them at the Yuma airport—Oct. 18, 1986—the U.S. Congress enacted the most sweeping revision of immigration law in more than 20 years and, in the process, neatly let the Quinteros off the hook. The critical change: a so-called amnesty provision inviting any illegal aliens who can prove they have lived continuously in the U.S. since Jan. 1, 1982 to apply for legal residency.

The Quinteros will have no trouble coming up with the proof. In fact, they slipped into the system with amazing ease. Unlike many other illegal

Economics Connection

The Sunbelt construction boom of the late 1970s and early 1980s initially enabled Quintero's carpet-laying enterprise to succeed. Construction in the Southwest slowed, however, and Quintero's profits decreased. Although he hoped to turn his business into a carpet distributorship, such an undertaking generally requires a significant capital outlay. At the time the story was written in 1987, he had hoped that legalization and citizenship would enable him to secure a loan to finance the business.

immigrants, who avoided leaving a paper trail for fear of being traced by the Immigration and Naturalization Service, the Quinteros filed taxes, paid their bills in their own name and kept the paperwork required by their business. . . .

Compared with most of the families enfranchised under the new law, the Quinteros have a considerable head start on the American dream. Their profitable business has two full-time employees, including Javier's younger brother Marcos, a legal resident. . . . The family owns their home, a trim, cinder-block ranch house in a blue-collar Mesa neighborhood. . . . Legalization will lift a tremendous burden of insecurity from the Quinteros. For the first time since they arrived, they will be free to plan for long-term goals, like college for the children, that seemed hopelessly distant before. . . .

Like generations of immigrants before them, the Quinteros got their start in the U.S. with the help of a relative already here. In this case, it was Javier's older brother Lazaro, a legal resident, who found Javier his first carpet-laying job in 1972 and eventually helped him set out as an independent contractor in 1980. Carpet-laying has proved to be an ideal enterprise for Javier; it requires no inventory and little capital outlay other than the cost of a pickup truck and about $3,500 for tools such as a power carpet stretcher and electrical generator. Since there is no set place of employment, the Quinteros never had to fear the raids that the immigration service occasionally runs on factories, restaurants and other places where illegal aliens usually work. . . .

The drive and energy that have taken the Quinteros this far trace back to childhoods spent in hardscrabble poverty. Both came from huge families—Javier is the fifth of 16 children, Juana the eighth of nine—where everyone had to work merely to survive. As a boy Javier had to miss about half of each school year to work in the cotton fields near his home in northwestern Mexico. Until he was 14 and his family moved to the border city of Mexicali, where he could work after school, he had never been a student long enough to finish third grade. When he left school for good at 18, he had completed only the eighth grade.

The memory of that poverty reinforced the couple's decision to emigrate after their marriage in 1979. At the time, Javier was making $76 a week driving a delivery truck in Mexicali; his brother Lazaro held out the prospect of making three times as much with him in the carpet business in Arizona. "It was sad leaving our families," says Juana through an interpreter, "but to make a better life for our children, we had no choice but to come here."

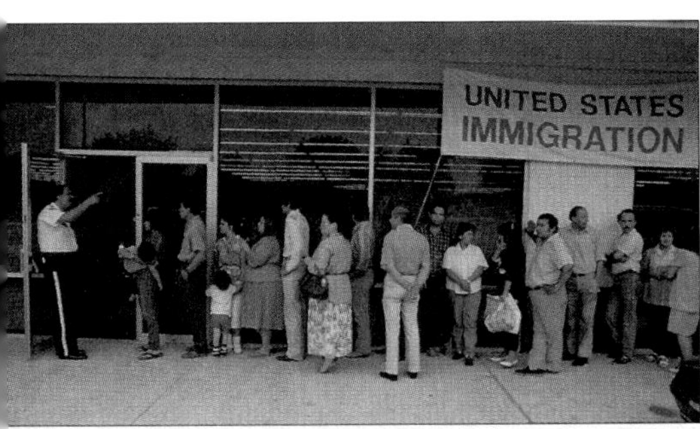

Applicants in Houston, Texas, wait to file for amnesty under the provisions of the revised immigration laws.

Setting the Stage Activity

Writing a Constitution

To help students understand what about the U.S. Constitution so appeals to people of other countries, ask them to complete this exercise. Have students review the Bill of Rights. Divide the class into four groups. Have each group choose the three amendments from the Bill of Rights that they think would be most important to an Eastern European country drawing up a constitution of its own, or that would convince a person from that country to immigrate to the United States. Have a volunteer from each group report to the class; then have students debate their choices.

Bonus Activity

Mapping Countries with New Constitutions

Countries worldwide have been inspired by the success of the U.S. Constitution in maintaining a stable, democratic government. Locate some of these countries on a world map: Poland, the Czech Republic, Slovakia, Hungary, Romania, Liberia, Zimbabwe, Bangladesh, the Marshall Islands, Fiji, and Peru.

Discussion

Stimulating Critical Thinking

1. Should anyone who wants to immigrate to the United States be allowed to do so, or should immigration be legally restricted? Explain. (Students should offer logical arguments for either side of the issue. Some may say that anyone who wants freedom should be allowed to share in the American Dream. Others may say that immigrants in the modern era take work from American citizens or that without work, they strain the already overburdened welfare system.)

2. Why might a country borrow ideas from several constitutions rather than simply copy the U.S. Constitution? (Most countries want a "home-grown product," one that takes the best ideas from other countries and adapts them to work in their own particular situation.)

3. Are there any circumstances in which one country's system of government would not work well in another country? (Where there are cultural differences success is less likely. For example, trying to impose trial-by-jury in countries where kings or chiefs traditionally dispense justice might not work.)

History Footnote

Recent years have seen several important American bicentennials: in 1976, the revolution; in 1987, the Constitution; and in 1991, the Bill of Rights. Since ratification of the Bill of Rights, only 17 other amendments have been added, a remarkable indication of how good a job our forefathers did. There have been 33 proposals approved by Congress, but several of these (including the Equal Rights Amendment, defeated in 1982) were not accepted by the required number of states. More than 10,000 other proposals were suggested but were rejected by Congress. Perhaps it is the solidity and longevity of the U.S. Constitution that makes it so appealing to other countries who are searching to establish that same stability and longevity in their own governments.

Madeleine Albright (right), U.S. Ambassador to the United Nations, and First Lady Hillary Rodham Clinton, wave to Prague citizens during a 1996 tour of the Czech Republic.

READING 15B

Exporting Constitutional Advice

One of the challenges that Eastern European countries faced after the communist regimes lost their one-party control of the government was writing new constitutions. Impressed by the success of the U.S. Constitution, officials in these countries asked American legal specialists for help. One of these experts, Professor Albert Blaustein of the Rutgers University School of Law, has been advising countries around the world on their constitutional systems since 1966.

Constitutional consultants, 1990

A handful of American constitutional law scholars are helping to write or revise constitutions for the new Governments in Poland, Hungary and Czechoslovakia. . . .

Although the collaborations have barely begun, several scholars are already immersed in the research and consultations that precede the writing of drafts. For professors like Albert P. Blaustein of Rutgers University School of Law, it is familiar territory: Professor Blaustein has worked with more than 40 governments on constitutional reform since 1966.

collaboration: process of working together

"Three-quarters of the world's constitutions have been written since 1965, many of them with American assistance," said Professor Blaustein, who has made more than 80 trips overseas to consult with foreign governments and constitutional scholars. The 68-year-old scholar has drafted the constitutions of Liberia and Fiji singlehandedly and contributed significant provisions to more than a dozen others, including Zimbabwe, Bangladesh and Peru. . . .

Helping countries write constitutions is not simply a matter of exporting the American Constitution, said Prof. Herman Schwartz of the American University in Washington, who recently left for Czechoslovakia to help a panel of constitutional scholars there. "We're not telling them what to do, nor do they want us to come in and simply replicate our own Constitution. They want to know what's worked for us and what hasn't."

replicate: repeat; duplicate

Constitution drafters say they are trying to avoid a repetition of the history in many post-colonial African countries in the 1960s, when departing colonial powers hastily imposed carbon copies of their own documents, which evolved from different cultural and historical backgrounds. . . .

Professor Blaustein said, "I ask them what they want, what values and heritage they want to see reflected in the document, and then I make suggestions, drawing on my knowledge of different constitutions from all over the world."

Readers' Theater

The story of the Quinteros will lend itself to treatment as a radio documentary. The immigration officer, Javier, and Juana are the only characters, but the rest of the text could be distributed among two to four narrators or announcers. Other voices might be used to sing or hum Mexican and American songs at appropriate places. Some of the material can be summarized or cut.

Borrowing from West Germany's postwar constitution, the professor said, he put an "anti-Hitler" clause in his draft for Liberia, making it illegal for Liberians to form extremist political parties. The clause was requested by the Government of Gen. Samuel K. Doe, who seized power in a 1980 coup.

Yet the American constitutional experience appeals to Eastern European constitutional scholars most of all. "Reformers in Europe know the American experience and admire its longevity," Professor Howard said. "The Hungarian revisers are particularly interested in the separation of powers, and in creating a strong independent judiciary. The model that is emerging in these early discussions is Madisonian." . . .

The scholars predict that some rights will be guaranteed more explicitly in the new Eastern-bloc constitutions than they are in the United States Constitution. "Our own document is too general, so we've had to fill in the blanks over the years with case law," Professor Blaustein said. "We can save others the trouble of all that by encouraging them to make explicit choices at the beginning and putting those choices into their constitutions."

"For Eastern European countries, the most important aspect to the right of free speech will be access to the television airwaves," said Professor Blaustein, who hopes to persuade Eastern European revisers to spell out this right. When he drafted the Liberian constitution, he said, he included a provision stating that the public's "access to state-owned media shall not be denied."

From 1978 to 1980, Professor Blaustein tried unsuccessfully to persuade the new leaders of Zimbabwe to include a version of the equal rights amendment in their constitution. "It was derailed," he said. "It went against tribal cultures."

For Fiji's constitution, Professor Blaustein drafted provisions proclaiming the rights to literacy, a job, health care, peace, and environmental protection.

"These are not easy rights to enforce," said Prof. Laurence H. Tribe of Harvard Law School, who wrote the constitution of the Marshall Islands in the Pacific in 1978, including clauses affirming the Government's obligation to provide minimum guarantees of shelter and employment.

A Closer Look

1. What difference did legalization make in the lives of the Quintero family?

2. What is a constitutional consultant? How have they been able to help many countries around the world?

3. Critical Thinking Imagine that you have been requested to help an Eastern European or African country draft a constitution. Which three features of the U.S. Constitution would you encourage that country to adopt? Explain.

Wrap-Up Activity

A New Face

To extend the lesson, explain to students that in 1920 approximately 90 percent of all Americans were of white European background. By the year 2050 this figure likely will be about 50 percent. Ask students to respond to the following questions in their history journals: Is the population shift that is predicted to take place by 2050 more likely to increase or decrease racial tension? Why? What might be done to help the nation adapt to its changing face?

A Closer Look

Answers

1. Legalization lifted a burden of insecurity from their lives. They would be able to work, save, and plan for their children's education and future.

2. Constitutional consultants are legal specialists who advise and help other countries draft constitutions. They have helped countries build constitutions that fit their specific needs.

3. Students' responses will vary. Some of the features of the U.S. Constitution that are proving popular among other countries are the separation of powers, an independent judiciary, and the right of free speech.

Teaching the Citizenship Lab

In this feature students learn about *Bush* v. *Vera,* a recent Supreme Court ruling dealing with the issue of race-based congressional district boundaries. The Court is struggling with the question of how to make sure minorities are represented while at the same time protecting the rights of the majority.

Have students read the entire feature before assigning the Understanding Civic Issues questions and the Hands-On Citizenship activity. The Bonus Activity in this Teacher's Edition may be used as an alternative to, or in addition to, the Hands-On Citizenship. The Discussion questions in this Teacher's Edition may be used at appropriate points during students' reading or afterward.

Objectives

- ★ Understand why congressional seats must be redistricted every ten years.
- ★ Explain how and why gerrymandering is such a common practice.
- ★ Identify the issues raised in race-based cases such as *Bush* v. *Vera.*
- ★ Interpret the effects of the Court rulings on elections.

Supreme Court Case: *Bush* v. *Vera*

Citizenship Lab

Must Election Districts Be Colorblind?

Since 1929 the size of the House of Representatives has been limited to 435 members. Each member is elected from a congressional district —a specific geographic area served by one representative. Because people in our country are always moving, it is not surprising that the populations of the states change over the years. For example, today the fastest growing states are in the Sun Belt—Florida and the states of the Southwest. At the same time, the populations of some of the industrial states of the Northeast—the so-called Rust Belt—are growing much more slowly. The Constitution requires that a census be taken every ten years. After each census, the congressional districts are reapportioned among the states. The 435 seats are redistributed among the states on the basis of their current populations.

The Constitution leaves it up to the state governments to decide how to draw the boundaries of the congressional districts in their states. Through the years, this has led to some strangely shaped districts. Districts often were drawn to favor the party that controlled the state legislature. Elbridge Gerry, who was governor of Massachusetts in 1812, drew the boundaries of the districts in his state to benefit his party. The result was that one of the districts ended up shaped like a salamander. From this episode, the practice of re-drawing voting districts to favor the party in power has became known as *gerrymandering.*

In recent years states have created some oddly-shaped districts in an effort to ensure that minorities are represented in Congress. They drew congressional district boundaries in such a way that the election of representatives sensitive to the needs of minorities were elected. Some non-

The term *gerrymandering* was born with the stroke of this cartoonist's pen.

History Footnote

Ruth Bader Ginsburg has consistently championed minority rights. Her strong feelings may be in part explained by her own experiences. Ginsburg grew up in a poor immigrant family during the Great Depression. She experienced prejudice because her family was considered foreign and she was a Jew. The way out of poverty was through education.

When Ginsburg graduated from law school, she had a hard time finding a job. She recalls that she had three strikes against her. She was "a woman, a Jew and a mother!" Eventually, she turned to teaching and became the first permanent female professor at Columbia Law School. In the 1970s Ginsburg argued many discrimination cases for the ACLU before the Supreme Court. In 1993 she was appointed to the Court.

minority voters have legally challenged the creation of these districts, arguing that they have been denied equal protection under the law as guaranteed by the Constitution.

The Court Takes a Harder Line on Race-Based Political Boundaries

The Supreme Court first dealt with race-based political boundaries in 1993. In *Shaw* v. *Reno,* the Court questioned "bizarredly shaped" districts. In 1995, in *Miller* v. *Johnson,* the Court threw out a map drawn by the Georgia legislature. It believed that race was the "predominant factor" in drawing the map and that this was unconstitutional. On June 13, 1996, the Supreme Court struck down a map drawn by the Texas legislature. In the *Bush* v. *Vera* decision the majority of the justices said the map was racial gerrymandering and therefore unconstitutional.

The Voting Rights Act of 1965 required states that had a history of racial discrimination, including Georgia and Texas, to have their districting map approved by the U.S. Department of Justice. The department pressured the states to redraw the boundaries of their congressional districts to increase the number of districts where minorities were dominant. *Bush* v. *Vera* stated that the department had gone too far and in the process violated the equal protection rights of white voters.

Ruth Bader Ginsburg and Sandra Day O'Connor

The Decision Shows the Court Is Sometimes Sharply Divided

Bush v. *Vera* was a 5-4 split decision. Justice Sandra Day O'Connor cast the deciding vote. She admitted "the Constitution does not mandate regularity of district shape." She went on to say that states can and should make special efforts to safeguard rights of minority voters under the Voting Rights Act. She recognized a

Setting the Stage Activity

To prepare for reading about Bush v. Vera, have students do quickwrites telling what they think the question at the top of the page means. Have students share their ideas and try to reach consensus. Later, they can assess the accuracy of their ideas.

Bonus Activity

Drawing Maps

Have students draw a map showing the reapportionment of congressional seats after the 1990 census. The students should label every state and indicate the number of representatives each state has and the total gain or loss compared to 1980. Using three different colors, students should indicate states that gained seats, states that lost seats, and states that stayed the same.

Discussion

Checking Understanding

1. Why is the number of seats in the House of Representatives limited to 435? (The House decided in 1929 that if the assembly grew larger, it would make it less efficient and more difficult to get anything done.)

Stimulating Critical Thinking

2. What can elected officials do to reach out to minority voters in their districts? (Answers will vary. Possible answers might include: appointing minorities to important staff positions, using community people as liaisons between the different groups in the district, creating more jobs and better schools, etc.)

Citizenship Footnote

In 1842 Congress passed a law that gave state legislatures the responsibility to draw their own congressional districts. Many state legislatures were controlled by rural areas. And they sometimes tried to preserve their power by creating districts with unequal populations. At times this meant that the rural vote was worth twice as much as the urban vote. In 1964, in *Wesberry* v. *Sanders*, the Court ruled that congressional districts must have equal populations. This principle has come to be known as the "one person, one vote" rule.

conflict, however: "The Voting Rights Act requires the states and the courts to take action to remedy the reality of racial inequality in our political system, sometimes necessitating race-based action, while the Fourteenth Amendment requires us to look with suspicion on the excessive use of racial considerations by the government." Chief Justice William Rehnquist and justices Anthony Kennedy, Antonin Scalia, and Clarence Thomas agreed with O'Connor.

Four justices disagreed—John Paul Stevens, Ruth Bader Ginsburg, David Souter, and Stephen Breyer. They believed states should have more flexibility regarding the drawing of district boundaries even if they are strangely shaped or largely based on race. In their opinions, this may be the only way of ensuring minority representation.

In her dissent, Justice Ginsburg wrote that the Miller ruling would create chaos in the redistricting process. Justice Souter expressed concern that the process would involve federal judges in the complex map-drawing. In Souter's opinion, Article 1 of the Constitution states this is the responsibility of state legislatures, not court judges.

Minority Leaders Attack the Court's Actions

More minorities than ever have won seats in Congress in recent years. This was in large part because of the creation of districts with majorities of minority voters. Some minority groups worried that the recent Court decisions would result in the loss of hard-won electoral victories. For example, Cynthia McKinney, U.S. Representative from Georgia, called the Court's actions "a setback to democracy." Donald Payne, U.S. Representative from New Jersey and chairperson of the Congressional Black Caucus, charged that the redistricting decisions threatened to "disenfranchise African Americans."

Donald Payne

Cynthia McKinney

Connections to Mathematics

The apportionment discussion offers an opportunity to integrate math and social studies. Have students calculate how many people are represented by each of their elected officials. Then have them compare the figures with that of a much smaller or larger state. To put population growth in perspective, have students draw comparative charts for different periods using census figures.

The Decisions Leave Many Unanswered Questions

Despite the recent Court decisions, many questions about the proper role of race in the districting process are left unanswered. It is still not clear when race is the "predominant" consideration and when it is just one of several factors that determine the shape of a district. O'Connor admitted that sometimes districts are legitimately drawn to favor the incumbent, the person who already holds a particular office. On other occasions, racial groupings might be the result of a community with shared political interests coming together. But the rulings in the cases fall short of providing the states with clear guidelines they can use in drawing their maps. In fact, the decisions have resulted in more court decisions. Recently, boundaries for predominantly Hispanic congressional districts in New York and Illinois have been challenged.

The Effects of the Court Rulings on Recent Elections

Six of the new "colorblind" congressional districts were tested in the 1996 election. Although it was widely predicted that many of the minority representatives in these districts would lose, all six of the African American candidates won reelection.

Understanding Civic Issues

1. Why must congressional district boundaries be redrawn from time to time?
2. In *Bush* v. *Vera*, what objections did the justices who disagreed with the majority have about the decision?
3. **Critical Thinking** Is racial or ethnic gerrymandering undemocratic or does it best serve the needs of generally underrepresented groups? Explain.
4. **Hands-On Citizenship** You and two classmates are members of an advisory group to one of the major political parties. The party leaders want your advice on how to increase minority representation in the party.

- Devise a strategy for the party. Discuss how you could increase minority representation yet still be fair to the majority.
- Discuss whether gerrymandering along racial or ethnic lines promotes or threatens democracy.
- Conduct a survey of at least 25 voters in your area. Ask: What qualities do you consider most important for an elected official to have? How important is the racial or ethnic background of an official?

Compile the results of your survey and analyze them. What conclusions can you draw from this activity?

Citizenship Lab Answers

1. The number of congressional seats is limited to 435, and the seats must be reapportioned on the basis of population changes.

2. The justices who disagreed believe states should have more flexibility regarding the drawing of district boundaries. Justice Ginsburg was concerned that the rulings would make redistricting chaotic. Justice Souter believed that the state legislatures and not the courts should draw the legislative maps.

3. Answers will vary. It could be argued that racial or ethnic gerrymandering is undemocratic because it does not treat all voters in the same way. Others will argue that racial and ethnic minorities are underrepresented in Congress and that their special needs are better understood by representatives of similar background.

Teaching the Hands-On Citizenship

Activities like this really help develop critical thinking skills. Among the skills you should be looking for and trying to develop in your students are: identifying central issues, making comparisons, determining relevant information, formulating appropriate questions, distinguishing fact from opinion, recognizing bias, drawing conclusions, identifying alternatives, and predicting consequences.

Teaching the

Link to Literature

Introduce *The House on Mango Street* by noting that although it is a work of fiction, it is rooted in Sandra Cisneros's own life. Cisneros is the only daughter among the seven children of a Mexican father and a Mexican American mother. Like the Cordero family, the Cisneros family lived in Chicago, was poor, and moved frequently. Like Esperanza, young Sandra attended Catholic schools. Asked whether *The House on Mango Street* is autobiographical, Cisneros says, "Every piece of fiction is based on something that really happened. On the other hand, it's not autobiography because my family would be the first one to confess: 'Well it didn't happen that way.'"

Literature Footnote

Sandra Cisneros has been hailed as a fresh, original voice in literature. She sees herself as a literary pioneer, saying, "I'm trying to write the stories that haven't been written. . . . I'm determined to fill a literary void." One way she does that is to focus on Hispanic characters, many of whom are as isolated from mainstream American culture as Cisneros sometimes feels herself to be. Cisneros's fiction often reads like poetry, while her poems often resemble short stories. She received the Before Columbus American Book Award for *The House on Mango Street* (Arte Público, 1984). Her other works include *Woman Hollering Creek and Other Stories* (Random House, 1991) and a collection of poems called *My Wicked Wicked Ways* (Third Woman Press, 1987).

Link to Literature

The House on Mango Street by Sandra Cisneros

In her novel, *The House on Mango Street,* author Sandra Cisneros tells her story through the eyes of Esperanza Cordero, a young girl growing up in the Latino section of Chicago. In a series of brief chapters, Esperanza vividly describes her family, friends, and neighborhood, and confides her hopes and dreams. The novel begins with the following passage.

We didn't always live on Mango Street. Before that we lived on Loomis on the third floor, and before that we lived on Keeler. Before Keeler it was Paulina, and before that I can't remember. But what I remember most is moving a lot. Each time it seemed there'd be one more of us. By the time we got to Mango Street we were six—Mama, Papa, Carlos, Kiki, my sister Nenny and me.

The house on Mango Street is ours, and we don't have to pay rent to anybody, or share the yard with the people downstairs, or be careful not to make too much noise, and there isn't a landlord banging on the ceiling with a broom. But even so, it's not the house we thought we'd get.

We had to leave the flat on Loomis quick. The water pipes broke and the landlord wouldn't fix them because the house was too old. We had to leave fast. We were using the washroom next door and carrying water over in empty milk gallons. That's why Mama and Papa looked for a house, and that's why we moved into the house on Mango Street, far away, on the other side of town.

They always told us that one day we would move into a house, a real house that would be ours for always so we wouldn't have to move each year. And our house would have running water and pipes that worked. And inside it would have real stairs, not hallway stairs, but stairs inside like the houses on T.V. And we'd have a basement and at least three washrooms so when we took a bath we wouldn't have to tell everybody. Our house would be white with trees around it, a great big yard and grass growing without a fence. This was the house Mama dreamed up in the stories she told us before we went to bed.

But the house on Mango Street is not the way they told it at all. It's small and red with tight steps in front and windows so small you'd think they were holding their breath. Bricks are crumbling in places and the front door is so swollen you have to push hard to get in. There is no front yard, only four little elms the city planted by the curb. Out

Literature Footnote

Partly because her family moved so often and partly because she was the only girl in the family, Sandra Cisneros was a shy and introverted child. She found comfort in reading and in writing her own poems and stories. After majoring in English at Loyola University in Chicago, she earned a master's degree through the University of Iowa Writers' Workshop. During one class at Iowa, her fellow students described their childhood homes—homes much nicer than the ones in which Cisneros had grown up. Cisneros suddenly realized that her Mexican American heritage and childhood poverty made her feel like a "yellow weed" among "hothouse flowers," but that she could put those feelings to work in her writing. "I decided I would write about something my classmates couldn't write about," she said.

Hermanas Juntas Sin Velo (Sisters Together Unveiled) **by Nivia Gonzalez**

back is a small garage for the car we don't own yet and a small yard that looks smaller between the two buildings on either side. There are stairs in our house, but they're ordinary hallway stairs, and the house has only one washroom. Everybody has to share a bedroom—Mama and Papa, Carlos and Kiki, me and Nenny.

Once when we were living on Loomis, a nun from my school passed by and saw me playing out front. The laundromat downstairs had been boarded up because it had been robbed two days before and the owner had painted on the wood YES WE'RE OPEN so as not to lose business.

Where do you live? she asked.

There, I said pointing up to the third floor.

You live there?

There. I had to look to where she pointed—the third floor, the paint peeling, wooden bars Papa had nailed on the windows so we wouldn't fall out. You live there? The way she said it made me feel like nothing. There. I lived there. I nodded.

I knew then I had to have a house. A real house. One I could point to. But this isn't it. The house on Mango Street isn't it. For the time being, Mama says. Temporary, says Papa. But I know how those things go.

A Closer Look

1. How does Esperanza feel about the house she lives in? How did she feel about the flat on Loomis?
2. What does Esperanza hope for?
3. Based on this passage, why do you think Cisneros uses a house as her central image?

Discussion

Checking Understanding

1. Should Esperanza's mother have kept her hopes about her dream house to herself? Explain. (Yes: raised expectations to the point that Esperanza is unhappy even though the house on Mango is an improvement over the flat on Loomis. No: sharing dreams with one's children is natural and desirable.)

2. Do you think the nun intended to make Esperanza "feel like nothing"? Explain. (Answers will vary. She was probably unable to hide her dismay that one of her students lived in such a place.)

A Closer Look

Answers

1. Although she is glad that the house belongs to her family, she is disappointed that it is not the house she dreamed of. She was ashamed of the flat on Loomis.

2. She hopes for a better house—one that she can point to with pride and want to live in forever.

3. She knows most people identify closely with their homes and that people tend to be judged by their homes.

Unit Survey

Making Connections

Answers

1. To keep communism from spreading. Economic aid, spying, NATO, buildup of nuclear arsenals, sending troops to other countries.

2. Some answers: Cold War led to a hunt for American Communists. Cost of Vietnam War undermined Great Society program funding. Support of Israel led to energy shortage in 1973. Iran hostage crisis helped Reagan become President.

3. Some answers: Coverage of McCarthy hearings turned Americans against him. Coverage of Vietnam War fueled opposition. Coverage of attacks on protestors led to demands that Congress protect civil rights of black Americans.

Teaching the Unit Project

If necessary, explain that "hippies" favored long hair, wire-rimmed glasses, bell-bottom jeans, and bright colors. In addition to music and dancing, students might play popular games of the decade or watch a movie from the decade.

Evaluation Criteria

The project can be evaluated according to the criteria listed below, using a scale for each: 4 = exemplary, 3 = good, 2 = adequate, 1 = poor.

Completing the task Students plan and have a decade theme party.

Knowing content All aspects of the party are accurate.

(Continued in top margin)

Thinking critically Students show good judgment in planning items and activities that reflect the decade.

Communicating ideas Students cooperate well. Invitations and other materials are clear and appealing.

Thinking It Over

Possible answers to first question: People find it comforting to escape their own lives for a few hours. Behaving like their parents and grandparents makes people feel closer to them. People enjoy learning tidbits about past daily life and popular culture. Answers to second question may range from "surfing the Internet" to shopping at malls to listening to rap music. Accept reasonable answers.

Unit Survey

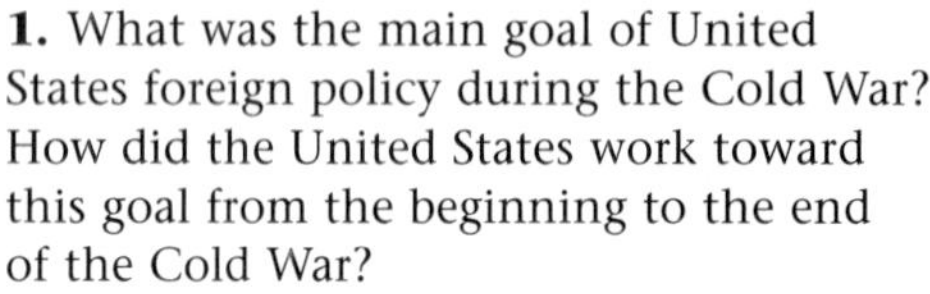

Making Connections

Review

1. What was the main goal of United States foreign policy during the Cold War? How did the United States work toward this goal from the beginning to the end of the Cold War?

2. Give four examples of developments in the United States that were closely linked to international events since World War II. Explain the links.

3. Support the following statement with evidence from the unit: *Television has had a major impact on the course of history since 1950.*

Linking History, Art, and Music

Project

A Fifties, Sixties, or Seventies Party

It may seem odd, but in the 1950s and 1960s, "Roaring Twenties" parties were extremely popular. Female guests dressed like "flappers," male guests tried to look like gangsters, and everyone danced the "Charleston" to loud jazz. Plan your own party centered on one of the following decades that you have read about: the 1950s, 1960s, or 1970s.

Project Steps

Work with a group.

❶ Choose the decade to center your party on. Select a date, time, and place for the party. Make up the guest list.

❷ Decide who in your group will do what in order to get ready for the party. Here is a list of tasks to get you started:

- Make invitations. They should ask guests to wear costumes appropriate to the decade. For example, guests might dress like "hippies" for a Sixties party. To help your guests plan their costumes, draw or photocopy pictures of people from the decade on the invitations.
- Plan and create decorations that relate to the decade. For example, put up authentic posters. Or make posters based on images you find in books about the decade or in magazines from the decade.
- Make arrangements for music. Gather recordings of popular music from the decade. If any group members play instruments, they can perform the decade's hits "live." Also, learn some dances of the decade so you can teach them to your guests.

❸ Carry out the preparations. Ask parents or other adults for ideas on making the party authentic and for help in learning dances. The adults may even have items such as clothing, posters, or recordings that you can borrow. Your library is another source of help.

❹ Have the party—and have fun!

Thinking It Over Someday, your children may attend Nineties parties in which they wear "costumes" like the clothes you wear and dance to "ancient" compact discs of the music you love. People of each generation enjoy this type of "time travel." Why do you think this is so? What do you suppose later generations will think of when they think of the 1990s? Why?

Tips for Teaching

Into the Future

The objectives for teaching the four pages entitled "Into the Future" are to:

- Make students aware of how futurists predict the future by studying the past.
- Engage students in writing scenarios about their own futures.

"Into the Future" can be effectively taught by having the class read and discuss pages 677–679 and then do the activity described on student page 680, individually or in small groups. The activity can be used as an alternative assessment. Evaluation criteria and a scoring rubric are provided on teacher page 680.

Epilogue

Into the Future

Imagine Waking Up in the Year 2025: A Scenario

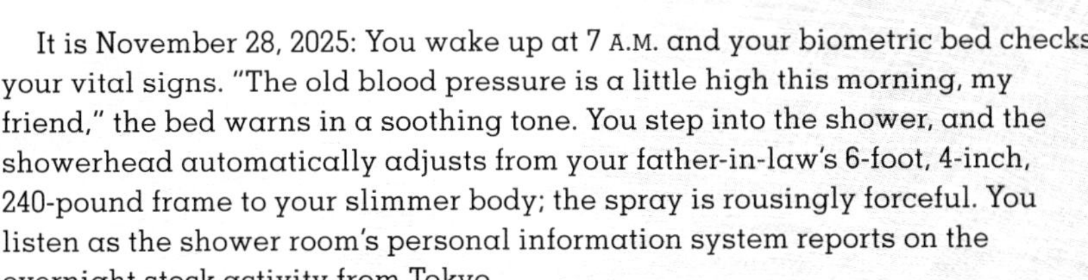

It is November 28, 2025: You wake up at 7 A.M. and your biometric bed checks your vital signs. "The old blood pressure is a little high this morning, my friend," the bed warns in a soothing tone. You step into the shower, and the showerhead automatically adjusts from your father-in-law's 6-foot, 4-inch, 240-pound frame to your slimmer body; the spray is rousingly forceful. You listen as the shower room's personal information system reports on the overnight stock activity from Tokyo.

As the shower douses you with antibacterial suds, you ask the information system for a quick personality assessment from the psychotherapeutic expert system you just installed. "Hey, relax! Try to image a sun-drenched beach," you're advised. "You'll be able to handle that marketing presentation much better." You smile, thinking about the fun you had on your last vacation in Hawaii as the shower's heat jets blast you dry. The robotic closet-valet brings out your color-coordinated, temperature-sensitive business suit, and you quickly dress. As you leave your bedroom, you sense the temperature going down behind you and the lights turning off automatically.

You peek into the kids' room to make sure they've transmitted their homework to school and have gotten dressed for their teleclass, which they "attend" for three hours in your home's media room during what used to be a long Thanksgiving holiday.

You are now ready to face an average workday in the 21st century.

The story above is called a scenario. A scenario is an imaginary account of happenings in the future. It is written by futurists—people who try to imagine what the future will be like. Futurists look at information from the past and the present. From that information they make predictions about what might happen in years to come and then draw up a scenario based on their predictions.

Introducing Into the Future

Point out that futurists, unlike science fiction writers, make their predictions on the basis of trends derived from careful analysis of information and statistics.

Setting the Stage Activity

Making a Prediction

Ask students to make predictions about an event or development that they think will take place before they are 30 years old. Ideas might include advances in technology affecting transportation, communication, medicine, or everyday life. Students may share their ideas with the class in written or oral form. Some may wish to include visual presentations.

Discussion

Stimulating Critical Thinking

1. Which parts of the scenario do you think would be possible with today's technology? (Some answers: a bed that checks blood pressure, a shower that sprays suds, heat jets, automatic lights and heat, televised classes.)

2. What would be the advantages and disadvantages of a "teleclass"? (Advantage: learning more in a shorter time without outside distractions; Disadvantage: not being able to interact with other students and teachers.)

Discussion

Stimulating Critical Thinking

1. Why do you think futurists expect people to move to southern and western states? (Students may note that the climate and the concentration of high technology industries in those areas would attract people.)

2. Do you think all schools in the future will be equipped with the latest technology? (Yes: they will need it if their students are going to be competitive in the business world. No: not all schools will be able to afford new technology.)

Bonus Activity

Predictions in the Media

To help students focus on predictions, have them find examples in newspapers and magazines and on radio and television to share with the class. For example, meteorologists predicting weather, economists predicting business trends, environmentalists speculating on long-range effects of a particular decision or activities, and politicians predicting the effects of a proposed policy. Discuss the examples, having students attempt to identify the basis for each prediction.

History Footnote

An early English futurist was Thomas Robert Malthus. In 1798 Malthus published a controversial pamphlet predicting that at its current rate of growth, the population of Britain would soon outstrip food production, resulting in mass misery and starvation. However, as Paul Kennedy points out in his book *Preparing for the Twenty-First Century,* Malthus's predictions did not prove accurate. He failed to foresee the effects of emigration, agricultural improvements, and the Industrial Revolution, which enabled Britain to support an expanding population with an improving standard of living.

Nevertheless, the race between population growth and food production continues to challenge futurists today as they attempt to gather data and analyze variables in an effort to predict the future.

Predicting the Future

To make a prediction, a futurist must first detect trends—patterns revealed over time by certain facts. In 1984, for example, 7 million Americans used computers at home. Over 30 million people did so in 1993. To note such an increase is to discover a trend.

To make predictions about the future of education, a futurist might look at—among other things—how many students graduate from high school and how that number has changed over the past 100 years. Having observed a trend, the futurist would try to predict whether more or fewer students will finish high school in the future. Using past and present facts, futurists have made the predictions on these pages.

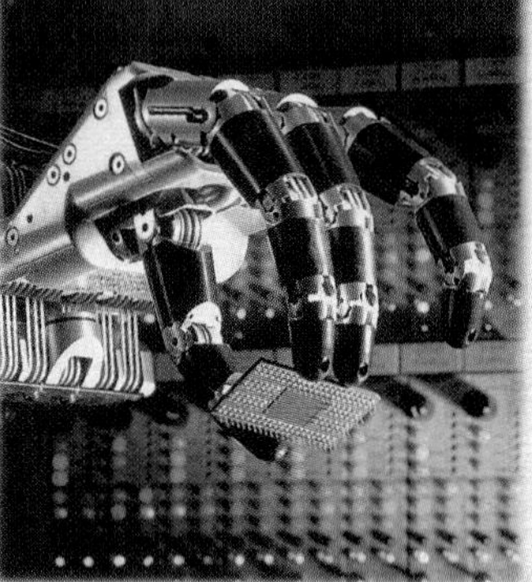

Robotic hand

City planners

Population Predictions

- The population of the United States is expected to rise from 260 million in 1994 to 390 million in 2050.
- By 2010, for the first time, more Americans will be over 55 years of age than under 18 years of age.
- Population will continue to explode in southern and western states. For example, California is expected to shoot up to 41 million people in 2010 from its 1995 population of 32 million.

Technology Predictions

- Smart technologies use computer chips to respond to changes in the environment around them. They can adjust a car's temperature or water the garden. With smart technologies, future cars might drive themselves while passengers watch television or take a nap.
- People will rely on information appliances, such as picture phones, computers, and faxes. Americans will increasingly turn to the Internet for information rather than to books and magazines.

Predictions About Education

- Use of information appliances will make individual instruction easier. Classmates will study different topics at the same time. One might watch a CD-ROM on volcanoes while others use computers to work on math problems or to write and illustrate a book.
- Students will learn in a variety of settings, from home to school to a museum. Schoolwork will be telecommunicated—sent by computer—between students and teachers.

History Footnote

The CD-ROM has brought changes to the ways we live and work. To demonstrate the storage capabilities and environmental advantages of the CD-ROM, Microsoft founder Bill Gates had 330,000 sheets of single-spaced typed paper stacked into two 55-foot columns, which closely resemble trees, outside his company. A single CD-ROM, he pointed out, could hold still more information.

Scientists at IBM are already developing a better CD-ROM with the ability to store information in as many as six layers on one disc. Physicist Hal Rosen, who leads the CD-ROM research team, hopes that one day they will be able to develop a disc with 20 layers. "That would be like putting a full public library at your doorstep," he says.

Predictions About Work

- The number of construction workers will increase. People working in service industries, such as teachers and doctors, will also find more opportunities. There will be 200,000 more lawyers by 2005, and 650,000 more waitresses and waiters.
- Jobs in farming and manufacturing industries, however, will decline in number. New technologies will be one reason behind the decline.
- More people will communicate at work through the Internet and videoconferencing than through face-to-face encounters or by telephone.

Teleconferencing

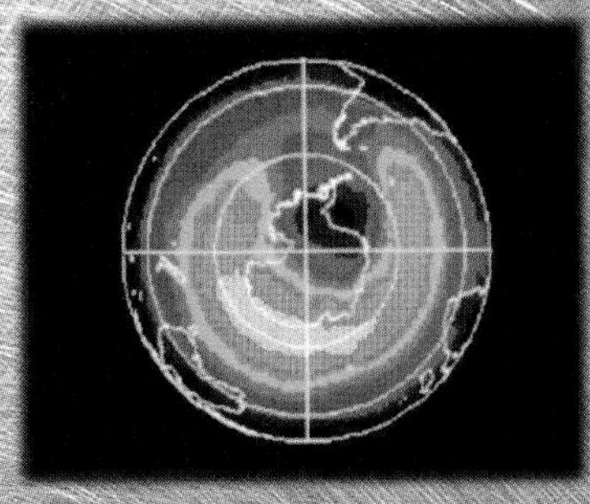
Ozone-layer image

Predictions About How We Live

- The world's population will become more urban. In 1900 only 1 in 40 people lived in cities. By 2000 at least 1 in 2 people will live in cities.
- English will be increasingly used as a major language throughout the world.
- Telecommuting will free workers from having to live near their workplaces. With one or both parents working at home, patterns of family life will change.
- Malls will add museums, theaters, and indoor botanical gardens to attract people who are looking for activities outside their homes.
- New forms of travel will be developed. Short-distance trips—from Boston to New York or Los Angeles to San Francisco—will be made easier by trains traveling 200 miles (320 km) an hour or faster.

Environmental Predictions

- As many as 50,000 types of plants and animals may die out during the first decades of the 21st century. By the time that century ends, two-thirds of all living species may be lost forever.
- The Amazon rain forest in South America may recover from the destruction that humans have caused. Satellite pictures reveal that new forests are already growing there.
- The "hole" in the ozone layer may begin to shrink in the near future. Such good news would result from the ban on chlorofluorocarbons (see page 657).

High-speed train

Discussion

Stimulating Critical Thinking

1. What kinds of skills do you think will be important in the future? (Students may suggest an ability to use new forms of technology; entrepreneurial skills; and an ability to work with a variety of people as the population expands and becomes more diverse, and as service industries increase in size.)

2. Why would English be used more, when it is a difficult language to learn? (Americans control much of the world's wealth and resources; people who want to do business with Americans will have to learn English.)

3. Will telecommuting help the environment? (Yes: less pollution from cars, less waste paper; people who telecommute from beautiful natural areas will want to help preserve them. No: more people moving to beautiful natural areas might mean destruction or more pollution in these areas.)

Teaching the

Creating a Scenario for 2025

This activity is appropriate for individual students, or for pairs or small groups of students. To help them generate and organize ideas for their scenarios, have them create a web. In the center they should put the name of their character. Radiating from the web should be details about the character's life, such as "interacts with teacher via computer." Once students have a wealth of ideas from which to choose, they can focus on doing research and bringing the best ideas together in a cohesive presentation.

Evaluation Criteria

The project can be evaluated according to the criteria listed below, using a scale for each: 4 = exemplary, 3 = good, 2 = adequate, 1 = poor.

Completing the task The scenario focuses on one day in the life of a 14-year-old in the year 2025. It provides at least ten details about his or her life inside and outside of the home.

Knowing content The scenario reflects an understanding of events and movements in the decades leading up to the present.

Thinking critically The student shows reasonable judgment in making predictions based on data and historical precedent.

Communicating ideas The student presents the scenario in a clear and engaging format.

History Footnote

Science fiction writers make their livings imagining what the future might hold. British writer H. G. Wells is considered by many to be the father of modern science fiction. Trained as a biologist, Wells turned to writing after an accident disabled him at age 21. Wells had hopes for the peaceful applications of scientific discoveries, and some of his novels reflect that hope. Others, however, such as *When the Sleeper Wakes: A Story of Years to Come* (1899), dramatize the potential dangers of technology.

In 1938 the American dramatist Orson Welles broadcast a radio play based on Wells's *The War of the Worlds*. The program was so convincing that it caused a nationwide panic among the many listeners who mistook it for a news report.

Creating a Scenario for 2025

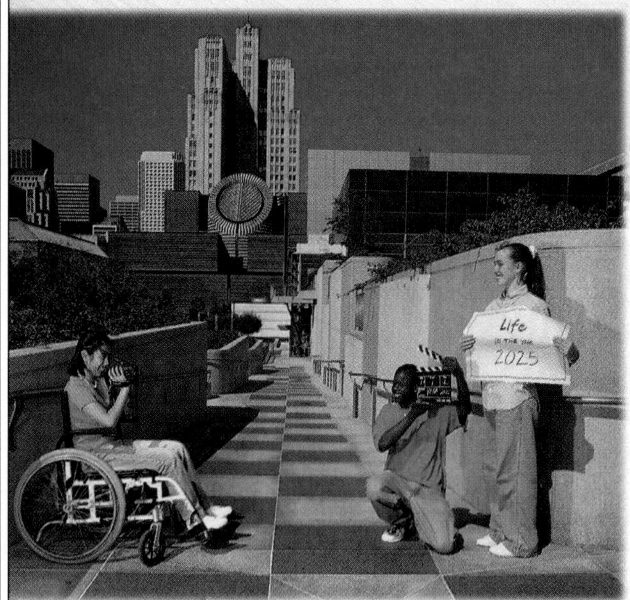

Imagine That You Have Been Hired as a Futurist

Your job is to create a scenario—an imaginary setting—of life in 2025. The scenario should present one day in the life of an average 14-year-old American student. She or he will be your main character. Follow the steps below to meet this challenge.

1. First, create the main character of the scenario in your mind. Imagine what one day in her or his life will be like. Think about the technologies that will be available. How will your character interact with people—parents, brothers and sisters, classmates, and teachers, among others? In your scenario describe the main character's life within the home and outside the home. Be sure to explain what schools will be like for young people in 2025.
2. Like any futurist, research your scenario by reviewing the trends of various topics you plan to include in your story. You can trace the changes in work done by Americans, for example, by reviewing information in this text and in other sources. Consider the current state of each topic, such as work, at this time in our history.
3. Present your scenario as a video or as an illustrated story on posterboards. Use both facts and fantasies in creating the script or captions, and in drawing the illustrations for your presentation.

Remember that an effective scenario is a prediction that is based on trends. On what trends will you base your scenario? Be prepared to explain them.

Reference Center

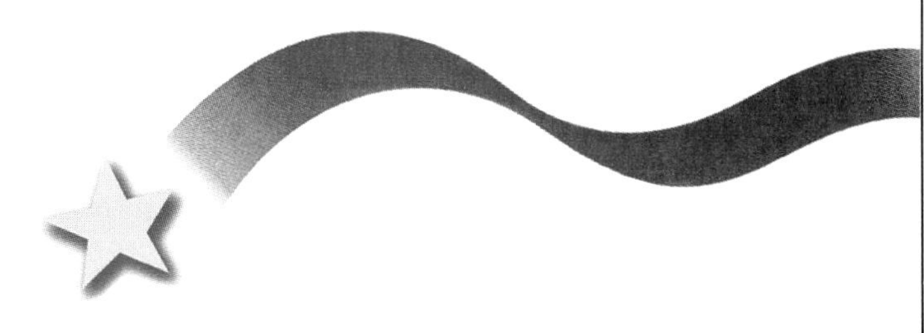

The World: Political

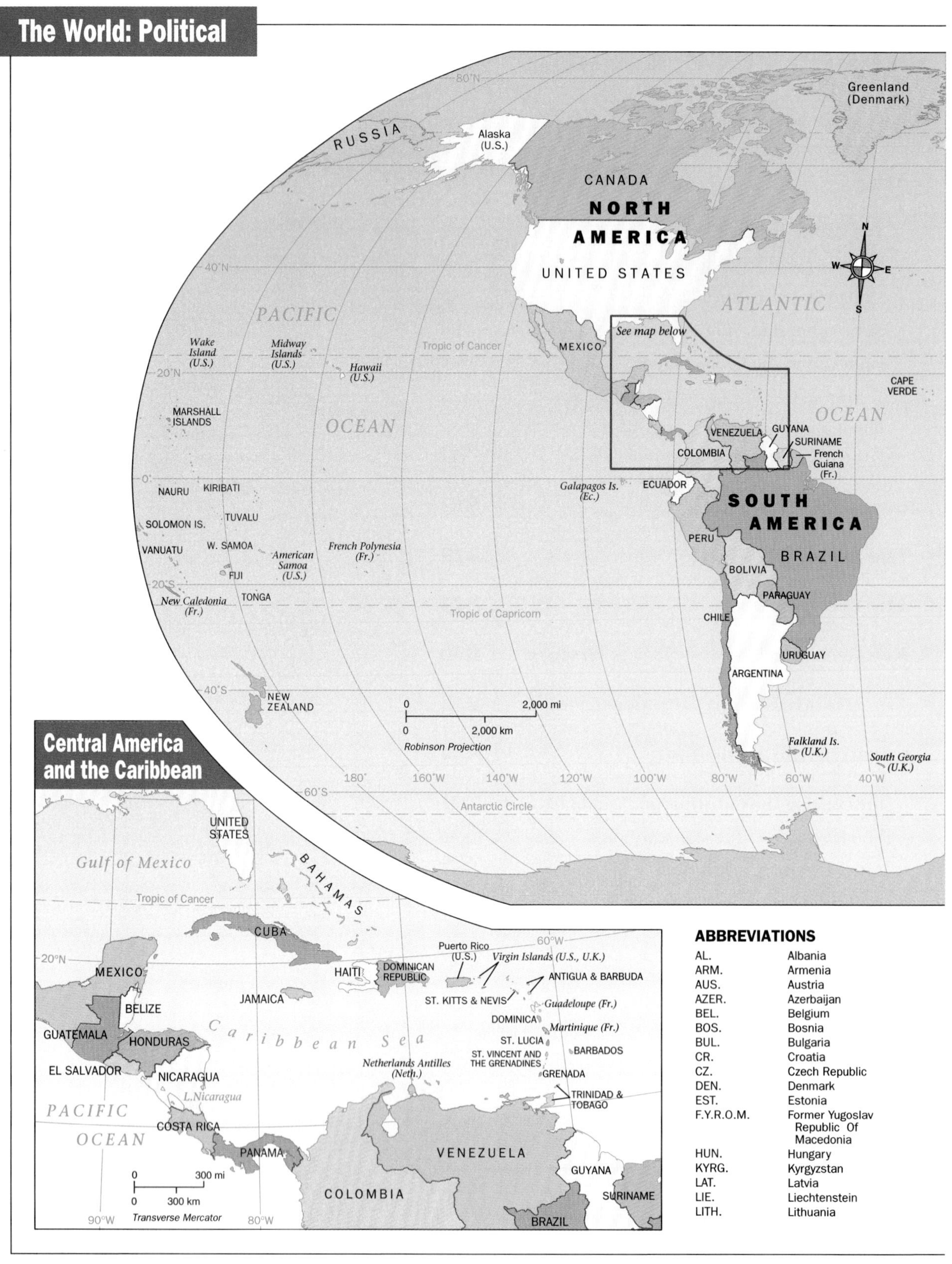

ABBREVIATIONS

AL.	Albania
ARM.	Armenia
AUS.	Austria
AZER.	Azerbaijan
BEL.	Belgium
BOS.	Bosnia
BUL.	Bulgaria
CR.	Croatia
CZ.	Czech Republic
DEN.	Denmark
EST.	Estonia
F.Y.R.O.M.	Former Yugoslav Republic Of Macedonia
HUN.	Hungary
KYRG.	Kyrgyzstan
LAT.	Latvia
LIE.	Liechtenstein
LITH.	Lithuania

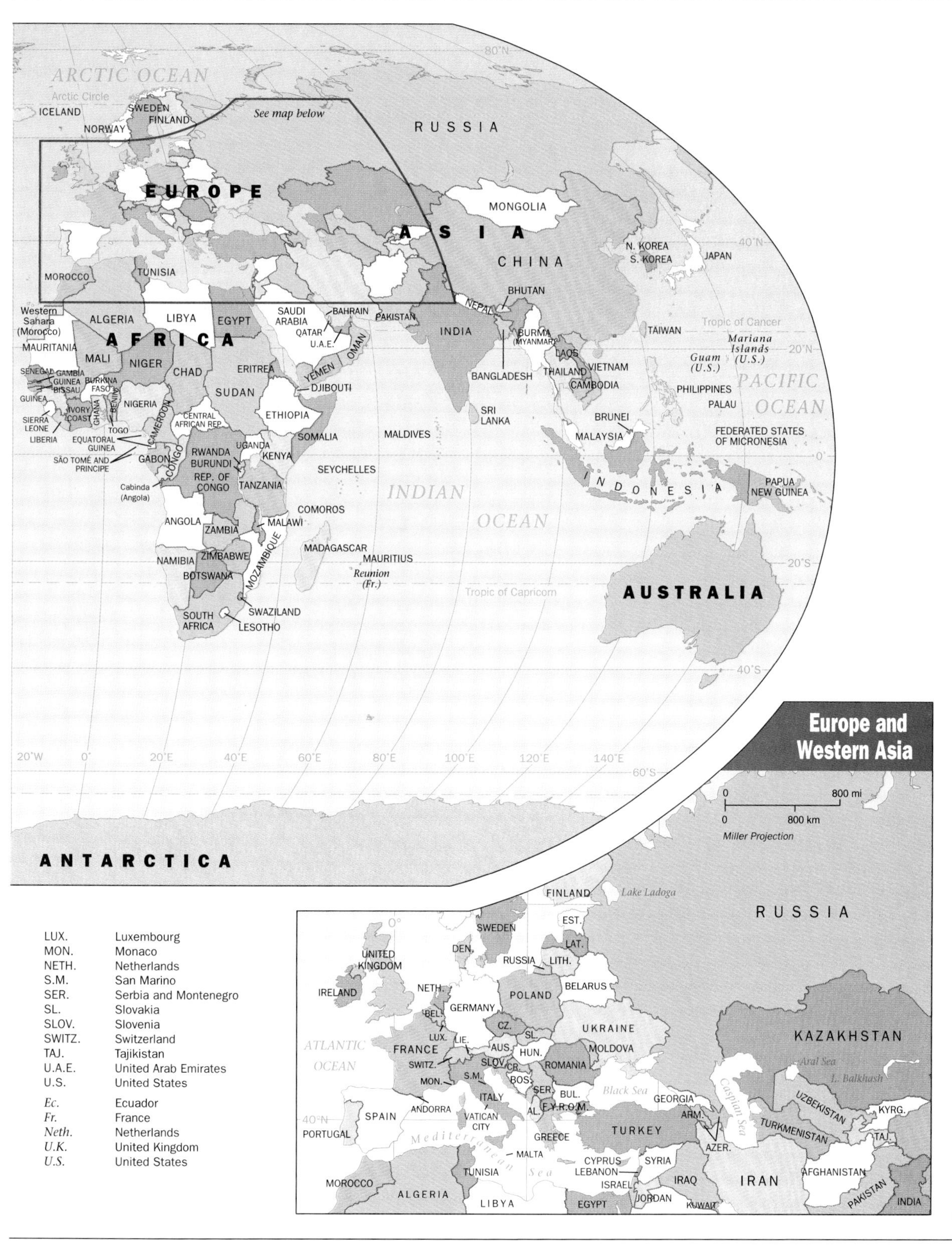
ARCTIC OCEAN
Arctic Circle
ICELAND
SWEDEN
FINLAND
NORWAY
See map below
RUSSIA
EUROPE
ASIA
MONGOLIA
N. KOREA
S. KOREA
JAPAN
CHINA
BHUTAN
NEPAL
MOROCCO
TUNISIA
Western Sahara (Morocco)
ALGERIA
LIBYA
EGYPT
SAUDI ARABIA
BAHRAIN
QATAR
U.A.E.
OMAN
YEMEN
PAKISTAN
INDIA
BURMA (MYANMAR)
BANGLADESH
LAOS
THAILAND
VIETNAM
CAMBODIA
TAIWAN
Tropic of Cancer
Mariana Islands (U.S.)
Guam (U.S.)
PHILIPPINES
PALAU
PACIFIC OCEAN
AFRICA
MAURITANIA
MALI
NIGER
CHAD
ERITREA
SUDAN
DJIBOUTI
SENEGAL
GAMBIA
GUINEA-BISSAU
GUINEA
BURKINA FASO
SIERRA LEONE
LIBERIA
IVORY COAST
GHANA
TOGO
BENIN
NIGERIA
CAMEROON
CENTRAL AFRICAN REP.
ETHIOPIA
SOMALIA
EQUATORIAL GUINEA
SÃO TOMÉ AND PRINCIPE
GABON
CONGO
UGANDA
KENYA
RWANDA
BURUNDI
REP. OF CONGO
TANZANIA
Cabinda (Angola)
SEYCHELLES
MALDIVES
SRI LANKA
BRUNEI
MALAYSIA
FEDERATED STATES OF MICRONESIA
INDONESIA
PAPUA NEW GUINEA
INDIAN OCEAN
COMOROS
ANGOLA
ZAMBIA
MALAWI
MADAGASCAR
MAURITIUS
Reunion (Fr.)
NAMIBIA
ZIMBABWE
BOTSWANA
MOZAMBIQUE
SWAZILAND
SOUTH AFRICA
LESOTHO
Tropic of Capricorn
AUSTRALIA
80°N
40°N
20°N
0°
20°S
40°S
60°S
20°W
0°
20°E
40°E
60°E
80°E
100°E
120°E
140°E
ANTARCTICA
Europe and Western Asia
0 800 mi
0 800 km
Miller Projection
FINLAND
Lake Ladoga
RUSSIA
SWEDEN
EST.
LAT.
DEN.
RUSSIA
LITH.
UNITED KINGDOM
IRELAND
NETH.
GERMANY
POLAND
BELARUS
BEL.
CZ.
SL.
UKRAINE
KAZAKHSTAN
ATLANTIC OCEAN
FRANCE
LUX.
LIE.
AUS.
HUN.
MOLDOVA
SWITZ.
SLOV.
CR.
ROMANIA
Aral Sea
MON.
S.M.
BOS.
SER.
BUL.
Black Sea
L. Balkhash
Caspian Sea
GEORGIA
UZBEKISTAN
KYRG.
ITALY
F.Y.R.O.M.
SPAIN
ANDORRA
40°N
PORTUGAL
VATICAN CITY
AL.
TURKEY
ARM.
TURKMENISTAN
TAJ.
GREECE
AZER.
Mediterranean Sea
MALTA
TUNISIA
CYPRUS
SYRIA
LEBANON
ISRAEL
IRAQ
IRAN
AFGHANISTAN
PAKISTAN
MOROCCO
ALGERIA
LIBYA
EGYPT
JORDAN
KUWAIT
INDIA
LUX. Luxembourg
MON. Monaco
NETH. Netherlands
S.M. San Marino
SER. Serbia and Montenegro
SL. Slovakia
SLOV. Slovenia
SWITZ. Switzerland
TAJ. Tajikistan
U.A.E. United Arab Emirates
U.S. United States
Ec. Ecuador
Fr. France
Neth. Netherlands
U.K. United Kingdom
U.S. United States

United States: Physical

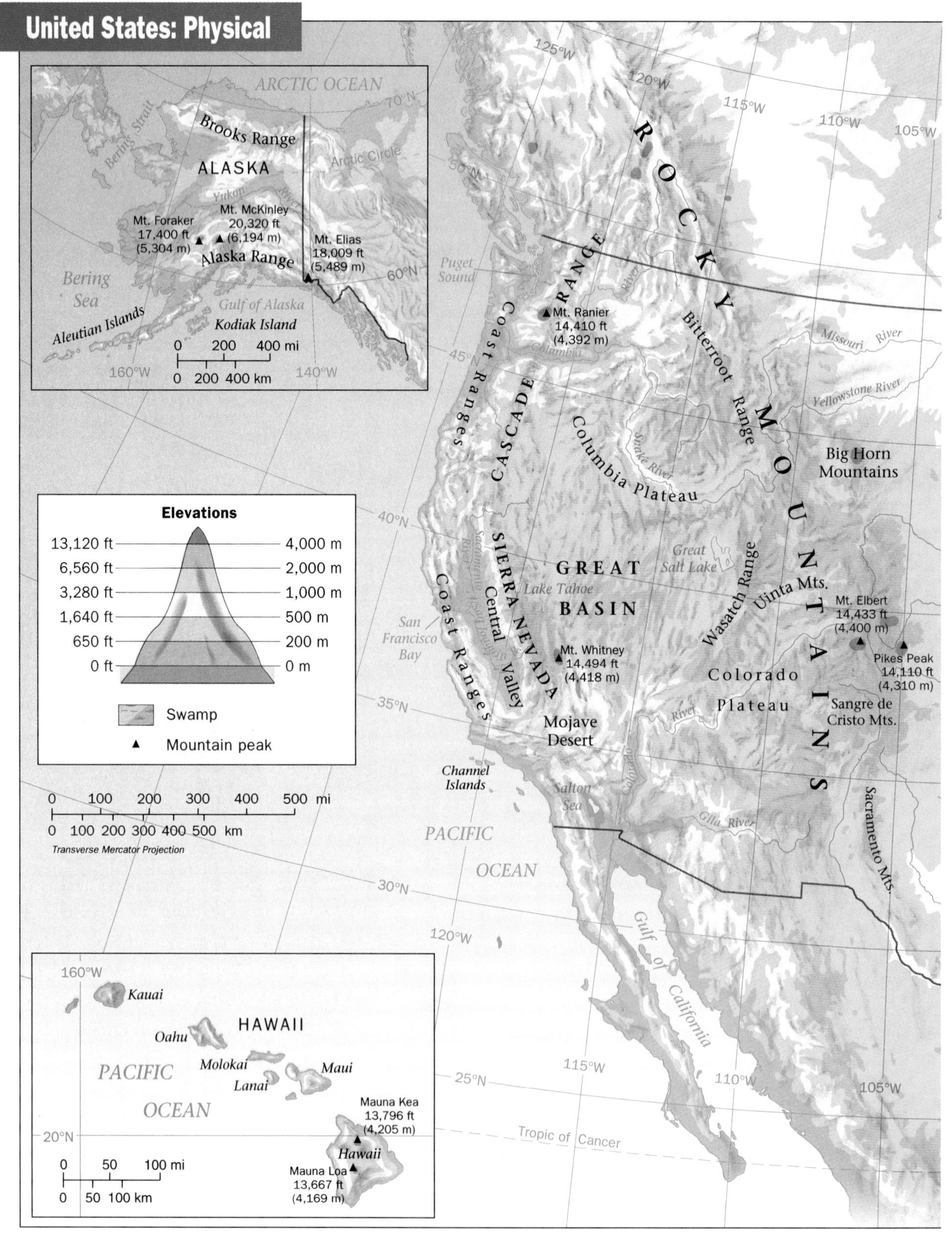

ARCTIC OCEAN
Brooks Range
ALASKA
Bering Strait
Arctic Circle
Yukon River
Mt. McKinley
20,320 ft
(6,194 m)
Mt. Foraker
17,400 ft
(5,304 m)
Alaska Range
Mt. Elias
18,009 ft
(5,489 m)
Bering Sea
Gulf of Alaska
Kodiak Island
Aleutian Islands
0 200 400 mi
0 200 400 km
70°N
60°N
160°W
140°W
Elevations
13,120 ft
6,560 ft
3,280 ft
1,640 ft
650 ft
0 ft
4,000 m
2,000 m
1,000 m
500 m
200 m
0 m
Swamp
Mountain peak
0 100 200 300 400 500 mi
0 100 200 300 400 500 km
Transverse Mercator Projection
125°W
120°W
115°W
110°W
105°W
50°N
45°N
40°N
35°N
30°N
25°N
ROCKY MOUNTAINS
Puget Sound
CASCADE RANGE
Mt. Ranier
14,410 ft
(4,392 m)
Columbia
Coast Ranges
Bitterroot Range
Missouri River
Yellowstone River
Big Horn Mountains
Snake River
Columbia Plateau
Great Salt Lake
GREAT BASIN
Lake Tahoe
Wasatch Range
Uinta Mts.
Mt. Elbert
14,433 ft
(4,400 m)
SIERRA NEVADA
Central Valley
San Francisco Bay
Mt. Whitney
14,494 ft
(4,418 m)
Pikes Peak
14,110 ft
(4,310 m)
Colorado Plateau
Sangre de Cristo Mts.
Mojave Desert
Channel Islands
Salton Sea
Gila River
Sacramento Mts.
PACIFIC OCEAN
Gulf of California
Tropic of Cancer
160°W
Kauai
Oahu
HAWAII
PACIFIC OCEAN
Molokai
Lanai
Maui
Mauna Kea
13,796 ft
(4,205 m)
Hawaii
Mauna Loa
13,667 ft
(4,169 m)
20°N
0 50 100 mi
0 50 100 km

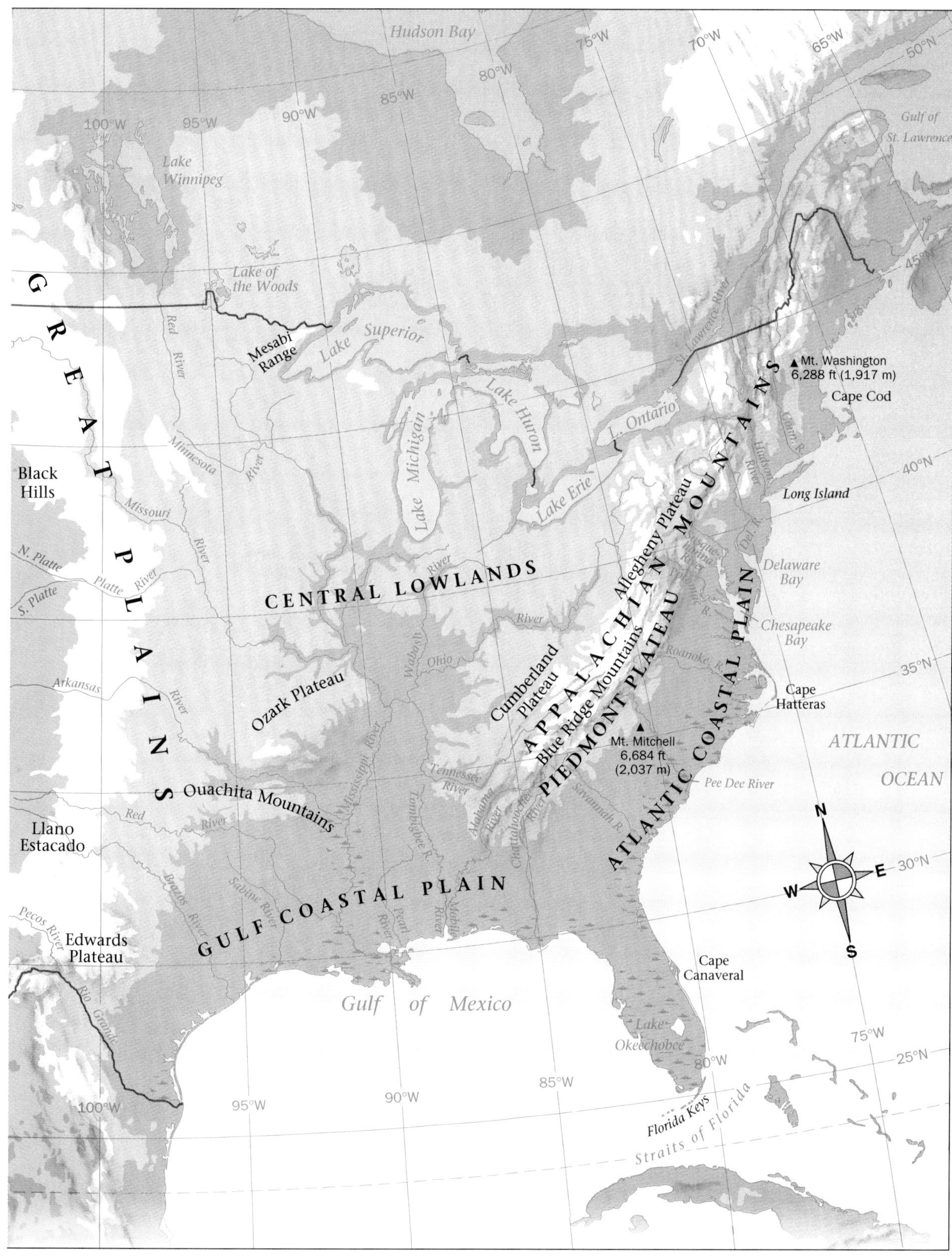
Hudson Bay
Lake Winnipeg
Lake of the Woods
GREAT PLAINS
Mesabi Range
Lake Superior
Lake Michigan
Lake Huron
L. Ontario
Lake Erie
Gulf of St. Lawrence
St. Lawrence River
Mt. Washington
6,288 ft (1,917 m)
Cape Cod
Long Island
Black Hills
CENTRAL LOWLANDS
Allegheny Plateau
APPALACHIAN MOUNTAINS
Delaware Bay
Chesapeake Bay
Cumberland Plateau
Blue Ridge Mountains
PIEDMONT PLATEAU
ATLANTIC COASTAL PLAIN
Ozark Plateau
Cape Hatteras
Mt. Mitchell
6,684 ft
(2,037 m)
ATLANTIC OCEAN
Pee Dee River
Ouachita Mountains
Llano Estacado
GULF COASTAL PLAIN
Edwards Plateau
Gulf of Mexico
Cape Canaveral
Lake Okeechobee
Florida Keys
Straits of Florida
N
S
E
W

United States: Political

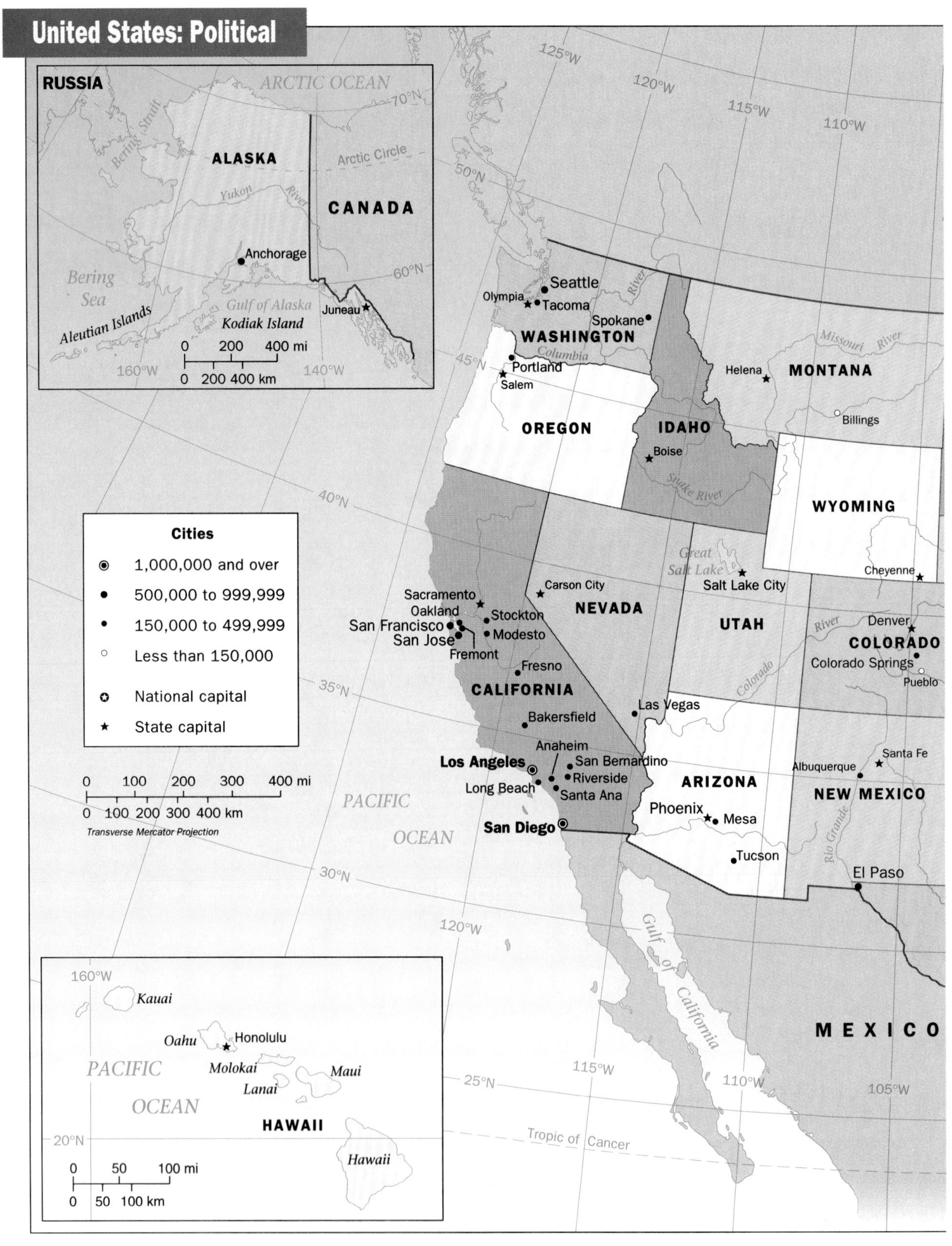
RUSSIA
ARCTIC OCEAN
ALASKA
CANADA
Arctic Circle
Bering Strait
Yukon River
Anchorage
Bering Sea
Aleutian Islands
Gulf of Alaska
Kodiak Island
Juneau
0 200 400 mi
0 200 400 km
160°W
140°W
70°N
60°N
125°W
120°W
115°W
110°W
50°N
45°N
40°N
35°N
30°N
25°N
105°W
Seattle
Olympia
Tacoma
Spokane
WASHINGTON
Columbia
Portland
Salem
OREGON
IDAHO
Boise
Snake River
MONTANA
Helena
Missouri River
Billings
WYOMING
Cheyenne
Great Salt Lake
Salt Lake City
UTAH
NEVADA
Carson City
Las Vegas
Sacramento
Oakland
Stockton
San Francisco
San Jose
Modesto
Fremont
Fresno
CALIFORNIA
Bakersfield
Anaheim
Los Angeles
San Bernardino
Riverside
Long Beach
Santa Ana
San Diego
ARIZONA
Phoenix
Mesa
Tucson
COLORADO
Denver
Colorado Springs
Pueblo
Colorado River
NEW MEXICO
Santa Fe
Albuquerque
Rio Grande
El Paso
PACIFIC OCEAN
Gulf of California
MEXICO
Tropic of Cancer
Cities
1,000,000 and over
500,000 to 999,999
150,000 to 499,999
Less than 150,000
National capital
State capital
0 100 200 300 400 mi
0 100 200 300 400 km
Transverse Mercator Projection
160°W
Kauai
Oahu
Honolulu
Molokai
Lanai
Maui
PACIFIC OCEAN
HAWAII
Hawaii
20°N
0 50 100 mi
0 50 100 km

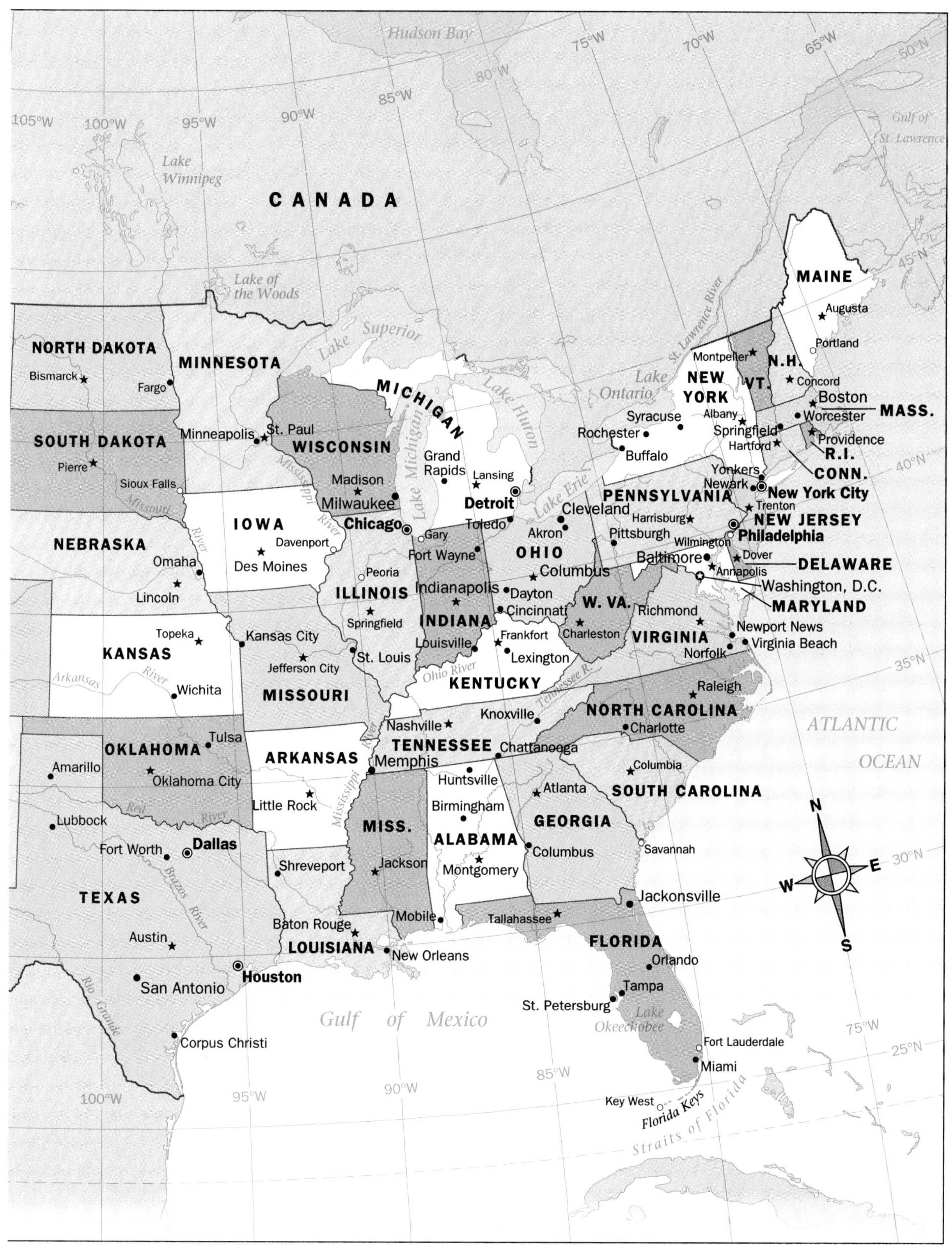

Hudson Bay
CANADA
Lake Winnipeg
Lake of the Woods
Lake Superior
Lake Michigan
Lake Huron
Lake Erie
Lake Ontario
Gulf of St. Lawrence
St. Lawrence River
NORTH DAKOTA
Bismarck
Fargo
MINNESOTA
Minneapolis
St. Paul
SOUTH DAKOTA
Pierre
Sioux Falls
WISCONSIN
Madison
Milwaukee
MICHIGAN
Grand Rapids
Lansing
Detroit
NEW YORK
Syracuse
Albany
Rochester
Buffalo
Yonkers
New York City
Montpelier
VT.
N.H.
Concord
MAINE
Augusta
Portland
Boston
MASS.
Worcester
Springfield
Hartford
Providence
R.I.
CONN.
PENNSYLVANIA
Harrisburg
Pittsburgh
Newark
Trenton
NEW JERSEY
Philadelphia
Wilmington
Dover
DELAWARE
Baltimore
Annapolis
Washington, D.C.
MARYLAND
IOWA
Davenport
Des Moines
NEBRASKA
Omaha
Lincoln
Chicago
Gary
Toledo
Cleveland
Akron
OHIO
Columbus
Dayton
Cincinnati
Fort Wayne
ILLINOIS
Peoria
Springfield
INDIANA
Indianapolis
Louisville
W. VA.
Charleston
Richmond
VIRGINIA
Newport News
Norfolk
Virginia Beach
KANSAS
Topeka
Wichita
Kansas City
Jefferson City
MISSOURI
St. Louis
Frankfort
Lexington
KENTUCKY
Ohio River
Tennessee R.
Mississippi River
Missouri River
Arkansas River
Red River
Brazos River
Rio Grande
Raleigh
NORTH CAROLINA
Charlotte
Knoxville
Nashville
TENNESSEE
Memphis
Chattanooga
OKLAHOMA
Tulsa
Oklahoma City
Amarillo
Lubbock
ARKANSAS
Little Rock
Huntsville
Birmingham
Atlanta
Columbia
SOUTH CAROLINA
GEORGIA
Savannah
MISS.
Jackson
ALABAMA
Montgomery
Columbus
Fort Worth
Dallas
Shreveport
TEXAS
Austin
San Antonio
Houston
Corpus Christi
Baton Rouge
LOUISIANA
New Orleans
Mobile
Tallahassee
Jacksonville
FLORIDA
Orlando
Tampa
St. Petersburg
Lake Okeechobee
Fort Lauderdale
Miami
Key West
Florida Keys
Straits of Florida
Gulf of Mexico
ATLANTIC OCEAN
N
S
E
W
105°W
100°W
95°W
90°W
85°W
80°W
75°W
70°W
65°W
50°N
45°N
40°N
35°N
30°N
25°N

ATLAS

Natural Vegetation of the United States

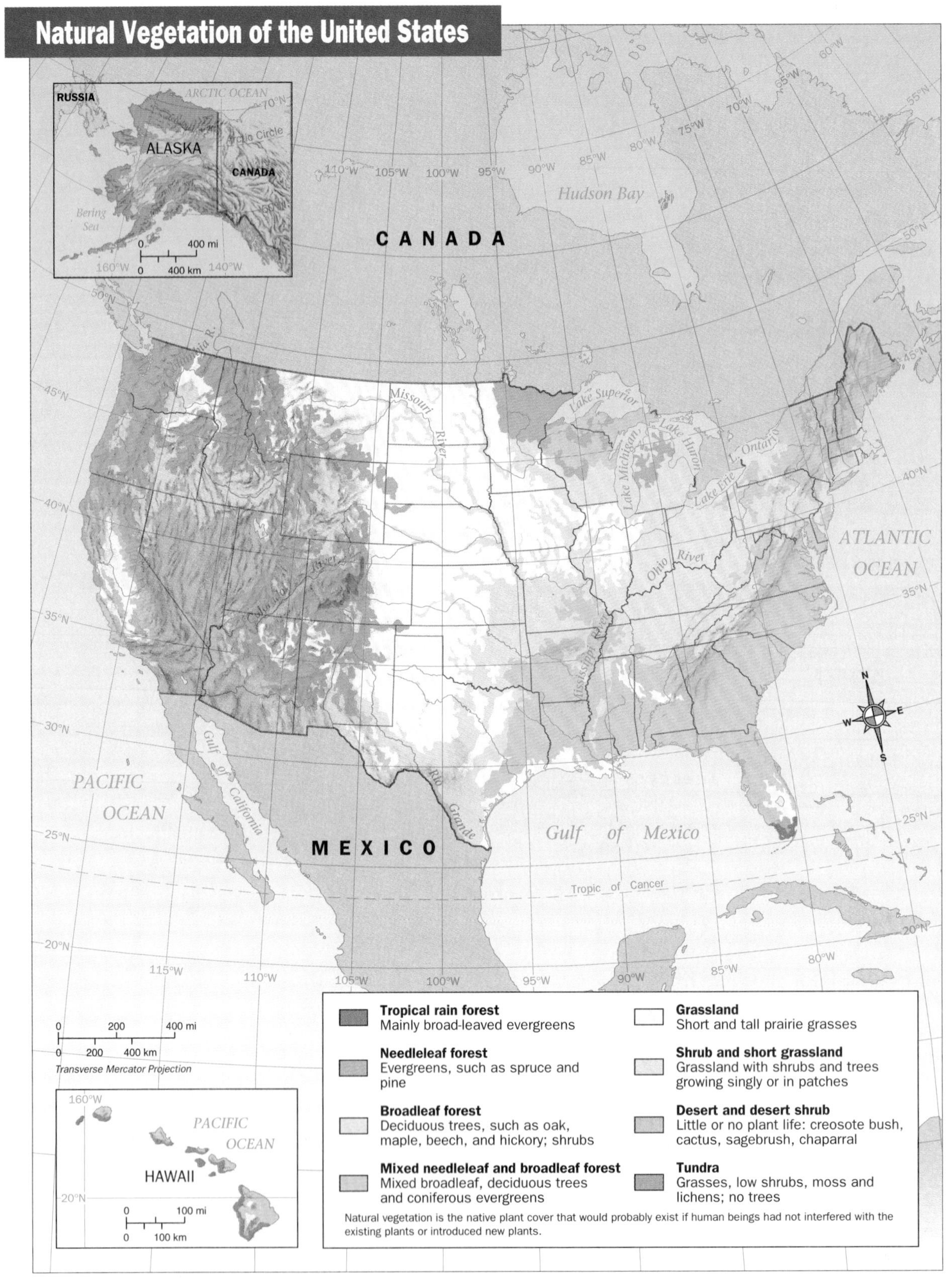
RUSSIA
ARCTIC OCEAN
ALASKA
CANADA
Arctic Circle
Bering Sea
0 400 mi
0 400 km
160°W
140°W
CANADA
MEXICO
Hudson Bay
PACIFIC OCEAN
ATLANTIC OCEAN
Gulf of Mexico
Gulf of California
Tropic of Cancer
Lake Superior
Lake Michigan
Lake Huron
Lake Erie
Lake Ontario
Missouri River
Mississippi River
Ohio River
Rio Grande
Columbia R.
Colorado River
0 200 400 mi
0 200 400 km
Transverse Mercator Projection
PACIFIC OCEAN
HAWAII
0 100 mi
0 100 km
Tropical rain forest
Mainly broad-leaved evergreens
Needleleaf forest
Evergreens, such as spruce and pine
Broadleaf forest
Deciduous trees, such as oak, maple, beech, and hickory; shrubs
Mixed needleleaf and broadleaf forest
Mixed broadleaf, deciduous trees and coniferous evergreens
Grassland
Short and tall prairie grasses
Shrub and short grassland
Grassland with shrubs and trees growing singly or in patches
Desert and desert shrub
Little or no plant life: creosote bush, cactus, sagebrush, chaparral
Tundra
Grasses, low shrubs, moss and lichens; no trees
Natural vegetation is the native plant cover that would probably exist if human beings had not interfered with the existing plants or introduced new plants.

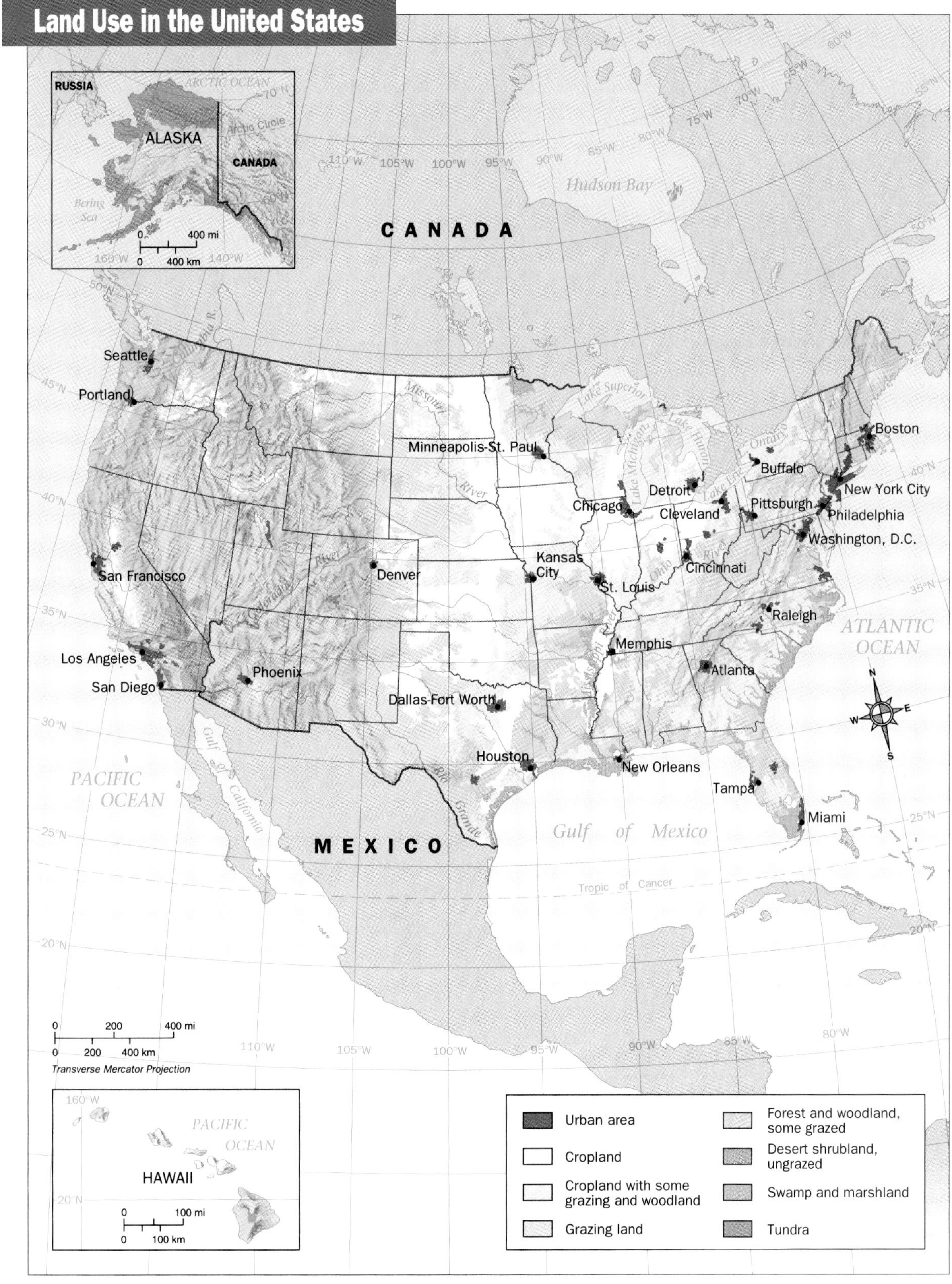
Land Use in the United States
RUSSIA
ARCTIC OCEAN
ALASKA
Arctic Circle
CANADA
Bering Sea
400 mi
400 km
CANADA
Hudson Bay
Seattle
Portland
San Francisco
Los Angeles
San Diego
Phoenix
Denver
Minneapolis-St. Paul
Kansas City
Dallas-Fort Worth
Houston
St. Louis
Memphis
New Orleans
Chicago
Detroit
Cleveland
Cincinnati
Pittsburgh
Buffalo
Boston
New York City
Philadelphia
Washington, D.C.
Raleigh
Atlanta
Tampa
Miami
ATLANTIC OCEAN
PACIFIC OCEAN
Gulf of Mexico
Gulf of California
MEXICO
Tropic of Cancer
Transverse Mercator Projection
HAWAII
PACIFIC OCEAN
Urban area
Cropland
Cropland with some grazing and woodland
Grazing land
Forest and woodland, some grazed
Desert shrubland, ungrazed
Swamp and marshland
Tundra

Territorial Growth of the United States

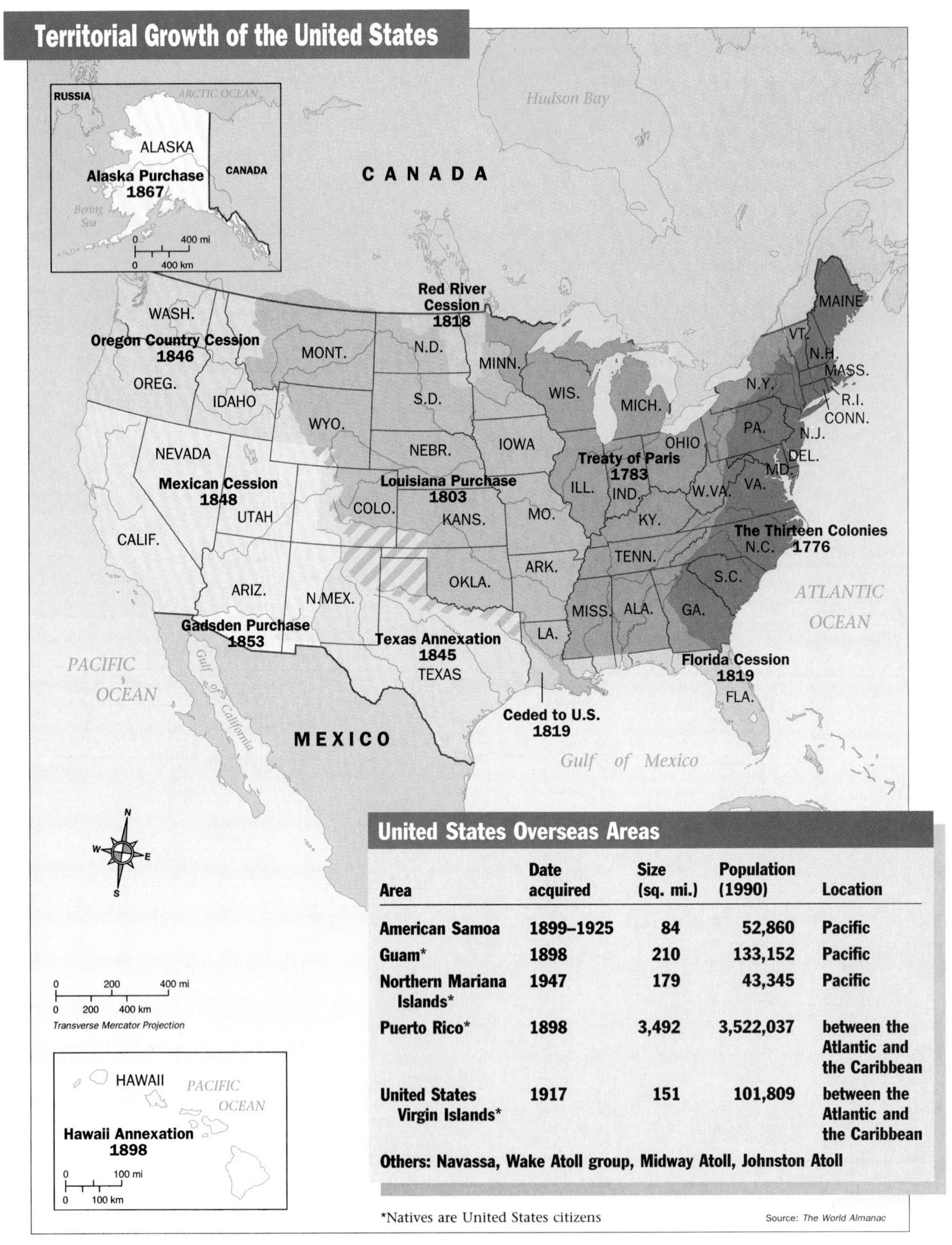

United States Overseas Areas

Area	Date acquired	Size (sq. mi.)	Population (1990)	Location
American Samoa	1899–1925	84	52,860	Pacific
Guam*	1898	210	133,152	Pacific
Northern Mariana Islands*	1947	179	43,345	Pacific
Puerto Rico*	1898	3,492	3,522,037	between the Atlantic and the Caribbean
United States Virgin Islands*	1917	151	101,809	between the Atlantic and the Caribbean
Others: Navassa, Wake Atoll group, Midway Atoll, Johnston Atoll				

*Natives are United States citizens

Source: *The World Almanac*

Population Density in the United States Today

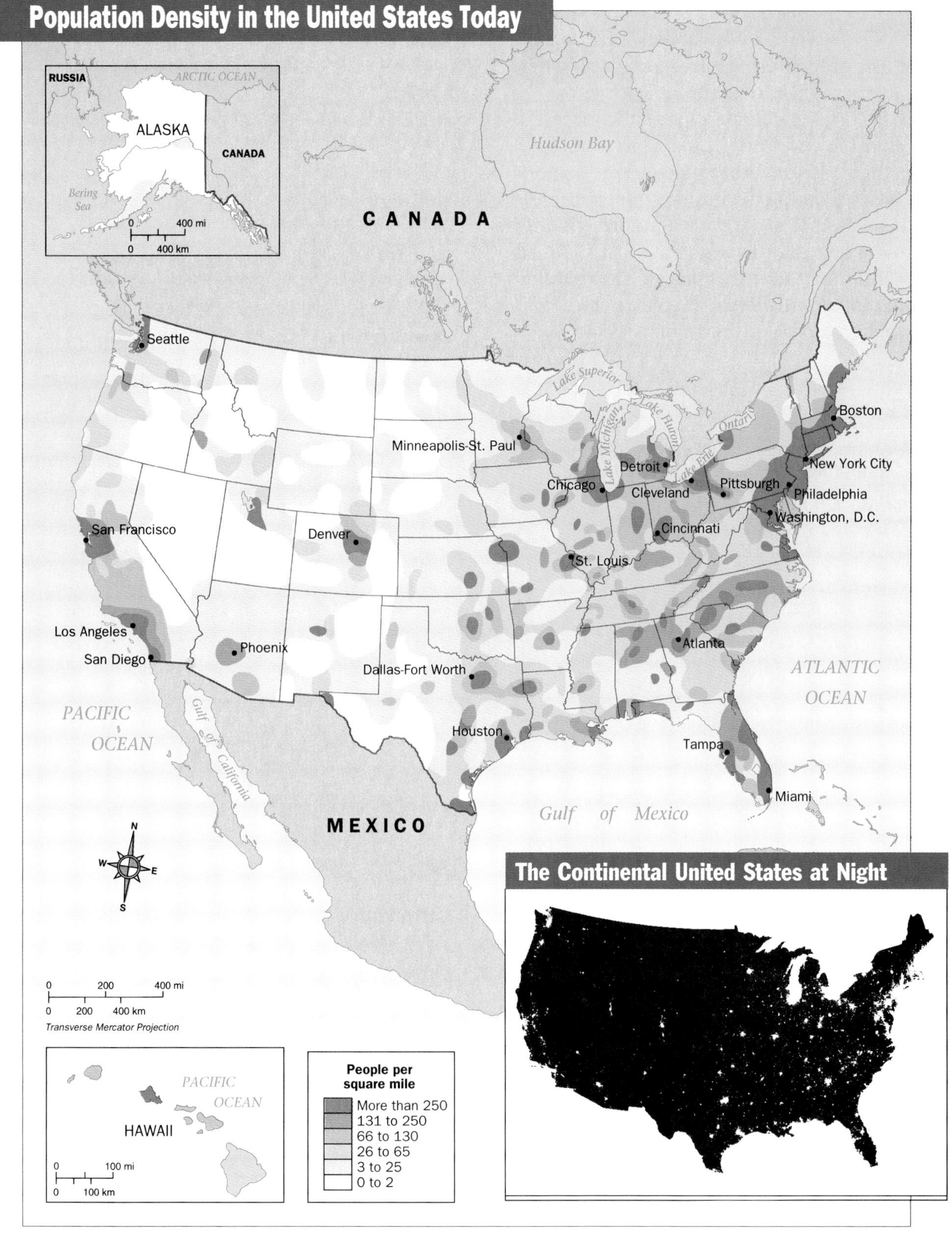

RUSSIA
ARCTIC OCEAN
ALASKA
CANADA
Bering Sea
0 400 mi
0 400 km
CANADA
Hudson Bay
Lake Superior
Lake Michigan
Lake Huron
Lake Ontario
Lake Erie
Seattle
Boston
Minneapolis-St. Paul
New York City
Detroit
Chicago
Cleveland
Pittsburgh
Philadelphia
Washington, D.C.
San Francisco
Denver
Cincinnati
St. Louis
Los Angeles
San Diego
Phoenix
Atlanta
Dallas-Fort Worth
ATLANTIC OCEAN
PACIFIC OCEAN
Gulf of California
Houston
Tampa
Miami
Gulf of Mexico
MEXICO
N
W
E
S
0 200 400 mi
0 200 400 km
Transverse Mercator Projection
PACIFIC OCEAN
HAWAII
0 100 mi
0 100 km
People per square mile
More than 250
131 to 250
66 to 130
26 to 65
3 to 25
0 to 2
The Continental United States at Night

ATLAS

Gazetteer

A gazetteer is a geographical dictionary. It lists geographic features and places where major events have occurred. Each entry includes a brief description of the place.

Entries with specific locations—cities, battlefields, and other sites—have locations given according to latitude and longitude. At the end of the entry is a number that refers to the text page on which the first significant mention of the entry appears. The number that follows the letter *m* refers to the page where the place is shown on a map.

A

Alabama southern state; part of the Confederacy during the Civil War (page 124, *m143*)

Alamo (29°N 98°W) former mission in San Antonio where Texans resisted Mexican troops in 1836 (*m79*)

Alaska state located in the far northwest of North America (page 3, *mR6*)

Antietam Creek (39°N 78°W) site where Confederate invasion of the North was stopped in 1862 (page 153, *m151*)

Appalachian Mountains mountain range in the Appalachian Highlands region of the eastern United States (page 14, *mR5*)

Appomattox Court House (37°N 79°W) Virginia town where Lee's surrender to Grant ended the Civil War in 1865 (page 166, *m163*)

Arizona southwestern state; once part of New Spain and Mexico (*mR6*)

Arkansas southern state; once part of the Confederacy (page 142, *m143*)

Atlanta (34°N 84°W) capital of Georgia; burned in 1864 by Union forces (page 165, *m163*)

Atlantic Coastal Plain coastal lowlands of the eastern United States; the plain grows wider in the South (page 14, *mR5*)

B

Backcountry in colonial times, a region of low, wooded hills extending from Pennsylvania to Georgia (page 55)

Baltimore (39°N 77°W) site of Fort McHenry; located at the upper end of Chesapeake Bay (page 69, *m69*)

Belleau Wood (49°N 3°E) site of an Allied victory that marked a turning point in World War I (page 418, *m418*)

Beringia land bridge that linked Asia and North America during the last Ice Age (page 24)

Berlin (53°N 13°E) city in Germany; split into East and West Berlin after World War II and reunited in 1989 (page 566, *m567*)

Birmingham (34°N 87°E) industrial city in north-central Alabama, where Martin Luther King, Jr., led civil rights demonstrations in 1963 (page 855, *mR7*)

Black Hills mountains in western South Dakota considered sacred by the local Sioux Indians and invaded by gold prospectors in 1874, leading to fighting between Indians and whites (page 232, *m232*)

Bosnia eastern European nation; broke away from Yugoslavia in 1991; scene of civil war and ethnic violence (page 406, *m408*)

Boston (42°N 71°W) capital of Massachusetts; center of colonial resistance to British rule (page 52, *m54*)

Brazil South American nation colonized by Portugal in the 1500s; it gained independence in 1822 (page 489, *mR2*)

Bull Run (39°N 77°W) site of two Civil War battles in northern Virginia; (page 148, *m151*)

C

California Far West state gained by the United States from Mexico in 1848 (page 111, *m116*)

Camp David the presidential retreat in Maryland about 70 miles from Washington, D.C.; site of the Middle East peace talks arranged by President Carter in 1978 between Sadat of Egypt and Benin of Israel (page 644)

Canada nation bordering the United States to the north; originally settled by both the French and English (page 3, *mR2*)

Canadian Shield lowland region that lies in north central United States and eastern Canada (page 267)

Canal Zone (9°N 80°W) Panama Canal and the land five miles on each side, governed by the United States from 1903 to 1978, and now governed by Panama (page 644, *m390*)

Chancellorsville (38°N 77°W) town in Virginia; site of Confederate victory in 1863 (page 161, *m163*)

Charleston (33°N 80°W) port city in South Carolina; site of Fort Sumter where the Civil War began (page 125, *m151*)

Chesapeake Bay large bay surrounded by the states of Virginia, Maryland, and Delaware (page 55, *m54*)

Chicago (42°N 87°W) third largest city in the United States; major railroad and shipping center in the 1800s (page 303, *mR7*)

China once a large empire in east Asia, now the most populous nation in the world (page 29, *mR3*)

Cincinnati (39°N 85°W) major city in Ohio; developed as a port on the Ohio River in the early 1800s (pages 552–553, *mR7*)

Cleveland (42°N 82°W) major city in Ohio on Lake Erie where John D. Rockefeller built a refinery in 1863 and began what would become the Standard Oil Company of Ohio (page 271, *mR7*)

Colombia South American nation (page 387, *m390*)

Colorado western state located in both the Rocky Mountain and Great Plains regions (page 230, *mR6*)

Columbia River explored by Lewis and Clark in 1805, this river separates Oregon and Washington (*m68*)

Concord (43°N 71°W) village near Boston and early battle site in the American Revolution (page 52, *m54*)

Connecticut New England state; first settled by the English in 1636 (page 40, *mR7*)

Cuba (22°N 80°W) country on the largest island in the West Indies; involved in fighting during Spanish-American War (1898) and U.S.–Soviet missile crisis (1862) (page 383, *m381*)

Czechoslovakia Eastern European nation created after World War I; split into two separate republics in 1992 (page 523, *m526*)

D

Dayton (36°N 85°W) city in east-central Tennessee; site of the 1925 Scopes trial over the teaching of evolution (page 136, *m122*)

Delaware Atlantic Coastal Plain state; first state to approve the United States Constitution (page 41, *mR7*)

Denver (50°N 105°W) Colorado city at the eastern edge of the Rocky Mountains that grew as a result of mining activity in the Rockies starting in the 1860s (page 227, *mR7*)

Detroit (42°N 83°W) founded as a French fort; now the largest city in Michigan (page 305, *mR7*)

District of Columbia, *see* **Washington, D.C.**

Dust Bowl large area of the western plains where droughts in the 1930s resulted in soil erosion and dust storms that carried away much of the topsoil (page 501, *m502*)

E

Egypt Middle Eastern nation (page 583, *m650*)

Ellis Island (41°N 74°W) small island in New York harbor; from 1891 to 1954 immigrants were examined there before entering the United States (page 299)

England southern part of the island of Great Britain (page 2)

Erie Canal waterway built in 1825 to link New York City and the Great Lakes (page 71)

F

Florida southern state; part of the Confederacy during the Civil War (page 124, *m143*)

Fort Laramie (42°N 104°W) fort located along the Oregon Trail in present-day Wyoming (page 225)

Fort McHenry (39°N 76°W) fort in Baltimore harbor; inspired Francis Scott Key's poem that later became "The Star-Spangled Banner" (page 69)

Fort Sumter (33°N 80°W) fort guarding the harbor of Charleston, South Carolina, where the first engagement of the Civil War occurred when Confederates bombarded the Union-held position in 1861 (page 125, *m151*)

GAZETTEER

Fort Ticonderoga (44°N 73°W) British fort on Lake Champlain raided by American troops in 1775 (*m54*)

France nation in western Europe that first colonized Canada (page 49, *mR3*)

Fredericksburg (38°N 77°W) Virginia town; site of Lee's victory over Union troops in 1862 (page 161, *m163*)

G

Georgia southern state; part of the Confederacy during the Civil War (page 124, *m143*)

Germany European nation; divided from the end of World War II until 1989 into East and West Germany (page 407, *m408*)

Gettysburg (40°N 77°W) Pennsylvania battle site where Lee was defeated and Lincoln made his Gettysburg Address in 1863 (page 161, *m163*)

Great Britain island nation established in 1707 and consisting of England, Wales, and Scotland (page 48)

Great Lakes Lakes Ontario, Erie, Huron, Michigan, and Superior; five large freshwater lakes on the border between the United States and Canada (page 4, *m5*)

Great Plains region of grasslands east of the Rocky Mountains and west of the Mississippi River (page 346, *mR5*)

Grenada Caribbean island nation; invaded by the United States in 1983 to end threat of Communist influence (page 646, *mR2*)

Greensboro (36°N 80°W) North Carolina city in which African American college students in 1960 staged the first sit-in to protest segregation in public facilities (page 612)

Guadalcanal (10°S 160°E) one of the Solomon Islands in the western Pacific Ocean; Japanese defeated there during World War II by U.S. forces (1942 and 1943) (*m533*)

Guam (14°N 143°E) island in the Pacific Ocean acquired by the United States from Spain as a result of the Spanish-American War in 1898 (381, *m381*)

Gulf of Mexico body of water that lies to the south of the United States (page 14, *mR5*)

H

Haiti at one time a French Caribbean colony; gained its independence after an 1801 revolt (page 644, *mR2*)

Harlem (41°N 74°W) New York City neighborhood that became the center of African American culture in the 1920s (page 458)

Harpers Ferry (39°N 78°W) West Virginia town where John Brown raided a federal arsenal in 1859 (page 122)

Hartford (42°N 73°W) Connecticut capital where New England Federalists met and demanded an end to the War of 1812 (*m69*)

Hawaii Pacific Ocean state made up of eight major islands; originally a kingdom established by 1795 (page 373, *mR6*)

Hiroshima (34°N 132°E) city in southern Japan; target of a United States atomic bomb in 1945 (page 536, *m539*)

Hollywood (34°N 118°W) a district of Los Angeles, California, that became the center of the American motion picture industry (page 471)

Homestead (40°N 80°W) industrial town near Pittsburgh, Pennsylvania; site of a violent strike against the Carnegie Steel Company in 1892 (page 278)

Horseshoe Bend (33°N 86°W) Alabama site where Creeks battled Andrew Jackson's troops in 1814 (page 69, *m69*)

Hudson River largest river in New York state; explored by Henry Hudson for the Dutch in 1609 (page 54, *m542*)

I

Idaho northwestern state; acquired by the United States as part of Oregon Country (*mR6*)

Illinois state in the Central Lowlands region; one of the states formed in the Northwest Territory; location of Lincoln–Douglas debates in 1858 (page 120, *mR7*)

Indiana Central Lowlands state; originally a part of the Northwest Territory (*mR7*)

Iowa Central Lowlands state; originally part of the Louisiana Purchase (*mR7*)

Iran Middle Eastern nation (page 569, *m650*)

Iraq Middle Eastern nation; Iraqi invasion of neighboring Kuwait drew United Nations involvement in 1991 (page 649, *m650*)

Israel Middle Eastern nation; formed in 1948 as a Jewish homeland (page 565, *mR3*)

Italy southern European nation; fought with the Allies in World War I and with the Axis in World War II (page 407, *m408*)

J

Jamestown (37°N 77°W) Virginia site where first English settlement in North America was founded in 1607 (page 38)

Japan densely populated industrial nation in East Asia; one of the Axis powers in World War II (page 372, *m381*)

K

Kansas Great Plains state; earlier a territory where proslavery and antislavery forces battled in the 1850s (page 116, *m116*)

Kentucky state in the Central Lowlands and Appalachians; birthplace of Abraham Lincoln (page 108, *m151*)

Korea East Asian nation; divided since World War II into North and South Korea; war there in the 1950s drew United States involvement (page 387, *m381*)

L

Lawrence (39°N 95°W) antislavery town in Kansas; set on fire by proslavery residents from Missouri in 1856 (page 117)

Lebanon Middle Eastern nation at the eastern end of the Mediterranean Sea; civil war there in the 1970s and 80s drew United Nations involvement (page 647, *mR3*)

Lexington (42°N 71°W) village near Boston where the War of Independence began in 1775 (page 52)

Leyte Gulf (11°N 125°E) gulf near the east central Philippine island of Leyte; site of World War II Battle for Leyte Gulf (Oct. 23–25, 1944) during which Japanese sea power was shattered (*m539*)

Liberia West African nation founded by former American slaves in 1821 and eventually established as a republic (*mR3*)

Little Bighorn River river in Wyoming and Montana; site of a famous battle between Sioux and Cheyenne Indians and the United States Cavalry (page 215, *m232*)

Little Rock (35°N 92°W) Arkansas city to which President Eisenhower sent federal troops in 1957 to help integrate public schools (page 611, *mR7*)

Louisiana southern state;part of the Confederacy during the Civil War (page 124, *m143*)

Louisiana Purchase land bought by the United States from France in 1803 that stretched from the Mississippi River to the Rocky Mountains (page 68, *m68*)

Lowell (41°N 83°W) Massachusetts city; early site of the Industrial Revolution in the United States (page 62)

M

Maine New England state; originally part of Massachusetts (page 40, *mR7*)

Maryland Atlantic coastal state; first of the English colonies to tolerate Catholic settlers (page 41, *mR7*)

Massachusetts New England state; site of first battles between the Patriots and the British in the War of Independence (page 50, *mR7*)

Menlo Park (40°N 74°W) community in the central part of New Jersey; site of Thomas Edison's laboratory (page 310)

Mexican Cession territory gained by the United States following the War with Mexico in 1848 (page 79, *m79*)

Mexico originally a center of Indian civilizations; now a nation that borders the United States to the south (page 3, *mR2*)

Michigan Central Lowlands state; originally part of the Northwest Territory (*mR7*)

Midway Islands (28°N 179°W) an area made up of two islands in a group of small islands in the Pacific Ocean; annexed by the United States in 1867; site of a World War II battle (June 1942) (page 372, *m533, m539*)

GAZETTEER

Minnesota state located in the Central Lowlands and Canadian Shield regions (page 110, *m143*)

Mississippi southern state; part of the Confederacy during the Civil War (page 124, *m143*)

Mississippi River longest river in the United States (page 55, *mR5*)

Missouri Central Lowlands state; admitted as a slave state in 1820 (page 72, *m72*)

Missouri River tributary of the Mississippi River and second longest river in the United States (page 37, *mR4-R5*)

Monmouth (40°N 74°W) New Jersey town where Patriots battled retreating British troops (*m54*)

Montgomery (32°N 86°W) Alabama city in which African Americans, led by Martin Luther King, Jr., organized a successful bus boycott in 1955 to protest segregation (page 612 *mR7*)

Montana western state; originally part of Oregon Country and the Louisiana Purchase (*mR6*)

N

Nagasaki (33°N 130°E) city in southern Japan; target of United States atomic bomb in 1945 (page 537, *m539*)

National Road first road built across the Appalachian Mountains (page 90)

Nebraska Great Plains state; part of the Louisiana Purchase (page 116, *mR7*)

Nevada western state; gained by the United States from Mexico in 1848 (*mR6*)

New England region in northeastern United States, includes the states of Maine, New Hampshire, Vermont, Massachusetts, Rhode Island, and Connecticut; named by English colonists for their homeland (page 70)

New Hampshire New England state; one of the original 13 states (page 41)

New Jersey Atlantic coastal state; first settled by the Dutch and Swedes; one of the original 13 English colonies and one of the original 13 states (page 41, *mR7*)

New Mexico southwestern state; settled by the Spanish in 1598 (page 78, *mR6*)

New Netherland Dutch colony along the Hudson River in the 1600s (page 41)

New Orleans (30°N 90°W) city founded by the French near the mouth of the Mississippi River; important port (page 69, *m69*)

New York Atlantic coastal state; settled by the Dutch in the 1600s; one of the 13 English colonies and one of the 13 original states (page 41, *mR7*)

New York City (41°N 74°W) largest city in the United States; founded by the Dutch as New Amsterdam (page 41, *mR7*)

Nicaragua nation in Central America; civil war there in the 1980s drew United States involvement (page 646, *mR2*)

Normandy Peninsula (49°N 1°E) peninsula in northwest France, part of Normandy province; site of European invasion by Allies in World War II (June 6, 1944) (page 534, *m535*)

North Carolina Atlantic coastal state; one of the 13 English colonies and one of the original 13 states (page 41, *mR7*)

North Dakota northern Great Plains state; location where Lewis and Clark spent their first winter (*mR7*)

O

Ohio Central Lowlands state; once part of the Northwest Territory (*mR7*)

Ohio River river that flows from Pittsburgh to the Mississippi River (page 47, *mR5*)

Ohio Valley region drained by the Ohio River (page 46)

Oklahoma southern Plains state; originally called the Indian Territory (page 77, *mR7*)

Omaha (41°N 96°W) city in Nebraska on the Missouri River; the eastern starting point of the first transcontinental railroad, begun in 1863 (page 227, *mR7*)

Oregon Pacific northwest state; first settled in the 1840s (page 78, *mR7*)

Oregon Country area in northwest United States; at one time also claimed by Spain, Britain, and Russia (page 78, *m68*)

Oregon Trail 2,000-mile route from Independence, Missouri, to Oregon Country (page 78)

Ottoman Empire, *see* **Turkey**

P

Panama nation in Central America; crossed by Balboa in 1513 (page 387, *m390*)

Panama Canal (9°N 80°W) a canal across the Isthmus of Panama connecting the Atlantic and Pacific oceans, completed in 1914 (page 387, *m390*)

Pearl Harbor (21°N 158°W) Japanese bombing of this United States naval base brought the United States into World War II (page 527, *m533*)

Pennsylvania eastern state; one of the original 13 colonies; founded in 1682 by William Penn (page 41, *mR7*)

Petersburg (37°N 77°W) city in Virginia; besieged by Grant's troops for nine months until Lee's troops fled in 1865 (page 165, *m163*)

Philadelphia (40°N 75°W) Pennsylvania city; capital of the United States from 1790 to 1800 (page 54, *m54*)

Philippines East Asian island nation; acquired by the United States in 1898; gained independence in 1946 (page 379, *m381*)

Piedmont Plateau hill country in the southeast United States; it lies upland from the Atlantic Coastal Plain (page 14, *mR5*)

Pittsburgh (40°N 80°W) city in western Pennsylvania where the Ohio River begins (page 268, *mR7*)

Plymouth (42°N 71°W) site of first English settlement in Massachusetts in 1620 (page 40, *m40*)

Poland east European nation (page 524, *m526*)

Portugal west European nation; first to begin large-scale overseas exploration in the 1400s (page 31, *mR3*)

Potomac River river dividing Maryland and Virginia on which Washington, D.C., is located (page 64)

Promontory Point (41°N 112°W) site in Utah at which the transcontinental railroad was completed (page 228, *m228*)

Prophetstown (41°N 90°W) center of Tecumseh's Indian alliance in 1811; located in present-day Indiana (*m69*)

Pullman (42°N 88°W) company town near Chicago (later a part of Chicago) built for workers at the Pullman Palace Car Company; site of a violent railroad strike in 1894 (page 279)

Puerto Rico (18°N 66°W) a self-governing commonwealth of the United States: a former Spanish colony annexed after the Spanish–American War (page 381, *m381*)

R

Rhode Island New England state; founded as a colony welcoming people of all religions (page 40, *mR7*)

Richmond (38°N 77°W) city in Virginia; capital of the Confederacy during most of the Civil War (page 142, *m151*)

Rio Grande river that forms part of the boundary between Mexico and the United States (page 3, *m5*)

Rocky Mountains high mountain range in western North America; reached by Lewis and Clark in 1805 (page 5, *mR4*)

S

St. Augustine (30°N 81°W) city in Florida founded by the Spanish in 1565; oldest continuous European settlement in the United States (page 37)

St. Lawrence River river that connects the Great Lakes and the Atlantic Ocean (*mR5*)

St. Louis (39°N 90°W) Missouri city from which Lewis and Clark set off to explore the West (*mR7*)

San Antonio (29°N 98°W) southern Texas city; site of the Alamo (*mR7*)

Sand Creek (38°N 103°W) site in Colorado of the Sand Creek Massacre of 1864 (page 230, *m232*)

San Francisco (38°N 122°W) northern outpost of New Spain; site of major earthquake in 1906; now a major city in California (page 306, *mR6*)

Santa Fe (36°N 106°W) present-day capital of New Mexico; established by the Spanish in 1609 (*mR6*)

Selma (32°N 87°W) city 40 miles west of Montgomery, Alabama; the site of civil rights confrontations in 1965 (page 614)

Serbia Balkan country in southeastern Europe (page 407, *m408*)

Shiloh (35°N 88°W) site of Union victory in Tennessee in 1862 (page 150, *m151*)

Somalia (5°N 47°E) eastern African nation; United States sent troops there in 1992-1994 to protect relief works who were distributing foot to starving people (page 649, *m650*)

South Carolina southern state;part of the Confederacy during the Civil War (page 41, *mR7*)

South Dakota northern Great Plains state; part of the Louisiana Purchase (*mR7*)

Stalingrad (49°N 44°E) city in former Soviet Union, on the Volga River; location of World War II battle that was the turning point of war in eastern Europe (page 534, *m535*)

T

Teapot Dome (43°N 106°W) oil reserve near Casper, Wyoming, involved in a political scandal during the 1920s (page 465)

Tennessee southern state; part of the Confederacy during the Civil War (page 150, *m151*)

Tennessee Valley the region extending over Tennessee and parts of six other states that is drained by the Tennessee River; site of the New Deal's Tennessee Valley Authority (page 493)

Texas southern state; part of Mexico until 1836; part of the Confederacy during the Civil War (page 124, *m143*)

Trenton (40°N 75°W) capital of New Jersey; site where Washington's army attacked Hessian troops in 1776 (page 54, *m54*)

Turkey Middle Eastern nation; formerly known as the Ottoman Empire (page 407, *m408*)

U

United Kingdom established in 1801 when Ireland was united with Great Britain (*mR3*)

Utah western state; first settled by Mormons (page 389, *mR6*)

V

Valley Forge (40°N 75°W) winter camp for Washington's troops in Pennsylvania from 1777 to 1778 (page 53, *m54*)

Vermont New England state located in the Appalachian Highlands (page 263, *mR7*)

Vicksburg (32°N 91°W) city in Mississippi; site of Union victory in 1863 that secured control of the Mississippi River for the North (page 164, *m163*)

Vietnam nation in Southeast Asia; conflict there drew United States involvement in the 1950s, 1960s, and 1970s (page 572, *m573*)

Virginia southern state; site of first permanent English colony in North America (page 39, *mR7*)

W

Washington state in northwestern United States; once part of Oregon Country (*mR6*)

Washington, D.C. (39°N 77°W) United States capital covering the entire District of Columbia; established on banks of the Potomac River in 1800 (page 64, *mR7*)

Watts (34°N 118°W) mostly African American suburb of Los Angeles,California; site of racial riots in 1965 (page 615)

West Virginia Appalachian Highland state; formed by pro-Union residents of Virginia during the Civil War (page 142, *m143*)

Wisconsin Central Lowlands state; originally part of the Northwest Territory (page 143, *m143*)

Wounded Knee Creek site of a clash between federal soldiers and a band of Sioux men, women, and children who had left their reservation in 1890; many Sioux were killed or wounded; now located on a Sioux reservation in southern South Dakota (page 234, *m232*)

Wyoming western state; located in the Rocky Mountain and Great Plains regions;the first territory to adopt women's suffrage (page 225, *mR6*)

Y

Yorktown (37°N 76°W) small Virginia port; site of British surrender to the colonists in 1781 that ended the War of Independence (page 55)

The States

Note: Population figures are 1995 estimates.

Alabama
Admitted: 1819
Capital: Montgomery
Population: 4,274,000
Area: 50,750 sq mi (131,443 sq km)
"Yellowhammer State"

Alaska
Admitted: 1959
Capital: Juneau
Population: 634,000
Area: 570,374 sq mi (1,477,269 sq km)
"The Last Frontier"

Arizona
Admitted: 1912
Capital: Phoenix
Population: 4,072,000
Area: 113,642 sq mi (294,333 sq km)
"Grand Canyon State"

Arkansas
Admitted: 1836
Capital: Little Rock
Population: 2,468,000
Area: 52,075 sq mi (134,874 sq km)
"Land of Opportunity"

California
Admitted: 1850
Capital: Sacramento
Population: 32,398,000
Area: 155,973 sq mi (403,970 sq km)
"Golden State"

Colorado
Admitted: 1876
Capital: Denver
Population: 3,710,000
Area: 103,729 sq mi (268,658 sq km)
"Centennial State"

Connecticut
Admitted: 1788
Capital: Hartford
Population: 3,274,000
Area: 4,845 sq mi (12,549 sq km)
"Constitution State"

Delaware
Admitted: 1787
Capital: Dover
Population: 718,000
Area: 1,955 sq mi (5,063 sq km)
"First State"

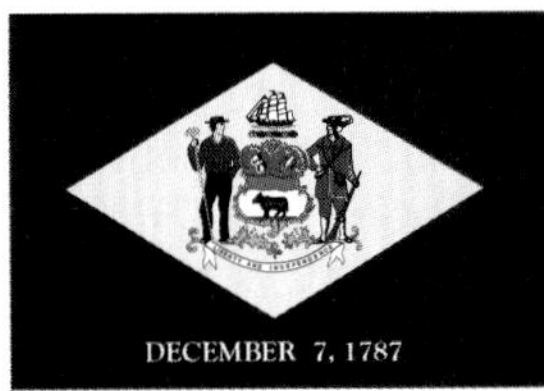

Florida
Admitted: 1845
Capital: Tallahassee
Population: 14,210,000
Area: 53,997 sq mi (139,852 sq km)
"Sunshine State"

Georgia
Admitted: 1788
Capital: Atlanta
Population: 7,102,000
Area: 57,919 sq mi (150,010 sq km)
"Peach State"

Hawaii
Admitted: 1959
Capital: Honolulu
Population: 1,221,000
Area: 6,423 sq mi
(16,636 sq km)
"Aloha State"

Idaho
Admitted: 1890
Capital: Boise
Population: 1,156,000
Area: 82,751 sq mi
(214,325 sq km)
"Gem State"

Illinois
Admitted: 1818
Capital: Springfield
Population: 11,853,000
Area: 55,593 sq mi
(143,986 sq km)
"Prairie State"

Indiana
Admitted: 1816
Capital: Indianapolis
Population: 5,820,000
Area: 35,870 sq mi
(92,903 sq km)
"Hoosier State"

Iowa
Admitted: 1846
Capital: Des Moines
Population: 2,861,000
Area: 55,875 sq mi
(144,716 sq km)
"Hawkeye State"

Kansas
Admitted: 1861
Capital: Topeka
Population: 2,601,000
Area: 81,823 sq mi
(211,922 sq km)
"Sunflower State"

Kentucky
Admitted: 1792
Capital: Frankfort
Population: 3,851,000
Area: 39,732 sq mi
(102,906 sq km)
"Bluegrass State"

Louisiana
Admitted: 1812
Capital: Baton Rouge
Population: 4,359,000
Area: 43,566 sq mi
(112,836 sq km)
"Pelican State"

Maine
Admitted: 1820
Capital: Augusta
Population: 1,236,000
Area: 30,865 sq mi
(79,940 sq km)
"Pine Tree State"

Maryland
Admitted: 1788
Capital: Annapolis
Population: 5,078,000
Area: 9,775 sq mi
(25,317 sq km)
"Old Line State"

Massachusetts
Admitted: 1788
Capital: Boston
Population: 5,976,000
Area: 7,838 sq mi
(20,300 sq km)
"Bay State"

Michigan
Admitted: 1837
Capital: Lansing
Population: 9,575,000
Area: 56,809 sq mi
(147,135 sq km)
"Wolverine State"

STATES

Minnesota
Admitted: 1858
Capital: St. Paul
Population: 4,619,000
Area: 79,617 sq mi
(206,208 sq km)
"North Star State"

New Hampshire
Admitted: 1788
Capital: Concord
Population: 1,132,000
Area: 8,969 sq mi
(23,230 sq km)
"Granite State"

Mississippi
Admitted: 1817
Capital: Jackson
Population: 2,666,000
Area: 46,914 sq mi
(121,507 sq km)
"Magnolia State"

New Jersey
Admitted: 1787
Capital: Trenton
Population: 7,931,000
Area: 7,419 sq mi
(19,215 sq km)
"Garden State"

Missouri
Admitted: 1821
Capital: Jefferson City
Population: 5,286,000
Area: 68,898 sq mi
(178,446 sq km)
"Show Me State"

New Mexico
Admitted: 1912
Capital: Santa Fe
Population: 1,676,000
Area: 121,364 sq mi
(314,333 sq km)
"Land of Enchantment"

Montana
Admitted: 1889
Capital: Helena
Population: 862,000
Area: 145,556 sq mi
(376,990 sq km)
"Treasure State"

New York
Admitted: 1788
Capital: Albany
Population: 18,178,000
Area: 47,224 sq mi
(122,310 sq km)
"Empire State"

Nebraska
Admitted: 1867
Capital: Lincoln
Population: 1,644,000
Area: 76,878 sq mi
(199,114 sq km)
"Cornhusker State"

North Carolina
Admitted: 1789
Capital: Raleigh
Population: 7,150,000
Area: 48,718 sq mi
(126,180 sq km)
"Tar Heel State"

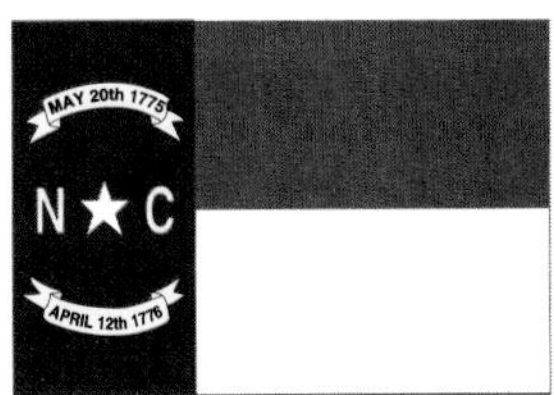

Nevada
Admitted: 1864
Capital: Carson City
Population: 1,477,000
Area: 109,806 sq mi
(284,398 sq km)
"Sagebrush State"

North Dakota
Admitted: 1889
Capital: Bismarck
Population: 637,000
Area: 68,994 sq mi
(178,694 sq km)
"Flickertail State"

Ohio
Admitted: 1803
Capital: Columbus
Population: 11,203,000
Area: 40,953 sq mi
(106,068 sq km)
"Buckeye State"

South Dakota
Admitted: 1889
Capital: Pierre
Population: 735,000
Area: 75,896 sq mi
(196,571 sq km)
"Coyote State"

Oklahoma
Admitted: 1907
Capital: Oklahoma City
Population: 3,271,000
Area: 68,679 sq mi
(177,879 sq km)
"Sooner State"

Tennessee
Admitted: 1796
Capital: Nashville
Population: 5,228,000
Area: 41,219 sq mi
(106,757 sq km)
"Volunteer State"

Oregon
Admitted: 1859
Capital: Salem
Population: 3,141,000
Area: 96,002 sq mi
(248,645 sq km)
"Beaver State"

Texas
Admitted: 1845
Capital: Austin
Population: 18,592,000
Area: 261,914 sq mi
(678,357 sq km)
"Lone Star State"

Pennsylvania
Admitted: 1787
Capital: Harrisburg
Population: 12,134,000
Area: 44,820 sq mi
(116,084 sq km)
"Keystone State"

Utah
Admitted: 1896
Capital: Salt Lake City
Population: 1,944,000
Area: 82,168 sq mi
(212,815 sq km)
"Beehive State"

Rhode Island
Admitted: 1790
Capital: Providence
Population: 1,001,000
Area: 1,045 sq mi
(2,707 sq km)
"Ocean State"

Vermont
Admitted: 1791
Capital: Montpelier
Population: 579,000
Area: 9,249 sq mi
(23,955 sq km)
"Green Mountain State"

South Carolina
Admitted: 1788
Capital: Columbia
Population: 3,732,000
Area: 30,111 sq mi
(77,987 sq km)
"Palmetto State"

Virginia
Admitted: 1788
Capital: Richmond
Population: 6,646,000
Area: 39,598 sq mi
(102,559 sq km)
"The Old Dominion"

Washington
Admitted: 1889
Capital: Olympia
Population: 5,497,000
Area: 66,581 sq mi
(172,445 sq km)
"Evergreen State"

Wyoming
Admitted: 1890
Capital: Cheyenne
Population: 487,000
Area: 97,105 sq mi
(251,502 sq km)
"Equality State"

West Virginia
Admitted: 1863
Capital: Charleston
Population: 1,824,000
Area: 24,087 sq mi
(62,385 sq km)
"Mountain State"

District of Columbia
Population: 559,000
Area: 61 sq mi
(158 sq km)

Wisconsin
Admitted: 1848
Capital: Madison
Population: 5,159,000
Area: 54,314 sq mi
(140,673 sq km)
"Badger State"

STATES

The Presidents

1. George Washington (1732–1799)
In office: 1789–1797
no official political party
Elected from: Virginia
Vice-President: John Adams

2. John Adams (1735–1826)
In office: 1797–1801
Federalist Party
Elected from: Massachusetts
Vice-President: Thomas Jefferson

3. Thomas Jefferson (1743–1826)
In office: 1801–1809
Democratic-Republican Party
Elected from: Virginia
Vice-Presidents: Aaron Burr, George Clinton

4. James Madison (1751–1836)
In office: 1809–1817
Democratic-Republican Party
Elected from: Virginia
Vice-Presidents: George Clinton, Elbridge Gerry

5. James Monroe (1758–1831)
In office: 1817–1825
Democratic-Republican Party
Elected from: Virginia
Vice-President: Daniel D. Tompkins

6. John Quincy Adams (1767–1848)
In office: 1825–1829
Democratic-Republican Party
Elected from: Massachusetts
Vice-President: John C. Calhoun

7. Andrew Jackson (1767–1845)
In office: 1829–1837
Democratic Party
Elected from: Tennessee
Vice-Presidents: John C. Calhoun, Martin Van Buren

8. Martin Van Buren (1782–1862)
In office: 1837–1841
Democratic Party
Elected from: New York
Vice-President: Richard M. Johnson

9. William Henry Harrison* (1773–1841)
In office: 1841
Whig Party
Elected from: Ohio
Vice-President: John Tyler

10. John Tyler (1790–1862)
In office: 1841–1845
Whig Party
Elected from: Virginia
Vice-President: none

11. James K. Polk (1795–1849)
In office: 1845–1849
Democratic Party
Elected from: Tennessee
Vice-President: George M. Dallas

12. Zachary Taylor* (1784–1850)
In office: 1849–1850
Whig Party
Elected from: Louisiana
Vice-President: Millard Fillmore

13. Millard Fillmore (1800–1874)
In office: 1850–1853
Whig Party
Elected from: New York
Vice-President: none

14. Franklin Pierce (1804–1869)
In office: 1853–1857
Democratic Party
Elected from: New Hampshire
Vice-President: William Rufus de Vane King

15. James Buchanan (1791–1868)
In office: 1857–1861
Democratic Party
Elected from: Pennsylvania
Vice-President: John C. Breckinridge

16. Abraham Lincoln† (1809–1865)
In office: 1861–1865
Republican Party
Elected from: Illinois
Vice-Presidents: Hannibal Hamlin, Andrew Johnson

*Died in office
†Assassinated

17. Andrew Johnson (1808–1875)
In office: 1865–1869
Democratic Party
Elected from: Tennessee
Vice-President: none

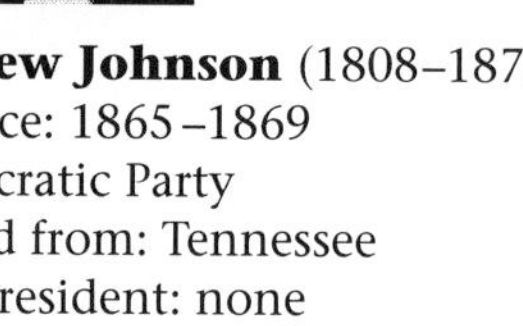

18. Ulysses S. Grant (1822–1885)
In office: 1869–1877
Republican Party
Elected from: Illinois
Vice-Presidents: Schuyler Colfax, Henry Wilson

19. Rutherford B. Hayes (1822–1893)
In office: 1877–1881
Republican Party
Elected from: Ohio
Vice-President: William A. Wheeler

20. James Garfield† (1831–1881)
In office: 1881
Republican Party
Elected from: Ohio
Vice-President: Chester A. Arthur

21. Chester A. Arthur (1829–1886)
In office: 1881–1885
Republican Party
Elected from: New York
Vice-President: none

22. Grover Cleveland (1837–1908)
In office: 1885–1889
Democratic Party
Elected from: New York
Vice-President: Thomas Hendricks

23. Benjamin Harrison (1833–1901)
In office: 1889–1893
Republican Party
Elected from: Indiana
Vice-President: Levi P. Morton

24. Grover Cleveland (1837–1908)
In office: 1893–1897
Democratic Party
Elected from: New York
Vice-President: Adlai E. Stevenson

† Assassinated

25. William McKinley† (1843–1901)
In office: 1897–1901
Republican Party
Elected from: Ohio
Vice-Presidents: Garret A. Hobart, Theodore Roosevelt

26. Theodore Roosevelt (1858–1919)
In office: 1901–1909
Republican Party
Elected from: New York
Vice-President: Charles Fairbanks

27. William H. Taft (1857–1930)
In office: 1909–1913
Republican Party
Elected from: Ohio
Vice-President: James S. Sherman

28. Woodrow Wilson (1856–1924)
In office: 1913–1921
Democratic Party
Elected from: New Jersey
Vice-President: Thomas R. Marshall

29. Warren G. Harding* (1865–1923)
In office: 1921–1923
Republican Party
Elected from: Ohio
Vice-President: Calvin Coolidge

30. Calvin Coolidge (1872–1933)
In office: 1923–1929
Republican Party
Elected from: Massachusetts
Vice-President: Charles G. Dawes

31. Herbert Hoover (1874–1964)
In office: 1929–1933
Republican Party
Elected from: California
Vice-President: Charles Curtis

32. Franklin D. Roosevelt* (1882–1945)
In office: 1933–1945
Democratic Party
Elected from: New York
Vice-Presidents: John Garner, Henry Wallace, Harry S Truman

*Died in office
†Assassinated

33. Harry S Truman (1884–1972)
In office: 1945–1953
Democratic Party
Elected from: Missouri
Vice-President: Alben Barkley

34. Dwight D. Eisenhower (1890–1969)
In office: 1953–1961
Republican Party
Elected from: New York
Vice-President: Richard M. Nixon

35. John F. Kennedy† (1917–1963)
In office: 1961–1963
Democratic Party
Elected from: Massachusetts
Vice-President: Lyndon B. Johnson

36. Lyndon B. Johnson (1908–1973)
In office: 1963–1969
Democratic Party
Elected from: Texas
Vice-President: Hubert Humphrey

37. Richard M. Nixon‡ (1913–1994)
In office: 1969–1974
Republican Party
Elected from: New York
Vice-Presidents: Spiro Agnew, Gerald Ford

38. Gerald R. Ford (b. 1913)
In office: 1974–1977
Republican Party
Elected from: Michigan
Vice-President: Nelson Rockefeller

39. Jimmy Carter (b. 1924)
In office: 1977–1981
Democratic Party
Elected from: Georgia
Vice-President: Walter Mondale

40. Ronald Reagan (b. 1911)
In office: 1981–1989
Republican Party
Elected from: California
Vice-President: George Bush

† Assassinated
‡ Resigned

41. George Bush (b. 1924)
In office: 1989–1993
Republican Party
Elected from: Texas
Vice-President: J. Danforth Quayle

42. Bill Clinton (b. 1946)
In office: 1993–
Democratic Party
Elected from: Arkansas
Vice-President: Albert Gore, Jr.

Key Events in United States History

by 20,000 B.C. Earliest inhabitants spread across North America
7000 B.C. Agriculture begins in the Americas
600 Mound Builders establish the city of Cahokia
1000s Anasazis build cliff dwellings
1300s Aztecs establish their capital, Tenochtitlán
1419 Prince Henry's ships start to explore West African coast
1492 Christopher Columbus reaches the Americas
1497 Search for the Northwest Passage begins
1513 Ponce de León explores Florida
1519 Cortés begins the conquest of Mexico
1519–1522 Magellan's expedition circles the globe
1565 Spain founds St. Augustine in Florida
1570 League of the Iroquois formed
1607 Jamestown founded
1608 Champlain founds Quebec for France
1610 Spanish establish Santa Fe, New Mexico
1619 Virginia House of Burgesses first meets
First Africans brought to Jamestown
1620 Mayflower Compact
Pilgrims land at Plymouth
1630 Puritans found Massachusetts Bay Colony
1644 Roger Williams establishes religious freedom in colony of Rhode Island
1675–1676 King Philip's War
1676 Bacon's Rebellion
1681 Penn plans "holy experiment" in Pennsylvania
1682 La Salle explores the Mississippi for France
1730s The Great Awakening begins
1732 Georgia becomes the last English colony
1754 French and Indian War begins
1763 France gives up claims in North America
1765 Stamp Act
1769 Spanish build first mission in California
1770 Boston Massacre
1773 Boston Tea Party
1774 First Continental Congress
1775 Battles of Lexington and Concord
Second Continental Congress
1776 Declaration of Independence
1781 Articles of Confederation ratified
British surrender at Yorktown
1783 Britain recognizes American independence in Treaty of Paris
1787 Constitutional Convention
Northwest Ordinance
1788 Constitution ratified
1789 **George Washington becomes first U.S. President**
1791 Bill of Rights ratified
1792 First political parties formed
1793 Eli Whitney invents the cotton gin
1797 **John Adams becomes President**
1798 Alien and Sedition Acts
Early 1800s Second Great Awakening sweeps the nation
1801 **Thomas Jefferson becomes President**
1803 *Marbury* v. *Madison*
Louisiana Purchase
1804–1806 Lewis and Clark expedition
1809 **James Madison becomes President**
1812–1815 War of 1812
1817 **James Monroe becomes President**
1819 United States acquires Florida
1820 Missouri Compromise
1821 William Becknell blazes the Santa Fe Trail
1823 Monroe Doctrine
1825 **John Quincy Adams becomes President**
Opening of the Erie Canal
1829 **Andrew Jackson becomes President**
1830 Indian Removal Act
1831 Nat Turner's Revolt
1832 Nullification Crisis
1833 American Anti-Slavery Society founded
1836 Texans declare independence from Mexico
First families on the Oregon Trail
1837 **Martin Van Buren becomes President**
1838 The Trail of Tears
1841 **William Henry Harrison becomes President**
John Tyler becomes President upon death of Harrison
1845 **James K. Polk becomes President**
United States annexes Texas
1846 United States declares war on Mexico
1848 Treaty of Guadalupe Hidalgo
Seneca Falls Convention on women's rights
1849 **Zachary Taylor becomes President**
California gold rush begins
1850 The Compromise of 1850
Millard Fillmore becomes President upon death of Taylor
1852 Harriet Beecher Stowe publishes *Uncle Tom's Cabin*
1853 **Franklin Pierce becomes President**
Gadsden Purchase
1854 Kansas-Nebraska Act
1857 **James Buchanan becomes President**
Dred Scott decision
1859 John Brown's raid on Harpers Ferry
1861 **Abraham Lincoln becomes President**
Civil War begins
1862 Homestead Act
Battle of Antietam
1863 Emancipation Proclamation
Battles of Gettysburg and Vicksburg
1864 Sherman's forces seize Atlanta
1865 Lee surrenders at Appomattox
Andrew Johnson becomes President upon assassination of Lincoln
Thirteenth Amendment abolishes slavery
1866 National Labor Union organized
1867 Congress passes Reconstruction Act
United States buys Alaska
1868 President Johnson's impeachment and trial
Fourteenth Amendment defines U.S. citizenship
1869 **Ulysses S. Grant becomes President**
1870 Fifteenth Amendment defines rights of voters
1877 **Rutherford B. Hayes becomes President**
Reconstruction ends
Great Railroad strike
1881 **James Garfield becomes President**
Chester A. Arthur becomes President upon assassination of Garfield

1882 Standard Oil trust formed
Chinese Exclusion Act
1885 **Grover Cleveland becomes President**
1886 Haymarket bombing
American Federation of Labor organized
1887 Dawes Act
1889 **Benjamin Harrison becomes President**
1890 Sherman Antitrust Act
1891 Populist party organized
1892 Homestead Strike
1893 **Grover Cleveland becomes President**
1894 Pullman Strike
1896 *Plessy* v. *Ferguson*
1897 **William McKinley becomes President**
1898 Spanish-American War
United States annexes Hawaii
United States acquires Philippines, Puerto Rico, and Guam
1899 Open Door policy in China
1901 **Theodore Roosevelt becomes President upon assassination of McKinley**
Progressive movement begins
1904 Construction of Panama Canal begins
Roosevelt Corollary to Monroe Doctrine
1909 **William H. Taft becomes President**
NAACP founded
1913 **Woodrow Wilson becomes President**
Federal Reserve Act
1914 World War I begins
1915 *Lusitania* sunk by German submarine
1916 U.S. troops sent to Mexico
1917 United States enters World War I
1919 United States rejects Treaty of Versailles
"Red Summer" and "Red Scare"
1920 Prohibition begins
Nineteenth Amendment gives women the vote
1921 **Warren G. Harding becomes President**
First immigration quota law passed
1923 **Calvin Coolidge becomes President upon death of Harding**
1929 **Herbert Hoover becomes President**
Stock market crash
1933 **Franklin D. Roosevelt becomes President**
Good Neighbor policy proclaimed
New Deal begins
1934 Indian Reorganization Act
1935 Wagner Act and Social Security Act
1938 Congress of Industrial Organizations formed
1939 World War II begins
1941 Japan bombs Pearl Harbor
United States enters World War II
1942 Japanese-American internment
1944 Allies invade France
1945 Yalta Conference
Harry S Truman becomes President upon death of Roosevelt
Germany surrenders
Atomic bombs dropped on Japan
Japan surrenders
UN charter goes into effect
1946 Philippines becomes independent
1948 Marshall Plan goes into effect
Berlin airlift begins
1949 NATO formed
1950 Korean War begins
1953 **Dwight D. Eisenhower becomes President**
Armistice in Korea signed
1954 *Brown* v. *Board of Education* decision
Army-McCarthy hearings
1955 Montgomery bus boycott
1956 Suez crisis
1961 **John F. Kennedy becomes President**
Peace Corps established
Berlin crisis
1962 Cuban missile crisis
1963 March on Washington for civil rights
Nuclear Test Ban Treaty
Lyndon B. Johnson becomes President upon assassination of Kennedy
1964 Civil Rights Act of 1964
1965 U.S. troop buildup begins in Vietnam
Voting Rights Act of 1965
Immigration quotas based on national origins ended
1966 National Organization for Women founded
1968 Martin Luther King, Jr., and Robert Kennedy assassinated
1969 **Richard M. Nixon becomes President**
American astronauts land on moon
1970 U.S. troops invade Cambodia
1971 Twenty-sixth Amendment lowers voting age to eighteen
1972 President Nixon visits mainland China
Watergate break-in
1973 Cease-fire agreement with North Vietnam
1974 **Gerald R. Ford becomes President upon resignation of Nixon**
1975 South Vietnam falls to North Vietnam
1977 **Jimmy Carter becomes President**
1978 Camp David Accords between Egypt and Israel
1979 Iranian hostage crisis begins
1981 **Ronald Reagan becomes President**
1983 U.S. troops invade Grenada
1986 Iran-Contra scandal
1987 INF Treaty
1989 **George Bush becomes President**
U.S. troops invade Panama
Communist governments in Eastern Europe fall
1991 Persian Gulf War
Soviet Union collapses
1992 Twenty-seventh Amendment gives voters a chance to review Congressional pay raises before they can take effect
1993 **Bill Clinton becomes President**
NAFTA established
1995 Republicans take over majority in Congress
Dayton peace agreement signed by warring parties of former Yugoslavia
1997 Madeleine Albright becomes first woman to be named U.S. Secretary of State

The Declaration of Independence

When, in the course of human events, it becomes necessary for one people to dissolve the political bands which have connected them with another, and to assume, among the powers of the earth, the separate and equal station to which the laws of nature and of nature's God entitle them, a decent respect to the opinions of mankind requires that they should declare the causes which impel them to the separation.

We hold these truths to be self-evident, that all men are created equal, that they are endowed by their Creator with certain unalienable rights, that among these are life, liberty, and the pursuit of happiness. That, to secure these rights, governments are instituted among men, deriving their just powers from the consent of the governed. That, whenever any form of government becomes destructive of these ends, it is the right of the people to alter or to abolish it, and to institute new government, laying its foundation on such principles, and organizing its powers in such form, as to them shall seem most likely to effect their safety and happiness.

Prudence, indeed, will dictate that governments long established should not be changed for light and transient causes; and, accordingly, all experience has shown that mankind are more disposed to suffer, while evils are sufferable, than to right themselves by abolishing the forms to which they are accustomed.

But when a long train of abuses and usurpations, pursuing invariably the same object, evinces a design to reduce them under absolute despotism, it is their right, it is their duty, to throw off such government, and to provide new guards for their future security. Such has been the patient sufferance of these colonies; and such is now the necessity which constrains them to alter their former systems of government. The history of the present King of Great Britain is a history of repeated injuries and usurpations, all having in direct object the establishment of an absolute tryanny over these states. To prove this, let facts be submitted to a candid world.

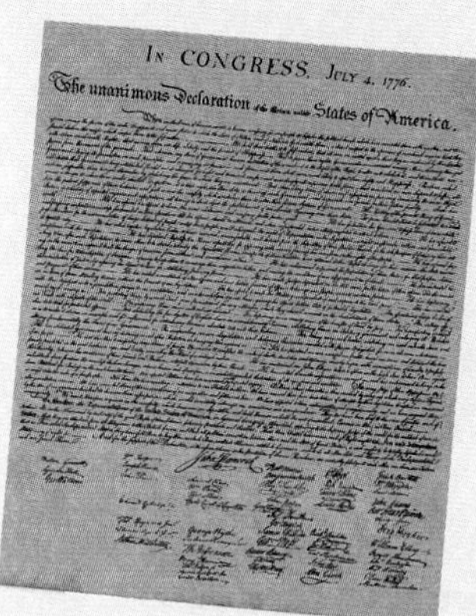

He has refused his assent to laws the most wholesome and necessary for the public good.

He has forbidden his governors to pass laws of immediate and pressing importance, unless suspended in their operation till his assent should be obtained; and when so suspended, he has utterly neglected to attend to them.

He has refused to pass other laws for the accommodation of large districts of people, unless those people would relinquish the right of representation in the legislature; a right inestimable to them and formidable to tyrants only.

He has called together legislative bodies at places unusual, uncomfortable, and distant from the depository of their public records, for the sole purpose of fatiguing them into compliance with his measures.

He has dissolved representative houses repeatedly, for opposing with manly firmness his invasions on the rights of the people.

He has refused for a long time, after such dissolutions, to cause others to be elected; whereby the legislative powers, incapable of annihilation, have returned to the people at large for their exercise; the state remaining in the meantime exposed to all the dangers of invasion from without, and convulsions within.

He has endeavored to prevent the population of these states; for that purpose obstructing the laws for naturalization of foreigners; refusing to pass others to encourage their migrations hither, and raising the conditions of new appropriations of lands.

He has obstructed the administration of justice, by refusing his assent to laws for establishing judiciary powers.

He has made judges dependent on his will alone, for the tenure of their offices, and the amount and payment of their salaries.

He has erected a multitude of new offices, and sent hither swarms of officers to harass our people, and eat out their substance.

He has kept among us, in times of peace, standing armies, without the consent of our legislatures.

He has affected to render the military independent of and superior to the civil power.

He has combined with others to subject us to a jurisdiction foreign to our constitution, and unacknowledged by our laws; giving his assent to their acts of pretended legislation:

For quartering large bodies of armed troops among us;

For protecting them, by a mock trial, from punishment for any murders which they should commit on the inhabitants of these states;

For cutting off our trade with all parts of the world;

For imposing taxes on us without our consent;

For depriving us, in many cases, of the benefits of trial by jury;

For transporting us beyond seas to be tried for pretended offenses;

For abolishing the free system of English laws in a neighboring province, establishing therein an arbitrary government, and enlarging its boundaries, so as to render it at once an example and fit instrument for introducing the same absolute rule into these colonies;

For taking away our charters, abolishing our most valuable laws, and altering fundamentally the forms of our governments;

For suspending our own legislatures, and declaring themselves invested with power to legislate for us in all cases whatsoever.

He has abdicated government here, by declaring us out of his protection, and waging war against us.

He has plundered our seas, ravaged our coasts, burnt our towns, and destroyed the lives of our people.

He is at this time transporting large armies of foreign mercenaries to complete the works of death, desolation, and tyranny already begun with circumstances of cruelty and perfidy scarcely paralleled in the most barbarous ages, and totally unworthy the head of a civilized nation.

He has constrained our fellow citizens, taken captive on the high seas, to bear arms against their country, to become the executioners of their friends and brethren, or to fall themselves by their hands.

He has excited domestic insurrections among us, and has endeavored to bring on the inhabitants of our frontiers, the merciless Indian savages, whose known rule of warfare is an undistinguished destruction of all ages, sexes, and conditions.

In every stage of these oppressions, we have petitioned for redress in the most humble terms. Our repeated petitions have been answered only by repeated injury. A prince, whose character is thus marked by every act which may define a tyrant, is unfit to be the ruler of a free people.

Nor have we been wanting in attentions to our British brethren. We have warned them from time to time of attempts by their legislature to extend an unwarrantable jurisdiction over us. We have reminded them of the circumstances of our emigration and settlement here. We have appealed to their native justice and magnanimity, and we have conjured them by the ties of our common kindred to disavow these usurpations, which would inevitably interrupt our connections and correspondence. They too have been deaf to the voice of justice and of consanguinity. We must, therefore, acquiesce in the necessity, which denounces our separation, and hold them, as we hold the rest of mankind, enemies in war, in peace, friends.

We, therefore, the representatives of the United States of America, in General Congress assembled, appealing to the Supreme Judge of the world for the rectitude of our intentions, do, in the name and by authority of the good people of these colonies, solemnly publish and declare, that these United Colonies are and of right ought to be free and independent states; that they are absolved from all allegiance to the British Crown, and that all political connection between them and the state of Great Britain is and ought to be totally dissolved; and that, as free and independent states, they have full power to levy war, conclude peace, contract alliances, establish commerce, and to do all other acts and things which independent states may of right do. And for the support of this declaration, with a firm reliance on the protection of Divine Providence, we mutually pledge to each other our lives, our fortunes, and our sacred honor.

Constitution Handbook

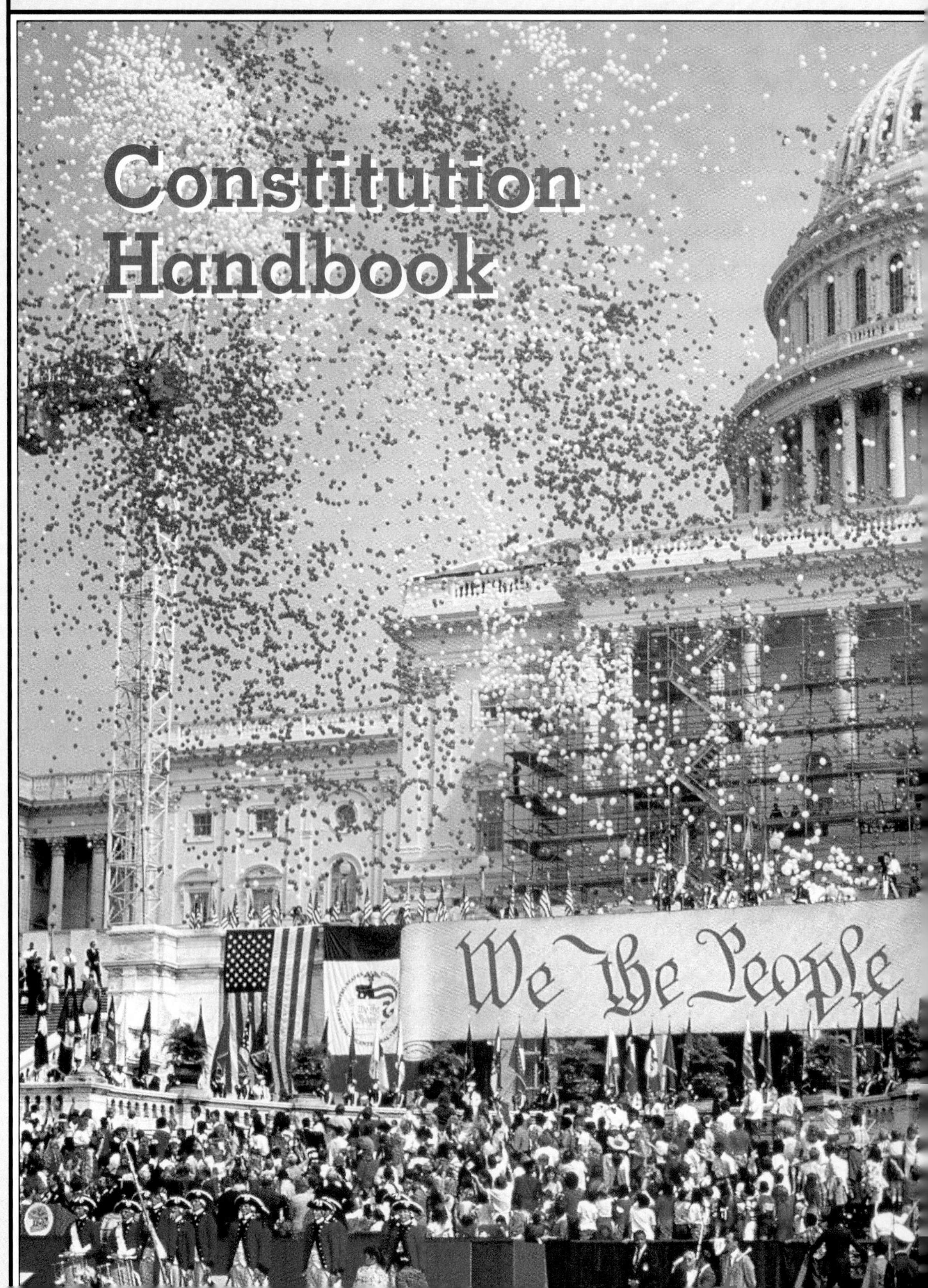

The Constitution, which was ratified in 1788, has seven articles, or parts. Since its ratification, 27 amendments have been added to the original document.

The Constitution is organized to serve as a user's manual for government. Long articles and amendments are broken into sections, each covering a single subtopic. Long sections are divided still further into clauses. This arrangement makes it easy to find your way around the Constitution.

Throughout this handbook, the original text of the Constitution appears in the right-hand column. Spelling and punctuation have been modernized where needed. The clauses have been numbered to help you identify them. You will see that some parts of the Constitution have lines drawn through them. These parts have been changed by amendments and are no longer in force.

The Constitution is written in a style of language that is more than 200 years old, making it difficult for people today to understand. To help you grasp its meaning, each section and clause has been rewritten in a simpler, more modern style. These translations appear in the left-hand column of each page, next to each section or clause.

On some pages, information appears below the Constitution text. There are explanations of what the Constitution means or how it works. Diagrams, tables, and photographs present interesting facts and help explain ideas.

Woven into the Constitution are three principles that shape how our government works:

- **Checks and Balances** Each branch of government can limit the powers of the other two.
- **Federalism** Power is divided between the federal government and the states.
- **Flexibility** General principles for running the government will survive the test of time better than specific details. If necessary, the Constitution can be changed through amendments.

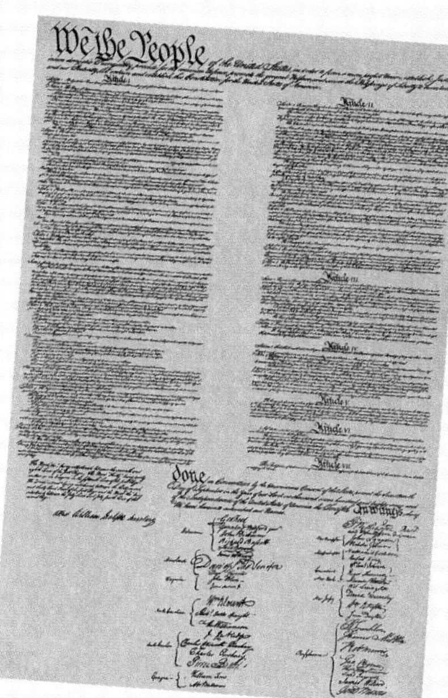

This handbook is organized to call your attention to these principles. You will see them, for example, in the titles of some explanations.

Guide to the Constitution

Introducing the Constitution Handbook

Begin by reading the student page with the class. As they read, have them refer to pages in the handbook to make sure that they can identify the original text of the Constitution (in right-hand columns), the rewritten version (in left-hand columns), and the explanatory and enriching material (at the bottom of the pages).

Next, ask students to skim the handbook to get acquainted with its contents. Point out that skimming involves looking at titles, headings, illustrations, captions, and sometimes the first sentences of paragraphs. This process will help give students an overview of the handbook. Once they have the big picture of how the Constitution and this handbook are organized, they will be better able to delve into the details.

Ask students to use the table of contents on this page as a guide when skimming. Have them go to the page on which each article begins and read the title of the article. A glance at the boldfaced heads will give them important topics in the article.

Bonus Activity

Reciting the Preamble

Memorizing the Preamble will help students identify the purposes of the Constitution. One of the basic rites of passage in American education has been to memorize and recite the Preamble to the Constitution. Divide the class into small groups of three or four for the purpose of working together to memorize and prepare a group recitation of the Preamble. Remind students that the Preamble has six purposes, or goals. They can count off each goal in their minds as they memorize the Preamble. Provide time for each group to recite the Preamble.

Constitutional Connections

Although the United States is a relatively new country, its Constitution is the oldest written national constitution in the world. It is very unlike the British constitution, which does not exist as a single written document. The British constitution consists of a variety of written documents and unwritten traditions establishing the powers of the monarchy, Parliament, and the courts. For example, the Magna Carta and the Declaration of Rights are two documents that are part of the British constitution. The form of constitution that Britain has is rare today. Most countries now have written constitutions that are single documents.

The Preamble to the Constitution

The Preamble

The Preamble is the introduction to the Constitution. It lists the six most important purposes of the new government. Those purposes are to:

- unify the states into a strong nation
- create a society based on law and justice
- keep peace among all Americans
- protect the nation from its enemies
- improve the lives of Americans
- ensure that all Americans, now and in the future, live in a free and democratic society

We the people of the United States, in order to form a more perfect Union, establish justice, insure domestic tranquility, provide for the common defense, promote the general welfare, and secure the blessings of liberty to ourselves and our posterity, do ordain and establish this Constitution for the United States of America.

Why the Preamble is Still Important

If your parents or grandparents went to school in the United States, the chances are that by your age they had memorized the Preamble to the Constitution. For generations, American schoolchildren began their study of the Constitution by committing these words to memory. The reason is simple. This one sentence tells us where the power comes from under our Constitution and how it should be used.

Look at first words of the Preamble: "We the people." They tell us that in this country, the power to govern comes from the consent of the governed. The Constitution was "ordained and established" in 1788 only after that consent was given by the people of the United States. It remains in effect today because we still choose to live under this framework of government.

The Preamble also says what the power is to be used for. The first purpose, "to form a more perfect Union," was dear to the hearts of all who had struggled with the very imperfect union created by the Articles of Confederation.

The remaining five purposes are as important today as they were in 1787. We still want to live in a just and law-abiding society. We still want to feel safe in our homes and communities. We still want to be protected from foreign enemies. We still believe that government should help make our lives better. We still treasure the opportunities, rights, and freedoms that are the blessings of liberty. In the pages that follow, you will learn more about the government created by the Constitution and how it serves these purposes.

Discussion

Checking Understanding

1. What is the introduction to the Constitution called? (The Preamble.)

2. What two houses make up the Congress of the United States? (Senate and House of Representatives.)

Stimulating Critical Thinking

3. What does "We the people" mean? (Suggests that government power comes from the people and can be taken away by them; suggests a democracy.)

4. Name an advantage and a disadvantage of having House members elected every two years. (Advantage: might be more responsive to citizens' wishes; disadvantage: might have to spend too much time running for re-election.)

Handbook Activity

Keeping a Log

As an ongoing activity to deepen understanding of constitutional principles, have students keep a Handbook Journal. Review the three guiding principles on page R35—checks and balances, federalism, and flexibility. As students read the handbook, have them record in their journals examples of each principle. In addition, encourage them to write down examples in action—in newspaper and magazine articles, TV reports, and other sources. When the journals are completed, have students share their examples.

Article 1: The Legislative Branch

The Legislative Branch	Article 1.
Section 1. A Two-Part Congress The legislative branch has the power to make laws. This power is given to both the Senate and the House of Representatives.	**Section 1.** All legislative powers herein granted shall be vested in a Congress of the United States, which shall consist of a Senate and House of Representatives.
Section 2. The House of Representatives **Clause 1. Election of Members** Members of the House are elected every two years by the people of the states. Short terms allow the people to quickly get rid of a representative they don't like.	**Section 2.** **Clause 1.** The House of Representatives shall be composed of members chosen every second year by the people of the several states, and the electors in each state shall have the qualifications requisite for electors of the most numerous branch of the state legislature.
Clause 2. Qualifications of Representatives A member of the House must be: • at least 25 years old • a U.S. citizen for at least seven years • a resident of the state from which elected	**Clause 2.** No person shall be a representative who shall not have attained to the age of twenty-five years, and been seven years a citizen of the United States, and who shall not, when elected, be an inhabitant of that state in which he shall be chosen.

Why Congress Comes First in the Constitution

The framers of the Constitution put the legislative branch at the center of the national government. Congress alone has the power to make laws. To indicate the importance of this branch, the framers put it first, in Article 1. Nearly half of the original Constitution deals with the organization and powers of Congress.

The structure of Congress is based on the Great Compromise of 1787. It is made up of two chambers: the House of Representatives, which represents the people, and the Senate, which represents the states.

The most important job of Congress is to make laws, the life blood of our political system. Laws do not just tell us what we can and cannot do. They also create government policies, programs, and agencies. Everything from the space agency to the school lunch program begins with a law passed by Congress.

Congress meets in the Capitol building in Washington, D.C.

Bonus Activity

Calculating House Representatives

To focus on how House representation can change over time, have students compare figures for their state after the 1980 and 1990 censuses. Provide national and state populations for each of those years, and then have students do the following steps for each year: (1) Divide the national population by 435 to find the number of people represented by each House member. (2) Take that answer and divide it into the state's population to determine the number of House members for your state following that census. Conclude by having students compare the 1980 and 1990 figures. To expand the activity, have students also do calculations for earlier censuses and summarize trends.

Constitutional Connections

Since the first national census in 1790, the government has conducted a census every ten years, as directed in Article 1, Clause 3. Although the framers intended the census for purposes of determining representation in the House, today the Bureau of the Census collects many kinds of data, including information about housing, agriculture, government, and economic matters.

In the first census, enumerators traveled the country on horseback to count the fewer than four million Americans. In 1990 the Bureau of the Census used a process of "self-enumeration" in which people responded to census questions by mail. It also used enumerators to collect data from people who did not respond by mail or who made mistakes. Altogether the 1990 census employed 565,000 temporary workers.

Article 1: The Legislative Branch

Clause 3. The Number of Representatives The number of representatives from each state is based on the state's population. Originally, slaves were counted as three-fifths of a person. When slavery was ended by the Thirteenth Amendment in 1865, the three-fifths rule became meaningless.	**Clause 3.** Representatives and direct taxes shall be apportioned among the several states which may be included within this Union, according to their respective numbers, ~~which shall be determined by adding to the whole number of free persons, including those bound to service for a term of years, and excluding Indians not taxed, three fifths of all other persons~~.
A census, or count of the people, must be taken every ten years. The results are used to apportion, or divide, House seats among the states. Each state must have at least one seat, no matter how small its population. Representatives within a state are elected from districts of roughly equal population. A typical House member now represents more than six hundred thousand persons.	The actual enumeration shall be made within three years after the first meeting of the Congress of the United States, and within every subsequent term of ten years, in such manner as they shall by law direct. The number of representatives shall not exceed one for every thirty thousand, but each state shall have at least one representative; ~~and until such enumeration shall be made, the state of New Hampshire shall be entitled to choose three, Massachusetts eight, Rhode Island and Providence Plantations one, Connecticut five, New York six, New Jersey four, Pennsylvania eight, Delaware one, Maryland six, Virginia ten, North Carolina five, South Carolina five, and Georgia three~~.
Clause 4. Filling Vacancies If a House seat becomes vacant between regular elections, the governor of that state can call a special election to fill the seat.	**Clause 4.** When vacancies happen in the representation from any state, the executive authority thereof shall issue writs of election to fill such vacancies.
Clause 5. Impeachment Power The Speaker of the House is the leading officer of the House. Only the House can impeach, or bring charges against, federal officials who have done wrong.	**Clause 5.** The House of Representatives shall choose their speaker and other officers, and shall have the sole power of impeachment.

Seats in the House of Representatives After the 1990 Census

The makeup of the House changed as a result of the census of 1990. Some states, mostly in the West and South, gained seats. The delegation from California, for example, swelled from 45 to 52 members. Other states, including New York, Ohio, Pennsylvania, and Massachusetts, lost seats.

Constitutional Connections

When the first Congress convened, the Senate had 22 members. By the time it adjourned, the Senate had 26 members. North Carolina and Rhode Island senators had joined the Congress after those states ratified the Constitution in 1789 and 1790, respectively.

Article 1: The Legislative Branch

Section 3. The Senate

Clause 1. Elections
The Senate is made up of two Senators from each state. Originally Senators were elected by their state legislatures. Amendment 17, ratified in 1913, calls for the direct election of Senators by the voters of each state.

Clause 2. Terms of Office
Senate terms overlap. Every two years, one-third of the Senators end their terms and must either leave or stand for re-election. As a result, there are always experienced lawmakers in the Senate.

Clause 3. Qualifications of Senators
A member of the Senate must be:

- at least 30 years old
- a U.S. citizen for at least 9 years
- a resident of the state from which elected

Clause 4. President of the Senate
The Vice-President serves as president of the Senate, but votes only in case of a tie.

Clause 5. Election of Officers
The Senate elects officers, including a temporary, or *pro tempore* president. The president pro tem leads the Senate when the Vice-President is absent.

Section 3.

Clause 1. The Senate of the United States shall be composed of two senators from each state, ~~chosen by the legislature thereof,~~ for six years; and each senator shall have one vote.

Clause 2. Immediately after they shall be assembled in consequence of the first election, they shall be divided as equally as may be into three classes. The seats of the senators of the first class shall be vacated at the expiration of the second year, of the second class at the expiration of the fourth year, and of the third class at the expiration of the sixth year, so that one third may be chosen every second year; ~~and if vacancies happen by resignation, or otherwise, during the recess of the legislature of any state, the executive thereof may make temporary appointments until the next meeting of the legislature, which shall then fill such vacancies.~~

Clause 3. No person shall be a senator who shall not have attained to the age of thirty years, and been nine years a citizen of the United States, and who shall not, when elected, be an inhabitant of that state for which he shall be chosen.

Clause 4. The Vice-President of the United States shall be president of the Senate, but shall have no vote, unless they be equally divided.

Clause 5. The Senate shall choose their other officers and also a president pro tempore, in the absence of the Vice-President, or when he shall exercise the office of President of the United States.

Giving States Equal Representation

The framers saw the Senate as a check on the House of Representatives. With longer terms in office and different interests in mind, Senators would see their role differently than Representatives. If the House passed a bill without fully considering its effects, the Senate might oppose it. When Thomas Jefferson asked George Washington why the delegates had established a Senate, Washington replied by asking, "Why do you pour your coffee into a saucer?" "To cool it," Jefferson answered. Washington replied, "Even so, we pour legislation into the senatorial saucer to cool it."

Discussion

Checking Understanding

1. How many senators are there from each state? (Each state has two senators.)

2. Who has a longer term—a senator or a member of the House? (Senator, whose term is six years, as opposed to two years for a House term.)

Stimulating Critical Thinking

3. Why do you think the framers decided that the number of representatives "shall not exceed one for every thirty thousand"? (To make sure that the number was not too large and unwieldy. Point out, however, that the Constitution does not specify a maximum number. With the growth of the nation's population, there would be over 8,000 House members today if each member still represented 30,000 people. To avoid such a situation, Congress has set the number of House seats at 435.)

4. What do you think Washington meant by saying, "We pour legislation into the senatorial saucer to cool it"? (Senators, who represent whole states and have longer terms, are not as subject to the fluctuations of public opinion. With their longer terms, they may gain more experience and thus vote more cautiously. In Washington's day, senators were elected by state legislatures, and thus were further removed from the daily demands of voters than were representatives.)

Constitutional Connections

The House of Representatives has voted articles of impeachment against 15 federal officials: 12 judges, 1 senator, 1 cabinet member, and 1 President. Of those, the 7 who were convicted were all judges. Students will read about President Andrew Johnson's impeachment and acquittal in Chapter 19 of the student text.

Article 1: The Legislative Branch

Clause 6. Impeachment Trials
The Senate serves as a jury in impeachment cases. A conviction requires a two-thirds vote of the members present.

Clause 6. The Senate shall have the sole power to try all impeachments. When sitting for that purpose, they shall be on oath or affirmation. When the President of the United States is tried, the Chief Justice shall preside. And no person shall be convicted without the concurrence of two thirds of the members present.

Clause 7. Penalty for Conviction
If an impeached official is convicted of wrongdoing by the Senate, that person is removed from office. The Senate cannot impose any other punishment. The convicted official can, however, be tried in a regular court.

Clause 7. Judgment in cases of impeachment shall not extend further than to removal from office, and disqualification to hold and enjoy any office of honor, trust, or profit under the United States; but the party convicted shall nevertheless be liable and subject to indictment, trial, judgment, and punishment, according to law.

Section 4. Elections and Meetings

Clause 1. Congressional Elections
Each state regulates its own congressional elections, but Congress can change the regulations. In 1872 Congress required that every state hold elections on the same day.

Clause 2. Meetings
Congress must meet once a year. Amendment 20, ratified in 1933, changed the first day of Congress to January 3.

Section 4.

Clause 1. The times, places, and manner of holding elections for senators and representatives shall be prescribed in each state by the legislature thereof; but the Congress may at any time by law make or alter such regulations, ~~except as to the places of choosing senators~~.

Clause 2. The Congress shall assemble at least once in every year, ~~and such meeting shall be on the first Monday in December,~~ unless they shall by law appoint a different day.

Checks and Balances: Impeachment

The framers worked hard to create a system of checks and balances that would keep any one branch of the government from misusing its power. One of the most important of those checks is the power of Congress to impeach and remove officials from office. To impeach means to accuse a government official of serious wrongdoing. Article 2, Section 4 defines such wrongdoings as "treason, bribery, or other high crimes and misdemeanors."

The first two offenses are clear. Treason is aiding the nation's enemies. Bribery involves giving gifts to a public official in exchange for special favors. Just what "high crimes and misdemeanors" means is less clear. The basic idea is that officials can be removed from office if they seriously abuse their power.

The House of Representatives has the power to impeach officials by charging them with such acts. Once impeached, an official is tried by the Senate. If found guilty by a two-thirds vote, the official is then removed from office.

Facing likely impeachment, Richard Nixon resigned from the presidency in 1974.

Constitutional Connections

In 1995, members of both houses of Congress earned an annual salary of $133,600. The president pro tempore of the Senate earned $148,400, as did the majority and minority leaders in the Senate. The Speaker of the House had an annual salary of $171,500, and the majority and minority leaders in the House of Representatives earned $148,400.

Discussion

Checking Understanding

1. Which house of Congress conducts the trial of an impeached official? (The Senate.)

2. What publication contains the written records of the House and Senate? *(The Congressional Record.)*

3. Who determines the salaries to be paid to members of Congress? (The members of Congress set their own salaries.)

Stimulating Critical Thinking

4. What advantages might there be to having the power of impeachment divided between the House and the Senate? (By reserving to the House the right to bring charges against a government official and to the Senate the right to try such an official, the framers of the Constitution probably increased the likelihood that the official charged would be granted a fair trial.)

5. What might be a reason for the employment restrictions in Section 6, Clause 2? (To avoid conflicts of interest for members of Congress and to ensure their objectivity about legislation before them.)

Section 5. Basics of Organization

Clause 1. Attendance
Each house can judge whether new members have been elected fairly and are qualified. A quorum is the minimum number of members who can act for all. While discussion can go on without a quorum, a quorum is required for voting.

Clause 2. Rules
Each house can:
- set up its own working rules
- punish members who misbehave
- expel a member with a two-thirds vote

Clause 3. Record-keeping
Each house must keep written records of what is done at meetings. Since 1873 the journals of the House and Senate have been published in the *Congressional Record.*

Clause 4. Ending Sessions
Both houses must agree to any adjournment, or ending of a session, for longer than three days.

Section 5.

Clause 1. Each house shall be the judge of the elections, returns, and qualifications of its own members, and a majority of each shall constitute a quorum to do business; but a smaller number may adjourn from day to day, and may be authorized to compel the attendance of absent members, in such manner and under such penalties as each house may provide.

Clause 2. Each house may determine the rules of its proceedings, punish its members for disorderly behavior, and, with the concurrence of two thirds, expel a member.

Clause 3. Each house shall keep a journal of its proceedings and from time to time publish the same, excepting such parts as may in their judgment require secrecy; and the yeas and nays of the members of either house on any question, shall, at the desire of one fifth of those present, be entered on the journal.

Clause 4. Neither house, during the session of Congress, shall, without the consent of the other, adjourn for more than three days, nor to any other place than that in which the two houses shall be sitting.

Section 6. Privileges and Restrictions

Clause 1. Salaries and Privileges
The members of Congress can set their own salaries. When Congress is in session, members cannot be arrested except on certain criminal charges. While working on congressional business, members can write or say anything about anyone.

Clause 2. Employment Restrictions
Members of Congress cannot create new federal jobs or increase the pay for old ones and then leave Congress to take those jobs. Nor can a member of Congress hold a job in one of the other branches of the federal government while serving in Congress.

Section 6.

Clause 1. The senators and representatives shall receive a compensation for their services, to be ascertained by law, and paid out of the Treasury of the United States. They shall in all cases, except treason, felony, and breach of the peace, be privileged from arrest during their attendance at the session of their respective houses, and in going to and returning from the same; and for any speech or debate in either house, they shall not be questioned in any other place.

Clause 2. No senator or representative shall, during the time for which he was elected, be appointed to any civil office under the authority of the United States which shall have been created, or the emoluments whereof shall have been increased, during such time; and no person holding any office under the United States shall be a member of either house during his continuance in office.

Constitutional Connections

The veto gives the President the power to reject bills passed by Congress. At present, the President cannot veto a portion of a bill, nor can the President veto constitutional amendments. Six Presidents, among them Jefferson and John Adams, vetoed no bills. Washington vetoed two bills. The record holder for number of vetoed bills is Franklin D. Roosevelt. He vetoed 635 bills.

Bonus Activity

Developing Vocabulary

To reinforce the meaning of the word *veto,* have students look up the origin of the word in a dictionary. Direct them to look for the etymology of the word and to record their findings. Have students write sentences relating the present meaning of the word to its original meaning. (The word *veto* comes from Latin and means "I forbid.")

Article 1: The Legislative Branch

Section 7. How Bills Become Laws

Clause 1. Tax Bills
All tax bills must begin in the House. The Senate, however, can thoroughly revise such bills.

Clause 2. Submitting Bills to the President
After Congress passes a bill, it goes to the President. The President can do one of three things at that point:

- Sign the bill, which then becomes law.
- Veto the bill and then return it to Congress with objections. If Congress overrides the President's veto by a two-thirds vote of both houses, the bill becomes law.
- Do nothing. In that case the bill becomes law after 10 days (not counting Sundays), provided Congress is in session. If Congress adjourns within 10 days, the bill dies. This method of killing a bill is called a pocket veto. A President may use it to avoid an open veto of a controversial bill.

Section 7.

Clause 1. All bills for raising revenue shall originate in the House of Representatives; but the Senate may propose or concur with amendments as on other bills.

Clause 2. Every bill which shall have passed the House of Representatives and the Senate shall, before it becomes a law, be presented to the President of the United States. If he approve he shall sign it, but if not he shall return it, with his objections to that house in which it shall have originated, who shall enter the objections at large on their journal and proceed to reconsider it.

If, after such reconsideration, two thirds of that house shall agree to pass the bill, it shall be sent, together with the objections, to the other house, by which it shall likewise be reconsidered, and, if approved by two thirds of that house, it shall become a law. But in all such cases the votes of both houses shall be determined by yeas and nays, and the names of the persons voting for and against the bill shall be entered on the journal of each house respectively.

If any bill shall not be returned by the President within ten days (Sundays excepted) after it shall have been presented to him, the same shall be a law, in like manner as if he had signed it, unless the Congress by their adjournment prevent its return, in which case it shall not be a law.

Checks and Balances: How the Veto Works

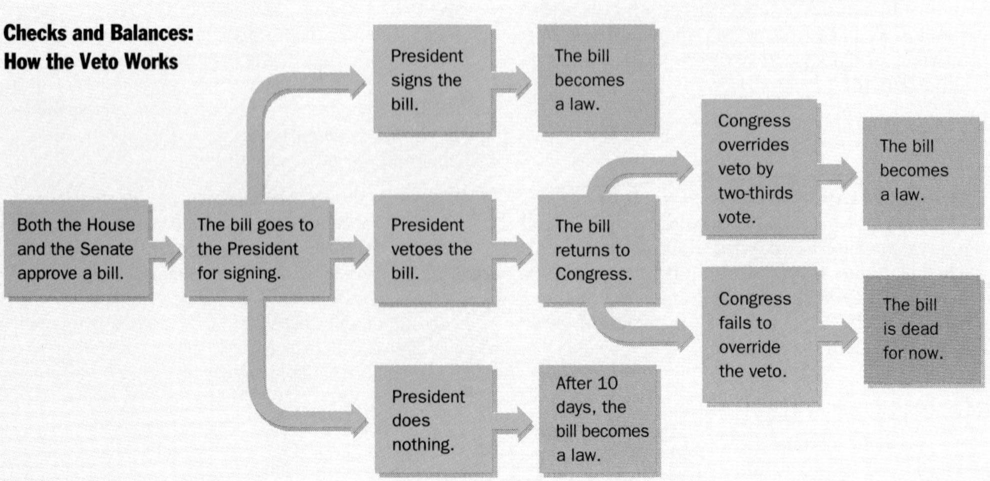

Article 1: The Legislative Branch

Clause 3. Submitting Other Measures Any other measures that require agreement by both houses must go to the President for approval. Congress cannot avoid submitting bills to the President by calling them orders or resolutions. When such measures reach the President, they are treated as bills.

Clause 3. Every order, resolution, or vote to which the concurrence of the Senate and House of Representatives may be necessary (except on a question of adjournment) shall be presented to the President of the United States; and before the same shall take effect, shall be approved by him, or being disapproved by him, shall be repassed by two thirds of the Senate and House of Representatives, according to the rules and limitations prescribed in the case of a bill.

Section 8. Powers of Congress

Congress has the power to:

Clause 1. Taxation
- impose and collect taxes and excises (taxes on products, such as cigarettes)
- collect duties (taxes on imported goods)

Clause 2. Borrowing
- borrow money as needed

Clause 3. Regulating Trade
- control trade with foreign nations, with Indian tribes, and between states

Clause 4. Naturalization; Bankruptcy
- decide how foreigners can become citizens, a process called naturalization
- pass bankruptcy laws for the country (laws for those unable to pay their debts)

Clause 5. Coining Money
- coin and print money
- define weights and measures so that they are the same across the country

Clause 6. Punishing Counterfeiting
- punish people who make fake money or government bonds

Clause 7. Providing Postal Service
- set up a postal system

Section 8.

The Congress shall have power:

Clause 1. To lay and collect taxes, duties, imposts, and excises, to pay the debts and provide for the common defense and general welfare of the United States; but all duties, imposts, and excises shall be uniform throughout the United States;

Clause 2. To borrow money on the credit of the United States;

Clause 3. To regulate commerce with foreign nations, and among the several states, and with the Indian tribes;

Clause 4. To establish a uniform rule of naturalization and uniform laws on the subject of bankruptcies throughout the United States;

Clause 5. To coin money, regulate the value thereof, and of foreign coin, and fix the standard of weights and measures;

Clause 6. To provide for the punishment of counterfeiting the securities and current coin of the United States;

Clause 7. To establish post offices and post roads;

Discussion

Checking Understanding

1. After Congress passes a bill, what three courses of action are open to the President? (The President can sign the bill, veto the bill, or do nothing.)

2. Who has the power to impose and collect taxes and duties? (Congress.)

3. What are the three ways in which a bill can become law? (**1.** If the President signs a bill that has been passed by both the House and Senate, the bill becomes law. **2.** If the House and Senate override a presidential veto by a two-thirds vote of both houses, the bill becomes law. **3.** If after ten days the President has neither signed nor vetoed a bill sent by Congress, the bill becomes law, unless Congress adjourns within that ten-day period.)

Stimulating Critical Thinking

4. Do you think the President should have the power to veto just a part of a bill (line item veto)? Explain. (Yes: parts added for special interests or as pet projects of legislators could be deleted without vetoing the whole act; parts added often have little or nothing to do with the main issues of the bill. No: the act was approved as it is and should be passed or vetoed in its entirety.)

Bonus Activity

Congress in the News

To reinforce understanding of the roles of Congress, have students find stories about Congress in current newspapers and bring them to class. For each story that discusses congressional powers, have students identify the clause of Section 8 that authorizes Congress to exercise the specific powers mentioned.

Constitutional Connections

In 1790, under powers granted in Section 8, Clause 8, Congress passed patent legislation to encourage inventors. As Secretary of State, Thomas Jefferson was the first patent officer. One of his last acts as patent officer was to write a letter to Eli Whitney, explaining that Whitney needed to submit a model as well as a sketch of his cotton gin before a patent could be granted.

Article 1: The Legislative Branch

Clause 8. Encouraging Invention • grant copyrights to authors and patents to inventors as a way of encouraging progress in science and the arts	**Clause 8.** To promote the progress of science and useful arts, by securing for limited times to authors and inventors the exclusive right to their respective writings and discoveries;
Clause 9. Establishing Courts • establish a federal court system	**Clause 9.** To constitute tribunals inferior to the Supreme Court;
Clause 10. Punishing Crimes at Sea • punish piracy and other crimes committed on the seas	**Clause 10.** To define and punish piracies and felonies committed on the high seas and offenses against the law of nations;
Clause 11. Declaring War • declare war • authorize private ships to attack and seize enemy ships	**Clause 11.** To declare war, grant letters of marque and reprisal, and make rules concerning captures on land and water;
Clause 12. Raising an Army • raise and support an army	**Clause 12.** To raise and support armies, but no appropriation of money to that use shall be for a longer term than two years;
Clause 13. Maintaining a Navy • establish and maintain a navy	**Clause 13.** To provide and maintain a navy;
Clause 14. Regulating the Armed Forces • make rules to govern the armed forces	**Clause 14.** To make rules for the government and regulation of the land and naval forces;
Clause 15. Calling Out the Militia • call out state militia units, now known as the National Guard	**Clause 15.** To provide for calling forth the militia to execute the laws of the Union, suppress insurrections, and repel invasions;
Clause 16. Regulating the Militia • organize, arm, and govern the National Guard. The states keep the power to appoint officers of state militias.	**Clause 16.** To provide for organizing, arming, and disciplining the militia, and for governing such part of them as may be employed in the service of the United States, reserving to the states respectively the appointment of the officers and the authority of training the militia according to the discipline prescribed by Congress;

Checks and Balances: Waging War

The Constitution gives Congress the sole power to declare war, to set up the armed forces, and to fund them. The framers gave these powers to Congress to make sure the nation would enter a war only if it was the will of the people. The President, however, was given the role of commander in chief of the armed forces. Under this authority, several Presidents have ordered American troops into battle without a declaration of war by Congress. In some of these cases, critics have charged that the President was going against the framers' intent.

Constitutional Connections

In 1790 George Washington selected a site on the Potomac River for a permanent national capital. Today Washington, D.C., has an area of approximately 70 square miles (180 sq km).

Discussion

Checking Understanding

1. What three reasons are given in Clause 15 for calling out the militia? (To execute the laws, suppress insurrections, and repel invaders.)

2. Why is Clause 18 called the "elastic clause"? (It provides flexibility by giving Congress the power to make all laws that are necessary to carry out the other powers given to Congress by the Constitution.)

Stimulating Critical Thinking

3. What might be the advantages of having the war-making power divided between Congress and the President? (It is more likely that war will be entered into cautiously and with time for reflection. The system of checks and balances makes it less likely that an impulsive act could launch the nation into a war that the people did not support.)

4. How might the President prevent Congress from abusing the "elastic clause"? (The President can veto bills, thus checking the power of Congress to stretch the elastic clause too far.)

Clause 17. Controlling Federal Property
- make laws for the District of Columbia and for federal land used for forts, naval bases, national parks, and other purposes. In 1974, Congress gave citizens of Washington D.C. the right to elect their own mayor and city council and run their own affairs. Still, Congress can overrule the council's actions.

Clause 17. To exercise exclusive legislation in all cases whatsoever over such district (not exceeding ten miles square) as may, by cession of particular states and the acceptance of Congress, become the seat of the government of the United States, and to exercise like authority over all places purchased by the consent of the legislature of the state in which the same shall be for the erection of forts, magazines, arsenals, dockyards, and other needful buildings; and

Clause 18. The "Elastic Clause"
- make all laws "necessary and proper" to carry out the powers listed above and any other powers of the federal government

Clause 18. To make all laws which shall be necessary and proper for carrying into execution the foregoing powers and all other powers vested by this Constitution in the government of the United States, or in any department or officer thereof.

Flexibility: The Elastic Clause

The last law-making power given to Congress is known as the "elastic clause" because it gives Congress the flexibility needed to carry out its other powers. For example, Congress has the power to coin and print money. To do so, however, it must pass laws to build mints, buy supplies, and hire workers. None of these powers are listed in the Constitution. Instead, such laws are considered "necessary and proper" under the elastic clause. Over the years the elastic clause has been stretched to allow Congress to do everything from build dams to outlaw some kinds of guns.

Congress has the power to decide how foreigners can become citizens. Here two new citizens attend a naturalization ceremony.

Constitutional Connections

A writ of habeas corpus is a court order commanding that a person held in custody be brought before a court to determine whether the detention is lawful. The purpose is to ensure that an accused person is granted due process under the law. Habeas corpus can be suspended only in time of rebellion or invasion. Early in the Civil War, President Lincoln used his constitutional power to suspend habeas corpus for pro-Confederate leaders in Maryland. As students will read in Chapter 18, this controversial action was part of Lincoln's strategy to prevent Maryland from seceding from the Union.

Article 1: The Legislative Branch

Section 9. Limits on Federal Power	Section 9.
Clause 1. Ending the Slave Trade As part of a compromise between northern states and southern states, Congress was forbidden to end the importing of slaves before 1808.	**Clause 1.** ~~The migration or importation of such persons as any of the states now existing shall think proper to admit shall not be prohibited by Congress prior to the year 1808, but a tax or duty may be imposed on such importation, not exceeding ten dollars for each person.~~
Clause 2. Suspending Habeas Corpus The government cannot take away a person's right to a writ of habeas corpus except in times of emergency. This right protects people from being held in jail without evidence.	**Clause 2.** The privilege of the writ of habeas corpus shall not be suspended, unless, when in cases of rebellion or invasion, the public safety may require it.
Clause 3. Unfair Laws Congress is forbidden from passing any: • bill of attainder, or law calling for the punishment of a particular person • ex post facto law, or law that makes an action done legally unlawful afterwards	**Clause 3.** No bill of attainder or ex post facto law shall be passed.
Clause 4. Taxing Individuals All taxes levied by Congress directly on land or people must be divided among the states according to their population. This was later changed by the Sixteenth Amendment.	**Clause 4.** No capitation or ~~other direct~~ tax shall be laid, unless in proportion to the census or enumeration herein before directed to be taken.
Clause 5. Taxing Exports Congress may not tax exports, or goods being sent to other countries.	**Clause 5.** No tax or duty shall be laid on articles exported from any state.
Clause 6. Regulating Trade Congress cannot favor one state over another in regulating trade and shipping.	**Clause 6.** No preference shall be given by any regulation of commerce or revenue to the ports of one state over those of another; nor shall vessels bound to or from one state be obliged to enter, clear, or pay duties in another.
Clause 7. Unlawful Spending The federal government can spend money only when Congress authorizes the spending. This clause is meant to keep government officials or employees from misusing federal funds.	**Clause 7.** No money shall be drawn from the Treasury but in consequence of appropriations made by law; and a regular statement and account of the receipts and expenditures of all public money shall be published from time to time.
Clause 8. Creating Titles of Nobility Congress cannot give anyone a title such as duchess or count. Federal officials cannot receive any gift of value from a foreign country. Such gifts are the property of the United States government.	**Clause 8.** No title of nobility shall be granted by the United States. And no person holding any office of profit or trust under them shall, without the consent of the Congress, accept of any present, emolument, office, or title of any kind whatever from any king, prince, or foreign state.

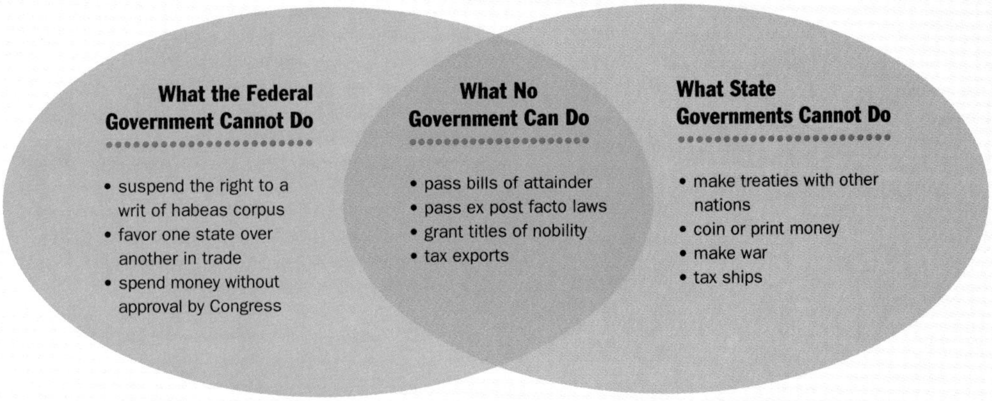

Discussion

Checking Understanding

1. Why did the Constitution's framers forbid Congress from ending the slave trade before 1808? (It was part of the compromise between the northern states and the southern states.)

Stimulating Critical Thinking

2. Why do you think Congress is forbidden to pass ex post facto laws? (It would be unfair to be punished for an act that was not illegal when performed.)

Article 1: The Legislative Branch

Section 10. Limits on State Power

Clause 1. Forbidden Actions
The states are not allowed to:
- make treaties with other nations
- coin or print money
- pass bills of attainder, ex post facto laws, or laws excusing citizens from carrying out contracts
- grant titles of nobility

Clause 2. Taxing Trade
A state cannot tax any goods entering or leaving the state. A state can charge a small fee, however, to pay for inspection of the goods.

Clause 3. Foreign Dealings
Without the agreement of Congress, states cannot tax ships that use their ports. Nor can a state prepare for war or wage war unless there is a military emergency.

Section 10.

Clause 1. No state shall enter into any treaty, alliance, or confederation; grant letters of marque and reprisal; coin money; emit bills of credit; make anything but gold and silver coin a tender in payment of debts; pass any bill of attainder, ex post facto law, or law impairing the obligation of contracts, or grant any title of nobility.

Clause 2. No state shall, without the consent of the Congress, lay any imposts or duties on imports or exports, except what may be absolutely necessary for executing its inspection laws; and the net produce of all duties and imposts laid by any state on imports or exports shall be for the use of the Treasury of the United States; and all such laws shall be subject to the revision and control of the Congress.

Clause 3. No state shall, without the consent of Congress, lay any duty of tonnage; keep troops or ships of war in time of peace; enter into any agreement or compact with another state or with a foreign power, or engage in war, unless actually invaded, or in such imminent danger as will not admit of delay.

Limits on State and Federal Power

Concerned that the federal government might become too strong, the framers of the Constitution spelled out the limits on federal power shown on the left. They also made sure to deny to the states the powers shown on the right. Some of these powers were reserved for the federal government alone. Others were denied the federal government as well.

What the Federal Government Cannot Do
- suspend the right to a writ of habeas corpus
- favor one state over another in trade
- spend money without approval by Congress

What No Government Can Do
- pass bills of attainder
- pass ex post facto laws
- grant titles of nobility
- tax exports

What State Governments Cannot Do
- make treaties with other nations
- coin or print money
- make war
- tax ships

Bonus Activity

Researching Vice-Presidents

To explore whether the vice-presidency is a stepping stone to the presidency, have students make a chart identifying all Vice-Presidents who later became Presidents. They may use information on Presidents and Vice-Presidents on pages R24–R29.

The chart should identify the Vice-Presidents who assumed the presidency upon the death or resignation of a President, those who became President by winning national elections, and those who did both (replaced a President and then ran successfully in the next election). Conclude the activity by having students speculate on why being Vice-President might or might not be an advantage to someone who wanted to become President.

Article 2: The Executive Branch

The Executive Branch

Section 1. The President and Vice-President

Clause 1. Term of Office
Executive power—power to carry out laws—is granted to the President, chief of the executive branch. The President serves a four-year term, as does the Vice-President.

Clause 2. The Electoral College
The people do not elect the President or Vice-President directly. Instead, both are chosen by a group of electors known as the electoral college. Each state legislature decides how electors are to be chosen in that state. Today electors are chosen by the voters. The number of electors from a state is equal to the number of senators and representatives from that state.

Clause 3. Electing a President
This clause describes the framers' original plan for electing a President and Vice-President. After the election of 1800 showed its weaknesses, the method was changed by the Twelfth Amendment. (See page R62 for more details.)

Vice-Presidents Who Have Taken Over for Presidents

Vice-President	President	Year
John Tyler	William Harrison	1841
Millard Fillmore	Zachary Taylor	1850
Andrew Johnson	Abraham Lincoln	1865
Chester Arthur	James Garfield	1881
Theodore Roosevelt	William McKinley	1901
Calvin Coolidge	Warren Harding	1923
Harry Truman	Franklin Roosevelt	1945
Lyndon Johnson	John Kennedy	1963
Gerald Ford	Richard Nixon	1974

Article 2.

Section 1.

Clause 1. The executive power shall be vested in a President of the United States of America. He shall hold his office during the term of four years, and, together with the Vice-President, chosen for the same term, be elected as follows:

Clause 2. Each state shall appoint, in such manner as the legislature thereof may direct, a number of electors, equal to the whole number of senators and representatives to which the state may be entitled in the Congress: but no senator or representative, or person holding an office of trust or profit under the United States, shall be appointed an elector.

~~**Clause 3.** The electors shall meet in their respective states and vote by ballot for two persons, of whom one at least shall not be an inhabitant of the same state with themselves. And they shall make a list of all the persons voted for and of the number of votes for each; which list they shall sign and certify, and transmit sealed to the seat of the government of the United States, directed to the president of the Senate. The president of the Senate shall, in the presence of the Senate and House of Representatives, open all the certificates, and the votes shall then be counted. The person having the greatest number of votes shall be the President, if such number be a majority of the whole number of electors appointed; and if there be more than one who have such majority, and have an equal number of votes, then the House of Representatives shall immediately choose by ballot one of them for President; and if no person have a majority, then from the five highest on the list the said house shall in like manner choose the President. But in choosing the President, the votes shall be taken by states, the representation from each state having one vote; a quorum for this purpose shall consist of a member or members from two-thirds of the states, and a majority of all the states shall be necessary to a choice. In every case, after the choice of the President, the person having the greatest number of votes of the electors shall be the Vice President. But if there should remain two or more who have equal votes, the Senate shall choose from them by ballot the Vice President.~~

Constitutional Connections

Every President, beginning with George Washington, has taken the same oath of office. Usually the Chief Justice of the Supreme Court administered the oath of office. Calvin Coolidge, however, was visiting his father in Vermont when he learned that President Harding had died. Coolidge's father, a local official, administered the oath of office. When the Attorney General pointed out that Coolidge's father had authority only in Vermont, Coolidge was sworn in a second time by a justice of the Supreme Court of the District of Columbia.

Article 2: The Executive Branch

Clause 4. Time of Elections
Congress sets the date for choosing electors, as well as the date for their voting. That date must be the same throughout the country.

Today Presidential elections take place every four years on the first Tuesday after the first Monday in November. Electoral votes are cast on the Monday after the second Wednesday in December.

Clause 4. The Congress may determine the time of choosing the electors and the day on which they shall give their votes, which day shall be the same throughout the United States.

Clause 5. Qualifications
Any American can be President who:
- is at least 35 years old
- is a natural born American citizen
- has lived in the U.S. for 14 years

Clause 5. No person except a natural-born citizen, or a citizen of the United States at the time of the adoption of this Constitution, shall be eligible to the office of President; neither shall any person be eligible to that office who shall not have attained to the age of thirty-five years and been fourteen years a resident within the United States.

Clause 6. Presidential Succession
This clause says that Congress can decide who should succeed, or replace, a President if the President dies, resigns, or is removed from office. In 1886 Congress said the line of succession would go from the Vice-President to members of the cabinet. In 1947 Congress changed it to go from the Vice-President to Speaker of the House, then to the president pro tempore of the Senate, and then to the cabinet. Amendment 25, ratified in 1967, prevents a long vacancy in the office of Vice-President. It also sets up procedures in case the President is disabled.

Clause 6. In case of the removal of the President from office, or of his death, resignation, or inability to discharge the powers and duties of the said office, the same shall devolve on the Vice-President, and the Congress may by law provide for the case of removal, death, resignation, or inability, both of the President and Vice-President, declaring what officer shall then act as President, and such officer shall act accordingly until the disability be removed or a President shall be elected.

Clause 7. Presidential Salary
The President gets paid like any other federal employee. That salary cannot be raised or lowered during a President's term in office. While in office, the President cannot receive any other salary from the U.S. government or a state government.

Clause 7. The President shall, at stated times, receive for his services a compensation, which shall neither be increased nor diminished during the period for which he shall have been elected, and he shall not receive within that period any other emolument from the United States or any of them.

Clause 8. The Oath of Office
Before taking office, the President must take an oath promising to carry out the duties of the Presidency and to preserve and protect the Constitution.

Clause 8. Before he enter on the execution of his office, he shall take the following oath or affirmation: "I do solemnly swear (or affirm) that I will faithfully execute the office of President of the United States, and will, to the best of my ability, preserve, protect, and defend the Constitution of the United States."

Discussion

Checking Understanding

1. Who directly elects the President and Vice-President? (The members of the electoral college.)

2. What are the qualifications for a President? (A person must be a natural born citizen, at least 35 years old, who has lived in the U.S. for 14 years.)

3. What must the President-elect do before officially becoming President? (He or she must take an oath promising to carry out the duties of President and to uphold the Constitution.)

Stimulating Critical Thinking

4. Do you think the Constitution should be amended to drop the age requirements for members of Congress to 18, the same as the voting age? (Yes: a person old enough to vote for an office is old enough to hold that office. No: the age requirements ensure that someone with experience will hold these offices.)

Bonus Activity

Finding Examples of Presidential Roles

To focus on the importance of presidential roles, have students find current examples. Divide the class into groups and assign one presidential role to each group. Ask each group to bring in newspaper or magazine articles that show the President playing that role. The class might make a bulletin-board display titled "The President's Many Roles."

Article 2: The Executive Branch

Section 2. Presidential Powers	**Section 2.**
Clause 1. Military and Executive Powers As head of the executive branch, the President has the power to: • act as commander in chief of all the armed forces • manage the federal bureaucracy • grant a reprieve, or delay of punishment, to a person convicted of a federal crime • grant a pardon, or excuse from punishment, to someone involved in a federal crime, except in impeachment cases	**Clause 1.** The President shall be commander in chief of the army and navy of the United States, and of the militia of the several states when called into actual service of the United States. He may require the opinion, in writing, of the principal officer in each of the executive departments upon any subject relating to the duties of their respective offices. And he shall have power to grant reprieves and pardons for offenses against the United States, except in cases of impeachment.
Clause 2. Treaties and Appointments The President also has the power to: • make treaties with foreign nations, with the approval of two-thirds of the Senate • appoint Supreme Court justices, with the approval of a majority of the Senate • appoint ambassadors and other important executive branch officials, with the approval of a majority of the Senate	**Clause 2.** He shall have power, by and with the advice and consent of the Senate, to make treaties, provided two thirds of the senators present concur; and he shall nominate, and by and with the advice and consent of the Senate, shall appoint ambassadors, other public ministers and consuls, judges of the Supreme Court, and all other officers of the United States whose appointments were not herein otherwise provided for, and which shall be established by law; but the Congress may by law vest the appointment of such inferior officers as they think proper in the President alone, in the courts of law, or in the heads of departments.
Clause 3. Other Appointments When the Senate is not in session, the President may make temporary appointments.	**Clause 3.** The President shall have power to fill up all vacancies that may happen during the recess of the Senate, by granting commissions which shall expire at the end of their next session.

Checks and Balances: The Advice and Consent of the Senate

The framers hoped that the Senate would act as sort of an advisory board for the President on appointments and foreign policy. The Constitution requires that the President submit all treaties and appointments to the Senate for its "advice and consent." This is one of the checks on the President's power.

President George Washington took the idea of seeking advice from the Senate quite seriously. On August 12, 1789, he went to the Senate to discuss a proposed treaty with the Creek Indians. The Senators wasted so much time arguing over details that the President finally left in disgust. This was the last time a President went to the Senate in person for "advice."

Constitutional Connections

Although the Constitution allows for a President or other officials to be removed from office for treason, there have been few prosecutions. One of the most famous trials involved Aaron Burr, the man who shot Alexander Hamilton and was a former Vice-President of the United States. Burr, accused of plotting to set up a separate country in the Southwest, was tried and acquitted.

Article 2: The Executive Branch

Section 3. The President's Duties

This section outlines the President's legislative duties. The President shall:

- Address Congress regularly on the nation's problems and recommend needed laws. This message is called the State of the Union Address.
- Call Congress into special session in times of national emergency.
- Adjourn Congress if needed.

The President shall also:

- Receive ambassadors from other countries. This duty puts the President in charge of the nation's foreign policy.
- Make sure the laws passed by Congress are "faithfully executed," or enforced.

Section 3.

He shall from time to time give to the Congress information of the state of the Union, and recommend to their consideration such measures as he shall judge necessary and expedient; he may, on extraordinary occasions, convene both houses, or either of them, and in case of disagreement between them with respect to the time of adjournment, he may adjourn them to such time as he shall think proper; he shall receive ambassadors and other public ministers; he shall take care that the laws be faithfully executed, and shall commission all the officers of the United States.

Section 4. Impeachment

The President, Vice-President, and other federal officials including department heads and federal judges can be removed from office by the impeachment process.

Section 4.

The President, Vice-President, and all civil officers of the United States shall be removed from office on impeachment for, and conviction of, treason, bribery, or other high crimes and misdemeanors.

The President's Many Roles

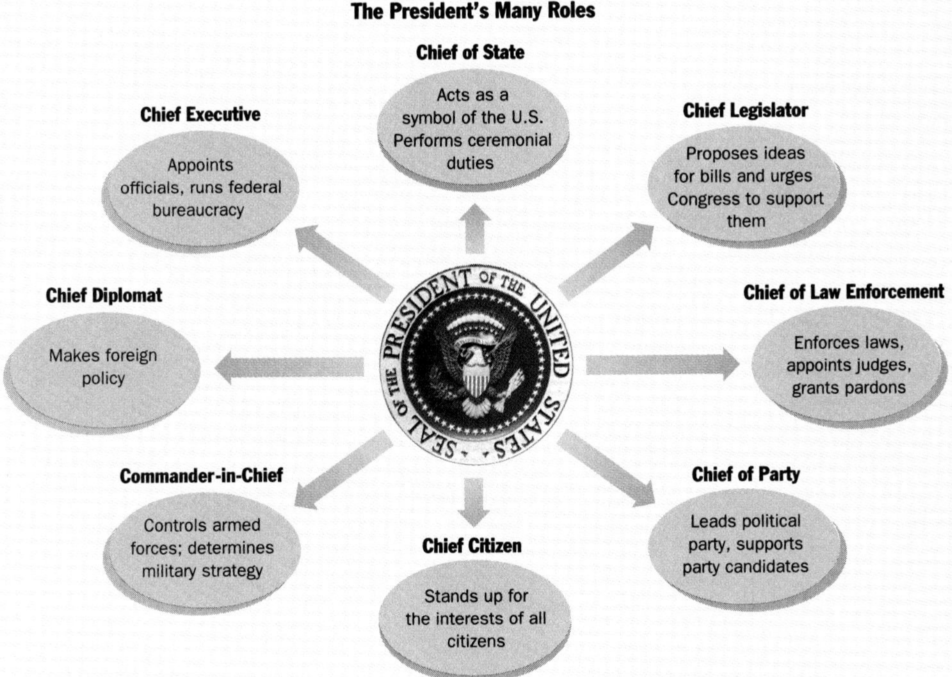
Chief of State
Acts as a symbol of the U.S. Performs ceremonial duties
Chief Executive
Appoints officials, runs federal bureaucracy
Chief Legislator
Proposes ideas for bills and urges Congress to support them
Chief Diplomat
Makes foreign policy
Chief of Law Enforcement
Enforces laws, appoints judges, grants pardons
SEAL OF THE PRESIDENT OF THE UNITED STATES
Commander-in-Chief
Controls armed forces; determines military strategy
Chief of Party
Leads political party, supports party candidates
Chief Citizen
Stands up for the interests of all citizens

Discussion

Checking Understanding

1. What is the State of the Union Address? (President's annual address to Congress on the nation's problems and goals.)

2. Who can be removed from office by the impeachment process? (President, Vice-President, and other federal officials, including department heads and federal judges.)

Stimulating Critical Thinking

3. Why does the President, rather than a military officer, serve as commander in chief? (In a democracy, decisions about war and peace should be made by someone answerable to voters. An officer in control of the armed forces might lead them in an attempt to overthrow the government.)

4. Why do you think Section 2, Clause 1, forbids the President from pardoning people who have been impeached? (Most officials subject to impeachment are presidential appointees; President might be likely to pardon his or her appointees.)

5. Why do you think the Constitution requires that the Senate approve appointments to the Supreme Court? (Maintains balance of power; if not, President could appoint supporters and the Court would not check presidential power.)

Bonus Activity

Drawing Symbols of Justice

To focus on the justice system, have students trace or draw common symbols of justice. They should first brainstorm a list of symbols, such as the blindfolded Themis, the scales of justice, and the Supreme Court building. Then they should locate pictures to trace or copy freehand. Conclude by asking them to explain what they think each symbol means.

Constitutional Connections

Perhaps the most important of the early Chief Justices was John Marshall, who presided over the Supreme Court from 1801–1835. Under his direction, the Court established many principles that continue to be observed today. For example, he established the principle of judicial review that enables the Supreme Court to review acts of Congress to determine their constitutionality.

Article 3: The Judicial Branch

The Judicial Branch

Section 1. Federal Courts

Judicial power is the power to decide legal cases in a court of law. This power is given to the Supreme Court and to lower federal courts established by Congress. A federal judge holds office for life unless impeached and found guilty of illegal acts. The salaries of judges cannot be lowered while they serve. This last protection prevents Congress from pressuring judges by threatening to cut their pay.

Section 2. Jurisdiction

Clause 1. Types of Cases
Jurisdiction is the power of a court to hear certain kinds of cases. The federal courts have jurisdiction over cases dealing with:

- the Constitution
- federal laws
- treaties with Indians or foreign powers
- ships and shipping on the seas
- disputes that involve the U.S. government
- disputes involving two or more states
- disputes between citizens of different states

Article 3.

Section 1.

The judicial power of the United States shall be vested in one Supreme Court, and in such inferior courts as the Congress may from time to time ordain and establish. The judges, both of the Supreme and inferior courts, shall hold their offices during good behavior, and shall, at stated times, receive for their services a compensation which shall not be diminished during their continuance in office.

Section 2.

Clause 1. The judicial power shall extend to all cases, in law and equity, arising under this Constitution, the laws of the United States, and treaties made, or which shall be made, under their authority; to all cases affecting ambassadors, other public ministers and consuls; to all cases of admiralty and maritime jurisdiction; to controversies to which the United States shall be a party; to controversies between two or more states; ~~between a state and citizens of another state;~~ between citizens of different states; between citizens of the same state claiming lands under grants of different states; and between a state, or the citizens thereof, and foreign states, ~~citizens, or subjects~~.

The Federal Courts and Judicial Power

The Constitution places judicial power in the hands of the Supreme Court and any "inferior courts" Congress decides to establish. Judicial power involves the authority to judge:

- **facts**—whether the accused violated the law
- **trials**—whether the case was tried properly
- **laws**—whether the law applied in the case is allowed by the Constitution

In the federal court system that has been set up since the ratification of the Constitution, there are two levels of "inferior" courts. The lowest level, made up of district and special courts, judges facts. The other level, made up of appeals courts, judges the fairness of trials. The Supreme Court is therefore left to judge matters of law, except in certain cases spelled out in the Constitution.

Constitutional Connections

The photograph at the bottom of the page shows Ruth Bader Ginsburg at a Senate confirmation hearing. She was subsequently appointed to the Supreme Court. This hearing was part of the process by which the President must seek the advice and consent of the Senate to appoint justices to the Supreme Court. Students might refer back to Section 2, Clause 2,on page R50 to review the President's obligation. This process of advice and consent takes the form of public confirmation hearings held by the Senate. They are frequently televised.

Discussion

Checking Understanding

1. Why is Congress not allowed to lower the salaries of federal judges while they are serving their terms? (To prevent members of Congress or other federal officers from pressuring judges by threatening pay cuts.)

2. How is the power of the Supreme Court checked? (The President appoints the justices, and the Senate approves or rejects the appointments; a constitutional amendment can override a Court decision; Congress can remove a Court justice for wrongdoing.)

Stimulating Critical Thinking

3. Why might trial by jury be seen as a basic democratic principle? (It ensures that the accused is tried, not by government officials, but by a group of fellow citizens. This protects the accused against persecution by government officials.)

Clause 2. Original and Appeals Cases
The Supreme Court has "original jurisdiction" in cases that involve the states or foreign countries. Such cases go directly to the Supreme Court. All other cases start first in the lower courts. The decisions of these courts may be appealed to the Supreme Court. Nearly all cases heard by the Supreme Court begin in the lower courts.

Clause 2. In all cases affecting ambassadors, other public ministers and consuls, and those in which a state shall be party, the Supreme Court shall have original jurisdiction. In all the other cases before-mentioned, the Supreme Court shall have appellate jurisdiction, both as to law and fact, with such exceptions and under such regulations as the Congress shall make.

Clause 3. Trial by Jury
Anyone accused of a federal crime has a right to a jury trial. The trial is to be held in the state where the crime was committed. The only exception to these rules is impeachment trials.

Clause 3. The trial of all crimes, except in cases of impeachment, shall be by jury; and such trial shall be held in the state where the said crimes shall have been committed; but when not committed within any state, the trial shall be at such place or places as the Congress may by law have directed.

Section 3. Treason

Section 3.

Clause 1. Defining the Crime
Treason is defined as making war against the United States or aiding its enemies. Convicting someone of treason is not easy. At least two witnesses must testify in court that they saw the accused commit an act of treason. Or the accused must confess to the crime in court. Talking or thinking about treason is not a crime.

Clause 1. Treason against the United States shall consist only in levying war against them or in adhering to their enemies, giving them aid and comfort. No person shall be convicted of treason unless on the testimony of two witnesses to the same overt act, or on confession in open court.

Clause 2. Limits of the Punishment
Congress decides how to punish treason. It can only punish the convicted traitor, however. Punishments cannot extend to that person's family.

Clause 2. The Congress shall have power to declare the punishment of treason, but no attainder of treason shall work corruption of blood or forfeiture except during the life of the person attainted.

Checks and Balances: Who Judges the Judges?

The power of the Supreme Court is checked in several ways. First, the other two branches of government decide who gets appointed to the Court. A candidate must first be nominated by the President and then approved by the Senate. Also, if Congress disagrees with the Court's interpretation of the Constitution, it can propose a constitutional amendment relating to the issue in question. If ratified, that amendment can overrule the Court's decision. Finally, Congress can remove a justice from office for wrongdoing.

Supreme Court nominee Ruth Bader Ginsburg answered questions at a Senate confirmation hearing in 1993.

Constitutional Connections

The nation's interstate highway system is a good example of federalism. The interstate highway system was built in the 1950s, during the Eisenhower administration. One of the largest public works programs in history, it would not have been possible without the cooperation of state and federal governments.

Bonus Activity

Describing Stamp Designs

To reinforce the state and national connection, have students write descriptions of stamp designs for their state. Have them examine the stamps commemorating Alaska's and Hawaii's entry shown on page R55. Ask them to think how their state is linked to the national government. Then have them describe a stamp that they would design to show the importance of their state to the Union.

Article 4: States and Territories

States and Territories

Section 1. Relations Among States

This section outlines the responsibilities of the states to each other in a federal system. Each state must give "full faith and credit" to the laws, official records, and court decisions of another state. This means accepting them as legal. A marriage in one state, for example, is legal in all states.

Section 2. Treatment of Citizens

Clause 1. Equal Privileges
A state cannot discriminate unreasonably against citizens from other states except in special cases. Such cases include residency requirements for voting and higher fees for out-of-state students at state colleges.

Clause 2. Return of Fugitive Criminals
Criminals cannot escape justice by running across state lines. Anyone accused of a crime in one state, who flees to another state and is caught, is to be returned if the government of the state where the crime took place makes such a request.

Clause 3. Return of Runaway Slaves
Runaway slaves could not become free by escaping to another state. They were to be returned to their owners. The Thirteenth Amendment made this clause invalid.

Article 4.

Section 1.

Full faith and credit shall be given in each state to the public acts, records, and judicial proceedings of every other state. And the Congress may by general laws prescribe the manner in which such acts, records, and proceedings shall be proved, and the effect thereof.

Section 2.

Clause 1. The citizens of each state shall be entitled to all privileges and immunities of citizens in the several states.

Clause 2. A person charged in any state with treason, felony or other crime, who shall flee from justice and be found in another state, shall, on demand of the executive authority of the state from which he fled, be delivered up to be removed to the state having jurisdiction of the crime.

~~**Clause 3.** No person held to service or labor in one state under the laws thereof, escaping into another, shall, in consequence of any law or regulation therein, be discharged from such service or labor, but shall be delivered up on claim of the party to whom such service or labor may be due.~~

Federalism: Cooperation Among the States

Before the Constitution was adopted, the original 13 states behaved almost like independent countries. For the new nation to endure, the states had to give up some of their independence and agree to cooperate, not only with the new federal government, but with one another.

The Constitution spells out only a few ways in which the states must cooperate with one another. Under the principle of federalism, however, the states have worked together for their common good in many ways. Building the nation's railways and interstate highway system, for example, would not have been possible without state cooperation.

Constitutional Connections

Puerto Rico is a Commonwealth of the United States, benefiting from the protection and assistance of the United States government. Its people are American citizens protected by the Constitution. In the 1960s, a commission studied whether to change Puerto Rico's status. Puerto Ricans have voted twice, in 1967 and 1993, to remain a Commonwealth rather than become a state.

Discussion

Checking Understanding

1. What happened to Section 2, Clause 3, of Article 4? (This clause was made invalid by the Thirteenth Amendment, which prohibits slavery.)

Stimulating Critical Thinking

2. What values or principles might the system of federalism encourage? (Cooperation would be vital to the success of a federal system, as would compromise, negotiation, and practicality.)

Section 3. New States and Territories

Clause 1. Admitting New States
Congress has the power to add new states to the Union. No new states can be formed by dividing up existing states, however, unless both Congress and the states involved agree to the changes.

Clause 2. Governing Territories
Congress has the power to govern federal land and property. This includes federal territory not organized into states and also federal land within states.

Section 3.

Clause 1. New states may be admitted by the Congress into this Union; but no new state shall be formed or erected within the jurisdiction of any other state; nor any state be formed by the junction of two or more states, or parts of states, without the consent of the legislatures of the states concerned as well as of the Congress.

Clause 2. The Congress shall have power to dispose of and make all needful rules and regulations respecting the territory or other property belonging to the United States; and nothing in this Constitution shall be so construed as to prejudice any claims of the United States, or of any particular state.

Section 4. Protection of the States

The federal government promises that each state will have some form of representative government. It also promises to protect each state from invasion. The federal government also stands ready to send help, when requested, to stop rioting within a state.

Section 4.

The United States shall guarantee to every state in this Union a republican form of government, and shall protect each of them against invasion, and, on application of the legislature or of the executive (when the legislature cannot be convened), against domestic violence.

From Territory to State

The framers of the Constitution realized the new nation was likely to continue expanding as Americans settled new lands. They made it possible for territories to become new states and created some basic rules for this process.

Thirty-seven new states have been admitted to the union since the Constitution was ratified. Most gained statehood in the 1800s. The two newest states are Alaska and Hawaii, both admitted in 1959.

The two most recent states to be admitted to the union were Alaska and Hawaii, in 1959.

Article 5: The Amendment Process

Amending the Constitution

Article 5 outlines the process for amending the Constitution. As the diagram below shows, there are two ways to propose an amendment and two ways to ratify it. Congress decides which method of ratification to use.

Article 5.

The Congress, whenever two thirds of both houses shall deem it necessary, shall propose amendments to this Constitution or, on the application of the legislatures of two thirds of the several states, shall call a convention for proposing amendments, which, in either case, shall be valid, to all intents and purposes, as part of this Constitution when ratified by the legislatures of three fourths of the several states, or by conventions in three fourths thereof, as the one or the other mode of ratification may be proposed by the Congress; provided ~~that no amendment which may be made prior to the year 1808 shall in any manner affect the first and fourth clauses in the ninth section of the first article; and~~ that no state, without its consent, shall be deprived of its equal suffrage in the Senate.

Flexibility: The Amendment Process

The amendment process makes is possible to change the Constitution to meet changing needs and demands. Since 1787, the Constitution has been amended 27 times. Each of these amendments was proposed by a two-thirds vote of both houses of Congress. All but one of these amendments were ratified by three-fourths of the state legislatures.

The exception was the Twenty-first Amendment. For the first time, an amendment was being proposed that would repeal an earlier one—the Eighteenth Amendment. In this case, Congress required ratification by state conventions and set a deadline for ratification of seven years.

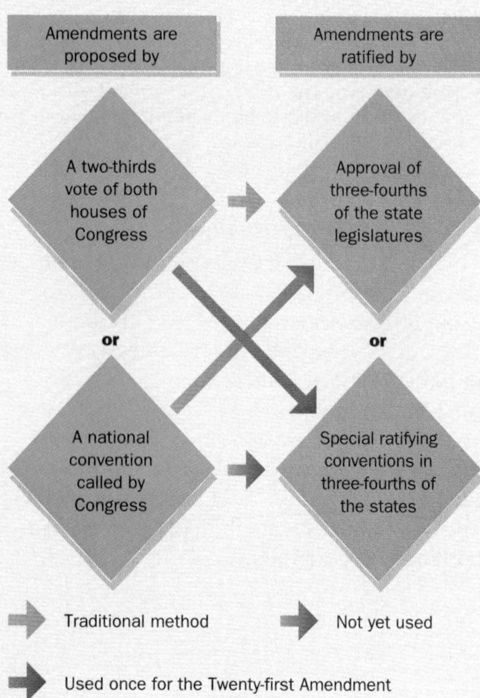

Amendments are proposed by
Amendments are ratified by
A two-thirds vote of both houses of Congress
Approval of three-fourths of the state legislatures
or
or
A national convention called by Congress
Special ratifying conventions in three-fourths of the states
Traditional method
Not yet used
Used once for the Twenty-first Amendment

Constitutional Connections

The Articles of Confederation provided the structure of the government before the adoption of the Constitution. The central government under the Articles was ineffective in conducting foreign policy, quelling domestic disturbances, and maintaining economic stability. Demand for a stronger, more centralized government led to adoption of the Constitution.

Articles 6 & 7: National Supremacy, Ratification

National Supremacy

Clause 1. Federal Debts
This clause promised that all debts owed by Congress under the Articles of Confederation would be honored by the United States under the Constitution.

Clause 2. The Supreme Law of the Land
The Constitution and federal laws or treaties made under it are the highest laws of the nation. When federal laws conflict with state laws or constitutions, state judges must follow the federal laws.

Clause 3. Government Oaths of Office
All federal and all state officials must promise to support the Constitution. No federal official may be required to meet any religious standards in order to hold office.

Ratification

Nine states had to ratify the Constitution before it could go into effect. By June 21, 1788, the necessary nine states had approved the new framework. The Constitution went into effect on April 30, 1789.

Article 6.

Clause 1. All debts contracted and engagements entered into before the adoption of this Constitution shall be as valid against the United States under this Constitution as under the Confederation.

Clause 2. This Constitution and the laws of the United States which shall be made in pursuance thereof, and all treaties made, or which shall be made, under the authority of the United States, shall be the supreme law of the land; and the judges in every state shall be bound thereby, anything in the Constitution or laws of any state to the contrary notwithstanding.

Clause 3. The senators and representatives before-mentioned, and the members of the several state legislatures, and all executive and judicial officers, both of the United States and of the several states, shall be bound by oath or affirmation to support this Constitution; but no religious test shall ever be required as a qualification to any office or public trust under the United States.

Article 7.

The ratification of the conventions of nine states shall be sufficient for the establishment of this Constitution between the states so ratifying the same.

The Ninth PILLAR erected !
"The Ratification of the Conventions of nine States, ſhall be ſufficient for the eſtabliſhment of this Conſtitution, between the States ſo ratifying the ſame." Art. vii.
INCIPIENT MAGNI PROCEDERE MENSES.
If it is not up it will riſe.
The Attraction muſt be irreſiſtible
DEL.
PEN.
N·JER.
GEOR.
CON.
MASSA.
MARY.
S° CARO.
N.HAMP.
VIRG.
N.YORK

This 1788 cartoon shows the first nine states that ratified the Constitution as upright pillars supporting a new national government.

Discussion

Checking Understanding

1. What does Article 5 of the Constitution cover? (It outlines the process for amending the Constitution.)

2. Which were the first nine states to ratify the Constitution? (Delaware, Pennsylvania, New Jersey, Georgia, Connecticut, Massachusetts, Maryland, South Carolina, and New Hampshire.)

3. What must state judges do when federal laws conflict with state laws? (They must follow the federal laws.)

Stimulating Critical Thinking

4. Why do you think the Constitution requires three-fourths of the state legislatures to ratify an amendment rather than a simple majority? (The requirement ensures that the proposed amendment has widespread and general support of the people.)

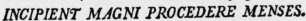

Bonus Activity

Sketches of Framers

To learn more about the framers of the Constitution, have each student prepare a biographical sketch of one of them. Each student should begin by creating an outline of the highlights of the person's life. The sketch should include basic information such as age when he signed the Constitution, his occupation, and the state he represented. Ask volunteers to present their findings to the class.

Constitutional Connections

Although many people contributed to the ideas and language of the Constitution, James Madison of Virginia was its chief author. He was also a chief author of *The Federalist Papers,* which argued for the adoption of the Constitution. In light of his influence on the Constitutional Convention, Madison has been called "the architect of the Constitution."

The Signers

Done in convention by the unanimous consent of the states present the seventeenth day of September in the year of our Lord one thousand seven hundred and eighty-seven, and of the independence of the United States of America the twelfth. In witness whereof we have hereunto subscribed our names,

George Washington—
President and deputy from Virginia

New Hampshire
John Langdon, Nicholas Gilman

Massachusetts
Nathaniel Gorham, Rufus King

Connecticut
William Samuel Johnson, Roger Sherman

New York
Alexander Hamilton

New Jersey
William Livingston, David Brearley, William Paterson, Jonathan Dayton

Pennsylvania
Benjamin Franklin, Thomas Mifflin, Robert Morris, George Clymer, Thomas FitzSimons, Jared Ingersoll, James Wilson, Gouverneur Morris

Delaware
George Read, Gunning Bedford, Jr., John Dickinson, Richard Bassett, Jacob Broom

Maryland
James McHenry, Dan of St. Thomas Jenifer, Daniel Carroll

Virginia
John Blair, James Madison, Jr.

North Carolina
William Blount, Richard Dobbs Spaight, Hugh Williamson

South Carolina
John Rutledge, Charles Cotesworth Pinckney, Charles Pinckney, Pierce Butler

Georgia
William Few, Abraham Baldwin

Signing the Constitution

On September 17, 1787, the delegates to the constitutional convention met one last time to approve their work. Many were still not satisfied with parts of the document. Knowing this, Benjamin Franklin made this final plea for their support:

> "Mr. President
>
> I confess that there are several parts of this Constitution which I do not at present approve, but I am not sure I shall never approve them. . . . I doubt, too, whether any other Convention we can obtain, may be able to make a better Constitution. . . . It therefore astonishes me, Sir, to find this system approaching so near to perfection as it does; and I think it will astonish our enemies.
>
> Thus I consent, Sir, to this Constitution because I expect no better, and because I am not sure that it is not the best. The opinions I have had of its errors, I sacrifice to the public good. . . . I can not help expressing a wish that every member of the Convention who may still have objections to it would, with me . . . put his name to this instrument."

Of the 42 delegates present on that day, only 3 refused to sign the Constitution. Time has shown the wisdom of Franklin's words. The Constitution is not perfect. That it comes "so near to perfection as it does," however, continues to astonish those who study it today.

Constitutional Connections

The Second Amendment to the Constitution continues to be a source of controversy. Some argue that the amendment gives citizens the right to own guns for personal use. The Supreme Court and lower courts, however, have consistently ruled that the amendment only guarantees the right of states to keep militia, now known as National Guard units. In other words, the courts have declared that individual citizens do not have a constitutional right to possess guns. That is why gun control measures, such as the 1994 Brady Bill, have not been declared unconstitutional.

Discussion

Checking Understanding

1. What are the first ten amendments called? (The Bill of Rights.)

2. What are the main freedoms identified in the First Amendment? (Freedom of religion, freedom of speech, freedom of the press, and freedom of assembly.)

Stimulating Critical Thinking

3. How do Benjamin Franklin's words on page R58 show his wisdom and common sense? (Franklin concedes that he does not approve of some parts of the Constitution, but he thinks it will be difficult to write a better Constitution. Further, he admits that he might be mistaken in his reservations about the document and thinks it sensible to sacrifice his minor objections to the public good.)

Amendments to the Constitution

The first ten amendments, called the Bill of Rights, were proposed as a group in 1789 and ratified in 1791. Other amendments were proposed and ratified one at a time. The dates in parentheses are the years of ratification.

Amendment 1 (1791) Religious and Political Freedoms

Congress cannot establish an official religion or pass laws that limit freedom of worship. It cannot make laws that keep people from speaking or writing what they think. Nor can Congress stop people from holding peaceful meetings or from asking the government to correct a wrong.

Amendment 1

Congress shall make no law respecting an establishment of religion or prohibiting the free exercise thereof, or abridging the freedom of speech or of the press, or the right of the people peaceably to assemble and to petition the government for a redress of grievances.

Amendment 2 (1791) The Right to Bear Arms

In order to maintain a state militia for their protection, citizens may own and use guns. Congress has outlawed the possession of certain firearms, however, such as sawed-off shotguns, machine guns, and assault rifles.

Amendment 2

A well-regulated militia being necessary to the security of a free state, the right of the people to keep and bear arms shall not be infringed.

Amendment 3 (1791) Quartering of Soldiers

In peacetime, citizens cannot be forced to provide a place in their homes for soldiers to stay. Even in wartime, this can only be done in a lawful manner.

Amendment 3

No soldier shall, in time of peace, be quartered in any house without the consent of the owner, nor in time of war but in a manner to be prescribed by law.

The Bill of Rights

Amendments 1–10

1. Freedoms of religion, speech, press, assembly, and petition
2. Right to bear arms in a state militia
3. No quartering of soldiers without consent
4. Protection against unreasonable searches
5. Right to due process of law
6. Rights of the accused
7. Right to a jury trial in civil cases
8. Protection against unreasonable fines and cruel punishment
9. Other rights of the people and seizures
10. Powers reserved to the states and to the people

Bonus Activity

A Bill of Rights Skit

To underscore protections in the Bill of Rights, have students work in small groups to prepare short skits. Each skit should illustrate a situation in which a protection in the Bill of Rights is being violated. For example, a group might act out a scene in which officers enter a person's home without a search warrant. After each skit, the class should identify the right or rights being violated and discuss what actions should have been taken to avoid violating those rights.

Constitutional Connections

One of the protections guaranteed by the Fifth Amendment is the right to refuse to incriminate oneself. This means that a person accused of a crime does not have to testify against him- or herself. Invoking the Fifth Amendment right implies neither guilt nor innocence.

Amendments 4 & 5

Amendment 4 (1791) Search and Seizure

People are protected from arrests, searches of their homes, or seizures of their property without good reason. Authorities must get a warrant, or legal document signed by a judge, before making a search or an arrest. To obtain a warrant, they must explain to the judge why it is needed, where the search will take place, and who or what will be seized.

Amendment 4

The right of the people to be secure in their persons, houses, papers, and effects against unreasonable searches and seizures shall not be violated, and no warrants shall issue, but upon probable cause, supported by oath or affirmation, and particularly describing the place to be searched and the persons or things to be seized.

Amendment 5 (1791) Due Process of Law

This amendment protects people from being abused by the legal system. It says:

- A person cannot be tried in a federal court for a serious crime without a formal indictment, or written accusation, by a grand jury. The grand jury decides whether there is enough evidence to make such an accusation.
- A person found not guilty of a federal crime cannot be tried again for the same offense in a federal court. This protection is known as the double jeopardy rule.
- Accused persons cannot be forced to say anything that might help convict them.
- The government cannot take away a person's life, liberty, or property without following correct legal procedures.
- The government cannot take away a person's property without paying a fair price for it. This power, called eminent domain, allows the government to acquire private property for public uses.

Amendment 5

No person shall be held to answer for a capital or otherwise infamous crime unless on a presentment or indictment of a grand jury, except in cases arising in the land or naval forces, or in the militia, when in actual service in time of war or public danger; nor shall any person be subject for the same offense to be twice put in jeopardy of life or limb; nor shall be compelled in any criminal case to be a witness against himself, nor be deprived of life, liberty, or property without due process of law; nor shall private property be taken for public use without just compensation.

Your Legal Rights and Protections

Before you are arrested, you are protected from:

- search without a warrant
- arrest without a warrant or sufficient cause (such as being caught in the act of committing a crime)

After your arrest, you have a right to:

- a writ of habeas corpus if held without charges
- remain silent
- consult a lawyer
- be indicted only by grand jury that weighs the evidence against you

(Continued on next page)

Amendment 6 (1791)
Rights of the Accused

Accused people have the right to:
- a prompt, public trial by a local jury
- know the charges against them
- face and question witnesses against them
- call witnesses to speak in their favor
- be represented by a lawyer

Amendment 6

In all criminal prosecutions, the accused shall enjoy the right to a speedy and public trial by an impartial jury of the state and district wherein the crime shall have been committed, which district shall have been previously ascertained by law, and to be informed of the nature and cause of the accusation; to be confronted with the witnesses against him; to have compulsory process for obtaining witnesses in his favor, and to have the assistance of counsel for his defense.

Amendment 7 (1791)
Right to a Jury Trial

When disputes involving more than $20 are tried in federal courts, either side can insist on a jury trial. If both sides agree, they can choose not to have a jury. Once a jury reaches a decision, it cannot be overturned simply because a judge disagrees with the jury's findings.

Amendment 7

In suits at common law, where the value in controversy shall exceed twenty dollars, the right of trial by jury shall be preserved, and no fact tried by a jury shall be otherwise reexamined in any court of the United States than according to the rules of the common law.

Amendment 8 (1791)
Bails, Fines, and Punishments

Bails, fines, and punishments must not be unreasonably high, cruel, or unusual. Bail is money or property given to the court by an accused person to guarantee that he or she will show up for trial. Usually, the more serious the crime, the higher the bail.

Amendment 8

Excessive bail shall not be required, nor excessive fines imposed, nor cruel and unusual punishments inflicted.

After you are indicted, you have a right to:
- know the charges against you
- reasonable bail
- a speedy trial by jury

At your trial, you have the right to:
- question witnesses against you
- call your own witnesses
- refuse to answer questions that might harm your case
- be represented by a lawyer

If you are found innocent, you are protected from:
- being tried again in federal court for the same crime

If you are found guilty, you are protected from:
- excessive fines
- cruel or unusual punishments

Discussion

Checking Understanding

1. What is a warrant? (A legal document signed by a judge.)

2. What is double jeopardy? (Putting a person on trial again for an offense after he or she was found not guilty of that offense.)

3. What does the Seventh Amendment guarantee? (It guarantees the right to a jury trial in civil cases where $20 or more is disputed.)

Stimulating Critical Thinking

4. Do you think the framers of the Constitution were more concerned about protecting the innocent or convicting the guilty? (Students might suggest that the framers' care in protecting the rights of the accused suggests that they were aware that the innocent are sometimes falsely accused and that it was very important to protect the rights of someone wrongly accused of a crime.)

Bonus Activity

Conducting a Bill of Rights Survey

To assess whether people know their rights, have students create questionnaires focusing on the Bill of Rights. For example, they might ask questions such as Does a person have complete freedom of speech?, or Can authorities search your house without a warrant? After questionnaires are completed, students should survey family members and neighbors. They can then compile the results and identify how well people know their constitutional rights.

Amendments 9, 10, 11, & 12

Amendment 9 (1791) Other Rights of the People

The listing of certain rights in the Constitution does not mean that these are the only rights the people have. Nor does it make those other rights less important.

Amendment 9

The enumeration in the Constitution of certain rights shall not be construed to deny or disparage others retained by the people.

Amendment 10 (1791) Powers Reserved to the States or the People

The federal government is granted certain powers under the Constitution. All other powers, except those denied to the states, belong to the states or to the people.

Amendment 10

The powers not delegated to the United States by the Constitution, nor prohibited by it to the states, are reserved to the states respectively, or to the people.

Amendment 11 (1795) Suits Against States

Citizens of other states or foreign countries cannot sue a state in federal court without its consent.

Amendment 11

The judicial power of the United States shall not be construed to extend to any suit in law or equity commenced or prosecuted against one of the United States by citizens of another state, or by citizens or subjects of any foreign state.

Amendment 12 (1804) Election of the President

The Twelfth Amendment was passed after both candidates in the election of 1800 received an equal number of electoral votes. This occurred in part because electors voted only for President, leaving the second-place candidate to be Vice-President. (See page 283 for more details.) This amendment calls for electors to cast separate votes for President and Vice-President.

Amendment 12

The electors shall meet in their respective states and vote by ballot for President and Vice-President, one of whom at least shall not be an inhabitant of the same state with themselves; they shall name in their ballots the person voted for as President, and in distinct ballots the person voted for as Vice-President, and they shall make distinct lists of all persons voted for as President and of all persons voted for as Vice-President and of the number of votes for each, which lists they shall sign and certify and transmit sealed to the seat of government of the United States, directed to the president of the Senate.

The president of the Senate shall, in the presence of the Senate and House of Representatives, open all the certificates and the votes shall then be counted.

Constitutional Connections

The Constitution does not specify the date of presidential elections. Article 2, Section 1, Clause 4 (page R49), says "Congress may determine the time of choosing the electors and the day on which they shall give their votes." Congress has set the election date as the first Tuesday after the first Monday in November. The electoral college votes on the Monday after the second Wednesday in December.

Amendment 12

If no presidential candidate receives a majority of electoral votes, the House of Representatives chooses a President from the top three candidates. In the House, each state gets one vote.

The person having the greatest number of votes for President shall be the President, if such number be a majority of the whole number of electors appointed; and if no person have such majority, then from the persons having the highest numbers not exceeding three on the list of those voted for as President, the House of Representatives shall choose immediately, by ballot, the President. But in choosing the President the votes shall be taken by states, the representation from each state having one vote; a quorum for this purpose shall consist of a member or members from two thirds of the states, and a majority of all the states shall be necessary to a choice. And if the House of Representatives shall not choose a President whenever the right of choice shall devolve upon them, ~~before the fourth day of March next following,~~ then the Vice-President shall act as President, as in the case of the death or other constitutional disability of the President.

If no candidate for Vice-President receives a majority of electoral votes, the election goes to the Senate. Two-thirds of either the House or Senate must be present when voting for President or Vice-President.

The person having the greatest number of votes as Vice-President shall be the Vice-President, if such number be a majority of the whole number of electors appointed, and if no person have a majority, then from the two highest numbers on the list the Senate shall choose the Vice-President; a quorum for the purpose shall consist of two thirds of the whole number of senators, and a majority of the whole number shall be necessary to a choice. But no person constitutionally ineligible to the office of President shall be eligible to that of Vice-President of the United States.

Electing a President

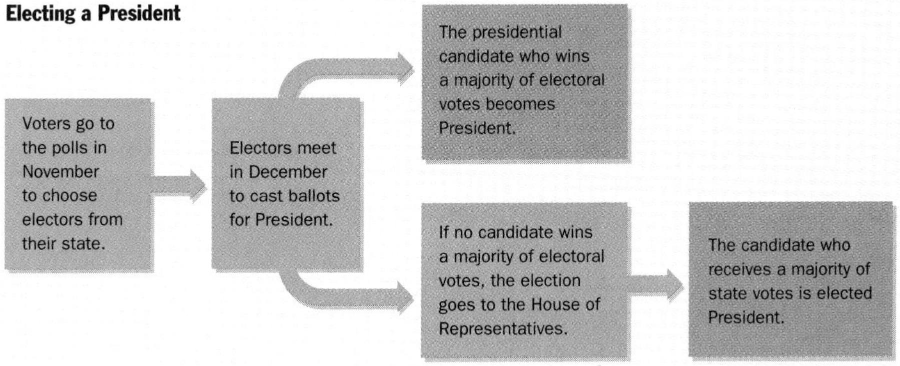

Voters go to the polls in November to choose electors from their state.

Electors meet in December to cast ballots for President.

The presidential candidate who wins a majority of electoral votes becomes President.

If no candidate wins a majority of electoral votes, the election goes to the House of Representatives.

The candidate who receives a majority of state votes is elected President.

The process outlined in this chart was established by Amendment 12.

Discussion

Checking Understanding

1. Which powers are reserved to the states or the people? (All powers not specifically given to the federal government by the Constitution are reserved to the states or the people.)

2. If no presidential candidate receives a majority of electoral votes, who decides the winner of the election? (The House of Representatives chooses a President from the top three candidates.)

Stimulating Critical Thinking

3. What do you think the "reserved powers" policy protects against? (It helps protect against the federal government taking too much power. It underscores that all power in the government flows from the people.)

Constitutional Connections

The "equal protection" clause of the Fourteenth Amendment continues to be important. It forbids states to discriminate against people on the basis of race, and also prohibits states from violating due process. The Supreme Court has interpreted the amendment to mean that states cannot make laws that prevent citizens from exercising rights under federal law.

Amendments 13 & 14

Amendment 13 (1865) Abolition of Slavery

This amendment was the first of three passed shortly after the Civil War. It ended slavery forever in the United States and its territories. No one may be forced to work unless ordered to by a court as punishment for a crime.

Amendment 13

Section 1.

Neither slavery nor involuntary servitude, except as a punishment for crime whereof the party shall have been duly convicted, shall exist within the United States or any place subject to their jurisdiction.

Section 2.

Congress shall have power to enforce this article by appropriate legislation.

Amendment 14 (1868) Civil Rights in the States

The Fourteenth Amendment was designed to give full citizenship rights to former slaves.

Section 1. Citizenship

All people born or naturalized in this country are citizens of both the United States and the state in which they live. States cannot make laws that keep people from enjoying their rights as citizens. States may not deprive citizens of life, liberty, or property without due process of law. Nor may states deny citizens "equal protection of the laws" by discriminating against any one group.

Section 2. Representation and Voting

This section replaced the old rule, by which slaves were counted as three-fifths of a person in determining a state's representation in the Congress, with a new one. If a state denied the right to vote to some male citizens over age 21—except as punishment for crime or rebellion—those citizens would not be counted in determining representation. The purpose of this new rule was to force states to let former slaves vote. If a state did not, it would lose representation in Congress. This new rule, however, was never enforced.

Amendment 14

Section 1.

All persons born or naturalized in the United States and subject to the jurisdiction thereof are citizens of the United States and of the state wherein they reside. No state shall make or enforce any law which shall abridge the privileges or immunities of citizens of the United States; nor shall any state deprive any person of life, liberty, or property without due process of law; nor deny to any person within its jurisdiction the equal protection of the laws.

Section 2.

Representatives shall be apportioned among the several states according to their respective numbers, counting the whole number of persons in each state, ~~excluding Indians not taxed.~~ But when the right to vote at any election for the choice of electors for President and Vice-President of the United States, representatives in Congress, the executive and judicial officers of a state, or the members of the legislature thereof is denied to any of the ~~male~~ inhabitants of such state, being ~~twenty-one years of age and~~ citizens of the United States, or in any way abridged, except for participation in rebellion or other crime, the basis of representation therein shall be reduced in the proportion which the number of such ~~male~~ citizens shall bear to the whole number of ~~male~~ citizens ~~twenty-one years of age~~ in such state.

Constitutional Connections

Although the Fifteenth Amendment was intended to protect the voting rights of African Americans, many states found ways to prevent them from voting. Two of the most commonly used means were the literacy test and the poll tax. A literacy test required voters to read and explain a difficult passage. If the readers failed to explain it to the satisfaction of the examiners, they could not vote. Some states also used a poll tax—a fee for voting. Since many African Americans were poor, this prevented them from voting. The Twenty-fourth Amendment abolished the poll tax in national elections. In 1966, the Supreme Court also outlawed the use of poll taxes in state and local elections. The Voting Rights Act, first passed in 1965 and later renewed, prohibited the use of literacy tests.

Section 3. Punishing Rebel Leaders

Former state and federal officials who had supported the South in the Civil War were barred from voting or holding office again. In 1898, Congress removed this barrier.

Section 3.

No person shall be a senator or representative in Congress, or elector of President and Vice-President, or hold any office, civil or military, under the United States, or under any state, who, having previously taken an oath as a member of Congress or as an officer of the United States or as a member of any state legislature or as an executive or judicial officer of any state to support the Constitution of the United States, shall have engaged in insurrection or rebellion against the same, or given aid or comfort to the enemies thereof. But Congress may by a vote of two thirds of each house remove such disability.

Section 4. Legal and Illegal Debts

This section dealt with debts left over from the Civil War. The only legal debt was the federal government's war debt. No government, state or federal, was allowed to pay off rebel war debts. No payment was to be made to slaveholders for the loss of their slaves.

Section 4.

The validity of the public debt of the United States, authorized by law, including debts incurred for payment of pensions and bounties for services in suppressing insurrection or rebellion, shall not be questioned. But neither the United States nor any state shall assume or pay any debt or obligation incurred in aid of insurrection or rebellion against the United States or any claim for the loss or emancipation of any slave; but all such debts, obligations, and claims shall be held illegal and void.

Section 5.

The Congress shall have power to enforce, by appropriate legislation, the provisions of this article.

Amendment 15 (1870) Voting Rights

This amendment was intended to protect the voting rights of the freed slaves. It said that neither the United States nor any state can deny citizens the right to vote because of their race or color, or because they were once slaves. Despite this amendment, many states did find ways to keep African Americans from voting. You can read more about this in Chapter 19.

Amendment 15

Section 1.

The right of citizens of the United States to vote shall not be denied or abridged by the United States or by any state on account of race, color, or previous condition of servitude.

Section 2.

The Congress shall have power to enforce this article by appropriate legislation.

Discussion

Checking Understanding

1. What did the Thirteenth Amendment accomplish? (It ended slavery forever in the United States and its territories.)

2. What did the Fourteenth Amendment do for former slaves? (It granted them full citizenship.)

3. What did the Fifteenth Amendment do for former slaves? (It was intended to protect their voting rights.)

Stimulating Critical Thinking

4. What did the so-called "Civil War amendments" have in common? (They all attempted to guarantee the political rights of the former slaves.)

Bonus Activity

Tax Options

Have students work in groups to brainstorm methods for raising revenue for the government. Methods might include an income tax with different percentages for varying income levels, a flat income tax, a national sales tax, and other methods students think of. Have each group discuss the pros and cons of each method and then recommend which method, or combination of methods, they think is most reasonable, and why.

Amendments 16 & 17

Amendment 16 (1913) Income Taxes

This amendment was passed to allow Congress to tax the incomes of individuals and businesses. The amendment was needed because Article 1, Section 9, Clause 4 says taxes levied on people must fall equally on the states based on their population. An income tax, however, taxes wealthy states more than poor states of equal population.

Amendment 16

The Congress shall have power to lay and collect taxes on incomes, from whatever source derived, without apportionment among the several states, and without regard to any census or enumeration.

Amendment 17 (1913) Direct Election Of Senators

Section 1. Regular Elections

The Constitution originally called for Senators to be elected by state legislatures. (See Article 1, Section 3, Clause 1.) This amendment gives the voters of each state the power to elect their Senators directly.

Amendment 17

Section 1.

The Senate of the United States shall be composed of two senators from each state, elected by the people thereof for six years; and each senator shall have one vote. The electors in each state shall have the qualifications requisite for electors of the most numerous branch of the state legislatures.

Section 2. Special Elections

If a senator dies or resigns before finishing his or her term, the governor must call a special election to fill that senate seat. The state legislature may let the governor appoint a temporary senator until such an election can be held.

Section 2.

When vacancies happen in the representation of any state in the Senate, the executive authority of such state shall issue writs of election to fill such vacancies, provided that the legislature of any state may empower the executive thereof to make temporary appointments until the people fill the vacancies by election as the legislature may direct.

Section 3.

This amendment shall not be so construed as to affect the election or term of any senator chosen before it becomes valid as part of the Constitution.

Sources of Federal Income 1995

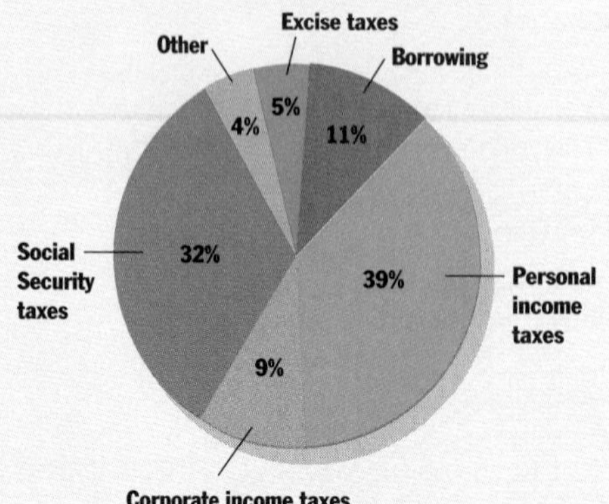

Source: Office of Management and Budget

The Federal Income Tax

The personal income tax is a progressive tax, which means that it taxes people with higher incomes at a higher rate than people with lower incomes. The theory is that the greater tax burden thus falls on the people who have the greatest ability to pay.

Constitutional Connections

Prohibition resulted in massive lawbreaking during the 1920s. Gangsters and racketeers made millions of dollars selling illegal alcohol, and many citizens who were otherwise law-abiding broke the law to obtain alcohol. The Twenty-first Amendment made the sale and distribution of alcohol a local or state matter.

Amendment 18 (1919) Prohibition of Alcohol

This amendment outlawed the making, selling, and transporting of alcoholic beverages in the United States and its territories. It was passed as part of a great reform effort to end the problems caused by the abuse of alcohol. The ban on alcohol, however, proved impossible to enforce. This amendment was repealed in 1933 by the Twenty-first Amendment.

~~Amendment 18~~

~~Section 1.~~

~~After one year from the ratification of this article the manufacture, sale, or transportation of intoxicating liquors within, the importation thereof into, or the exportation thereof from the United States and all territory subject to the jurisdiction thereof for beverage purposes is hereby prohibited.~~

~~Section 2.~~

~~The Congress and the several states shall have concurrent power to enforce this article by appropriate legislation.~~

~~Section 3.~~

~~This article shall be inoperative unless it shall have been ratified as an amendment to the Constitution by the legislatures of the several states, as provided in the Constitution, within seven years from the date of the submission hereof to the states by the Congress.~~

Amendment 19 (1920) Suffrage for Women

Until the passage of this amendment, most women in the United States were denied suffrage, or the right to vote. The Nineteenth Amendment says that women and men have an equal right to vote in both state and national elections.

Amendment 19

Section 1.

The right of citizens of the United States to vote shall not be denied or abridged by the United States or by any state on account of sex.

Section 2.

Congress shall have power to enforce this article by appropriate legislation.

This 1919 cartoon, entitled "Almost Through the Dark Alley," criticizes senators who opposed woman suffrage. Many supporters believed that once the amendment was finally approved by Congress, ratification would follow quickly.

Discussion

Checking Understanding

1. What is suffrage? (The right to vote.)

2. What did the Sixteenth Amendment authorize? (An income tax on individuals and businesses.)

3. What did the Eighteenth Amendment outlaw? (The making, selling, and transporting of alcohol.)

Stimulating Critical Thinking

4. Analyze the cartoon on page R67. What does it imply were the reasons for opposing suffrage for women? What do you think the senators feared? (The cartoon identifies prejudice and tradition as two of the forces that led some senators to oppose suffrage for women. Fear of how woman suffrage might affect traditional roles of men and women may have caused many to oppose it. Students might suggest that the senators feared losing their jobs or having to address issues that were important to women.)

Constitutional Connections

The term "lame duck" originally referred to a stockbroker or trader who could not pay his losses. William Makepeace Thackeray used the term in this sense in his novel *Vanity Fair:* "I don't like the looks of Mr. Sedley's affairs. . . . He's been dabbling on his own account I fear. . . . unless I see Amelia's ten thousand down you don't marry. I'll have no lame duck's daughter in my family."

Later the term came to mean anyone who defaulted on debts or who was disabled. Today, it is used almost exclusively in reference to a defeated elected official who continues to hold political office before the inauguration of a successor.

Amendment 20

Amendment 20 (1933) **The "Lame-Duck" Amendment**	**Amendment 20**
A "lame duck" is someone who remains in office for a time after his or her replacement has been chosen. The outgoing official is considered "lame," or without much power and influence. The main purpose of Amendment 20 was to reduce the amount of time "lame ducks" remained in office after national elections.	
Section 1. New Term Dates	**Section 1.**
In the past, a new President and Vice-President elected in November waited until March 3 to take office. Now their terms begin on January 20. In the past, new members of Congress waited 13 months between election and taking office. Now they are sworn in on January 3, which is just a few weeks after their election.	The terms of the President and Vice-President shall end at noon on the 20th day of January, and the terms of senators and representatives at noon on the 3rd day of January, of the years in which such terms would have ended if this article had not been ratified; and the terms of their successors shall then begin.
Section 2. Meetings of Congress	**Section 2.**
Congress must meet at least once a year, beginning on January 3. Congress may, however, choose a different starting day.	The Congress shall assemble at least once in every year, and such meeting shall begin at noon on the 3rd day of January, unless they shall by law appoint a different day.
Section 3. Death of a President-elect	**Section 3.**
If a newly elected President dies before taking office, the Vice-President-elect will become President.	If, at the time fixed for the beginning of the term of the President, the President-elect shall have died, the Vice-President-elect shall become President. If a President shall not have been chosen before the time fixed for the beginning of his term, or if the President-elect shall have failed to qualify, then the Vice-President-elect shall act as President until a President shall have qualified; and the Congress may by law provide for the case wherein neither a President-elect nor a Vice-President-elect shall have qualified, declaring who shall then act as President, or the manner in which one who is to act shall be selected, and such person shall act accordingly until a President or Vice-President shall have qualified.

Section 4. Death of a Presidential Candidate in a House Election

Amendment 12 says that if no candidate for President wins a majority of votes in the electoral college, the House of Representatives must choose a President from the three leading candidates. If one of those candidate dies before the House votes, Congress can decide how to proceed.

Similarly, Congress can decide how to proceed in case a vice-presidential election goes to the Senate and one of the leading candidates dies before the Senate makes its choice.

Section 4.

The Congress may by law provide for the case of the death of any of the persons from whom the House of Representatives may choose a President whenever the right of choice shall have devolved upon them, and for the case of the death of any of the persons from whom the Senate may choose a Vice-President whenever the right of choice shall have devolved upon them.

Section 5.

Sections 1 and 2 shall take effect on the 15th day of October following the ratification of this article.

Section 6.

This article shall be inoperative unless it shall have been ratified as an amendment to the Constitution by the legislatures of three fourths of the several states within seven years from the date of its submission.

Amendment 21 (1933) Repeal of Prohibition

Section 1. Repeal of Amendment 18

Amendment 18, which established a national prohibition of alcohol, is repealed.

Section 2. Protection for "Dry" States

Carrying alcohol into a "dry" state—a state that prohibits alcoholic beverages—is a federal crime.

Section 3. Ratification

Because this was such a controversial amendment, Congress insisted that it be ratified by state conventions elected by the people. This was the only time this system of ratification had been used since the Constitution itself was ratified.

Amendment 21

Section 1.

The eighteenth article of amendment to the Constitution of the United States is hereby repealed.

Section 2.

The transportation or importation into any state, territory, or possession of the United States for delivery or use therein of intoxicating liquors, in violation of the laws thereof, is hereby prohibited.

Section 3.

This article shall be inoperative unless it shall have been ratified as an amendment to the Constitution by conventions in the several states, as provided in the Constitution, within seven years from the date of submission hereof to the states by the Congress.

Discussion

Checking Understanding

1. When did a new President and Vice-President take office before and after the Twentieth Amendment? (In the past a new President and Vice-President elected in November took office in March; after the Twentieth Amendment passed, they began taking office in January.)

2. If a newly elected President dies before taking office, who becomes President? (The Vice-President-elect.)

3. What did the Twenty-first Amendment do? (It repealed the Eighteenth Amendment.)

Stimulating Critical Thinking

4. Why do you think the Eighteenth Amendment was repealed? (It proved difficult to enforce. It resulted in massive lawbreaking and thereby led to disrespect for the law. Possibly most people came to feel that the use of alcohol in moderation should not be a crime.)

Bonus Activity

Taking Sides on Term Limits

To review opinions about term limits, have student groups take positions for or against them. They should identify their positions and support them with reasons. A group may choose to take different stands on term limits for the President and term limits for members of Congress. Have each group summarize their position for the class.

Constitutional Connections

Much of the original impetus for the Twenty-second Amendment came from Republicans who were unhappy with Franklin D. Roosevelt's long tenure. A proposal to limit the President to a single six-year term in office has also been made. Some proponents for a single-term presidency believe that the President could then make decisions without concerns about re-election.

Amendment 22

Amendment 22 (1951) Presidential Term Limits

This amendment made the long tradition that Presidents limit their stay in office to two terms part of the Constitution. It says that no person can be elected President more than twice. If a Vice-President or someone else succeeds to the presidency and serves for more than two years, that person is limited to one additional term.

Amendment 22

Section 1.

No person shall be elected to the office of the President more than twice, and no person who has held the office of President or acted as President for more than two years of a term to which some other person was elected President shall be elected to the office of the President more than once. But this article shall not apply to any person holding the office of President when this article was proposed by the Congress, and shall not prevent any person who may be holding the office of President or acting as President during the term within which this article becomes operative from holding the office of President or acting as President during the remainder of such term.

Section 2.

This article shall be inoperative unless it shall have been ratified as an amendment to the Constitution by the legislatures of three fourths of the several states within seven years from the day of its submission to the states by the Congress.

The Presidential Two-Term Tradition

1796
George Washington declines to run for a third term, beginning the two-term tradition.

1808
President Thomas Jefferson follows Washington's example by retiring after two terms.

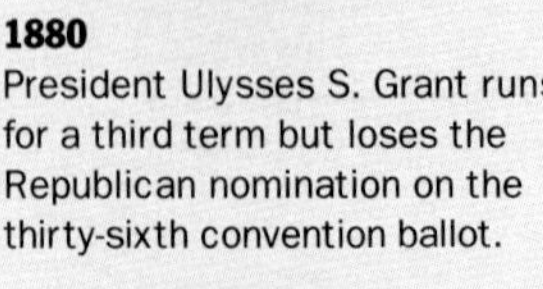

1880
President Ulysses S. Grant runs for a third term but loses the Republican nomination on the thirty-sixth convention ballot.

1940
Democrat Franklin Roosevelt wins for a third and then a fourth term. Republicans begin pushing for a two-term amendment, which is ratified in 1951.

1985
After winning a second term, Ronald Reagan says: "I see no reason why the Twenty-second Amendment shouldn't be repealed."

Amendment 23 (1961)
Voting in the District of Columbia

This amendment allowed residents of the District of Columbia to vote in Presidential elections. The District is given the same number of electors it would be entitled to if it were a state. But that number cannot be greater than the number of electors from the state with the smallest population.

At the time this amendment was ratified, more than 781,000 people lived in Washington, D.C. Capital residents paid taxes like all other citizens, but did not have the right to vote in national elections.

Amendment 23

Section 1.

The district constituting the seat of government of the United States shall appoint in such manner as the Congress may direct: A number of electors of President and Vice-President equal to the whole number of senators and representatives in Congress to which the district would be entitled if it were a state, but in no event more than the least populous state; they shall be in addition to those appointed by the states, but they shall be considered, for the purposes of the election of President and Vice-President, to be electors appointed by a state; and they shall meet in the district and perform such duties as provided by the twelfth article of amendment.

Section 2.

The Congress shall have power to enforce this article by appropriate legislation.

Amendment 24 (1964)
Abolition of Poll Taxes

A poll tax is a tax people have to pay in order to vote. For decades, poll taxes were used by some southern states to discourage poor people, especially poor black people, from voting. The Twenty-fourth Amendment says that neither the United States nor any state can require a citizen to pay a poll tax in order to vote in national elections.

Amendment 24

Section 1.

The right of citizens of the United States to vote in any primary or other election for President or Vice-President, for electors for President or Vice-President, or for senator or representative in Congress, shall not be denied or abridged by the United States or any state by reason of failure to pay any poll tax or other tax.

Section 2.

The Congress shall have power to enforce this article by appropriate legislation.

Why Did It Take an Amendment to Outlaw Poll Taxes?

Congress can outlaw many things by passing a bill into law. In the case of poll taxes, however, Congress faced a constitutional barrier. The Constitution gave the states authority over how to hold federal elections. So, if poll taxes were to be forbidden, an amendment specifically outlawing them had to be proposed and ratified.

Discussion

Checking Understanding

1. Why did Republicans push for a two-term amendment for Presidents? (Because Franklin Roosevelt had served for more than two terms, Republicans wished to prevent the possibility of a future Democratic President staying in office for so long.)

2. What did the Twenty-third Amendment offer the residents of the District of Columbia? (The right to vote in presidential elections.)

3. What was the purpose of poll taxes? (They were used to discourage poor African Americans from voting.)

Stimulating Critical Thinking

4. Do you think the two-term restriction on Presidents is reasonable? Explain. (Yes: helps guard against a President becoming overly confident in his or her use of power. No: voters should have the right to decide when a President has served long enough.)

Constitutional Connections

President Woodrow Wilson suffered a disabling stroke in September of 1919. He never fully recovered from the stroke, limiting his ability to serve as President. During the time he remained in office, a number of people made presidential decisions and exercised great influence over public affairs. Among them were unelected advisors such as Colonel E. M. House and Wilson's wife, Elizabeth Bolling Galt Wilson. Had the Twenty-fifth Amendment been in effect during his administration, the Vice-President could have acted as President.

Amendment 25

Amendment 25 (1967) Presidential Disability and Succession

Section 1. Replacing the President

If the President dies, resigns, or is removed from office, the Vice-President becomes President.

Section 2. Replacing the Vice-President

The President appoints a new Vice-President if that office becomes empty. That appointment must be approved by both houses of Congress.

Section 3. Temporary Replacement with the President's Consent

If the President notifies Congress in writing that he or she is unable to perform official duties, the Vice-President takes over as Acting President. The President may return to office after notifying Congress that he or she is again able to serve.

Section 4. Temporary Replacement Without the President's Consent

If a President is disabled and cannot or will not notify Congress, the Vice-President and a majority of the cabinet (or some other group named by Congress) can send such notice. The Vice-President will then become Acting President.

The Vice-President will step down when the President sends Congress written notice of renewed ability to serve. If the Vice-President and others disagree, they must notify Congress within four days.

Amendment 25

Section 1.

In case of the removal of the President from office or of his death or resignation, the Vice-President shall become President.

Section 2.

Whenever there is a vacancy in the office of the Vice-President, the President shall nominate a Vice-President who shall take office upon confirmation by a majority vote of both houses of Congress.

Section 3.

Whenever the President transmits to the president pro tempore of the Senate and the speaker of the House of Representatives his written declaration that he is unable to discharge the powers and duties of his office, and until he transmits to them a written declaration to the contrary, such powers and duties shall be discharged by the Vice-President as Acting President.

Section 4.

Whenever the Vice-President and a majority of either the principal officers of the executive departments or of such other body as Congress may by law provide, transmit to the president pro tempore of the Senate and the speaker of the House of Representatives their written declaration that the President is unable to discharge the powers and duties of his office, the Vice-President shall immediately assume the powers and duties of the office as Acting President.

Thereafter, when the President transmits to the president pro tempore of the Senate and the speaker of the House of Representatives his written declaration that no inability exists, he shall resume the powers and duties of his office unless the Vice-President and a majority of either the principal officers of the executive department or of such other body as Congress may by law provide, transmit within four days to the president pro tempore of the Senate and the speaker of the House of Representatives their written declaration that the President is unable to discharge the powers and duties of his office.

Congress must meet within 48 hours to discuss whether the President is still disabled. They have 21 days to decide the issue. If two thirds or more of both houses vote that the President is disabled, the Vice-President remains in office as Acting President. If they do not, the President resumes official duties.

Thereupon Congress shall decide the issue, assembling within forty-eight hours for that purpose if not in session. If the Congress, within twenty-one days after receipt of the latter written declaration, or, if Congress is not in session, within twenty-one days after Congress is required to assemble, determines by two-thirds vote of both houses that the President is unable to discharge the powers and duties of his office, the Vice-President shall continue to discharge the same as Acting President; otherwise, the President shall resume the powers and duties of his office.

Amendment 26 (1971) Eighteen-Year-Old Vote

Neither the United States nor any state can deny the vote to citizens of age 18 or older because of their age. The effect of this amendment was to lower the voting age in most state elections from 21 to 18.

Amendment 26

Section 1.

The right of citizens of the United States, who are eighteen years of age or older, to vote shall not be denied or abridged by the United States or by any state on account of age.

Section 2.

The Congress shall have power to enforce this article by appropriate legislation.

Amendment 27 (1992) Congressional Salaries

If members of Congress vote to change their own salaries, that change cannot go into effect until after the next Congressional election. This change gives voters a chance to speak out on pay raises.

Amendment 27

No law varying the compensation for the services of the senators and representatives shall take effect until an election of representatives shall have intervened.

The 26th Amendment passed mainly because many people believed that if 18-year-olds were old enough to fight for their country, they were old enough to vote.

Discussion

Checking Understanding

1. What main topics does the Twenty-fifth Amendment address? (Presidential disability and succession.)

2. What did the Twenty-sixth Amendment do? (It lowered the voting age from 21 to 18 years.)

Stimulating Critical Thinking

3. Do you think the Twenty-seventh Amendment will help check congressional pay increases? Why or why not? (Yes: voters can express their displeasure at increases by voting members of Congress out. No: incumbents have name recognition that helps them win elections even though they may vote themselves unpopular pay increases.)

Wrap-Up Activity

Writing an Essay

To review and reflect on the Constitution, have students write essays explaining why the Constitution is important to them as individuals. Their essays might focus on specific articles or amendments, or on the Constitution in general. Conclude the activity by having volunteers read their essays to the class.

Glossary

The Glossary defines terms that are important in the understanding of United States history. The page number at the end of the definition refers to the page in the text on which the term is first defined.

Pronunciation Key

In the text, words that are difficult to pronounce are followed by a respelling in parentheses. The respelling helps the reader pronounce the word. For example, Antietam (see page 140) has been respelled as an-TEET-uhm. A hyphen separates the syllables. Syllables in large capital letters are stressed the most; syllables in small capital letters are stressed in a weaker tone.

The pronunciation key appears below. Letters used in the respelling of words are listed on the left side of each column. On the right side are commonly used words that show the pronunciation.

Pronounce				
a	as in	hat	*j*	jet
ah		father	*ng*	ring
ar		tar	*o*	frog
ay		say	*ō*	no
ayr		air	*oo*	soon
e, eh		hen	*or*	for
ee		bee	*ow*	plow
eer		deer	*oy*	boy
er		her	*sh*	she
ew		new	*th*	think
g		go	*u, uh*	sun
i, ih		him	*z*	zebra
ī		kite	*zh*	measure

A

abolition putting an end to slavery (page 82)

amendment a change that is made or added to a constitution, law, bill, or motion (page 56)

anarchism the idea that all forms of government are bad and should be done away with (page 454)

annex to take control of a territory and add it to a country (page 78)

anthropologists scientists who study human beings and how they live in groups (page 25)

anti-Semitism hatred and persecution of Jews (page 298)

appeasement giving in to another nation's demands just to keep peace; policy followed before World War II by Britain and France to avoid conflict with Hitler (page 523)

arbitration using a third party to settle a dispute (page 278)

archaeologists anthropologists who search for clues to how human beings lived in the past (page 25)

armistice a truce (page 419)

arms race a competition between countries for more and better weapons (page 520)

artifacts objects made by human work (page 25)

assembly line a factory system in which the product moves from worker to worker, each of whom performs one task (page 467)

assimilate to be absorbed into the main cultural group (page 301)

B

bill of rights a list of the rights and freedoms guaranteed to the people of a state or nation; first ten amendments to the United States Constitution adopted 1791, which include a declaration of fundamental rights held by U.S. citizens (page 56)

black codes laws passed by white southern politicians after the Civil War that limited the rights and opportunities of African Americans (page 187)

blockade a shutting off of a place by ships or troops to prevent supplies from reaching it (page 50)

boycott a refusal to buy something as a form of protest (page 48)

C

cabinet the department heads of the executive branch of government who advise the President and help carry out the nation's laws (page 64)

capital money used to produce goods (page 269)

carpetbaggers northerners, including teachers, ministers, businesspeople, and former Union soldiers, who moved to the South after the Civil War to gain political or economic advantages (page 191)

cash crops crops that are raised to be sold for a profit (page 42)

casualties soldiers killed, wounded, captured, or missing (page 150)

cede to give up territory (page 48)

checks and balances the system by which each branch of government can check, or limit, the power of the other two branches (page 58)

civilization a society in which a high level of art, technology, and government exists (page 25)

civil rights the rights guaranteed to all Americans by the Constitution (page 608)

civil service the body of government workers who are hired rather than elected (page 338)

closed shop a workplace in which only union members can be hired (page 602)

Cold War the struggle for power between Communist and non-Communist countries; the rivalry between the Soviet Union and the United States that began after World War II; carried on by political and economic means rather than direct military action (page 564)

collective bargaining the process by which the representatives of a union and a business discuss and reach agreement about wages and working conditions (page 278)

colony settlement made by a group of people in a distant place that remains under the control of their home country (page 30)

communism a system in which property is owned by society as a whole instead of by individuals (page 453)

confederation an alliance of independent states (page 56)

conquistadors Spanish conquerors in the Americas during the 1500s (page 36)

conservation protecting natural resources and using them wisely (page 355)

consolidation combining several companies into one large company (page 265)

constitution plan of government; a system of principles according to which a nation, state, or group is governed (page 56)

containment the policy of blocking Communist expansion (page 565)

corporation a type of business that raises money by selling shares of stock to investors (page 269)

corruption when public office is used for illegal purposes (page 193)

credit a system in which a buyer takes home a product and then makes monthly payments until it is paid for (page 468)

culture the way of life of a group of people, including arts, beliefs, inventions, traditions, and language (page 27)

D

deficit the amount by which the government's spending is greater than its income (page 648)

détente a relaxing of tensions between nations (page 582)

dictator a person with complete control of a government (page 521)

diplomacy conducting relations with other nations (page 387)

direct primary an election, open to all members of a party, to choose candidates to run for office instead of having political party leaders choose for them (page 350)

discrimination unfair treatment of a group of people compared with another group (page 80)

diversity variety (page 42)

dividends part of the profits of a corporation earned by stockholders (page 269)

draft system that requires men to serve in the military (page 158)

due process of law following the legal steps in a court of law (page 57)

durable goods goods meant to last, like machinery and locomotives (page 489)

E

emancipation freeing of slaves (page 94)

embargo to halt trade with one or more other nations (page 66)

ethnic neighborhoods areas where people who share the same languages and culture live (page 299)

executive branch the branch of government that carries out the laws (page 56)

expedition a journey organized for a definite purpose (page 29)

exports goods sent out of one country to sell in another (page 38)

extermination total destruction (page 229)

F

fascism a political system that appeals to racism and nationalism and is ruled by a dictator and a single political party (page 521)

federalism system of government in which power is shared between state governments and a national government (page 58)

freedmen former slaves, both women and men, who lived in the South during the Reconstruction period (page 98)

free enterprise the economic system in which businesses are free to compete without government rules (page 266)

G

glaciers vast slow-moving masses of ice (page 24)

grandfather clause statements in southern voting laws, used to deny blacks the vote but allowing the vote to whites who had voted before 1867 or who had fathers or grandfathers who had the right to vote then (page 198)

H

habeas corpus right that protects people from being held in prison unlawfully (page 142)

homesteaders people who claimed land under the Homestead Act (page 241)

I

impeach to accuse the President of wrongdoing and bring him to trial (page 96)

imperialism the policy of taking control of governments and resources of other countries in order to build an empire (page 373)

imports products brought in from another country to be sold (page 43)

inauguration the ceremony that installs a new President (page 64)

income tax tax on money people earn from work or investments (page 159)

indentured servants people who signed a contract agreeing to work a certain number of years without pay for the person who paid their passage to England's American colonies (page 44)

Industrial Revolution the shift of production from hand tools to machines and from homes to factories; the era in which such a change took place (page 70)

infectious diseases illnesses that can be passed from one person to another (page 32)

initiative the process by which citizens can propose new laws (page 350)

injunction a court order (page 280)

integration the process of ending segregation (page 611)

Internet a web of computer networks linked through telephone lines (page 659)

interstate commerce business between states (page 266)

invest to use your money to help a business get started or grow, with the hope that you will earn a profit (page 30)

isolationism a principle or policy of staying out of foreign affairs; term often used to describe U.S. diplomatic policy in years between World War I and World War II (page 520)

J

Jim Crow laws segregation laws passed in the South after Reconstruction (page 98)

judicial branch the branch of government that judges laws and decides legal cases. The courts are in the judicial branch of government. (page 56)

L

legislative branch the branch of government that makes the laws. Congress is the legislative branch of the national government. (page 56)

legislature a group of people chosen to make the laws for a state or nation (page 48)

leisure free time (page 311)

M

martial law rule by the army instead of by the usual government officials (page 142)

memoirs a person's written remembrances of the events of his or her life (page 102)

mercenaries soldiers who fight for money for a country other than their own (page 52)

militia citizens trained to fight in an emergency (page 51)

minutemen militia volunteers in New England at the beginning of the War of Independence, so called because they were ready to fight on short notice (page 52)

monopoly complete control (page 50)

N

nationalism a strong feeling of pride in one's nation (page 68)

nativism belief that immigrants threaten traditional American culture and institutions (page 80)

navigation the science of getting ships from place to place (page 43)

nomads people with no permanent home who move in search of food (page 24)

O

open range thousands of miles of unfenced grassland used for grazing (page 238)

P

pacifists people who are against war under any circumstance (page 417)

Patriots strong supporters of American independence (page 53)

pension retirement income (page 496)

persecution a series of injurious actions—for example, attacking, imprisoning, torturing, or killing—carried out against members of a group for their beliefs (page 41)

plantation a large estate where a single crop that requires a large labor force is grown for profit (page 36)

platform a statement of beliefs by a political party (page 118)

political machine the organization of a political party that granted favors in return for votes (page 307)

political parties groups of voters who have similar ideas about government and who organize to elect members to public office, operate government, and determine public policy (page 64)

poll tax a fee enacted by state governments in the South that charged citizens for the right to vote and that successfully prevented black southerners from voting (page 98)

popular sovereignty the pre–Civil War principle or policy of allowing voters who lived in a newly organized territory to decide whether or not to allow slavery there (page 88)

prairie eastern part of the Great Plains, where the grasses grow tall (page 241)

proclamation official announcement (page 48)

Prohibition the banning of the manufacture, transport, and sale of liquor (page 462)

propaganda the spreading of ideas that help one cause and hurt another (page 412)

proprietary colonies colonies in which the owners, known as proprietors, organized the colonies, controlled the land, and appointed governors (page 41)

protectorate a nation protected and controlled by another nation (page 383)

R

ratify to adopt or formally approve, as in to approve a plan of government or an amendment (page 56)

rationing limiting the amount of scarce goods that people can buy (page 529)

rebates refunds to the buyers of part of the fees or prices for purchased products or services (page 265)

recall a process by which the people can vote to remove an elected official from office before the end of his or her term (page 350)

Reconstruction the task of bringing Confederate states back into the Union after the Civil War; the period when it was done (page 96)

referendum the process by which citizens can approve or reject a law passed by a state legislature (page 350)

regulate make rules for (page 266)

reparations payments for war damages (page 423)

repeal to do away with a law (page 50)

representatives people who are chosen to speak and act in government for their fellow citizens (page 33)

republic a government run by elected representatives of the people (page 73)

reservations areas of land set aside for Indian nations (page 230)

revival a renewed interest in religion; a stirring up of religious faith (page 82)

S

scalawags white southerners who joined the Republican Party during Reconstruction (page 190)

secede to withdraw formally from an organization or a nation, as in a state breaking away from the United States (page 91)

sectionalism devotion to the interests of one's own section of the country over those of the nation as a whole (page 91)

segregation the forced separation of races in public places and housing (page 98)

self-determination the right of the people of a certain nation to decide how they want to be governed without the influence of any other country (page 421)

settlement house a community center that provided services—from English-language classes to hot meals—to the poor (page 308)

sharecropping a system where tenant farmers pay a part of their crop as rent, rather than using cash (page 197)

socialism the belief that government, rather than individuals, should own a nation's major industries (page 281)

social reform the effort to make society better and more fair for everyone (page 82)

sod the thick mat of roots and earth beneath the prairie grasses (page 241)

spheres of influence areas in one nation in which other nations claim exclusive rights to trade and invest (page 385)

spoils system the practice of rewarding political supporters with government jobs (page 76)

stalemate deadlock; a situation in which no action can be taken (page 409)

stockholders investors who own stock in corporations (page 269)

strategic arms weapons designed to strike at an enemy's military bases and industrial centers (page 583)

suburbs communities on the outskirts of cities (page 460)

suffragists people who supported the right of women to vote (page 351)

T

temperance moderation in drinking habits (page 82)

tenant farmers people who pay rent for the use of land on which they grow crops (page 197)

tenements apartment houses where large families shared one or two rooms, often without heat or water (page 305)

Tidewater waterways in the Atlantic Coastal Plain affected by the tide (page 42)

totalitarian state a country in which the government controls all areas of its citizens' lives (page 521)

total war war against armies and also against a people's resources and their will to fight (page 95)

transcontinental railroad a rail line extending across the continent from coast to coast (page 115)

trust a form of business combination in which a board of trustees, or managers, controlled the member corporations (page 272)

tyranny the harsh use of power (page 43)

U

urbanization the movement of people into cities (page 304)

V

vaudeville a stage show that combined songs, dance, opera, and comedy (page 312)

Index

The purpose of the Index is to help you quickly locate information on any topic in this book. The Index includes references not only to the text but also to special features, illustrations, and maps. *Italicized* page numbers preceded by an *f, i,* or *m* indicate a feature, an illustration, or a map. **Boldface** page numbers indicate pages on which glossary terms first appear.

A

I N D E X

B

C

INDEX

F

J

K

L

M

INDEX

Q

R

INDEX

T

Y

Z

Acknowledgments

Quoted Material

Chapter 1: 130–132 Excerpts from James W. C. Pennington, *The Fugitive Blacksmith,* 1849. **133** "The Kansas Emigrants" by John Greenleaf Whittier, 1854.

Chapter 2: 170–171 From *Bull Run* by Paul Fleischman. Copyright © 1993 by Paul Fleischman. Reprinted by permission of HarperCollins Publishers. **172** Excerpts from *The Rise of American Civilization* by Charles and Mary Beard. Copyright 1927 The Macmillan Company; copyright renewed © 1955 by Mary R. Beard. Reprinted with permission of Macmillan Publishing Company. **173** Excerpts from *The Repressible Conflict, 1830–1861* by Avery Craven. Louisiana State University Press, 1939. Reprinted by permission. **174** Excerpts from *Battle Cry of Freedom: The Civil War Era* by James M. McPherson. Copyright © 1988 by Oxford University Press, Inc. Reprinted by permission.

Chapter 3: 206 Excerpts from Frederick Douglass, "What the Black Man Wants," 1865. **207** Excerpts abridged from the preface to *The Tragic Era* by Claude Bowers. Copyright © 1929 by Claude G. Bowers. Copyright renewed 1957 by Claude G. Bowers. Reprinted by permission of Houghton Mifflin Company. **208** From *The Era of Reconstruction, 1865–1877* by Kenneth M. Stampp. Copyright © 1965 by Kenneth M. Stampp. Reprinted by permission of Alfred A. Knopf, Inc. **209** Excerpt from *Reconstruction: America's Unfinished Revolution* by Eric Foner. Copyright © 1988 by Erik Foner. Reprinted by permission of Harper & Row, Publishers, Inc.

Chapter 4: 248–249 From *Dragon's Gate* by Laurence Yep. Copyright © 1993 by Laurence Yep. Reprinted by permission of HarperCollins Publishers. **250–251** Excerpts from *A Bride Goes West* by N. T. Alderson and H. H. Smith by permission of University of Nebraska Press. Copyright © 1942 by Farrar & Rinehart, Inc. **252–253** Excerpt from *Wild Bill, the Pistol Deadshot; or, Dagger Don's Double* by Prentiss Ingraham. Number 168 of Beadle's Dime Library. (New York: Beadle & Adams). 1882.

Chapter 5: 284–285 Excerpts from *The Life Stories of Undistinguished Americans: as Told by Themselves* edited by Hamilton Holt. New York: James Pott & Company, 1906. **285–286** Excerpts from "Fincher's Trades' Review," Oct. 14, 1865. Cited in *Bread and Roses:* "Labor Standard," 1872. **286–287** Excerpts from *Seventy Years of Life and Labor* by Samuel Gompers. Copyright 1925 by E. P. Dutton & Co., Inc.: renewal © 1953 by Gertrude Gleaves Gompers. Reprinted by permission of the publishers, E. P. Dutton & Co., Inc. **287** Excerpts from *Addresses and Writings of George F. Baer* collected by William N. Appel. (Lancaster, PA: Privately Printed). 1916.

Chapter 6: 318–320 Excerpts from *A Bintel Brief* by Isaac Metzker. Translation Copyright © 1971 by Isaac Metzker. Reprinted by permission of Doubleday & Company, Inc. **320–321** Excerpts from *An American in the Making* by Marcus E. Ravage. (New York: Harper & Bros.), 1917.

Chapter 7: 360–362 Excerpts from "Jane Addams" from *Some Dissenting Voices* by Arthur and Lila Weinberg. Copyright 1970 by Arthur and Lila Weinberg. The World Publishing Company. **362–363** Excerpts from Florence Kelley's address to the Massachusetts Woman Suffrage Association, 1903.

Chapter 8: 394–395 Excerpts from James D. Richardson, ed., *A Compilation of the Messages and Papers of the Presidents, 1789–1897* (Washington, 1899) 9: 460–472. **396–397** From Stephen Crane, *War Is Kind,* 1899.

Chapter 9: 440–441 From *After the Dancing Days* by Margaret I. Rostkowski. Copyright © 1986 by Margaret I. Rostkowski. Reprinted by permission of HarperCollins Publishers.

Chapter 10: 474 "I, Too, Sing America": From *Selected Poems* by Langston Hughes. Copyright © 1926 by Alfred A. Knopf Inc. and renewed 1954 by Langston Hughes. Reprinted by permission of the publisher. **475** "Juke Box Love Song": From *Collected Poems* by Langston Hughes. Copyright © 1994 by The Estate of Langston Hughes. Reprinted by permission of Alfred A. Knopf Inc. "The Dream Keeper": From *The Dream Keeper and Other Poems* by Langston Hughes. Copyright © 1932 and renewed 1960 by Langston Hughes. Reprinted by permission of Alfred A. Knopf Inc. **476–478** Excerpt from *Bario Boy* by Ernesto Galarza. Copyright © 1971 by University of Notre Dame Press. Reprinted by permission.

Chapter 11: 508–509 Excerpts from "Children of the Grapes of Wrath" by Jerry Stanley, first appeared in *The American West,* 1986. Reprinted by permission of the author.

Chapter 12: 546–547 From *Brave Men* by Ernie Pyle. Copyright 1943, 1944 by Scripps-Howard Newspaper Alliance. Copyright 1944 by Ernie Pyle. Copyright © 1971 by Holt, Rinehart and Winston. Reprinted by permission of Henry Holt and Company, Inc. **548** Excerpt from *Decision to Drop the Bomb* by Len Giovannitti and Fred Freed. Copyright © 1965 by Len Giovannitti and Fred Freed. Reprinted by permission of Coward, McCann & Geoghegan, Inc., and Methuen and Co. Ltd. **549** Excerpts from *Memoirs by Harry S Truman: Years of Decision,* Vol. 1, Doubleday & Company, Inc. Copyright © 1956 by Time, Inc. Reprinted by permission.

Chapter 13: 590 Excerpt from "The Revolution in U.S. Foreign Policy" by Hans J. Morgenthau, *Commentary,* February 1957. Reprinted by permission of Mathew Morgenthau. **591** Excerpts from *The Limits of Power* by Joyce

Kolko and Gabriel Kolko. Copyright © 1972 by Joyce and Gabriel Kolko. Reprinted by permission of Harper & Row, Publishers, Inc. **592** Excerpts from *Soviet-American Confrontation: Postwar Reconstruction and the Origins of the Cold War* by Thomas G. Paterson, pp. 260–261. Baltimore, Maryland: The Johns Hopkins University Press, 1973.

Chapter 14: 630–631 Excerpts from "Letter from Birmingham Jail" from *Why We Can't Wait* by Martin Luther King, Jr. Copyright © 1963 by Martin Luther King, Jr. Reprinted by permission of Harper & Row, Publishers, Inc. **632–633** Excerpt abridged from "A Passion for the Covert: The Response to the Threat of Discovery" by Carl Bernstein and Bob Woodward from *The Fall of a President.* Copyright © 1974 by The Washington Post Company. Reprinted by permission.

Chapter 15: 666–667 Excerpts from "Here to Stay at Last" by Eric Schurenberg is reprinted from *Money Magazine* by special permission. Copyright 1987 The Time Inc. Magazine Company. **668–669** "Constitution Anyone? A New Cottage Industry," by Liz Wiehl, *New York Times,* February 2, 1990. Copyright © 1990 by the New York Times Company. Reprinted by permission. **674–675** From *The House on Mango Street.* Copyright © 1991 by Sandra Cisneros. Published by Vintage Books, a division of Random House, Inc., New York and originally in hardcover by Random House, Inc. Reprinted by permission of Susan Bergholz Literary Services, New York. All rights reserved.

Photos

Unless otherwise acknowledged, all photos are the property of Scott Foresman – Addison Wesley. Page positions are as follows: **T** (Top), **C** (center), **L** (left), **R** (right), **INS** (inset).

Front Matter: ii Terry Ashe*; **xxiv** J. L. Atlan/Sygma

Prologue: 1BR From *Virginia, A Pictorial History,* by Parke Rouse, Jr.; **1BL** Copyright the British Museum; **1 Background** Randy Wells/Tony Stone Images; **2** John Shaw/Tom Stack & Associates; **4** Tom Algire/Tom Stack & Associates; **5** Ray Richardson/Animals Animals; **6** Culver Pictures Inc.; **7** Museum of Art, Rhode Island School of Design; **8** Culver Pictures Inc.; **9** Phelps Stokes Collection/Prints Division/New York Public Library, Astor, Lenox and Tilden Foundations; **10B** Library of Congress; **10T & 11** Chicago Historical Society; **12** Culver Pictures Inc.; **13** Brown Brothers; **14** Courtesy of the California Historical Society, San Francisco, CA; **15** Culver Pictures Inc.; **15INS** James H. Karales/Peter Arnold, Inc.; **16B** Brian Parker/Tom Stack & Associates; **16TR** Culver Pictures Inc.; **16TL** Western History Collections, University of Oklahoma Library; **17** National Museum of American Art/Art Resource

Review (Section 1): 20 Jerry Jacka; **21T** New York State Historical Association; **21B** Copyright Yale University Art Gallery, Trumbull Collection; **22T** Scala/Art Resource; **22B** Jon Levy/Gamma-Liaison; **23** Library of Congress, Geography & Maps Division; **24L** Corbis/Bettmann Archive; **24R** Erich Lessing/Art Resource; **25L** Peter French/Bruce Coleman Inc.; **25CL** Boltin Picture Library; **25CR** St. Louis Museum of Science and Natural History, Photo: Dirk Bakker; **25R** Boltin Picture Library; **26T** Scala/Art Resource; **26B** Kenneth Garett/Woodfin Camp & Associates; **28L** Michael Holford; **28R** Corbis/Bettmann Archive; **29CR** Giraudon/Art Resource; **29BL** Corbis/Bettmann Archive; **29CL** Robert Harding Picture Library; **29BR** Rare Book Room & Manuscript Division/New York Public Library, Astor, Lenox & Tilden Foundations; **30L** Robert Frerck/Odyssey Productions; **30R** John Carter Brown Library at Brown University; **31L** Francisco Erize/Bruce Coleman Inc.; **31C** Germanisches National Museum, Nurnberg; **31R** Tate Gallery, London/Art Resource; **32T** National Museum of American Art, Washington, D.C./Art Resource; **32C** Courtesy Department of Library Services/ American Museum of Natural History

Review (Section 2): 34T National Portrait Gallery, Washington, D.C., Smithsonian Institution; **34B** Corbis/Bettmann Archive; **35** Aldo Tutino/Art Resource; **36L** Giraudon/Art Resource; **36R** Oakland Museum History Department; **37T** Laura Platt Winfrey, Inc.; **37BL** Jim Schwabel/Southern Stock Photo Agency/Index Stock Photography; **37BC** Corbis/Bettmann Archive; **37BR** Paul Mellon Collection/National Gallery of Art, Washington, D.C.; **38L** Colonial Williamsburg Foundation; **38R** Culver Pictures Inc.; **39T** Colonial National Historical Park/Eastern National Parks & Monuments Association; **39BR** Corbis/Bettmann Archive; **39BC** Philadelphia Museum of Art, Given by John T. Morris; **39BR** American Antiquarian Society, Worcester, MA; **40** Metacomet, Shelburne Museum, Shelburne, VT; **41** Ad for Virginia Settlers, New York Public Library, Astor Lenox & Tilden Foundations; **42L** American Antiquarian Society; **42R** Massachusetts Historical Society; **43L** National Portrait Gallery, London; **43C** Yale University Art Gallery/Franklin Collection; **43R** Rare Books and Manuscripts Division/New York Public Library, Astor, Lenox and Tilden Foundations; **44T** National Maritime Museum, London; **44B** Maryland Historical Society, Baltimore

Review (Section 3): 46T Washington and Lee University, Lexington, Washington/Curtis/Lee Collection; **46B** Culver Pictures Inc.; **47** Anne S. K. Brown Military Collection/Brown University Library; **48L** Library of Congress, Geography & Map Divison, National Geographic Society, Photo by Breton Littlehales; **48R** Colonial Williamsburg Foundation; **49L** Museum of Fine Arts Boston, Boston, Deposited by the City of Boston; **49C** American Antiquarian Society; **49R** Library of Congress; **50** Library of Congress; **52L** Robert Weinreb/Bruce Coleman Inc.; **52C** Corbis/Bettmann Archive; **53TL** Corbis/ Bettmann Archive; **53TR** Corbis/Bettmann Archive; **53BR**

National Archives; **53BC** Corbis/Bettmann Archive; **53BL** Corbis/Bettmann Archive; **54** Delaware Art Museum, Howard Pyle Collection; **55** Michael Anderson/Folio, Inc.; **56** National Archives; **57L** National Portrait Gallery/Smithsonian Institution; **57C** Independence National Historical Park Collection; **57R** Collection of the New-York Historical Society, New York City

Review (Section 4): 60 Chicago Historical Society; **61T** National Museum of American Art/Bequest of Sarah Carr Upton/Art Resource; **61B** Chicago Historical Society; **62T** Print Division, Miriam and Ira D. Wallach DIvision of Arts, Prints and Photographs/New York Public Library; **62B** Yale University Art Gallery, The Mabel Brady Garvan Collection; **63** The Hermitage, Home of Andrew Jackson, Nashville, TN; **64L** National Portrait Gallery, Smithsonian Institution/Art Resource; **64R** Jefferson campaign broadside, New York Historical Society; **65TL** National Portrait Gallery, Smithsonian Institution/Art Resource; **65TR** Copyright the White House Historical Association, photography by National Geographic Society; **65BL** Corbis/Bettmann Archive; **65BC** Collection of the New-York Historical Society; **66BL** Collection of the Supreme Court of the United States; **66BR** Smithsonian Institution, Photo 83.7221; **67TL** Collection of the New-York Historical Society; **67TR** Private Collection: photo courtesy of Monticello, Thomas Jefferson Memorial Foundation; **67TC** Earl Gregg Swem Library, College of William and Mary; **67TB** Monticello, Thomas Jefferson Memorial Foundation; **67BL** Culver Pictures Inc.; **67BC** Collection of the New-York Historical Society; **67BR** Smithsonian Institution, Photo 83.7221; **68L** Oregon Historical Society, Neg. # OrHi 38090; **68R** Oregon Historical Society, Neg. # OrHi 38091; **70L** Slater Mill Historic Site, Pawtucket, Rhode Island; **70R** National Museum of American History/Smithsonian Institution, photo #73-11287; **71TC** Giraudon/Art Resource; **71TR** Culver Pictures Inc.; **71BL** I. N. Phelps Stokes Collection/Miriam and Ira D. Wallach Division of Arts, Prints and Photographs/New York Public Library, Aster, Lenox and Tilden Foundation; **71BC** Library of Congress; **71BR** National Portrait Gallery, Smithsonian Institution/Art Resource; **72** New York Public Library, Astor, Lenox & Tilden Foundations

Review (Section 5): 74T J. R. Eyeman/Time Life Inc.; **74B** From the collection of the Madison County Historical Society, Oneida, NY; **75** Corbis/Bettmann Archive; **76L** National Numismatic Collection, Washington, D.C./Smithsonian Institution; **76R** Gift of the Seawanhaka Corinthian Yacht Club/Museum of the City of New York, Neg. 52.11; **77BL** Hood Museum of Art, Dartmouth College, Hanover, NH, Gift of the artists; **77BCL** Stock Montage, Inc.; **77BCR** Philbrook Museum of Art, Tulsa, OK; **77BR** Political History Dept./Smithsonian Institution; **78L** Rare Book Division, New York Public Library, Astor, Lenox & Tilden Foundations; **78R** Buffalo Bill Historical Center/Gift of the Coe Foundation; **79BL** U.S. Postal Service; **79BC** National Museum of American Art, Smithsonian Institution, Washington, D.C./Gift of Bryant Baker/Art Resource; **79BR** National Archives; **80L** National Museum of American Art, Washington, D.C. Gift of the Harmon Foundation/Art Resource; **80R** Culver Pictures Inc.; **81T** Culver Pictures Inc.; **81TC** Culver Pictures Inc.; **81BC** New York Public Library, Astor, Lenox and Tilden Foundations; **81BL** National Maritime Museum, London; **81BC** Smithsonian Institution, Neg. # 27979; **81BR** Corbis/Bettmann Archive; **82L** Abby Aldrich Rockefeller Folk Art Center, Williamsburg, VA; **82R** New York Public Library, Astor, Lenox & Tilden Foundations; **83T** Flip Schulke/Black Star; **83BL** Corbis/Bettmann Archive; **83BC** Culver Pictures Inc.; **83BR** Culver Pictures Inc.; **84L** Culver Pictures Inc.; **84R** Publisher: Currier and Ives/Museum of the City of New York, The Harry T. Peters Collection

Review (Section 6): 86T National Archives; **86BL** Culver Pictures Inc.; **86BR** Granger Collection; **87T** Newberry Library; **87B** Culver Pictures Inc.; **88L** Corbis/Bettmann Archive; **88R** Dept. of Special Collections and University Archives/Stanford University Libraries; **89T** Corbis/Bettmann Archive; **89TC** Chicago Historical Society; **89TB** Collection of the New-York Historical Society; **89BL** Corbis/Bettmann Archive; **89BC** Boston Athenaeum; **89BR** The Museum of the Confederacy, Richmond, VA, Photo by Katherine Wetzel; **92L** Corbis/Bettmann Archive; **92R** Library of Congress; **93T** (hat) From *Echoes of Glory: Arms & Equipment of the Union.* Collection of Chris Nelson, photo by Larry Scherer. ©1991 Time-Life Books Inc.; **93T** (tin cup) The Museum of the Confederacy, Richmond, VA., Photo by Katherine Wetzel; **93T** (canteen) The Museum of the Confederacy, Richmond, VA; **93T** (shoes & silverware) From *Echoes of Glory: Arms & Equipment of the Union.* Collection of Chris Nelson, photo by Larry Scherer, ©1991 Time-Life Books Inc.; **93BL** *Forever Free,* 1933 by Sargent Claude Johnson. Wood with lacquer on cloth, 36 x 11-1/2 x 9-1/2 in. San Francisco Museum of Modern Art, Gift of Mrs. E. D. Lederman; **93BC** The West Point Museum, United States Military Academy, West Point, New York. Photo by Karen Willis; **93BR** Library of Congress; **94** Library of Congress; **95** Sam Abell, © National Geographic Society; **96L** Corbis/Bettmann Archive; **96R** Library of Congress; **97T** Rutherford B. Hayes Presidential Center; **97BC** Library of Congress; **97BR** Corbis/Bettmann Archive; **98T** Library of Congress; **98B** Elliott Erwitt/Magnum Photos; **100** Terry Ashe*; **101** Courtesy Fred Veil; **102** Library of Congress; **103** Cheryl Fenton*

Unit 1: 104–105 Chicago Historical Society

Chapter 1: 106L The Bettmann Archive; **106R** Department of Special Collections and University Archives, Stanford University Library; **107T** Library of Congress; **107BL** The

Bettmann Archive; **107BC** Boston Athenaeum; **107BR** The Museum of the Confederacy, Richmond, Virginia, photo by Katherine Wetzel; **108** Meserve-Kunhardt Collection; **109** *The Railsplitter,* 1860. Chicago Historical Society. Gift of Maibelle Heikes Justice; **111** Collection of The New-York Historical Society, New York City; **112** The Granger Collection, New York; **113TL** Collection of The New-York Historical Society, New York City; **113TR** The Bettmann Archive; **113BL** Meserve-Kunhardt Collection; **113BR** Chicago Historical Society; **115L** Smithsonian Institution; **115R** Schlesinger Library, Radcliffe College; **117** Kansas State Historical Society, Topeka, Kansas; **118** The Granger Collection, New York; **120** *Dred Scott,* 1881, by Louis Schultze. Missouri Historical Society; **121L** *Lincoln-Douglas Debate at Charleston, Illinois* (detail) by Robert Marshall Root. Henry Horner Lincoln Collection, Illinois State Historical Library; **121R** Ira Wyman/Sygma; **123** *John Brown Going to His Hanging,* 1942 by Horace Pippin. The Pennsylvania Academy of the Fine Arts, Philadelphia. John Lambert Fund; **127** Robert Llewellyn; **130** Library Company of Philadelphia; **131** State Historical Society of Wisconsin; **132** North Carolina Department of Cultural Resources, Division of Archives & History; **133** Kansas State Historical Society, Topeka; **134** National Archives; **135** Frank Leslie's *Illustrated Newspaper,* June 27, 1857; **136–137** Library of Congress

Chapter 2: 138L The Bettmann Archive; **138R** Library of Congress; **139T** Private Collection; **139BL** *Forever Free,* 1933 by Sargent Claude Johnson. Wood with lacquer on cloth, 36 x 11 1/2 x 9 1/2 in. San Francisco Museum of Modern Art. Gift of Mrs. E. D. Lederman; **139BC** *First Day of Gettysburg* (detail) by James Walker. The West Point Museum, United States Military Academy, West Point, New York. Photo by Karen Willis; **139BR** Library of Congress; **140** National Archives; **141** The Bettmann Archive; **144T** (hat) From *Echoes of Glory: Arms & Equipment of the Union.* Collection of Chris Nelson, photo by Larry Scherer. ©1991 Time-Life Books Inc.; **144T** (tin cup) The Museum of the Confederacy, Richmond, VA., Photo by Katherine Wetzel; **144T** (canteen) The Museum of the Confederacy, Richmond, VA; **144T** (shoes & silverware) From *Echoes of Glory: Arms & Equipment of the Union.* Collection of Chris Nelson, photo by Larry Scherer, ©1991 Time-Life Books Inc.; **145** Library of Congress; **146** *Sounding Reveille,* 1865 by Winslow Homer. Oil on canvas, 13 1/4 x 19 1/2 in. Private Collection, photo courtesy of Gerald Peters Gallery; **149** *An August Morning with Farragut: The Battle of Mobile Bay, August 5, 1864,* 1883 by William Heysham Overend. Wadsworth Atheneum, Hartford. Gift of the citizens of Hartford by Subscription, May 24, 1886; **152TR** National Archives; **152TC** The Bettmann Archive; **152CL** Meserve-Kunhardt Collection; **153** Library of Congress; **155** Library of Congress; **157TL** The Granger Collection, New York; **157B** Culver Pictures; **157TR** Eleanor S. Brockenbrough Library/The Museum of the Confederacy, Richmond, Virginia; **158** Library of Congress; **159** National Archives; **160** Cheryl Fenton*; **161** *Stonewall Jackson at the Battle of Winchester, VA.* by L. M. D. Guillaume. R. W. Norton Art Gallery, Shreveport, Louisiana; **162** *First Day of Gettysburg* by James Walker. The West Point Museum, United States Military Academy, West Point, New York. Photo by Karen Willis; **164** Sam Abell, © National Geographic Society; **165** *Surrender at Appomattox* by Tom Lovell. © National Geographic Society; **167** David Muench; **170** Stephen Frisch*; **171** Culver Pictures; **173** Gettysburg National Military Park; **175** Library of Congress; **177** Museum of Fine Arts Boston

Chapter 3: 180L The Bettmann Archive; **180R** Library of Congress; **181T** The Newberry Library; **181BR** *William Edward B. Du Bois* by W. Reiss. The Bettmann Archive; **181BC** Library of Congress; **182** Photographs and Prints Division, Schomburg Center for Research in Black Culture/The New York Public Library, Astor, Lenox and Tilden Foundations; **183** Cook Collection/Valentine Museum, Richmond, Virginia; **185** Cook Collection/Valentine Museum, Richmond, Virginia; **188–189** Culver Pictures; **191** David Butow/Black Star; **193** Library of Congress; **194** Rutherford B. Hayes Presidential Center; **195** Cheryl Fenton*; **197** Brown Brothers; **199** *Aspects of Negro Life: From Slavery through Reconstruction* by Aaron Douglas. Photo by Manu Sassoonian. Arts and Artifacts Division. Schomburg Center for Research in Black Culture. The New York Public Library; Astor, Lenox and Tilden Foundations; **200** Elliott Erwitt/Magnum Photos, Inc.; **201** Library of Congress; **203** Old Court House Museum, Vicksburg, MS; **206** *Harper's Weekly,* November 16, 1867; **206** *Harper's Weekly,* June 4, 1870; **207** *Harper's Weekly,* April 24, 1875; **208** Florida State Archives; **211** Library of Congress; **212T** Costa Manos/Magnum Photos; **212B** Library of Congress; **213B** Ed Clark/Time Life Inc.; **215** James Woodcock/Billings Gazette; **216** NAA/Smithsonian Institution; **217** Scott Rutherford, © National Geographic Society

Unit 2: 218–219 Library of Congress, Geography and Maps Division

Chapter 4: 220L John Deere; **220R** Union Pacific Museum Collection; **221T** John Livzey/Tony Stone Images; **221BL** Negatives/Transparencies #3273(2), courtesy Department of Library Services, American Museum of Natural History; **221BC** Courtesy Frederic Remington Art Museum, Ogdensburg, NY; **221BR** Rod Planck/Tony Stone Images; **222** Photo by Hutchins and Lanney, 1892. NAA/Smithsonian Institution; **223** Smithsonian Institution; **224** *Herd of Bison, Near Lake Jessie* by John Mix Stanley © Smithsonian Books, photo by Ed Castle; **225** National Archives. Photography by PhotoAssist; **227INS** José Fuste Raga/The Stock Market; **227** Photo by W. G. Chamberlain, 1860. Denver Public

Library, Western History Department; **228** Union Pacific Museum Collection; **231** Oklahoma Historical Society; **233** Library of Congress; **235L** Library of Congress; **235C** National Museum of the American Indian, Smithsonian Institution; **235R** National Museum of the American Indian, Smithsonian Institution; **237** National Archives. Photography by PhotoAssist; **239** The Bancroft Library, University of California, Berkeley; **240** Library of Congress; **241** Corbis/Bettmann Archive; **242** Library of Congress; **243** Solomon D. Butcher Collection, Nebraska State Historical Society; **245** Western History Collections, University of Oklahoma Library; **248** California State Railroad Museum; **249L** California State Railroad Museum; **249R** Kentucky Historical Society; **250** Nebraska State Historical Society, Solomon D. Butcher Collection; **253** Western History Collections/University of Oklahoma Libraries, University of Oklahoma; **254** Museum of Church History and Art, Salt Lake City, Utah; **255** Union Pacific Museum Collection; **256** Corbis/Bettmann; **257** AP/Wide World

Chapter 5: 258L Corbis/Bettmann; **258R** Library of Congress; **259T** UPI/Corbis-Bettmann; **259BL** Brown Brothers; **259BC** The George Meany Memorial Archives; **259BR** Library of Congress; **260** Culver Pictures; **261** Bethlehem Steel Corporation; **264** Sears, Roebuck and Co.; **265L** Randall Hyman; **265R** Library of Congress; **266** Culver Pictures; **267T** John Elk III/Stock, Boston; **267B** Minnesota Historical Society; **269** Culver Pictures; **272L** The Granger Collection, New York; **272R** Brown Brothers; **274** Cheryl Fenton*; **276L** The Texas Collection, Baylor University, Waco, Texas; **276TR** Photo by Lewis W. Hine. George Eastman House Collection; **276BR** Brown Brothers; **276C** Photo by Lewis W. Hine. Library of Congress; **278** UPI/Corbis-Bettmann; **279** Library of Congress; **280** *The Ironworkers' Noontime* (1880) by Thomas Pollock Anshutz. The Fine Arts Museums of San Francisco, Gift of Mr. and Mrs. John D. Rockefeller 3rd, 1979.7.4; **284** Brown Brothers; **286** Brown Brothers; **287** Library Company of Philadelphia; **288** Chicago Historical Society; **289** New-York Historical Society, New York City; **291** Reprinted by permission: Tribune Media Services

Chapter 6: 292L Brown Brothers; **292R** Corbis-Bettmann; **293T** Danilo G. Donadoni/Bruce Coleman Inc.; **293BL** Chuck Pefley/Stock, Boston; **293BC** Phil Degginger/Bruce Coleman Inc.; **293BR** *Triangle Fire, 1911* (detail), by Victor Joseph Gatto. Oil on canvas, 19 × 28 inches. Gift of Mrs. Henry L. Moses, Museum of the City of New York; **294** Culver Pictures; **295** Photograph by Jacob A. Riis. The Jacob A. Riis Collection. Museum of the City of New York; **297** Library of Congress; **299** The Staten Island Historical Society. Photo by E. Alice Austen; **301** RG 85, Records of the Immigration and Naturalization Service, National Archives—Pacific Sierra Region; **302** Jacques Chenet/Woodfin Camp & Associates; **305** Chicago Historical Society, neg. #ICHi-04191; **306** Patricia Layman Bazelon/Lauren Tent, Buffalo, New York; **311L** Susan Lina Ruggles/Third Coast Stock Source; **311R** Culver Pictures; **312** Collection of The New-York Historical Society, New York City; **313** *Central Park, 1901* by Maurice Prendergast. Watercolor on paper. 14 3/8 × 21 5/8 in. (36.5 × 54.9 cm.) Collection of Whitney Museum of American Art. Purchase 32.42. Photograph Copyright © 1996: Whitney Museum of American Art, New York; **318** Ella Gallup Sumner and Mary Catlin Sumner Collection/ Wadsworth Atheneum, Hartford, CT; **319** Library of Congress; **321** Courtesy, Minnesota Historical Society; **323** Culver Pictures Inc.; **324T** International Museum of Photography/George Eastman House; **325T** Albin O. Kuhn Library and Gallery, University of Maryland, Baltimore; **324–325** Michael Schwarz/Image Works; **327** Library of Congress; **328L** Library of Congress; **328R** Lewis W. Hine Collection, U.S. History, Local History and Genealogy Div., The New York Public Library, Astor, Lenox & Tilden Foundations; **329** Cheryl Fenton*

Unit 3: 330–331 *The Fleet Entering the Golden Gate, May 6, 1908* (Detail) by Henry Reuterdahl, U.S. Naval Academy Museum

Chapter 7: 332L Stanley King Collection; **332R** *The Purposes of the Grange* (detail), 1873 lithograph. Library of Congress; **333T** Library of Congress; **333BL** The Granger Collection, New York; **333BC** The Granger Collection, New York; **333BR** Schomburg Center for Research in Black Culture, The Research Libraries, The New York Public Library; **334** University of Illinois at Chicago, The University Library, Jane Addams Memorial Collection; **335** Brown Brothers; **337** Library of Congress; **338** Bob Daemmrich/Stock, Boston; **339L** Division of Political History/National Museum of American History/Smithsonian Institution; **339C** Division of Political History/National Museum of American History/ Smithsonian Institution; **339R** The Oakland Museum History Department; **340T** Cheryl Fenton*; **340B** Culver Pictures; **342** Library of Congress; **343** (portrait) The Kansas City Star Company; **343** (border) The Kansas State Historical Society; **344** S.S. Archives, Shooting Star; **345** Division of Political History/National Museum of American History/ Smithsonian Institution; **346** Grant Heilman/Grant Heilman Photography; **348** Corbis-Bettmann; **349** The Granger Collection, New York; **351L** UPI/Corbis-Bettmann; **351R** Brown Brothers; **352INS** Schomburg Center for Research in Black Culture, The Research Library, The New York Public Library; **352R** UPI/Corbis-Bettmann; **354** Culver Pictures; **355** Culver Pictures; **356** Culver Pictures; **361** Chicago Historical Society; **362** Library of Congress; **363** Child laborer, George House Eastman, International Museum of Photography; **364** Library of Congress; **365** AP/Wide World; **366–367** AP/Wide World

Chapter 8: 368L National Archives; **368R** Stanley King Collection; **369T** From *Harper's Pictorial History of the War with Spain,* 1899; **369L** *The Fleet Entering the Golden Gate, May 6, 1908* (Detail) by Henry Reuterdahl, U.S. Naval Academy Museum; **369C** Private Collection; **369R** Library of Congress; **370** Brown Brothers; **371** Theodore Roosevelt Collection, Harvard College Library; **373** The Granger Collection, New York; **374** Collection of the New-York Historical Society, New York City; **378** Collection of the New-York Historical Society, New York City; **379** Chicago Historical Society; **380** Library of Congress; **382** Charles Phelps Cushing/H. Armstrong Roberts; **384** Cheryl Fenton*; **385** The Granger Collection, New York; **386L** The Metropolitan Museum of Art, Gift of Paul J. Sachs, 1916 (16.2.9); **386R** The James A. Michener Collection, Honolulu Academy of the Arts (HAA20,799); **388L** Library of Congress; **388R** Harvey Lloyd/The Stock Market; **389** The Granger Collection, New York; **394** Library of Congress; **395** Hawaii State Archives; **396L** Newark Public Library photo; **396R** New York Public Library, Astor, Lenox & Tilden Foundations; **397** Trustees of the Imperial War Museum, London; **399** Culver Pictures Inc.; **400L** Supreme Court Historical Society; **400R** Culver Pictures Inc.; **401** Corbis/Bettmann

Chapter 9: 402L Austrian National Tourist Office; **402R** Brown Brothers; **403T** The American Numismatic Society; **403BL** Library of Congress; **403BC** National Archives; **403BR** Detail from *The Signing of Peace in the Hall of Mirrors, Versailles, 28th June,* 1919 by Sir William Orpen. By courtesy of the Trustees of the Imperial War Museum, London. Photo by Larry Burrows; **404** Brown Brothers; **405** Culver Pictures; **406** Corbis-Bettmann; **409** Brown Brothers; **413** The West Point Museum Collections, United States Military Academy; **414** UPI/Corbis-Bettmann; **415** Corbis-Bettmann; **416** *The Rope Dancer Accompanies Herself with Her Shadows,* 1916, by Man Ray. Oil on canvas, 52" × 6'1-3/4" (132.1 × 186.4 cm). The Museum of Modern Art, New York. Gift of G. David Thompson. Photograph © 1996 The Museum of Modern Art, New York; **417** Library of Congress; **420T** Cheryl Fenton*; **420C** Poster by W. A. Rogers; **420B** Library of Congress; **424** UPI/Corbis-Bettmann; **426T** Culver Pictures Inc.; **426BL** UPI/Corbis/Bettmann; **426BR** Corbis-Bettmann; **427TL** National Archives; **427TR** FPG International Corp.; **427BL** National Archives; **427BR** National Archives; **428–429 Background** National Archives; **428L** National Archives; **428R** National Archives; **429TL** National Archives; **429TR** UPI/Corbis/Bettmann; **429B** Dennis Brack/Black Star; **433** Library of Congress; **434** Lawrence, Jacob. "Industries attempted to board their labor in quarters that were oftentimes very unhealthy. Labor camps were numerous." Panel 46 from "The Migration Series," (1940–41; text and title revised by the artist, 1993). Tempera on gesso on composition board, 18 x 12' (45.7 x 30.5 cm). The Museum of Modern Art, New York. Gift of Mrs. David M. Levy. Photograph ©1995 The Museum of Modern Art, New York.; **435T** Phillips Collection, Washington, D. C.; **435B** Phillips Collection, Washington, D.C.; **436** New Jersey Historical Society; **437** Corbis/Bettmann; **439** Drawing by P. Steiner; ©1993 The New Yorker Magazine, Inc.; **440** The West Point Museum Collections, United States Military Academy, photo by Joshua Nefsky*; **441** The Imperial War Museum, London; **443** U.S. Air Force; **444TL** National Archives; **444TR** National Archives; **444B** Cheryl Fenton*; **445** Cheryl Fenton*

Unit 4: 446-447 Copyright The Dorothea Lange Collection, The Oakland Museum of California, The City of Oakland. Gift of Paul S. Taylor

Chapter 10: 448L *Bartolomeo Vanzetti and Nicola Sacco* by Ben Shahn from the Sacco-Vanzetti series of twenty-three paintings (1931–32). Tempera on paper over composition board, 10 1/2 × 14 1/2" (26.7 × 36.8 cm.). The Museum of Modern Art, New York. Gift of Abby Aldrich Rockefeller. Photograph © 1996 The Museum of Modern Art, New York. © 1997 Estate of Ben Shahn/Licensed by VAGA, New York, NY; **448R** Corbis-Bettmann; **449T** Brown Brothers; **449BL** Corbis-Bettmann; **449BC** Brown Brothers; **449BR** Brown Brothers; **450** Courtesy, Estate of Carl Van Vechten, photo from the Schomburg Center for Research in Black Culture; The New York Public Library; Astor, Lenox and Tilden Foundations; **451** Culver Pictures; **453** Brown Brothers; **454** UPI/Corbis-Bettmann; **455** Brown Brothers; **457** Corbis-Bettmann; **458** UPI/Corbis-Bettmann; **459** © 1969 by James Van Der Zee. All Rights Reserved; **461** Corbis-Bettmann; **462** Culver Pictures; **463** Corbis-Bettmann; **464** Cheryl Fenton*; **466T** Iowa Department of Transportation Library; **466C** Culver Pictures; **466B** Culver Pictures; **467** Brown Brothers; **468** Caufield & Shook Collection, Photographic Archives, University of Louisville; **469** R. Maiman/Sygma; **471** The Holland House, Lone Pine, CA; **474** *Langston Hughes* by Winold Reiss (c. 1925, pastel on artist board, 30 1/16 × 21 5/8 in.), National Portrait Gallery, Smithsonian Institution/ Art Resource, NY; **475L** UPI/Corbis-Bettmann; **475R** From *The Dream Keeper and Other Poems* by Langston Hughes, illustrated by Brian Pinkney. Original copyright © 1932. Illustrations copyright 1994 by Brian Pinkney. Reprinted by permission of Alfred A. Knopf, Inc. Photo by Cheryl Fenton*; **477** Kraushaar Galleries, New York City; **478** From *National Police Gazette*/New York Public Library, Astor, Lenox & Tilden Foundations; **479** Culver Pictures Inc.; **481T** Stephen Agricola/Stock Boston; **481B** David Young-Wolff/PhotoEdit; **482** Joseph Nettis/Stock Boston

Chapter 11: 484L Icon Communications/FPG International; **484R** Leon Carlin, illustrator. Courtesy Vanity Fair. Copyright © 1934 (renewed 1962) by the Condé Nast Publications Inc.; **485T** Brown Brothers; **485BL** Poster by Vera Bock, New York,

NY, 71 × 56 cm (28 × 22 in.) Library of Congress, Prints and Photographs Division; **485BC** Library of Congress; **485BR** Archives of Labor and Urban Affairs, Wayne State University; **486T** Franklin D. Roosevelt Library; **486B** UPI/Corbis-Bettmann; **487** UPI/Corbis-Bettmann; **488** UPI/Corbis-Bettmann; **490L** Corbis-Bettmann; **490R** Franklin D. Roosevelt Library; **493L** Corbis-Bettmann; **493R** UPI/Corbis-Bettmann; **495** UPI/Corbis-Bettmann; **496** Drawing by Robt. Day; © 1933, 1961 The New Yorker Magazine, Inc.; **497** Cheryl Fenton*; **500** Archive Photos; **501** Library of Congress; **502** Culver Pictures; **505T** Lee Rentz/Bruce Coleman Inc.; **505C** Terry Donnelly/Tom Stack & Associates; **505B** Inga Spence/Tom Stack & Associates; **509** Jerry Stanley; **510** From the Collection of the Memory Shop; **512** Library of Congress; **513** Daniel Robert Fitzpatrick/St. Louis Post-Dispatch; **514** Library of Congress

Chapter 12: 516L UPI/Corbis-Bettmann; **516R** Judah L. Magnes Museum; **517T** Hulton Deutsch Collection Ltd./Woodfin Camp & Associates; **517BL** National Archives; **517BC** National Portrait Gallery, Smithsonian Institution/Art Resource, NY; **517BR** U.S. Air Force; **518** UPI/Corbis-Bettmann; **519** UPI/Corbis-Bettmann; **521** UPI/Corbis-Bettmann; **522** Margaret Bourke-White/LIFE Magazine © Time Inc.; **525** UPI/Corbis-Bettmann; **527** The Granger Collection, New York; **528** Cheryl Fenton*; **530** National Archives; **531** National Archives; **532** Myron Davis/LIFE Magazine © Time Inc.; **535** Brown Brothers; **537** Corbis-Bettmann; **540Background** National Archives; **540INS** Russell Lee/Magnum Photos; **541CL** UPI/Corbis/Bettmann; **541BL** National Archives; **541R** Collection of Delton Lee Johnson, Santa Paula, CA; **542T** U.S. Coast Guard; **542B** Photograph by Toni Frissell, Courtesy Frissell Collection, Library of Congress; **543Background** Defense Dept. Photo; **543T** Superstock, Inc.; **543B** AP/Wide World; **547** U.S. Army photo; **548** Library of Congress; **549T** Lanois/Black Star; **549B** AP/Wide World; **550** National Archives; **551** National Archives; **552** From Mine Okubo, "Citizen 13660," Columbia University Press, NY, 1946; **553** Krutein/Gamma-Liaison; **555** Courtesy of Dr. Herman Viola; **556** Courtesy of Dr. Herman Viola. Photos by Cheryl Fenton*; **557** Cheryl Fenton*

Unit 5: 558–559 Johnson Space Center/NASA

Chapter 13: 560L United Nations; **560R** Carl Mydans/LIFE Magazine © Time Inc.; **561T** Sovfoto/Eastfoto; **561BL** LIFE Magazine © Time Inc.; **561BC** Dick Swanson/Black Star; **561BR** Patrick Piel/Gamma-Liaison; **562** UPI/Corbis-Bettmann; **563** Cornell Capa/Magnum Photos, Inc.; **566** Fenno Jacobs/Black Star; **569** Gillhausen-Stern/Black Star; **570L** Michael Barson/Archive Photos; **570R** UPI/Corbis-Bettmann; **571** Dirck Halstead/Liaison Agency; **574** James Pickerell/Black Star; **575** UPI/Corbis-Bettmann; **576T** Sylvia Johnson/Woodfin Camp & Associates; **576INS** Les Stone/Sygma; **578T** UPI/Corbis/Bettmann; **578B** Larry Burrows/Time Life Inc.; **579L** UPI/Corbis/Bettmann; **579TR** Paul Fusco/Magnum Photos; **579C** UPI/Corbis/Bettmann; **579B** Printed with permission of Another Mother For Peace; **580–581Background** Robert Ellison/Black Star; **580T** Philip J. Griffiths/Magnum Photos; **580B** John P. Filo; **581T** UPI/Corbis/Bettmann; **581C** UPI/Corbis/Bettmann; **581B** Markel/Gamma-Liaison; **582** Wally McNamee/Woodfin Camp & Associates; **584** Robert Trippett/Sipa Press; **585** Vladimir Sichov/Sipa Press; **587** Cheryl Fenton*; **591** Ben Shahn, *Liberation, 1945* (detail), © 1996 Estate of Ben Shahn/Licensed by VAGA, New York, NY; **592** Vaughn Shoemaker; **593** Copyright ©1982 by Samuel Tower/ Reprinted by permission of Julian Messner, a division of Simon and Schuster, Inc.; **595** UPI/Corbis/Bettmann; **596** UPI/Corbis/Bettmann; **597** PACH/Corbis/Bettmann

Chapter 14: 598L AP/Wide World Photos, Inc.; **598R** UPI/Corbis-Bettmann; **599T** Carl Iwasaki, LIFE Magazine © Time Inc.; **599BL** Fred Ward/Black Star; **599BC** From *The Herblock Gallery* (Simon & Schuster, 1968); **599BR** Sven Simon; **600** Fred Ward/Black Star; **601** Bob Adelman/ Magnum Photos, Inc.; **603L** UPI/Corbis-Bettmann; **603INS** Calvin D. Campbell/Black Star; **605** Brown Brothers; **606** Bill Pogue/Tony Stone Images; **608** Photo by Abraham Zapruder, courtesy National Archives. Copyright 1967 by LMH Company. ALL RIGHTS RESERVED; **609** Photo by Cecil Stoughton/John F. Kennedy Library; **610** © 1997 Robert Rauschenberg/Licensed by VAGA, New York, NY; **612** UPI/Corbis-Bettmann; **613** AP/Wide World Photos, Inc.; **614** Charles Moore/Black Star; **615** Wide World Photos, Inc.; **617T** George Ballis/Take Stock; **617INS** Victor Alemán; **618L** Schomberg Center for Research in Black Culture; **618C** AP/Wide World; **618R** National Portrait Gallery Washington, D. C.; **619TL** Carl Iwasaki/Life Magazine © Time Warner, Inc.; **619BL** John Moore; **619TR** UPI/Corbis/Bettmann; **620–621Background** James H. Karales © 1965 LOOK Magazine/Library of Congress; **620L** UPI/Corbis-Bettmann; **620R** Bruce Davidson/Magnum Photos; **621TL** Bruce Davidson/Magnum Photos; **621TR** *Ebony* Magazine/Johnson Publishing Co.; **621B** UPI/Corbis/Bettmann; **624** Ivan Massar/Black Star; **625T** From *Herblock: A Cartoonist's Life* (Macmillan, 1993); **625B** Corbis-Bettmann; **627** Cheryl Fenton*; **630** AP/Wide World; **631** AP/Wide World; **633** Englehardt/St. Louis Post-Dispatch; **634** AP/Wide World; **635L** Supreme Court Historical Society; **635R** Supreme Court Historical Society; **636T** Russ Kinne/Photo Researchers; **636B** Michal Heron/Woodfin Camp & Associates

Chapter 15: 638L UMI; **638R** Magnum Photos, Inc.; **639T** Ken Hawkins/Sygma; **639BL** Roddey E. Mims/Sygma; **639BC** Bob Daemmrich/Stock, Boston; **639BR** Chamussy/Sipa Press; **640** Tony Friedkin. Copyright © 1993, FASE; **641** Andy Freeberg; **643** Wally McNamee/Woodfin

Camp & Associates; **644** Alain Mingam/Gamma-Liaison; **645** Michael Evans/Sygma; **646** Toshi Matsumoto/Sygma; **647** Jack Higgins with permission of the Chicago Sun-Times, Inc. © 1986; **652** Diana Walker/The Gamma-Liaison Network; **653T** Dirck Halstead/Gamma-Liaison; **653B** F. Carter Smith/Sygma; **654Background** John Ficara/Sygma; **654BL** Wally McNamee/Sygma; **654BR** Cynthia Johnson/Liaison (Gamma); **655T** MacDonald Photography/ Envision; **655BL** MacDonald Photography/Envision; **655BR** Dave Bartruff/ Stock, Boston; **657Background** Lance Nelson/The Stock Market; **658TL** Jim Corwin/Stock, Boston; **658TC** David Ulmer/Stock, Boston; **658TR** Stephen Kraseman/DRK Photo; **658BL** Spencer Swanger/Tom Stack & Associates; **658BC** Kirk R. Tuck; **658BR** Stephen J. Krasemann/DRK Photo; **660** Geri Engberg/Stock Market; **661** © Art by Juana Alicia and Susan Cervantes, photo by Jim Prigoff; **663** Cheryl Fenton*; **666** Max Aguilera-Hellweg/Onyx; **667** Dan Ford Connolly; **668** AP/Wide World; **670** American Museum of Natural History; **671** Ken Heinen; **672L & 672R** AP/Wide World; **675** *Hermanas Juntas Sin Velo* by Nivia Gonzalez, San Antonio, Texas. © 1990

Epilogue: 677 Masahiro Sano/The Stock Market; **678T** John Madere/The Stock Market; **678B** Brownie Harris/The Stock Market; **679T** Jon Feingersh/The Stock Market; **679C** NASA; **679B** Michael J. Howell/Rainbow; **680** Jenny Thomas*

Back Matter: R11 United States Department of Commerce, Bureau of the Census; **R24TL** *Portrait of George Washington (1732–1799), 1st President of the United States,* by Rembrandt Peale. National Portrait Gallery, Smithsonian Institution/Art Resource, NY; **R24TCL** Independence National Historical Park Collection; **R24BCL** *Thomas Jefferson* by Rembrandt Peale. Copyrighted by the White House Historical Association; photograph by National Geographic Society; **R24BL** *Portrait of James Madison* by Gilbert Stuart, oil on canvas, ca. 1820. Accession #1945.82. Mead Art Museum/ Amherst College. Bequest of Herbert L. Pratt, Class of 1895; **R24TR** *Portrait of James Monroe after an oil painting by John Vanderlyn,* by James Herring. National Portrait Gallery, Smithsonian Institution/Art Resource, NY; **R24TCR** *John Quincy Adams* by George Caleb Bingham. National Portrait Gallery/Smithsonian Institution/Art Resource, NY; **R24BCR** *Andrew Jackson* by James Tooley, Jr. National Portrait Gallery/Smithsonian Institution/Art Resource, NY; **R24BR** *Martin Van Buren* by George Peter Alexander Healy. Copyrighted by the White House Historical Association; **R25TL** *William Henry Harrison* by Albert Gallatin Hoit. National Portrait Gallery/Smithsonian Institution/Art Resource, NY; **R25TCL** *John Tyler* by George Peter Alexander Healy. National Portrait Gallery/Smithsonian Institution/Art Resource, NY; **R25BCL** *James Knox Polk* by Max Westfield after painting by George Peter Alexander Healy. National Portrait Gallery/Smithsonian Institution/Art Resource, NY; **R25BL** *Zachary Taylor* by James Reid Lambdin. National Portrait Gallery/Smithsonian Institution/Art Resource, NY; **R25TR** *Millard Fillmore* by George Peter Alexander Healy. Copyrighted by the White House Historical Association; **R25TCR** *Franklin Pierce* by George Peter Alexander Healy. Copyrighted by the White House Historical Association; **R25BCR** *James Buchanan* by George Peter Alexander Healy. National Portrait Gallery/Smithsonian Institution/Art Resource, NY; **R25BR** Library of Congress; **R26TL** Library of Congress; **R26TCL** Library of Congress; **R26BCL** Library of Congress; **R26BL** National Archives; **R26TR** Library of Congress; **R26TCR** National Archives; **R26BCR** Library of Congress; **R26BR** National Archives; **R27TL** Library of Congress; **R27TCL** Library of Congress; **R27BCL** Library of Congress; **R27BL** Library of Congress; **R27TR** Library of Congress; **R27TCR** Library of Congress; **R27BCR** Library of Congress; **R27BR** Reuters/Bettmann; **R28TL** The Bettmann Archive; **R28TCL** UPI/Bettmann Newsphotos; **R28BCL** Bachrach Studios; **R28BL** Arnold Newman/L. B. Johnson Library Collection; **R28TR** Nixon Presidential Materials/ National Archives; **R28TCR** Gerald R. Ford Library; **R28BCR** Jimmy Carter Library; **R28BR** Ronald Reagan Library; **R29T** National Archives; **R29C** The White House; **R28B** The White House; **R34** J. L. Atlan/Sygma; **R37** Andre Jenny/ International Stock; **R40** Fred J. Maroon/Folio, Inc.; **R45** Elliott Smith; **R53** Dennis Brack/Black Star; **R55** Cheryl Fenton*; **R57** The Bettmann Archive; **R67** *Almost through the Dark Alley,* 1919 by Kenneth Chamberlain. Black crayon, pen and ink on paper. Grunwald Center for the Graphic Arts, University of California, Los Angeles. Gift of Mr. & Mrs. Kenneth Chamberlain; **R70TL** *Portrait of George Washington (1732–1799), 1st President of the United States,* by Rembrandt Peale. National Portrait Gallery, Smithsonian Institution/Art Resource, NY; **R70TR** *Thomas Jefferson* by Rembrandt Peale. Copyrighted by the White House Historical Association; photograph by National Geographic Society; **R70C** Library of Congress; **R70BL** Reuters/Bettmann; **R70BR** Ronald Reagan Library; **R73** Bob Daemmrich/The Image Works

Front cover and back cover inset: National Archives (Declaration of Independence); Wes Thompson/The Stock Market (flag); Randy Taylor/Liaison International (people)

Back cover: Dr. Viola photographed by Terry Ashe for the publisher.

Scholar's Tool Kit backgrounds and Epilogue backgrounds: Cheryl Fenton*

*Photographed expressly for the publisher.

Art

Russ Charpentier **270–271, 410, 494**
Nea Hanscomb: Time lines, stars, and banners
Peg Magovern **27**
Ortelius Design **658**
Sarah Woodward **300, 623**
Map on page **303** from *Historical Atlas of the United States, Centennial Edition,* National Geographic Society, 1988, p. 248. Copyright © 1988 National Geographic Society.
Based on data from *Residents of Hull House, A Social Settlement, Hull House Maps and Papers: A Representation of Nationalities and Wages in a Congested District of Chicago, Together with Comments and Essays on Problems Growing Out of the Social Conditions* (NY: Thomas Y. Crowell, 1895); *Hull House Yearbook* (Chicago: Hildmann, 1916).

Maps: Maryland CartoGraphics

Using the Internet for Social Studies Research

Just what is it about this new tool, the Internet, that has all of us so excited? What's grabbing our attention is the Internet's unique ability to connect people and to allow them to gain access to information. And, if you're an educator, you can't resist finding out how to bring this tool on board for your students! That's because education is about communicating and sharing information. With the Internet, students can collaborate not only with classes in other schools, but with those in other countries as well. They can get up-to-the-minute information that their textbooks don't include. They can publish their own ideas for the world to see. Teachers can share tips and lesson plans. And it doesn't really matter when you or your students want to work—the Internet is ready for action 24 hours a day!

When it comes to social studies, this new tool is a natural. Vital skills such as acquiring information, thinking critically, and using information to make decisions or ask more questions are reinforced via Internet exploration, especially when students find resources that they would otherwise not have access to using traditional methods.

Glossary of Internet Terms

Here are some terms and definitions to help you find your way around on the Internet.

AUP Acceptable Use Policy: an agreement between students, teachers, and parents that sets the rules for Internet use in the school.

Bookmark Used by your browser to record the location of your favorite Web sites for access at a future time.

Browser A software application that enables a computer to search, or "browse," the World Wide Web. The browser makes documents that are coded in the HyperText Markup Language (html) viewable on the screen to the user.

Cyberspace A word coined by novelist William Gibson to describe the data created by the millions of computers connected worldwide via online communications.

Download To receive a file sent from another computer.

E-Mail Electronic mail, or messages sent from one computer to another.

Home Page The first file that you see when you go to a Web site; usually functions much like a book's table of contents.

Hotspot A portion of an image that changes the cursor from an arrow to a hand with a pointing finger, indicating the location of a hyperlink. You can click on a hotspot to find out more information or go to a linked Web page.

Html HyperText Markup Language: a programming language that relies on internal "tags" to indicate how documents should appear on the screen.

Http HyperText Transfer Protocol: a communication standard used by computers on the World Wide Web. You'll see it at the beginning of URLs.

Hyperlink A connector that takes you to a different document. Hyperlinks usually appear on the screen as colored or underlined text or as icons. The new document may come from the same computer as the document containing the hyperlink or from a different computer.

Hypermedia The joining together of video, sound, graphics, animation, and other elements through links or hotspots to form an association of independent yet interrelated topics. You can jump from subject to subject in search of information on related topics. Allows for nonlinear movement through topics.

Internet A global computer network that began in the 1960s as a U.S. Department of Defense project linking university computer science departments. It has since grown to include millions of business, governmental, educational, and individual computers around the world. Often called the Net, for short.

Internet Explorer Widely used browser that allows World Wide Web users to view html documents (those with graphics as well as text).

IRC Internet Relay Chat: allows for text-based real-time group conversation on the Internet .

LAN Local Area Network: network in which groups of computers are connected within an office or building.

Link See *Hyperlink.*

Listserv An electronic mailing list of subscribers who have chosen to receive information about a specific topic.

Modem A device that allows computers to communicate with one another via telephone lines.

Mosaic A popular browser that allows users to view documents on the World Wide Web.

Multimedia Describes a computer or computer program that uses sound with animation and/or video.

Netscape Navigator Widely used browser that allows World Wide Web users to view html documents (those with graphics as well as text).

Newsgroup An electronic bulletin board providing the ability to view messages without an e-mail account—usually related to a specific topic.

Online Connection to another computer through telephone lines or a network.

Online access provider An organization that provides access to the Internet. AOL, Prodigy, and CompuServe are examples of private-service providers.

Protocol Set of standards assuring that different network products can work together. Any product using a given protocol should work with any other product using the same protocol.

Search Engine A tool used to help locate information on the Internet. Examples include Yahoo, Alta Vista, and Webcrawler.

Upload To send or transmit a file to another computer.

URL Universal Resource Locator: an Internet address. The URL is embedded within a hyperlink, so that when you click on the link, your computer knows where to find the file you want. You can also find a Web site by typing its URL in the locator box.

Webmaster A person who manages a Web site.

Web Site Electronic files created by an individual or organization.

World Wide Web Usually called the Web, for short; a service on the Internet that weaves information and resources together through the use of hyperlinks.

Searching Successfully

How can you make the most of your and your students' online time? Online search engines, such as Yahoo, Alta Vista, and Webcrawler, are tools that can help you find information on the Internet quickly. They use programs that periodically scan the Internet. From their searches, these programs build their own database, or index, of information. When you visit a search engine site and enter a key word or phrase, you are really searching the database built by the search engine. Each search engine works a little differently from the others, and no single search engine contains all of the contents of the Internet, so it's a good idea to use more than one search engine when doing your research. If you don't know where to start, both Netscape and Internet Explorer have "Search" buttons that will take you to a page with several search engines from which to choose. Here are some search tips:

• Before you search, plan ahead. Think about what key words you can use.

• The more specific you can be, the more likely it is that you will find relevant information. Instead of a broad subject category such as *automobiles,* type in *Model T* or *Henry Ford.*

• Think of synonyms for your words. If the first key word you type in doesn't yield a good response, try a synonym.

• Accurate spelling counts! Search engines look for matching "strings" of letters; a spelling error can derail your search.

• Don't forget those Boolean operators. Never heard of them? Sure you have! They are the words *and, or,* and *not.* For example, if you type in *John Smith,* the search engine will list pages of Web listings containing the word *John* and pages of listings containing the word *Smith.* Type in *John and Smith* and all listings will contain *John Smith.*

(For some background on George Boole, mathematician and educator, visit this Web site: http://www.digitalcentury.com/encyclo/update/boole.html.)

The Internet and Information Literacy

Think of the Internet as a library, but one in which *anyone* can place his or her writings. How can you and your students distinguish the valid, accurate information on the Internet from the junk? Just as it has always been important to know how to evaluate your resources using conventional methods, it is especially true with online resources. Evaluating information has always been a crucial part of information literacy and is an important life skill for students to gain. Here are some tips:

• Consider the source. Is the source an academic, government, commercial, or personal site? Commercial sites can be valid sources of information, but be wary of any hidden agendas.

• Is the information presented in an objective manner? Have all sides of the issue been covered? Does there seem to be a bias?

• How old is the information? One way to tell is to find out when the site was last updated.

• What do you know about the author of the information? Can the author be contacted?

If your students use the Internet for research, share these tips with them and help them evaluate the information they find. You may want to use this as a springboard to a discussion of propaganda or bias.

Use Bookmarks

You've found a terrific Web site with lots of information about your topic—and lots of links to other Web sites on the page, too. Before you do anything else, bookmark that terrific Web site. It only takes clicking on one link every time you come to a new page before you find yourself far away from your original page. You can also click backward to where you started using the browser's *Back* button.

Using the Internet in Your Social Studies Classroom

Why We Remember brings alive the events, people, ideas, and places of the past for today's young people. The Internet can bring the world of today—and tomorrow—to students' fingertips. Using the ever-changing wealth of information on the Internet in your social studies classroom helps students connect the lessons of United States history with up-to-the-minute events in the community, the state, the country, and the world.

Depending on time and computer availability, you can have students work individually, in pairs, or in small groups to do research on the Internet. Their findings can be shared with the class or become part of written assignments. If you have only one computer in your classroom, or only one Internet account, you may want to do research as a whole-class activity. Since an important goal of such research is to familiarize students with Internet skills, have individual students take turns at the computer keyboard. Remember that some Web pages, especially those with graphics, can take several minutes to download completely. You may want to take this opportunity to have class members predict what they think they will find when the site is reached.

Learning Links—Social Studies

Here are just a few of the many resources available to you for use in your social-studies classroom. Many of the sites include links to other related Web Sites.

Note: Scott Foresman-Addison Wesley has reviewed the Web sites listed below for appropriate content and suitability for students. However, Web sites do change—and even disappear. Scott Foresman-Addison Wesley cannot be held responsible for the content of these sites. It is strongly advised that you review the sites yourself first to ensure their appropriateness for your students.

The American Civil War Home Page

http://funnelweb.utcc.utk.edu/~hoemann/warweb.html

Provides a gateway to hundreds of resources related to the Civil War.

Black History Month

http://www.kn.pacbell.com/wired.BHM/AfroAm.html

A variety of Internet-based activities related to African American history and issues.

Chicano Latino Net

http://latino.sscnet.ucla.edu/

Links to hundreds of Web sites related to Hispanic Americans.

Colonial Williamsburg

http://www.history.org

A vast array of resources for understanding life in eighteenth-century America.

Congressional E-Mail Addresses

http://ast1.spa.umn.edu/juan/congress.html

Find out the name of your congressional representative by typing in your zip code, and then send him or her an e-mail message.

ERIC

http://ericr.syr.edu

A database that enables educators to search all education journals for articles of interest.

Federal Election Commission

http://www.fec.gov/press/pac18ctr.htm

Learn about elections, political action committees, and more.

Historical Documents

http://lcweb2.loc.gov/const/mdquery.html

Search important historical documents, such as the U.S. Constitution, to find specific information.

The History Net

http://www.TheHistoryNet.com/

Produced by the National Historical Society, this site includes interviews, personality profiles, eyewitness accounts, and articles from *American History* magazine.

The History Place

http://www.historyplace.com/

Contains features on various social studies topics, such as Abraham Lincoln, World War II, and John F. Kennedy.

History/Social Studies Web Site for K–12 Teachers

http://execpc.com/~dboals/govt.html#

Links to a multitude of resources for social studies teachers.

Kids Web: A World Wide Web Digital Library for Schoolkids

http://www.npac.syr.edu/textbook/kidsweb

Includes links to Web sites related to history and geography.

Library of Congress—State and Local Governments

http://lcweb.loc.gov/global/state/stategov.html

Links to indexes of state information, including individual states' home pages. Many states include "virtual field trips" at their sites.

The National Council for Social Studies

http://www.ncss.org

Information about workshops, publications, events, and news related to social studies.

PBS Online

http://www.pbs.org>

Contains background information on historical programs produced by public television, including resource guides for teachers and parents.

Social Studies School Service

http://writingco.com/

A clearinghouse of information and links related to social studies.

Student Links to Twentieth-Century History

http://www.geocities.com/Athens/3344/history.htm

Annotated links to sites related to twentieth-century topics, including Theodore Roosevelt, Ellis Island, aviation, the Jazz Age, and World War II.

The Supreme Court

http://oyez.at.nwu.edu/oyez.html

Online audio files of complete oral arguments of many landmark cases argued before the U.S. Supreme Court. Background information, the constitutional question involved, and the voting record are provided.

TeachNet

http://www.teachnet.org

This site for teachers is sponsored by IMPACT II—The Teachers Network, a nonprofit organization that supports innovative teachers.

Thomas: Legislative Information on the Internet

http://thomas.loc.gov/

Named after Thomas Jefferson, this site includes up-to-date information on legislation in Congress.

Virtual Tour of the Capitol

http://senate.gov/capitol/virtour.html

Take a tour of the U.S. Capitol and learn about the seat of government.

Welcome to the White House

http://www.whitehouse.gov/WH/Welcome.html

Find out about the White House and the families who have lived there.

White House Briefing Room

http://www.whtehouse.gov/WH/html/briefroom.html

Visit the White House Briefing Room to find out "Today's Top Issue."

Women's Suffrage in America

http://www.cc.rochester.edu:80/SBA/95-75/

The Web site for the Susan B. Anthony Center in Rochester, NY.

The Education Network makes it easier than ever to bring quality online experiences into your classroom.

Visit Scott Foresman-Addison Wesley's Web site at

http://www.sf.aw.com

Be a part of The Education Network! Send us a brief review of your favorite Web site, listserv, or news group. We'll publish reviews in our Global Links area. When you send your review, be sure to include the following information:

- your first and last name
- your city, state, and school
- your review
- a photo of yourself (optional)

E-mail your review to:

sfawonline@aw.com

Or write to:

Scott Foresman-Addison Wesley Online
1900 East Lake Avenue
Glenview, IL 60025

We welcome your input!